WORLD DRAMA

FROM ÆSCHYLUS TO ANOUILH

BY

ALLARDYCE NICOLL

PROFESSOR OF ENGLISH LANGUAGE AND
LITERATURE IN THE UNIVERSITY OF
BIRMINGHAM
FORMERLY PROFESSOR OF THE HISTORY OF DRAMA
AND DRAMATIC CRITICISM
AND CHAIRMAN OF THE DEPARTMENT OF DRAMA YALE UNIVERSITY

With Sixty-four Plates in Half-tone

T, BRACE AND COMPANY
NEW YORK

TO
MY WIFE

WORLD DRAMA

PREFACE

THIS book attempts to provide a general conspectus of the drama's development from its earliest days in ancient Greece down to latest times. Confessedly it is prejudiced, since without prejudice no essay of this kind can be other than a mere record of facts, and the endeavour here is to present something beyond a collection of statistical information.

Judgments on individual plays and on the work of various playwrights are, therefore, coloured by the light in which the entire progress of the theatre is viewed. Still further, it must be emphasized that these judgments are based on standards or values independent of particular times and places. In a volume devoted to a period of dramatic activity restricted both in time and in place certain plays may justifiably be selected for praise because they rise above the general tone of their companions: in a book dealing with the whole development of the drama such plays may, with equal justification, be omitted or dealt with cursorily. If we take Sophocles and Shakespeare, Aristophanes and Shaw, as our standards, many lesser authors, although perhaps important for their own time and country, must of necessity be ignored.

An attempt, of course, has been made to refer to many plays which, because of their historical significance, are worthy of notice even though they may no longer make appeal to us, but always my object has been to make a distinction between such historical significance and intrinsic value. Should any reader in another country feel that I have not done justice to authors whose local fame is greater than their general esteem, I refer to my treatment of certain periods of English dramatic history, wherein numerous plays of decided interest have been weighed against others of greater importance and found wanting.

Particular difficulty has arisen, naturally, in dealing with contemporary contributions to the stage. In this region there is no perspective supplied by time to aid us; yet modern efforts are those which most attract our attention. Because of these considerations I have devoted to the dramatic work of the twentieth century perhaps greater space than would have been accorded to it had this book been written, not in 1949, but in 2049—and certainly greater space than a strict balancing of worth with that of earlier times might warrant.

In this connexion another thing must be emphasized. A purely factual account of theatrical development would presumably treat of plays in all countries, East and West, according to their position in time; and it would, moreover, seek to deal with all manifestations of the art dramatic no matter where they were exhibited. Thus, for example, in a work of

1

presentation of statistical information, although it is too much to hope that, with so wide a scope, errors have been entirely avoided.

For aid in locating elusive documentary evidence I have to thank many of my colleagues and friends, at the University of Birmingham, at other British universities, in the United States of America, and in continental Europe. The Cultural Attachés at the Embassies of the U.S.S.R. and Norway have also been most kind in helping me in this task. For all such assistance I am deeply grateful.

Some of the translated quotations from plays have been specially prepared for the present book, but many have been taken from already published versions. For permission to include both extracts from these versions and quotations from original works by British and American authors I have to thank the following:

Messrs ACTAC (Theatrical and Cinematic), Ltd, for extracts from Christopher Fry's *Venus Observed* (Oxford University Press).

Messrs George Allen and Unwin, Ltd, and Messrs Alfred A. Knopf, Inc., for an extract from Arthur Waley's *The Nō Plays of Japan* (copyright 1922).

Messrs George Allen and Unwin, Ltd, and the Oxford University Press, Inc., New York, for extracts from Dr Gilbert Murray's translations of Euripides' *The Trojan Women* and *Bacchæ* (from *Euripides: Five Plays*; copyright 1906, 1910, 1915, by the Oxford University Press, Inc., New York).

Messrs George Allen and Unwin, Ltd, and Messrs Random House, Inc., for extracts from J. M. Synge's *Riders to the Sea* and *The Playboy of the Western World.*

Messrs G. Bell and Sons, Ltd, for extracts from E. P. Coleridge's translations of Euripides' *Orestes*, *Hecuba*, and *Helen*; from Sir George Young's translation of Sophocles' *Œdipus at Colonus*; from F. M. Stawell's translation of Euripides' *Iphigenia in Aulis*; from B. B. Rogers' translations of Aristophanes' *The Acharnians* and *The Birds*; and from Sir Theodore Martin's translation of Schiller's *William Tell.*

Signor Ugo Betti for an extract from his *Frana allo Scalo nord.*

The Executors of the late Dr Gordon Bottomley and Messrs Constable and Co., Ltd, for an extract from Dr Bottomley's *Fire at Callart.*

Mr James Bridie for extracts from his *Tobias and the Angel* and *The Sleeping Clergyman.*

Messrs Curtis Brown, Ltd, for an extract from Barrett H. Clark's translation of Sardou's *La Patrie.*

The Syndics of the Cambridge University Press for an extract from F. L. Lucas's translations of Seneca's *Thyestes* and *Hercules Furens* appearing in that author's *Seneca and Elizabethan Tragedy* (1922).

Messrs Chatto and Windus for an extract from C. St John's translation of the *Plays of Roswitha.*

Mr Barrett H. Clark for extracts from his translations of Beaumarchais and Dumas appearing in his *European Theories of the Drama*, and for an extract from Ethel van der Veer's translation of *The Chalk Circle.*

The Columbia University Press, Inc., for an extract from A. E. Zucker's translation of *The Redentin Easter Play*.

Messrs J. M. Dent and Sons, Ltd, and Messrs E. P. Dutton and Co., Inc., for an extract from Barker Fairlie's translation of Hebbel's *Maria Magdalena* ("Everyman's Library"), for extracts from Pirandello's *Six Characters in Search of an Author*, *Clothing the Naked*, and *Each in his Own Way* (translated by the present author).

Messrs Dennis Dobson, Ltd, and Messrs Alfred A. Knopf, Inc., for an extract from Harold Clurman's *The Fervent Years*.

Messrs Doubleday and Co., Inc., for an extract from C. H. Meltzer's translation of Gerhart Hauptmann's *The Sunken Bell*.

Messrs Gerald Duckworth and Co., Ltd, and Messrs Charles Scribner's Sons for extracts from E. Björkmann's translations of Strindberg's *The Dance of Death* and Introduction to *The Dream Play* in *Eight Famous Plays*, by A. Strindberg (*Plays by August Strindberg*, copyright 1912).

Mr S. A. Eliot, Junior, for an extract from his translation of Hans Sachs' *Wandering Scholar*.

Messrs Faber and Faber, Ltd, and Messrs Harcourt, Brace and Co., Inc., for an extract from T. S. Eliot's *Murder in the Cathedral*.

The Librairie Gallimard for an extract from Albert Camus' *Caligula*.

The Executors of John Galsworthy, Messrs Gerald Duckworth and Co., Ltd, and Messrs Charles Scribner's Sons for an extract from John Galsworthy's *Justice* (copyright 1910).

Mme Jean Giraudoux for an extract from Jean Giraudoux' *Electre*.

Messrs Harcourt, Brace and Co., Inc., for an extract from D. Fitts' and R. Fitzgerald's translation of Sophocles' *Antigone*.

Messrs A. M. Heath and Co., Ltd, Victor Gollancz, Ltd, and Random House, Inc., for an extract from Clifford Odets' *Golden Boy*.

Messrs William Heinemann, Ltd, for extracts from William Archer's translations of Ibsen's *Emperor or Galilean*, *Pillars of Society*, *The Wild Duck*, and *When We Dead Awaken*.

Messrs William Heinemann, Ltd, and Messrs Doubleday and Co., Inc., for an extract from Noel Coward's *Private Lives*.

Messrs John Lane, The Bodley Head, Ltd, for an extract from Roy Campbell's translation of Krog's *Triad*.

Messrs John Lane, The Bodley Head, Ltd, and Messrs William Sloan Associates, Inc., New York, for an extract from Maxwell Anderson's *Winterset*.

The Editors of the Loeb Classical Library for extracts from F. Storr's translation of Sophocles' *Electra* and from Arthur S. Way's translation of Euripides' *Electra*.

Messrs Longmans, Green and Co., Inc., New York, for an extract from M. P. Baker's translation of Molnar's *The Swan*.

Mr Eugene O'Neill, Messrs Jonathan Cape, Ltd, and Messrs Random House, Inc., for extracts from Eugene O'Neill's *The Hairy Ape*, *All God's Chillun got Wings*, and *Mourning becomes Electra*.

The Princeton University Press for an extract from Lacy Lockert's translation of Racine's *Andromaque*.

Messrs Random House, Inc., for extracts from the translations of Aristophanes' *Acharnians*, *The Clouds*, and *The Wasps* appearing in *Complete Greek Drama* (ed. Whitney J. Oates and Eugene O'Neill, Junior), and from Paul Landis's translation of Corneille's *Cinna* and Robert Henderson's translation of Racine's *Phèdre* appearing in "The Modern Library."

Mr Elmer Rice for an extract from his *Counsellor-at-Law*.

Messrs Rinehart, Inc., New York, and Messrs Victor Gollancz, Ltd, for an extract from Marc Connelly's *Green Pastures* (copyright 1929 by Marc Connelly).

Messrs Routledge and Kegan Paul, Ltd, for an extract from L. A. Post's translation of Menanders' *Arbitration*.

M. Armand Salacrou for extracts from his *L'Archipel Lenoir* and *La terre est ronde*.

Messrs Charles Scribner's Sons for extracts from J. G. Underhill's translations of Lope de Vega's *The King the Best Alcalde*, *Fuente Ovejuna*, and *El perro del hortelano*, and of Benavente's *Bonds of Interest*.

Mr George Bernard Shaw for extracts from his *Too True to be Good*, *St Joan*, *Cæsar and Cleopatra*, and *Man and Superman*.

Messrs Simon and Schuster, Inc., for an extract from H. Thayer Kingsbury's translation of Rostand's *Cyrano*.

Mrs Bella and Samuel Spewack and Messrs Victor Gollancz, Ltd, for an extract from *Boy Meets Girl*.

The Executors of August Strindberg and Messrs Jonathan Cape, Ltd, for extracts from E. Classens's translation of *Lucky Peter's Travels*, and from C. D. Locock's translations of *The Saga of the Folkungs* (*Master Olof and Other Plays*), and the Introduction to *Lady Julia*.

Mr Louis Untermeyer for an extract from his translation of Toller's *Man and the Masses* (produced by the Theatre Guild at the Garrick Theatre, April 14, 1924).

The Viking Press, Inc., New York, for extracts from translations of Gerhart Hauptmann's *Before Sunrise* and *Schluck und Jau*, appearing in *Dramatic Works of Gerhart Hauptmann*, translated by Ludwig Lewisohn (copyright 1913, 1915, by B. W. Huebsch; 1941, 1943, by Ludwig Lewisohn).

The University of Washington Press, Inc., for an extract from Edward N. Stone's translation of *Adam*.

The Yale University Press and the Oxford University Press for an extract from C. W. Mendell's *Our Seneca*.

Mrs W. B. Yeats, Messrs Macmillan and Co., Ltd, and the Macmillan Co., New York, for extracts from W. B. Yeats' *At the Hawk's Well* and *The King's Threshold*, from *Collected Plays of W. B. Yeats* (*Four Plays for Dancers*).

A. N.

CONTENTS

PART I

FROM ATHENS TO ROME

7

PART II

RELIGIOUS DRAMA AND PROFANE DURING THE MIDDLE AGES

PART III

THE DRAMA OF THE RENAISSANCE

PART IV

THE DRAMA OF THE RENAISSANCE: ENGLAND

PART V

THE TRIUMPH OF CLASSICISM

PART X

THE DRAMA OF THE ORIENT

Contents

PART XI

ENTERING THE TWENTIETH CENTURY

PART XII

DRAMA BETWEEN TWO WARS

PART XIII

THE THEATRE IN THE MIDST OF WAR, AND AFTER

PART XIV

CONCLUSION

ILLUSTRATIONS

17

PART I

FROM ATHENS TO ROME

THE FIRST DRAMATIST: ÆSCHYLUS

FOR US the theatre may be said to begin about the year 490 B.C., when the first extant drama by Æschylus, *The Suppliants*, was performed before an audience of Athenian citizens.

It is possible that dramatic entertainment existed hundreds, perhaps thousands, of years before this date; it is probable that Æschylus and the other early playwrights of Greece owed a considerable debt, both for the content and the form of their plays, to priestly performers of sacred dramas in ancient Egypt; it is certain that Æschylus was no inventor of tragedy, but merely elaborated upon a growing Greek tradition which gradually brought the theatre as we know it to full fruition. But in all of these realms we move darkling, unable to do more than guess at what may be around us.

What forms were assumed by mimetic dances in prehistoric communities we can only vaguely conjecture; we do not know whether the tellers of tales, the acrobats, and the singers of songs amid these tribes mingled dramatic material with their own wares. However strongly we may suspect that the dances took on something approaching a theatrical appearance, and that the popular entertainers made their contributions to later dramatic artistry, there is no evidence available by which we can formulate any assured statements.

Egypt offers us a trifle more, yet, despite all our wealth of knowledge concerning this ancient empire, we are barely better off, in so far as our knowledge of the theatre is concerned, than when we contemplate prehistoric times. There was, we are aware, an *Abydos Passion Play* existent in the second, perhaps even in the third, millennium before Christ. This drama celebrated the death of Osiris, and apparently told how his limbs were torn apart, to be brought together again by Isis, his sister and his wife; but no text survives, and its action can be only tentatively reconstructed from a record by one Ikhernofret, who refashioned older material for a presentation before Secostris III (1887-1849 B.C.). Even after such a tentative reconstruction, however, we remain unsure whether this presentation was truly dramatic—whether it may not have been, after all, merely a piece of expanded ritual. And if we are in doubt concerning the *Abydos Passion Play*, still greater doubt attends any consideration of the "Pyramid Texts" and the so-called "Memphite Drama." We are in the presence of a kind of dramatic exercise here, undoubtedly; yet there is so little evidence of a concrete nature that regretfully we must leave these ritual plays aside. For the specialist their exploration is fascinating, but to the specialist they must be left.

Safer and firmer ground is reached when we move to Greece. The tragic dramas of Æschylus and his successors sprang from the ancient dithyramb, a choral song chanted in honour of Dionysus. Again, however, even although the way be clearer, certainties are lacking, and we can but guess at the probable line of development. At first the dithyramb was, in all probability, an improvised affair, words and music alike issuing from the excitement of the festival occasion. At first, too, the dithyramb must have been largely or wholly narrative in form, telling some legend relating to the god. Gradually changes came. At least by the days of Arion of Methymna (between the seventh and sixth centuries B.C.) individual poets were composing lines for the celebrants; and at the same time the separation of a choral leader (the *exarchos*, ἔξαρχος) from the crowd led to the possibility of genuine dramatic action—or, rather, for the transformation of narrative into direct representation.

Then came the truly decisive step, traditionally attributed to Thespis (sixth century B.C.), when an actor (as distinct from a choral leader) was introduced. With the use of masks—whereby the single actor might impersonate several characters during the course of the action—the way was opened for the exploitation in dramatic form of many and complex themes.

With Thespis we move close to Æschylus, for this actor-dramatist seems, after having exhibited his plays in his native Icaria, to have transferred his activities to Athens about the year 560 B.C. Precise records are wanting, but such evidence as remains tends to suggest that from this date Thespis gave public performances of his works in the city, and it is certain that when Pisistratus established the first dramatic festival in 534 B.C. he won the prize for one of his tragedies.

His activities, aided by the incentive of the festival-contests, immediately had their effect. Other dramatists followed his lead: the fecund Choirilos, who is credited with some hundred and sixty plays, and who is said to have improved on the masks introduced by Thespis; Pratinas, who specialized in the 'satyric' drama; Phrynichos, the inventor of women's masks, a writer famous in his own days, yet, unlike the happier Æschylus, without a single one of his works extant.

There is no doubt here: these men wrote plays similar in form to those which have been preserved from the hands of other dramatists. Yet consideration of their activities helps us nothing in our endeavour to see the history of the theatre as a whole, for we have naught save scattered allusions, a few historical records, and a handful of fragments of their writings to assist us. We see faint streaks of light amid the darkness, and dim, silhouetted outlines begin to become apparent; but not until we reach Æschylus does the sunrise come.

THE FIRST THEATRE: "THE SUPPLIANTS"

It is sunrise, and a great crowd of Athenian citizens is gathered on the bare hillside below the Acropolis, some standing, some squatting among the rocks, some seated on rudely constructed tiers of wooden benches. Below them the slope of the hill levels out, and on the small plateau thus formed a great circle has been marked out, in its midst an altar. Near by the dim light reveals the outline of a temple.

The crowd is expectant and eager, though physically tired. Already there have been days and nights of ecstatic festivity, beginning with a solemn procession, during which the statue of Dionysus has been carried from its temple down towards the Academy on the road to Eleutheros, and including a tumultuous torchlit return, when the god's statue has been placed, where it is now visible, beside the great orchestral circle. There has been sacrifice and ritual, flute music and the chanting of hymns, solemnity and ribald laughter, in the atmosphere of release and reverence.

Now once more the crowd has gathered, in this dawn, anxious to see the presentations which are to be placed before them in further honour of Dionysus.

A sudden silence descends as the nightingale-clear tones of a flute issue from the half-darkness below, and vaguely can be seen a group of fifty figures robed in white garments with strange embroideries moving into the circle's precincts and arranging themselves about the altar. Among them is one man, clad in rich robes, high-soled boots on his feet, with a venerable mask which towers upward about his temples in a kind of crown.

For a moment there is silence, and then a choral chant begins:

> Zeus! Lord and guard of suppliant hands!
> Look down benign on us who crave
> Thine aid—whom winds and waters drave

From where, through drifting, shifting sands,
   Pours Nilus to the wave.
From where the green land, god-possest,
Closes and fronts the Syrian waste,
We flee as exiles, yet unbanned
By murder's sentence from our land;
But—since Ægyptus had decreed
His sons should wed his brother's seed—
Ourselves we tore from bonds abhorred,
From wedlock not of heart but hand,
Nor brooked to call a kinsman lord!

Only one section of the chorus has been singing; now another takes up the tune:

   And Danaus, our sire and guide,
   The king of counsel, pond'ring well
   The dice of fortune as they fell,
   Out of two griefs the kindlier chose,
   And bade us fly, with him beside,
   Heedless what winds or waves arose,
   And o'er the wide sea waters haste,
   Until to Argos' shore at last
   Our wandering pinnace came.

Already sufficient has been told to permit the attendant audience of Athenian citizens, their minds fed with the legends of their land, to know that the stalwart man in the orchestral circle is Danaus, and that the fifty women in the chorus are his daughters. All the spectators know the bare outline of their fate. Danaus was the brother of Ægyptus, two princes descended from a union of the god Zeus and the poor tormented Io. The fifty sons of Ægyptus had proferred marriage with, and had later threatened violence upon, Danaus' daughters, who in terror had taken ship with their father to seek Io's native land, Argos, and beg the protection of its king, Pelasgus.

The audience, then, know the antecedents of the action about to be unfolded before them, and are even aware of the course to be taken by the coming scenes. They ask no thrill of novelty in the plot: unhindered by ignorance of the events, they give their whole minds to listening to the poet's words and to appreciating his skill in handling this age-old theme.

Through complex strophe and antistrophe, in subtle melody the chorus has continued its chant, accompanying the stanzas with intricate dance movement. Now, their voices and their bodies stilled, the maidens gather close to the altar, while Danaus, left alone at the edge of the circle, addresses them, warning them to be wary, and telling them that they must expect the arrival of the King of Argos and his soldiers:

> Adore this altar consecrate
> To many lesser gods in one; then crouch
> On holy ground, a flock of doves that flee,
> Scared by no alien hawks, a kin not kind,
> Hateful, and fain of love more hateful still. . . .
> Take heed, draw hitherward,
> That from this hap your safety ye may win.

At this the actor playing Danaus remains silent, while his active rôle is taken by another, clad in a royal mask. Addressing the chorus, this second actor announces himself as Pelasgus, comments on the strange Eastern robes of the chorus, and asks why they are come to Argive land.

Eagerly the audience listen, for now is come a scene of crisis. How will these maidens defend themselves? What will the King of Argos say? The answer to the first question is soon given. "Short is my word and clear," declares the leader of the chorus. "Of Argive race we come." Pelasgus stands amazed, unable to credit that women so strange in attire should be of his country, but gradually, as the choral leader retells the story of Io and the fortunes of her descendants, he becomes convinced; and thereupon the chorus breaks out into a wild chant pleading for protection and justice. Through the clear air, in the brilliant light of morn, the words come singing to the crowd above:

> Justice, the daughter of right-dealing Zeus,
> Justice, the queen of suppliants, look down,
> That this our plight no ill may loose
> Upon your town!
> This word, even from the young, let age and wisdom learn:
> If thou to suppliants show grace,
> Thou shalt not lack Heaven's grace in turn,
> So long as virtue's gifts on heavenly shrines have place.

This is the maidens' plea: what now of Pelasgus' reply? It comes equally short and direct:

> Not at my private hearth ye sit and sue;
> And if the city bear a common stain,
> Be it the common toil to cleanse the same:
> Therefore no pledge, no promise will I give,
> Ere counsel with the commonwealth be held.

And, hearing these words, the crowd stirs eagerly, for this audience belongs to a democracy, proud that common opinion, not the will of tyrants, rules its fate; and this ancient Argos over which Pelasgus is chieftain is the land of Athens. Thus is the antique tale brought close to them in spirit.

With the threat in his ears that these maidens will hang themselves should succour be refused, the Argive king retires, while the chorus chants melodiously a hymn to Zeus. To the audience gathered there the five strophes and antistrophes take but a brief space of time, yet, as the song is being sung, winged imagination accompanies Pelasgus on his mission, pictures him summoning his free council of citizens, creates in fancy the scene wherein the case is set and argued. With no shock of surprise or resentment, the spectators see Danaus return and hear him announce the verdict: time is foreshortened here in this highly conventional presentation of bygone action:

> With one assent the Argives spake their will,
> And, hearing, my old heart took youthful cheer.
> The very sky was thrilled when high in air
> The concourse raised right hands and swore their oath:
> *Free shall the maidens sojourn in this land.*
> *Unharried, undespoiled by mortal wight:*
> *No native hand, no hand of foreigner,*
> *Shall drag them hence.*

Immediately the chorus break into a passionate song of thankfulness to the gods; but no sooner is this ended than Danaus, gazing down the hillside towards the sea far beneath him, cries out that he discerns there the ship of their pursuers. Danaus leaves the stage, while the maidens cluster miserably round the altar, uttering cries of fear:

> O land of hill and dale, O holy land,
> What shall befall us? whither shall we flee,
> From Apian land to some dark lair of earth? . . .

> For the race of Ægyptus is fierce, with greed and with malice afire;
> They cry as the questing hounds, they sweep with the speed of desire.

In a moment a new figure enters, the Herald of Ægyptus. Rudely he attempts to force the women from the altar; the air is rent with their cries, all is tumult and dismay. Then suddenly Pelasgus appears, and with him hope:

> Know that if words unstained by violence
> Can change these maidens' choice, then mayest thou,

With full consent of theirs, conduct them hence.
But thus the city with one voice ordained—
No force shall bear away the maiden band.
Firmly this word upon the temple wall
Is by a rivet clenched, and shall abide:
Not upon wax inscribed and delible,
Nor upon parchment sealed and stored away.—
Lo, thou hast heard our free mouths speak their will:
Out from our presence—tarry not, but go!

At this, but threatening war, the Herald withdraws, and the chorus, overjoyed, release their emotions in a passionate song in praise of Argos, in praise of the land of Athens:

Pass and adore ye the Blessed, the gods of the city who dwell
Around Erasinus, the gush of the swift immemorial tide.

So rings out one pæan, to be caught up excitedly by another:

Chant ye, O maidens; aloud let the praise of Pelasgia swell;
Hymn we no longer the shores where Nilus to ocean doth glide.

So ends the play, the first drama known to us, *The Suppliants* of Æschylus.

The audience, however, does not move. There is a restless moment of intermission, but soon expectancy and silence once more fall upon the crowd: once more the sound of a flute, playing a fresh melody, comes from below; once more the maidens of the chorus flock into the orchestra. A new play begins.

We do not possess this second drama, but its content is easily to be reconstructed. Here is shown the rape of the daughters of Danaus by Ægyptus' sons. Nor is this even the end, for the second play in turn is followed by a third, which tells their final fate—tells how all the maidens but one (Hypermnestra, moved by new-won love for her Lynceus) slay their hated husbands. Only then does the dramatic movement reach its conclusion.

Thus, for those gathered on the bare hillside by the little Athenian town, the single drama of *The Suppliants* becomes by a strange paradox at once a complete dramatic whole and yet only part of a trilogy, a single act in a larger unity.

THE DRAMATIC CONVENTIONS OF GREECE

The space thus given to *The Suppliants*, even although that play cannot be counted the greatest of Æschylus' works, is justified by the facts that this is the first extant drama that the history of the theatre yields to us and that it well exemplifies the stage which the young Æschylus inherited from Thespis and his immediate followers.

As yet there is hardly any theatre as such: as yet only rude provision is made for the audience, and the actors all move within the level circle of the orchestra, with no background save what is provided by the open sky and the long, noble landscape stretching far below. The drama is close to the form of its origin, the dithyramb; action is kept to a minimum, and the chorus, these daughters of Danaus, become, as it were, a collective protagonist; of individual portraiture there is virtually nothing. This is drama, certainly, and not ritual, but it is drama of the most rudimentary kind.

Already, however, the main conventions of the Greek stage have been set. Very soon a stage-building, designed at once to give the actors opportunity for the changing of mask and dress and to provide for them an architectural background, is to come into being, but even in its absence the conditions of performance for *The Suppliants* are characteristic of the entire course of the Greek theatre. This theatre was never at any time more than a collection of parts—the auditorium remained separate from the orchestra and the orchestra from the stage—and always the central part was the great complete circular level assigned to the chorus. Out of the chorus the drama had originally sprung, and with the chorus (albeit at the end a trifle unwillingly) it remained until the tragic spirit vanished completely.

This hillside theatre of *The Suppliants* was already a festival theatre, in which plays were presented, in competition, by actor-dramatists who trained their own performers and found the cost of the production defrayed by some rich citizen who gladly accepted the onus of payment as a kind of religious offering, or at least as a public duty. Already the system of appointing judges by lot had been established; already the dates had been set for the two great Athenian dramatic festivals, the City Dionysia, in the spring (March), and the Lenæa, in the winter (January). The actors were costumed as they were to be costumed for the entire space of the production of Greek tragedy, and their dress was virtually the creation of Æschylus himself. Basing his model upon antique traditional forms, he was responsible for the theatrical adoption of the long-sleeved robe, generally embroidered more richly than was the attire of the contemporary Athenian and, when occasion offered, assuredly taking advantage of barbaric ornament. In *The Suppliants*, for example, Pelasgus at once recognizes that the fifty women of the chorus come from some strange, far-off land, and we may presume

ÆSCHYLUS
From the original in the Museo
Capitolino, Rome.
Photo Anderson

SOPHOCLES
From the original in the Museo
Laterano, Rome.

Photo Anderson

THE THEATRE AT EPIDAURUS

This theatre is among the best preserved and the most beautiful of the earlier type.

Photo E. P. Co.

that Egyptian motifs appeared on their flowing draperies. To Æschylus, too, the stage owed the utilization of the *cothurnus* (κόθορνος), or high-soled boot worn in tragedy. This gave greater stature to the actors, provided means of giving a hero-king an appearance more impressive than that of his companions, and must have introduced a fine contrast between the majestic-seeming chief figures of the tragedy, solemn and statuesque in their proportions and movements, and the fleet-footed characters in the chorus. That solemn and statuesque appearance, too, was increased by the use of the *onkos*, the relic of an ancient method of dressing the hair, by which long tresses were bound up over the top of the head. In the tragic masks this crown of hair was exaggerated and added to the height of the actor. In general it seems that Æschylus' object was, by the use of the majestic theatre dress, the *cothurnus*, and the large masks with *onkos* for which he was responsible, to create an impression of idealized nobility, of magnificence and of grandeur.

The Suppliants was originally part of a trilogy, and we must remember that, from the time of Æschylus at least, the poets who entered into the festival competition were compelled to present, not one play, but four plays—a tetralogy, consisting of three tragedies (a trilogy) and a satyr play. Æschylus' habitual method was to use the trilogy for the purpose of revealing a dramatic story —as that of the daughters of Danaus—extending in action over a considerable period of time. Theoretically each individual drama had a fictional action corresponding to the time of representation: the presence of the chorus in the orchestra from the beginning to the end seemed to make this obligatory. In practice, however, two devices could be used to obviate the severe limitations thus imposed. The use of the trilogy enabled Æschylus to show the daughters of Danaus in Argos, later—after the passage of many months—in Egypt, and still later—again after the passage of months—at their final death-scene. Between the parts of a trilogy, as between the acts of a modern play, time might lapse. In addition to this device was another, once more exemplified in *The Suppliants*. These dramas of Æschylus were poetic dramas, not bound by the petty restrictions of the realistic stage: the actual might therefore easily be forgotten in the contemplation of the imaginative. For the audience there was no shock, or wrenching of the mind, when, during the chanting of a few verses by the chorus, it was presumed that Pelasgus, the king, had journeyed back to his palace, had summoned his council, had explained the problem set before him, had received their answer, and had travelled back again to

B

the sea-shore. Ideal time, not real time, rules in the Greek tragic theatre.

The fourth part of the tetralogy was a satyr play. This is a peculiar form of drama, the characteristic property of the Greek stage, about which we know but little. Only one complete work of the kind has come down to us—the *Cyclops* of Euripides, presumably performed about the year 410 B.C.—but another, the *Ichneutæ*, or *Trackers*, of Sophocles (about 460 B.C.), has fairly recently come to light in incomplete form. From these, and from some representations on vases, it would seem that the typical play of this kind was a drama in which the chorus were satyrs, dressed in pieces of skin, with attached tails, round their middles, led by old Silenus himself. The themes must have been tales of adventure, involving a fair amount of merriment and ending happily. The *Cyclops* tells how Odysseus (Ulysses) out-tricks the one-eyed giant who seeks to destroy him; the *Trackers* is the earliest detective-drama on record, in which the chorus take in hand the search for Apollo's stolen cattle and discover the culprit in Hermes. In view, however, of the facts that so little is extant of this kind of play and that it is so dependent upon the ancient and forgotten cult of Dionysus, lord of the satyrs, we may pass it rapidly by; although, in any endeavour to reconstruct in our minds the conditions of an Athenian festival performance, the inclusion of these satyr shows should always be remembered. They formed part of the offerings of the tragic poets.

The chorus, as *The Suppliants* amply reveals, was the original core of the tragic drama. Here in this play the number of performers was fifty, and that number, the established size of the dithyrambic chorus also, appears to have been the traditional chorus strength when tragedy first took shape. Very soon, however, modifications were introduced. Perhaps because it was difficult for the performers to train themselves in the intricate melodies and in the complex dance movements demanded in the four parts of the tetralogy, Æschylus was responsible for splitting the fifty performers into four groups of twelve each; and twelve remained the stable size of the chorus until, some years later, Sophocles increased the number to fifteen. If the reduction of the chorus to twelve persons was due to practical considerations it has been presumed that the subsequent increase to fifteen was due to æsthetic reasons. Since the chorus was always split into parts, with a general chorus-leader and subsidiary leaders for the separate portions, the presence of fifteen performers permitted the entry of three lines of five persons each, and at the same time allowed the main chorus-leader to detach himself on occasion from his fellows, leaving still a balanced array of two half-choruses each consisting of seven persons.

On the rôle of the chorus it is wise to concentrate when reading the Greek drama, for the modifications introduced in its theatrical function provide a kind of record of the development of the tragic concept from the beginnings in Æschylus to the end in Euripides. In *The Suppliants*, as we have observed, the chorus is virtually the protagonist. This is the earliest, most primitive form, when the drama is dragging itself with difficulty out of the dithyramb. Sporadically, similarly composed plays are to be found much later in date, but in general the history of the Greek stage shows a gradual reduction of the chorus's participation in the dramatic action. It never disappears completely—that with which Æschylus started remains to the very conclusion—but less and less, as the years go by, does it play the major part assigned to it in earliest times.

At the very beginning Thespis drew drama out of the dithyramb by placing a single actor in opposition to the choral group and to its *exarchos*, or leader. When we speak of a single actor, however, two things must be understood. First, by the use of different masks and dress, one performer might, within the course of a single drama, assume various parts. And, second, the reference to a single actor does not imply that the Greek drama, from beginning to end, did not make free theatrical use of other, but mute, persons. In imaginatively reconstructing the productions of these dramas we must think of a king, Pelasgus or Menelaus or Agamemnon, entering the stage powerfully and richly attended; we must think of the Herald in *The Suppliants* as accompanied by many warriors ready to lay hands on the petitioning women; we must, too, be prepared to accept the appearance of named characters, often of some considerable importance, who, in excess of the stipulated number of 'actors,' come on the stage in silent rôles.

The allusion to 'stipulated number of actors' reminds us that Thespis' single player was soon given companions. Very hesitantly, as *The Suppliants* shows, Æschylus brought in a second actor—so hesitantly, in fact, that, with the slightest of changes, the entire action of this drama might have been carried through with the utilization of one performer only. There are only two scenes—when Danaus speaks to Pelasgus and when Pelasgus confronts the Herald—that positively demand the presence of two speaking actors on the stage at one time.

With this second actor Æschylus remained content until Sophocles, his younger contemporary, introduced a third speaking part. This, however, was the limit to which the Greek stage moved. Even the rebellious Euripides dared not go further, but was prepared to make use of diverse dramatic devices to cover up the consequences of the restriction in speaking rôles. A good example appears in his *Orestes*. During the earlier scenes Pylades appears as the traditional friend of the hero. At the close of the drama, however, the author needs to have on the stage Menelaus, Orestes, and the god Apollo, three actors all with speeches to deliver; in addition he needs the presence of a girl, Hermione, and of Pylades. There is no difficulty in leaving Hermione mute, but a slight problem arises in connexion with Pylades. Silent he stands throughout the scene, and then Menelaus turns to him with a question.

> Art thou too, Pylades, a partner in this bloody work?

he asks, and Orestes quickly intervenes with the words

> His silence says he is; so my saying it will suffice.

Later, to get him off the stage, Orestes gives his friend a cue for exit:

> Ho there! fire the palace from beneath, Electra; and, Pylades, my trusty friend, kindle the parapet of yonder walls.

Thus bidden, the mute hastily retires.

Conventions such as these must obviously be fully understood if we are to appreciate the Greek drama aright—although at the same time, despite these conventions born of a stage so unlike our own, we must ever stand amazed at the likeness between the dramatic concepts and methods of this age and those operative more than two thousand years later. The dramatist's task was essentially the same then as now: the presence of particular theatrical conventions creates no chasm between Æschylus and O'Neill, between Sophocles and Shaw.

THE STALWART WARRIOR: "THE PERSIANS"

Æschylus, author of *The Suppliants*, was born at Eleusis in the year 525 B.C., at the very time when Cambyses, monarch of Persia, led his victorious forces down into Egypt. Great things were happening as he grew to boyhood: the shuttle of destiny was weaving a glorious future for the city of his adoption, the little sea-town of Athens, although for a time the oracles seemed dark. Closer and closer came the looming power of Persia. When the dramatist-to-be was aged thirteen Darius, the successor of Cambyses, swept down over the Balkan peninsula; when he was thirty-five years old, even while *The Suppliants* was being performed at Athens, he stood alongside his brother and a band of his countrymen at Marathon, a plain on the eastern coast of Attica, and there helped to shatter the Persian hosts sent to destroy his city. The event was long remembered, and the poet's prowess on the occasion became almost legendary. When, an old man of sixty-nine, as he lay dying, afar off from his own land, in Sicily, he wrote his epitaph he recalled the event in bold Miltonic words. "Here Æschylus lies," he wrote:

> Here Æschylus lies, neath Gela's fertile soil, a guest
> From the Athenian land he loved the best:
> How stalwart in the fight was this Euphorion's son
> May the long-tressed Persian tell that fled from Marathon.

These were the words they carved in honour on his tomb.

Marathon, however, did not end the struggle. Ten years later, at Thermopylæ, a pass leading from Thessaly to the south, an heroic company of Spartans fought a long and weary battle with the invaders and were eventually overwhelmed by the force of numbers. Athens soon was in flames, and its memory would have perished had not the city's tiny ships, anticipating the great fight of the Armada, battled with the mightier Persian fleet at Salamis and so shattered the encroaching power of the East. Rebuilt, the Athenian state was freed to produce its inspiration for the world.

Remembering these things, we need feel no surprise that in the works of Æschylus there appears a grandeur, an elemental strength, that gives to his plays a quality of monumental majesty. He was, we feel, close to Olympus in his heroic stature and conceptions. Legend said that he was inspired by the god Dionysus, and it is known that he had been initiated into the mysteries of his native Eleusis, the mysteries that brought men near to the power of Demeter, the goddess of the Earth. In his plays the human seems very close to the godlike, the gods walk like men, and we breathe the air of ecstasy.

Nor need we feel surprise that in his second extant play, *The Persians*, produced in 472 B.C., eight years after the battle of Salamis, he has presented us with a drama at once unique in the annals of the Greek stage because of its adoption of contemporary subject-matter, and almost unique in the entire history of the theatre because it succeeds in viewing a stirring contemporary struggle from an almost Olympian height. This was no catchpenny theatrical exploitation of recent war; by his extraordinary strength Æschylus has attained to what might have appeared the impossible—the contemplation of living events, in which he himself had been directly and physically involved, *sub specie æternitatis.*

It is a magnificent achievement this. Set in distant Susa and thus removed from the contemporary spectators in space if not in time, rich in sonorous Persian names, which give to it an element of strangeness, it introduces a chorus of Persian Elders at a period shortly after the battle of Salamis. Xerxes, the son of Darius, is in Greece with his army, and the chorus expresses anxiety concerning the king's return and his "arm'd host blazing with gold." Atossa, the queen-mother, joins them in their talk, and this gives the author dramatic opportunity for the introduction of a reference to Athens and what that city stands for. Atossa inquires, "Where, in what clime, the tow'rs of Athens rise?" and the choral leader answers her:

LEADER: Far in the west, where sets th' imperial sun.
ATOSSA: Yet my son will'd the conquest of this town.
LEADER: May Greece through all her states bend to his power!
ATOSSA: Send they embattled numbers to the field?
LEADER: A force, that to the Medes hath wrought much woe. . . .
ATOSSA: From the strong bow wing they the barbed shaft?
LEADER: They grasp the stout spear, and the massy shield.
ATOSSA: What monarch reigns, whose power commands their ranks?
LEADER: Slaves to no lord, they own no kingly power.

A messenger now enters and relates, in memorable words, the progress of that battle of Salamis in which Æschylus himself had participated. A long catalogue of fallen Persian nobles is recited, but to the intensely dramatic query of the queen,

> Who is not fallen?
> What leader must we wail? What sceptred chief
> Dying hath left his troops without a lord?

the Messenger is able to reply,

> Xerxes himself lives, and beholds the light—

small comfort when the flower of Persian youth is gone.

After a long dirge by the chorus Atossa now calls upon the spirit of Darius, and that king's ghost rises from the tomb. This gives Æschylus the opportunity of introducing his basic tragic concept: the disaster fallen upon Persia has been wrought by *hubris*, overweening pride and ambition:

> With what a winged course the oracles
> Haste their completion! With the lightning's speed
> Jove on my son hath hurl'd his threaten'd vengeance:

> Yet I implor'd the gods that it might fall
> In time's late process: but when rashness drives
> Impetuous on, the scourge of Heav'n uprais'd
> Lashes the fury forward; hence these ills
> Pour headlong on my friends.

At the end of the drama, tattered, weary, worn, Xerxes enters. In the lament chanted by him and the chorus there is no idle indulgence in triumph, on Æschylus' part, over a defeated enemy. Rather is there a profound sympathy with the despair that has come upon this land through pride and a deep, tragic appreciation of the meaning of these contemporary events.

The Persians is a 'static' drama in that but little or no action occurs in it and that there is no real conflict involved in the presentation of the characters, yet its majesty of conception gives it an intensity that makes up for any absence of movement. The greatness of Æschylus is revealed nowhere more clearly than in this play wherein he invests the immediate and the topical with almost mythological grandeur.

AMONG THE GODS: "PROMETHEUS BOUND"

In Æschylus' thought the relation of God to man was ever paramount. It was, indeed, through this preoccupation that he succeeded with such power in establishing the tragic form of drama, for tragedy is in essence the theatrical representation of themes wherein man is set in relation to the universe. It is an essay, not in social relationships, but in the eternal problem of good and evil. Its quality is metaphysical. In tragedy the supernatural becomes, as it were, part of the natural: man and fate become one.

How deeply Æschylus was obsessed with such considerations is revealed in *Prometheus Bound* (c. 470 B.C.), a baffling drama in view of the fact that we have in it only a fragment of a trilogy and can but guess at the solution. We do not even know whether this play was a first part or a second. Presumably it was preceded by an action showing Prometheus—who, although a mortal, had been admitted to the secrets of Olympus—defying the anger of Zeus and bearing the precious treasure of fire to man, but of this we may not be sure. All that is certain is that the end of the trilogy must have introduced some kind of a reconciliation between the god and his enemy: beyond this we may only vaguely conjecture. Our feet are on sure ground nowhere save on the basis of the one extant portion of the greater whole.

This drama, since it showed Prometheus bound by Zeus' orders to a crag in the Caucasus, presented to the poet a serious problem in dramaturgy, and a measure of Æschylus' skill is to be found in a consideration of the manner in which he keeps our interest alive in the necessarily static action. At the beginning two symbolic characters, Force and Power, enter with the blacksmith god Hephaistos, commissioned to nail Prometheus to the rocks. Their attitude towards the task assigned to them immediately captures our attention: although compelled to do Zeus' bidding, Hephaistos shrinks from its necessity: "It must needs be done," he says to Power, "yet urge me not overmuch." In the contrast between these two figures the essential problem of the tragedy is set. Prometheus has betrayed his trust and therefore must be punished, yet even a god may feel pity at his fate, for his crime was motivated by pity for mankind.

Left alone, Prometheus cries out to the elements, and as he cries the chorus, consisting of the daughters of Oceanus, enter the orchestra. "What murmur hovereth near?" asks Prometheus:

> Once more the murmur
> I hear as of hovering birds;
> And the air is whirring with quick
> Beating of wings. For me
> There is fear, whatever approaches.

The chorus, however, is come in sympathy with the hero, and the skill of the dramatist is shown in the manner by which he thus draws a sharp contrast first between the dark, mighty figure of the man nailed to the rock and these women, light and free as the ocean's waves, and, second, between the gloom of the Caucasian rocks, elements of earth, and the bright elemental sprites of water. In a moment their father, Oceanus, appears, and once more contrast is afforded, since this monarch of the seas is presented as a good-willed but craven-hearted time-server, who is eager to give advice, unwilling to take any risks. In a choral chant Prometheus tells of his hopes for mankind, and again his words are broken by the appearance of the wretched Io, another victim of divine wrath, half demented as she flees from land to land pursued by a gadfly. Akin to her in misery, Prometheus reveals that Zeus' power cannot last for ever, and dares the gods' anger a second time by counselling her to a certain yet perilous way of escape. Still further contrast is provided by the entry of Hermes, the impertinent herald of Zeus: Prometheus remains obdurate, and at the end of the drama, amid lightning from heaven, the entire crag to which Prometheus has been bound sinks downward out of sight.

How to explain this tragedy it is difficult to say. One thing alone seems certain—that Æschylus viewed Zeus in what may be styled a progressive light. In his thought Zeus becomes a character, domineering and tyrannical at first, and later wrought, through experience and its accumulated wisdom, to assume the benign and just features of the monarch to whom pray the daughters of Danaus. Prometheus because of pride has done wrong in breaking his trust, yet his opposition to the tyrannical power is worthy of admiration. His pride and the cruel implacability of the god will alike be modified and tempered in the final reconciliation.

Perhaps, with its wealth of mythological reference, this drama set at the very beginning of time may not make as great appeal to modern readers as others among the plays of the Greeks, yet its majestic proportions allied to the skill by which the contrasting characters are endowed with vitality reveal, more than any other of his plays, the essential secret of Æschylus.

THE TALE OF THE HOUSE OF ATREUS: THE "ORESTEIA"

Out of all the poet's ninety plays only seven remain, but among these seven there is fortunately one complete trilogy, the *Oresteia* (458 B.C.), comprising *Agamemnon*, *The Choephori*, and *The Eumenides*. Of another trilogy we possess the final part, *The Seven against Thebes* (467 B.C.), but, being nothing save an act in a larger drama, this deserves less attention than the later complete work.

Before commencing to read *Agamemnon* one must have in clear view those antecedent events which would have been known to practically every Greek spectator, and the knowledge of which placed the tragic dramatist in a peculiar position with respect to his subject-matter. In a fragment of one of Antiphanes' comedies, *Poetry*, we listen to a comic playwright complaining:

> The writer of tragedy is a lucky fellow! The audience always knows the plot as soon as his play begins. All the poet has to do is to give a jog to their memories. He just says "Œdipus": they know all the rest—father, Laius; mother, Jocasta; daughters, sons, what's to come and what is past. If he but utter the one word "Alcmeon," the very children at once repeat: "He went mad and killed his mother; in a minute Adrastus will come in a rage and go out again. . . ." We can't do that, we have to invent everything—new names, the action before the play begins, the present situation, the climax, the opening. If a

comic character forgets any of this, he's hissed off the stage, but a tragic character can forget as much as he likes.

This complaint, exaggeratedly as it may be expressed, is basically justified, and in our reading of the tragic dramas we must make full imaginative allowance for this body of common knowledge on the part of the spectators. Thus, in witnessing a play on Agamemnon, the memories of the audience would have carried them far back in time to the story of two brothers, Atreus and Thyestes, sons of Pelops. Thyestes sins by seducing his sister-in-law, and Atreus takes a grisly vengeance. Pretending to be reconciled, he bids Thyestes to his house and sets before him a rich banquet—a banquet, however, which he reveals to be composed of the bodies of his brother's own children, thus served up before their father. As a result a curse has descended on the house of Atreus. Agamemnon, son of Atreus, has married Clytemnestra, and, when the former is absent in Troy, his wife is seduced by Ægisthus, son of Thyestes. Living in Agamemnon's palace, the pair of lovers await the return of its lord. It is at this moment in time, ten years after the departure of Agamemnon for Troy, that the trilogy begins.

When we turn to the *Oresteia* we immediately recognize that the drama has moved far from the early days of *The Suppliants* and *Prometheus Bound*, and, in particular, that three changes have occurred to influence its composition. The first is a change in physical representation. *The Suppliants* was set on a lonely sea-coast, *Prometheus Bound* amid the Caucasian wilds; *Agamemnon* opens before a palace front. By this time the scene-building, or the *skene* (σκηνή) —which gave us our word 'scene'—has been added to the early auditorium and orchestra. No doubt simpler in appearance than was the *skene* of later theatres, it still must have had some slightly raised platform in front and a background consisting of a wall, ornamented with columns and broken by one large centre door of entrance, together with two smaller doors placed at the sides. From now on there was a tendency on the part of the dramatists to choose for their fictional localities the courtyard of a palace or of a temple: rudimentary scene-painting already had been introduced —it is said at the inspiration of Æschylus—but the playwrights found their easiest path was to accept the wall and the columns as they stood and to utilize these directly.

The second change concerns the actors. About the year 470 B.C. Sophocles appeared as a successor to Æschylus, and very soon after his début he added a third to the two speaking parts allowed by his predecessor. This immediately made for a rapid development of dramatic dialogue as opposed to choral chant; it offered greater opportunities for interplay of character; it permitted variety of incident; above all, it induced the playwrights to consider more closely the question of dramatic technique.

This development of dramatic technique is the third great change that had come into being under the influence of Sophocles. The Greek tragedy now assumed a definite form and was divided into a number of recognized parts. First came the prologue introducing the theme, indicating the locality, sometimes even the time of day; this was followed by the entrance-song of the chorus, known as the *parodos*; thereafter followed five 'episodes,' portions of dialogue, separated by five choral odes; finally, the drama was brought to a conclusion with the exodus, or exit-song, of the chorus. From this division of parts came, in later Hellenistic times, the traditional five acts of drama.

These altered circumstances must be taken fully into account as we turn to the *Oresteia*.

The *Agamemnon* opens in front of a palace, and in the dim light of dawn we can discern a lonely figure on the roof. His words at once proclaim the palace to be the home of Agamemnon, son of Atreus, and we learn that he himself is a Watchman, placed here by Clytemnestra to give news when a beacon-fire appears on a distant height. This will be the herald of Troy's fall. Suddenly a distant light is seen, and the Watchman retires to present his tidings, while the chorus enter singing of the house of Atreus, of the long, ten-year absence of their lord, and particularly of one episode of the Trojan expedition—when the Greek fleet was held back by contrary winds, and when Agamemnon, the leader of the host, sacrificed his own daughter Iphigenia that the gods might be propitious:

> And so he steeled his heart—ah, well-a-day—
>   Aiding a war for one false woman's sake,
>   His child to slay,
>   And with her spilt blood make
> An offering, to speed the ships upon their way!
>
>   Lusting for war, the bloody arbiters
> Closed heart and ears, and would not hear nor heed
>   The girl-voice plead,
> "Pity me, Father!" nor her prayers,
>   Nor tender, virgin years.
>
>   So when the chant of sacrifice was done,
>   Her father bade the youthful priestly train
> Raise her, like some poor kid, above the altar-stone,

From where amid her robes she lay
Sunk all in swoon away—
Bade them, as with the bit that mutely tames the steed,
Her fair lips' speech refrain,
Lest she should speak a curse on Atreus' home and seed.

"Lest she should speak a curse on Atreus' home and seed"—these words give us our first clue to Æschylus' treatment of the Agamemnon story. Outwardly there is a curse upon this house; in a certain sense all the characters are doomed by fate, have no choice but to pursue paths allotted to them. Yet a strange paradox exists here. Already it is evident that this absent king, Agamemnon, has committed a crime, and, since, immediately after these words, the queen, Clytemnestra, appears, our imagination connects the story of Iphigenia with her: she, queen and mother, has been sadly wronged that thus her daughter has been sacrificed in order that a fleet might sail. In this paradoxical sense character is destiny: whatever happens to Agamemnon in this ill-fated house will be of his own creation.

In their chant the members of the chorus have revealed themselves to be old men—"grey dishonoured eld, feeble of frame, unfit . . . to join the warrior array that then went forth unto the fray." Once more, in providing a contrast between the woman Clytemnestra and these aged men—a contrast similar to that between the man-god Prometheus and the daughters of Oceanus—Æschylus has shown his innate dramatic sense. She tells them of the meaning of the beacon-fire: Troy is fallen. Some there are who doubt her word, think she may be deluding herself; there is a confusion of thought and of talk, when, in this idealized time of Greek tragedy, a Herald arrives to announce the truth of the tidings and to say that Agamemnon, homeward bound, has been separated from the rest of his fleet. With fine dramatic irony the chorus now sings of the woe fallen upon Troy through a woman, and hints unknowingly at what is to come to this palace and its occupants:

Woe springs from wrong, the plant is like the seed—
While Right, in honour's house, doth its own likeness breed.
Some past impiety, some grey old crime,
Breeds the young curse, that wantons in our ill,
Early or late, when haps th'appointed time—
And out of light brings power of darkness still,
A master-fiend, a foe, unseen, invincible;
A pride accursed, that broods upon the race
And home in which dark Atè holds her sway—
Sin's child and Woe's, that wears its parents' face.

Again in the world of idealized time, Agamemnon now appears, royally attended, seated in a chariot, while another chariot bears the person of Cassandra, daughter of Priam and dedicated vestal, to touch whom is impiety, and yet whom Agamemnon has reft away from her altar and her home. With a rather heavy, bombastic speech he addresses the chorus and is greeted in honeyed words by Clytemnestra, who, to honour him, spreads rich crimson tapestries from the chariot to the palace. Agamemnon knows that such honour is fit only for the gods, refuses to set foot on the "rich dyes," but, puffed up with self-esteem and guiled by her flattery, at length consents and walks over the crimson cloth into the palace. As he goes he adds another to the grievances of Clytemnestra by bidding her care for his mistress, Cassandra.

Left alone, the chorus gives expression to its dark foreboding:

> Wherefore for ever on the wings of fear
>> Hovers a vision drear
> Before my boding heart? a strain,
> Unbidden and unwelcome, thrills mine ear,
>> Oracular of pain.

Immediately thereafter Clytemnestra comes from the palace and cruelly, rudely, addresses Cassandra, bidding her also go within. Although she maintains silence in the presence of the queen, as soon as Clytemnestra departs Cassandra, the priestess-prophetess, dismally foreshadows what is to follow. First, in dark words, she shows her awareness of the bloodstained story of the house of Atreus, and then her chanting ecstasy hints at what must be:

> God! a new sight! a net, a snare of hell,
> Set by her hand—herself a snare more fell!
>> A wedded wife, she slays her lord,
>> Helped by another hand!

The chorus chides her for her boding speech, but becomes disturbed as her words continue, and still more disturbed when, after she has entered the palace, a loud cry is heard from within. There follows a highly dramatic scene where the individual members of the chorus speculate confusedly on the meaning of the cry—confusion stilled when Clytemnestra appears, blood on her forehead, and when the palace doors open to display the slain bodies of Agamemnon and Cassandra. The queen exults in her crime, the while the chorus upbraids her: their words are full of love and honour for their dead lord, hers emphasize the foul wrongs done to her by his faithlessness and by his sacrifice of Iphigenia. A moment later Ægisthus

comes upon the stage, proud of having avenged himself upon the
son of the man who had set the ghastly banquet before Thyestes.
So incensed is he by the reproaches of the old men of the chorus
that he is about to fall upon them when Clytemnestra intervenes.
She will have no more of killing and stays Ægisthus' angry hand:
in her words as she addresses him one senses a hint of weariness:

> Nay, enough, enough, my champion! we will smite and slay no
> more.
> Already have we reaped enough the harvest-field of guilt:
> Enough of wrong and murder, let no other blood be spilt. . . .
>   Let the cur-pack growl and yell:
> I and thou will rule the palace and will order all things well.

Her speech is instinct with unconscious dramatic irony, for the next
play, *The Choephori*, is to tell of the vengeance fallen on the murderers: murder is not, as Clytemnestra thinks, an end, but is merely
a beginning. Before turning to the second drama, however, it is
essential to survey Æschylus' dramatic purpose as revealed in
Agamemnon. That this play is executed with consummate skill and
majestic mastery is at once apparent. The tension is subtly built up
and varied: the calm opening in the darkness before dawn, with the
sleepy Watchman at his weary vigil; the sudden glow of the
beacon; the nervous excitement of Clytemnestra; the doubts of
the chorus; the triumphant entry of Agamemnon, and his wife's
steel-lipped greeting; the insulting of Cassandra, followed by the
priestess's ecstatic ravings; Clytemnestra's defence after the murder,
and the approach towards a physical struggle between Ægisthus
and the chorus—all these give to the play a dramatic movement
intense and absorbing. In the midst of the movement characters
shine forth brightly: Clytemnestra nursing her wrongs; Ægisthus,
love-besotten and querulously intent on vengeance; Agamemnon,
of true heroic stature, yet guilty of the sin of pride, willing to step
like a god into his house, willing like a god to make the dedicated
Cassandra his mistress. This intent upon character-delineation
makes *Agamemnon* a much more human play than any we have so
far considered; yet we must not lose sight of the fact that here we
are confronted with no domestic drama: here we are in the presence
of essential tragedy, metaphysical, baffling, infinite in its implications. The problem of evil is that on which Æschylus sets his gaze,
and the gods are ever in his mind as he deals with the human
action.

The story, of course, is not yet done. When Clytemnestra greets

Agamemnon she makes excuse for the absence of his son, the boy Orestes. This Orestes is the hero of *The Choephori*, so called because the chorus is composed of a band of 'Libation-bearers,' who are the companions of Orestes' sister Electra. The action opens before the tomb of Agamemnon. Two men, seen from their dress to have travelled from afar, enter the stage and reveal themselves as Orestes, now grown to manhood, and his close friend, Pylades. On the altar the former reverently places two locks of his own hair. This prologue scene is followed by the entry of the chorus, together with Electra: at the altar she finds the locks, and immediately recognizes them as belonging to her brother. Orestes reveals himself to her, and, after a moment of doubting suspicion, tearfully she embraces him and learns that he has come at the god Apollo's command to seek vengeance. A great wave of ecstatic song from the chorus ensues, and Orestes hastily outlines his plan of action. He enters the palace; the cry of Ægisthus in his death-agony is heard; and at last the vengeful son confronts his mother. A moment's compassion comes to him:

CLYTEMNESTRA: Woe, woe! Ægisthus, spouse and champion, slain!
ORESTES: What, lov'st the man? then in his grave lie down,
   Be his in death, desert him nevermore!
CLYTEMNESTRA: Stay, child, and fear to strike. O son, this breast
   Pillowed thine head full oft, while, drowsed with sleep,
   Thy toothless mouth drew mother's milk from me.
ORESTES: Can I my mother spare? speak, Pylades.
PYLADES: Where then would fall the hest Apollo gave
   At Delphi, where the solemn compact sworn?
   Choose thou the hate of all men, not of gods.

Thus bidden, Orestes drives Clytemnestra within, but hardly has she been slain before the murderer sees what is visible to him alone —a grisly throng of "Gorgon shapes" with "dusky robes and hair unwound," the Furies sent to torment him.

It is difficult to interpret *The Choephori* aright. Brilliant as is the conception and glorious the language, one has the impression that Æschylus is not as deeply interested in this part of the theme as he was in *Agamemnon*. He is inclined, as it were, to hurry on with the action, laying no stress, for example, on such potentially dramatic scenes as the recognition by Electra of the brother she has not seen for so long or the confronting of Clytemnestra by her son. The whole of the action might almost be regarded as merely the necessary preliminary for that which is to follow—the expiation and reconciliation of spirit revealed in *The Eumenides*.

The Furies form the final chorus in this third play. The scene now is the temple at Delphi, to which Orestes, worn with suffering, has at last come in his wanderings. A Pythian priestess goes to the shrine and shrinks back in terror: at the central altar she has seen a tattered, bloodstained figure, and

> Lo, in front of him,
> Crouched on the altar-steps, a grisly band
> Of women . . . not like women they,
> But Gorgons rather . . . black, and all their shape
> The eye's abomination to behold.

At this the main doors of the temple open, showing the scene as the priestess has described it, and revealing also the god-figure of Apollo. The ghost of Clytemnestra rises, awakening the Furies from their sleep; they demand their prey while Apollo tries to protect his suppliant. Sternly he admonishes them:

> Know, that above the marriage-bed ordained
> For man and woman standeth Right as guard,
> Enhancing sanctity of troth-plight sworn;
> Therefore, if thou art placable to those
> Who have their consort slain, nor will'st to turn
> On them the eye of wrath, unjust art thou
> In hounding to his doom the man who slew
> His mother.

Pallas, he declares, Pallas, the goddess of reason, shall decide.

After this the scene is supposed to change. In all probability Orestes and the Furies simply move over to one of the side-doors and imaginatively are presumed to have made the long journey from Apollo's temple at Delphi to the temple, in Athens, of Pallas Athene. Thus in this movement time and place are alike truncated: both exist in an imaginatively ideal world. Before the goddess Orestes and the Furies put their case. For the latter the old law of implacable vengeance alone has validity:

> When from womb of Night we sprang, on us this labour
> Was laid and shall abide.
> Gods immortal are ye, yet beware ye touch not
> That which is our pride!
> None may come beside us gathered round the blood-feast—
> For us no garments white
> Gleam on a festal day; for us a darker fate is,
> Another darker rite.

That is mine hour when falls an ancient line—
 When in the household's heart
The God of blood doth slay by kindred hands,—
 Then do we bear our part:
On him who slays we sweep with chasing cry:
 Though he be triply strong,
We wear and waste him; blood atones for blood,
 New pain for ancient wrong.

Athene decides that the case must be tried and argued before the twelve judges of the Areopagus, the highest court in Athens. On the one side, the Furies mutter and grumble:

 Now they are all undone, the ancient laws,
  If here the slayer's cause
 Prevail—

while, on the other, Apollo comes as witness in Orestes' defence. The judges place their votes in an urn, and it is found that they are equally divided—whereupon Athene gives her voice for Orestes, and to the threatening chorus, who cry that they have been dishonoured by the younger gods, she offers a new rôle: if they agree to follow her they will win honour as spirits of mercy. After some hesitation they accept, and the play ends with a kind of mystical chant as the Furies, now become Eumenides, figures of goodwill, leave the stage:

 With loyalty we lead you; proudly go,
 Night's childless children, to your home below!
  (*O citizens, awhile from words forbear!*)
 To darkness' deep primeval lair,
 Far in Earth's bosom, downward fare,
  Adored with prayer and sacrifice.
  (*O citizens, forbear your cries!*)
 Pass hitherward, ye powers of Dread,
 With all your former wrath allayed,
  Into the heart of this loved land;
 With joy unto your temple wend,
 The while upon your steps attend
  The flames that feed upon the brand—
 (*Now, now ring out your chant, your joy's acclaim!*)
  Behind them, as they downward fare,
  Let holy hands libations bear,
   And torches' sacred flame.
  All-seeing Zeus and Fate come down
  To battle fair for Pallas' town!
 Ring out your chant, ring out your joy's acclaim!

This is the very apotheosis of patriotism. For Æschylus the problem of evil, which he sought to explore in the *Oresteia*, is to be explained only by taking it to the uttermost extremes—to primeval times before the birth of history when the universe was peopled by titans and by gods, and to the conditions of his own age, into the very halls of the Areopagus. That final chorus chant of *The Eumenides* is a fitting epilogue to his entire dramatic achievement, with its supernatural figures of the old law, led by Pallas Athene, trooping downward towards the elements that gave them being, and with its direct appeal to those citizens, the fellows of the poet, who sit watching the first performance of his tragic trilogy. Fitting, too, is the concept they embody. Evil has been set loose in the world; death and torment and darkness have come in its wake, and Clytemnestra's hope that by the mere exercise of the human will it can be, at any point, given an end has been proved naught save an idle dream; yet the end does come, and out of the suffering new vision arises: the Furies are transformed into the spirits of mercy.

The first dramatist whose work has come down to us was a mighty master.

CHAPTER II

THE GLORY OF THE GREEK THEATRE: SOPHOCLES

ÆSCHYLUS was obviously a pioneer: he was compelled to forge the very instruments from which his art was fashioned, and there must ever be amazement that, thus handicapped, he was able to accomplish so much. His position in relation to the theatre of his time bore many parallels to that of Marlowe in the Elizabethan Age. If he wrought deeper and finer things than Marlowe in the course of his brief existence was permitted to create, like him he served as a forerunner to one, if not greater, at least more fortunately circumstanced than himself. If Æschylus is Marlowe, Sophocles is Shakespeare.

When Sophocles was born in the lovely town of Colonus about 495 B.C. the struggle with Persia was at its fiercest, but by the time he was a boy of fifteen Athens had secured her independence. Events were moving rapidly in these distant days, and there was a world of difference between the man who, at forty-five, fought at Salamis and the youth, thirty years his junior, who was chosen for his beauty and his skill in music to lead the chorus of boys who sang a pæan of joy round the trophy erected to commemorate that victory. The one spent his early years in conflict, the other was destined to reap full advantage of the peace which brought Athens to its greatest glory. Under Pericles he saw the Parthenon rise majestically: he was privileged to gaze on the wonders of Pheidias' art when these were fresh and young.

Contemporary records tell of his wide accomplishments. Extraordinarily handsome, he was a noted athlete; the gifts of learning were his; for his dancing and his musical talents he was famous. Surrounded by friends, esteemed by his countrymen, he lived a life of even tenor, balanced, calm, and classically triumphant. He was καλὸς κ'ἀγαθός—beautiful and good—the ideal of perfection. Even in his death he was fortunate, for, passing away at eighty-nine years of age, he was spared seeing the might of the Athenian navy annihilated at Ægospotami in 405 B.C. This was the decisive battle in the Peloponnesian War and the ominous sign that Athens' brief flowering was near its end.

Amid these surroundings Sophocles might readily have become an easy sentimentalist, but the basis of his city's culture was not of so light a kind. There was strength here, and thought, and passion. Above all, there was deep interest in man and in man's relations to the universe. The dark and the terrible formed part of the woof of Greek philosophy. Of a consequence most of Sophocles' dramas, instead of dealing—as they might well have done—with the easy loveliness of life, take us through the world of suffering: Antigone dies immured in a rock and the eyes of Œdipus are cruelly torn out. The tragic sense was deeply implanted in him, and his calm was not won by a refusal to contemplate suffering. It was this fortunate man who wrote: "Never to have been born is much the best."

As a dramatist he necessarily benefited much from the pioneering efforts of his predecessor Æschylus. To the latter's two actors, as we have seen, he added a third, and the consummate skill with which he handled his dialogue showed that he had learned much from the earlier works. Æschylus had improved the stage: Sophocles improved it further and gave it flexibility. Contemporary record testifies to his inventions in the field of scene-painting, and there is reason to believe that he was the first to provide the persons of his tragedies with a defined background. A still more significant step was taken when he discarded the Æschylean trilogy and substituted therefor separate dramas, each with its own beginning, middle, and end, works self-inclusive and self-complete. By taking this step he moved the early theatre vastly nearer the dramatic form of the later Western stage.

Æschylus had been, like his immediate predecessors, the entire director of his own writings. It was expected then that the poet, besides penning his lines, should provide the accompanying music, train the chorus, and even take the leading histrionic rôles. With Sophocles, despite his varied accomplishments, we begin to see the breaking-up of these functions: the actor becomes an interpreter of the poet's words, the musician is a separate artist, and the chorus may be trained by one other than the author. Perhaps this breaking-up of theatrical functions came by chance. Although record tells of Sophocles' magnificent performance in the parts of the maiden Nausikaa, when he held an audience spellbound as he gave an exhibition of expert ball-playing, and of the youthful lyric Thamyras, it is known that his voice was too weak for weightier rôles. As a result, he was forced to depend on the services of another.

At the same time, this separation of actor and poet was a natural development. In the early days of Æschylus there were no trained actors, and the poet was consequently forced to be his own interpreter, but when Sophocles came to write there must have been a number of men in Athens with stage experience, and clearly it was to the author's advantage to relieve himself of this part of the performance in order to concentrate on his writing and on general direction. Here is the true beginning of professional playing, and it is interesting to observe that in the Greek age the actor, instead of being the despised slave of Roman times or a person only half removed from an Elizabethan vagrant, held a high position in public esteem.

THE HOUSE OF ATREUS AGAIN: "ELECTRA"

Of all Sophocles' one hundred and twenty dramas only seven have come down to us complete, together with a sorry yet precious fragment of one of his satyr plays. Although he first appeared in 471 B.C. and had already won a victory over Æschylus in 468 B.C., the first of these seven tragedies, the *Antigone*, was not written until about the year 441, when his position was fully established. About the same time came his *Ajax*; *Œdipus Tyrannus* dates from about ten years later; *Electra* and the *Trachiniæ* must have come between 420 and 414, *Philoctetes* in 409, when the playwright was eighty-six years old; while *Œdipus at Colonus* was presented posthumously in 402.

Of these *Antigone* is perhaps the most appealing to the modern consciousness, but, before dealing with this drama, we may do well to examine the later *Electra*, since this treats of the same theme as Æschylus' *Oresteia*, and in its modifications well indicates the essential differences between the two playwrights.

In this *Electra*, as at the beginning of the *Agamemnon*, it is time of dawn. Three figures appear before us—an aged Tutor, Orestes, and Pylades. Orestes has returned to effect his revenge and is discussing his plans with the old man when a cry from within the palace reminds him of the sister whom he has not seen for so many years. Electra now enters with a chorus of women of Mycenæ, the latter sympathetic but counselling her to forget her woes and to give stay to her self-torment. Suddenly a new character enters—Chrysothemis, Electra's sister. Anxiously she advises caution and the acceptance of authority:

Sister, why com'st thou once more to declaim
In public at the outer gate? Has time
Not schooled thee to desist from idle rage?
I too, my sister, chafe no less than thou
At our sad fortunes, and had I the power,
Would make it plain how I regard our masters.
But in the storm 'tis best to reef the sail,
Nor utter threats we cannot execute.
I would thou wert likeminded; yet I know
Justice is on thy side, and I am wrong.
Yet if I am to keep my liberty,
I needs must bow before the powers that be.

At once, in a flash of anger, Electra displays her true temper. "O shame," she cries,

that thou, the child of such a sire,
Should'st him forget and take thy mother's part! . . .
Shall we to all our ills add cowardice?

Her spirit is implacable; unshakeable the devotion she bears to the memory of her father.

After this scene follows a scene between Electra and her mother. It is apparent that there is deadly enmity between them; their words to each other are bitter, smouldering in hate. Now the Tutor appears, in accordance with the plan devised by Orestes. Pretending to have been sent by a Phocian known to Clytemnestra, he tells her that Orestes is dead, that his ashes are in the urn he bears. While Electra sinks in woe, Clytemnestra is troubled by mingled passions:

CHORUS-LEADER: Alas, alas! our ancient masters' line,
                So it appears, hath perished root and branch.
CLYTEMNESTRA: Are these glad tidings? Rather would I say
                Sad, but of profit. Ah, how hard my lot
                When I must look for safety to my losses!
TUTOR: Why, lady, why downhearted at my news?
CLYTEMNESTRA: Strange is the force of motherhood; a mother,
                Whate'er her wrongs, can ne'er forget her child.
TUTOR: So it would seem our coming was in vain.
CLYTEMNESTRA: Nay, not in vain. How canst thou say "in vain,"
                If of his death thou bring'st convincing proof,
                Who from my life drew life, and yet, estranged,
                Forgat the breasts that suckled him, forgat
                A mother's tender nurture, fled his home,
                And since that day has never seen me more,

CLYTEMNESTRA:	Slandered me as the murderer of his sire
	And breathed forth vengeance?—Neither night nor day
	Kind slumber closed these eyes, and immanent dread
	Of death each minute stretched me on the rack.
	But now on this glad day, of terror rid
	From him and her, a deadlier plague than he,
	That vampire who was housed with me to drain
	My very life blood—now, despite her threats
	Methinks that I shall pass my days in peace.

Left alone as Clytemnestra and the Tutor enter the palace, Electra gives vent to expression of her woe. The chorus in vain endeavours to comfort her, and bitter gall comes when Chrysothemis arrives, eager and excited, to say that Orestes must have returned, for she has found his locks on the altar. Miserably Electra tells her of the news of their brother's death, but warns her that, although he is gone, she is determined to act unaided: Chrysothemis, who a moment before had been saying she would assist Electra to the limit of her power, now shrinks back, looks timorously around to see if her words have been overheard, advises caution—while the chorus adds to her prudent arguments. Electra, however, is adamant:

CHORUS-LEADER:	Hearken! for mortal man there is no gift
	Greater than forethought and sobriety.
ELECTRA:	'Tis as I thought: before thy answer came
	I knew full well thou wouldst refuse thine aid.
	Unaided then and by myself I'll do it,
	For done it must be, though I work alone.

A choral chant follows, and immediately after it is completed Orestes and Pylades enter: Electra takes the urn supposed to contain the ashes, and there is a scene of gentle pathos as brother and sister, she not knowing who he is, converse together, until at last he reveals himself:

ELECTRA:	Ah! woe for thee, Orestes, woe is me,
	If I am not to give thee burial.
ORESTES:	Guard well thy lips; thou hast no right to mourn.
ELECTRA:	No right to mourn a brother who is dead!
ORESTES:	To speak of him in this wise is not meet.
ELECTRA:	What, am I so dishonoured of the dead?
ORESTES:	Of none dishonoured; this is not thy part.
ELECTRA:	Not if Orestes' ashes here I hold?
ORESTES:	They are not his, though feigned to pass for his.

[He gently takes the urn from her

ELECTRA:　Where then is my unhappy brother's grave?
ORESTES:　There is no grave; we bury not the quick.
ELECTRA:　What sayst thou, boy?
ORESTES:　　　Nothing that is not true.
ELECTRA:　He lives?
ORESTES:　　　As surely as I am alive.

In joy she embraces him, and eagerly they discuss what they shall do—too eagerly, for now the Tutor comes to warn them:

TUTOR:　Fools! madmen! are ye weary of your lives?
　　　　Or are your natural wits too dull to see
　　　　That ye are standing, not upon the brink,
　　　　But in the midst of mortal jeopardy?
　　　　Nay, had I not kept watch this weary while,
　　　　Here at the door, your plot had slipped inside
　　　　Ere ye yourselves had entered.

Orestes, Pylades, and the Tutor enter the palace while Electra remains to guard against the return of Ægisthus: Clytemnestra cries out in death agony, and Orestes comes on the stage once more—a wisp of doubt in his mind:

ELECTRA:　How have ye sped, Orestes?
ORESTES:　　　　　　All within
　　　　Is well, if Phœbus' oracle spake well.

On the arrival of Ægisthus the doors are opened to display the shrouded corpse of Clytemnestra, which he believes to be that of Orestes, and a tensely dramatic scene ensues:

ÆGISTHUS:　Take from the face the face-cloth; I, as kin,
　　　　I too would pay my tribute of lament.
ORESTES:　Lift it thyself; 'tis not for me but thee
　　　　To see and kindly greet what lieth here.
ÆGISTHUS:　Well said, so will I. [*To* ELECTRA] If she be within,
　　　　Go call me Clytemnestra, I would see her—
ORESTES:　She is beside thee; look not otherwhere.
　　　　　　[ÆGISTHUS *removes the face-cloth from the corpse.*
ÆGISTHUS:　O horror!
ORESTES:　　　　Why dost start? is the face strange?
ÆGISTHUS:　Who spread the net wherein, O woe is me,
　　　　I lie enmeshed?
ORESTES:　　　　Hast thou not learnt ere this
　　　　The dead of whom thou spakest are alive?
ÆGISTHUS:　Alas! I read thy riddle; 'tis none else
　　　　Than thou, Orestes, whom I now address.

ORESTES: A seer so wise, and yet befooled so long!
ÆGISTHUS: O I am spoiled, undone! yet suffer me,
        One little word.
ELECTRA: Brother, in heaven's name
        Let him not speak a word or plead his cause.
        When a poor wretch is in the toils of fate
        What can a brief reprieve avail him? No,
        Slay him outright and having slain him give
        His corse to such grave-makers as is meet,
        Far from our sight.

Ægisthus is driven within and dies. The end has come.

Even from such a brief summary as the above it must be immediately apparent that Sophocles' *Electra* moves in a world different from that of Æschylus' *Oresteia*. Quite apart from the subtler building of dramatic climaxes, we see that his purpose is entirely distinct from what his predecessor had aimed at. There is no doubt expressed concerning the justice of Orestes' action: a very slight ironic hint is in the words he speaks after the murder of his mother—"All within is well, if Phœbus' oracle spake well"—but that is all. The whole action of the play has been taken down from the elemental world, closer to the world of ordinary life. Condensed as the conversations are, they approach reality more closely than those of Æschylus, and the practical considerations of common life now play their part. In Æschylus' plays the characters stand and speak in idealized isolation; Sophocles causes the Tutor to warn the brother and sister that their words might have been overheard in the palace. We are in the world of men here, not in the world of eternity.

Sophocles' aim is to explain the legendary story in human terms, and to effect this aim he concentrates, not on the theme itself, but on one character. All else is subordinated to Electra. The chorus does not take any dominant position; Orestes and the Tutor are but broadly outlined. In Electra, however, there is a psychological study such as appears nowhere in any of Æschylus' works. Her position in this household is clearly indicated, and as scene follows scene her personality unfolds before us. If any persons stand beside her they are Chrysothemis and Clytemnestra—for this is a tragedy of women rather than of men—but even they are largely foils for the heroine. What Sophocles is interested in is the situation in which one main and two subsidiary characters appear: the mother, unable to hate her son yet living in deadly terror of his return; one daughter, devoted to her father's memory and passing her days in impotent hate; the other, sympathetic towards Electra, yet timorous, prudent, cautious. The drama is one composed of a single fully drawn portrait set against a background of interplay of character.

Electra is a much more assured piece of dramatic art than *The Choephori*, yet something essential has been lost. The metaphysical has ceded place to the natural, and, despite the high idealization in the treatment of the story, we feel that we have drawn somewhat away from the presence of majesty, that we are coming tremblingly near to the realm of the domestic drama.

THE HUMAN LAW AND THE LAW OF THE SPIRIT: "ANTIGONE"

The scene between Electra and Chrysothemis has a close parallel in an earlier and a greater play by Sophocles. *Antigone* presents what *Electra* lacks.

In approaching this drama, once more the preceding events associated with a doomed house must be appreciated. The house is the house of Laius in Thebes. Laius has sinned, and upon his son Œdipus the curse has descended. After many torments Œdipus dies, leaving behind him two sons, Eteocles and Polyneices, who, quarrelling, die by each other's hands in battle. The lordship of Thebes is taken by Creon, who gives the body of Eteocles all due rites, but issues a proclamation to the effect that the body of his brother—because he led an alien host against his native city—shall remain unburied. Of the children of Œdipus only two are left, the girls Antigone and Ismene, the former betrothed to Creon's son, Hæmon.

In the prologue to Sophocles' drama the two sisters enter. Antigone has heard of the proclamation, and, although she knows that death is decreed for anyone who defies the proclamation, she is determined to give honour to her brother's corpse. In a few short lines the personality of the pair is searingly revealed to us—Antigone, devoted to her brother, obdurately intent on her self-appointed mission, herself perhaps half in love with easeful death, Ismene, more fragile, afraid of what her sister's obstinacy may bring. "Listen, Ismene," says Antigone,

> Creon buried our brother Eteocles
> With military honours, gave him a soldier's funeral,
> And it was right that he should; but Polyneices,
> Who fought as bravely and died as miserably—
> They say that Creon has sworn
> No one shall bury him, no one mourn for him,
> But his body must lie in the fields, a sweet treasure

> For carrion birds to find as they search for food.
> That is what they say, and our good king Creon is
> To announce it publicly; and the penalty—
> Stoning to death in the public square!
> > > > There it is,
> And now you can prove what you are:
> A true sister, or a traitor to your family.

In Ismene's reply her character is enshrined: "Poor Antigone! But what can I do about it?" How can Polyneices' body be buried, she inquires: "You have just said the new law forbids it. . . . Think of the danger! Think what Creon will do!" Equally characteristic are Antigone's words:

> > > > If that is what you think,
> I should not want you, even if you asked to come.
> You have made your choice, you can be what you want to be.
> But I will bury him; and if I must die,
> I say that this crime is holy: I shall lie down
> With him in death, and I shall be as dear
> To him as he to me.
> > > > It is the dead,
> Not the living, who make the longest demands:
> We die for ever.

Ismene's terror is partly for herself, but largely also for her sister:

ISMENE:	Antigone,
	I am so afraid for you!
ANTIGONE:	You need not be:
	You have yourself to consider, after all.
ISMENE:	But no one must hear of this, you must tell no one!
	I will keep it a secret, I promise!
ANTIGONE:	Oh, tell it! Tell every one!
	Think how they'll hate you when it all comes out
	If they learn that you knew about it all the time!

To this last cry Ismene's reply is once again revealing, but now rather of Antigone than of herself: "You are so on fire with a plan so ghastly cold!"

The entry-song of the chorus follows, and the isolation of the heroine is increased when we realize that this chorus is made up, not of women or even of youths, but of old men, grown chill and cautious with age. With fine irony they chant of the Theban success in battle; this will be a day of joy:

> Our temples shall be sweet with hymns of praise,
> And the long night shall echo with our chorus.

Creon now comes on stage and, in a kind of parody of a political oration, pompously announces his proclamation. No sooner is this done than, in a comic scene, a half-crazed soldier tells of his finding Polyneices' body with earth sprinkled upon it. In a burst of anger, Creon lashes out with fury: rejecting contemptuously the chorus's suggestion that this deed might have been done by the gods, he declares his belief that some one has been bribed to do it. That every man has his price and that 'money talks' is the mainspring of his thoughts:

> Money!
> There's nothing in the world so demoralizing as money.
> Down go your cities,
> Homes gone, men gone, honest hearts corrupted,
> Crookedness of all kinds, and all for money!

The choral song that follows anticipates a famous passage in *Hamlet*. "What a piece of work is a man" forms its theme:

> Numberless are the world's wonders, but none
> More wonderful than man; the storm grey sea
> Yields to his prows, the huge crests bear him high;
> Earth, holy and inexhaustible, is graven
> With shining furrows where his plows have gone
> Year after year, the timeless labour of stallions.

And its conclusion is a plea for reason:

> O clear intelligence, force beyond all measure!
> O fate of man, working both good and evil!
> When the laws are kept, how proudly his city stands!
> When the laws are broken, what of his city then?
> Never may the anarchic man find rest at my hearth,
> Never be it said that my thoughts are his thoughts.

From this moment the tragedy rushes swiftly on. The soldier returns triumphant with the culprit, Antigone. "You dared defy the law?" inquires Creon incredulously, and her reply is calm:

> I dared.
> It was not God's proclamation. That final Justice
> That rules the world below makes no such laws.
>
> Your edict, King, was strong,
> But all your strength is weakness itself against
> The immortal unrecorded laws of God.
> They are not merely now: they were, and shall be,
> Operative for ever, beyond man utterly.

In a passion, Creon orders Ismene also to be brought before him, and, with the skilled dramatist's sensitive use of the unexpected, she professes to have been a co-partner in her sister's guilt, even while Antigone in her pride wishes to suffer alone:

ISMENE: Yes, if she will let me say so. I am guilty.
ANTIGONE [*coldly*]:   No, Ismene. You have no right to say so.
            You would not help me, and I will not have you
                help me. . . .
                Save yourself. I shall not envy you.
            There are those who will praise you; I shall have
                honour too.

The chorus now sings of impending doom; the gods are at work; "Man's little pleasure is the Spring of Sorrow." Hæmon, the betrothed of Antigone, comes to plead her cause. On Creon's side is the argument that law and order must be preserved; on Hæmon's the argument that no single man, however wise, can be absolutely sure of the rightness of his judgments. "The State is the King!" cries Creon, to which Hæmon's answer is: "Yea, if the State is a desert." The monarch remains resolute, although, again with a touch of the unexpected, he announces that he will spare Ismene, while the chorus sings of the power of love over intellect, the force that has made Hæmon dare to brave his father's wrath. Antigone goes to her doom, ordered to be walled up in a rock, but hardly has she been taken away before the old blind Tiresias, the seer, approaches Creon, warning him that he stands "once more on the edge of fate." The king rejects his counsel, claiming that he too has been bribed, but his mind becomes troubled as the prophet lashes out with a dark prediction of disaster. The words are so solemn that suddenly Creon reverses his decision and commands his attendants to rescue the girl he has condemned. By this time, however, it is too late. A messenger tells how Antigone has been found hanged and how Hæmon in misery has committed suicide, while Creon's wife, Eurydice, broken by the death of her son, perishes also. A shattered Creon is left standing lonely on a dark stage.

In *Antigone* there is obviously present a quality the presence of which in *Electra* we seek for in vain. Here, too, emphasis is upon human character, but, even although no supernatural beings appear among the other *dramatis personæ*, the gods have come mysteriously close to the action. The human persons, together with their actions, are illuminated by the light of a basic theme, a theme essentially metaphysical. Throughout the entire play runs a refrain, the refrain of the two laws. For Creon reason and civic order are of paramount import; for Antigone, led by faith and emotion, the spiritual commandment is all. Between these conflicting forces Sophocles holds an even course, for this is no propaganda play. True, our deepest sympathies are for Antigone and for Hæmon, yet, as she is drawn in clear terms before us, she is not ideally perfect. In her pride she is selfish, and about her clings a neurotic robe of world weariness: she is almost enamoured of death.

Unquestionably this is the finest and most delicately balanced of all the tragedies the Greek stage has to offer us.

THE HOUSE OF LAIUS: "ŒDIPUS TYRANNUS" AND "ŒDIPUS AT COLONUS"

The story of the Theban kingdom was one that had deep attractions for Sophocles. Shortly after writing *Antigone* he created his terrible *Œdipus Tyrannus*, and four years after his death his *Œdipus at Colonus* was performed.

The former is perhaps the play by which he is most widely known, and one must agree that its planning is magnificent, its dialogue supremely fashioned, its revelation of character profound. Before the action begins much of basic significance for an understanding of the plot has occurred, but with great skill the dramatist makes allusion to these events in the process of unfolding his story, so that past and present become interfused. Œdipus has now been monarch of Thebes for several years, having married the widow of Laius, Jocasta. In reality Jocasta is his mother, and Laius has died, although Œdipus knows it not, by his son's hand. A plague has descended on the city, and the king, desperately anxious for the fate of his kingdom, has sent Creon, his brother-in-law, to the oracle in an endeavour to find what sin has brought this ruin upon them.

The oracle declares that the plague is due to the presence in Thebes of the murderer of Laius, and Œdipus pledges himself to discover this criminal. He summons the blind seer Tiresias, who darkly accuses him, but whom Œdipus curtly and angrily dismisses as suborned by Creon. An angry scene between the king and his brother-in-law is interrupted only by the hurried entry of Jocasta from the palace. Left alone with Œdipus, she laughs aside Tiresias' accusation by describing the way in which Laius was killed, by robbers, "at a place where three highways meet." From this moment the tragedy develops rapidly. Œdipus is aghast, for the description of the spot tallies with his own memory of an event when, in anger, he once slew a wayfarer who obstructed his path. Jocasta comforts him by pointing to the oracle's declaration that Laius should die by the hand of his own son, arguing that clearly therefore the murder of this king cannot be true to prophecy. Further comfort arrives when a messenger announces the death of Polybus, whom Œdipus thinks to be his father and from whose presence he had departed in order that another oracle might not be fulfilled.

"Thou dreadest to be stained with guilt through thy parents?" inquires the Messenger:

> ŒDIPUS: Even so, old man—this it is that ever affrights me.
> MESSENGER: Dost thou know, then, that thy fears are wholly vain?
> ŒDIPUS: How so, if I was born of those parents?
> MESSENGER: Because Polybus was nothing to thee in blood.
> ŒDIPUS: What sayest thou? Was Polybus not my sire?
> MESSENGER: No more than he who speaks to thee, but just so much.

With inexorable logic the truth is gradually revealed. Œdipus was found as a child by a shepherd and reared by Polybus as his son. By this time Jocasta has divined the terrible secret, tries to stay him from obtaining the final proof from the old shepherd, but is powerless to stop the progress of events. She commits suicide, while Œdipus in torment tears out his own eyes and prepares to leave the city.

The entire play is executed with masterly precision, event following on event, the passion continually on the build. Because of its dramatic skill Aristotle, when he sought for support of his arguments in his *Poetics*, took it as the prime example of tragedy. There is hardly a line that is unnecessary in the dialogue, hardly an opportunity that has been missed for the creation of emotional tension. As in *Electra* and *Antigone*, the chief emphasis is on character—on Creon, the honest courtier; on Jocasta, half-wife, half-mother; on Œdipus, noble and magnanimous, yet cursed with too quick a temper, obstinate and rash. By his well-nigh perfect handling of the theme Sophocles has been able to let us see the story in a kind of double vision. Externally considered, this is a tragedy of fate; the oracles prove true in the end; whatever Œdipus and Jocasta do to escape, fate twists and turns their lives to their own undoing. On the other hand, as Œdipus is delineated here he was responsible for the events which prove the oracles true. The sudden anger directed against Tiresias and, more particularly, against the faithful

Creon is symbolic of what formed a basic weakness in his character: the aged Laius would never have been slain had the young prince not been possessed, then as now, of ungovernable fits of anger. Nor does he plead ignorance in defence at the close of the play. Very easily he might have indulged in self-pity, laying the entire blame on the curse that thwarted his every action: instead he accepts full responsibility, for once more character is being shown as destiny. Contemplation on the strangeness of life's passage is the mood with which we are left as the chorus departs from the stage:

> While our eyes wait to see the destined final day, we must call no one happy who is of mortal race, until he hath crossed life's border, free from pain.

The slightest error may have the most grievous consequence.

Once again, at the very close of his life, Sophocles turned to the Œdipus story, showing the aged king, as self-appointed exile for many years from his home in Thebes, blind and feeble, led from land to land by his faithful Antigone. The plot possesses at once a grand simplicity and a peculiarly complex structure. We are now at the moment in time when Eteocles is preparing to meet the great Argive army that Polyneices has gathered against his brother, and when an oracle has declared that Thebes will prove fortunate only if the exiled Œdipus dies there, that if his body is buried in Attica the city of Athens will flourish instead. It is at Colonus, in Attica, by the grove sacred to the Furies, or Eumenides, that Œdipus is found.

The action of the play shows Creon endeavouring to trick the old man into returning to Thebes, the while Theseus offers him protection. But it is not the action that is important: the prime quality of this drama consists in its depiction of peace of spirit won out of suffering. In the Œdipus presented here breathes a nobility such as could come to no man who has not plumbed the very depths of despair and risen triumphant above them. And at the end an almost mystical scene rivets our attention. Rising to his full height, the grey figure of the king stands facing his daughters and King Theseus; blind though he is, he knows he will find his final resting-place unaided, guided not by human hands but by the light of his own new-found inner strength:

> I will inform thee, son of Ægeus,
> Of what shall be in store for this thy city
> Beyond the harm of time. Of my own self,

ANDROMEDA
Attic vase, Berlin.
From Margarete Bieber,
*The History of the Greek and
Roman Theater*, Fig. 63.

MASK OF A TRAGIC HERO
From Margarete Bieber,
*Die Denkmäler zum Theaterwesen im
Altertum.*

TWO DRUNKEN MEN

Terra-cotta group, Berlin.

From Margarete Bieber, *The History of the Greek and Roman Theater*, Fig. 87.

A MAN AND A WOMAN

Terra-cotta in the Kunstgeschichtliches Museu Würzburg University.

Photo Rudol Hartzold

A COMIC HERAKLES

Terra-cotta statuetre, Berlin.

From Margarete Bieber, *The History of the Greek and Roman Theater*, Fig. III.

A WORRIED SLAVE

Terra-cotta statuette.

By courtesy of the Metropolitan Museum of Art, New York

65

Without a hand to guide me, presently
I will explore a spot where I must die. . . .
Now—to the place! The message from on high
Urges me forth; let us not linger now.
Here, follow me, my daughters! in my turn.
Look, I am acting as a guide to you,
As you were mine, your father's. Come along!—
Nay, do not touch me; let me for myself
Search out the hallowed grave where, in this soil,
It is my fate to lie. . . .
O Light—my Dark—once thou wast mine to see;
And now not ever shall my limbs again
Feel thee! Already I creep upon my way
To hide my last of life in Hades. Thou,
Dearest of friends—thy land—thy followers—all,
May you live happy; and in your happiness
Fortunate ever, think of me, your dead!

The last words of the chorus form a fitting conclusion to this
drama: "Come, cease lamentation, lift it up no more; for verily
these things stand fast."

In these mystically conceived scenes once more appears an
apotheosis of patriotism, but gentler, and perhaps for that reason
even more profound, than in the work of Æschylus. No lines are
more lovely in the play than the choral ode in honour of Attica:

Stranger, thou art come to rest
Where the pasturing folds are best
Of this land of goodly steeds
In Colonos' glistening meads,
Where the clear-voiced nightingale
Oftenest in green valley-glades
Loves to hide her and bewail;
Under wine-dark ivy shades,
Of the leafy ways, untrod,
Pierced by sun or tempest never,
Myriad-fruited, of a God;
Where in Bacchanalian trim
Dionysus ranges ever
With the Nymphs who fostered him.

In these last days of his life Sophocles turned in fond recollection to
"white Colonos," city of his birth, and to praise of the Attica that
had reared him. The golden words shimmer in the sunlight of
memory, and the present scene becomes tinged with the radiance
of eternity.

C

THE DREAM OF LIFE: "AJAX" AND "PHILOCTETES"

Among the dramatist's early works is his *Ajax*, among his latest the *Philoctetes*. Basically, these are far apart from each other, the one instinct with passion, tempestuous and fierce, the other tinged with an almost romantic strangeness of quiet mood. Yet these two plays, taken together, help to reveal an essential quality in Sophocles' outlook upon the world and help to explain the atmosphere of his *Œdipus at Colonus*.

The former drama is a terrible study of tragic error. Ajax, one of the most renowned warriors among the Greeks, deems that a prized honour, the arms of Achilles, should fall to his lot. These arms are, however, given to Odysseus, and Ajax, bitterly wounded in his pride, sets out by night to murder the leaders of the expedition, Agamemnon and Menelaus, whom he believes responsible for this insult.

Angered at this exhibition of overweening pride, the goddess Athene comes from Olympus, and darkens his mind with madness so that he falls upon the army's flock of sheep in the fond delusion that he is slaying his enemies. In the end, having recovered from his frenzy, and consumed by shame, he commits suicide.

As a study in character the tragedy possesses great force, but beyond the character-portrayal resides a peculiar quality of even greater import. The opening scene displays this clearly. Athene appears above and speaks to Odysseus, but, although he hears her voice, she remains to him invisible. After a short conversation between the man and the goddess she summons forth the crazed Ajax from his tent. Cruelly she mocks him, leading him on from pathetic boast to boast, while Odysseus the wise stands silent, wondering. At last, when Ajax has again retired, he gives expression to his thoughts. "I know none nobler," he declares,

> and I pity him
> In his misery, albeit he is my foe,
> Since he is yoked fast to an evil doom.
> My own lot I regard no less than his,
> For I see well, nought else are we but mere
> Phantoms, all we that live, mere fleeting shadows.

The thought that life is but a dream is one that has haunted the minds of several of the greatest playwrights in the theatre's history: that this thought was first expressed by Sophocles over two thousand years ago indicates the quality of his genius. In this scene of madness and of wonder is, as it were, the adumbration of Shakespeare's vision in *The Tempest* and of Calderón's in *Life's a Dream*.

The spirit of *The Tempest* is recalled even more potently in the drama of *Philoctetes*, written when Sophocles was nearing ninety years of age. Strange is the story of this drama and strange its atmosphere. The scene is the lonely isle of Lemnos, where for years Philoctetes, deserted by the Greeks when he had had the misfortune to be stung by a serpent and consequently to suffer from a loathsome disease, has been living in a cave; his life he has preserved only because he possesses the famous bow and arrows of the heroic Herakles. Although there are many complications in the plot, briefly the drama tells how Neoptolemus, the youthful son of the dead Achilles, and the wily Odysseus arrive at Lemnos, sent thither by the leaders of the Greek forces at Troy because an oracle had declared that success would come to them only if they could obtain possession of the Herakles arms.

For Odysseus all that matters is the acquiring of this bow; pity stirs him not, and he is entirely content to trick the helpless Philoctetes in the pursuit of this one object. For the young Neoptolemus, however, the matter is not so simple: the calm nobility of the dweller upon this island casts its spell on him, so that questions of honour and loyalty conflict with Odysseus' single-minded expediency.

Throughout the whole play an atmosphere of wonder enwraps the action. From the moment Odysseus and Neoptolemus set foot on the shore of this "sea-girt Lemnos, desart and forlorn, where never tread of human step is seen, or voice of mortal heard," we are caught in the spell. By skilled words Sophocles conjures up before us an image of the desolate spot, so that we seem to feel the very silence of the place, disturbed until now only by the breaking of waves upon the rocks and by the sighing of the pitiless winds. With consummate art the dramatist weaves his tapestry of human character set against this scene; contrasts the conscienceless intrigues of Odysseus both with the fresh bloom of Neoptolemus' enthusiasm and the nobility, rendered greater through suffering, of Philoctetes; sets the physical torment of the hero against the healing balm of sleep:

> Sleep, thou patron of mankind,
> Great physician of the mind,
> Who dost nor pain nor sorrow know,
> Sweetest balm of ev'ry woe,
> Mildest sov'reign, hear us now:

Hear thy wretched suppliant's vow;
His eyes in gentle slumbers close,
And continue his repose;
Hear thy wretched suppliant's vow,
Great physician, hear us now.

We are close to Shakespeare here, with his deep appreciation of nature, his wide observation of mankind, his sense of the intermingling of fate and of character, his profound realization of the suffering of life, and his concept of the nobility of spirit that comes when the human soul has been tested and tried by pain. Sophocles, more than the rugged Æschylus, approaches near to us. His dramas may be bound by the strict conventions of the Greek stage, but no conventions, however strange, can conceal the essential humanity which breathes out of his lines.

CHAPTER III

THE DAWN OF REALISM: EURIPIDES

WHEN WE turn to the plays of Euripides as presented, for example, in the translations of Gilbert Murray and read the lyrical chants of their choruses, it is somewhat difficult to think of them in relation to the term 'realism'; yet, placed in comparison with the work of Æschylus or Sophocles, they undoubtedly reveal, on careful examination, qualities which bring them close to the characteristic theatrical form of our time. If Sophocles shows himself akin to Shakespeare, Euripides, with his prevailing intellectualism and disillusionment, frequently reminds us of Shaw.

For this mood in him there were causes in the conditions of his life. True, he was born only ten years after Sophocles, but these ten years were fateful. In 480, as we have seen, Æschylus was a man of middle age fighting at Salamis, Sophocles was a youth of fifteen leading a chorus in honour of the victory. Euripides was a child of only five years. The relationship between Sophocles and Euripides in connexion with the Peloponnesian War is also instructive: they both died about the same time, but when the first part of this long struggle broke out in 431 B.C. the former was already an old man, while Euripides was still in full manhood— not so much older, indeed, than Æschylus at the time of the battle of Salamis. By then Sophocles was already moving towards the mysticism of his final years, while his younger contemporary was actively interested in the political affairs around him.

Euripides seems to have addressed himself primarily to the young intelligentsia of his time. Scepticism was in the air about the middle of the fifth century, and the Sophists came to exercise much influence on the young. The older idealism was fading; expedient calculations rapidly were taking its place. To this school of thought Euripides belonged. For him the gods were no longer the awful forces they had been in the imagination of Æschylus; the old legends of Athens were scanned now with doubting eyes; the heroic was reduced to terms of the common life of the day. There is an ugly modern word that saw much service in the twenties of the present century —'debunking': it might well be applied to much of Euripides' work.

His tendency to doubt the truth of the ancient legends, to question the wisdom of the past, presented him with a peculiar dramatic problem, and through his solution to that problem he drew the theatre still nearer to our age. For the most part the playwright was restricted to choice among a limited number of legendary histories, and, even although Euripides sought more widely than his predecessors, the restriction still kept him within fairly narrow bounds. Two things, however, Euripides was eager to do—to make the characters real and ordinary, and to use them for the purpose of 'philosophizing' on the events. From these two endeavours came his changes in dramatic structure. Obviously the chorus was a theatrical element out of keeping with his central idea, and, as a consequence, in most of his plays he tended to reduce its participation in the main action until it became nothing save a detached group of singers indulging in the presentation of chants only slightly related to the major theme. To compensate for what was thus lost Euripides provided brilliant and beautiful lyrics for this group to sing, and at the same time steadily enriched the musical accompaniments, but the fact remains that in the majority of his plays our attention is concentrated almost entirely on the 'episodes' involving the main characters: his plays are dramas in which appears a collection of choral interludes rather than dramas built from the interplay of chorus and characters.

A further modification in dramatic structure was necessitated by his individualistic attitude towards the legendary themes. Not seldom he found himself compelled to introduce, at the very beginning of his plays, explanatory matter designed to give the audience the information essential for an understanding of his point of view; hence evolved the typical Euripidean 'prologue,' in which a single person becomes almost the mouthpiece of the poet himself. Had Euripides lived at a later age he would have written prefaces.

If this was obligatory at the beginning of the piece, a similar device was needed at the end. So boldly did he deal with the ancient stories that often there remained no possible solution for the complicated action that would have been acceptable on the Greek stage. As a result Euripides fell back on the trick ever afterwards associated with his name—the use of the *deus ex machina*. The 'machine' in question was a theatrical device introduced towards the close of the fifth century by which a deity could be lowered from the roof of the scene-building. Since Euripides frequently used the device to huddle his drama to an illogical end—the god announcing his divine commands to the characters below—the phrase about the *deus ex machina* came to bear the transferred significance which it has to-day. Even when the gods are gone Euripides' practice remains.

In noting these innovations, however, we must not think that all of Euripides' eighteen or nineteen extant plays are of one kind or that he did not have within him both sincerity of purpose and depth of feeling. Although he frequently sinks to sentimentalism and is driven to the exploitation of the sensational—the two curses that ever dog the footsteps of the realistic playwright—he does have the power at times of rising to true tragic perceptions. However much he would wish to belittle the mystery of man, the impress of his age was sufficiently strong on his spirit to make him present, in at least some of his plays, profound expression of the problems of evil and of good.

"ELECTRA"

It may be well to start an examination of his work by choosing a play which stands, as it were, in the middle of his dramatic career and which provides opportunities for comparison with kindred dramas by Æschylus and Sophocles. *Electra* was presented about the year 413 B.C., when he was seventy-two years of age, and, as its title indicates, it deals with the same theme as that of Sophocles' similarly named tragedy and that of *The Choephori*. A scrutiny of its structure is revealing.

Instead of a palace courtyard, we stand before a peasant's hut, from which the owner comes dressed in poor raiment, a figure worn by toil. In his prologue speech he rapidly reviews the events leading to Agamemnon's murder, and then turns to tell of subsequent events. Electra has grown of an age to marry, and all the princes of Greece seek her hand, but Ægisthus, afraid lest she bear a high-born son to wreak vengeance upon him, would not betroth her to any—would, indeed, have slain her had his hand not been held back by Clytemnestra. At last he conceived a wily scheme: he married off the girl to a poor peasant, believing that no low-born son could give him cause to fear. For himself, this peasant declares, he has ever respected her maidenhood.

As he finishes his talk Electra enters with a water-pitcher on her head. Asked why she toils in this manner, she replies that she does so because of the peasant's kindness:

> High fortune this, when men for sore mischance
> Find such physician as I find in thee,

I ought, as strength shall serve, yea, though forbid,
To ease thy toil, that lighter be thy load,
And share thy burdens.

Immediate comment is demanded on this scene. The effect created is obvious. Electra, heroic in the hands of Æschylus and idealized in those of Sophocles, becomes an ordinary girl going to the well for water. The antique legend is dragged down to earth. Besides this, the characters are, as it were, related now to a real environment. While the peasant talks of taking his steers to the fields to sow his crop, Electra speaks of keeping the house in order so that the labourer at the day's end will find comfort. Not only is the legend dragged down to earth, it is being made domestic. At the same time an implicit comment is being made. Euripides is a kind of socialist before his time, and his presentation of noble qualities in this poor toiler seems designed to indicate that high thought and passion are not the exclusive property of those kings and princes who are the persons of early myth. That such was indeed his purpose is clearly indicated later when Orestes makes direct reference to the magnanimity of mind enclosed in an outward form so impoverished. Above all, the new situation invented by the dramatist provides an opportunity for the arousing of pity: pathos is one of Euripides' main devices; if he does not know how to express that hardness of temper so characteristic of Æschylus, he is adept at causing tears to flow.

The following scene introduces us to Orestes and his friend Pylades. Electra and a chorus of Argive maidens come on the stage, and when their chant is done Orestes detains her, tells her he has news of her brother, and indulges in a lengthy conversation with her, during which her love for her brother is fully displayed, and the information is given to the audience that, were Orestes to return, only one person, an aged servant who tended him as a child, would recognize his features. The pathetic note is increased. "Since thou dost wake the tale," says Electra:

> I pray thee, stranger,
> Report to Orestes all mine ills and his.
> Tell in what raiment I am hovel-housed,
> Under what squalor I am crushed, and dwell
> Under what roof, after a palace-home;—
> How mine own shuttle weaves with pain my robes,—
> Else must I want, all vestureless my frame;—
> How from the stream myself the water bear;—
> Banned from the festal rite, denied the dance.

If this contributed added pathos, added realism appears when the peasant returns and complains that it is unseemly for a woman to stand talking with young men, while she begs him not to be "suspicious." Being satisfied, he then chides her for not bidding the strangers welcome to his hut, and Orestes makes the comment on natural nobility:

> Lo, there is no sure test for manhood's worth;
> For mortal natures are confusion-fraught,
> I have seen ere now a noble father's son
> Proved nothing-worth, seen good sons of ill sires,
> Starved leanness in a rich man's very soul,
> And in a poor man's body a great heart.
> How then shall one discern 'twixt these and judge?
> By wealth?—a sorry test were this to use.
> Or by the lack of all?—nay, poverty
> Is plague-struck, schooling men to sin through need.
> To prowess shall I turn me?—who, that looks
> On spears, can swear which spearman's heart is brave?
> Leave Fortune's gifts to fall out as they will!
> Lo, this man is not among Argive's great,
> Nor by a noble house's name exalted,
> But one of the many—proved a king of men!
> Learn wisdom, ye which wander aimless, swoln
> With vain imaginings: by converse judge
> Man, even the noble by their daily walk.
> For such be they which govern states aright
> And homes: but fleshly bulks devoid of wit
> Are statues in the market-place.

Obviously this is extra-dramatic material, the reflections of the author rather than of the character, material for preface rather than for play.

The scene continues in the same strain. Electra criticizes her husband for asking such noble strangers to so poor an abode, but, since he has made this social error, she bids him send for Orestes' old servant; he will aid in entertaining the guests and at the same time take joy in hearing of his young master.

A choral ode, beautiful but inconsequent, gives time for this old man to arrive. He says a few words to Electra, and then starts to examine Orestes' figure and features, declaring eventually that here in person is Electra's brother. She at first doubts (in terms that show Euripides ridiculing the recognition scene in Sophocles' *Electra*), but becomes convinced when the old man points out a scar on the young man's brow, the result of a fall in childhood's days. All now sit down to discuss plans. The palace is closely guarded, and only careful strategy may prevail. It is settled that Orestes will go to Ægisthus where he is sacrificing at an altar outside the palace, while Electra, who cries that she will make preparation for her mother's slaying, proposes to entice Clytemnestra to her hut by sending false news that she has been delivered of a son.

The chorus sings another lyrically lovely but obscure song, when a noise is heard in the distance. Electra is in despair, thinking Orestes has been detected and slain, but news soon comes that it is Ægisthus who is dead. Orestes returns with the body, and Electra, after a moment's hesitation, indulges in a brutal reviling of the corpse; her hate knows no bounds, and in her long tirade we guess at the long-pent-up emotions that have for so many years seared her spirit.

This done, Clytemnestra is seen approaching. Orestes trembles at thought of completing his vengeance:

ORESTES: What shall we do? Our mother—murder her?
ELECTRA: How? Hath ruth seized thee, seeing thy mother's form?
ORESTES: Woe!
How can I slay her—her that nursed, that bare me?
ELECTRA: Even as she thy father slew and mine.
ORESTES: O Phœbus, folly exceeding was thine hest.
ELECTRA: Nay, where Apollo erreth, who is wise?
ORESTES: Who against nature bad'st me slay my mother!
ELECTRA: How art thou harmed, avenging thine own sire?
ORESTES: Arraigned for a mother's murder—pure ere this.
ELECTRA: Yet, impious if thou succour not thy sire.
ORESTES: Her blood-price to my mother must I pay.
ELECTRA: And *Him*!—if thou forbear to avenge a father.
ORESTES: Ha!—spake a fiend in likeness of the God?—
ELECTRA: Throned on the holy tripod!—I trow not.
ORESTES: I dare not trust this oracle's utter faith!
ELECTRA: Wilt thou turn craven—be no more a man?
ORESTES: How? must I lay the self-same snare for her?
ELECTRA: Ay! that which trapped and slew the adulterer!
ORESTES: I will go in. A horror I essay!—
Yea, will achieve! If 'tis Heaven's will, so be it.
Oh bitter strife, which I must needs hold sweet.

By this treatment Euripides is completely rewriting the age-old scene. Clytemnestra's murder is placed last, with ample time given for reflection. Instead of killing her in the heat of passion, Orestes is made to sacrifice her in the light of reason. The new situation permits the dramatist to emphasize his conception of Electra, a starved soul rendered neurotic by hate and thwarted love, dominating her brother through the intensity of her passion. It also permits him to cast characteristic doubt upon the ways of the gods: confronted by his terrible task, Orestes goes so far as to question whether the inviolate oracle may truly be trusted.

Equally characteristic is the debate between Clytemnestra and her daughter that immediately follows. The queen justifies herself, while Electra castigates her as the mere wanton. "Child," says Clytemnestra, not unwisely and rather pathetically,

> Child, still thy nature bids thee love thy sire.
> 'Tis ever thus: some cleave unto their father,
> Some more the mother than the father love.
> I pardon thee. In sooth, not all so glad
> Am I, my child, for deeds that I have done.

These are almost her last words, for, entering the hut to do sacrifice —"take care that my smoke-grimed walls soil not thy robes," remarks Electra in cruel sarcasm—she is slain by Orestes. No sooner is she dead, however, than a great revulsion of feeling descends upon Electra; in tears she and Orestes think of her pitiful words to them; they are abjectly conscience-stricken—and at last when it is hard to see how the playwright can reach a fitting conclusion a heavenly vision appears. Castor and Pollux descend in the machine. They declare the deed to be unrighteous, and Castor confirms Orestes' suspicions by himself condemning Apollo's command:

> Thou, thou hast sinned;
> And Phœbus—Phœbus—since he is my king,
> I am dumb. . . . He is wise:—not wise his hest for thee!
> We must needs say "'Tis well."

Things being as they are, the twin gods bid Electra to marry Pylades (a nice sentimental tying-up of knots), while Orestes is to journey to Argos that Athene may release him from the torment of the Furies. In a final pathetic scene, when Electra throws her arms tearfully about her brother's neck, Orestes bids a last farewell to his native land.

The fate of Orestes is the same as that in *The Choephori*, yet in spirit we are here far indeed from Æschylus' high concept. Tears, not emotions too deep for tears, afflict us; and in place of an attempt to justify the ways of god to man is a sneering at religious belief: the divine Apollo is treated as a fool.

SOME STUDIES OF WOMEN:
"ALCESTIS," "MEDEA," "HIPPOLYTUS,"
"ANDROMACHE," "HECUBA," "THE TROJAN WOMEN"

Having gained some conception of Euripides' dramatic style, we may now turn to examine his other plays briefly in their chronological sequence. In the *Electra* all attention is concentrated upon the heroine, and it may be said that in general this dramatist was more interested in his women characters than in his men. He understood well the neurotic types; their presentation gave him opportunity for the exploitation of those pathetic scenes he so dearly loved. Not without considerable justification did Aristophanes satirically depict him as the playwright most detested by womenkind, because he had revealed to the world many of their innermost secrets.

With the exception of the *Cyclops*, his solitary extant satyric drama, the first play we have from his pen is *Alcestis*, produced in 438 B.C. Strangely, it was the fourth element in a tetralogy—a position usually taken by a satyr drama—and very probably its romantic, almost fairy-tale-like quality, together with its comic scenes, is explainable by reference to its original purpose. Nevertheless the characteristic elements of the Euripidean play are already amply apparent. The plot deals with an ancient legend which told how King Admetus of Thessaly was promised by the Fates, through the intervention of Apollo, that death would spare him for a time if only he could find some person willing to go to Hades in his place. With complete lack of heroic nobility, Admetus hurries from kinsman to kinsman, seeking help in his predicament and finding aid from none save his wife, the loyal Alcestis. As the play opens she is just on the point of going to her doom, calm, matter-of-fact, but with just a faint tremor that betrays her humanity.

What precise purpose Euripides had in writing this drama is hard to tell: perhaps he had no thought other than that the story gave him a pathetic situation, romantic in colouring; that it allowed him to reveal, not too blatantly, his utter scepticism concerning the gods; and that it offered opportunity for subtle revelations of human character. "The King will not know his loss until he suffers it," is an appropriate comment, made by a servant to the leader of the chorus, on his attitude towards Admetus. This monarch is depicted as a thoroughly respectable, convention-loving middle-class citizen. To Alcestis he makes all the proper promises: he will look after the children, he will not marry again, gone for ever are the merry drinking-parties that used to send their music through the house. He is desperately anxious lest she should decide not to carry the business through to the bitter end, yet he is as desperately afraid to be left alone. He is mightily affronted by his father, Pheres, who counsels him sarcastically to "woo many women, so that more may die for you," yet there is more than a trifle of shame-facedness in his talking about the whole matter to Herakles. As for Herakles, he is presented as a kind of softened version of the comic caricature that passed under his name on the farcical stages of the time—a self-assured braggart who goes out to wrestle with death for Alcestis, not unfortified with wine and somewhat uncertain in his gait. Beautiful as portions of *Alcestis* are, disbelief and cynicism appear to be the mainsprings of its action.

Far different in character is *Medea* (431 B.C.), a sensational tragedy of love turned to hatred, and the first drama extant written on the theme of miscegenation. Medea is a princess of distant Colchis and a sorceress, a strange barbaric figure from the mysterious East. She has aided Jason to obtain the Golden Fleece, and, later, wedded to him, she has contrived the death of his uncle, Pelias, in an endeavour to place her husband on the throne of his native land. The plot, however, miscarries; Jason, Medea, and their two sons have to flee into exile; and there Jason deserts her, marrying the daughter of Creon, monarch of Corinth.

This, then, is a study of ill-mated husband and wife. Jason is nothing but a self-seeking, self-deluding male, willing to accept the results of any crime committed on his behalf by his wife, but absolutely incapable of accepting any joint responsibility. His love for her is an intoxicated affair, the desire for physical possession of her body, in no wise a true marriage. She, on the other hand, is the barbarian who gives her whole being to the man she loves, and when that love fails finds herself consumed by a hate no less fierce and incandescent. Tremble though she may at the thought of killing her children, this sacrifice, in her mind, must be made to expiate the treachery to which she has been exposed. In the end, and not inappropriately, she flies from human sight in a magical chariot drawn by dragons.

The intensity of this play, its bold presentation of the two main characters, its theme of sex-strife accentuated by racial disparities, and also, be it said, its inherently sensational qualities have made it the happy hunting-ground for modern playwrights of the realistic school. It strikes an inherently 'modern' note, and, if that modern note possesses less power than the ancient strength of Æschylus, less calm than the assured mastery of Sophocles, our regret at the loss can avail us nothing.

Hippolytus (428 B.C.), which, in spite of its title, again focuses attention upon a heroine rather than on a hero, has something of the same elements. *Medea* is the first of its kind of drama; *Hippolytus* is the earliest-known full-length study of criminal passion—the love of Phædra, wife of King Theseus, for her husband's illegitimate son Hippolytus. As Euripides traces the course of the action we watch the young queen struggling against her infatuation and finally succumbing to it; we see Hippolytus, the cold, uprighteous youth, incapable of even faintly appreciating the power that wraps her in its folds. The contrast between these two is the more stressed in that Artemis and Aphrodite, the symbols of chastity and love, appear in person to provide a kind of symbolic commentary on the course of events and upon the personalities of the two opposed human figures. Between them stands Theseus, troubled of mind, credulous, an inefficient judge of character. When Phædra, scorned by the pure Hippolytus, accuses him of making love to her, and when he, for his father's sake, remains silent under the accusation, the king all too readily accepts his wife's word and puts such a curse upon him as to lead him to his death. While obviously Euripides was most interested in the heroine here, we might perhaps agree that the tragedy is one produced by three conflicting types, each with its own peculiar failing: Theseus, finding his youthful incontinence the ultimate cause of his present miseries, and obtusely unable to deal with any circumstances beyond the ordinary commonplace affairs of daily life; Phædra, consumed by her fatal passion; and Hippolytus, wrapped up in the dignified silence of his own self-esteem and frigidity of spirit. If ever Euripides came close to capturing the true tragic spirit it was in this play; although, even in the making of this statement, one must recognize that only in one or two of his scenes does he rise above the depiction of the psychological and reach a metaphysical plane.

About the same time came his *Hecuba* (about 425 B.C.) and *Andromache* (about 430 B.C.). The latter reveals clearly two of Euripides' chief failings—his tendency towards contriving complex incident and allowing plot to dominate over other dramatic elements, and his corresponding tendency towards exaggeration of pathos. In *Andromache* is a whole tangle of incident. Andromache, widow of the Trojan hero Hector, is shown as the slave and mistress of Neoptolemus, son of Achilles. Neoptolemus has married Hermione, daughter of Menelaus, and she, consumed with jealousy, plots to murder both Andromache and her son. There is intrigue in the device by which the unhappy widow is tricked by Menelaus and Hermione; there is pathos in the scene wherein she stands helpless and bound while her little son vainly clings to her robes. Almost as though this were a nineteenth-century melodrama, this situation is saved by the opportune arrival of Peleus, who unties her bonds and rescues the child. Virtually the dramatic action is now over, but suddenly a fresh movement begins. Hermione is tormented by the thought of what she had intended to do, when suddenly Orestes makes his appearance, claims that she had been betrothed to him, leads her off the stage, murders Neoptolemus. Finally comes the usual Euripidean *deus ex machina*—Thetis this time—who gives commands for the care of the corpse, and orders Andromache, without any previous warning, to be married to Helenus.

Little may be honestly said in praise of this tissue of sensational and pathetic episodes. Likewise sharply split into two parts, *Hecuba* deserves a somewhat different judgment. Here also a slave-queen appears—Hecuba, formerly ruler of Troy along with Priam, now the captive property of Agamemnon. First, we are shown the sacrifice of her daughter Polyxena, whom the Greeks slay as a sacrifice to the spirit of Achilles; next we are introduced to the murder of her son Polydorus and to the cruel revenge she takes upon the treacherous perpetrator of this deed, Polymestor.

In order to understand this play, we need to remember that already Athens had become involved in the Peloponnesian War and that Euripides was becoming obsessed with the thought of war's follies in general. Hecuba's plight is the result of the long, disastrous struggle round Troy; and as the aftermath of war youth perishes, evil is let loose. With bitter irony the dramatist puts into Agamemnon's mouth the last words of the play. He, who was to have such a dismal homecoming, turns to the wretched Hecuba:

> Go thou, unhappy Hecuba, and bury thy two corpses; and you, Trojan women, to your masters' tents repair, for lo! I perceive a breeze just rising to waft us home. God grant we reach our country and find all well at home, released from troubles here!

During this period Euripides may have suffered deeply from divided loyalties. In the *Herakleidæ* (about 430 B.C.) and *The Suppliants* (about 421 B.C.) he indulges in some patriotic tub-thumping, vastly different from the calmly assured praises of Athens that came from the lips of Æschylus and of Sophocles (although in *The Madness of Herakles* (about 421 B.C.) he succeeds in striking a surer patriotic note), but in *The Trojan Women* (415 B.C.) he turns once more to the mood of *Hecuba*, and seems to have become so immersed in it that all sense of dramatic structure is lost. There is in reality no play here, simply one long lament over the consequences of war and an eloquent lyrical cry of despair. No special power of divination is required to see reflected in it the image of contemporary events. The year before it was produced the Athenians had attacked neutral Melos and with unparalleled savagery had put all its men to the sword: the same year saw the laying of plans for the ill-fated Sicilian expedition and demonstrated clearly the total lack of concerted purpose among the new rulers of Athens. From the very beginning of his career Euripides had been a doubter and a sceptic: now his doubts and scepticism overflowed. As the flames light up the ruined city of Troy the chorus is left on the stage uttering its miserable cries:

> Woe, woe, woe!
> Thou of the Ages, O wherefore fleest thou,
>   Lord of the Phrygian, Father that made us?
> 'Tis we, thy children; shall no man aid us?
> 'Tis we, thy children! Seest thou, seest thou?
>
> He seeth, only his heart is pitiless;
>   And the land dies: yea, she,
> She of the Mighty Cities perisheth citiless!
>   Troy shall no more be!

From disbelief in the gods Euripides is moving towards belief in a cruel and pitiless universe.

SENSATIONALISM AND DISILLUSIONMENT: "HELEN," "IPHIGENIA IN TAURIS," "ORESTES"

Probably induced by reflection on these contemporary events, Euripides produced in his latter years a series of plays of a peculiarly baffling kind. *Helen* (412 B.C.) may be selected as an extreme example. Every one knows the legend of Helen, how she, the wife of Menelaus, was taken to Troy by Paris and caused that proud city to fall. She is the supreme *femme fatale* of ancient myth. In the hands of Euripides her whole story becomes a jest, for he has seized upon, and elaborated, a story far different from that hallowed by the Homeric epic. According to this, Helen never went to Troy: the pother of the ten years' siege of that city was not over a real woman, but over her wraith, a mere phantom semblance of her person. All the time that Paris thinks he has possessed her, all the time that Menelaus has been afflicted with jealous pangs, the real Helen has lived a pleasant and blameless life in Egypt under the protection of King Proteus. As the play opens, however, she reveals in her prologue address to the audience that since Proteus' recent death conditions in Egypt are beginning to change; his son, Theoclymenus, wishes to marry her, and she is troubled by his unwanted attentions. Shortly thereafter Menelaus enters, tattered, worn, shipwrecked on this Egyptian shore while on his journey home from Troy. With him he has brought Helen from Troy— that is to say, the wraith of Helen—and has concealed her in a cave, but now he learns from a rude portress at the palace that some one is living here in Egypt under Helen's name. The poor man is at an utter loss, the more particularly since he is depicted here as a rather obtuse and dull-witted individual. Had he been a clown, we might have said he goggled at the news. Suddenly he spies the real Helen:

MENELAUS: Who art thou? whom do I behold in thee, lady?
HELEN: Nay, who art thou? the self-same reason prompts us both.
MENELAUS: I never saw a closer resemblance.
HELEN: Great God! Yea, for to recognize our friends is of God.
MENELAUS: Art thou from Hellas, or a native of this land?
HELEN: From Hellas; but I would learn thy story too.
MENELAUS: Lady, in thee I see a wondrous likeness to Helen.
HELEN: And I in thee to Menelaus; I know not what to say.
MENELAUS: Well, thou hast recognized aright a man of many sorrows.
HELEN: Hail! to thy wife's arms restored at last!
MENELAUS: Wife indeed! Lay not a finger on my robe. . . .
HELEN: In me thou beholdest no spectre of the night, attendant on the queen of phantoms.
MENELAUS: Nor yet am I in my single person the husband of two wives.
HELEN: What other woman calls thee lord?
MENELAUS: The inmate of yonder cave, whom I from Troy convey. . . . Herein is my dilemma; I have another wife.

Helen, thus spurned, is in despair. The situation seems to offer no remedy, when suddenly one of Menelaus' attendants rushes in excitedly to announce that the lady in the cave has vanished into thin air, being so thoughtful, before her departure, as to give an unsolicited testimonial to Helen's purity. Husband and wife fall into each other's arms.

Grievous thoughts, however, soon assail the pair. If Theoclymenus hears of Menelaus' arrival the Greek prince undoubtedly will be slain; and that he will be informed of the arrival appears certain, since his sister is Theonoe, a damsel gifted with the power of divination, one who knows all. As a last resort Helen falls on her knees before this lady, begging her not to tell her brother, and, somewhat to her own surprise, receives the promise of silence. This hurdle surmounted, she devises a plan of escape: she will tell Theoclymenus that Menelaus has perished at sea, beg from him a funeral ship so that she may offer the dead man's spirit the appropriate rites, and so bid good-bye to Egypt. The plot succeeds; Helen and Menelaus step on board the proffered vessel, the sails are set, and the miserable Theoclymenus is left raging on the strand, impotent, until the Dioscuri descend from heaven to pacify him.

There is an air of *The Private Life of Helen of Troy* about this play: there is a flavour of melodrama, at times even a flavour of farce. It is unlikely, as some have thought, that here Euripides was burlesquing his own tragic style: what he was doing was to provide the audience with excitement and adventure and stage thrill in a colourful setting, and at the same time express his cynical view both of the gods and of the ancient myths. We are far from the spirit of tragedy, yet we are not in the presence of burlesque; rather we inhabit the world of tragic comedy and come close indeed to the atmosphere of *Cæsar and Cleopatra* or *The Man of Destiny*.

Closely akin to *Helen* stands *Iphigenia in Tauris* (about 414 B.C.), where a similar situation is dealt with. This too is a romantic tale of adventure with a happy ending, and, like *Helen*, it deliberately exploits a variant legend of a famous event in the history of the house of Atreus. It will be recalled that when the Greek fleet was stayed by contrary winds in its expedition against Troy Agamemnon had sacrificed his young daughter Iphigenia on the altar of the gods. Euripides supposes that, like Helen, the girl was in reality saved, carried off by divine power to a distant land—the land of the Taurians—while a mere phantom was placed upon the altarstones. In this land of Tauris she has lived for many years, a dedicated priestess in a temple, where all strangers who set foot in the barbarian country are cruelly sacrificed.

All goes reasonably well until Iphigenia's brother, Orestes, and his friend Pylades arrive. In a tense scene of recognition, specifically praised by Aristotle as a prime model of its kind, brother and sister are united after their many years of separation, only to realize that they stand in mortal peril. Once the presence of these travellers is known it will be her duty to prepare them for sacrificial death. The greater part of the drama is taken up with an account of the trick, very close to that used by Helen, through which Iphigenia deceives Thoas, King of the Taurians, and saves them all. Delineation of character is here, but again Euripides' main object would seem to have been the creation of a kind of romantic escape play, half serious and half cynically amused.

Closely akin in spirit is the strange *Orestes* (408 B.C.), which, after a brilliant opening wherein Electra is seen tending her brother in his madness after Clytemnestra's murder, degenerates into a perplexing farrago of sensational incident and undramatic argumentation. There is truth in the depiction of his abnormal state of mind, falsity in the succeeding events. Orestes, Pylades, and Electra are condemned to death by an Argive court, but, in a series of exciting scenes, they seize Helen as a hostage and murder her, later lay hands on Menelaus' daughter, Hermione, and set fire to the palace. The tumult subsides only when the inevitable *deus ex machina* creaks down from the roof and reconciles all strife.

What Euripides was aiming at here is quite uncertain; perhaps his sensationalism was merely going to seed. This sensationalism, we should remember, must have been accompanied in those times by increasing sensationalism in the scenic production. Again and again in reading such plays as those just dealt with one feels that Euripides was relying upon stage effects, and this impression is confirmed by diverse contemporary evidence.

The stage was certainly becoming more spectacular: painted scenery was more freely employed, and machines of all kinds were being introduced. The device for lowering gods from above was one of these; another was the frequently used *ekkuklema* (ἐκκύκλημα) a sort of turn-table set in the doorway of the scene-building, through which might be displayed the bodies of characters murdered behind the scenes. In all probability, too, the actors' costumes had been made richer, while at the same time realistic touches appeared in harmony with the familiar quality of many of his scenes. How these actors seemed to their original audiences we are, fortunately, able to tell with a certain amount of assurance, since a number of painted vases of the latter part of the fifth century B.C. were obviously made by artists who had been witnesses of the theatrical events they depicted.

One such vase shows us the characters in the *Iphigenia in Tauris*. In the background we get a glimpse of the noble temple front, its great doors slightly ajar. Iphigenia is there, clad in her finely embroidered theatrical robes, with an attendant priestess behind her. Before her sits forlorn the wretched Orestes, dressed in rags, and near by Pylades stands, leaning on a staff.

Even more revealing of the appearance these dramas assumed in his own times is a scene from his lost drama, *Andromeda*. The central figure here is the heroine herself, a barbarian princess, as is at once indicated by the Eastern crown upon her head: her dress is peculiarly ornamented, and her arms are spread wide in the gesture which the artist had seen in the theatre, for she has been chained to a rock and awaits a dismal fate at the mercy of a sea-monster. To her right sits her father, Kepheus, a royal staff in his hands and on his head a crown of the same pattern as that worn by his daughter. Towards her comes Perseus, with a skull-cap showing that he has voyaged far, bearing in his hand the curved sword with which he had slain Medusa: behind him the goddess Aphrodite, much bejewelled, is crowning him for his exploits in the name of love. Particularly interesting is the maiden seated at the extreme left: with great naturalness her mask shows her to be an Ethiopian, and we may presume that she was one of a dark-skinned chorus designed to give an atmosphere of strangeness to this drama of romantic adventure.

The whole impression here is of an ornate stage, far different from the simple orchestral circle that satisfied Æschylus not a hundred years before; in looking at these vases we realize that we are well on our way towards the decorated theatres of modern times. The fact reminds us that the history of the drama presents one unassailable truth: when the drama declines scenic adornment begins to flourish. Perhaps we might even say that when scenery and show become dominant poetry and passion are forced to retire. The theatre cannot nobly feast the ear if the eye is distracted.

THE FINAL DRAMAS: "PHŒNISSÆ," "BACCHÆ," "IPHIGENIA IN AULIS"

Fortunately we do not need to take our farewell of Euripides with *Helen* and *Orestes* in our minds. During his last years the aged playwright seems to have had a fresh vision and discovered a hitherto untapped fount of strength. From this time three plays come before us, each of great interest.

In the extraordinarily lengthy *Phœnissæ* (about 409 B.C.) he struck a new note—new in many ways. The canvas is greater than that of any other Greek drama, and even approaches the scope of a modern play; the chorus occupies a peculiar position, being formed of a group of Phœnician girls sanctified to the cult of Apollo who happen to be in Thebes at the time of the action and who therefore act as observers of the events displayed before them; the characters are dealt with sincerely and with deepened vision.

For a Greek play the character list is enormous. Here we meet the blind Œdipus and his aged queen-mother, Jocasta; here are his sons, Eteocles and Polyneices; here is Jocasta's brother, Creon, and his son, Menœceus; here is the blind seer, Tiresias, and his guardian child; here is the ill-fated Antigone. The whole story of Thebes is caught up into one single play.

There is much to attract our attention in the *Phœnissæ*, but perhaps, despite its brilliance in portraiture and some of its incisive scenes, it must be regarded as a comparative failure. This failure, however, is of a kind different from that of *Orestes*, for it comes from the very largeness of the attempt made by the playwright. The weaknesses are the weaknesses of supreme genius, not those of mediocre talent.

Genius too breathes throughout that most puzzling of all Greek plays, the *Bacchæ*, written presumably after the poet had departed in exile from his native city, and produced posthumously. No one will ever be able to say what this strange drama intends; but no one can deny its power, its intensity, and its beauty. Fundamentally it is a study of religious frenzy. Set in Thebes during the time of King Pentheus, it shows the city caught up in hysterical orgies in honour of Dionysus, and the god himself not only speaks the prologue, but plays an important rôle in the action.

The scenes are complex, but briefly the story told is that of Pentheus' attempt, in the name of reason, to combat the frenzy that has gripped all the citizens. Between the god and the king stand the old Tiresias and Cadmus, rather contemptuous of the follies of the worshippers, yet prepared to pursue a cautious path. Resolutely Pentheus sets forth to rid his kingdom of the Dionysiac rites, but is confronted by the magic-working god, is himself seized by a group of intoxicated women, including his own mother, Agave, and killed. Peculiarly intense is the scene wherein this Agave, who holds her son's head in her hands under the delusion that it is a lion's head, comes slowly back to reason and realization of the truth:

Enter from the Mountain AGAVE, *mad, and to all seeming wondrously happy, bearing the head of* PENTHEUS *in her hand. The* CHORUS MAIDENS *stand horror-struck at the sight; the* LEADER, *also horror-struck, strives to accept it and rejoice in it as the God's deed.*

AGAVE: Ye from the lands of Morn!

LEADER: Call me not; I give praise!

AGAVE: Lo, from the trunk new-shorn
    Hither a Mountain Thorn
    Bear we! O Asia-born
      Bacchanals, bless this chase.

LEADER: I see. Yea; I see.
    Have I not welcomed thee?

AGAVE [*very calmly and peacefully*]:
    He was young in the wildwood:
    Without nets I caught him!
    Nay, look without fear on
    The Lion; I have ta'en him!

Cadmus enters and argues her back to sanity:

AGAVE [*troubled*]: I know not what thou sayest; but my will
    Clears, and some change cometh, I know not how.

CADMUS: Canst hearken then, being changed, and answer, now?

AGAVE: I have forgotten something; else I could.

CADMUS: What husband led thee of old from mine abode?

AGAVE: Echion, whom men named the Child of Earth.

CADMUS: And what child in Echion's house had birth?

AGAVE: Pentheus, of my love and his father's bred.

CADMUS: Thou bearest in thine arms an head—what head?

AGAVE [*beginning to tremble, and not looking at what she carries*]:
    A lion's—so they all said in the chase.

CADMUS: Turn to it now—'tis no long toil—and gaze.

AGAVE: Ah! But what is it? What am I carrying here?

CADMUS: Look once upon it full, till all be clear.

AGAVE: I see . . . most deadly pain! Oh, woe is me!

CADMUS: Wears it the likeness of a lion to thee?

AGAVE: No; 'tis the head—O God!—of Pentheus, this!

As will be realized, it is indeed difficult to discern Euripides' purpose. The most likely explanation is that, as in the *Hippolytus*, he is suggesting imaginatively that the extreme of reason and frigidity is as false as the extreme of passion. There is no jeering at the gods now: their terrible power has been amply revealed, and the final words of the chorus testify to their omnipotence:

    There be many shapes of mystery.
    And many things God makes to be,

Past hopes or fear.
And the end men looketh for cometh not,
And a path is there where no man thought.
So hath it fallen here.

Finally we reach *Iphigenia in Aulis,* perhaps the last dramatic effort of Euripides' career and one completed by his son. The scene of the maiden's sacrifice forms its subject-matter, but, although it provides a sort of prelude to the story of *Iphigenia in Tauris*, it displays a greater depth and a higher seriousness. Euripides' interest seems concentrated less on the story and more on the characters, and it is interesting to observe that, whereas in his earlier dramas, the playwright had tended to fix his attention on a limited group of main persons, sometimes merely on one outstanding hero or heroine, here he depicts interplay of human personalities.

The central character is Agamemnon, a good-willed but feckless individual, obsessed by thought of his position as general of the Greek forces, easily influenced by his restless brother, Menelaus, who, fretting at the delay in recapturing Helen and so at restoring his honour, eggs him on to follow the advice of the seer Calchas that he shall sacrifice his daughter, Iphigenia. After some hesitation Agamemnon sends a missive to Clytemnestra declaring that Achilles wishes to marry their daughter, and bidding her bring the girl to the camp. Hardly has this missive gone, however, before he suffers from afterthoughts and dispatches a second message countermanding the first. Unfortunately it miscarries; Clytemnestra and Iphigenia arrive, much to Agamemnon's dismay, and the scene wherein they greet him not only exhibits high dramatic skill in the handling of an ironic situation, but throws brilliant light on all their characters:

CLYTEMNESTRA: There comes your father! Let us greet him, girl!
Most honoured lord, King Agamemnon, hail!
We came at your behest.

IPHIGENIA: O mother, blame me not! Let me go first
And put my arms about my father's neck.

CLYTEMNESTRA: Go, go, my girl. You have always loved your father
More than the other children.

IPHIGENIA: Father, how glad it makes my heart to see you!
It is so long since you have been away!

AGAMEMNON: Yes, and mine too; your words are for us both!

IPHIGENIA: How good it was of you to send for me!

AGAMEMNON: No, child, not good; and yet there's good in it.

IPHIGENIA: Why, what is it? There's trouble in your face,
Your eyes are sad. You are not glad to see me.

AGAMEMNON: A general and a king has many cares.
IPHIGENIA: O, stay with me now; send your cares away!
AGAMEMNON: Why, all my cares are only for your sake.
IPHIGENIA: Then smooth your face, unknit your brows, and
                  smile!
AGAMEMNON: I am as glad as I can be, my child.
IPHIGENIA: And all the while the tears are in your eyes!
AGAMEMNON: The parting that must come will be for long.
IPHIGENIA: O, father dear, I do not understand.
AGAMEMNON: Had you the sense I should but suffer more.
IPHIGENIA: Then I'll talk nonsense, if that pleases you.

Here breathes a spirit of pathos vastly different from what we have
met with in others of Euripides' plays: the pity here arises not
from the situation itself, but from contemplation of the characters
involved.

Step by step Agamemnon treads deeper in the mire of his own
deceit. With difficulty he satisfies the questioning of Clytemnestra,
but a moment later the queen encounters Achilles, addresses him
as the future husband of her daughter, and is met by his blank
wonder at her words. Finally a faithful old servant reveals to her
the dire secret, while she in turn tells it to Achilles. In the preceding
scenes Euripides had already given sufficient hints to indicate that
no true harmony existed between Agamemnon and his wife; now
Clytemnestra throws off the veil completely in a magnificent
tirade:

> Then hear me now. I'll speak the naked truth,
> No dark hints now! By force you wedded me,
> I never loved you! Tantalus you slew,
> My first dear husband; and my little son,
> You tore him from my breast. And when my brothers,
> The sons of God, flashed to me on their steeds,
> My father pitied you, his suppliant,
> Gave me to you for wife. And a true wife I was,
> Yes, chaste and true, and cared well for your home.
> Such wives are not so common!—
> Three girls I bore you and a son, and now
> You rob me of the first! Your reason, pray,
> If men should ask it? Oh, I'll answer that,—
> To win back Helen! Your own child for a wanton,
> Your dearest for a foe! A proper bargain!
> If you do this, if you are long at Troy,
> What will my heart be like, think you, at home,
> When I look on my daughter's empty chair,
> And empty room, sitting there all alone,

Companied by my tears, still muttering,
"Your father killed you, child, killed you himself!"
What will your wages be when you come back?
We who are left, we shall not want much urging
To greet you with the welcome you deserve!
O, by the gods, drive me not thus to sin,
Nor sin yourself!
If once you killed your child, how could you pray?
What good thing ask for? Rather for defeat,
Disgrace, and exile! Nor could I pray for you:
We make fools of the gods if we suppose
They can love murderers. If you come home,
Will you dare kiss your girls? Or they dare come,
That you may choose another for the knife?
Have you once thought of this? Are you a man?
Or nothing but a sceptre and a sword?
You should have gone among the Greeks and said,
"You wish to sail for Troy? Good, then draw lots,
And see whose child must die." That had been fair;
Or Menelaus should have slain his own,—
Hermione for Helen. But I, the chaste,
I must be robbed, and she come home in triumph
To find her daughter! Answer, if I am wrong!

The human heart is crying here; the vision of the woman's heart thus bared is brilliant with incandescent tensity.

Iphigenia, terrified, flings herself at her father's feet, but the plans for the sacrifice go on. Achilles, who had tried to save her, is stoned for his pains, and at last the girl, wearied out with the confusion, breaks down and pitifully accepts the fact of her coming death.

It is good to end our survey of Euripides' work on this high note. A puzzling, and at times irritating, dramatist, he contributed much towards the decay of the tragic theatre at the end of the fourth century B.C., but in him too there were brave, translunary things. The only regret is that the world outside of Greece seized on his writings rather than on those of Sophocles or Æschylus for imitation, and, among these writings, often tended to select the most sensational.

CHAPTER IV

ARISTOPHANES AND THE OLD COMEDY

CONSIDERATION of the further fate of tragedy in classical times must be put aside for the moment until we gain a general picture of the comedy that developed during the period from the appearance of Æschylus to the death of Euripides. Greek audiences were capable of appreciating deep, tragic sensations: they could listen spellbound to the sonorous words given to choruses and actors in the serious plays; but they also enjoyed their merriment, and enjoyed it to the full. They were alert for beauty and wit and bawdry alike.

Comedies were first admitted to the Dionysiac Festivals in the year 486 B.C., but for many decades before that the comic form had been slowly evolving out of a diverse series of popular entertainments and rituals. In its earliest shape it was, indeed, a strange admixture, and for long it betrayed, in its absence of a precise structure, the variety of the elements out of which it had been wrought.

Its foundation was the Attic *comus* (κῶμος), a popular ritual wherein a group of revellers organized processions and sang songs of doubtful propriety in honour of Dionysus. From this *comus* comedy takes its name. Often the *comus* group wore masks, or dressed themselves up in a kind of animal masquerade, appearing as birds, horses, or frogs, and this element also was incorporated into the literary comedy when finally that assumed an independent existence. The near-by town of Megara, too, contributed something to the general joy by providing burlesque sketches of a rudely farcical kind, while hilarious dances, such as the licentious *kordax*, contributed to the total ensemble.

The general result was the creation of that type of play which came to be known as the Old Comedy—grotesque, wanton, vulgar, sharp with stinging wit, and richly lyrical; a fantastic exhibition in which the latest gossip of the city was intermixed with material of the most imaginative sort; in which serious political and philosophical purpose jostled with buffoonery of the lowest. This is the Gilbert and Sullivan opera in a land where no Victorian taboos were set upon playwrights or performances, where anything might be said and almost anything done. The shriek of the magpie and the chattering of apes mingle here with the exquisite melodies of the nightingale.

In performance everything was done to make this an hilarious occasion. Animal figures freely appeared in the chorus, and for the main actors there was a rude comic dress. Tights were worn on the legs; a kind of jerkin was exaggeratedly padded; over this a short cloak barely came down to the non-existent waist; and prominently displayed was the indecent *phallus*, the emblem of fertility. The masks were equally exaggerated, rollicking in their distortion and caricature, yet underneath all the slapstick costuming, underneath the unbridled hilarity, there was always the sense of significant purpose, often the unexpected appearance of beauty.

COMEDIES OF WAR, PHILOSOPHY, AND PEACE

Of this Old Comedy we know much from extant vases and statuettes, but the only literary relics that have been spared for us are the eleven precious plays written by Aristophanes. He was not the earliest nor was he any by means the only exponent of the form, but contemporaries recognized him as the greatest, so that this treasure not only has the value of displaying to us the content of the Old Comedy, but also, and more importantly, of revealing it at its best.

Aristophanes was born about 448 B.C., and the first play of his that we possess was produced in 425, at the time when Euripides was oppressed by bitterness on account of the Peloponnesian War and the decline of the democratic principle in Athens. In his opposition to the conduct of the war itself Aristophanes was at one with his elder contemporary, but the two differed violently in their basic philosophies. Where Euripides belonged to the coterie of young, advanced thinkers and in disillusioned spirit sought to discredit the legends of the past, Aristophanes, for all his boisterous fun, was made of Æschylean marble, and endeavoured, with every power that in him lay, to recall the degenerating citizenry of his age to the virtues of their predecessors. His is the conservatism of faith; Euripides fed on a rather superficial disbelief and a facile liberalism.

Since the structure of Old Comedy presents features unique and peculiar, it may be of service to take the first of Aristophanes' plays, *The Acharnians*, and rapidly review its contents. The scene we must suppose to be the Pnyx at Athens, with three doors representing the entrances to the houses of an ordinary citizen Dicæopolis, of the poet Euripides, and of the military general Lamachus (the last two being, of course, prominent contemporaries of the comic dramatist). On to the stage wanders Dicæopolis alone; in his prologue speech he grumbles about the discomforts consequent upon the current war, and declares that when the assembly meets he will press for peace. His aim, however, is thwarted when the officers of the court rudely repress another citizen, Amphitheus, who rises to raise the same issue, and when a group of ambassadors, newly returned from Persia and all togged-up in Eastern fineries, enter to present their reports. With burlesqued dignity the envoys explain that they went on their mission on a miserable salary of two drachmas a day, that they "suffered horribly on the plains of the Cayster, sleeping under a tent, stretched deliciously on fine chariots, half dead with weariness," and were "forced to drink delicious wine out of golden or crystal flagons." In vain Dicæopolis tries to expose the lies with which they flatter the assembly, and disgustedly he sends off Amphitheus to conclude a private truce with Sparta on behalf of himself, his wife, and his children. Meanwhile another ambassador returns, dressed in Thracian costume, and Dicæopolis, to put an end to the business, announces an omen: he pretends he has just felt a drop of rain. Immediately the court is adjourned, while Amphitheus runs in, panting, with a group of angry Acharnians at his heels, irate because of the proposed truce.

All of this provides the first part of the action, and the way is now clear for the *parodos*, or entrance-song, of the chorus. They enter, a group of Acharnian charcoal-burners, and after their first chant proceed to assail Dicæopolis. By the burlesque trick of taking a basket of coal from the house and threatening to destroy it, he commands their attention, and then proposes that he should be permitted to present his defence. At the same time he knows that if he is to prevail he must arouse their pity, and a brilliant thought occurs to him: off he goes to seek Euripides, in order to borrow some of the realistic stage rags worn by characters in that poet's pathetic plays. Knocking at the door, he is answered by a slave:

SLAVE [*opening the door and poking his head out*]: Who's there?
DICÆOPOLIS: Is Euripides at home?
SLAVE: He is and he isn't: understand that, if you can.
DICÆOPOLIS: What's that? He is and he isn't?
SLAVE: Certainly, old man; busy gathering subtle fancies here and there, his mind is not in the house, but he himself is; perched aloft, he is composing a tragedy.

DICÆOPOLIS: Oh, Euripides, you are indeed happy to have a slave so quick at repartee! Now, fellow, call your master.

SLAVE: Impossible!   [*He slams the door.*

DICÆOPOLIS: Too bad. But I will not give up. Come, let us knock at the door again. Euripides, my little Euripides, my darling Euripides, listen; never had man greater right to your pity. It is Dicæopolis of the Chollidian Deme who calls you. Do you hear?

EURIPIDES [*from within*]: I have no time to waste.

DICÆOPOLIS: Very well, have yourself wheeled out here.

EURIPIDES: Impossible.

DICÆOPOLIS: Nevertheless . . .

EURIPIDES: Well, let them roll me out; as to coming down, I have not the time.

[*The ekkuklema turns and presents the interior of the house.* EURIPIDES *is lying on a bed, his slave beside him. On the back wall are hung up tragic costumes of every sort, and a multitude of accessories is piled up on the floor.*

Dicæopolis asks for the costume of one of the tragic poet's most wretched characters. After refusing some that are proffered to him he selects those of Telephus, which the slave finds on top of the rags of Thyestes and mixed with those of Ino. Holding this costume up for the audience to see, he soliloquizes:

Oh! Zeus, whose eye pierces everywhere and embraces all, permit me to assume the most wretched dress on earth. Euripides, cap your kindness by giving me the little Mysian hat, that goes so well with these tatters. I must to-day have the look of a beggar; "be what I am, but not appear to be"; the audience will know well who I am, but the Chorus will be fools enough not to, and I shall dupe them with my subtle phrases.

He now bothers Euripides for a whole set of hand-properties—a beggar's staff, a little pot with a sponge for a stopper; these, to get rid of the nuisance, Euripides gives him, although he complains that Dicæopolis is stealing an entire tragedy.

Now comes Dicæopolis' speech, in which he gives a grotesque yet not essentially false account of the origins of the war, with the result that the chorus splits into two parts, those for him and those against. The latter call to their aid the general Lamachus, who enters in full warlike panoply and acts the braggart, but, rather discomfited by Dicæopolis' words, soon retires.

This leaves the stage free for what was a cardinal element of the Old Comedy, the *parabasis*, wherein the chorus wheeled round and made direct address to the audience in a long melodic ode. There follows a series of detached episodes. Dicæopolis marks out a square in front of his house and declares that this will be a market-place where all but Lamachus may trade. A starved Megarian enters, followed by a well-fed Bœotian, and in their farcical scenes further comment is made both on the effects of the war and on the political dangers within the city. Dicæopolis, prospering in his own peaceful little market-square, prepares himself a fine feast, and while he does so the braggart Lamachus comes out of his house to get ready for a military expedition commanded by the General Staff. The scene in which the joyous Dicæopolis sits at one side of the stage and the gloomy Lamachus at the other is replete with ironic comedy:

LAMACHUS: Bring me the plumes for my helmet.

DICÆOPOLIS: Bring me wild pigeons and thrushes.

LAMACHUS: How white and beautiful are these ostrich feathers!

DICÆOPOLIS: How fat and well browned is the flesh of this wood-pigeon!

LAMACHUS [*to* DICÆOPOLIS]: My friend, stop scoffing at my armour.

DICÆOPOLIS [*to* LAMACHUS]: My friend, stop staring at my thrushes.

LAMACHUS [*to his slave*]: Bring me the case for my triple plume.

DICÆOPOLIS [*to his slave*]: Pass me over that dish of hare.

LAMACHUS: Alas! the moths have eaten the hair of my crest.

DICÆOPOLIS: Shall I eat my hare before dinner?

Both soon go off, but immediately re-enter—Lamachus wounded and woeful, Dicæopolis gloriously drunk, accompanied by two pretty girls.

The whole comedy is spattered with indecent references, and there is much vulgar by-play, yet its serious purpose is amply apparent. Aristophanes does not like the new school of thought represented by Euripides, and he detests the political developments in his city. There is no doubt about his mission, or about his consciousness of it. In the parabasis to this play of *The Acharnians* the chorus specifically points out to the audience what the poet is trying to do and what benefit will accrue to the city if attention is given to his words:

> He therefore affirms,
> In confident terms,
> That his active courage and earnest zeal
> Have usefully served the common weal . . .
> . . . He for his part
> Will practise his art
> With a patriot heart,
> With the honest views
> That he now pursues,

And fair buffoonery and abuse;
Not rashly bespattering, or basely beflattering,
Not pimping, or puffing, or acting the ruffian;
Not sneaking or fawning;
But openly scorning
All menace and warning,
All bribes and suborning:
He will do his endeavour on your behalf;
He will teach you to think, he will teach you to laugh.
So Cleon again and again may try;
I value him not, nor fear him, I!
His rage and rhetoric I defy.
His impudence, his politics,
His dirty designs, his rascally tricks
No stain of abuse on me shall fix.
Justice and right, in his despite,
Shall aid and attend me, and do me right:
With these to friend, I ne'er will bend,
Nor descend
To an humble tone
(Like his own),
As a sneaking loon,
A knavish, slavish poor poltroon.

That he was permitted in the midst of a serious war to produce this stinging anti-war comedy, to refer to the "tricks and plotting" of the popular leader Cleon, and to bring a burlesque Lamachus on the stage testifies to the fact that the Athenian democracy was still, in spite of all he said, healthy and robust. To think of a modern parallel to *The Acharnians* one would have to imagine a bitingly anti-war play of, say, 1943, in which an Eisenhower or a Montgomery were ridiculed in person, and in which a Roosevelt or a Churchill were openly attacked: it would have to be, too, the success of the season, for Aristophanes' comedy was awarded the first prize when it was produced at the Lenæan Festival in 425.

The attack was continued in *The Knights* (424 B.C.), which unfortunately no amount of admiration of Aristophanes' style can make us call a good play; in it indignation has banished laughter. Why it also gained the first prize we cannot tell; nor can we tell why *The Clouds* was rated lowest in the competition of the following year. In this latter work Aristophanes turns from politics to philosophy, and an assessment of its merits is rendered difficult in view of the fact that as his chief figure he has chosen the person of Socrates, presented in such a distorted caricature as to leave the original far behind. If our attention is fixed mainly on the subject of the caricature, then we are bound to deem this play unjust, absurd, and even crassly stupid; but if, as seems the more proper approach, we consider it as a comedy designed to ridicule the follies of the new sophistries then in fashion, with the person of Socrates conveniently taken in symbolic wise, the drama becomes one of prime importance, full of pleasant sallies and amusingly plotted. The story tells of an old man, Strepsiades, who is much worried because of the debts incurred by his son's addiction to horse-racing. Creditors are pressing for their money, and the idea occurs to him that if only the youth will study for a time under the guidance of Socrates he will learn how to argue his way out of paying what he owes. The son, Pheidippides, refuses, whereupon the aged Strepsiades himself determines to go to school. Approaching Socrates' Thought-shop, he finds the philosopher strung up in a basket contemplating the heavens (a burlesque of the tragic *deus ex machina*), and is treated to a discourse in which the Clouds, and not the gods, are made the authors of all things. The Chorus of Clouds now appears, and Socrates explains how everything has a cause that goes back to them:

STREPSIADES: But you have not told us what makes the roll of the thunder.

SOCRATES: Have you not understood me, then? I tell you, that the Clouds, when full of rain, bump against one another, and that, being inordinately swollen out, they burst with a great noise.

STREPSIADES: How can you make me credit that?

SOCRATES: Take yourself as an example. When you have heartily gorged on stew at the Panathenæa, you get throes of stomach-ache, and then suddenly your belly resounds with prolonged rumbling.

STREPSIADES: Yes, yes, by Apollo! I suffer, I get colic, and then the stew sets to rumbling like thunder and finally bursts with a terrific noise. At first, it's but a little gurgling *Pappax, pappax!* then it increases, *Papapappax!* and when I take my crap, why, it's thunder indeed, *papapappax! pappax! papapappax!* just like the clouds!

After the chorus has sung its odes Socrates comes out again, exhausted with the attempt to teach anything to Strepsiades: the latter's mind is set on learning nothing but "the art of false reasoning," but he is incapable of study. The philosopher bids him lie down on a pallet and cogitate. "Well, now!" he inquires. "What are you doing? Are you reflecting?"

STREPSIADES: Yes, by Poseidon!

SOCRATES: About what?

STREPSIADES: Whether the bugs will entirely devour me.
SOCRATES: May death seize you, accursed man!

At last Socrates can stand it no longer, and Pheidippides is persuaded to come in the old man's stead, and we are regaled with a long debate between "Just Reason" and "Unjust Reason"—which might be interpreted as Valid Argument and Specious Argument. So well does Pheidippides prosper that, returning home, he is able to give his father a thorough thrashing, and prove that in taking this course with his parent a son is completely justified.

Purposeful laughter becomes at once gayer and more deeply loaded with serious ore in *The Wasps*, which won the first prize in 422 B.C. The attack returns again to Cleon, and specifically to the large juries which, under his administration, consumed much precious time and proved a political danger. In the first portion of the play we find an elderly gentleman, Philocleon, shut up in his house by his son, Bdelycleon, because of his inordinate love of serving in the courts. Vainly the old man tries, by every trick he can think of, to get away: he pretends he is smoke coming out of the chimney, he attempts to escape by clinging to the belly of an ass, he gets on the roof and endeavours to persuade his gaolers that he is a bird. To his aid come a chorus of his fellow-jurymen, costumed as wasps, but eventually he is persuaded to stay at home, provided he can set up his own private law-court. Here the trial is begun of the house-dog Labes, flagrantly caught in the act of stealing a Sicilian cheese, who is accused by a fellow-dog. There is no doubt about the defendant's guilt, but Bdelycleon puts up a spirited argument on his behalf.

BDELYCLEON: Gentlemen of the jury, it is a difficult thing to speak for a dog who has been calumniated, but nevertheless, I will try. He is a good dog, and he chases wolves finely.
PHILOCLEON: He is a thief and a conspirator.
BDELYCLEON: No, he is the best of all our dogs; he is capable of guarding a whole flock.
PHILOCLEON: And what good is that, if he eats the cheese?
BDELYCLEON: What? he fights for you, he guards your door; he is an excellent dog in every respect. Forgive him his larceny! he is wretchedly ignorant, he cannot play the lyre. . . . Take pity on the unfortunate. . . . Have pity, Father, pity, I adjure you; you would not have him dead. Where are his puppies? [*A group of children costumed as puppies comes out.*] Come, poor little beasties, yap, up on your haunches, beg and whine!

Partly by this moving address and partly by a trick, Philocleon is

D

persuaded to do what he has never done before, acquit the accused
—whereupon he faints from shame and is revived only on his son's
promise of a lively banquet.

The parabasis of the chorus follows, a stirring ode in which the
praise of the jurymen of old is sung, of the men who saved Athens
at Marathon. In rich melodies the music takes the audience back
in memory to the days of Æschylus, when the city repelled the
barbarian might of Persia.

Not yet, however, is the comedy over. The old man Philocleon
has to be tutored in social graces by his son, and this gives occasion
for further digs at Cleon:

BDELYCLEON: The flute-player has finished the prelude. The guests
are Theorus, Æschines, Phanus, Cleon, Acestor. . . . You are with
them. Shall you know exactly how to take up the songs that are
started?
PHILOCLEON: Quite well.
BDELYCLEON: Really?
PHILOCLEON: Better than any born mountaineer of Attica.
BDELYCLEON: That we shall see. Suppose me to be Cleon. I am the
first to begin the song of Harmodius, and you take it up: "There
never yet was seen in Athens——"
PHILOCLEON: "—such a rogue or such a thief."
BDELYCLEON: Why, you wretched man, it will be the end of you if
you sing that. He will vow your ruin, your destruction, to chase
you out of the country.

Having gone to the banquet, Philocleon gets thoroughly drunk,
and the comedy ends in an hilarious dance.

The next year, 421 B.C., Aristophanes' theme was once again
the Peloponnesian War; his *Peace* is a lyrical cry for a cessation of
the stupid internecine conflict which was destroying both Athens
and Sparta. Emulating Dicæopolis, a certain worthy Athenian
citizen, Trygæus by name, has determined on ending the fight,
and at the beginning of the play there is a glorious scene in which
he and his slaves are busily engaged in feeding dung to a large
beetle which he hopes will become sufficiently large to carry him
up to the heavens, where he intends to solicit the aid of Zeus.

At last all is ready. Up he goes in his beetle-machine (another
hit at Euripides), and discovers that most of the gods, tired and
wearied at contemplation of the follies of men, have gone off,
leaving War to do his worst. For his part, War has made a huge
mortar in which he proposes "to pound up all the cities of Greece."
When he has departed Trygæus realizes that the only hope lies in

rescuing Peace from the deep cave into which War has thrust her, and he summons a chorus of Greek peasants and workmen to aid him in this task. After many difficulties they get her out and, again amid difficulties, prepare for a wedding feast. A prophet angrily declares that to war there can be made no end, while an Armourer, equally angry, protests that if peace comes he will be utterly ruined—all his helmets and spears will have to be scrapped or sold at a loss. There is, of course, a happy ending, as Trygæus sings:

> While eating and drinking deep draughts of wine,
> continue to repeat: Oh! Hymen! oh! Hymenæus!
> Oh! Hymen! oh! Hymenæus! Hail, hail, my
> friends. All who come with me shall have
> cakes galore!

The whole play, written just before the deceptive Peace of Nicias, is full of joyousness, and the choral odes, with their lyric praise of the peaceful countryside, are trembling with ecstasy.

FROM "THE BIRDS" TO "THE FROGS"

The beetle-flight of *Peace* was followed by the aerial delights of *The Birds*, but between these two plays six long years had elapsed. *The Birds* appeared in 414 B.C., and the delusive hope of a truce in the Peloponnesian War had gone: indeed, the time was rapidly approaching when Athens was to experience her heaviest blows and to see her democracy overthrown. Small wonder is it, therefore, that Aristophanes sought refuge in a dream-world of his own creation, and endeavoured to find expression for his disgust at the real in the building for himself of an imaginative, fantastic world of Utopian quality.

Again we are introduced to the ordinary sensible Athenian citizen, this time presented by a couple of figures, Euelpides and Peisthetærus, who, wearied out with the discomforts of war and the follies of human politics, set off to consult Epops, the hoopoe. Arrived at his habitation, they suddenly have a brilliant idea: why, they inquire, should the birds not be made masters of all things, building a city in the air in such a strategic situation as might permit them to overawe the gods by controlling the sacrificial smoke from the altars and to rule men by having power over the earth's weather?

Epops is impressed by the grandeur of the plan and summons all the birds to counsel. At first they are prepared to attack the humans who have invaded their sanctuary, but gradually order prevails; they endorse the proposal and indulge in an exquisitely beautiful

chant, in which the notes of the nightingale form a lovely refrain
—so lovely and so gay it must be quoted almost in full:

> O darling! O tawny-throat!
> Love, whom I love the best,
> Dearer than all the rest,
> Playmate and partner in
>   All my soft lays,
> Thou art come! Thou art come!
> Thou hast dawned on my gaze,
> I have heard thy sweet note,
> Nightingale! Nightingale!

Thou from thy flute   Softly sounding canst bring
Music to suit   With our songs of the spring.
>   Begin then I pray
> Our own anapæstic address to essay.

Ye men who are dimly existing below, who perish and fade as the
    leaf,
Pale, woebegone, shadowlike, spiritless folk, life feeble and wingless
    and brief,
Frail castings in clay, who are gone in a day, like a dream full of
    sorrow and sighing,
Come listen with care to the Birds of the air, the ageless, the deathless,
    who flying
In the joy and the freshness of Ether, are wont to muse upon wisdom
    undying. . . .
>   O woodland Muse,
>   *tio, tio, tio, tiotinx,*
Of varied plume, with whose dear aid
On the mountain top, and the sylvan glade,
>   *tio, tio, tio, tiotinx,*
I, sitting up aloft on a leafy ash, full oft,
>   *tio, tio, tio, tiotinx,*
Pour forth a warbling note from my little tawny throat,
Pour festive choral dances to the mountain mother's praise,
And to Pan the holy music of his own immortal lays;
>   *totototototototototinx,*
>   Whence Phrynichus of old,
> Sipping the fruit of our ambrosial lay,
> Bore, like a bee, the honied store away,
>   His own sweet songs to mould.
>   *tio, tio, tio, tio, tiotinx.*

Is there any one amongst you, O spectators, who would lead
With the birds a life of pleasure, let him come to us with speed.

All that here is reckoned shameful, all that here the laws condemn,
With the birds is right and proper, you may do it all with them.
Is it here by law forbidden for a son to beat his sire?
That a chick should strike his father, strutting up with youthful ire,
Crowing, "Raise your spur and fight me," that is what the birds
    admire.
Come, you runaway deserter, spotted o'er with marks of shame,
Spotted Francolin we'll call you, that, with us, shall be your name.
You who style yourself a tribesman, Phrygian pure as Spintharus,
Come and be a Phrygian linnet, of Philemon's breed, with us.
Come along, you slave and Carian, Execestides to wit,
Breed with us your Cuckoo-rearers, they'll be guildsmen apt and fit.
Son of Peisias, who to outlaws would the city gates betray,
Come to us, and be a partridge ("cockerel like the cock," they say),
We esteem it no dishonour knavish partridge-tricks to play.

      Even thus the swans,
        tio, tio, tio, tiotinx,
   Their clamorous cry were erst up-raising,
   With clatter of wings Apollo praising,
        tio, tio, tio, tiotinx,
   As they sat in serried ranks on the river Hebrus' banks.
        tio, tio, tio, tiotinx,
Right upward went the cry through the cloud and through the sky.
Quailed the wild-beast in his covert, and the bird within her nest,
And the still and windless Ether lulled the ocean-waves to rest,
      totototototototototinx.
   Loudly Olympus rang!
Amazement seized the kings; and every Grace
And every Muse within that heavenly place
     Took up the strain, and sang.
      tio, tio, tio, tio, tiotinx.
Truly to be clad in feathers is the very best of things.
Only fancy, dear spectators, had you each a brace of wings,
Never need you, tired and hungry, at a Tragic Chorus stay,
You would lightly, when it bored you, spread your wings and fly
    away,
Back returning, after luncheon, to enjoy our Comic Play. . . .
If a gallant should the husband on the Council-bench behold
Of a gay and charming lady, one whom he had loved of old,
Off at once he'd fly to greet her, have a little converse sweet,
Then be back, or e'er ye missed him, calm and smiling in his seat.
Is not then a suit of feathers quite the very best of things?

The city is now a-building and named Nephelococcygia—Cloud-
cuckoo-town—but soon its founders are confronted by a set of self-

seeking Athenians. A poet ready to pen civic odes, a seer who would provide it with oracles, a town-planning expert, an inspector, and a law-maker are dealt with summarily; but a herald announces that there is a positive bird-mania down below, that thousands are applying for wings, and once again a series of objectionable characters flocks in—a Parricide who wants to live in Nephelococcygia because there, he thinks, he can kill his father with impunity, Cinesias the poetaster, and an Informer, who thinks his professional pursuits would be the better carried out if he could fly from place to place. Finally creeps in a heavily cloaked figure who turns out to be Prometheus, traditional friend of man: he brings news that the gods are in a sorry state since the founding of the city, and that they may be forced to accept whatever terms may be imposed.

Thus ends a joyous and a lovely play in gladness and in mirth.

Three years later (411 B.C.) *Lysistrata* repeats the mirth, although the gladness is more than a trifle bitter. This magnificent comic conception, in which Lysistrata, a woman of Athens, plans to stop the war by swearing all the wives of the warring states to refrain from intercourse with their husbands until the latter abandon their stupidities and call a truce, has the brilliance of simplicity. The fortunes of the women's revolution are related with gusto—both the anxieties of the men to have their wives back, and the pathetic little tricks employed by the weaker among the sisterhood, who wish to escape from the austere fervour of Lysistrata, are handled with consummate ease and obvious enjoyment. Here Aristophanes' inventive powers are at their finest; scene follows scene in unflagging merriment. The oath that the revolutionaries rather dismally are forced to swear; the almost pitiful combat between the chorus of old men, who bear faggots to the Acropolis in the hope of smoking out Lysistrata's friends, and the chorus of old women, who bear buckets wherewith to douse the flames; the discomfiture of the Athenian magistrate; the comic misery of Cinesias as he attempts to recapture his wife, while she tortures him beyond endurance; followed by the equally comic misery of the Spartan herald— episode after episode is daringly vulgar and gloriously amusing.

The same season (411 B.C.) Aristophanes offered to the public another comedy of women, the *Thesmophoriazusæ*, in which the theme of war is laid aside and the poet returns to the attack, begun many years before, on Euripides. Again, the comic invention is boldly and brilliantly simple. The tragic dramatist has learned that the women of Athens are to try him in their meeting at the Thesmophoria, accusing him of betraying the secrets of their sex; and, terrified of what may happen, he determines he must have an advocate to speak in his defence. First, he approaches his effeminate tragic colleague, Agathon, begging him to dress up as a woman and go on his behalf to the Thesmophoria, but fails to find the assistance he needs. Now, however, unexpected aid comes from a kinsman, Mnesilochus, who, after a comic shaving scene, gets himself ready. At the meeting all would have been well had this advocate not chosen to deliver a hearty but exceedingly tactless oration, pleading that the assembly should remember how many feminine sins and failings Euripides had *not* revealed. Infuriated, the women set upon him; he is found to be a man and placed under strong guard pending the announcement of his doom.

There follows a series of delicious episodes in which the wretched Mnesilochus tries device after device from the plays of his kinsman in an attempt to escape. Remembering how Œax in the (now lost) *Palamedes* had carved messages on wooden oars, he tries to send word of his fate to Euripides by similarly carving on small wooden images. Next he starts reciting from the *Helen*, while Euripides enters in the part of Menelaus, and there is fine merriment when Mnesilochus, whose face is lacerated from his shaving, quotes Helen's line: "My cheeks show the marks of the insults I have been forced to suffer." A magistrate enters and causes him to be bound to a post, but Euripides, retiring, declares he will never abandon him "as long as I draw breath and one of my numberless artifices remains untried." Given a cue, the prisoner sings a doleful ditty from *Andromeda*, while Euripides, peering round the edge of the scene-building, pretends to be Echo, and later poses as Perseus. All these tricks, however, fail, and in the end the dramatist has to forget his dramas, is forced to dress up as an old bawd and come in leading two pretty girls. These he parades across the stage, thus distracts the guardian policeman, and is enabled to release Mnesilochus.

The comedy is replete with good-humour and incisive wit, and its episodes are instinct with the sense of the ludicrous.

To Euripides Aristophanes returned some years later in *The Frogs* (405 B.C.), a short time after the tragic dramatist had died. Dionysus, god of the theatre, is worried lest the stage be left without any good plays and determines to go to Hades to try to get the deceased Euripides back. Remembering that Herakles had once made the journey to the nether regions with impunity, he goes with his slave Xanthias to seek advice from that hero:

DIONYSUS: Just tell us what's the best and quickest road to Hades. And, please, give us the most comfortable route.

HERAKLES: Well, let's see. Now, which would be best? Oh, yes, I have it. Get a sturdy seaman to tug a hawser round your neck.

DIONYSUS: A chokey sort of journey, that.

HERAKLES: Well, then, there is one very quick way—smoothly pounded up in a mortar.

DIONYSUS: The road of hemlock?

HERAKLES: Precisely.

DIONYSUS: Too cold for me. I'm freezing already.

HERAKLES: What about a short steep road?

DIONYSUS: That would suit me fine. I'm not a great walker.

HERAKLES: Then just walk down to Ceramicus——

DIONYSUS: Yes?

HERAKLES: Ascend the tower there——

DIONYSUS: That's all right: and then?

HERAKLES: Wait till they start the races down below, lean over till they give the signal to go, and then go.

DIONYSUS: Where?

HERAKLES: Over.

At last, after this badinage, the pair set out, Dionysus dressed in Herakles' skin and bearing his club. He is ferried across Charon's lake of the dead while Xanthias pants round the edge, and a group of frogs raucously chants the "Brekekekex koax koax" chorus. Ludicrous scenes occur in Hades and gradually work up to the climax, when Æschylus and Euripides contest to see which of them is the weightier playwright by placing lines from their dramas on a great pair of scales. Although the latter displays wit, subtlety of argument, and an ability to anger his opponent by his sophistries, the scales weigh down on Æschylus' side, and he is chosen to return to earth. Even as a contemporary, Aristophanes realized how far Euripides was injuring the spirit of tragedy: only a return to Æschylean passion could save it from complete ruin.

Thus is enclosed, between the bird chorus and the chorus of frogs, the gayest, the most serious, the wittiest, and the most lyrical period of Aristophanes' genius.

THE LAST PLAYS: "ECCLESIAZUSÆ" AND "PLUTUS"

In the year 405 B.C. the doom of Athens had been firmly engraved by the hand of destiny and the foolish hands of its citizenry. The great fleet was routed at Ægospotami, and the once proud city-state surrendered ignominiously to Sparta; the Piræus and the Long

Walls were razed, only twelve ships were permitted to remain in her navy, her foreign possessions all were lost. Very soon the Thirty Tyrants took control, the moderate Theramenes was murdered, and the brief-lived despotism was overthrown by a violent revolution under Thrasybulus. Amid these events the civic life of the state inevitably altered: excesses were rife and the old freedom had gone. Socrates, instead of merely being laughed at on the stage, was grimly forced to take the chilly hemlock road to Hades jokingly recommended to Dionysus by Herakles.

Under such conditions the spirit of comedy gradually changed; the Old Comedy was transformed into what was known as the Middle Comedy. In this, it would seem, the licences of the earlier Aristophanic style were curbed, political references were cautiously introduced, and the general structure was changed through the influence of Euripides, but largely, too, because rich men no longer were prepared to defray the high costs of production of these pieces. In the *Ecclesiazusæ* (392 B.C.) the familiar Aristophanic fantasy is still apparent, but subdued in tone. Like the *Lysistrata*, it deals with a women's revolution, led by Praxagora, designed to establish a genuine communist state, in which property belongs to all and where free love is allowed—with modifications, the chief of these being that the old women and the ugly are given priority over the young and the lovely. This piece of legislation furnishes the principal merriment at the end, when a young man, attracted by a girl, finds he must satisfy first an elderly woman; rescued from her, he is captured by one yet older; and finally, a second time rescued, he finds himself in the clutches of a hideous and aged harridan.

The spirit is the spirit of the Old Comedy, but the form is changing. Gone is the central element in the more ancient type of play, the parabasis of the chorus, and although the basic action is fantastic, the language is more nearly akin to the speech of common life. That we are entering a new world is revealed, too, in one character name, Chremes, which in the New Comedy, soon to follow, was destined to become a stock title for the comic old man.

Aristophanes' last play is the peculiar *Plutus*, presented in 388 B.C., a kind of morality drama, in which the blind god of riches, Plutus, is protected (incognito) by the worthy citizen Chremylus, at length is cured, and regains his sight. The spectre of Poverty rises and enters into a debate by trying to prove that she, not Plutus, has most aided mankind; discomfited, she retires, and the god is left to dispense his blessings more equably than in the past. The play has some quality, and a few flashes of the Aristophanic humour irradiate the dialogue, but, compared with the outpouring of invention in *The Birds* or the roistering joy of *Thesmophoriazusæ*, it is a tame, and rather dull, affair. The time of unbridled, uproarious, purposeful laughter had gone for Aristophanes, for Athens, and, one might even say, for the world.

FROM MENANDER TO THE MIMES

THE STYLE known as the Middle Comedy endured from the first quarter of the fourth century to about 330 B.C., but concerning its qualities we can but make broad guesses. The literary evidence consists of no more than a number of fragments, and our chief guide is a set of statuettes which evidently reproduce the stage appearance of its characters. From these we may hazard the conjecture that the Middle Comedy was basically a transitional form of drama, inheriting some of the features of the Old Comedy, but definitely tending towards an entirely different concept of the comic.

The costumes worn by the characters still bear traces of the attire of the actors in the fifth century, with the padded stomachs, the tights, the short cloak, but when we examine the figures in greater detail we realize that the exaggeration of feature has been softened and that the characters represented must have been much closer to the living persons to be seen on Athens' streets than the grotesques beloved by Aristophanes. There are still some burlesque mythological persons, such as the braggart Herakles, but most of the statuettes represent a series of stock types of the day—an old woman holding a child, a modest-seeming courtesan, old men and young men, rascally slaves, some seated in impertinent attitude on altars where they have sought sanctuary. We receive the impression—fortified from other sources—that the actions in which these characters were involved must have been of a more domestic kind than the earlier fantasies and that their behaviour must have been much more realistic.

A CHANGING THEATRE

Meanwhile both audience and theatre were in process of change. The old gusty days of the Athenian democracy were gone, and a bourgeois civilization had taken its place. Civic interests had ceded to domestic. Having argued the gods out of existence, men had no other deity than Plutus, god of wealth. The ancient culture was sufficiently strong to leave its deep impress on all the peoples of the Mediterranean basin, but its vitality had been dissipated; the culture had become polite.

Gradually Athens ceased to be the core of this civilization. Power passed from state to state, and it was not to be long before Alexander the Great, Greek in outlook but a monarch of Macedon, became lord of the ancient world. Nor was it to be long after that before this civilization was to find its chief home in Egypt, at Alexandria under the Ptolemies.

All over the Greek countries there was the building of new theatres and the remodelling of old during this time, for the impetus of the three great Athenian tragic dramatists and of Aristophanes was powerful enough to maintain prime interest in the stage; but the forms assumed by these new theatres were different from those of the fifth century. True, the Greek playhouse to the very end retained its chief characteristic feature—the combination of three essentially separate parts, auditorium, orchestra, and scene-building. At the same time the functions of these parts were being altered. The great sweep of stone seats tended to approach more nearly to the shape of a semicircle. Although the orchestra still kept its central position, the reduced importance of the chorus permitted an encroachment upon its area, with the *skene* pushing itself forward; in some theatres, even, such as those at Assos and Priene, the circular form was deliberately abandoned, and the new orchestra took the shape of a semicircle extended by lines drawn at right angles to the diameter.

It was, however, the scene-building that altered most, taking shape as a structure clearly modelled on the richer domestic architecture of the time. Because the chorus and the actors were now separate, with more emphasis placed upon the individual characters in the dramas presented, the way was open for the erection of a high stage. Normally, this high stage was placed upon a long line of low pillars and jutted out in front of the *skene* proper: it was, accordingly, styled the proscenium (*proskenion*), literally signifying that which was before the *skene*. Behind it was the second storey of the *skene*, with a row of columns supporting a roof and providing a kind of rear or inner stage in the space between the columns and the front wall of the scene-building.

In this new type of theatre scenery could be, and was, more freely used than in the past, and we must think of the actors appearing against backgrounds of panels (*pinakes*), painted either to give the suggestion of walls and doors or more elaborately to convey an impression of buildings in perspective. We must think, too, of these actors becoming more and more important, until Aristotle could observe that in theatrical productions they were generally of greater consequence than the dramas they interpreted. This is a playhouse intended not for those who have come to a religious exercise, intent upon listening to rich words, but for those who see in the theatre a place of entertainment merely, whose interests are more mundane and whose eyes need showy scenes.

THE NEW COMEDY: MENANDER

The characteristic dramatic genre in this theatre was the New Comedy, established, during the time of Alexander the Great, about 330 B.C. Even had we possessed nothing but the terracottas and other visible records of the actors in these plays, we could have made a fair guess at its tone and contents. Gone is the old grotesque comic dress; the mythological types have vanished. Instead on the stage now appear figures garbed in the costumes of the day. Here are the fathers and sons of Hellenistic society, the slaves and the cooks and the musicians, the old gossips and the parasites, the young wives, and, above all, the courtesans. Some of the masks still retain an element of grotesquerie, but in general the features are closely modelled on the real.

Happily some literary record also remains, and this enables us to corroborate the impression received from contemplation of the little histrionic statuettes and to round out our imaginative reconstruction of the productions. Apart from fragments from a number of authors of the New Comedy style, a happy discovery at Cairo has given us some four thousand lines of the writing of the most famous of these authors, Menander, amply sufficient to allow us to shape general conclusions concerning the entire development of this comic style.

One of a group of playwrights including Philemon, Diphilus, Poseidippus, and Apollodorus, Menander was born in 343 B.C. (he died in 292), the nephew of a Middle Comedy dramatist, Alexis. Well-born, he was interested in social manners and the graces of culture; the life of the city appealed to him, and its types he studied with sympathetic care. The contemporary and friend of Epicurus, he imbibed some of that philosopher's ideas, while from Theophrastus he probably acquired his interest in the delineation of character types.

Before turning to an examination of those works of his which are still, though fragmentarily, extant, we may do well to consider, in general terms, the style of play which he was largely responsible for establishing on the stage. This style of play is essentially realistic. Aristophanes' fantasies are forgotten, and the characters are familiar; nor need we be surprised, since the comedies were penned for a bourgeois civic audience, to find that, despite the changed conventions of life, a peculiarly 'modern' note is struck in the dialogue. When we hear the persons of New Comedy speaking about 'gold-digging' and 'shop-keeping minds' we recognize the world we are in.

With the fantastic has vanished, too, the old uproarious laughter. Menander seldom allows more than a smile to curve his lips. Indeed, we encounter here a quiet, contemplative mood which might almost have seemed more proper to the tragic stage.

> When you wish to know what you are, look at the tombs in the cemeteries. There are bones there, and the ashy dust of men who were monarchs, tyrants, sages, men proud of their birth and their riches, their estates and their handsome figures. Naught of these defended them against Time: Death comes to all things mortal. Look on these and learn what you are.

Passages such as this remind us that we are far off from boisterous comedy, that we are in the world of a realistic, reflective, sentimental comedy of human manners.

And here the influence of Euripides upon the New Comedy becomes clearly apparent. From Euripides two great streams of influence are to be traced. His inspiration was a dominant influence on all the tragic playwrights who followed him. This was a direct channel, but no less direct was the passage from his dramas to those of Menander. In Euripides' plays certain characteristic features attract attention: his suppression of the chorus, his emphasis upon character (particularly the characters of women), his carefully wrought plots with their complications, his reflective, rhetorical tone, his introduction of love-themes, his development of a kind of tragi-comedy. The chief trend of his art was from the heroic to the realistic, from the ideal to the ordinary, from the rigours of tragedy to the sentimentalities of the drama of ideas. Already, in *Helen* and other plays, these features have been amply revealed, but there still remains at least one of his works to be considered, and this may now be glanced at, since it demonstrates in an extreme form qualities later on to be taken up by the comic playwrights of the fourth century. The date of *Ion* is unknown, but almost certainly it came late in Euripides' career; with one or two changes its plot might easily have been the plot of one of Menander's plays. The familiar situation is here—a girl ravished in the dark and a child exposed with trinkets; only here the girl is a princess, Creusa, the ravisher is a god, Apollo. As the plot proceeds we find Creusa married to a king, Xuthus; the couple are childless and go to Delphi for aid. Apollo's oracle declares that the first person whom Xuthus meets as he leaves the temple will be his son; this person is, in reality, Ion, the child of Creusa. Not knowing who he is, Creusa, enraged, determines to destroy him, is prevented, and discovers the boy's real paternity by means of the jewels she herself had left with the exposed babe. Gods appear in this story, and princesses, but they behave like middle-class citizens; bourgeois romance surrounds them, sentimentalism colours their actions, the atmosphere in which they dwell is not that highly charged mountain air out of which tragedy is wrought, but the quiet, reflective comic air of the plains. Tragedy is rapidly becoming drama.

Fundamentally, then, we may say that the style of Menander and his fellows was wrought out of the Euripidean manner. In their structure, in their romantic theme, in their concentration on the domestic, and in their rhetorical quality a direct link exists between the tragedies of the one school and the sentimental comedies of the other.

The first play from which we have fragments of Menander's writing is *Samia* (*The Girl from Samos*), which, although more carefree, perhaps one might almost say farcical, than his other extant works, nevertheless reveals the typical features of his art. Only a small portion of the text has come down to us, sufficient, however, for a reconstruction of the plot. Romantic love is the core, with misunderstandings complicating the action, providing opportunity for character portrayal and creating scenes of laughable disorder. Moscion, son of the kindly, good-willed Demeas, is deeply in love with Plangon, daughter of the poor, irascible, touchy Niceratus. She has a child, and, fearing her father's wrath, has it taken by Chrysis, Demeas' mistress and housekeeper, who gives out that it is her child by her guardian. The complications may be imagined: Demeas suddenly rendered jealous when he imagines that Chrysis has been unfaithful with his own son; Niceratus so hasty in his passions that he will not listen to reason; slaves trying to conceal secrets and making confusion worse confounded by their efforts. There is in some lines a sort of brittle wit, as when the slave Parmeno addresses the Cook:

Cook, I'm damned if I know why you carry knives with you. Your
chatter would reduce anything to mincemeat.

There is abundance of comic irony when characters blunder over
issues quite plain to the audience. There is pathos, as in the scene
where the unfortunate and falsely suspected Chrysis is driven out-
of-doors by her protector.

Misunderstandings—symbolized by the abstract figure of Mis-
apprehension—teem also in *Perikeiromene* (*The Girl with Shorn Hair*),
a comedy of separated twins, Glycera and Moschion. Abandoned
in infancy, the former has been brought up by a poor woman and
later finds a protector in the soldier Polemon, while the latter has
been adopted and lavishly cared for by a wealthy old lady, Myrrhine.
From the scene in which Polemon, enraged by ill-founded jealousy,
shears off Glycera's hair the play takes its title, but jealous rages of
such sort do not long endure in Menander's comedies, and, of
course, the pair are reconciled; of course Glycera and Moschion
discover their relationship; of course the pair are united to their
long-lost father. It is all very pretty, very romantic, and yet at the
same time very close to real life.

How far Menander carried the comic drama along these lines is
revealed even more patently in *Epitrepontes* (*The Arbitration*), still
another play of love, in which pathos battles with laughter as to
which shall win. Since more of this comedy has been preserved
than of any other of Menander's works, and since in this New
Comedy the true basis is to be found for the characteristic modern
theatre, its plot may be more fully summarized.

In the first act we are introduced to a young wife, Pamphila,
daughter of the hard-fisted Smicrines, and her strait-laced husband,
Charisius, a very serious and proper youth. There has just been a
crisis in the household. Barely five months after her marriage
Pamphila has borne a son, and we learn that this was the result of
an attack made upon her, before her wedding, by a drunken man
at one of the city's festivals: since the assault was in the dark, she
has no idea of the identity of her seducer. The child has been taken
by a slave to be exposed, and all would have been well had not
Onesimus, Charisius' slave, revealed the secret. Charisius is shocked
but, being genuinely in love with his wife, he does not cast her off:
instead, he leaves the house and indulges in extravagant orgies in
which a girl harpist, Habrotonon, figures largely.

The second act opens with the appearance of Smicrines, who,
not knowing about the child, is in a rage at his son-in-law, not so
much for having deserted Pamphila as for squandering his fortune

MENANDER WITH
HIS MASKS
From the original in the
Museo Laterano, Rome.
Photo Anderson

112

A SCENE FROM THE NEW
COMEDY

From the original in the
Museo Nazionale, Naples.

Photo Anderson

OLD MAN AND SLAVE

Phlyax vase at Bari. From Margarete Bieber,
Die Denkmäler zum Theaterwesen im Altertum,
Taf. LXXXV, I.

THE BIRTH OF HELENA

Phlyax vase at Bari. From Margarete Bieber,
Die Denkmäler zum Theaterwesen im Altertum,
Taf. LXXX.

ZEUS VISITING ALCMENA

Phlyax vase in the Vatican.

Photo Alinari

ZEUS VISITING ALCMENA

Phlyax vase in the British Museum.

THE THEATRE AT
ORANGE
"Picture Post" Library

113

on riotous living. His reflections are interrupted when a slave, Davus, and Syriscus, a charcoal-burner, enter in lively and acrimonious argument. They agree to put their case to arbitration and beg Smicrines to be the judge. Davus explains that some time ago he found an exposed babe along with some trinkets:

> I picked it up and went back home with it and was going to raise it. That's what I intended then. In the night, though, like everybody else, I thought it over to myself and argued it out: "Why should I bring up a baby and have all that trouble? Where am I to get all that money to spend? What do I want with all that worry?" That's the state I was in. Early next morning I was tending my flock again, when along came this fellow, he's a charcoal-burner, to this same spot to get out stumps there. He had made friends with me before that. So we got talking together and he saw that I was gloomy and said: "Why so thoughtful, Davus?" "Why indeed," said I, "I meddle with what doesn't concern me." So I tell him what had happened, how I found the baby and how I picked it up. And he broke in at once, before I had finished my story, and began entreating me: "As you hope for luck, Davus," he kept saying, "do give me the baby, as you hope for fortune, as you hope for freedom. I've a wife, you see," says he, "and she had a baby, but it died." Meaning this woman who is here now with the child. Did you entreat me, Syriscus?

The charcoal-burner admits this, but, having heard about the trinkets, he claims he ought to have them. In a spirited speech he argues that these trinkets must go with the child:

> Perhaps this babe is better born than we. He may, though brought up among labourers, look down on our condition, seek his own native level, have pluck to ply some noble occupation, hunt lions, bear arms, take part in races at the games. You have seen actors, I am sure, and all these things are familiar to you. A certain Neleus and Pelias, the famous ones, were found by an aged goat-herd clad in a goat-skin just like mine. When he saw that they were nobler born than he, he told them all, how he found and picked them up, and he gave them a wallet full of tokens and from that they found out everything about themselves for certain and, goat-herds before, now became kings.

Convinced by such arguments, Smicrines immediately commands Davus to hand over the trinkets. As Syriscus examines his booty Onesimus enters, and at once recognizes a ring as belonging to his master, Charisius.

The third act reveals, through the words of Onesimus and Habrotonon, that Charisius, despite his semblance of rioting, is really pining for his wife and curses the day he was told her secret

—so much so that Onesimus is afraid to reveal the secret of the ring to him. He knows Charisius lost it at a festival, and he is almost sure he must have assaulted some girl there; before taking further action he wishes to find that girl. Here Habrotonon comes to his aid: she was at the festival, she says, when a young girl was apparently attacked:

ONESIMUS: You were there?
HABROTONON: Yes, last year at the Tauropolia. I was playing the lute for some young ladies, was joining in the sport myself; at that time I hadn't—I mean I didn't know yet what a man is. [ONESIMUS *smiles knowingly*.] Indeed I didn't, by Aphrodite.
ONESIMUS: Yes, but do you know who the girl was?
HABROTONON: I could ask. She was a friend of the women that I was with.
ONESIMUS: Did you hear who her father was?
HABROTONON: I don't know anything about her except that I should recognize her if I saw her. A good-looking girl, goodness, yes, and rich too, they said.
ONESIMUS: Perhaps it's the same one.
HABROTONON: I don't know about that. Well, while she was with us there, she strayed off and then suddenly came running up alone, crying and tearing her hair. She had utterly ruined a very fine Tarantine shawl, and delicate, my goodness. Why, it was all in tatters.

It is arranged between them that Habrotonon will wear the ring and, if Charisius notices it, will profess to have been the wronged maiden. The plot works: Charisius acknowledges the child and is prepared to pay heavily in order to secure Habrotonon's liberty; while Smicrines, outraged, determines to take his daughter home with him.

In the fourth act Pamphila protests to her father (Charisius overhearing her words) that, despite all the ill-usage she has received, she will not desert her husband. A moment later she meets Habrotonon and receives the joyous news that Charisius is the father of her child, while as for Charisius himself, the words of Onesimus are sufficient testimony:

He's not quite sane. By Apollo, he's mad. He's really gone mad. By the gods he *is* mad. My master, I mean, Charisius. He's had an atrabilious stroke or some such thing. How else can you explain it? He spent a long time by the door inside just now craning his neck and listening. His wife's father was having a talk with her about the business, I suppose. The way he kept changing colour, gentlemen, I don't even care to mention. Then he cried out: "O darling! what a wonderful thing to say!" and beat his head violently. Then again after a while: "What a wife I had and now have lost, alas!" And to cap it all, when he had heard them to the end and had gone in at last, inside there was groaning, tearing of hair, continual frenzy. Over and over again he'd repeat: "Criminal that I am, when I had myself done a thing like that, when I had myself got an illegitimate child, to be so unfeeling, so utterly unforgiving to her in the same unhappy situation. No humanity; no mercy." He calls himself names as hard as he can, his eyes are bloodshot with fury. I'm shaking in my shoes; I'm all wilted with terror. If he catches sight of me, who told on her, anywhere, while he's in this state, he'll maybe kill me. That's why I've quietly slipped out here. Where am I to turn though? What can I think of? It's all over. I'm done for. He's at the door coming out. O Zeus Saviour, help me if you can.

Poor Charisius now comes in, berating himself for his superiority and determining to make amends to Pamphila. Learning that she is really the mother of the child, his self-abasement knows no bounds, his new-found resolve no limits.

The last act shows the discomfiture of Smicrines, who, arriving in a passion to abduct his daughter by force, is suddenly deflated by the truth. "By all the gods and spirits," he cries, and Onesimus cynically questions him:

ONESIMUS: Do you believe, Smicrines, that the gods can spare the time to mete out daily to every individual his share of good or evil?
SMICRINES: What's that?
ONESIMUS: I'll make it quite plain. The total number of cities in the world is approximately a thousand. Each has thirty thousand inhabitants. Are the gods busy damning or saving each of them one by one? Surely not, for so you make them lead a life of toil. Then are they not all concerned for us, you'll say. In each man they have placed his character as commander. This ever present guardian it is that ruins one man, if he fails to use it aright, and saves another. [*Indicating himself*] This is our god, this is the cause of each man's good or evil fortune. Propitiate this by doing nothing absurd or foolish, that good fortune may attend you.

Thus ends *The Arbitration*, on a strangely modern note. All the ingredients are here for the drama of to-day—the emphasis on manners, the mingled smiles and tears, the growth of character in the persons represented, the concept of the single moral law for men and for women alike, even, we may say, the building of the entire play about an idea, for Menander's comedy is, in essence, a problem drama.

THE MIMES, ROUGH AND REFINED

The style of Menander was handed on and taught to Rome, but before we turn to the Latin playwrights we must consider, very briefly, the characteristics of a largely unliterary theatre which, taking many and diverse shapes, ran its course from earliest days to latest, independently of the Old, Middle, and New Comedy traditions.

It will be recalled that the Aristophanic kind of drama owed something to the burlesque, farcical episodes put upon the stage at Megara. Down through the years from Aristophanes to Menander, and beyond, dim relics of these popular farces may be traced, sometimes very faint and uncertain, sometimes firm and sure. An example of the latter is the stage of the so-called Phlyakes (Φλύακες) of Southern Italy and Sicily, as depicted on numerous vases and revealed in contemporary record. In the pieces played by these actors a wooden stage was used, sometimes at least with an upper gallery which could serve as an acting-area. Their costumes were based on the costumes of the Old Comedy (themselves probably derived from the Megarean farce), and the basis of their efforts was burlesque.

Some authors, whose names are preserved for us by commentators—such as Rhinthon, who flourished about 300 B.C.—lent their talents to the penning of plays for the Phlyakes, but one gets the impression, on studying the vase paintings in which the players appear, that most of this activity was unliterary, perhaps largely improvised. In most of the scenes depicted the gods and the heroes are unmercifully mocked. Zeus is a pathetic creature, Herakles a brutal savage, Apollo an effeminate æsthete; Zeus appears dragging a ladder with which to mount to Alkmena's window, Apollo takes refuge on the top of his own temple from the threats of Herakles. Scenes of ordinary life are here too, burlesqued in like manner; old men are stupid, slaves ridiculous; life's amusing panorama is broadly set before us.

This *mimus*, or mime, as it came to be styled, spread out in two directions, the one untheatrical and literary, the other becoming ever more and more popular. For back in the fifth century the Sicilian Epicharmus won fame for his handling of this kind of play, and later came Herodas, a native of Kos, who apparently lived and wrote in the third century B.C. Of the former's works nothing save titles and a few fragments remain, but fortune has preserved eight sketches by Herodas—lively, frank little studies of life. About the same time were composed the mimes of Theocritus, in which a polished style and a delicate refinement in the handling of subject-matter cannot conceal the popular origin of the idyllic poetry.

In these, however, we are being steadily drawn away from the stage, and for our purposes it is much more important to trace the movement of the mimic drama in its more definitely theatrical forms. From Sicily the mime seems to have moved northward, through the Greek settlements on the Italian peninsula, to Tarentum and Pæstum, and thence it reached the Oscans, producing a kind of associated drama which the Romans called the *fabula Atellana*— a name derived from the Campanian town of Atella. Little is known of the *fabula Atellana*, but certain facts seem clear: it was inspired by Greek models, apparently of the Phlyakes type; it became popular in Rome as early as the third century B.C., and was the genre particularly favoured by Pomponius of Bononia and by Novius a couple of centuries later; it introduced a set of stock characters among whom the stupid Bucco, the Punch-like Dossennus, the greedy Maccus, the senile Pappus, are clearly indicated. In tone the spirit of these Atellan plays cannot have been far removed from that of the Sicilian popular drama.

THE COMIC WORLD OF PLAUTUS

The Greek inspiration in the development of the Atellan farce is a symbol of a general truth regarding the entire development of Roman literature and Roman theatre alike. The Greek genius was inventive; the Romans knew best how to adapt: the Greeks felt an innate demand for spiritual expression; the Romans delighted more in practical things. The result is that the Roman theatre is built out of what the Greeks created, and the Latin plays were based confessedly on Athenian models. At the same time we must ever bear in mind the fact that, while Rome did not introduce anything fundamentally new, the manner in which it took over and firmly stamped the older forms made it, and not Athens, produce the models on which the whole of the subsequent Western stage is based.

So far as the theatre building is concerned, certain dominant features are worthy of special attention. To Rome the theatre came late, but when it did it took characteristic shape as a single architectural structure; the three separate parts of the Greek theatre (auditorium, orchestra, and stage) were crushed within continuous

containing walls. The effect was achieved by making the first and
second elements exact semicircles and by elaborating the *skene* so
that it occupied the entire diameter. Thus the spectators, entering
such a playhouse, no longer sat watching a performance in which
the actors were at least partly revealed against a natural background
of sea and mountainous landscape, but, instead, remained enclosed
by the lofty theatre's retaining structure. Plays, as it were, became
more indoor affairs, and the impression was no doubt intensified
by the roofs, which in some buildings jutted out over the stage,
and by the awnings, which could even be spread, as occasion
demanded, above the audience. No longer was there any advantage
in erecting theatres on lofty positions, and, therefore, in Roman
times the followers of Thespis brought their baggage down from
the hillsides and performed on the plains. In such playhouses scenery
could be more effectively introduced than in any of the early
Greek structures, and scenic display, we know, was freely presented
on the lofty, ornate façades against which the actors were revealed.
There even came into use the theatrical front curtain, raised on posts
at the side of the stage and lowered into specially prepared trenches
at the rear of the attenuated orchestra.

The development of these structures, with their characteristic
Roman features, was, however, mainly the result of architectural
activity during the period of the Empire; the plays of Plautus, the
first Latin playwright known to us, and, indeed, virtually the first
Roman author, were produced in no such grandiose structures.
For him simple wooden erections, apparently based on the kind of
stage used by the Phlyakes, had to suffice.

Titus Maccius Plautus was born about 254 B.C. and died, at the
age of seventy, in 184. Reared in poor circumstances and forced
to make a living by hard labour, he seems to have turned to the
theatre in the hope of easing his lot, and consequently all his works
have a strongly popular flavour: he wanted success and was fully
prepared to give the audience precisely what it wanted. Rough
and ready, he sought no literary esteem and was content if he
could make his audience laugh.

His inspiration was twofold. First, he was well acquainted with
the writers of the Greek New Comedy, Menander in particular,
and from them he freely borrowed plots, character, and dialogue.
For an ordinary Roman audience, however, the refinements of
Menander's style would have been too dull, and therefore this
author, with an eye on the public, freely borrowed also from the
Atellan farces, themselves based on the Sicilian Phlyakes, which in

turn have at least a nodding acquaintanceship with the work of Aristophanes. His middle name, Maccius or Maccus, he took from the stock character of the greedy fool of the *fabula Atellana*. The general result is a strange admixture of diverse elements. In the plays of Plautus there are scenes modelled on Menander's sentimental realism, farcical scenes in the style of the mime, burlesque like that introduced into the Sicilian comedy. He reflects the style of Menander's comedy of manners, of the mime's realistic scenes, and even (as in *Amphitryon*) of the ancient burlesque drama. The very form of his comedies is mixed—a jumbling together of spoken dialogue (*diverbium*) and lyrics (*cantica*)—reminding us of the forms assumed by the ballad opera in the eighteenth century.

Naturally his pieces exhibit wide diversity, for all was fish that came to his net; but throughout run certain dominant qualities. The characters are for the most part broadly delineated types. Chief of all is the comic slave, an intriguing, bustling, impertinent fellow, ever in danger of a whipping or worse, ever meddling, ever ingenious. In nearly every one of the extant twenty comedies he is the moving spirit of the piece. Old men also figure prominently; some are irascible, some are kindly, most are willing to have a gay time if they can. 'Mother,' as Edith Hamilton so aptly emphasizes, is a prominent influence in these plays, and her romanticized figure reminds us of the very strong sentimental concept which colours so many of the Plautan scenes. Indeed, his characteristic recipe for a successful piece seems to have been a sentimentally romantic plot, with a touch of heart-interest and an occasional stock reflection, intrigue in plenty, with many a dash of farcical episode. The formula for the modern drama is being set.

For the most part he avoids the use of surprise: little is kept concealed from his simple-minded spectators, who are thus flattered by being made little gods watching the blunderings of characters immersed in a slough of misapprehensions. By this means he has been able to make what, in the end, may perhaps be regarded as his principal contribution to drama—the development of comic irony. The device was, of course, more ancient than he. It appears markedly in Menander's work, and Aristophanes makes free use of it in individual scenes—as, for example, in that ludicrous if indecorous episode when the wretched Cinesias in *Lysistrata* thinks his wife, Myrrhine, is to give him satisfaction, while we know that by her delays she is intent merely on increasing his wretchedness. But it was in Plautus that the device was first used to its fullest extent. His characteristic method is to let the audience fully into the secrets of his plot at the very beginning and allow them to take delight, not from the unexpected in action, but from the mistakes and errors resultant from the fact that what the audience knows remains unknown to the characters.

Some of his pieces are little more than uproarious farce. Of these the *Miles Gloriosus* (*The Bragging Soldier*) may be taken as an example. The plot is complex, but is reducible to a simple plan: all depends upon the follies of Pyrgopolinices, the braggart, who, full of strange oaths, is discomfited in love and deflated in spirit. The very first words of the play introduce him as he addresses one of his men:

> See that my shield be polished so that its sheen is more resplendent than the noon-day sun. When the battle is joined, it must dazzle the eyes of the fierce ranks of the enemy before me. But ah! my sword: how doleful and sad is its spirit, lamenting its long disuse! How eagerly it pines to make havoc of my foes!

In the final scene we see him wretchedly cudgelled and abject in his protestations: "By Venus and Mars," he swears, "I bear no malice for this affront. You were quite right, entirely right. If you let me off now, I'll consider it just punishment and let it go." The merriment creaks a trifle nowadays, yet we must remember the influence of this and other Plautan plays on the later course of the theatre: the *miles gloriosus* was a popular figure on the Renaissance stage, and had Pyrgopolinices not been created we might not now be laughing at Falstaff's gay and scoundrelly bombast.

Of somewhat similar sort, and equally popular among later dramatists, is the *Menæchmi* (*The Menæchmuses*), from which Shakespeare wrought his *Comedy of Errors*—extracting fun from the misadventures caused by the presence in one city of long-separated twins. In the *Asinaria* (*The Comedy of the Asses*) a young man, Argyrippus, applies to his father, Demænetus, for some money wherewith to purchase a pretty young courtesan, Philenium. The father, also attracted by the girl, gladly gives his aid, but unfortunately has no ready cash, since his wife, Artemona, holds the purse-strings tight: hence comes the main intrigue of the farce, in which money due to the wife for the sale of some asses is transferred, by devious means, into his control. At the end of the play the elderly gentleman, greatly pleased with himself, is sitting pleasantly with Philenium and about to amuse himself with her caresses, while the wife, apprised of the affair, listens, fuming, in concealment, until, unable to control her temper, she bursts in and drags him off home.

Financial intrigues designed for the same purpose—this time to enable Calidorus procure his beloved Phœnicium—provide the theme for *Pseudolus*; although there is one well-drawn character here, Ballio the procurer, the trickery, ingenious as it is, wears a trifle thin. Money, it may be noted, plays a major rôle in these plays, and its constant presence serves as a reminder, if that were needed, of the materialistic and bourgeois character of the audience whom Plautus is addressing. *Trinummus* is entirely taken up with the subject of treasure buried under a house and of the transactions by which the house is sold; *Curculio* concerns itself with an impoverished young man who, desiring to purchase a slave-girl, Planesium, is induced to steal a ring from another *miles gloriosus*, Therapontigonus by name; in the *Bacchides*, a sort of female *Menæchmi*, money is extracted by the slave Chrysalus from the old Nicobulus on behalf of the latter's son, Mnesilochus (once more for an identical end); buried treasure reappears in the *Aulularia* (*The Comedy of the Little Pot*), in which the portrait of the aged miser Euclio imprinted itself on the imagination of many later dramatists, especially of Molière: Harpagon in *L'avare* is Euclio Parisianized.

In this last-mentioned Plautan comedy occurs a close parallel to one part of the plot of Menander's *Arbitration*. Euclio's daughter, Phædra, has been ravished, at the feast of Ceros, by a young man, Lyconides. This youth, repentant of his behaviour and now genuinely in love with the girl, desires to marry her, and such scenes as are not devoted to showing the old man's frantic devices for the concealment of his money are concerned with this affair. Like the audience whom Menander addressed, the Roman audience of Plautus' time was apt to welcome a romantic theme with strong sentimental colouring, provided always that this portion of the story did not take away too much from the farcical merriment. Certainly this romantic, sentimental element must not be forgotten amid the raucous merriment and the play of comic irony. It suffuses, for example, the entire drama called *Rudens* (*The Rope*), one of the most interesting among Plautus' productions, in which is told the pathetic story of Palæstra, an earlier Marina, who, having been stolen from her home in childhood, has fallen into the clutches of the procurer Labrax. How a storm has been raised by the star-god Arcturus, how Palæstra is cast up from a shipwrecked vessel on the very shore where her father has his house, how a fisherman drags from the deeps a box containing Labrax' gold and the trinkets proving the girl's identity, how she is restored to her father and to her lover, Plesidippus, is a tale told in scenes not unreminiscent of the style of Shakespeare's later comedy. Akin in its sentimentalism is the *Captivi* (*The Captives*), which relates the fortunes of the two sons of Hegio, seized in their boyhood, the one by pirates and the other by a runaway slave. Through a number of almost serious scenes, enlivened by misunderstandings, the plot is carried forward until the old man recovers the two youths, ironically finding that one of them is a slave of his own whom he has been punishing severely. The *Cistellaria* (*The Casket*) brings a foundling girl back to her parents (again by means of trinkets), and something of the same theme appears in *Casina*, while in *Pœnulus* (*The Little Carthaginian*) two girls are restored to their home. *Epidicus* combines the theme of the long-lost daughter with the tricks by which a cunning slave draws an old man's money into the hands of his son.

Comedy after comedy rings the changes on farce and sentiment, romantic love and carnal love, trickery and caricature. In *Mercator* (*The Merchant*), as typical as any, a young man brings back with him from abroad a lovely Rhodian girl; his father spies her and determines to have her for his own, persuades a friend to buy her on his behalf, and sets in train a series of ludicrous misunderstandings and errors. The scene in which old Demipho reveals his infatuation to his neighbour Lysimachus has true comic spirit:

DEMIPHO: How old do I look?

LYSIMACHUS: One foot in the grave: a broken-down, decrepit old fellow.

DEMIPHO: Oh, you're not looking at me right. I'm just a child, Lysimachus, seven years old.

LYSIMACHUS: What's all this nonsense? A child?

DEMIPHO: Really just a child.

LYSIMACHUS: Oh, I see. Lost your senses: second childhood, eh?

DEMIPHO: No, no, not that at all. I'm twice as lusty as I've ever been.

LYSIMACHUS [*getting bored*]: Is that a fact? Excellent.

DEMIPHO: And I can see much better now than before.

LYSIMACHUS: That's good.

DEMIPHO [*shyly*]: I'm almost ashamed to tell you——

LYSIMACHUS: What?

DEMIPHO: May I?

LYSIMACHUS: What?

DEMIPHO: Well, then.

LYSIMACHUS: Come on, man.

DEMIPHO: I've been going to school to-day, Lysimachus. I've learned four letters already.

LYSIMACHUS [*puzzled*]: What's that? Four letters?

DEMIPHO: L O V E.

Much as Lysimachus laughs at his friend, however, he goes to the dock and purchases Pasicompsa on his behalf, and we meet the pair coming back to town. The girl is in tears:

LYSIMACHUS [*aside*]: Well, I've done what he asked. He wanted me to buy her, and here she is. [*To* PASICOMPSA] You now belong to me. Come on. Stop blubbering. [*More kindly*] Really, it's quite stupid your spoiling these lovely eyes. There's more reason for laughter than tears.

PASICOMPSA: Please, sir, do tell me.

LYSIMACHUS: Ask me what you like.

PASICOMPSA: Why did you buy me?

LYSIMACHUS: Why? To do what you're bidden. [*After a pause, slyly*] But then what you bid, I'll do.

PASICOMPSA: I'm ready, I'm sure, to give every satisfaction.

LYSIMACHUS: Of course, I shan't ask you to do anything very hard.

PASICOMPSA: My goodness, I hope not. I haven't learned, sir, to do hard work.

LYSIMACHUS: If you promise to be a good girl, you'll be all right.

PASICOMPSA: My gracious, that's terrible.

LYSIMACHUS: What do you mean?

PASICOMPSA: Where I come from it was the bad girls that had a good time.

LYSIMACHUS [*aside*]: By Jove, her talk itself's worth all I paid for her.

This is followed immediately by a characteristic Plautan scene of equivoque. Pasicompsa is in love with and is loved by Demipho's son, and in the ensuing conversation she refers to the latter, while Lysimachus speaks of his elderly friend:

LYSIMACHUS: Can you spin?

PASICOMPSA: Yes, sir.

LYSIMACHUS: Fine, and coarse?

PASICOMPSA: There's not another who's my match at spinning.

LYSIMACHUS: You've been well brought up, my dear.

PASICOMPSA: Yes, I was well taught, sir.

LYSIMACHUS: Well, then, what do you say if I give you a sheep of your very own, sixty years old.

PASICOMPSA [*laughing*]: As old as that?

LYSIMACHUS: Pure Greek breed. If you take care of it, you can shear it very easily.

PASICOMPSA [*not understanding, a trifle puzzled*]: It's very good of you, sir. Thanks a lot.

LYSIMACHUS: To put it quite straight, you're not mine, so don't think you are.

PASICOMPSA [*astonished*]: Then whose am I?

LYSIMACHUS: I've bought you for your own master. He asked me to.
PASICOMPSA: That's fine.
LYSIMACHUS: You'll get freed, I'm quite sure. He's madly in love with you.
PASICOMPSA: Yes, it's two years we've been lovers.
LYSIMACHUS [*amazed*]: What? Two years?
PASICOMPSA: Sure it is. We pledged ourselves, him and me: he wasn't to look at any other girl, I wasn't to look at any other man.
LYSIMACHUS [*nonplussed*]: My goodness gracious! What about his wife?
PASICOMPSA: He's not got a wife.
LYSIMACHUS: I wish he hadn't. Goodness gracious me, he's been committing perjury.
PASICOMPSA: I don't love any young man as much as him.
LYSIMACHUS [*slowly*]: Young man? Well, yes, of course he really is a child, my dear.

In *Persa* (*The Persian*) sport is made of the outwitting of a procurer; in *Truculentus* (*The Churl*) a courtesan makes hay while the sun shines; in *Mostellaria* (*The Ghost*) an astute slave causes an old man to believe that his house is haunted; a hungry parasite is held up to ridicule in *Stichus*. All the familiar doings of Rome are here, treated in a spirit of wanton levity: of the grandeur of the Republic there is no sign—that was left to the historians to depict; Plautus was interested in the characters of his day, not when they donned their togas, when they fought or philosophized, but rather when they stepped out of their front doors in undress and indulged in domestic strife instead of battle, in bickering instead of noble oratory.

TERENCE AND THE YOUNG MEN ABOUT TOWN

If Plautus wrote to please the crowd, his successor Terence sought the esteem of the intelligentsia; if Plautus derived his comic style from many sources, Terence tried to follow only the one master, Menander. Between the two men, although frequently their names are linked together, there was a world of difference.

Publius Terentius Afer was born about 195 B.C. and died in 159. A native of Carthage, he was probably negroid in origin and had been brought, in his youth, to Rome as a slave. Educated by his master, he seems to have become the protégé of a little circle of literary wits, and for their delectation rather than for the plaudits of the crowd he confessedly penned his comedies. In all, six of his pieces are extant—*Andria* (166 B.C.), *Hecyra* (165 B.C.), *Heautonti-*

morumenos (163 B.C.), *Eunuchus* (161 B.C.), *Phormio* (161 B.C.), and *Adelphi* (160 B.C.).

This "half-Menander" (*dimidiate Menander*), as Cæsar styled him, based all his art upon the New Comedy, deliberately revealing the sources of his plots, and making no claims to anything beyond purity of style and skill in the weaving together of plots taken from the Greek plays: "Nullum est iam dictum quod non dictum sit prius," he cheerfully remarks. "There's nothing new under the sun; everything one says has been said before." Like Menander, he aims at arousing smiles, not laughter; and like his master, he is a sentimentalist. Perhaps the essential difference between him and Plautus is revealed most clearly by a consideration of the general orientation of their works. Whereas the latter brings his merchants, his young sons, his slaves, his pimps, and his courtesans in a tumultuous, seething mass on stage, Terence endeavours to secure an exact perspective, and this perspective has as its focal-point the elegant young Roman gentleman. Highly trained, eminently conscious of the value of good manners (or at least of the manners considered good by his society), eager for enjoyment, and more than a little annoyed by the fretting restraints put upon his freedom by men less youthful than himself, this Roman gallant is the centre of every Terentian play; here is his image, and the actions are those in which, at least, he would like to have been involved. "What partial judges of all sons are fathers!" soliloquizes Clitipho in *Heautontimorumenos* (*The Self-tormentor*),

> Who ask grey wisdom from our greener years,
> And think our minds should bear no touch of youth;
> Governing by their passions, now kill'd in them,
> And not by those that formerly rebell'd.
> If ever I've a son, I promise him
> He shall find me an easy father; fit
> To know, and apt to pardon his offences!

These young gallants, like the gallants of the Restoration period in England, savour fine phrases and delight in epigram, and Terence must have endeared himself to them not only by the fond picture he gives of their lives and aspirations, but also by his skill in forging the delicate phrase—"quot homines, tot sententiæ," "hinc illæ lacrimæ," "amantium iræ amoris integratiost"—these, and other have become proverbial.

Andria (*The Girl of Andros*), his first drama, is as representative as any, and it may be of value to follow its plot act by act. First, we have conversations between Simo, father of Pamphilus, and his devoted slave Sosia. The old man explains that his son, a youth of infinite perfection and promise, has of late been devoting himself to a certain girl, Glycerium by name, sister of the courtesan Chrysis. So open has this scandal become that old Chremes, who had been willing to have his daughter marry Pamphilus, now refuses to go through with the match. In order to catch his son, Simo is, however, pretending to go on with the preparations for the wedding. Having retired, he leaves the stage free for Pamphilus, who enters in desperation, and whose words have the true romantically sentimental ring of Menander. To Glycerium's maid, Mysis, he protests his undying devotion:

MYSIS: I only know
        That she deserves you should remember her.
PAMPHILUS: I should remember her? O Mysis, Mysis!
        The words of Chrysis touching my Glycerium
        Are written in my heart. On her death-bed
        She call'd me. I approach'd her. You retir'd.
        We were alone; and Chrysis thus began:
        My Pamphilus, you see the youth and beauty
        Of this unhappy maid: and well you know
        These are but feeble guardians to preserve
        Her fortune or her fame. By this right hand
        I do beseech you, by your better angel,
        By your tried faith, by her forlorn condition,
        I do conjure you, put her not away,
        Nor leave her to distress. If I have ever,
        As my own brother, lov'd you; or if she
        Has ever held you dear 'bove all the world,
        And ever shown obedience to your will—
        I do bequeath you to her as a husband,
        Friend, guardian, father: all our little wealth
        To you I leave, and trust it to your care.
        She join'd our hands, and died. I did receive her,
        And once receiv'd will keep her.

This pathetic narrative out-Menanders Menander in its sentimental implications: it even introduces the golden-hearted courtesan.

The second act introduces another character, Charinus, a friend of Pamphilus, who, it appears, loves Chremes' daughter, Philumena, as much as Pamphilus detests her. He is cheered by his friend's frank declaration of disinterest in the girl, while Pamphilus receives the welcome news, from Davus, his slave, that the marriage preparations are all a pretence. As a result Pamphilus, for his part, pretends to agree to a wedding. Unfortunately Simo becomes apprised that Glycerium has had a child and that Pamphilus has acknowledged himself the father, but the day is saved when, in his self-conceit, he refuses to believe that this is anything more than a device designed to trick him. Davus takes his cue and anxiously helps to confirm the old man in his belief; but in this the slave overreaches himself, since Simo immediately communicates the news to Chremes and once more rearranges the marriage.

In the course of the fourth act all is in confusion. Charinus is enraged at what he regards as Pamphilus' perfidy: Mysis is in despair because she thinks her mistress deserted. The ever-resourceful Davus, however, has a device: he takes Glycerium's child and convinces old Chremes that he is being deluded by Simo. Meanwhile a new character, Crito, arrives, and through him it is discovered (we almost guess it at the beginning) that, of course, Glycerium is a well-born Athenian girl—none other, in fact, than the daughter of Chremes himself. She is thus free to marry her beloved Pamphilus, while Charinus is allowed to wed her sister.

In general terms, the plot is similar to that of many a Plautan comedy, but the atmosphere is vastly different. Here all is refined, toned down, softened. No broad farcical scenes shatter the atmosphere of well-to-do politeness, of romantic sentiment, and of moral reflection. The young men are more worthy than their Plautan brothers, the old men far less ridiculous, the jests of the slave are more subdued, and the (supposed) courtesan's maid becomes a pretty little Columbine whose one thought is of her mistress's happiness.

The closeness of Terence to Menander—and yet at the same time the gulf that separates them—is well revealed in his second play, *Hecyra* (*The Step-mother*), the plot of which is a variant of that of *The Arbitration*. Pamphilus, the hero, has, very unwillingly, been persuaded to abandon his mistress Bacchis and marry Philumena. Trouble breaks out between the young wife and her stepmother, and the latter ferrets out a dark secret—that shortly after her wedding Philumena has given birth to a child. It turns out, of course, that, like Menander's heroine, the girl had been violated in the darkness of night, and, by means of a ring, the violator is proved to have been Pamphilus himself. Fundamentally the plot is the same, but the manners are Roman. The awful power of the Roman mother is patently revealed, and above all there is the excessive sentiment associated with the golden-hearted courtesan. Although Pamphilus, after swearing that he would never marry, has deserted

Bacchis, the happy discovery at the end is made largely through that young lady's disinterested efforts. "What joy have I procur'd to Pamphilus by coming here to-day!" she reflects.

> What blessings brought him!
> And from how many sorrows rescu'd him!
> His son, by his and their means nearly lost,
> I've sav'd; a wife, he meant to put away
> I have restor'd. . . . That I've been
> The instrument of all these joys I'm glad,
> Tho' other courtesans would not be so;
> Nor is it for our profit and advantage
> That lovers should be happy in their marriage.
> But never will I, for my calling's sake
> Suffer ingratitude to taint my mind.
> I found him, while occasion gave him leave,
> Kind, pleasant and good-humour'd: and this marriage
> Happen'd unluckily I must confess.
> Yet I did nothing to estrange his love,
> And since I have receiv'd much kindness from him,
> 'Tis fit I should endure this one affliction.

Another Bacchis appears in *Heautontimorumenos* (*The Self-tormentor*), where again the sentimental is laid on thickly. The self-tormentor is Menedemus, who toils and sweats in voluntary penance for the harsh treatment he had meted out to his son Clinia. "Homo sum: humani nihil a me alienum puto," says his friend Chremes. "I am a man and feel for all mankind"—and the epigrammatic phrase has become a proverb—as he seeks out his secret sorrow and chides him gently:

> You I believe a tender parent, him
> A duteous son, if govern'd prudently.
> But you were unacquainted with his nature,
> And he with yours: sad life, where things are so!
> You ne'er betray'd your tenderness to him,
> Nor durst he place that confidence in you
> Which well becomes the bosom of a father.
> Had that been done, this had not happen'd to you.

Thus are the fathers romantically conceived by the world of youth that Terence represents: thus fathers ought to behave were life ordered properly. Clinia's sole fault was that he had fallen in love with Antiphila, the supposed daughter of a poor Corinthian woman. On this basis the plot develops. Clinia returns to his native town and stays with his friend Clitipho (Chremes' son), who is spending

THE THEATRE AT
TAORMINA
Photo Alinari

128

A SLAVE
Terra-cotta statuette, Berlin. From
Margarete Bieber, *The History of the
Greek and Roman Theater*, Fig. 416.

A MONEYLENDER (?)
Terra-cotta statuette in the British
Museum.

A ROMAN ACTOR
Bronze statuette.
*By courtesy of the
Museum of Fine Arts,
Boston*

A POTTER (?)
Terra-cotta statuette in
the British Museum.

his money freely on the courtesan Bacchis. Says Bacchis to
Antiphila:

> Well, I commend you, my Antiphila:
> Happy that you have made it still your care
> That virtue should seem fair as beauty in you!
> Nor gracious Heaven so help me, do I wonder
> If ev'ry man should wish you for his own;
> For your discourse bespeaks a worthy mind.
> And when I ponder with myself, and weigh
> Your course of life, and all the rest of those
> Who live not on the common, 'tis not strange
> Your morals should be different from ours.
> Virtue's your int'rest; those with whom we deal
> Forbid it to be ours—for our gallants,
> Charm'd by our beauty, court us but for that,
> Which fading, they transfer their love to others.
> If then meanwhile we look not to ourselves,
> We live forlorn, deserted and distressed.
> You, when you've once agreed to pass your life
> Bound to one man, whose temper suits with yours,
> He too attaches his whole heart to you:
> Thus mutual friendship draws you each to each;
> Nothing can part you, nothing shake your love.

At the end of this sentimental drama the virtuous Antiphila is, of
course, found to be Chremes' long-lost daughter.

A courtesan, Thais, who is anxious to return a free-born girl to
her family, figures as a prominent character in *Eunuchus* (*The
Eunuch*), where also is included a braggart soldier, Thraso, and a
rather delightful parasite, Gnatho, in addition to the usual collection
of young men. The main episode, which gives its title to the play,
concerns the device by which the young Chærea, enamoured of the
girl who is being befriended by Thais, poses as a eunuch in order to
find an opportunity for ravishing her: when she turns out to be one
of the collection of long-lost daughters a marriage is, of course,
immediately arranged. Witty, reflective, epigrammatic, the style
here is even more polished than in Terence's earlier plays, and for
this reason it has ever maintained a high position in the list of this
dramatist's work.

Nearer in plot to a Plautan comedy is *Phormio*, in which a young
man, Antipho by name, marries a poor orphan (who turns out to
be the daughter of Chremes), and another young man, Phædria,
aided by the astute parasite who provides the title for the comedy,
goes to extraordinary lengths to secure money wherewith to purchase

E

a music-girl with whom he is in love. The plot is complicated by the fact that old Chremes, while away on a journey, has been having an *affaire* of his own, and in his endeavours to recover some money inveigled from him by Phormio this *affaire* is, to his dismay, brought to light.

Perhaps more thoroughly Terentian is the *Adelphi* (*The Brothers*), in which a sentimentally conceived plot is worked out almost in the style of a modern problem drama. Demea, a harsh old disciplinarian, has two sons: one, Ctesipho, he himself rears in the country, the other, Æschinus, is cared for, in town, by his kind-hearted, genial, indulgent uncle, Micio. As might have been expected from the pen of one who so persistently takes the side of youth, Æschinus, although for a time under a considerable cloud owing to his own kind-heartedness, is revealed as a man of the best intentions and the warmest feelings, while Ctesipho, who had been hypocritical enough to deceive his father into thinking him the very model of moral discretion, is shown to be a profligate. In essence the whole comedy is an essay in education, a propaganda piece designed on the part of the young gentlemen about town to persuade their fathers that liberality and lack of discipline will, in the end, produce the best results. We are well on our way here towards modern romantic concepts of how to bring up the young: "Apply the rod and spoil the child" is Terence's motto. Here the modern sentimental drama is becoming fully formed.

SENECA AND THE END OF THE ROMAN STAGE

In the *Hecyra* Terence mournfully relates how at the first performance of his play the audience had given it no attention:

> When I first
> Began to play this piece, the sturdy boxers—
> The dancers on the rope expected too—
> The increasing crowds, the noise and women's clamour
> Obliged me to retire before my time.

The truth is that the Roman public had but little taste for the drama. Give them raucous horse-play of the Plautan sort, and they would suffer a comedy, but their interests lay rather in watching rope-dancers, boxers, and the still more brutal displays presented in their one original type of entertainment-building, the amphitheatre.

If for comedy they had but little use, they had practically none for tragedy. From the Hellenistic period, indeed, tragedy's fate seems to have been but a sorry one. Throughout the fourth century and onward writer after writer sought to assume the mantle of Euripides, but Aristophanes had been in the right when he made his Dionysus believe that the only hope of preserving the tragic stage was to make the dangerous journey to Hades and to bring back the ghost of one of the old giants.

Although virtually nothing remains either of the later Greek efforts in tragedy or of those made later in Rome, we know sufficient to realize that rhetoric was being substituted for vibrant poetry, artificialities for living texture, sensationalism for passion. As creative writing declined actors became famous and, again anticipating the ways of the present age, insisted on altering the works of the classical masters in order to make their own individual rôles the more effective. By the third century they had their own trades unions (the guilds of the Dionysiac artists, οἱ περὶ τὸν Διόνυσον τεχνῖται), through which they succeeded in escaping both from military service and the payment of taxes. From extant vase-paintings and terracottas we can imagine that their styles of performance were much more muscular, much more gesticulatory, than had been those of their predecessors, and that they contributed towards forcing the remnants of tragic drama along the channel of sensationalism. One particular vase-painting of the fourth century gives us a vivid picture of a production of a play on the theme of *Medea*, written probably some fifty years after Euripides' death. The stage is filled with action; the dresses are rich; there is a suggestion of scenic effect in Medea's dragon-borne car. A sense of restlessness is here in sharp contradiction to the impression of monumental calm in the preceding century.

In Rome the actors, too, took a prominent place, especially about the first century B.C. Although at first recruited from the ranks of slaves, they won social prominence, became 'stars' in their own time, and even—as with Roscius—had their names reverently handed down to after-ages as masters of their art. In watching the actors' tricks the spectators were apt to forget the dramatist.

There being no indigenous Latin tragedy, the first steps towards establishing this form were made by the preparing of translations, and even the earliest of these were made, not by a native of Rome, but by a man who, born at Tarentum (a Greek settlement), was, like Terence, a slave. Between 240 and 207 B.C. Livius Andronicus thus introduced to a Latin-speaking public some of the plays of Sophocles and Euripides, and one of these, presented in the former year, was the earliest tragedy to be produced in the Eternal City.

About the same time a certain Nævius, a native of Campania and a naturalized Roman citizen, took the next steps by preparing what seem to have been original dramas based on the Greek (called, because of the use in their production of the Hellenic cloak, or *pallium, fabulæ palliatæ*), and by writing tragedies on Roman historical or legendary themes (named *fabulæ prætextæ*, from the togas in which the actors were dressed). During the second century B.C. the impact of Athens became even more pronounced, and three tragic dramatists, all of whom were influenced by Euripides, have had their names, if not their works, preserved for posterity— Ennius, Pacuvius, and Accius.

As the years wore on, so interest declined in this newly discovered form. Still-existing mosaics and similar records prove that on special occasions tragedies continued to be performed both in Rome and the provinces until at least the end of the second century A.D., but all the evidence seems to indicate, firstly, that the performances were sporadic, secondly, that they were not widely popular, and, thirdly, that they were weakened by pathetic sensationalism and suffocated by show. When the *Clytemnestra* of Accius was produced at the opening of Pompey's theatre in 55 B.C. we are informed that five hundred mules and three thousand chariots, besides elephants and giraffes innumerable, took hours to pass over the stage: they formed a processional spectacle of the trophies borne from ruined Troy. Thinking of some modern efforts in this direction, Terence's dictum comes to mind again: there truly is nothing new under the sun, and it is not only the theatre of to-day that has been taught to ruin creative writing by a passion for spectacle.

In the midst of these sporadic theatrical activities the nine or ten tragedies of Seneca stand out as a puzzle and an enduring, if not wholly worthy, monument. Lucius Annæus Seneca, a native of Corduba, in Spain, was born about 4 B.C. and took his own life, by Nero's command, in A.D. 65. A kind of earlier Bacon, he was a noted writer of philosophical and scientific works, and, like Bacon, did not always permit his moral sentiments to coincide with his practical political actions. The plays were probably composed late in his life, and include nine dramas on traditional Greek themes— *Hercules Furens, Medea, Troades, Phædra, Agamemnon, Œdipus, Hercules Œtæus, Phœnissæ, Thyestes*—with one *fabula prætexta, Octavia*, on a Roman topic. This tenth tragedy is often denied to his pen, and several scholars believe it to be a work of considerably later date.

The puzzle is to determine whether these plays were intended for stage representation or whether they were designed merely as literary exercises suitable for private 'readings.' That Seneca did take an interest in the theatre and had studied the art of acting is certain from one of his letters, and it has been observed that the spirit of his verses is not unlike that expressed in contemporary reproductions of tragic scenes. On the other hand, the custom of reading tragic compositions aloud before small literary coteries was then well established, and it is easier to explain many peculiarities in the Senecan structure by treating the plays as literary exercises than by regarding them as intended for the theatre. Most of the external evidence, corroborated by examination of the works themselves, appears to show that Seneca was the first-known closet playwright.

If the puzzle leaves much uncertain, there is no doubt about the solidity of the monument. It was at the fount of Seneca that the early dramatists of the Renaissance fed, and without the influence of his writings we might never have had, in their existing form, the tragedies of Shakespeare. For an entire century, at the most formative period in the development of the modern drama, his was the model towards which all young writers reverently gazed. His mantle may be a trifle tattered now and his bust more than a little tarnished, but for what he meant to the dramatic authors of the sixteenth century he can never be forgotten or completely despised.

To examine Seneca's plays in detail would be useless, for in his treatment of the old themes he introduced no intrinsically worthy elements. All we need do is consider the principal features of his dramatic work, and in particular those characteristics which exerted most influence upon the playwrights of the new world born in the Renaissance.

Although he based his conceptions on Euripides, little of the Greek tragedian's realism appears in Seneca's scenes. Rather does he seize upon, and exaggerate, the sensational, melodramatic qualities which existed along with that realism in such plays as *Medea* and *Orestes*. Blood, torment, and the sense of impending doom delight him: all he feels is a mood—dark, gloomy, fateful. He adores an out-and-out villain, whose mind is set on naught but the accomplishment of his crimes. In *Thyestes* Atreus thus soliloquizes:

> Fall now this mighty house of famous Pelops,
> And crush me, so it crush my brother too.
> Come dare, my heart, a crime no age shall pardon,

> But no age e'er forget. Venture some deed
> Bloody and fell, such as my brother would
> Wish to be *his*. Nothing avenges crimes
> But what surpasses them.

So, too, he adores a dramatic figure who, for no apparent reason, is conscious of a terrible future, of one who invokes the divinities of hell. Thus does Medea introduce her story:

> Ye gods of wedlock and thou guardian queen
> Lucina, watcher o'er the marriage couch,
> And thou that taughtest mankind to master ships
> To dominate the sea, thou ruler fierce
> Of all the vasty deep, thou Titan too
> Dividing with thine orb the coursing days,
> Thou Hecate of triple form whose beams
> Glance at all secret rites, ye gods by whom
> Jason once swore to me and whom methinks
> 'Tis seemlier far Medea should invoke:
> Chaos of night eternal, realms the gods
> See not, all impious shades and thou the lord
> Of blackest hell and thou its mistress too—
> I call ye all with my ill-omened cry.

Characteristic of the Senecan bombast is the way in which a single metaphor or simile is monotonously carried through a long speech; characteristic also is the vast amount of equally monotonous moralizing. A heavy cloud of pessimism weighs down upon these plays, but it is a pessimism which lacks vitality, which dully creeps and heavily drags its slow length along. Darkness can be inspiring; ebony's blackness may have almost the quality of light: Seneca's gloom is merely oppressive.

It cannot, however, be denied that, within his own chosen field of rhetorical expression, the Roman playwright had more than common skill. In his interminable tirades, in his rapid fire of dialogue, and in his contemplative choruses alike he was able to strike out sparks which, although they perhaps themselves had no warmth, had the power later of producing passionate flame. In *Hercules Furens* the hero thus declaims:

> What Tanais, what Nile or swirling flood
> Of Persian Tigris, what wild Rhine or Tagus,
> Rolling in spate the rich Iberian gold,
> Will wash this right hand clean? Though cold Mæotis
> Should deluge me with all her Arctic waves,
> Or all the Ocean flood across these hands,
> The stain of blood will stay.

The flint has struck the steel here; the spark is cold yet, but the flame comes from it:

> Will all great Neptune's ocean wash this blood
> Clean from my hand? No, this my hand will rather
> The multitudinous seas incarnadine,
> Making the green one red.

In the form of his plays Seneca, together with Terence, established a structure which was destined to endure up to the nineteenth century. His dramas are all cast in five formal acts, and the old Greek prologue is incorporated into the action; Terence's plan is fundamentally the same, although he takes the further step of separating the prologue from the body of the drama and of making it, like the Aristophanic parabasis, a mouthpiece for the poet. The five-act shape for tragedy and comedy alike was thus definitely set.

The chorus Seneca retains, but in retaining it he carries to further limits the trends already noted in the works of Sophocles and, more particularly, of Euripides. The choral odes in his tragedies, some of them gifted with a cold loveliness, are in general unrelated, or at best only slightly related, to the events narrated in the main action. Fundamentally the chorus has now become merely a purveyor of interludes.

In the dialogue long speeches tend to alternate with passages of a kind of battledore-and-shuttlecock quality, wherein two characters thrust and parry through some fifty or sixty staccato lines. Thus it is in *Hercules Furens*:

> LYCUS: Art thou so proud of a husband lost in Hell?
> MEGARA: He entered Hell, that he might scale the Heavens.
> LYCUS: Well, now he's crushed beneath the massive earth.
> MEGARA: The back that bore the sky *no* load can crush.
> LYCUS: I'll force thee.
> MEGARA: None is forced that dares to die.
> LYCUS: Nay, tell me, what royal gift shall I prepare
>   To grace our bridals?
> MEGARA: Thy death or mine own.
> LYCUS: Fool, thou shalt die.
> MEGARA: So I shall meet my lord.
> LYCUS: Dost prize a slave above our royal crown?
> MEGARA: How many kings that 'slave' has sped to death!
> LYCUS: Then why serves he a king, and bears a yoke?
> MEGARA: Remove all harsh commands: and what is virtue?

Such dialogue, the so-called *stichomythia*, based on the Greek but made exaggerated, played its part, too, in the creation of the Elizabethan tragic style.

With Seneca the impulse that began with Æschylus and his immediate predecessors reached its lurid end—at least in so far as the direct line of development from Athens to Rome was concerned. It is true that a kind of side-stream carried the current of the Greek theatre to Byzantium, where apparently the Euripidean influence succeeded in producing a series of dramas based in structure and style on the Greek, but intent on Christian themes. Of these plays one, Χριστος πάσχων (*Christ's Suffering*), dating from the eleventh century A.D., has come down to us. This stream of dramatic activity, however, interesting though it is, has no direct bearing on the main growth of the Western stage. From Rome the early writers of the Renaissance received their first introduction, at second hand, to the theatre of Greece; Seneca, Terence, and Plautus were the masters whom they acknowledged and followed.

One further development of the Roman stage, on the other hand, may have combined with the dramas of these three men to make an impress on the later playhouse. Between the second and the fourth centuries of our era Rome produced little or nothing of dramatic literature, but the mimes energetically and successfully pursued their popular activities. Out of tragedy came the *pantomimus*, a kind of ballet, in which a chorus chanted words while an actor mimed the parts one after another. This *pantomimus* seems to have been mainly a toy of the degenerate imperial Courts, but the *mimus*, or comic mime, certainly appealed to a wider public. With mingled memories of the Atellan farces and of the indigenous mimes of Greece, these shows were diversified in character, sometimes taking shape as burlesque knock-and-tumble comedy, sometimes presenting dramas of a tragi-comic sort, sometimes capable of being performed by a small troupe of half a dozen itinerant entertainers, sometimes demanding the services of companies as large as those called for in a modern musical comedy.

When Rome fell before the invading might of the barbarians at the beginning of the fifth century these mimic actors were freely presenting their shows throughout the entire extent of the Empire. Under the new conditions of life no doubt they fell on evil days. The Goths, the Vandals, and the Huns were hardly equipped to appreciate even their crude dramatic efforts, and the Christian church, wrathful at the manner in which its rites had been burlesqued on the stage, ceased not to fulminate at the iniquities of the mimes. Nevertheless they seem to have carried on their profession into the ages of darkness: one of our last pictorial records of the classical theatre is a sixth-century ivory tablet with a scene in relief showing a mimic hero amid a group of comic, bald-headed gesticulating slaves. To this had the heritage of Æschylus come, and yet out of this was later to arise a new flowering of the popular stage. If there is any dramatic continuity between the world of the Greek and Roman temples and the world dominated by the fantastic imagination of the Gothic cathedral we must look for it in the pitiful and despised gesturings of the mimes.

PART II

RELIGIOUS DRAMA AND PROFANE DURING THE MIDDLE AGES

RELIGIOUS DRAMA AND PROFANE DURING THE MIDDLE AGES

THE MIMIC actors thus take their itinerant way into the darkness. Occasionally we catch half-glimpses of them, entertaining gaping village crowds and the rude denizens of medieval castles with their jests, their juggling, their acrobatic tricks, but the path they tread is a long, a dim, and a tortuous one before they come clearly before us again. Their grimacings and their gesticulations are lost in the night of the Dark Ages.

Here and there, in monastery cell or in nunnery, a black-robed figure will turn from the Scriptures and the theological commentaries and take down from the heavy oak presses a manuscript of Terence, appeasing his conscience by remembering that a good Latinity is next to godliness and that Terence is a master of style. Sometimes a worthy clerk, or even a pious nun, will dare a little more and attempt, afar off, to imitate Terence by a few pages of dramatic dialogue, and it is possible to imagine the occasional reciting of these lines of dialogue within the closed walls of a convent, the hearts of the little audience fluttering with a conflict of emotions—the joy of daring to participate in exercises so closely associated with the pagan, the fear that this might be but another bait of Satan's designed to trap the unwary.

Such reading and imitation of Terence is attested for us by the naïve playlets of a certain tenth-century nun of Gandersheim, in Saxony: Hrotswitha or Roswitha she called herself. Concerning the inception of her dramatic work she leaves us in no doubt; her desire is to give to her sisters, worthily, holy matter in the form used by the Roman comedians for their doubtful stories of love and intrigue:

> There are many Catholics, and we cannot entirely acquit ourselves of the charge, who, attracted by the polished elegance of the style of pagan writers, prefer their works to the holy scriptures. There are others who, although they are deeply attached to the sacred writings and have no liking for most pagan productions, make an exception in favour of the works of Terence, and, fascinated by the charm of the manner, risk being corrupted by the wickedness of the matter. Wherefore I, the strong voice of Gandersheim, have not hesitated to imitate

in my writings, a poet whose works are so widely read, my object being to glorify, within the limits of my poor talent, the laudable chastity of Christian virgins in that self-same form of composition which has been used to describe the shameless acts of licentious women.

The plays themselves are exceedingly short, and it is difficult to tell whether they were intended for performance. The fact, however, that there are scenes which require their action to be visualized before they can be understood seems to suggest that the nuns of Gandersheim may have enlivened their winter evenings with attempts to act them in person. Thoroughly typical of the series is *Dulcitius*, which narrates the martyrdom of the Christian maidens Agape, Chionia, and Irena. These girls are first shown rejecting the order of the Emperor Diocletian that they should marry; in anger he throws them into prison under the control of the governor Dulcitius. The latter is enflamed by their beauty and commands his soldiers to place them in a room more easy of access, "the one leading out of the passage where the pots and pans are kept." There he goes to ravish them, but by a miracle he is led to believe that the pots and pans are the girls; fervidly he kisses them, gets his face thoroughly blackened, and is thus made a laughing-stock. Other miracles of a like kind follow, but in the end the Christian maidens are executed by the Count Sisinnius, Agape and Chionia being burned, Irena shot to death by arrows.

The admixture of tragedy and comedy has a definitely theatrical flavour, and, if we believe that these plays were indeed intended for amateur performance, we recognize that—at least afar off—the spirit of Terence was being kept alive in surroundings which were vastly different from those he had enjoyed in pagan Rome. The tenth century has nothing to show us more interesting or more revealing.

Such dramatic activities, however, as are exemplified in the plays of Hrotswitha do not illustrate the main current of dramatic development. They may have contributed towards the growth of the medieval stage, but it was from another source, and in an even humbler manner, that the new Western drama arose.

THE LITURGY AND THE DRAMA

The story of the evolution of drama out of the liturgy has often been told; although some portions of it remain dark, and although, after all the attention devoted to it, some puzzles remain, the main lines of progress are clearly to be traced. It is now recognized that, after all the wealth of Greek endeavour and of imitation of the Greek in Rome, the theatre in the tenth century made a fresh start in the form of a tiny, four-line playlet inserted into the Easter service. The cue is taken from the Bible. In the Gospel according to Mark we read:

> And entering into the sepulchre, they saw a young man sitting on the right side, clothed in a long white garment; and they were affrighted. And he saith unto them, Be not affrighted: ye seek Jesus of Nazareth, which was crucified: he is risen; he is not here; behold the place where they laid him. But go your way, tell his disciples and Peter that he goeth before you into Galilee: there shall ye see him, as he said unto you.

Here is the plot, as it were, and thus the play takes shape. One priest, clad in a white robe, sits near the altar, where a cloth has been laid over a cross: three other priests advance towards him, and he addresses them: "Quem quæritis in sepulchro, O Christi-colæ?" ("Whom do ye seek in the sepulchre, O Christian women?") At this the others reply in unison: "Jesum Nazarenum crucifixum, O cælicola!" ("Jesus of Nazareth who was crucified, O Heavenly One!") Raising the cloth, the first replies: "Non est hic: surrexit sicut prædixerat. Ite, nuntiate quia surrexit de sepulchro." ("He is not here: He has risen even as He said. Go, announce that He has arisen from the sepulchre.")

This is the entirety of the drama, but, short as it is, there can be no doubt of its being a play. A locality is clearly indicated—the sepulchre; the short dialogue, moreover, in its additions to the Gospel texts adds just those words that are so necessary in drama, demonstrating to the spectators the rôles that are being interpreted by the actors and suggesting appropriate action. The three priests are no longer priests, but Christian women—the three Marys; the single priest has become, for the space of the brief action, an angel.

Thus was born the *liturgical drama*, that form of medieval play wherein the dialogue and the movement formed part of the regular liturgy or service of the day. Even from the very beginning it must have begun to expand in several ways; by the introduction of mimetic action, by the utilization of properties and appropriate dress; and by the expansion of the simple plot through the addition of related episodes. Being part of the liturgy, these plays were written in Latin, and we must presume that their representation always retained a hieratical character: at the same time, there is plentiful evidence to demonstrate that as the years went by elaboration in form drew them out of their simple four-line shape into something much more complex.

Already in the tenth century instructions are given for the behaviour of the clerical actors. The first priest must approach the sepulchre without attracting attention, and sit there quietly with a palm in his hand; the others must walk up the nave, "stepping delicately as those who seek something," and come to the sepulchre "like folk lost." Later the rubrics to various texts show how this mimetic action becomes enlarged, while at the same time additional Latin words are given to the actors. Here, for example, is a specimen of a text, still liturgical, that well illustrates both developments. The three Marys are lamenting:

> MAGDALEN [*here she turns to the men with her arms extended*]: O my brothers! [*Here to the women*] O my sisters! Where is my hope? [*Here she beats her breast.*] Where is my consolation? [*Here she raises her hands.*] Where is my whole well-being? [*Here, head inclined, she throws herself at Christ's feet.*] O my Master!
>
> MARY MAJOR [*here she points to* MARY MAGDALEN]: O Mary Magdalen, [*here she points to* CHRIST] sweet disciple of my Son, [*here she embraces* MAGDALEN, *putting both her arms round her neck*] weep with me, in grief, [*here she points to* CHRIST] over the death of my sweet Son, [*here she points to* MAGDALEN] and the death of your Master, [*here she points to* CHRIST] the death of Him [*here she points to* MAGDALEN] who so loved you, [*still pointing to* MAGDALEN] who all your sins [*here she lets her arms fall*] has taken from you. [*Here she embraces* MAGDALEN, *as before, while she says*] Most sweet Magdalen.
>
> MAGDALEN [*here she greets* MARY *with her hands*]: Mother of Jesus crucified, [*here she weeps*] with you do I weep over the death of Christ.
>
> MARY, MOTHER OF JAMES [*here she makes a wide gesture over the audience and then puts her hands before her eyes*]: Who is there here who would not weep, seeing the Mother of Christ [*here she beats her breast*] in such misery?

The stage directions indicate here a highly stylized approach towards the interpretation of the parts, and this is precisely what we should expect so long as the play remained within the walls of the church, was connected with the ecclesiastical services, and was performed by the clergy.

The reference above to the early tenth-century liturgical playlet comes from an English manuscript; the very first record we have of the "Quem quæritis" issues from France; the last quotation given here is taken from an Italian text several centuries later. These facts illustrate, firstly, the extensive geographical distribution of the liturgical drama, and, secondly, the lengthy period of time during which it remained a feature of the Church's celebrations. Everywhere the Catholic creed was established the liturgical drama developed, and in all probability expansions of the primitive dialogue, together with the addition of fresh episodes, were being introduced now here, now there, and carried from country to country by the last of the true internationalists—those clerks who acknowledged themselves the servants of no particular country, and whose universal Latin tongue made them as much at home in Paris or Winchester as in Rome itself.

The accretions that grew around the simple sepulchre scene can easily be imagined. At the close of the original four-line dialogue the Marys are told to announce the arising of Christ: it was natural that the carrying out of this command should be the first additional scene, wherein the choir becomes, as it were, the body of Christ's disciples or wherein two members of the choir take the rôles of Peter and John. But the Gospel narrative tells us how these two apostles hurry to the tomb, how John "did outrun Peter, and came first to the sepulchre." This at once adds materially to the dramatic action. Still a further episode is the appearance of the risen Christ to Magdalen, who mistakes him for a *hortolanus*, or gardener. Later comes a scene showing the Marys purchasing perfumes and spices from an *unguentarius*, or spice-seller.

Thus grew the liturgical play, and, growing, it gradually created its own characteristic method of staging. At first no locality is demanded save the altar, taken for the sepulchre, or the erection within the church of a special structure representing this sepulchre. Even then, however, the entirety of the nave has to be considered part of the 'theatre,' since the three Marys come from a supposedly distant point and move slowly up to the Angel. The episode of the Announcement calls for movement to a second locality, that of the garden for a third, and when the Marys stop to buy their spices something representing a stall has to be supplied for the *unguentarius*. Thus, without any conscious planning, the earliest medieval theatre is evolved with three main characteristic features: (*a*) the mingling of audience and actors; (*b*) the establishment of a series of platforms or small structures indicating special localities (sepulchre, garden, spice-seller's booth); and (*c*) the utilization of the space between these platforms or structures as an acting area. On these principles was the entire medieval stage to develop during the course of the centuries from the tenth to the fifteenth.

THE LITURGICAL PLAYS BREAK THEIR BONDS

Obviously, the original intention of the clergy in thus introducing the liturgical drama was to make the chief episode in the Christian story more real and more vivid for the assembled congregation. The effect must, we imagine, have exceeded their expectations: for the people of the early medieval period, starved of entertainment of all kinds, the little shows were assuredly things not only of devotion but also of delight; and no doubt the clergy themselves found a secret joy in participation in the exercise of amateur theatricals. Pressure from within and without, therefore, guaranteed the rapid elaboration of the new-found stage.

After dealing with the Easter story it was natural that the story of Christmas should similarly be exploited, with the substitution of the opening line, "Quem quæritis in præsepe, pastores, dicite?" ("Whom seek ye in the manger, shepherds, say?") for the original "Quem quæritis in sepulchro, O Christicolæ?" Here progress was even more rapid. We hear of priests appearing "quasi obstetrices" ("like midwives"), we hear of the introduction of an ox and an ass, even of simple theatrical machinery, such as a movable star. Herod becomes a character; the three Magi are introduced. The play is expanded into a drama of many scenes.

The next step is also an obvious one. Scenes are written, still in Latin, for separate performance; they belong yet to the church, but they are no longer extensions of the church service, and, as they become more elaborate, they are brought out of the church itself and played in the open. Here for the first time in the medieval theatre do we encounter anything of genuine dramatic worth—the twelfth-century Anglo-Norman *Adam*—and fortunately the stage-directions in the original manuscript of this drama give extraordinarily clear indications of the way in which it was intended to be performed.

We must imagine ourselves standing outside a great Norman cathedral. On the steps leading to the west door a platform has been built, "with curtains and cloths of silk hung round it at such a height that persons" there "may be visible from the shoulders upward." This place represents Paradise, and here appears God, rather peculiarly named the Figura, or Figure. He is clothed in a dalmatic, and before him come Adam, in a red tunic, and Eve, dressed in a woman's robe of white, with a white silk cloak. The author is exact in his demands.

wide sleeved
tunic or robe
A medieval state Robe

ADAM *must be well trained when to reply and to be neither too quick nor too slow in his replies. And not only he, but all the personages must be trained to speak composedly, and to fit convenient gesture to the matter of their speech. Nor must they foist in a syllable or clip one of the verses, but must enounce firmly and repeat what is set down for them in due order. Whoever names Paradise is to look and point toward it.*

The direction regarding 'pointing' reminds us of the stylized hieratic gesture demanded for the Marys: obviously the acting required here is akin to that of the priests before their altars.

The Figura gives his commands to Adam and Eve and departs into the church, while they "walk about Paradise in honest delight." At the same time a number of devils run out "per plateas"—that is to say, on the open ground, or *platea*, immediately in front of the Paradise platform. Adam is tempted, but remains loyal to the Figura's behest, whereupon the chief devil,

> *sadly and with downcast countenance, shall leave* ADAM, *and go to the doors of Hell, and hold council with the other demons. Thereafter he shall make a sally amongst the people, and then approach Paradise on* EVE'S *side, addressing her with joyful countenance and insinuating manner.*

It is clear that the liturgical principles of staging are being observed: there must be a distinct place representing Hell, the open ground between this and Paradise is an acting area, and the spectators are almost involved in the action: the devil makes "a sally amongst the people."

Now comes a scene of true dramatic insight:

DEVIL: Eve, hither am I come, to thee.
EVE: And prithee, Satan, why to me?
DEVIL: Seeking thy weal, thine honour, too.
EVE: God grant it!
DEVIL: Then thy fears eschew.
          Long since, I've mastered by my pains
          Each secret Paradise contains;
          A part of them to thee I'll tell.
EVE [*her curiosity aroused*]:
          Begin, then, and I'll listen well.
DEVIL: Thou'lt hearken to me?
EVE: Hearken?—yea,
          Nor vex thy soul in any way.
DEVIL: Thou'lt keep it hidden?
EVE: Yea, in truth.
DEVIL: Nor publish it?
EVE: Not I! forsooth.

DEVIL:　Then, to this contract I'll agree,
　　　　Nor further pledge require of thee.
EVE:　　Might'st safely trust my promise, though.
DEVIL:　Thou'st been to a good school, I trow!
　　　　Adam I've seen—a fool is he.
EVE [*considering*]:　A little hard.
DEVIL:　　　　　　　　　　　　He'll softer be;
　　　　But harder now than iron is.
EVE:　　A noble man!
DEVIL:　　　　　　　A churl! I wis.
　　　　Thought for himself he will not take;
　　　　Let him have care, e'en for thy sake.
　　　　Thou art a delicate, tender thing,
　　　　Thou'rt fresher than the rose in spring;
　　　　Thou'rt whiter than the crystal pale,
　　　　Than snow that falls in the icy vale.
　　　　An ill-matched pair did God create!
　　　　Too tender thou, too hard thy mate.
　　　　But thou'rt the wiser, I confess;
　　　　Thy heart is full of cleverness.

At this, of course, Eve begins to consider the devil a very discerning young man and is all ready to listen when he tells her of the wonders of the forbidden fruit. "What savour hath't?" she asks, and is told, "'Tis heavenly food!":

　　　　To thy fair body, to thy face,
　　　　Most meet it were to add this grace:
　　　　That thou be queen of the world—of this,
　　　　Of the firmament, and of the abyss—
　　　　And know all things that shall befall,
　　　　And be the mistress of them all.

Carefully she reviews the situation, but, womanlike, delays. Only when the serpent arrives does she taste of the fruit and bring it to Adam. When he demurs she taunts him with cowardice and munches the apple, declaiming at its delicious taste; and at last he consents to eat of it. Immediately, however, he takes "knowledge of his sin," bows down out of sight behind the curtains, and changes his fine dress for "poor garments of fig-leaves sewn together." His lament is pitiful:

　　　　And whom shall I beseech for aid,
　　　　When mine own wife hath me betrayed,
　　　　Whom God gave me my fere to be?
　　　　An evil counsel gave she me!
　　　　Alas! O Eve!

The Figura returns, "wearing a stole, and looking about him, as if seeking to know where Adam is. But Adam and Eve shall be hidden in a corner of Paradise, as if conscious of their wretchedness." Adam confesses his sin as the terrible figure ironically denounces the miserable pair:

> Didst reckon thus my peer to be?
> I do not think thou'lt jest with me! . . .
> Didst think through him to be my peer?
> Hast learned to make things hidden clear?
> Erstwhile thou heldest sovereignty
> Over all living things that be;
> How quickly hast thou lost thy crown! . . .
> I'll render thee thy just desert;
> Thy service I will thus repay.

They are driven out of Paradise and toil wearily. Adam turns upon his wife with bitter sarcasm, crying:

> O wretched Eve! How seemeth it to thee?
> This hast thou gained thee as thy dowery—

while she expresses her contrition pathetically:

> Forgive me!—no atonement can I see,
> Else would my sacrifice be offered free . . .
> I gave it thee, to serve thee was mine aim . . .
> The fruit was sweet, bitter will be the pain!

This tense treatment of the Fall is followed by a great scene of diablerie:

> *Then shall the devil come, and three or four other devils with him, bearing in their hands chains and iron shackles, which they shall place on the necks of* ADAM *and* EVE. *And certain ones shall push them on, others shall drag them toward hell; other devils, however, shall be close beside Hell, waiting for them as they come, and these shall make a great dancing and jubilation over their destruction; and other devils shall, one after another, point to them as they come; and they shall take them up and thrust them into Hell; and thereupon they shall cause a great smoke to arise, and they shall shout one to another in Hell, greatly rejoicing; and they shall dash together their pots and kettles, so that they may be heard without.*

After this comes a scene of Cain and Abel, and when the latter has been slain there follows a great procession of the Prophets, ending with a dialogue between Isaias and an unnamed Jew:

JEW: Now, Sir Isaias, answer me:
          Is this a tale or prophecy?
          This thing thou'st told—pray, what is it?
          Didst it invent, or is it writ?
          Thou'st been asleep—didst dream the rest?
          Speak'st thou in earnest, or in jest?
ISAIAS: This is no tale, 'tis very truth!
JEW: Then, let's know all of it, forsooth!
ISAIAS: What I have spoke is prophecy.
JEW: Writ in a book?
ISAIAS: Yea, verily,
          —In Life's! I've dreamed it not, but seen!
JEW: And how?
ISAIAS: Through grace of God, I ween.
JEW: Thou seem'st to me a dotard grey,
          Thy mind and sense all gone astray!
          A soothsayer thou seem'st, indeed,
          Skilled in the glass, perchance, to read;
          Come, read me now this hand, and tell
          [*then shall he show him his hand*]
          Whether my heart be sick or well.
ISAIAS: Thou hast sin's murrain in thy soul,
          Ne'er in thy life shalt thou be whole.

The last words of the drama are a vision of the Redeemer:

> His face shone, full of majesty,
> The Son of God he seemed to be!

We are in the presence here of something quite extraordinary. There is a simple passion and a sly, humorous observation in *Adam* that is hard to match in the entire course of the medieval drama until we reach, at the very end of its development, that other anonymous play of quiet faith, *Everyman*.

THE GREAT MYSTERY CYCLES

In *Adam* the setting is close to a church; Latin anthems are sung; and, although the first two episodes are written wholly in the Anglo-Norman vernacular, Latin appears, along with the vulgar tongue, in the speeches of the Prophets, as in the words of Isaias:

> Egredietur virga de radice Jesse, et flos de radice eius ascendet, et requiescat super cum spiritus Domini.

> Or vus dirrai merveillus diz:
> Jesse sera de sa raïz.

Verge eu istra, qui fera flor,
Qui ert digne de grant unor.
Saint esprit l'avra si clos,
Sor cest flor iert sun repos.

The play, though attached still to the Church, is straining towards the people.

Gradually the final step is made; the ties are broken; the drama becomes entirely vernacular and belongs to the laity. When this finally occurred vast expansion became possible—indeed, imperative. Hundreds of worthy medieval citizens wanted, like Bottom and his crew, to amuse themselves with the delightful new toy, and consequently there grew into being those vast collections of separate playlets known as the *Mystery Cycles*, the word 'mystery,' from *ministerium* (service or office), still denoting the religious origin of these pieces.

The actors now were, for the most part, the ordinary burghers and artisans of the towns and countryside. In England the trades guilds undertook the performance of the plays, especially after the establishment of the Corpus Christi festival in 1311, a feast set apart specifically for the performance of these pieces. The guilds defrayed the expenses for the costumes and scenery, and from their members came the acting personnel. In France arose special organizations, amateur groups, named *confréries*, of which the most famous was the Confrérie de la Passion at Paris, founded in 1402, although there the craft corporations also concerned themselves with theatrical performances. In certain parts of Italy the actors were youths who formed themselves into devotional associations named after their patron saints—la Compagnia di San Francesco or la Compagnia dell' Agnesa.

There is no festival competition here, as in the Greek theatre, and, although there may have been a sincerity in the presentation of the parts, we must assume that in many instances the interpretation was naïve and ludicrously inadequate. At least in one district of France in the sixteenth century record declares that the performers of mystery plays

> are an ignorant set of men, mechanics and artisans, who know not an A from a B, untrained and unskilled in playing such pieces before the public. Their voices are poor, their language unfitting, their pronunciation wretched. No sense do they have of the meaning of what they say.

Nevertheless they took their job seriously. They were willing to rehearse for long hours, to be up betimes at 4.30 in the morning, and, although their labours were freely interspersed with collations of ale and beef, the task they set themselves must have been a hard one.

For the presentation of their pieces they followed, and expanded, the stage principles established by the liturgical drama, setting up a series of decorated platforms, now named 'mansions,' before the audience in a straight line, in a semicircle, or, as in Cornwall, in a circle. Each mansion represented a distinct and separate locality, while the open space in front or in the middle, the *platea*, could be used much in the manner in which it had formerly served when the drama was in the hands of the clergy.

Already in the twelfth century a *Conversion de l'apôtre Saint Paul* (*Conversion of St Paul*), of French composition, shows the principle in full development. Instructions are there given for the preparation "in a convenient place of a platform for the Prince of Priests: this will stand for Jerusalem. Another platform must be prepared also, where a young man dressed as Saul will be seated, with armed guards before him." At the other side are platforms representing Damascus, one for Judas and one for the Prince of the Synagogue, and in addition to these there is a bed for Ananias. This system of 'multiple staging' or 'simultaneous setting' was the characteristic medieval contribution to the art of the theatre, although in some places, notably in England and Flanders, another device was adopted whereby individual mansions were set upon wheels (and named pageants) and drawn from group to group of spectators.

As the years went by the productions became more and more elaborate. Guild vied with guild, confraternity with confraternity, in enriching the mansions, while at the same time machinery and 'effects' were freely introduced, especially in France. The great director's script of the mysteries played at Mons gives us a clear insight into the marvels shown to the public, and the impression made upon a contemporary is well revealed in an account of a production at Valenciennes in 1547:

> The effects associated with Heaven and Hell were veritably prodigious and might well have seemed to the audience the result of magic. One saw Truth, the Angels and diverse characters descend from a great height. . . . From Hell, Lucifer rose, how one could not tell, on a dragon's back. Moses' staff, dry and withered, suddenly burst forth with flowers and fruit; the souls of Herod and Judas were borne into the air by devils. . . . Water was seen to change into wine, so extraordinarily that one could hardly credit it, and more than a hundred persons tasted the wine; the five loaves and two fish were

multiplied and distributed to more than a thousand people, yet notwithstanding there were a dozen baskets over. . . . The eclipse, the earthquake, the shattering of rocks and other miracles that accompanied the death of Our Lord were represented with still further miracles.

While we cannot assume that in all districts such wonders were reproduced—while in some areas the plays certainly must have been presented in a very humble manner—we must not lose sight of the fact that those who lived at least in the later medieval period were acquainted with theatrical effects of no mean kind.

The plays thus produced essayed to tell the entire Biblical story from the Creation of the World to the Last Judgment. In many countries they took shape in fundamentally similar forms. The Italian *sacre rappresentazioni* were akin to the French *mystères*, the *mystères* to the German *Passionsspiele*, and those to the English 'miracle plays' and to the Cornish *guary* plays. Taking days to perform, the cycles consisted of thirty, forty, fifty, and even more separate dramas, each telling some salient portion of the Bible's account of events human and supernatural. In England there are still extant the cycles of York, Wakefield, Coventry, Chester; in France there are riches innumerable, from the early thirteenth-century plays of a Chantilly manuscript to the later vast *Passions* of Eustache Marcadé, Arnoul Greban, and Jehan Michel, and to the *Mystère du Vieil Testament*; other lands similarly add their quota to the total treasury.

In the composition of the dramas clearly a variety of different impulses was at work. First was the basic object of presenting dramatically the Biblical story, with accretions from apocryphal gospels as well as from the writings of commentators. In this sense the mystery cycle was an historical drama. But truth to the original narrative frequently was permitted to give way to a desire for symbolic and allegorical treatment of persons and events. Mary Magdalen, for example, thus becomes, not so much a real woman as an abstract figure representing sin repentant. This trend towards symbolism is, of course, a general characteristic of medieval art, but it is intensified here because these plays, besides being drama of an historical and symbolic kind, are also propaganda theatre, designed to instruct men to avoid vice and cling to virtue. Even when the mysteries strayed farthest from the Church, their devotional, or, at least, instructorial, quality remained dominant.

Beyond all of this, however, there was something else. All the marvels involved in the production of the plays were designed obviously to delight the audience, and we recognize that those concerned with their presentation were fully aware of what we should now call their 'entertainment value.' This awareness led to the invention of subject-matter for which no valid authority was forthcoming. In general it assumed certain clearly defined forms: the introduction of realistic elements, of comic scenes, and of sensational scenic devices such as those indicated in the staging of the later French *mystères*. While possibly all of these were natural developments such as might have been expected to arise unbidden within the mystery-play framework, there is more than a suspicion that as the amateurs pursued their path and sought for new ways of delighting their audiences they may have turned to professional entertainers—the minstrels and *jongleurs*, who were the descendants of the mimes—for aid and inspiration. The comic elements brought into the plays were of just that kind in which the early mimics had delighted, and there is undoubtedly a professional touch in the magical wonders described for us by contemporaries. The realistic element, too, provides further suggestions of a similar kind: it is, for example, noteworthy that in precisely those portions of the mystery cycles to which the entertainers might have been expected to contribute their skill—the scenes of the devils and the comic episodes—the characters, instead of being left anonymous (first, second, third devil or first, second, third soldier), are provided with names and to a certain extent at least are given individual rôles. In all countries do we find this feature. Mak, the good-humoured predecessor of Autolycus, appears in England; Italy brings its Nencio, Bobi, and Randello, its Filino, Schirnio, and Thesino; France its Aloris, Ysambert, and Pellion. Looking at these, we may well suspect that the secularization of certain scenes in these prevailingly devotional plays was materially aided by the activities of those obscure descendants of the *mimi* who strutted forth, on the fall of Rome, into the Dark Ages.

To reach a valid appreciation of the artistic quality of the mystery cycles is difficult. We are inclined to do no more nowadays—unless we are specialized students of literature—than read a few selected examples of individual plays in anthologies; yet we must always bear in mind that for contemporary audiences the entire cycle, and not merely separate portions of it, was the object of attention. The cycle, on the other hand, possessed no formal unity: playlets might be added to or extracted from the collection at will. If there is a unity, it is such as we find in a Gothic cathedral, wherein Norman elements are set side by side with the work of later builders, where there need be no symmetry, where elaboration in one transept may be in no wise paralleled in another, where the very pillars of the nave may be of the most diverse forms. The unity here is rather a unity of impression than one of formally associated parts.

Within the various countries of Europe different elements were stressed in these productions, even although the main features were the same in all lands. The Germans loved grotesque, nightmarish scenes of devils, were adept at Jew-baiting, and enjoyed a kind of rude realistic satire in which contemporary personalities were set cheek-by-jowl with figures from the Bible. An excellent example is provided in the fifteenth-century *Redentiner Osterspiel* (*Redentin Easter Play*), a work which, despite the extraordinary diversity of its material, illustrates well the Gothic unity referred to above as well as the characteristic qualities of the German medieval mind. Divided into two parts, the play first tells, with some rude-handed humour and broad satire, how the Jews beg Pilate to see that Christ's body is not taken from the tomb: their efforts fail, and Jesus rises to effect the harrowing of Hell. The devils are in dismay; and consternation is among the soldiery appointed by Pilate to guard the tomb. In the second part of the drama Lucifer is shown lamenting; Hell must be repopulated, and Satan is sent to gather in as many souls as he can. "Bring the poor and the rich," he is ordered,

> And let none escape from you:
> The usurer and also the robber;
> The counterfeiter and the milk-thief;
> The magician and the pastry-cook;
> The liar and the dog-trainer;
> The brewer, the maltster,
> And also the dealer in tripe.

Then comes a long procession of miserable sinners—a baker who has cheated his customers, a shoemaker who has left his leather untanned, a tailor who has stolen cloth, a barmaid who has given short measure:

> Why should I try to cover it up?
> I don't think I could deceive you anyway.
> I was always able to make a lot of beer,
> Chiefly for this reason:
> I used an ample quantity of water—
> Otherwise my need for water was small.
> Also, when I sold beer or wine,
> Then this was my custom:

I put my thumb into the glass
And served beer with a lot of foam.
Whenever I measured out beer for some one,
I believe that I never once forgot
To serve part from the second boiling;
And thus I earned many a penny.

The procession continues, with a weaver, a butcher, a huckster, a robber, and, finally, a priest—all depicted in vivid contemporary terms. Obviously here, although the aim is highly moral, the story of Christ is being forgotten amid the clamour of the devils and their prey.

Farcical satirical scenes are frequent in other of the German plays of the time. In the *Wiener Osterspiel* (*Vienna Easter Play*), for example, the episode of the unguent-seller is much elaborated. He is represented as a quack doctor, just arrived from Paris with a stock of tinctures and drops. He is worried because his assistant has left him. Luckily, however, the rascally Rubin appears—a thief and a rogue—and accepts the vacant position. The whole scene is a vivid picture of contemporary life. From the realistic trend which gave it birth also derives a number of scenes of more serious import. Thus in the *Hessisches Weihnachtsspiel* (*The Hessian Christmas Play*) there appears a remarkable and touching picture of the homeless Joseph and Mary wearily seeking a humble lodging. The appeal made by their words springs from the same source as gives vitality to the quack doctor's bargaining with Rubin.

The vast mystery cycles of France are broader in their scope, and in general one is inclined to regard them as unnecessarily prolix. Rhetoric and intellectual argument only too often are substituted in them for dramatic passion. They too, however, possess their characteristic interest. Diablerie is much stressed here, as in the German plays, but what most attracts our attention is the occasional appearance of an intensely lyrical note and of scenes as realistic as the German, but more polished and refined. Even the usually tedious Greban can thus rise to his song of Hell, with its refrain,

La dure mort éternelle
C'est la chanson des damnés—

and to the haunting appeal of Christ's prayer to His Father:

Heavenly Father, sovereign creator,
Who first adorned these beautiful heavens,
Who know all in Thy infinite wisdom,
Look on me, Thy lowly human son,

> Bowed down with an intolerable burden
> Such as heart of man cannot guess at.

As representative of the realistic note we may take the lively scene in Marcadé's *mystère* in which Magdaleine is shown, before her conversion, with her waiting-maids Pasiphée and Perusine:

PASIPHÉE:	You are all the rage;
	They talk of nothing else but you. . . .
MAGDALEINE:	I must get myself ready,
	Dressed, laced, made-up:
	I must look my best.
PASIPHÉE:	There's not a lady your equal;
	You're so lovely
	You don't need make-up. . . .

[MAGDALEINE *washes her face and looks in her mirror.*]

MAGDALEINE:	Have I not a radiant face?
PERUSINE:	Indeed, yes.
	You're quite a picture.
MAGDALEINE:	And my bonnet?
PERUSINE:	The latest fashion.

A trifle more polished, and this might have been an episode from a comedy of manners.

The English mystery plays, compared with the German and the French, seem more subdued, but perhaps because of that there may be justification for those who believe that their contents have more structural harmony and more directness of appeal than any of the others. Here the devils play just such a part as they ought and no more; here comedy appears rather as a relief and a contrast than as an entity by itself; here at times there is a simple passion and a naïve tenderness of a strangely appealing sort. There is a peculiarly restrained emotional impact in the scene where Abraham unwillingly prepares to sacrifice his son:

ABRAHAM:	Oh, my son! I am sorry
	To do thee this great annoy,
	God's commandment do must I,
	His works are aye full mild.
ISAAC:	Would God, my mother were here with me!
	She would kneel upon her knee,
	Praying you, father, if it might be,
	For to save my life.
ABRAHAM:	Oh, comely creature, but I thee kill,
	I grieve my God, and that full ill:
	I may not work against his will
	But ever obedient be. . . .

ISAAC: Is it God's will I should be slain?
ABRAHAM: Yea, son, it is not for to layne;
   To his bidding I will be bane,
    Ever to his pleasing.
   But that I do this doleful deed,
   My Lord will not quit me my meed.
ISAAC: Marry, father, God forbid
    But you do your off'ring.
   Father, at home your sons you shall find
   That you must love by course of kind.
   Be I at once out of your mind,
    Your sorrow may soon cease.
   But you must do God's bidding.
   Father, tell my mother of nothing.

A homely quality is present in the gentle Coventry Nativity Play, with its lovely shepherds' song:

  As I outrode this enderes' night,
  Of three jolly shepherds I saw a sight,
  And all about their fold a star shone bright;
   They sang, Terli, terlow—
  So merrily the shepherds their pipes can blow.

In the Torturers of the Towneley Crucifixion appears a grim humour, and a gay atmosphere surrounds Noah's wife in the Chester Deluge. She is a true artisan's wife, and her words are racy as she flouts her husband:

  Yea, sir, set up your sail
  And row forth with evil heale,
  For, without any fail,
  I will not out of this town.
  But I have my gossips every one,
  One foot further I will not go.
  They shall not drown, by Saint John,
  If I may save their life.
  They loved me full well, by Christ!
  But thou wilt let them in thy chest,
  Else row forth, Noah, whither thou list,
  And get thee a new wife.

And, of course, above all others, there is the famous Wakefield *Second Shepherds' Play*, the first part of which presents an incisive picture of the three shepherds, cold and weary, watching their flocks as they grumble about the exactions of the "gentlery men" and their minions. The thievish Mak comes and steals one of their flock, carries it to his home, and, aided by his wife Gill, puts it in a cradle and swaddles it with clothes. Found out at last, Mak is "tossed for his sins," and immediately after this merriment an Angel's voice is heard sweetly intoning the announcement of Christ's birth. The contrast is severe, yet the quiet scene by the manger gains in simple dignity, not loses, from this sharp juxtaposition with the comic episodes preceding it. Although the author of this play may have been untutored, he possessed an innate sense of the dramatic.

For us to-day the medieval mystery plays may have historic rather than intrinsic interest. We still flock to Oberammergau, but the mood in which these pieces were written is gone; at best we can be but spectators at, not participators in, the performance. On the other hand, the historic interest is no ordinary one, for this vast endeavour of the Middle Ages is, as it were, the rock upon which Shakespeare's palaces and towers were firmly erected. It is possible, of course, to argue that, since Christ is a perfect character and a symbol rather than a man, the mystery play could offer no basis for the later secular tragic drama, but such arguments seem to lose sight of the most important contributions of this form to the theatre. The tragic drama depends fundamentally on what we may call high seriousness; it is an exploration of the deepest, the most fundamental problems of the universe; the slightest breath of cynicism is fatal to its being. So far as form is concerned, the mystery plays had nothing to give to the later theatre, but their spirit is the illimitable landscape against which the tragic figures of the Elizabethan stage stand gloriously illumined. Their atmosphere of unquestioning faith, their breadth of scope, and the variety of tone through which they contrasted the solemn with the ludicrous all contributed materially towards building the strength that reached its culmination in Shakespeare.

THE THEATRE OF THE SAINTS

In many respects the mystery cycles were inhibited from the possibility of organic growth. Once a cycle had been composed additions and alterations might be, and, indeed, were, undertaken, but there was no incentive or opportunity for the building of things new. Partly this was due to the fact that the Biblical material was the be-all and the end-all for the dramatists; partly it was due to the fact that the actors were amateurs who engaged in the presentation of the plays only once a year. For the preparation of fresh dramatic compositions there was the impulse neither of the Athenian competitions nor of professional needs. Apart from this, the cycle itself weighed heavily upon the theatre: too vast to be lightly rewritten, it prohibited the growth of a more readily perceivable unity. A new playwright might on occasion substitute another "Abraham and Isaac" or "Deluge" for those which had been previously performed, but in general he was fettered by the thought that these separate dramas could be no more than parts of a very much larger whole. The process could be little beyond the exercise of a modern dramatist engaged in the rewriting of a single scene—the thirtieth or fortieth part—of an already existent tragedy or comedy.

Besides the Biblical play, however, the medieval stage had plays of the saints, and these offered some more promising possibilities. Although owing their being to the development of the liturgical drama, these miracle plays early sprang into being alongside the mysteries, and exhibited not so much a development from as a growth parallel to the others. As early as the beginning of the twelfth century a chance accident provides us with a record of a play of *St Catherine* (*ludus de Sancta Katarina*) performed at Dunstable. The accident occurred to a certain Norman clerk named Geoffrey who had borrowed some vestments from the abbey for the performance; fire broke out in his house, the ecclesiastical property was destroyed, and the poor man, conscience-stricken, became a monk. For Geoffrey the ill-wind had the advantage of bringing him in time to be the abbot of St Albans; for us it has given us our first authentic record of a saint's play, or miracle, in Europe.

This record will illustrate some of the problems confronting a student of the medieval theatre. Although the twelfth century thus reveals the existence of a play of St Catherine in England, and although later allusions testify to the flourishing of miracles alongside the mysteries, there is virtually no single text of an English play of the kind now extant. For our knowledge of what the saint's play provided we must turn to other lands, notably to France, where fortunately so much has been preserved, from the thirteenth to the sixteenth century, that a clear picture both of the growth of the genre and of its diverse manifestations is readily obtainable.

Le jeu de Saint Nicolas (*The Play of St Nicholas*) is known to have been written by a certain Jean Bodel, and, since he died in 1210, its date can be at least approximately determined. Its trailing plot

MIMIC FOOLS
Terra-cotta statuettes in the British Museum.

A MIMIC FOOL
Bronze (probably Greek).
*By courtesy of the Metropolitan Museum
of Art, New York*

TERRA–COTTA MASKS
From the originals in the British Museum.

STAGING OF THE MYSTERY PLAY AT VALENCIENNES

Hubert Cailleau, National Library, Paris.

From Dr Hans Heinrich Borcherdt, *Das Europäische Theater im Mittelalter und in der Renaissance*, Fig. 22.

MEDIEVAL DEVILS' MASKS
Collection in the Ferdinandeum, Innsbruck.
Photo Ferdinandeum

BICCI DI LORENZO: MIRACLES OF ST NICHOLAS AT BARI. THE THREE PICKLED BOYS

By courtesy of the Metropolitan Museum of Art, New York

BICCI DI LORENZO: MIRACLES OF ST NICHOLAS AT BARI. THE THREE GOLDEN BALLS

By courtesy of the Metropolitan Museum of Art, New York

well exemplifies some of the elements which were later to be so fully exploited in this kind of drama. The background is that of the Crusades, romantic, adventurous, with a King of the Pagans, surrounded by his "amiraus," or emirs; there is noise of battle and slaughter of the Christians; there are effective prayers to St Nicholas and an overthrowing of the great idol Terragan. But there also appear scenes of a different character—scenes in an inn, with rollicking, racy dialogue born of the Arras soil. *Le jeu de Saint Nicolas* is ostensibly a religious drama, and it ends with the singing of the *Te Deum*; but it is at least half-secular, a mixture of an adventure story and a comedy of ordinary life.

From the same period comes an even more interesting play, *Le miracle de Théophile* (*The Miracle of Theophilus*), the work of a thirteenth-century minstrel, Rutebeuf. The plot here deals with the tale of the man who gives his soul to the devil. Dissatisfied with his lot, Théophile, a clerk, effects the sale of his immortal being through the office of a magician named Salatin, "who talks to the devil as often as he wants." The hero is not untroubled by doubts, and the devil, for his part, is treated, amusingly, as a character much annoyed by the way in which he is continually being tormented by human conjurations, and very cautious in this transaction because he has so frequently been cheated in the past. After a career of sin, suddenly, without any warning, Théophile repents, prays to the Virgin, is first repulsed and then aided by her. She succeeds in recovering the paper that Théophile had signed; he takes it triumphantly to his bishop, who indulges in some suitable moralizations; and the play ends with the *Te Deum*.

Here we are approaching the great treasury of the French miracles —the wonders wrought by Our Lady—which was to produce the lengthy series of diverse dramas entitled *Les miracles de Nostre-Dame* (*The Miracles of Our Lady*). Already in *Théophile* the shape of these pieces has been determined. Each play is now a separate entity, and, even when miracle cycles develop, the component parts remain independent: the cycle now is not a lengthy story stretching from Creation to Resurrection, but merely a collection of individual dramas. These dramas consist of two parts, showing first the sins of the protagonists and secondly the wonder-working miracle, the repentance, the finding of the true way; and since the miracle comes necessarily at the conclusion of the plot, it is to be understood that the greater part of the story is concerned with secular, and often comic, material.

The variety of such material is astounding. In general, one may

F

divide the *Miracles de Nostre-Dame* into three groups: (*a*) those in which the miracle is the climax of the plot, in which the playwright has tried to build his tale towards the final wonder; (*b*) those in which the miracle, while necessary for the resolving of the plot, tends to be overshadowed by the secular material; and (*c*) those in which the miracle is a mere appendage to an entirely secular theme. A few examples will illustrate the types.

In *Jehan le Paulu* an anchorite is tempted by the devil, who poses as his servant, and when the king's daughter comes to his cell after losing her way during a hunt he ravishes and kills her at the demon's suggestion. The body is thrown into a pit. Repenting, he vows he will make penance by going on all-fours like a beast and feeding himself on roots. Seven years pass, when the king revisits the place where his daughter was lost. Word from heaven comes to Jehan saying he is pardoned; he rises, confesses his crime, prays that the princess be restored. The prayer is granted, and all the company thanks the Virgin for her intercession. Although the plot has an element of romantic wonder about it, clearly its design has been determined by the fact of the miracle; the end is anticipated in the beginning.

Somewhat different is the *Miracle de Nostre Dame, comment elle guarda une femme d'estre arse* (*The Miracle of Our Lady: how She protected a Woman from being burned*). The first part of the story is a domestic melodrama. Guillaume, the mayor of Chiefvi (Chivy), and his wife, Guibour, live happily with their daughter and their son-in-law, Aubin, until rumour starts to whisper that Guibour and Aubin are lovers. Informed of this, she comes to a terrible decision: Aubin must die. Two harvesters are commissioned to trap him as he goes to his wine-cellar and to strangle him. A brilliantly conceived scene follows when the mayor cheerily prepares for the family meal and sends his daughter to call Aubin, while Guibour astutely conceals her guilty knowledge. After the arrival of officers of justice it is discovered that the youth has been murdered; the whole family is arrested; Guibour confesses and is sentenced to be burned alive. The play might now be considered finished, but the marvel is still to come. So well does she pray to the Virgin that a miracle is wrought: the cords that bind her are consumed by the flames, but her body remains untouched.

With this drama we are well on the way to the secular theatre, and when we move to the miracles of the third type we are almost wholly within that sphere. Here we encounter a variety of themes of diverse moods. In *La femme du Roy de Portugal* (*The Wife of the*

King of Portugal) a king proposes to a girl, but declares that, since the marriage day has to be delayed, he will die if he does not have her immediately. She pleads the cause of honour, then succumbs and gives him the key of her room, with the words: "You have in your hands now the key of my honour, and of your own." This is a plot of ordinary life, not a religious exercise. The story of *Amis et Amille* appears here, a tale of friendship in the realm of chivalry. *Robert le Diable* makes his entry. There are stories of romantic pathos and adventure, such as *La fille du Roy de Hongrie* (*The Daughter of the King of Hungary*), in which is told how a monarch, in order to keep his vow to his now dead wife that he will never remarry save it be to "a woman of her likeness," obtains the Pope's blessing for a wedding with his own daughter. The girl, to escape incest, dares her father's wrath, is condemned to death, escapes, marries the King of Scotland, is accused by her mother-in-law of faithlessness to her husband and set adrift on the sea in a small boat. From a dismal fate she is saved by intercession of Our Lady. The same story, it may be noted, although wrapped up in pseudo-classical robes, appears in the interesting fifteenth-century Latin *Comœdia sine nomine* (*The Comedy without a Title*).

So much has been lost of this kind of drama that it is difficult to assess rightly its true significance in the development of the romantic stage. A few years ago we should have been inclined to believe, for example, that England had nothing to offer in this kind, but towards the beginning of the present century there was discovered a manuscript, written about 1380, containing the part of an actor who took the chief rôle in a play which may be called *Duke Moraud*. Penned in stanza form which is similar to the form of the miracles, it tells a melodramatic story of a duke who conceives an incestuous passion for his own daughter; his wife threatens to expose them and is killed by the girl; a child is born of the liaison, and, at the duke's command, it too is slain. At the end he is shown joyous at the thought that now their secret is safe, but, going to church, he becomes conscious of his sin, falls into a decline, and dies begging Christ to have mercy upon him. Here in the fourteenth century is a wholly secular drama, with as sensational a theme as any of those exploited by the later Elizabethans.

One after another these plays ring the changes on episodes and characters akin to those familiar to us in the worlds of romance and balladry, and we realize that the genre of the miracle play was offering to the playwrights of the time innumerable opportunities for the exploitation of new material. There are no inhibitions in this realm, as there were in the realm of the mystery dramas; the tales of miracles were legion, and if necessary it was a simple feat to take any theme, no matter whether grave or gay, sordidly realistic or replete with romantic wonder, and tack on to its close a miracle of the Virgin. If the mysteries provided the element of high seriousness and vastness of conception, the miracles taught men how to give theatrical expression to domestic scenes and legends of adventure.

THE MORALITIES

In the mystery plays we occasionally meet with personifications among the Biblical and invented characters, and it is probable that the growth of yet another type of medieval drama, the *morality play*, was inspired from this source. In the moralities all the persons introduced upon the stage are abstract figures, most of them representing vices and virtues. Already in the twelfth century Germany could show, in the *Ludus de Antichristo*, a morality-type drama introducing Paganism and Synagogue, Hypocrisy and Heresy, as speaking characters.

At first glance it would seem as though this were a retrograde movement in the theatre, a moving away from living characters to characters of a purely symbolic cast; but examination of the plays themselves must lead us to beware of too hasty judgments. The typical morality handles a plot in which a central figure, called Mankind or Humanum Genus or Infans, is tempted, falls, and comes again to grace. The pens of some of the playwrights may be heavy and dull and uninspiring; others may permit their moralizing aims to suppress dramatic tensity; but in general it will be found that this basic theme aids rather than hinders the medieval dramatist in the writing of vividly conceived scenes, many of them based on the life he has seen around him.

Of all the moralities the Anglo-Dutch *Everyman*, or *Elckerlijk*, is both the most typical and the best. Its story is well known. God summons Everyman by ordering Death to take him for his own:

> Go thou to Everyman,
> And show him in my name
> A pilgrimage he must on him take,
> Which he in no wise may escape;
> And that he bring with him a sure reckoning
> Without delay or any tarrying.

Everyman pleads delay, and then seeks around for anyone who may bear him company. First he turns to Fellowship:

EVERYMAN: Well met, good Fellowship, and good morrow!

FELLOWSHIP: Everyman, good morrow by this day.
Sir, why lookest thou so piteously?
If anything be amiss, I pray thee, me say,
That I may help to remedy.

EVERYMAN: Yea, good Fellowship, yea,
I am in great jeopardy.

FELLOWSHIP: My true friend, show to me your mind;
I will not forsake thee, unto my life's end
In the way of good company.

EVERYMAN: That was well spoken, and lovingly.

FELLOWSHIP: Sir, I must needs know your heaviness;
I have pity to see you in any distress;
If any have you wronged ye shall revenged be,
Though I on the ground be slain for thee,—
Though that I know before that I should die.

EVERYMAN: Verily, Fellowship, gramercy.

FELLOWSHIP: Tush! by thy thanks I set not a straw.
Show me your grief, and say no more.

When, however, he hears what is wanted he quickly draws back. A similar answer is given by Kindred and Goods; Knowledge, Confession, Beauty, Strength, Discretion, Five-wits, all fail Everyman; in the end only Good Deeds, although faint and "lying cold" in the ground, is prepared to stand at his side.

The quality of this drama has deservedly rescued it from oblivion. In the original form and in the rather voluptuously expanded German *Jedermann* it has seen many performances during recent years and has always worked its magic on its audiences. This magic derives, of course, largely from the universal appeal of its theme, but it is contributed to by the manner in which the unknown playwright has made his figures, despite their abstract names, vital human characters—and this is true of all the moralities. Even in the dullest of these pieces there are flashes of this quality. Sensual Appetite is one of the deadly sins, but he becomes a man when he meets Studious Desire in *The Four Elements*:

SENSUAL APPETITE: Aha! now good even, fool, good even!
It is even thee, knave, that I mean.
Hast thou done thy babbling?

STUDIOUS DESIRE: Yea, peradventure, what then?

SENSUAL APPETITE: Then hold down thy head like a
                  Pretty man, and take my blessing.
                  Benedicite! I grant to thee this pardon
                  And give thee absolution
                  For thy sooth saws. Stand up, jackdaw! . . .
                  Make room, sirs, and let me be merry,
                  With huffa, gallant, sing tirl on the berry
                     And let the wide world wind!
                  Sing friska jolly, with hey trolly lolly,
                  For I see well it is but a folly
                     For to have a sad mind.

In France the 'morality' went even further, and, although it preserved its ethical colouring, actually sloughed off the personifications and substituted real or type names in their place. Thus, for example, we find a *Nouvelle moralité d'une pauvre fille villageoise, laquelle ayma mieux avoir la teste coupée par son père que d'estre violée par son seigneur, faicte à la louenge et honneur des chastes et honnestes filles* (*A New Morality of a Poor Village Girl who chose rather to have her Head cut off by her Father than be violated by her Lord, in honour of all Chaste and Honest Maids*). The plot reveals to us, first, a poor domestic interior, with a widower, Le Père, and his beloved daughter, Eglantine, without whom his life would be dark. Into this humble setting comes Le Seigneur, who has been informed of her beauty by his valet. The Seigneur demands to have her, but father and daughter prefer to brave his threats. In order to escape him and at the same time to avoid the punishment of eternal damnation on account of suicide, she begs her father to slay her, hands him the sword herself. But the Seigneur has overheard her pitiful plea and steps forward in time to prevent this action, crying:

                O venerable creature!
                I renounce my former folly.
                Pardon me, gentle maid.

Thus converted, he makes atonement by appointing the father the governor of his territory, and places a "crown of chastity" on Eglantine's head. All ends happily, and the valet presents the moral in terms that the sentimental Richardson would have approved:

                Good comes to her who favours good:
                Maidens, take good heed!

Before taking leave of these edifying dramas one aspect of their production requires attention. Although some, like the English *Castle of Perseverance*, called for a simultaneous setting akin to that which served the mysteries, the majority, both French and English, asked for no more than a single simple platform. This meant that they could step out of the world of the amateurs with their elaborate, cumbersome, and costly mansions or pageants and adapt themselves to the needs of those small professional companies which came into being towards the end of the fifteenth century. The morality, therefore, formed the true link between the medieval theatre and the modern. Shakespeare almost certainly witnessed performances of mystery plays in his youth, but there was a vast gulf between the stages they demanded and the London stages upon which he became an actor. On the other hand, whatever company he first joined almost certainly must have had some moralities in its repertoire. When Sir Thomas More is shown, in the drama to which he gives his name, greeting, like Hamlet, a group of comedians who come to his house, he finds on inquiry that their plays include *The Cradle of Security, Impatient Poverty, Lusty Juventus,* and *The Marriage of Wit and Wisdom.* In carrying such plays with them these comedians in *Sir Thomas More* were undoubtedly typical of all their fellows.

FARCES AND INTERLUDES

Lusty Juventus is extant, and is called in the original text "An Interlude." The interlude is a term difficult to define: here, for example, it is applied to what unquestionably is a morality, and from the diversity of its use it might almost be taken to mean a short play of any kind, and particularly one suited for professional production. While the word does have this wider significance, however, it also bears a narrower and more specialized significance, indicating in the more particular sense a short play of purely secular nature, without any very obvious ethical moral, and usually farcical in tone. The existence of this form reminds us that just as the miracle play rapidly tended to transform itself into romantic drama of adventure, the morality gradually threw off its ethical attire and came to exist entirely for sheer entertainment.

These farces or interludes of the late medieval and early Renaissance periods are of prime importance in the history of the theatre. In many countries they arose. Germany had her Nuremberg Shrovetide Plays (*Fastnachtsspiele*), out of which sprang the farces of Hans Sachs, a prolific and not untalented author who set an individual seal on the anonymous forms of his predecessors. One cannot claim him as a genius, but undoubtedly he did succeed in writing scenes of a not unamusing if rough sort. There is, for instance, considerable good humour and a nice sense of dramatic contrasts in his *Der fahrende Schüler im Paradies* (*The Wandering Scholar from Paradise*, 1550). The story is a simple one. A Wife, whose first husband is dead, dreams fondly of the days when he was with her; her new husband is a surly brute; she did not appreciate her first as he deserved. To her comes a wandering student. He tells her he has just come from Paris, and she, a creature illiterate and credulous, thinks he said Paradise. Immediately she inquires whether the Student has seen her old man; all he had when he died, she says, was a blue hat and a winding-sheet. The Student soon catches on and declares that the poor man is a perfect sight in heaven:

> He goes about there without boots,
> Breeches, or smock—or substitutes!
> As queer as he was laid in earth!
> Cock his hat as he may, or girth
> His shroud around him,—when others feast
> He stays outside, penniless, fleeced,
> Lingering there with longing eyes,
> Living on alms the rest despise—
> Dirty and wretched beyond expression!

The tale is so moving that the Wife gets together a bundle of her husband's clothes and begs the Student to take these, together with a purse of gold, to the poor man when next he goes to Paradise. The Husband comes home, and there is a pleasant scene in which she, glad-eyed, twittering with excitement, tells him of this wonderful piece of good-fortune:

> WIFE [*beginning to realize the miraculous nature of her news*]:
> Oh, how shall I the marvel say?
> A strolling scholar, to still my sighs,
> Came by here out of Paradise!
> There he had seen my former man—
> And swears that he is poorer than
> The meanest, without shirt or shoes
> Or money—nothing he can use
> But hat and sheet! Think!—nothing save
> What we thrust with him in the grave!
> HUSBAND [*with a grim smile*]:
> Wouldst thou not send him something fit?
> WIFE [*surprised at the suggestion from him, accepting it eagerly*]:
> Oh, husband dear, I did!

With excitement he asks what road this man has taken, and sarcastically adds:

> Thou gav'st him far too little money
> For thy dead husband's alimony!
> He cannot well live long therewith!
> Go, have the fast horse saddled forthwith.

The Wife takes these words literally and blesses him for his thought-
fulness, while he dashes off in pursuit of the Student. Arriving at
a muddy patch of ground, he encounters his quarry, but the astute
Student, after dropping his pack, pretends to be a peasant, sends
the Husband on foot over the mire, and gaily steals his horse.
Returned home, the good man haltingly explains to his Wife that
out of kindness he has given away the horse, but counsels her to
keep the whole affair quiet:

> WIFE [*jubilantly*]: Nay, the whole parish knows and agrees!
> HUSBAND [*much startled*]: Eh? Who told them of it so quick?
> WIFE: Why, before thou hadst reached yon rick
> I had told them all from beginning to end:
> What to my husband I would send,
> With all respect, to Paradise.
> And everybody was so nice—
> Laughed aloud and made sport with me.

This little playlet is but one among many others. In *Der Rossdieb
zu Fünsing mit den tollen Bauern* (*The Horse Thief*, 1553) three
farmers are deliberating about the hanging of a horse thief. They
decide the execution shall be on Monday, and then recall that, if
it takes place then, the corn in their fields will be spoiled: the crowds
will trample it down. To save the crops and at the same time to
avoid the cost of feeding the thief they eventually determine to
free him on his promise that he will return to the gaol four weeks
hence—after the harvest. The thief, hearing of their proposal,
soon estimates with whom he has to deal. Shall it be said, he asks,
that the village was so mean as to leave him to find his own food
during the time of waiting? They are all impressed by this argument and quickly collect money for his keep, while he leaves a
worthless cap in pledge. Gaily he proceeds to steal right and left,
sells his booty to others in the village, and finally has them all
soundly belabouring one another. *Das heisse Eisen* (*The Hot Iron*,
1551) has a similar mood. A Wife wonders, first, why she no longer
loves her husband as passionately as she did at first, and, secondly,
whether he is faithful to her. She determines to test his virtue by
the trial of the hot iron. When she proposes this to him he at once

feels suspicious and begins to wonder whether she perhaps may not be leading a double life. For himself he prepares to pass the test by concealing a piece of wood in the hand that is to hold the red-hot iron. His trick succeeds beautifully, and at once he turns the table. Now that he has submitted to the trial, he says, she must follow suit. In horror she confesses that she has had an *affaire* with the chaplain:

> HUSBAND: The Devil take the chaplain!—well;
> He was a priest, and threatened Hell.
> I give you up the priest. Now take
> The iron for thy honour's sake.

At this she blubbers out that there were two others, and then asks him to forgive her "four more men—all, as I live!" The four soon grow to seven, and at the end she is abject in submission. The play closes with the Husband, duly virtuous, exulting in a new-found authority in his household.

These farces of Hans Sachs are akin to many another similar playlet produced about this time. From Holland comes a set of peasant comedies of kindred spirit. In one a foolish Lippijn is cheated by his slatternly wife; in another an old farmer is tricked by a quack at the fair; in still another a dull-witted Rubben whose wife bears a child three months after marriage is persuaded by her relations that all is well. Italy gives us the farces of Giorgio Allione da Asti; Spain produces its *Dialogo entrel Amor y un Viejo* (*Dialogue between Love and an Old Man*).

Most prolific in this field, however, were France and England. In the former, amid the many *sotties* presented by those associations of 'fools'—*sots* or *fous*—that flourished in the later Middle Ages, there are several works which, because of their dramatic structure, characterization, and individual spirit may truly be brought among the theatre's masterpieces. Such a play is the famous *Pierre Pathelin* (c. 1469), an anonymous work, vivid and gay, in which the hero, Pathelin, succeeds in cozening a draper out of a roll of cloth, and then, feeling proud of his skill, instructs a shepherd how to get out of paying his debts, only to find that his seemingly stupid pupil has learned so well that he is able to escape from tendering a fee to his mentor. The trickster is himself tricked. Here is something more than mere peasant buffoonery: the farce is coming close to comedy.

Even more true is this of the peculiar plays written many years before, in the thirteenth century, by Adam de la Halle (or Adan de la Hale), extraordinary achievements for their time, at once reaching back towards Aristophanes and stretching forward towards the modern world. One of these dramas, which might almost be regarded as the earliest of comic operas, is named *Robin and Marion* after its two chief persons, a shepherd and his shepherdess. The pastoral opens with a song by Marion, testifying to her love:

> Robin m'aime, Robin m'a;
> Robin m'a demandée, il m'aura.

A Chevalier arrives, makes love to her, even offers violence, and departs; Marion sings out to her Robin, who comes running, and there is a pleasant little rustic interlude. The Chevalier returns, but Marion says her lines so prettily that he is discomfited, and the play charmingly ends, as it had begun, on the note of pastoral song and dance. To find such delightful scenes in the thirteenth century is surprising, but even more surprising is the same author's *Jeu de la feuillée* (*The Play of the Greenwood*), in which the real and the fantastic are inextricably intermingled, and in which the spirit of Aristophanes is recalled by the sharp juxtaposition of satire directed at contemporaries and of soaring adventures in the world of the imagination. Adam himself comes on stage, and with him his father, Maistre Henris de la Halle, but the play also includes a kind of dream scene, a vision of the land of fairy. Whether there were other plays of this age akin in spirit to the *Jeu de la feuillée* we cannot tell; as it stands, it is unique; but even if nothing like it existed at that time it testifies to a potential dramatic power that awaited only the coming of the Renaissance to break free and enlarge itself. The oak that was Molière already existed in the acorn of *Pathelin* and the plays of Adam de la Halle.

From the same century comes an English fragment, the *Interludium de clerico et puella* (*The Play of a Clerk and a Girl*), in which a Clerk, failing to win the love of a Girl, goes off for aid to an old bawd, Mome Helwis. Later the century that produced *Pathelin* also produced the interludes of the first writer of English comedy, John Heywood. To this author, who lived in the early part of the sixteenth century, are assigned six plays: *A Play of Love*, *A Dialogue of Witty and Witless*, *The Play of the Weather*, *The Pardoner and the Freer*, *The Four PP*, and *Johan Johan*. If these are indeed all by the same author it is easy to see how he advanced both in dramatic skill and in his sense of the comic. The first is nothing but a debate among four abstractly named characters: Loved-not-Loving, Loving-not-Loved, Neither-Loved-nor-Loving, and Both-Loved-and-Loving. In *The Four PP* a similar debate makes its appearance, but with more point, the Palmer, the Pardoner, the Pothecary, and the Pedlar vying with each other as to which is the most skilled in lying. The prize goes to the Palmer, who, after listening to the Pardoner's tale of a shrew in Hell, innocently remarks that he is much surprised to hear it—since in all his wanderings he has never yet known a single woman out of patience.

Something more of dramatic movement enters into *The Play of the Weather*, wherein Jupiter, worried because of human complaints regarding the weather he supplies to the world, commissions Merry-report to conduct an investigation. After hearing a Gentleman ask for days

> Dry and not misty, the wind calm and still,

a Merchant request suitable gentle winds for his ships, a Ranger seek "blustering and blowing," a Water Miller demand rain and a Wind Miller no rain at all, a Gentlewoman pray for weather undamaging to her complexion, and a Launderer bright sunshine, and finally a Boy (described as "the least that can play") beg for frost,

> And plenty of snow to make my snowballs,

Jupiter decides to let matters stand as they have been in the past. Although there is nothing but a succession of entries here, at least some action appears; characters come and go on their cues instead of merely standing still and debating. Action becomes more pronounced in *The Pardoner and the Freer*, while in *Johan Johan* a fully outlined plot is developed.

This last play is easily the best of all that Heywood had to give to the stage. Its complete title, *A Mery Play, betwene Johan Johan, the Husbande, Tyb, his Wyfe, and Syr Jhan, the Priest*, introduces the three characters whose interrelations provide the comic episodes. At the start appears Johan Johan, the henpecked husband, but for the moment irate and boastful:

> God speed you, masters, every one!
> Wot ye not whither my wife is gone?
> I pray God the devil take her,
> For all that I do I cannot make her—
> But she will go a-gadding very much
> Like an Antony pig with an old witch
> Which leadeth her about hither and thither—
> But, by Our Lady, I wot not whither.
> But, by Goggis' blood, were she come home
> Unto this my house, by our Lady of Crome,
> I would beat her ere that I drink.

In a lengthy tirade he permits his fancy to imagine all he would do, but on her entry his tone changes:

TYB: Why, whom wilt thou beat, I say, thou knave?
JOHAN: Who? I, Tyb? None, so God me save.
TYB: Yes, I heard thee say thou would'st one beat.
JOHAN: Marry, wife, it was stockfish in Thames Street,
        Which will be good meat against Lent.
        Why, Tyb, what had'st thou thought that I had meant?

The wife pretends to be satisfied and, announcing that she has made a fine pie, sends Johan off to bid the priest, Sir Jhan, to partake of the fare. The scene now changes to the priest's house; Johan gives his message; and once more we are back in his dwelling. Thinking to sit down and eat of the pie, he is rudely disillusioned; first, he is sent out to get some water; next, it is discovered that the pail has a hole in it; after that, he has to sit by the fire chafing wax wherewith to mend it. And all the while the priest and the wife make merry at the table:

SIR JHAN: What dost, Johan Johan, I thee require?
JOHAN: I chafe the wax here by the fire.
TYB: Here is good drink, and here is good pie.
SIR JHAN: We fare very well, thanked be Our Lady.
TYB [*aside to* SIR JHAN]: Look how the cuckold chafeth the wax
                that is hard,
            And for his life dareth not look hitherward.
SIR JHAN: What doth my gossip?
JOHAN: I chafe the wax—
  [*aside*] And I chafe at it so hard that my fingers cracks,
            And eke the smoke putteth out my eyes two.
            I burn my face and ray my clothes also—
            And yet I dare not say one word,
            And they sit laughing yonder at the board.

So the scene proceeds until, unable to stand it any longer, Johan Johan kicks over the traces, smashes down the pail, and chases Priest and Wife out of the house.

It is a simple and perhaps crude playlet, but true comedy is peering round the side-wings of farce.

PART III

THE DRAMA OF THE RENAISSANCE

COMEDY, TRAGEDY, AND MELODRAMA IN ITALY

ALREADY, at the time when these farces of Heywood were being written and performed, a new movement was afoot in the world of the theatre. *Johan Johan* looks back to the medieval comic realm that Chaucer so well knew how to depict; perhaps indirectly and afar off it has connexions with the work of the wandering mimes, but certainly it exhibits no tie with the literary comedy of Rome or of Greece.

By the end of the fifteenth century, however, the whole of Europe was being changed by the impact of that revolution of spirit to which has been given the name of the Renaissance. Essentially it was a forward-looking development, in which new concepts—political, religious, and artistic—came to supplant those which had so long served men's needs. It is true that the more its diverse manifestations are studied the more we realize how much the men of the sixteenth century unconsciously incorporated into their new philosophies the core of medieval thought, how freely they made use of medieval forms in their ecstatic searching for fresh means of expression. Certainly strength came from the incorporation of the long tradition of the Middle Ages; but now the medieval elements were incorporated into something else, not pursued in their original forms: in the process of combination with elements different from themselves they suffered a complete transmogrification. Shakespeare, the brightest star in this firmament, owes his being to a subtle fusing of three forces: the classical influence contributes to his sense of structural form, the spirit of his age is strong upon him, and beyond these stretches the powerful tradition of the medieval theatre. Out of those three something entirely new has been created.

THE THEATRES OF ITALY

How necessary for absolute success was a fusing of the three forces is amply demonstrated by a comparison of the Italian theatre with the theatres of Spain and of England during the sixteenth and seventeenth centuries. The union that so gloriously was effected in England, and that gave strength to Spain, in Italy failed of realization, largely because diverse groups laid their hands on particular elements and attempted to develop these independently.

The story starts with the endeavour, at several Italian Courts, during the last years of the fifteenth century, to put plays by Plautus, Terence, and Seneca upon the stage. At this time we must not think of 'Italy,' but merely of a collection of Italian states, each under its own ruler and each, although maybe allied with its neighbours, existing in tremulous or passionate rivalry among the rest. Only one thing brought them together—love of art and admiration of the classics. Amid conditions of life dangerous and often depraved, amid the clashing of arms and the perilous intrigue of palace politics, this passion ruled in every city, and princes vied with one another in attracting to their service men of literary and pictorial genius, philosophers, scholars. In Rome the Popes and Cardinals were the patrons, in Florence the Medici, in Milan the Sforza; Ferrara owed its esteem to the efforts of the Este, Mantua to those of the Gonzaga, and Urbino to those of the Della Rovere.

At the start Rome and Ferrara took the lead. Under the inspiration of Julius Pomponius Laetus, Latin plays were given before specially invited audiences in the Eternal City, while Duke Ercole I eagerly encouraged similar efforts at Ferrara. This was an amusement that appealed to all. Princes gained esteem from the performances they sponsored; scholars were delighted to assist in presenting the texts they studied; painters and architects found in the stage new opportunities for the exercise of their skills.

From first to last these activities put firm stress on the visual effects to be secured, and in general two main lines of development are to be traced. The one was the endeavour to recreate the form of the classical stage in an indoor hall; the other was the attempt to achieve in three-dimensional terms the effects currently aimed at two-dimensionally by the artists of the time. For the early productions at Rome and Ferrara apparently no more was done than the building of what has come conveniently to be known as "the bathing-box" stage, illustrated in some fifteenth-century editions of Terence. Here a platform some four or five feet high was raised upon trestles, and at the rear was a façade formed by pillars supporting round ornamented arches and by curtains between the pillars. Each entry was supposed to be the 'house' of a particular character, and on occasion the curtains might be drawn to reveal small interiors within. The classical façade with its doors of entrance is thus interpreted in a manner not unreminiscent of the contemporary simultaneous setting used for the production of the mystery plays.

Soon, however, more was attempted. In 1484 the work of the Roman architect and author Vitruvius was discovered, and when men read of the scenery devised in ancient times for tragedy, comedy, and satyr play, and when they found plans for the arrangement of auditorium, orchestra, and stage, they set happily to work in diverse directions. One series of experiments culminated in the famous Teatro Olimpico (1584) of Vicenza, wherein a semicircular auditorium faces a long, narrow stage backed by a richly designed façade with one large central opening and with four other doors of entrance. Here the attempt to reproduce the Roman theatrical form comes to its logical end.

Beyond the entrance-ways of the Teatro Olimpico, however, were set what no Roman theatre had known, perspective vistas of city streets; these, designed by the architect Vincenzo Scamozzi, belong to the other tradition—the tradition of the artists, not of the scholars. Easy to trace is the development of these pictorial scenes from the type of fixed settings illustrated in Serlio's *Architettura* (1551) on to the elaborate displays, so fashioned as to admit of sudden breathtaking changes, popular at the Courts in the early seventeenth century. Easy, too, is it to see how, with these settings, a proscenium frame—no doubt not uninfluenced by such large central openings as that which appears in the Teatro Olimpico— became necessary. At first these frames were merely flat and painted, each constructed especially for its own production, but by 1618 had come into being the great Teatro Farnese at Parma, with its elongated auditorium and its richly sculptured proscenium arch. Thus the modern theatre was born.

In watching the progress of this theatrical architecture three things are worthy of special note. First, the playhouses thus described were essentially courtly. Most of them were built within the vast halls of the princely palaces of the Renaissance, and the rest, like the Teatro Olimpico, were the efforts of academies closely associated with and sponsored by noble patrons. Into them entered no ordinary spectators: when they were used for the performance of plays the audience was a splendid one of princes and their guests. Secondly, they were all closed structures, so that a theatrical element unknown in the past, lighting, made its first appearance and was destined to play, later at least, an important rôle. Thirdly, the forms assumed by these theatres did not provide a harmony between the needs of the time, its dramatic theory, and its creative effort.

This last aspect is the most important and deserves some further attention. With the rediscovery of ancient Greece and Rome came the finding of Aristotle, and the scholars of the sixteenth century had a pretty time poring over his *Poetics* and enunciating theatrical laws which they fondly thought were based on his injunctions. Thus came into being the famous or notorious Rule of the Three Unities, which demanded that a play should have unity of action (with a single plot), unity of place (permitting no change of scene), and unity of time (the fictional action being restricted to twelve or twenty-four hours). These were fettering laws, yet the age was one of adventuresome existence, vivid in colour, when men sought rich show and rapid movement. The validity of scholarly theory, firmly set on the unassailable rock of Aristotelian authority, could not be denied, while at the same time the whole desire of the time was for an expansive display fundamentally opposed to these circumscribing limitations.

No organic solution for the problem thus set was reached in Italy. Instead the theatre found itself hopelessly divided at heart. The dramatists were compelled to accept the unities and to fashion their scenes within one setting, while the desires of the century, craving for change and excitement, called for, and obtained, satisfaction in the presentation of richly spectacular shows between the acts of comedy or of tragedy. The result may readily be imagined: dramatists found that their efforts were bound by the restrictive laws, at the same time as licence revelled tumultuously about them; spectators, bored with the plays, gave all their attention to the *intermedii* (or *intermezzi*) between the acts. The words of the poet were lost in a riot of show.

ITALIAN COMEDY

Of the two dramatic forms, comedy and tragedy, the former obviously had more chance than the latter to preserve some vitality under these conditions, but even the laughing muse, although at first promising liveliness of spirit, soon languished and miserably died.

The first signs of life came from Ferrara, where Tito Livio dei Frulovisi wrote an interesting series of Latin plays of Plautan flavour and romantic sentiment (1432–34), and where, later, Lodovico Ariosto, the Court poet, applied himself energetically to the stage, producing plays which, although too heavily imitative of Latin models, suggested that from this beginning much might come.

Despite the fact that his comedies were composed only a few years after the first experiments in the presentation of the Plautan and Terentian originals, he showed an eye keenly observant of contemporary manners and a hand apt to infuse into the classical material the qualities of his own time.

Ariosto's first extant play, *La cassaria* (*The Casket*, originally (1508) written in prose and later (1529) recast in verse), reveals the dramatist at his apprentice stage. The plot is a tissue of episodes culled from Latin sources, telling how Erofilo and Caridore, loving two slave-girls owned by the bawd Lucrano, are involved in a series of escapades and misunderstandings in their attempt to obtain the wherewithal to purchase them. There is nothing original in this story, but the language is crisp and direct, while some of the characters bear features that give them individuality. In *I suppositi* (*The Counterfeits*, also originally written in prose (1509) and reworked (1529) in verse), translated by George Gascoigne as *The Supposes* (1572) and used by Shakespeare for *The Taming of the Shrew*, the *dramatis personæ*, although still heavily bound by their classical fetters, are making more determined efforts to break free. The episodes may be borrowed from Plautus' *Captivi* and the *Eunuchus* of Terence, but the scene is set in Ferrara, the spirit is that of Ariosto's own time, and the characters are drawn from the life of his day. The story tells how Erostrato, a Ferrarese student, has dressed as his own servant in order to gain entry to the house of Damone, father of Polimnesta, a girl wooed also by the old Cleandro, who offers two thousand ducats as her dowry. Since Erostrato cannot cap this offer, his servant Dulipo (dressed as his master) induces a Sienese traveller to pose as the young man's father. The complications attendant upon the arrival of the real father, and upon the discovery of Polimnesta's relations with the supposed servant (Erostrato in disguise), may be left to the imagination: it is not these that challenge our attention. What is noteworthy is the vividity and ease of the style. Ariosto commands an easy pen and is as happy when allowing Dulipo to recount his intrigue with the stranger from Siena as when devising the flow of talk among the masters and their attendants.

Ariosto's other three plays, *La lena* (*The Bawd*, 1529), *Il negromante* (*The Charlatan*, 1520), and *La scolastica* (*The Academic Comedy*, left uncompleted at the author's death and finished by his brother about 1543), show considerable developments along similar lines. For *Il negromante* both the plot and the principal character, the charlatan Jachelino, seem to have been the invention of the poet:

the whole spirit of the play, with its adumbration of Jonson's *Volpone*, breathes of the sixteenth century, when astrologers and quacks abounded, feeding luxuriously on popular credulity. Satire of modern life appears in a different guise in *La lena*, with its prostitute and its complacent husband, while in *La scolastica* we find a gay dramatic record of contemporary academic life. Here the chief persons are a couple of students who have come from Paris to the University of Ferrara, and their adventures with their lady-loves provide many scenes of hilarious comedy.

When we consider that *La cassaria* is the first true modern comedy, and that consequently Ariosto had to create his own style, his achievement indeed must be deemed remarkable. The episodes are lively, the language is crisp, the characters have vitality, and the atmosphere of Plautus is subtly altered so that what was in his hands a comedy of crude sexual appetite tends to take shape as a comedy of romantic adventure. One might readily have thought that with this beginning the Italian stage was due to exhibit wonders.

Nor was Ariosto alone. Already in 1513 his friend, Cardinal Bernardo Dovizi da Bibbiena, had produced his *La Calandria* (*The Comedy of Calandro*) at Urbino. Based on Plautus' *Casina* and *Menæchmi*, it introduces a pair of twins, Lidio and Santilla, the former dressed as his sister, the latter dressed as her brother. Although lacking Ariosto's grace and, like *La cassaria*, heavily indebted to its classical models, this play too presents a vivid picture of sixteenth-century life. And about the same time came Niccolò Machiavelli's deliciously salacious exposure of contemporary stupidity and corruption, *La mandragola* (*The Mandrake*; Florence, *c.* 1520). The action here concerns the journey of Callimaco from Paris to Florence for the purpose of seeing the famed beauty of Lucrezia, wife of Messer Nicia Calfucci. Consumed with passion for this lady, he seeks the aid of the parasite Ligurio, who devises a subtle trick. Knowing that Messer Nicia is concerned because he has no heir, and, at the same time, knowing his abject credulity, he induces Callimaco to pose as a wonder-working doctor. The latter advises that the wife be given a potion of mandragola, but warns that the first man to lie with her must, because of the potion, inevitably die; whereupon he further proposes that they shall kidnap some young fellow after dark and bring him to Nicia's house for the purpose of taking off the effects of the medicament. On hearing that the King of France and his leading nobles have consented to adopt just such procedure, the silly little husband agrees, and the more he is drawn into the device the more eager he becomes. To persuade Lucrezia to accept the plan they call on the aid of her mother and her confessor. In tears she is won by their arguments: Callimaco is, of course, the supposed kidnapped stranger, and at night he wins Lucrezia's heart by declaring his passion and demonstrating the crass stupidity of her husband. The comedy ends in satiric laughter:

NICIA: Master, take my wife here by the hand.
CALLIMACO: Gladly.
NICIA: Lucrezia, here's the man who will be responsible for our having a staff to support our old age.
LUCREZIA [*demurely*]:   I hold him very dear, and I hope he'll be our friend.
NICIA: Now bless you! And I want him and Ligurio to come and dine with us to-day.
LUCREZIA: Of course.
NICIA [*with a sudden new thought, beaming fatuously*]:   I want to give them the key to the ground room by the loggia, so that they can come here just to suit their convenience. . . .
CALLIMACO: I accept it, and I'll use it when I can.

Although by far his finest work is *La mandragola*, Machiavelli proved in his companion plays, *La Clizia* (1506) and his unnamed *Commedia in prosa*, that he possessed a wide and varied power of comic invention. *La Clizia* in particular is memorable for its mordantly satirical portrait of the old Messer Nicomaco.

After this brilliant start in romantic comedy and in satire, although nearly all the prominent writers of the time turned their hands to the stage, and although the classical episodes came to be mingled with invented material and with material taken from the *novelle* of the time, comedy, unfortunately, shows little progress. Plays such as Trissino's *I simillimi* (*The Identical Twins*; Venice, 1548) and Lodovico Dolce's *Il capitano* (*The Captain*; Venice, 1545) we may neglect as being little more than reworkings of Plautan themes, but it is strange that more life was not infused into others in which contemporary events were exploited, and particularly into those written by authors intent on shaking off the undue influence of the classics. Even in such a play as Dolce's *Fabrizia* (1549), where an attempt is made to break away from overgreat reliance on the classical, the intrigue is apt to creak.

In many ways the devices for arousing the spirit of comedy were here being expanded, as, for instance, in Lorenzino de Medici's interesting portrait (*L'Aridosia, The Play of Aridosio*; Florence, 1536) of a timid, prevaricating miser, or in Agostino Ricchi's use of foreign

speech (*I tre tiranni, The Three Tyrants*; Bologna, 1530) for the arousing of laughter, yet as a whole these plays remain lifeless and dull.
Even Antonfrancesco Grazzini (called Il Lasca), despite his "proud
Florentinity" and his aggressive modernism, failed. His *La gelosia*
(*Jealousy*; Florence, 1550) has interest in that it introduces the trick
which plays such a vital part in Shakespeare's *Much Ado about
Nothing*, but its scenes, although full of invention, rarely have
sparkle. Grazzini may justly lay claim (as he specifically does for
this comedy) that he is introducing fresh matter to the stage, but
he may hardly be accounted one of those who, by their wit and
vigour, have advanced comedy's cause. Much the same verdict
must, regretfully, be passed on *La spiritata* (*The Possessed*; Florence,
1560), although for us it has considerable historical value, both
because of its Elizabethan adaptation as *The Bugbears* and because of
the frequent later use of its plot—wherein a girl, to escape the
unwanted attentions of an undesirable suitor, pretends to be
possessed or mad. Perhaps the most amusing of his plays is *La
pinzochera* (*The Devotee*; printed 1582), which entertainingly tells
how old Gerozzo, a henpecked husband, tries to win the favour of
Diamante, wife of Alberto Catelani. A rascally servant makes him
believe that the lady would agree were it not that she fears discovery, and gives Gerozzo a couple of supposedly magic cherry-
stones which, it is claimed, will make him invisible. When they
have been put in the old man's mouth the servant and his associates
pretend they cannot see him; off he goes on his love-tryst, with
the expected result that he is soundly beaten for his pains.

Another author who sought to break new ground, but with
hardly greater success, was the self-styled Scourge of Princes, Pietro
Aretino. Of all his work perhaps *La cortigiana* (*The Play of the
Court*; Venice, 1534) is the best—a bitter attack on the Papal Court,
containing an excellent picture of little Messer Maco, who comes to
Rome full of piety and is gradually taught to do as Romans did in
the sixteenth century. All his work, however, has interest, from the
vividity of the farcical scenes in *Il marescalco* (*The Blacksmith*; printed
1533) to the satirical sallies of *L'ipocrito* (*The Hypocrite*; Venice, 1541).

Angele Beolco, nicknamed Il Ruzzante, essayed still another
path in trying to wed a native Paduan farcical style to the comic
style of Plautus: an interesting example of this mixed form of
comic invention is to be found in his *L'Anconetana* (*The Girl of
Ancona*, c. 1530), in which romantic and classical elements are intermingled. Still freer in subject-matter and tone are *La moschetta* (*The
Sting*, c. 1520) and *La Fiorina* (*The Little Flower*, c. 1520), both of

which take their inspiration from the Paduan countryside and deal realistically with rustic love affairs. How strongly the impress of the age was striving to substitute a contemporary romantic for a classical seal is to be seen when we compare, for example, the two plays of Gigio Artemio Giancarli: *Capraria* (*The Comedy of the Goats, c.* 1540) is almost entirely Roman in concept, whereas *La zingana* (*The Gipsy, c.* 1550) is rich in the life of the day. The movement too is easily traceable in the various comedies written by a better-known author, Giambattista Della Porta. *La Cintia* (*c.* 1560), with its girl dressed as a boy and its man dressed as a girl, is thoroughly imitative; when we come to *L'astrologo* (*The Astrologer,* 1570), however, we find a classic plot enlivened by the introduction of a strongly drawn portrait of a fake astrologer whose actions and words are those of the sixteenth century; while in *I due fratelli rivali* (*The Two Rival Brothers, c.* 1580) we are in the midst of romantic subject-matter with only a few vague echoes of Plautus and Terence, and the atmosphere of romance is still further developed in *La furiosa* (*The Desperate Girl, c.* 1590) and *Il moro* (*The Moor;* printed 1607). The student life of the time, which had attracted Ariosto's attention in *La scolastica,* is treated in *La Cecca* (*c.* 1550) by Girolamo Razzi, author of an extraordinary drama of sentimental heroics named *La Gostanza* (printed 1564). A playwright such as Raffaello Borghini can deal in tragi-comic manner with a Romeo and Juliet theme in *La donna costante* (*The Constant Lady;* printed 1582); and a Francesco d'Ambra can make vivacious some scenes of *I Bernardi* (*The Bernardos,* 1547) by allowing popular elements to intrude into his imitative plot. The list of dramatic works is impressive in quantity if not in quality. Niccolò Secchi comes forward with his *Gli inganni* (*The Cheats,* 1549), introducing some reasonably lively scenes based on the ancient theme of long-lost children, and with his farcical *L'interesse* (*Self-interest;* printed 1584); an anonymous author gives us the rather delightful *Gli ingannati* (*The Cheated,* 1531), to which, perhaps, Shakespeare owed a debt in *Twelfth Night;* to Plautan intrigue Giovanni Maria Cecchi adds some witty dialogue in *Gli incantesimi* (*The Charms;* printed 1550); in *Flora* (1555) Luigi Alamanni attempts to regularize the contemporary stage by reference back to classic models; a fairly graceful style marks Giambattista Gelli's story of an elderly lover in *L'errore* (*The Error, c.* 1550) and the not dissimilar story told by Agnolo Firenzuola in *I Lucidi* (*The Lucidos,* 1549); in *Il Granchio* (1566) of Lionardo Salviati echoes of folk speech are substituted for polish of phrase. There is variety here; there is the desire to achieve things of value; there is obviously superabundant energy. Yet, despite this infusion of new material, not one of these plays possesses enduring quality.

What it was that prevented these plays from achieving richer proportions than they were in fact able to realize is difficult to determine. One restrictive element was, of course, the impress of the classics, and, in particular, the rule of the unities which forced the playwrights to fit their themes to a Procrustean bed of fixed time and place; but this in itself cannot be cited as the sole explanation. More important, perhaps, was the fact that all these comedies were being written for highly select audiences unleavened by what existed outside the courtly halls—indeed, by the fact that, even so, the audiences were not those of one centre but of several independent cities, each small and almost parochial in spirit. If Ariosto's Ferrara could have been united with Bibbiena's Urbino, Grazzini's Florence, and Aretino's Venice, more might have come from these endeavours. Chief of all, however, was the failure of the dramatists to create that world of romance which permitted Shakespeare and Lope de Vega such wide opportunities. There is a hint of it in Ariosto's scenes, but no more than a hint; it appears, but dully expressed, in Alessandro Piccolomini's *L'amor costante* (*Constant Love*; Siena, 1536) and in his *Alessandro* (1543); but for the most part all these plays are dull and antiquated. Love, ideal and romantic yet close to earth, was the major theme of the time, but whereas the Elizabethan drama incorporated that theme into the harmony of its comedy, Italy allowed it to be endlessly and tiresomely discussed in her philosophical *dialoghi d'amore* while her stage fed, not on the spirit of poetry, but on the physical intrigues of prose.

THE TRAGEDIES

The tale of tragedy during these years is much similar to that of comedy, although here the rules were more insistent in their demands, and the models—the plays of Seneca—less inspiring.

Early in the fourteenth century Albertino Mussato was responsible for a Latin tragedy *Ecerinis* (1315), in which the story is told of a fairly recent Paduan tyrant, Ezzelino III, in Senecan terms. The following century produced Antonio Commelli's *Filostrato e Panfila* (Ferrara, 1499), the first tragedy written in Italian wherein elements of the mystery plays were combined with suggestions taken from the Roman playwright—a drama of illicit love and horror, the theme of which had been narrated by Boccaccio in his tale of Gismonda.

Soon came severer efforts at classical imitation, heralded by the first 'regular' tragedies, the *Rosmunda* (1515) of Giovanni Rucellai, in which Seneca is taken as a guide, and the *Sofonisba* (1515) of Gian Giorgio Trissino, who went beyond Seneca back to Greek models. *Sofonisba* is an important work historically, but, despite contemporary esteem which praised it even above the *Œdipus* of Sophocles, incredibly dull. The themes of *Ecerinis*, *Filostrato e Panfila*, and *Sofonisba* indicate that the same spirit was at work as operated in the realm of comedy: playwrights, although dominated by admiration of the classics, were prepared to exploit subject-matter distinct from that used by the authors of Rome and of Athens, but once more failed to produce any work of a truly noteworthy sort.

In vain, for example, did Giraldi Cinthio, at Ferrara, endeavour to establish a new form based on the Senecan by developing the theme of romantic love and sensational horrors. Of the latter element his *Orbecche* (1541) is full. The prologue promises the spectators "tears, sighs, anguish, terrors and frightsome deaths," and the five acts that follow, introduced by the ghost of Selina, former wife of Sulmone, clamouring for revenge, do not disappoint that promise. Apparently Selina had been executed because of her incestuous relations with Sulmone's son, discovered through the intermediary of that young man's sister, Orbecche. Orbecche is now secretly married to the humbly born Oronte—which gives the ghost her chance. Gradually the tension increases until in the fourth act we are informed that Sulmone has cut off Oronte's hands, murdered his children, cut off his head, put the head and the bodies into vases for some obscure purpose. The Chorus guesses that these vases will perhaps be sent to Orbecche. The guess is justified: Orbecche kills her father, Sulmone, cutting off his head in turn, and finally stabs herself—leaving the ghost of Selina presumably the only satisfied character in the play.

Obviously little promise could come from such efforts (although we must remember that the young Shakespeare started his career with the equally bloody *Titus Andronicus*), but Cinthio by no means confined his writing to this style. His most interesting dramas, indeed, are those in which he exploited the material of romance and contrived to bring tragic material to a happy close. Thus, for example, his *Arrenopia* (printed 1583) frankly deals with the world of the adventuresome, narrating how Arrenopia, a princess of Scotland, is secretly married to the King of Ireland, and how her husband, having become infatuated with another lady, plans to murder her. Confusion follows confusion until, in an atmosphere not unreminiscent of that of such a play as *Cymbeline*, the plot is brought to a fortunate conclusion.

The reference to *Cymbeline* reminds us that Cinthio, more than any of his companion dramatists, was making a contribution to the Elizabethan comedy of romance. This is even more marked in *Gli antivalomeni* (*The Interchanged*; printed 1583), where we learn of children of a king exchanged for the children of a usurper, of girls donning men's clothes, of threatened death and sudden recognitions. We might almost, but for the lack of poetic magic, be in a Forest of Arden, a mythical Thebes, or a fantastic Sicily.

Unhappily there were none to follow his lead. The *Canace* (1542) of Sperone Speroni, a famous work of its day, outdoes the gruesome follies of *Orbecche*, opening with a speech uttered by the ghost of a child not born until the third act. Lodovico Dolce brings in a slightly new element by introducing, in his *Marianna* (1565), the theme of jealousy for the first time into tragedy, while Luigi Groto crowds into *La Dalida* (1572) all the horrors of which his fevered imagination can dream. Other playwrights, with no more dramatic skill, essayed to explore the realms of chivalric romance, but mostly their scenes are dull, as in Torquato Tasso's *Il Re Torrismondo* (*King Torrismondo*, 1587), or replete with artificial absurdities, as in the ludicrous *Almerigo* (1590) of Gabriele Zinano. Even the interesting experiments made by Giovanni Maria Cecchi in his 'religious dramas' can hardly be said to offer anything of enduring import.

There is but little good to be said of this field of endeavour. Once more we feel the impress of the classical, the frantic endeavours to escape, and the resultant disharmony of effort.

PASTORALS AND OPERAS

The audience before whom such plays were presented had interests which found satisfaction in more artificial realms of dramatic expression than tragedy could, or should, offer. Far back, in 1471, Angelo Poliziano produced at Mantua his *Orfeo*, and in this play he achieved a finer unity of effect than anything attained by the tragic dramatists of the period. There is a fantastic charm here and a delicacy of utterance which rings truer than many a comic scene of the time or the mouthing rhetoric of the serious dramas. Although *Orfeo* is hardly a pastoral, in its scenes the pastoral is being born. The line of development from this play to the *Aminta*

(Ferrara, 1573) of Torquato Tasso and the *Pastor fido* (*The Faithful Shepherd*, 1585) of Battista Guarini is a direct one. In these works the Italian Renaissance theatre comes as near as anywhere to perfection of expression: yet neither of the works can be styled a great play. Charm they have, and smiles, rippling verse and artificiality of sentiment, but to these they add none of those qualities which make for true strength in the theatre. Here is the world of escape. Shakespeare entered this world too in *As You Like It*, but his shepherds and shepherdesses are treated in a mood of ironic amusement, while Touchstone and Jacques arouse thoughts far other than those appropriate to idyllic joy and bucolic simplicity.

The pastoral virtually closed its career with *Il pastor fido*, although many other plays in the same style, such as the not uncharming *L'amoroso sdegno* (*Lovers' Trials*; printed 1597), by Francesco Bracciolini, were still to be written and performed, but a kindred form of drama, closely connected with it in origin, was destined to develop rapidly in this time and to have a long and distinguished career. During the latter years of the sixteenth century the age of madrigals discovered that the Greek plays were originally chanted, and this discovery led to the desire to present modern plays in the same way. In 1574, at Venice, a tragedy was "produced in the manner of the ancients"; it had music composed by Claudio Merulo, and "all the actors sang in most pleasant harmony, both in solos and in choruses." Already Poliziano's *Orfeo* had made a gesture towards the opera, while the *intermezzi* usually added a musical element to their preponderating element of scenic decoration. This last step, therefore, was not without its forerunners, and the manner in which the 'melodrama'—or musical drama—met the desires of the time is indicated by its immediate popularity.

For the full establishment of the form a group of Florentine enthusiasts was responsible. Under the presiding genius of Giovanni Bardi, Count of Vernio, a little academe gave its anxious thought to the development of the music-drama. Here was Vincenzo Galilei, father of the famous Galileo, Giulio Caccini, an able musician, Jacopo Peri, the composer, and Ottavio Rinuccini, the poet. After much talk and many experiments the first true opera took final shape in 1594—a *Dafne*, with libretto by Rinuccini and music by Peri. A short time later came Peri's *Euridice* and Caccini's *Il ratto di Cefalo* (*The Rape of Cephalus*)—and the opera was well launched on its early lines of classical mythology.

The Bardi group had always intended to achieve a true marriage of poetry and music; but the charm of novelty lay in the singing, and it is easy to see how, as the 'melodrama' developed and became the 'opera, or work, in music,' the libretto more and more faded in importance. Within a few years a composer of genius, Claudio Monteverde, had seized on the newly devised dramatic genre and stamped it as the property of the musician, not of the poet. In the year 1607 appeared at Mantua his *Orfeo*, followed the next year by *Arianna*, in both of which the restrained academic character of Peri's efforts was discarded in favour of a full-blooded theatricality. The bored intellectuals at the Courts eagerly cast aside dull tragedy and trivial comedy in order freely to embrace the new form. From Mantua the vogue of opera spread among the principalities and dukedoms of Italy, penetrated into bourgeois Venice (where the first public opera-house was opened in 1637), crossed the Alps into France and Austria, becoming ever more and more ornate. All that lavish theatre-building of the seventeenth century, all that labour expended in creating majestic settings, all that inventive power applied to the devising of stage machinery, was associated, not with drama, but with opera. Words were lost in the splendour of the scene and in the harmonies of the music. During the seventeenth century Italy has nothing to give us of worth in the realm of the literary play. The opera had triumphed.

THE POPULAR PLAY: THE COMMEDIA DELL' ARTE

INSTEAD of sitting in a palace hall, let us imagine ourselves standing in the great square of Venice about the year 1600.

It is spring-time, and the lazy Italian sun is falling gently on the flagstones, on the roofs of the surrounding buildings, on the gay façade of the Cathedral of San Marco.

At one corner of the square a platform stage has been erected; in front of it are benches for specially privileged spectators; around, in a widely expectant semicircle, stands a jostling, excited crowd. The comedians are about to present a play, announced as *Arcadia incantata (Enchanted Arcady)*.

Of scenic decoration there is little. Two little box-like side-wings are set at the sides of the stage, and at the rear is a backcloth painted with trees to represent a wood.

Suddenly an actor steps forward, and the crowd is silent. His heavy robe is decorated with astrological signs; he bears a heavy, leather-bound volume and leans upon a peculiarly carved staff; obviously he is a magician. Alone on the stage he addresses the audience, declaring that by his art he has become lord of this island of Arcadia and of its silly inhabitants, the shepherds and the nymphs of the woods; but now he has learned by his magic skill that the privacy of his lonely retreat is about to be broken: strangers are approaching.

At this he departs, and the backcloth of the forest is changed to represent a stormy sea with, in the distance, a ship foundering upon rocks. From one of the side-wings staggers in a strangely dressed creature, hump-backed, with a dark half-mask showing a sharply curved nose and a wrinkled receding brow on which a large wart is prominent. There is no doubt about his identity, for he has appeared in countless other plays; his name is Pulcinella. Gaspingly he tells us that he has just escaped from the wreck; alone of all his companions he has been saved.

As he is speaking, from the other side comes in a second character, also masked but even more grotesque, with a long, drooping nose and exaggeratedly large spectacles perched precariously on its bridge. His dress consists of a jacket, flapping trousers, a short cloak, and a beret with two long, curving feathers. He too is immediately recognizable as Coviello. In a kind of echo of Pulcinella's words, he also relates how he, alone of all his companions, has escaped a watery grave.

Gradually the pair move over towards the centre of the stage until, the one looking to the right and the other to the left, they bump into each other, start back in fear, take one another for ghosts, make as if to run away, then cautiously, timorously, draw near again, put out tremulous fingers, touch each other's arms, and finally, realizing the truth, embrace ecstatically. This done, they move aside in doleful converse over the loss of the others.

Meanwhile the same scene is repeated with another pair—the first, bespectacled like Coviello, and the other, older and ridiculously pompous, dressed like a savant of the University of Padua—Tartaglia and the Dottore. First, these two recognize each other as Coviello and Pulcinella had done, and then the two couples go through the scene of fear as a foursome. The more the crowd laughs at their ridiculous antics the more absurd their gestures become, until at last, the tumult over, they sit down and, talking all at once, gabble excitedly about their adventures. Then the thought of food comes into their minds; they are all hungry, and with one accord they decide to go off on a foraging expedition.

The scene now changes back to the wood, and four pastoral figures enter—the shepherd Silvio, who tells us he is in love with the shepherdess Clori, who tells us she is in love with Fileno, who tells us he is in love with Filli, who tells us she is in love with Silvio. Blundering into the midst of this idyllic tangle comes Pulcinella, and they all run off. Pulcinella has become separated from his companions, and, having failed to stay the shepherds, he is delighted when a company of richly costumed Priests enters. He begs them for food, and they ask him to come to their temple—where, they explain to the audience, they intend to sacrifice him.

Again the scene changes, this time to a temple. A great procession of Priests and Shepherds comes in, with Pulcinella, ludicrously unaware of the fate intended for him, borne on a chair. In a scene of equivoque he asks for food, while they exhort him to make a good end. At last he realizes what is intended; the knife is just descending when the Magician makes an impressive entry, bids them desist, and, when they prove obdurate, calls up two fiery Spirits who drive the whole crowd off the stage.

The first act is now over, and, after a pause, the scene is altered

SCHOOL OF MANTEGNA: THE TRIUMPH OF DEATH
Influenced by a similar set of 'Triumphs' painted for the theatre at Mantua, 1491.

SCHOOL OF MANTEGNA: THE TRIUMPH OF DIVINITY

SCHOOL OF MANTEGNA: THE TRIUMPH OF FAME

SCHOOL OF MANTEGNA: THE TRIUMPH OF LOVE

SCHOOL OF MANTEGNA: THE TRIUMPH OF CHASTITY

SCHOOL OF MANTEGNA: THE TRIUMPH OF TIME

THE TEATRO
OLIMPICO, VICENZA,
1594
Photo Alinari

193

to the wood again, with a large property fruit-tree set in front of the backcloth. The Dottore, Tartaglia, and Coviello wander in, abjectly miserable, hungry, and lost. Wild beasts have terrified them in the forest, and they fear that Pulcinella has been eaten by one of these. At this moment Pulcinella dashes across the stage convulsed with fear. Forcibly they stay him, and in stammering words he relates his adventures in the temple, while they laugh at his words, thinking he has gone off his mind through lack of food. Suddenly the Dottore spies the fruit-tree and calls the attention of his companions, whereupon, with ridiculously cautious movements, they start to peer into every corner of the stage to see if anyone is looking; satisfied at last, they approach to take the fruit —only to be terrified at the rising of flames, which consume the tree and drive them back. As they are going a shepherdess, Silvana, enters complaining about a shepherd, Dameta, who, having loved, has left her. All the four comic characters at once fall in love with her, and there is a ridiculous struggle among them, when the Magician enters with words of reproof. Thinking him powerless in the face of their numbers, they are about to attack him, but he charms them into immobility and releases them only if they promise to be good. Off they go with the kind-hearted Silvana to have some supper.

Once more there is a pastoral interlude, Fileno lamenting the cruelty of Filli, Clori suing Fileno, Silvio in despair, and Filli making vain love to him. Now the Magician places a magic garland on a tree, explaining that if anyone puts it on his temples he will seem to be the person beloved by another.

First comes Pulcinella, satisfied after having had a good repast: he sees the garland, puts it on, and is immediately taken for Clori by Silvio. Pulcinella jeers at him, and he goes off; but a moment later Filli enters and takes Pulcinella to be Silvio; then Fileno thinks he is Filli, while Clori deems him Fileno. As Pulcinella stands amazed at this madness his companions enter, assume that he is Silvana, and attempt to embrace him; and matters become more complicated when, in the resultant confusion, the Magician enters invisible and shifts the garland from head to head.

At last he desists and carries the garland away; Silvana comes on stage and, hearing them all woo her, declares she cannot belong to all four, but will marry the one who is the best sleeper—whereupon all settle themselves down to display their prowess in repose, only to be awakened by four Spirits who chase them off the stage. Thus ends the second act amid cries of fear and strange noises.

G

The third act opens with the pastoral characters, all of whom are bearing gifts to the temple and propose to pray for success in love. Coviello, who has overheard their words, immediately outlines a plan to his companions: the Dottore shall dress as Jove, Tartaglia as Venus, Pulcinella as Cupid, and Coviello as a Priest; seated in the temple, they will be able to appropriate all the rustic sacrifices for themselves. In a richly ludicrous scene this project is realized, and the four conspirators set themselves down for a good feast. Again, however, Pulcinella becomes separated from the other three and, when they depart, remains alone.

The Magician now enters and creates him King of Arcadia, handing to him the magic book, the crown, and the sceptre. Pulcinella opens the book, and at once a Spirit appears and declares he is at his lord's service. Just at first Pulcinella is terrified, but he soon gains assurance, bids the Spirit bring him a chair, and seats himself royally upon it. Silvio enters, jeers at him, is beaten for his pains by the Spirit, begs for pardon, and is admitted to Pulcinella's retinue: and a similar scene is enacted with Fileno, Clori, Filli, and Silvana. Finally the Dottore, Tartaglia, and Coviello come on stage and mock him unmercifully, until in a rage he opens his book and a Spirit appears. First he orders them to be beaten, and they are duly chastised; then he commands them to be hanged. Ropes are put round their necks, while they weep and implore, and the execution is about to take place when the Magician enters, stops the Spirit, chides Pulcinella, and marries off Silvio to Clori, Fileno to Filli, and Silvana to Dameta.

So the play ends.

THE PROFESSIONAL PLAYERS

Clearly this is something entirely different from the tragedies and comedies, the *intermezzi* and the *opere*, acted at Court. The performers are professionals, not courtly amateurs; and, were we able to go backstage, we should find that their entire method of approach towards the play is different from that familiar in the palace theatres. There a poet composed his drama and the actors learned their lines. Here, search where we will, we shall find no written text. All that the manager of the company has is a brief scenario, specifying entries and exits, with a summary indication of what is to be done in each scene; all that the actors have is a short set of instructions pinned up behind the wings. When, for example, Pulcinella and Coviello are to make their first appearance on the stage they

have as guidance only a general sketch of what they are expected
to do and to say:

> *Enter* PULCINELLA, *from the sea; he speaks of the storm, the shipwreck and
> loss of his master and his companions. At this enter* COVIELLO, *from the
> other side; he speaks of the same things as* PULCINELLA; *they see one another
> and make the lazzi of fear. At last, after lazzi of touching one another, they
> realize that they have been saved and speak of the loss of their comrades and
> their master.*

The players, therefore, were expected to be their own authors,
providing in their various scenes such dialogue as might appear
necessary. Thus the type of performance illustrated by *Arcadia
incantata* could be carried out only by men and women trained for
long years in a special kind of acting technique; and consequently,
in contradistinction to the *commedia erudita*—the 'erudite,' or
'amateur,' play of the Court—men were accustomed to speak of
this other sort of drama as the *commedia dell' arte*, the play of 'the
quality' (as the Elizabethans would have said), or, as we say now,
of '*the* profession.'

Even for well-trained professionals, however, the creation of
such scenes could not have been effectively realized without the
acceptance of a number of conventions. The *commedia dell' arte*
plays were improvised, certainly, so that no two performances of
any given scenario could be quite the same in action and in dialogue,
but the players were aided in diverse ways towards the successful
securing of their ends. While it is true that over eight hundred
scenarios have come down to us from the sixteenth, seventeenth,
and eighteenth centuries, and that we must presume this number
to have been but a small proportion of those originally in existence,
we must observe, first, that many of these are almost duplicates,
and, second, that any single company would have been content to
use only a dozen or score out of the entire list.

Besides this fact, there is another still more important. In play
after play of this kind the same characters put in an appearance and
similar scenes occur. Each company was made up of a limited
number of actors, each of whom, in every play, interpreted the same
stock rôle. Normally there were four lovers, dressed either as
gallants and ladies of the day or, as in *Arcadia incantata*, as shepherds
and their nymphs. Alongside these were two old men, Pantalone,
the Venetian merchant, and Dottore, the Paduan academic. Then
came the Capitano, a boasting soldier, and an indeterminate number
of so-called *zanni*, servants or clowns, each with his own particular
name and characteristics—Pulcinella, Tartaglia, Coviello in *Arcadia*

incantata, or elsewhere Arlecchino, Brighella, Bertolino, Fritellino, Pedrolino—together with a clownish maid or two, Colombina or Arlecchina. Occasionally other types appeared; occasionally the Capitano took the rôle of one of the *zanni* or Pantalone played the part of another old man (as probably he did in *Arcadia incantata*); but generally the dramatic characters were fixed and constant.

This meant that each actor from experience could build up for himself a long range of set speeches suitable for particular occasions: the lover might memorize Petrarchan sonnets for quoting to his lady; the Dottore might at leisure compose and learn long rigmaroles full of Latin tags; the Capitano might rehearse at length his mouth-filling oaths and rhadamontades. Business, too, could be established and used on different occasions. In the scenario of *Arcadia incantata* reference is made to the 'lazzi of fear,' and whenever we come across that word *lazzi* (and no scenario is without it) we recognize that we are in the presence of stock business. If the manager bade two *zanni* to do a scene with the *lazzi* of fear they knew precisely what was required of them; they had enacted this scene together many times before, and their comic tricks were all ready to hand.

In this way a *commedia dell' arte* performance took shape as a repatterning of well-established, familiar stock-types and of well-known 'acts' or 'turns' similar to those we associate now with circus clown and music-hall comedian. A modern Christmas pantomime, although the words are here provided for the actors, is not dissimilarly composed: from the music-hall come the players with their diverse turns, and these are incorporated into the framework provided by the theme of a *Cinderella* or a *Puss-in-Boots*.

The performers in these companies set their eyes mainly upon broadly popular audiences. It is true that often, indeed, generally, the larger troupes were attached to particular Courts and that some of the actors were on such familiar terms with the dukes and princes that they might dare to address their lords with impertinent levity: regularly, *commedia dell' arte* productions were given in palace halls, while the time and energy of ambassadors were occupied in trying to persuade the sovereigns to whom they were accredited to grant leave for foreign tours of the troupes acting under their licence. At the same time the roots of even the most famous companies ran deep into the common soil; most of their performances were given before the people of the cities they visited. No doubt they purchased their trinkets out of moneys allotted to them by Court treasurers; but their bread and butter came from the takings at public performances. And beside these more famous troupes, with skilled actresses, like Isabella Andreini, who were the companions of queens and the stars of poets, with expert *zanni* like Drusiano Martinelli or Giuseppe Domenico Biancolelli, honoured guests at Court, were dozens of smaller companies, some engaged solely in producing plays, some merely appendages to the booth of some quack or charlatan, eager, through their antics, to gather gaping spectators apt to buy his nostrums.

THE FORTUNES OF THE COMMEDIA DELL' ARTE

No one knows for certain whence the *commedia dell' arte* arose. It may have been born independently out of the social conditions of sixteenth-century Italy; on the other hand, there seems to be sufficient evidence to suggest that in this Renaissance form of entertainment we may trace the inspiration of medieval *jongleurs*, who themselves were the inheritors of the tradition of the Roman mimes.

All that is sure is that about the middle of the sixteenth century we begin to catch glimpses of dramatic shows which included some of the later stock characters—the Venetian Pantalone, the Bolognese Dottore, and the *zanni*—and that with extraordinary rapidity these small early groups of players expanded into the internationally renowned troupes of the Gelosi, the Confidenti, and the Fedeli.

At first their activities were confined to Italian cities, but before the sixteenth century had drawn to a close they were giving performances in France, while during the following century their fame spread widely over the entirety of Europe, where the various countries welcomed them and gradually modified their stock personages. In German lands Hanswurst is a native type born of Italian inspiration; France created the pathetic Pierrot out of Pedrolino, and refined the early rough Colombina into the dainty Columbine; in England Pulcinella became Punch, and the pantomime clown was born out of the Italian *zanni*. For nearly two hundred years the *commedia dell' arte* was the most popular form of dramatic entertainment in most countries of the Continent.

In itself, of course, it has vanished; these improvised plays have left no record of their original productions such as come from the production of written dramas. Yet the debt of the theatre to the *commedia dell' arte* cannot be exaggerated. Continually, in the pictorial records of the stage during the time of the Renaissance, an

Arlecchino or a Dottore is peering impertinently from the wings, and in the writings of even the greatest authors of the time the spirit of the lost improvised comedies is to be traced. The theme of *Arcadia incantata* is so close to that of *The Tempest* that we are almost bound to assume a connexion between Shakespeare's last comedy and some similar piece played by the Italians; in *The Taming of the Shrew* Gremio is specifically named as the 'pantalowne,' while the *zanni*, or zany, well known to the English playwright, seems to have left his impress on more than one Elizabethan clown. Nearly a century later Molière was finding his genius stimulated by the *commedia dell' arte*, while a few decades after that Goldoni began his artistic career among these players.

There can be no doubt concerning the influence of the *commedia dell' arte* upon the drama, yet this very influence serves to indicate why the Renaissance in Italy failed to produce great plays. To create worthy tragedies and comedies an age requires to put all its strength into the theatre; part of its effort will not do. In Italy the stage was split. The literary qualities were reserved for the *commedia erudita*, and that remains lifeless or dull. There is a closet atmosphere, a preciousness, a smell of the wax candle, about every one of these Court productions, and their very weakness led to the expenditure of excessive effort upon costly scenic production. The atmosphere they breathe is so heavy with perfume, their surroundings are so stiff with brocade, that one sighs for at least a faint whiff of good honest garlic and the feel of homespun. In exchange for a few sincere kersey 'yeas' and 'noes' we would willingly sacrifice much of their artificial and turgid rhetoric.

Yet when we turn to the popular play we find something, instinct with life, no doubt, but like life mortal. Of the elements making for permanence in art there was none. Hence the strange double paradox: that, although the Italian stage has left us virtually no memorable play from this time, it established the form of theatre which still endures to-day, and that it created a dramatic form which, though evanescent, appealed throughout the whole of Europe not only to popular audiences, but also to the greatest dramatists of the seventeenth and eighteenth centuries. There was no lack of theatrical inspiration in Renaissance Italy, but the delicate balance of forces out of which alone a great dramatic expression can come was absent. Only rarely, and then without the power of a Goldoni, did any Italian author of this time succeed in fusing the literary and the popular. Although Giovan Battista Andreini, the son of the famous actress Isabella Andreini and himself an actor in the *commedia dell' arte* tradition, essayed the task in such plays as *Amor nello specchio* (*Love in the Looking-glass*; printed 1622) and *Le due commedia in commedia* (*The Two Plays within a Play*; printed 1623) with spirit and a certain grace, he failed, partly because his own talents were not equal to the occasion, partly because already it was too late to hope for the achieving of an end which, if it were to have proved fruitful, ought to have been secured nearly a century before.

FRENCH ROMANTICISM AND CLASSICISM

THE STORY of the stage in France during these years is at once similar and dissimilar. Here, as in Italy, imitation of the classics led to the writing of independent tragedies and comedies; here too there is virtually nothing of worth produced from the beginnings of the new movement in the theatre up to the middle of the seventeenth century. If there is this agreement, however, there are three marked differences: the French theatre presents no vital popular movement such as is marked in the *commedia dell' arte*, but, on the other hand, it does exhibit the development, albeit crude, of a kind of drama more appealing to ordinary tastes than the Senecan tragedies and the Plautan comedies, and it was destined, at a time when the Italian stage had sunk to its lowest ebb, to flourish forth gloriously towards the end of the seventeenth century. In a sense, the rather dull record of the French theatre from 1500 to 1650 is but the preliminary introduction to the glories of Molière and Racine.

THE CLASSICAL TRADITION

In the Courts and academies of France the same restless search for classical inspiration is to be traced as aroused the Courts of Italy— and, since the Italians had begun their questing at an earlier date, it was but natural that the French should often have approached their Seneca and their Terence through transalpine intermediaries.

Seneca appeared in Paris in 1485; Greek tragedy in Latin dress was represented by Erasmus' translations of two Euripidean dramas in 1506; by the middle of the sixteenth century these, or similar, plays were being issued in French versions. At the same time Italian tragedy was being introduced to Gallic readers through the renderings of Trissino's *Sofonisba* by Mellin de Saint-Gelais (1559) and Claude Merinet (1585), while the *commedia erudita* made its bow before French royalty as early as 1548, when Bibbiena's *La Calandria* was performed at Lyons, by Italian players, at the command of Henri II.

The real start of the French 'literary' drama was made in 1552 when Étienne Jodelle produced his historically significant, but intrinsically worthless, *Cléopâtre captive* (*Cleopatra Captive*), in which the old classical chorus is retained, the unities are preserved, and rhetoric rules.

The model thus established, other academically minded amateurs eagerly pursued the same path. The ghost of Seneca sits heavily on the *Médée* (1555) of La Péruse (Jean Bastier) and Jacques Grévin's *Jules César* (1558), on Gabriel Bounin's *La Soltane* (*The Sultan*, 1561) and André de Rivaudeau's *Aman* (1561). These are all hopelessly dull; in the kindred works of Robert Garnier a faint spark of light illuminates the darkness, although on them, too, the oppressive influence lays its sterile hand. Look where we will—at the early *Porcie* (printed 1568), *Hippolite* (printed 1573), and *Cornélie* (printed 1574), or at the later *Bradamante* (printed 1582) and *Les Juifves* (*The Jews*; printed 1583), we find but little to excite our admiration. Contemporaries—at least those who belonged to the intelligentsia —thought his work marvellous; he was lauded above Seneca, above the Greeks; his plays ran into an enormous number of editions. Yet the truth is that before the tribunal of time he stands shorn of his glory, exposed as a poor imitator of Seneca and as one who sacrificed dramatic effect for rhetorical commonplace. It is indeed difficult for us to realize what the men of his time, however besotted with passion for the 'rules,' saw in his dramas to admire so much. Almost the only element in his work which calls for special note is the manner in which he applied (as, for example, in *Bradamante*) the classical form to subject-matter derived from romantic sources, going so far, indeed, as to allow this subject-matter to break the rule of exact genres and to evolve a tragi-comic kind of drama.

A similar tale, only slightly more encouraging, is to be told of the efforts to establish regularized comedy during these years. The active and indomitable Pléiade, bent on reforming French literature, set out from the beginning to substitute for the medieval farces and moralities a more consciously artistic form of comic expression, based, of course, on the familiar Terence and Plautus. Already by 1500 the latter's *Amphitryon* had been translated by Jean Meschinot; the former's *Andria* appeared in French dialogue in 1537; two years later (1539) came *Le Grant Térence tant en rime qu'en prose*, a collection of renderings by diverse hands.

Then, as in Italy, arrived the time for the writing of plays, heavily influenced by the classic authors, but more or less independent— and almost wholly valueless. In 1552 was produced the *Eugène* of Étienne Jodelle, who thus takes rank as the creator, not only of the first regular tragedy in France, but also of her first Renaissance comedy, although in this satirical piece the traces of the long-established medieval farce are clearly to be seen beneath the framework ostensibly erected in an entirely different manner. Others soon followed: Jacques Grévin, whose *Jules César* was among the earliest of French tragedies, contributed to the comic stage his *Maubertine, ou la trésorière* (*Maubertine; or, The Paymistress*, 1558) and his *Esbahis* (1560), in both of which he attacked the older models and declared his determination to set up new. In his theatre, he asserts, the audience will not "see either farce or morality," but instead true comedy based on the Roman pattern. Jean de la Taille, author of an interesting critical tract entitled *De l'art de la tragédie* (printed as the preface to his *Saül le furieux*, 1573), brought forward *Les corrivaux* (*The Rivals*) in 1562, a comedy in prose; in 1567 appeared *Le brave* (*The Boaster*), by Antoine le Baïf, based mainly on Plautus' *Miles Gloriosus*.

Already the classical inspiration was being confused and inter-mingled with that of Italy. Translations of the *commedia erudita,* such as de la Taille's version of Ariosto's *Il negromante* (1573), were creeping in among the renderings of the Roman plays. The double force of Roman comedy and of the Italian *commedia erudita* is well illustrated in the writings of that author who, before Corneille and Racine, was perhaps the most important playwright this Renaissance French theatre had to offer—Pierre de Larivey, an Italian by origin, but born in Troyes, who set himself the task of introducing the transalpine plays to the audiences of Paris and the provinces. Six plays were published in 1579 and another three in 1611—of which the best-known is *Les esprits* (*The Wits*), based on Lorenzino de Medici's *L'Aridosia*, and destined to be used later by Molière in *L'avare*, Regnard in *Le retour imprévu*, and Montfleury in *Le comédien poète*. The very fact that it was thus employed by later authors testifies to Larivey's skill in translating the Italian scenes into French vestments. His style is easy; he has a true sense of the theatre; and his feeling for gentle comedy is assured. In *Les esprits* and in its companions—*Le laquais* (*The Lacquey*; from Lodovico Dolce's *Il ragazzo*), *La veuve* (*The Widow*; from Niccolò Buona-parte's *La vedova*), *Le morfondu* (*The Abashed Lover*; from Anton-francesco Grazzini's *La gelosia*), *Les jaloux* (*The Jealous Couple*; from Vicenzio Babbiani's *I gelosi*), *Les escolliers* (*The Students*; from Girolamo Razzi's *La Cecca*), *La constance* (*Constancy*; from the same author's *La Gostanza*), *Le fidelle* (*The Faithful Lover*; from Luigi Pasquaglio's *Il fedele*), and *Les tromperies* (*The Tricks*; from

Niccolò Secchi's *Gli inganni*)—he provided the stage with livelier examples of comic material than had been produced by his predecessors. The Italian plays he used were perhaps not brilliant comedies, but at least they had more grace than the original French comedies composed before his time, and his influence is to be widely traced in the following years. In the sprightly *Les contens* (*The Merry Ones*, 1580?) of Odet de Turnèbe reminiscences of Italian comedy are present, but are becoming transformed more definitely into French shapes: its delightfully drawn Louise and her daughter Geneviève, its bombastic soldier, Rodomont, and its inimitable old Françoise are characters well worthy of remembrance. This play can be honestly praised, yet, when one considers how few companions it has, one realizes the essential poverty of this French classical stage of the sixteenth century. The foundations are being laid for something to come, but in itself this ambitious activity, this endeavour to establish a regular tragedy and comedy in Paris, failed as the kindred endeavours in Italy had failed.

THE PUBLIC THEATRES

To a large extent this was due to a similar cleavage between the 'intellectual' and the 'popular,' although we must also recognize that the political conditions in France, amid the heat of religious controversies and the ever imminent threat of civil war, were not propitious to the producing of a vital drama.

During the time when the young academicians were intenlty eager upon establishing a regularly composed literary drama plays of another sort were being performed before less precious audiences than normally attended the productions of classic tragedy and comedy. In 1402 the Confrérie de la Passion had been granted a royal privilege virtually establishing them as the sole acting group in Paris, their special mission being to present annually the great medieval mysteries, which they had been created to interpret. A hundred years later, however, conditions had changed: both Catholics and Protestants were looking askance at the Biblical plays, and as a consequence came a decree of 1548 sternly forbidding the setting upon the stage of religious dramas, but, instead, establishing the Confrérie as controllers of whatsoever secular forms of entertainment might be given in the city. From being an association of amateurs engaged in performing the mystery cycles, therefore, the Conrérie became a corporation of theatre managers, with the rare good fortune of having absolute monopoly in their own field.

They hurriedly fitted up a theatre in the famous Hôtel de Bourgogne and prepared themselves to receive the high rent they were determined to exact from its occupants.

For years this theatre was leased by a variety of troupes—French players acting those farces and moralities so severely frowned upon by the intellectuals, English and Spanish actors appearing for brief spells with their characteristic repertoires, and, most importantly, Italian comedians—among them the outstanding Gelosi—introducing to Parisian audiences the style of improvisation already popular in their native cities. Only with the beginning of the seventeenth century did a relatively permanent troupe settle itself within its walls, when Valleran Le Conte, after performing at Court, established himself there with a company he named Les Comédiens du Roi (The King's Men), which included the then popular favourites among Parisian actors—"Gros-Guillaume" (Robert Guérin), the fat, farcical clown, "Gaultier-Garguille" (Hugues Guéru), the comic old man, and "Turlupin" (Henry Le Grand), the rascally servant. As the prominence of these performers indicates, the Comédiens du Roi were adapted for the interpretation, not of academic drama, but of essentially popular scenes rougher in fabric.

At the Hôtel de Bourgogne medieval traditions still lingered. Two methods of staging were used there, and both stemmed from the Middle Ages. The first, employed for the production of farces, was a simple adaptation of the open platform used by the popular actors of the late fifteenth century and carried on by those troupes (the most renowned of which was the company headed by Tabarin) permitted to give their out-of-doors performances at the fairs. The other, more complex, interestingly showed an adaptation of Italian scenic method to more ancient principles. In this the medieval device of the separate 'mansions,' with foreshortening of space, was translated into terms suitable for a small stage set at the end of an indoor hall and for the utilization of the perspective wings evolved by the Italian architects. At first, no doubt, the remnants of the scenery used for the mystery plays were put to profaner use, and in all probability there was a time of transition when back-curtains, with openings for entrances and exits, served the players, but certainly by 1633, as the well-known *Mémoire* of the scene-directors Mahelot and Laurent amply testifies, the stage was being set for divers plays by means of side-wings representing the most widely separated localities, backed by a cloth indicating either a distant prospect or still another specific locality. Thus, for the earliest of the productions noted by Mahelot—that of Rotrou's *Les occasions perdues* (1633)—the setting shows, at the rear, a palace in a garden, with practicable windows, doors, and stairs, and, at the two sides, a fountain in a wood and a ruined building—places which in the play are supposed to lie far apart from one another.

Just how far this method of stage-setting was in use during the early years of the seventeenth century cannot now be determined with any surety, but the fact that, although it adopts the style of scene-painting habitual in Italy, its basis is unquestionably to be traced back to the medieval 'mansions' gives us assurance for believing that the forms so fully illustrated in the *Mémoire* are the final results of a continuous tradition from the time when, in 1548, the Hôtel de Bourgogne had turned from the religious to the secular drama.

The interest of this device rests in its attempt to find a compromise suited to the needs of the time. As we have seen, the Italian theatre failed in this respect, so that two sharply opposed principles clashed with one another and never found harmony. On the other hand, there was the set perspective scene, providing a background for plays which, theoretically at least, preserved the unity of place, and on the other was the open, generally undecorated platform of the *commedia dell' arte*. The age, however, demanded more liberty than the severer classicists would allow, and hence the Court theatres lost themselves in the riotous display of the *intermezzi* while the *commedia dell' arte* troupes fumblingly experimented with crude scenic changes. In the type of decoration associated with the work of Mahelot we see an endeavour to find another solution for the problem—the adoption of the architectural side-wings and backcloth familiar in Italy, but the arrangement of these in such a manner as to put three, four, or even five different localities on the stage at one time.

EARLY ROMANTICISM

The appearance of this staging method reminds us that the French public, fed with the restlessness of the Renaissance spirit, was by no means inclined to endure the dull classic immobility of the tragedies and comedies written by the academicians. They loved their free farces, and when they turned to more serious fare they demanded that the scene should be full of action and that the dramatic tales should be restrained by no artificial bonds.

As a result, the first French professional dramatist, Alexandre

Hardy, found his *métier*, not in the realm of the unities, but in a land of romantic adventure where change of locality was frequent and no bars were set against the presentation, in full view of the audience, of scenes of violence. It has been said that "Hardy was irregular enough to have become a Shakespeare, had he had the genius," but irregularity in itself presents no highroad to mastery of the theatre, and, although perhaps we may find a trifle more of interest in his plays than in those of his predecessors, we recognize that the path he trod was not one likely to yield greatness. A man with no resources save what might come from the exercise of his pen, he early attached himself to a provincial troupe of comedians, and throughout several decades wrote feverishly in an attempt to keep body and soul together with the meagre sums then offered to a practising playwright. In all he penned over six hundred dramas (of which only forty-one are extant), some of them composed, rehearsed, and produced within a period of three days.

Obviously little could be expected from such conditions, and the expectation is not out of harmony with the reality. Most of his works are tragedies or tragi-comedies, and although they move their stories forward with commendable vigour, they lack all the qualities making for dramatic power. Their sole interest for us now is that they were the earliest professional plays written in France, and that they indicate a desire on the part of the public for a type of drama utterly at variance with that cultivated by Garnier and his companions. Love themes are frequently exploited here, and sensationalism is not absent; the classical elements are well concealed under romantic trappings.

From his work stems a long but not particularly inspiring line of similarly romantic plays—the Marquis de Racan's pastoral *Les bergeries* (*The Pastoral Comedy, c.* 1619), Théophile de Viau's tragic *Pyrame* (1621), the various dramas of Jean Mairet and of Jean de Rotrou, the last of whom was claimed by Voltaire to have been "le véritable fondateur du théâtre français."

Mention of Rotrou in this company reminds us, however, that the style which these men had cultivated—the drama of romance —was nearing the end of its not very glorious career, for he was one of the famous group of 'Five Poets' commissioned by Cardinal Richelieu to reform the French stage by leading it back to classicism. In taking this course Richelieu displayed true judgment. The age had passed the excitements of Renaissance passion, and the quality of romanticism was becoming tarnished. There might have been the hope of a virile, untrammelled French drama had Hardy come, not in the seventeenth century, but towards the middle of the century preceding: as it was, his example arrived too late; and although Mairet and Rotrou endeavoured to pursue the path he had trod, that path itself was becoming so entangled by the briers of undisciplined fancy that it could give no promise of reaching any worthy goal. A different way, as Richelieu (with surprisingly correct judgment) realized, had to be taken: instead of an irregular Shakespeare, France was to have a most regular Racine.

During all these years the French drama was handicapped, and the handicaps, not uninterestingly, throw light on what qualities are demanded if a theatre is to produce work of permanent worth. It took long before Paris became the prime centre of the world of the stage, and even when that time arrived the dramatic activities of the city were inhibited by cluttering restrictions. All through these years the theatre was looked upon with not a little disdain by those who esteemed themselves on account of their wealth or intellectual attainments; all through, the dramatists were wretchedly remunerated. Despite experimentation, the stage itself never succeeded in evolving a form truly suited to the needs of the age: the modification of the medieval simultaneous setting was, at best, a cumbersome device and unimaginative.

Looking at these facts, we may perhaps suggest that a vital theatre requires to have a geographical focus, relative freedom, the support of both the populace and the intellectuals, the provision of encouragement for the professional author, and, at the same time, a stage-form adapted to the time's demands. None of these prerequisites was satisfied in France until the reforms of Richelieu had established a fresh tradition.

THE SPANISH STAGE UNDER LOPE DE VEGA AND CALDERÓN

The FAILURE of Italy and France is made the more pronounced when we contrast it with the success of Spain and the triumph of England.

Concerning the remoter developments of the stage in Spain not much need, or perhaps can, be said. Most of what must once have existed has now perished, and such fragments as remain have no more than an historical interest. Nothing is worthy of engaging our attention until we reach the rather crude 'Comedias' written by Bartolomé de Torres Naharro, confessedly under Italian inspiration, and the better-known works of Lope de Rueda, the latter of whom may be regarded, despite the more earthy quality of most of his writings, as the true founder of that style of play which was destined to become the characteristic expression of the Spanish genius—free from restraint, romantic in tone, lyrical in medium, and in texture weaving together the serious and the comic. At the same time attention should be called to the work of the Portuguese Gil Vicente, particularly to his trilogy of the *Barca do Inferno* (*The Boat of Hell*, 1517), the *Barca do Purgatorio* (*The Boat of Purgatory*, 1518), and the *Barca do Gloria* (*The Boat of Glory*, 1519)— devotional morality-type presentations that certainly had a considerable influence in the development of the Spanish religious plays.

When Lope de Rueda was composing his *comedias* professional playing was at its most primitive. "The whole apparatus of a manager," wrote Cervantes,

> was contained in a large sack, and consisted of four white shepherds' jackets, turned up with leather, gilt and stamped; four beards and four sets of hanging locks; and four shepherd's crooks more or less. . . . The theatre was composed of four benches, arranged in a square, with five or six boards laid across them, providing a platform a few feet from the ground. . . . The furniture of the theatre was an old blanket drawn aside by two cords, making what they call a tiring-room, behind which were the musicians, who sang old ballads without a guitar.

Before more could be expected of the drama this theatre had to reach nobler proportions.

THE THEATRES OF SPAIN

Fortunately the audiences and the playwrights of Madrid and Seville had not long to wait, and when the theatre was set up on a firmer foundation it assumed a form at once more fitting and more flexible than that of the French or Italian stages.

The model was that of the *corrales*, or courtyards, where the earliest dramatic troupes had been accustomed to play. We must imagine for ourselves a square formed by the walls of houses, with windows and balconies providing box-accommodation for privileged spectators. In the yard there was standing-room for the less fortunate, while some tiers of benches at the side opposite the stage offered seats for the gentlemen, and above these a wooden gallery, nicknamed the *cazuela*, or stewpan, was apportioned to women of the poorer classes. Already in 1574 a troupe of Italian *commedia dell' arte* players at Madrid had fitted up such a theatre at the Corral de la Pacheca, while a few years later (1579 and 1582) the success attending the production of plays inspired the erection, in the manner of those improvised in the *corrales*, of two permanent houses, the Corral de la Cruz and the Corral del Príncipe.

For the actors there was a long, rather narrow platform, without any front curtain, but curtained at the back and at the sides in such a way that, when necessary, a kind of inner stage could be revealed. Above, a gallery extended over the acting-platform, and this was employed regularly for the representation of the upper window of a house or of a city wall. It is obvious that essentially this stage was built on the same principles as those operative in contemporary London, and the fact that the two were almost identical suggests that the dramatic strength developed in these two lands was at least partly dependent upon the harmony thus reached between the desires of the time and the opportunities offered to the actors. Here was a theatre where the players' rich clothes presented a continually moving panorama of kaleidoscopic colours before the spectators; here was a stage well adapted for the uttering of poetic lines; here the imagination of the audience was called actively into play. Only later, in the seventeenth century, did scenic effects and machinery begin to be put to frequent use, with the result that, as Lope de Vega observed, the true spirit of the drama started to evaporate: when "the managers avail themselves of machinery," he said, then "the poets avail themselves of the carpenters and the auditors of their eyes."

No doubt there were many shortcomings in these theatres and

many abuses; no doubt managers, actors, and playwrights had justification for their occasional grumblings; but fundamentally the conditions were well adapted for the production of a vital drama. Spain was not dominated, as Italy was, by the supposedly classical rules of the academic theorists; artisans and aristocrats joined together in their love of the stage; the actors had free opportunity for movement; and the authors found that their flights of poetry could be spoken to good effect on the open stage for which they wrote. Once a fitting medium of expression was devised the way was open for a rich, flamboyant drama such as these men and women of the Renaissance were avid to receive.

LOPE DE VEGA

After the first efforts of Lope de Rueda a number of other writers eagerly attempted to exploit the theatrical form, each—like the immediate predecessors of Shakespeare—contributing something to the creation of a national drama, so that when, in 1585, Lope Felix de Vega Carpio attached himself to the stage he found not only a well-established playhouse but a reasonably lively and inspiring literary tradition to give him aid.

Interestingly, the career of this author and the career of Shakespeare exhibit a strange parallel. Born in 1562, Lope was two years older than his English contemporary, but both came to attach themselves to the stage about the same time—towards the middle of the second-last decade of the sixteenth century. Separated by that vast gulf which is symbolized historically by the Spanish Armada, each ignorant of the other's very existence, their positions in their respective countries were virtually the same, and their writings, diverse though they are, display many features in common. Only in the length of their lives and in the extent of their contributions to the stage do they essentially differ; Shakespeare, dying at the age of fifty-two, left thirty-seven dramas behind him; Lope lived to be seventy-three and is estimated to have written, in addition to several hundred miscellaneous entertainments, no fewer than 1700 plays. Although the greater proportion of these has vanished, even so over 470 of his dramas are still extant. No poet has ever displayed greater ease and fertility.

Nor are these works merely imitative. Much in Lope's plays may be inspired by the efforts of his predecessors, but the greater part was his own, and to him the Spanish theatre owes many of its most characteristic features. His concept of tragic action set its

impress on the work of his successors; his style of tragi-comedy
was that accepted by others; it was he who developed the thoroughly
representative genre of *comedias de capa y espada*—the cloak-and-
sword drama—tending sometimes towards romantic incident, sometimes towards the style of the comedy of manners; recently we have
become aware of his surprising invention of what has been acclaimed
as a true proletarian theatre; even particular stage characters, such
as the *gracioso*, or humorous clown, although adumbrated before,
were virtually of his creation.

In writing his plays Lope set above all other things the desire to
capture the attention of his auditors, and one imagines that if
Shakespeare had found time to put down his critical precepts in
essay form they would have been expressed very similarly to the
way the Spanish dramatist expounds his aims in the *Arte nuevo de
hacer comedias en este tiempo* (*The New Art of Writing Plays in this
Age*, 1609). The tone of this short discourse is clear and uncompromising—I know all the rules, says Lope, but

> when I have to write a comedy I lock in the precepts with six keys, I
> banish Terence and Plautus from my study . . . and I write in accor-
> dance with that art which they devised who aspired to the applause of
> the crowd.

He was intent on pleasing first, and the theatre was his testing-place.
He might have wished to write more 'correct' dramas, but in
practice he was prepared to give his audience what obviously it
wanted.

His plays are lyrical in tone, for the Spanish audiences of the
'Golden Age,' like those in contemporary England, loved to listen
to words instinct with passion and rich in melody. There is realism
in Lope's work, but it is realism inspired and deepened by the
imagination—not the dull, pale, miserable thing which creeps
pitifully into many a modern scene. Here is true theatre—bold,
emotional, built on terms appropriate to the theatre's conventionalism, and made powerful by strong contrasts.

For the most part Lope's dramas defy exact classification. Nearly
all include elements high and low, tragic and comic, some veering
more in the one direction, some more in the other. Many of the
plots are based on history, but the historical events are rendered
theatrical; many are derived from romances, but the romantic
matter is made vital by effective portraiture. All we can say is that
within the course of his work we find certain dramas which we may
call tragedies, because in them the greatest stress is laid on dark

actions conditioned by the social codes then universally maintained by the aristocracy; that we find others in which the dark and the light provide a tragi-comic impression; that still others emphasize the interests of the peasantry or the gallantries of youth or the clowneries of the ignorant. At moments we are in the presence of a *Twelfth Night*, at moments we are conversing with Bottom, at moments we approach the mood of a *Romeo and Juliet*. The ranges of Shakespeare and Lope are not far different from each other: what is lacking in the latter is the intensity of a *Hamlet* and the wonder of a *Tempest*. With Lope we move from the spirit of *Love's Labour's Lost* through *Much Ado about Nothing* to *All's Well that Ends Well*; we have much of the atmosphere of the histories, too; but of the tragic temper and the metaphysical tone there is but little in his plays.

The darker side of his work is well illustrated by *El castigo sin venganza* (*Punishment without Revenge*; printed 1635), which tells the story of a Duke of Ferrara, whose illegitimate and beloved son, Federico, falls in love with the young Duchess. On discovering this liaison the Duke's mind is cast into a torment of conflicting passions, but at last he devises a scheme whereby vengeance—and, more important, the clearing of his honour—will be secured without his own hands being dipped in blood. In a darkened room he binds up his wife, casts a cloth over her, and tells Federico that a trapped traitor is seated there. The son stabs his stepmother-mistress, and is himself slain by men outside the palace when the Duke informs them that the Duchess has been murdered. Basically the plot is that of a sensational melodrama, but Lope—although he wants the power to conjure forth the spirit of tragedy—contrives by his bold delineation of consuming emotion and by the sombre passion of his verse to give the theme enduring interest. With sympathetic understanding is revealed the course of the illicit intrigue; with flashing grandeur the twisted mentality of the Duke is bravely illuminated.

More commonly, however, the potentially tragic atmosphere in such plays is converted, generally by means of surprising intrigue, into a tragi-comic sentiment. Jealousy and love, for example, suggest that the plot of *Lo cierto por lo dudoso* (*A Certainty for a Doubt*; printed 1625) must end in disaster. The King, Don Pedro, is consumed with jealousy of his brother, Don Enrique, who is the accepted lover of Doña Juana; in turn, Juana's lady-in-waiting, Doña Inés, devoted to Don Enrique, strives to get him for her own. The action threatens royal displeasure, decrees of banishment, and death, yet in the end, by a rather conventional trick, Enrique and

Juana are married, while the King casts off his earlier humour and accepts the event:

> What is done
> Admits no remedy. I pardon him,
> And I confirm the match.

So far as the movement of the dramatic story is concerned, there is little here of value, but once more the play takes life from the intimate and penetrating relations of human character presented in its various scenes. On the one hand, there are the little wisps of doubt in the faithful Juana's mind when she weighs the passion of Don Enrique against the joy of being a queen; on the other, there is the contorted jealousy of the King, who is led to lay suit to Juana only because he knows her the object of his brother's attentions. As a whole, the tragi-comedy has but small intrinsic interest, yet its action is carried on with vigour, and life pulsates beneath the inanimate mask. Much the same judgment may be passed on such plays as *Los embustes de Celauro* (*Celauro's Machinations, c.* 1600), where a villainous Iago is foiled in his plans to wreck connubial happiness, and *El halcón de Federico* (*The Falcon of Federico*; printed 1620), based on the same story of Boccaccio's on which is founded Tennyson's *The Falcon*.

Of particular interest, because of its theme, among these tragi-comedies is *Castelvines y Monteses* (*The Castelvines and the Montagues, c.* 1608), Lope's treatment of the story of Romeo and Juliet, a strange mixture of lyrical ecstasy and clownish merriment. The drama opens with the ball at which Roselo Montes first meets his Julia, but the action is complicated by the fact that Julia is also beloved by her cousin Otavio, and that, after giving Roselo some token of her affection, she is inclined cautiously to withdraw her words, only reluctantly being persuaded by his protestations:

ROSELO: I'd have thee all mine own sweet star,
          In secret, if thou wilt: a close friendship
          With a holy friar I have, and he, I know,
          Will aid us; but should his conscience scruples hold,
          I'll find some subtle means of cure.
JULIA: My very soul doth tremble at thy words.
ROSELO: What fears my dearest Julia?
JULIA: More than a thousand ills.
ROSELO: They are but fancied ills; once wed,
          All rivalry would cease, all hatred should be dead.
          Love beckons by this safe and secret road
          To hold our houses free from hate,
          And through our love shall smile everlasting peace....

JULIA: Look that thou no promise dost forget.
ROSELO: Nay, this I swear; forgetting such,
           May heaven desert me at my need.
JULIA: Swear not, for I have read
           That ready swearers have
           Scant credit with the world or God.
ROSELO: What shall I say, sweet maid?
JULIA: Say that I am thy heart's desire.

Immediately after their secret wedding a broil springs up between
the two houses, in the midst of which Otavio is slain by Roselo,
who is forthwith banished. During his journey to Ferrara the latter
hears that Julia has promised to marry Count Paris, while she,
forced by her father to give consent, finds her only remedy in a
philtre concocted by the friar and supposed by Julia herself to be a
deadly poison. In the vault she wakens and there meets Roselo;
both proceed in disguise to her father's house, where they are
engaged as servants. Shortly after Julia calls out to her father from
an upper room, persuades him that the voice he hears is that of an
angel, and acquaints him with the truth of the marriage: the result
is that when Roselo, discovered, is about to be executed for his
breaking the order of banishment the old father pleads for him,
Julia reveals herself, and all ends happily.

Perhaps the basic theme of *Romeo and Juliet* is more suited for
romantic tragi-comic than for tragic treatment, and in so far Lope's
handling of the story is more harmonious with the events than is
that of Shakespeare; yet, even granting this, we must recognize
how much he has sacrificed for the sake of plot intrigue and stage
thrill. There is nothing here that corresponds to the homely
garrulousness of the Nurse or to the exquisitely youthful fancies of
the debonair Mercutio; all is on a level—the level of intrigue and
of sensational events.

Something worthier of esteem enters into *La estrella de Sevilla*
(*The Star of Seville, c.* 1615)—although in dealing with this play one
must draw attention to the fact that recent study tends to deny it
to Lope. The basic theme concerns the action of a Spanish knight
who, bidden by his monarch, slays a man who is not only his
friend, but also the brother of the girl whom he is on the point of
marrying. Although the King attempts to protect him after this
deed has been committed, the judges refuse to allow the law to be
tampered with by arbitrary practice, and at length the hero escapes
death only when his royal master makes full confession. The
important element is the presentation of the final scenes of the play

We are living here in a world wherein the courtiers are all but slaves of their king, wherein they will not, even to escape execution, betray the secrets of their lords, yet beyond the walls of the palace another world is suggestively revealed. Even the King himself must bow to a force greater than his own—the force of justice, incorruptible and supreme.

The existence of this world gives to certain of Lope's plays a peculiar intensity. Among these may be singled out *El mejor alcalde el Rey* (*The King the Best Alcalde*; printed 1635) and *Fuente Ovejuna* (*The Sheep Well*, c. 1614). The plots of both are worthy of careful scrutiny. At the opening of the first drama Sancho soliloquizes on his pastoral love of Elvira, daughter of the farmer Nuño. In a delightfully playful scene he obtains Nuño's blessing, provided that his lord, Don Tello, will promise to give him a gift or offer him constant employment. All is rustic joy and jollity. The next scene shows Don Tello just returned from hunting; he is pleased with the world and, on hearing Sancho's request, gladly gives him a marriage gift of twenty cows and a hundred sheep. When, however, he graces the betrothal with his presence he is consumed with passion for Elvira, and, with the aid of his minion Celio, raids Nuño's house and carries her off. In the second act Don Tello is shown trying to persuade the girl to become his mistress; Sancho and Nuño come and seek his aid, but are driven out by his servants. They have, however, one other course open to them; Sancho goes to the Court of the King and solicits his justice, eventually obtaining from him an order for Elvira's release—only to find that Don Tello treats it with contumely. On hearing his news the King decides to go in person to Galicia:

KING: Though all the world should question who I am,
    You are to say a noble of Castile,
    And lay your hand upon your mouth like this—
    Take heed and mark me well—and never be
    Without these first two fingers on your lips. . . .

SANCHO: Consider, Sire, a peasant's humble honour
    Touches you not so near. Despatch some judge,
    Some just Alcalde to Galicia
    To do your will.

KING: The King the greatest Alcalde!

At the very time when Don Tello is preparing to force Elvira to his will the monarch arrives at Nuño's house: kindly he greets the farmers, the labourers, the shepherds, and then proceeds to Tello's palace, announces himself, condemns the seducer to death, but decrees that first he shall marry Elvira in order that she, as an honest woman, may wed Sancho with a dower of half his "lands and hoarded revenues."

Lope's sympathetic treatment of the peasantry is even more pronounced in *Fuente Ovejuna*, in which he unconsciously develops a dramatic form later to be associated with experiments in the 'proletarian' theatre. Essentially the hero of this play is, not one person, but a crowd of peasants in the village of Fuente Ovejuna. The Commander (Fernán Gómez de Guzmán) is a libertine, who, in seeking to seduce Laurencia, is threatened and foiled by the base-born Frondoso. Enraged, he seizes the wretched youth, beats Laurencia's father, and carries off this maid. The villagers thereupon gather to take council:

ESTEBAN: Is the Town Board asembled?

BARRILDO: Not a person can be seen.

ESTEBAN: Bravely we face danger!

BARRILDO: All the farms had warning.

ESTEBAN: Frondoso is a prisoner in the tower, and my daughter Laurencia in such plight that she is lost save for the direct interposition of heaven. [JUAN ROJO *enters with the* SECOND REGIDOR.

JUAN ROJO: Who complains aloud when silence is salvation? Peace, in God's name, peace!

ESTEBAN: I will shout to the clouds till they re-echo my complaints while men marvel at my silence. [*Enter* MENGO *and* PEASANTS.

MENGO: We came to attend the meeting.

ESTEBAN: Farmers of this village, an old man whose grey beard is bathed in tears inquires what rites, what obsequies, we poor peasants, assembled here, shall prepare for our ravished homes, bereft of honour? And if life be honour, how shall we fare since there breathes not one among us whom this savage has not offended? Speak! Who but has been wounded deeply, poisoned in respect? Lament now, yes, cry out! Well? If all be ill, how then say well? Well, there is work for men to do.

The peasants are inclined to caution, when Laurencia enters, her hair dishevelled, after having been ravished by the Commander, and in a stirring speech rouses them to action:

My face is bruised and bloody in this court of honest men. Some of you are fathers, some have daughters. Do your hearts sink within you, supine and cowardly crew? You are sheep, sheep! Oh, well-named, Village of Fuente Ovejuna, the Sheep Well! Sheep, sheep, sheep! Give me iron, for senseless stones can wield none, nor images, nor pillars—jasper though they be—nor dumb living things that lack the tiger's heart that follows him who steals its young, rending the hunter limb from limb upon the very margin of the raging sea, seeking the pity of the angry waves.

> But you are rabbits, farmers,
> Infidels in Spain,
> Your wives strut before you
> With the cock upon their train!
> Tuck your knitting in your belts,
> Strip off your manly swords,
> For, God living, I swear
> That your women dare
> Pluck these fearsome despots,
> Beard the traitors there!
> No spinning for our girls;
> Heave stones and do not blench.
> Can you smile, men?
> Will you fight?

The crowd storms the palace, and the Commander is slain by Esteban. Knowing that this crime cannot remain unavenged, the villagers, in a highly interesting scene, rehearse what they will do when the officers of justice arrive, and all agree that, even under torture, they will assert that the Commander was killed by the entire populace, by Fuente Ovejuna itself. This is followed by another scene, in which Frondoso and Laurencia listen to the examination of their fellows; the royal judge, in another chamber, takes them one by one:

JUDGE [*within*]: Old man, I seek only the truth. Speak!

FRONDOSO: An old man tortured?

LAURENCIA: What barbarity!

ESTEBAN [*within*]: Ease me a little.

JUDGE [*within*]: Ease him. Who killed Fernando?

ESTEBAN [*within*]: Fuente Ovejuna.

LAURENCIA: Good, Father! Glory and praise!

FRONDOSO: Praise God he had the strength!

JUDGE [*within*]: Take that boy there. Speak, you pup, for you know! Who was it? He says nothing. Put on the pressure there.

BOY [*within*]: Judge, Fuente Ovejuna.

JUDGE [*within*]: Now by the King, carls, I'll hang you to the last man! Who killed the Commander?

FRONDOSO: They torture the child, and he replies like this?

LAURENCIA: There is courage in the village.

FRONDOSO: Courage and heart.

JUDGE [*within*]: Put that woman in the chair. Give her a turn for her good.

LAURENCIA: I can't endure it.

JUDGE [*within*]: Peasants, be obstinate and this instrument brings death. So prepare! Who killed the Commander?

PASCUALA [*within*]: Judge, Fuente Ovejuna.

JUDGE [*within*]: Have no mercy.

FRONDOSO: I cannot think: my mind is blank!

LAURENCIA: Frondoso, Pascuala will not tell them.

FRONDOSO: The very children hold their peace!

JUDGE [*within*]: They thrive upon it. More! More!

PASCUALA [*within*]: Oh, God in heaven!

JUDGE [*within*]: Again, and answer me! Is she deaf?

PASCUALA [*within*]: I say Fuente Ovejuna.

JUDGE [*within*]: Seize that plump lad, half undressed already.

LAURENCIA: It must be Mengo! Poor Mengo!

FRONDOSO: He can never hold out.

MENGO [*within*]: Oh, oh, oh!

JUDGE [*within*]: Let him have it.

MENGO [*within*]: Oh!

JUDGE [*within*]: Prod his memory.

MENGO [*within*]: Oh, oh!

JUDGE [*within*]: Who slew the Commander, slave?

MENGO [*within*]: Oh, oh! I can't get it out! I'll tell you——

JUDGE [*within*]: Loosen that hand.

FRONDOSO: We are lost!

JUDGE [*within*]: Let him have it on the back!

MENGO [*within*]: No, for I'll give up everything!

JUDGE [*within*]: Who killed him?

MENGO [*within*]: Judge, Fuente Ovejuna.

Hardly another scene in Renaissance drama is more surprising than this, and the surprise is the greater when we remember that it comes, not from an England where already democratic sentiment was growing in power, but from proud, aristocratic Spain.

Although so far little attention seems to have been paid to another of Lope's plays, *La bella mal casada* (*Marriages of Convenience*; printed 1621), it would seem worthy of being associated with the dramas just discussed, since in effect it is the very first theatrical work on record which deals, almost in the style of an eighteenth-century *drame*, with the theme of love and money. Strangely modern is its subject. Lucrecia, impelled partly by poverty and partly by her mother's ambitions, finds herself forced to abandon Don Juan, the man she loves, for a Milanese millionaire. He dies after a few years and leaves her his wealth provided that she marries his nephew, a weak, malformed youth, and only fortunate circumstances enable her to escape from an even more disastrous second marriage and to unite herself to the man whose image has been in her mind all these

years. Hardly any play of this period more startlingly attests to
Lope's originality: some of its scenes might have been written in
1900. Almost equally extraordinary is the strangely philosophic *El
villano en su rincón* (*The Peasant in his Acres*; printed 1617), which,
set in an idealized France, presents as hero a rich peasant Juan
Labrador who, though loyal to his king, prides himself on being a
king in his own acres. When he is called to Court it is evident that
instead of depending on the monarch, it is the monarch who depends
on him. Still another surprise comes in *Las famosas asturianas* (*The
Famous Asturian Women*; printed 1623), where nearly all the dialogue is cast in an out-of-date form of speech—obviously in an effort
at a kind of historical realism.

Among the many plays written by Lope de Vega, works of
another kind abound—comedies of love and gallantry, charmingly
light essays in the display of manners. Of these *El perro del hortelano*
(*The Gardener's Dog, c.* 1615) may be taken as an example. The plot
of this play, artificial, delicate, and gracious, toys with the characters
as a juggler with his balls. Teodoro, the handsome secretary to
Diana, Countess of Belflor, makes love to Marcella, and the
Countess, led, like numbers of Lope's men and women, to love
through jealousy, finds him attractive. She first pretends to aid his
suit of Marcella, then—on the ground that their embracements are
too public—locks the maid in her room. Love combats in her
breast with the sense of honour, and not the least sign of Lope's
originality lies in the solution he finds. Teodoro claims to a rival
that he is a Count's son: both he and Diana know this to be false,
but she is willing to let the lie remain, since this will allow her to
marry him. If others think he is noble all is well. We are far on
the way here towards the world of Pirandello.

Lope's skill is nowhere more clearly displayed. Nothing could
be better, theatrically, than the opening scene, a room in the
Countess's palace, at night. Teodoro and Tristan cross the stage
at a run:

TEODORO: Quick, Tristan! Run!
TRISTAN: Who's there?
TEODORO: Discovered!
TRISTAN: Down quickly!

As they vanish Diana enters:

DIANA: Stay, sir, stay! Such effrontery before my door? Turn, stop,
stay! Up, my people! Not a man astir in the house? I have seen a
solid shade, no wisp of dreams. Hello! Does the Palace sleep?

[*Enter* FABIO.

FABIO: My lady calls——

DIANA: You are as cool by my troth as I hot by my call. Run, fool, thou quintessence of folly, and bring me the scoundrel's name who this moment passed my door.

FABIO: I see no scoundrel, lady.

DIANA: Reply by speed. Fly quickly!

FABIO: I vanish.

DIANA: His name on your life!

FABIO: In this wicked world? . . . Ah me!

[*Exit. Enter* OTTAVIO, *the majordomo.*

OTTAVIO: Though I heard your voice, I could not believe that at this hour your Excellency called so loudly.

DIANA: O thou Flicker of the Faltering Flare, at what hour crept you to sleep? You rouse from a soft bed right smartly. There are men in my house making the dark hours hideous even at the very portal of my chamber! Can such insolence be, Ottavio? And when I call, like a faithless squire you nod in my extremity.

OTTAVIO: Though I heard your voice, I could not believe that at this hour your Excellency called so loudly.

DIANA: No, I did not call. Back to bed! To dream! Repose!

Again and again in Lope's comedies the seeming is contrasted with the real, the belief with the actuality. His lovers in *El premio del bien hablar* (*The Prize for Good Speech*, 1625) are wrapped in a maze of doubts and suppositions; conventional regard wars with true sentiment in the gay *Las bizarrías de Belisa* (*Belisa's Tricks*, 1634), in which the heroine, Belisa, gifted with teeming fancy and independence of spirit, wins Don Juan de Cardona from her rival, Lucinda; there is even, as in Pirandello, the contrast between sanity and madness: in *La boba para los otros y discreta para sí* (*There's Method in't*, c. 1630) a witty Diana pretends to be a simpleton in order to gain her own ends, while in *Los locos de Valencia* (*The Lunatics of Valencia*, c. 1600) there are real madmen, pretended madmen, and some folk deemed mad.

Love themes are dominant in these plays, and it is interesting to observe that the social codes that form the basis of so many Spanish tragedies are habitually turned here into the cause of merriment. Jealousy becomes a thing of laughter, and ladies indulge in escapades which, in other dramas, would have been deemed ample cause for their public dishonouring, if not of their death. *Los melindres de Belisa* (*Belisa's Caprices*; printed 1617), also known as *La dama melindrosa* (*The Capricious Lady*), shows a pair of lovers taking menial positions in a rich household and occasioning much disturbance thereby. A jealous lover in ¡ *Si no vieran los mujeres!* (*If Women didn't see!*, c. 1631) is forced to confess that he really has less interest in the code of honour than in the love of his mistress, and in *El mayor imposible* (*The Greatest Impossibility*, 1615) the title of the play refers to what is seen to be the utmost in folly—the belief that any power on earth can constrain a woman if her heart is set upon a man.

With infinite ease Lope plays variations on such themes, continually startling us by the introduction of some unexpected reflection or some quick turn in the development of what seems to be a conventional situation. In other comedies, such as *El acero de Madrid* (*Madrid Steel*; written 1603), heroines restrained by dragon-like chaperones find means of meeting their lovers: in this particular play Belisa, infatuated with Lisandro, escapes the clutches of Teodora by getting Lisandro's servant Beltran to pose as a doctor and to prescribe for her residence in Madrid, where she must drink a medicine compounded of water strongly impregnated with iron ("agua de acero") and take long walks in the city, when, of course, she has ample opportunity for meeting her sweetheart. *Amar sin saber a quién* (*Loving without knowing Whom*; printed 1630), with its complex story of Don Juan and Leonarda, typically presents Lope's skill in handling stage intrigue; the character of Fenisa in *La discreta enamorada* (*The Clever Girl*; printed 1618) adds to the same kind of intrigue something of character-portrayal; while the similarly named but vastly different heroine of *El anzuelo de Fenisa* (*Fenisa's Bait*; printed 1617) demonstrates that when he desired Lope could depict men and women with sure and subtle touches.

In the midst of these gay, artificial works we are suddenly encountered by that peculiar play *La Dorotea* (printed 1632), in which Lope, evidently incorporating into it much of his own life's story, almost anticipates Musset in his delicate analysis of the unpredictable movements of the human heart. This story of Dorotea, a married woman attached to the poet Fernando, yet faithless both to lover and husband—this story of the poet-devotee who tries to escape from his infatuation, now by fleeing to another city, now by joining the Armada in its expedition against England—shows a power of psychological observation and spiritual subtlety well-nigh unique in its time.

A final judgment on his work is difficult to arrive at. There can be no doubt but that he is a dramatist of amazing invention and extraordinary fecundity. This is a teeming world he sets before us, widely diversified and rich in colour. Yet he exhibits many defects. No man could write as much as he did and hope that his work might possess that final perfection which is the mark of highest genius. Only too often his plots betray the haste of their planning, and his scenes present rather an inspiring suggestion of what might have been had he had more time to develop lines and characters. Perhaps that is why his plays have had a rather peculiar fate outside of Spain. Productions of his work have been rare, yet his influence has been strong on many another dramatist. The Parisian stage did not wish to present his plays as they stood, although Rotrou and Molière owed much to his writings: on the English stage he is virtually unknown, but there too his scenes peer through numberless dramas from the time of Fletcher onward. In approaching Shakespeare men have felt the harmony between content, conception, and execution; with Lope they have rather experienced a wonder at the inventive powers displayed and an accompanying disappointment with the manner in which the dramatic material has been handled.

On the other hand, there is a chance that after so many years of neglect by the public abroad he may now be coming to his own. Recent study has revealed afresh the almost incredible diversity of his work, and dramas—such as *Fuente Ovejuna*—which had remained known only to a few specialists are now being translated and presented in their original forms. All too few are to be found in English dress, but the way is being opened, and it is possible that the coming years will make him more than he has been hitherto—a name attached to works unknown.

CALDERÓN

Lope's immediate successor, Pedro Calderón de la Barca, has had more favourable fortunes, both because his Court position offered him financial security and because, not having to invent so much as the earlier dramatist and not attempting to emulate his fertility, he had more time to polish and refine his work. Even so, however, his output of plays was larger than that of most theatrical authors: in 1680 his own list included 111 dramas, together with 70 *autos* (plays on religious themes), and to these a fair number of other writings for the stage must be added.

In turning from Lope's theatre to his we are struck primarily by its greater elevation of tone and by what might almost be styled its stiffness. Lope reflects the severe code of behaviour which dominated Spanish life in these decades, but there is about him a breezy naturalness which constantly brings the air of nature into his palace interiors. With Calderón all is mannerism; his nature is nature methodized into courtly convention; he is orientating himself, we feel, towards the aristocrats rather than towards a general audience. The result is that, while unquestionably we feel ourselves more in the presence of a finished artist, the glow of vitality that comes from a perusal of Lope's plays is absent. Despite the often misplaced enthusiasm of the romantics for his writings, Calderón is seen as a lesser genius than Lope. It has been said that "Lope de Vega incarnated the genius of a nation; Calderón expresses the genius of an age"—but maybe the truth might be rephrased: Calderón expresses the genius of a nation at a particular epoch in its development, while in Lope's work common humanity, timeless and unchangeable, peers through the contemporary masks of his characters.

Symbolic of this difference between the two men is the fact that, while Lope's plays are based mainly on the theme of love, Calderón's frequently concentrate on a peculiar and restricted concept of honour. The first makes universal appeal; the second is based entirely upon the social conventions operative in Calderón's own time. When Lope's peasants in *Fuente Ovejuna* speak of honour their words are those of men; when Calderón's characters talk of honour their accents are narrowly Castilian.

At the same time, we cannot escape from the respective fortunes of these two playwrights: Calderón has achieved an international reputation, while Lope remains largely unknown outside of Spain. Perhaps there is a lesson for us here. Lope has ebullience, vigour, keenness of eye, but his writing is careless, and it is this carelessness that has formed a barrier to his fuller appreciation. The theatre needs the qualities he brought to it, but on these alone it cannot subsist. Its conventional nature cries out continually for form and precision. Had Shakespeare been the utterly careless artist so many have thought him we should not now be esteeming his plays so highly. Lope fails because his form is deficient; Calderón's reputation is founded on his skill as a craftsman. Although deficient in the eager understanding of theatrical values so patent in all Lope's plays, he has been able by his sense of balanced form and by his delicate lyricism to conceal weaknesses left manifest by his fellow-dramatist.

Beyond this there is a further distinction to be made between the two authors. Both Lope and Calderón lay great stress on the stories they have to tell, and this is entirely right: but, whereas the former is content, in the main, with plot and character, Calderón introduces what might be called a 'philosophical' note. Where the drama rests on plot and character it can never attain greatness: only when these elements are illuminated by an informing purpose can the true heights be reached.

The 'philosophical' quality in Calderón is well exemplified in the success of his *autos*, a peculiarly characteristic kind of play that flourished in Spain and found in him its greatest exponent. While the word *auto* (from the Latin *actus*) has a wide interpretation, in application to this dramatist it generally bears a particular significance and refers to the *autos sacramentales* presented on Corpus Christi Day in honour of the Mystery of the Blessed Eucharist. These plays were allegorical; their characters, like the characters of the moralities, were usually abstractions.

The occasion of their performance was a religious procession. In the year 1654 a Dutch visitor to Madrid left a detailed account of the manner of their production. The festival started with a great parade, in which the king, his nobles, the common people, and grotesque statues of giants, in strange array, accompanied the sacrament as it was carried through the streets. After an intermission the *autos* were played, the more privileged spectators seated in balconies, the others standing on the ground below.

To gain some idea of the way in which these shows were produced we cannot do better than turn to George Ticknor's account of *El divino Orfeo* (*The Divine Orpheus*, 1663):

It opens with the entrance of a huge black car, in the shape of a boat, which is drawn along the street toward the stage where the auto is to be acted, and contains the Prince of Darkness, set forth as a pirate, and Envy, as his steersman; both supposed to be thus navigating through a portion of chaos. They hear at a distance sweet music, which proceeds from another car, advancing from the opposite quarter in the form of a celestial globe, covered with the signs of the planets and constellations, and containing Orpheus, who represents allegorically the Creator of all things. This is followed by a third car, setting forth the terrestrial globe, within which are the Seven Days of the Week, and Human Nature, all asleep. These cars open, so that the personages they contain can come upon the stage and retire back again, as if behind the scenes, at their pleasure—the machines themselves constituting, in this as in all such representations, an important part of the scenic arrangements of the exhibition. . . .

On their arrival at the stage, the Divine Orpheus, with lyric poetry and music, begins the work of creation, using always language borrowed from Scripture; and at the suitable moment, as he advances, each Day presents itself, roused from its ancient sleep, and clothed with symbols indicating the nature of the work that has been accomplished;

THE TEATRO
FARNESE, PARMA,
1618
Photo Alinari

224

SBARCO DI VENERE E DELLA SVA CORTE CONDOTTA DA ZEFFIRO NELLE SPIAGGE TIRRENE

Alfonso Parigius delj: et fecit 1628

ALFONSO PARIGI · "THE DISEMBARKING OF VENUS" SETTING FOR AN INTERMEZZO after which Human Nature is, in the same way, summoned forth, and appears in the form of a beautiful woman, who is the Eurydice of the fable. Pleasure dwells with her in Paradise; and, in her exuberant happiness, she sings a hymn in honour of her Creator, founded on the hundred and thirty-sixth Psalm. . . .

The temptation and fall succeed; and then the graceful Days, who had before always accompanied Human Nature and scattered gladness in her path, disappear one by one, and leave her to her trials and her sins. She is overwhelmed with remorse, and endeavouring to escape from the consequences of her guilt, is conveyed by the bark of Lethe to the realms of the Prince of Darkness, who, from his first appearance on the scene, has been labouring, with his coadjutor Envy, for this very triumph. But his triumph is short. The Divine Orpheus, who has for some time represented the character of our Saviour, comes upon the stage, weeping over the fall, and sings a song of love and grief to the accompaniment of a harp made partly in the form of a cross; after which, rousing himself in his omnipotence, he enters the realms of darkness, amidst thunders and earthquakes; overcomes all opposition; rescues Human Nature from perdition; places her, with the seven redeemed Days of the Week, on a fourth car, in the form of a ship, so ornamented as to represent the Christian Church and the mystery of the Eucharist; and then, as the gorgeous machine sweeps away, the exhibition ends with the shouts of the actors in the drama, accompanied by the answering shouts of the spectators on their knees wishing the good ship a good voyage and a happy arrival at her destined port.

With this may be compared *El gran teatro del mundo* (*The Great Theatre of the World, c.* 1645) in which the Author (God), in a gorgeous starry cloak, addresses the World He has created, and summons representatives of humanity—the rich and the poor, the king and the slave, the beautiful and the learned. Some of the characters object to their parts, but the Author stills their complaints; these actors must play their rôles without rehearsal, even without knowing the precise times of their entrances and exits. Appropriate garments and properties are furnished for all, and the World utters a kind of prologue:

> Since the stage is now supplied
> With its motley company,
> For I there a monarch see
> With his kingdoms broad and wide,
> And a beauty that with pride
> Of her charms all senses awes,
> Great men having great applause,
> Clownish hinds and beggars bare,

H

Or who in still cloisters fare,
All brought forward for this cause
That the persons they may play
Of this present comedy,
To whom I a stage supply,
Fit adornments and array,
Robes or rags, as suit it may,
Oh look forth, the pageant see,
Divine Author, which to Thee
Mortals play; this earthly ball
Let unfold, for there of all
That is done, the scene must be.

Two great globes now open simultaneously, the one with a throne for the Author, the other with a stage, at each end of which are doors, painted respectively with representations of a cradle and a coffin. The Author seats Himself, the Law of Grace makes ready to act as prompter, and a morality play is presented. As the characters utter their lines the Law of Grace keeps up a kind of refrain. Beauty and Discretion part company; the Beggar complains of his lot, while the Rich Man boasts:

RICH MAN:	How shall I make ostentation
	Best of all my wealth?
BEGGAR:	My woe
	How shall I best endure?
LAW OF GRACE:	*Doing well; for God is God.*
RICH MAN:	Oh, how that voice wearies me!
BEGGAR:	Oh, how that voice me consoles!

"What do *I* need in the world?" inquires the King, and to him comes the voice of the Law of Grace: "*To do well; for God is God.*"

So they play their parts, while one after another is summoned towards the door of death. At last the stage is left empty save for the World, who now seeks to claim from each of the actors the properties lent for the purposes of the action. The King is miserably stripped of crown and rich array—"for naked they must go, who naked came"; Beauty loses her loveliness, the Labourer gives up his spade—and all the actors prepare to pass in to a great banquet beyond:

DISCRETION:	All of us are equal now,
	Having laid aside our garments;
	For in this poor winding-sheet
	No distinction more remaineth.
RICH MAN:	Do you go before me, villain?

LABOURER: Leave this foolish dream of greatness;
For, once dead, thou art the shadow
Of the sun which thou wast lately.

RICH MAN: Some strange fear in me the prospect
Of the Author's presence wakens.

BEGGAR: Author of the earth and heaven,
All Thy company, the players,
Who that briefest comedy
Played of human life so lately,
Are arrived, of that they promise
Mindful, of that noble banquet.
Let the curtains be drawn back,
And Thy glorious seat unveilèd.

Closely associated with the *autos* are Calderón's religious dramas, mostly concerned with miracles of the saints. These include *La devoción de la cruz* (*The Devotion of the Cross*, c. 1633)—a tale of the saving of a sinner because of his worshipping of whatever is cruciform; *El purgatorio de San Patricio* (*The Purgatory of St Patrick*, 1635) —in which also a sinner reaches salvation and is instrumental in converting a heathen court to Christianity; *Los dos amantes del cielo* (*The Two Lovers of Heaven*; printed 1636)—wherein a peculiarly lyrical tone enwraps a theme presenting the conflict between paganism and the Christian faith; and the better-known *El mágico prodigioso* (*The Wonder-working Magician*, 1637)—a drama distinguished through the translation of several of its scenes by the poet Shelley. The plot of the last work deals with the life of St Cyprian, who in the first scene is shown as still a heathen, but one searching for the ultimate truth: he has retired for solitary contemplation while

with glorious festival and song
Antioch now celebrates the consecration
Of a proud temple to great Jupiter,
And bears his image in loud jubilee
To its new shrine.

In the midst of his deliberations the Devil enters, dressed as a courtier, pretending to have lost his way in the forest. He offers to debate on any topic that Cyprian cares to choose, and an argument on the essential nature of God ensues. In this Cyprian outwits his opponent, but the Devil now tries another plan. Floro and Lelio prepare to fight a duel over the poor but beautiful Justina; staying their hands, Cyprian agrees to adjudicate their quarrel, visits Justina, and immediately falls in love with her. After returning in

perturbation of spirit to a lonely sea-shore he is again confronted
by the Devil in another guise, that of a shipwrecked mariner:

DÆMON: And who art thou, before whose feet my fate
Has prostrated me?

CYPRIAN: One who, moved with pity,
Would soothe its stings.

DÆMON: Oh, that can never be!
No solace can my lasting sorrows find.

CYPRIAN: Wherefore?

DÆMON: Because my happiness is lost.
Yet I lament what has long ceased to be
The object of desire or memory,
And my life is not life.

CYPRIAN: Now, since the fury
Of this earthquaking hurricane is still,
And the crystalline Heaven has reassumed
Its windless calm so quickly, that it seems
As if its heavy wrath had been awakened
Only to overwhelm that vessel—speak,
Who art thou, and whence comest thou?

DÆMON: Far more
My coming hither cost, than thou hast seen
Or I can tell. Among my misadventures
This shipwreck is the least. Wilt thou hear?

CYPRIAN: Speak.

DÆMON: Since thou desirest, I will then unveil
Myself to thee;—for in myself I am
A world of happiness and misery;
This I have lost, and that I must lament
Forever. In my attributes I stood
So high and so heroically great,
In lineage so supreme, and with a genius
Which penetrated with a glance the world
Beneath my feet, that, won by my high merit,
A king—whom I may call the King of kings,
Because all others tremble in their pride
Before the terrors of His countenance,
In His high palace roofed with brightest gems
Of living light—call them the stars of Heaven—
Named me His counsellor. But the high praise
Stung me with pride and envy, and I rose
In mighty competition, to ascend
His seat and place my foot triumphantly
Upon His subject thrones. Chastised, I know
The depth to which ambition falls; too mad

DÆMON: Was the attempt, and yet more mad were now
Repentance of the irrevocable deed:—
Therefore I chose this ruin, with the glory
Of not to be subdued, before the shame
Of reconciling me with Him who reigns
By coward concession—— Nor was I alone,
Nor am I now, nor shall I be alone;
And there was hope, and there may still be hope,
For many suffrages among His vassals
Hailed me their lord and king, and many still
Are mine, and many more perchance shall be.
Thus vanquished, though in fact victorious,
I left His seat of empire, from mine eye
Shooting forth poisonous lightning, while my words
With inauspicious thunderings shook Heaven,
Proclaiming vengeance, public as my wrong,
And imprecating on His prostrate slaves
Rapine, and death, and outrage. Then I sailed
Over the mighty fabric of the world,—
A pirate ambushed in its pathless sands,
A lynx crouched watchfully among its caves
And craggy shores; and I have wandered over
The expanse of these wide wildernesses
In this great ship, whose bulk is now dissolved
In the light breathings of the invisible wind,
And which the sea has made a dustless ruin,
Seeking ever a mountain, through whose forests
I seek a man, whom I must now compel
To keep his word with me. I came arrayed
In tempest, and although my power could well
Bridle the forest winds in their career,
For other causes I forbore to soothe
Their fury to Favonian gentleness.

His curiosity excited, Cyprian leagues himself with this magician, who in the meantime proceeds to torment the poor Justina's mind with thoughts of love. She, however, is a Christian devotee, and although the impress of passion is on her heart, she remains firm. In the end, after many trials, Cyprian and she reach peace of spirit and are martyred for their faith. The Dæmon is vanquished.

The concept of purity of spirit thus presented in *El mágico prodigioso* finds a strange metamorphosis in the concept of honour introduced into many of his secular dramas. Perhaps *El médico de su honra* (*The Physician of his own Honour*, 1635) may be taken as a prime example. This play tells of a lady, Doña Mencía de Acuña, who is the wife of Don Gutierre Alfonso de Solís. Before her marriage she had been the object of the affections of Don Enrique, the King's brother, and this prince, against her will, pays her a visit. The husband's suspicions are aroused: interrupted while writing a letter to Don Enrique bidding him trouble her no more, she faints, and on recovering finds that her husband has written on the paper the fatal words:

> Love adores thee, but honour abhors thee; and thus while one condemns thee to death, the other gives thee this admonition: thou hast but two hours to live—thou art a Christian—save thy soul, for as to thy life it is impossible to save it.

In terror she calls on her maid: no one answers. She rushes to the door: it has been locked. The windows are stoutly barred. Within two hours' space the husband returns with a blindfolded surgeon. "Come," he says,

> Look within this chamber:
> What do you see in it?
>
> SURGEON:　　　An image
> Of pale death—an outstretch'd body
> Which upon a bed is lying:—
> At each side a lighted candle
> And a crucifix before it,—
> Who it is I cannot say,
> As the face is covered over
> With a veil of taffeta.
>
> GUTIERRE: To this living corse—this body
> Which you see, you must give death.

On threat of his own demise if he disobeys, the surgeon is compelled to bleed the wife to death, and is led blindfold back to his house again. There follows an amazing series of scenes. The surgeon finds the place to which he had been conducted and hastens to inform the King. In order to protect his honour—that is to say, in order not to let anyone know the cause of his crime—Gutierre claims that his wife's death was an accident, whereupon the King immediately commands him to marry Doña Leonor, a lady to whom he had made promises in the past. Hinting at what has happened, he inquires what he should do after a second wedding if he were to find Don Enrique disguised at night within his house:

> KING: Do not give faith to mere suspicion.
> GUTIERRE: And if behind the very arras
> Of my bed, I find the dagger
> Of the Infante Don Enrique?

KING: Remember there are thousand servants
In the world by gold corrupted.
And thy better self invoke.

GUTIERRE: How many times then must I do so,
If night and day I see him haunting
The very precincts of my house?

KING: Complain to me . . .

GUTIERRE: And, if, unto my house returning,
I find a certain letter, asking
The Infante not to go?

KING: There is a remedy for all things.

GUTIERRE: What! Is it possible? For this one?

KING: Yes, Gutierre.

GUTIERRE: What, my lord?

KING: It is your own.

GUTIERRE: What is it?

KING: Bleeding!

Gutierre gives his hand to Leonor, warning her it is bathed with blood, but she does not flinch:

LEONOR: 'Tis no matter: that doth neither
Wake my wonder nor my fear.

GUTIERRE: Remember, too, I am Physician
Of my own Honour, and my skill
Is not forgotten.

LEONOR: Cure with it
My life, when deadly danger threatens.

This scene, so popular in the Spanish theatre, amply demonstrates how alien to almost all other sentiment is the social code on which Calderón built his scenes.

A kindred play is *El pintor de su deshonra* (*The Painter of his own Dishonour*, c. 1645), in which a queer romantic story is told of Serafina, who has married, at her father's command, Don Juan Roca, although her memory still holds fondly the love of Álvaro, whom she thinks dead. Álvaro unexpectedly returns and forcibly abducts her. The husband slays them both and is applauded for the deed by the fathers of the wife and the lover (Don Pedro and Don Luis). As the Prince and other characters enter upon the tragic scene Don Juan Roca stands boldly forward:

JUAN: A picture
Done by the Painter of his own Dishonour
In blood.
I am Don Juan Roca. Such revenge
As each would have of me, now let him take,

JUAN: As far as one life holds. Don Pedro, who
Gave me that lovely creature for a bride,
And I return to him a bloody corpse;
Don Luis, who beholds his bosom's son
Slain by his bosom friend; and you, my lord,
Who, for your favours, might expect a piece
In some far other style of art than this.
Deal with me as you list; 'twill be a mercy
To swell this complement of death with mine;
For all I had to do is done, and life
Is worse than nothing now.

PRINCE: Get you to horse,
And leave the wind behind you.

LUIS: Nay, my lord,
Whom should he fly from? not from me at least,
Who lov'd his honour as my own, and would
Myself have help'd him in a just revenge,
Ev'n on an only son.

PEDRO: I cannot speak,
But I bow down these miserable grey hairs
To other arbitration than the sword;
Ev'n to your Highness' justice.

not funny like pope

Jealousy and an exaggerated belief in honour—these form staple themes in Calderón's work. In *El mayor monstruo del mundo los celos* (*No Monster like Jealousy*, c. 1634) he deals horribly with Herod's determination to have his beloved wife, Mariamne, slain lest she become another's after his death, while in *A secreto agravio, secreta venganza* (*For a Secret Wrong, Secret Revenge*, 1635) a tale hardly less terrifying is narrated.

In strange contrast to such pieces, revolting in their calm delineation of tortured emotions, are Calderón's romantic comedies, delightful in their gay humour. In *Nadie fíe su secreto* (*Keep your own Secrets*, c. 1624) Prince Alexander explains to Don Arias how he has suddenly become smitten with love for Doña Anna; he had seen her often, but not till now has he looked upon her with passion:

Know you not
That not an atom in the universe
Moves without some particular impulse
Of heaven? What yesterday I might abhor,
To-day I take delight in: what to-day
Delight in, may as much to-morrow hate.
All changes; 'tis the element the world,
And we who live there, move in.

This philosophy of love is soon further extended. He is informed that this lady and his secretary, Don César, are betrothed. "Oh, wretched fate!" he cries,

> Desperate ere jealous—jealous ere in love!
> If César but loved her, I could, methinks,
> Have pardon'd, even have advanc'd, his suit
> By yielding up my own. But that *she* loves,
> Blows rivalry into full blaze again.

To torment César he draws him into his company at the very hour when he had trysted his Anna; he tells Anna's brother that a kinsman of his own desires the lady in marriage; he harries César by his commands, and at the end bids him bear a letter to the brother purporting to make arrangements for the wedding with the rival prince. When, however, this letter is read they discover that, with princely magnanimity, César's name is set as that of the bridegroom.

A similar atmosphere breathes through *El secreto a voces* (*The Secret in Words*, 1662), with its gay group of ladies—Florida, the Duchess of Parma, Laura, Flora, and Livia—and its sprightly lyric dialogue of passion, in which the characters vie with one another in describing and evaluating the various states of the heart—loving and loved, loving not loved—in a manner reminiscent of Heywood's interlude. So too in *Guárdate del agua mansa* (*Beware of Smooth Water*, 1649) the scenes are tremulous with happy though conflicting emotion; ludicrous intrigue, although not without the threat of dark consequence, dominates in *Antes que todo es mi Dama* (*My Lady First of All*, c. 1636), the charming *La banda y la flor* (*The Scarf and the Flower*, c. 1632), and the hardly so charming *El astrólogo fingido* (*The Feigned Astrologer*; printed 1633).

As in Lope's works, so in Calderón's, the aristocratic code is frequently shattered when comedy is in view. The *Casa con dos puertas mala es de guardar* (*It's Difficult to guard a House with Two Doors*, 1629) shows a heroine evading the angry eye of her brother, and *No siempre lo peor es cierto* (*Don't always believe the Worst*, c. 1650) gleefully attacks just such excessive jealousy as was condoned in *The Physician of his own Honour*. No play shows this trend better than the delightful *La dama duende* (*The Fairy Lady*, c. 1629), with its charming portrait of the mischievous and unconventional Doña Angela. This lady, by means of a concealed secret door between her apartments and those of Don Manuel, succeeds in persuading the latter's servant, Cosme, that she is a goblin and is mightily perplexing the master. It is true that in this play honour

is rampant, and two duels are introduced into its action, but the
defiance of conventions by Angela infuses its scenes with a delicious
gaiety.

Still a further class of play is illustrated in *El príncipe constante*
(*The Constant Prince*, 1629). The opening scene has a haunting
loveliness. We are in the gardens of the King of Fez, and some
Christian captives enter with Zara, attendant upon the Princess:

ZARA:	Sing, from out this thicket here,
	While the beauteous Phenix dresses;
	Those sweet songs, whose air expresses
	Fond regrets; which pleased her ear
	Often in the baths,—those strains
	Full of grief and sentiment.
FIRST CAPTIVE:	Can music, whose strange instrument
	Was our clanking gyves and chains—
	Can it be, our wail could bring
	Joy unto her heart? Our woe
	Be to her delight?
ZARA:	'Tis so;
	She from this will hear you; sing.
SECOND CAPTIVE:	Ah! this anguish doth exceed,
	Beauteous Zara, all the rest—
	Since from out a captive's breast
	(Save a soulless bird's indeed)
	Never has a willing strain
	Of music burst.
ZARA:	But have not you
	Yourselves sung many a time?
THIRD CAPTIVE:	'Tis true;
	But then it was no stranger's pain
	To which we hoped some ease to bring;
	It was our own too bitter grief
	For which in song we sought relief.

Thus set in an atmosphere of captivity, the action proceeds. The
hero is Don Fernando, who, although taken prisoner and suffering
the worst indignities, is stalwart in his determination not to win
his ransom from the Moors by ceding the city of Ceuta—the price
of his freedom. His fixed resolution remains firm even unto death,
and, although much romantic nonsense has been written concerning
the virtues of the play, it must be agreed that Calderón has here
succeeded in painting an arresting picture of inflexibility of purpose
and devoted gallantry.

Two other dramas deserve attention. In *El alcalde de Zalamea*

(*The Mayor of Zalamea, c.* 1640), based on a similarly named play by Lope, he comes closer perhaps to that author than in any other of his plays, dealing with a theme that recalls the story of *Fuente Ovejuna*. There is, however, an essential difference. Lope had daringly made the entire population of the village a collective hero; the quality of his work ultimately depends on the memorable scene in which they all unite in accepting common responsibility for the crime that has been committed. In *The Mayor of Zalamea* all stress is laid on one man, Pedro Crespo, a farmer who has been elected *alcalde* and who, low-born though he is, dares to avenge his daughter's violated honour by executing Don Álvaro de Ataide. There can be no doubt but that Crespo is an interestingly delineated character and that here, as in Lope's play, we are made aware of the sense of justice which transcends the pride of the aristocrats, but the story is one treated on a plane by far less interesting than that on which *Fuente Ovejuna* is based.

Finally we reach *La vida es sueño* (*Life's a Dream, c.* 1636), the true triumph of Calderón's art. Outwardly this play is but another romantic tale, set this time in Poland, with a heroine, Rosaura, and a miserable captive, Segismundo; but what gives the whole action its distinction is the way in which the author has, as it were, imposed a theme upon his plot. Segismundo is being kept in durance because an oracle had declared that he, the true prince, would prove a fatal enemy to his father and his country. As the King, his parent, grows old, however, remorse comes to him, and he determines that his son shall be granted a trial. Given a potion, the young man is brought, drugged, to the palace, and when he opens his eyes he finds himself surrounded by the trappings of royalty. Almost at once, however, he betrays ungovernable brutality of spirit even while he wonders in his mind whether all of this may not merely be a dream. His actions are so savage and arbitrary that once more he is returned to his dungeon, and there he reflects, now with regret and horror, on what he is convinced must have been an hallucination:

> And let us then restrain
> This the fierceness of our pride,
> Lay this wilfulness aside,
> Lest perchance we dream again:
> And we shall so, who remain
> In a world of wonder thrown,
> Where to live and dream are one.
> For experience tells me this,

Each is dreaming what he is,
Till the time his dream is done.
The king dreams himself a king,
And in this conceit he lives,
Lords it, high commandment gives,
Till his lent applause takes wing,
Death on light winds scattering,
Or converting (Oh, sad fate!)
Into ashes all his state:
How can men so lust to reign,
When to waken them again
From their false dream death doth wait?
And the rich man dreams no less
'Mid his wealth which brings more cares,
And the poor man dreams he bears
All his want and wretchedness;
Dreams, whom anxious thoughts oppress,
Dreams, who for high place contends,
Dreams, who injures and offends;
And though none are rightly ware,
All are dreaming that they are
In this life, until death ends.
    I am dreaming I lie here,
Laden with this fetter's weight,
And I dreamed that I of late
Did in fairer sort appear.
What is life? a frenzy mere;
What is life; e'en that we deem;
A conceit, a shadow all,
And the greatest good is small,
Nothing is, but all doth seem,
Dreams within dreams, still we dream.

With these words, in their intensity and spiritual exploration beyond anything Lope ever wrote, we may take leave of Calderón. Had he but been granted some of his predecessor's verve and his theatrical sense, had he not been bound and fettered by the narrow code of honour that dominated his age, he might have been another Shakespeare. As it is, despite his skill and the beauty of much of his work, he just fails to achieve ultimate dramatic greatness. The concept of *Life's a Dream* is universal, but all too much of Calderón's writing is tied to a particular place and time, thus preventing his scenes from making such appeal to all ages and races as is made by the dramatist of Elizabethan England.

CERVANTES, MORETO, AND OTHERS

Lope de Vega and Calderón are sun and moon of the firmament of the Spanish theatre, but beside them glitter—gaily or ominously—many another star.

The names of the early playwrights are many, and the influence of their works is not inconsiderable. *La comedia de Calisto y Melibea* (known also as *Celestina*; printed 1499), probably written by Fernando de Rojas, although unsuited for theatrical representation, won international repute and inspired numerous other dramas. The author of *Don Quixote*, Miguel de Cervantes Saavedra, turned to dramatic composition, although without much distinction in style or concept. As yet the secular play had not thrown off the trammels of the morality; even his best drama, the *Numancia* (c. 1587), is a strange, rambling affair, with abstract characters jostling historical personages; his *entremeses* are little more than farces in the medieval mode; and, when he tries to handle romantic material, as in *La gran sultana* (*The Great Sultana*; printed 1615), his treatment of characters and events often becomes ludicrous.

The great period of the Spanish stage came much later, between 1620 and 1665; from this age derive numerous writers of worth. During these years flourished Augustín Moreto y Cavaña, a man who vied in popularity with Lope himself. Thoroughly conversant with the theatre, his scenes have life, vigour, and interest. Less successful in serious efforts, he has left several comedies which, because of their skilful planning and interesting character portraits, have been instrumental in inspiring later playwrights. His rôle was that of the elaborator and refiner rather than that of the inventor, and most of his pieces—such as *El desdén con el desdén* (*Scorn for Scorn*; printed 1654), *No puede ser* (*You Can't*, c. 1660), *De fuera vendrá quien de casa nos echara* (*The Cuckoo in the Nest*; printed 1654), and *El lindo Don Diego* (*Don Diego the Fop*, c. 1662)—are based on plays by Lope and others. As typical of Moreto's work the last-mentioned play may be briefly noted. Don Diego is a foolish provincial booby who gives himself absurd airs, and when Doña Inés finds herself betrothed to him against her will she and her sweetheart, Don Juan, play upon his pretensions, finally exposing him after he has laid suit to a supposed countess, who is really Inés' maid in disguise. Moreto delighted in such farcical situations and knew well how to handle them: he knew, too, how to enliven his scenes with a delicate, fresh, and vivacious wit.

Allied to Calderón rather than to Lope is Francisco de Rojas

Zorilla, who carries both romantic intrigue and the idea of honour—as diversely exemplified in the popular *Del rey abajo ninguno* (*All Equal below the King*), *Entre bobos anda el juego* (*The Boobies' Sport*), and *Lo que son mujeres* (*What Women are*) (all printed 1640-54)—to an extreme.

From Tirso de Molina (Gabriel Téllez) comes the dramatic story of Don Juan. This author, almost as prolific as Lope, has among his four hundred odd plays *El burlador de Sevilla y convidado de piedra* (*The Deceiver of Seville and the Stone Guest*; printed 1630), the first presentation of the legendary libertine on the stage. Although the play is episodic and chaotic in form, the author has the power to reveal to us a sinner whose very daring and flamboyancy charm our senses. No doubt we agree with the retribution that comes to him in the end, but until that time arrives we are held intent by his prodigious villainy and the spell of his personality. Like Lope and Calderón, Tirso de Molina also has a number of witty comedies of intrigue, best known among which are *Don Gil de las calzas verdes* (*Don Gil of the Green Trousers*; printed 1635), in which Don Gil is found to be a lady less fortunate than, but as mischievous as, the heroine of *La dama duende*, and *El vergonzoso en palacio* (*The Timid Fellow at Court*; printed 1621), which transports a clown into aristocratic circles. Perhaps one of the best is *Marta la piadosa* (*Martha the Devotee*; also known as *La beada enamorada*, *The Blessed Mistress*; printed 1634), in which a girl, in order to escape an unwished marriage, feigns to have received a heavenly call.

With these go other plays that demonstrate in the author a range of interests almost as wide as Lope's. *La villana de Vallecas* (*The Peasant Woman of Vallecas*; printed 1620) tells a pathetic story of intrigue in which a ravished maiden, Violante, after disguising herself as a peasant, succeeds in discovering her seducer. Not least powerful among them all is the religious drama *El condenado por desconfiado* (*Damned for Lack of Faith*; printed 1635), distinguished by the fact that, through the concrete story of a hermit, Paul, it introduces to the theatre discussion of theological problems deeper and more abstract than those essayed by other playwrights.

Somewhat more original in concept, but less virile, is Juan Ruiz de Alarcón y Mendoza, a native of Mexico, among whose twenty-seven dramas a few stand out either for their strong characterization or for their themes. *La verdad sospechosa* (*Truth Suspected*; printed 1628) interestingly deals with a hero, Don García, whose ready wit, keen fancy, and careless disposition cause him to tell so many lies that no one will believe him. He falls in love with a girl, Jacinta, but he labours under the impression that she is really

Lucrecia, while he lays official suit to the true Lucrecia under the name of Jacinta. Normally in a comedy of this kind one would have expected to find this lover relieved of his tangles in the end, but Alarcón takes the unconventional course of causing his hero to marry Lucrecia, with whom he is not in love, because of his failure to distinguish between truth and reality. At the opposite pole this author produces such a study of loyalty, treachery, and passion as *La crueldad por el honor* (*Cruelty for Honour*, c. 1625) or such an 'heroic' play as *Ganar amigos* (*Gaining Friends*, c. 1630), which glorifies generosity of spirit in its story of how a noble marquis, by conquering his own passions, gains a devoted friend in Don Fernando, and how the latter proves true to the loyal Doña Flor. While Alarcón clearly bases his style on that of Lope and Calderón, equally clearly demonstrated in his work is an individual sincerity of purpose.

In between these two comes such a play as *El examen de maridos* (*The Husband's Examination*; printed 1632), where the heroine, Inés, who has loudly proclaimed her intention of testing her suitors before making choice of a husband, falls in love and is, unwillingly, forced to impose the examination she would now fain dispense with. For its character delineation the comedy is noteworthy.

A somewhat similar originality of treatment appears in *Las paredes oyen* (*Walls have Ears*; printed 1628), in which the hero, Don Mendo, is severely punished both for his vacillation in affection and for the stories he tells about his two lady-loves. Juan Ruiz de Alarcón has severe moral standards, and the logic with which he applies these in comedy give him an undoubted, but a rather unsympathetic, distinction among his fellows.

All these authors became known, at least to playwrights if not to the general public, beyond the boundaries of Spain, and there were many others who, although noted among their fellow-citizens, have remained outside of the Iberian peninsula nothing but names—Álvaro Cubillo de Aragón, Antonio Coello, Antonio de Solís y Ribadeneira, Fernando de Zárate y Castronovo, Juan Bautista Diamante, Juan de la Hoz y Mota, and others. The galaxy of talent is as great, and as diversified, as that which graced the English theatre during the reigns of Elizabeth and her Stuart successors. Without question the Spanish drama is the closest rival to the Elizabethan, and was prevented from vying with it more closely only by the carelessness of texture that mars so much of Lope's work and by the provincially Castilian code on which Calderón based so many of his writings.

THE INTERNATIONAL THEATRE OF THE JESUITS

BEFORE leaving the Renaissance theatre of Europe we must cast at least a fleeting glance on what was, in effect, the last relic of the international stage of the medieval mysteries. In the year 1540 St Ignatius of Loyola, a Spanish soldier turned ecclesiastic, succeeded in obtaining Papal approval for his new religious order, the Society of Jesus. Designed to combat the heresies of the Reformation, the order of the Jesuits eagerly seized on all devices likely to be of use in testifying to the glory of the Church, and among such devices the theatre, because of its appeal to eye and ear, was particularly favoured. Especially in the Germanic territories and in the lands of Eastern Europe, this Jesuit drama flourished, serving at once as a continuation of the medieval and as a forerunner of secular drama to come.

The Jesuits were thoroughly eclectic. For their stage and plays they took suggestions from a diversity of sources. The mysteries, miracles, and moralities, of course, provided them with many ideas, but they were not prepared to rest on ancient traditions. Nothing if not modern, they looked around them on the contemporary stages and infused new material into old forms. In especial, they gazed with favour upon the 'school-drama,' and upon the tableau type of production which had grown up in the Netherlands.

The school-drama was a direct result of those early amateur productions of Roman comedies and tragedies which ushered in the theatre of the Renaissance. Performed for the most part simply on an open hall-stage backed by curtains or by a skeleton façade, the original Latin plays soon were succeeded by Latin dramas of later vintage. Dozens of learned authors, in places as diverse as Western Oxford and Eastern Vienna and Cracow, turned their pens towards the creation of scenes, usually but not always on sacred subjects, imitated from Plautus or from Terence. Although hardly any one of these early efforts is worthy of special attention (unless it be for historical reasons), their collective influence was by no means negligible, for they brought to their restricted publics examples of the new methods of dramaturgy. Their subject-matter may have been the same as that of the mysteries: their technique was entirely different.

From these school-dramas the early Jesuit authors took many ideas for their later Latin plays. In addition, they saw and took advantage of opportunities presented to them in the Netherlands. There two theatrical developments are of interest to us. The first is the long series of *tableaux vivants*, presented usually on platforms framed by archways and revealed by the drawing of curtains, which, while not restricted to Dutch cities, especially flourished there. The second, and more important, is the dramatic activities associated with the Rederyker Kamers, or "Chambers of Rhetoric," that played such a vigorous rôle in the sixteenth century. These companies of Rederykers were collections of amateur enthusiasts who banded themselves together into societies, each distinguished by a particular emblem, linked loosely together by means of annual competitions. Much of their energy was spent on the arranging of processions, the reciting of poems, and the singing of songs: nevertheless the dramatic art was the real core of their being, and to this style of literary composition they gave themselves eagerly.

Usually for the competitions a general theme or problem was set, sometimes of a theological or moral kind, more commonly based on humanistic learning. As a natural result the Rederyker plays were all flavoured strongly with the atmosphere of the moralities, and, because bound by abstract interests, never succeeded in creating anything of permanent worth. (Almost the only Dutch play of this time calling for special mention is the satirically comic *De Spaanische Brabander* (*The Spanish Citizen of Brabant*, 1617), by Gerbrand Adriaanszoon Bredero, which contains some racy scenes of contemporary life.) If, however, the subject-matter was abstract and framed in the style of the moralities, the appeal to the eyes was vivid, colourful, and realistic. Generally an outdoor platform with a façade at the rear served their purposes: this façade had archways concealed by curtains which could be drawn to reveal the scenes within them, the revelation being often preceded by a 'Precursor's' speech. It was from these and similar productions that there arose, in 1638, the famous Schouburgh of Amsterdam.

From this source, too, the Jesuits took material for their religiously inspired dramas, but in taking over they characteristically elaborated, so that what at the beginning was tied closely to the school performances and to the *tableaux vivants* in the end was almost indistinguishable from the opera. The first step was the extension of the curtained façade so that the spectators were presented with a series of arched frames, each with its own stage, and all capable of being used at once if occasion demanded. Thus the earlier Terence façade or that used in the Netherlands was adapted for the use of representational scenery, while at the same time the traditions of the medieval 'simultaneous setting' were pressed again into service. From this type of stage, established by the third quarter of the sixteenth century, to the adoption of the single proscenium opening favoured by seventeenth-century Italian architects was an easy progress. In this later form of Jesuit stage relics of the old frequently remain in the shape of small (and by then useless) side-arches, but the visual appeal is concentrated on the central picture.

Naturally the plays presented by the Jesuits were didactic. An authoritarian order, its self-appointed mission was to display the glories of the true Church and to demonstrate to men the evils of free thought. Against the individualism expressed in the Reformation, it set forth to deny the right of man to think for himself, and, like some dictators, richly extolled the virtues of authority. Loyalty to the Church and loyalty to a king were its two main virtues. On the other hand, in order to exhibit these virtues most effectively and appealingly, the Jesuits were willing to employ all means of attracting attention, and hence their drama has interest not only for the potentially romantic material incorporated into its being, but also for the impetus it gave to the development of scenic decoration already richly sponsored by the opera.

Most of the playwrights have no more than a minute value, but two or three deserve to be remembered, and it must be confessed that under the bare Latin exteriors of their scenes there rests a quality of significance and distinction. Jakob Gretser merits mention, partly because he was among the first of his school with the composition of his *Comœdia de Timone* (*Timon*) in 1584, partly because he succeeds in many of his scenes in striking a note of genuine passion. His power, however, rests much inferior to that of his follower, Jakob Bidermann, a writer of unquestioned talent. Among his nine dramas one stands out pre-eminent, the *Cenodoxus* of 1602. This tragedy, which interestingly begins with a comic episode and is as free in construction as any secular romantic play, puts Heaven and Hell upon the stage, uses almost every stage device known to contemporary theatre-workers, and definitely opens the way towards the still more elaborate functioning of the Jesuit playhouses during the course of the seventeenth century. In its dramatic concretion of the struggle between free thought and divine faith, it obviously made tremendous appeal in its own day and was frequently reproduced in the later Jesuit repertory.

Cenodoxus is a kind of morality play of Faustian flavour. Others among Bidermann's plays seize on historical subject-matter, on material from the Bible, and on themes of romantic style (for example, *Philemon*, which deals with the ancient tale of the Roman comedian who suffers martyrdom, and *Cosmarchia* or *Mundi Respublica*, with its folk-tale, 'life-is-a-dream' structure). In all of these the religious author shows himself possessed of an innate dramatic sense, of a skill in character-portrayal, and of a true concept of the tragic.

Of his immediate companions Joseph Simeons (*alias* Emanuel Lobb), an English Jesuit, perhaps comes nearest to him in power of expression, with his five tragedies printed in 1656—*Zeno sive ambitio infelix* (*Zeno; or, Unfortunate Ambition*), *Mercia sive pietas coronata* (*Mercia; or, Piety Crowned*), *Theoctistus sive constans in aula virtus* (*Theoctistus; or, Virtue Constant at Court*), *Virtus sive Christiana fortitudo* (*Virtue; or, Christian Fortitude*), and *Leo Armenius sive impietas punita* (*Leo Armenius; or, Impiety Punished*). Of his followers most important was Nikolaus of Avancini, author of over thirty plays —allegories, mysteries, miracles, and the like. His varied style is characteristically revealed in his *Susanna Hebræa*, *Cyrus*, *Dei bonitas de humana pertinacia victrix sive Alphonsus X* (*The Goodness of God Victorious over Human Obstinacy; or, Alfonso X*), and *Pietas Victrix sive Flavius Constantinus Magnus* (*Piety Victorious; or, Flavius Constantinus the Great*).

Nor was it only in the Germanic lands that the Jesuit theatre won some dramatic success. In Sicily Orazio Scamacca produced a long series of such plays, and the impulse that brought these into being lasted well into the eighteenth century, when minor masterpieces appeared in *La santa infanzia di Gesù Cristo* (*The Holy Infancy of Jesus Christ*; printed 1708), by Presepio Presepi (Giuseppe Antonio Patrignani), and *Eustachio* (printed 1758), by Agostino Palazzi. Still further, it must be observed that the Jesuit theatre did not always remain within the walls of the colleges. In 1644 Sforza Pallavicino urged in the 'discourse' prefaced to his *Martire Ermengilda* (*Hermengild the Martyr*) the general adoption of religious themes such as the Jesuit authors dealt with, pleading that the fate of martyrs was more fitting material for tragedy than the subjects of classical myth. The way in which this influence worked may be traced too in the works of the German Andreas Gryphius. His *Catharina von Georgien, oder bewährte Beständigkeit* (*Catharine of*

Georgia; or, True Constancy; printed 1698) is a drama of martyrdom cast in the style that the author had learned from his early association with the Jesuit stage. No doubt the choice of theme in *Carolus Stuardus, oder die ermordete Majestät* (*Charles Stuart; or, Majesty Murdered*; printed 1698) was selected because Charles I could be regarded as a martyr; but *Cardenio und Celinde* (printed 1657) is a tragedy of love, while in *Die geliebte Dornrose* (*The Beloved Thorny Rose*, 1660) Gryphius was able to write not merely an imaginative comedy of intrigue, but a comedy composed almost entirely in dialect, thus pointing forward to dramatic developments that as yet lay far in the future.

The early influence of the humanist stage and of Italian theatrical activities, followed by the later influence of the Jesuit stage, is to be traced in diverse localities during the sixteenth and seventeenth centuries. Typical are the plays that came into being in the vicinity of Ragusa (or Dubrovnik) on the shores of the Adriatic. Here flourished a native Croat drama, inspired by Italian example yet instinct with individual vitality. Already in the sixteenth century playwrights were at work, and one of them, Martin Držić, succeeded in creating comic scenes which even yet retain their appeal on the stage; in the following century came the still more notable epic and tragic poet Ivan Gundulić, a man who symbolized his age and time by dealing both with classical themes and with themes culled from the legend and history of his own land. Slightly later the Jesuit Latin theatre induced other writers to turn to the composition of plays moral and religious. Although all this vigorous flourishing of the dramatic form was destined soon to wither and vanish, it deserves notice both for such intrinsic excellence as it attained and for its testimony to the strength and widespread appeal of Renaissance enthusiasm for the theatre.

There can be no doubt but that the activities of the Jesuits were of prime importance in developing dramatic interest among lettered audiences, particularly in the countries to the east of Europe, and that everywhere they had a widespread influence on theatrical form. Even although their dialogue was commonly in Latin, and even although their basic philosophy was destined to be confronted with philosophies alien and antagonistic to the Papal Court they aimed to extol, they too set their seal on the stage of the time. To neglect the school-drama and this its offshoot is to omit an essential chapter—albeit a short one—in the history of the modern playhouse.

PART IV

THE DRAMA OF THE RENAISSANCE: ENGLAND

THE POPULAR BEGINNINGS

IF ONLY because of Shakespeare, the English drama of this time demands treatment apart from that of Italy, France, and Spain. It has its close ties with all of these, yet it stands apart by its realization of a broader spirit and of a richer harmony than its companions succeeded in attaining.

THE FIRST ATTEMPTS

At the beginning it showed no more promise than any of the others; indeed, for many decades it seemed to be lagging grievously behind the drama of Italy. Before 1560—and even much later—England could show nothing to compare with Ariosto's clean-cut comedies of contemporary life or with Machiavelli's penetrating satire. In 1583, when Sir Philip Sidney, writing his *Apology for Poetry*, utterly condemned the contemporary popular stage, no one, whether academically classical in trend or romantically revolutionary, could have dared to dream that the English theatre would, within the course of a few decades, produce such riches as to make even the gold of Greece seem less glorious a treasure. After the event, of course, it is easy to discern in the early works the shadows cast by what was to come, but if the development of the English stage had suddenly ceased in 1580 one would have said that here, as in Italy and France, was interesting material utterly failing to find adequate realization in artistic form.

The fact remains, however, that the London theatres did succeed in reaching this realization and that their magnificent contribution to the drama was not due simply to the fortuitous appearance of one author or of a group of authors. Something in the conditions of the English stage permitted the growth stifled in Italy, stunted in France, and only partly developed in Spain. In our survey obviously one of our chief tasks must be to suggest what these conditions were.

To England the Renaissance came as it did to other lands. There was a great stirring of spirit and an eager-eyed enthusiasm; the wonders of the long-lost classical world were being suddenly revealed to men's wondering gaze. At the Court of Henry VIII Latin plays were presented, just as they had been elsewhere.

There was, however, an essential difference in the atmosphere in which these performances were set. They were being given, not at a variety of different Courts, as in Italy, not against a background of civil war, as in France, not in the midst of a narrowly repressive *milieu*, as in Spain. It is true that many years were to pass before the burning hatreds between Catholics and Protestants in England began to smoulder down—after Henry VIII was to arise the bloody Mary; but, fundamentally, Henry's reforms became the established tradition of the land, and most men, no matter what their private beliefs, gradually united in a common good. It was a Catholic who commanded the little English fleet confronting the might of the Catholic Armada. For England the Renaissance meant not merely the rediscovery of the classics and the opening up of fresh vistas for art, but also the finding of a new sense of national unity, expressed clearly in the establishment of a national Church, but embracing all—even those who would not bow to the reformed creed—within its folds. Italy and France lacked that unity, while in Spain the sense of common purpose was vitiated by obscurantism.

And by more than obscurantism. To a large extent Spain was living on its past. At a time when hardly anyone thought of England seriously as a power Spanish galleons were sailing home laden with untold wealth, the whole of the New World was in the grasp of her monarchs, and over much of the Old World they had set their imperial seal. In the sixteenth century the English were just becoming conscious of their strength; their eyes were on the future. It is characteristic that, while in England a new national Church was born, with the sweeping away of so many cluttered and outworn traditions, Spain endeavoured through the Inquisition to stamp out the new by force of rack and fire. No doubt the new Church was created as a political device by the astute Henry VIII, but, whatever its inception, it met the needs of the time and succeeded because it accorded with the will of the people; and it was a symbol of an England realizing her own promise.

In another way, too, these early performances of Latin plays were placed against a different setting. Much as men in England paid homage to the classic civilization, there was always in England a healthy spirit of scepticism. The other three countries could never forget that they were forged out of the Roman Empire and that their Romance tongues were but Latin vulgarized. Despite the long centuries of Roman occupation of Britain, this mould of form was never so deeply felt in the land where successive invasions had left a race, and a language, which owed its being to many diverse cultures. Even beyond that there were Englishmen who prided themselves in the fact, or in the belief, that their ultimate being derived not from proud Rome and haughty Greece, but from the ancient land of Troy. The belief was, perhaps, no more than a pleasant fiction even for those who expressed it most warmly, but its very existence as a fiction is also symbolic. Dreams are woven out of desires.

The result is that we search almost in vain during the early years for any faithful reproduction of classical dramatic forms in English dress. Sir Philip Sidney, in 1583, deplored the fact that even *Gorboduc*, the only tragedy that might in any respect be regarded as regular, was manifestly impatient of the rules. Only later did a number of academically minded playwrights endeavour to provide stricter examples, but by that time the popular theatre had grown to full stature and its course was not to be stayed. The voices of the little group of English Senecans were drowned by the accents of Shakespeare and his fellows—whereas had they been uttering their Aristotelian notes fifty years before they might well have altered the entire development of the English drama. In Italy the model presented by *Sofonisba* came very early; England had no such model until the years had passed when it might have been an object of reverent admiration.

It is true, of course, that the same kind of amateurism as flourished abroad also played an important part in London, but the Court plays were at once less elaborate and more closely associated with professionalism than was common in Italian palaces. Elizabeth's parsimony held expenses down, so that, although scenery assuredly was used at Court, we may be sure it was kept simple. At the Inns of Court, at the Universities, and in the schools young men and boys amused themselves with acting, but rapidly the Queen and her Court came to depend rather upon the skilled services of professional players than upon the exhibitions of the amateurs. From the year 1493 we have record of a troupe of "Lusores Regis" (the King's Players), and these are known to have given regular performances before royalty during the early part of the sixteenth century, while the companies of boys (the Children of Paul's, the Children of the Chapel and the Queen's Revels, and the Children of Windsor) became, in Elizabeth's reign, virtually professionals. The account of Court performances during the middle of the century shows the performance of many masques by the amateurs, but of comparatively few plays; these were given by those of 'the quality,' and necessarily included, for the most part, popular dramas.

As a consequence the list of purely 'classical' plays in England during this era is a meagre one, while at the same time there is a goodly show of dramatic works, even those amateur in origin, in which elements taken from Seneca, Plautus, and Terence are subordinated to the needs of audiences unapt to welcome the severer forms beloved of the academics.

In comedy Plautus' *Amphitruo* is just faintly discernible beneath the careless vesture of *Jacke Juggler* (printed 1555), described as "A new Enterlude for Chyldren to playe," while the learned authors of the *Ryght Pithy, Pleasaant and merie Comedie: Intytuled Gammer gurtons Nedle* (*c.* 1550–53; printed 1575) and *Roister Doister* (1553–54; printed 1556) were not prepared to allow their knowledge of classical methods to prevent them from producing work of a popular sort. *Gammer Gurton's Needle* is a gay and good-humoured farcical comedy, much of it written in rustic dialogue, with the characters firmly rooted in an English village; while *Roister Doister*, although a trifle more imitative, not only shows the delineation of contemporary types, but also borrows largely from the native morality tradition.

The same is true of the gestures made in the direction of tragedy. *Gorboduc* (1562), by Thomas Norton and Thomas Sackville, is certainly 'classical' when compared with some other dramas of the time, but it displays a healthy independence and a native power of invention. The plot is taken, not from the writings of some Greek or Roman historian, but from the legendary material of Geoffrey of Monmouth; the unities are disobeyed; there is a flavour of the morality in the development of its theme; and the use made of the dumb-show at the beginning of the acts is apparently unique.

Other plays of kindred provenance during these mid-years of the sixteenth century exhibit similar features. Thomas Hughes follows the authors of *Gorboduc* in going to Geoffrey of Monmouth for the plot of *The Misfortunes of Arthur* (1588), and Robert Wilmot discovers in Boccaccio the material for his *Tancred and Gismund* (1567–68). And alongside these comedies and tragedies is a large number of dramas indeterminate in kind, and in spirit romantic. In *Fulgens and Lucrece* (printed 1497) romantic love is the theme of the anonymous poet; George Whetstone's *Promos and Cassandra* (printed 1578) is akin in spirit; in the hands of John Pikeryng the tale of Orestes is transformed into a tragi-comedy with a Cockney accent as *A Newe Enterlude of Vice, Conteyninge the Historye of Horestes* (printed 1567); in *The Commody of the most vertuous and Godlye Susanna* (printed 1578)—a play discovered only a few years ago—the Biblical story is told in terms of a morality, with a character-list including the Devil, a Vice named Ill Report, and such persons as Voluptas and Sensuality. All these plays delight in action, and perhaps none is more typical than Thomas Preston's *Lamentable Tragedie, mixed full of plesant mirth, containing the life of Cambises King of Percia* (probably 1561). The plot is based on ancient history, but the numerous characters include such abstract figures as Councell, Murder, Commons Cry, and Cruelty, as well as such humorous characters as Huf, Ruf, and Snuf, companions of Ambidexter the Vice. Although the parts include no fewer than thirty-eight speaking rôles, the author has been careful to arrange them so that a company of but six men and two boys can perform the play, while this evidence of his keen attention to its theatrical possibilities is corroborated by the numerous racy stage directions running throughout its length. Ambidexter enters "with an old capcase on his head, an olde paile about his hips for harnes, a scummer and a potlid by his side, and a rake on his shoulder"; he "swinges" Huf, Ruf, and Snuf; a Meretrix comes in, and there is a ludicrous brawl in which Ruf "falleth downe; she falleth upon him, and beats him, and taketh away his weapon." There is a constant impression of movement here: Commons Cry comes "running in," and after speaking his verse goes "out againe hastily." We are told of drinking, kissing, shooting, executions; the hands of Cruelty and Murder are "bloody." No reticence is shown; no attempt is made to avoid displaying scenes of violence; rather are these freely exploited for the merriment or the thrilling of the audience. Lamentable tragedies mixed full of pleasant mirth may later have become somewhat ridiculous, retaining their hold only on the Bottoms of the last years of the sixteenth century, but they were healthily unrestrained, and, despite Shakespeare's good-humoured but satirical allusions to them, were to prove the model on which his comedy of romance and even his tragedy were fashioned.

THE GROWTH OF PROFESSIONAL DRAMA AND PUBLIC THEATRES

In the Christmas season of 1567-68 Queen Elizabeth had eight plays acted for her delight—*As Plain as can be, The Painful Pilgrimage, Jack and Jill, Six Fools, Wit and Will, Prodigality, Orestes, The King of Scots*. When the authors of *Sir Thomas More* pictured a group of actors, consisting of four men and a boy, presenting their repertoire to the hero of that drama, they listed *The Cradle of Security, Hit Nail o' th' Head, Impatient Poverty, The Four PP, Dives and Lazarus, Lusty Juventus,* and *The Marriage of Wit and Wisdom.*

These titles may be taken as fairly typical of what the professional actors were engaged in performing about the middle of the century. By far the majority of the plays are moralities—nine out of a total of fourteen; *As Plain as can be, Jack and Jill,* and *Hit Nail o' th' Head* sound as though they were comedy farces; *Orestes* is presumably the *Horestes* mentioned above among the early tragi-comedies; only one tragedy, and that an historical play, appears in either list. We receive the impression of a repertoire composed mainly of late medieval or early humanist moralities and interludes, with a faint infusion of popular romantic drama based on classical legend and of chronicle history. From what we know of the extant examples we can assert with assurance that all these dramas must have been crude affairs, but they possessed what the theatre of Italy lacked— a sound foundation and a tradition. The moralities brought into the sixteenth century the high seriousness of the medieval stage and the interludes its sense of fun.

As the years went by certainly new plays were added to the store. In the Court records of the seventies titles of a different kind begin to appear: *Lady Barbara, Iphigenia, Fortune, Alcmæon, Quintus Fabius, The Painter's Daughter, The Three Sisters of Mantua, The Cruelty of a Stepmother,* and *Murderous Michael*—titles suggestive of a dual development of classical themes and of realistic material. Along with these, however, plays of a thoroughly romantic sort seem to predominate: *Cloridon and Radiamanta, Theagenes and Chariclea, Perseus and Andromeda, Predor and Lucia, Mamillia, Herpetalus the Blue Knight and Perobia, The Solitary Knight, The Irish Knight.* None of these have come down to us, but one precious example of a kindred play almost certainly demonstrates their general characteristics.

This is *The Historie of the two valiant Knights, Syr Clyomon Knight of the Golden Sheeld, sonne to the King of Denmarke And Clamydes the white Knight, sonne to the King of Suavia.* Although not printed until 1599, there can be no doubt but that it belongs to a period about 1570 and that it represents the kind of chivalric adventurous drama which, from the evidence of the titles of plays given at Court, we may assume to have been popular then.

A stranger farrago of diverse elements has hardly ever been included in a single set of scenes. In the old 'fourteener' measure—

"Well," says Quince to Bottom, "we will have such a prologue; and it shall be written in eight and six"—the author concentrates on the story of his two knights, but introduces along with them personages of the most diverse kinds. The opening lines might almost have been uttered by the artisans in the enchanted wood near Athens. Clamydes enters:

> As to the weary wandering wights, whom waltering waves environ,
> No greater joy of joys can be than when from out the ocean
> They may behold the altitude of billows to abate,
> For to observe the longitude of seas in former rate—
> And having then the latitude of sea-room for to pass,
> Their joy is greater through the grief than erst before it was.

Shortly afterwards Sir Clyomon comes on stage to enact a comic scene with Subtle Shift the Vice. Crude intrigue and excitement follow at the Court of the King of Suavia, and then suddenly we are confronted by "King Alexander the Great, as valiantly set forth as may be, and as many soldiers as can." Soon he is associated with a giant, Bryan Sans Foy, and with Patranius, "King of the Strange Marshes." There is fighting, there is love-making, there are horn-pipes and funerals.

The whole drama is almost as ludicrous as "Pyramus and Thisbe," yet within it is embedded the seed out of which grew the rich flourish of the Elizabethan stage. Alexander and Bryan and Subtle Shift meet on one platform: the classic age unites with chivalric romance and with the spirit of the moralities. *Clyomon and Clamydes* is absurd, but it is absurd in the right way. Its tissue of diverse elements is no more ridiculous than the mingling together of a mythical Theseus and Hippolita, a King and Queen of Fairy, and a group of Elizabethan artisans in a wood near Athens. Shakespeare knew this, realizing that the best in this kind are but shadows, and the worst are no worse if imagination amend them.

With plays such as these the players delighted their audiences. They began, too, to exploit the realm of the history play. Before 1548 John Bale had penned his *Kynge Johan*, in which the morality drama with its abstractions was beginning to assume a new form. King John is paired in this play with Cardinal Pandulph and the Pope, but their companions are England, Clergy, Private Wealth, Dissimulation, Usurped Power, and Treason. Not more than forty years later we hear of the comic actor Tarlton doubling the parts of a judge and a clown in a play of Henry V, and there is some reason to believe that in *The Famous Victories of Henry the Fifth* (printed 1598) we may have a mangled text of the very drama in which, as one of the Queen's Men, he appeared on that occasion.

The Famous Victories, well known because of its connexions with Shakespeare's later trilogy, is the earliest dramatic chronicle extant, and no doubt gives a fair picture of what its lost companions were like. As it has come down to us it possibly represents a rough running-together of a pair of plays, but, faulty as its text may be, its general tone, we may believe, reflects the spirit in which such works were written. Comic scenes preponderate, and in the serious portions nothing more is attempted than a bare presentation of sentiment. A barrenness in language and concept is everywhere evident. Yet the scenes have movement, and it is easy to understand how appealing this panorama of history must have proved to audiences as yet untutored in the possibilities of the poetic drama.

The episode recorded of Tarlton took place "at the Bull in Bishopsgate," and this fact reminds us that the rapidly growing professional companies were now giving regular performances in London and elsewhere. Just as the Spanish actors seized upon the convenient *corrales*, their English contemporaries found the Elizabethan inn-yard excellently suited to their purposes. The main archway provided an entrance where money could be taken by door-keepers; the galleries offered more comfortable accommodation for those who desired to be separated from the crowd in the yard below; a platform stage could readily be erected on trestles at the farther end, and to this access was easy from the inn-doors themselves. We may imagine *Clyomon and Clamydes* and *The Famous Victories* presented in such surroundings, without scenery, but with full appeal made to the imaginations of the audience.

In the year 1576 a long step forward was made. The Red Lion Inn, the Bull, the Bell, the Bel Savage, and the Cross Keys found the actors moving into a newly erected building just outside Bishopsgate: the work of James Burbage, it was called the Theatre. Immediately successful, this first permanent home of theatrical entertainment in London was soon followed by the near-by Curtain (1577), by Newington Butts (before 1580), by the Rose (1587), south of the river, by the Swan (c. 1595), and by the famous Globe (1599).

For the model of his theatre Burbage might have gone to the kind of staging utilized by the boy-players associated with the Court. The same year that the Theatre was opened (1576) a room in the ancient Blackfriars monastery was converted into a playhouse by Richard Farrant, Master of the Children of Windsor Castle and deputy to the Master of the Children of the Chapel

Royal. Here, apparently, they established the type of production which was already familiar to them in their command performances —wherein various localities were, as in France, set upon the stage at the same time.

The device was liable and congruent, as Holofernes might have said, and we could very easily imagine its being adapted by Burbage for his first theatrical venture. Happily, it was not. Had it been, the development of the Elizabethan drama would almost certainly have been seriously retarded. What was needed by the age was freedom and an air of expansiveness: the restrictions imposed by the simultaneous setting might well have proved fatal to the genius of Shakespeare and his companions.

Instead a highly effective compromise was—by design or not we cannot tell—arrived at. A great open platform provided ample scope for movement; beyond was an inner stage, which could serve, when occasion demanded, as a particular locality; while above, a gallery divided by pillars and curtains gave opportunity for vertical action as opposed to the horizontal action on the stage below. Intimacy between audience and actors was effected; the actors were not tempted to ruin themselves by spending vast sums on scenery; the imagination of the spectators was freely called into play; and the authors were left free to develop their themes as they cared, with the knowledge that here was an excellent platform for the speaking of noble lines and that such noble lines were imperatively demanded from them if the imperfections of the stage were to be overcome. There was a challenge to the poet here, and an incentive.

Basically, as we have already suggested, this Elizabethan stage was similar in principle, and even in particular form, to the Spanish, but there was one essential difference. The *corrales* appear always to have been makeshift affairs, and even in the time of Calderón the arrangements made for both actors and audiences were crude. When foreign visitors came to London—even those who were acquainted with the theatres of Italy—they agreed that the English playhouses were sumptuous. They possessed a dignity and a distinction lacking in Spain. The players attained an appropriate home, and, although there were Puritans who grumbled, the acting profession secured a position of no mean rank. Servants of lords, even of royalty, Shakespeare's fellows were no vagabonds; the poet-actor could write himself gentleman and retire in his latter years to the best house in his native town; his contemporary, Edward Alleyn, could establish the College of God's Gift at Dulwich.

With the erection of the Theatre in 1576 the scene was set, with every augury propitious. As yet the English drama had produced nothing of any significance, but, if an Ariosto and a Machiavelli were wanting, the conditions were such as to provide fertile soil for the flourishing of genius. In a united kingdom looking eagerly towards the future men of all ranks were displaying interest in the stage—in the one stage, that of professional actors. Love of words was universal, and audiences were eager to listen to high-astounding terms. No single writer had appeared, as in Italy, to stamp his impress too soon on dramatic material; no critics of any consequence were giving laws to the liberty-loving age. In the theatre a new stage form had been evolved, with its potentialities still to explore, and orientated not towards the scenic decorator, but towards the actor interpreting the playwright's words.

Where the playhouse of Italy was ruined by its cleavage into amateur and professional, by the weight of classical theory, and by the dispersed interests of its Courts; where that of France was inhibited by the confining political conditions of the time, by the failure to develop a suitable stage, and by the late appearance of its first professional dramatist, Hardy; where that of Spain, despite the near approach it made to complete success, was prevented from reaching the highest levels because of its provincialism and because its greatest author came at a time when already the force of the Renaissance was being dissipated; the stage in England in 1580 found itself most fortunate. There was now a home for the drama, while a group of eager young university men were preparing themselves for the exercise of playwriting in popular terms. Robert Greene was then twenty-two years of age, Thomas Lodge twenty-three, John Lyly twenty-six, George Peele twenty-three; with them was associated Thomas Kyd, a learned if not an academic man, aged twenty-two; while there were another two youths, both then aged sixteen, the one a student at St John's College, Oxford, and the other possibly acting as assistant to his wool-dealing father, who were soon to join the ranks of London's dramatists. Again, fortunately, the former of the latter pair, Christopher Marlowe, hurried to the theatre a few years before his companion, so that the young William Shakespeare, coming to the stage at about twenty-eight years of age, arrived not only in time to catch the Renaissance spirit at its most glorious, but with models immediately behind him unstaled by custom and awaiting his refinement.

CLOUD MACHINES AT TURIN IN THE SEVENTEENTH CENTURY

INIGO JONES: SETTING FOR "THE SHEPHERD'S PARADISE"

By courtesy of the Duke of Devonshire

SHAKESPEARE AND HIS PREDECESSORS

WILLIAM SHAKESPEARE began and ended his work with comedies. At the beginning of his career stand *Love's Labour's Lost* (c. 1594), *The Taming of the Shrew* (1594), and *The Comedy of Errors* (c. 1593); at its conclusion stands *The Tempest* (1611). He it was who gave colour and composition to the comedy of romance, but many suggestions for its development he owed to his younger contemporaries.

THE COMEDY OF ROMANCE

The romantic comedy ultimately takes its tone from the tragicomic efforts of the kind exemplified in *Clyomon and Clamydes*, but plays of this kind clearly had two outstanding weaknesses: they were dominated by no general mood and in style they were deplorably weak. They lacked both form and spirit.

About the year 1584 a young Oxford student named John Lyly became associated with the boy-players of the Chapel Royal and St Paul's, and for them he wrote a play, *Campaspe*, described on the title-page as "A most excellent Comedie" and in the title-headings to individual pages as "A tragical Comedie." The same year saw the appearance of a second drama, *Sapho and Phao*, and shortly after came *Galathea*. In these works appeared a tone at once old and new.

The author quite clearly is one who knows his classic authors; there is no jumbling of Alexander and Subtle Shift here. The scene of *Campaspe* is Athens, and the characters are all suitably named. He is, too, a man interested in style. The old fourteeners have vanished, and in their place appears a highly artificial form of elegant prose: "Parmenio," says Clitus, at the very beginning of the play,

> Parmenio, I cannot tell whether I should more commend in Alexander's victories courage or courtesy, in the one being a resolution without fear, in the other a liberality without custom. Thebes is razed, the people not racked; towers thrown down, bodies not thrust aside a conquest without conflict, and a cruel war in a mild peace.

I

This may sound stilted, and the antithetical balancing of the phrases seem tedious; but at least there is no mere blundering and floundering here. The author of *Clyomon and Clamydes* stamps his way through the world of words ignorant of his goal; Lyly is sure-footed, and, certain of his purpose, he steps delicately.

The style accords with the contents. Tragic elements are here softened, comic scenes are made less clownish; over all is spread a strange illumination, so that high and low lose their contrasts, so that thrill is reduced to interest and laughter to delight. Listen to three servants talking—Manes, attendant upon the crusty Diogenes, Granichus, upon Plato, and Psyllus, upon Apelles, the painter:

MANES: I serve instead of a master a mouse, whose house is a tub, whose dinner is a crust, and whose bed is a board.

PSYLLUS: Then art thou in a state of life which philosophers commend: a crumb for thy supper, a hand for thy cup, and thy clothes for thy sheets—for "*Natura paucis contenta.*"

GRANICHUS: Manes, it is pity so proper a man should be cast away upon a philosopher; but that Diogenes, that dog, should have Manes, that dog-bolt, it grieveth nature and spiteth art: the one having found thee so dissolute, I would say—in body, the other so single—singular—in mind.

Their accents are different, but their tone is the same as that of Apelles while he stands at his canvas painting the fair Campaspe:

APELLES: I shall never draw your eyes well, because they blind mine.

CAMPASPE: Why then, paint me without eyes, for I am blind.

APELLES: Were you ever shadowed before of any?

CAMPASPE: No: and would you could so now shadow me that I might not be perceived of any!

There can be no possibility of claiming that Lyly was a great genius, but in his application of form and style to the popular tragi-comedy he laid the foundation-stone for the later comedy of romance. He showed that this tragi-comedy could be made truly effective only by creating a particular mood in the minds of the audience, and he indicated how an appreciation of classical forms could be put into service for the creation of a kind of drama of which neither Rome nor Greece could even have dreamed.

His plays, however, were written for the boy-players, and although these boys were virtually professionals too, the strength of the new theatre lay in the hands of the adult companies. Lyly's delicately graceful comedies were suited for boyish treble; the other actors sought for deeper tones. For the Children of the Chapel George Peele penned his *Arraignment of Paris* about the same time as Lyly wrote his *Campaspe*, and in its verse, delicate and fantastic though it be, we hear these deeper tones being sounded. They become more pronounced in *The Old Wives' Tale* (*c.* 1591), while they sound clearly enough in the plays written for the adult actors by his friend Robert Greene—*Friar Bacon and Friar Bungay* (*c.* 1589) and *James the Fourth* (*c.* 1591). In these the tradition of *Clyomon and Clamydes* is perhaps more apparent than in Lyly's writings, yet at the same time there is both a firmer handling of dramatic tools and a greater variety of material. The main scenes of *James the Fourth* concern love and intrigue at the Court of Scotland, but the whole action is preceded by an introduction in which figure Oberon, King of the Fairies, and a misanthropic Bohan: in *Friar Bacon and Friar Bungay* the supernatural joins with the natural; in both we move from high to low, from clownery to romantic seriousness. The staple instrument for dialogue here is the blank-verse medium, a form introduced many years before by the poet Surrey and put to dramatic use, but dully and awkwardly, in *Gorboduc*. In Greene's hand blank verse begins to give out some of its true melodies. Individual lines, such as

> Why, thinks King Henry's son that Margaret's love
> Hangs in the uncertain balance of proud time?

exhibit ease and strength, while throughout the measure is employed effectively for the give-and-take of dramatic speech. "My lord," asks Ida, "why are you thus impatient?" and Ateukin replies:

> Not angry, Ida, but I teach this knave
> How to behave himself among his betters.
> Behold, fair countess, to assure your stay
> I here present the signet of the king,
> Who now by me, fair Ida, doth salute you;
> And since in secret I have certain things
> In his behalf, good madam, to impart,
> I crave your daughter to discourse apart.

There is no distinction in these lines, but there is here something of great significance—an instrument for dramatic language capable of almost any note that a greater poet may care to play.

In his earliest essays in comedy the young Shakespeare shows himself a follower of these men, but as yet a trifle unsure. We do not know the precise order of his first plays, but the impression we have is of a young man experimenting. *Love's Labour's Lost* is satirical and impertinent, the work of a youth who looks with amused contempt at the follies around him; *The Taming of the Shrew* is a gay flight on the wings of Italianate farce; in *The Comedy of Errors* homage is paid to the spirit of Plautus. Yet, if we look with care, the quality which enriches the later dramas is to be discerned here in embryo. The satire in *Love's Labour's Lost* turns in upon itself; laughing at Berowne, Shakespeare smiles at his own follies, and even Holofernes is not merely an objectively conceived figure of fun, a butt for the intellectuals. There is a warmth here and an originality in concept unlike anything contributed by the preceding playwrights; the structure may be somewhat mechanically composed, the characters may want depth, and the merriment may be more than a little forced, but, imperfect as these comedies are, we recognize in them the presence of a distinctive atmosphere.

From these plays alone, however, we could not have told what course in the realm of comedy this dramatist would pursue. The satire of *Love's Labour's Lost*, the farcical laughter of the other two plays, might indeed have suggested that this young recruit to the stage was likely to depart from the line of romantic comedy and to aim rather at the creation of scenes instinct with wit and replete with ludicrous situation.

Soon, however, comes the full achievement, and all doubt is set at rest. In *A Midsummer Night's Dream* (c. 1595) there is complete technical mastery and a brilliant development of the romantic mood through which Lyly and Greene had been able to harmonize diverse elements. The heroic Theseus, the commonplace Ægeus, the lovers, the fairies, the artisans, are all swept into one pervasive melodic pattern. We are in a world of dreams where everything seems double: the fanciful and the real may barely be separated, and a charm is wrought upon our senses. Nothing quite like this has previously appeared in the history of the drama.

In *A Midsummer Night's Dream* the fancy-weaving imagination is given free play, but Shakespeare is not prepared to make this a model for his other romantic comedies. Oberon is not to find a companion until, at the close of the dramatist's career, Ariel is created to minister to Prospero's magic. The main line of development is marked much more clearly in a less distinguished play, *The Two Gentlemen of Verona* (c. 1593). With its Sir Eglamour, the squire of dames, with its fancifully conceived outlaws, and with its basic theme of friendship and love, its chivalric-romantic origins are manifest, and with its choice of an Italian setting it is linked with most of the comedies immediately to follow. For background

Lyly had selected a vaguely classical world of history or legend, Greene had chosen an equally vague pseudo-historical realm. It would seem as though the young Shakespeare quite deliberately had decided, after experimenting with the legendary in *A Midsummer Night's Dream*, to make Italy the spiritual home of his comic characters. The device has certain obvious advantages. It provides distance, but not too great distance: the events are taking place in a far-off land of music, of colour, and of sunshine, and yet, by the exercise of the imagination, they may be conceived of as almost contemporaneous. There is the opportunity here for the creation of what, after all, is the basic paradox of the theatre—the arousing of a mood of strange wonder and at the same time the making of this wonder seem real and true.

The *Merchant of Venice* (c. 1596), *Much Ado about Nothing* (c. 1598), *Twelfth Night* (c. 1601)—all of these take Italy for their scene, and in all the quality of romantic realism is dominant. To keep this quality in perfect equilibrium, however, is a task hard even for one of Shakespeare's genius; sentimental romanticism is easy of attainment, but realistic romanticism demands for its preservation and development such delicate handling of characters and of actions as to make the path of any dramatist essaying its creation fraught with perils. *Much Ado about Nothing* and *Twelfth Night* catch the mood perfectly, but *The Merchant of Venice* and *Measure for Measure* (c. 1604) show signs of its shattering. Even if we are prepared to see in the portrait of Shylock nothing more than a comic composition or to view the theme of *Measure for Measure* merely as a kind of fairy-tale, we must recognize that the presence of evil and the ever-looming threat of death tend to disrupt the quiet mood and the good-humoured laughter. There are accents here as threatening as those which rudely interrupt the pastoral grace of *Lycidas*.

The spirit of Shakespeare's comedy of romance is something entirely new, differing alike from the ecstatic abandonment of Aristophanes, from Plautan scenes of hilarious merriment, from Terence's sophisticated sentimentalism, and from the crudities of medieval farce. There is a kind of transcendentalism here, where the objective and the subjective meet; where the author is at one with his characters and yet, godlike, above them; where intellectual laughter becomes emotional; where clowns become wise and wise men fools. We scoff at ridiculous absurdities in these plays and discover that we are mocking ourselves; in superior manner we look down on the Dogberries and find that they alone hold the true secrets in their clumsy hands. Over all breathes an atmosphere of natural beauty wherein the common flowers of the fields have ideal implications and the hedgerows are invested with a strange unwonted grace.

This is not mere pastoralism, such as was being exploited by Guarini and Tasso. Its difference from that, indeed, is seen nowhere more clearly than in Shakespeare's one play of shepherds and their nymphs—*As You Like It* (*c.* 1600). Superficially considered, the comedy seems an ordinary pastoral, with its banished lords in the leafy greenwood, its Corins and its Sylviuses, yet throughout all its scenes runs a strain that is the very antithesis of pastoralism. With consummate art Shakespeare plays upon his rustic pipes, and then, in a single line, reveals smilingly that he realizes not only the rusticity, but also the artificiality, of his instrument. "Pray you, no more of this," cries Rosalind after she has taken part with Phebe and Sylvius in a highly artificial melodic dialogue; "'tis like the howling of Irish wolves against the moon." We listen to pleasant praise of the free life of the forest and are almost persuaded that the author would wish for himself nothing better than a bed of leaves and a drowsy peace far from the busy hum of men, when suddenly, on news that the banished exiles may return to their homes, the Duke turns from extolling "this life more sweet than that of painted pomp," and from protestations that he would change his condition on no account, to frank admission of the unhappiness of his existence and of the "shrewd days and nights" he and his companions have suffered in their enforced retirement. All through the course of the play a gentle ironic scepticism irradiates its sentiments: Shakespeare loves the greenwood, but no one is more conscious of its prickly discomforts.

Although the scene of these dramas be the Forest of Arden, or antique Athens, or an Italian city, the characters are all recognizably Elizabethan, and little attempt is made to disguise their native habiliments. At the same time, Shakespeare reveals a power far beyond that of Lope de Vega or Calderón, who also peopled their strange localities with persons of their own age and clime. To a supreme measure, the English dramatist possessed knowledge of basic human nature, so that where the Spanish playwrights were unable or unwilling to distinguish the temporary from the eternal and that which depends on social convention from that which is essential, he is granted the skill to present, in his Elizabethan persons, figures of permanent interest. We need no knowledge of life in sixteenth-century London or Stratford to understand a Rosalind or a Viola; Touchstone wears a vanished motley, but his thoughts are not of one age; Claudios and Dogberries, Lysanders and Bottoms, are as common to-day, and everywhere, as they were in Shakespeare's time.

If an exquisite sense of balance, poising these plays between the two extremes of reality and the ideal, distinguishes the characters and the themes, no less is this sense of balance evident in the medium employed. Taking over the blank verse of his immediate predecessors, Shakespeare gives it flexibility in body and spirit. It hovers between rich lyricism and the common speech of men. At moments the dialogue sings melodiously, at others it has the simple directness of familiar utterance. The blank verse may be richly stocked with ore, or it may descend to such phrases as: "When are you married, madam?—Why, every day, to-morrow. Come, go in"; "If you go on thus, You will kill yourself"; "Away! I will not have to do with you." For further variety there is the medium of prose itself, with its diverse stops capable of making it the appropriate utterance of a Doll Tearsheet or of Hamlet's reflections upon man. Here too is a distinction between the English and the Spanish stages. The measures that Lope de Vega and Calderón knew were supple, but their artificiality could not permit of the scope that the Elizabethan blank verse and prose can give. The former are inclined to tinkle, where the latter yield subtle harmonies and deep diapasons. In the end drama is a creation in words, and for its development it depends more than perhaps we are accustomed to realize upon the provision of a suitable instrument—an instrument which may be exquisitely attuned to one age, but which may not serve for another. Shakespeare's genius must have been aided considerably by the fortunate circumstances that he found such an instrument—the potentialities of which had not yet been fully explored—apt in its accord with the ordinary language of his time.

THE LATER TRAGI-COMEDIES

With *Measure for Measure* the series of Shakespearian comedies of romance comes to an end, although some of its tones were to be sounded again, with variations, in the tragi-comedies of his last years. *Cymbeline* (c. 1609), *The Winter's Tale* (c. 1610), and *The Tempest* (1611) are plays difficult to assess aright. Some readers find in them a groping towards a newer, and more 'philosophical,' form of theatre; others see them merely as essays made by the aging Shakespeare in the style of his younger contemporaries Beaumont and Fletcher; by some they are treated as deeply symbolic; others are equally certain that they are mere fairy-tales.

Three things are incontrovertible: that they differ markedly in spirit from the early comedies, even although we may trace likenesses in themes and in characters; that they do betray kinship of mood with the plays of Beaumont and Fletcher; and that in this mood they come closer than any of the other plays to the spirit of the Spanish stage. What is not sure is the precise relationship between Shakespeare's work and that of his companions, and to that is added the still greater doubt concerning the purpose which impelled him to adopt this style of drama.

In *Cymbeline* the atmosphere of *King Lear* has turned tragi-comic. We are back in Roman Britain, and villainy unadulterated reveals itself; a heroine self-reliant as Cordelia, and as tender, is the centre of the plot. Whereas, however, in the one drama the tempest of passion rises until it engulfs all the characters, in the other looming clouds suddenly part and sunshine descends on the world. If *Cymbeline* reminds us of *Lear*, *The Winter's Tale* recalls *Othello*. The passion of Leontes almost parallels that of the Moor, but again the sun shines forth and the tragic gloom is dissipated: the maligned wife is condemned to death, but lives, through seventeen long years, to bless with her forgiving smiles the repentant husband. It is as though a Desdemona of forty were greeting with mature love an Othello with silver in his hair. Both these plays agree in having extensive canvases, in time and in place, but in the third of the series, *The Tempest*, we encounter a drama almost as strict in its retention of the unities as even the severest of the classicists would have wished. This fact alone separates it from its companions, and that separation is increased by its basic theme. Where they recall the tragedies, this is reminiscent of the early comedies. Prospero has no kinsman in all Shakespeare's work save Oberon, Ariel none save Robin Goodfellow. The mood in which the three plays were written must have been fundamentally the same, yet perhaps we do wrong to treat them together as though they were all manifestations of an exactly similar spirit. A subtle difference divides them: *Cymbeline* and *A Winter's Tale* are the creation of a tragic dramatist prepared to ease the tensity of his passion; in *The Tempest* we have a drama written by a comic playwright whose vision of life has been deepened, enriched, and made more solemn. There is, indeed, justification for interpreting this play of Prospero as a deliberately conceived farewell to the stage.

THE HISTORY PLAYS

From *The Tempest*, at the close of Shakespeare's career, return must now be made to the very start of his apprentice work. At the same time as he was experimenting in comedy he also found exercise for his pen in the composition of drama based on the history of England. Unfortunately, once more the relationship between his work in this kind and that of his contemporaries is unsure. *Henry VI* is now tending to be credited wholly or largely to his pen, rather than to those of his elder contemporaries. *Richard III* probably, but not certainly, came in 1592 or 1593, *King John* about 1595, and *Richard II* either the same or the following year. Peele's *Edward I* was printed in 1593, but it is impossible to say what time elapsed between its composition and its publishing; Marlowe's *Edward II* was printed the following year, and may be dated about 1592. All we can say with assurance is that the history play, probably in a crude form, was being exploited in the years before Shakespeare came to London, but that the development of the form seems to have been his own characteristic contribution to the theatre. He may have owed in inspiration to Marlowe, but just as easily can we argue for his impress on that author's single history drama.

Whether or not *Edward II*—not the most interesting but decidedly the best-fashioned of all the plays left by that rebellious and ill-starred genius of the Renaissance, Christopher Marlowe—was written before Shakespeare presented the stage with his first history dramas, it serves a useful purpose for comparison with these. In Marlowe's hands the story of Edward's reign becomes an isolated study of conflicting temperaments, with an analysis of kingly weakness. Opposite the astute, ambitious, and ruthless Mortimer is placed the figure of the dissolute, perverted monarch, gifted with a certain royalty of character, but fatally irresolute in his purposes. The scenes have undoubted strength, yet a reading of them leaves us unsatisfied. Edward's death does not arouse the tragic passions; rather do we experience a feeling of pitiful contempt as the gay king at the end lies in his unsavoury dungeon and goes miserably to his death. If it came first, Shakespeare could have gained from this work a conception of the manner in which the old chronicles might be vivified by the interpretation of their chief characters, but for the characteristic quality of his own histories he had to rely on his own genius.

That characteristic quality is suggested, if but crudely, in the three parts of *Henry VI* (*c.* 1592), where, on a vast canvas, the story of

Henry's reign is discursively told, leaving Edward as the reigning king, but with threats of future disaster in the ominous person of Richard, Duke of Gloucester. There is not much of highest praise that can be given to this rambling trilogy, yet we recognize an element in it lacking in *Edward II.* Whereas that was an isolated drama, these plays, besides dealing with that cardinal fact in English medieval history—the cleavage between the red rose and the white, with the resultant Wars of the Roses—suggest, at least vaguely, an action preceding the opening scenes of the first part, and very definitely hint at what is to come after the close of the third part's final scene. The initial lines bewail the death of King Henry V; at the end there is sharp juxtaposition of Gloucester's self-confessed villainy and of King Edward's dream of happiness:

> And now what rests but that we spend the time
> With stately triumphs, mirthful comic shows,
> Such as befits the pleasures of the court?
> Sound drums and trumpets! farewell sour annoy!
> For here, I hope, begins our lasting joy.

When these lines were written, it would seem, *Richard III* (c. 1593) was already in the author's mind, and with this play we enter a new realm. Here the discursive arrangement of scenes has vanished, and in its stead all concentration is placed on the personality of one man. Richard is a demon incarnate, made sympathetic only by the very flamboyance of his evil, by his flashes of sardonic humour, and by that rift in his armour of baseness which eventually causes his assurance to crack and crumble. Already Shakespeare has achieved, at least in rough terms, his vision of tragic action, with the forces of hell let loose upon the world, only to dissipate themselves in their self-destroying hate, leaving us worn with travail yet conscious that a new era is to begin. When Henry of Richmond ascends to Richard's throne there is an anticipation of Malcolm's succession to *Macbeth.* In addition, Shakespeare has made his characteristic contribution to the history play—the creation of a drama with its own unity which is yet merely part of a larger concept.

Why, after thus creating *Richard III,* the dramatist turned to the isolated *King John* (c. 1595) we cannot tell: perhaps it was merely because his fellows in the theatre desired to have a reworking of an older drama on this monarch's reign; perhaps he had boyish memories of Worcester, where John lies buried, to urge him on. In handling his material he has striven to paint a picture of an irresolute monarch who, however, possesses sufficient royalty to summon forth the devoted service of the only truly living person in the play, the Bastard Faulconbridge.

The irresolution of John is paralleled, but with a notable variation, in the king who gives his name to *Richard II* (1595–96), a play in which is inaugurated another and a greater tetralogy. The three parts of *Henry VI* and *Richard III* had narrated events following the death of Henry V; *Richard II* is the initial section of a second dramatic sequence telling of the actions which led to the reign of the hero of Agincourt. Once more Shakespeare has created a tragedy, although of a sharply diverse kind. Where Richard of Gloucester was a villain and the moving spirit in the circle within which he moved, Richard II is depicted as a man of worth placed in circumstances false to his nature. He is a poet who loves to play with fancies, not a man of action such as a king should be. His irresolution, unlike that of King John, is at once motivated and made dramatically arresting.

In misery Richard goes to his death, overawed and overpowered by the masterful Henry Bolingbroke, Duke of Hereford, who ascends to the throne as King Henry IV. The play, like *Henry VI* ends on a continuing note of ironic content. Mourning the Richard whom he has slain, Henry declares:

> I'll make a voyage to the Holy Land,
> To wash this blood off from my guilty hand:
> March sadly after; grace my mournings here;
> In weeping after this untimely bier.

The first part of *Henry IV* opens with the King's reference to the conflicts which have prevented him from fulfilling his vow; a moment of peace has come, and now he proposes at last to seek "the sepulchre of Christ." No sooner have these words been uttered, however, than news comes of the breaking out of fresh trouble in Wales, and there is the commencement of a fresh unfolding of evil strife.

Yet in the second scene we are suddenly carried into a world utterly alien to anything in the earlier histories. With the first line spoken by a greasy, corpulent, white-haired knight—"Now, Hal, what time of day is it, lad?"—we move unexpectedly out of the tragic into the comic world. For this Shakespeare had the cue in the earlier drama, *The Famous Victories of Henry V*, already mentioned, but its crude farce is here deepened into a humour pre-eminent among all the comedies of the age. With consummate mastery Shakespeare keeps these Falstaff scenes as a foil to the serious action, and at the same time makes use of them to reveal the humanity of the man who was to be the hero of this tetralogy —Prince Hal, the later Henry V. There is an almost epic sweep in this series of plays, from the lyrically poetic and tragic tone of *Richard II*, through the variegated spirit of *Henry IV*, on to the triumphant conclusion, when the son of Bolingbroke reveals the true kingly qualities so lacking in all the other monarchs whose failures Shakespeare had previously depicted.

This, except for the later *Henry VIII* (*c.* 1610), possibly written in collaboration with Fletcher, marks the close of Shakespeare's career as a writer of history plays, and it was virtually the close of the Elizabethan history play itself. The great reigns of the past had been exhausted, and the devastating Wars of the Roses had been given profound theatrical presentation. For others there was but little left to do. Here and there, sporadically, a history drama made its appearance during the years immediately following, but since Shakespeare had given such consummate expression to the form, the excitement of invention, the joy of exploration, had gone.

THE TRAGEDIES

If Shakespeare owed much to his predecessors for his comedy of romance and no less for his exploitation of the history play, and if, paradoxically, these two genres were his own creation in their final achievement, the same paradox is equally true of his tragedy. That came from his predecessors, yet was unmistakably his own.

In the complete realization of the tragic spirit exemplified in the four great dramas written between 1602 and 1606 several distinct elements are fused into unity. These elements may be described as the medieval-philosophical, the morality, the Marlovian, and the Kydian.

By the medieval-philosophical is intended that concept of tragedy which sees it as any story (not necessarily dramatic) showing great princes at the height of their estates about to fall calamitously to disaster. The moralists declared that the mission of these stories was to demonstrate the vanity of earthly happiness or to warn us of the instability of fortune. Basically such a definition of tragedy agrees with that of the early classical critics, who found the criteria of the tragic in its disastrous conclusion and in its concentration upon royal personages.

The morality tradition, while by no means directly concerned with the arousing of the tragic mood, laid stress upon the eternal conflict of good and evil, while in practice it set forth, crudely but not ineffectively, the inner struggle within man of these two forces. Here good was always triumphant in the end, but that end might come—and generally did come—only at the very conclusion of each drama, so that essentially the morality play was concerned with an exhibition of evil rampant against a field of eternity)

In the hands of the authors of *Gorboduc, Tancred and Gismund,* and their like attempts had been made to create a native English tragedy, but all evidence seems to show that until about 1587 the popular stage had failed to produce anything of worth in this kind. Rude tragi-comedies, not tragedies, satisfied the general audiences to whom the early dramatists made their appeal. That these general audiences, however, were ready to welcome something sterner is proved conclusively by the immediate success of Marlowe's plays.

Christopher Marlowe, born in the same year as Shakespeare, was a more fiery spirit than his greater contemporary. Where Shakespeare's genius manifested itself comparatively late in his career and continued to burn steadily through two decades, Marlowe's flared forth in rich splendour and vanished, with his own death, after a brief few years. No one, of course, can say what he might or might not have accomplished had he lived, but the very brilliance of the flower suggests—though it cannot prove—that its endurance might have been slight. It burned too fiercely to have lasting qualities.

Of the brilliance of the torch he held Marlowe was thoroughly conscious. Throughout the plays of Shakespeare there is little evidence of any flamboyant vainglory; there is no indication that he himself realized the extent to which he was recreating the material he found to hand. He may have known his own power, but of such knowledge no indication is given in his writings. The very first words of Marlowe uttered on the stage are a declaration of defiance and of self-assurance. From jigging veins of rhyming mother-wits he loudly promises to bring us to the high-astounding terms in which his *Tamburlaine (c.* 1587) is expressed.

This was precisely what the age had been waiting for: the stage in 1587 needed a man sure of his aims and deliberately intent on dramatic reform. Before Shakespeare, with consummate ease, could consolidate and give culminating expression to the spirit of the Elizabethan audiences a forerunner had to blaze a bold trail for his feet to tread.

Tamburlaine is not a great play, but it was an inspiration. In terms apt to catch the attention of the spectators it set forth in glowing words an heroic theme with consistent seriousness. Marlowe proved that admiration and wonder alone could hold a crowded theatre silent, that no vulgar clownage was necessary as a sop to the public, and that lofty rhetoric, expressed in impassioned lines suited for an actor's delivery, held a charm of potent worth.

The success of *Tamburlaine* was followed by that of an entirely different kind of play, *Dr Faustus* (c. 1588), in which a closer approach was made to the familiar tragic form. Fundamentally the former drama had depended upon a record of achievement rather than a display of disaster. It called on men to gaze in wonderment at the power of a man who might from humblest origins rise to greatest heights; in *Dr Faustus* we are bidden to look upon a human being whose ambition leads him to uttermost ruin, and, furthermore, we are shown this hero encircled about with the insidious spirit of evil. So different was *Tamburlaine* from all preceding concepts of the tragic that men might have failed to relate it to earlier essays in this form; about *Dr Faustus* there could be no doubt: it is definitely, as the first quarto of the play states, a "tragical history."

Its innovations are many. First, it utterly defies authority and practice by abandoning completely the convention of royalty. The central figure makes not the slightest pretensions to princely lineage. He is naught but a poor scholar, distinguished from his companions solely through the extent and the intensity of his learning. Tamburlaine, if not born a king, at least becomes one, and the greater part of the drama in which he appears bears the trappings of a monarch's Court: from first to last Faust moves within the orbit of his study.

This revolutionary conception of the hero is of profound significance, since it led men to substitute a spiritual, or an inner, for an external, or a material, interpretation of the tragic essence. So long as the kingly rank was sufficient qualification the playwrights were offered no incentive to do other than clothe a dummy with ermine and gold; now Marlowe showed them that the true spirit of tragedy lay within and that the presentation of even the humblest character could arouse the deepest emotions.

The second innovation is the uniting of the tragic elements with the elements of the morality play. In every respect *Dr Faustus* is an example of the dramatic movement that produced *Everyman*. The one difference—and it is, of course, an essential difference—lies in the fact that, whereas the hero of *Everyman* is every man, the hero for the criminals is dictated, not by any desire to clear his injured name, but by a human passion—independent of time and place—to bring to justice those who have destroyed his happiness.

In introducing this type of revenge play to the stage, Kyd unwittingly did tremendous service. To win success in this genre a dramatist must pay close attention to the weaving of his scenes, and in a period as dominated by the inconsequences of the earlier style of tragi-comedy the new authors required, above all other things, experience in strict dramatic construction. Nothing could have been better adapted for the purpose of urging them towards such exercise than the play of revenge.

Thus was the stage set for Shakespeare. At first, as in comedy, the young writer failed to indicate the path he was later to take. In *Richard III* he had concentrated on a Marlovian superman, melodramatically evil as the Jew of Malta, ambitious as Tamburlaine; in *Titus Andronicus* (1594) he waded into a sea of horror and of blood. From that he moved, with startling suddenness, to *Romeo and Juliet* (*c.* 1595), which is to his tragedy what *Love's Labour's Lost* is to his comedy. Instinct with the spirit of youth, its lyric ecstasy attempts to wrest the tragic mood from a pitiful romantic tale, but the quality which animates a *Hamlet* or a *Lear* is absent from its scenes. Basically its story is akin to such plots as Shakespeare was currently using for his comedies, and although he has enwrapped the action in an atmosphere of fate or of adverse fortune, and although the very intensity of his poetic utterance carries us onward in a torrent of words, there can be no doubt but that the final impression leaves us without the soul-searing experience which comes from contemplation of the deepest forms of the tragic.

In *Richard II*, perhaps, a clearer advance towards this deeper tragic concept may be discerned. Richard's disaster springs not from the influence of external stars but from within, and this failing which leads to his downfall is closely and intimately related to the circumstances in which he finds himself. He is by no means a despicable character, but the very qualities that might otherwise have won our admiration are the cause of his ruin. Moreover, the failing in his nature, when related to the circumstances by which he is surrounded, releases an evil force engulfing both him and his country. In dim form and as yet not fully expressed the essential foundations of the later tragedies are outlined—as they were not outlined in *Romeo and Juliet.*

With *Hamlet* (*c.* 1601) the tragic idea is clear and the form exact:

Shakespeare has found that for which he had been seeking and has succeeded in welding together harmoniously all the various elements passed on to him by his predecessors. The close connexion with Kyd's revenge tragedy is patent: it is even possible that an early *Hamlet* may have come from his pen. Marlowe contributes the feeling of admiration with which the Prince's person is invested. Hamlet in a sense is Everyman, and the general plot of the play would make it fit with ease into the early definitions of the tragic.

No play has attained to greater fame than this of Shakespeare's, and its universal appeal is seen to rise from the manner in which the poet-creator has infused into a story of apparently peculiar circumstance qualities of common and eternal import. Age after age has seen itself reflected in the hero of this play, because Shakespeare, in depicting this central figure, has seized upon human qualities of wide diffusion. The result is a strange paradox: we feel admiration for Hamlet; here is the courtier, the scholar, the soldier, the man who was eminently fitted for kinghood; and at the same time we feel that Hamlet is a representative of ordinary humanity; in Hamlet is something of ourselves.

This is the effect that Lope de Vega and Calderón so frequently missed: in their heroes the inessential and the temporary concealed the basic and the eternal.

In *Othello* (c. 1604) Shakespeare turned to attempt a somewhat different kind of theme. *Hamlet*, with its extensive canvas, is unquestionably romantic; the tightness of *Othello's* structure has a classic simplicity. In *Hamlet* a prince is the hero; *Othello* takes us more into the realm of the ordinary: its setting is republican Venice and its hero a man who, although general of the Doge's forces, is placed before us mainly in his domestic capacity. Powerful as this play is, its quality is less than that of *Hamlet*. Only Shakespeare could have conceived the latter, whereas *Othello*, while possessing a strength of poetic passion, might have been conceived by another. We are moving here on a less exalted plane, and the element of mystery is absent.

King Lear (1605–6) swings us tempestuously back into the realm of the metaphysical and the exalted. As a play calculated for the stage, its virtues are perhaps below those of *Othello*, but in majesty of concept and in tensity of emotion it attempts heights far beyond. The word 'elemental' has frequently been applied to this play, and the epithet is just. In *Othello* the force of evil was symbolized in a single human figure—that of Iago; in *King Lear* the whole of nature seems to become impregnated with the vapours of hell.

The fury of the heavens contrasts markedly with the ironically calm Italian skies that vault Othello and Desdemona.

Better than any other drama the tragedy of Lear indicates those qualities which mark out Shakespeare's power. In this play the superficial sources are readily to be traced. The plot has affinities both with the typical themes of the early tragi-comedies and of the histories; bold, flamboyant portraiture appears as in Marlowe's plays, and the gloomy intrigue of Kyd is not lacking; in structure and concept, too, the spirit of the moralities is evident. Yet *King Lear* is like none of these; a new being has been wrought out of the many forces fused into one. No tragic drama had sought to achieve so much in the course of its action, and, if there is less that is strictly theatrical in its structure than there is in *Othello*, the reason lies in the fact that Shakespeare is here moving over to the very boundaries of the stage, is straining the walls of the Globe until they groan and crack.

Reference to the Globe reminds us that this, above all other plays by Shakespeare, must be visualized in terms of the stage for which he wrote. To see its illimitable conceptions degraded to the pettiness of canvas scenery is certain ruin to the idea it expresses. Here Shakespeare is calling for the fullest possible exercise of the imagination on the part of his audience, and any attempt to reproduce in artificial terms the forms surrounding the characters immediately conflicts with, and destroys, the spell of his poetic utterance. If the storm scene is enacted on a bare stage it can achieve its effect; if painted scenery is set behind the aged Lear his figure becomes tawdry and his words mere rant. If an actor succeeds in conquering such hindrances the victory is merely a personal *tour de force*.

With *Macbeth* (1605-6) we reach the end of this magnificent series of tragic dramas, and once more—although almost certainly in mangled form—there is placed before us a play of elemental scope. Already in *Julius Cæsar* (1599) Shakespeare had essayed the presentation, in theatrical form, of evil let loose upon the world, consuming and destroying in its terrible path. The earlier play, however, did not provide him with the fullest scope for the development of this conception, largely because of the presuppositions which any spectator inevitably must bring with him to a drama on such a well-known story, but partly also because the historical material could not permit of apt moulding to the dramatist's basic theme. The result was an effective theatrical piece, but not a play of deepest import.

For *Macbeth* Shakespeare could work as he willed. True, the plot was 'historical,' but only vaguely so: no member of the audience would be likely to know much of almost legendary Scottish chronicles, and the way was thus entirely open for the (creation of characters and episodes best calculated to reveal the cardinal idea that called the tragedy into being. This cardinal idea was the release of evil through an individual crime, its sweeping course of destruction, and its final self-destruction, leaving a world shattered and broken, yet in some strange way the richer for its experience) Magnificently as the central characters are placed before us, it is the theme rather than the persons that seizes on our imagination and stirs our emotions. As de Quincey so clearly realized and so brilliantly put into words, this is a play of hell in which Macbeth's dark castle, with its great doors shutting out the world of humanity, is endowed with a symbolic significance:

All action in any direction is best expounded, measured and made apprehensible, by reaction. Now apply this to the case of Macbeth. Here . . . the retiring of the human heart, and the entrance of the fiendish heart, was to be expressed and made sensible. Another world has stepped in, and the murderers are taken out of the region of human things, human purposes, human desires. They are transfigured: Lady Macbeth is "unsexed"; Macbeth has forgot that he was born of woman; both are conformed to the image of devils; and the world of devils is suddenly revealed. But how shall this be conveyed and made palpable? In order that a new world may step in, this world must for a time disappear. The murderers, and the murder, must be insulated—cut off by an immeasurable gulf from the ordinary tide and succession of human affairs—locked up and sequestered in some deep recess; we must be made sensible that the world of ordinary life is suddenly arrested—laid asleep—tranced—rocked into a dread armistice; time must be annihilated; relation to things without abolished; and all must pass self-withdrawn into a deep syncope and suspension of earthly passion. Hence it is that, when the deed is done, when the work of darkness is perfect, then the world of darkness passes away like a pageantry in the clouds: the knocking at the gate is heard; and it makes known audibly that the reaction has commenced; the human has made its reflux upon the fiendish; the pulses of life are beginning to beat again; and the re-establishment of the goings-on of the world in which we live, first makes us profoundly sensible of the awful parenthesis that had suspended them.

Such comment on *Macbeth* well illustrates the gulf that separates Shakespeare from Calderón and Lope de Vega. They were skilled dramatists with easily moving pens, but not a single one of their works, not even the philosophically conceived *autos*, bears a quality worthy of contemplation in this way. Their ideas are surface ideas, readily appreciated and capable of interpretation in intellectual terms; for the interpretation of Shakespeare an imaginative process is demanded, and intellectually conceived words must fail in the attempt to indicate his meaning.

The effect he produces is achieved by the utilization of every device offered to him by the theatre, from the physical movement of his actors upon the stage to the subtlest use of poetic imagery. In *Antony and Cleopatra* (*c.* 1606), for example, he takes a story of grand passion which had already been told and retold both by historians and by playwrights and invests it with a quality of his own. Even he, perhaps, cannot wrest out of its material a tragic atmosphere so intense as that of *Hamlet* or *Macbeth*, but, by the pervasive imagery through which he excites our minds into conceiving illimitable spaces and the very vastness of the universe, he takes a tale of consuming sexual passion, all too human, and gives it superhuman proportions. Here the temporary is wrought into the eternal.

EARLY SEVENTEENTH-CENTURY TRAGEDY AND COMEDY

A CHANGING THEATRE

By the time that Shakespeare retired from the stage the theatre was beginning to change its form. James VI of Scotland travelled southward in the year 1603 to assume the throne left vacant by Elizabeth's death, and very soon he showed that the royal parsimony which had prevented the fuller development of Court theatricals in the sixteenth century was to be replaced by lavish expenditure on scenic productions. Under the direction of the architect-designer Inigo Jones the masque rapidly assumed a position of importance.

Like the *intermezzi* and later operas of Italy, these masques existed more for show than for sense. Care no doubt went into their composition; at least one author, Ben Jonson, never ceased to press the claims of poetry, while another, John Milton, produced in *Comus* (1634) a work of delicate literary art. But, fundamentally, appeal to the eyes was inherent in the genre. When the courtiers gathered at Whitehall to witness one of these productions they forgot the words in the wonder of the scenery, the richness of the costumes, and the glittering lights with which Inigo Jones and his assistants bespangled the stage.

In the published texts of the masques we may find many lovelinesses. There are lyrics with words that sing, delicate fancies, and charmingly turned phrases, but, with the exception of *Comus*, there is not a single example in this kind, from Jonson's *Masque of Blackness* (1605) on to the elaborate productions of the reign of Charles I, culminating in Sir William D'Avenant's *Salmacida Spolia* (1639–40), which possesses any true dramatic worth. It may be amusing to revive one of these pieces for an occasional performance, yet the amusement can go little beyond historical interest and dilettante curiosity.

What is significant in the development of the Court masque is the change it wrought in the shape of the public theatre. To Whitehall Inigo Jones brought the perspective scenery of Italy, with its proscenium stage, its wings, its backcloths, its 'machines,' and its indoor lighting. The novelty was too great and too alluring not to be without its influence abroad. As the seventeenth century advanced we can easily trace a change in the typical theatre audiences, with the gradual retirement of the puritanically inclined middle classes and the taking over of the stage by the Cavaliers. That which had been in 1590 a genuinely popular entertainment, attracting all classes of the community, became by 1640 an almost exclusively courtly delight. Thus, increasingly, the same spectators as joyed in the production of the masque at Whitehall came to form the greater part of the audiences in the public playhouses: and, this being so, it would have been strange indeed had they not sought to introduce, or had they not inspired the introduction of, theatrical effects similar to those with which they were familiar at Court.

Thus is explained the general shifting from the open air to the roofed-in theatre during the early years of the seventeenth century. By 1608 Shakespeare's company was using the closed Blackfriars theatre as their winter headquarters; by 1617 the Phœnix in Drury Lane had been established, and by 1629 the Salisbury Court Playhouse. These were the typical theatres of the Caroline period, and in these scenery could be, and was, introduced—perhaps tentatively at first, but nevertheless in such a manner as to indicate that the bare, flexible stage that Shakespeare knew would soon be superseded.

DOMESTIC AND HORROR TRAGEDY

Amid these changing conditions new forms of drama necessarily arose, but, since the process of change was slow, the qualities we may call 'Elizabethan' maintained their integrity well into the reign of James I, and of these qualities two call for particular attention here.

Already about the year 1590 the public stage had witnessed the production of a tragedy called *Arden of Feversham*, in which is presented, not a story of a kingdom's downfall, but a tale of the murder of a Mr Arden by his wife, Alice. Nothing could be further removed from the principles of the 'classic' drama, yet no theatrical development could have been more natural in the circumstances of the romantic theatre. In Spain a similar set of conditions produced *The Physician of his own Honour*; although this has a courtly background and deals with aristocratic figures, the weaving of tragic scenes out of ordinary domestic circumstances is fundamentally the same as that which inspired the unknown Elizabethan author to pen his tragedy of middle-class passions. Out of romantic fervour and liberty the realistic drama was being born.

Although only one drama of this kind in England—Shakespeare's *Othello*—reaches any great height (and even this tragedy veers from the true 'domestic' scene to exploit a background of Venetian splendour and of Eastern war), the vogue of plays dealing with common characters has unquestioned interest for us as we survey the development of dramatic art in the early seventeenth century. Various records show that many dramas of domestic sort must have perished, while even those which have been preserved form a goodly little company. A flash of lurid genius illuminates *A Yorkshire Tragedy* (c. 1606); the murder of a "Master George Sanders of London, Merchant," is narrated in *A Warning for Fair Women* (printed 1599); while *Two Lamentable Tragedies* (printed 1601) tells of several similar crimes. Here, definitely, is middle-class realism, with all the sensational and moral qualities associated with that style of composition.

The middle-class atmosphere enwraps many of the works of two authors of this time—Thomas Dekker and Thomas Heywood—both of whom added to the mere delineation of murders an element which pointed unmistakably towards the problem drama of later times. The latter started his career with a peculiar romantic play entitled *The Four Prentices of London* (c. 1592), and in the course of a long journeyman's service in the theatre turned out dozens of diverse pieces exploiting historical and legendary themes; among these stand out two domestic dramas—*A Woman killed with Kindness* (1603) and *The English Traveller* (c. 1627). The former presents a happily married, fairly well-to-do gentleman, Frankford by name, who generously offers hospitality to a friend, Wendoll, and is betrayed by him. At first he will not allow his suspicions to fall on his wife; then as he watches them doubts arise in his mind, until certainty eventually is forced upon him. It is at this stage in the development of his theme that Heywood shows his originality. Instead of stabbing the guilty lovers when he finds them in each other's arms, Frankford refrains from vengeance and, in broken accents, dreams passionately and fondly for ignorance of his wife's guilt:

> O God! O God! that it were possible
> To undo things done—to call back yesterday—
> That Time could turn up his swift sandy glass,
> To untell the days and to redeem these hours;
> Or that the sun

> Could, rising from the west, draw his coach backward—
> Take from the account of Time so many minutes
> Till he had all these seasons called again,
> Those minutes and those actions done in them,
> Even from her first offence, that I might take her
> As spotless as an angel in my arms.
> But Oh! I talk of things impossible
> And cast beyond the moon!

As punishment for her sin she is sent to a neighbouring house, there to be well cared for, but condemned never to see him or her children again. Her conscience will not, however, permit her to live; gradually she fades, and as she lies dying her husband comes to see her, and, calling her wife and mother, bids her a sad farewell:

> Both those last names I do restore thee back,
> And with this kiss I wed thee once again.

That a prolific but not particularly outstanding playwright could conceive such scenes testifies to the inherent strength of the Elizabethan theatre.

The English Traveller, although marred by a comic sub-plot, has a somewhat similar atmosphere. The hero of the play, young Geraldine, returns from abroad and meets again a love of his boyhood, now the wife of the elderly Wincott. He realizes that he is still passionately in love with her, yet his fineness of temper will not allow him to wrong the husband. In a peculiarly emotional scene he pledges chastity, although the wife and he vow to marry when the old man has died. Here, as in *A Woman killed with Kindness*, Heywood introduces an original twist in the plot. By chance Geraldine discovers that this woman whom he adores is playing false with a young gallant, Delavile. His rage is that of an injured husband, but, like Frankford, he forbears from taking a bloody revenge, while she, broken by the nobleness of his spirit, dies of shame.

Thomas Dekker was a dramatist somewhat akin to Heywood, author of a large number of plays, tinged with a similar middle-class colouring, but possessed too of a romantically poetical quality. *Old Fortunatus* (1599), with its strange allegorical scenes, is a queer farrago of episodes illuminated by passages of melodious verse; *The Shoemaker's Holiday*, produced the same year, presents a racy, 'realistic' picture of master-journeymen and their apprentices in late-Elizabethan London. These first two plays of his indicate the wide range of Dekker's style, a style which led him to not ineffective satire in *Satiromastix* (1601), to exploitation of the morality play in *The Whore of Babylon* (*c.* 1605), and to the depiction of common scenes of contemporary life in such works as *Westward Ho!* (1604), *Northward Ho!* (1605), and *The Roaring Girl* (*c.* 1610). Many of these plays were written in collaboration with others, as was *The Honest Whore* (*c.* 1604–5), a drama in two parts written with Thomas Middleton. Typical of several similar theatrical writings of the time, this last work infuses into a plot of palace intrigue a story of common life. Bellafront is the courtesan referred to in the title; falling in love with Hippolito, she declares she will "prove an honest whore in being true to one, and to no more," but is rejected angrily by the man on whom she has set her affections. The second section of the drama reverses the situation, for here Hippolito sues her to be his mistress, while she, having been converted by his earlier words, refuses his suit. Although not strictly like the other domestic plays already noted, the treatment of this part of the story shows Dekker influenced partly at least by the realistic tragedies and tragi-comedies of the time.

Under the new conditions operative in the theatre, however, this vogue of bourgeois scenes rapidly disappeared, and the tragic stage more and more was given over to sensationalism and the presentation of horror. Palace intrigue rather than domestic pro-blems interested the courtly audiences: the theme of revenge, which already had attracted attention in the Elizabethan period, now be-came of greater interest, while the bold passions that had served the earlier theatres were supplanted by strange and tortured emotions.

Playwrights such as George Chapman, Philip Massinger, and Thomas Middleton form a link between the old and the new. The first of these won some virtue out of the writing of historical tragedies with philosophic content, failing to reach the highest levels only because of a lack of variety in his utterance and by a failure to develop unity out of his diverse material. Listening to Chapman's words, we have the impression of hearing Marlowe's boldly vigorous terms turned incoherent, of passion that has become forced, and of scenes framed rather for their intellectual than for their theatrical content. There is strength in the flamboyant *Bussy d'Ambois* (1604); there are flashes of true insight in the two parts of *Charles, Duke of Byron* (1608); there is an interesting attempt to present a wholly virtuous hero in *Chabot, Admiral of France* (*c.* 1613); but not a single one of these leaves us with a clear picture. The stage is cluttered with useless characters; never do we feel that Chapman is thorough master of his own conceptions.

The rhetorical note so strongly sounded in Chapman's plays becomes intensified in those of Massinger, while the glaring colours to which Dryden objected in *Bussy d'Ambois* are rendered still more blatant. With Dekker he collaborated in *The Virgin Martyr* (*c.* 1620), exploiting all the current love of spectacle and sensation. The main theme concerns the constancy of the Christian maid Dorothea, but about her circle a motley collection of wonders, from the 'fearful shape' of the devil Harpax to the heavenly Angelo, while full use is made of the dire torments meted out at the end to the heroine and her fellow-martyrs. Although six hundred years separate the two plays, *The Virgin Martyr* is strangely akin, in its mingled buffoonery and concentration upon pagan rage, to Hrotswitha's primitive little *Dulcitius*.

Rhetoric, horror, sensationalism, mar all of Massinger's other tragic dramas. Character is sacrificed to effect, and self-conscious argumentation takes the place of self-revealing lines. *The Duke of Milan* (printed 1623) is full of surprises and grisly episodes; we can take no interest in it as a whole, since sensational scenes crowd upon each other in such wise that any possibility of capturing a dominant central emotion is utterly lost. Incest and murder form the theme of *The Unnatural Combat* (*c.* 1620); torture and torment are freely exploited in *The Roman Actor* (1626).

Thomas Middleton has something of greater worth to offer. His atmosphere may be dark, with flashes of lurid light, but there is a passionate tensity in his writing that holds our attention. He too could sup on crude horror, as in *The Witch* (*c.* 1616), but a more serious purpose animated some of his other works, and, where Chapman and Massinger showed a failure to grasp their material firmly, he displays a concentration of power and an insistence in aim that reminds us of the Shakespearian model. In *Women beware Women* (*c.* 1620) the darkness of passion is almost unrelieved. One plot tells of an incestuous relation between Hippolito and his niece Isabella; another relates how Bianca, wife of Leantio, is seduced by an amorous Duke of Florence. In the end Leantio is slain in a duel, while Hippolito, Isabella, the Duke, and Bianca all perish in a masque presented in a manner reminiscent of that in *The Spanish Tragedy*. Sensationalism is beginning to run riot here, yet there is a strength, albeit tormented with loathing, inherent in the succession of dismal scenes. More impressive is *The Changeling* (1622), in which Middleton collaborated with William Rowley, a play akin to *Macbeth* in its delineation of evil breeding evil. Falling in love with Alsemero, a girl, Beatrice Joanna, commissions a needy gentleman, De Flores, to murder the man whom her father bids her marry. Although she does not know it, De Flores lusts after her and gladly accepts the task. The murder done, he returns to claim his reward; she offers him money, only to learn that it is herself he desires. In a magnificently planned scene Middleton reveals the capricious, proud, aristocratic woman, who has imagined that she can easily control this insignificant creature, gradually forced to a sense of the terrible reality. "Why," she cries, in incredulous accents,

> Why, 'tis impossible thou canst be so wicked,
> Or shelter such a cunning cruelty,
> To make his death the murderer of my honour!
> Thy language is so bold and vicious
> I cannot see which way I can forgive it
> With any modesty.

The imperious words, just faintly broken by a trembling fear, are stilled by his reply:

> Pish! You forget yourself!
> A woman dipped in blood, and talk of modesty!

When she speaks of "the distance that Creation set 'twixt thy blood and mine," she finds for answer only his contemptuous

> Look but into your conscience, read me there:
> 'Tis a true book; you'll find me there your equal.

She has truly become, as he says, "the deed's creature"—and the deed will not let her rest. Relentlessly she is driven on until she is slain by her minion.

Something of the same quality appears in *The Maid's Tragedy* (c. 1611) by Beaumont and Fletcher, two playwrights whose work in the field of tragi-comedy will call for further treatment. With a simple plot, the authors drive steadily towards their goal, and although there is here no dominant theme illuminating the actions, the characters stand out in bold and vital terms. Evadne, the King's mistress, is married by royal command to the loyal courtier Amintor, who is thus forced to abandon his first love, Aspatia. Coldly she informs him after the wedding of the truth, and he, although fired with anger, cannot lift his hand against his monarch. Evadne, however, finds herself oppressed by his reproaches and by those of his friend Melantius; secretly she prepares to destroy her royal lover, binds him to the bed in which he lies, and stabs him. Expecting Amintor's praise, she is dismayed at his horror of her deed and dies by her own hand. Unfortunately, with that tendency towards sentimentalism which becomes so patent in the plays of the seventeenth century, the authors have followed these truly impressive scenes with others in which the fragile Aspatia, dressed as a man, challenges Amintor to a duel and perishes by his hand.

Many plays of this time might merit consideration here, but obviously selection must be made if proportion is to be kept. That the dramatic urge which produced Shakespeare maintained some of its power during the reigns of James I and Charles I is certain, yet when the tragedies written during this time are put to the highest test we must admit that, brilliant though individual scenes may be, they fall far short of perfection. Sense of character-drawing becomes increasingly weaker; larger compositional values are lost; novelties in the exploitation of sensational incident grow more and more frequent; almost frenzied rhetoric and splenetic outbursts replace the rich sounds of balanced poetic utterance; for boldness of passion appears subtly degenerate emotion.

Out of the run of the earlier tragedies stand *The White Devil* (c. 1610) and *The Duchess of Malfi* (1613–14) of that dark genius John Webster. The 'White Devil' is Vittoria Corombona, wife of the spiritless Camillo, whose tempestuous desire for power causes her to encompass the murder both of her husband and of the innocent Isabella, wife of the Duke whose mistress she has become. Her character is brilliantly drawn, and her resolute will receives ample illumination in the scene wherein, brought to justice, she clearly renders herself intellectual master of the Court. As in so many other of these Jacobean dramas, the stage becomes cluttered here with inessentials and with a very plethora of horrors, but no one can deny that Webster has with singular skill created an atmosphere of courtly evil or that he has succeeded in presenting to us one of the most memorable, although at the same time one of the most unsympathetic, heroines in the entire course of the drama.

The mood of *The Duchess of Malfi* is similar, but the personality of the heroine is vastly different. She is here presented as a woman of highest lineage, offering her love to, and marrying, a low-born steward. Her action enrages her brothers—one a great Cardinal, the other a Duke. They engage a villainous agent for their purpose in the criminal Bosola; they torment her with grim pageants, culminating in a cruel dance of madmen; they proceed to strangle her and her children. Webster's genius is shown nowhere more clearly than in the famous line with which her brother the Duke turns from the cold corpses of his victims. He has displayed no feeling when Bosola reveals them to him, but finally breaks when he looks closer at his sister:

> Cover her face: mine eyes dazzle: she died young.

In the final act complete eclipse descends on this palace interior. The Cardinal is slain by his own brother; Bosola and the Duke fall by each other's hands. This indeed is, in Webster's own words, a "gloomy world," a "deep pit of darkness."

An even deeper pit is dug by Cyril Tourneur, author of *The Atheist's Tragedy* (c. 1607) and probably of *The Revenger's Tragedy* (c. 1607). The latter is immeasurably the finer work, and, despite the fact that its conglomeration of sensational scenes becomes almost ludicrous for a modern reader, its ghastly impressiveness cannot be denied. There is a grim tragic irony in the development of the plot; a refulgent beauty appears in its unrelieved delineation of fathomless evil. From the moment when, at the very beginning of the drama, we listen to Vindice apostrophizing the skull of his murdered mistress to the very last scene a kind of evil spell is wrought upon us. Few authors of the time could rise to that sombrely bitter denunciation of sexual passion delivered in searing words by Vindice as he gazes on the skull:

> Does every proud and self-affecting dame
> Camphire her face for this? And grieve her maker
> In sinful baths of milk—when many an infant starves—
> For her superfluous outside, all for this?
> Who now bids twenty pounds a night, prepares
> Music, perfumes and sweet meats? All are hushed:
> Thou may'st lie chaste now! It were fine, methinks,
> To have thee seen at revels, forgetful feasts
> And unclean brothels. Sure, 'twould fright the sinner
> And make him a good coward, put a reveller
> Out of his antic amble
> And cloy an epicure with empty dishes.
> Here might a scornful and ambitious woman
> Look through and through herself. See, ladies, with
>   false forms
> You deceive men, but cannot deceive worms.

Such frenzy, as is obvious, could not long maintain its intensity, and when we trace the fortunes of the tragic drama in England up to the closing of the theatres in 1642 we clearly see how the dark sensationalism of the earlier years becomes a mere mannerism, and how the fiery bitterness of spirit is reduced to a staleness of utterance. One author of the later years, John Ford, retains elements of the pristine strength, but the worm is upon his pages, the rose is cankered; we are out of the honest breath of heaven breathing hot-house air. *'Tis Pity she's a Whore* (*c.* 1624) ventures daringly into the realm of incest: with hardly a backward thought Giovanni woos his sister, Annabella, gains her love, and calmly watches her being married off (for the purpose of preserving her 'honour') to a gentleman named Soranzo. Knowing that the husband plans revenge, Giovanni kills Annabella, and in a scene of sensational incident dashes in among Soranzo's assembled guests with her heart impaled on his dagger, stabs him, and is himself slain. Despite the fact that the author has inserted here and there some pious reflections of a suitable moral tendency, there seems to be no doubt but that he was flaunting his daring theme before a jaded public for whom ordinary passions had well-nigh lost their savour. Degenerate sensuality, wrapped in an intoxicating riot of words, casts its orchidian clamminess over every scene.

Sensationalism of a like kind flourishes in *The Broken Heart* (*c.* 1629), where two lovers, Orgilus and Penthea, are separated by Ithocles, who forces the latter to marry the noble blackguard Bassanes. Under the stress of her emotions she goes mad and finally dies, while Orgilus plans vengeance on Ithocles. Trapping him in a specially devised chair with movable arms, he stabs him to death. At this point in the drama we suddenly discover, to our astonishment and dismay, that Ford's main purpose is to concentrate attention, not upon any of these characters, but upon the princess Calantha who had been betrothed to Ithocles: it is she who dominates the latter part of the tragedy. Such disruption of interest reveals strikingly the inherent weakness in the later Jacobean and Caroline drama. The authors have lost the virtue of simplicity, because their audiences, affected and blasé courtiers, are not content with the consistent dramatic development of a single story. Each scene has to have its horror or excitement; each act has to have its catastrophe and climax.

After Ford little remains worthy of mention. The stages are closed by Puritan ordinance on the violence and strained passions of James Shirley and Sir William D'Avenant. The former's *The Traitor* (1631) and *The Cardinal* (1641) and the latter's *Albovine* (1626) and *The Cruel Brother* (1627), each presenting, in Shirley's words, a "heap of tragedies," show the Elizabethan fervour at its last panting gasp. Phrenetic emotions, allied to madness, infect these plays: were it not for their obvious mannerism and artificiality they would be unbearable; as it is, save for a few individual scenes, they are merely dull. Renaissance romanticism had here run its course.

THE GROWTH OF REALISTIC COMEDY: BEN JONSON

One man had stood out stalwartly against romanticism during the first years of the seventeenth century. Ben Jonson, although largely self-educated, made himself one of the best classical scholars of his time, and tried with desperate seriousness to convert the stage to imitation of the models he so deeply admired. Had he been born twenty years earlier, he might have altered the entire course of the Elizabethan drama—and, incidentally, might have denied us the works of Shakespeare; as it was, his comparatively late appearance permitted the Elizabethan romanticism to develop unchecked while it served the salutary purpose of revivifying the spirit of comedy, which, after Shakespeare, otherwise would certainly have exhibited signs of progressive debility.

In his attempt to establish 'classical' tragedy among the courtly audiences of his time he failed utterly. *Sejanus* (1603) and *Catiline* (1611) are ponderously dull, and their heavy solemnity pleased not at all the spectators before whom Shakespeare's own company presented them. Far diverse was the fate of his comedies. At a time when men were seeking for new styles in their scenes of merriment Jonson stepped forward with a self-conscious, deliberately planned programme which caught the attention of men who inclined to look on the Shakespearian comedy of humour as more than a trifle old-fashioned, and perhaps even lacking in gentility.

Fundamentally this programme of Jonson's was based on three precepts: he sought for precision of form, condemning the discursiveness of the romantic mood; he wanted 'realism,' believing that it was the mission of comedy to depict contemporary life with moral intent, not tell pleasing tales of fairies and Calibans; he believed in the presentation of boldly conceived types, each representative of some folly or vice, in order that through the resultant satire men might laugh and be cured of their errors. The age was ready for satire, and thus Jonson rolled forward gloriously on the crest of the wave.

Like Marlowe before him, but with greater explicitness, Jonson announced his purposes in prologue and 'induction.' He sought to give in his plays

INIGO JONES: FOUR COSTUME DESIGNS

By courtesy of the Duke of Devonshire

INIGO JONES: SETTING
FOR "OBERON"

*By courtesy of the
Duke of Devonshire*

tectum

porticus

orchestra

mimorum ædes

ingressus

proscænium

planities sive arena

THE SWAN THEATRE,
1595

WILLIAM SHAKESPEARE: FRONTISPIECE TO THE FIRST FOLIO, 1623
British Museum photograph

> Deeds and language such as men do use,
> And persons such as Comedy would choose
> When she would show an image of the times
> And sport with human follies, not with crimes.

His plots were to be "near and familiarly allied to the time," and not concerned with romantic incident:

> As of a Duke to be in love with a Countess, and that Countess to be in love with the Duke's son, and the son to love the Lady's waiting-maid—some such cross-wooing, with a Clown to their serving-man.

Above all, the characters in these realistically conceived plots were to be based on the 'humours' of men, their eccentricities. The word 'humour,' connected etymologically with our modern 'humid,' is to be explained by the belief that in the human body coursed four separate fluids (or 'humours'); in proper balance and proportion these produced even perfection, but when one or more were in excess the character concerned was carried out of the level path and became obsessed or dominated by melancholy, choler, and the like. Jonson insisted strongly that he was concerned, not with mere mannerism, but with basic human traits. For him 'humour' arose

> When some one peculiar quality
> Doth so possess a man that it doth draw
> All his affects, his spirits and his powers
> In their confluctions all to run one way.

"This," he declares, "may be truly said to be a humour," but it is "more than most ridiculous" to imagine that a 'humour' is to be found when a gallant sports some strange fashions in clothes: this is merely an external affectation and does not indicate any inner quality.

The result is that Jonson's comedies are more closely tied to the London world in which he lives than are the typical comedies of Shakespeare (although the comic scenes of *Henry V* and *The Merry Wives of Windsor* approach towards the former's ideal), and at the same time are concerned not so much with the presentation of rounded characters as with the delineation, almost caricature-wise, of living eccentricities. Instead of drawing a man, Jonson takes a 'humour' and invests it with seemingly human form, so that, in one sense, Greed and Folly and Jealousy, not living persons, stalk his stage.

Were his programme all, we should not now be regarding him as

K

Shakespeare's greatest rival in dramatic art; fortunately, to his deliberateness of purpose he added a full-blooded, lusty strength, a keen eye, and a style incisive and theatrical. His inventive power is rich, his vigour unsurpassed: in his plays there crowd before us a great gathering of grotesques whom he has invested with vitality, presenting a vast and motley panorama of caricature, boldly coloured, unforgettable.

Towards his final aim he seems to have moved slowly, although ponderously and surely. Before 1600 he had written several plays, now lost, which from their titles must certainly have been in the romantic manner; *The Case is Altered*, which may date from this period, shows his style by no means fully fashioned; and even *Every Man in his Humour* (1598), as first composed, had an Italianate, not an English, scene.

This is the play, however, in which he realized his peculiar strength, and, after listening to the author's pronouncement of aim, we find it something of a shock when we discover that its quality depends by no means entirely upon the 'classical' plan that Jonson designed for himself. It is true that in the relation between the testy Knowell and his poetic son there is a clear utilization of Plautan and Terentian comedy scenes, but the central figure in the play, the inventive Brainworm, is much more than adaptation to modern conditions of the intriguing slave of Rome. This character, who is singled out by the wise and kindly Justice Clement as the best fellow of them all, gains his vitality more from the tradition of the morality Vice than from that of the Latin *servus*. His gusto is medieval rather than classical.

The whole racy action, vaguely based though it may be on Jonson's knowledge of the ancients, is instinct with the life of his own time. The jealousy of Kitely, the pretence of Cob, the absurdities of the 'gulls' Matthew and Stephen, the melancholy grandeur of Bobadil—all these derive from native sources and Jonson's own imaginative power.

As his art developed, we become conscious both of the possibilities of this new form of comedy and of the dangers inherent in it. A man with a programme may incline both towards overweening self-esteem and towards exaggeration of purpose; and such inclinations unquestionably prevented Jonson from achieving more than he did. *Every Man out of his Humour* (1599) pushes his ideas too far; *Cynthia's Revels* (1600) and *The Poetaster* (1601), brilliant though some of their scenes may be, are marred by the incursion of personal bitterness; in the plays of his latter years determination to keep to his self-appointed plan makes the aging dramatist falter and stumble, become incoherent and dull.

But all of the complete or partial failures count as nothing against the brilliance of four plays of his maturity—*Volpone; or, The Fox* (1606), *Epicœne; or, The Silent Woman* (1609), *The Alchemist* (1610), and *Bartholomew Fair* (1614). The first of these is incomparably the greatest, rising from the merely laughable to levels worthy of comparison with tragedy itself. With magnificent conception Jonson here presents a play with which there is none to compare in that age save the contemporary dramas of Shakespeare. The author's grasp is sure; his delineation of character types is superb; his weaving of plot and theme indicates the presence of theatrical genius.

The scene is Venice and the central figure the luxurious, cynical, contemptuous Volpone. Aided by his rascally servant Mosca, he pretends to be on his death-bed in order to tempt a miserable crew of self-seekers—Corbaccio, Corvino, Voltore—to make him presents of gold and jewels in the expectation of being named his heir. Volpone's active mind, his sensuality, his overweening belief in his own cunning and his underrating of the intelligence of all mankind, will not, however, let him rest with such a simple piece of ironic villainy. He becomes enamoured of Corvino's beautiful young wife, Celia, and in his attempt to seduce her oversteps himself. Ordered before the Venetian courts, he has himself brought in on a litter, and Mosca claims he is so enfeebled he cannot even open his mouth to speak. This trick has its effect; his detractors are silenced; while he, intoxicated by success, is induced to attempt a more daring device still: he gives out that he is dead, and that Mosca is his heir. In his savage joy at the discomfiture of his dupes he does not see the danger into which he has blundered: Mosca, invested with his riches, calmly refuses to part with his booty; Volpone's only course left is to reveal the trick, and this leads to his punishment and disgrace.

There is an intensity and a directness in this play which give it uncommon distinction. Its vision of a world of rapacious birds and beasts of prey has the simplicity and the searing light of true genius.

The play that immediately followed, *Epicœne*, is more mirth-provoking. Taking as his central figure an elderly Morose, whose ears can brook no noise, Jonson devises an intrigue of the kind he knew so well how to manage. Tricked into marrying an apparently ideal, soft-spoken wife, poor Morose is dismayed to find he has

brought a loud-tongued termagant into his household, and is
released from the torment (by the discovery that the supposed wife
is in reality a boy) only after he has agreed to make suitable provision for his nephew Dauphine. The whole piece is masterly in
its handling of a complex and amazing intrigue, although it is to be
questioned whether Jonson was wise in avoiding Plautan practice
and in endeavouring to keep the audience as much in the dark as
the main characters of the play.

From the merriment of *Epicœne* he next turned to a milder and
less bitter essay in the *Volpone* style. In *The Alchemist* the scene is
plague-stricken London, when many a rich householder fled the
city, leaving their houses tenanted only by servants. One such house
is being looked after by Face, who, in order to make some money
on the side, leagues himself with a charlatan-alchemist, Subtle, and a
prostitute, Dol Common. Into their spider's web come a variegated
collection of stupid flies—the young tobacconist, Abel Drugger;
Dapper, a clerk; Sir Epicure Mammon, a would-be millionaire;
Ananias and Tribulation Wholesome, the needy Puritans.

With consummate skill Jonson handles his types and their characteristic speech. The play is full of racy idiom, slang, and spurious
'alchemical' jargon, but the author succeeds in making the entire
action richly fraught with interest and meaning, even although much
of the language must have been almost as obscure to a Jacobean
audience as to Georgian readers. Indeed, the very obscurity points
to a peculiar paradox in Jonson's work as a whole. With his learning
and his 'classical' leanings, it might have been thought that his
writings would have yielded more in the study than on the stage,
whereas precisely the opposite is true. When we read the lines of
Abel Drugger we may find it hard to understand why David
Garrick chose this rôle for himself, or how, having chosen it, he
succeeded in winning such acclaim for its interpretation. Any
theatrical production will explain the conundrum: on the stage
Jonson's lines achieve an individuality, a verve, and a significance
which are hard to wrest from them when they are merely conned
on the printed page.

The final drama in this great quartet is *Bartholomew Fair*, an
uproarious, breezy delineation of low life in London, where character and plot alike become subordinate to the noisy clamour of
the Fair itself. There is, indeed, in this play no 'plot' in the ordin-
arily accepted sense of that word; the persons, from Lantern, the
maker of toys and verses, and Rabbi Zeal-of-the-Land Busy to the
sweaty pig-woman Ursula and the thievish Edgeworth, move in

and out of the scenes, passing from raucous booth to booth, as though they truly lived.

Here Jonson's realism is stretched to its farthest limits.

ROMANCE AND WIT: FROM BEAUMONT AND FLETCHER TO SHIRLEY

During the years that Jonson was thus fighting to establish a realistic, 'classical' form of English comedy Elizabethan romance continued to flourish in the hands of many playwrights, although gradually the romantic elements were taking such new shapes that eventually they coalesced with his style and, combined with that, produced a new comedy of manners.

A typical author of the early years of the century, John Day, illustrates well the way in which the Jonsonian plan was being tentatively fused with the romantic. *The Blind Beggar of Bethnal Green* (1600), with its plethora of disguises, need not detain us, but *The Isle of Gulls* (1606) and *Humour out of Breath* (1607–8), although not great works of art, deserve some brief attention. The story of the first, dealing with a Duke of Arcadia and chivalric adventure, is thoroughly in the 'Elizabethan' mood, but the fact that all the characters are 'gulled' at the close brings the comedy near to *Every Man in his Humour*; chivalric adventure, general challenges offered to the world, provide the chief stuff of the second play also, but when the witty Florimell engages in a duel of wits with the melancholic hero Aspero we come at last to the threshold of another world, a world of realistic vision and sharp repartee.

The comedies of Thomas Heywood and Thomas Dekker likewise display transitional features, middle-class realism here marrying with sentimental and romantic fancies; *The Fair Maid of the West* (printed 1631) and *The Roaring Girl* (c. 1610) reveal these amply. The latter comedy was written by Dekker in collaboration with Thomas Middleton, an author who, besides contributing largely to the sensational domestic tragedy, made characteristic contribution to the realistic comedy. His affiliations with the earlier comedy of romance may easily be traced in *The Old Law* (1599) and *Blurt Master Constable* (1601–2). In the former a Duke of Epire publishes a decree condemning to death all men over eighty, all women over sixty, and as a result several characters are led to ludicrous intrigue. Simonides rejoices because his aged father will go; Eugenia receives suitors since her husband will be eighty in a few months; Gnatho the clown suborns a clerk to alter his wife's date of birth. With considerable verve the scenes are vividly brought before us, and the dialogue is frequently amusing. "When dies thy husband?" says one wife to another. "Is't not July next?" The second play provides us with a strange admixture of elements reminiscent of *Romeo and Juliet* and *Much Ado about Nothing*, with humours of a Jonsonian sort.

Something different, however, appears in *A Trick to catch the Old One* (c. 1605), with its group of gallants who live on their wits. Here, as in others of Middleton's realistic comedies, the Jonsonian element is heavily emphasized, but to that element a new quality is being added. Jonson's humours depend almost entirely on their own natures; in Middleton the humours are beginning to be related to the classes to which the various persons belong. A social note is being introduced.

With *A Trick to catch the Old One* may be associated the much darker comedy of Philip Massinger, and in particular *A New Way to pay Old Debts* (c. 1620) and *The City Madam* (1632). Both of these have the downrightness which was an inheritance from Elizabethan days, but both breathe a new air. The former is distinguished by the magnificently drawn portrait of Sir Giles Overreach, a man of money who has risen from lowly rank; he is a Sir Epicure Mammon without that character's voluptuousness—hard, cruel, self-seeking. Here Massinger clearly shows his awareness of social conditions apart from, yet operative on, character. In *The City Madam* it is a woman, Lady Frugal, who seeks to rise in the social scale, and Massinger spares nothing in listing her absurdities.

All of these plays bear about them an unmistakably bourgeois flavour, but the new audiences in the theatre, now predominantly courtly, were waiting for something of a different kind. Before that something different could come, however, there was needed both a fresh instrument and a fresh concept. An easy, witty style was required and a self-conscious presentation of aristocratic manners. Both of these were furthered in the plays written by John Fletcher in collaboration with Francis Beaumont and others. In these the English stage begins to assume the colouring of the Spanish. Tragicomic episode is frequent, often with patent absurdities, but the manner in which the aristocrats are depicted is realistic, and their codes are unhesitatingly adopted as the correct behaviour. Courtly love begins to triumph over natural love, and much is being said of honour. Witty gallants come to take centre stage, and laughter is meted out to those not born to the manner who strive to ape the ways of the palace.

In *Wit at Several Weapons* (printed 1647) Wittypate Oldcraft is a young gallant who lives on his wits; he is companioned by several others in *Wit without Money* (c. 1614; printed 1639), in which, characteristically, the hero, Valentine, esteems intelligence, quickness of fancy, and ease in conversation above wealth; in *The Nice Valour; or, The Passionate Madman* (printed 1647) Shamont is "a superstitious lover of reputation," reminiscent of Spanish types: we are stepping now out of the old Globe into the new Drury Lane.

The enormous variety of the 'Beaumont and Fletcher' plays makes any kind of classification difficult, and perhaps all we need to do is to note a few examples typical of their style. Some are frankly satirical in a farcical way—such as *The Little French Lawyer* (c. 1620), with its brilliantly incisive picture of La Writ, who comes to imagine himself a great duellist because in the first combat he attends he has the almost unbelievably good fortune to disarm two of his opponents. Others concentrate most on tragi-comic incident, as in *The Woman Hater* (c. 1606), which the printer "dare not call Comedy or Tragedy; 'tis perfectly neither; a Play it is." Since this work excellently illustrates the complexity of intrigue introduced in dramas of this kind, the two strands of its plot may summarily be indicated. In the first appears a mischievous girl, Oriana, not unlike the heroine of *La dama duende*. Although beloved by the Duke of Milan, she forces herself on Gondarino, the womanhater, in order to plague him. In return he slanders her reputation, and she is in danger of utter disgrace when a fortunate turn saves her. The second element in the plot centres on Lazarillo, a poor courtier whose eccentricity it is to dote on strange viands. Hearing of a rare fish which has been given to the Duke, he struggles to get an invitation to the palace; successful in this, he finds the fish has been presented to Gondarino, who in turn has handed it over to his Mercer, who gives it to a Courtesan; in order to taste it, Lazarillo agrees to marry the last-named.

In these and similar plays the authors of the 'Beaumont and Fletcher' comedies have, quite unconsciously, achieved certain ends. They have stressed unconditionally the world of fashionable youth, making the witty gallant their main character. They have introduced a gay, high-spirited aristocratic maiden to be fit match for him. They have suggested, but only slightly, an opposition to the citizen class, and have transferred the quality of humours from character defects to social manners. Above all, they have forged a new instrument of dialogue—delicate, intellectual, acute: in their scenes we listen to the quick repartee of the superficially brilliant Cavaliers in tavern and salon.

The comedy of manners was thus nearly formed. A further step taken towards its perfection was made by one of Jonson's protégés, Richard Brome, a man of no great talent, but one who more clearly than Fletcher recognized both the inherent opposition of the citizens and the Cavaliers and the existence of a special code of manners on which the society of the latter was founded. Where Fletcher unconsciously reflected this code, Brome consciously exploited it. Here satire directed at citizens who dare to ape the courtly manners—as in *Sparagus Garden* (1635), *A Mad Couple well matched* (printed 1653), and *The New Academy* (printed 1658)— derives, not only from a sense of the ridiculous, but still more from an awareness of social values.

Then came James Shirley, and the search was ended. In some of his comedies, such as *The Constant Maid* (printed 1640) and *The Gamester* (1634), Elizabethan features are predominant, but even in these class-consciousness is strongly marked. In the latter play Hazard asks Old Barnacle why, since he is a citizen, he does not bring up his nephew in his own way of life; the answer is clear:

> We that had·
> Our breeding from a trade—cits, as you call us,
> Though we hate gentlemen ourselves, yet are
> Ambitious to make our children gentlemen.

Three plays in particular reveal Shirley's true accomplishment— *The Witty Fair One* (1628), *Hyde Park* (1632), and *The Lady of Pleasure* (1635). Here the comedy of manners is fully shaped and awaits only perfection in style to reach culmination. The fundamental basis of these plays is ease of courtly manners. Equally fundamental is the equality of men and women, and the frank, realistic appraisal of an intellectual duel of the sexes. Everywhere there is emphasis on polished wit, and brilliant conversation carries each scene. It is noteworthy, for example, that such a play as *Hyde Park* presents not a single 'comic' character as such figures were conceived in earlier years: the interest is concentrated almost entirely on the erratic and fanciful Mistress Carol and her three lovers—not so much on the intrigue which brings her into Fairfield's arms at the end, but on the display of wit occasioned by their wooing.

Shirley lived on into the period of the Restoration, and thus was an elder contemporary of Dryden and of Etherege: it was his style that they adapted and wrought into the finely aristocratic form, graceful and graceless, which eventually found its culmination in Congreve's *The Way of the World*—the world of Society, the world of manners, the world of artificiality and polish and scintillating wit.

PART V

THE TRIUMPH OF CLASSICISM

CHAPTER I

RACINE AND THE TRAGEDY OF SENTIMENT

BEFORE pursuing farther the fortunes of the English stage and examining the heroic drama and the comedy of manners produced at the Court of Charles II we must once more return, and in happier circumstances, to the theatre of Paris. Only two countries in Europe during the latter half of the seventeenth century produced dramatic writing of any significance, and of these two France is without even a film of doubt vastly the superior. She had failed utterly to create anything of real value during the period of the Renaissance, but now, under conditions far more propitious for her than those of 1600, her stage rapidly assumed an assurance and a power which made it the immediate inspiration for other lands, and which nourished the genius of two authors, Molière and Racine, who have been universally recognized as prime masters of their art, the one supreme in comedy, the other in tragic drama.

THE REVIVAL OF THE FRENCH STAGE

The change in conditions came slowly yet with determined sureness as the seventeenth century was approaching its middle years. Throughout the whole of the Western world a longing for order and settled social state was supplanting the hardy adventurings, the bold individualism, and the emotional excitements of the Renaissance. England was still to plunge herself into civil war and execute her king, but even there the impress of the age was sufficiently strong to make men welcome the firm rule of Oliver Cromwell and, later, to induce them to call back the son of the monarch whom they had tried and condemned to death. Romanticism ruled at the beginning of the century: fifty years later the world was ready for classical precision and control.

Whereas England won through to acceptance of this spirit only after years of bloody conflict, France steadily moved forward from social chaos to order. The fury of the wars of religion died away, and under the astute hands of Cardinal Richelieu, from 1624 to 1642 the chief Minister of Louis XIII, the troublesome power of the nobles was reduced and the foundation was laid for a strong monarchical rule. Had his efforts been less sure, serious strife might well have broken out afresh when Louis XIII, dying in 1643, left his throne to a child of but five years of age, but the basis he had built was laid upon rock, and, despite the Fronde, it proved not impossible for his successor, Cardinal Mazarin, trained by Richelieu himself, to tide over the dangerous years until Louis XIV was able to assume control and in his long and glorious reign to become famous as the 'Grand Monarque' and 'Le Roi Soleil.'

Thus the particular conditions in France harmonized perfectly with the temper of the world in which she played her part. That part too was to prove a major rôle. With the coming of national unity, national greatness followed, and in the affairs of Europe French politics exercised decisive sway. To the sense of new-found unity, therefore, there was added something of the aspiration that had animated England fifty or sixty years before.

This aspiration was political, but it was also cultural. From the thirties of the century, when Richelieu was beginning to reap the certain fruits of his efforts, on to the latter years of Louis XIV, there was evident in Paris a desire to create a national literature, to penetrate the secrets of taste, to devise sure standards of critical judgment; and the success that attended these endeavours is attested by the dominant position French culture assumed in the other countries of Europe. For the authors of England, of Germany, of Russia, French writers provided the models of literary excellence.

So far as the stage in particular was concerned, the path of achievement was made the smoother by the fact that, while the provinces still retained independent interests, Paris rapidly came to be the centre of cultural activities. Theatres might flourish in other cities; dramatic authors and actors might train themselves there; but Paris was their ultimate goal, and from Paris alone the artists could receive final, assured acclaim.

To this may be added another consideration. The French stage of the mid-seventeenth century was assisted materially by its very poverty in the years immediately preceding. The age needed, and sought for, adequate means of expression in classical form, and the absence of any great romantic models permitted freer scope to the Parisian authors than they would have had if the shadow of romantic genius had fallen on their pages. If the French theatre had possessed a Shakespeare, even a Marlowe or a Webster, the task would have been infinitely harder. As it was, the new generation of classically minded authors started their work largely unimpeded. The tragi-comedies and farces with which they were surrounded could call forth little or no critical esteem, and thus no temptations offered themselves for the infusion of romantic elements in their classical conceptions. This meant, too, that in seeking for a fresh kind of tragedy and comedy the authors were not simply acting negatively, opposing old forms with new; their efforts were positive, uninhibited, and free.

With the development of the classical drama the names of princes and their Ministers are closely associated. Louis XIV was the patron of Molière and Racine, and during the earlier, formative years Richelieu, by his direct personal encouragement, was responsible for the creation of the new theatre. Interested generally in the development of French literature, Richelieu was particularly intent on the drama. Partly at least through his influence the stage came to abandon the old type of simultaneous setting and to adopt the Italian proscenium frame with its perspective scenery. The theatre known as the Palais Cardinal, and later as the Palais Royal, established under his direct orders by the architect Mercier, opened with the performance of *Mirame* in 1641, and was the model that finally and definitely ousted the old. In place of the multiple settings that had been used for the popular tragi-comedies at the Hôtel de Bourgogne, and that trailed with them memories of the Middle Ages, men now were provided with classically simple, unified stage-scenes created by means of side-wings and backcloths, framed by a deep proscenium arch as though in a picture-frame. Although the Palais Cardinal was originally a courtly playhouse, its influence was widely spread among the public theatres that followed. Another Court theatre that had considerable influence was the great Salle des Machines, built by Vigarani in the Tuilleries (1661)—so large and with such vast space for scenic equipment that in 1763, when the Palais Royal was burned, the architect Soufflot created an entirely new and sufficiently commodious playhouse out of its stage alone.

At the same time the more settled conditions of life and the growth of Paris as the capital of France permitted the development of more permanent companies than had commonly prevailed in the past. The Hôtel de Bourgogne came under settled management, and its company gradually evolved into the Théâtre Français, playing in various houses, including the Théâtre Guénégaud (1670) and, later, a new Théâtre Français, converted out of a tennis-court in 1689; its rivals, the company of the Théâtre Marais, boasted the attraction of the great tragic actor Mondory; the Comédie Italienne now attention for its gay freedom and its vitality; above all, there was the famous Illustre Théâtre, formed by the young Molière in 1643, which after many vicissitudes in the provinces achieved glory on its return to Paris in 1659.

Although there were numerous abuses in the theatre during those days, the general conditions were right for the development of fruitful creative activity, and it is by no means surprising that France, producing Corneille, Racine, and Molière, became the leader of the world dramatic.

THE FORERUNNER: PIERRE CORNEILLE

The drama that first gave distinction to the French tragic stage was *Le Cid* (1636), the work of Pierre Corneille. Its author, a lawyer of Rouen, had been impelled towards the theatre by the visit to his native city of the Marais troupe, and when, in 1629, Mondory returned to Paris he carried with him the manuscript of a comedy, *Mélite*, by the young author. During the succeeding years Corneille trained himself in the penning of comedy, and then set all literary Paris in an uproar with his heroic drama on a Spanish theme.

At the time that this drama appeared classic theory and practice had not as yet fully established itself. Tragi-comedies were still being produced by men such as Rotrou and Benserade, and for some years these dramatists were to remain moderately popular. Along with their vogue was a vogue for dramas on English history —a kind of gesture on the part of romantic playwrights to the claims of tragedy. Here came La Calprenède's *Jeanne, Royne d'Angleterre* (printed 1638) and Regnault's *Marie Stuard, Royne d'Écosse* (printed 1639). Already, however, the classical style was making headway. In 1634 Jean Mairet came forward with his *Sophonisbe*, the first tragedy in France truly based on the rules, and it was followed by a series of dramas which treated ancient themes in accordance with the critical precepts supposed to be found in Aristotle's *Poetics*. Mairet himself followed his *Sophonisbe* with *Marc Antoine, ou la Cléopâtre* (c. 1635), Scudéry produced his *La mort de César* (*The Death of Cæsar*, 1635) and Pierre Corneille his *Médée* (*Medea*, 1634-35).

At the same time the critics were eagerly discussing the precepts that should be followed. Some men of independent judgment followed François Ogier in objecting to the stricter application of the rules, but the majority welcomed Mairet as the leader of the classical legion. As yet, however, the debate was rather abstract, since no really important tragic drama, whether classically inclined or the reverse, had appeared to provide a concrete issue. It was precisely such a concrete issue that *Le Cid* gave to Parisian society. No one could deny its power; the question was whether that power was secured by legitimate means.

The plot of Corneille's drama was derived from a Spanish source. Chimène is the daughter of Don Gomès, and is the love of the gallant Rodrique. Unfortunately Don Gomès insults and strikes Rodrique's father, and the young man, at the very moment of his wedding, is forced to challenge the former; in the ensuing duel Don Gomès is slain. Chimène now is in turn forced to wish Rodriuqe's death, and he, rather than commit suicide, takes command of a small troop of soldiers prepared to attempt the apparently forlorn hope of preventing the advance of a great Moorish army. Instead of perishing on the field, however, Rodrique is triumphant, and returns home in glory. Still impelled by her sense of loyalty to her dead father, Chimène causes Don Sanche, who seeks her hand in marriage, to challenge Rodrique, but, on hearing that he proposes to let himself be killed, she herself bids him to use his strength in order to obtain victory—even although (or because) she is aware that by the King's order she must marry the survivor. Rodrique wins the duel, and the lovers are united.

The storm that broke around this drama may at first seem inexplicable; but consideration of *Le Cid* in its setting dissipates all difficulty. Its brilliant, forceful verse and its bold, arresting presentation of character marked it out as a tremendous achievement. Here was a literary effort that could not be ignored, and in this period when men were so eagerly searching for the true road the question as to whether Corneille, by his very genius, might not be leading the world astray became a theme of profound significance.

Externally the author keeps the rules. All the action is supposed to take place within a period of twenty-four hours, and the entire action is pursued near the royal palace. Yet the five acts of the drama are crowded with incident, straining dangerously our sense of probability, and the end, instead of being tragic, bears a happy conclusion. Several questions were paramount for the dramatic authors of that time: Was probability or retention of the rules the more important? Could these two be reconciled, and, if so, in what way? What was the true end of the tragic drama? *Le Cid* provided a practical test for the establishing of opinion.

Anyone who wades through the spate of controversy which

flooded upon *Le Cid* at that time may well deem that the critical comments are frequently weak, absurd, and beside the point; yet a general understanding of the situation shows that, although the authors were frequently arguing about problems of lesser import, their passionate advocating of even trivial views ·sprang from a consciousness of the ultimate importance of the quarrel.

Almost immediately following its presentation on the stage, Mairet (perhaps stung by jealousy) and others started debating its merits, and so bitter did the debate prove that within a few months the Academy was formally asked to judge the issue, with the result that Jean Chapelain, assisted by the learned institution to which he belonged, soon published the famous *Sentimens de l'Académie Françoise sur la tragi-comédie du Cid*.

Much space is taken up in the *Sentimens* with criticism of minor points, and even more with what seems utterly futile—the moral questions involved. In particular, the authors of that essay fix their attention on the impropriety of causing Chimène to marry the man who has slain her father, of allowing her to permit love to sway her heart above the dictates of duty. Unquestionably this appears to be but foolish criticism, yet · perhaps unconsciously, the *Sentimens* here have, although rather crudely, concentrated their attention upon what is ultimately the core of the entire controversy. Corneille, while he bows formally to the unities, has in reality a romantic soul. There is a strength about him that rebels against restraint: into the age of classicism he carries a bold, truculent individualism. But individualism of this sort is exactly that which the age was seeking to restrain, and in the criticisms directed at Chimène's conduct the Academy was, in effect, testifying to its desire for order, restraint, and social unity. Marlowes and their like could find place in the Renaissance; in this later age no room might be allowed to them.

The emphasis laid upon the improbabilities of the action of *Le Cid* also has deeper implications. The old tragi-comedies had extended actions, but their structure was formless. Form was needed, hence the inculcation of the unities. At the same time form must harmonize with content, and the truth is that Corneille, despite the vigour and beauty of his work, failed to secure such harmony. In plays of romantic structure it may be proper to have variety of incident; in plays of classical restraint the subject-matter, and the passions, must be so conceived as to accord with the conventions employed. The Academy, rightly, recognized that what Corneille aimed at was a type of drama which could not provide the age with what it needed. Some of its members may have been animated by personal jealousies, some may have been too academic to recognize true genius when it appeared; but basically the general criticism of the *Sentimens*, in the light of what was then demanded of the theatre, must be deemed fully justified. The path indicated by Corneille could have led to nothing but chaos; the way of the *Sentimens* leads towards the work of Racine.

That Corneille himself took the lesson to heart is indicated in his later dramas. In *Horace* (1640) he selects a classical subject and attempts to deal with it more simply than he had treated the content of *Le Cid*. Basically this tragedy deals with conflicting loyalties. Rome is at war, and against the background of the conflict the dramatist sets Horace, the patriot of untroubled mind; Sabine, his wife, and a native of the enemy country; Camille, his sister, in love with a soldier, Curiace, also of that country. Each character, clearly etched, is presented without any inner conflict. Horace is so assured of the rightness of his views that he slays his sister when he finds her cursing her own country; for Camille nothing matters save love of Curiace. There is a noble grandeur about the entire conception; and with subtle sensitivity Corneille has been able to hammer out lines of almost Roman brevity, pith, and grandeur: "Qui veut mourir ou vaincre est vaincu rarement"; "Et qui veut bien mourir peut braver les malheurs"; "Mais Rome ignore encor comme on perd des batailles"—these and other epigrammatic lines linger in the memory.

Yet *Horace*, even although its author has taken the *Sentimens* to heart, still fails to point in the true direction. Its very boldness is too strong for the temper of the age, and its lack of inner conflict causes it to miss an opportunity such as Racine knew later how to embrace.

In *Cinna, ou la clémence d'Auguste* (*Cinna; or, The Clemency of Augustus*, c. 1641) Corneille turned once more to a tragedy with a happy ending, but, as in *Horace*, simplified the contents of the work. Auguste is the all-powerful Emperor, and among his closest protégés are Emilie, burning with a desire to avenge her father's death; Cinna, induced to join in a conspiracy against Auguste because of his love for Emilie; and Maxime, another member of the conspiracy and also secretly in love with the heroine. With admirable conciseness and economy of means Corneille reveals these characters in their relations with the Emperor, and rises to a magnificent conclusion in Auguste's decision to pardon the offenders. Peculiarly effective is the monarch's soliloquy in the fourth act, which might be regarded as the classical equivalent of the romantic soliloquy put into the mouth of Henry V by Shakespeare:

> O Heaven, to whom is it your will that I
> Entrust my life, the secrets of my soul?
> Take back the power with which you have endowed me,
> If it but steals my friends to give me subjects,
> If regal splendours must be fated ever,
> Even by the greatest favours they can grant,
> To foster only hate, if your stern law
> Condemns a king to cherish only those
> Who burn to have his blood. Nothing is certain.
> Omnipotence is bought with ceaseless fear. . . .

Polyeucte (*c.* 1642) carries us into a different world, for here Corneille moved from pagan character to Christian. Polyeucte is a descendant of Armenian princes who has accepted the material power of Rome and is married to the daughter of the Governor, Pauline. A quality of mystical faith enters in here, for the author is intent upon showing how this man, becoming dedicate to a higher law, is forced to a way of life different from that of his companions. The contrast is well revealed in his relations with Pauline. This Roman lady has married him only at her father's command; in reality her heart has been given to a fellow-Roman, Sévère. Faithful to her husband, the other love cannot be stilled, but when, towards the close of the tragedy, she finds Polyeucte, recognizing her passion, offering her happiness with Sévère when he himself is dead, while Sévère tacitly accepts the proposal, a sudden new light floods in upon her. She becomes a Christian in order that, even in death, she may be with the heroic soul whose virtues have thus been revealed to her.

The qualities displayed in these dramas are reproduced in the succeeding tragedies of Corneille—*Pompée* (1642), *Rodogune, Princesse des Parthes* (printed 1646), *Héraclius* (1646), and *Nicomède* (1650–51), as well as the later works, *Œdipe* (1659), *Sertorius* (1662), and *Sophonisbe* (1663)—but the times were rapidly leaving him as a monument of the past. His stalwart figure, strayed out of the Renaissance, stood somewhat awkwardly among the polite and delicate gallantries of the age. His characters were rough-hewn, bold in their proportions, massive; what the ladies and gentlemen of the Paris Court desired was something subtler and more polished. These audiences had the power to be aroused by "greatness of soul," as Charles Saint-Évremond expressed it, but even more they sought "tender admiration." There is a rugged masculinity about

Corneille; more appropriate to the age were Racine's sensitive heroines.

THE NEW TRAGEDY: RACINE

Jean Racine was born in 1639; by 1664 he had produced his first play, and before his death in 1699 he had established himself as the supreme master in that particular style of French classicism which distinguished the age of Louis XIV.

Unlike Corneille, he was content to mould his own desires absolutely to the form of his age—or perhaps it might be said that basically his desires were harmoniously attuned to the desires of the Parisian society in which he found himself. Behind him were many models, each of which offered something of inspiration, but in the dramas of his maturity he so wrought the elements he had taken from others to his own image that they became converted into shapes far other than those they had originally exhibited, and everywhere the mould was formed in the image of his times.

Chief of his predecessors was, of course, Pierre Corneille, but before *La Thébaïde, ou les frères ennemis* (*The Theban; or, The Enemy Brothers*) appeared in 1664 there were other writers who had essayed the tragic path, and even while he was engaged in producing his series of classical plays numerous companions vied with him for supremacy. Thomas Corneille, younger brother of Pierre, stalwartly contributed a series of tragedies to the stage, but even the best of these, *Timocrate* (1656), lacks brilliance. Philippe Quinault also pursued the Corneillian way, but soon, in collaboration with Lulli, was drawn into the sphere of opera, when among other works he produced his famous *Armide* (1686), one of the tragedies most influential in establishing 'Grand Opera' in France. None of the tragic plays produced during the years immediately before Racine's appearance had given any indication of true greatness: *Le Cid, Horace,* and *Cinna* still remained the finest serious dramas that the French stage had created.

To the theatre of his time Racine brought certain qualities which immediately distinguish him from his companions. The beauty of his verse is dependent not so much upon vigorous utterance as upon delicacy and precision. Corneille's dialogue is that of a romantic constrained to speak in classical tones; Racine's lines are perfectly adjusted to the general speech-character of his age. His epigrams are chiselled to perfection, where Corneille's are heavily and sometimes even impatiently hammered out. This verse he made both eminently theatrical—so that it has been acclaimed by generations of French actors—and dramatic, in that it is at once the expression of character and expresses character with almost epigrammatic poise. The single line in Racine may carry a weight that only a paragraph of Corneille could counterbalance. The very simplicity of Hermione's cry in *Andromaque*—

> Where am I? What have I done? What ought
> I to do now? What fury sways me? What
> Anguish devours my heart? All aimlessly
> Hither and thither through this palace I
> Have rushed. Alas! Is there no way I can
> Know if I love or hate?

—has a quality far beyond its ordinary meaning. Lacking flamboyant features, Racine's verse is virtually untranslatable. Its delicacy depends on the author's exquisite sensibility to the tones of his own tongue; and when other tongues attempt to reproduce his forms they falter with embarrassment.

To this simplicity of language Racine adds simplicity of action. He knew, as Corneille did not, how to adjust his plots to the requirements of current conventions. No improbabilities mar his scenes: it seems eminently proper—nay, inevitable—that what he shows us should take place in a few hours and in one place. There are no digressions here, and the directness which is appropriate to the classic style finds perfect realization.

His greatest achievement, however, was the evolving of a pattern suited to the classical tendencies of his particular time. Corneille had aimed at the arousing of heroic admiration for his characters, and although the theme of love played a considerable part in his dramas, he specifically stated his belief that in tragedy the love element should be made subordinate to other issues. "The dignity of tragedy," he stated in his discourse of 1660,

> needs some great state interest or passion nobler and more virile than love, such as ambition or vengeance, which leads us to expect greater misfortune than the loss of a mistress. It is fit to mix love in it because it always has much attraction and can serve as a basis to those other interests and other passions of which I speak. But it must content itself with second rank in the poem and leave the first to the other.

Unquestionably in setting forth this point of view Corneille was correctly estimating the general requirements of the tragic genre, but the age in which he lived was one of gallantry, where the theme of love was of paramount importance and where the sterner emotions of which he spoke could make little appeal. Racine realized that if tragic drama were to be truly successful in this time the passion of love must form the centre, or at least the determining element, in the composition.

This in turn implied the exercise of greater subtlety than Corneille commanded. His figures were simply and boldly fashioned: Racine set out to secure interest and develop interest by means more delicate. Inner conflict became obligatory, and this spectator of the human heart knew well how to weave a tissue of conflicting passions in such a manner as to arouse a feeling of almost unbearable tension. He began to search down into the domain below consciousness, and in effect laid the basis for the modern 'psychological' drama.

As his aim was not to encourage heroic admiration or to deal pre-eminently with other emotions than love, he wisely took another step. Corneille had concentrated most of his attention upon his heroes; Racine explored a fresh realm by emphasizing his heroines. Nor was it the heroines of hard, almost masculine quality that most attracted his attention—an Electra consumed by hate or a Medea tormented by the desertion of her husband: the heroines he displayed were women of more tender structure. Where Æschylus reveals the classical tragic style at its most masculine, where Corneille's genius is romantically masculine, subdued and restricted by the impress of classic form, Racine's spirit is essentially feminine.

To a realization of his mission he came but slowly. In the preface to *La Thébaïde* he drew attention to the fact that he had practically neglected the love element, deeming lovers' tenderness and jealousies to have no legitimate place amid the severities of the plot he had selected. Moreover, in *Alexandre le Grand* (1665) he followed Corneille, and to a certain extent Quinault, in dealing with a theme calculated to call forth admiration for the heroic qualities of his hero.

Two years later, however, he showed that these were but trial essays by producing his first feminine tragedy, the *Andromaque* (*Andromache*, 1667). Here the simple classical framework was definitely established: not only were the unities preserved and the story stripped of every vestige of extraneous matter, but the very movement of the actors on the stage was reduced to a minimum. There are but four persons of any interest in the play—Oreste, in love with Hermione, Hermione in love with Pyrrhus, Pyrrhus in love with Andromaque, and Andromaque herself, with her devotion set upon her dead Hector. Their names are Greek; but they step forth before us as idealized portraits of ordinary human types. Rising and falling in intensity, the five acts of the tragedy are given over to an analysis of the torments of these four love-intoxicated persons. The ancient Greek tale is retold in delicate terms; Andromaque's mind is in conflict because of the clash between self-dedication to the memory of her first husband and devotion to her living son; Hermione hardly knows whether to love or hate, can barely distinguish these passions in her soul. "Hate him, Cleone?" she asks:

> All my dignity,
> My honour, is at stake, such kindness I
> Have shown to him, whereof all memory
> He yet hath lost—yea, e'en he that was so
> Dear to me, and who could betray me. Oh,
> Too much I have loved him, not to hate him now!

Oreste stands lost in his melancholy abstraction, enfeebled both by his obsession for Hermione and by his sense of being doomed by the gods to disaster:

> I understand. My doom
> Is this: that Pyrrhus hath thy heart; thy head,
> Orestes.

We are far here from the world of the heroic: Andromaque calls for our sincere admiration, but the others are tortured souls, each disturbed within its own being, and each selfishly intent upon its own desires, its own miseries. The difference between Corneille's aims and Racine's is perhaps revealed most characteristically in the contrast between Chimène and Hermione: the former is prepared to seek, or at least to sanction, her lover's death because the claims of honour demand it; the latter is led only by her own inner rage to bid Oreste slay Pyrrhus.

For Racine, now sure of his own powers and of the path he wished to travel, tragedy had assumed clear proportions: it was to be "a simple action, charged with little matter, as becomes an action which occupies a single day, advancing gradually to its end, and sustained by the interests, the sentiments, and the passions of the characters." In *Britannicus* (1669) he essayed, brilliantly, a drama more in the manner of Corneille, but adapted to his own peculiar pattern—almost as though he were determined to demonstrate that the theme of love did not embrace the entire range of his conceptions. Corneillian influence of the same kind is traceable in *Bajazet* (1672) and *Mithridate* (1673), but in *Bérénice* (1670), *Iphigénie* (1674), and *Phèdre* (1677) he moved firmly on his own elected soil. In *Bajazet*, dealing with an almost contemporary event, he tried to secure tragic 'distance' by treating of life in a far-off Oriental world, painting excellent portraits of the politician Acomat and of the impassioned Roxane—indeed, it is Roxane who becomes the central figure in the play, and Racine assuredly was wise in concentrating, in his three classically derived dramas, upon the character of a woman.

These three tragedies boldly announce in their titles the predominating feminine interest. *Iphigénie* presents a delicate interplay of character and carries its action to a happy conclusion, although the atmosphere throughout is serious and threatening disaster. Central in the composition stands the frail, lovely Iphigénie, firm in her constancy both to her lover, Achille, and to her father, Agamemnon. On one side she is flanked by her weak, ambitious, vacillating parent, desperately anxious not to lose his post as commander-in-chief of the Greek forces, yet almost equally anxious not to stir up domestic trouble—a man whose absence of will makes him take what seems the easier of two disturbing alternatives, and whose mind changes and shifts with every breeze. On the other side is Clytemnestre, desperately intent on saving the life of her child, balanced against her husband by her fixity of purpose, stronger than he in character, yet rendered impotent by circumstance. And in sharp contrast to Iphigénie are the young Achille and Ériphile—the former a blunt, single-minded man of action, the latter a pathologically miserable girl, jealous of others and suicidal in tendency. It is, indeed, by her self-inflicted death that Racine succeeds in giving a fortunate conclusion to his action, for the seer Calchas declares that she may be accepted instead of Iphigénie as the victim-sacrifice demanded by the gods.

This play naturally challenges comparison with Euripides' *Iphigenia in Aulis*, and it must be confessed that it stands up well in the test. It does not possess the boldness with which even Euripides—so much less monumental in his work than Æschylus—knew how to invest his characters, but such boldness in execution is not its aim. Racine seeks to probe into secret recesses of the soul, while Euripides attempts to present a picture classically etched.

Bérénice had preceded *Iphigénie* by four years, but consideration of the latter first is justified in view of the fact that it more clearly shows Racine's full mastery of his peculiar tragic style. In a sense *Bérénice* may be regarded as transitional, since although the theme is love and the chief figure is a woman, the dictates of duty and the 'state' quality demanded by Corneille are clearly present. Rome imperiously calls upon Titus for abandonment of his passion for Bérénice, yet the claims of her beauty batter down his resolution, while Antiochus, sent by his master to give her the stern command to leave the city, falls dangerously under her spell. *Bérénice*, like *Andromaque*, is a drama of conflicting love; it differs from the latter in introducing the clash between love and honour; yet the fact that duty triumphs cannot conceal from us the dominant power of passion or take from the pervading atmosphere of tenderness. One line spoken by Antiochus might be taken as typical of its whole mood:

> Je cherchais en pleurant les traces de vos pas.

In rejecting the Corneillian pattern, and in penning such a drama of renunciation, Racine undoubtedly strikes a note that appears strangely modern.

In *Phèdre* Racine exhibits to the full both his strength and his weakness. The dialogue has an exquisite delicacy beyond almost anything he had previously accomplished, and the figures of the drama stand out in clearly limned perfection. For his plot the French author once more has turned to Euripides, and reveals the encroaching obsession of Phèdre, wife of Theseus, for her husband's son by a former marriage, Hippolyte. In order to help her mistress, the faithful Œnone, believing that Theseus has died on a foreign expedition, counsels Phèdre to disclose her passion to the stepson. Indignantly he rejects her offer of love, but when, on Theseus' unexpected return, he is accused by Œnone of having tried to seduce Phèdre he refuses to say a word: cursed by his father, he goes to his doom, while Phèdre herself, overwhelmed by mingled shame and grief at her loss, commits suicide.

With consummate artistry, the dramatist has presented an unforgettable portrait of a woman whose very being is consumed by a fire she cannot quench. Her first entry shows her pitifully weakened. "Yes, this is far enough," she says to Œnone:

> Stay here, Œnone.
> My strength is failing. I must rest a little.
> I am dazzled with the light; it has been long
> Since I have seen it.

Before she confronts Hippolyte he is displayed to us as having fallen in love with Aricie: he confesses that to him, the scorner of the tender passion, has come an unwonted emotion:

> I leave your presence:—leaving, I find you near,
> And in the forest's darkness see your form.
> Black night, no less than daylight brings the vision
> Of charms that I avoid. All things conspire

> To make Hippolytus your slave. The fruit
> Of all my sighs is only that I cannot
> Find my own self again.

The tension rises steadily up to Phèdre's great speech in the fourth act, in which she thinks with bitterness of that which she cannot have. When Œnone asks her, "What fruit can they desire from fruitless love?" her reply reveals the torment of her spirit:

> That love will stay,
> And it will stay for ever. While I speak—
> O dreadful thought—they laugh and scorn my madness
> And my distracted heart. In spite of exile,
> In spite of that which soon must come to part them,
> They make a thousand oaths to bind their union.
> Œnone, can I bear this happiness
> Which so insults me? I would have your pity.
> Yes, she must be destroyed. My husband's fury
> Against her hated race shall be renewed.
> The punishment must be a heavy one.
> Her guilt outruns the guilt of all her brothers.
> I'll plead with Theseus, in my jealousy—
> What do I say? Oh, have I lost my senses?
> Is Phædra jealous? Will she, then, go begging
> For Theseus' help? He lives—and yet I burn.
> For whom? Whose heart is this I claim as mine?
> My hair stands up with horror at my words,
> And from this time, my guilt has passed all bounds!
> Hypocrisy and incest breathe at once
> Through all I do.

The tempestuous passion, despite her will, cannot be controlled.

At this point in Racine's career a new mood came upon him. Not, as some have supposed, because of the disgraceful attacks of his ill-wishers, but because of a genuine religious conversion, he left the theatre. In the peace of faith he found refuge from the torments of the characters of his own creation, and he abandoned the public stage. One great play, however, he still had to give to the world. At the age of fifty-two, in 1691, he produced his Christian drama, *Athalie*. The theme of love is now far off, and a bare lyric grandeur takes the place of the earlier searchings of spirit. Its simple plot contrasts the ambitious queen Athalie, her hands stained with blood, and the youthful Joas, heir to the true vision. This story of faith and purpose he has exhibited with much the same subtlety as, but with calmer assurance of spirit than, he had revealed the tormented emotions of *Phèdre* and *Andromaque*, achieving, however, a deeper impression because of the way in which the individual characters are silhouetted against the background provided by a chorus of maidens. The first choral ode celebrates the power of God:

> His glory fills the universe sublime,
> Lift to this God for aye the voice of prayer!
> He reign'd supreme before the birth of Time;
> Sing of His loving care.

And the final words of this choral group are devoted to the same subject: in a sense the invisible God is the hero of the play. The hand that created such concise, memorable lines for the delineation of Andromaque and Phèdre has lost none of its skill: such a person as Joad, for example, is put before us with peerless simplicity in less than a dozen words; when, shortly after his first appearance, he utters the line

> Je crains Dieu, cher Abner, et n'ai point d'autre crainte,
> —I fear my God, and know no other fear,—

his entire rôle in the play is indicated in a single illuminating flash. In its own time *Athalie* won little esteem, but the nineteenth-century romantics, in spite of their general reaction against Racine's classicism, found qualities in this play lacking in the others, so that for many it has come to stand as his highest achievement.

To assess Racine's position aright is a hard task. That he cannot be compared with the very greatest dramatists is certain, since his range and his style are both limited. Shakespeare and Sophocles, despite the power and the subtlety of their poetic medium, still retain much of their quality even in translation: the very precision and simplicity of Racine make his plays somewhat dull and bare when the poise of their original language is rendered into other tongues. Allied to this is the fact that they imperiously demand a particular kind of theatrical interpretation, and certainly do not offer either to actor or to director the rich possibilities that have given the Shakespearian tragedies their triumphant career upon the stage. As a result, the performance of Racine's dramas outside of France—and even there very largely only by the company which inherited the traditions of the age of Louis Quatorze—is rare: French actresses for over two and a half centuries have won fame in the rendering of Racine's rôles, but it is seldom that these rôles receive stage realization abroad.

These are limiting factors, but against them may be placed other considerations—and among such considerations the most significant is the power that Racine exhibits to achieve dramatic interest and tension by the simplest possible means. He demonstrated that violent action and richness of incident were not necessary to engage an audience's attention, that excitement could be induced by concentrating upon the delicate delineation of inner movement, that subtle suggestion could play a part almost as forceful as bold enunciation. He showed how the dramatist could exhibit characters whose whole beings are consumed by desires beyond their reach, so that with the impossibility of satisfying these desires life becomes empty and death is a merciful deliverance. Through these qualities he taught much to the stage, and his influence, indirect if not direcit is far-flung. The entire development of the modern psychologcal, drama owes much to his inspiration.

MOLIÈRE AND THE COMEDY OF MANNERS

THE GROWTH of classical tragedy in France moved steadily forward alongside a corresponding growth of comedy. Racine himself inserted among his serious dramas a witty *Plaideurs*, and Pierre Corneille started his theatrical career with a comic *Mélite*. The very fact that classical theory stressed the purity of genres, or kinds, induced men to seek expression now in the tragic style, now in the comic, and this stress on purity led towards the creation of comic scenes of peculiar excellence and individual quality.

THE PRECURSORS OF MOLIÈRE: PIERRE CORNEILLE

In the year 1638 there was published—with, rather extraordinarily, a dedication to Sir Kenelm Digby—a play manufactured under highest auspices. It had been especially commissioned by Richelieu himself, and for its composition he had selected five authors— Boisrobert, Colletet, Corneille, l'Estoile, and Rotrou. His object was to set up a model for a new comedy.

In harmony with his political desires, which sought order, precision, and unity, Richelieu definitely approved of those critics who endeavoured to apply the pseudo-classic rules. The formlessness of the popular tragi-comedy was to him anathema, and all his efforts to encourage the drama were orientated towards the creation of pure comedy and tragedy, towards simplicity, and towards the preservation of the unities. The play he had commissioned, and of which he was, indeed, part-author, *La comédie des Tuilleries*, was designed to show what comedy of this kind should be.

Of the five authors of the piece the only man of true genius was Corneille. With his *Mélite* of 1629 he had shown himself possessed of genuine dramatic skill, apt in the delineation of manners, and interested in depicting social life in a realistic manner. Between the composition of this play and the *Comédie des Tuilleries* came several other similar works from his pen—*La veuve* (*The Widow*, 1633), *La galerie du palais* (*The Palace Gallery*, 1634), *La Place Royale* (1634), and *L'illusion comique* (*The Comic Illusion*; printed 1639)— all of which marked him out as a writer of promise.

It cannot be claimed that the experiment in joint authorship was a signal success, yet there can be no doubt but that Richelieu's emphasis on classical precision, concretely exemplified in the simple plot and symmetrically balanced scenes of his comedy, was in accord with the needs of the time, was to prove of prime importance in the development of the French theatre, and was not alien to the genius of Corneille himself, who, although a trifle restive under the excessive strictness which some critics would have desired to impose upon the stage, was well equipped to experiment in the style of classic comedy.

In so far as these comic efforts of his are concerned, however, we must admit that Corneille was a precursor, not a thoroughly accomplished master. In *Mélite* he demonstrated to contemporaries how the pattern of real life, the life of society, could with propriety and delicacy be reproduced in dramatic form; in *L'illusion comique* he created a comic spirit richer than anything that had hitherto been shown on the Parisian stage; and in his later comedies—particularly *Le menteur* (*The Liar*, 1644), based on *La verdad sospechosa*, in which he opened up the way for a true comedy of character—he led the van of those among his companions who discovered fresh inspiration in the Spanish theatre.

This Spanish influence on the French comic writers of the time is a force which must be fully appreciated. Paul Scarron's *Jodelet, ou le maître valet* (*Jodelet; or, The Man the Master*; printed 1645), Thomas Corneille's *Les engagements du hazard* (*Fortune's Favours*; printed 1657), the same author's *Le feint astrologue* (*The Feigned Astrologer*; printed 1650), and the anonymous *L'amour à la mode* (*Love à la Mode*; printed 1653)—all of them full of wit and vitality, and all destined to inspire other plays abroad—are derived from this source. So too is what must be regarded as among the very best of these mid-seventeenth-century comedies, Scarron's *L'héritier ridicule* (*The Foolish Heir*; printed 1650), a gay dramatic picture of cross-purposes in love, with its amusing scenes in which Filipin poses grandiloquently as Dom Pedro de Buffalos.

THE ADVENT OF MOLIÈRE: THE EARLY FARCES

During the decades immediately to follow the stage was well supplied by comic authors. The earlier group, headed by the two Corneilles and by Paul Scarron, soon were succeeded by others such as Philippe Quinault, whose very first play, *Les rivales* (*The Rivals*; printed 1655), was a comedy, and who produced in *La comédie sans comédie* (*The Comedy without Comedy*; printed 1657) a work of genuine interest; Samuel Chappuzeau, a restless spirit who contributed several lively pieces to the contemporary stage; Racine, whose *Les plaideurs* (*The Litigants*, 1668) is an amusing satire on lawyers; and Raymond Poisson, an actor who wrote a number of farcical comedies not without merit.

All the comic authors of the second half of the seventeenth century, however, fade into insignificance when we turn to Jean-Baptiste Poquelin, who, under the name of Molière, stood forward in this time as one of the greatest masters in the art of comedy that the world has known. However, it was not until 1655, when he was thirty-three years of age, that his first important work, *L'étourdi, ou le contretemps* (*The Blunderer; or, The Mishaps*), was written and acted. Up to that time he had been gaining experience in the playhouses. His own company, L'Illustre Théâtre, had been formed in 1643, and since then had been touring the provinces with a repertory consisting mainly of farce; now the future author of *Tartuffe*, trained in his profession of actor, felt himself ready to add to that repertory by plays in which his sense of the stage and his wide observation of life could find free scope.

Before *L'étourdi* it is possible, even likely, that Molière had written one or two short farces; if so, we have a suggestion of their style in two pieces, *La jalousie du Barbouillé* (*The Jealousy of Le Barbouillé*) and *Le médecin volant* (*The Flying Doctor*), first published in 1819 from an early manuscript. Clearly based on the style of the *commedia dell' arte*, yet displaying affinities with medieval farce, they well illustrate the manner in which their author may have served his apprenticeship, drawing strength and assurance from the popular French tradition, and enlivening that with material taken from Italian sources. The former play introduces to us a jealous fool, Le Barbouillé, married to Angélique. At a loss to know what to do, he consults a doctor, who, refusing to listen to him, gives him a long discourse on his own merits. In the end, thinking to trap his wife as she returns home late from a party, he is himself locked out of his house and severely chided by Angélique's father. Equally slight is the plot of *Le médecin volant*. Here also a doctor appears, but in this case a pretended one. Gorgibus, father of Lucile, does not wish his daughter to marry Valère, whereupon the young man's servant, Sganarelle (played by Molière himself), takes upon him to dress as a doctor, and, despite his ridiculous patter, completely dupes Gorgibus and is thus enabled to effect the union of the lovers. Gorgibus greets him:

GORGIBUS: Doctor, I am your very humble servant. I sent for you to come and see my daughter who is ill; I put all my hopes in you.

SGANARELLE: Hippocrates says, and Galen, too, with strong reasoning, argues, that a person does not feel well when he is ill. You are right to put all your hopes in me, for I am the greatest, the cleverest, the wisest doctor in the vegetable, animal and mineral faculty.

GORGIBUS: I am delighted to hear it.

SGANARELLE: Do not imagine that I am an ordinary doctor, a common doctor. All other doctors compared to me are abortions. I possess wonderful talents; I am a master of many secrets. *Salamec, salamec.* "Hast thou courage, Rodrigo?" *Signor, si; signor, non. Per omnia sæcula sæculorum.* Still, let us see a little. [*Feels* GORGIBUS' *pulse.*

SABINE: Eh! He is not the patient; it is his daughter who is ill.

SGANARELLE: It does not matter: the blood of the father and that of the daughter are the same; and by the deterioration of the blood of the father, I can know the illness of the daughter.

GORGIBUS: Ah! doctor, I am greatly afraid that my daughter will die.

SGANARELLE: S'death! she must not! She must not indeed have the pleasure of dying before she has the doctor's prescription.

The title of the farce comes from the fact that in the course of his intricate deception Sganarelle is forced to impersonate not only the doctor, but also his own supposed twin brother—all of which necessitates his flying on and off the stage in disguise and out.

For the longer and more pretentious comedy of *L'étourdi* Molière passed from the *commedia dell' arte* to the *commedia erudita*, choosing for inspiration *L'inavvertito* (*The Indiscreet Man*), by Nicolò Barbieri, already used by Quinault for his *L'amant indiscret.* The plot is little more than a series of episodes. Lélie is in love with Célie, and in order to win her agrees that his servant, Mascarille, should indulge in a series of stratagems. To the disgust of this witty and ingenious rogue, however, Lélie destroys plot after plot by his blunderings. Sometimes he wrecks his servant's plans through ignorance of what is being arranged, sometimes through excessive honesty, sometimes through his own love obsession. There is an undoubted advance here upon the style of the short farces, but dramatic intricacy is lacking, the characters are as yet only surface-drawn, and there is no sign of that comedy of social criticism which later was to prove Molière's greatness.

After the series of episodes in this play we move to a mass of complication in *Le dépit amoureux* (*Lovers' Spite*; acted first at Béziers in 1656), another work based on an Italian comedy— *L'interesse* (*Self-interest*), by Niccolò Secchi. Although it can hardly be esteemed to show an advance upon *L'étourdi*, individual scenes exhibit a widening of the author's dramatic skill. Such episodes, for example, are the lovers' quarrels, which are the core of the play, and the scene in which Albert tries in vain to get the attention of the pedant Métaphrase:

MÉTAPHRASE: *Mandatum tuum curo diligenter.*

ALBERT: Master, I wish to——

MÉTAPHRASE: Master is derived from *magister*; it is as if you said "three times greater."

ALBERT: May I die if I knew this. But let it be. Master, then——

MÉTAPHRASE: Proceed.

ALBERT: I will proceed, but do not you proceed to interrupt me thus. Well then, master (mark, this is the third time!), my son causes me some anxiety. You know that I love him dearly, and that I have always carefully brought him up.

MÉTAPHRASE: It is true: *filio non potest præferri nisi filius.* . . .

ALBERT: He seems to me to have set his heart against matrimony, and whatever match I propose to him he is cold and indifferent, and rejects my offer.

MÉTAPHRASE: Perhaps he is of the temper of the brother of Marcus Tullius, who discoursed about it to Atticus; and as the Greeks also say that: "*Athanaton*——"

ALBERT: For Heaven's sake, you irrepressible pedagogue, leave in peace the Greeks, the Albanians, the Sclavonians, and all the other nations you want to talk about. What can my son have to do with them?

MÉTAPHRASE: Very well, then, your son——?

ALBERT: I often wonder if some secret love does not burn within him. For certainly there is something on his mind; and, unnoticed by him, I saw him yesterday, alone in a part of the wood where nobody ever goes.

MÉTAPHRASE: In the remote part of the wood, do you mean to say? a solitary spot, in Latin, *secessus*; Virgil says, *est in secessu locus*——

In the end his disquisitions are cut short only when Albert brings in a large bell and rings it loudly at his ear.

THE PURSUIT OF MASTERY

Towards the end of the year 1658 Molière brought his company to Court and won royal favour with a repertoire of farces, his own and others'. To those he added, in 1659, *Les précieuses ridicules* (*The Affected Ladies*)—also a farce, but a farce with a mighty difference. Here for the first time the individual style of the author becomes apparent, for *Les précieuses ridicules* is in essence a social

LOPE DE VEGA
From *Lopé de Véga*, by Marcel Carayon (Presses Universitaires de France, Paris, 1929).

SETTING FOR A PLAY BY CALDERÓN, 1690

From *Lopé de Véga*, by Marcel Carayon (Presses Universitaires de France, Paris, 1929).

comedy. The externals of the plot are not unlike those of many earlier plays—the disguising of a witty servant—but in this case the servant's masquerading has a different dramatic purpose. When Mascarille parades as a marquis it is not in order to cheat an old man and win a lady for his master, but to expose the absurd affectations of the ladies themselves. In the cult of preciosity, fed by the interminable romances of the time, Molière saw an object well worthy of the laughter of social comedy; he sought to entertain, and to reform through entertainment. The Marquis has himself carried directly into the house, and the girls at once are infatuated with his elegant hauteur and languid grace. "My dear," says Cathos, "we should call for chairs"; "Almanzor," replies Madelon to her page, "convey me hither at once the appliances of conversation." To cover her mistake in thus vulgarly alluding to chairs, Cathos turns to the Marquis: "For pity's sake," she begs,

> do not be inexorable to that armchair which for the last quarter of an hour has stretched out its arms to you; satisfy the desire it has of embracing you.

The attack on what was then a fashionable diversion of Parisian Society soon had various ladies of the Court protesting violently, and, although Molière assured them that he was but aiming his shafts at absurd provincials, he found that the hornets' nest he had aroused suggested the taking of more cautious steps for at least the immediate future. In *Sganarelle, ou le cocu imaginaire* (*Sganarelle; or, The Cuckold in his own Imagination*, 1660) he accordingly produced an innocuous, and a highly successful, farce in which the citizen Sganarelle thinks his wife unfaithful and yet cannot rouse up courage enough to seek vengeance on her supposed lover. He considers the claims of honour, lets prudence calm his rage, and then, with anger once more rising, comes to his final conclusion. He will address himself to some manly action:

> Yes, my blood is up, I will revenge myself on the scoundrel, I will be no coward! And to begin with, in the heat of my passion, I am going to tell every one everywhere that he is living with my wife.

After a somewhat unfortunate excursion into the field of tragicomedy (*Don Garcie de Navarre*, 1661) the actor-dramatist once more swung back to social comedy in *L'école des maris* (*The School for Husbands*, 1661), the first truly great comedy from his pen, and one destined for a lengthy career. Although lacking the ease and organic structure of some of his later works, this comedy, based on Terence's *Adelphi* and on Lope de Vega's *Discreta enamorada*, exhibits clearly the qualities that give him his real title to fame— (the development of a social comedy in which excesses are ridiculed wittily, good sense is enthroned, and the golden mean is made the prize of man's endeavour.) Externally this comedy is, like Ben Jonson's, classically realistic; like the English dramatist, Molière endeavours to present in imaginative terms deeds and language such as men do use; yet there is an essential difference between the two. Jonson bent all his energies to the creation of satire, and the things he satirized were those follies that touched him nearly; for Molière the task was to shed comic laughter on follies he deemed inimical to the social structure. Jonson was ego-centred; Molière's orientation was towards the society to which he belonged.

The School for Husbands is somewhat mechanically planned, but Molière's typical approach is well exemplified in its scenes. The two main characters are set before us at the very beginning—Ariste, who argues that one should bow to the ways of society, and Sganarelle, his brother, who churlishly insists on the expression of his own individuality. "We should always fall in with the majority," says Ariste, "and never cause ourselves to become conspicuous. All excesses are offensive, and every truly wise man ought not to display affectation either in his dress or his language, but willingly follow the changing customs of his time." These two men are revealed in relation to their wards, Isabelle in the charge of Sganarelle and Léonore in the charge of Ariste. Where the socially amenable Ariste allows Léonore her freedom, the puritanically individualistic Sganarelle insists on imposing his will upon Isabelle. The greater part of the play is devoted to showing how this girl, irked by the restrictions imposed upon her, eventually tricks her guardian and marries Valère, while at the end Léonore expresses her willingness to marry Ariste, whose kindness has won her heart. Poor Sganarelle, the misanthropist, is left alone cursing the female sex and the more strongly confirmed in his misanthropy.

Following *The School for Husbands* came the rather slight sketch entitled *Les fâcheux* (*The Bores*), which formed a *comédie-ballet* presented before the King in 1661. *L'école des femmes* (*The School for Wives*, 1662) soon followed, and in this Molière made a notable advance in his comic art. The serious element is over-pronounced in *The School for Husbands*: brilliant as are many of the scenes, the play is written to a thesis. Far greater freedom and more liveliness in the character delineation animate its successor. The difference between the two comedies may be realized when we contrast the

Ariste and Sganarelle of the one with the other's Chrysalde and
Arnolphe. Basically they represent the same types, but here the
types are made richer and more delicately humanized. Arnolphe is
also a surly individualist, but instead of having a philosophy on
which his actions are dependent, he is presented as an ambitious,
self-confident egotist. Similarly, Chrysalde appears not as a mouthpiece for a particular view of life, but as a good-humoured, cynical
man of the world. When the play begins we are shown Arnolphe
(who, to shine in society, calls himself M. de la Souche) planning
to marry his innocent ward Agnès, a girl as yet wholly ignorant of
the world. He explains his belief that if a man is to avoid being
made a cuckold he should marry such an ignorant maiden, and keep
her ignorant. His assurance is complete: "I am up to all the cunning
tricks and ingenious devices which women employ to deceive us,"
he declares. "As I know that we are always duped by their dex-
terity, I have taken my precautions against mishaps, and she who is
to be my wife has all the ignorant simplicity needed to save my
forehead from evil influence." In vain Chrysalde presents before
him his worldly wisdom; in vain he argues that no man can count
himself safe, and that, if one needs must marry, the best plan is not
to worry overmuch about it; the only certain course is not to
marry at all. As the play develops we are introduced to this innocent
Agnès, whose simple little heart is stirred into love by the gentle
courtship offered her by Horace. This young gentleman, however,
is rather like the hero of *L'étourdi*, and nearly ruins his own chances
by confiding to Arnolphe (whom he does not know to be Agnès'
guardian) the whole progress of his love-affair. The first important
scene in which Agnès and Arnolphe are shown together is perfect
in its simplicity:

ARNOLPHE: It is very pleasant walking.

AGNÈS: Very pleasant.

ARNOLPHE: What a fine day!

AGNÈS: Very fine.

ARNOLPHE: Well, and what news?

AGNÈS: The kitten is dead.

ARNOLPHE: That's a pity: but we are all mortal, and every one must
think of himself. Has it rained here during my absence in the
country?

AGNÈS: No.

ARNOLPHE: Did you feel dull?

AGNÈS: I never feel dull.

ARNOLPHE: What have you done during these nine or ten days?

AGNÈS: Six nightshirts, I think, and six nightcaps too.

Prompted, she tells frankly and openly of her having seen Horace from her balcony, and of her later meeting with him. Arnolphe then announces that he intends to marry her immediately, and reads her a passage from a book entitled *The Maxims of Marriage; or, The Duties of a Wife: with her Daily Exercises.* As her love grows, so Agnès throws off her simple folly; from a desire to have her as his wife because of her innocence, Arnolphe moves to a deeper devotion, but all is in vain; by a sudden turn of the plot Agnès is made free to marry her Horace.

The play immediately made a stir, and there were not wanting moralists and literary critics who attacked its contents and its style, whereupon Molière made dramatic history and added to his stock of comic scenes by penning the first play upon a play—*La critique de l'école des femmes* (*The School for Wives criticized*, 1663). Climène, a *précieuse*, feels faint with disgust after seeing it; Uranie protects it against her strictures; Élise satirically agrees with Climène; a marquis thinks it must be altogether silly because it has proved so popular; the poet Lysidas feigns to praise, but easily allows himself to reveal his belief that such pieces are not true comedies. Into the mouth of Dorante Molière has put his own defence. He argues that the general applause given to the drama is a testimony to its value and to good sense, that the "rules of art" cannot be taken as definitive laws. "I should like to know," he remarks, "whether the greatest rule of all rules is not to please, and whether a piece which has gained that end has not followed the right road."

The controversy continued. Edmé Boursault gave to the Hôtel de Bourgogne his *Le portrait du peintre, ou la contre-critique de l'école des femmes,* whereupon Molière replied with *L'impromptu de Versailles* (*The Impromptu at Versailles,* 1663), in which his actors are gathered together for a rehearsal. Here, again, Molière seems to have been making dramatic history: the play within the play was a well-known device, but this seems to be the first 'rehearsal' piece on record. Ironically he hits out at the style of acting at the Hôtel de Bourgogne. Once more a single individual, Brécourt, is introduced to put forward the claims of common sense. The comic author does not present satirical portraits, he argues: "The business of comedy is to represent in a general way all the defects of men, and particularly those of our own age"—and consequently he ought to remain free from the strictures of those petty individuals who fail to see that in his work is to be found a corrective for society.

THE TRIUMPH OF THE ART OF COMEDY

Immediately after these plays came a couple of slight *comédies-ballets*—*Le mariage forcé* (*The Forced Marriage*) and *La Princesse d'Élide* (*The Princess of Elis*), both acted in 1664, the one at the Louvre and the other at Versailles. Neither deserves much attention, although the former—which shows Sganarelle anxious to marry, and then, having seen his future wife's flirtatious propensities, at the end aghast at the thought of the wedding—is written with verve and gaiety.

A third time Molière was asked during this year to contribute in the diversion of the Court, but instead of these two flimsy shows his chief offering to the gorgeous spectacle at Versailles, entitled the *Plaisirs de l'île enchantée*, was the first version of his deepest and his bitterest comedy, *Tartuffe, ou l'imposteur* (*Tartuffe; or, The Impostor*). We cannot tell precisely, of course, what relationship this bears to the drama we now possess, but the fact that, after its Court performance, it was not again given until 1667, and then was forbidden public representation until 1669, suggests that basically it contained the same material as that with which we are now familiar.

Here was the most complete fusion of comedy and purpose. From the portraits of folly Molière now turns to vice. Tartuffe is a sensual, self-seeking hypocrite who trades on credulity. Fastening upon the dull-witted Orgon, he insinuates himself into his household and threatens to bring it to complete disaster. Only his own lust and his over-confidence, brought to betrayal by the innate honesty of Orgon's wife, result in his unmasking, discomfiture, and punishment. Technically the comedy is a true work of genius. For two entire acts Tartuffe himself does not appear before us, yet a powerful impression of his personality is built up through the references to him on the part of the other characters: thus the looming character of his personality comes upon us with the greater force, while his eventual entry is made the more impressive. In the first scene the bigoted Madame Pernelle, mother of Orgon, gives him praise, while his true nature is hinted at in the words of Damis, her grandson, and the maid, Dorine. The whole family is set before us in inimitably etched lines, so that we are thoroughly acquainted with their personalities before ever the main figure appears—and his appearance is effectively contrived. Dorine, the maid, is on the stage when he enters. Catching sight of her, he immediately turns to his servant:

TARTUFFE: Laurent, lock up my hair-shirt and my scourge, and pray
Heaven ever to enlighten you with grace. If anybody comes to see
me, say that I am gone to the prisons to distribute my alms. . . .
[*Turning to* DORINE] What is it you want?

DORINE: To tell you——

TARTUFFE [*taking a handkerchief out of his pocket*]: Ah! Heaven! before
you speak to me, take this handkerchief, pray.

DORINE: What's the matter?

TARTUFFE: Cover this bosom, of which I cannot bear the sight. Such
objects hurt the soul, and are conducive to sinful thoughts.

Almost at once we see him making love to Élmire, Orgon's wife;
Damis, her son, tells his father, and Tartuffe shows his genius by
refusing to deny the specific accusation; instead, he piously declares
that he is "a wicked, guilty, miserable sinner," and, when Orgon
angrily turns on his son, magnanimously chides his patron:

Ah! let him speak; you blame him wrongfully, and you would do
better to believe what he tells you. Why should you be so favourable to me in this instance? Do you know, after all, what I am capable
of doing? Do you, brother, trust to the outward man; and do you
think me good, because of what you see? No, no, you are deceived
by appearances, and I am, alas! no better than they think. Everybody
takes me for a good man, no doubt; but the truth is, I am worthless.
[*To* DAMIS] Yes, dear child, speak; call me perfidious, infamous,
reprobate, thief, and murderer; load me with still more hateful names;
I do not gainsay them, I have deserved them all; and on my knees
I will suffer the ignominy due to the crimes of my shameful life.
[*Kneels.*]

His unmasking comes only when Orgon is persuaded to listen while
he makes further love to Élmire and seeks speciously to argue that
she may without sin lie with him because of "the purity of the
intention." Even then he is not defeated and almost succeeds in
ruining Orgon, who is saved only by direct intervention of the King.
There is an atmosphere here closely akin to that of Jonson's
Volpone, but, whereas in the English play there is hardly a worthy
character among all the *dramatis personæ*, and whereas all these
dramatis personæ are exaggerated caricatures, Molière's domestic
interior, although treated idealistically, is true to life, and good shines
among the bad. Madame Pernelle is the typical old bigot, Orgon
the besotted fool, Élmire the wife who would rather suffer incon-
veniences than have trouble in the house, Dorine the keen-eyed
little maid, Damis the honest youth who has not tact enough to
make his honesty known. In reading *Volpone* we are not con-

cerned with the interests of society; in *Tartuffe* Molière seeks to
arouse laughter that he may warn his fellows of an insidious danger.

Tartuffe was a hypocrite: in *Don Juan, ou le festin de pierre* (*Don
Juan; or, The Banquet of Stone*, 1665) Molière delineated the atheist
for whom no conventional morality has any meaning, the brave
soul whose daring leads him to disaster. There is a mood of continual dissatisfaction about his hero; like Faust, although in another
way, he seeks for the unattainable:

> The true pleasure of love consists in its variety. It is a most captivating
> delight to reduce by a hundred means the heart of a young beauty;
> to see day by day the gradual progress one makes; to combat with
> transport, tears and sighs, the shrinking modesty of a heart unwilling
> to yield; and to force, inch by inch, all the little obstacles she opposes
> to our passion; to overcome the scruples upon which she prides her-
> self, and to lead her, step by step, where we would bring her. But
> once we have succeeded, there is nothing more to wish for; all the
> attraction of love is over, and we should fall asleep in the tameness of
> such a passion, unless some new object came to awake our desires and
> present to us the attractive perspective of a new conquest. . . . I have
> in this the ambition of conquerors, who go from victory to victory,
> and cannot bring themselves to put limits to their longings.

Accompanied by the timorous Sganarelle, he is revealed in diverse
aspects, in the end—like Tartuffe—donning the garb of the hypocrite in order to effect his purposes, and after this final evil being
consumed in hell-fire, while Sganarelle, true to the spirit of comedy,
can think only of the money owed him and now lost to him for
ever:

> Oh! my wages! my wages! His death is a reparation to all. Heaven
> offended, laws violated, families dishonoured, girls ruined, wives led
> astray, husbands driven to despair, everybody is satisfied. I am the
> only one to suffer. My wages, my wages, my wages!

An apparently more joyous play followed—*L'amour médecin*
(*Love is the Best Doctor*), acted in 1665 as part of an elaborate *comédie-
ballet*—but the bitter tone apparent in the two dramas immediately
preceding cannot quite be concealed by its gaiety. The plot is a
simple one. Lucinde, daughter of Sganarelle, pretends illness in
order to further her love-affair with Clitandre. Four pompous
doctors are called in to attend her, and spend most of their time in
boring talk about the social aspects of their profession. Eventually
Clitandre dresses as a physician, declares that Lucinde's trouble is
mental, and persuades Sganarelle that she must be humoured:

CLITANDRE: However, as one must flatter the imagination of patients, and as I see in your daughter signs of distress of mind that would be dangerous if prompt remedies were not administered, I have made use of her own fancies and have told her that I was here to ask her of you in marriage. Then her face changed in a moment, her complexion cleared up, and her eyes brightened. If you keep up that delusion in her for a few days, you will see that we shall save her.

SGANARELLE: Indeed, I am most willing.

CLITANDRE: After that we will use other remedies to cure her entirely of these fancies.

SGANARELLE: Quite right!—Well, my daughter, here is a gentleman who wishes to marry you, and I have told him that I am most willing.

LUCINDE: Alas! is it possible?

SGANARELLE: Yes.

LUCINDE: But really?

SGANARELLE: Yes, yes.

LUCINDE [*to* CLITANDRE]: What! are you willing to be my husband?

CLITANDRE: Yes.

LUCINDE: And does my father consent to it?

SGANARELLE: Yes, my child.

LUCINDE: Ah! I am truly happy, if it is really so!

CLITANDRE: Do not doubt it for one moment; my love for you does not date from to-day, and I have long wished to be your husband. I came here on purpose, and if you wish to know the whole truth, this dress is but a mere disguise, and I only acted the doctor that I might better obtain what I desire.

LUCINDE: You give me marks of real affection, and I am as grateful as I can be.

SGANARELLE [*aside*]: Oh! the foolish, foolish, foolish girl!

LUCINDE: You are willing, then, Father, to give me this gentleman for my husband?

SGANARELLE: Yes, yes; come, give me your hand. Give me yours also, sir.

CLITANDRE [*holding back*]: But, sir——

SGANARELLE [*choking with laughter*]: No, no, it is to—[*stifling his laugh*] to soothe her mind. Shake hands, both of you. There, the affair is settled.

CLITANDRE: Accept as a gage of my faith this ring, which I give you. [*To* SGANARELLE] It is a constellated ring, which cures all delusions of the mind.

LUCINDE: Let us write the contract, then, so that nothing be wanting.

CLITANDRE: Alas! I will do so, if you like. [*Aside to* SGANARELLE] I will call up the man who writes my prescriptions, and tell her he is a notary.

SGANARELLE: Very well.

CLITANDRE: Ho! there! send up the notary I brought with me.

LUCINDE: What! you had brought a notary with you?

CLITANDRE: Yes.

LUCINDE: How pleased I am!

SGANARELLE: Oh! the foolish, foolish, foolish girl!

L'amour médecin was followed by what many critics regard as Molière's greatest play, *Le misanthrope* (1666), in which his comic view of life becomes darker and his consideration of man more philosophic. Basically this is a study in the opposition in the human being between his own individuality and his needs as a social animal. The central figure is Alceste, a character akin to the individualist of *L'école des maris*, but more intimately and effectively delineated. The empty politenesses that accompany social life arouse his anger and annoyance; why, he asks, should he praise a wretched sonnet on which his opinion is requested or bow and smile to a man whom he has no intention of seeing again? To his own disgust he finds himself emotionally attracted by the young widow Célimène, a gay, flirtatious coquette, and the greater part of the comedy is occupied with tracing his repulsion to her follies and his paradoxical desire to possess her. Contrasted with him is the good-humoured, complacent Philinte, who, while recognizing the absurdities of the world, is prepared to accept its manners and to comply with its conventions. The two sides of the picture are presented with scrupulous balance. Alceste is undoubtedly a figure that stirs in us both admiration and sympathy; compared with Célimène, he possesses an honesty and integrity wholly worthy. Yet the individualist is an ever-potent menace to his companions; the only logical course for him and for the society to which he belongs is to have him sent out in loneliness to a desert. This, indeed, is the end of Alceste. Célimène's frivolity has been amply demonstrated, but even a realization of her pettinesses cannot kill the love for her he has in his heart: he consents to forgive her, on condition that she will follow him into the solitude where he has vowed to live. "What!" cries Célimène, "renounce the world before I grow old, go and bury myself in the wilderness?" Alceste argues with her:

> But if your love answers to mine, what can be to you all the rest of the world; are not all your desires centred in me?
>
> CÉLIMÈNE: Solitude at twenty years of age frightens me. I do not find in my heart greatness and self-denial enough to yield to such a fate; if the gift of my hand can satisfy your wishes, I am willing; and marriage——

This offer Alceste indignantly rejects, and the play ends with his departure, while Philinte and Éliante prepare for their common-sense wedding, and Célimène retires, no doubt to capture other hearts. These characters are sensible, yet to the very conclusion the balance is preserved: there is a moving quality in the hero's final words:

As to myself, betrayed on all sides and crushed with injustice, I will escape from a gulf where vice triumphs, and look in all the earth for a desert place where one may be free to be a man of honour.

MOLIÈRE'S LAST PLAYS

Laughter, gay and uninhibited, comes again in *Le médecin malgré lui* (*The Doctor in spite of Himself*, 1666), in which a woodcutter, Sganarelle, is mistakenly forced to act as a physician. At the beginning he is cudgelled into his profession, but as he proceeds he finds that he has the audacity sufficient to carry off the trick, and decides that doctoring is better than woodcutting. His patient pretends she is dumb, and Sganarelle is talking with Géronte, her father, who seeks to know the cause of her malady:

SGANARELLE: There is nothing easier; it is caused by her having lost her speech.

GÉRONTE: Yes. But the cause, if you please, for her losing her speech?

SGANARELLE: All our best authors will tell you that it comes from an impediment in the action of her tongue.

GÉRONTE: But still, what is your opinion on this impediment in the action of her tongue?

SGANARELLE: Aristotle, on that subject, says—marvels!

GÉRONTE: I believe you.

SGANARELLE: Ah! he was a great man!

GÉRONTE: Undoubtedly.

SGANARELLE: Altogether a great man. [*Raising his arm above his head*] Greater than I am by all this. To come back to our reasoning, then; I hold that this impediment in the action of her tongue is caused by certain humours, that is to say—peccant humours; for, as the vapours formed by the exhalations of the influences which arise in the region of diseases coming—as it were—to—— Do you understand Latin?

GÉRONTE: Not in the least.

SGANARELLE: You don't understand Latin?

GÉRONTE: No.

SGANARELLE [*with enthusiasm*]: *Cabricias, arci thuram, catalamatus, singulariter, nominativo, hæc musa*, the muse, *bonus, bona, bonum. Deus sanctus, est-ne oratio latinas? Etiam.* Yes. *Quare?* Why? *Quia substantivo, et adjectivum, concordat in generi numerum et casus.*

GÉRONTE: Ah, that I had studied Latin!

JACQUELINE [*the Nurse*]: See what a clever man he is!

LUCAS [*her husband*]: Sure enough, that's so fine that I can't make out never a bit of it.

SGANARELLE: Now, these vapours of which I have been speaking to you, in passing from the left side where the liver is, to the right side where the heart is, it happens that the lungs, which we call in Latin *armyan*, communicating with the brain, which we call in Greek *nasmus*, by the means of the concave vien, which we call in Hebrew *cubile*, meets on its way the said vapours, which fill the ventricles of the omoplate; and as the said vapours—— Follow closely this reasoning, I beg of you—— And as the said vapours have a certain malignancy—— Listen to this, I beseech you.

GÉRONTE: Yes.

SGANARELLE: Have a certain malignancy which is caused—— Be attentive, if you please.

GÉRONTE: I am so.

SGANARELLE: Which is caused by the acrimony of the humours engendered in the concavity of the diaphragm. It so happens that these vapours—*Ossabandus, nequeis, nequer potarinum, quipsa milus*. This is precisely the cause why your daughter is dumb.

When Géronte remarks that he has placed the heart wrongly on the right side Sganarelle can rise gloriously to the occasion with his famous "*Nous avons changé tout cela*":

Yes, it was, formerly; but we have altered all that, and we now practise medicine in quite a new way.

GÉRONTE: I did not know that, and I beg you will excuse my ignorance.

Many plays were still to follow, although some, such as *Le Sicilien, ou l'amour peintre* (*The Sicilian; or, Love the Painter*, 1667)—an anticipation of the *opéra-comique*—may be disregarded. *Amphitryon* (1668), except for the vivacious part of Sosie (written for himself), does not add much to the body of his work, and *Georges Dandin, ou le mari confondu* (*George Dandin; or, The Baffled Husband*, 1668), although replete with verve, is little more than an elaboration of *La jalousie du Barbouillé*, with development of character and the provision of a firmer social background.

In *L'avare* (*The Miser*, 1668), as in *Amphitryon*, Molière sought his theme among the plays of Plautus, selecting for this purpose the *Aulularia*. Although this play is superior to the other two presented during the same year, it betrays a falling off from the brilliance of *Tartuffe* and *Le Misanthrope*. The miser, Harpagon, is rather farcically conceived, and the plot tends to be confused. One has the double impression that Molière, unlike Ben Jonson, is not at his happiest in dealing with miserliness and that his skill of hand is declining. What is of interest, however, is the manner in which the French dramatist has departed from his original by associating the old man with a large household instead of leaving him an isolated recluse. Within that household, too, there is one person, Maître Jacques, who is a masterpiece of comic portraiture. He is both cook and coachman, and keeps two coats ready for his assumption of either of his two duties. A somewhat stupid but good-willed fellow, he provides much of the laughter of the play.

A *comédie-ballet* entitled *Monsieur de Pourceaugnac* followed in 1669—a merry record of the painful adventures suffered by a provincial lawyer among the professional sharks of Paris. In this piece Molière experimented upon, and considerably improved, the comic-opera style already tried in *L'amour médecin*. The mediocre *Les amants magnifiques* (*The Magnificent Lovers*, 1670) was of the same character, as was also the joyous *Le bourgeois gentilhomme* (*The Bourgeois Gentleman*), produced during the same year. The picture painted of M. Jourdain is superb. A middl -class shop-keeper who has amassed a small fortune, he determines to figure in the world of Society. He enters in dressing-gown and nightcap, having been told that in this wise aristocrats hold their morning levees; amid the dancing- and music-masters whom he has sum-moned to instruct him he meanders along in simple-minded delight. Soon the professional teachers are at each others' throats, each claiming the superiority of his own subject, until the exponent of philosophy, flying at his companions, remains lord of the stage. "*Nam sine doctrina vita est quasi mortis imago*," declares the philo-sopher. "You understand this, and you have no doubt a knowledge of Latin?" "Yes," replies M. Jourdain; "but act as if I had none. Explain to me the meaning of it." "The meaning of it is that 'without science life is an image of death.'" "That Latin is quite right," says M. Jourdain. A ludicrous lesson follows, and rises to a culmination in Jourdain's famous discovery that he has been speaking prose all his life without knowing it. Into this world of the fantastically real the Turkish episode at the end fits with perfect harmony: M. Jourdain is made a Mamamouchi by a group of men disguised to hoodwink him, and the play ends with the simple, foolish, and rather pathetic little shopkeeper thoroughly pleased with himself and entirely ignorant of the figure of fun he has become.

In *Les fourberies de Scapin* (*The Tricks of Scapin*, 1671) a return is made to that admixture of *commedia dell' arte* and native farce with which Molière began his work, with Scapin keeping the scenes in constant movement by his skilful impostures. Provincial pretensions are satirized in the rather slight *La Comtesse d'Escarbagnas* (1671), and then, somewhat surprisingly after these efforts, comes the magnificent *Les femmes savantes* (*The Learned Ladies*, 1672). Here the theme is that of education for women. Central in the picture is the pedantic Philmainte, the middle-aged wife of the honest bourgeois Chrysale, who neglects her home for the sake of philosophy. She has two daughters, Armande, a prudish *précieuse*, and the common-sense Henriette. Clitandre is the lover, once the wooer of Armande, but, disgusted by her affectations, now the avowed adorer of her sister. Philaminte deems him too unlearned to marry one of her daughters, preferring the wit Trissotin. On this basis the comedy proceeds. Armande professes repugnance at the thought that Henriette can even dream of marriage—although secretly and almost unknown to herself she is consumed with jealousy. Poor Chrysale tries from time to time to put in a word, but the masterful Philaminte ever bears him down. One hilarious occasion occurs when the maid Martine is being dismissed. Chrysale tentatively inquires the cause, but is soon forced to berate the girl without knowing why: he eventually discovers that she has been guilty of using a word disapproved of by a famous grammarian. Towards the very conclusion of the drama, when Philaminte seems certain to compel Henriette to marry Trissotin, a *deus ex machina* appears in the person of Chrysale's brother, Ariste, who falsely announces that the family has lost all its money: Trissotin immediately backs out of his pretensions to Henriette, while Clitrandre nobly offers the household all he possesses. Anticipating many a later sentimental heroine, Henriette now refuses to wed Clitandre, because she would not burden him with their poverty, when Ariste reveals the fact that his news was merely a device to expose Trissotin. The last words are spoken by Chrysale, anxious at last to assert his authority: turning to the notary, he bids him, "Execute my orders and draw up the contract in accordance with what I said."

The brilliance of this comedy cannot be denied, and yet that last sentimental note is troublesome: it is an indication that a new world is approaching. Molière's own career, however, was now near its end. Suffering from a disease he knew would soon bring his end, he ironically penned his last comedy, *Le malade imaginaire* (*The Imaginary Invalid*, 1673), at the fourth performance of which he collapsed and died. Argan here is a hopeless hypochondriac who surrounds himself with doctors and apothecaries, and it is his person who dominates in the play. Opposed to him is the gay maid Toinette, whose frank enjoyment of life and refusal to think of the morrow provides a vivid contrast to his dark thoughts. A further foil is established in Argan's brother, Béralde, who, mocking the hypochondriac's fancies, counsels a visit to the theatre to see some of Molière's plays. It is in this scene that Béralde quotes the author himself as saying that he will have nothing to do with the doctors:

> He is certain that only strong and robust constitutions can bear their remedies in addition to the illness, and he has only just strength enough to endure his sickness.

Thus closed Molière's career. During its course he had succeeded in creating a comic world which places him among the greatest of comic playwrights. Building from the individual, yet concerned with the presentation of types, he wrote plays in which an inimitable gallery of memorable portraits is placed before us. His fundamental attitude is one of common sense; frankly he accepts the world, and strives to show that excesses of all kinds are fatal to the even tenor of social life. Although his plays include many farces, and even his darkest comedy contains much of hilarity, his greatest power lies in his skill in arousing what has been called 'thoughtful laughter,' where a smile takes the place of the guffaw and in the mind is left a dominant concept. Logical proportion, avoidance of extremes, honest acceptance of the facts of life, the application of reason to social affairs—these were the messages which Molière constantly preached to his fellows even as he contributed richly to their entertainment.

THE RESTORATION COMEDY OF MANNERS

SINCE Racine and Molière were so closely associated with the Court of Louis XIV, we might have thought that France would have produced during this time a drama prevailingly aristocratic. It is true that the former's tragedies reflect the modes of High Society and that the orientation of the latter's comedies is towards the manners set by the King and his courtiers; yet both Racine and Molière refuse to be bound by the aristocratic *milieu*. Molière's main strength, indeed, comes from the fact that the interests of the middle class play a part equal to that of the Court's interests; the family that is nearly wrecked by the machinations of Tartuffe is essentially bourgeois, and the numerous Sganarelles are worthy citizens, not noble gallants. The "bon bourgeois," although he may often be placed in a ridiculous setting, is in a sense the true hero · of these comedies; if he is exposed to the stings of satire it is for the good of his own soul, not because he seems to a well-born author an object of contempt.

Despite the royal patronage accorded to Molière, therefore, and despite the writing of several of his plays specifically for the delectation of the Court, the strength of this classical French drama rests in its power to take into account all classes in the community. The peasant and the shopkeeper, the coachman and the maidservant, are fully as important as the marquises and the wits, nor is the ridicule devoted to the aristocratic follies a whit less than that devoted to the follies of the others.

For a truly aristocratic theatre in this age we must, peculiarly, go to that country which had dared to set on trial and to execute its sovereign. During the time of the Commonwealth Puritan opposition to the stage had succeeded in closing the theatres, so that for eighteen years the only dramatic performances in England were surreptitious productions liable to be interrupted at any moment by the incursion of Cromwell's soldiery, or else, at the very end of the period, simple shows disguised as musical entertainments. Sir William D'Avenant obtained licence to present 'operas' where he would have failed to get leave for the giving of 'plays.' In 1660,

however, the King, Charles II, came back to his own again, and
the playhouses were reopened—but under conditions far different
from those that prevailed during the days of Elizabeth. The great
mass of the citizenry, still dominated by Puritan sentiment, avoided
them; the auditorium became filled with courtiers and their
attendants.

THE RESTORATION PLAYHOUSES

The quality of this audience is the cardinal and determining factor
in the development of the Restoration drama. It explains the fact
that from 1660 to 1682 only two theatres could keep their doors
open in London—and then often at a loss—while from 1682 to 1695
but one stage was active. Innumerable records of these forty years
indicate that the courtiers regarded the playhouses as toys of their
own; the theatres became almost like clubs attached to Whitehall.
Assignations were made there; gallants wandered into the auditorium in search of friends or mistresses; quarrels sprang up while
plays were in progress, and duels even were fought upon the stage.
In structure and equipment these stages stood as transitional
between the Elizabethan and the modern. The new houses, like
those of France, were modelled on the long, narrow, rectangular
tennis-court of the time, with the actors placed, not in the midst of
the audience, but at one end of the hall; indoor conditions introduced lighting as a theatrical element; memories of the Court
masques presented during the days of Charles I, added to the
theatrical knowledge acquired by Charles II's little wandering group
of courtiers during the time of the Commonwealth, led to the
regular presentation of plays with scenic accompaniment. At the
same time Elizabethan traditions could not be forgotten. In place
of the sharp stage-line characteristic of most Continental theatres,
the Restoration playhouse had a curving projection beyond the
curtain—technically known as the 'apron,' and obviously the relic
of the platform stage of earlier times. Besides this relic another
appeared in the presence of two, and sometimes four, doors of
entrance set in the proscenium façade. Through these the actors
commonly moved on to the stage, and through them they made
their exits. Since the apron brought the players nearer to the
audience, and since the doors opened on to the apron, we may
believe that the greater part of the action took place on the forward
area and that the scenery for long remained little more than a background to the actors. It was to be many years before these actors

gradually moved back and were content to perform within, instead of against, the settings provided for them.

While there were some particularly spectacular productions during the Restoration period, we must believe also that most of the scenes were simple and that but little endeavour was made to paint new flats for new plays. All the evidence available suggests that the playhouses possessed stock sets of wings and back-shutters, which were used variously in the presentation of their repertoire, and it is noticeable that the writers both of tragedy and of comedy were inclined to fashion their plays in such a manner as to permit of the use of these stock scenes. Unquestionably the introduction of scenery points towards theatrical realism, but the realism of the Restoration stage was by no means particularized. In tragedies the grove, the temple, and the palace hall follow each other in almost monotonous succession, while in comedy appears the corresponding series of bedroom, boudoir, and park.

The audience was self-centred and fashionably noisy, of that we may be sure; and as a consequence histrionic style in serious drama was apt to become bombastic. These young gallants were not qualified to appreciate tragic drama, and a Betterton could capture their attention only by means of flamboyance of utterance. For comedy, on the other hand, they were ready to attend; a scene of wit could rivet their eyes and ears on the stage, for on conversational wit they fed in their daily lives, and a dramatist's skill in sharp repartee, an actor's ease in the delivery of polished lines, immediately aroused their interest.

Here was the aristocratic playhouse *par excellence*—not the temporary Court theatre of the Renaissance with a privileged invited audience, but a public theatre, set in the midst of a relatively small but bustling community, which yet attracted to its performances only those who clustered around the palace either by right of birth or, like Pepys, by reason of their occupations.

THE HEROIC DRAMA

Despite the fact that at least one author of eminence and two or three others of fitful genius applied themselves to the writing of serious drama during the latter years of the century, absolutely nothing of sterling excellence in this kind was produced by the Restoration theatre. In France Racine won through to the creation of an adequate form of expression for this age of classical sentiment, but in England conditions were not so propitious. France had no distracting romantic traditions to haunt the imaginations of her playwrights. English playwrights could never forget the glories of Shakespeare's tragedies. The result was that all the efforts made in London to devise a new tragic form were vitiated by confusion of form and uncertainty in orientation.

Typical is Thomas Otway, an author of more than mediocre talent, who made determined attempts to develop a tragic style suited to the conditions of his time. Racine laid a spell upon his spirit, and his early plays, notably *Alcibiades* (1675) and *Don Carlos* (1676), obviously strove (and failed) to capture classical form, yet the Shakespearian influence could not be gainsaid. After a pitiful experiment in trying to turn *Romeo and Juliet* into a Roman *Caius Marius* (1679) he reverted completely to native English models, producing a kind of romantically emotional domestic tragedy in *The Orphan; or, The Unhappy Marriage* (1680) and another romantic tragedy with an Italian setting, *Venice Preserved; or, A Plot Discovered* (1682), which almost achieved true greatness. The age, however, could not cultivate that sternness of spirit out of which the Elizabethan tragedy was wrought, and consequently, noble as is Otway's attempt, the quality of pathos takes from its would-be tragic grandeur. Considered in relation to the development of Restoration drama alone, *Venice Preserved* must be accounted a great play, but when it is set against the background of the theatre as a whole we have regretfully to dismiss it as but a very modest eminence amid surrounding mountain heights.

At the beginning of the Restoration period John Dryden, a worthy successor to the literary giants of the earlier part of the century, sought to evolve a form of 'heroic drama,' penned in couplet verse, harmonious with the classic predilections of his contemporaries. The conflict of love and honour was its staple theme; intellectualism ruled the conduct of its scenes; and inflated bombast was employed in a vain endeavour to arouse that mood of admiration which the tragic drama demands. There are some magnificent things in these plays of Dryden—in *Tyrannic Love; or, The Royal Martyr* (1669), in *The Conquest of Granada by the Spaniards* (1670), in *Aureng-Zebe* (1675)—but their whole atmosphere is false and their conception confused. The Duke of Buckingham had ample justification for his satirical burlesque of the form in his famous *Rehearsal* of 1671.

The failure of this form of drama was tacitly recognized by Dryden himself when he turned, in 1677, to write his blank-verse *All for Love; or, The World well Lost* on the theme of Antony and

Cleopatra. The structure here is classical, but the selection of a theme which Shakespeare had enriched indicates an awareness of the impossibility of producing anything of worth in the purely 'heroic' style. Thereafter, for the last quarter of the century, the tragic drama oscillated precariously and uncomfortably among the ideals of classic precision, heroic sentiment, pathetic interest, and Shakespearian grandeur. John Crowne essayed classicism dully in several dramas; Nathaniel Lee mingled mad absurdities with searing flashes of real genius; from John Banks came a series of tragedies in which heroines took the leading rôles—*Virtue Betrayed; or, Anna Bullen* (1682) and *The Island Queens; or, The Death of Mary, Queen of Scotland* (printed 1684) being the best—without, however, in the slightest degree suggesting the subtlety with which Racine had handled similar material.

Surveying this long range of bombastic and pathetic dramas, we must confess that the Restoration genius had but little to offer to the realm of tragedy. The power that had invested the Elizabethan period was gone, yet there did not exist that singleness of aim and precision in form out of which alone strength could emerge from the classic style. Racine's greatness is seen clearly outlined when presented against the array of these works.

RESTORATION COMEDY: JOHN DRYDEN AND OTHERS

If, however, the Restoration audiences could not foster an effective tragic drama they were well qualified to summon forth the comic spirit. The one thing on which their minds were set was social brilliance; fine manners ruled, witty conversation was practised and admired, intrigue formed the daily business of the gallants and their ladies.

To a large extent conditions at the English Court were similar to those at the Court of Versailles, but there was one fundamental difference. Despite the haughty tone of the French nobility, Molière could, as we have seen, bring within his circle the world of the middle class and as a consequence produce a comedy broad in its implications. For the courtiers who thronged Drury Lane, Lincoln's Inn Fields, and Dorset Garden the middle class simply did not exist; these courtiers were interested in their own exclusive affairs, and everything outside was neglected. Thus came into being an entirely new type of play—the comedy of aristocratic manners; and, although it does not have the breadth of appeal which attaches to any dramatic form wider in its range, the accomplishment of the

Restoration comic authors is by no means negligible. We may decide that the style of comedy they produced has but limited interest, but in the handling of their material they were undoubtedly accomplished, if characteristically careless, masters.

Already before the theatres closed in 1642 comedy, as has already been suggested, was moving steadily from the humour of Shakespeare and the satire of Jonson to the gay presentation of the witty Cavalier's existence. In the plays of Shirley the atmosphere of the Restoration is clearly adumbrated. When the return of Charles II permitted the actors once more to go about their business the time and the conditions were ripe for the fuller development of the genre sketched in these earlier plays. The courtly society was even more than previously a coherent unity, conscious of its own peculiar principles. By the introduction of scenery a suggestion of immediate reality could be given to the episodes of daily life. The substitution of actresses for boy players permitted a richer development of the sex-duel which formed the basis of so many of these episodes. In the hands of diverse authors the ornate Elizabethan prose periods were giving way to a new, crisp, intellectual prose style admirably equipped to deal with comic dialogue. Above all, there was the model set in France. During the sixties Molière was rapidly making himself the outstanding dramatist of his time, and, although his earliest introduction to the English stage was in a burlesque scene of *The Playhouse to be Let* (probably written by Sir William D'Avenant in 1663, but possibly a burlesque, penned by an unknown author, of his theatrical efforts), there is plentiful evidence in the plays of the time that his works were eagerly and appreciatively read by English dramatists. They found his plots too simple; they rejected much that he had to offer; but for structure and for comic invention they ransacked his writings. Without doubt, despite the difference between his spirit and theirs, he contributed much to the Restoration dramatists of manners.

Even here the theatre is not entirely sure of its aims. There were playwrights such as Thomas Shadwell, who, although presenting scenes in the style of the comedy of manners, fundamentally looked back to the Jonsonian comedy of humours. In *The Sullen Lovers; or, The Impertinents* (1668) this author won an instant success; both his skill and his range of comic invention were displayed in *The Humourists* (1670), *Epsom Wells* (1672), *The Squire of Alsatia* (1688), and *Bury Fair* (1689). In these the teeming world of Restoration London is set before us, its wit and its folly, its uglinesses and its graces; but in writing his plays Shadwell explored no new territory. His model was Jonson, and to the style of that author's comedy he added nothing. Other playwrights, like Mrs Aphra Behn, pursued the comedy of intrigue, especially the Spanish variety beloved of Charles II. In her *The Rover; or, The Banished Cavaliers* (1677; second part 1680) and *Sir Patient Fancy* (1678), as in John Crowne's surprisingly sprightly *Sir Courtly Nice; or, It cannot be* (1685), we have little of delicacy in the dialogue, but much intricacy of episode and bold caricature.

Still other writers, while making passing contributions to the characteristic comedy of manners, displayed a strange eclecticism, indicating their lack of certainty as to what they wished to achieve. Of these, unfortunately, John Dryden is one. Without doubt the witty lovers of his early comedies—*The Wild Gallant* (1663), *An Evening's Love; or, The Mock Astrologer* (1668), *Marriage à-la-mode* (1672)—as well as such pairs as Celadon and Florimel (*Secret Love; or, The Maiden Queen* 1667,) from his tragi-comedies, did something towards consolidating the first experimental essays in the new style, but in all of these there is a lack of distinction; the delineation of manners is confused by association with scenes cast clearly in imitation of Jonson and with episodes inspired by the Spanish comedy of intrigue.

THE COMEDY OF MANNERS

For its development the true comedy of manners requires single-ness, and sureness, of aim, and this first was indicated in the work of Sir George Etherege, a gentleman of fashion, to whom the depiction of the aristocratic world came easily. His first essay, *The Comical Revenge; or, Love in a Tub* (1664), in which he mingled comic scenes with heroic, marked a false start, but in *She Would if She Could* (1668) and *The Man of Mode; or, Sir Fopling Flutter* (1676) he brilliantly outlined the main features which were to be adopted by all those who applied themselves to this comic kind. Of these features most significant is the emphasis laid on the young gallants in their prime quest of amorous adventure. In the comedy of Shakespeare the lovers generally are not particularly interesting, and, although in Benedict and Beatrice there is a faint suggestion of what was to come, it is not so much of the lovers themselves we think when considering his lighter plays as of the atmosphere in which they appear. Jonson was too intent on his satirical purposes to allow this element free play, and in Molière it is more commonly the wit of a servant than the liveliness of a gallant that captures our attention. Spanish comedy, it is true, had made the lover and his mistress central figures, but always the code of manners in that country prevented the full development of repartee between the man and the woman—between the lover who tried to cover emotion with a veneer of scepticism and the lass who, though coy and affected, would fain be won. During the entire history of the drama this was the first time when conditions of social life and of the theatre were propitious for the development of such scenes as Etherege had to display.

In presenting these lovers to us Etherege paints them in terms of his age. Courtall and Freeman in *She Would if She Could* are portraits of such men as the audience knew—or, rather, we might perhaps say that they were such as the gallants in the audience would have wished to be. This comedy is realistic in that its setting is London and its characters types of that city's men and women, yet it is idealistic in that the dramatist uses his skill to give its life a polish, a grace, and a turn of phrase which but rarely could have been met with in reality. Here is a dream-world of the witty courtier, not fantastic, but based on the familiar and the known.

There is no thought of the past or of the future in this comedy; its men and women live entirely for the present—a present of indolence and pleasure. "Well, Frank," says Courtall at the opening of *She Would if She Could*, "what is to be done to-day?" and Freeman's answer is typical:

> Faith, I think we must e'en follow the old trade: eat well and prepare ourselves with a bottle or two of good Burgundy that our old acquaintance may look lovely in our eyes—for, for aught as I see, there is no hopes of new.

Having thus placed his two heroes, Etherege hastens to introduce us to his heroines—Ariana and Gatty. "My dear Ariana," cries the latter, "how glad am I we are in this town again!" and at once their talk turns to risky adventures. They express envy of the men:

GATTY: How I envy that sex! Well! we cannot plague 'em enough when we have it in our power for those privileges which custom has allowed 'em above us.

ARIANA: The truth is, they can run and ramble here and there and everywhere, and we poor fools rather think the better of 'em.

GATTY: From one playhouse to the other playhouse, and if they like neither the play nor the women, they seldom stay any longer than the combing of their perriwigs, or a whisper or two with a friend, and then they cock their caps and out they strut again.

Very soon the couples have met, the girls masked and the men encountering them in the park:

COURTALL: By your leave, ladies——

GATTY: I perceive you can make bold enough without it.

FREEMAN: Your servant, ladies——

ARIANA: Or any other ladies that will give themselves the trouble to entertain you.

FREEMAN: 'Slife, their tongues are as nimble as their heels.

COURTALL: Can you have so little good nature to dash a couple of bashful young men out of countenance, who came out of pure love to tender you their service?

GATTY: 'Twere pity to balk them, sister.

ARIANA: Indeed, methinks they look as if they never had been slipped before.

FREEMAN: Yes, faith, we have had many a fair course in this paddock, have been very well fleshed and dare boldly fasten.

> [*They kiss their hands with a little force.*

The same ease and gaiety attends all their meetings:

COURTALL, FREEMAN: Your servant, ladies.

ARIANA: I perceive it is as impossible, gentlemen, to walk without you as without our shadows; never were poor women so haunted by the ghosts of their self-murdered lovers.

GATTY: If it should be our good fortunes to have you in love with us, we will take care you shall not grow desperate and leave the world in an ill humour.

ARIANA: If you should, certainly your ghosts would be very malicious.

COURTALL: 'Twere pity you should have your curtains drawn in the dead of the night and your pleasing slumbers interrupted by anything but flesh and blood, ladies.

This ease and this gaiety reach even finer precision in *The Man of Mode*. The title character, a delicious caricature of a fop, is cleverly withheld from us until the play is half-way through; but he is not the mainspring of the comedy: the true figures of importance are Dorimant and his Harriet. The former is characteristically introduced in the first scene, clad in dressing-gown and slippers, soliloquizing over a letter he has penned to a mistress of whom he had grown tired:

What a dull insipid thing is a billet-doux written in cold blood, after the heat of the business is over! It is a tax upon good nature which I have here been labouring to pay, and have done it, but with as much regret as ever fanatic paid the royal aid or church duties.

Harriet is a lady well his match in wit. Both play easily with delicate intellectual fancies, and at heart both feel the force of love, more powerful than their ready scepticism. By convention Dorimant offers his protestations; by convention she conceals her emotions; but the protestations now are sincere, and nothing can quite hide the impress that he has made upon her. She keeps her flippancy to the end, but when Dorimant agrees, in order to see her, to leave his loved town and endure the miseries of the country we know that their marriage is assured: the sprightly blade has been caught and his mistress's armour pierced. Lady Woodvil tells him he will be welcome at her manor if he cares to visit it:

HARRIET: To a great rambling lone house, that looks as it were not inhabited the family's so small. There you'll find my mother, an old lame aunt and myself, sir, perched up on chairs at a distance in a large parlour; sitting moping like three or four melancholy birds in a spacious volary. Does not this stagger your resolution?

DORIMANT: Not at all, madam. The first time I saw you, you left me with the pangs of love upon me, and this day my soul has quite given up her liberty.

HARRIET: This is more dismal than the country!

The painting of this world of fashionable manners requires the most delicate balance, and it is not surprising that few were able to follow Etherege's lead. Individual scenes in the plays of his contemporaries and successors catch his well-poised grace, but of the dramatists belonging to the Court of Charles II only William Wycherley succeeded in capturing his style—and even he exhibited elements alien to this kind of comic expression and dangerously apt to shatter its fragile being. Etherege was born to the manner of the time; Wycherley acquired it. No doubts or fears entered into the former's mind; Wycherley was always liable to view the fashionable world from without rather than from within, and he was, too, always liable to indulge in exaggeration. An accomplished dramatist, with a sure sense of character-drawing, he just failed to move with unthinking ease in the world he chose to depict.

Love in a Wood; or, St James's Park (1671) and *The Gentleman Dancing-master* (1672), his earliest experiments, present gaily the gallants, the fops, and the fools on whom Etherege fixed his attention, but it is not for these plays that he is remembered. In *The Country Wife* (1675) and in *The Plain Dealer* (1676) he produced comedies which at once were recognized as the work of a strong and arresting personality, individual in its outlook. The former of these plays is obviously based on Molière, but there is a vast chasm between the spirits of the English and the French play-wrights, just as there is a chasm between the spirits of Etherege and Wycherley. This story of Horner, who, in order to carry on his intrigue among the ladies unhindered by their jealous males, pretends that he has been castrated, has a viciousness lacking in Molière and a sensuality wanting in Etherege. Dorimant and his companions are libertines, yet there is a grace in their lives which gives them distinction: Horner dwells on another plane. Etherege's wit is expended on social raillery; Wycherley's applies itself almost entirely to sexual affairs. There is brilliance here, as in the scene in which the country wife writes her letter to her lover or as in the famous 'china' scene, yet this brilliance is of a kind less airy and more brutal than that which renders the meeting of Freeman and Courtall with Ariana and Gatty a joyous masquerade.

Recognizing these qualities in Wycherley's work, we need feel no surprise in turning from *The Country Wife* to *The Plain Dealer*. Once more Molière is the model, but, whereas in *Le misanthrope* the hero is presented as a man irritated at the follies and insincerities of social life, as one who feels his individuality threatened by the conventions of the world he moves in, Wycherley's hero, Manly, is one obsessed by sexual thoughts. It is not irritation at social conventions that inspires him, but disgust at infidelity. The very plot of the play indicates its difference from *Le misanthrope*. Manly is the misanthrope, whose faith in humanity hangs slenderly on two threads—reliance on his friend, Vernish, and trust in his mistress, Olivia. Returning from a journey abroad, he finds that Olivia has married Vernish, and his fury at the world rises almost to lunacy—would, indeed, have ended in madness had he not discovered that his page is in reality a lady, Fidelia, who has followed him faithfully because of her devotion to him. There is something of an Elizabethan quality in this plot, and the language often reminds us more of Middleton than of either Etherege or Molière. We are being carried in *The Plain Dealer* far from *The Man of Mode*.

The spirit of Etherege, however, had not died; indeed, at the very end of the century it was to reach its fullest expression in the work of William Congreve. Here perfection was attained both in poised acceptance of the social world and in precision of utterance. The very first lines of *The Old Bachelor* (1693) illustrate this fully. Bellmour and Vainlove meet:

BELLMOUR: Vainlove! and abroad so early! Good morrow. I thought a contemplative lover could no more have parted with his bed in a morning than he could have slept in't.

VAINLOVE: Bellmour, good morrow. Why, truth on't is, these early sallies are not usual to me: but business, as you see, sir [*showing letters*]. And business must be followed, or be lost.

BELLMOUR: Business! And so must time, my friend, be close pursued, or lost. Business is the rod of life, perverts our aim, casts off the bias and leaves us wide and short of the intended mark.

VAINLOVE: Pleasure, I guess you mean.

BELLMOUR: Ay, what else has meaning?

The plot much concerns Heartwell, "a surly old bachelor, pretending to slight women," who falls in love with Vainlove's discarded mistress, Silvia, agrees to marry her, and is saved only by a trick at the end. This theme, however, is merely the material fabric of the play: its spirit depends on the adventures of Vainlove and his Araminta; he intoxicated with delight in the chase, but immediately chilled when the object of his attentions shows any fondness, and she, aware of his capricious foibles, dallying gracefully with him. They are in love with each other, this pair, yet the mood of their time keeps them delightfully apart.

In *The Double-dealer* (1693) a similar combination is presented. The action is kept moving through the machinations of Lady Touchwood and Maskwell, and through the follies of Lord Froth, "a solemn coxcomb," his *précieuse* wife, Lady Froth, and the "pert coxcomb," Brisk, but the quality of the comedy depends upon the relations between the young gallant Mellefont and Cynthia, his mistress. In their conversations the wit flows easily and fancies abound:

MELLEFONT: You're thoughtful, Cynthia?

CYNTHIA: I'm thinking, though marriage makes man and wife one flesh, it leaves 'em still two fools; and they become more conspicuous by setting off one another.

MELLEFONT: That's only when two fools meet and their follies are opposed.

CYNTHIA: Nay, I have known two wits meet and by the opposition of their wit render themselves as ridiculous as fools. 'Tis an odd game we're going to play at. What think you of drawing stakes and giving over in time?

MELLEFONT: No, hang't, that's not endeavouring to win, because it's possible we may lose. Since we have shuffled and cut, let's e'en turn up trump now.

CYNTHIA: Then I find it's like cards; if either of us have a good hand it is an accident of fortune.

MELLEFONT: No, marriage is rather like a game at bowls. Fortune indeed makes the match, and the two nearest, and sometimes the two farthest, are together, but the game depends entirely upon judgment.

A certain darkness of spirit lightly clouds *The Double-dealer*; though perhaps a faint shadow yet remains in *Love for Love* (1695), this comedy displays Congreve in the process of fully mastering his instrument. Valentine and Angelica here are the lovers. Because of his extravagance the hero has fallen under the displeasure of his father, Sir Sampson Legend; in a thoughtless moment he agrees to sign a bond, whereby Sir Sampson engages to pay his debts on the understanding that the inheritance will be handed over to his brother Ben, a sailor. Repenting of his action, he later pretends insanity, and is saved, partly through Ben's rough manners, partly through Angelica's presence of mind and wit. This simple plot is complicated by the introduction of many finely etched and amusing characters—Scandal, Valentine's free-spoken friend; the garrulous Tattle; superstitious old Foresight; Mrs Frail, Foresight's amorous sister-in-law; and Miss Prue, a gawky young country girl. There are comic scenes between the irascible Sir Sampson and Foresight, between Ben and Miss Prue, between Mrs Foresight and Mrs Frail. The last-mentioned characters, indeed, provide one of the most exquisite episodes in the play. They are sisters, and the former upbraids the latter for going in a coach to Covent Garden and meeting a friend there. "But can't you converse at home?" she inquires:

> I own it, I think there's no happiness like conversing with an agreeable man. I don't quarrel at that, nor I don't think but your conversation was very innocent; but the place is public, and to be seen with a man in a hackney-coach is scandalous. What if anybody else should have seen you alight, as I did? How can anybody be happy while they're in perpetual fear of being seen and censured? Besides, it would not only reflect upon you, sister, but me.
>
> MRS FRAIL: Pooh, here's a clutter! Why should it reflect upon you? I don't doubt but you have thought yourself happy in a hackney-coach before now. If I had gone to Knightsbridge, or to Chelsea, or to Spring Garden, or Barn Elms with a man alone, something might have been said.
>
> MRS FORESIGHT: Why, was I ever in any of those places? What do you mean, sister?
>
> MRS FRAIL: Was I? What do *you* mean?
>
> MRS FORESIGHT: You have been at a worse place.
>
> MRS FRAIL: I at a worse place, and with a man!
>
> MRS FORESIGHT: I suppose you would not go alone to the World's End?
>
> MRS FRAIL: The World's End? What, do you mean to banter me?
>
> MRS FORESIGHT: Poor innocent! You don't know that there's a place called the World's End? I'll swear you can keep your countenance purely; you'd make an admirable player.

MRS FRAIL: I'll swear you have a great deal of confidence, and in my mind too much for the stage.

MRS FORESIGHT: Very well, that will appear who has most. You never were at the World's End?

MRS FRAIL: No.

MRS FORESIGHT: You deny it positively to my face?

MRS FRAIL: Your face? What's your face?

MRS FORESIGHT: No matter for that, it's as good a face as yours.

MRS FRAIL: Not by a dozen years' wearing. But I do deny it positively to your face then.

MRS FORESIGHT: I'll allow you now to find fault with my face—for I'll swear your impudence has put me out of countenance. But look you here now: where did you lose this gold bodkin? Oh, sister, sister!

MRS FRAIL: My bodkin!

MRS FORESIGHT: Nay, 'tis yours, look at it.

MRS FRAIL: Well, if you go to that, where did you find this bodkin? Oh, sister, sister! Sister every way.

In this comedy as in the others, however, it is the lovers, Valentine and Angelica, whose wooing and whose wit give characteristic tone to the scenes as a whole. The other characters provide merriment, but they form the focus of the dramatist's attention.

Valentine and Angelica are transformed, and enriched in the transformation, into Mirabell and Millamant of *The Way of the World* (1700), Congreve's last and finest comedy. The plot is an intricately confused one, but whatever puzzlements, inconsistencies, and improbabilities occur in the story need trouble us little; Congreve has atoned amply for these in the scenes he has written about the gay Mirabell, in love despite himself, and the affected, coquettish Millamant, jealous of her freedom, yet fain to be won. Well is her entry prepared for. She is so talked of in the first act that we get a glimpse of her from afar, and then in the middle of the second act, as Mirabell puts it, "she comes i'faith full sail, with her fan spread and streamers out, and a shoal of fools for tenders"—or at least with one fool, Witwoud. She is the perfect lady of fashion. Accused of being late for her appointment, she confesses "Ay, that's true,"

O but then I had—Mincing, what had I? Why was I so long?

MINCING: O mem, your La'shap staid to peruse a packet of letters.

MILLAMANT: O ay, letters—I had letters—I am persecuted with letters —I hate letters—no body knows how to write letters, and yet one has 'em, one does not know why—they serve to pin up one's hair.

WITWOUD: Is that the way? Pray, madam, do you pin up your hair with all your letters? I find I must keep copies.

MILLAMANT: Only with those in verse, Mr Witwoud. I never pin up
my hair with prose. I think I tried once, Mincing?

MINCING: O mem, I shall never forget it.

MILLAMANT: Ay, poor Mincing tift and tift all the morning.

Rising and falling, the wit flows steadily on until at last love conquers, albeit with effort, the affectation of indifference:

MIRABELL: "Like Daphne she, as lovely and as coy." Do you lock
yourself up from me to make my search more curious? Or is this
pretty artifice contrived to signify that here the chase must end and
my pursuit be crowned, for you can fly no further?

MILLAMANT: Vanity! No—I'll fly and be followed to the last moment;
though I am upon the very verge of matrimony, I expect you should
solicit me as much as if I were wavering at the grate of a monastery,
with one foot over the threshold. I'll be solicited to the very last,
nay and afterwards.

MIRABELL: What, after the last?

MILLAMANT: O, I should think I was poor and had nothing to bestow
if I were reduced to an inglorious ease, and freed from the agreeable
fatigues of solicitation.

There follows the delicious proviso scene. "Positively, Mirabell,"
she says,

I'll lie abed in a morning as long as I please.

MIRABELL: Then I'll get up in a morning as early as I please.

MILLAMANT: Ah! idle creature, get up when you will. And d'ye hear,
I won't be called names after I'm married—positively I won't be
called names.

MIRABELL: Names!

MILLAMANT: Ay, as wife, spouse, my dear, joy, jewel, love, sweetheart, and the rest of that nauseous cant in which men and their
wives are so fulsomely familiar—I shall never bear that. Good
Mirabell, don't let us be familiar or fond, nor kiss before folks . . .
nor go to Hyde Park together the first Sunday in a new chariot, to
provoke eyes and whispers—and then never be seen there together
again, as if we were proud of one another the first week and ashamed
of one another ever after. Let us never visit together, nor go to a
play together, but let us be very strange and well bred. Let us be as
strange as if we had been married a great while, and as well bred as if
we were not married at all.

It is all very pretty and very fantastic, the last curtsy of aristocratic
fashion before the new world is ushered in.

PART VI

THE AGE OF GENTILITY, PHILOSOPHY. AND SENTIMENTALISM

THE AGE OF GENTILITY, PHILOSOPHY,
AND SENTIMENTALISM

BY THE time Congreve was writing a new age was already waiting
to take control of the stage. In France and in England alike the
serried ranks of the aristocracy were being broken. While the
young gallants busied themselves with pleasure, worthy and unworthy scions of middle-class houses occupied themselves with
business less witty but more serious, so that the beginning of the
eighteenth century found the circle of the élite impoverished and a
new circle of *nouveaux riches* ready to pay attention to something
more than their counting-houses. When young aristocrats discovered
that they could obtain the wherewithal to live only by espousing
daughters of the wealthy bourgeoisie the barriers between the
classes were shattered, the exclusive families had to admit aldermen
and their wives into their drawing-rooms, and the newly arrived
guests eagerly, if at first somewhat ludicrously, applied themselves
to acquiring the manners of society and to taking an interest in the
diversions of the cultured.

This process was, of course, slow in its development. Already
in Molière's comedies and in the plays of pre-Commonwealth
English dramatists hints are given of what was to come, but only
in the eighteenth century does the movement reach a culmination.
In France the tax-collectors, made rich through the foolish policies
of the Court, established a new class of financiers; in England, less
spectacularly, the men of business had built up pretty fortunes from
trade and, later, from diverse escapades in the East.

The general result was a new theatrical public, destined to call
for dramatic fare different from what had pleased their predecessors.
Since, however, this public was not so coherent as that, for example,
in Restoration London or so assured in its judgments, the eighteenth-
century drama exhibits a strange variety of form. Plays of the
most diverse kinds appear on the stage, and at first it seems almost
impossible to determine the main currents by which the theatre
was carried from the precision of Racine to the romantically melodramatic spectacularism of Pixérécourt. Yet these currents may,
with effort, be distinguished and viewed apart, even if they appear
at times to mingle their waters confusedly.

M   353

One such current may be called *the traditional*, carried forward, although with slackening force, from the seventeenth century. The pseudo-classic tragedy and the comedy of manners continued to persist amid conditions rapidly changing.

The manners, however, were not quite the same. Much as the middle-class members of the audience tried to admire what aristocratic society admired, they could neither appreciate the aristocratic delicacies of style nor quite forget their own moral code. The result of this was that they sought for something more sensational than Racine could give them in tragedy, and that in comedy they were uneasy when polite manners became *risqué*. A man born to the manner may hazard much, for he stands on the firm footing of his birth; a middle-class merchant, admitted on sufferance to this society, has to play safe and is apt to be shocked by freedoms unknown in his own circle. Hence a second main current of the age is that of *the genteel*, insensibly altering the old forms into forms of a new devising.

Beside this is another force. By habit and training the aristocratic society had come to base itself upon precision and convention, and this emphasis on precision and convention it carried over to its literary tastes. Exact comedy and exact tragedy pleased it, and it was quite content to see both presented with a kind of formalism. Not so with those born of the middle class. For them conventions tended to be alien and irksome; they took delight in mixed forms and constantly sought, without conscious purpose, for reality. Realism in itself is obviously hostile to the dramatic tendency to separate plays into diverse genres, for life presents tears alongside laughter and rarely rises for more than a passing moment to either; if tragedy be black and comedy white, then common existence usually manifests itself in a neutral grey. This current of *realism*, even although we may now deem the realism hopelessly artificial, is a potent power in the eighteenth-century theatre.

Allied to that is the current that may be styled *philosophic*. In the past many critics and some playwrights had attempted to demonstrate the moral and even the social value of drama, but they did so only in the broadest and the most general of terms. When we enter the eighteenth century we begin to find, for the first time in modern Europe, a definitely propagandist theatre. Men were beginning in these days to think very seriously about social life; from Addison's gentle essays in *The Spectator* to the revolutionary enthusiasms of Rousseau the age showed itself 'philosophic' in this sense, displaying an almost pathetic belief in the power of reason.

Apart from this, and on a more practical plane, the middle-class audience demanded from the theatre the inculcation of those virtues from which—despite attempts to embrace the code of aristocratic society—the bourgeoisie could not escape. The middle-class fortunes had been built up by hard work and application to business; they depended on efforts extending over periods of years; hence the careless freedom of the aristocratic gallants—their concentration on the pleasures of the moment, their destructive duelling and reckless gambling—were to the merchants anathema. What these merchants wanted was a series of plays in which such vices were condemned and the bourgeois virtues lauded. Consequently the drama of the time becomes filled with highly moral 'sentiments,' and, since these sentiments were commonly both facile and superficial, the provision of stock sentiment easily passed into the sentimental colouring which is so typical of those days.

In endeavouring to trace their currents we must observe that in this century the theatre rapidly becomes more international than it had been during the sixteenth and seventeenth centuries. Not only do diverse countries find a drama awakening in their midst, but there is more interflow of ideas and forms throughout the whole of Europe. It is true that Shakespeare knew of Italian drama, but the influence was one way only; during the eighteenth century the thought and the creative achievement of England, France, Germany, and other lands move more freely across individual frontiers. Hence the study of the theatre in this time demands, not so much the discussion of national achievements, as the tracing of broad movements within the various countries treated as a whole.

CHAPTER I

TRAGEDY AND OPERA

THE FATE of tragic drama during the eighteenth century was but a sorry one. Despite the fact that playwright after playwright attempted to emulate the triumphs of his predecessors in this kind, the conditions were so unpropitious that but little of worth emerged. Opera, on the other hand, flourished, precisely from the same causes as occasioned tragedy's decline: the audience that could not be moved by austerity or aroused to sincere admiration of tragic grandeur found joy in the less exacting emotions of the operatic, revelled in the splendour of the scenes and the rich music of the orchestra. It was mainly the opera that encouraged the building of new theatres.

THE THEATRE OF THE EIGHTEENTH CENTURY

This was the period when the modern type of theatre structure definitely assumed its characteristic form; it was also a period of considerable expansion in stage affairs, not only in the capital cities of the larger countries, but in the provincial centres as well.

In England the patent monopoly established by Charles II in 1662 endured until the nineteenth century overthrew its restrictions, but it is plentifully evident that the growing audiences of the period, swelled by middle-class recruits, were capable of supporting more than Drury Lane and Covent Garden (which supplanted the theatre at Lincoln's Inn Fields). Not only were the patent theatres periodically enlarged within these hundred years, not only did they find more accommodation for spectators by cutting down the 'apron' and putting seats in the space thus saved, but various attempts were made to establish other playhouses in the metropolis. An opera-house in the Haymarket (1705) marked the start of the vogue for musical performances; a smaller theatre in the Haymarket eventually secured a 'summer licence' (1766) under the direction of Samuel Foote: minor theatres, such as Goodman's Fields and Sadler's Wells, succeeded at various times in evading the law and in opening their doors to paying patrons. At the same time the old touring actors of the circuits took on unwonted dignity. All over the country Theatres Royal were being built, and within their walls stock companies presented fare not dissimilar from that which delighted London audiences. By the end of the century hardly a city of importance lacked its theatre, and the stage of the metropolis was constantly being fed by actors who had served their apprenticeship in the provinces.

This was an age of great actors. No doubt David Garrick towered above them all, but the general histrionic quality of the period is indicated by the existence of a brilliant group of players during the first years of the century—including the eccentric Colley Cibber, the sparkling Anne Oldfield, and the tragedian Barton Booth—who handed on the torch to the tempestuous Charles Macklin, the delicate Kitty Clive, and the affected Peg Woffington, until eventually they ceded place to the 'incomparable' Sarah Siddons and her brother John Philip Kemble.

At the same time the French stage likewise gathered to itself a galaxy of splendid performers. Adrienne Lecouvreur won fame for her successful endeavour to supplant earlier rhetorical styles by more realistic interpretation of her rôles; in this she was followed by Mlle Dumesnil (Marie-Françoise Marchand)—although Mlle Clairon (Claire-Josèphe Léris) brought the stage back again to artificial heroics in the grand manner, an effort in which she seems to have been aided by Voltaire's protégé Lekain (Henri-Louis Caïn).

These actors, however, appear to have been less happy in their conditions than their English colleagues. True, they had a national theatre, but their esteem in the eyes of the public was less than Garrick and Mrs Siddons were to enjoy. Yet increase of the French audiences is as clearly marked as increase of the English. Paris had three theatres in 1700; the number was five in 1754, and that had doubled in 1784, when a royal edict gave monopolistic rights to the Comédie Française and the Académie Royale de Musique; in 1791, with freedom restored, fifty-one houses were opened in the metropolis. Meanwhile the provinces showed their own interest in the stage. Almost every large town proceeded to erect theatres of ever greater proportions and richer embellishment. To mention many examples would be tedious; sufficient be it to cite, as illustrative of the general trend, the majestic new playhouse built at Lyon in 1754 and the even more majestic structure of which Bordeaux boasted in 1780. It is indeed a far cry from these monumental edifices to the simple, tennis-court stages of little more than a century previously.

In Spain theatrical affairs were less fortunate. Isabella Farnese, the second queen of Philip V, caused an opera-house to be constructed in 1737, and this, it is true, did have the effect of persuading the managers of the public theatres (still *corrales* in the open air) to think of improving conditions for their audiences; as a result the Theatre of the Cross was established in 1743 and the Prince in 1745. But the spectators at these public theatres were rude and unlettered, and the eighteenth century saw the Spanish drama fall sadly from the heights it had attained in the Golden Age.

Italy too was dominated by opera, and most of the magnificent baroque and classic houses built there were intended for this purpose. Here was constructed the lovely Teatro Filarmonico of Verona (after designs by Francesco Galli-Bibiena), the Teatro San Carlo of Naples (1737, designed by Antonio Medrano), and Milan's famous Scala (1778). For operatic use, too, were intended the rich scenes and the surprising machine effects which Italian architects and designers wrought from their inventive minds. The Galli-Bibiena family of Bologna spread their influence wide, not only throughout their native land, but over the entire European world, and they were companioned by many another artist of rich talent —Filippo Juvarra of Messina, Giovanni Servandoni of Florence, Vincenzo Re of Naples, Giambattista Piranesi of Venice, the various members of the Galliari family of Andorno, whose work, carrying into the nineteenth century, vied with that of the Bibiena. There was, however, in Italy—and especially in Venice—still a dramatic theatre of some general interest, and, although, as in Spanish society, the social vogue was mainly for the opera, just sufficient encouragement was given to the playwrights to keep them creatively productive.

Meanwhile other theatres were awakening in many lands. No doubt patronage was commonly given in most of these countries to the opera, but stages intended for the spoken word arose alongside those intended for recitative and aria. Noble houses designed for the opera were erected through princely enterprise in the Germanic territories—almost every Court of distinction deemed itself uncultured until it had engaged an architect to build it an elaborate operatic stage—but at the side of the companies of singers dramatic troupers were winning their way, surely if comparatively slowly. During the seventeenth century visits of English actors (the *Englische Komödianten*) and of Italian *commedia dell' arte* players prepared the path for native professional troupes. By the twenties of the century following the talented actress Karoline Neuber was establishing her reputation; before the third quarter of the century had been reached the playhouses of Hamburg and of Weimar were welcoming men of such eminence as Lessing and Goethe. In 1800 Berlin had its Royal Theatre, a structure soon to be rebuilt on interestingly new lines under the inspiration of the architect Karl Friedrich Schinkel. Vienna saw the establishment of the famous Burgtheater's tradition in 1752, and this house was soon to be followed by the opening, in 1780, of the Leopoldstadttheater.

About the same time (1782) Stockholm's citizens were introduced to their new National Theatre; Copenhagen's Royal Theatre was opened in 1725; Norway was beginning at the same time to show a faint interest in that form of art from which her greatest writer was to arise. Eastward Russia and other Slavonic lands were wakening to the joys of the stage. Already in 1672, during the reign of Tsar Alexis, amateur performances had been given in the Imperial Palace: further enthusiasm for the drama was witnessed under the inspiration of Tsarina Anna and Tsarina Elizabeth; and finally the great Catherine, herself a dramatic author, thoroughly accustomed her nobles to theatrical productions. At first the playhouses were either built within the Court or regarded as appendages to the Court; soon, however, what the nobles enjoyed was handed down to the bourgeoisie. The history of the great Bolshoi Theatre in Moscow goes back to 1776, and, although the building of this house did not come until the nineteenth century, the official sanction for its establishment is symbolic of its age. Petersburg's Bolshoi, or Kamenni, Theatre was opened in 1783.

In 1765 Poland acquired a public theatre. In Prague a playhouse was opened in 1783 for performances of plays and operas, although in that city a long time had to pass before representations in Czech took the place of those in German and Italian.

If thus it was in the East, so was it too in the West. Far off amid the young American colonies, which were to break their ties with England towards the close of this period, stage-playing had begun, and in the rapidly growing cities theatres were being erected. By the middle of the century several of these cities welcomed more or less permanent playhouses: in 1767 New York had its John Street Theatre, and the end of the century saw the opening of the important Park Theatre, destined to be the first of many imposing houses in the commercial and cultural, if not the political, capital of the United States.

This brief conspectus of stage activities from 1700 to 1800 may provide a clue towards an understanding of the drama produced during this age. Everywhere the Courts were sponsoring the opera, and through their sponsorship ever richer scenery and more effective stage machines were being introduced; everywhere the middle classes were beginning to take an interest in the performances of plays. A new audience and new forms were in process of creation.

THE FATE OF CLASSICAL TRAGEDY

This new audience was not well fitted to take delight in the austere virtues of the tragic drama. It is true that in all countries bewigged and brocaded actors strutted their way across the boards and mouthed speeches replete with impeccable tragic sentiment, but the entire century—at least until the arrival of romantic passion towards its very close—has hardly more than three or four dramas of this kind worthy to be seriously considered. Shakespeare and Racine between them had so far exhausted the possibilities of the dramatic forms they exploited that little remained for their successors to accomplish, while at the same time the social conditions of the period offered but half-hearted encouragement to authors willing to essay this style of composition.

In England at the beginning of the century there was a flutter of excitement over Joseph Addison's *Cato* (1713), but the excitement was political rather than æsthetic. About the same time Nicholas Rowe sought to emulate Racine by penning a series of 'she-tragedies'—*The Fair Penitent* (1703), *Jane Shore* (1714)—but without achieving more than a rather chill pathos. No finer were the works of his followers: *The Distrest Mother* (1712) of Ambrose Philips is only a dull translation of *Andromaque*; the *Zara* (1736) and *Alzira* (1736) of Aaron Hill are fashioned after Voltaire; James Thomson has a trifle more of vigour, yet his classically conceived *Sophonisba* (1730) and *Edward and Eleonora* (1739) hardly make inspiring reading to-day; even the great Samuel Johnson failed when he tried to awaken the tragic spirit with his *Irene* (1749). There was ample justification for those satirists—the Duke of Buckingham, with his *The Rehearsal* (1671), and R. B. Sheridan, with *The Critic* —who turned their caustic pens upon the contemporary tragic theatre.

The Spanish serious drama was at an even lower ebb. The native style descended from the vigour of Calderón to the depths of absurdity, and the attempt made by Agustín de Montiano y Luyando, with his *Virginia* (printed, in 1750, with a lengthy essay "sobre las tragedias españolas"), to introduce the exacter model of Racine utterly failed to meet the needs of the time; nor did his later Visigothic *Athaulpho* (printed 1753) improve upon his first experiment. Twenty years passed before a tragedy based on the French style, Nicolás Fernández de Moratín's *Hormesinda* (1770), appeared on the boards; its influence was insignificant.

In Germany there were slight stirrings of the dramatic spirit, but the country was divided into small principalities and racked by strife—conditions hardly propitious for the production of any work of value. During the seventeenth century Italian and English players carried their wares to many Courts, and, stimulated partly by their efforts, partly by the work of the Jesuit playwrights, Andreas Gryphius composed a series of largely religious tragedies, thus establishing this form in his native tongue. Thereafter numerous attempts were made in the same direction, all without the slightest grace or consequence. On the popular stages flourished bombastic melodramas—the Haupt- und Staatsaktionen—mere mixtures of gory incident, meaningless mouthings, and such conceits as clownage keeps in pay. Only with the appearance of Johann Christoph Gottsched was any conscious attempt made to encourage higher effort. Realizing the formlessness of the German drama, he concentrated upon the pseudo-classic 'rules' and sought to impose French fashions on the theatre of his time. He translated plays by Racine and others and imitated their style in such works as *Der sterbende Cato* (*The Dying Cato*, 1732). Because of his energy and enthusiastic sense of purpose, and because he succeeded in associating himself with a competent group of actors, among whom Karoline Neuber and Heinrich Koch were the most important, his influence was widespread, and up to the time of Lessing the German intelligentsia aped nothing but the French. Little of value came of his efforts, but no doubt this period of apprenticeship was necessary before maturer achievements could come towards the end of the century.

To Russia, as to other countries, the French influence penetrated, and Alexander Petrovich Sumarokov for long was the arbiter of dramatic fashion with his classically inspired *Khorev* (1747) and his *Zemir* (1751). It is worthy of note that he was responsible for introducing *Hamlet* (1748), through a French adaptation, to the Russian public. His successor, Iakov B. Kniazhnin, pursued the same path in his *Vadim* (1789), influenced by both Racine and Voltaire.

It is, of course, to France that we should look for developments in the realm of classical tragedy, but the French genius had all but exhausted itself in Racine: although her tragic stage offered a trifle more than either that of England or Germany, the record of serious plays presented during the latter half of the seventeenth and the entire course of the eighteenth century is rather a sorry one. Dramatist after dramatist essayed to assume Racine's mantle, but it would fit none with ease. Except for the work of one author, it produced merely that dull combination of classic chill and of gory incident which formed the staple recipe of the once famous Prosper Jolyot de Crébillon. The single exception is Voltaire (François-Marie Arouet), who won both his contemporary laurels and his later fame more by his incisive sense of purpose than by his theatrical skill: if he made a real contribution to the theatre it was less in form and concept than in extension of subject-matter. His earliest effort, *Œdipe* (1718), was an obvious imitation of Racine's style with suggestions from the Greek, and these influences endured throughout his entire career. He did, however, try both to recall tragedy from its concentration upon love-themes and to widen the range of tragic material beyond the limits of the classical. *Brutus* (1730), *La mort de César* (*Cæsar's Death*, 1735), and *Mérope* (1743) illustrate the first endeavour, while the second is demonstrated by such dramas as *Zaïre* (1732), *Alzire* (1736), *Zulima* (1740), *Le fanatisme, ou Mahomet le prophète* (*Fanaticism; or, Mahomet the Prophet*, 1741), *L'orpheline de la Chine* (*The Orphan of China*, 1755), and the medieval *Tancrède* (1760). Of these *Zaïre* may be taken as typical. Set in Orosmane's seraglio in Jerusalem, it introduces a heroine, Zaïre, who is loved by and loves the sultan. She is in reality a Christian maid, and, unknown to herself, the sister of Nérestan, a youth who has been released from Saracen slavery so that he might return to France in order to raise money sufficient for the rescue of his fellow-captives. Nérestan returns with just sufficient to buy the freedom of Zaïre and a few other prisoners: for himself he proposes that he should remain in durance. Orosmane, however, meets his offer with noble magnanimity, pledging the release of himself and of a hundred Christians, but declaring that the aged Lusignan and Zaïre cannot be of their number. It is at this point that the true tragic conflict begins. Lusignan is discovered to be the father of Nérestan and Zaïre; she is torn between love of Orosmane and desire to follow her Christian heritage; Orosmane is tortured by the fear that Nérestan is her lover. In the end the sultan stabs her, learns the truth, gives orders for the liberation of all the Christian captives, and commits suicide.

All the chief characteristics of Voltaire's tragic style are here. The Eastern setting gives him opportunity for the introduction of an element of colourful wonder; and perhaps one of his chief contributions to the tragic stage was the introduction of subject-matter apart from the almost exhausted treasury of classical material. Even farther East did he go in *L'orpheline de la Chine*, while in *Alzire*, the sub-title of which is "Les Américains," he voyaged westward to distant Peru at the time of the Spanish Conquest. In *Zaïre* the theme of Christianity and Mohammedanism allows ample chance for the expression of philosophical opinion. There can be no doubt but that there is strength here—yet that strength is not as the strength of Racine. The characters are sentimentally conceived in that their motives spring rather from externally determined principles than from their own inner beings. For revelation of personality in subtle words rhetoric is substituted. It is true that Voltaire had sufficient power to make his plays success-ful in their own day and capable of retaining their hold in the repertoire of the Comédie Française: he lacked, however, the larger qualities which alone can carry a dramatist's work over the boun-daries of his own land. These tragedies certainly did make their appeal to English (and other) contemporaries: they can make little appeal to us to-day.

Typical of his failure is the fact that, while refusing to concentrate entirely on the theme of love in the Racine manner, he yet could not escape from introducing this theme—and, because it did not receive main stress, inrtoducing it unsatisfactorily. In *Mérope*, for example, the principal plot is 'political,' yet Mérope's devotion to her son almost assumes the characteristic of the more familiar forms of love-interest: so too in *Brutus* the austerity of the Roman political scene is softened by Titus' passion for Tullia. Voltaire was, in fact, struggling unsuccessfully against those limitations which Racine had so easily accepted; his sardonic genius was unfitted for the fetters worn so tranquilly by his predecessor.

The truth was, of course, that classical tragedy in France had temporarily run its course. The old 'rules,' certainly, were to continue for years to lay their skinny fingers upon the stage, and even when Shakespeare was first imported across the Channel he was forced by Jean-François Ducis to permit a classic curb upon his romantic fervour: the *Hamlet* that appeared in 1769 and the *Lear* of 1783 were but grinning shadows of their real substance. Never-theless the domination of the pseudo-classic manner was at its close; it had no longer in it the spirit to inspire new works of quality, and soon it was to be supplanted by other aspirations.

As in England, Germany, Spain, and Russia, the French influence swept into Italy. Her earlier attempts at the development of the classical style had not proved very propitious (for example, the *Medoro* (1630) of Giovanni Delfino), and later there is not much of praise that can be given to such dramas as the *Marco Tullio Cicerone* (1715) of Pier Jacopo Martello, but, with the flowing in of French influence, something more promising made its appearance. In the *Merope* (1713) of Francesco Scipione di Maffei a tragedy was written in a style which showed that the Italian theatre possessed potentiality of greatness. The time was ripe. France's greatness was behind her; England could not forget Shakespeare; Spain's theatre was debased; Germany's just becoming aware of itself; whereas Italy was now free to experiment freshly and interestingly in the classical form. *Merope*, although not one of the greatest masterpieces of the theatre, has a quality denied to most works of a similar kind produced during the eighteenth century, a quality so marked that it was deemed worthy of imitation by Voltaire himself. There is true character delineation here, and passion is not concealed by cold rhetoric.

After Maffei there came a lull, with the sporadic appearance of tragic essays such as the *Marco Bruto* (1743) and *Druso* (1747) of Antonio Conti or the *Giovanni di Giscala* (1754) of Alfonso Varano, all of them possessing merely minor interest; then appeared the only true master in that age of the classic drama, Count Vittorio Alfieri, who succeeded in infusing new life and force and grace into the old forms. Fundamentally his strength comes from the fire of his own heroic, if undisciplined, emotions and from his drinking deeply at the prime fount of the Greeks. Racine's artificial delicacy, so hard to imitate, is here cast aside in favour of an idealized reality; further strength comes to his work from the way in which he conceives his scenes in terms of the political enthusiasms of his time. There is a drive here, and a fire, lacking in almost all other similar works written during this age.

Alfieri himself has left a clear critical statement of his aims. The tragic, he believed, should concern itself with the most powerful passions, but reveal these in a form of the simplest and most repressed kind. For themes the finest models were to be found among the legends of the Greeks; in exploiting those there was an opportunity for uniting "artistic truth with moral truth, beauty with morality." In his opinion the theatre ought to be a school in which men should learn to be "free, strong, generous, transported by true virtue, impatient of every oppression, dominated by love of their country, truly aware of their individual rights and in all their passions keen, noble and magnanimous." To secure this end he deliberately renounced the use of secondary characters, of tender emotions, of all that savoured of mediocrity.

Among his earliest dramas—there are twenty-one in all, extending from the *Cleopatra* of 1775 to *L'Alceste seconda* of 1798—is an interesting *Filippo* written on a theme chosen because of the opportunity it gave for the presentation of the liberal-minded Don Carlos in opposition to his father, Philip II of Spain. His masterpieces, however, with the exception of *Saul* (1782) and *Mirra* (1789), are to be found among the groups of plays composed on themes already dealt with by the dramatists of Greece. Of these *Antigone* (1783), contrasting the revolutionary heroine with the tyrannical Creonte, possibly shows his intense political sentiments at their best, but undoubtedly the most powerfully conceived is his *Oreste* (1776). In both, the antique stories are given a new and an interesting development. The first shows Argia, Adrasto's daughter and the widow of Polinice, come to Thebes for the purpose of bearing with her the ashes of her husband. Secretly entering the Theban Court by night, she hopes she may encounter Antigone, and the two women do meet, reveal their identities to each other, and league themselves to undertake the burial specifically banned by Creonte. They are seized by guards; Antigone boldly confesses her action; they are condemned to die, the while Emone, in love with Antigone, pleads for mercy. Discovering his son's infatuation, Creonte changes his plan and offers Antigone the choice of death or marriage to Emone. Stung by pride and determined not to bow to a tyrant's will, she chooses the former. In anger he decrees that she shall be buried alive, but, in carrying out the decree, he finds he has lost his son. Emone enters at the head of an armed band, denies that he has a father, and in misery moves off to his own death, bearing the body of Antigone. In its fundamentals the plot is almost the same as that of Sophocles' drama, but the interpretation of the characters is coloured by modern sentiment; beneath the flow of individual passions runs a powerful political current.

The way in which Alfieri seeks to give reality to the classical legends is well demonstrated in *Oreste*. Even after its treatment by Æschylus, Sophocles, and Euripides, he still is able to find a new approach. Oreste enters after having slain Egisto and also, unwittingly, his mother Clitennestra. Elated, he holds his sword on high, while Pilade trembles at the thought of what will happen when he realizes the truth. "Where is Clitennestra?" he asks, and Pilade evades an answer. Oreste presses him:

ORESTE: Tell me;
             What is't?
PILADE: Stabbed . . .
ORESTE: By whom?
PILADE: Come; let us go . . .
ELETTRA: Thou hast killed her.
ORESTE: I? A parricide? . . .
PILADE: Thy sword
         Has pierced her breast, as thou, unconscious, blind
         In thy rage, dashed upon Egisto. . . .
ORESTE: Oh, what
         A fear enfolds me! I have killed her? That sword,
         Pilade, give it me. I must . . .
PILADE: It shall not be.
ELETTRA: My brother . . .
PILADE: Wretched Oreste!
ORESTE: Who calls me brother?
         Thou impious woman, perhaps, who hast to life
         And to the murder of my mother saved me?—
         Give me that sword, that sword . . . Oh, Furies?—What
         Have I done? . . . Where am I? . . . Who is by me? . . . Who
         Torments me? . . . Oh, where, where shall I fly? . . . Where
         Shall I hide my miserable self? . . . My father!
         Dost thou glare at me? Thou askedst blood;
         And here is blood . . . for thee alone I spilt it.
ELETTRA: Oreste, Oreste . . . O miserable brother! . . .
         He hears us not; . . . his sense is gone. . . . Ever must we,
         Dear Pilade, stand by his side. . . .
PILADE: Cruel
         Inevitable law of fearful destiny!

Alfieri came near towards revitalizing the classical tragic drama,
but already by the time he was writing the forces of romanticism
were at work—and, indeed, his own passion for liberty was part
of the revolutionary movement which animated men's minds
towards the end of the century. His influence upon the Italian
dramatists who immediately followed him was strong, but little
of prime worth emerged from their efforts, and some of these
efforts showed clearly that the romantic theme was nearer to the
age than the classic. Vincenzo Monti closely imitated Alfieri's
style in his *Caio Gracco* (1802) after displaying some faint signs of a
romantic spirit in his fundamentally classical *Aristodemo* (1786) and
Galeotto Manfredi (1788), based on a not entirely unworthy drama of
the same name by Carlo de' Dottori (printed in 1670); in the work
of Giovanni Pindemonte and of Niccolò Ugo Foscolo, on the other

hand, the Alfierian passions were channelled into diverse courses. The former's *Ginevra di Scozia* (*Ginevra of Scotland*, 1795) is thoroughly romantic in concept, while Foscolo is recognized now as one of the stalwarts of the Italian romantic movement. The time was too late to hope for virtue from the pseudo-classic stage.

THE OPERA, SERIOUS AND COMIC

Tragic sentiment more easily in that age found its expression in the softened beauties of the opera. This form of drama, born of the Renaissance, rapidly sped from splendour to splendour. Kings and princes vied with one another in building theatres for its production, and during the eighteenth century both courtly and middle-class audiences found it precisely to their taste. Its appreciation required no intellectual effort or exercise of passion; its scenic beauties pleased the eye and its lyrics the ear. Over the whole world it spread, leaving a trail of rich 'opera-houses' in its wake, although for all this period its prime inspiration remained Italian. Giovanni Battista Lulli may have so identified himself with the Paris Court that he became a Frenchman as Lully, but his birth and training belonged to the land whence the opera had originally sprung. Other composers, such as Henry Purcell and G. F. Handel, although introducing original qualities into their compositions, freely fed from this fount.

The story of opera, of course, does not properly belong in a volume of this kind, yet it may hardly be neglected completely. For music Dryden wrote some of his dramas; *The Beggar's Opera* and the later Savoy operas form part of the record of the ordinary theatre; in a poet such as Metastasio the operatic stage found a dramatist of genius; from the opera descended the plebeian melodrama. In order to understand the course of dramatic history from the seventeenth century to the nineteenth century, therefore, it is necessary to glance at least at the development of the musical theatre.

In Apostolo Zeno, Court poet to the Emperor Charles VI at Vienna, the opera acquired a formalizer who sought to refine and polish the work of his predecessors. A learned man, he aimed at giving to the musical drama a dignity and a regularity akin to what was possessed by the classical tragedies, and, although his own talents were not outstanding, he succeeded in his sixty-odd operas in bringing distinction to a form that hitherto had lacked any true sense of proportion. In this task he was aided by his greatest

successor, Pietro Metastasio (Pietro Trapassi). Metastasio's writings
were universally admired in his own time; Voltaire put him alongside Racine, and most contemporaries would have been prepared
to echo the praise of Rousseau: "He is the only poet of the heart,
the only genius apt to move us by the charm of his musical and
poetical harmony"; even now we can recognize, in the words of
Carducci, that he was the finest Italian poet since Tasso and that
his lyric talent was not rivalled by any other European poet of his
age. To us now his work may seem unduly formal, yet, particularly
in those pieces which he wrote during his so-called 'second period'—
notably *Adriano* (1731), *Issipile* (1732), and *La clemenza di Tito* (1734)
—we find a fine lyrical quality and an economy of means that mark
him out as a writer of unquestioned talent.

What, however, is also to be observed is a certain monotony in
the character presentation of these works. All are alike in their
pattern, and when we note that that pattern always introduces a
noble-minded hero, a frail and unfortunate heroine, and a dark
villain we realize how fatally easy was the passage from courtly
operatic realms to the rudeness of the melodrama. At the same
time the fact that his operas could be, and sometimes were, performed as spoken tragedies without the aid of music testifies to the
fact that they possessed a quality of which most *libretti* are innocent.

Except for this later development of the melodrama and for the
encouragement given to the elaboration of scenic decoration and
machinery, the serious opera left comparatively little impress on
the drama. Metastasio was a lonely lyric genius, and most of the
other *libretti* of the time offer nothing of merit: Paolo Rolli's work
makes sad reading after Metastasio's. More and more the composers seized the upper hand. Handel in England, Gluck and
Mozart in the German lands, these were the men who dominated
in the operatic world. It is also to be remembered that throughout
this period the Italian language was universally regarded as the sole
tongue fit for chorus and aria, with the result that in no country
outside Italy was there any encouragement offered by the serious
musical drama to native writers.

The story of comic opera, however, is another affair. The
beginnings of this form seem ultimately traceable to Naples, where
the exalted courtliness of the grand opera found a rival in a gay,
realistic world, of peasants instead of princes, of farce instead of
formality. When Gennarantonio Federico wrote the words and
Giovanni Battista Pergolesi the music for *La serva padrona* (*The
Maid the Mistress*, 1733) the Neopolitan *opera buffa* acquired an

SETTING FOR "PANDOSTE" AT THE HÔTEL DE BOURGOGNE, ABOUT 1632

A PERFORMANCE IN
LE PALAIS-ROYAL,
PARIS

Bibliothèque Nationale

CLASSICAL TRAGEDY IN
FRANCE

SIR PETER LELY:
"NELL GWYN"

Photo National Portrait Gallery,
London

369

FRANCIS HAYMAN:
"PEG WOFFINGTON"

Photo National Portrait Gallery,
London

international reputation. On its own it proceeded to produce works of spirit and of gaiety, culminating in the magnificent *Socrate immaginario* (*Socrates in Imagination*, 1775), in which Giambattista Lorenzi collaborated with the composer Giovanni Paisiello in presenting a delightfully satirical portrait of the classical enthusiast Don Tammaro Promontorio; at the same time it spread abroad, and, in the form of the French *opéra-comique*, rapidly was accepted by ordinary theatre audiences (as opposed to the more courtly or more affectedly social spectators who flocked to listen to the more ambitious compositions in the tragic style). The *opéra-comique* found a friendly home in Paris, while in England it produced hundreds of musical plays of the lighter kind, from regular comic opera—or 'comedies in music'—to the more interesting ballad operas. Indeed, for a time it seemed as though the ballad opera, in association with related forms, was destined to create a characteristic kind of dramatic expression apt to meet the needs of the new middle-class English audiences of the time.

When John Gay presented *The Beggar's Opera* in 1728 at the small theatre in Lincoln's Inn Fields he took London by storm, and for the next few years the most popular performances were those of pieces similarly composed or of farcical burlesques, mostly with a political colouring, such as Henry Fielding's *The Author's Farce* (1730), *The Tragedy of Tragedies* (1731), *Pasquin* (1736), and *The Historical Register* (1737). In these the age was being given what it wanted. These middle-class audiences did not seek for, and perhaps were incapable of appreciating, delicacy of form; they liked to listen to music; they could relish burlesque; and they were actively interested in political personalities even if political principles were not deeply relished. Gay and Fielding between them went far towards supplying dramatic works well calculated to meet these requirements. *The Beggar's Opera* owed its success partly to its burlesque atmosphere, partly to its gay lyrics, and partly to the fact that, skilfully though it may be constructed, it exhibits none of that precision in pattern which marked the writings of Congreve. Had the ballad opera and the associated political burlesque favoured by Fielding been permitted free range, something of worth might well have arisen from these efforts, but unfortunately governmental action soon brought its uproarious career to an untimely end. Sir Robert Walpole had been keenly touched in the sallies made by Gay and Fielding, and, determined not to permit further attacks upon his person, he succeeded in obtaining Parliamentary approval for the famous Licensing Act of 1737, by the terms of which the activities of the little theatres (such as had housed the efforts of the offending dramatists) were suppressed, and no plays were permitted to be performed until they had first been approved by the Lord Chamberlain or by his deputy. The ballad opera continued its career, but with marked lack of enthusiasm, while Fielding in disgust turned from the stage to become the first of a great line of English novelists.

THE GROWTH OF BOURGEOIS COMEDY

SOME of the interests of the middle-class audiences of the eighteenth century had been met in the work of Gay and Fielding, but these authors did not in any wise reflect what, above all others, was the prevailing characteristic of the time.

With the entry of the bourgeoisie into the theatre new demands were being made. The cavaliers and gallants at the Court of Charles II were content to live for the day, to relish carefree laughter, to ignore contemptuously all that did not come within the privileged circle of their aristocratic society. When this circle was broken and daughters of wealthy merchants, marrying scions of the nobility, brought their families into the playhouses, a clearly marked change in audience attitude, and a corresponding change in drama, became apparent. No doubt the bourgeois spectators were willing, in order to keep up with social tone, to simulate enjoyment—if not actually to enjoy—something at least of the manner of Restoration comedy, but, as we move from the seventeenth into the eighteenth century, we observe, first, that the aristocratic atmosphere is being slowly yet definitely restrained, and that the middle classes, less sure of their foothold in society than those born of noble houses, display an anxious concern with respect to all kinds of excesses. A young gallant of Etherege, because he is absolutely certain of his position in society, may permit himself to do anything; a member of a bourgeois family who seeks to keep in society must ever be cautious, lest he be accused of vulgarity and ostracized. Hence the comedy of aristocratic manners gradually evolves, during the eighteenth century, into the genteel comedy.

This, however, represents merely a negative influence exerted by the new audience. Its power was sufficiently great to call forth a positive influence as well. Where the young Restoration gallant was prepared to follow only the pleasure of the moment and to regard money solely as a means of realizing that pleasure, the middle-class spectator, trained in the way of trade, could never escape thinking of the morrow, and certainly might never avoid seeing money as a commodity not carelessly to be dissipated. For

371

him the future came to mean almost as much as the present, and the wisdom of age to be as important as the sprightliness of youth. Still further, this spectator was concerned mainly, not with daring flights of wit, but with material things: he tended to be practical-minded, utilitarian in his philosophy, and realistic in his outlook on the world. Hence he sought for a kind of play utterly diverse from anything that had been produced in the past.

He was prepared to savour a dash of comedy, but not too much; he was willing, indeed, eager, to welcome pathetic situations and to indulge in the luxury of pity, but not to arouse himself to combat with the austerities of tragedy; he demanded a treatment on the stage of what he conceived to be real life; he desired his plays to be replete with moral sentiment; and he relished seeing in them some not too difficult and not too complex social problem. Hence arose, out of these demands, the characteristic sentimental drama of the eighteenth century, and with its establishment the modern problem drama or play of ideas was adumbrated.

THE FIRST STEPS IN ENGLAND AND IN FRANCE

When we survey the plays written during the first years of the eighteenth century in England and in France it is easy to see the gradual and tentative approaches that are being made in those years towards the sentimental drama of the mid-century.

These approaches are, of course, very faint at first. Congreve was followed by Sir John Vanbrugh and by George Farquhar, and at first the two men seem to be nothing but inheritors of the Restoration tradition. Closer scrutiny of their work, however, indicates that both were breathing a new air. Vanbrugh carries us into the country—territory anathema to the town-loving gallants—and his sense of fun is vastly different from Congreve's play of wit; in *The Provoked Wife* (1697) he shows a woman ill-treated by her spouse who yet remains faithful to him, while in *The Provoked Husband* (1728) a reckless and extravagant 'wife is cured of her follies by her husband's threat of divorce. No less indicative of changing moods are the plays of Farquhar. Both in *The Beaux' Stratagem* (1707) and in *The Recruiting Officer* (1706) the scene is rustic, and there is an evident undercurrent of human feeling below the badinage that marks the arrival of a new style.

In this period, moreover, when Jeremy Collier was startling the theatrical world with his forthright *Short View of the Immorality and Profaneness of the English Stage* (published in 1698), a different class of dramatic author was arising. The successor of the gay Sir George Etherege was the plebeian Colley Cibber, whose *Careless Husband* (1704), in which the libertine Sir Charles Easy is brought to contrition when he discovers that his wife's faithfulness to him is due, not to ignorance of his lapses, but to true love, well displays both the mood of the genteel comedy and the beginnings of sentimental moralizing. At the same time honest Dick Steele (Sir Richard Steele), co-partner with Joseph Addison in the mildly philosophic and essentially middle-class *Spectator*, carried the style a further stage. In *The Funeral; or, Grief à la Mode* (1701), a highly moral play, he concentrates on the elderly Lord Brampton, who pretends to be dead in order to discover the truth in his family circle, thus finds out that his wife has been jealously maligning her stepson to him, and in the end realizes this son's true devotion. *The Lying Lover; or, the Ladies' Friendship* (1703), founded on Corneille's *Le menteur*, didactically attacks the practice of duelling—a delight of aristocrats, but alien to the interests of the bourgeoisie—while *The Tender Husband; or, The Accomplished Fools* (1705) and *The Conscious Lovers* (1722) are full of the most worthy of moralizations and the most pathetic of scenes. Quite clearly we are entering here into a different world, more decorous, more serious, and intent rather on social problems than on character-portrayal or the effervescence of wit.

Similar, although by no means entirely parallel, trends are observable in France. There the comedy of Molière had never exhibited the aristocratic exclusiveness cultivated by the English dramatists of the Restoration, and hence there was no need to react against a tone antagonistic towards the spirit of the new age. Yet even here the middle-class audiences were making new demands. In Molière's plays social conditions are usually neglected, save when they are absolutely necessary for the development of the plots: in those of Jean-François Regnard, his successor and imitator, not only is the range of portraiture widened, but the social *milieu*, especially in its monetary aspects, is considerably more deeply stressed. True, Regnard is a laughing dramatist, not a sentimental, and there are some who, despite his skill in handling intrigue and dialogue, would dismiss his works as mere farce; but the impress of his age is nevertheless upon him. Of his many comedies the earliest were written for the Théâtre Italien, the latest for the Comédie Française. They include the lively *La coquette* (1691), the racy *La foire Saint-Germain* (1695), and the charming *Le bal* (*The Ball*, 1695, renamed in 1696 *Le bourgeois de Falaise*), as well as the better-known *Le joueur* (*The*

Gamester, 1696), *Le distrait* (*The Absentminded Lover*, 1697), and
Le légataire universel (*The Residuary Legatee*, 1708). *Le joueur* tells
the story of an inveterate gambler, Valère, who through his excesses
loses his Angélique and is left disinherited as the curtain falls. The
style and the theme alike recall the plays of Steele. In *Le distrait*
the absentminded Leandre complicates a theme of love and jealousy
by his truly comic tactlessness. The flavour of Steele's plays also
pervades *Le légataire universel*, although the atmosphere is more
bitter than in any of the English dramatist's works. We are introduced here to a world of self-seekers. Old Geronte is obviously
near his end, and with eager eyes his relatives gaze upon his wealth.
In particular his nephew, Eraste, endeavours, by his assiduous
attentions, to become his uncle's heir. In love with Isabelle, this
Eraste learns to his dismay that the old man proposes to marry the
girl, and this proposal is formally approved by her avaricious
mother, Madame Argante. By a somewhat strained device, however, Eraste succeeds in persuading this mercenary lady to agree to
alter her plans, on the assurance that he will be able to obtain a will
from Geronte in his favour; but the young man's hopes are once
more dashed when he hears that his uncle intends to leave large
sums to a penniless Norman gentleman, his nephew, and to his
niece, the wife of an equally penniless baron. This gives excuse for
the main scenes of the play, in which Eraste's servant, Crispin,
impersonates these relatives; thoroughly successful, he persuades
the old man that he ought to leave his money to Eraste. All seems
well, when once more the young man's hopes are dashed by news
of Geronte's death. Only one solution for the problem remains:
Crispin, daringly and a trifle apprehensively, poses before the
attorney as Geronte himself and executes a will—and then is dismayed to learn that Geronte has awakened from his death-like
trance. Only with difficulty is the old man made convinced that in
this trance he has forgotten his immediately preceding actions and
is tricked into approving of the false will.

Much of this is, indeed, farce, but beneath the surface we may
discern a new current flowing. This current is still more clearly
marked in the *Turcaret* (1709) of Alain-René Lesage, wherein
money is the sole motive-force, and the French financier (the type
of man who had acquired wealth in collecting the king's taxes) is
vigorously held up to ridicule. Turcaret, the central figure, is a
man astute in his business affairs, but a fool with women. What he
earns he lavishly presents to the Baroness, a widow, a coquette, and
in reality nothing more than a fashionable courtesan, who, in turn,

gives of her money freely to the specious Knight, her lover. As in *Le légataire universel*, there is not a single amiable character in the entirety of this comedy: all are rogues or fools, and the curtain descends on the servant, Frontin, proud of having tricked his master of a formidable sum of money, boasting that Turcaret's reign is now over and his own begins. In spite of the farcical scenes, *Turcaret* is a bitter comedy, and it is interesting to observe how the style of the comedy of intrigue, which, as is clearly shown by such a play as *Crispin rival de son maître* (*Crispin Rival of his Master*, 1707), Lesage learned from the *commedia dell' arte*, could be turned to purposes of moral import.

Money matters also figure largely in the farcical pieces of Florent-Carton Dancourt, whose plays, if individually of lesser value, collectively provide a magnificent caricature of contemporary society. His *Les bourgeoises à la mode* (*The Citizens' Wives in the Fashion*, 1692; first performed as *Les femmes à la mode*), and *Le chevalier à la mode* (*The Man of Mode*, 1687), and *Les bourgeoises de qualité* (*The Citizens of Quality*; first performed in 1700 as *La fête du village*, and retitled in 1724) may be taken as characteristic. The first shows two middle-class women who render themselves ridiculous by their aping of aristocratic manners, and a couple of husbands made equally foolish by their grasping avarice and arrant credulity. A brilliantly satirical picture of a genteel libertine who courts three women at once appears in the second play. The cynical delineation of social stupidities is carried even farther in the third comedy, where a thin, indeed, barely traceable, plot is used by the author for the purpose of presenting four trenchantly drawn portraits of middle-class characters, each of whom seeks to obtain a title. No dramatist of the time has given a more lively, or a more cruelly mordant, display of a society racked by confusion and rapidly sinking into disintegration.

Reflection of changing social modes appears in the plays of Dancourt's companions, Charles-Rivière Dufresny and David-Augustin de Brueys, but, even although the latter's *Le grondeur* (*The Grumbler*, 1691) once received high praise, we can hardly find other than historical interest in their dialogue and action. These writers need not detain us, but at one author we must pause. Dancourt and Dufresny have no living interest now: Marivaux still retains vitality.

If Lesage is bitter Marivaux (Pierre-Carlet de Chamblain de Marivaux) is genteel. In this author appeared something fresh. Other writers had, without question, accepted Molière as a master:

Marivaux sought for a new style in comedy. To describe this new style is somewhat difficult; its very virtue lies in its subtlety; but fundamentally it may be said to depend upon a translation of Racine's tragic method into comic terms and a polished adaptation of the spirit of the Italian *commedia dell' arte.* Already in the seventeenth century, as has been seen, the Italian players won success in Paris, and towards the end of the century a notable development occurred in their repertory when they called in diverse French playwrights to pen scenes intended to be presented in the midst of their improvised action. Many of these compositions were preserved in the famous collection edited by the actor Evaristo Gherardi, and from these it is plain that the French authors—Nolant de Fatouville, Eustache Lenoble, Jean Palaprat, Regnard, and others— eagerly seized on this opportunity of producing realistic pictures of Parisian manners in a fantastic framework. Typical of such pieces are *L'isle des Amazones* (*The Isle of the Amazons*), in which Arlequin and Pierrot are captured, threatened, and then embraced by the lusty Marphise and Bradamante, and *Arlequin invisible* (*Harlequin Invisible*), in which the *commedia dell' arte* hero has gay adventures through the magic device granted him by Asmodée. The whole of French society parades here, from its aristocrats and its wealthy bourgeois citizens to the dregs of the underworld, and the verve with which many of the scenes is written well justifies those who point to the Gherardi collection as containing some of the best comic material between the work of Molière and that of Marivaux.

In 1697 the Italians encountered royal disfavour and their theatre was closed, but they once more appeared at Paris in 1716, and immediately sought to perform plays specially written for them by French authors. By thus as it were naturalizing themselves the 'Italiens' subtly altered the style of the older *commedia dell' arte*: the originally rough serving-maid was transmogrified into the pert and delicate Columbine, the clownish Pedrolino became a sentimentalized Pierrot, and the whole of the action assumed a misty Watteauesque quality. It was here that Marivaux found his spiritual home.

What he did was to take Racine's intimate searching into the human heart, transform it into comic terms, place it against the fanciful background of the *commedia*, use every endeavour to polish and refine his dialogue, and create out of these elements and qualities a new kind of psychological comedy. Racine had dealt with the ardours and passions of fierce love; Marivaux traced the gentle beginnings of affection charmingly, sympathetically, amusingly.

The whole process of his art is already revealed in one of his earliest plays, *La surprise de l'amour* (*The Unexpectedness of Love*, 1722), in which we are introduced to a group of five characters—Lélio, the Countess, Arlequin, Colombine, and Jacqueline. Lélio and the Countess have both renounced love, and the whole plot concerns the gradual awakening in them of a new, and largely unwished for, affection.

The pattern is varied in other comedies, but the basic model remains. In *La double inconstance* (*The Double Inconstancy*, 1723), the two main characters think they are in love, but gradually discover their error when true love enters their lives. Arlequin and Silvia are affianced to each other, but the Prince chooses the latter for his bride, and Arlequin discovers that, in truth, it is Flavinia whom he adores. Another, and a still finer, experiment on the same lines is *Le jeu de l'amour et du hasard* (*The Game of Love and Chance*, or *Love in Livery*, 1730), which tells of the device by which Silvia changes places with her maid, Lisette, and Dorante with his servant, Arlequin. As might be expected in a comedy of this kind, Silvia finds herself disgusted by her supposed lover (Arlequin masquerading as Dorante), while at the same time, to her dismay, she is attracted by one whom she believes far beneath her in station. Concurrently Dorante (dressed as Arlequin) discovers, also to his dismay, that he has come to adore the girl whom he thinks a maid. By a tortuous process, in which the emotions are delicately revealed, Silvia and Dorante are enabled to find their true selves. Equally delicate is *Les fausses confidences* (*False Confidences*, 1737), which reveals the way in which an impoverished Dorante wins the heart of a rich widow.

In some of his plays there is an extension of subject-matter beyond such themes, and these bring his work close indeed to the characteristic sentimentalism of his century. *L'isle des esclaves* (*The Isle of Slaves*, 1729) is of a different sort. Here an Athenian general, a lady, Arlequin, and a maid are wrecked on a lonely island, and are forced to change places: Arlequin and the maid become master and mistress, while the general and the lady become slaves. We are entering the world of social ideas here, and in that world we remain throughout the scenes of such dramas as *Le triomphe de Plutus* (*The Triumph of Plutus*, 1728), where the evils of wealth are displayed. Marivaux was no revolutionary, yet in his mingling of the genteel and the social he was unquestionably reflecting an age for which the methods of Molière in comedy were becoming a trifle out of date. In his works, and in the works of his companions, the eighteenth century was feeling its way towards a new form of theatrical expression. On Marivaux' plays much later endeavour was to be based. We shall have several occasions for observing the influence both of his delicately artificial, fantastic style and of his intimate revelations of sentiment.

GOZZI AND GOLDONI

Meanwhile the *commedia dell' arte* in Italy itself was producing something of related interest. Throughout the seventeenth century the improvising comedians flourished, retaining their traditional vigour, but, as good showmen, ever showing a willingness to introduce such modification in subject-matter, characters, and theatrical tricks as were likely to prove popular among the changing audiences of the time. Increasingly the literary comedy of the baroque age showed clear signs of the impress made by their performances, and these signs appeared both in the writings of authors who applied themselves to the development of dialect comedy and in those of other authors who sought expression in the standard Tuscan speech. Carlo Maria Maggi thus made much of the type-figure of Meneghino in his Milanese pieces, using the theatrical stock person for the purpose of enunciating concepts of a kind far beyond the reach of the popular comedians with their improvised merriment: typical is *Il falso filosofo* (*The False Philosopher*, 1698). Equally patent traces of the *commedia's* influence are to be seen in the writings of Girolamo Gigli, Jacopo Angelo Nelli, and Giovan Battista Fagiuoli, all of whom eschewed in general the use of dialect forms. The first two of this trio perhaps are of little importance, but Fagiuoli, although no genius, merits some individual attention. Even towards the beginning of his career he could produce a vivid study of contemporary manners in *Ciò che pare non è vero, ovvero il cicisbeo sconsolato* (*Appearance isn't Truth; or, The Disconsolate Gallant*, 1708), and this liveliness continues with him even when his themes grow more serious, as in *La forza della ragione* (*The Power of Reason*, 1736), wherein the rational is made to triumph over the emotional, or *Il marito alla moda* (*The Fashionable Husband*, 1735), with its almost problem theme. His *Gli amanti senza vedersi* (*Love Unseen*, 1737) is an interestingly novel comedy that tells how Lelio, in love with Isabella, seizes her and locks her in his house. Her cries are heard by Federico, who speaks to her in the darkness of the night through a window. As a result of this conversation the couple, without having seen each other, fall in love. Sad puzzlement, however, comes to Federico when he returns in daylight. Lelio has died suddenly, and in the house besides Isabella are his brother, Orazio, and another girl, Lucinda: between the pair of girls poor Federico cannot decide which is the lady of whom he has become enamoured, and only after diverse scenes of 'equivoque' is the tangle straightened out. Another entertaining play by the same author is *L'aver cura delle donne è pazzia* (*Trying to Control Girls is Folly*, 1735), where the story of the young Cintia, determined to have the man on whom her heart is set, proves the truth of the proverbial title.

Even at their best, however, these three comic writers are second-rate and must immediately cede place to two men of unquestioned genius who were their immediate followers—Count Carlo Gozzi and Carlo Goldoni—both deeply imbued with the Italian popular comic tradition, both reared in the midst of the city, Venice, where the *commedia dell' arte* had its deepest roots, yet hopelessly opposed to each other in their ideas as to the use that should be made of this native material.

For Gozzi the *commedia dell' arte* means fantasy and delight. Less delicate than Marivaux, more keenly satirical, and much more apt to fly into a world of wonder and enchantment, he yet is to a certain extent the French dramatist's Italian counterpart. There are no intimate psychological searchings in his plays, but unquestionably the artificiality of the popular comedy appealed to both men in the same way. Each saw in it a pattern into which they might weave their dreams: each eagerly seized on the opportunity it gave them for securing an imaginative contrast between the ideal and the real.

Gozzi's most representative writings are his so-called *fiabe*—fairy-tales with a purpose—grotesque, absurd, full of theatrical wonder, and, at the same time, closely in contact with the real, humorously ironic in concept, interfused with literary satire. Of his first important composition, *L'amore delle tre melarance* (*The Love of the Three Oranges*, 1761), nothing remains save a 'reflective analysis' (*analisi riflessiva*) presenting the outline of the plot, but even this meagre record is sufficient to indicate its quality, and has proved capable of inspiring later theatrical effort of noteworthy quality. The story tells of a melancholic prince, Tartaglia, who, under the curse of Fata Morgana (in league with the traitors Leandro and Clarice), is doomed to die unless he can be made to smile. The faithful Pantalone persuades King Silvio to introduce the laughter-moving Truffaldino to Court in the hope of curing the young invalid, but his utmost efforts fail until Fata Morgana, an old woman, is knocked head over heels by the acrobatic Truffaldino. At this the prince roars with merriment, and the whole Court is rejoiced. His troubles, however, are only beginning. Enraged, Morgana puts a fresh curse upon him: he is doomed to pine for the Three Oranges. These are kept in an enchanted castle many leagues away, and the prince, attended by Truffaldino, sets forth on the perilous journey. Fortunately aided by the magician Celio—Morgana's rival—he obtains the Oranges, gives them to Truffaldino to carry, and is separated from his companion. Although he knows that the Oranges must not be cut open unless a fountain of water is near by, the foolish Truffaldino, consumed with thirst, opens one. A young girl appears from it, piteously pleading for a draught of water. In terror, Truffaldino cuts open the second Orange, intending to give her the juice, and another young girl comes from this, too: both die of thirst. Just as he is about to cut the third Tartaglia enters, angrily takes it from him, opens it and, when a beautiful maiden appears, gets water from a lake, revives her, and learns that she is a princess, the daughter of Concul, King of the Antipodes. The Prince promises to marry her, but, while he goes off to arrange for the wedding, the wicked Smeraldina, a Moorish girl, causes the Princess Ninetta to be turned into a dove and herself takes her place. It seems as though Tartaglia, bound by his promise, must espouse this dark-skinned girl, when Truffaldino succeeds in bringing Ninetta back to her human form, and the play ends happily.

On the surface this is simply a child's fairy-tale, the theme for a sentimental pantomime. It must, however, be remembered that Tartaglia, Truffaldino, Pantalone, and others are characters of the *commedia dell' arte*, performed by actors to whose personal skill was added a rich inheritance from tradition. To them Gozzi makes magnanimous praise-offering. Describing the scene in which Tartaglia finds Truffaldino with the lifeless bodies of the two young girls who have issued from the Oranges, he declares that no words can adequately convey the effect created by the performers. "The witty actors of the *commedia*," he comments, "in scenes like these improvise such graciously pleasing dialogue and action as may not be expressed in written terms and could not be emulated by any dramatic author."

To appreciate *L'amore delle tre melarance*, therefore, we must use every effort of our imagination to reconstruct for ourselves the original conditions of performance. We must also realize that into this framework Gozzi has infused a kind of philosophic content. His chief aim is to entertain, to offer the comic actors a vehicle of wonder for the exercise of their talents, but throughout the action sly satire plays its part. Fata Morgana and the magician Celio are creators of marvels in this fairy-tale: they are also caricatures of those two contemporary playwrights whom Gozzi most detested —Carlo Goldoni and Pietro Chiari. He disliked their sentimental moralizings, he thought they were murdering the theatre of laughter, and, accordingly, in this guise he held them up to ridicule. He held up to ridicule too the dull, bombastic, tragic style of the age, thus making his entire piece, to use his own words, a "fantastic parody."

The same qualities animate all his later *fiabe* (although in these he provided more written dialogue than he had allowed himself in his earliest effort). *Il corvo* (*The Crow*) followed in 1761, and in 1762 came *Il re cervo* (*The King Stag*), *Turandot*, and *La donna serpente* (*The Woman Serpent*). In *La Zobeide* (1763) tragi-comedy ceded to grotesque tragic scenes. This was followed by *I pitocchi fortunati* (*The Fortunate Beggars*, 1764), *Il mostro turchino* (*The Turkish Wonder*, 1764), and *L'augellin belverde* (*The Magic Bird*, 1765), the last characteristically described as a "philosophic *fiaba*," and introducing a poverty-stricken couple, Renzo and Barbarina, who breathe the most moral sentiments of the new French philosophy until they become rich, when all their noble professions of faith vanish in pride, ingratitude, and deliberate evil.

In all of these plays some scenes are left for the improvisation of the actors, but most of the action is fully prepared, with dialogue in prose and verse, by the author. Contrast of every kind is eagerly sought—contrast between the fairy-tale atmosphere and reality, between serious scenes and hilarious, between the imaginative and the satiric, between colloquial prose and delicate verse, between the standard Tuscan tongue and the dialects of Venice or Naples— above all, between scenes apparently designed solely for entertainment and scenes clearly based on philosophic reflection.

These qualities are excellently revealed in *Il re cervo*. The plot tells of a King Deramo who has been given two wonder-making marvels by the magician Durandarte. The first of these is a statue which makes signs to its master when he is being told an untruth. Vainly the monarch has been seeking for a bride: every princess and noble lady brought to his chamber has had her duplicity revealed by the statue's movements, and now at last the King has decided to interview anyone, no matter how poorly born, who may care to seek an interview. Among these candidates he includes one who has sought to escape the ordeal—Pantalone's faithful daughter, Angela. She alone passes the test, and, to her joy (for she is secretly devoted to her lord), is chosen to be the bride. This action, however, enrages Tartaglia, who, besides himself loving Angela, had hoped his daughter, Clarice, would have been the queen. Through his machinations the King is transformed, by means of the second marvel, into a deer; he is nearly slain, would, indeed, have perished had the magician Durandarte, in the likeness of a Parrot, not opportunely given him his aid.

All means are taken to enchant the audience. The prologue is spoken by Durandarte's servant, Cigolotti, who hints at the wonders to come; the scenes, constantly changing, present a rich and beautiful variety; Pantalone's homely Venetian dialect breaks in upon Tartaglia's Machiavellian Florentinity; and Angela's devotion is revealed sharply against the duplicities of her companions. Although German romanticists sadly erred in praising Gozzi as a supreme genius (sometimes placing him even above Shakespeare), they were right in recognizing that, in the midst of an increasingly lachrymose age, this author's keen wit and sense of wonder possessed a virtue well worthy of attention and of praise.

Gozzi was an ironic philosopher; Carlo Goldini tended to be a sentimental one. The former was an aristocrat who might have found himself more happily situated a century before his own time, who contrasted in his mind the courtly ideals of a past age and the hypocritical bourgeois beliefs that animated the intellectuals of the eighteenth century; the latter was born of the bourgeoisie in a bourgeois period. Like Gozzi, he started his dramatic career by writing for the players of the *commedia dell' arte*, but he early came to believe that such buffooneries and fairy-tale wonders as delighted his companion were unworthy of serious attention. His whole inclination was towards the realistic theatre; he came to despise the native popular Italian tradition (even when its impress was laid upon him most strongly) and sought for models in France and elsewhere; despite his overflowing good humour, his spiritual home was rather in the territory of the sentimental drama than in that inhabited by Pantalone and his companions. The very fact that, after an apprenticeship in Venice and Rome, he moved to France in 1762 and spent many years in writing for the Parisian Théâtre Italien is indicative of the trend of his talents.

Goldoni is an author whose merits are difficult to assess. His pen was ever on the move, and among the two hundred and fifty odd plays of his composition there are many which deserve no attention. Even his best works fail to measure up against the masterpieces written by those—particularly Molière—whom he took as his models. He has an infectious sense of fun which gives vividity to his scenes, but his power of observation is shallow. He senses the force of the new philosophical ideas that are transforming Europe, yet his own moralizations are petty, and his solutions for the problems he introduces often absurd. Fundamentally optimistic, he misses much that gave substance to Molière's work. At the same time hardly any dramatist has shown greater fertility in invention, hardly any has so enriched the stage with scenes of genuine comic spirit, hardly any has given such a variegated and vitally delineated panorama of his age.

His essential aims appear most clearly expressed in a critical work he presented in 1750—*Il teatro comico* (*The Comic Theatre*), in which a troupe of actors, under their leader Orazio, is engaged in rehearsing a Goldoni farce entitled *Il padre rivale del figlio* (*The Father a Rival to his Son*). Here are enumerated the various evils of the stage as the author saw them—the foolish and disturbing claims of individual performers, the interlarding of improvised words by the comic players, the introduction of senseless vulgarity just for the sake of arousing merriment, the lack of moral purpose in contemporary plays. From all of this it is obvious that Goldoni, forced though he was to write for actors of the *commedia dell' arte* tradition, dreamed of a stage in which the dramatist gave words to the performers, in which the comic spirit was employed for noble ends, and in which the purely fantastic was replaced by scenes based on observation of life.

This critical presentation of his attitude towards the stage came, of course, some time after he had applied himself to the theatre, and at an early date he had succeeded both in imposing some of his reforms upon the actors and in sketching out the style he wished to follow. By 1743 he had already written his first comedy with completely expressed dialogue, *La donna di garbo* (*The Worthy Woman*), and succeeding plays reveal his chief interests. In *La putta onorata* (*The Honest Girl*, 1748) the social world of his day forms a vivid background to a story which tells of the devotion of the heroine, Bettina, to the man of her choice, despite the evils that surround her. Although he does not dare to come forth too boldly, the dramatist obviously believes that virtue is to be found rather under the humble dress of the poor than under the brocades of the aristocracy. Such a concept runs through the greater part of his work, reaching culmination in a play like *La famiglia dell' antiquario* (*The Family of the Antiquary*, 1749), in which Goldoni's refashioning of the character of Pantalone is most trenchantly revealed. In earlier days Panaltone had been nothing save a comically conceived caricature of a Venetian merchant, wealthy but stupidly amorous and a fit butt for others' wit. In *La Bancarotta ossia il mercante fallito* (*Bankruptcy; or, The Ruined Merchant*, 1741) Goldoni had treated him in such a way, and even in *La putta onorata* relics of his original character still trailed about him, but already in the sequel to that play, *La buona moglie* (*The Good Wife*, 1748), they are beginning to fall away: through Pantalone's sympathetic efforts harmony is restored in a household nearly wrecked by dissension. From this time on Pantalone becomes in Goldoni's hands a sentimentally drawn character, often proving the means by which the happy conclusion ends a series of confusing and even potentially tragic scenes. In *La famiglia dell' antiquario*, although much of the action concerns the follies of the passionately devoted collector of antiques, the basic theme concerns the fate of Pantalone's daughter, Doralice, married into a rather decadent and impoverished aristocratic household. It is only the virtue, the common sense, and the magnanimity of Pantalone that bring all to rights as the curtain falls. It is only old Pantalone's sympathetic aid that prevents the action of *Il giocatore* (*The Gamester*, 1750) from developing into a distressful drama.

In another comedy produced in the same year, *L'avvocato veneziano* (*The Venetian Lawyer*), the author's serious aims are equally clearly displayed. The hero is the lawyer Alberto, who is engaged to defend Florindo in a suit against Rosaura: with her he falls in love, and is consequently torn between his passion and his duty. Fortunately for him Rosaura loses her case, but is persuaded to find in him a devoted and sincere husband. Although Goldoni cannot resist the introduction of rich and hearty laughter in many of the scenes, the basic theme obviously deals with a subject of moderately serious import involving a moral problem.

If these comedies illustrate certain cardinal characteristics of Goldoni's style, the conflicting elements in his comic conception of life are even more widely exemplified in the total range of the famous set of sixteen plays which, with truly amazing facility, he produced during the one season of 1750–51. Among them are charming pieces, such as *Il bugiardo* (*The Liar*) and *La bottega del caffè* (*The Coffee House*), in which merriment derived from intrigue is mingled with not-inexpert delineation of contemporary manners. Witty dialogue gives colour to the scenes of *Il cavaliere di buon gusto* (*The Gentleman of Good Taste*). The character of Ottavio in this play and that of the aristocratic scandalmonger, Don Marzio, in *La bottega del caffè*, are expanded and diversified in *I pettegolezzi delle donne* (*The Women's Gossip*), where the gay depiction of social

METZETIN
Etching in J. Callot's
I Balli de Sfessania.

TWO CAPTAINS
Etching in J. Callot's
I Balli de Sfessania.

RAZULLO AND
CUCURUCU
Etching in J. Callot's
I Balli de Sfessania.

FRANCATRIPPA
AND FRITELLINO
Etching in J. Callot's
I Balli de Sfessania.

OPEN–AIR PERFORMANCE
IN VENICE
Painting by Gabriele Bella
in the Pinacoteca Querini,
Venice.
Photo T. Filippi

385

life is invested with a slight touch of sentimental purpose. In turn, this sense of purpose becomes more patent in the plot of *L'avven-turiero onorato* (*The Honest Adventurer*), and eventually finds itself responsible for the entire colouring of *Pamela nubile* (*Pamela the Maid*), based on Samuel Richardson's famous novel. If Richardson's influence is apparent here, that of Molière is still more potent. After all, Goldoni was a laughing dramatist, and we are not surprised to find among these sixteen comedies both *La finta ammalata* (*The Pre-tended Invalid*), based on *L'amour médecin*, and *Molière*—the latter an open testimony to Goldoni's sense of indebtedness to his French master.

Perhaps the total spirit investing this extraordinary run of plays, in which Goldoni ran the gamut from seriousness to farcical merri-ment, is best expressed in *La castalda* (*The Housekeeper*, 1751), with its engaging portrait of Corallina, and in an immediately succeeding comedy, *La locandiera* (*The Mistress of the Inn*, 1753), with its still more engaging portrait of Mirandolina, who astutely benefits from the attentions of the decayed nobleman the Marchese di Forlipopoli and the rich *parvenu* Conte di Albafiorita, gaily plagues the miso-gynist Cavaliere di Ripafratta, and finally gives her hand to her humble and faithful servitor. Deservedly this has come to be regarded as one of his true masterpieces.

In *La locandiera* another, and a highly significant, quality of Goldoni's art makes its appearance. Although attention is given to the characters, in a sense the comedy has as its chief hero the inn itself, and, noting this, we recall that among the plays men-tioned above is one called *La bottega del caffè*, where the locale assumes almost as much theatrical appeal as the persons who frequent it. In a sense, we may say that Goldoni's comedies take the whole of Venice for their subject, and that in his diverse scenes he casts the spotlight now on a building and now on a social group within the larger community, instead of concentrating, as Molière did, on individuals. The very titles of later plays, such as *Il campiello* (*The Public Square*, 1756), *Il festino* (*The Party*, 1754) and *La villeggiatura* (*The Trip to the Country*, 1756), demonstrate how consistently he exploited this device in so far as localities are concerned, and to these should be added others in which the main effect comes from the delineation of particular segments of Venetian society: the house-hold of the would-be gentleman in *Le femmine puntigliose* (*The Punctilious Ladies*, 1750), the boudoir life of *Il cavaliere e la dama* (*The Gentleman and the Lady*, 1749), and of *La dama prudente* (*The Prudent Lady*, 1750), the teeming city life of *Il cavalier Giocondo* (*Giocondo*

N

the Gentleman, originally acted as *I viaggiatori, The Tourists*, 1755), the rustic vignettes of *Il feudatorio* (*The Peasant*, 1752), the carnival excitements of *Le morbinose* (*The Merry Ladies*, 1758), or the back-stage world at the ballet in *La figlia ubbidiente* (*The Obedient Daughter*, 1752). As typical as any is a scene from *La putta onorata*:

A view of the Grand Canal with gondolas. At one side a wooden booth at the entrance to the theatre. Farther in, the exit-door of the theatre and the little window where tickets for the performances are sold. A BOY *shouts out from time to time: "Get your tickets, sirs, ten soldi each. Here's the cashier, sirs." At the other side a long bench for four people. Here and there lamps such as are usual outside theatres.*

Several masks go by; some go to buy tickets and enter the theatre; some go without tickets and walk off.

NANE, *the gondolier, enters with a lantern, conducting masks to the theatre.*

A servant, also with a lantern, conducts the MARCHESA BEATRICE, BETTINA, *and* CATE. MENEGO CAINELLO *ushers in the* MARCHESE OTTAVIO *and four other men, who go into the theatre. During this time the* BOY *calls out from time to time: "Take your tickets," etc.*

From inside a voice is heard: "This is the way out."

A door opens, and MENEGO *and* NANE *come out with their lanterns.*

MENEGO: Nane! How are you?

NANE: How are you, Menego?

MENEGO: All's well, then?

NANE: What's the matter?

MENEGO: That bit of quarrel we had.

NANE: It's gone clean out of my head, I assure you.

MENEGO: We're enemies aboard, but ashore we're friends and brothers.

NANE: A bit of a row is sometimes necessary just to keep up one's reputation, even although it doesn't mean anything.

MENEGO: Why do you think I didn't give you right of way? Because of my master? Not at all. Simply because fifty gondoliers were looking on, and of course I had to put up a show.

NANE: You've brought your master to the play?

MENEGO: Yes.

NANE: I'm here with a stranger who arrived this morning. I've served him before, and he treated me well.

As they chatter away the chill night air begins to enter their bones, and while their masters enjoy themselves they think of their own pleasures:

NANE: The wind's rising. I'm cold.

MENEGO: We'll put that to rights with a bottle of wine. [*To the* BOY] Come here, you, ticket boy!

BOY: What do you want?

MENEGO: We're cold here: get us a bottle of wine. Tell the waiter that Cainello has sent you and that he's to give you what he gives to his friends. Understand?

There is vigorous theatrical skill displayed in the presentation of the teeming life outside the doors of a Venetian water-fronted theatre and in the manner by which this general background is used as an animated setting for the particular persons of the play— its servants and its gondoliers, its gallants and its ladies.

Still a further general characteristic of Goldoni's work is revealed in the comedies already rererred to. Their very titles indicate how greatly interested he was in the comic presentation of women: *dama* and *donna* are words frequently on his lips. The little follies that accompany the feminine, the gossip in the boudoir, the contrast between outward flattery and inner jealousy—these all caught his observant eye, and some of his most effective scenes are those in which his heroines take a principal part. In *Le smanie per la villeggiatura* (*The Craze for the Country*, 1761), for example, the liveliest and the most delicate episodes are those which show the barbed arrows lurking underneath the outwardly affectionate greetings of Victoria and Giacinta. The consuming, Pandora-like qualities of the feminine heart provide practically all the plot and the interest of *Le donne curiose* (*Female Curiosity*, 1753), wherein a group of women make every endeavour to penetrate into an exclusively male club run by Pantalone and his friends; the title of *Le donne gelose* (*The Jealous Women*, 1752) tells its own story, and the same theme of feminine jealousy appears in *Gli innamorati* (*The Lovers*, 1759); the desire of a lady to have a little court of admirers is the main theme of *La donna bizzara* (*The Capricious Lady*, 1758). In noting the atmosphere of these plays, however, we must contrast it with another atmosphere less satirical. If Goldoni saw feminine follies he did not close his eyes to feminine virtues, and his men are often as petty-minded as his women. Already in the Corallina of *La castalda* and the Mirandolina of *La locandiera* he had drawn sympathetic pictures of capable, attractive, hard-working heroines; and these pictures are paralleled by others, such as that of Giulia in *La donna di maneggio* (*The Housekeeper*, 1760). Besides this, the author's undercurrent of sentimentalism led him to depict the honesty and sincerity of an Eleonora in *Il cavaliere e la dama*, as well as the almost pathetic distresses of a Corallina in *La donna vendicativa* (*The Revengeful Lady*, 1753).

Goldoni's period of richest invention came during the forties and the fifties of the eighteenth century. In 1758 he left Venice and wandered far, first to Rome and later to Paris. Some of his plays written after this date, such as the rather farcical *La donna di governo* (*The Intriguing Woman*, 1758), suggest that his powers were failing, but others amply testify that even after all his early prolific activity he still had strength for considerable comic invention. In *I rusteghi* (*The Boors*, 1760) he presents the excellently drawn figures of the self-opinionated Simon, the stupidly obstinate Lunardo, and the sour old Canciano. *La casa nova* (*The New House*, 1761) pursues the plan of taking a locality and giving it animation: the plot here tells of the troubles of a young husband, Anzoletto, when his thoughtless bride, Cecilia, runs him into debt because she wants her new house to be fashionably elegant, but somehow it is less the married couple than, so to say, the personality of the house itself that comes to true life. Into *La buona madre* (*The Good Mother*, 1761), with its story of the widow Barbara and the way she protects her children, guiding them to socially successful marriage, the inherent sentimentalism of the theme is concealed by sympathetic character-drawing; while in the Venetian-dialect *Le baruffe chiozzotte* (*The Quarrels in Chioggia*, 1762) Goldoni carries to its farthest limits his interesting experiment in the weaving of comedy out of entire social groups—in this instance the inhabitants of a small fishing village.

In France the aging author continued to pour forth his wares. *Il ventaglio* (*The Fan*, 1765) is one of his best-known plays, in which is employed the novel device of making an inanimate object—in this case the fan itself—form the core of the action. Passing from hand to hand, it connects the characters and gives vividity to the complex plot. In *Le bourru bienfaisant* (*The Kindly Boor*, 1771) he even turned to pen a comedy in French, depicting a crabbed old Géronte, who, however, hides a sentimentally sympathetic heart beneath his rough exterior. Another play in French, *L'avare fastueux* (*The Ostentatious Miser*), followed in 1773, and here sentimentalism triumphs in the fate meted out to the miserly count who is its central figure.

With this play Goldoni's career was at an end. That he had succeeded in making real contribution to the stage is certain, yet outside of Italy he remains—and probably is destined to remain—a name rather than a living presence in the theatre. He possessed true ability and an amazingly fecund invention, but for the deeper qualities that go to make the true masterpiece we seek vainly in his work. In his comedies is to be found charm rather than strength. The charm, however, is not a fleeting thing: springing directly from the vivacious author's own character, it irradiates all his works with the sole exception of those dull, serious dramas, so ill-suited to his genius, that he wrote at the beginning of his career. The sunlight of eighteenth-century Venice shines here for those who will take the trouble to search it out. To neglect his work is to neglect something very delightful, gay, and vivacious.

Both Gozzi and Goldoni were a trifle unfortunate in their circumstances. They both had genius: in both that genius was thwarted. Gozzi found the kind of theatre he wanted in the *commedia dell' arte* —and no doubt recognized, albeit unwillingly, that the style of that comedy had become by his time a thing outworn. For such fairytales as he knew so well how to narrate the serious philosophers had but little sympathy. In the *commedia dell' arte* for which he was forced to pen his plays Goldoni sensed only a hindrance to the development of what he wished to give to the world. Had another histrionic style existed in the Venice of his time he might not have had to waste so much valuable energy in effecting the 'reforms' so solemnly expounded in *Il teatro comico*. As it is, instead of achieving what might easily have been a series of pre-eminent masterpieces, each has left little more than a delightful memory of laughter in an age that was becoming so soberly serious.

THE AWAKENING OF THE NORTH: HOLBERG

In the year 1720 a company of French actors established themselves at the Copenhagen Court; two years later, in 1722, another Frenchman, René Montaigu, obtained permission to gather a troupe of Danish players and started his season with a Danish version of Molière's *L'avare*. The same season saw the production of five original comedies by Ludvig Holberg, an author who had already acquired a reputation for his burlesque epic *Peder Paars*, and whose residence in France and in England had given him first-hand experience of what the theatres of these two countries were producing.

It is tempting to find praise for this writer, and when one realizes that he was in effect creating not only Danish drama but Danish literature, one is indeed led to treat his works in a kindly spirit. To call him the Northern Molière, however, is to reject all critical values, and it is better to see in him a stalwart soul who, amid many difficulties, succeeded in providing for his native country a series of plays which the kindliest of criticism cannot call great, but which formed a worthy beginning for the Scandinavian stage.

Holberg suffers from many defects. He satirizes broadly, but rarely does he exhibit any clear orientation in his satire. His mind is confused, and amid the changing social conditions of his time he finds it impossible to take a clear stand. Although we feel that in his comedies he desired to arouse his compatriots to improve their somewhat backward cultural state, and although we recognize that in this aim he was aligning himself with Molière, we are bound to confess that he shows himself wholly unsure concerning the nature and quality of the improvements to be sought. The same lack of certainty is exhibited both in the structure and in the characterization of his comedies. There is liveliness in his presentation of bourgeois Danish types, and he has a number of effective scenes; yet the scenes are often ill-harmonized, and frequently opportunities for the enriching of the characters are sadly neglected.

These defects, along with Holberg's genuine virtues, are well revealed in the two plays by which he is best known outside of Scandinavia—*Jeppe paa Bjerget, eller Den forvandlede Bonde* (*Jeppe of the Hill; or, The Peasant Metamorphosed*), one of his earliest works, performed in 1722, and *Erasmus Montanus*, a later play, printed in 1731. The former is closely related to the 'induction' of Shakespeare's *The Taming of the Shrew*, in that it shows a poor peasant, Jeppe, taken up by a laughter-loving nobleman and persuaded that he is indeed a man of rank and wealth whose memories of a poverty-stricken existence are nothing but hallucination. There are social implications here, but when we compare Holberg's treatment of this plot with Calderón's not dissimilar *Life is a Dream* we realize by how much it fails to achieve greatness. Like the hero of the Spanish drama, Jeppe proves tyrannical, boorish, and cruel when he thinks he is a lord; what is lacking completely is Calderón's philosophic reflections and the conclusions he draws from his action. With the one drama we soar into the realms of the imagination; with Holberg's we plod, not unentertainingly but a trifle heavily, over much miry ground. In *Erasmus Montanus* an interesting theme is developed. The plot here deals with a peasant who has been sent to the university and returns to his native village full of wisdom and Latin saws. He can wield the instrument of logic: he knows that the earth is round; he has mastery over books. Unfortunately for him, however, he runs into opposition. The villagers do not take well to his pedantries, while local dignitaries (such as the deacon and the sheriff) are much disturbed lest he take from their importance. Many scenes are amusing in their satirical display of the foolish academicism of the hero, and presumably Holberg's purpose is to indicate that, while there is no merit in ignorance, there is no greater merit in arid learning. On the one hand, Erasmus is right in most of his beliefs, and an infiltration of knowledge could be expected to raise the boorish standards of the village culture; on the other, he himself is made an arrant fool, without enough common sense to avoid being pressed for the army, and is contrasted with his brother, into whose mouth the author puts expressions, evidently sympathetically conceived, of homely wisdom.

Perhaps we shall do best to regard Holberg as we regard a 'documentary.' There is no doubt but that in his plays is presented a lively picture of social conditions in eighteenth-century Denmark. *Hexerei, eller Blind Allarm* (*Witchcraft; or, The False Alarm*; printed 1731) gives an excellent view of the superstitions prevailing in his backward land. Various other plays reveal by incisive touches the growth of a newly enriched bourgeoisie, with all the pretensions of the newly enriched, no matter where they may appear; in *Den ellefte Junii* (*The Eleventh of June*, 1723) he turns to show the effects of enrichment on a boorish peasantry; in *Mester Gert Westphaler, eller Den meget talende Barbeer* (*Master Gert Westphaler; or, The Very Loquacious Barber*, 1722) and *Den politiske Kandstøber* (*The Pewterer a Politician*, 1722) he ridicules, firstly, the affectations of an uneducated man who, having travelled slightly, wishes to dazzle his friends by his conversation, and, secondly, the absurdities of a tradesman suddenly bitten by the desire to shine in the realm of politics. In all of these are presented vivid pictures of the life of Holberg's day, although rather in a series of jerky scenes than in harmonious weaving of plot.

Only in two respects did Holberg make real contributions to dramatic conceptions. Most of his characters are obviously Danish versions of types already dealt with on the stage by Molière and others, but in drawing one figure he achieved real originality. The hero of *Den Stundesløse* (*No Time to Waste*, 1728) is a man who is continually buzzing about, flitting from one job to another, trying to do three things at once, never possessed of a moment of leisure: and in his oddities he is distinctly entertaining. Here, at least, the Danish author was painting straight from life. Something of the same originality enters into the portrait of the heroine in *Den Vægelsindede* (*The Weathercock*, 1722) and into the rehandling of *commedia dell' arte* material in *De Unsynlige* (*The Masked Ladies*, 1725), where Harlequin's stupid aping of Leandro's affected love affairs serves to show up fashionable follies. Nor did he have a model for the interesting device employed in *Hexerei*, where several of his own *dramatis personæ* culled from earlier plays are introduced for the purpose of protesting against their having been ridiculed on the stage. The trick almost suggests the style of Pirandello (although, obviously, Holberg makes no subtle use of it), and indicates that this author, awaking the cold and silent North to the joys of the theatre, was not content merely to adapt scenes and characters from French or English masters.

In himself, perhaps, Holberg does not warrant overmuch attention, but he stands forth as a symbolic figure. With the growth of the middle classes the stage is being carried rapidly into lands which had barely felt the impress of the Renaissance, and from those lands was soon to come new strength and fresh inspiration. Holberg, although he applied himself to the Danish drama, had been born in Norway, and not so many generations were to pass before that country produced its giant figure of Ibsen. It is true that the immediately following years offered but little of any value, yet the line from Denmark's first dramatist, through Johan Herman Wessel, sentimental Johannes Ewald, and classically inclined Nordahl Brun, on to the masters of the nineteenth century, is clear. Nor must the influence of Holberg outside his native country be forgotten. It was, for example, his inspiration that produced one of the earliest comedies in far-off Finland—the *Nummisuutarit* (*The Country Shoemaker*, 1864), by Aleksis Kivi.

It was not only in Scandinavia and the North that the awakening was to be found. In Holland were appearing such comedies as the *Wederzijdsch Huwlijksbedrog* (*Lovers' Deceits*, c. 1712) of Pieter Arenz Langendijk, where Lodewijk, a penniless man of quality, lays suit to a girl, Charlotte, born of poor parents: she is described to him by her maidservant, Klaar, as abounding in riches, while he pretends to be a wealthy Polish count. Underneath the framework of intrigue is obvious an appreciation of social manners and their bearing upon character. In Hungary György Bessenyei produced his rather interesting sentimental satire of sentimentalism in *Philosophus* (*The Philosopher*, 1790). The early theatres of Russia, somewhat later in the century, were seeing the foundations laid for the stage that was to welcome a Chekhov, and their dramatic offerings will later claim our attention. Across the long wastes of the Atlantic, too, a stirring of dramatic desire was leading towards the establishment of a native American drama.

THE LAST FLICKERS OF COMEDY: SHERIDAN, GOLDSMITH, BEAUMARCHAIS

By the year 1750 bourgeois interests had introduced a new type of comedy into France and England. However, before this new style engulfed the comic stage entirely there was one last flickering of laughter, and maybe it is fitting to contemplate this before turning to examine the growth of the drama of sentiment.

There were, of course, many men during that age who saw the inherent follies of sentimentalism, and some among them tried to stay its course. For such an endeavour three possible means suggested themselves: satirical attacks and parodies, the creation of an entirely new style of comedy, and the revival of one of the older styles submerged by the wave of sentimentalism.

The first of these was tried, but without much effect. In England the cynical Samuel Foote, who became owner of the 'summer theatre' in the Haymarket, turned out *The Handsome Housemaid; or, Piety in Pattens* (1773), in which he ridiculed the morality of such works as Richardson's *Pamela*, and others joined him in directing occasional barbs at the lachrymose drama. It is, however, difficult to trace any sure influence of the parodies cast in this mould: men laughed, no doubt, and a few may have heartily sympathized with the effort, and that was all. Sentimentalism pursued its course unchecked.

As we have seen, *The Beggar's Opera* had suggested the possibility of finding a new form for the expression of a comic mood harmonized with the interests of the eighteenth-century audience. This movement was stayed by the Licensing Act of 1737, and the later record of the ballad-opera presents a series of disappointments. The endeavour to evolve a fresh comic style was frustrated.

Something more, however, came from the determined attempt to revive older forms; out of that attempt came half a dozen masterpieces in France and in England, and, even if we are forced to confess that these masterpieces did not establish a tradition, there can be no doubt but that we must welcome and esteem them for their intrinsic accomplishment.

Both Oliver Goldsmith and Richard Brinsley Sheridan were utterly opposed to the mawkishly sentimental, and both looked back with nostalgic regret at the vanished comedy of the past. We must not, however, assume that the gaze of each was directed at the same object. Goldsmith exhibits in his writing something of Shakespeare's mood: humour, not wit, is the instrument he best knows how to wield; and accordingly, in searching for a model to be used in his own dramatic efforts, he fixes his eyes on the romantic comedies of the latter years of the sixteenth century. It is their spirit he wishes to revive. His *Essay on the Theatre; or, A Comparison between Laughing and Sentimental Comedy* (1772) puts his position clearly. He deplores the growth of the sentimental comedy—"a kind of *mulish* production, with all the defects of its opposite parents, and marked with sterility"; he pleads for the return of "humour" and, with it, a franker attitude towards life, a banishing of that fastidiousness which came with genteel comedy and was exaggerated in the sentimental.

His first endeavour to supply a "laughing comedy," *The Good-natured Man* (1768), showed the hand of an apprentice, but its emphasis was unmistakable, and some of the more polite among his audience were inclined timorously to condemn it as "low." This was followed by the brilliant *She Stoops to Conquer; or, The Mistakes of a Night* (1773). Although it is possible to dismiss this play as merely a mild farce, its characterization and its delicacy of dialogue deservedly make it one of the most popular of eighteenth-century comedies. Marlow, "one of the most bashful and reserved young fellows in the world," is drawn adeptly for the rôle he is to play; Hardcastle, the crusty but kind-hearted country gentleman, has vitality and interest; Miss Hardcastle is a heroine of whom even the exquisite Marivaux need not have been ashamed; and Tony Lumpkin is twin-brother to Shakespeare's clowns. Despite the fact that the author obviously finds it hard to maintain credibility in the results of the original mistake (by which Marlow enters Hardcastle's house under the belief that it is an inn), these persons keep our interest alive in the plot. Goldsmith, like Shakespeare, was less intent upon verisimilitude in action than upon the creation of humorous scenes and the evoking of mood.

If Goldsmith discovered his spiritual home in the romantic comedies of the Elizabethan era, Sheridan lived in spirit with the wits who surrounded Charles II. His endeavour was to revive the comedy of manners. At the same time he was an opportunist and himself a theatrical manager, with the consequence that, fundamentally opposed though he was to sentimentalism, he permitted a faint flavour of that style to colour scenes penned mainly for their laughter, and, moreover, soon abandoned the effort to emulate Etherege and Congreve.

His first dramatic work, *The Rivals* (1775), patently revealed what he wanted to do. The hero is Captain Absolute, a witty young gentleman; the heroine is the fair Lydia Languish, whom reading of books from the lending library has made affected and sentimentally absurd. The plot, complicated by the absurd pretensions of the inimitable Mrs Malaprop, the fiery passions of Sir Lucius O'Trigger, and the good-natured blunderings of Bob

Acres, eventually leads to Lydia's surrender to reality. We are, no doubt, far off from the cynical libertinism of the Restoration dramatists; if Sheridan calls any to mind it is the late Vanbrugh and Farquhar, in whose works the atmosphere of the comedy of manners was being transformed into shapes which could easily be moulded into the genteel and the sentimental; yet the indebtedness of the author of *The Rivals* to the graceless author of *The Man of Mode* is easily to be traced.

This early essay was followed by *The School for Scandal* (1777), a masterpiece of dramatic construction. Although the basic plot illustrates the way in which Sheridan was prepared to bow to contemporary sentimental tastes, the spirit of wit is admirably sustained throughout. Like many a duller playwright of his age, Sheridan here presents a hero who, although guilty of many follies and even stained with vices, is shown at the end to be a man whose honesty of heart deserves our approbation. This young gentleman, Charles Surface, is contrasted with his hypocritical brother, Joseph. The former loves Maria, the wealthy ward of Sir Peter Teazle; the latter makes suit to the girl in the hope of obtaining her money while at the same time he pursues Lady Teazle, Sir Peter's wife. As the play develops a *deus ex machina* arrives in the person of Sir Oliver Surface, uncle of the two brothers; by his means Charles' nobility and Joseph's duplicity are amply demonstrated, and concurrently Lady Teazle is made to realize the dangers into which she has so nearly fallen.

The School for Scandal is too well known to require lengthy analysis, yet such analysis it fully deserves; rarely has a comic playwright wrought a complicated plot with such exquisite skill.

Both *The Rivals* and its successor were welcomed by the contemporary theatre, but Sheridan, ever an easy-going character, must have realized that esteem of them arose in spite of and not because of their relationship to the mood of the time. As a result, nothing in the same style followed from his pen. *The Critic; or, A Tragedy Rehearsed* (1779) is a magnificent satire of many follies in the theatre of his day; only in its attempt to evoke laughter, however, can it be related to the two earlier comedies. *St Patrick's Day; or, The Scheming Lieutenant* (1775) is but a flimsy piece; *The Duenna* (1775), although it includes some lively scenes, does not exhibit much merit; *A Trip to Scarborough* (1777) is nothing more than a genteel version of Vanbrugh's *The Relapse*.

The truth is that the age did not really want the comedy of wit or the comedy of humour; and Sheridan knew it. Some other authors of the time tried to persuade the audience to like plays in which a strong dash of sentimentalism accompanied scenes cast in another manner; thus Arthur Murphy penned *The Way to Keep Him* (1760) and George Colman the Elder his amusing *Jealous Wife* (1761), while the latter joined David Garrick, playwright as well as actor, in writing *The Clandestine Marriage* (1766), one of the best of these mixed comedies. Along with these works may be mentioned the not unamusing American comedy of sentimentalized manners, *The Contrast* (1787), by Royall Tyler—the first play from across the Atlantic that really calls for serious attention. Meanwhile others, among whom Samuel Foote was the most successful, kept turning out short farces in an effort to keep laughter in the theatre. All of this, however, was of little avail. Men at the close of the eighteenth century were acclaiming George Colman the Younger as Sheridan's successor, and it is depressing to note that this prolific author aimed rather at the development of qualities later to serve the melodrama than at the cultivation of wit.

Much the same story is to be told of Beaumarchais (Pierre-Augustin Caron) in France. Like Goldsmith and Sheridan, he was a lonely figure, without true successors; like Sheridan—as his *Eugénie* (1767) shows—he stood in somewhat doubtful relationship to the sentimental drama; like both, he had a free sense of fun and a genuine dramatic talent.

So far as comedy is concerned, his name will be remembered for two works, *Le barbier de Seville* (*The Barber of Seville*, 1775) and *Le mariage de Figaro* (*The Marriage of Figaro*, 1784). The theme of the first is a simple one. Old Bartolo wishes to marry his ward, Rosine, who for her part loves a gentleman, Lindoro, who is really the Count Almaviva. To the help of the young couple comes the Barber of Seville, Figaro, and the plot is carried forward partly by his intrigues and partly by the various devices by which Almaviva insinuates himself into Bartolo's house. In essence the play is thus a comedy of intrigue, with action similar to that of hundreds of other pieces; it would have remained undistinguished from them had it not been for two qualities it possessed. Beaumarchais was an author with a precise and delicate pen: his dialogue—like Molière's, excessively difficult to translate—gives animation to scenes of action which otherwise might have appeared artificially dull. The second quality concerns the characterization of Figaro. The Barber is no ordinary valet; he is a man of the people; and into his mouth Beaumarchais has placed a number of such common-sense reflections on the ways of the aristocracy as were to give to *The Barber of*

Seville an almost revolutionary significance in the changes which so soon were to overturn French society.

Both qualities are marked again in *The Marriage of Figaro*, written obviously in order to capitalize on the success of the former play, and equally obviously invested with greater social bitterness. The Count and his Rosine are now viewed several years after marriage. They are drifting apart. Figaro, the Count's servant, is preparing to marry Suzanne, the soubrette, but Almaviva demands that, in return for favours he has done to Figaro, she should first become his mistress. When foiled in this effort he capriciously tries to marry off the faithful Figaro to the elderly Marceline, while poor Figaro is further plagued because, without his knowledge, the Countess has persuaded Suzanne to agree to an assignation (intending to meet the Count herself and thus endeavour to effect a reconciliation). Peace comes to the troubled household only when the Count is unmasked and when the discovery is made that Marceline is in reality Figaro's mother.

There is much of laughter in this play, but there are darker sounds as well. The plot gives Figaro the opportunity for passing many trenchant remarks on the pride, the worthlessness, and the exactions of the aristocracy. He becomes a figure of honest, sturdy, plebeian heroism, and unquestionably audiences were expected not merely to laugh, but to feel with him as well. Although Beaumarchais may be justifiably regarded as a not undistinguished descendant of Molière, even these two merry dramas bear clear indication of having been composed in a spirit alien to that of the comedy of manners. The last words of *The Barber of Seville* are "Je me presse de rire de tout, de peur d'être obligé d'en pleurer" ("I am anxious to laugh at everything lest I be forced to weep").

The truth, of course, is that Beaumarchais was fully immersed—for all his laughter—in the sentimental stream. His first play, *Eugénie* (1767), with its characteristically English characters, is a seriously composed drama, while *Les deux amis* (*The Two Friends*, 1770) is thoroughly bourgeois in spirit. With two entirely diverse moods thus fighting within him, he provides an excellent means of transition from the old to the new.

THE WAVE OF SENTIMENTALISM

WITH HIS *Eugénie* Beaumarchais published an *Essai sur le genre dramatique sérieux*, in which he set forth as clearly as any the basic principles of the sentimental cult. He notes that there are some people who deplore the partiality of the public for the 'serious drama.' To them he answers, first, that the audience must ever be the master of what is provided in the theatre, secondly, that no appeal to ancient models can be allowed, and, thirdly, that it is "permissible to interest a theatre audience and make it shed tears over a situation which, if it occurred in everyday life, would never fail to produce the same effect upon each individual in that audience." The ancient tragedies are barbaric; the persons of the heroic drama rarely appeal to the heart; a prince is a stranger to us, and we can be truly moved only by contemplating the relationship between man and man. "What," he inquires,

> What do I care, I, a peaceful subject in an eighteenth-century monarchy, for the revolutions of Athens and Rome? Of what real interest to me is the death of a Peloponnesian tyrant, or the sacrifice of a young princess at Aulis? There is nothing in that for me; no morality which is applicable to my needs. For what is morality? It is the fruitful result and individual application of certain mental deductions occasioned by an actual occurrence. What is interest? It is the involuntary sensation by which we adapt that occurrence to our own ends; it puts us in the place of him who suffers, throws us into the situation for the time being.

Folly, he thinks, can be ridiculed in laughter, but only too often we are betrayed by comedy into sympathizing with moral vice because of our delight in witty lines and stage tricks. To attack vice men need an emotional drama, a serious drama, moving us "by true and natural means," which may call forth our tears.

THE BASIS OF THE SENTIMENTAL DRAMA

These words of Beaumarchais reveal trenchantly that the two essential foundations upon which the serious drama is set are truth to reality and didactic moralization. Both of these, however, are relative terms, and, as a result, much that seemed realistic to the eighteenth century appears now to be highly artificial, while a great deal that the age regarded as profoundly philosophical has become in our eyes shallow and mawkish. In spite of the aims of the playwrights, the serious philosophical lachrymose drama of the eighteenth century has produced little, if anything, that does not seem absurd and laughable. The word 'sentimental,' which we commonly apply to the genre, is an indication of our awareness of the follies and inadequate reflections which crowd into these scenes.

Originally sentimentalism was adumbrated in England, although it was soon to be taken over by Continental playwrights and given firmness of form. Already in the first years of the century Steele's attacks on duelling and his interest in domestic harmony were didactically pointing forward towards a serious treatment of social evils; even before that diverse comedies had been introducing scenes of a deliberately pathetic kind, so that long ere men were aware of the existence of a new form of drama in their midst many of the technical devices and much of the sentimental mood had been clearly adumbrated. In 1740 Samuel Richardson won popularity for his sentimental novel, *Pamela*, to be followed within a few years by *Clarissa* (1747–48), and from that date the theatre fed freely from the fount of narrative fiction.

It must sadly be confessed that there is not a single English play written in this style during the eighteenth century which is worthy of serious criticism. Author after author applied himself to this genre, and all failed dismally. Men like Hugh Kelly and Richard Cumberland won fame for such works as *False Delicacy* (1768) and *The West Indian* (1771); later came Thomas Holcroft with *The Road to Ruin* (1792) and the prolific Mrs Elizabeth Inchbald with her *Such Things are* (1787) and her adaptation from Kotzebue, *Lovers' Vows* (1798).

Although each of these authors brings his own peculiar qualities to the development of character and of scene, a common style appears in all. Each writer strives to be realistic, and each falls far short of his goal: each is interested in preaching, and deliberately designs his action in order to make his moralistic point; each mingles laughable scenes with serious, although quite clearly he will be better pleased if the audience weep at his comedy than roar with merriment. As an example, and a single example will serve, we may take a scene in Mrs Inchbald's *Every One has his Fault* (1793). Lady Eleanor has come to the home of her father, Lord Norland, to beg his clemency on her husband's behalf: in this house lives her little son, who has been adopted in infancy by his grandfather:

She is following the Servant; EDWARD *walks softly after her, till she gets near the door; he then takes hold of her gown, and gently pulls it; she turns and looks at him.*

EDWARD: Shall I speak for you, Madam?

LADY ELEANOR: Who are you, pray, young Gentleman? Is it you, whom Lord Norland has adopted for his son?

EDWARD: I believe he has, Madam; but he has never told me so yet.

LADY ELEANOR: I am obliged to you for your offer; but my suit is of too much consequence for *you* to undertake.

EDWARD: I know what your suit is, Madam, because I was with my Lord when Hammond brought in your message; and I was so sorry for you, I came out on purpose to see you—and, without speaking to my Lord, I could do you a great kindness—if I durst.

LADY ELEANOR: What kindness?

EDWARD: But I durst not—— No, do not ask me.

LADY ELEANOR: I do not. But you have raised my curiosity; and in a mind so distracted as mine, it is cruel to excite one additional pain.

EDWARD: I am sure I would not add to your grief for the world. But then, pray do not speak of what I am going to say. I heard my Lord's lawyer tell him just now, "that as he said he should not know the person again, who committed the offence about which you came, and as the man who informed against him was gone off, there could be no evidence that he did the action, but from a book, a particular pocket-book of my Lord's, which he forgot to deliver to his servant with the notes and money to return, and which was found upon him at your house: and this, Lord Norland will affirm to be his." Now, if I did not think I was doing wrong, this is the very book. [*Takes a pocket-book from his pocket.*] I took it from my Lord's table; but it would be doing wrong, or I am sure I wish you had it. [*Looking wistfully at her.*

LADY ELEANOR: It will save my life, my husband's and my children's.

EDWARD [*trembling*]: But what is to become of me?

LADY ELEANOR: That Providence, who never punishes the deed, unless the *will* be an accomplice, shall protect you for saving one, who has only erred in a moment of distraction.

EDWARD: I never did anything to offend my Lord in my life;—and I am in such fear of him, I did not think I ever should. Yet, I cannot refuse *you*;—take it. [*Gives her the book.*] But pity me, when my Lord shall know of it.

LADY ELEANOR: Oh! should he discard you for what you have done, it will embitter every moment of my remaining life.

EDWARD: Do not frighten yourself about that. I think he loves me too well to discard me quite.

LADY ELEANOR: Does he indeed?

EDWARD: I think he does; for often, when we are alone, he presses
me to his bosom so fondly, you would not suppose. And, when
my poor nurse died, she called me to her bedside, and told me (but
pray keep it a secret)—she told me I was—his grandchild.

LADY ELEANOR: You are—you are his grandchild—I see—I feel you
are; for I feel that I am your mother.   [*Embraces him.*

Thus did the sentimental drama seek to display reality.

For the most part it was simply 'serious drama' or 'lachrymose
comedy,' but a few attempts of a bolder kind were made during
the age to substitute for the older tragedy of royal associations a
tragedy of bourgeois proportions. In this sphere George Lillo
easily comes first with his mediocre, yet revolutionary and widely
influential *The London Merchant; or, The History of George Barnwell*
(1731). Already in Shakespeare's time experiments had been made
in the writing of middle-class tragic scenes, but these had been long
forgotten, and Lillo's play came as a surprise and a shock to his
contemporaries. They were thrilled to find a hero in an ordinary
London apprentice and to discover tragic sentiment in a sordid
story of his intrigue with a prostitute, of his sinking ever deeper
into the abyss, and finally of his murdering an uncle who has ever
been his guardian and friend. Typical of the style of this drama is
the scene in which the latter walks to his doom: it is night on a
lonely lane:

UNCLE: If I was superstitious, I should fear some danger lurked unseen,
or death were nigh. A heavy melancholy clouds my spirits; my
imagination is filled with ghashly forms of dreary graves and bodies
changed by death—when the pale lengthened visage attracts each
weeping eye and fills the musing soul at once with grief and horror,
pity and aversion. I will indulge the thought. The wise man prepares himself for death by making it familiar to his mind. When
strong reflections hold the mirror near and the living in the dead
behold their future selves, how does each inordinate passion and
desire cease or sicken at the view? The mind scarce moves; the
blood, curdling and chilled, creeps slowly through the veins—fixed,
still and motionless, like the solemn object of our thoughts. We
are almost at present what we must be hereafter, till curiosity awakes
the soul and sets it on inquiry. [GEORGE BARNWELL *enters at a distance.*]
O death, thou strange mysterious power, seen every day, yet never
understood but by the incommunicative dead—what art thou?
The extensive mind of men, that with a thought circles the earth's
vast globe, sinks to the centre or ascends above the stars, that worlds
exotic finds or thinks it finds—thy thick clouds attempt to pass

in vain, lost and bewildered in the horrid gloom, defeated she returns more doubtful than before, of nothing certain but of labour
lost.

[*During this speech* BARNWELL *sometimes presents the pistol and draws it
back again. At last he drops it, at which his* UNCLE *starts and draws his
sword.*

BARNWELL: Oh, 'tis impossible!

UNCLE: A man so near me, armed and masked!

BARNWELL: Nay, then, there's no retreat.
[*Plucks a poniard from his bosom and stabs him.*

UNCLE: Oh, I am slain! All gracious Heaven regard the prayer of thy
dying servant. Bless with thy choicest blessings my dearest nephew;
forgive my murderer; and take my fleeting soul to endless mercy.

[BARNWELL *throws off his mask, runs to him, and, kneeling by him, raises
and chafes him.*

BARNWELL: Expiring saint! Oh, murdered, martyred Uncle! Lift
up your dying eyes and view your nephew in your murderer. Oh,
do not look so tenderly upon me! Let indignation lighten
from your eyes and blast me ere you die! By Heaven, he weeps
in pity of my woes! Tears! Tears for blood! The murdered, in
the agonies of death, weeps for his murderer! Oh, speak your pious
purpose—pronounce my pardon then and take me with you. He
would, but cannot. Oh, why with such fond affection do you press
my murdering hand? What, will you kiss me?
[*Kisses him.* UNCLE *groans and dies.*

Such scenes seemed marvellous to the age, and hardly any play of
the time was better known, either in England or abroad, than
The London Merchant. It shared with Richardson's novel *Pamela*
the honour of promoting that veritable 'anglomania' which swept
over the Continent towards the middle of the century.

On the Continent sentimentalism grew much as it had done in
England, but there it rapidly became more philosophical and conscious of its purposes. In diverse ways these earlier dramatists to
whom reference already has been made—Regnard, Lesage, and
Marivaux—contributed towards its formation. To their efforts
were added those of Philippe-Néricault Destouches, who rather
dully strove to clothe moral sentiments in theatrical costumes. His
best play is *Le glorieux* (*The Conceited Count*, 1732), in which is
clearly marked the opposition between the old aristocracy and the
newly rising middle class, although his most influential was the less
skilful *Le philosophe marié* (*The Married Philosopher*, 1727), with its
strongly moralizing strain. Characteristic of the international style
of the new movement in drama, and of the cross-currents that
eventually brought it to port, are the facts that Destouches not only

wrote this play in England but showed himself inspired by English authors, and that, when adapted by John Kelly as *The Married Philosopher* in 1732, it exercised a powerful force in developing later English sentimentalism.

From Destouches it is an easy step to Nivelle de la Chaussée, who is frequently regarded as the true father of the *comédie larmoyante*, because of such plays as *La fausse antipathie* (*The False Antipathy*, 1733), *Le préjugé à la mode* (*Fashionable Prejudice*, 1735), and *L'homme de fortune* (*The Man of Fortune*, 1751), and even if we decide that the fullest expression of this type of drama was still to come, we must agree that in his writings the orientation was clearly towards that new species of composition which, hovering between the tragic and the comic, seemed most nearly to meet the demands of contemporary audiences.

The sentimental *drame*, however, first received adequate expression in the once famous *Le fils naturel, ou les épreuves de la vertue* (*The Natural Son; or, The Trials of Virtue*) of Denis Diderot. This work, published in 1757, was first acted in 1771. Its author was the central figure in the combination of writers (including Voltaire) who made history through the publication, during the seventies, of the vast, many-volumed *Encyclopédie, ou Dictionnaire raisonné des sciences, des arts et des métiers*, a work destined to have enormous influence on the growth of such 'philosophical' thought as was ultimately to lead to the Revolution. *Le fils naturel* and the accompanying *Le père de famille* (*The Father of the Family*, 1758) were composed much in the spirit of the *Encyclopédie*. They were animated by a didactic aim and sought to teach by moving the emotions of the audience. From Diderot the whole of the French *drame* took its colouring: even the Théâtre Italien was influenced, and a new kind of sentimental comic opera came into being. Play after play concentrated on the enunciation of moral truths, preached the sermon of natural virtues and the crimes of civilization, aroused tearful pity for those cruelly oppressed, and held up the serious middle-class merchant as an object of supreme admiration. Author after author came forward in this style—unhappily for the most part with pieces of little intrinsic excellence even although of contemporary popularity. Michel-Jean Sedaine was among the best with his well-executed *Le philosophe sans le savoir* (*A Philosopher without knowing it*, 1765)—a drama of merchant morality directed against the practice of duelling—and the musical *Le déserteur* (*The Deserter*, 1769). Of great contemporary significance, Louis-Sébastien Mercier presented his *Jennéval, ou le Barnevelt français*

(*Jennéval; or, The French Barnevelt*; printed 1769) and his *Le juge* (1774).

Mercier was the author of an important *Essai sur l'art dramatique* (1773), and this fact reminds us of the close association of critical exposition with creative effort in France during these years. Beaumarchais' essay has already been mentioned, and to his work and Mercier's is to be added the notable letter written by Diderot in 1758—*De la poésie dramatique, à Monsieur Grimm*. The reference to Grimm further reminds us that the critical discussion of the new form was rapidly being pursued in Germanic lands as well; soon, indeed, the torch that had passed from England to France was to be transferred to that country.

Diderot's essay is designed as an effort to give philosophical justification for the "serious comedy, whose office it is to depict virtue and the duties of man." With enthusiasm he discovers the rudiments, at least, of the serious type of play in the comedies of Terence, which, he avers, hardly raise laughter, but present "touching scenes based on events, natural in character and harmonized with the customs of the time." Probably the most revealing in all critical documents of this time is the set of arguments set forth by Carl Wilhelm Ramler in the fourth edition (1774) of a translation of a work by l'abbé Charles Batteux (originally published in 1750). Bourgeois drama, Ramler asserts, is in harmony with the middle-class tastes of the audiences and can more easily draw those audiences to sympathy with the characters; it deals with common events and not with far-off Court intrigues; it is easier for actors to portray familiar characters and for dramatists to find such characters fitting dialogue. The stress here is on utilitarian values, not on æsthetic ones; the playwrights of the time constantly confused, as has been said, "the pattern of drama with the pattern of reality itself."

Soon, however, the incipient realism of the sentimental play was to receive a rude check. That check came, not as the result of endeavours to re-establish the laughing comedy, but as the consequence of a force that, absorbing the sentimental into its being, gave to the lachrymose scenes a new direction. Sheridan and Goldsmith failed to alter the course of the drama in England, just as in Italy Goldoni's gaiety was inclined to become confused with moral seriousness, and his followers (for example, Francesco Albergati Capacelli, with his comic gallery of *Il ciarlatore maldicente, The Malicious Prattler*, c. 1785, or Simeone Antonio Sografi, with his vividly depicted backstage world in *Le convenienze teatrali, Theatrical*

Conventions, 1794), could not stem the tide of sentimentalism. That sentimentalism spread everywhere. Alongside *Il ciarlatore maldicente* stands the pathetic *Il delatore* (*The Informer*, 1799) of Camillo Federici, where, instead of a social gossip, we are confronted with a kind of noble traitor. The plot of this play, indeed, shows how far authors were prepared to go in devising tearful situations. A poor old woman, Teodora Benamati, is ill, and her two sons, Pietro and Lorenzo, are desperate in their search for money wherewith to aid her. Suddenly an opportunity offers itself. A man has been killed and a reward offered for information regarding his murderer; whereupon Pietro accuses his brother, dashes home with the reward, and as quickly dashes back to the prison, demanding to be substituted for Lorenzo. Only the discovery of the true criminal prevents both of these most noble-minded youths from dire punishment. A similar atmosphere pervades another typical 'comedy' of this time, *La dama di spirito* (*The Lady of Spirit*, c. 1790), by Francesco Cerlone; here the story is told of a Beatrice who loves Don Luigi, but is separated from him because he has killed her father in a duel. Much distressed, she is saved from the clutches of a wicked duke, Orione, by the fortunate return of her lover, only to find that he has now got engaged to a rich widow. As in Federici's play, happiness comes in the end only through an unexpected discovery—in this case the sudden turning up of the widow's husband, whom all had believed to be dead.

So, in Spain, Gaspar Melchor de Jovellanos produced his characteristically titled *El delincuente honrado* (*The Honest Criminal*; printed 1787, written 1774), a dismal tale of self-sacrifice, remorse, and concepts of humanitarian honour. Less darkly, a similar sentimentalism enwraps the plays of Moratín the Younger (Leandro Fernández de Moratín)—for example, the not uninteresting *El viejo y la niña* (*The Old Man and the Maid*, 1790) and *El sí de las niñas* (*The Feminine 'Yes,'* 1806)—although this author not only conceals much of his sentimentalism under a mask of laughter, but also is capable of turning out amusingly satirical plays such as *La comedia nueva, o el café* (*The New Play; or, The Coffee-house*, 1792). In Germany dramas of a dull and uninspired, if morally worthy, kind—such as Otto von Gemmingen's *Der deutsche Hausvater* (*The German Father of a Family*, 1782)—developed in the hands of Lessing and Schiller into something far beyond the sentimental achievements of other European theatres.

The mention of Schiller's name, however, at once brings us back to realization of the fact that the sentimentally realistic was fated to be swallowed up in a force greater than itself. Many of those very qualities that characterized the serious comedy and the bourgeois tragedy had within them the germs of romanticism, and with the arrival of strong romantic passions during the latter years of the century the sentimental moralizings were rapidly channelled into fresh courses. The historical, even if often ludicrously interpreted, swept back into the playhouse, and domestic interior sets gave way to ancient abbey scenes and scenes placed in the gaunt halls of medieval castles. Without difficulty the sentimental comedy was transformed into the melodrama.

PART VII

THE ROMANTIC THEATRE

THE ROMANTIC THEATRE

THE ROMANTIC movement may be traced far back into the eighteenth century, where it assumes form as an endeavour to break away, now in one direction and now in another, from the classical style which, having temporarily exhausted itself, no longer could offer the inspiration required for the creation of new works of vital artistry.

Classicism fundamentally implies an attempt to delineate the typical and the representative, to show reality through the revealing of such common qualities as are shared by objects of a like nature. The classic artist tends, as far as is possible, to avoid the handling of detail: he is suspicious of the visionary; and he seeks to simplify. At its highest the classic spirit will produce the art of a Sophocles; at its lowest it will yield the formalized 'rules' of the lesser critics.

Obviously, in searching for a method of artistic creation opposed to this classic method, the romantic artist casts aside all the formalized 'rules,' and eschews the attempt to reduce things to simple terms. He is inclined both to rely upon his own individual genius and to find in elaboration of his material an intrinsic virtue. Where the classicist hammers out for himself a straight road, running Roman-like across undulating plain and over steep mountainside, the romanticist finds a joy in deviation, in the tortuous path that curves and bends, that often seems to lose the very sense of direction.

While such a course is characteristic of nearly all romantic art, from the very beginning of romanticism a cleavage within the ranks of the writers makes itself apparent. The opposition to the classic cult of typical form may, and does, assume two distinct shapes: one of these, cultivating the presentation of detail, leads ultimately towards naturalism; the other, making search beyond and behind the world of material reality, eventually loses itself in a realm of the subjective imagination.

At the very beginning of the romantic movement we may thus recognize the realistic poet Crabbe and the visionary Blake as joining in common fight against the classical style, even while at the same time we are fully conscious of the thoroughly divergent trends in their artistry which keep them distinct. And throughout the entire course of this period we can easily see how the spirit animating Crabbe constantly bends ever more and more inward until it reaches the *impasse* of Surrealism.

Although these two strains are of almost equal importance in the development of the nineteenth-century theatre, it is obvious that, in the first flush of revolutionary enthusiasm heralding the break-away from outworn classic models, the more flamboyant tendencies of the romantic mood found freer expression and almost over-whelmed the realistic. Both made their appearance at the same time in all forms of literature, so that, for example, the epoch-making *Lyrical Ballads* took shape as an amalgam of Wordsworth's poems of common life and of Coleridge's visionary essays; but when we think of the drama of this time it is the latter mood that clearly takes predominance. Reflections of the mood that created *The Rime of the Ancient Mariner* are apparent everywhere: many years were to elapse before the theatre was to welcome the mood that inspired Wordsworth. What confronts us in the playhouse of the nineteenth century is, first, a wild surge of 'gothicism,' with poetic tragedy, melodrama, opera, and fantastic extravaganza carried on its waves, next, a realistic swell gradually gathering force, and, finally, at the end of the period a bitter conflict between the two, during which each current strives to assert its superior force, and frequently the two find their waters mingling in a confused flood.

Socially, the world was at this time passing through a ferment. The French Revolution, combined with the successful establish-ment of an independent republic in the United States of America, ushered in an era of revolt. Country after country felt the urge towards freedom, and, in evolving a national consciousness, dis-covered in the theatre a means of arousing sentiments of a patriotic kind. Italian poets thus turned to the drama with fresh enthusiasm, and even in lands where the theatre had had no previous existence revolutionary knights-errant applied their energies to establishing native stages. Hungary provides a good example. Not until 1791 was there a public performance of a play in the national tongue: a few years later, in 1802, a Transylvanian National Theatre was founded, and in 1837 came a Hungarian National Theatre. Con-ditions elsewhere in Eastern Europe exhibited similar features. The first performance of a Czech play was given in 1785, and a series of successive ventures throughout the century led ultimately to the setting up, in 1862, of a 'Provisional Theatre' for dramas in the native language and, in 1883, to the opening of a National Theatre.

It was not, however, only patriotic sentiment that was being aroused. Social classes that had previously been submerged or had failed to become vocal were now demanding a share in the general life of the community. The old aristocracy and the new wealthy bourgeoisie still maintained their hold in most lands, but the working men were beginning to stir, and even underneath the apparently placid surface of life in Victorian England heavy currents were on the move.

This meant, for the theatre, a new audience and a new liberty. Although the complete freedom given to the French theatres during the first flush of revolutionary enthusiasm was soon curbed, and although the English playhouses were not officially released from the ancient patent monopoly until 1834, the hard control of theatrical affairs was almost everywhere being lightened, and new houses were being built to accommodate a rapidly increasing public. Men who would never have thought of entering a theatre half a century before now demanded their entertainment, and as the industrial cities grew so grew a fresh body of spectators anxious to savour the delights of the stage. From north to south, from east to west, the drama was exercising a novel fascination.

FROM TRAGEDY TO MELODRAMA

THROUGHOUT this period almost every poet, major and minor, sought to contribute to a new drama that should be richer than the old, and every one of them gazed with reverent eyes upon the majesty of Shakespeare. Translations of his works multiplied themselves in profusion; on the stage his dramas won wide acclaim; philosophers and critics found in his scenes a wealth of imaginative magic. This being so, we might have thought that the new romantic drama would have attained its greatest achievements in the land of Shakespeare's own tongue and that from the poets of the English romantic revival would have come masterpieces based on his inspiration.

THE FAILURE OF THE ENGLISH POETS

It is true that every one of these poets made valiant efforts to achieve greatness in the dramatic form. From the earliest group of writers to the latest all tried their hands at theatrical composition. William Wordsworth produced *The Borderers* (composed 1795–96); Robert Southey and Samuel Taylor Coleridge collaborated in *The Fall of Robespierre* (1794), and the latter later penned his *Remorse* (1813). Lord Byron has numerous dramas, including the once-popular *Manfred* (1817), among his other works; John Keats wrote an *Otho the Great* (1819), and Percy Bysshe Shelley a *Cenci* (1818). Concerning the will towards the theatre exhibited by these men there can be no doubt.

Yet every one of them failed. We may, if we will, discern some virtue in Byron's dramatic efforts, particularly in his *Marino Faliero* (1820) and *Sardanapalus* (1821), and some erratic praise has been given to the *Cenci*, but not the most ardent of romantic critics have dared to find in any of the other dramas matter of abiding interest; even the laudatory comments made by some on Byron's and Shelley's dramas clearly betray a determination to find something to laud, rather than a genuine critical enthusiasm.

This failure to create a vigorous romantic drama cannot be attributed to one cause alone. Byron's plays have much in them that is good, and if we were engaged here in a consideration of the English drama alone we might be prepared to give them greater consideration. What prevents them from assuming higher power is the intensely subjective tendency of Byron's own genius. This was a common feature of the romantic temper, but when seeking for the basic reasons for the weaknesses in the plays of his companions perhaps we ought to give more weight to other considerations.

One such consideration is the cleavage between the poets and the theatre, due partly to defects in the audience, partly to the aloofness of those who would fain have had their plays put upon the boards. Audiences were rough in those years and their tastes vulgar; the poets were inclined towards solitariness; the two trends, reacting upon each other, served to drive the pair apart. The poets came to despise the contemporary stage; the spectators could find no joy in the rather dull poetic dramas which from time to time were set before them. The divorce between literature and the playhouse was well-nigh complete.

Above all, however, was the fact that the English poets were so thoroughly immersed in the Shakespearian style that all their efforts were remote from the spirit of their own age. Imitation of his works was inevitable, yet his style, so perfectly harmonized to the conditions of the Elizabethan age, could not provide the stage utterance needed by an age two centuries distant from Shakespeare's time, while the fact that the author of *Hamlet* had so deeply plumbed the resources of the romantic theatre meant that imitation of his work, in his own tongue, was bound to seem shallowly apish. Audiences and readers familiar with *Lear* and *Macbeth* and *Othello* could not be expected to feel a thrill of wonder and delight in the contemplation of works so closely akin to these in general aim and yet so far removed from them in freshness of imaginative power and execution. The excitement of novelty and the achievement of original form could come only in countries where no looming native colossus cast its heavy shadow on the poets, and where the influence of Shakespeare could enter as a freshening and invigorating breeze from afar.

THE ROMANTIC DRAMA OF GERMANY: LESSING AND GOETHE

Such a country was Germany. Thus far the diverse Germanic principalities had accomplished nothing particularly noteworthy in the dramatic form, and, although Gottsched had succeeded in imposing a trifle of shapeliness on a hitherto inchoate stage, the shapeliness was of a classic mould ill-fitted to meet the needs of a new generation. The time was ripe here for a great awakening.

That awakening was foreshadowed in the work of Gotthold Ephraim Lessing. In the year 1765 the Hamburg National Theatre was established, destined to become, two years later, the German National Theatre, and with it came a hitherto undreamed-of periodical. Lessing had been appointed *Dramaturg* to the ambitious young playhouse, and, with the sponsorship of its controllers, he started to issue what is the world's first house-organ, the periodical essays issued collectively in 1769 as the *Hamburgische Dramaturgie*.

These essays were not simply occasional reviews of current productions. Throughout Lessing engaged himself in an endeavour, by means of direct criticism, to inspire young writers to turn to the composition of plays and thus to lay the foundations of a national theatrical art. His aim was at once practical and revolutionary: he ever kept the practical stage in view, and at the same time he ever sought to suggest that the pseudo-classic models favoured by Gottsched were not such as his age required. "The one thing we can never forgive in a tragic poet," he writes, "is coldness: if he arouses our interest it does not matter what he does with the petty mechanical rules." What he searches constantly for is form—organic form springing vitally from a genuine harmony between the subject-matter and the poet's untrammelled inspiration; and in his search he preaches the dual truth that the so-called 'rules' were right and proper for the Greek stage, false and improper for ours, and that, whereas the Greeks properly observed certain restrictions precisely because they were organic developments of their theatre form, the French classic authors were forced, while giving lip-service to the restrictions, to seek for means of circumventing them. By such observations and by the general power of his critical thought Lessing was able not merely to accomplish the negative task of destroying the pseudo-classic cult, but also to provide a firm basis for creative artistry of a new and different kind.

He himself endeavoured to put his own theories into execution in a series of carefully wrought plays, but unfortunately we cannot esteem Lessing the dramatist as highly as we may Lessing the critic. The *Hamburgische Dramaturgie* is worthy almost of being placed alongside Aristotle's *Poetics*, but the dramas—*Miss Sarah Sampson* (1755), *Minna von Barnhelm* (1767), *Emilia Galotti* (1772), and *Nathan der Weise* (*Nathan the Wise*, 1779), although all deserving of individual attention, and although vastly superior to anything produced contemporaneously in England, never succeed in capturing that elusive quality from which true greatness springs. All are heavily oppressed by the philosophy of the 'enlightenment' which cast such a spell over the author's mind, and are rather expansions of the sentimental than plays suggestive of a fresh endeavour. *Miss Sarah Sampson*, by the very choice of an English domestic theme and setting, betrays its close association with the bourgeois drama of London, while *Minna von Barnhelm* exploits a sentimental situation such as had already served half a dozen other playwrights of this school. Here the hero, Zellheim, penniless on his discharge from the army, refuses to marry his wealthy love—the heroine who gives her name to the play—and a happy solution is found only when a lost fortune is discovered, and Minna herself, giving out that she has become poor, pretends to refuse him in turn. There is a sense of character in the comedy and a skilful development of the theme, without, however, the creation of anything of first-rate value.

Emilia Galotti has somewhat greater worth. The story is clearly taken from the age-old Roman tale of Virginia, stabbed by her father in order to save her from a tyrant's lascivious embraces; but the girl is now presented as a member of the bourgeoisie, her would-be seducer is a member of the aristocracy, and a new turn is given to the theme when Emilia is shown by no means unmoved by the lover's advances. Although there are scenes here that speak to us far more powerfully than anything in *The London Merchant*, yet this play too savours of the dramatic style that gave birth to Lillo's tragedy.

A similar judgment must be passed on *Nathan der Weise*, the subject of which had seen a faint anticipation in one of this author's juvenile works, a one-act drama called *Die Juden* (*The Jews*; printed 1755). Its sincerity of aim is unquestionable. Taking Nathan the Jew as his hero, Lessing shows this man, basing his whole life on such a 'natural religion' as was sought after by Diderot and his companions, infinitely superior in morality and in nobleness of mind to those who base their actions upon established creeds. Nathan is a Jew only in name; in himself he embraces all the virtues and none of the vices inherent in the tenets of Judaism, Christianity, and Mohammedanism. By the romantic device of introducing Rebecca, the supposed daughter of a Christian crusader, who falls in love with a Templar—only to discover that both he and she (brother and sister) are in reality the long-lost children of a kinsman of the Sultan Saladin (who had become a Christian just before his death)—Lessing strives to give concrete dramatic expression to his dissatisfaction with all existing creeds and, at the same time, to his belief that in all the creeds reside some elements of divine wisdom. This argument is further pursued when Nathan presents before Saladin his parable of the rings, a parable designed to demonstrate that the only true religion is that which most benefits humanity. The expression of this concept, however, does not equal the vision, or perhaps it would be more true to say that the vision so cumbersomely preponderates that what ought to excite and arouse us remains uninvested with that theatrical fire we look for in the greatest works of dramatic art.

What Goethe said of Schiller might be applied specifically to Lessing and generally to the entire school of dramatic writing that he inaugurated. "Philosophy," said the poet, "injured his poetry, because this led him to consider the idea far higher than all nature; indeed, thus to annihilate nature. He believed that what he was able to conceive must happen, whether it were in conformity with nature or not." Ironically, this criticism applies to its own author as potently as to any. Johann Wolfgang von Goethe was certainly one of the greatest authors of his age; as certainly, he was not one of its greatest playwrights. For one who was so keenly interested in the theatre and so actively engaged in stage affairs his dramas betray a peculiar lack of theatrical sense: his service as director of the Weimar Court Theatre seemed to teach him nothing. Ideas tend to rule in his plays, and intellectual discussions to take the place of action; the true transcendence of the dramatist is lost in the romantic subjectiveness of his art.

With Goethe's works we move into the full flush of romanticism, into the atmosphere of that movement which took its name from the title of a tempestuous drama of Friedrich Maximilian von Klinger called *Sturm und Drang* (*Storm and Stress*, 1776). Goethe's first work for the stage was the equally tempestuous *Goetz von Berlichingen* (1773), with its revolutionary hero battling against the forces of oppression in his day. This tragedy became a kind of Bible for all the young spirits of Europe animated by passion for 'gothicism'; among the earliest of Sir Walter Scott's writings is a translation of its rather turgid dialogue. In its patent imitation of Shakespearian methods of composition, notably the union of tragic and comic scenes, it served to direct attention away from the style of the would-be realistic domestic drama, and in its choice of a medieval theme it led to the vast wave of historical writing that flooded the stage of the time.

NICOLAS LANCRET:
"LA CAMARGO
DANCING"

By courtesy of
the National Gallery
of Art, Washington,
Mellon Collection

417

Goethe's next drama, *Clavigo* (1774), dealing with the tragic consequences resultant when the hero decides to break his engagement to Maria lest marriage with her should injure his career, has but slight merit, but *Stella* (1775), destined to be taken by English opponents of the 'German theatre' as the very epitome of immorality, calls for attention if only for the boldness of its theme, which shows a hero, Fernando, loving two women almost equally and finally settling down to an unconventional *ménage à trois*. (It is interesting to observe that in a later reworking the conclusion was utterly changed, and, with greater psychological probability, Fernando and the heroine find a solution for their troubles in self-inflicted death.)

The endeavour to preach a message, so clearly marked in *Stella*, becomes even more pronounced in *Iphigenie auf Tauris* (*Iphigenia in Tauris*; begun in 1779, completed 1787), yet perhaps in the end this may be regarded as Goethe's most successful theatre work. With interesting deviations from the original Greek treatment of the theme, he concentrates on the problem confronting Iphigenia. If she saves her brother by a trick—as she may—she will have given over her soul to lying; instead, therefore, she boldly tells the barbarian king who Orestes is, and endeavours, by working on his sympathy, to persuade him to permit the taking away of the statue of Artemis from the temple. Obviously her action is symbolic, but for once Goethe has succeeded in making the symbol concrete and in clothing a living character with the robes of the idea.

Not so much can be said of *Torquato Tasso* (begun in 1780, completed in 1790), which is little more than a psychological study of a morbidly sensitive poet, not dramatized, but merely cast in dialogue form. Tasso, the hero, becomes almost frenzied in his imaginative passions, is tormented by his hatred of the calm statesmanship of Antonio Montecatino, and at the end comes to realize and to admire the very qualities that had driven him to the verge of madness. The last lines, so full of autobiographical implication, by themselves reveal the undramatic nature of the entire work. As Antonio takes his hand Tasso speaks:

> Oh, noble man! thou standest firm and calm,
> While I am like the tempest-driven wave.
> But be not boastful of thy strength. Reflect!
> Nature, whose mighty power hath fixed the rock,
> Gives to the wave its instability.
> She sends her storm, the passive wave is driven,
> And rolls and swells and falls in billowy foam.

O

Yet in this very wave the glorious sun
Mirrors his splendour, and the quiet stars
Upon its heaving bosom gently rest.
Dimmed is the splendour, vanished is the calm,
In danger's hour I know myself no longer,
Nor am I now ashamed of the confession.
The helm is broken, and on every side
The reeling vessel splits. The riven planks,
Bursting asunder, yawn beneath my feet!
Thus with my outstretched arms I cling to thee!
So doth the shipwrecked mariner at last
Cling to the rock whereon his vessel struck.

Similarly undramatic is *Egmont* (1787), a play, set in the midst of the Inquisition, which deals mainly with the passions of the character who gives it his name. Although a Catholic, Count Egmont deplores the oppressions imposed, in the name of the Church, upon the Netherlands, but fails in his effort to relieve the suffering because his benevolent goodwill is not enough in a world of hard reality. And, finally, there is *Faust* (1808, 1831), a vast amalgamation of lyric and dramatic episode, of psychological probing, and of recondite philosophy. Difficult indeed is the task of discussing such a drama in the present context. Unlike any work in dialogue that had preceded it, the enormous scope of the play renders it unfit for any but a few experimental stage productions, and in this way it cannot be given such rank in the history of the drama as is accorded to the works of Sophocles or Shakespeare. On the other hand—and quite apart from the pre-eminent position the poem holds in the world's literature—there can be no doubt but that its vastness of scope proved a theatrically inspiring force, indirectly if not directly. By it men were taught to see that the dramatic form need not be used only for the presentation of themes narrowly circumscribed in content, and the way was opened for a vast extension of the stage.

Faust opens in Heaven and shows Mephistopheles gaining permission to attempt the destruction of Faust's soul: this permission is granted by God in the belief that, even if Mephistopheles succeeds in his evil intent, Faust will gain in spiritual wisdom through the trial. Then follows the first part of the play—a clear, dramatic story, in which Faust gives his soul to Mephistopheles provided that the latter can grant him a passing minute of perfect joy. The young Margaret is seduced; Faust kills her brother; she loses her mind, destroys her child, and miserably perishes. From this we move to the richly imaginative and exceedingly difficult second part, wherein the image of Helen of Troy is summoned from the dark backward and abysm of time. From her union with Faust is born Euphorion, who ultimately vanishes into thinnest air. Later Faust, growing old, becomes intent on reclaiming some submerged land, and in this task comes to recognize the truth that only through aiding others can real joy be found. In making this confession he acknowledges that Mephistopheles has won, for a moment of perfect satisfaction has come to him: at the same time, paradoxically, Faust too has gained the victory, and his soul passes upward into bliss.

The general philosophical purpose is plain, even if details remain obscure or hard of interpretation. This questing spirit of humanity represented in Faust seeks sensual, worldly pleasure and finds it inadequate; higher it searches in the realms of ideal loveliness (Helen) and of poetry (Euphorion), only to discover the delights of these worlds evanescent; and eventually, on the highest plane, it reaches to ultimate fulfilment of purpose in renunciation of self and thought for others. The mystical concept is a direct development of the concepts out of which were built *Iphigenia auf Tauris*. We are here in the presence of an imaginative vision which, if expressed in a form beyond the scope of the purely theatrical, obviously soars far above the mediocre philosophizings of the contemporary stage.

THE TRIUMPH OF SCHILLER

Less gifted with imaginative power, Goethe's friend Johann Christoph Friedrich von Schiller succeeded theatrically where he had failed. There can be no doubt that since the times of Shakespeare, Molière, and Racine no greater dramatist had appeared on the horizon and that his works deserve to be placed, if not on a level with the writings of these men, at least close in their company. There is a comprehensive sweep here that marks the hand of an expert and masterly playwright.

Like Goethe, he commenced his literary career in the midst of an atmosphere of 'Sturm und Drang,' full of dark medieval fancies, the gloom of pessimism, and turbulent revolutionary sentiment. Out of this grew *Die Räuber* (*The Robbers*, 1781), an extraordinary work for a youth of twenty-two, and one that, in spite of some absurdities, has held the stage from its original production at Mannheim until to-day. The robber-hero (conceived in the spirit of a Robin Hood who flees to the forest because of the exactions of tyranny) was popular at the time when the drama was composed, and Schiller acted astutely in choosing as his central figure Karl von Moor. This man, noble in soul, becomes the captain of a band of outlaws, whose sincerity of spirit is contrasted with the evils and chicaneries of the palace hall, symbolized in Karl's ill-souled brother, Franz. The combination of 'gothicism' in the setting, romantic incident in the development of the scenes, and implicit revolutionary sentiment made the drama an immediate success throughout many European lands. Schiller's star, blazing thus brightly on its first arising, was not destined to wait for later discovery.

Immediately following this triumph came *Fiesko* (1783) and *Kabale und Liebe* (*Intrigue and Love*, 1784), both born of the same mood, and produced during the years when the young rebel, having fled from his native Württemberg, was acting as *Dramaturg* at the theatre of Mannheim. Neither adds very greatly to the achievement of *The Robbers*, although both show the poet gaining in his grasp of the stage and in his handling of character. The former is again revolutionary in spirit. Set in Genoa in the year 1547, it concentrates upon the brutal Gianettino Doria, heir to the dominion of his aged uncle, Andreas Doria, and upon the handsome, dashing figure of the hero, Fiesko, Count of Lavagna, one who, in spite of his excellent qualities, is cursed with the sin of pride, and who conceals an element of selfish deceit beneath his noble exterior. In *Intrigue and Love* Schiller turns from the past to try his hand at domestic tragedy cast in the Lessing mould, telling the dismal story of the fair Louisa, a simple civic musician's daughter, who loves and is loved by Major Ferdinand, son of the aristocratic President von Walther. By the intrigue of this proud old nobleman the loves of the young officer and the common maid are destroyed; Louisa pitiably dies, Ferdinand follows her, and the President is left in despair, his household shattered and his character publicly ruined. Although it may be admitted that *Kabale und Liebe* is not one of the world's greatest plays, we must recognize that it was the first domestic drama in Europe to reach something approaching majesty of proportion.

All these plays had been written in prose, but Schiller essentially was a poet, and in his next play, *Don Carlos* (1787), he turned to verse dialogue, producing a work which, despite its inordinate length, indicates a marked advance in dramatic concept. A political theme is here wrought with a tragedy of love. Philip II, the King of Spain, is a brutal tyrant, and against his cruelties, particularly in the Netherlands, his son and heir, Don Carlos, is in sharp revolt. At the same time this prince finds his heart sorely torn, for Philip has married Elizabeth de Valois, to whom Carlos himself had been betrothed and with whom he is still passionately in love. Carlos is the hero of the play, not perfect in his character, but endowed with basic nobility and majesty of soul; at his side stands the devoted Marquis de Posa, his friend and the character through whom Schiller most clearly reveals his purpose. Carlos can think only in terms of passion and violent revolution; the Marquis is a man who sees the world as yet unripe for his ideal, who realizes that "the rage for innovation but serves to increase the heavy weight of chains it cannot break," and who yet succeeds, by the powerfulness and sincerity of his arguments, in arousing the King's conscience when opposition had merely hardened his tyrannical will. As his first flush of success begins to fade and Carlos seems bound for destruction, the Marquis bravely sacrifices himself, although by that time the force of circumstance has pressed too far to permit his sacrifice to be other than vain. In a trenchant scene the King stands before the Grand Inquisitor, abject in front of a power greater than his own, and gives his son over to the terrible arm of Rome:

GRAND INQUISITOR: I am not minded, King,
To seek such interviews again.
KING: But one—
One service more—the last—and then in peace
Depart. Let all the past be now forgotten—
Let peace be made between us. We are friends.
GRAND INQUISITOR: When Philip bends with due humility.
KING [*after a pause*]: My son is meditating treason.
GRAND INQUISITOR: Well!
And what do you resolve?
KING: On all, or nothing.
GRAND INQUISITOR: What mean you by this *all*?
KING: He must escape,
Or die.
GRAND INQUISITOR: Well, Sire! decide.
KING: And can you not
Establish some new creed to justify
The bloody murder of one's only son?
GRAND INQUISITOR: To appease eternal justice, God's own Son
Expired upon the cross.
KING: And can you spread
This creed throughout all Europe?

GRAND INQUISITOR:	Ay, so far
	As the true cross is worshipp'd.
KING:	But I sin—
	Sin against nature. Canst thou, by thy power,
	Silence her mighty voice?
GRAND INQUISITOR:	The voice of nature
	Avails not over faith.
KING:	My right to judge
	I place within your hands. Can I retrace
	The step once taken?
GRAND INQUISITOR:	Give him up to me!
KING:	My only son!—For whom then have I labour'd?
GRAND INQUISITOR:	For the grave rather than for liberty.
KING [*rising up*]:	We are agreed. Come with me.
GRAND INQUISITOR:	Monarch! Whither?
KING:	From his own father's hands, to take the victim.

In this drama of *Don Carlos* Schiller demonstrated what he sought in the exploitation of tragic historical themes. A strong philosophical purpose constantly animated his mind, and in his scenes, without having recourse to any overt symbolic devices, he strove to present the truth as he saw it. Aristotle's declaration that the poet presents a more philosophical conception of events than ever the historian can would have won his complete approbation, and in the several plays he was yet to write on records of the past he consistently endeavoured to weld his material into an imaginative pattern. As a moralist, he believed that herein lay the ultimate justification for the dramatic form.

This sense of philosophical purpose is to be seen nowhere more clearly than in his next play, in which he turned from a Spanish to a German theme. *Wallenstein* is a trilogy consisting of *Das Lager* (*The Camp*, 1798), *Die Piccolomini* (*The Piccolomini*), and *Wallensteins Tod* (*Wallenstein's Death*; both in 1799). Nothing equal to this in scope and performance had appeared since the writing of Shakespeare's history plays, and, despite the fact that Schiller has not proved able to condense his plot sufficiently, we must recognize in these three connected dramas one of the greatest achievements of the stage. There is a sweep here, and a force, which rarely has been paralleled in theatrical composition.

The Camp is to be regarded as a prologue, introducing none of the main characters, but providing instead a magnificent picture of the army commanded by Count Albrecht von Wallenstein, in the name of the Emperor Ferdinand II—a motley collection of men of all nations, held together by the will and genius of their general.

The Piccolomini shows the growing cleavage between Wallenstein and the Imperial Court. Intrigue is at work, and, now that the army has driven back the Swedes, the palace has begun to look with suspicion and fear upon the instrument of its might. Realizing that a definite break is inevitable, Field-Marshal Illo and Count Terzky by a trick persuade almost all the officers to sign a document pledging their loyalty to Wallenstein alone, hoping thereby that he will be persuaded to take definite action, repudiate the Emperor, and establish an independent state in league with the Swedes. Meanwhile, however, the Imperial Envoy von Questenberg has found an ally in the ambitious Lieutenant-General Octavio Piccolomini, who, pretending to be one of Wallenstein's most devoted followers, is hoping that he himself may become the commander-in-chief. His son, Max, colonel of a regiment of cuirassiers and an upright, noble figure, finds himself torn in spirit. He detests his father's intrigues, yet is tied to him in filial affection: loyalty to the Emperor clashes with his boundless admiration of Wallenstein and with his love of the general's daughter, Thekla. The last part of the trilogy shows Wallenstein driven desperately to throw over his allegiance and deserted by most of his officers through the machinations of Octavio Piccolomini, who, at the very close of the play, achieves his reward in being created a prince.

The entire work is a complex study in pride and ambition. Piccolomini intrigues in order that he may be ennobled, the Irish officer Butler, hitherto faithful to Wallenstein, is persuaded to desert him and to engineer his assassination because of a slight; Wallenstein's own failing is the taint of overweening pride and belief in his ascendant star. One of the most revealing and dramatic scenes is that in which the Countess Terzky plays on the hero's failings and wins him to rebellion:

WALLENSTEIN: If there were yet a choice! if yet some milder
Way of escape were possible—I still
Will choose it, and avoid the last extreme.
COUNTESS: Desirest thou nothing further? Such a way
Lies still before thee. Send this Wrangel off.
Forget thou thy old hopes, cast far away
All thy past life: determine to commence
A new one. Virtue hath her heroes too,
As well as fame and fortune. To Vienna
Hence—to the Emperor—kneel before the throne;
Take a full coffer with thee—say aloud,
Thou didst but wish to prove thy fealty;

COUNTESS: Thy whole intention but to dupe the Swede. . . .
                On some morrow morning
        The Duke departs; and now 'tis stir and bustle
        Within his castles. He will hunt, and build;
        Superintend his horses' pedigrees,
        Creates himself a court, gives golden keys,
        And introduceth strictest ceremony
        In fine proportions, and nice etiquette;
        Keeps open table with high cheer: in brief,
        Commenceth mighty King—in miniature. . . .

WALLENSTEIN [*in extreme agitation*]: Take her away.
        Let in the young Count Piccolomini.

COUNTESS: Art thou in earnest? I entreat thee! Canst thou
        Consent to bear thyself to thy own grave,
        So ignominiously to be dried up?
        Thy life, that arrogated such a height
        To end in such a nothing! To be nothing,
        When one was always nothing, is an evil
        That asks no stretch of patience, a light evil;
        But to become a nothing, having been——

WALLENSTEIN [*starts up in violent agitation*]:
        Show me a way out of this stifling crowd,
        Ye powers of Aidance! Show me such a way
        As *I* am capable of going. I
        Am no tongue-hero, no fine virtue-prattler;
        I cannot warm by thinking; cannot say
        To the good luck that turns her back upon me,
        Magnanimously: "Go; I need thee not."
        'Cease I to work, I am annihilated.
        Dangers nor sacrifices will I shun,
        If so I may avoid the last extreme;
        But ere I sink down into nothingness,
        Leave off so little, who begun so great,
        Ere that the world confuses me with those
        Poor wretches, whom a day creates and crumbles,
        This age and after ages speak my name
        With hate and dread. . . .

COUNTESS: What is there here, then,
        So against nature? Help me to perceive it!
        O let not Superstition's nightly goblins
        Subdue thy clear bright spirit! Art thou bid
        To murder?—with abhorr'd, accursed poniard
        To violate the breasts that nourish'd thee?
        That *were* against our nature, that might aptly
        Make thy flesh shudder, and thy whole heart sicken.

COUNTESS: Yet not a few, and for a meaner object,
            Have ventured even this, ay, and perform'd it.
            What is there in thy case so black and monstrous?
            Thou art accused of treason—whether with
            Or without justice is not now the question—
            Thou art lost if thou dost not avail thee quickly
            Of the power which thou possessest. Friedland! Duke
            Tell me where lives that thing so meek and tame,
            That doth not all his living faculties
            Put forth in preservation of his life?
            What deed so daring, which necessity
            And desperation will not sanctify?

WALLENSTEIN: Once was this Ferdinand so gracious to me;
            He loved me; he esteem'd me; I was placed
            The nearest to his heart. Full many a time
            We, like familiar friends, both at one table
            Have banqueted together. He and I—
            And the young kings themselves held me the basin
            Wherewith to wash me—and is't come to this?

COUNTESS: So faithfully preservest thou each small favour
            And hast no memory for contumelies?
            Must I remind thee, how at Regensburg
            This man repaid thy faithful services?
            All ranks and all conditions in the empire
            Thou hast wronged to make him great—hadst loaded
                on thee,
            On *thee*, the hate, the curse of the whole world.
            No friend existed for thee in all Germany,
            And why? because thou hadst existed only
            For the Emperor. To the Emperor alone
            Clung Friedland in that storm which gather'd round
                him
            At Regensburg in the Diet—and he dropp'd thee!
            He let thee fall! he let thee fall a victim
            To the Bavarian, to that insolent! . . .

WALLENSTEIN: I never saw it in this light before;
            'Tis even so. The Emperor perpetrated
            Deeds through my arm, deeds most unorderly,
            And even this prince's mantle, which I wear,
            I owe to what were services to him,
            But most high misdemeanours 'gainst the Empire. . . .
            Send Wrangel to me—I will instantly
            Despatch three couriers——

And the die is cast. In the long scene of which the above is but a
fragment the Countess has played upon his pride and superstition

until he is forced, albeit almost against his will, to take decisive action—the action that his enemies were waiting for and that is to lead to his death.

Than *Wallenstein* Schiller never achieved anything more masterly or more majestic, yet still, despite his rapidly failing health, he had power left to create some plays worthy of regard.

Maria Stuart came in 1800. Imprisoned in England, Mary has a faithful servant in young Mortimer and a weak, innately deceitful one in Leicester. In the key scene of the play, and one by no means without power, the two queens confront each other, and with skill Schiller contrasts them—Elizabeth wary, cautious, apparently frank, Mary apt to let her passions guide her. Almost wearily the latter offers to resign her pretensions to the English throne:

> Then, sister, not for all this island's wealth,
> For all the realms encircled by the deep,
> Would I exchange my present lot for yours.

Such, however, is not sufficient for Elizabeth, and with politic art she flings taunts apt to put into Mary's mouth words destined to doom her:

> And you confess at last that you are conquer'd?
> Are all your schemes run out? No more assassins
> Now on the road? Will no adventurer
> Attempt again, for you, the sad achievement?
> Yes, madam, it is over. You'll seduce
> No mortal more. The world has other cares—
> None is ambitious of the dang'rous honour
> Of being your fourth husband. You destroy
> Your wooers like your husbands.

Despite Mary's cry,

> Sister, sister!
> Grant me forbearance, all ye pow'rs of heav'n!

she is goaded into a wild outburst of fury:

> A bastard soils,
> Profanes the English throne! The gen'rous Britons
> Are cheated by a juggler, whose whole figure
> Is false and painted, heart as well as face!
> If right prevail'd, you now would in the dust
> Before me lie, for I'm your rightful monarch!

Elizabeth retires, and Schiller astutely makes the Scottish queen wholly unconscious of what she has done. All she can think of is her triumph in having abased Elizabeth, and in the glow of the besotted Mortimer's praise she ignores the tremulous fears of her other counsellors and fails to see the axe she has herself poised above her head. In scenes such as these Schiller reveals his strength, and, though, like all dramatic authors who have dealt with Mary Queen of Scots, he is sentimentally intoxicated with the romantic legend which is hung about her name, these scenes give real distinction to his tragic theme.

Maria Stuart was followed in 1801 with another 'she-tragedy,' *Die Jungfrau von Orleans* (*The Maid of Orleans*), and one, unhappily, still more deeply soaked in romantic tears. Despite the fact that for years it proved popular on the German stage, we cannot esteem it a great play: no valid central idea gives life to the historical record, no power irradiates the character of the sentimentally conceived Joan of Arc. This study of high idealism, sullied by the world and eventually finding self-purification, fails to achieve its object.

As though he himself were aware of the softening of his romantic mood, Schiller turned in his next play, *Die Braut von Messina* (*The Bride of Messina*, 1803), to a would-be classic style—going so far, indeed, as to imitate the Greeks in the use of the chorus. By introducing this element he believed he was declaring "open and honourable warfare against naturalism in art"; by its means, he pleaded, the modern poet might "transform the commonplace actual world into the old poetical one"; through it lyricism might once more return to the stage. In his idea the chorus should and could be "a general conception . . . represented by a palpable body which appeals to the senses with an imposing grandeur." Unfortunately, for all the beauty wrought into this play, we cannot regard it as a real triumph. The old cloying, romantic sentiment vitiates the strength of its tale of fraternal jealousy between Don Manuel and Don Cæsar, both in love with a girl who turns out, tragically, to be their own sister.

His last play was *Wilhelm Tell* (1804). Basically it is a drama apt to make popular appeal, yet in it are clearly to be seen the defects which prevented Schiller from completely rivalling the earlier masters. The desire to inculcate an idea—the determination to resist oppression and to oppose tyrannical power—leads the author into dividing his characters sharply into the good and the bad, the white and black, so that subtlety is lost and didacticism pervades the treatment of the scenes. Even more serious is the fact that, as the play advances, the hero is left without a genuinely tragic choice. At the beginning Tell is confronted with the necessity of electing death or the trial of his skill by shooting an arrow at an apple on his son's head; bravely he seizes on the former. The test, however, is rendered spuriously melodramatic, since Tell learns that if he does not make the trial both he and his son will perish. Perhaps, however, Schiller inwardly imagined his theme not so much in terms of the romantic trial itself as in terms of the contrast introduced in the last act. Immediately after Tell's famed skill with the bow has vindicated itself he lies in wait for the cruel Governor Gessler and slays him, conscious that he has acted in the interest of his fellows. Later a man clad in monk's robes comes to his house:

MONK: Are you that Tell that slew the governor?

TELL: Yes, I am he. I hide the fact from no man.

MONK: You are that Tell! Ah! it is God's own hand
That hath conducted me beneath your roof.

TELL [*examining him closely*]: You are no monk. Who are you?

MONK: You have slain
The governor, who did you wrong. I, too,
Have slain a foe, who late denied me justice.
He was no less your enemy than mine.
I've rid the land of him.

TELL [*drawing back*]: Thou art—oh, horror!
In—children, children—in without a word!
Go, my dear wife! Go! Go! Unhappy man,
Thou shouldst be——

HEDWIG: Heav'ns, who is it?

TELL: Do not ask.
Away! away! the children must not hear it.
Out of the house—away! Thou must not rest
'Neath the same roof with this unhappy man!

HEDWIG: Alas! What is it? Come! [*Exit with the children.*

TELL [*to the* MONK]: Thou art the Duke
Of Austria—I know it. Thou hast slain
The Emperor, thy uncle, and liege lord.

JOHN: He robbed me of my patrimony.

TELL: How!
Slain him—thy King, thy uncle! And the earth
Still bears thee! And the sun still shines on thee!

JOHN: Tell, hear me, ere you——

TELL: Reeking with blood
Of him that was thy Emperor, and kinsman,
Durst thou set foot within my spotless house?
Show thy fell visage to a virtuous man
And claim the rights of hospitality?

Although he fails to integrate his material successfully, it would seem that Schiller deliberately wrote his entire play for this conclusion; and when we realize this we realize, too, that here, as in all his plays, the idea is predominant. Neither Tell nor Duke John is a real character in the final episode of *Wilhelm Tell*: they are symbols of conflicting interpretations of right and justice. In thus stressing the idea Schiller weakened his own dramatic expression, yet he was at the same time laying the basis for the later development of the nineteenth-century theatre. When we place alongside his dramatization of the philosophical concept those mass scenes in *Wallenstein's Camp* and the scenes of the Swiss mountaineers in his last play—scenes in which the corporate crowd becomes, as it were, a theatrical entity—it is obvious how much the dramatists of the modern era owed to his inspiration. We may smile now at his romantic enthusiasms and recognize their adolescent sentimentalism; but no such smiling can conceal from us their innate, even if not fully developed, strength.

SCHILLER'S SUCCESSORS

Following Schiller came a long line of German playwrights who tried, generally without much success, to exploit the resources of the romantic drama, and as we contemplate their work we see romanticism gradually becoming ever more and more tempestuous, ever more and more absurd. Morbid themes attract the attention of the playwrights, and the concept of fate, at first held in bounds, is carried to lengths truly ridiculous. Where the extreme of pseudo-classicism ends in chill sobriety the extreme of romanticism ends in dissipated excess: the fate of the minor pseudo-classic writer is to be dull, the fate of the minor romanticist is to be absurd.

Absurdities troop lugubriously on the stage of the German *Schicksalstragödien*, the tragedies of fate, that were so dear to Schiller's successors. Adolf Müllner turns out his *Der neunundzwanzigste Februar* (*February the Twenty-ninth*, 1812), so called because the family of an incestuous forester is slowly cut down one by one, the victims being summoned to their dooms as the extra days of succeeding leap years bring with them their inevitable call of death. In his *Die Schuld* (*The Crime*, 1816) is to be found a very compendium of all the ridiculously gloomy elements beloved of romantic melancholy. A trifle less absurd, but equally sensational, is Zacharias Werner's *Der vierundzwanzigste Februar* (*February the Twenty-fourth*, 1809), in which the hoary tale is told of a poor aged couple who murder a stranger youth only to discover that he was their long-lost son; and in his unfinished *Das Kreuz an der Ostsee* (*The Cross on the Baltic*, 1806), despite the presence of some scenes powerfully imagined, we wallow rather dismally in a world of pagan sentiment and early Christianity. So exaggerated is the *Alarcos* (1801) of Friedrich von Schlegel that it has been called a parody of tragedy; hardly less of a parody is *Die Gründung Prags* (*The Founding of Prague*, 1814), by Clemens Brentano, with its hopeless conglomeration of witchcraft and sensational incident. There are scenes in these works no less amusing than those in the satirical travesties of August von Platen-Hallermünde—*Der romantische Œdipus* (*The Romantic Œdipus*, 1829) and *Der verhängnisvolle Gebel* (*The Fatal Fork*, 1826).

Even those authors gifted with richer qualities sank into the morass, and the fashion spread outward so as to embrace the Austrian as well as the German theatre. A good example of this appears in the work of Franz Grillparzer, some of whose Viennese dramas may hardly be distinguished from the type of play being turned out contemporaneously by the intoxicated poets in the Germanic states. Just before Grillparzer's arising a change had been coming over the Austrian stage. Up to the middle of the eighteenth century it had given welcome, on the one hand, to the great Court operas, largely Italian in inspiration, and, on the other, to crude, if racy, popular farces. In 1752 the great Burgtheater housed a French company, and under its influence the styles of Molière and Racine came to predominate. Then, in the seventies, German actors came to replace the French, and the way was opened for the introduction of the romantic genres cultivated by Schiller. Grillparzer is the first native Austrian dramatist to essay the new forms.

The immediate result was his *Die Ahnfrau* (*The Ancestress*, 1817), wherein a crime committed against a woman of the house of Count Borotin is shown bringing its curse down upon the living Bertha and Jaromir, until the former poisons herself and the latter, after killing his own father, is slain by a fatal kiss bestowed on him by the ghost of the 'ancestress.' Although this drama exhibits a certain skill in the evocation of the eerie, obviously its theme is basically absurd. All Grillparzer's plays are thus wrapped in romantic sentiment. *Sappho* (1819) deals fervently with the love of the Greek poetess for Phaon, a youth who tragically discovers that his supposed passion for the lady was no more than an admiration for her poetic gifts. His awakening true love for the maid Melitta brings the action to a suitably tragic close. Despite the beauty of some of the language, the trilogy of *Das goldene Vlies* (1822) makes rather tedious reading, and as a drama not much can be said of *Des Meeres und der Liebe Wellen* (*The Sea's Waves and Love's*, 1840), in which another classic tale, that of Hero and Leander, is told with romantic fervour. A certain vigour appears in *Die Jüdin von Toledo* (*The Jewess of Toledo*; written 1837, acted 1888); there are excitingly contrived scenes in *König Ottokars Glück und Ende* (*The Fate and Fall of King Ottokar*, 1824); and an inner sensitiveness distinguishes the treatment of *Libussa* (*c.* 1848)—but we cannot esteem the author of these dramas an outstanding artist of the theatre. He is poet rather than dramatist.

More of worth is to be discovered in the writings of the erratic Heinrich von Kleist, who, besides his contributions to comedy, turned out some tragic dramas of a strangely tortured kind, in which the delineation of the passions almost anticipates the studies of similar passions made by modern playwrights. *Die Familie Schroffenstein* (*The Schroffenstein Family*, 1803) treats, rather untheatrically, the subject of the vicious influence exerted by two self-willed old men upon their children. In *Penthesilea* (1808) a morbid, brooding spirit surrounds the Amazon queen, who, consumed by love of her conqueror, finally murders him amid a weltering torrent of emotion. *Das Kätchen von Heilbronn* (1810), which succeeded in attracting some considerable contemporary attention, is equally morbid, depicting, with amorous gloom, a heroine willing to endure every insult and every indignity that her lover cares to put on her. More interesting is *Der Prinz von Homburg* (*The Prince of Homburg*; written 1811), in which a strange story is strangely told. Opening with a peculiar half-symbolical scene of a life-is-a-dream atmosphere, it pursues a love-story alongside a tale of honour and duty. With a perplexing admixture of irony and serious purpose, tension is built up to the striking scene in the third act where the heroic Prince, arrested and condemned to death for a breach of military discipline, suddenly loses courage in the face of death and, like Claudio in *Measure for Measure*, begs abjectly for the right to live. In his terror he is prepared to humble himself before the Electress, and even to abandon the love which has been awakened in his heart for Natalie. What gives distinction to this drama is not its almost mystic exaltation of Prussianism, but the way in which Kleist, departing from the straightforward method employed by other romantic historical playwrights, has invested his scenes at once with fantasy, psychological penetration, and humour. With this drama may be associated another, not dissimilar, historical study, *Die Hermannsschlacht* (*The Battle of Arminius*; written 1808, printed 1821). Here Kleist, following the lines set by F. G. Klopstock in his earlier proto-romantic trilogy of *Hermanns Schlacht* (1769), *Hermann und die Fürsten*

(*Arminius and the Princes*, 1784), and *Hermanns Tod* (*The Death of Arminius*, 1787), mingles treatment of passion (sometimes skilful, sometimes jejune) with a conscious and dominating political aim.

None of these plays is a masterpiece, yet in each one there appears a frenzied strength that marks them out as the work of a man of genius who himself realized that that genius was flawed by defects.

Vast conceptions apt to shatter the walls of the theatre buzzed in the minds of these men. Typical are the extraordinary productions of Christian Dietrich Grabbe, whose *Napoleon oder die hundert Tage* (*Napoleon; or, The Hundred Days*, 1831) suggests a continent for a stage, and for the actors an entire army. Grabbe's other romantic-historical works—extending from classical themes, such as *Marius und Sulla*, through the fantastic, as in *Don Juan und Faust*, to the realm of German history, as in the 'cycle' of *Die Hohenstaufen*, are all extensive in scope and, although of some literary interest, are not particularly suited for the stage. Among them, however, may be noted the *Hannibal* (1835), distinguished by its interesting attempt to develop a kind of 'one-man' drama and by the vigour of many of its scenes.

There can be no doubt but that within the field of this romantic theatre we can find many elements which were to be seized upon and developed by later writers, but, in general, historical rather than intrinsic interest attaches even to the best of the plays written during these early decades of the nineteenth century. The poetic imagination of their authors was apt to carry them outside the frame of the stage.

THE TREND TOWARDS MELODRAMA: KOTZEBUE

The German romantic movement tended to burn itself out and, as it progressed, to split in two directions. One of these directions is forcibly indicated by that strange theatrical figure August Friedrich Ferdinand von Kotzebue. Generally despised by the literary critic and often neglected even by the historian of the stage, his was an influence of profound importance in the growth of early-nineteenth-century drama. He was the instrument by which Schiller's poetic style was reduced to popular terms, and with Guilbert de Pixérécourt he shares the honour of creating the most characteristic playhouse genre of the time, the melodrama.

Perhaps there is nothing good that can be said of his literary powers; perhaps his philosophy was insincere; but we cannot escape from the fact that hardly any other German dramatist was more popular, in his native country and abroad, than he. Of his many plays no fewer than thirty-six were translated into English during these romantic years, and of the thirty-six twenty-two were given stage representation. Among them were the immensely popular *Pizarro* (1799), adapted by R. B. Sheridan from *Die Spanier in Peru, oder Rollas Tod* (*The Spaniards in Peru; or, The Death of Rolla,* 1796), and the much discussed *Stranger* (1798), a version of his *Menschenhass und Reue* (*Misanthropy and Repentance*; printed 1789). Between 1790 and 1800 there was a positive Kotzebue mania in London, and for most people 'the German theatre' meant his works. He himself was much influenced by Voltaire and Rousseau, and to their native France he returned their ideas, Germanized and made theatrical: his vogue in London was hardly less intense than his vogue in Paris.

In dramatic composition Kotzebue was the complete eclectic. Nearly all his plays are deeply coloured by sentimental philosophizing, but he permitted only so much of this element as he knew his audience would endure. Of theatrical effect he was a consummate master, and for sensationalism, stage thrill, he was prepared to sacrifice much. He took from his fellow-romantics their historical, often medieval, themes, and from the *philosophes* of France their humanitarian interests. His range carried him everywhere—from the world of the gothic past to the conquest of Peru, from familiar domestic interiors to scenes theatrically built around his own experiences in Russia. His was a restless pen.

His characters were composed in terms of romanticized sentimentalism, and it is through these characters, added to his sensational development of plot, that he becomes one of the founders of the melodrama. The stock figures, the thrilling episodes, the artificially conceived conclusions of his plays, almost cry out for musical accompaniment, and it is easy to see how the impress of his style was laid upon that type of play which formed so much of the world's dramatic fare during the early years of the nineteenth century.

To attempt any analysis of his works would be futile. At the same time attention must be drawn at least to a few which proved particularly popular or received special comment in their time. First comes a group of dramas, including *Menschenhass und Reue*, *Armuth und Edelsinn* (*Poverty and Nobleness of Mind*; printed 1795), *Der Opfertod* (*Family Distress; or, Self-immolation*, 1798), and *Das Kind der Liebe* (*The Child of Love*; printed 1791), which excited attention because in them Kotzebue, with a skilled hand, carried the bourgeois stage beyond the position it had reached with Lessing and his companions. In the first he was sufficiently bold to adumbrate that popular late-nineteenth-century heroine, the lady with a past; in the second the tale is told of a man who has rejected the child whose birth caused the death of his dearly loved wife; the third, opening with an effective scene showing a poverty-stricken room in which lives an old blind woman, hitherto used to the constant attention of servants, who is unaware of the change that has come upon the house, deals with a wife, faithful to her husband in his distress and yet deeply in love with another man; the last treats of the fate of a natural child. Such themes for their time were indeed audacious; we can understand how shocking they appeared to some, how daringly novel to others.

In telling these tales Kotzebue makes full use of his theatrical craft and teaches many a trick to the later melodramatists. Here, for example, is the ending of *Poverty and Nobleness of Mind*, as it appeared to English readers in the year 1799. The bereaved father tells of his devotion to the memory of his dead wife:

PLUM: Yes, here she lives—I feel her presence—she is near me—how else could I feel myself so well? On this chair she has sat [*looking on the back of it*]. Here is still a little powder out of her hair, I have carefully preserved it. At this table she has sat and wrote, with this same pen, so many tender epistles to her happy husband! Here are her letters! Every one is a remembrance of her excellent heart! her faithful love! these gloves she knit for me—this waistcoat was a present from her on my birthday—this lock of hair was cut off after her death. Ah! and here is her picture!

[*He tears away the curtain.*

LOUISA [*with uplifted hands at the foot of the picture*]: My mother!

PLUM [*starts trembling back*]: Girl, what are you doing?

LOUISA [*wildly*]: My mother! my mother!

PLUM [*trembling, in unspeakable agitation*]: Speak! who are you?

LOUISA: She was my mother.

PLUM: Louisa!

LOUISA: Your daughter.

[PLUM *wishes to precipitate himself on her, his knees fail, he sinks back in a chair.*

LOUISA [*hastens to him and embraces his knees*]: My father! forgiveness!

PLUM: Are you really my daughter?

LOUISA: Does not your heart say, Yes?

PLUM [*on her neck*]: Yes, you are!

LOUISA: My letters were in vain; I was determined to try if I could not personally succeed in gaining your affection.

PLUM: You have succeeded! ...

LOUISA: You forgive me?

PLUM: Do you forgive *me*? Oh, how could I so long deny myself this comfort! [*He lifts* LOUISA *from the ground.*] Beloved child! help me up—my knees tremble—lead me under the picture of your mother, that I there may bless you!

Such sentimental scenes, with just a dash of what to the period was riskily daring, brought Kotzebue much fame, even as similar scenes brought fame to his contemporary, August Wilhelm Iffland, who, less gifted than his contemporary, pursued this path in *Die Jäger* (*The Foresters*; printed 1785) and *Die Mündel* (*The Nephews*; printed 1785). Kotzebue, however, had many other strings to his bow. Another set of his dramas gives expression to the very best of Rousseauesque sentiments and effectively plays with humanitarian feelings. In *La-Peyrouse* (printed 1798) is depicted the fate of a man cast upon a desert island, who, while falling in love with a "young female Savage," Malvina, still retains his devotion for his wife, Adelaide. The conclusion is typical:

MALVINA [*turning affectionately, yet with trembling, to* ADELAIDE]: I have prayed for thee, and for myself—let us be sisters!

ADELAIDE: Sisters! [*She remains some moments lost in thought.*] Sisters! Sweet girl, you have awakened a consoling idea in my bosom! Yes, we will be sisters, and this man shall be our brother! Share him we cannot, nor can either possess him singly. [*With enthusiasm*] We, the sisters, will inhabit one hut, he shall dwell in another. We will educate our children, he shall assist us both—by day we will make but one family, at night we will separate—how say you? will you consent? ... [*Extending her arms to* LA-PEYROUSE] A sisterly embrace!

Similar in spirit is *Die Negersklaven* (*The Negro Slaves*, 1795), in which the objects of compassion, as has been said, "show a remarkable acquaintance with eighteenth-century philosophy."

Closely akin to such plays, but more romantically sensational, are those written on the conquest of the Americas. Here *Die Spanier in Peru* stands out pre-eminent. From these it is an easy step to dramas of the type of *Johanna von Montfaucon* (printed 1800), and thence to those in which Kotzebue makes use of Russian themes—notably *Graf Benyowsky, oder die Verschwörung auf Kamtschatka* (*Count Benyowsky; or, The Conspiracy of Kamtschatka*; printed 1795). With constant variety he keeps his audiences interested and alert, providing for his successors both suggestions regarding form and hints for later plot development.

THE MELODRAMA IN FRANCE AND ENGLAND: PIXÉRÉCOURT AND HIS SUCCESSORS

During these years when the German theatre was displaying such sudden and unexpected strength Paris had but little of worth to offer to the stage, and the reason is to be sought—apart from the political confusions of the time—largely in the determined retention by the major theatres of the classical ideal. The age was ripe for the cultivation of romanticism, yet Racine, buttressed by all the extensive library of pseudo-classic theory, forbade the development of a new literary style fit for the expression of the changing concepts animating an altered civilization.

At the same time audiences were anxious to see presented on the stage dramas of a kind different from those hallowed by critical approval, and hence arose that peculiar form of play soon to become familiar under the name of the *mélodrame*. Originally the word 'mélodrame' was introduced to France from Italy as a synonym for 'opera,' but by the beginning of the nineteenth century it had acquired its later specialized significance—signifying a popular play, with a sensationally serious plot broken by comic scenes, and accompanied throughout by incidental music. In this kind of production no attempt is made at securing depth of purpose or literary grace; hence the melodramatic characters tend to become a series of stock types, presented in simple terms of white and black, while the author frankly allows action to preponderate over dialogue. In developing and establishing this new genre chief credit must go to the Kotzebue of France, Guilbert de Pixérécourt, who, first coming before the public with his *Sélico, ou les nègres généreux* (*Selico; or, The Magnanimous Slaves*) in 1793, soon formulated all the elements of which his successors were to make free use.

Like Kotzebue, Pixérécourt was an eclectic writer, and, like him, he displayed wide variety in the choice of his themes. Popular novels gave him many a plot: *Les Maures d'Espagne* (*The Spanish Moors*, 1804) and *La muette de la forêt* (*The Dumb Girl of the Forest*, 1828) are from French sources; how far he ranged is shown in *Robinson Crusoë* (1805), *Les chefs écossais* (*The Scottish Chiefs*, 1819), and *Le château de Loch-Leven* (*The Castle of Loch Leven*, 1822). Emulating Kotzebue, he turned out a *Pizarre* (1802) and a *Christophe Colomb* (1815), and even fared eastward (again like his German companion) in *Les mines de Pologne* (*The Mines of Poland*, 1803).

None of these works exhibits any quality worthy of particular examination, yet a judgment must be passed on them similar to that passed on the writings of Kotzebue. Although they have hardly value as literature, their influence on the stage may not be minimized. Pixérécourt's theatrical skill joined with Kotzebue's in forming the brilliant technique of Scribe, and from the spirit of both was born the English melodrama. Although Goethe was no doubt right in resigning from the Weimar Court Theatre when Pixérécourt's *Le chien de Montargis* (*The Dog of Montargis*, 1816) was produced there—believing it beneath his dignity to be associated with a drama in which a dog was a hero—the fact remains that Pixérécourt knew his public and recognized that dogs were precisely to their taste.

It is easy to see how Pixérécourt built his success out of a determined formalization of elements already existent in the Parisian theatres towards the close of the eighteenth century; equally easy is it to trace the movement on the English stage towards the melodramatic form, years before his influence dominantly asserted itself. In 1802 Thomas Holcroft, already possessed of a reputation as an author of sentimental plays, adapted the French author's *Cœlina, ou l'enfant du mystère* (*Cœlina; or, The Child of Mystery*, 1800) as *A Tale of Mystery*, and thereby inaugurated the vogue for the new genre. At the same time the various elements making up this genre are amply displayed in such earlier works as the sensational *Castle Spectre* (1797) of M. G. Lewis or the *Columbus* (1792) and *Zorinski* (1795) of Thomas Morton. The fact is that the theatre, inadequately supplied by the literary authors with dramas of a modern tone, craved for and, in craving, created a popular form fitted to its mood. Pixérécourt and Kotzebue were not so much innovators as creatures of their time, extraordinarily sensitive to the current demands.

In England the melodrama flourished with particular success because of the long-standing monopoly that gave to the two 'winter' theatres (Drury Lane and Covent Garden) and the one 'summer' theatre (the Haymarket) exclusive rights in the spoken drama. Audiences were increasing; many members of these audiences demanded fare beyond that which was provided in the patent houses; and an escape was found by the opening of other places of entertainment—soon to be familiarly classified as the 'minors'—which were enabled to circumvent the law by presenting plays accompanied by music. Thus the melodrama met not only a spiritual need but also a practical need of the time.

In addition it met a theatrical need. Most of the efforts of the romantic poet were vitiated by their being too classical (Alfieri,) too Shakespearian (Schiller) or too abstract (Goethe). The new type of modern playhouse called for a correspondingly new technique, and this the poets were little fitted to provide. Before any further advance in dramatic writing could come there was needed a fresh approach to the purely theatrical devices which might be put to the use of the playwrights—and here precisely the Kotzebues and the Pixérécourts were able to give suggestions of a vital kind. It is not too much to say that the line of development towards Ibsen proceeds from the fount of melodrama. What the early authors in this style gave to the stage was taken over by Scribe and later by Sardou; they brought the mechanics of play production almost to a science; and, although the distance from Scribe to Ibsen is indeed a far cry, technically the later author could not have composed his dramas with such ease had his undistinguished predecessor not made the path smooth for him. The melodrama may have nothing to give us of depth of thought or intensity of emotion, but it exerted a potent force in the development of the modern stage.

THE SPREAD OF ROMANTIC TRAGEDY

While the melodrama thus swept over the popular stages of England and France, other countries, some of them for the first time proudly tasting the joys of the theatre, made noble, but in general fruitless, efforts to produce tragic works of majesty and distinction. For the most part these efforts, being pursued by poets out of harmony with the stage of their time, yielded plays which, although possessing literary quality of varying degrees of excellence, are to be regarded rather as texts for the reading than as scripts designed for histrionic interpretation. In view of the fact that our prime interest here is the playhouse, it were needless to linger lengthily over these many tragedies in diverse tongues: all that is necessary is a rapid glance at some of the more characteristic and intrinsically worthy contributions made in the various lands.

In Italy, where the Shakespearian style never took easy root, the mantle of Alfieri, after being handed to Giovanni Pindemonte, whose *Ginevra di Scozia* (1795) shows romantic sentiment imposing itself on classical forms, and whose *Lucio Quinzio Cincinnato* (1800) begins to display awareness of other methods than those established by the followers of Racine, passed into the possession of the great Alessandro Manzoni, whose *I promessi sposi* is one of the finest of the world's historical novels. For the stage Manzoni wrote his early drama *Adelchi* (printed 1822), set in eighth-century Lombardy, with half-real, half-symbolic figures, of whom chief are the King, Desiderio, a man who knows no law save the barbaric rule of the sword, Adelchi, his son, whose nature is transformed by Christianity, and the gently noble heroine Ermengarda. A second theatrical work, *Il conte di Carmagnola* (*The Count of Carmagnola*, 1820), presents a vivid study of a noble general who, enveloped in political intrigue, is condemned by the Venice he has served so well.

These two plays might have been thought capable of reviving Italy's tragic drama, but after Manzoni comes a long, dreary patch of territory stretching onward to the close of the nineteenth century. With his *Polissena* (1810) Giovanni Battista Niccolini had endeavoured without much success to arouse his countrymen to follow the original Greek models rather than those of Racine and Alfieri. This playwright's most significant work is *Arnaldo da Brescia* (1843), wherein is depicted the effort of the hero, aided by Ostasio, Count of Campania, to break the power of the Pope and establish a popular republic on antique lines: Arnaldo's effort is wrecked, partly by the overwhelming power sent against him, partly by his betrayal through the unwilling complicity of Ostasio's wife, Adelaide. In this drama, as in the earlier over-rhetorical *Antonio Foscarini* (1827) and *Giovanni da Procida* (1830), Niccolini's political aims are clearly delineated. Another political author, Silvio Pellico, famed for his fight in the cause of Italian freedom and for the vividly penned record of his life, *Le mie prigioni*, produced in *Eufemio da Messina* (1820), *Ester d'Engaddi* (1832), and *Tommaso Moro* (1833) three similarly conceived works. Patriotic sentiment also colours the *Buondelmonte e gli Amadei* (*Buondelmonte and the Amadei*, 1827) and the *Lodovico Sforza* (1833) of Count Carlo Marenco; neither of these last two plays has much virtue, although the former, set in thirteenth-century Florence, possesses a certain interest because of its not ineffective portrait of the almost saint-like hero. Among the many dozens of similar plays that made their appearance during these years mention may be made of one other—the *Beatrice di Tenda* (printed 1825) of Carlo Tedaldi Fores, who, despite a mixed style compounded of borrowings from authors as far apart as Shakespeare and Alfieri, also succeeds in presenting a portrait of nobility in the figure of his heroine.

Political fire rather than theatrical glows in these dramas. The poets, as elsewhere, are seen to be removed from contact with the popular stage, where audiences who could have found no satisfaction in this rarer philosophic atmosphere eagerly inhaled the cruder air of the romantic opera and the clowneries of farce.

Other countries likewise failed to give any truly noteworthy contributions to the theatre in this style, although it is important to note the fact that it was largely from the romantic movement that diverse lands which so far had lain dormant found inspiration for the awakening of their dramatic genius. Even if little of consequence emerged within these years, the impulse thus provided is obviously of some considerable interest and importance.

Thus, for example, was Scandinavia beginning to stir restlessly in anticipation of an Ibsen to come. In Denmark arose Adam Gottlob Oehlenschläger. Stimulated largely by the influence of Schiller, he produced a defence of barbaric religion in *Haakon Jarl* (*Earl Hakon*, 1807), a tragic treatment of Teutonic myth in *Palnatoke* (1809), and a medieval love-drama in *Axel og Valborg* (*Axel and Valborg*, 1810), crowning these achievements with a not uninteresting work, written in German, *Correggio* (1809). This story of the almost saint-like artist, Antonio Allegri, amid his companions, is infused with much romantic sentiment, in which art is viewed as a kind of counterpart to religion. It is of interest to observe that here may be found the source of those many nineteenth-century plays that base their plots on artists' lives. Through his application to the historical stage Oehlenschläger's influence was widespread and powerful on nearly every one of the later-nineteenth-century Scandinavian playwrights: his dramas, although marked by common romantic weaknesses, had vigour and strength sufficient to make them appeal to minds greater than his own.

Sweden produced Bengt Lidner, whose *Grefvinnan Spastaras Död* (*The Death of Countess Spastara*, 1783) was once highly praised, and he was companioned by Erik Johan Stagnelius, with his poetic *Martyrerna* (*The Martyrs*, 1821–22) and his tragic *Bacchanterna* (*The Bacchanals*, 1822)—both men adding to the inspiring force of Oehlenschläger.

Similarly, an awakening is to be sensed in the far-off Russian realms. Although nearly all the dramatic works produced there before the middle of the century were comedies, we may by no means neglect the long line of efforts made in an endeavour to establish a serious poetic and a tragic stage. The earlier level of development is marked in the activities of Alexander Petrovich Sumarokov, an ardent admirer of the French theatre, deeply influenced by Corneille, Racine, and Voltaire. By the close of the eighteenth century, however, German influence was beginning to modify this Gallic trend, and shortly after came a still further impulse gained through knowledge both of Shakespeare and of Byron. With Vasili Andreevich Zhukovski and Ivan Andreevich Krylov the way was being prepared, and finally a major author appeared in the person of Alexander Sergeevich Pushkin, more important perhaps as a lyric writer than as a dramatist, yet distinguished also in the latter field by his *Boris Godunov* (composed 1825, printed 1831). Obviously inspired by Shakespeare, Pushkin has here succeeded in presenting a vivid picture of the ambitious pretender who moves to the throne of Ivan the Great by murdering the heir, Dmitri, and is racked, like Macbeth, by the whisperings of his conscience. While not well adapted for performance, the qualities that Pushkin introduced into this drama—notably the treatment of the crowd and the deep moral tone infusing the entire action—render it worthy of highest praise. Unfortunately, beyond this one work Pushkin gave nothing to the drama: compositions such as *Mozart and Salieri* are poetic essays rather in the style of Browning's 'dramatic lyrics' than in that suited for stage interpretation.

With Pushkin is associated the almost contemporary Mikhail Yurevich Lermontov, also deeply influenced by German and English romanticism. Schiller dominates over his *Ispantsi* (*The Spaniards*, 1830) and Shakespeare over *Maskerad* (*Masquerade*, 1835). Neither is a masterpiece, although the poet's own lyrical passion has given to the latter a quality capable of arousing interest in the theatre. In this bitter story of a man who, loving his wife yet possessed of an almost demoniacal fury, thinks she has been unfaithful to him, poisons her, and, when confronted by the truth, loses his reason, resides a psychological penetration of more than common appeal. Even in our own times *Masquerade* has proved successful on the stage.

Corresponding to the political poets of Italy, Ladislav Alexandrovich Ozerov sought to use the classical tragic form in *Dmitri Donskoi* (1807) for the expression of patriotic sentiment; while, later, Alexei Stepanovich Khomiakov seized upon the romantic style, as in *Ermak* (1827) and *Dmitri samozvanets* (*Dmitri the Pretender*, 1832), for similar purposes. Their efforts were followed by not a few authors of lesser import. These works may be neglected, but if only for Pushkin's *Boris Godunov* the Russian contribution to romantic drama is of considerable significance.

In Poland, too, the romantic spirit found exponents. The stage there had produced nothing of serious worth since Jan Kochanowski's sixteenth-century Senecan and Euripidean *Odprawa posłów greckich* (*The Discharge of the Greek Ambassadors*, 1578)—a play dealing with the Trojan war. Now came the work of Alojzy Feliński, with his

Barbara Radziwiłłówna (1811), followed, first, by the writings of Józef Korzeniowski, author of *Piękna kobieta* (*A Beautiful Woman*, 1834), and, later, by those of Juliusz Słowacki, a poet who assumes a position only less high than that of Pushkin. Like his Russian contemporary, Słowacki too was largely inspired towards the stage by his discovery of Shakespeare's genius, and his finest dramas all reveal the strong impress of the Elizabethan technique. *Mindowe* (1833) reflects both *Richard III* and *Hamlet*; *Balladyna* (1839) similarly calls upon *Macbeth* and *Lear*; *Mazepa* (1840) has echoes of *Othello*. While we cannot rate Słowacki highly as a playwright, his scenes display poetic power, and the later development of the Polish stage owes much to his inspiration.

Precisely the same Shakespearian seal was set on the Hungarian poets. It was after studying the English plays that József Katona produced his *Bánk Bán* (*Viceroy Bank*) in 1819. This not unimpressive tragedy, set in the thirteenth century, tells how Andreas II leaves the governorship of the kingdom in the hands of the Bán or Count Bank, who becomes involved in a frenzied drama of domestic and political passion. The same theme, it may be noted, was treated by Franz Grillparzer in *Ein treuer Diener seines Herrn* (*A True Servant to his Lord*, 1828), and in noting this we may also admit that Katona's handling of the tragic situation contrasts favourably with that of his Austrian contemporary. A couple of years after the appearance of *Bánk Bán* Karoly Kisfaludy produced his *Irene* (1821), another landmark in the development of the Hungarian drama.

Of a significance still greater than all of these was the slow arising of the theatre in America. Up to 1830 the youthful States had produced nothing of fundamental importance, but clearly a giant was in the making. Its first beginnings may be traced back to the start of the eighteenth century (perhaps even beyond that date); definite advance came immediately after 1750; and with the establishment of the Republic there was a great expansive movement, during which theatres rapidly arose in the principal cities and touring companies brought their wares to the farthest frontiers. In the earlier years the actors had been but waifs and strays from London's minor houses; by the middle of the century American-born players were joining companies with some claims to distinction; when the nineteenth century opened many such companies were in existence, and the most prominent stars (Edmund Kean among them) were glad to make tours across the Atlantic.

Naturally the repertory was at first entirely composed of English classics and of more recent London successes; nor did this kind of repertory alter much during the romantic years. As in London, the comedy of Vanbrugh and Farquhar ceded place to the sentimental drama, and that in turn was swallowed up in the great melodramatic wave that came after 1800. Signs, however, were not wanting that this young playhouse desired to try its hand at the production of native works, and, although nothing much came of those desires, the urge was one later to prove fruitful. America's first native tragedy, Thomas Godfrey's *The Prince of Parthia* (1765), was dully neo-classical in the strain of Addison's *Cato*, and equally dull was the first native play on an American theme, *Ponteach; or, The Savages of America* (1766), by Robert Rogers. With William Dunlap arrived the influence of Kotzebue and Pixérécourt, and soon playwrights were nosing around restlessly amid spectacular Indian themes. James Nelson Barker produced his *The Indian Princess; or, La Belle Sauvage* (1808), while John Augustus Stone, capitalizing on this initial effort, won a measure of justifiable success for his *Metamora; or, The Last of the Wampanoags* (1829). In those same years John Howard Payne, famous as the author of *Home, Sweet Home*, was turning out melodramas, such as *Julia; or, The Wanderer* (1806), and more ambitious 'tragedies,' such as *Brutus; or, The Fall of Tarquin* (1818); while more literary authors of the type of Robert Montgomery Bird, with his *The Gladiator* (1831), were trying to give dignity to the poetic stage. From his efforts stemmed the later and more worthy plays of George Henry Boker, whose *Francesca da Rimini* (1855) is perhaps as vigorous a dramatic work as any produced by the English poets of the age.

Even *Francesca da Rimini*, however, is artificial and lifeless. The American theatre then, and for half a century to come, could do no more than try its hand awkwardly at dramatic composition and give birth to writings of promise rather than of assurance.

Here, as elsewhere, the romantic theatre had little to offer. In the writing of drama control is necessary, and powerful scenes cannot be wrought out of enthusiasm alone. The poets had their minds inflamed and disturbed by political and imaginative visions, which made them incapable of paying due attention to the requirements of the stage; their despised companions, the melodramatists, knew how to pen effective stage pieces, but of higher purpose they had none. Looking at the drama throughout the world from 1800 to 1830, one can see only slender hope for better things; when, however, we take it in conjunction with what was to follow we realize that the seeds were at this time being planted which were destined, fifty years after, to germinate and to flourish.

COMEDY AND EXTRAVAGANZA

DURING this period of romantic gloom and political ferment men still knew how to laugh. The intellectuals at times were inclined to be somewhat ponderous, but the common folk, at least, still retained their good, hearty, healthy sense of fun. As in the realm of the tragic drama, so here a distinction is to be made between the more literary efforts in the field of high comedy and those in less dignified genres intended for popular consumption. To the melodrama corresponds the vaudeville, the extravaganza, and the musical burlesque.

SOCIAL SATIRE IN RUSSIA: GRIBOEDOV AND GOGOL

Pride of place, for originality of conception and grace of execution, must go to two Russian comedies—*Gore ot uma* (literally *Woe from Wit*, also known as *Too Clever by Half*; first acted posthumously in 1831), by Alexander Sergeevich Griboedov and *Revizor* (*The Inspector-General*, 1836), by Nikolai Vasilievich Gogol. In these appears a spirit entirely at variance with anything contemporaneously produced by other European writers—a spirit in which may be discerned the genuine basis of a characteristically Russian comic realism.

Already in the eighteenth century hints had been given of the potentialities of a native satiric comedy. Even Catherine the Great found time from amorous intrigue and the issuing of ukases to pen (in French or Russian) eleven comic scenes, and in them, despite the German origin of their imperial authoress, a peculiarly Russian kind of ironic satire makes its tentative appearance. In *Peredniaia znatnavo boiarina* (*A Great Lord's Antechamber*, 1772) we are presented with a sketch in which a number of optimistic petitioners have their interviews and depart dejected or irate. *O vremia!* (*O Time!*, 1772) castigates provincial affectations and follies in the persons of three pretentious ladies, Khanzhakhina, Vestnikova, and Chudikhina. With genuine comic verve she ridicules absurd superstition in the person of Kalifalkzherston (a caricature of Cagliostro), the chief character of *Obmanshchik* (*The Impostor*, 1786), ridicule that is pursued farther in *Shaman sibirskii* (*The Siberian Sorcerer*, 1786).

That the quality exhibited here—the tendency to look directly at life and to portray its oddities; the desire to display the follies, duplicities, and, especially, the absurdities of men in society; the predilection to prefer a sketch of life to a formalized development of plot—was not confined to Catherine may be realized when we turn to glance at the *Brigadir* (*The Brigadier*, 1766) of Denis Ivanovich Fonvizin. In this entertaining comedy plot counts for far less than depiction of character and atmosphere. There is, certainly, an 'intrigue' by which Ivanushka, the retired Brigadier's son, is betrothed to Sofia, daughter of a Counsellor, while, with his own father for rival, he lays suit to the Counsellor's wife (like him, an ardent reader of French romances); but the real interest of the play, and the source of its comic spirit, rests in its vivid depiction of manners. Fonvizin has another comedy almost equally good, *Nedorosl* (*The Booby*, 1782), where appears a stupid young Mitrofanushka, a gentleman who wants to get married, "to-night if possible" to no matter whom, placed against the appropriate background of his ridiculous family, the Prostakovs. Thoroughly typical of this author's style, too, is his slighter sketch *Vibor guvernera* (*The Choice of a Tutor*, c. 1790), which gaily, if a trifle crudely, caricatures the absurd pretensions of an almost illiterate Count and Countess, who, in seeking to engage a tutor, prefer a French manicurist to a Russian scholar.

Only a few years later came the *Yabeda* (*Chicanery*, 1798) of Vasili Yakovlevich Kapnist, a play that delineates ironically and with a keenly realistic touch the trickeries of provincial magistrates. Another author who took the same path was Mikhail Matinski, whose *Gostinii dvor* (*The Bazaar*, 1791) indulges in similar satire and serves still further to develop the resources of that kind of native comic realism first exploited by Catherine.

Out of this tradition stemmed directly Griboedov's *Gore ot uma*, written in delicate, witty verse, deriving its strength from earlier pictures of life, but giving to these portraits a fineness and a precision such as the Russian drama had not hitherto known. Started in 1821, the comedy did not receive even a partial performance until ten years later, and a rigid censorship prevented its complete stage presentation until the sixties. Nevertheless it was eagerly read, and unquestionably did much to further the progress of the Moscow theatre. In form the play is little more than a series of comic scenes, but the vividness with which these are etched gives genuine distinction to Griboedov's writing. His hero, Chatski, the young man who is annoyed with the follies of society, moves forward with amusing grace to his final discomfiture. True humour is here, and sprightliness, and that peculiar element, so clearly marked in Gogol's work, of laughter concealing tears. Although Chatski obviously expresses many of the ideas of his creator, his intellect and his appreciation of society's faults do not save him; and at the end he remains a lonely figure, bereft of his beloved Sophie. In Famusov, Sophie's father, Griboiedov depicts the worldly-wise functionary, against whose subservience Chatski rebels. The latter has just proclaimed his refusal to take a position at Court. "There you are!" cries Famusov,

> you're all so proud nowadays! You ought to inquire how your forefathers behaved: from their example you could profit mightily. Take, for instance, my late uncle Maksim Petrovich. He dined not on silver but on gold. He had a hundred servants in his house. He was positively covered with decorations. He rode in a six-horse carriage. His whole life he spent at Court—and what a Court! The past wasn't like the present. He served Catherine. In those days every one was a somebody. . . . And my uncle! What prince or count could compare with him? Though dignified and austere, he knew when to bow and bend. Once at a levée he tripped and stumbled, nearly breaking his neck. The old man groaned and was rewarded with a smile from Her Imperial Highness—she even laughed. And what did he do? He rose, adjusted his clothes, bowed—and fell again. This time on purpose. His fall was greeted with a roar of laughter, so down he fell a third time. What did everybody think? They thought he was very clever. His fall may have caused him pain, but it caused him to rise. After that, who was most sought after at the whist-table? Maksim Petrovich. Who received the most cordial greetings at the palace? Maksim Petrovich. Who received most attention? Maksim Petrovich. Who led in rank? Who was given a pension? Maksim Petrovich. You modern braggarts are pigmies compared with him.

After this Chatski's famous last speech comes with the force of a blow. "I'm sorry," he says to Famusov,

> every one is trying to explain to me something I cannot understand . . . I seem to be moving in a dream. [*With passion*] What a blind fool I was! From whom did I hope to get a reward for all my pains? I rushed: I ran: I flew! I trembled, for I thought that happiness was near! [*To* SOPHIE] To whom did I whisper tender words of love? And you! Oh, my God, whom did you choose instead of me? When I think of it, my brains go numb. Why didn't you tell me straight

out that you had turned the past into ridicule?—that you had ripped from your memory all the devotion that bound our hearts together? For me, no distance, no amusement, no alteration of place has made me forget, even for a moment, the days of our youth. I lived and breathed and joyed in the past! . . . And you, sir, father of this daughter, you who adore orders and decorations, I shall leave you happily dozing in your folly. I shall not upset you by asking for your daughter's hand. Another more worthy will come along to bend and bow his way to fame—one who may equal the talents of his future father-in-law. Now my illusions are gone and I am calm. The scales have fallen from my eyes: I am awakened from my dream. . . . You have unanimously proclaimed me mad—you, the amorous fools, the spiteful boobies, the sharp-tongued old women, the decrepit old men tittering with senile mirth. And you're right! A man can spend a day with you and not suffer for it; but he who breathes for a time the atmosphere you live in is bound to sink into permanent stupefaction. Away from Moscow! I shall come here no more! I shall speed without rest to seek a corner in the world where my tormented soul can find peace. My carriage! My carriage!

And the final word is spoken by Famusov: "What will Princess Maria Aleksandrovna say?"—the Russian equivalent of the English inquiry about Mrs Grundy.

Out of this atmosphere steps that greatest of all early Russian comedies, *Revizor* (*The Inspector-General*), by Gogol. The hero of this piece is no Chatski. Khlestakov is a young intellectual stranded, for want of money, in a remote provincial town: he is not either an idealist or a thoroughgoing rogue—merely a lively fellow, rather simple, but with an eye on the main chance, and endowed both with a sense of fun and a keenly observant eye. By chance the various officials of the town, expecting the visit of a governmental inspector, come to the conclusion that this young gentleman is that functionary arrived incognito. In the ensuing scenes Gogol, in a riot of laughable episodes, reveals the chicaneries and the peculations of the provincials, who, feeding on bribes themselves, thrust sums of money and other presents upon him, gleefully reflecting that the fact of their acceptance guarantees immunity for themselves. One by one they come before us—the timid Superintendent of Schools, the lazy Judge, the prying Postmaster, the ignorant District Doctor, and, above all, the terrified but forceful Chief of Police. With them other figures are associated—the Chief of Police's intriguing wife and coquettish daughter, the garrulous and stupid country squires, Dobchinski and Bobchinski, even representatives of the peasantry—for in *Revizor* the whole of Russia is depicted. At the end a letter written by Khlestakov and opened by the Postmaster reveals the self-imposed trick to the dismayed crowd, and in the midst of recriminations a servant announces, with due dignity, the arrival of the true inspector.

There is here a peculiar quality, hard to analyse. The satire and the realism alike remove *Revizor* from the range of Shakespeare's comedies, yet Gogol unquestionably shares some of the English writer's humour. A delicate measure is in his laughter; bitter as is the satire, sympathy intrudes. The characters are fools and rogues, but they are our fellow-creatures. When Gogol printed the play he inserted a motto: "The mirror mustn't be blamed if your face is at fault."

The same mood predominates in *Zhenitba* (*Marriage*; printed 1847), in which, farcically—though, by a paradox, realistically— the timorous bachelor Podkoliossin makes arrangements with a professional matchmaker for a bride, persuades a friend to make the proposal, and, after all has been satisfactorily settled, climbs out of a window and escapes—too terrified to go through with the ceremony. With gaiety, and yet with an undercurrent of emotion, the ridiculous situation is presented in such a manner as to throw emphasis not on the episodes themselves, but rather on the characters and, particularly, on the social *milieu* against which these characters are set.

It is interesting to observe that another Slavonic country, Serbia, produced during this time, in the plays of Jovan Sterija Popovič, an atmosphere closely akin to the Russian: his *Laža i paralaža* (*The Liar and his Mate*, 1830) typically deals with the affectations of a girl who, after having received an education in the city, returns to her country home despising what she deems to be rustic ignorance and vulgarity; she is suitably shocked into sense when a Baron Holić, who has been flattering her fancies, is unmasked as a mere trickster. As in the Russian plays, the comic spirit derives, not from intrigue, but from the analysis of character relationships and from the presentation of social *milieu*.

THE WORLD OF FAIRY AND OF FOLK

During these years, when Russia was slowly shaping a character-istic form of comic expression, some dramatists elsewhere were developing a dramatic style which, although all too frequently we neglect it in our consideration of the nineteenth-century stage, must be regarded as one of the most potent and fruitful forces of the time.

THE TEATRO FILARMONICO, VERONA
Reconstructed on the original plans of Francesco Galli Bibiena.
From *La Scenografia Italiana*, by Corrado Ricci (Fratelli Treves Editori, Milan, 1930).

ITALIAN OPERA SETTING BY FRANCESCO GALLI BIBIENA, ABOUT 1730

Uffizi Gallery, Florence.

By courtesy of the Superintendent of the Florence Galleries

ITALIAN OPERA SETTING BY BERNARDINO GALLIARI, ABOUT 1780

By courtesy of the Ministero della Pubblica Istruzione, Rome

When we think of romanticism it is its serious 'gothicism' that comes to our mind. We are inclined to forget that the imaginative fantasy which produced the many poetic tragedies was channelled also into comic territory, where it served to irrigate the soil of fantastic extravaganza.

In Germany, within the decades that were giving birth to the tragedies of fate and the melodramas of Kotzebue, two interesting comic forms make their appearance. The one is the half-fantastic, half-realistic ironic treatment of the actual; the other is the exploitation of an impossible fairy-tale world in terms that institute a relationship between the fantastic and the real. For examples we need go no farther than the experiments in comedy made by two authors whose names we usually associate with work of a serious romantic trend.

Heinrich von Kleist's tragic dramas have already been referred to, but in addition to these he wrote *Der zerbrochene Krug* (*The Broken Jug*, 1811). The jug that gives the title to the play is the precious possession of Frau Marthe Rull, and when it is found broken a lawsuit follows. Before the single act is over it is discovered that the judge is the true culprit and that all the confusion has sprung from his libidinous attempt to engage in an amorous intrigue with Frau Rull's daughter. Outwardly we inhabit the real world here, but careful investigation reveals that beneath the actuality rests a kind of metaphysical basis whereby the hilarious plot serves symbolically to demonstrate a deeper theme. Something of the same is true of the farcical *Die Gouvernante* (*The Governess*, 1813) of Theodor Körner and even of *Der Datterich* (*The Braggart*, 1840) by the dialect poet Johann Elias Niebergall.

This comedy may be taken as illustrating one trend. The other appears in the writings of Ludwig Tieck. His *Leben und Tod der heiligen Genoveva* (*The Life and Death of the Holy Genoveva*; printed 1811), although once highly praised, is not very impressive: its tale of a maligned medieval lady who lives six years in a forest cave before she is restored to her husband reeks of the romantic-sentimental. The very similar plot of *Kaiser Octavianus* (printed 1804), despite the adroitness shown by the author in the rhythmic forms of his dialogue, yields hardly more of value. There is, however, an entirely different story when we turn from these serious efforts to the series of fantastic, fairy-tale satires that start with *Blaubart* (*Bluebeard*), *Der gestiefelte Kater* (*Puss-in-Boots*), and *Die verkehrte Welt* (*The World Upside Down*)—all printed in his *Volksmärchen* of 1797—and proceed farther with *Zerbino, oder die Reise*

P

nach dem guten Geschmack (*Zerbino; or, The Search for Good Taste*), *Leben und Tod des kleinen Rotkäppchens* (*The Life and Death of Little Red Riding Hood*), both published in 1799, and the later *Fortunat* (*Fortunatus*, written 1815). In these Tieck does several interesting things. First, he follows Gozzi in investing fairy-tale subject-matter with satirical content. Second, he breaks down the frontiers between the audience and the actors, so that we have here a kind of romantic intellectual adumbration of yesterday's riotous *Hellzapoppin*. And, thirdly, there arises out of these two things a clear expression of that 'irony' so characteristic of Tieck and his circle. In *Blaubart* elements of terror, of symbolic portraiture, and of literary satire are inextricably intermingled. Satire directed against eighteenth-century 'Enlightenment' appears in *Der gestiefelte Kater* along with hilarious scenes in which actors and audience almost come to blows. In *Die verkehrte Welt* spectators actually do storm the stage in order to take sides in the fight between Apollo and the usurper Skaramuz. The plot of *Zerbino* tells how this sentimentally inclined prince sets out on a journey to find good taste and returns home to discover that his house-dog, Stallmeister, has become the Court philosopher: when he calls the dog a dog all are scandalized and he is locked up as a madman. Even more interesting is the treatment of the Little Red Riding Hood story, where the heroine is depicted as the daughter of corrupt parents (her mother is a rationalist and her father a drunkard) and consequently tainted by her environment: she is obstinate, self-satisfied, and overweening, so that when she is gobbled up by the wolf it is as a result not of childish innocence but of innate stupidity. The wolf himself is drawn within this circle: he too is the victim of circumstance, an idealist who has become embittered through disillusionment.

With these plays may be associated another. Among his romantically serious works Christian Dietrich Grabbe has a strange *Scherz, Satire, Ironie und tiefere Bedeutung* (*Farce, Satire, Irony, and Deeper Purpose*; written 1822), in which appears a wild admixture of characters—the Baron von Haldungen, his niece, Liddy, the poet Rattengift, a writer on natural history, the Devil with his Grandmother, and Grabbe himself. Perhaps this is an extreme example, yet in its very eccentricities it well illustrates the mood out of which these gambollings of the poets, no less than the ruder extravaganzas of the popular hack writers, were born.

In contemplating the development of this fantastic comedy, we recall the intense enthusiasm aroused in Germany by the discovery of Gozzi's *fiabe* as well as by such Spanish plays as Calderón's

Life is a Dream. Among Schiller's works is a version of *Turandot*; Schlegel produced, in addition to his famous translation of Shakespeare, two volumes of the *Spanisches Theater* (1803–9); Grillparzer not only translated Calderón's dream play, but also penned his own, independent *Der Traum ein Leben* (*Dreaming is Life*, 1834), in which an Eastern hero, Rustan, instead of experiencing events which he later believes to have been a dream, dreams in such a way that his real life is influenced by what he has experienced when asleep. This drama, it is true, is hardly a comedy, while the heavy-handed daubing of philosophical concepts in the same author's *Weh' dem der lügt!* (*Woe to the Liar!*, 1840) almost completely removes it from the realm of the laughable, but the spirit that animates these works is not far removed from that which appears in more gaily fantastic essays of the time.

Finally we may turn to the less pretentious and more popular stage pieces of two Viennese authors, Johann Nestroy and his more brilliant earlier contemporary Ferdinand Raimund. In Nestroy appears a combination of elements to be fully, and perhaps sometimes rather tiresomely, exploited during the half-century following his time. His plays are thoroughly irreverent, indulging in much burlesque of the tragic efforts of the time: they frankly exist for the purpose of entertainment and make no apologies for introducing the impossible and the absurd; their style is marked by an accumulation of sometimes amusing, but more commonly over-elaborated, puns. Taking the already existent *Zauberpossen*, or fairy-tale farces, popular on the Viennese stage, Nestroy fashions his sixty-odd comedies either out of folk-tale elements—such as *Eulenspiegel, oder Schabernack über Schabernack* (*Eulenspiegel; or, Trick after Trick*, 1830) or *Der böse Geist Lumpazivagabundus, oder Das liederliche Kleeblatt* (*The Evil Spirit Lumpazivagabundus; or, The Disreputable Trio*, 1833)—or out of non-supernatural material treated in a manner akin to that used for the handling of the miraculous. The latter style led almost to the threshold of the Pirandellesque drama of a century later. For example, in *Der Zerrissene* (*The Broken Man*, 1834) the hero, thought to be dead, lives among his old friends, while in *Zu ebener Erde und im ersten Stock, oder Die Launen des Glücks* (*Basement and First Floor; or, The Whims of Fortune*, 1825) the wealthy man living in a rich upper-floor apartment is forced down to the basement and the poor man vacates the latter to enjoy life upstairs. There is an atmosphere here of the wonderful and the fantastic, even if outwardly the scenes are realistic and all the characters persons of the day.

The *Zauberpossen*, however, gained its greatest exponent in the person of Ferdinand Raimund, a man possessed of a dramatic skill far beyond that of Nestroy, and one, too, imbued with a richer vision. In 1823 Raimund produced his first play, *Der Barometermacher auf der Zauberinsel* (*The Barometer-maker on the Magic Island*), the title of which immediately indicates its style. In it a fairy gives three magical treasures to Quecksilber, a Viennese barometermaker, much in the manner that wizards and supernatural beings bestow their favours in Gozzi's dramas, although the purposes of the gifts imagined by the two playwrights are different. For Raimund the device is employed in order to reveal the worth of good, honest, homespun integrity: despite the facts that Quecksilber has had annoyances in Vienna and that on his magic island all luxuries are provided for him, he is eager, when the time comes, to return to his humble home.

The next year saw the appearance of *Der Diamant des Geisterkönigs* (*The Diamond of the King of Spirits*, 1824). Here the story is told of a young man, the son of a magician, who is promised a statue of diamond if he can find a girl who has never told a lie. After many adventures and many a weary search he discovers this paragon, falls in love with her, and is granted her as wife—a gift that is "the finest diamond" that could be given him.

With increased mastery, Raimund pursues the theme of *Der Barometermacher* further and more effectively in *Der Bauer als Millionär, oder, Das Mädchen aus der Feenwelt* (*The Peasant a Millionaire; or, The Maid from the World of Fairies*, 1826). The entire plot here is concerned with a peasant hero, Fortunatus Wurzel, who is suddenly granted almost unlimited wealth—wealth that brings evil effects both upon his health and upon his character. Misfortune after misfortune comes, until at last his adopted daughter (really a fairy in disguise) flees his house so that she may escape a loveless marriage Wurzel is trying to force upon her. Left alone, the man who at the beginning of the play had been hale and hearty and who now is brokenly aged, repents and goes back to the rude and simple existence that had brought him peace of mind and the sense of security. Although the main emphasis is, as the title indicates, thrown on the peasant hero, the actions relating to him are bound up with fairy-tale material and with material which almost recalls the subjects of ancient moralities. The adopted daughter is a fairy-child, and the riches that come to Wurzel are due to the fact that this girl's enemy is none other than Neid (Envy) himself.

This play at once reveals the essential difference between Raimund and Gozzi. In outward form the writings of these two men have much in common. Although the Viennese author does not make use of any stock characters (such as those of the *commedia dell' arte*), he follows a model akin to that of his Italian predecessor, mingling the world of the folk-tale with the world of reality, and seizing every opportunity of employing the contrast for the purpose of commenting upon contemporary life. Beyond this, however, the two differ fundamentally. Gozzi is an aristocrat who looks back nostalgically to the times of chivalry; Raimund is a good, honest bourgeois. The question of money hardly enters into the *fiabe*: as in *Der Bauer als Millionär*, it continually plays a potent part in Raimund's writings. In *Der Alpenkönig und der Menschenfeind* (*The King of the Alps and the Man-hater*, 1828) the central figure, Rappelkopf, has come to detest the society of his fellows, partly because of his unsuccessful matrimonial adventures—he has buried three wives—but mainly because some of his investments have gone wrong. The plot tells how he sets off for a life of solitude, meets the King of the Alps, becomes terrified, and decides to return home to his latest wife (an embodiment of all the virtues). There, however, the King of the Alps follows him in his own likeness—or, rather, in the likeness he had before he set out on his adventures. By means of the double manifestation of his personality at the end of the play the author develops his philosophy in symbolic wise. The false Rappelkopf —that is, the King of the Alps transformed into the Rappelkopf that was—is in utter despair because he sees himself faced with financial disaster, while the true Rappelkopf, now cured of his hatred of mankind and living an existence based on values higher than the material, tries vainly to dissuade him. When the false Rappelkopf dies the latter has been completely cured of his follies.

Obviously the motivation here depends almost wholly on monetary matters, and the same emphasis appears in most of Raimund's work. The very title of *Der Verschwender* (*The Spendthrift*, 1834) indicates how basic to Raimund's creations was the question of money and its effect upon human character. This play is almost a secular, fairy-tale *Everyman*, in which Julius von Flotwell, a reckless spendthrift, is the hero, accompanied by a devoted servant, whose moral qualities may be taken as representing the author's own ideal. Through the interest of his good angel, the fairy Cheristane, a strange beggar appears before him at certain moments in his career, and when, at the age of fifty, he finds himself utterly ruined it is the alms which he has given to this outcast that bring him joy and promise of a new life.

A play produced the following year, *Die unheilbringende Krone* (*The Cursed Crown*, 1829), brought the fairy element into a fresh atmosphere. The chief character here is a general, Phalarius, who, angered at his King, Creon, accepts from Hades a magic crown which will give him unlimited power over man and nature. As he puts this to evil use, the fairy protecting Creon discovers that the crown's fatal power can be counteracted if she obtains three things —a crown belonging to a king without a kingdom, a crown belonging to a hero lacking courage, and a crown belonging to a woman who, while not beautiful, seems so. The way in which these are secured provides most of the action of the play, and in this action, involving the ambitious Phalarius, the easily satisfied Simplicius, and the poetically fanciful Ewald, we recognize that here Raimund's tendency towards the symbolic has reached its extremest expression.

There can be no doubt but that Raimund expresses in vivid and delicate forms certain qualities inherent in the spirit of the age. In his writings is reflected a mixture of elements which appear and reappear in many a comedy of these years—the fantastic Gozzi-like flavour, the world-is-a-dream motif, the sense of life's pathos, and that other mood which delights to contrast the marionette and man —the mood that finds expression, for example, in the *Lustiges Komödienbüchlein* of Count Franz von Pocci, wherein irrepressible Kasperle brings mingled laughter and meditation.

As with the historical poetic plays, so with these comedies of folk and fairy we can find cognate works in almost every country. There is a breath of Nestroy and Raimund in *Kong Salomon og Jörgen Hattemager* (*King Solomon and Jörgen the Hatmaker*, 1826), *Aprilsnarrene* (*The April Fool*, 1826), and *En Sjæl efter Döden* (*A Soul after Death*; printed 1841), by the Danish playwright Johan Ludvig Heiberg. Typical is the last-mentioned comedy, wherein, by means almost Aristophanic, the worthy citizens of Copenhagen are reflected in scenes depicting the best circles of Hell. Akin in spirit is Heiberg's *Elverhöj* (*The Hill of the Elves*, 1828), one of Denmark's most popular romantic dramas. Here a racy fantasy colours a tale of misunderstandings, and lyric sincerity is combined with episodes ironically conceived. The main plot concerns Albert Ebbensen, who, loving Agnes, is bidden by his King (Christian IV) to wed Elizabeth. Fortunately Agnes is a friend of the elves, and to her aid troop all the supernatural inhabitants of the fairy mount. Only when Christian himself arrives is their power arrested, but they have already won their victory because, in delaying the marriage, they have given time for the King to discover that, by a change effected years ago in the nursery, Agnes is really Elizabeth and Elizabeth Agnes. The same fanciful quality appears in the Swedish *Lycksalighetens ö* (*The Isle of Happiness*, 1824) by Daniel Amadeus Atterbom—a work clearly influenced by Tieck's fairy-tale style.

In Poland comic peasant material was freely and amusingly exploited by the first truly notable playwright of that country, Count Aleksander Fredro. Some of his writings, such as *Mąż i żona* (*Husband and Wife*, 1822), are clearly based on Western models, but the greater part of his contribution to the stage consists of native farces, such as *Nowy Don Kiszot* (*The New Don Quixote*, 1826) and *Damy i huzary* (*Ladies and Hussars*, 1826), or of more ambitious comedies with a peculiarly individual flavour. Of the last group the finest and most characteristic piece is unquestionably *Pan Jowialski* (*Mr Jowialski*, 1833). This play, which might almost be called "Mr Jolly," is a minor masterpiece, in which an interesting twist is given to a *Taming of the Shrew* plot. The part of Sly is here taken by a novelist who willingly accepts the trick imposed upon him in order to gain insight into the beings of his companions —the members of Pan Jowialski's family circle. Full of fun and thoughtful laughter, *Pan Jowialski* is one of the numerous dramas of the time that deserve translation into English. This comedy is well companioned, too, by *Zemsta* (*The Revenge*, 1835), in which are presented lively portraits of two neighbours, Cześnik Raptusiewicz and the notary Milczek, who, quarrelling over a boundary fence, are involved in complex intrigue which at once springs from and serves to illuminate their characters.

For Italy the development of fantastic comedy presented no problem, since the tradition of the *commedia dell' arte* was still vital there; but it is to be noted that for the moment this strain was confined to the cruder efforts of the dialect theatres. Later the fantastic spirit was to blossom forth in the *teatro del grottesco*, out of which Pirandello sprang; during these early decades of the century Italian comedy of a more literary sort was, rather strangely, in the hands of such men as Alberto Nota, with his sentimental *Atrabiliare* (1812), characteristically set in London, his mechanically plotted *L'ammalato per immaginazione* (*The Invalid in his own Imagination*, 1813), his pathetically conceived *La novella sposa* (*The Newly Married Wife*, 1827), and his sentimental *La fiera* (*The Fair*, 1829). A somewhat similar atmosphere enwraps the plays of Nota's less well-known companion, Francesco Augusto Bon, an author who hardly got beyond the rather feeble satire of current romantic sentiment presented in the person of the *précieuse* Antonia in *La donna e i romanzi* (*The Lady and the Novels*, 1819). Bon's best work is his series of 'Ludro' plays, starting with *Ludro e la sua gran giornata* (*Ludro and his Great Day*, 1833). Still another minor playwright worthy of brief mention is Giovanni Giraud: typical of his writings is *I gelosi fortunati* (*The Happy Jealous Couple*, 1808), where a husband and a wife, each confessing to jealousy, discover that the green-eyed monster is, after all, only an instrument in Cupid's service. Here in Italy was potentiality rather than effective immediate production.

Into France the play of wonder was introduced and won particular success through the association with it of the popular music of Jacques Offenbach: the *féerie* is one of the recognized dramatic genres of the Parisian stage. And with these French plays are closely connected the teeming extravaganzas of the English J. R. Planché, who in turn passes on the tradition to W. S. Gilbert later in the century. In forms both crudely popular, replete with devastating puns and all the roughest kinds of absurdity, and symbolically ironical, the extravaganza spirit thus found expression nearly everywhere, providing at once what is perhaps the most pleasing dramatic compositions of these particular years and the basis for much interesting effort yet to come.

PART VIII

FROM THE MEDIEVAL TO THE MATERIALISTIC

FROM THE MEDIEVAL TO THE MATERIALISTIC

BY THE year 1830 vast changes both in the social world and in the world of the theatre were in process of accomplishment. It is true that we cannot select a single year or a single decade to mark the frontier between one period and another; it is also true that the work of many significant writers extends over the early decades into the middle of the century; nevertheless there is every justification, particularly in so far as the theatre is concerned, for treating the four decades from 1830 to 1870 as a unit. During these years earlier suggestions for fresh dramatic paths were courageously explored, and during these years still further paths were, in turn, pointed out to the playwrights of the century's final decades.

The full flush of 'gothic' romanticism had passed away by 1830, and a new romanticism was in process of formation. Browning followed Shelley, and Tennyson Keats. Scientific invention, applied in diverse ways, was changing alike the lives of the theatre's spectators and the fabric of the theatre itself, and necessarily the drama, in accordance with new demands, altered its shape, devised for itself a new structure, adopted a fresh orientation.

Fundamentally this period was characterized by rapid industrialization and the coming to power of the bourgeoisie; the trends in those directions evident from the seventeenth century onward now reached culmination. This meant, first, an uneven conflict between the relics of the old aristocracy and the growing power of the middle class; second, concentration upon the city rather than upon the country; and, third, a long, slow movement of political reform. The dying world of Trollope was being engulfed, both physically and spiritually.

In so far as theatre organization was concerned, perhaps the two most potent forces were the substitution of the railway for earlier means of travel and the introduction of gas lighting. The first destroyed the relative independence of provincial theatres, aided the development of touring companies (utterly distinct from the touring actors of the 'circuits'), helped in the extraordinary growth of the principal cities, and brought the theatres of Europe much closer together than ever they had been in the past. Associated with the

459

omnibus, the railway proved a practical means whereby the teeming middle classes could flock into the playhouses, and, as a result, city after city found its houses of entertainment multiplying themselves. Save where national theatres, such as the Comédie Française, were enabled by their special regulations and opportunities to preserve the repertory system, this in turn meant the establishment of the long run and the rapid commercialization of the theatre. There was money in entertainment, and as a result the playhouses more and more became buildings owned by men whose only interests lay in financial returns, while the companies using these playhouses were, with increasing frequency, collections of actors engaged for the performance of a particular play, to be disbanded just as soon as its popularity waned and a new piece had to be substituted for the old.

To a certain extent the actor-manager system that played such an important rôle in England and in America proved a check to the complete commercialization of the theatre during these three decades, but the handwriting was on the wall, and even the triumphs of a Charles Kean or, later, of a Henry Irving could not conceal the main trends of the age.

Gas lighting was first used theatrically towards the beginning of these forty years, and soon a profound revolution was effected by its means. So long as candles and lamps remained the only resources at the command of actors all attempts at realism were bound to be half-hearted and ineffectual. It is true that from the sixteenth century onward men interested in the production of plays had sought to devise methods of controlling stage illumination, and that during the second half of the eighteenth century considerable progress in this direction had been made: when all is said, however, the fact remains that before the introduction of gas lighting any devices of this kind were bound to be cumbersome and that the sources of the light—candles and lamps—were bound to remain basically intractable.

The introduction of gas lighting meant, first, that the auditoria of the theatres could easily be darkened, and, second, that the means of illumination could be completely and readily controlled. Hence the gradual movement towards the separation of actors and of audience—a movement evident over a period of two hundred years—now became not only possible but apparently logical, and with this separation the curtain took on new significance. The curtain became both the symbol of the separation itself and the means by which a new stagecraft could come into being.

In minor theatres the older staging methods, with the habitual use of side-wings and back-cloths, persisted well into the modern era, but along with these methods new principles were coming into operation. In the main these new principles may be associated together (despite their variety and apparent diversity) as all aiming at the creation of theatrical realism. Throughout these thirty years, and for decades thereafter, the public took a naïve delight in seeing presented before them stage pictures which simulated such objects as were familiar to them in their daily lives, and by an extension of this delight they rejoiced in watching the re-creation, in correct terms, of the life of past ages. Approaches towards both present and historical realism had, of course, been made even in the eighteenth century, but it was only within this time that full opportunities were given for the execution of such effects and that the process was carried to its fullest extent. We need do no more than consider the English theatre and cast a glance, on the one hand, at the historical scenes so carefully devised by Charles Kean and, on the other, at the 'reforms' of Tom Robertson to recognize the truth of this assertion.

A further result is to be observed. Both because of the growth of the occasional company, in which actors were assembled for the playing of a particular drama, and because of the increasing importance of the stage picture, a demand was made for the presence in the theatre of a new functionary, the 'stage-manager' or producer. In the old days actors performing in repertory were so familiar with one another that there was little need of the services of such a person; a leading player or a prompter could readily act as the convener of rehearsals, and the performance of a play take shape as a kind of collective effort. Now, however, inspired alike by sheer necessity imposed by changed conditions and by desires different from those in the past, this new figure arose and rapidly came to assume an almost god-like stature, co-ordinating all the activities of the stage, determining the type of scenery to be employed, and instructing the actors in the interpretation of their rôles. Within the realm of ordinary productions the stage-manager became a necessary part of a theatrical enterprise which, however humble, was much more complicated than had been generally known in the past, while within other realms—such as those of the Saxe-Meiningen company or Wagner's Bayreuth—he invested himself with Prospero's mantle and became a wonder-working artisan.

Under these changing conditions several kinds of dramatic effort flourished. In the main realism was dominant, although it is necessary to distinguish several movements within this larger field. At the lowest level we may note how the old melodrama, persisting in its hold on the public, gradually moved from the exploitation of the imaginatively romantic to that of the sensationally familiar. Wicked lords of medieval vintage give way to evil squires, and heroines become simple village maidens or, later, honest factory girls. Here realism of effect takes the form mainly of child-like imitations of the actual—snowstorms and the like—or of equally child-like introduction of real objects—live geese or pigs or hansom-cabs. A higher level is marked in the plays written by Scribe's successors, where the formula of the well-made play is applied to episodes and problems of contemporary existence and where the characteristically 'modern' play of ideas is adumbrated. On the third level something much profounder is attempted. In Germany Hebbel aims at the utilization of the realistic principle for the communication of ideas far beyond the reach either of the melo-dramatists or of the followers of Scribe, while Zola tries to carry realism to logical extremes and invents the drama which is, in truth, a slice of life.

Although these realistic activities form the most typical endeavour of the age, we shall err if we concentrate all attention upon them alone. The older forms of romanticism, delighting in the depiction of past epochs, still persisted, if in changed shape, and won success. Indeed, the application of realistic methods of production to the older forms gave to the romantic play a fresh lease of life. And alongside of this we must remember that in this utilitarian age when scientists were busy ousting the elves there remained a strange, persistent, almost nostalgic love of fairyland. Fancy, despised of science, became a familiar stage character during these four decades, and the impossibilities of the extravaganza, summoned forth by her magic wand, were welcomed along with the increasingly grim depiction of the real.

THE REALM OF FANCY

PERHAPS it may not be unfitting to consider the extravaganza first, and in doing so we may extend our gaze beyond the stricter limits of these forty years in order to see, if not its culmination, at least its highly characteristic expression in the work of Gilbert. Although the extravaganza is by no means the most representative dramatic trend of the age, so frequently do we permit ourselves to forget the fairy element in our contemplation of austerer realism that there is virtue in thus fixing in our minds what was without doubt a potent theatrical force—one that produced some of the most enduring stage pieces during the age in question and that was destined to influence considerably the course of the drama in the twentieth century.

THE EXTRAVAGANZA AND THE FAIRY PLAY

The extravaganza did not by any means die out with the first decades of the century, and in many countries—particularly England, the United States, and France—burlesques and similarly conceived pieces were popular until near the close of the century. Most of these, it is true, have but little worth. Hack writer after hack writer turned out these works with crudely conceived scenes and with little more than wild collections of puns to maintain the merriment.

In the writings of J. R. Planché, however, we can discern an effort to make of the extravaganza form something of more enduring worth. Planché was no genius, yet his limited measure of success and the fact that he is the lineal ancestor of Gilbert give him a measure of importance. Of particular significance in his work is the conscious exploitation of the fairy play. Although he does not have the power of a Raimund to invest his scenes with a moral purpose, and although his touch is heavier and less expert than that of Gozzi, he has a verve of his own, and his tinkling dialogue, replete with fantastic puns, proved vastly popular in his time. From his first burlesque of 1818, *Amoroso, King of Little Britain*, to his final lyrics in the fairy spectacle of *Babil and Bijou* in 1872 he kept the stage supplied, frequently through material derived from the Countess de Murat's *Cabinet des fées*, with a constant series of extravagant fancies. A common sentiment was expressed in a letter to this author by J. Hamilton Reynolds in 1850. "What I like about your fairy dramas," he wrote,

> is their truth in delicate humour, and the perfect understanding you shew of the nice art of Burlesque *in flower*. . . . You inform grown-up beings how they may be reflected in fairy mirrors. . . . You put with an elegant manner *our* household words into mouths, and our habits and foolish manners into persons and places I don't know how far off, or how *very* out of sight, and we laugh at, and enjoy ourselves, and our own delectable nonsenses, all because it pleased a French Countess to be a delicate fairy humourist, and you to be a man of a poetical mind who knew how to translate her into the rarest English burlesque. . . . Oh, that you and I, and a few others (*not many*) could charter a vessel for the latter quiet sea-girt retreat. Where is it? *I* do not know. It *must* be somewhere in the Pacific!

For these were the days when the Pacific seemed far away, and atomic bombs were things undreamed of.

With some slight modifications Reynolds' words might even more appropriately have been applied to W. S. Gilbert, who carried on, expanded, and perfected the Planché tradition during the last years of the century. Although a consideration of his work carries us far beyond the period at the moment under survey, the dependence of these plays and operas upon what immediately preceded them and the manner in which they bring to a culmination what had been fully adumbrated before Gilbert's own time justifies an analysis of their characteristics here.

Gilbert started his career by practising in the style of the fairy play, and, in these, outwardly at least, he acts the sedulous ape to his predecessors. He makes a few excursions into farce, it is true, but his representative writings up to the start of the Savoy operas are pieces such as *The Palace of Truth* (1870) and *The Wicked World* (1873). That which distinguishes these essays from the fairy plays of Planché is the personal mood introduced into the treatment of scenes and characters. Reynolds, contemplating the latter's extravaganzas, wished that he and a few boon companions could sail off to an idealistically conceived Pacific; the sense of world-weariness implied in this desire is increased a thousandfold in Gilbert. A concealed sadness gives distinction to his most humorous scenes, and his famous topsy-turviness springs ultimately from a loathing for the things he finds around him. The fever and the fret of mankind weigh heavily on his senses, and, while we must confess that the decorous conventions of Victorianism prevent his achieving such a range and such a freedom as was attained by an Aristophanes, there can be no doubt but that he succeeded in creating a comic realm of his own not entirely unworthy of comparison with that of the Greek master.

To-day, of course, he is known chiefly through the later operas, in which his versifying skill was combined with the kindred musical skill of Sir Arthur Sullivan. The spirit of these operas, however, was no new thing: it was merely a further development of that which had animated his earlier plays. *Iolanthe; or, The Peer and the Peri* (1882) uses the fairy machinery familiar in these works, and the mood of *Broken Hearts* (1875) reappears in *The Yeomen of the Guard; or, The Merryman and his Maid* (1888). It is easy to accept the operas simply as delightful entertainment—and no doubt such is the prime reason for their being—yet we shall be wrong if we close our eyes to their ironic intent. On the surface *H.M.S. Pinafore; or, The Lass that loved a Sailor* (1878) is a carefree extravaganza replete with all the most orthodox patriotic sentiments of Victorian England; on the surface *The Pirates of Penzance; or, The Slave of Duty* (1879) is only a fantasy, in which the wicked buccaneers throw down their weapons in the name of the Queen. Underneath, however, both of these have an ironic tang. It is not so much that Gilbert was writing with his tongue in his cheek as that he could not quite conceal a mood that passed beyond the outward appearances of his scenes. Whereas outwardly his scenes appear to be invested merely with easy laughter and the delicate play of a punning wit, in reality they are informed by a kind of world-weariness. When royalty severely frowned upon *Utopia Limited; or, The Flowers of Progress* (1893) royalty, from its own point of view, was right. In *Utopia Limited* Gilbert had lowered the veil a little too far, and what was seen beyond did not seem so amusing. All the vaunted progress of the century was revealed as a thing of doubtful value, and the whole of life was presented darkly. The royal box may have lost its occupants ostensibly because a Privy Council meeting was turned into a Christy Minstrel show, but Gilbert's barb went deeper than burlesque of such a kind: fundamentally he was guilty of looking with eyes of laughter upon the benefits of science and of mocking that on which Victorian society was founded—the very concept of progress.

THE INHERITANCE OF MARIVAUX: MUSSET

The concealed melancholy, masked by mocking laughter in Gilbert's writings, assumed a peculiar and a strangely appealing form in the hands of a French author who added to the spirit of fancy a penetrating interest in the human heart. It may seem foolish to associate Gilbert with Alfred de Musset, yet when we think that the latter owes his being to Marivaux, and that Marivaux' genius springs from the *commedia dell' arte*, perhaps the connexion of their names may seem not so extraordinary after all. Although Musset's plays present nothing of the topsy-turvy humour characteristic of the Savoy operas, the fantastic atmosphere is potent in their scenes.

The influence of Marivaux had been hovering in the wings of the Parisian theatres since the beginning of the eighteenth century, prompting the playwrights even while the spirit of Molière held the stage, and it was no wonder that at last a successor came to carry on his style. Not that Musset realized in his earliest efforts what precisely he wanted to do: he began as a serious romantic dramatist, penning works of minor interest, heavily tinged with dark sentimentalism. *La nuit Vénitienne* (*A Venetian Night*, 1830) was deservedly hissed; *André del Sarto* (printed 1833) is boringly verbose, with little credibility in its portrait of the aging painter; *Lorenzaccio* (printed 1834), although better wrought, is romantically diffuse.

These writings we may ignore, but something different enters with *Les caprices de Marianne* (*Marianne's Whims*; printed 1833) and *Fantasio* (printed 1833). In the former a young man, Célio, falls in love with a married woman, Marianne. She in turn finds her heart moved by his friend, Octave, and through a caprice inadvertently causes Célio's death. The play ends with Octave and Marianne standing by the dead man's tomb: she offers her affections to Octave, but his simple words close the action: "I do not love you, madam: it was Célio who loved you." In *Fantasio* is presented a young hero who, living for pleasure, can yet find no pleasure in anything he does. In a kind of romantic renunciation of the world he dons the dress of a Court fool, and in this rôle succeeds in breaking off a proposed match between his Princess and a boorish Prince.

The plots of these two plays have no other purpose than to provide the author with an opportunity of delving into the human heart and of presenting whimsical contrasts in human value. In a sense the action is real; at the same time, as *Fantasio* demonstrates, the world of the imagination easily superimposes itself upon the world of actuality.

From such pieces it is an easy step to *On ne badine pas avec l'amour* (*No Trifling with Love*; printed 1834), and in taking this step we move into Musset's characteristic realm, that of the *proverbe dramatique* or *comédie-proverbe*. This theatrical genre explains itself in its title. The author here selects a familiar proverb and develops an action illustrative of its significance. Although Musset is its most famous exponent, he was by no means its inventor; indeed, as a number of plays in several tongues cited above must have indicated, it was one of the most popular kinds of drama during the eighteenth century. Even during the period of the Renaissance a tendency to select proverbial titles may be observed among English and Spanish playwrights, and it was a simple task for Louis Carmontelle, a painter whose activities carried him into the sphere of the aristocratic amateur stage, to evolve from earlier suggestions the typical form assumed by the French *comédie-proverbe* in the salons—short, condensed, epigrammatic playlets of comic spirit with serious undertones. His *Proverbes dramatiques*, published in eight volumes between 1768 and 1781, set the pattern for the similar writings of Théodore Leclercq and his companions. Thus was the fashion passed down to Musset.

In his hands the dramatic proverb was refined and made delicately penetrating. *On ne badine pas avec l'amour* introduces as central figure a proud and testy Baron who plans a marriage between his son, Perdican, and his niece, Camille. Like Marianne, this girl has her caprices: she refuses Perdican and yet is stung when he makes a show of indifference, while he, in turn, devotes half-hearted affection to a country girl, Rosette. Irritated and inwardly loving him, Camille engages in a series of contradictory devices—inducing Perdican to confess his devotion to her, laughing at him when he does so, and attempting to prevent his marriage to Rosette. At the end Perdican surprises her in tears, and through this their mutual love becomes apparent to both: they embrace, only to be confronted by the fact that Rosette, the tragic pawn in their love-duel, has perished of a broken heart and thus presents an inescapable barrier to their union. "She is dead. Adieu, Perdican," are Camille's last, simple words. By means of this plot of turns and counter-turns Musset succeeds in painting a memorable portrait of his heroine and of revealing delicately the strange paradoxes of the human heart, and, as a fine contrast to the serious action, he balances these baffled lovers with an amusing group of humorous figures—

Perdican's tutor, Maître Blazius, Camille's governess, Dame Pluche, and the little village priest, Maître Bridaine. Hardly any play of the nineteenth century is subtler than this, or more graciously alert in its analysis of passion.

Le chandelier (*The Decoy*; printed 1835) tells a somewhat similar story of love, with Jacqueline, the amorous wife of the besotted Maître André, as heroine. Her lover is the conceited soldier Clavaroche, and in order to distract her husband's suspicions from him she pretends a display of affection for the adolescent clerk Fortunio. Unfortunately this idealistic young poet takes her advances seriously, while she for her part is momentarily attracted by his devotion. In the end tragedy ensues, the scenes moving inexorably, with fine precision and with nervous tension, to their close.

A year later came *Il ne faut jurer de rien* (*You can't be sure of Anything*; printed 1836). Again the plot is simple: no more than the story of a young gallant, Valentin van Bruck, who sets out to seduce a girl, Cécile, and ends by offering her his true devotion. Love here, as in all Musset's plays, is the mainspring of human life, even of the universe. In the final scene of the comedy Cécile and Valentin are seated in a glade by moonlight. "How vast the sky is!" she says; "how happy the world! How calm and kindly is nature!"

> VALENTIN: Do you want me to talk to you of science and astronomy? Tell me: in this dust of worlds, is there one star that knows not its path, that has not received its mission when it was first created, that is not willing to die in fulfilment of that mission? Why are these vast heavens not motionless? Tell me, if there ever was a moment in time when everything was created, by virtue of what force have these restless worlds been impelled to move?
> CÉCILE: By eternal thought.
> VALENTIN: By love eternal. The hand suspending them in space has written but one word in letters of fire. They live because they seek each other: these stars would crumble into dust were one of them to cease to love.

In *Un caprice* (*A Whim*; printed 1837) further development of character appears, not so much in the depiction of the faithful Mathilde and of her erring husband, Chavigny, as in that of Madame de Léry, with her infinitely amusing garrulity and her kindness of heart. Eight years later came *Il faut qu'une porte soit ouverte ou fermée* (*A Door should be either Open or Shut*; printed 1845), where the action consists merely in the fact that a Count pays a social call on a Marquise and ends by offering her a declaration of marriage.

And finally there is *Carmosine* (printed 1850), in which Musset's peculiar atmosphere of real unreality reaches its peak. This tale of a maid who loves a King and of a Queen who is so magnanimous as to send her lord to comfort her exists in the world of the ideal, yet paradoxically the sentiments and characters assume a concreteness and an interest of which, in theory, we might well have deemed them incapable.

It is hard, indeed, to give any impression, by a mere outlining of basic plots, of Musset's extraordinary dramatic quality. His triumph lies in the excessive refinement of his style, in the clarity and intimacy of his portraiture, in the strange air of imaginative fantasy with which he invests his scenes, and in his presentation of a kind of modern disillusioned reflection of Marivaux' gracefully artificial and sentimental analyses of the human heart.

THE ROMANTIC POET IN PARIS

Musset began his career, as has been seen, with a series of romantically conceived tragedies, and his experiments in this style are part of a general movement that swept over Paris literary circles in the thirties. So far France had failed to respond, within the theatre at least, to the romantic enthusiasm of Europe, but a store of explosive material was being gathered during the early years of the century, and a match, lit innocently enough by a company of English actors, set this off in a blaze of flamboyant splendour.

It was in the season of 1827–28 that Paris was visited by the English troupe—a distinguished body of players who presented, among other works, the four great tragedies of Shakespeare. There was an immediate furore. At first glance the excitement thus occasioned seems inexplicable. Shakespeare had been known in France for many years, and although the earlier translations had been sadly defective, draping the robust Elizabethan limbs in the respectably dignified robes of pseudo-classicism or in the more tight-fitting garments of decent bourgeois sentiment, a complete edition of his plays had been issued in 1821 under the combined direction of Guizot, de Barante, and Pichot. Furthermore, the first of these editor-translators, Guizot, had published a capable analysis of the objectives of Shakespeare's art and had made, at least by implication, a defence of his romantic style. Only three years later Stendahl (Marie-Henri Beyle) issued an essay, *Racine et Shakespeare*, in which, albeit with admirable confusion, the cudgel was deliberately lifted in opposition to classicism. The impress made by the

English company would appear, therefore, as though beyond the reach of explanation.

The explanation, however, is there. Not only was this the first opportunity granted Parisian audiences to see the plays in their original form, it was the first opportunity these audiences had had of seeing them, even in mangled shapes, presented with an appropriate acting technique. Edmund Kean had served to reintroduce histrionic passion on the London boards, and as a result the performances came before the public not simply as 'Shakespeare,' but as something such as no auditor, however well acquainted he might have been with Shakespeare's text, could possibly have imagined.

In the theatre, watching these productions, was a young French littérateur, Victor Hugo, and immediately he was inspired to work a reform, based on what he had seen, in his native theatre. Already in 1824 he had penned his amorphous *Cromwell*, and now in 1827 he issued it to the public accompanied by a fiery preface which was in effect a trumpet-call to revolution. Basically his argument is that drama is the greatest form of artistic expression, that Shakespeare is "its poetic summit," and that the quality of his genius is to be found in the "grotesque," the characteristic mood of the modern world—"so complex, so diverse in its forms, so inexhaustible in its creations, and therein directly opposed to the uniform simplicity of the ancients." From this he deduces that the drama, instead of being, as some have said, a mirror of life, is "a concentrating mirror, which instead of weakening, concentrates and condenses the coloured rays, which makes of a mere gleam a light, and of a light a flame."

From this preface Hugo proceeded to example. It is worthy of note, however, that his first experiment was an historical drama, *Marion Delorme* (1831; originally written in 1829 as *Un duel sous Richelieu*), in which, however, the story of a courtesan, although draped in romantic robes, has about it an element of the realistic: the pressure of the real and the actual could deflect even this flamboyant medievalist from his purposes. It was in *Hernani* (1830) that romanticism truly flourished. All Paris recognized the challenge: the classicists mustered in droves, intent upon hissing it out of existence and ridiculing its life away; the young, ardent spirits of Montmartre came to applaud and cheer. It is said that for a hundred performances the scenes were constantly interrupted by the conflicting cries of derision and of praise, that frequently the lines spoken by the actors could not be heard in the confused turmoil. The cause of the excitement is perhaps just as difficult for us to appreciate, a century after the event, as the impress made on Paris by the English players. To us, maybe, the plot of the play seems even a trifle absurd. Blood-and-thunder here holds the stage. Centrally placed is Donna Sol de Silva, the ward of Don Ruy Gomez de Silva, who desires to marry her himself. For her hand, however, there are other suitors, the romantic outlaw Hernani and Don Carlos, Prince of Spain. Amid confusion, the story passes from thrilling episode to thrilling episode. Hernani and Don Carlos pursue their rivalry, and at one point the former would have been doomed to destruction had not the old de Silva concealed him, while the hero pledges his life to his protector in pawn. Later Don Carlos becomes not only King of Spain, but Holy Roman Emperor as well, displays his imperial greatness by pardoning Hernani, and is thwarted by de Silva's calling on Hernani's pledge. The conclusion is suitably tragic. Seizing a phial of poison, Donna Sol drinks of the liquid:

HERNANI: That philtre leads thee to thy grave.
DONNA SOL: Was not this head to sleep upon thy breast
To-night? What matters where it sinks to rest?
HERNANI: My father, thy revenge is just—that I
Forget.   [*He raises the phial to his lips.*
DONNA SOL [*throws herself upon him*]: Forbear! Forbear!
'Tis hard to die!
The poison lives, and round the heart it hangs,
Like a fell serpent with a thousand fangs.
Oh, drink it not! Alas! I could not tell
That earthly pain could match the fires of hell—
He drinks!
HERNANI [*drinks and throws away the phial*]: 'Tis done.
DONNA SOL: Come then to meet thy fate—
Come to these arms. Is not the torture great?
HERNANI: Not so.
DONNA SOL: Behold, our marriage couch is spread!
Am I not pale for one so lately wed?
Be calm. I suffer less. Our wings expand
Towards the blest regions of a happier land—
Together let us seek that world so fair—
One kiss—and one alone.
DON RUY: Despair! despair!
HERNANI: Blest be the Heaven which from my birth pursued
My life with misery, and in blood imbued—
For it permits me, ere I part, to press
My lips to thine, and die on thy caress.
DON RUY: They still are happy!

HERNANI:	Donna Sol, 'tis night.
	Dost thou still suffer?
DONNA SOL:	No.
HERNANI:	See'st thou the light?
DONNA SOL:	Not yet——
HERNANI:	I see it.
DON RUY:	Dead!
DONNA SOL:	Not so; we rest.

He sleeps. He's mine—we love, and we are blest.
This is my marriage couch. What happier spot
Can the world show? Lord Duke, disturb us not.
              [*Her voice gradually sinks.*
Turn thee towards me—nearer yet—'tis well.
Thus let us rest.   [*Dies.*

DON RUY: Both dead! Receive me, hell!   [*Kills himself.*

Obviously the main appeal of this drama to its contemporaries lay in its highly coloured setting, in its bold presentation of romantic love, and, above all, in the quality of its bandit hero. Of subtle character portrayal there is none: indeed, the persons in this lurid tragedy so frequently act contrary to their natures that a reader or spectator must often remain in perplexed puzzlement. Yet the individual scenes are sensationally thrilling, and some of the verse, freed from the excessive technical restrictions of the classicists, mightily thunders in the index. Its very clamour was what gave it distinction and inaugurated the full flow of romanticism in France.

In his next play, *Le roi s'amuse* (*The King takes his Pleasure*, 1832) —the basis of the opera *Rigoletto*—the romantic pattern was further filled in by displaying a Court jester, Triboulet, who avenges himself on his lord, Francis the First, for a wrong done to his beloved daughter. Here revolutionary sentiment is added to the general scheme of fierce passion and sensational incident.

Hugo's next efforts were in prose—*Lucrèce Borgia* (1833), *Marie Tudor* (1833), and *Angelo* (1835)—but with the shedding of the verse little remained save melodrama of the crudest sort. We may be prepared to accept inconsistencies amid the flowing speeches of *Hernani*; when we encounter such inconsistencies in plays written without the magic of poetic utterance we can only dismiss the dramas in which they appear as of little worth. The poetry, however, returns in *Ruy Blas* (1838) and once more sweeps us off our feet. Follies and absurdities are here in plenty, but these are forgotten in the surge of the verse and in the exploitation of the 'grotesque' so dearly loved by its author. The same intoxicating vigour appears also in *Les Burgraves* (1843), a drama consisting of a collection of scenes, divided into three episodes, illustrative of life in the time of Barbarossa.

In all these plays Hugo reveals his deep understanding of the stage's requirements. His appreciation of the quality and interests of the contemporary audience is clearly outlined in the preface to *Ruy Blas*:

> Three sorts of spectators compose what we are accustomed to call the play-going public—first, women; secondly, the intellectuals; and thirdly, the general crowd. That which the last-named group principally seeks in a dramatic work is action; what most attracts women is passion; what the thoughtful seek above all else is the portrayal of human nature. . . . All three groups look for pleasure—the first, visual pleasure, the second, gratification of emotional sentiments, the last, mental enjoyment. Accordingly in my play appear three distinct kinds of material, the one common and inferior, the two others illustrious and superior, but all answering to a demand—melodrama for the crowd, tragedy that analyses passion for the women, and for the thinkers, comedy that depicts human nature.

The recipe is truly Shakespearian, and that Hugo did not reach Shakespeare's level is due, not so much to a failure on his part to comprehend the true aim of the tragic dramatist, as to the fact that his genius was less fortunately adjusted than Shakespeare's to the conditions of his time. Had Hugo lived in the Elizabethan period he might still not have risen to Shakespearian heights, but he certainly would have proved a mighty rival to Marlowe.

Hugo's chief contribution to the stage of his time was an element that we may call vitality. There is nothing petty in his vision. Though he may often sink to bathos, it is because he aims at, and often attains, the grand style. From the time when he produced *Hernani* the careful precision of Racine's plays ceased to be the paramount model of the French stage. Hugo may not himself have been able to set up a new god, but at least he destroyed some idols.

As a companion he had another young writer, destined like himself to become famous as a novelist, Alexandre Dumas, whose *Henri III et sa cour* (*Henry III and his Court*) appeared in 1829. Less ambitious in his revolutionary aims, Dumas is content to use the melodramatic mould of his predecessors and to make no effort to establish a new poetic theatre. The force that inspired him, however, was the same as that which occasioned the preface to *Cromwell*. He has left on record an account of the impression made upon him by the English performances of Shakespeare's tragedies, when he suddenly realized that the Elizabethan dramatist "was the greatest creator after God himself."

And, however melodramatic, *Henri III et sa cour* is a play planned according to the best recipes of the new romanticism. The realistic tendency enters in and causes the author to paint his background not only in general terms but in particular: his courtiers are faithfully depicted in the fashions of their time, and even the games with which they disport themselves on the stage are historically correct. From the melodrama he takes his technical skill and, unlike Hugo, weaves a plot which, however conventional it may appear on analysis, carries the spectator forward with breathless interest. The same qualities made the later *La Tour de Nesle* (*The Tower of Nesle*, 1832) a success such as is paralleled by hardly another play of the time; scarcely less exciting or less skilful in their exploitation of popular romantic elements are *Don Juan de Maraña* (1836), *Kean* (1836), and *Mademoiselle de Belle Isle* (1839).

Just as Hugo veered in one play towards the contemporary realistic, so Dumas interrupted his series of historical dramas to write his *Antony* (1831), a drama set in the surroundings of his time and introducing characters of the middle class. It is particularly interesting because it indicates how easily the powerful romantic passions could be transferred to another *milieu*. This tale of illicit love, with its dark hero, has clear ties with earlier melodrama: it also points forward, and as clearly, towards the sensationally naturalistic drama to come. When the hero, having ravished the heroine, stabs her in order to save her honour, crying "She resisted me and I killed her!" he is at once imitating melodramatic gestures and anticipating the gestures of a later style of play.

Others of the young romantic group essayed the same path. Alfred de Vigny, for example, made fame for himself when his translation of *Othello* (*Le More de Venise*) was performed in 1829, and when, later, his drama, *Chatterton*, was presented in 1835. Despite its apparent following of classic precept, *Chatterton* belongs in spirit to the revolutionary and noisier tragedies of Hugo and Dumas, and its despondent young hero accords exactly, though in sentimentalized manner, with the Byronic figures of his contemporaries. One thing does, however, give this drama very considerable historical significance. As is shown in the prefatory "Dernière nuit de travail," Vigny essayed to establish a new kind of play— the drama of thought ("le drame de la pensée"). Drawing attention to the simplicity of his plot, he asserts that here "the moral action is everything: the action is within a soul delivered over to dark

tempests." In this way Vigny therefore becomes the unacknowledged ancestor of the 'impressionistic' theatre of our own century.
In his emphasis upon the manner in which an individual can be
ruined by society—a theme mordantly dealt with in the one-act
'comedy' *Quitte pour la peur* (*Let Off with a Fright*, 1833)—he likewise anticipates much that was to come.

Although the grandiose emotions so characteristic of Hugo
could not be expected to dominate the stage for long, and although
even Vigny's subtler presentation of passion found but few followers, the romantic style thus colourfully set upon the stage
continued to make its popular appeal for a number of years to come.
François Ponsard, it is true, had some success in his endeavour to
re-establish the classical forms with his *Lucrèce* (1843), yet even in
his writings the romantic note intrudes (as in *Agnès de Méranie*,
1846, and *Charlotte Corday*, 1850). The same is true of several other
similarly inclined authors. Although the French romantics of the
Hugo school may have burned themselves out by the forties, the
impulse that created their works maintained its force for long and
could never quite be forgotten.

THE CONTINUED SPREAD OF THE ROMANTIC

Partly developing from independent sources, partly inspired by
the Hugo revolt, this second wave of romanticism swept over the
whole of Europe.

While England, for example, had nothing to offer at this time
worthy of much praise, something of the same romantic fervour
gripped the minds of her poets and even the minds of her lesser
hack writers. On the 'literary' level the Poet Laureate, Alfred
Lord Tennyson, applied himself, without too great distinction, to
his *Queen Mary* (1876), *The Falcon* (1879), *Harold* (1876) and
Becket (1879), while his fellow-poet Robert Browning turned out
his *Strafford* (1837), *The Return of the Druses* (1843), and *A Blot in
the 'Scutcheon* (1843). Most of these plays were produced by prominent actor-managers—Macready, Irving, and the Kendals—but
none created any particular stir: an audience that knew Shakespeare
could hardly be expected to become excited over such works. On
a slightly lower plane popular romantic plays were being composed
by others. Edward Bulwer-Lytton (Lord Lytton) won an immediate and lasting success with *The Lady of Lyons* (1838) and an almost
equally resounding success with *Richelieu; or, The Conspiracy* (1839).
Earlier James Sheridan Knowles had valiantly endeavoured to keep

the poetic flag flying with his long run of historical dramas, of which one, *William Tell* (1825), deservedly achieved popularity; later Tom Taylor interspersed among his melodramas a few plays of more ambitious intent, while Dion Boucicault, ever adept at sensing the tastes of the audiences of his time, extended the romantic subject-matter in his series of Irish melodramas—such as *Arrah-na-Pogue* (1864).

There is, perhaps, little here worthy of remembrance on account of intrinsic quality: on the other hand, in later viewing the growth of realism on the stage within these forty years, we must not lose sight of the fact that a great deal of the current stage fare, both then and later, was in the romantic style. Sir Henry Irving's most characteristic play was *The Bells* (1871), as adapted by Leopold Lewis from *Le juif polonais* (a melodrama by 'Erckmann-Chatrian' —the joint pseudonym of Émile Erckmann and Alexandre Chatrian), while the last years of the century saw audiences flocking in their thousands to joy in theatrical representations of *The Prisoner of Zenda* (1896) and *The Sign of the Cross* (1895).

In Spain, as in France although less forcefully, romanticism wrought something of moderate value, worthy of at least passing attention. Throughout the eighteenth century the inheritance of Lope de Vega and of Calderón had been sadly dissipated, and such playwrights as Ramón de la Cruz, author of several hundred stage pieces, popularly exploited the resources of farce and early melodrama. Pseudo-classic models, of the kind set forth in Montiano's *Virginia* or Moratín the elder's *Hormesinda*, produced nothing of consequence, and the earlier sort of romanticism produced nothing better than the mediocre *El duque de Viseo* (*The Duke of Viseo*, 1801), by José Quintana. As a result, when the impress of later romanticism was felt in the peninsula it came as a sudden revelation and as an inspiration.

Influenced by the French school was Francisco Martínez de la Rosa, whose *Abén Humeya, ó la rebelión de los Moriscos* (*Aben Humeya; or, The Rebellion of the Moors*, 1830) not only coincided in date with Hugo's efforts, but was originally written in French and produced in a Parisian theatre. While the dramatic quality of this piece is not particularly outstanding, its historical value is considerable: the author accomplished something of import in applying the new romanticism to a native Spanish theme in scenes wherein is shown the vengeful onslaught against the Castilians led by a Moorish hero. An intrinsically finer work by this author is his later *La conjuración de Venecia* (*The Venetian Conspiracy*), presented in his native country in 1834. These plays created no great stir, but excitement came when Ángel de Saavedra, Duke de Rivas, released his bold *Don Álvaro, ó la fuerzo del sino* (*Don Alvaro; or, The Force of Destiny*) in 1835. This drama, concocted according to the fondest prescriptions of the 'grotesque,' immediately captured public attention, and achieved fame outside of Madrid when it was taken by Verdi as the basis of his opera *La forza del destino* (1862). Although less popular than this drama, more poetic power is to be found in Saavedra's later *El desengaño en un sueño* (*The Disabusing in a Dream*; printed 1842), wherein the spirit of Calderón's famous dream-reality play is reborn. Another highly successful opera of Verdi's, *Il trovatore* (1853), was taken from *El trovador* (*The Troubadour*, 1836), by de Rivas' contemporary Antonio García Gutiérrez; this drama, cast in the same style and presented so near in date to *Don Álvaro*, served to consolidate the new romantic movement in the Spanish theatre.

Season by season the stage of Madrid was fed with the work of young poets, their heads filled with Byronic fancies and all anxious to create a romantic masterpiece. *Ni el tío ni el sobrino* (*Neither Uncle nor Nephew*), by José de Espronceda, appeared in 1834. José Zorrilla y Moral brought out his *Don Juan Tenorio* in 1844—a Don Juan play wherein the hero truly falls in love with one of his intended victims and is saved by her prayers. In 1837 came *Los amantes de Teruel* (*The Lovers of Teruel*), by Juan Eugenio Hartzenbusch, followed in 1838 by his complex and passionate *Doña Mencía, ó la boda en la Inquisición* (*Donna Mencia; or, Marriage in the Inquisition*). And eventually arrived a man who, gifted with a genuine theatrical power and well versed in the European literature of the romantic revival, succeeded in consolidating on the efforts of his predecessors. The aim of Manuel Tamayo y Baus was to re-establish a truly national Spanish drama, and through his vigorous contributions he succeeded in bringing to the theatre of Madrid something at least approaching the quality it had possessed in earlier times. Schiller influenced him in his *Juana de Arco* (*Joan of Arc*, 1847) and Alfieri in his *Virginia* (1853); the spirit of both, added to a characteristic strain of his own, appears in *La locura de amor* (*Love's Fool*, 1855). Perhaps his most interesting drama was the un-Calderón-like *Un drama nuevo* (*A New Play*, 1867), in which he showed Shakespeare with his companions rehearsing and presenting a new drama. What is particularly noteworthy here is that Pirandello has been anticipated in his juxtaposition of theatrical sentiment and real passion: the skill with which Tamayo y Baus has dealt with the theme has caused his play long to hold the boards. In the work of this author the door was being opened for the modern flowering of the Spanish theatrical genius.

Meanwhile in neighbouring Portugal, a country singularly undramatic, Visconde João Baptista Almeida-Garrett produced his *O alfageme de Santarem* (*The Armourer of Santarem*, 1842), a drama politically conceived and containing a powerfully drawn portrait of the armourer, Ferrando Vaz, a stout proponent of the people's rights. Although extraordinarily successful, this author's other well-known drama, *Frei Luiz de Souza* (1843), with its story of a long-lost husband who returns to a wife now married to another man, can hardly be esteemed to have any great general interest.

Less fruitful than Spain, Italy, after her contributions to the earlier romantic theatre, has less to offer. Melodrama flourished fitfully, but only rarely do we encounter there the work of even mediocre talent in this style. Almost the only author deserving of particular mention is Pietro Cossa, who exhibits some slight quality of virtue in his historical plays—notably *Monaldeschi* (1864), *Sordello* (1865), *Nerone* (1871), *Lodovico Ariosto e gli Estensi* (*Lodovico Ariosto and the Estensi*, 1875), and *I Borgia* (*The Borgias*, 1878). His companions rarely display any worth, although occasionally interesting qualities are to be found in portions of a few individual plays—as, for example, the broad sweep in some acts of *Elisabetta, regina d'Inghilterra* (*Elizabeth, Queen of England*, 1853), by Paolo Giacometti, and the warmth animating certain scenes of *Il fornaretto di Venezia* (*The Venetian Baker Lad*, 1855), by Francesco Dall' Ongaro.

To Germany the new movement came in the characteristic form of a campaign styled *Das junge Deutschland*. One of its chief leaders in the theatre was Karl Gutzkow, and he well expressed the strange mixture of liberal and national sentiments animating this circle of writers. Here the excesses of the 'Sturm und Drang' period are rejected; there is a certain trend towards the naturalistic; and philosophical sentiment once more dominates. Of all Gutzkow's numerous works most characteristic and most notable for the sincerity of its utterance is *Uriel Acosta* (1846), a drama which, in the introduction of a Jewish but free-thinking hero, demonstrates how *Das junge Deutschland* moved back beyond the earlier romanticism to the style of Lessing. Besides Gutzkow, one other dramatic author merits attention—Georg Büchner. During recent years his *Dantons Tod* (*Danton's Death*, 1835) has been signalled out for praise, and it may be confessed that in this work by a young disillusioned revolutionary there is unquestioned power. Jerkily composed, it yet suggested to later dramatists fresh methods of achieving their effects. In place of the restrained pseudo-classical style based on the example of Racine or the sweeping romantic style inspired by Shakespeare, Büchner endeavoured, not without success, to adopt a new method. His tale of the French Revolution—and his portrait of a man who, having helped to stimulate rebellion, bitterly regrets his action—is presented by means of a series of staccato scenes almost film-like in composition. In his general concept of the historical drama, too, Büchner makes interesting deviations from earlier practice. For Schiller the historical play was a means of presenting moral truths; for Büchner it was a literary medium for the depiction of the truth of past events. Thus, in writing of the Revolution, he refused to delineate the leaders of the time as other than they were—"bloody, energetic, cynical."

The potential power of this young author (he died at the age of twenty-four) is also shown in his unfinished realistic tragedy *Woyzeck* (written 1836), with its flashes of inspired but erratic language and its strange lunatic theme. A pessimist who came to see men as mere playthings of a mechanistic fate, Büchner joins the earlier von Kleist in anticipating much in the drama that was later to be fully developed. Perhaps his actual achievements have been somewhat overpraised by recent critics, but we cannot deny that in these two dramas are, somewhat strangely, combined the seeds both of the naturalism and of the expressionism to come.

Apart from these two men, Germany did not have much to offer, at this time, in the new romantic style. Writers such as Heinrich Laube, author of *Prinz Friedrich* (1845), a drama which traces the relations between Frederick William I of Prussia and his son much as Kleist had dealt with his Elector and the Prince of Homburg; Emil Brachvogel, whose *Narziss* (*Narcissus*, 1856) once was widely popular; Friedrich Halm (Baron Eligius von Münch-Bellinghausen, author of the equally popular *Der Sohn der Wildnis* (*The Son of the Wilderness*, 1843); and Salomon Hermann Mosenthal, author of *Deborah* (also known as *Leah the Forsaken*, 1850), turned out dozens of capably written acting vehicles or passable romantic reading-plays, but not any of their works possess permanent value.

Meanwhile other countries were taking up the challenge. During these decades Russia felt the first stirrings of liberalism. The Byronic spirit was rampant in Pushkin, and Pushkin's mantle fell on Count Alexei Konstantinovich Tolstoi, whose *Smert Ivana Groznavo* (*The Death of Ivan the Terrible*, 1866), *Tsar Feodor Ivanovich* (**1868**), and *Tsar Boris* (1870) present a colourful and emotionally arresting panorama of Russian history. The intrinsic quality of this trio of dramas has been well attested by the success that attended their production by the Moscow Art Theatre. No other Russian romantic playwright vies with him at this period; although Ostrovski tried his hand at the style, his efforts are mediocre by comparison; such a writer as Dmitri Vasilevich Averkiev is little more than a sentimental dreamer with a commercial flair; while Apolloni Nikolaevich Maikov, whose rather dull *Dva mira* (*Two Worlds*), a study of paganism and Christianity, appeared in 1873, can be regarded only as a second-rate poet with rather vague philosophical aspirations.

In Poland Count Zygmunt Krasiński composed his powerful *Nie-boska komedja* (*The Undivine Comedy*; written over a series of years during the thirties and forties), which symbolically presents the class-struggle between the relics of the old feudal nobility and the rising proletariat. Not penned specifically for the stage, it has yet achieved theatrical success in modern times, as has the even more poetic *Irydjon* (1836). These poetic dramas are of greater significance than those of Józef Szujski, even although the latter author pursued the self-appointed mission of trying to give vitality to the Polish historical drama. More important for the history of the stage are the plays of Cyprjan Kamil Norwid, whose *Wanda* (printed 1860) and *Krakus* (printed 1860) not only give expression to Polish romantic sentiment, but point forward to later romantic practice— particularly in the application of the theory of 'silence' as a force in play construction. Even if his actual accomplishments hardly measure up to his aspirations, Norwid was, in theory, far in advance of his times.

The Jugoslav stage produced its Laza Kostich, with his *Maxim Crnojević* (1866), based on local legends and influenced by Shakespeare. Schiller's style animates the *Tugomar* (1876) of the Slovene Josip Jurčich, while the spirits of both Schiller and Shakespeare haunt the scenes of the Slovak Jonáš Záborský and Ján Palárik. The best work of the latter, *Dimitrij samozvanec* (1863), has a certain intrinsic worth. Like this drama, most of these plays select source material from Slav legends, but occasionally there is a searching farther afield, as in the *Fântâna Blanduziei* (*The Bandusian Spring*, or *Fons Bandusiæ*, 1884), a drama dealing with the life of Horace, by the Rumanian Vasile Aleksandri.

In almost every country national historical dramas and dramas cast in romantically symbolic moulds flourished apace, although perhaps the only play of such kind worthy of special praise is the

BACKSTAGE AT THE DROTTNINGHOLM THEATRE
From *Bilder från Slottsteatern på Drottningholm* (Malmö Ljustrycksanstalt, 1942).

DRURY LANE THEATRE, LONDON, IN THE YEAR 1792

DRURY LANE THEATRE IN 1813

From *Edmund Kean*, by Harold Newcomb Hillebrand (Columbia University Press, 1933).

Hungarian equivalent of the Polish *Undivine Comedy*—*As ember tragoediája* (*The Tragedy of Man*, 1862), written by Imre Madách. Obviously dependent upon Goethe's influence, its theme is based on Lucifer's attempt to destroy man's faith by showing him the growth of corruption and vice in human society. Here the concept of progress, so potent a force in nineteenth-century thought, is being seriously challenged. With this drama may be noted another Hungarian work, by Mihály Vörösmarty—*Csongor es Tünde* (*Csongor and Tünde*; printed 1831), a symbolic work that recalls both the *fiabe* of Gozzi and Raimund's *Zauberpossen*.

Denmark's contribution came through the writings of Frederik Paludan-Müller and Henrik Hertz. The former's lyrical *Amor og Psyche* (*Amor and Psyche*, 1834) and *Kalanus* (1857) have poetic beauty if not theatrical strength; the latter won some contemporary fame for his *Kong Renés Datter* (*King René's Daughter*, 1845), as well as for his *Svend Dyrings hus* (*The House of Svend Dyring*, 1837).

In general this new wave of romanticism between 1830 and 1870 is to be viewed as important not so much for its positive contributions to dramatic literature as for its awakening inspiration. National spirit was everywhere aroused through these efforts, and from the glowing fire of that spirit new theatres arose, enshrining dreams for the future. The impulse, of course, was not so powerful in some countries as in others, and England in particular gained little of worth from the plays either of her Sheridan Knowles or of her Tennyson; in some lands, however, this romantic endeavour meant the very creation of a national literature or else the revivification of that literature with the introduction of new forms and fresh concepts.

OPERA AND THE 'MYSTIC CHASM': WAGNER

Already it has been noted how many of the romantic dramas of this time were transformed into operas, and this reminds us how mightily the romantic cause was served by the musical stage. The equivalent of the fairy play is to be found in the work of Mozart, especially, of course, in *Don Giovanni* (*Il Dissoluto punito*, 1787) and the *Zauberflöte* (*The Magic Flute*, 1791); more clearly can be seen the correspondence between romantic tragedy and the operas of the nineteenth century. Out of a typical theme of melodrama arose, in the early years, the French 'rescue-opera,' in which a hero (or heroine) is encompassed by perils while in the clutches of the villain, to be nobly and miraculously released just before the final curtain. Beethoven's *Fidelio* (1805) manifestly follows this pattern.

Q

Rossini produces now his *William Tell* (1829), and romance comes sweeping in with Donizetti's popular *Lucia di Lammermoor* (1835). Historical eras are ransacked for subject-matter, from ancient Druidic days in Bellini's *Norma* (1831) and early Egypt in Rossini's *Mosè in Egitto* (*Moses in Egypt*, 1818) to more recent times in Meyerbeer's *Les Huguenots* (1836). The world of magic intrudes into the notorious *Der Freischütz* (*The Charmed Bullets*, 1821) of Weber, while Verdi freely rifles the dramatic literature of many lands for his long series of still popular operatic works—*Ernani* (1844) from Hugo, *Macbeth* (1847) from Shakespeare, *Il Trovatore* (1853) from Saavedra, *La Traviata* (1853) from Dumas *fils*.

All of these works kept audiences freely familiar with romantic themes, and, when we bear in mind the rapidly increasing public for the opera, we recognize that here indeed was a powerful instrument for the maintenance and propagation of such sentiment. It was, however, in the creative and critical work of Richard Wagner that operatic romanticism reached its climax. An ugly, domineering, aggressive figure, his theories were as noisy as his drums, and since he beat the latter with considerable power, he succeeded in permanently hypnotizing his fellow-countrymen and for a time at least in stunning all men's ears.

His early operas need not concern us, but very considerable historical importance attaches to the lengthy, pretentious series of works that stretch from *Tannhäuser* in 1845, through *Lohengrin* (1850), *Die Meistersinger* (*The Mastersingers*, 1867) on through *Der Ring des Nibelungen* (*The Ring of the Nibelung*; in four parts, 1869 to 1876) and *Parsifal* (1882). In these he tried to create an entirely new concept. His chief general aim was to make the musical theatre a synthesis of all the arts, with the specific object of rendering it a kind of mystic temple of Germanic aspiration. His opera, first of all, was to be national, and how far he succeeded in this endeavour has been only too blatantly demonstrated by German history during the past dozen years. Apart from this, however, is the larger purpose of creating in the operatic form a kind of theatrical performance such as the stage had never known, had never even dimly approached since the time of the Greeks. His opera was to be a unified work of art (*Gesammtkunstwerk*), in which poetry and music, composed by one and the same hand, would be fused in a single harmony.

In attempting to realize this aim, Wagner, despite all his grandiloquent protestations of originality and despite all the mystic mumbo-jumbo with which he invests his inventions, shows himself the inheritor of earlier traditions. Nietzsche was intuitively right when he averred that the master of Bayreuth was, in essence, a French romanticist. From the tensions of Hugo and Dumas he freely imbibed, and his structural power he derived from that most despised of popular playwrights, Eugène Scribe.

That he had immense power cannot be questioned; perhaps he might well be accepted as the greatest genius of his age. But genius can work for different ends, and Wagner's end is, in reality, a betrayal. When we compare him with the exquisite Mozart or the lyric Beethoven he suddenly takes shape as a middle-class charlatan who is using his god-given talents for a spurious objective. Here romanticism is channelled into false courses, and the very spate of his power turns these courses into dangerous torrents. When Nietzsche further observes that "Wagner as a musician is reckoned among painters, as poet among musicians, as artist generally among actors," he is bitterly expressing his own sense of sorrow at the misuse of this genius's potentialities and eternally castigating his unforgivable artistic treachery. The *Gesammtkunstwerk*, instead of being a new creation, with its own inner being, is seen to be a shoddy jumble of music and words, flapping canvas and flickering lights. The true work of art, no matter by whom it is composed—whether in a monarchy or in a proletarian state—is always aristocratic: its very precision breathes pride of breeding: Wagner's operas are incoherently middle class.

His influence on the theatre, however, was profound. From his theories derive many of our modern conventions. Although we are not accustomed to prate Germanically about a 'mystic chasm' between audience and actors, created by an illuminated stage separated from a darkened house by means of proscenium arch and curtain, we have taken from him the habitual lowering of the auditorium lights as the play begins. To a certain extent, it is obvious, Wagner was here but carrying one of the implications of the proscenium-frame stage to its logical conclusion. He did not seek like others to present naturalistic scenes in such a way as to suggest that a fourth wall had been miraculously left out of a room; his endeavour was rather to hypnotize his audience into imagining that, by the exercise of wizardry, they were privileged initiates gazing into the sanctuary of a Teutonic holy of holies: but, however different his work from that of his naturalistic companions, the emphasis put by him upon the 'mystic chasm' proves him the eldest child of the theatre of yesterday.

In another way too he is typical of his time. During these years the more ambitious dramatic authors were rapidly losing the power to laugh; and Wagner is unquestionably stigmatized by his utter and abject lack of humour. The romantics were a solemn crew, whether they turned to depict reality with drab dismalness or colourfully sought to evoke an historical past; and of them all Wagner is the solemnest.

For all the stormy wonder of his music, the work produced by this man cannot, as drama, be deemed worthy of high esteem. In his over-seriousness of purpose and in his absorption in grandiose concepts he sacrificed that subtlety which can come only from the seeking for perfection in a strictly defined sphere of theatrical activity. The history of opera will always record his name with reverence; but the progress of the drama, in spite of the influence he has had on the stage, was destined to be inspired towards fresh efforts by men whose interests and aims and techniques were far other than his.

THE COMING OF REALISM

THE REALISTIC MELODRAMA

WHILE Wagner was invoking Nibelungs humbler playwrights were more modestly engaged in preparing the ground for the new realism, destined to be the most characteristic theatrical form of the century.

At the start melodrama had been for the most part sensationally removed from the ordinary world. Deliberately the authors sought to find themes which, because of their strangeness, might capture the attention of the popular audiences thronging the theatres. As we have seen, however, about the year 1830 a change begins to become apparent: the wicked feudal count is transmogrified into the moustache-twisting squire, the forester's virgin daughter wears a new dress as a contemporary village maid, and the hero, instead of being a sympathetic outlaw, is a sailor or a soldier home on leave. In many a melodrama in many a country during the thirties and forties breathes an air of contemporary rusticity, and interest is maintained partly by the surprises of the plot, partly by the all-pervading sentimentalism, and partly by the increasing introduction on to the stage of real objects. Vincent Crummles rules in this domain.

A decade passes, and for the country scene are being substituted scenes in the city. A wealthy financier, as often as not, takes the place of the village squire, the heroine now is a poor working lass, a sempstress or a mill-hand, the hero is a working lad; and in place of pigs and geese brought alive upon the boards real hansom-cabs are wheeled in, and the scenic effects attempt to suggest train-wrecks or fires in factories.

By these steps the melodrama moves forward. It remains romantic in the basic sense of that term, only it passes from the world of the past to the world of the present; it sheds medievalism and becomes material. The process, of course, is a slow one, and the strides forward tentative, often halting. Not until the last years of the century does the train-wreck melodrama—to take a single example—reach its culmination. But, however hesitant and lacking in deliberate purpose is the advance, there can be no doubt of the direction of the general current with which the professional dramatists were content to glide.

Now that the melodramatic form had been established by men such as Kotzebue and Pixérécourt, there was no need for the arising of other authors of independent spirit and invention in this field. For all essential purposes the melodramatic authors of the mid-century may remain anonymous, and to a large extent they may remain stateless. Any attempt to trace the development of melo-drama in more than one country during this time would result merely in repetition. In endeavouring to get an idea of the kind of development within this general realm we may, therefore, rest con-tent with the English stage: another would have served equally well.

The movement from such favourites as *The Castle Spectre* (1797; by M. G. Lewis) and his successors on to pieces like *Luke the Labourer; or, The Lost Son* (1826; by J. B. Buckstone) may easily be traced from 1800 to 1830. Thereafter, although colourful romance still holds its own, the 'realistic' rapidly gains in strength, and as it proceeds on its course it attracts to its composition authors of slightly more ambitious aims. Dion Boucicault is no literary genius, but he makes some higher pretensions than Buckstone or Edward Fitzball, and in those melodramatic works in which he dealt with Irish and American themes he clearly tried to secure a tone beyond that of his earlier *Vampire* (1852). Such plays as *The Octoroon; or, Life in Louisiana* (1859) and *The Colleen Bawn; or, The Brides of Garryowen* (1860) were successful beyond other more ephemeral productions precisely because they were more carefully and more skilfully constructed. The same judgment is true of Tom Taylor's long-remembered *Still Waters Run Deep* (1855). It is worthy of note that both this and *The Octoroon* deal with problems of sex—a theme taboo in earlier specimens of the kind—and equally worthy of note is the introduction in the former of the world of criminality. Crimes, naturally, had been common in all the melodramas, but it is only when we come to plays like *Still Waters Run Deep* that we find ourselves introduced to the police-court, only in plays like the same author's *Ticket-of-leave Man* (1863) that we find a detective a principal person among the characters. The detective is a city figure, and from this time on the street rather than the hedgerow lane is the typical locale. *Jim the Penman* (1886), by Sir Charles Young, is a logical development from Taylor's play, as is *The Silver King* (1882), by Henry Herman and Henry Arthur Jones.

With Jones, however, we have entered another sphere, for this author, associated with Sir Arthur Pinero, is by common consent regarded as one of the true founders of the modern literary drama. Perhaps the strength of this modern movement in the theatre lies in the fact that we are able to enter its confines not merely through one broad entrance nobly escutcheoned with the arms of literature, but, as it were, through an obscure wicket set unobtrusively in a side-wall. To get at the *Cenci* only the one approach is possible; to come to *The Second Mrs Tanqueray* (1893) a quite legitimate, although not commonly traversed, path is from *The Castle Spectre*.

SCRIBE AND THE WELL-MADE PLAY

Meanwhile a significant development in dramatic technique was being evolved in France. This came partly through the practice of the melodrama and of its associate, the *comédie-vaudeville*, partly through trends in the sphere of comedy.

From the time of the Revolution to the thirties of the nineteenth century French comedy had been unsure of itself. The famous decree of 1791 established complete freedom for the theatres; decrees issued fifteen years later, in 1806 and 1807, not only limited the number of playhouses, but once more set up a censorship; still other decrees, continually changing the regulations, left those concerned with stage affairs never certain by what rules they would next be bound. Such were not conditions favourable for the flourishing of comedy, nor were the general moods of the age apt to encourage the thoughtful laughter of Molière. If, however, little of intrinsic worth was produced, two movements deserve attention.

The first of these may be described as the mechanization of comic-character portrayal. This is marked particularly in the work of Charles Étienne and of Louis-Benoît Picard. As an example may be taken the latter's *Un jeu de la fortune, ou les marionettes* (*Play of Fortune; or, The Marionettes*, 1806), wherein men are depicted as creatures whose actions are determined by the pulling of invisible strings. In a sense this trend may be regarded as the unconscious comic counterpart of the emphasis on fate in the poets' dismal tragedies.

The second movement is that towards realism. Such a play as *Un moment d'imprudence* (*An Imprudent Moment*, 1819), by Alexis-Jacques-Marie Wafflard, shows a new realistic comedy in the making. Life is treated here with interesting vividity, and the adventures of Monsieur and Madame d'Harcourt are dealt with skilfully. These adventures, ultimately determined by economic causes, are given theatrical complexity through the person of Madame de Montdésir, who lives a double life under her own name and under that of Madame d'Ange: to Madame d'Harcourt she is known in the latter guise, while her husband is acquainted with her in the former. Not without some true virtue, and informed with the same materialistically realistic spirit, is *Les comédiens* (*The Comedians*, 1820) of Casimir Delavigne, an author more famous for his rather melodramatic *Les vêpres Siciliennes* (*The Sicilian Vespers*, 1819).

Into this atmosphere stepped Eugène Scribe. A practical man of the theatre, he realized that for the attainment of success a new, foolproof dramatic technique was required, a technique suited for a theatre so vastly different in potentiality and form from those that had housed the plays of Shakespeare or even the tragedies of Racine.

For Scribe that which matters in a play is the plot, and consequently he looks back, not towards Marivaux, whose stories were merely slim excuses for an opportunity to probe the heart and reveal sentiments, but towards Beaumarchais, who, although he knew how to delineate character, was fundamentally interested in intrigue and action.. Being a practising writer for the theatre, Scribe realized that a popular audience wants, in the first instance, a vividly told dramatic tale; he realized, too, that many of the devices used in the telling of theatrical tales in the past no longer suited the changed stages of his time; and he set for himself the task of devising a formula by which narratives of all kinds—melodramatic, comic, and farcical—could, with a minimum of effort, be rendered appealing when presented on the boards. His success in this task may be gauged from the fact that he was able to set up what amounted to a play-factory, in which stories were found, invented, or paid for and turned, like sausages, into comestibles for which the public was eager to expend its money.

As Alexandre Dumas *fils* saw clearly, Scribe had no "inspiration of idea" and no sincerity save what he devoted to his commercial values. For Musset a play has an artistic being and, however fantastic, an inner reality: for Scribe a play is a play, to be prepared according to a mechanical plan, a thing without organic life. "No one," comments Dumas,

knew better than M. Scribe—who was without conviction, without simplicity, without any philosophic end in view—how to set into action if not a character or an idea, at least a subject, and above all a situation, and to extract from that subject and that situation their logical theatric effect; none better than he understood how to assimilate the latest ideas and adapt them to the stage, sometimes on a scale and in a spirit absolutely opposed to the combinations of the one from whom he received the idea. . . . He was the most extraordinary improviser we have had in the history of our drama; he was the most expert at manipulating characters that had no life. He was the shadow-Shakespeare.

From this description of Scribe's ability Dumas proceeds to compare him with Musset:

If, among the four hundred plays he wrote, either by himself or in collaboration, you place *Il ne faut jurer de rien*, or *Un caprice*, or *Il faut qu'une porte soit ouverte ou fermée*—that is to say, a tiny *proverbe* written by the most naïve and inexpert of dramatists—you will see all Scribe's plays dissolve and go up into thin air, like mercury when heated to three hundred and fifty degrees; because Scribe worked for his audience without putting into his labour anything of his soul or heart, while Musset wrote with heart and soul for the heart and soul of humanity. His sincerity gave him, though he was unaware of this, all the resources which were the sole merit of Scribe.

While this is true—that Scribe's many plays go up into thin air when compared with dramas written from the heart—Dumas was too wise to fail to see that the technical skill of the popular dramatist had its own value. The conclusion, he remarks, is that the playwright who knows *man* as Balzac (or Musset) did, "and the *theatre* as Scribe did, will be the greatest of the world's dramatists."

Just as Musset perfected the work of his immediate predecessors, so Scribe, looking only at theatrical form, perfected the work of others. Fundamentally, his inspiration comes from the writers of melodramas—who, eschewing character studies, were forced to pay particular attention to action—and from those of the vaudeville-farce, a genre which became increasingly popular during the early decades of the nineteenth century. His earliest piece, *Une nuit de la Garde Nationale* (*A Night with the National Guard*, 1815), was called a *tableau-vaudeville*, and the vaudeville technique remained with him to the end of his career. This sketch already shows the main elements of his craft. The play begins with a clear presentation of the background, economically but firmly implants in the audience's mind knowledge of the facts on which the subsequent episodes are founded. These facts known by his public, all the author has to do is to start pulling the strings of his puppets: in and out they go, and the resultant intrigue holds the attention, almost makes us forget that they are puppets without life of their own. And the illusion is made the greater by the free use made by the playwright of material taken from the life of the day. Scribe, as Dumas noted, was nothing if not up-to-date.

This does not, of course, imply that Scribe always took his scenes from material familiar to, or closely associated with, the life of the time. Many of his pieces introduce historical matter—however unhistorically treated—and quite a number escape into the world of the fantastic. Towards the very beginning of his career he varied his pattern with a *folie-vaudeville* entitled *L'ours et le pacha* (*The Bear and the Pasha*, 1820), with exciting scenes in the seraglio, designed to titillate the public, and all the mechanism of Oriental wonder.

By this time the talented young author was the rage of Paris; by this time he had become sure of his art and was capable of applying it to subject-matter of any description. The formula of the well-made play—*la pièce bien faite*—was complete. Thenceforward for a period of thirty-odd years he kept the playhouses supplied with a constant series of dramas, nearly all accompanied by music, in which scenes serious, comic, and farcical were wrought into a skilful theatrical pattern. One after another his five hundred plays followed in a constant stream. Here were the sketches from life, such as *La petite sœur* (*The Little Sister*, 1821), *La seconde année* (*The Second Year*, 1830), and *Le chaperon* (*The Hood*, 1832); here were *drames*, such as *Rodolphe, ou frère et sœur* (*Rodolphe; or, Brother and Sister*, 1823) or (turn it about) *Camilla, ou la sœur et la frère* (*Camilla; or, The Sister and the Brother*, 1832); here were sentimental 'tragedies,' such as the once-famous *Adrienne Lecouvreur* (1849), penned in collaboration with Ernest Legouvé, and (with a happy ending) these two authors' *La bataille des dames, ou un duel en amour* (*The Ladies' Battle; or, A Duel of Love*, 1851); here were fantasies, such as *La chatte métamorphosée en femme* (*The Cat metamorphosed into a Woman*, 1827), *Le diable à l'école* (*The Devil at School*, 1842) or *La fée aux roses* (*The Rose Fairy*, 1849); here were Oriental spectacles, such as *Haÿdée, ou le secret* (*Haydee; or, The Secret*, 1847); here were pseudo-historical pieces, such as *La sirène* (*The Syren*, 1844) or *Marco Spada* (1852). With spirit, gaiety, and a sense of the sensational Scribe makes each one of these exciting and entertaining fare; there is hardly a real character in any, but, as many another author of the time discovered, there is a multiplicity of action and, above all, an almost infallible recipe for the production of similar works. As he showed so clearly in the extraordinarily popular *Une chaîne*

(*A Chain*, 1841), Scribe was able to make people believe in his almost wholly synthetic situations, and naturally his companions eagerly examined the secrets of his art. The immediate imitators of Scribe are legion.

What is more important is that his formula for the construction of a *comédie-vaudeville* was found to be applicable also to the writing of more serious dramas. It is not too much to say that, mediocre though his own creations may be, he provided for others precisely what an age of romanticism most needed—a mould into which dramatic thought and passion might be poured. The romantic mind tends to be diffuse and sometimes vague, but diffuseness and vagueness are untheatrical qualities. Scribe accomplished an important task—albeit unwittingly—by emphasizing the importance of action and by showing how necessary for success is careful and deliberate planning of effect.

While the influence of Scribe's works was widespread, extending far beyond the boundaries of France, it is important to remember that even where the impress of his style is patent dramatists of many European lands preserved at least the main elements in their own native traditions and allowed the Scribe formula, when they employed it, merely to make more strongly theatrical qualities stemming from a different source.

Thus, for example, in Spain the Argentinian Ventura de la Vega, in introducing knowledge of the new style to Madrid, incorporated in it features of a purely Castilian sort: his *El hombre del mundo* (*The Man of the World*, 1845) owes its vigour to such a combination of forces. In these efforts he was companioned by Mariano José de Larra, whose *No más mostrador* (*Closing the Shop*, 1831) is confessedly an adaptation, with Spanish elements, of the French 'master.' In Italy, similarly, the spirit of Goldoni and of the *commedia dell' arte* prevented a merely slavish following of Paris models. There is a true breath of Venetian air in *La donna romantica e il medico omeopatico* (*The Romantic Lady and the Homeopathic Doctor*, 1858), by Riccardo Castelvecchio (Giulio Pullé), which deals, rather delightfully, with a young bride, Irene, who is wrapped in dismal sighs contracted from a reading of the best French love-romances.

Poland finds its characteristic spirit expressed in the various writings of Kazimierz Zalewski, with his *Bez posagu* (*Without a Dowry*, 1869), *Małżenstwo Apfel* (*The Apfel Marriage*, 1887), and other dramas of domestic interests. In Czechoslovakia the Scribe style is given an individual twist by Emanuel Bozděch, with his popular

Zkouška státníkova (*The Politician's Trial*, 1874), and in Austria it is handled by Eduard von Bauernfeld in such plays as *Die Bekenntnisse* (*The Acknowledgments*, 1834) and *Bürgerlich und romantisch* (*Simple and Romantic*, 1835). Hungary too presents a peculiar comedy-drama variant of its own in such plays as the lively *A kérök* (*The Suitors*, 1819) and *Csalódások* (*Illusions*, 1828), by Károly Kisfaludy, and *Szökött katona* (*The Deserter*, 1845), by Ede Szigligeti, although the latter author is probably better known for his *A trónkeresö* (*The Pretender*, 1867), a tragic drama set in the thirteenth century. *Csalódások* is notable for its portrait of the blundering Mokány, *Szökött katona* for its effective pictures of peasant life. From Sweden comes *Ett resande teatersällskap* (*The Touring Company*, 1842), by August Blanche, a play confessedly built on a French foundation, yet made thoroughly Scandinavian in atmosphere and characters.

In looking at such plays it is evident that we must endeavour at once to estimate the force of that powerful French influence which made so many plays in so many lands merely pieces taken "from the French" and which is the expression of a mechanistic philosophy of the theatre, and to give full weight to the enduring national strains which even that influence could not completely banish from the stages of Europe.

'SARDOODLEDUM'

Through a kind of amalgam of Scribe's technique, the suggestions given by the early experiments in mechanistic comedy and the resourcefulness of the melodrama—now directing its attention to materialistic themes—a new form of drama gradually came into being. From Lytton to Robertson in England, and from Augier to Sardou in France, diverse playwrights were engaged in preparing the theatres for what was to come—and, paradoxically, establishing a style against which later writers might react. Although the progress of realism is constant and uninterrupted during these years, yet the realism of one decade has ever seemed absurd to the realists of the next, and accordingly advance has taken the form continually of unacknowledged influence associated with public expressions of contempt. To Robertson Lytton appeared old-fashioned, and to Pinero Robertson was outmoded; nevertheless the line from the first author to the last is absolutely unbroken. Sardoodledum was both an inspiration and a menace for the dramatic authors at the end of the century.

It is, indeed, the prolific and successful Victorien Sardou who, although so much of his work belongs to the final years of the century, provides one of the chief links between the earlier styles and those that were to come. If we take a bird's-eye view of dramatic development in France and England within this period we can easily discern three main currents meandering downward and eventually forming one great stream. One is the melodramatic, represented by Sardou in France and by Boucicault in England. The second is the transformation of comedy-farce: here Eugène Labiche and H. J. Byron may be taken as representative. The third is the tentative introduction of contemporary themes—in particular those of marriage and money—not confined to one author or to one group of authors, but, as it were, welling up from the soil in diverse places almost imperceptibly until suddenly they take shape as a constantly flowing rivulet.

Victorien Sardou was a faithful disciple of Scribe, and his one endeavour was to produce plays likely to prove successful on the stage; he soared to success in 1860 with *Les pattes de mouche* (*A Scrap of Paper*), which long held popular esteem. Accordingly he ranges over vast territory, embracing in his wanderings both the romantic-historical and the realistic. Plot is of more concern to him than either character or idea, and theatricality predominates in his writings. This very theatricality, however, has its values, since he succeeded in enlarging the Scribe formula so as to make it apply to a stage which was becoming increasingly rich in its resources. He knew well how to make use of new scenic effects, and he was even capable of making his own innovations—such as the dramatic use of crowds, the employment of groups of persons not as automaton-supers but as dynamic forces in the action. In this and other ways he prepared the path for his successors.

His historical pieces, such as *Théodora* (1884), *La Tosca* (1887), *Robespierre* (1899), *Madame Sans-Gêne* (written with Émile Moreau, 1893), and *La sorcière* (*The Witch*, 1903), need not detain us, although some of these are to be remembered because they were written for, and provided highly characteristic rôles for, Sarah Bernhardt. This sphere of playwriting, moreover, provided Sardou with what was one of the most successful and certainly one of the best among his plays, *La patrie* (*The Fatherland*, 1869), in which he piles melodramatic sensation upon realistic scenes and both of these upon the exhibition of tragic, tortured love. Typical is the scene in which Karloo discovers that his revolutionary friends have been betrayed through the ministry of Dolorès. Her husband is going to his death on the scaffold as Karloo and she plan to flee the country together, when suddenly the truth is revealed:

KARLOO: That woman—at the Duke's—this morning! That woman —at the Duke's—last night!

DOLORÈS: Last night?

KARLOO: It is she.

DOLORÈS: No!

KARLOO: It's you. It's you! You have betrayed us! You miserable—— Dare you deny that you are the one?

DOLORÈS: Ah, Karloo!

KARLOO: Leave me—don't touch me!

[*He disengages himself and darts towards the right, where he falls into a chair.*

DOLORÈS: Pity me.

KARLOO: God's vengeance! And I have been looking for her! And here she is. Who else?

DOLORÈS [*who has fallen to the floor*]: Ah, Karloo! Don't curse me! Let the others do that—not you.

KARLOO: Fiend—traitress—coward—coward!

DOLORÈS [*on her knees, making her way towards him*]: You don't know all, my Karloo. He wanted to kill you. When he left me he said: "I am going to kill him!" I was mad with terror—stark mad— Karloo! I swear I was raving mad! I only tried to save you—I loved you so much! It was for your sake, for you!

KARLOO [*taking her hands in his*]: Your love. Your love has made me a perjurer and a traitor! Your fatal love has brought these poor wretches to the scaffold, and a whole nation to its ruin! Your love is hellish, deadly! I *do* curse you! I execrate, I hate you!

[*He casts her to the floor.*

DOLORÈS: Ah, Karloo, you are killing me!

KARLOO: No, not yet!

DOLORÈS: What are you going to do?

KARLOO [*dragging her to the window*]: Come here, Madam! First, look at your work.

DOLORÉS: Pity me!

[*The windows are red with the reflected light of the faggots. Screams and murmurs of horror are heard.*

KARLOO: Look at it! Look at your faggot-heap—it's burning!

DOLORÈS: Pity me!

KARLOO: Look—count your victims!

DOLORÈS: Karloo—ungrateful——

KARLOO [*raising her and forcing her to look*]: You must accustom yourself to flames—you must have some notion of what hell is like— hell, where your love is dragging us!

DOLORÈS: Mercy!

KARLOO: Listen! They have caught sight of me! Listen now, listen!

THE PRISONERS: Karloo—traitor! Traitor!

KARLOO: Do you hear?

DOLORÈS: My God!

KARLOO: And do you not also hear the dead man crying out: "Re-member your oath"?

DOLORÈS [*rising in terror*]: No. No.

KARLOO: "No matter who the guilty one may be, strike, have no mercy!"

DOLORÈS: Karloo, would you strike me?

KARLOO [*drawing his dagger*]: My oath!

DOLORÈS [*wild with terror, as she struggles to free herself*]: With your own hand—no! You wouldn't do that! Pity me—I'm afraid!

KARLOO [*losing his self-control*]: I have sworn!

DOLORÈS: No, no—don't—leave me!

KARLOO: I have sworn, I have sworn! [*He plunges the dagger into her.*

DOLORÈS [*falling to the floor*]: Now go—you have killed me. And I loved you so! I loved you so. [KARLOO *throws his dagger down.*

KARLOO [*nearly out of his mind*]: I have killed you! I! I!

DOLORÈS: At least you can join me, now! Come.

KARLOO [*falling to his knees before her, an inanimate mass, and covering her with kisses, while he sobs*]: I will come with you—I am so miserable! Dolorès, my sweetest love! O God! O God!

DOLORÈS: Come, then.

KARLOO [*standing*]: Wait! I am coming! [*He runs to the window, stands in it, and cries out.*] Executioner [*excitement in the Square*]—you lack one man! Make way for me on your faggot-heap!

DOLORÈS [*rising in order to see him*]: Ah!

KARLOO [*to* DOLORÈS, *his voice full of loving tenderness*]: You see? I am coming, I am coming! [*He goes swiftly from the room.* DOLORÈS *dies.*

What popular audience would not be thrilled by such a scene? What lover of truth in the theatre can refrain from a smile or a sneer?

Play after play is cast in the same mould. *Spiritisme* (*Spiritualism*, 1897) exploits current interest in the occult by showing a young wife, Simone, angered at her husband's absorption in spiritualistic research, first taking a lover and later giving herself out as dead. Deserted by the lover, she finds a friend who so works on the husband's mind as to persuade him to summon her spirit back from the shades—whereupon, of course, the real Simone appears. This is the situation of *Much Ado about Nothing* without the poetry. Equally theatrical is *Marcelle* (1896), which, dealing with the story of a woman with a past, characteristically brings her safely out of her troubles to a conclusion vastly happier than any of the realists would have allowed her.

Yet this very theatricality was to be put to good use, both by Sardou himself and by his immediate followers, in the service of the realistic drama. Of such plays his *Daniel Rochat* (1880) may be regarded as typical. Here a free-thinking, 'atheist' hero marries, by a civil ceremony, an Anglo-American girl, Léa, but jibs at following this by a ceremony in church. The entire play is taken up with the struggle between these two, and in the end a somewhat unsatisfactory conclusion is reached. Although not by any means a masterpiece, and although now seen to be replete with many spurious sentiments, this drama illustrates well how the Scribe technique, applied in new ways, was being adapted to the requirements of contemporary themes. In himself Sardou is nothing but a later edition of Kotzebue or of Pixérécourt; as a 'barometer' of Parisian playhouse taste his works have prime historical value; for those who came after him he was a model to be imitated and an idol to be overthrown.

Closely associated with Sardou in his endeavour to feed the stage with successful entertainments is Eugène Labiche. Instead, however, of cultivating the melodramatic, he relies mainly upon comedy farce, applying the now familiar Scribe formula to plays designed mainly for the purpose of arousing laughter. Although he succeeded in presenting a delightful series of amusing pictures of contemporary life, most of his works have little intrinsic value. On the other hand, a few of them—notably *Le voyage de M. Perrichon* (*M. Perrichon's Journey*, 1860) and *La poudre aux yeux* (*Dust in the Eyes*, 1861)—betray qualities of a further kind. The former presents a definite thesis, suggesting that men are apt to detest those who do them a good turn, that their affection goes out rather to those whom they themselves have assisted. In *La poudre aux yeux* the plot is based on the idea of being and seeming—the complications arising from the social masks worn by the diverse characters. Perhaps Labiche does not contribute in these works much of great importance for the later development of the play of ideas, yet this incursion of a sense of purpose into the realm of farce is not unworthy of notice. Most of his work, however, is of the delightfully irresponsible kind represented by *Le chapeau de paille d'Italie* (*The Italian Straw Hat*, 1851), in which a worthy young hero is thrown into a maze of unexpected comic trials all because his horse happens to eat a straw hat that has been hung up on a tree.

Along with these two currents we must observe how topics based on contemporary conditions were beginning, even before 1829, to receive dramatic treatment. Two thoroughly minor playwrights, for example, Édouard-Joseph Mazères and Adolphe Empis, collaborated in this very year to produce *La mère et la fille* (*Mother and Daughter*, 1830), a play dealing with marriage in relation to money, while four years later they brought out *Une liaison* (1834), in which appeared a theme later to be more fully exploited—that of the prostitute in the family circle. Even before these dates another minor writer, Casimir Bonjour, wrote his *L'argent, ou les mœurs du siècle* (*Money; or, The Manners of the Age*, 1826), which by its very title indicates its interests.

These are early dramas: Sardou, starting his career in 1854, carries us on into the present century; the work of Labiche appears mainly in the sixties and seventies. Although diverse in date, the three streams may be viewed together if we regard Sardou not so much for himself as for what he symbolized, and if we see Labiche merely as the perfector of a line of comedy-farce the tradition of which he inherited. The realistic melodrama, the realistic farce, and the introduction of the 'thesis' in both laid the foundations of the typical drama of the latter half of the century.

POPULAR REALISM IN FRANCE

The fusion of these is well revealed in the work of Émile Augier. Starting in the mood of imaginative romanticism, tinged with melodramatic sentiment, pursuing technically the methods of Scribe, he became one of the principal founders of the new style. In 1844 he first came before the public with a verse drama, *La ciguë* (*Hemlock*), an unimportant piece, followed shortly afterwards by a couple of other works in the same medium, *L'aventurière* (*The Adventuress*, 1848) and *Gabrielle* (1849). The interest of these two dramas rests in their subject-matter. *L'aventurière* presents a picture (set in an historical past) of a prostitute, Clorinde, whose entire being is transformed because of her newly awakened love, and draws a sharp contrast between the good sense of the bourgeoisie and romantic follies: in it we are close to *La dame aux camélias*. In the second a definite thesis is introduced. The whole purpose of the play is to prove that it is better for a woman to extract joy and romantic pleasure from living respectably as a wife than to snatch at the illusory delights of being a mistress: here we have entered the sphere of the drama of ideas.

As yet, however, the form by no means harmonized with the content. The scenes, characters, and ideas belong to the social life of the mid-nineteenth century, but the tinkling verse carries us into the atmosphere of another age. Soon, however, Augier, no doubt inspired by Dumas *fils*, was prepared to find a truer harmony; and as a result of his determination came *Le gendre de M. Poirier* (*The Son-in-law of M. Poirier*), in 1854, written in collaboration with Jules Sandeau, from whose novel *Sacs et parchemins* its plot is derived. There can be no question but that this is a minor masterpiece. Its effervescent wit, allied to a serious purpose, gives it a distinction above most of its companions. Fundamentally, the story is based on the clash between two ideals. On the one hand stands the Marquis de Presles, representative of the ancient aristocracy; on the other is the wealthy, middle-class M. Poirier. The latter has caused his daughter, Antoinette, to marry Gaston, a scion of the noble house: Gaston is just on the point of coming to appreciate the virtues of his *parvenu* bride when Poirier starts to retrench, to speak vulgarly of money, to display all his lack of gentility. The conflict between the proud aristocrat, living in the past, idle, domineering, yet gifted with magnanimous qualities, and the hardworking, yet essentially vulgar, bourgeois is delineated with admirable balance and fine restraint. Perhaps the end may appear a trifle sentimental, when Antoinette's native dignity and nobleness of mind succeed in converting Gaston to look upon her with love, but until the very last scenes this play is innocent of the vices which so cluttered up and falsified the dramas of the eighteenth century. Here is a modern spirit: *Le gendre de M. Poirier* can still be read or seen with interest and profit.

Augier's stress on moral ideas is perhaps his greatest contribution to this mid-nineteenth-century realistic movement, and the moral idea becomes even more pronounced in *Le mariage d'Olympe* (*Olympia's Marriage*, 1855), which may be regarded as a kind of answer to *La dame aux camélias*. Augier had been prepared in *L'aventurière* to accept the concept of the reformed prostitute, but he was not prepared to allow her to stain family honour. His Olympe is a woman who, after a life of sin, allows her former life to vanish from memory by the device of taking another name. In her new rôle she marries Henri, nephew of the Marquis de Puygirou, by whom she is welcomed into the aristocratic circle. Her nature, however, is wholly evil: she yearns for the excitements of her early life, and through sheer boredom she starts a scandal concerning the innocent Geneviève. By her own actions she is revealed, and at the end the old Marquis, to protect the honour of his line, shoots her and is shown reloading his pistol, for the purpose of committing suicide, as the curtain falls.

Throughout the course of his later work Augier kept emphasizing his common-sense views on life. He was no revolutionary, and romantic excesses seemed to him a potent danger; his mission, as he regarded it, was to draw lifelike pictures of contemporary society and to plead for the basic virtues. The evils of city life are delineated both in *La jeunesse* (*Youth*, 1858), and *Les lionnes pauvres* (*Dissipation*; written in collaboration with Édouard Foussier, 1858); in *Les effrontés* (*The Impertinents*, 1861) he attacks the enormities of the modern newspaper and the power it puts into the hands of single men; discussion of politics and clericalism made *Le fils de Giboyer* (*Giboyer's Son*, 1862) a *succès de scandale* in its day; divorce is the theme of *Madame Caverlet* (1876). Finer than these is *Les Fourchambault* (1878), in which a study is made of an upper middle-class household, with a vulgar Mme Fourchambault, a libertine son, Léopold, who yet has some good in him, a poor relation, Marie, and a *deus ex machina* in the person of an illegitimate son, Bernard, who sentimentally saves the family from bankruptcy and wins the fair Marie's hand as the curtain falls. In all of these there is a skilful and interesting handling of character as well as a philosophy which, although maybe somewhat shallow, gives to the scenes an individual quality. The plays of Augier proved that the theatre could well serve as a platform for the enunciation of ideas, made interesting because of their incorporation in plots narrated with the technical brilliance which Scribe had taught his followers to cultivate.

Augier's chief companion in this sphere was Alexandre Dumas *fils*, whose career extends from the famous *La dame aux camélias* of 1852 to *Francillon* in 1887. Like Augier, he was serious in his intent; like him, he based his technique on that of Scribe, although to Scribe's influence in this way he added a strength based apparently on careful study of Corneille's style; like him, he set out to explore the reaches of contemporary life. In his writings, however, more clearly than in those of Augier, the characteristic trend of nineteenth-century realism becomes apparent. His persons are treated as creatures of their surroundings, puppets rudely battered as they are jerked to and fro by unseen strings in the blind power of circumstance, and there is a tendency in his writings to assume that the realistic resides only in the darker spheres of life. In their reaction against the prevailing themes of their romantic predecessors, the romantic realists of the age were impelled to abandon the colourful for the sordid.

His characteristic qualities are well revealed in that earliest of his plays, *La dame aux camélias* (played frequently as *Camille*), in which a prostitute, Marguerite Gautier, is made the heroine. Following the Scribe formula, the first act is devoted almost entirely to presenting the general *milieu* in which she moves. This set, the play is then made to march on towards its fatal conclusion. For the first time Marguerite's heart has been touched by love, and she arranges to go off with her Armand to spend the summer in the country. His father arrives, and by his skilful pleading persuades her that, if she truly loves him, it is her duty to give him up. Hereupon she makes the great sacrifice, writing to Armand that she has decided to leave him for another. In drunken anger he insults her publicly, and she, worn out from the passions of these events, falls into a decline. Just as the repentant Armand, having learned the truth, takes her to his arms she dies.

Like a thunderbolt this play descended upon Paris. The whole of the theatre public wept and sighed over the poor Marguerite, and when Augier tried to arouse consideration of other aspects of the problem his *Mariage d'Olympe* had short shrift. This particular kind of realistic drama was firmly established.

It was even more fully established in *Le demi-monde*, of 1855, a play that in its title introduced a new word into the French—indeed, into the international—vocabulary. The 'demi-monde' is the asylum of all those who have left their own social environment, welcoming alike men and women of rank whom fortune has cast down and other men and women who, usually for their own advancement, have climbed up the rungs of the social ladder, but have been unable to enter the closed windows of high life. In this world lives Suzanne, a self-seeking beauty whose one thought is of herself. She entangles in her snares the young hero, Raymond de Nanjac, who is, however, sternly warned of the menace by his gay and cynical friend, Olivier de Jalin, a former lover of Suzanne. A quarrel ensues between the two men, and a duel is fought; but in the end Suzanne's duplicity is revealed, and for the hero all is well.

What attracts our attention here is the manner in which Dumas has concentrated his attention almost entirely on environment. The stress of the play is not so much on the persons as on the social world in which they live: the demi-monde itself, rather than de Nanjac, may be regarded as the central character in the play.

La question d'argent (*A Question of Money*, 1857) followed a couple of years later. Here, instead of developing a *milieu*, Dumas turns to exploit a problem. Fundamentally, this problem is that of the rightness or wrongness of capitalistic finance. The story of the poor-born Giraud, who is prepared to marry Élisa de Roncourt simply for the purpose of obtaining a respectable position in life, does not matter in comparison with the basic question—whether a man has the right to employ duplicity (in this case a pretended absconsion designed to lower the value of company stocks) in order to make an enormous profit from his investments. The theme has been so frequently dealt with since Dumas' time—it has now even invaded the realm of the detective story—that it has ceased to make much impress on our minds, and maybe we must agree that in its structure *La question d'argent* does not exhibit such skill as was revealed in the earlier plays of this author; at the same time, we may readily imagine the impression made on contemporaries by this bold presentation of a problem, adumbrated before, but never so trenchantly expressed.

With *Le fils naturel* (*The Illegitimate Son*, 1858) comes something new: it is now commonly recognized that in this work the modern 'thesis-play' was created. And it was created with conscious deliberation. "'Art for art's sake?'" cries Dumas. "Words devoid of meaning!" And he proceeds to enunciate his belief that it is the mission of the dramatist to preach. The sermon in *Le fils naturel* is illegitimacy, and one of the chief virtues of the drama is that the preacher, instead of merely giving his congregation what it expected to hear, dares to present an idea of his own. Through an exceedingly complex plot Dumas traces the fortunes of the base-born Jacques de Boisceny, who through his own fine qualities succeeds in becoming an outstanding political figure of his time. His father is Charles Sternay, a self-seeking individualist, who has deserted his mistress in order to marry into an aristocratic family. At first Sternay is merely annoyed when his paternity of Jacques is revealed, but as the young man becomes of greater and greater importance in the world of affairs he seeks, in vain, to recognize him as his son. Unquestionably the audience would have expected a sentimental reunion for the final curtain: Dumas, however, has caused his hero to adopt his mother's name and remain unreconciled.

After a number of largely insignificant plays Dumas proceeded to enlarge the scope of his new dramatic invention in *Les idées de Madame Aubray* (*Madame Aubray's Ideas*, 1867), in which appears a kind of study of true Christianity in modern social surroundings. The central character is Madame Aubray, a woman who believes in following the dictates of her own charitable soul rather than the codes of the world in which she lives. Her dearly beloved son, Camille, falls in love with a girl, Jeannine, a presumed 'widow' and in reality an unmarried mother. When Camille asks for his mother's approval Madame Aubray refuses, but after Jeannine, in a moment of noble renunciation, pretends to Camille that she has had many lovers she is so deeply touched that she gives the girl to her son. This is undoubtedly an interesting play, and Dumas has exhibited great skill, not only in revealing the mind of Madame Aubray herself, but, more importantly, in suggesting the influence of her character upon those with whom she comes into contact. Sentimentalism, no doubt, colours the general picture, and the situations are sometimes twisted to accord with the author's purpose, but among the plays of ideas written in the sixties and seventies this stands out for its directness of aim and its sincerity af purpose.

There follows a series of rather conflicting plays on the subject of illicit relations. In the ironical *Une visite de noces* (*A Honeymoon Call*, 1871) a husband is shown attracted towards a former mistress when he thinks she has had many lovers, but immediately repelled when he finds out that she is faithful to his memory: he prefers, rather than resume an illicit attachment to a woman of this kind, to remain with his wife. In *La Princesse Georges* (1871) the irony is of a different sort and bitter. Séverine's husband, a prince, has a liaison with Sylvanie, wife of the Count de Terremonde. Loving her husband, the injured woman informs the count, and then is dismayed to learn that he intends to kill his rival when he comes for his assignation. A shot is heard; Séverine is in despair; then suddenly it is revealed that the slain man is not her husband, but a wretched youth, de Foudette, to whom also Sylvanie had opened her arms and who had, all unwittingly, walked into the trap. The solution is clever—perhaps too clever; for, although in our minds we are prepared to recognize that the author has found an interesting twist for a hackneyed plot—even although we may admit that his purpose is being pursued by indication of the blind fate that operates in this world of the illicit in sex relations—the unexpectedness of the final scene undoubtedly invokes in us an impression of artificiality. Like so many plays of the same kind still to come, there is too much brain-work here.

It is of interest to note—especially when we compare Dumas' career with that of authors immediately following him—that from these purely realistic plays he now turned to a kind of drama which, although maintaining outward realism, became invested with a kind of mystical atmosphere. In his address to the public prefacing *La femme de Claude* (*Claude's Wife*, 1873) he speaks of his latest work as "purely symbolic." "Claude does not murder his wife," he declares; "the dramatist does not murder a woman; together they destroy a Beast." Written after the outbreak of war with Prussia, *La femme de Claude* mingles a spy theme with that of adultery. Césarine is the thoroughly dissipated wife of a great inventor; she becomes involved in the toils of a German agent, Cartagnac, and turns the head of her husband's brilliant assistant, Antonin. In the end, just after she has been foiled in her attempt to steal some military plans, Claude shoots her dead—symbolically with the new rifle invented by Antonin—and the Beast is vanquished.

The symbolic style, no less than that of *La Princesse Georges*, shows at once Dumas' source of weakness and his source of strength. The strength lies in his mastery of what may be called theatrical logic. Although analysis may demonstrate the spurious sentiment apparent in many scenes of *La dame aux camélias*, that irresistible sweep accompanied by economy of means which the author learned from Scribe has made it a popular favourite. Above all other things, Dumas knew how to arrest and to hold the attention of his audiences. At the same time, in this strength lies potential weakness. So long as the dramatist keeps to the level of *La dame aux camélias* all is well; but when he tries to become profound the very artificiality inherent in the 'well-made-play' formula proves his undoing. The scaffolding and the machinery suddenly reveal themselves to us blatantly, and illusion is dispelled.

With Augier, Dumas may be accepted as one of the most influential members of that dramatic group which was intent on establishing the new realism, on introducing social problems into the playhouse, and on using the stage for the purpose of inculcating ideas; but neither was a genius.

Dozens of other writers applied themselves to the new style and wrote abundantly of the problems (mainly marriage and money) of the bourgeoisie. Among them are François Poinsard with his *L'honneur et l'argent* (*Honour and Money*, 1853), Paul Arène with his *Pierrot héritier* (*Pierrot the Heir*, 1865), Theodore Barrière with his *Malheur aux vaincus* (*Woe to the Vanquished*, 1870), Jacques Bornet with his *L'usurier* (*The Usurer*, 1870), Victor Séjour with his *L'argent du diable* (*The Devil's Coin*, 1854). Of such authors few deserve special note. Honoré de Balzac has quality, but even he warrants much more attention for his *Comédie humaine* than for his plays—*La marâtre* (*The Stepmother*, 1848) and *Mercadet* (1851)— although the latter is an incisively written study of financial chicanery, with some excellent scenes. So, too, individual mention may be made of the interesting *La révolte* (*The Revolt*, 1870) of Count

Philippe de Villiers de l'Isle-Adam, a not ineffective anticipation of *A Doll's House*.

There are works of minor interest here, but the real triumphs of the realistic stage were still to come.

REALISTIC GROPINGS IN ENGLAND

While the English stage produced no Dumas or Augier, the same movements as dominated in Paris can be traced in London.

In the year 1840 appeared a play called *Money*, by Lord Lytton, and its very title tells its story. Here is the direct equivalent of those French plays which, then and later, explored the problems of wealth and sought to reveal some of the vices of bourgeois society. The scene in which the will of the rich Mr Mordaunt is read indicates its tone. The relatives are gathered, all eager and expectant, with, among them, the poor hero, Evelyn, and his love, Clara. One after another of the richer members of the company are woefully disappointed, and then comes the shock as the laywer reads on:

SHARP: "And, with the aforesaid legacies and exceptions, I do will and bequeath the whole of my fortune, in India Stock, Bonds, Exchequer bills, Three Per Cent. Consols, and in the Bank of India (constituting him hereby sole residuary legatee and joint executor with the aforesaid Henry Graves, Esq.) to Alfred Evelyn [*pause— a movement on the part of everybody but* SHARP], now or formerly of Trinity College, Cambridge [*universal excitement*], being, I am told, an oddity, like myself—the only one of my relations who never fawned on me; and who, having known privation, may the better employ wealth." And now, sir, I have only to wish you joy, and give you this letter from the deceased. I believe it is important.

[*All rise.*

EVELYN [*looking over to* CLARA]: Ah, Clara, if you had but loved me!

CLARA [*turning away*]: And his wealth, even more than poverty, separates us for ever!

LADY FRANKLIN: I wish you joy.

OMNES [*crowding round to congratulate* EVELYN]: I wish you joy.

SIR JOHN [*to* GEORGINA]: Go, child—put a good face on it—he's an immense match! My dear fellow, I wish you joy; you are a great man now—a very great man! I wish you joy.

EVELYN [*aside*]: And *her* voice alone is silent!

GLOSSMORE: If I can be of any use to you——

STOUT: Or I, sir——

BLOUNT: Or I? Shall I put you up at the clubs?

SHARP: You will want a man of business. I transacted all Mr Mordaunt's affairs.

SIR JOHN [*rushing to centre of crowd, and pushing them aside*]: Tush, tush! Mr Evelyn is at home *here*—always looked on him as a son! Nothing in the world we would not do for him!

EVELYN: Lend me ten pounds for my old nurse!

OMNES: Certainly! Certainly!

[*Chorus put their hands into their pockets, producing purses, and offering them eagerly.*

No more than this brief extract is required to indicate *Money's* position in the history of the theatre. Without doubt it stems from the sentimental tradition: the situation in which Evelyn and Clara find themselves is similar to that of many an eighteenth-century hero and heroine. At the same time, its dialogue has not the strained artificiality associated with the names of Cumberland and Kelly, while its theme definitely aligns it with the work of the new realists.

In this way the play stands as an excellent example of transitional drama. Lytton was a writer who, like Scribe himself, was apt in sensing the trend of public taste. *Money* he wrote because he realized the craving for the realistic in measured doses: he was also the author of the immensely popular 'gentlemanly melodrama' *The Lady of Lyons* (1838) and the romantically historical *Richelieu; or, The Conspiracy* (1839), because he realized that the same public that craved for realism also craved for romance.

The contributions of Boucicault, Reade, and Taylor have been noted above, but something new enters into the theatre with the work of Tom Robertson (T. W. Robertson). It must be confessed that his plays have little intrinsic importance: he wrote no *Dame aux camélias* or *Gendre de M. Poirier*. On the other hand, the significance of his writings was, for the English stage, of very considerable extent, and accordingly their innovations must be surveyed, if not for their own worth, at least for what they meant to others.

Fundamentally Robertson, who started as a romantic melodramatist, was the first man in England to conceive of stage realism as a complete whole. Others before him had penned scenes taken (more or less) from ordinary life; others too had introduced real objects, or their theatrical semblances, to the boards. It remained for him to co-ordinate these efforts. He not only set forth to write plays in which he tried to reflect the ways of common life; he endeavoured to provide for those plays such settings and such interpretation as fitted their lines. He sought for actors prepared to abandon the old bold manner appropriate to melodrama and the romantic play; he insisted that his doors should have real knobs on them and not simply painted forms.

An excellent, and an essentially truthful, picture of his struggles was presented by his successor, A. W. Pinero, in *Trelawny of the 'Wells'* (1899), and nowhere better could one find an indication both of what Robertson set out to accomplish and what he sought to banish from the playhouse. If this later comedy is read as a comment on his own works we shall have a clear mental image of his achievements. After a kind of transitional play, *David Garrick* (1864), he created in *Society* (1865) a drama that immediately fluttered Victorian audiences, and followed this with a series of similar pieces—*Ours* (1866), *Caste* (1867), and *School* (1869). Of these *Caste* shows his qualities at their best and most characteristic. Whiffs of sentimentalism and romance are to be breathed here certainly. The Honourable George D'Alroy is almost as pure as a hero of melodrama, and Esther Eccles is a true heroine. Beyond this, however, there is a flavour in this comedy-drama of which the melodrama remained innocent. Esther is in danger, but not from any dark-moustached villain: the menace to her life is the snobbery of D'Alroy's aristocratic family. Noting this, we realize that in *Caste* Robertson has moved into an entirely different mental and emotional world. Although he makes use of melodramatic devices, the service to which they are put is far other than that of a few decades before. The very title of his play shows his purpose: above and beyond the characters and the plot there exists a theme, and that theme is 'Caste.' In his own way Robertson was doing for London what Augier and Dumas *fils* were doing for Paris.

One further comment may be made on his significance for the modern stage. Not alone, certainly, yet nevertheless powerfully, he aided in the development of the present-day producer. As the drama increased its scope during the nineteenth century and as the theatres came to enjoy practical resources of which they had no knowledge in the past, the need arose for the appointment of officials responsible for co-ordination of effect. Such need came with the 'historical' productions of Shakespeare's plays by Charles Kean; it presented itself to Dion Boucicault with his new-style melo-dramas; Gilbert found it essential to exercise control of this kind in the production of his comic operas. Robertson was one of the first in England to demonstrate the need with respect to the realistic stage.

This, of course, is not to say that he achieved anything akin to what was accomplished by the German players who acted under the direction of the Duke of Saxe-Meiningen and whose methods so deeply impressed contemporary theatre workers, but his tentative efforts were in the same direction as theirs. In its tours during the seventies and eighties this company revealed in final form what the stage had been groping towards during the immediately preceding decades. The director became all-important, and every effort was made to secure unity of impression, whether in the presentation of Shakespeare's plays in revival or in the production of the new realistic drama.

THE REALISM OF HEBBEL AND THE NATURALISM OF ZOLA

Germany had something else to offer to realism in the theatre.

This was a period when Prussia under the Hohenzollerns was forging an unwieldy collection of dukedoms and principalities into a coherent whole; and with startling rapidity the Reich thus created swelled to giant proportions, stepped beyond its boundaries, and shattered the proud power of France. Perhaps most effort during these decades was devoted to the building of material strength and to the provision of a philosophy, mystical in its quality, likely to serve as a kind of national religion, but the theatre too played its part in the development of nationalism.

Its greatest and most characteristic growth was that of the Wagnerian opera.

At the same time the surge of national enthusiasm could not entirely conceal the concurrent development of social thought, and in Friedrich Hebbel the stage found an author of more than common vision and depth of purpose. A tortured soul inclined by nature and circumstance towards introspection, he succeeded in accomplishing something much more profound than anything achieved either by Augier or by Dumas *fils*. In his earliest drama, *Judith* (1841), the potentialities rather than the actualities of power were displayed: although this rather chaotic, artificially constructed, and bombastically executed tragedy has won some considerable applause from his countrymen, we must deem it nothing save the immature promise of Hebbel's genius. His second important work, however, fully revealed his strength. *Maria Magdalena* (1844), despite its title, was no tragedy based on a Biblical theme. The scene is set in a German joiner's house. This joiner, Anthony, a hard and rigorous although well-meaning man, has a daughter, Clara, and a son, Karl. With grim realism Hebbel traces their fortunes until the girl is forced to cast herself into a well. The end of the play is typical of its general mood. A secretary, in love with Clara, has just come in wounded after fighting a duel with her seducer: Karl has rushed out after a rumour that a woman has killed herself:

KARL [*comes back*]: Clara's dead. Her head's all broken in by the edge of the well, when she—— Father, she didn't fall in, she jumped in. A girl saw her.

ANTHONY: Let her think well before she speaks. It is too dark for her to have seen that for certain.

SECRETARY: Do you doubt it? You'd like to, but you can't. Just think of what you said to her. You sent her out on the road to death, and I, I'm to blame that she didn't turn back. When you suspected her misfortune, you thought of the tongues that would hiss at it, but not of the worthlessness of the snakes that own them. You said things to her that drove her to despair. And I, instead of folding her in my arms, when she opened her heart to me in nameless terror, thought of the knave that might mock at me, and—I made myself dependent on a man who was worse than I, and I'm paying for it with my life. And you, too, though you stand there like a rock, you too will say some day: "Daughter, I wish you had not spared me the head-shakes and shoulder-shruggings of the Pharisees: it humiliates me more that you are not here to sit by my deathbed and wipe the sweat of anguish from my brow."

ANTHONY: She has spared me nothing. They saw her.

SECRETARY: She did what she could. You were not worthy that she should succeed.

ANTHONY: Or she, perhaps! [*Noises without.*

KARL: They're bringing her. [*Going.*

ANTHONY [*standing immovable till the end, calls him back*]: Into the back room with her, where her mother lay.

SECRETARY: I must go to meet her. [*Tries to get up and falls.*] Oh, Karl! [KARL *helps him out.*

ANTHONY: I don't understand the world any more. [*Stands thinking.*

All the ingredients of the later naturalistic play are here—the drab, lower middle-class atmosphere, the sensationalism, the tendency towards moralization, the conflict of man and society.

In one sense this drama is unique among Hebbel's works, since all his other plays have historical or legendary themes, but in this mingling of the contemporary with the mythical he proved himself a companion of the later Ibsen and Strindberg. He proved their companion, too, in striving to attain a philosophy of the theatre in its relation to social life. In his critical pronouncements he develops, albeit in a strangely crabbed Germanic style, the concept of a new kind of tragedy—the tragedy, not of the individual (conflicting with forces outside himself or within his own being), but of society. Despite all the verbiage with which he invests this idea, it is obvious that basically it is both pessimistic and authoritarian. In *Agnes Bernauer* (1855), for example, he shows his fifteenth-century hero, Albrecht, Prince of Bavaria, resolutely sacrificing his love for the heroine, the barber's daughter who is nicknamed "the angel of Augsburg," in the stern interests of the state which he is destined to rule. For Hebbel the ultimate Universal is human society, and tragedy is developed when a man or a woman attempts to set his or her individual will against the basic Idea. Yet the concepts of this individual, paradoxically, may be those which the Universal, at a later date, will embrace within its own being. *Agnes Bernauer* thus, in the words of the author,

> simply represents the relation of the individual to society, and accordingly illustrates in two characters, one of the highest, the other of the lowest class, the fact that the individual, however splendid and great, however noble and fair, must under all circumstances yield to society. For in society and its necessary formal expression, the state, humanity lives as a whole, while in the individual only one single phase of it is unfolded.

Irony lies in the fact that, to quote this author again, "all tragedy lies in destruction and proves nothing but the emptiness of existence."

The distinctive quality of Hebbel's historical dramas lies in their expression of this philosophy and in their distinctively 'modern' development of motivation. If they were stripped of their decorative costumes the characters might stand forth as persons of the dramatist's own time. In *Judith* there is a probing of the heroine's soul; in *Genoveva* (1843) is an examination of the fate of a woman falsely accused of unfaithfulness; in *Herodes und Mariamne* (*Herod and Mariamne*, 1850) is an exploration of religious sentiment. Later came *Gyges und sein Ring* (*Gyges and his Ring*, 1855), in which a Greek atmosphere is transformed into German. The story of Kandaules, King of Lydia, who causes Rhodope, his queen, to appear disrobed, with the consequent vengeance taken by the injured woman, is here (somewhat absurdly) invested with would-be philosophical significance. A final proof at once of Hebbel's intimate association with his own time and of his power of anticipating things to come may be found in his trilogy entitled *Die Nibelungen* (1862), professedly designed to draw the "great national epic dramatically nearer to the public"—a romantic monument as florid and pretentious as Wagner's. Including an introductory act,

Der gehörnte Siegfried (*The Horned Siegfried*), and two complete dramas, *Siegfrieds Tod* (*Siegfried's Death*) and *Kriemhilds Rache* (*Kriemhild's Vengeance*), it forms a vast, lumbering, effusive, two-day production.

What Hebbel lacked was a sense of form. Like Kleist and others, his language tends to be tormented—a chaotic flow illuminated at times by lurid flashes of mighty splendour. Like Wagner, his soul was essentially middle-class. At the same time hardly any other dramatic author of his own time can be accounted his equal. We may detest his philosophy, deplore his cloudy rhetoric, smile at some of his tragic tensions, but we cannot deny his genius.

During these same years another kindred German author was striving to develop a new modern tragic expression. Otto Ludwig shared Hebbel's tendency towards theorizing and his associations with Kleist and the earlier 'Sturm und Drang.' He too feels deeply the fate of the modern artist, denied the free, untrammelled lyricism of the primitive poet and forced to bring intellect into the sphere of the imagination. He too is a soul broken by an inner dichotomy. His interests are almost equally divided between the romantic and the materialistic, and in his critical discussion of the latter he tends to give away the basic secret of much failure in the realistic theatre. "It is no little thing," he pompously remarks, "to keep your eye on eight characters all at the same time." The statement is no doubt true, but the fact, of course, is that the truly great dramatist does not 'keep his eye' on his characters: by a strange imaginative magic he *becomes* those characters: he is the god who has created them and in whom mystically he has his being. In their concentration upon philosophies the realistic playwrights have constanlty tended to abrogate their divinity and become spectators of the events they describe—or else they have sought, Byron-wise, to make all their dramatic characters mere replicas of parts of themselves.

Ludwig's concrete contributions to the theatre are *Die Makkabäer* (*The Maccabees*, 1854) and *Der Erbförster* (*The Forester*, 1850), but only the latter has any real significance. This grim tale of crime and passion, in which an old hereditary forester, his mind filled with exaggerated ideas of his own rights, clashes fatally with his choleric master, with its technique confessedly based on the author's own intimate analysis of Shakespeare's methods, undoubtedly established one more trenchant model for the realistic dramatists to come. Such a work, when taken with Hebbel's *Maria Magdalena*, at once reveals to us what qualities the new realists desired to substitute for the artificialities of the Scribe pattern. No doubt neither achieved more than a partial success, but they both point the way unerringly to Ibsen.

Although the dramatic work of Émile Zola takes us into the seventies of the century, it may be well to consider his naturalistic aims along with these German efforts. In himself Zola is not important as a playwright, but he has tremendous importance on account of the æsthetic philosophy which he tried to establish on the stage. Fundamentally, what he sought was the extreme of objectivity, applied—characteristically enough—only to the gloomiest spheres of human life. In the realm of prose fiction, of course, rests his greatest fame, but of hardly less significance is his contribution to the theatre. *Thérèse Raquin* (1873) inaugurated a style utterly different from anything attempted by Augier, Dumas *fils*, and their companions. The plot is not particularly remarkable—a story of a woman, Thérèse, and her lover, Laurent, who decide to murder her husband, accomplish their crime, and find that they are driven by force of conscience to end their own lives in a suicide pact. It is the way in which this gloomy tale is presented that grants the play its peculiar significance. What Zola wanted was a type of drama which should, without twisting facts in order to prove a thesis, be absolutely true to existence. Where Augier had tried to be realistic Zola endeavoured to be naturalistic. The 'drama of ideas,' the *pièce à thèse*, tacitly assumes that the author devises a plot in such a way as to prove his argument: such an author may present a setting true to the actual in every respect, he may adopt a kind of dialogue faithful to the terms of contemporary speech, but his basic purpose implies that he must so order his material as to accord with his preconceived idea. Zola wanted complete objectivity, the depiction of the real with almost photographic exactitude. He sees his characters as case-studies; he wishes the drama to submit to follow the methods of science by studying men dispassionately. He attacks the old romantic theatre, but at the same time has no desire to revive the classic. "There should no longer be any school," he cries, "no more formulas, no standards of any sort: there is only life itself, an immense field where each may study and create as he likes." The recipe for the well-made play he rejects: "Naturalism is already stammering its first accents on the stage. . . . The drama will either die, or become modern and realistic. . . ." In writing *Thérèse Raquin* he attempts so to present his characters against the background of their environment as to make them "not *play*, but rather *live*, before the audience."

THE REALISM OF OSTROVSKI AND TURGENEV

Both Hebbel and Zola, each in his own way, exercised a wide influence on the drama of Western Europe. A third force, working during the same years, was destined for long to remain unknown save in the land of its birth. Hebbel's was German realism, Zola's was French: meanwhile, in Russia, further advances were being made towards the creation of the style that culminated in Chekhov. Moscow had its writers such as Alexei Feofilaktovich Pisemski, author of the Tolstoi-like and powerful *Gorkaia sudbina* (*Bitter Destiny*, 1859)—in which a peasant murders the child born of his wife to a libidinous landowner—who were influenced deeply by current theatrical developments abroad and who sought to construct their dramas according to the recipes popular in Paris or Berlin; but far more important is the gradual evolution of the characteristic methods adumbrated by Gogol and Griboedov. In this field two men, writing during the middle years of the century, are of supreme significance.

The work of Alexander Nikolaevich Ostrovski is not well known outside his own country, yet he is unquestionably one of the most important and interesting dramatists of his epoch: without Ostrovski, Chekhov the dramatist might not have been. His first claim to attention is the fact that he was the first Russian author to apply himself exclusively to a professional stage career. Gogol and Griboedov had entered the theatre lightly, airily; Ostrovski made of playwriting his entire life's work. In himself he thus symbolized the Russian theatre's coming of age. This, of course, merely gives him historical significance; intrinsic significance is provided by the quality of his writings. Intensely Slav in sentiment, he seized upon and developed the native realistic style cultivated by his predecessors. Instead of concentrating upon plot, he followed them in exploring character; instead of stressing ideas and problems, he set out to depict the life around him, satirically yet with infinite sympathy. Characteristic of all this school of writing is the peculiar orientation of the poet-creator to the objects of his creation. From one point of view we might be tempted to regard Ostrovski's plays as based on the 'slice-of-life' pattern. Their lack of exact structure and the tendency to prefer a series of loosely related scenes to the logical exposition of a theme would seem to give justification for such a point of view. No less than three of his dramas, instead of being called comedies or dramas, are described as "Scenes" or "Sketches" of Moscow or village life—*Prazdnichnii son—do obieda*

THE ROYALTY THEATRE, LONDON, IN THE YEAR 1787: INTERIOR

THE ROYALTY THEATRE, LONDON, IN THE YEAR 1787: AUDITORIUM

(a) MISS YOUNGE AS ETHELINDA   (b) MISS YOUNGE AS MEROPE
(c) MRS YATES AS JANE SHORE   (d) MRS MELMOTH AS QUEEN
ELIZABETH

(*A Holiday Dream—before Dinner*, 1857), *Vospitannitsa* (*The Ward*, 1859) and *Ne vse kotu maslianitsa* (*After the Dinner comes the Reckoning*, 1871). Looking at these, we might indeed be tempted to suppose that Zola's naturalism was here being put into practice. Such a conception, however, would be false: the looseness of structure is apparent merely, and on examination proves itself, like the structure of Chekhov's plays, to be carefully designed. Carefully designed, too, is that quality which so often has puzzled Western critics of this Russian realistic theatre—its seeming uncertainty of mood. Very often we do not know whether to laugh or to cry, whether to praise or to condemn: a character whom we feel to be despicable may suddenly assume admirable virtues; the coarse merchants whom Ostrovski so frequently flays may, in some scenes, be put forward as heroes. The explanation, of course, is that this author, like his companions, is composing his work under the impulse of a peculiar kind of humour: he is satiric, certainly, yet for the things satirized there is in his heart infinite compassion. This is the realm of the so-called *bytovaia komedia*—an almost untranslatable term signifying a play which depicts a way of life—the dramatic expression of the Russian literary movement to which was given the title *Byt*.

With the exception of *Snegurochka* (*The Snow Maiden*, 1873) and his unimportant historical dramas, all Ostrovski's plays are realistic, and, with the exception of *Groza* (*The Thunderstorm*, 1860), *Grekh da beda na kovo ne zhivet* (*Sin and Sorrow are Common to All*, 1863), and *The Ward*, they are comedies in the sense that they end happily, even though their happiness be bitter. Although among the exceptions stands his best-known play, *The Thunderstorm*, his genius was not well adapted to deal with potentially tragic material. *Sin and Sorrow*, which tells the story of Krasnov, a shopkeeper, married to Tatiana Danilovna, who starts an *affaire* with a young landowner, has little incisiveness of purpose, and the stabbing of the wife by her husband seems to have no inevitability. Infinitely superior is *The Thunderstorm*, yet even it leaves us unsatisfied. Here a similar plot is used. A young wife, Katia, finds herself neglected by her husband and gives way to a handsome lover. In the end the lover abandons her, and, terrified of the husband's wrath, she commits suicide. Death is avoided in *The Ward*, but the atmosphere is no less dark; the last words are spoken by a maidservant who has been a spectator of all the events—"What's fun for the cat is sorrow for the mouse." The ward is Nadia, and basically the entire action which leads towards her betrothal to a man she detests is designed

R

to reveal the evil unconsciously perpetrated by the rich, domineering, self-righteous old dowager, the lady Ulanbekov.

Bespridannitsa (The Poor Bride, 1879) may be taken as transitional between these and the comedies. To a certain extent the plot is tragic in that a girl without a dowry is forced into a loveless marriage, yet the fact that she takes a joy in sacrificing herself, together with the exceedingly vivid manner in which the dramatist deals with the preparations for the wedding, gives the play an atmosphere different from that of *Sin and Sorrow.* Another transitional work is *Bednost ne porok (Poverty is no Crime,* 1854), distinguished by the character of Liubim Karpich Tortsov, a sad rogue and a drunkard, albeit lovable, who reveals the pettiness and meanness of his merchant-brother's household and who serves as *deus ex machina* in joining the hands of Liubov and the poor, honest clerk Mitia.

This type of character was a favourite one on the Russian stage, largely because it enabled a contrast to be made with the dull, convention-ridden life of the middle class. Not dissimilar is the Neschastlivtsev of *Les (The Forest,* 1871), an actor who, though not as successful on the stage as he had hoped, prefers his way of life to that of his bourgeois relations. The rogue, however, is not always presented in such pleasing form as he assumes in the person of Liubim Tortsov. Among Ostrovski's most successful comedies is his very first, *Svoi liudi—sochtemsia* (1850; with an almost untranslatable title: *It's a Family Affair—We'll settle it Ourselves* is literal, but loses idiomatic significance; perhaps *Birds of a Feather* would best express the theme). In effect, this play is a kind of middle-class Russian *Volpone.* In order to enrich himself a merchant, Bolshov, arranges with a rascally attorney, Rispolozhenski, to fake a bankruptcy: since he has long had loyal service from his clerk, Podkhaliuzin, he decides to pretend to make over certain of his property to him. Podkhaliuzin, however, at once sees and seizes his opportunity, holds on to the assets and finds in Olimpiada, Bolshov's daughter, a kindred spirit. The cold-blooded pair marry, and the wretched Bolshov, all his schemes awry, is hoist with his own petard. Typical of the style are the daughter's long opening soliloquy as she reviews in memory the season's dances, and the final words spoken by Podkhaliuzin. The latter has just indulged in his final trick, bilking the dishonest lawyer, who departs muttering enraged curses and accusing his tormentor of many crimes. Thereupon the hero turns to the audience. "Don't you believe him," Podkhaliuzin says,

I mean him who was talking, gentlemen—that's all lies. He's just inventing. Perhaps he only dreamt it. The wife and I, gentlemen, intend to open a little shop: do please favour us with your patronage. If you send your little son to us for an apple, you may be sure he shan't be given a rotten one.

Here the villain-rogue triumphs, although in another kindred work, *Na vsiakovo mudretsa dovolno prostoti* (*Enough Silliness in Every Wise Man*, or, *The Diary of a Scoundrel*, 1868), the trickster is outwitted by forces more honest than his own. A comparison of the two plays shows how difficult it is to pin down Ostrovski to any particular moral code: unlike the French dramatists of the ideological school, he is elusive as life itself.

The comedies mentioned above are thoroughly characteristic of Ostrovski's work as a whole, and perhaps are the best of his writings. In the others the picture of Russian life—sometimes realistically displayed, sometimes coloured with the garish tints of caricature— is expanded along similar lines. *Dokhodnoe mesto* (*A Lucrative Job*, 1856) reveals the weakness of the Civil Servants; *Beshenie dengi* (*Rabid Money*, 1870) deals with those financial questions which so worried all authors in this age: in one play after another Ostrovski essayed to reveal some fresh aspect of Moscow society. In all he showed himself a master in portraiture—one who perhaps hardly possessed Chekhov's power of universalizing the particular, yet nevertheless a dramatic artist whose worth has not been sufficiently realized outside his own land.

As a companion he had another author who, despite the fact that his best work was accomplished in the realm of prose fiction, materially contributed to the development of the Russian drama. Where Ostrovski concentrated his attention mostly on representatives of social classes, Ivan Sergevich Turgenev dealt mainly with the intricacies of the heart. It is true that *Provintsialka* (*A Provincial Lady*, 1851) charmingly makes use of such material as that on which Ostrovski drew for his plots, but the orientation is different. Here Daria Ivanovna, wife of a provincial Civil Servant, is a true creation. We learn that she had been, like Ostrovski's heroine in *The Ward*, a protégée of a rich woman, who had married her off at an early age to the rather stupid, hard-working Stupendev. In her little home she dreams of the joys of life in the great house where she had spent her girlhood, and when she learns that her patroness's son, Count Liubin—now an elderly dandy, but with whom she once had had a flirtation—has arrived in town she eagerly entices him into her net. Turgenev's genius is shown in the masterly comic manner by which he leaves us guessing whether her affections are really aroused or whether all of her sly advances have been made in a spirit of fun. That she wants the Count to obtain a Moscow post for her husband is certain, but how far she is attracted towards the dandy we cannot tell. It is a comedy she is playing, and playing well, as the Count realizes. When he compliments her on her skill her reply is ambiguous: "Count, you know one can only play a comedy well when one feels one's part. . . ."

Not always was Turgenev so gay. In the plays that he wrote during his 'dramatic' years, mostly between 1847 and 1850, the mood varies from laughter to tears. There is a seriousness of purpose in *Razgovor na bolshoi doroge* (*A Conversation on the Highway*), which contrasts an impecunious aristocrat and an honest old servant, while *Mesiats v derevne* (*A Month in the Country*) ends in darkness. This undoubtedly is the greatest of his plays, and at once demonstrates how much Chekhov owed to his predecessors. In dramatic technique and in atmosphere alike the Chekhovian manner is amply apparent. The plot is complex, yet lacking entirely the tight intrigue of Scribe: the characters are revealed, not directly but by implication. In the centre of the picture stands Natalia Petrovna, the twenty-nine-year-old wife of a wealthy landowner, Islaev. She does not really love her husband, nor does her love of Rakitin, her husband's friend, go beyond mild affection and a sense of comfort derived from his constant and unselfish devotion. Trouble enters her life when a young student, Beliaev, is engaged as tutor for her boy Kolia, and when her seventeen-year-old ward, Vera, falls in love with him. Subtly Turgenev shows his heroine inflamed by a passion which her reason tells her is absurd, but which she cannot control.

Had this play been written by a contemporary French playwright it would have been made into a drama of the grand passion or else presented as a social problem; certainly the young man with whom the heroine falls in love would have been made into a hero. In Turgenev's hands the tutor Beliaev is pictured as a most ordinary fellow, himself callow and uninterested in either Natalia or Vera. The result is that opportunity is given for developing psychological studies of the two women: Natalia so loses herself in her frenzied passion that she is even prepared to marry off Vera to an elderly and stupid neighbour; from being an innocent child Vera develops before our eyes into a woman.

In a French play too all the 'intrigue' would have been concentrated and made economic with respect to means: Turgenev not only introduces numerous scenes of no importance for the development of the plot, but brings in lengthy speeches utterly unrelated, except by emotional implication, to the main story. Typical is the opening of the play, with four characters playing at cards, while Rakitin sits reading *The Count of Monte Cristo* to Natalia. The conversation ebbs and flows fitfully, providing atmosphere merely. This is followed by the equally characteristic long narrative of the doctor, Shpigelski, apparently entirely unconnected with the theme of the drama and yet later aiding us in the building-up of a total imaginative impression.

A kindred spirit prevails in *Nakhlebnik* (*A Poor Gentleman*). The plot here is of the simplest. A newly married couple, Pavel Niko-laevich Eletski and Olga Petrovna, come to the bride's estate. In the evening the husband and some of his friends, for their amuse-ment, cause a poverty-stricken old man, Kuzovkin, to become drunk. Becoming conscious of their taunts, he suddenly declares that he is in fact Olga's father. It is not, however, the plot that really matters: what Turgenev is interested in are his characters, and particularly he is concerned with the relationships of these characters—the wretched, broken-down Kuzovkin; the steel-like Eletski; the sympathetic Olga; Tropachov, the boorish land-owner; Karpachov, his toady; even the self-effacing and timorous Ivanov, Kuzovkin's friend. The social *milieu* plays its part; but it is what men are and what they may become, it is the contrast between what man dreams of being and what he actually is, that interests Turgenev. When the author devotes so much space to recounting Kuzovkin's dreams of recovering his lost estate he is not wasting time, for herein lies the symbolic core of his play; and typical Russian irony results when the dream is made true, not in the way which Kuzovkin had imagined, but through the fact that his drunken indiscretion forces him to leave the Eletski household—and, inciden-tally, the daughter whom he loves.

Like Ostrovski, Turgenev played infinite variations on this theme. In *Bezdenezhe* (*Insolvency*) the young Zhazikov plans, in imagina-tion, a new livery for his servant Matvei, even while he is forced to keep in hiding from his creditors. Another aspect of the same con-trast between the dream and the reality appears in *Gde tanko, tam i rvetsa* (*It breaks where it's Thin*), which shows the ineffective Gorski losing the girl of his heart because he cannot summon up sufficient resolution to win her hand. Often the contrast leads to a half-resignedly sad, half-happy conclusion, as in *Kholostiak* (*The Bachelor*), where a self-seeking young Petrusha becomes the fiancé of Maria, a ward of Moskin's. When, however, an acquaintance complains she is not sufficiently cultured he throws her over, and we are left to understand that she will marry her guardian. The contrast here is between kind-heartedness and self-interest, between passion and sentiment, between dreams of ecstatic devotion and homely affection.

In these plays Ostrovski and Turgenev, building on the foundations set by Gogol and Griboedov, wrought an entirely new kind of comedy. Hebbel's is the realism born of Byronic romanticism: it is bold and blatant. Zola's realism is that which strives to depict a section of life photographically, and, since so many photographs are of the Christmas-card variety, the French naturalist tries to select the darker, cruder scenes of life on which to turn his lens. In the Russian plays we seek in vain either for the boldness of the German or for the external faithfulness of the French; rather do we move within the characters and their environment, exploring spiritual spheres no camera can reach, spheres which boldness of utterance cannot hope to reveal. The result is that even while Ostrovski and Turgenev are realists, their realism induces a kind of poetic mood: the delicate balancing of implications is almost like the poet's balancing of images. We are in the presence of life here, but it is as though, instead of watching the events through a non-existent fourth wall, we were paradoxically at once outside and inside the scenes, watching the characters as they move about and at the same time entering into them. Zola's drama, and Hebbel's too, is the drama of the spectator; Ostrovski's and Turgenev's is the drama of the spectator-participant.

PART IX

REALISM'S TRIUMPH

REALISM'S TRIUMPH

BY THE year 1870 sufficient experiments had been conducted in the realistic style to provide a firm foundation for the work of a culminating master. So far no unquestioned genius in this style had appeared; so far no attempt had been made to select from the diverse forms assumed by the new drama and to establish one single form exactly suited to the requirements of the age. The time for the appearance of such a genius, however, and for such a task of selection was now ripe.

Hebbel had contributed a crude strength; Augier and Dumas *fils* had shown how ideas could effectively be realized; Zola had presented a new naturalistic pattern; while Scribe and Sardou, despised though they might be by the superior spirits in the theatre, had taught men how the common speech of men and the ordinary events of their lives might be given appealing shape in the playhouse.

At the same time two developments were contributing materially towards the culmination of the new style. In France various critics had discussed the qualities to be desired in realistic plays, while in Germany one theorist, Hermann Hettner, a friend of Hebbel's, had produced a slim volume, entitled *Das moderne Drama* (1850), which was destined to prove of considerable importance in furthering the interests of its subject. Fundamentally Hettner's thesis is that Hebbel was pointing the way towards a great dramatic revival, but that he had failed to oring his achievement to the height of his aims; that in the struggles within the social fabric lay the materials for a new form of tragedy; and that in the development of this new form playwrights must strive at once to concentrate on psychological truth and on a deep understanding of social forces. Ibsen himself has left on record a testimony to the impress made upon his mind by this critical essay: it opened up for him fresh avenues of thought and stirred him to new effort.

The social forces on which Hettner laid such stress were, of course, the preponderating power in this age, largely because of the rapid development of scientific activities both pure and applied. The impact of a machine civilization on human beings tended to put man at the mercy of forces beyond his own individual strength, while scientific thought led towards the belief that the human being, so far from having mastery of his fate, is a creature of circumstance, conditioned by his environment, and hence not even possessing a native personality of his own. With the sweeping away of religious and moral concepts came a conviction on the part of many writers that all they could do was to observe life, depicting the miserable sorrows of reality; while other authors saw drama and literature generally, not as the instrument of expressing eternal values (for these were assumed not to be more than figments), but as an instrument designed to ameliorate the conditions of life.

The second development was that of the theatre itself. During these latter years of the century the stage was acquiring equipment by which it could present much more realistic settings than anything achieved in the past. The gas lighting that had been introduced about 1820 remained for many years a crude device, but within the years 1870–1900 the addition of many improvements (such as the new lime-light), together with superior methods of control, rendered it an instrument capable of producing most of the effects desired by the directors. And towards the very end of the period electricity came, gropingly at first, to supplant the earlier source of illumination and to offer still greater flexibility of control. Gradually too the traditional use of wings and back-cloths was giving way to the execution of box-sets for interiors and of built-up sets for exterior scenes. With the disappearance of the repertory system in many theatres, obviously greater care could be given to the scenic backgrounds than was usual, or feasible, in days when the bill was changed nightly. When Charles Kean, during the fifties, devoted anxious labour, first, to research into the historically correct dress and surroundings of Shakespeare's plays and, next, to endeavours to reproduce in realistic form the results of his research, he was pointing the way forward with unerring finger.

Even when the repertory system was abandoned, however, the new desires of the directors and of the scenic artists demanded changes in theatrical equipment. It is during these years that machinery enters the stage. In New York that inventive genius Steele MacKaye opened the Madison Square Theatre (1881) and displayed to wondering audiences a double elevator stage by means of which entire sets, with their actors ready placed, could be raised or lowered into position. Shortly before, in 1880, the Opera House at Budapest was equipped with a sectional stage and hydraulic elevators. At the Staatstheater in Munich and the Opera House at Dresden Adolf Linnebach was soon to be engaged in perfecting mechanical devices suggested by these and other efforts as well as in inventing new devices of his own. Thus was the machine age adapting itself to stage requirements: the fresh means were all ready to produce spectacularism or realism, whichever might at the moment be demanded.

One further innovation at this time is worthy of particular note. Realism was obviously desired by the public, and in all countries its sombre joys were exploited. At the same time, in most centres of theatrical activity the enthusiasts forged sadly ahead of the great mass of their contemporaries, so that by the nineties there existed a very considerable gap between what ordinary spectators were prepared to accept and what the more ardent spirits wished to impose upon the stage. The result was the introduction into the theatrical realm of an entirely novel element—the growth of the 'independent' theatre. In 1889, largely owing to the inspiration of Otto Brahm, the Freie Bühne was opened in Berlin, and throughout its career specialized in the presentation of realistic plays too extreme for public representation. Two years earlier a young French devotee of naturalism, André Antoine, succeeded, by the sheer drive from within him, in opening the Théâtre Libre in Paris. This lasted from 1887 to 1894: when it closed much of the enthusiasm that had inspired its efforts was transferred to the Théâtre de l'Œuvre, opened by Alexandre Lugné-Poë in 1893. Again under the inspiration of one man—in this instance J. T. Grein—the Independent Theatre Society was established in London in 1891. While it is true that the effect of these efforts was perhaps felt rather through their offshoots in our own century, we must give them all credit for their experimental aims, for the way in which they spread among their members knowledge of what was being accomplished in countries other than their own, and for their encouragement to new playwrights: Strindberg, Hauptmann, Brieux, and Shaw all stand in debt to the 'independents.'

CHAPTER I

THE TRIUMPH OF REALISM: IBSEN

ABOVE all other dramatic authors of this age towers the rocky figure of Henrik Ibsen, one who suddenly brings the hesitant Norwegian theatre to a position rivalling that of other lands with lengthier stage traditions and far richer heritage of accomplishment.

Not only does Ibsen display a greater combination of assured theatrical strength, of penetrating vision, and of determined purpose than any of his companions, he reveals himself as a kind of massive symbol of all that his age sought for and achieved in dramatic form. Within the course of his works we can see, as though in a concentrating mirror, an image of his age's countenance.

THE HISTORICAL PLAYS

When we think of Ibsen now it is usually the author of *Ghosts* who comes to our mind, and we conceive him as a man who wrought a realistic form for himself almost unaided. The first thing we ought to remember is that, as *Dramaturg* and director of the little theatre at Bergen, he had much to do with presenting the plays of Scribe, and that his own primal effort was a romantically conceived *Catilina* (1850). In his apprentice days he was most deeply influenced by the romantic strain of his century, and the first task he set for himself was that of creating a powerful form for historical drama concerned with the traditions of his native Norway. Scribe offered suggestions in so far as technique was concerned; Shakespeare presented visions of greatness; the efforts of the many romantic dramatists from the time of Schiller onward provided immediate inspiration; while the attempts already made by preceding dramatists to put Scandinavian themes on the stage pointed out to him the path he should take.

In 1850 appeared the relatively unimportant *Kjæmpehöjen* (*The Warrior's Barrow*), in which the influence of Oehlenschläger is amply apparent; five years later came the first truly significant piece from his pen, *Fru Inger til Östråt* (*Lady Inger of Östråt*, 1855), where the spirits of Schiller and Scribe vie for pre-eminence. There is strength here, and a sense of character in the depiction of an ambitious woman who succeeds by her machinations only in ruining her son. Individual scenes display unquestioned skill in the composition, although the play's plan as a whole indicates that as yet the young Ibsen had not gained mastery. When the Stranger is suddenly introduced at the close of Act I and Lady Inger faints we can realize how thrillingly effective the apprentice dramatist must have imagined this 'curtain' to be; yet it is equally obvious how ill-adapted the device is to stage requirements. What Ibsen has forgotten is that an audience must know the circumstances of an action before it can be moved; he has yet to learn to put himself out of his study into the auditorium.

Lady Inger of Östråt ushered in a long line of dramas on Scandinavian themes, each succeeding play demonstrating the author's advance in theatrical craftsmanship and in grasp of character. *Gildet paa Solhaug* (*The Feast at Solhaug*, 1856) and *Olaf Liljekrans* (1857) are not of any importance, but *Hærmændene paa Helgeland* (*The Vikings at Helgeland*, 1858) and *Kongsemnerne* (*The Pretenders*, 1864), although neither proved an immediate success, fully demonstrated his growing power. Based on the same sagas as were to animate the soul of Wagner, the former deals mainly with Sigurd the Strong and his beloved Hiördis, foster-daughter of Örnulf of the fiords, and the attempt is made, albeit with not a trifle of romantic sentimentalizing, to reproduce in modern form the atmosphere of the world of ancient myth. In *The Pretenders* the tale is told of two contrasting men—Håkon, sure of himself and with an objective in whose rightness he has not a shred of doubt, and Skule, his mind filled with visions, but timorous and hesitant. Although in the latter is a god-given strength lacking in the former, it is Håkon who becomes King and ruler of a united Norway. Both plays have vital plots, but clearly *The Pretenders* is a much greater drama than its predecessor, precisely because in it Ibsen has concentrated on the inner beings of his characters.

EARLY SYMBOLISM

In these plays is evident, besides the increasing psychological power, an increasing sense of purpose: to a certain extent *The Pretenders* may be regarded as a symbolic tragedy. This symbolic purpose is even more deeply marked in other works written about this time—diverse in nature yet all contributing towards the deeper harmonies of Ibsen's composition. In *Kjærlighedens komedie* (*Love's*

Comedy, 1862) the symbolic is carried close to the author's own time. An essay on sex relations, it preaches a gospel alien to that of conventional society: "If you want to marry," says Ibsen, "don't be in love; if you love, part." This thesis is presented by means of a series of couples, each, as it were, in gradation. First comes the clergyman Straamand and his wife, in both of whom domesticity has destroyed all vision; next are Styver, the law-clerk, a visionless creature, and Fröken Skjaere; following them are Lind, a divinity student who dreams of being a missionary, and his Anna: and finally there are the poet Falk and Svanhild. Through these pairs Ibsen endeavours to show that inevitably marriage brings with it a dulling of aspiration and a supine acceptance of conventional codes. For such as Styver and Fröken Skjaere there may be no loss in this, but in marrying Anna, Lind is sacrificing his missionary dream, while for the lyrical Falk marriage would be the death of his poetic power and his revolutionary ardour. Ironically, the truth is shown to this poet by the merchant Guldstad, and, true to her romantic name, Svanhild gives him up at the end of the play: the stage is left peopled by the Straamands and their numerous progeny, while Falk's voice is heard in poetic triumph as he tramps off for a life of adventure with a group of gay, ardent youths.

Although *Love's Comedy* seems to occupy a peculiar place among Ibsen's works, it is a play the understanding of which is necessary for an understanding of the dramatist's entire development and outlook upon the world. Ibsen was by way of being a prophet, and this bitter comedy is an expression of his faith, a challenge cast down to the Philistine, a declaration of his intention to keep unsullied and unimpaired the visions and the dreams that were in him. Clearly it links up with his next three dramas—*Brand* (1866), *Peer Gynt* (1867), and the last of his historical works, *Kejser og Galilæer* (*Emperor and Galilean*, 1873).

After having displayed a caricature of a spineless, worldly-minded, hopelessly conventional clergyman in *Love's Comedy*, in *Brand* Ibsen shows his opposite. The hero of this play, young and vigorous in his faith, goes to a small remote town. Determined not to sacrifice by a tittle the integrity of his vision, he proceeds to follow the dictates of his inner voice even although all are against him—the civic officials of the little community, the whole mass of his parishioners, even men who might have been supposed to sympathize with his point of view. The play is a difficult work to understand, for the likelihood is that in it the young author, now coming to his full powers, wrote more and better than he knew. On the surface *Brand* is a violent outburst on the part of an irate individualist against all the pettiness, triviality, and spiritual squalor of his surroundings. It breathes the spirit of Kierkegaard, whose whole philosophy, opposed to the idealistic absolutism of Hegel, laid stress on individuality and on the painful relation of each individual to his god. Brand looks with horror on his mother, who, having made a marriage of convenience, finds her heart dead and her whole being submerged in the world's common greed. Nobly, he dares to face the dangers that others will not face in an endeavour to aid those in distress, but the very intensity of his passion brings sorrow upon himself. By believing that his duty lies in remaining with his people he virtually destroys his own loved child, who, ailing, could have been saved only by being taken southward to a more clement atmosphere. In the end he stands among the mountains virtually alone with the God whom he has so sternly endeavoured to serve, and, as an avalanche is about to descend upon him, he cries out in misery—his very soul overwhelmed with a weight of doubt as his body will be overwhelmed by the snows—asking bitterly whether "the uncompromising assertion of man's will" cannot bring him salvation. From the empyrean above the answer thunders over the roar of the avalanche: "*Deus caritatis.*"

God is love: this pronouncement at the close of the tragedy in itself suggests that, perhaps without being fully conscious of it, Ibsen saw that his Brand was not a wholly worthy figure. "Brand dies a saint," says Bernard Shaw, "having caused more intense suffering by his saintliness than the most talented sinner could possibly have done with twice his opportunities." Even although Ibsen the prophet did often lack the saving grace of humour and often posed in attitudes ridiculous rather than sublime, one can hardly credit that he was so naïve as to take his hero seriously, all on trust. There can be no doubt that Ibsen detested many elements in the bourgeois society surrounding him, that he found himself frequently thwarted by that society, and that he sought to arouse men towards the freer expression of their own beings, but even if we admit so much we cannot avoid seeing in *Brand* something perhaps just a trifle humorous: this clergyman is as much a caricature as the clergyman of *Love's Comedy*.

In *Peer Gynt* symbolism, serious purpose, a sense of tragedy, and a spirit of fun jostle each other through five long, hell-bubbling acts. There is much here that might well have been omitted; there is much here that reminds us of Goethe's rather clumsy attempts at comedy, as though an elephant, clad in canvas frills, were solemnly

trying to emulate on his hard hoofs the graceful pirouettes of a
ballet-dancer; yet, when all has been said, *Peer Gynt* remains one
of the greatest plays produced in the nineteenth century. It is
strange that, despite the facts that when this play was written Ibsen
was nearing his fortieth year and that he was exhibiting a technical
ability of assured competence, here and in *Brand* individual scenes
remind us of the work of an adolescent. The very crudity of the
central ideas in both these dramas suggests youth rather than
maturity, and the 'symbolism,' which elsewhere is subtle and
imaginative, frequently sinks to the juvenile quality of the scene
of the four merchants in *Peer Gynt*. There a Frenchman, a Swede,
a German, and an American stand aghast after having heard Peer
explain that he is supporting the Turks against Greece:

MONSIEUR BALLON: I saw myself a conqueror,
                  by lovely Grecian maids encircled.
TRUMPETER STRÅLE: Grasped in my Swedish hands, I saw
                  the great, heroic spur-strap-buckles!
VON EBERKOPF: I my gigantic Fatherland's
                  culture saw spread o'er earth and sea!
MR COTTON: The worst's the loss in solid cash.
                  God dam! I scarce can keep from weeping!
                  I saw me owner of Olympus.[1]

This is the sort of thing we might have smiled at had we found it in
a play by a youth of twenty: in the composition of a man nearly
twice that age the crudity of the satire seems almost unforgivable.

Yet, when all is said, *Peer Gynt* remains a masterpiece of extravagant fancy. With enormous verve Ibsen traces his hero from his
early days, when he fills his mother's ears with wild tales of impossible adventure and abducts the bride of a neighbour, to the time
when, greyed and failing, he finds his soul being weighed in the
scales of judgment. At the beginning he is a graceless rascal for
whom we cannot but feel a certain amount of sympathy: his very
lies suggest a power of imagination in him, and his escapades, if
reprehensible, have a daring quality. This sympathy accompanies
him when, having made advances to the troll-king's daughter, he
is shown in the hobgoblin Court of that monarch. There then
follow a contest with the great Boyg, a figure of crass vulgarity,
and a sentimental scene in which a girl, Solveig, innocent and truly
loving, comes to share his exile in the mountains. Peer, too, loves
her as he has loved no other woman, but, remembering the stains
that are on his spirit, he deliberately renounces the idyllic delights of

---

[1] The quotations from *Peer Gynt* are from the translation of W. and C. Archer.

life in companionship with her: she is to him fairest, purest gold, and no alloy can be permitted. In the scene of renunciation the best that is in his character becomes revealed. He remembers that the Boyg had monotonously reiterated the advice to "go roundabout":

PEER: The Boyg said, "Go roundabout!"—so one must here.—
There fell my fine palace, with crash and clatter!
There's a wall around her whom I stood so near,
of a sudden all's ugly—my joy has grown old.—
Roundabout, lad! There's no way to be found
right through all this from where you stand to her.
Right through? Hm, surely there should be one.
There's a text on repentance, unless I mistake.
But what? What is it? I haven't the book,
I've forgotten it mostly, and here there is none
that can guide me aright in the pathless wood.—
   Repentance? And maybe 'twould take whole years,
ere I fought my way through. 'Twere a meagre life, that.
To shatter what's radiant, and lovely, and pure,
and clinch it together in fragments and shards?
You can do it with a fiddle, but not with a bell.
Where you'd have the sward green, you must mind not
   to trample.
   'Twas nought but a lie though, that witch-snout
      business!
Now all that foulness is well out of sight.—
Ay, out of sight maybe, not out of mind.
Thoughts will sneak stealthily in at my heel.
Ingrid! And the three, they that danced on the heights!
Will they too want to join us? With vixenish spite
will they claim to be folded, like her, to my breast,
to be tenderly lifted on outstretched arms?
Roundabout, lad; though my arms were as long
as the root of the fir, or the pine-tree's stem,—
I think even then I should hold her too near,
to set her down pure and untarnished again.—
   I must roundabout here, then, as best I may,
and see that it bring me nor gain nor loss.
One must put such things from one, and try to forget.—
      [*Goes a few steps towards the hut, but stops again.*
Go in after this? So befouled and disgraced?
Go in with that troll-rabble after me still?
Speak, yet be silent; confess, yet conceal——?
      [*Throws away his axe.*
It's a holy-day evening. For me to keep tryst,
such as now I am, would be sacrilege.

SOLVEIG [*in the doorway*]: Are you coming?
PEER [*half aloud*]: Roundabout!
SOLVEIG: What?
PEER: You must wait.
        It is dark, and I've got something heavy to fetch.
SOLVEIG: Wait; I will help you; the burden we'll share.
PEER: No, stay where you are! I must bear it alone.
SOLVEIG: But don't go too far, dear!
PEER: Be patient, my girl;
        be my way long or short—you must wait.
SOLVEIG [*nodding to him as he goes*]: Yes, I'll wait!

The final episode in this section of the drama is the magnificently
conceived death-scene of Peer's mother. Miserably he tries to
forget that her poverty has been caused by his extravagance. "Now,
mother," he says,

                    we'll chat together;
               but only of this and that,
            forget what's awry and crooked,
               and all that is sharp and sore.—
            Why see now, the same old pussy;
               So she is alive then, still?

He tells her a tale, quietly but with conviction, and the old woman,
entranced by his eloquence as he sits astride a chair with a string for
reins, imagines herself riding with him far up into the air. The
story becomes more and more vivid, ending with a loud and
triumphant laugh. Peer turns to his mother:

PEER: Ay, didn't I know what would happen?
          Now they dance to another tune!
          [*Uneasily*]
          Why, what makes your eyes so glassy?
          Mother! Have you gone out of your wits——?
                              [*Goes to the head of the bed.*
          You mustn't lie there and stare so——!
            Speak, mother; it's I, your boy!
          [*Feels her forehead and hands cautiously; then throws the string
            on the chair, and says softly.*
          Ay, ay!—You can rest yourself, Granë;
            for even now the journey's done.
                              [*Closes her eyes, and bends over her.*
          For all of your days I thank you,
            for beatings and lullabys!—
          But see, you must thank me back, now—
                              [*Presses his cheek against her mouth.*
          There; that was the driver's fare.

When next we see him Peer is middle-aged, a prosperous merchant who has made himself rich by trading Negro slaves to Carolina and idols to China and who has dreams of becoming the world's emperor. Deserted by his companions, he turns in abject fear to thoughts of the religion he has ever spurned, but these he soon forgets when luck comes his way again. His life is now, however, a constant decline: he is tricked by a Moorish maiden, caged in a Cairo lunatic asylum, nearly drowned as he sails homeward. The final scenes are mainly concerned with the episode of the Button-moulder, an instrument of divine wisdom, who has come to melt his soul down in a ladle. Desperately Peer argues with him:

> PEER: But these, my good man, are most unfair proceedings!
> I'm sure I deserve better treatment than this;—
> I'm not nearly so bad as perhaps you think,—
> I've done a good deal of good in the world;—
> at worst you may call me a sort of a bungler,—
> but certainly not an exceptional sinner.
> THE BUTTON-MOULDER: Why, that is precisely the rub, my man;
> you're no sinner at all in the higher sense;
> that's why you're excused all the torture-pangs,
> and land, like others, in the casting-ladle.

To his horror Peer learns that he is neither an heroic sinner nor a virtuous saint and, being neither one thing nor the other, must lose his identity. "Bless me, my dear Peer," remarks the Button-moulder,

> there is surely no need
> to get so wrought up about trifles like this.
> Yourself you never have been at all;—
> then what does it matter, your dying right out?

Given a little time, Peer searches desperately to prove that he has had a true self, and fails. He even cannot fathom what this really means, and stands somewhat puzzled when the Button-moulder tells him that "to be oneself is—to slay oneself." Only at the end does he come upon Solveig again: he casts himself in repentance at her feet, and is pardoned. To her he propounds his riddle:

> Canst thou tell where Peer Gynt has been
> since we parted?
> SOLVEIG: Been?
> PEER: With his destiny's seal on his brow;
> been, as in God's thought he first sprang forth!
> Canst thou tell me? If not, I must get me home,—
> go down to the mist-shrouded regions.

SOLVEIG [*smiling*]: Oh, that riddle is easy.
PEER: Then tell what thou knowest!
        Where was I, as myself, as the whole man, the true man?
        where was I, with God's sigil upon my brow?
SOLVEIG: In my faith, in my hope, and in my love.

It is common to speak of *Brand* as a drama in which Ibsen puts forward a hero who asserts his individuality even at the expense of others, and of *Peer Gynt* as a companion piece in which "the poverty of spirit and half-heartedness that Ibsen rebelled against in his countrymen" were embodied in the character who gives his name to the play. To a certain extent, but to a certain extent only, this is true: what we should realize, however, is that its imaginative vision goes far beyond such a concept. It is, indeed, impossible in logically framed words to define its precise imaginative scope, and just because it does proceed beyond the intellectually logical it assumes its own peculiar quality of greatness.

Ibsen soon was to turn to the exploitation of realism, but before the coming of *Ghosts* he made one last effort in the historic and poetic style. During a visit to Rome his mind became deeply impressed by the presence there of two distinct civilizations—the ancient pagan grandeur and the later medieval grandeur of the Christian Church. Out of this grew a strange work which, while cast in terms beyond those of the stage, may perhaps be regarded—as he himself regarded it—as the most powerful demonstration of his genius. In *Kejser og Galilæer* (*Emperor and Galilean*, 1873) there is a sweep and a vigour that surpasses anything in his other writings. The drama—divided into two parts—is at once an essay in imaginative philosophy and a lengthy study of character, and, in ways similar to those that make *Peer Gynt* so complex, both are presented with peculiar subtlety. At the beginning we are introduced to the main character, Prince Julian, living during the reign of an Emperor who favours Christianity. He is a handsome, brilliant youth, proud of his skill in debate, in love with life and beauty. At the same time the greatness of his spirit causes him to be dissatisfied with such learning as he has acquired, and anxiously, eagerly, he seeks out teacher after teacher, ever striving to reach the innermost core of thought's mysteries. Eventually he encounters the mystic Maximus, who, calling up spirits from the vasty deep, shows him a vision of the 'Third Empire.' Maximus explains:

                There are three empires.
JULIAN: Three?

MAXIMUS: First that empire which was founded on the Tree of Knowledge; then that which was founded on the Tree of the Cross——
JULIAN: And the third?
MAXIMUS: The third is the empire of the great mystery; that empire which shall be founded on the Tree of Knowledge and the Tree of the Cross together, because it hates and loves them both, and because it has its living sources under Adam's grove and under Golgotha.

When Julian becomes Emperor he endeavours to establish a reign of tolerance, although, in order to make a break with the immediate past, he himself pours libations to the ancient pagan gods. Gradually, however, he is forced into persecutions real and imagined: since most of the Court officers are Galileans of a time-serving and corrupt sort, he dismisses them, and is accused of attacking the Church; while ardent enthusiasts, eager for martyrdom, act in such a way as to call forth sternest measures. In watching Julian's progress throughout the latter part of the drama we see a man in desperation striving to crush a spirit that is unconquerable and eventually destroying himself in the process. Madness descends on him during a disastrous expedition into Persia; the thought of Christ haunts him wherever he goes and intrudes into whatever he does. Tricked by a Persian spy, he gives orders for the imperial fleet to be burned, and, as the flames mount, bursts out exultantly:

Yes, the fleet is burning! And more than the fleet is burning. In that blazing, swirling pyre the crucified Galilean is burning to ashes; and the earthly Emperor is burning with the Galilean. But from the ashes shall arise—like that marvellous bird—the God of earth and the Emperor of the spirit in one, in one, in one!

Darkness descends deeper and deeper on his spirit: the oracles that Maximus consults on his behalf are silent. In the end he is slain by his boyhood friend Agathon, and dies in the knowledge that the Galilean has triumphed, that the vision of sun-bathed loveliness, of pagan joy, has betrayed him. At the same time we are given the sense that in his failure he has been a tool in the hands of a power greater than either Christ or the old pagan deities:

MAXIMUS: Led astray like Cain. Led astray like Judas.—Your God is a spendthrift God, Galileans! He wears out many souls.
    Wast thou not then, this time either, the chosen one—thou victim on the altar of necessity?
    What is it worth to live? All is sport and mockery.—To will is to have to will.
    Oh, my beloved—all signs deceived me, all auguries spoke with a

double tongue, so that I saw in thee the mediator between the two empires.

The third empire shall come! The spirit of man shall re-enter on its heritage—and then shall offerings of atonement be made to thee. . . . [*He goes out.*

BASIL: It dawns on me like a great and radiant light, that here lies a noble, shattered instrument of God.

We may, if we will, ridicule Ibsen's philosophy here; we may even detest it; but we cannot avoid judging *Emperor and Galilean* a worthy peer of *Faust* and *The Dynasts* in its epically dramatic proportions.

THE COMING OF REALISM

Already, before the composition of this historical and symbolic tragedy, Ibsen had shown signs that he was preparing to experiment in a new style. In 1869 came the tempestuous presentation of *De unges forbund* (*The League of Youth*), a highly topical 'comedy' in which the author castigated local politics and, in particular, the liberal party. Even yet Ibsen was the disciple of Scribe, and in the rather mechanical structure of this piece, with its irritating mixture of farce and melodrama, the impress of the 'well-made play' is amply apparent. On the other hand, the realistic dialogue and the portraits of the opportunist Stensgård, of the spirited Selma, and of the pompous Councillor Bratsberg may easily be related to other less mechanically composed dramas to be written shortly afterwards. Once more the comedy scenes seem to be elephantine and the concept diffusely presented, but we may accept the play for what it is worth—an excellent introduction to Ibsen's most characteristic dramatic work.

Eight years later appeared *Samfundets stötter* (*Pillars of Society*, 1877), in which again the influence of Scribe and the satirical presentation of social conventions predominates. Not yet has he succeeded in shedding all his adolescent fancies. Much better constructed than *The League of Youth*, *Pillars of Society* essays to expose small-town morality. One of the pillars is the ultra-respectable, wealthy Consul Bernick, whose wife's brother, Johan, is spoken of in scandalized tones by local gossips because he is supposed to have had an *affaire* with an actress and to have stolen some public money, and whose stepsister, Lona Hessel, is looked upon as an immoral character. Unfortunately for Bernick, Lona and Johan return to their native town from America, and it is revealed, mainly through the persistence of the former, that not Johan but Bernick himself had been the criminal. At the same time this worthy's selfish plan for self-aggrandizement through the building of a railway is exposed, and, touched by conscience, he publicly confesses his errors. The story is told not without sentimentality, and the curtains—like that at the end of Act I ending with Lona's "I will let in fresh air, Pastor" —are frequently designed rather for theatrical effectiveness than for their character values. The satire, also, exhibits often the heavy-handed quality which is so patent in Ibsen's earlier plays—as, for example, when Hilmar utters bold words to the little Olaf as the child is showing him his bow:

HILMAR: Ha—there we have the rising generation nowadays! Goodness knows there's plenty of talk about pluck and daring, but it all ends in play; no one has any real craving for the discipline that lies in looking danger manfully in the face. Don't stand and point at me with your bow, stupid; it might go off.

Ibsen obviously was finding it hard to throw off his youth; perhaps, indeed, he never quite grew up.

The following year, in Rome, he was jotting down notes for a new play, a "modern tragedy":

There are two kinds of spiritual law, two kinds of conscience, one in man and another, altogether different, in woman. . . . The wife in the play ends by having no idea of what is right or wrong: natural feeling on the one hand and belief in authority on the other have altogether bewildered her.

A woman cannot be herself in the society of the present day, which is an exclusively masculine society, with laws framed by men and with a judicial system that judges feminine conduct from a masculine point of view.

She has committed forgery, and she is proud of it; for she did it out of love for her husband, to save his life. But this husband with his commonplace principles of honour is on the side of the law and regards the question with masculine eyes.

Spiritual conflicts. Oppressed and bewildered by the belief in authority, she loses faith in her moral right and ability to bring up her children. . . . Love of life, of home, of husband and children and family. Here and there a womanly shaking-off of her thoughts.

Sudden return of anxiety and terror. She must bear it all alone. The catastrophe approaches, inexorably, inevitably. Despair, conflict and destruction.

Krogstad has acted dishonourably and thereby become well-to-do; now his prosperity does not help him, he cannot recover his honour.

Thus was *Et dukkehjem* (*A Doll's House*, 1879) born, and additional papers from Ibsen's study reveal clearly how it grew. First came a scenario, in which the bare outlines of the plot were presented. Next was a full draft of the play itself, in which mere suggestions in the scenario were brought to life and enriched. From this draft evolved the play as we know it, taut in construction, character-revealing in its subtly framed dialogue. Throughout, the handling of the speech and the planning of the scenes display a masterly hand at work. The story of the play is, of course, too well known to require a précis, but we may pause to consider wherein it soars beyond all previous attempts at the creation of realistic drama. First, there is the skill in the use of words: Ibsen has conquered what, after all, is the basic problem of the realistic playwright—the problem of combining language which shall at once seem natural and be dramatically appropriate. After his long apprentice-ship he has at last succeeded in achieving that inner harmony without which the situations must remain bare or artificial. In addition to this, he has learned how to modify the Scribe formula so as to retain the thrillingly effective and at the same time to hide the presence of the machinery. His curtains, looked at objectively, are of the same kind as those employed in the earlier dramas, but the fact that they are built out of character and imaginatively integrated with the basic situation makes us forget the deliberate craftsmanship determining their being. The third element might be described as Ibsen's thought. In France the playwrights could not get beyond themes of marriage and money conceived in conventional terms: to the question of marriage and money Ibsen gives a startlingly new interpretation. The French plays had rung the changes on the social relations between aristocrats and members of the wealthy bour-geoisie, on love opposed to convenience, on the eternal triangle, and on the problems of illegitimacy. Fresh air blew into this salon and café world when Ibsen took a loving husband as his hero and as his heroine a childish creature, adoring her husband and yet, when her eyes are opened to his character, determining that she must leave his house. This is the old theme of marriage and money certainly, but presented with such a difference as to make it seem absolutely new. *A Doll's House*, because of this novelty of concept, served as a clarion-call to the younger generation of dramatic realists.

If this play was a clarion-call, *Gengangere* (*Ghosts*, 1881) was a long-drawn-out fanfare. Here Ibsen dared to deal with a topic absolutely taboo, and wrought his modern theme to the pattern of a Greek tragedy. In those ancient plays a fatal curse hung inexorably over a house doomed to the third and fourth generation: in adopting this dramatic situation, for his fatal curse Ibsen substitutes an in-

herited venereal disease and peoples his drama with ghosts that are
no less powerful because they are unseen. To a certain extent
Ghosts is now an outmoded drama: it is always the fate of the
innovator to find that the very qualities that caused such a stir
when his works first appeared lose their interest as others exploit
the same or similar themes. Indeed, this drama would have proved
to be no more than an historical curiosity had Ibsen not cast into it
a wealth of character delineation. The portrait of Mrs Alving
combines all the solidity demanded of a strong theatrical rôle with
subtle implications which make her seem a living character. She
is a frigid, conventional woman, whose husband has had *affaires*
with other women: in order to preserve the respectability of her
household she remains with him. Venereal disease contracted by
the father is passed on to his son, Oswald, and as the play ends the
latter is shown rapidly sinking into insanity. It rests a moot point
whether his mother is to give him poison rather than let him suffer
in misery. The very fact that Ibsen himself has left us to guess is
in its own way indicative of the gulf between him and his French
predecessors; whereas they were inclined to tie all their knots tightly
and to leave no untidy ends, Ibsen's dramas, like all great works of
the theatre, permit at least a little room for our imaginative fancies
to play in. Once, when William Archer asked Ibsen whether he
intended Mrs Alving to give her son poison or not, the author
"smiled and said thoughtfully: 'I don't know. Each one must find
that out for himself. I should never dream of deciding so delicate
a question. But what is your opinion?'"

THE INTRUSION OF THE SYMBOLIC

With *Ghosts*, 'Ibsenism' became an affair of battle. Young
enthusiasts in many a land fanatically ranged themselves under the
standard thus set up, while the more conservative employed every
weapon in an endeavour to destroy what they regarded as a godless
and immoral force. In looking back now at records of the strife
we are almost reminded of the bitter and unruly theological bicker-
ings at the time of the Reformation.

Meanwhile Ibsen himself showed that his was a nature not content
to win acclaim among the ranks of ardent youth by continuing to
deal with subjects hitherto denied entry into the playhouse. In his
subsequent career, indeed, he succeeded not a little in dismaying
and perplexing his followers; some were shaken in their beliefs,
and others speculated seriously on the sad falling off of their master's

power. Just for a moment, in fact, it seemed as though his own angry spirit and a revival of that adolescent naïveté which is so marked in some of his earlier dramas were to lead him astray. *En folkefiende* (*An Enemy of the People*, 1882) is a good acting-piece, but it is written too irately to be taken seriously. Attempts have been made to suggest that the author himself saw the fun in this story of a Dr Stockman who makes a vast philosophic issue of the contaminated swimming-baths in a small Norwegian town, but the truth is that here the juvenility of Ibsen's mind was once again dominant—a fact that he himself recognized when, in later age, he described his hero as "*ein grotesker Bursche und ein Strudelkopf*" ("an extravagant immature fellow and a hot-head").

Two years later, however, came *Vildanden* (*The Wild Duck*, 1884), and at once we recognize that Ibsen has won through to an entirely new vision, building a structure finer than anything hitherto achieved in the realistic style. There is no petty anger here; instead, a wealth of sympathy, such as had appeared in no other of his plays, enwraps the characters in its folds. Ordinary men and women are frail and pitiable figures as Ibsen now sees them, and in order that they may live they require to have their dreams: for them a word of truth may be fatal. This theme is revealed through concentration on a single domestic interior—the household of the unsuccessful and well-intentioned, although fundamentally selfish, Hjalmar Ekdal. In poverty the members of this household carry on their lives with a certain measure of happiness, their illusions being symbolized in the strange secret of the attic—where a crippled wild duck is kept by the daughter, Hedwig, and her old grand-father: opening the door to that room, they enter into a world of fond dreams and inhabit for a space the mountains and the moors. Into this circle comes the crass young idealist Gregers Werle, who has been so fed by modern theories as to believe that truth must be served at all costs, and that it is impossible for a man to be himself unless he resolutely refuses to allow untruth to clutter his own life or the lives of others. As a result of this 'idealism,' Werle reveals to Hjalmar that his wife, Gina, had been the mistress of Werle's own father, and that Hedwig is not his child; he further persuades Hedwig that it is her duty to make sacrifice of her precious wild duck, with the consequence that the child, all her illusions broken, kills herself with the pistol Werle has practically thrust into her hands.

In this play of infinite compassion Ibsen reaches a dramatic power beyond anything he had hitherto revealed. The characters have a peculiar depth, and the skill with which the plot is unfolded shows a command of material such as could be matched by no other contemporary author. For the secret of his strength we must look to his infinite patience, his painstaking care, and the refusal to be satisfied with anything less than perfection. "I have just completed a play in five acts," he wrote to a friend in 1884, "that is to say, the rough draft of it; now comes the elaboration, the more energetic individualization of the persons and their modes of expression." What that process of elaboration entailed is made amply apparent by a comparison of the happily preserved first writing of the play and the final version. A single example will serve to illustrate this. In the finished play very considerable dramatic significance attaches to weakness of eyesight: Hedwig is threatened with blindness and her father suffers from failing vision. The device has several values: not only does it possess something of a symbolic nature, it also helps simultaneously to reveal the plot and to expose character. Hedwig's relationship to her father is hinted at before the discovery is actually made, and to that relationship is given at least a suggestion of the heritage theme which dominates in *Ghosts*. In addition Hedwig's plight serves to make her the more appealing, while Hjalmar's selfishness is illuminated by his permitting her to injure her eyes further over retouching work that he himself should have carried out. Looked at from these different angles, the stress on this element is realized to be a key to the understanding of the entire drama—from the old Werle's entry in the first scene "passing his hand over his eyes" and being warned that it is very bad for him to stare at the gaily lighted ballroom, to the remarks, so replete with unconscious irony, that Gregers addresses to Hedwig in the last act:

> Oh, if only your eyes had been opened to that which gives life its value—if you possessed the true, joyous, fearless spirit of sacrifice, you would soon see how he would come up to you.

Yet the fact is that not a word is said about weakness of eyesight in the early version: although *The Wild Duck* seems almost to rest on this foundation, the device—symbolic, plot-aiding, and character-revealing—was an afterthought, the result of the process of "elaboration." Nothing, perhaps, better shows Ibsen's imaginative genius at work.

From *The Wild Duck* it is but a step to *Rosmersholm* (1886), in which the outward semblance is realistic, the inner core spiritually symbolic, and in which Ibsen turned to give his attention to the modern emancipated woman. In *A Doll's House* Nora is just becoming free; Rebecca West has no ties to bind her, no soil into which she may cast down roots. A housekeeper in the family of the liberal Johannes Rosmer, a man of breeding and the owner of Rosmersholm, she has set out to become his second wife and inspirer; to achieve her ends she has so worked upon the mind of Beata, his first wife, as to drive her to suicide. It is at this point that the play starts, and through its four acts we are shown the spectacle of this iron-minded female, goading on Rosmer to glorious battle with the entrenched forces of the conservative clergy, gradually broken down by a force greater than she possesses. The spirit of Rosmersholm enters into her being; in the end she and Rosmer go out hand in hand to meet death in the same place and by the same means as carried off the wretched Beata.

There is a peculiar haunting quality about this drama, and Ibsen's delineation of at least one type of the 'new woman' is subtle. As he advanced in his art he was becoming more and more conscious of emotional values, less and less animated by the rather jejune enthusiasms of his earlier years; and perhaps a grim, slightly cynical smile is touching the lips which before had been set in the hard revolutionist's lines.

Most assuredly that grim smile appears in another 'tragic' drama composed four years later and also presenting a portrait of a self-seeking woman—*Hedda Gabler* (1890). In one sense Hedda is the opposite of Rebecca; for she is a woman of birth who thinks she has married beneath her, not one who aims to rise by her marriage; yet fundamentally they are sisters at heart. With consummate artistry (although not without showing to the critical eye evidence of lessons in craftsmanship learned from Scribe) Ibsen reveals this woman to us in the first act, and draws her inevitably to her end in the succeeding scenes. Married to Tesman, she is possessed of a demonic passion for the young genius Eilert Lövborg, and because of the follies into which this brings her she finds herself in the power of the cynical and libidinous Judge Brack, who, when he hears that she has shot herself, sinks back in his chair, crying, "Heaven help us—people don't *do* such things!" With certain reservations, Brack is right, and his words form a motto to the drama, for this is no high tragedy, as some Ibsen enthusiasts would have us believe. Obviously a sentiment such as Brack expresses could never have found a place at the close of the scene when Œdipus tears out his eyes or of the scene when Hamlet sinks to rest; it is entirely appropriate to *Hedda Gabler* precisely because, instead of aiming at the tragic, Ibsen has written what in effect is a high comedy. If we try to interpret all the talk about "vine-leaves in the hair" seriously we immediately find ourselves straining to give solemn interpretation to things at which the comic muse is gazing quizzically; only by realizing that in penning this case-study of a modern neurotic Ibsen is essaying the path taken centuries before by Jonson in his *Volpone* can we really appreciate this masterpiece aright. Hedda is really not frightening: she is mordantly funny.

Before writing *Hedda Gabler* Ibsen had written another study of a woman in *Fruen fra havet* (*The Lady from the Sea*, 1888), in which a not uninteresting story of an idle woman's hallucinations is made just a trifle ridiculous by the pomposity of the symbolism with which the entire action is wrapped. That Ibsen was on the right track in seeking to invest his realistic subject-matter with material of deeper imaginative import is certain; the difficulty is, however, that what so easily may be introduced into a poetic play often becomes rather absurd when it is attached to prosaic dialogue. In *The Tempest*, as in *King Lear*, the symbolism is implicit rather than explicit; we are hardly aware of it consciously, and we realize how powerful it is only after a careful analysis of the scenes. In *The Lady from the Sea*, and in the kindred *Bygmester Solness* (*The Master Builder*, 1892), the symbols stand out aggressively as though they had been intellectually instead of imaginatively conceived, as though they had been nailed on to the text instead of being organically fused with it. The plot of *The Lady from the Sea* tells of a woman, Ellida, who is possessed of a haunting attraction towards the ocean, and this attraction becomes concretized in the debt she imagines she owes towards the Stranger, a man whom she had known in her youth, who has been a seafarer, and who now returns to claim her from her husband, Dr Wangel. In so far as this story is concerned, we have merely a skilful dramatic study of a peculiar neurosis; but, besides that tale, there are two elements in the play of more questionable import. The first is the somewhat naïve solution of Ellida's problem. At the end, after much discussion and bandying to and fro of argument, Wangel suddenly decides to allow his wife freedom of choice, whereupon the lady who feels the sea-waves lapping in her heart equally promptly decides to give up her Stranger:

WANGEL: And therefore—therefore I—I cancel our bargain on the spot. So now you can choose your own path—in full—full freedom.
ELLIDA [*gazes at him awhile as if speechless*]: Is this true—true—what you say? Do you mean it—from your inmost heart?
WANGEL: Yes; from the inmost depths of my suffering heart, I mean it.
ELLIDA: And *can* you do it? Can you carry out your purpose?

WANGEL: Yes, I can. I can—because I love you so deeply.

ELLIDA [*softly and tremblingly*]: So closely—so tenderly have you come to love me!

WANGEL: The years of our union have taught me to.

ELLIDA [*clasps her hands together*]: And I—I have been blind to it!

WANGEL: Your thoughts took other directions. But now—now you are fully freed from me and mine. Now your own true life can return to its—its right groove again. For now you can choose in freedom; and on your own responsibility, Ellida.

ELLIDA [*clasps her head with her hands and gazes fixedly towards* WANGEL]: In freedom—and on my own responsibility? Responsibility too?— That transforms everything! [*The steamer bell rings again.*]

THE STRANGER: Do you hear, Ellida? They are ringing for the last time. Come away?

ELLIDA [*turns towards him, looks fixedly at him, and says with decision in her voice*]: I can never go with you after this.

Intellectually considered, the conclusion is logical: it remains to be wondered, however, whether it has emotional justification. The truth seems to be that Ibsen has allowed himself to become so hopelessly enamoured of his fine symbol that he has subordinated all else to it. By the time we are half through with *The Lady from the Sea* we become rather tired of mermaids and fish-eyes, and Ellida's fancies seem to us excessively boring.

The same dominance of a symbolic concept weighs heavily on *The Master Builder*; indeed, the symbol, here as in the former drama, assumes such a blatant form as to make it seem immature and consequently almost laughable. All the talk in these scenes is of houses built for God or for people to live in, of architects' dreams, of trophies to be placed on high scaffoldings—and the import of this talk is akin to that about brackish waters, seaweed, and drowned sailors on the beach. The plot itself is simple. Halvard Solness is a builder, a man of late middle years, hearty yet feeling the effects of age, and terrified by the thought that youth will come and supersede him. Into his life comes a young girl, her mind gloriously and selfishly set on inspiring him to do great things. Although he knows that his head is not good for heights, he forces himself to climb up to the top of one of his recently constructed buildings, turns sick, and crashes down to his death. Perhaps the story is autobiographical, and, if so, then certain weaknesses in it would be explained. There is strength and there is interest here, yet *The Master Builder*, like others of Ibsen's dramas, appears not a little absurd; it lacks the calm objectivity of true greatness, and its ideas are somewhat shallowly based. At the end of a recent performance a man was heard to remark, "Crude, of course, but a promising play for a young man. The author *is* very young, isn't he?"—and the comment embodies an essential truth. When Ibsen wrote *The Master Builder* he was, technically, a master craftsman; spiritually, he was a middle-aged adolescent.

Lille Eyolf (*Little Eyolf*, 1894) is equally peculiar and equally oppressed by the symbolic. Fundamentally written to show the selfish Allmers and his wife, Rita, finding a new vision after the death of their crippled child,. it fails to reach imaginative tensity. We may, if we will, interpret the little child as passive and suffering humanity, Allmers as self-conscious egoism, Rita as unconscious egoism, and the half-sister, Asta, as beneficent love, but the effort hardly enriches our appreciation of the play. What is an inherent weakness in the realistic drama is revealed by a comparison of the original draft for *Little Eyolf* and the finished version. In the former is little more than a straightforward and rather dull domestic tragedy concentrating on a mother's hatred of her sick child; in the latter this theme is complicated by symbolic content. Neither is satisfactory: the one is bare and the other is artificially decorated. Nor can we see any way by which the bare could be made richer or the artificially decorated given vitality. Once more the symbol fails to integrate itself into the organic whole, and the failure is due, not to Ibsen's weakness, but to the intractability of the form in which he is working.

John Gabriel Borkman (1896) displays a greater imaginative power, perhaps because in it the symbolic is, except in a few episodes, laid aside. Instead Ibsen presents a study of a man and of his surroundings. Borkman's vision had been one of wealth and power—not so much in and for itself as for what it could achieve. He had been truly and genuinely inspired by the thought of harnessing the hidden forces of the earth in the service of mankind: he was, in fact, the very image of the great modern industrialist, the Carnegie, whose vast undertakings are dominated by a tangle of inextricably intertwined motives, from selfish love of riches to grandiose dreams of bettering humanity's lot. The man who first markets safety-razors no doubt thinks at one and the same time of gashless chins and the chink of gold. Like many a great industrialist, Borkman has crashed heavily, and after a long incarceration he has returned to his home—to his hard wife, Gunhild, whose one aim is to encourage her son, Erhart, to amass money and so mend the family fortunes, and to her sister, Ella, whom Borkman years ago had loved and left. With powerful intensity, Ibsen shows the broken giant living in his study, waiting vainly day by day for the call which he thinks is sure to come to him from his former colleagues, befriended only by the weak little clerk Foldal, who visits him merely because he finds that Borkman is the one person who will flatter his secret passion to be considered a poet. Perhaps the most poignant scene in the entire play is that wherein Borkman is suddenly stung into revealing the truth and bluntly telling Foldal he has no use for his "poetical nonsense," and wherein Foldal, angered in turn, informs Borkman that he can never hope to come back to the position he once held. The picture is etched firmly and harshly.

One other play was still to come—*Naar vi döde vaagner* (*When We Dead Awaken*, 1899). In this we may see Ibsen's final testament. The hero here is a sculptor, Arnold Rubek, married to a sensuous, empty-headed Maia, younger than he, "with a vivacious expression and lively, mocking eyes, yet with a suggestion of fatigue." Neither is happy. Back into his life comes a woman, Irene, one who had served as model for his greatest piece of statuary and whom Rubek had regarded as no more than an instrument towards the achieving of an artistic result. Hearing him thank her for a "priceless episode," she had left him and had gone about the world as a kind of living corpse; his coldness had slain her:

IRENE: I . . . swore . . . that I would serve you in all things——
RUBEK: As the model for my art——
IRENE: —in frank, utter nakedness——
RUBEK [*with emotion*]: And you did serve me, Irene—so bravely—so gladly and so ungrudgingly.
IRENE: Yes, with all the pulsing blood of my youth, I served you!
RUBEK [*nodding, with a look of gratitude*]: That you have every right to say.
IRENE: I fell down at your feet and served you, Arnold! [*Holding her clenched hand towards him*] But you, you,—you——!
RUBEK [*defensively*]: I never did you any wrong! Never, Irene!
IRENE: Yes, you did! You did wrong to my innermost, inborn nature——
RUBEK [*starting back*]: I——!
IRENE: Yes, you! I exposed myself wholly and unreservedly to your gaze—[*more softly*] And never once did you touch me.
RUBEK: Irene, did you not understand that many a time I was almost beside myself under the spell of all your loveliness?
IRENE [*continuing undisturbed*]: And yet—if you had touched me, I think I should have killed you on the spot. For I had a sharp needle always upon me—hidden in my hair—[*Strokes her forehead meditatively.*] But after all—after all—that you could——

Mr PHELPS as CORIOLANUS. No. 70.
London.Published by J.REDINGTON 7. Hoxton Street. Formerly called 208.Hoxton Old Town.

THE WATER KING IN
"THE SILVER PALACE"

THE WATER KING in the SILVER PALACE.
London Pub. by REDINGTON 208.Hoxton Old Town & sold by WEBB.75. Central St.S.t Luke

GATTIE AS M. MORBLEU

Mr C. PITT, AS CHARLY WAG.

London by J. REDINGTON 208 Hoxton Old Town & sold by J. Webb 78 Brick Lane St Lukes.

PITT AS CHARLY WAG

SETTING FOR "NORMA," BY LUIGI BAZZANI

By courtesy of the Ministero della Pubblica Istruzione, Rome

545

RUBEK [*looks impressively at her*]: I was an artist, Irene.
IRENE [*darkly*]: That is just it. That is just it.

Bitterly she claims that she had given him her "young, living soul"——

And that gift left me empty within—soulless. . . . It was that I died of, Arnold.

In the end, among the mountains, the pair are caught in a storm, but, instead of seeking safety by descending, they agree, like Rosmer and Rebecca, to mount upward towards certain death. The full significance this work held for Ibsen will never be known, but it would seem that thus, at the end of his life, he had come to believe that fullness of emotional existence was all that man should seek in the world, and that devotion to art or industry, if it interfered with that existence, was an evil.

It is hard indeed to estimate Ibsen's spirit aright. As a craftsman his position is secure. Trained in the school of Scribe, he evolved a powerful technique suited to the modern stage; what had been mechanical he made organic. In his casting aside of the older methods of exposition, in his attempt to allow character gradually to evolve as the action proceeds, and in his demonstration of what can be achieved by means of strict economy of form he was followed by many a successor. Besides these things that he taught to others, he was responsible for breaking the ancient five-act division, for suggesting the potential value of the retention of the unity of place, and for pointing out how much a realistic dramatist may convey to actor and reader through carefully worded stage directions. In the field of social and character concepts he wrought a veritable revolution, so that his influence on the intellectual world from 1880 to 1920 can hardly be fully assessed: Shaw's *Quintessence of Ibsenism* is a clear testimony to the impress made by the aging, rugged Norwegian upon the younger spirits of other lands.

His plays have a power beyond that of nearly all other realistic dramas of his time. Partly this is due to the fact that in him a poetic spirit sang lyrical tunes even while he was engaged in handling material of sordid reality: principally it is due to the fact that not one of his principal characters is ordinary or commonplace. It was the professed object of Zola, the confirmed practice of Augier and Dumas *fils*, to depict familiar situations and such persons as in no wise deviated from the regular run of men and women. Ibsen's characters are of an entirely different category. He may depict scenes of middle-class life, but the creatures who inhabit these scenes

S

are not of the middle range of humanity. When we think of them
we think of human beings *possessed*. Nora is no ordinary child-
wife: she has heard a call that comes from the mountains, not from
the market-place. Rebecca West is enthralled, as is Hedda: Solness
has heard sirens' songs; Ellida belongs to the sea; and Hedwig is a
queen of an enchanted attic. Something from outside, something
that suggests the operation of a magic spell, holds these persons in
fee. The result is that while outwardly Ibsen's scenes are 'ordinary'
and materialistically conceived, inwardly they are extraordinary and
at times breathe the atmosphere of Peer Gynt's adventures in the
hobgoblin's court.

This gives greatness and enduring interest to his work. At the
same time his plays, when placed against the greatest achievements
of the theatre, are seen to lack that balance and poise out of which
alone the highest dramatic achievements can come. Perhaps for
this the historical position in which he found himself was to blame.
He was forced to devote his energies to the cultivation of the
realistic stage, yet the realistic stage could not offer him the scope
desired. As a result, his imaginative development was, to a certain
extent, thwarted. Had he grown in the poetic concept his spirit
would have expanded: as it was, he lived on into old age a strangely
adolescent soul. His writings still have power to appeal to us, yet
that appeal is waning. Of the measure of Sophoclean and Shakespearian greatness he has none.

STRINDBERG AND THE PLAY OF THE SUBCONSCIOUS

OF PARTICULAR interest to us, when we consider the history of the theatre as a whole, is the fact that Ibsen does not stand alone. Just as Athens produced Æschylus, Sophocles, Euripides, and Aristophanes, as Elizabethan London produced Marlowe, Shakespeare, Jonson, and a score of others, as Spain produced Lope de Vega, Calderón, and their companions, as seventeenth-century France produced Corneille, Racine, and Molière, so the Scandinavian dramatic movement out of which Ibsen sprang brought to birth other talents worthy of being associated with his own.

BJÖRNSON AND HIS COMPANIONS

The prevailingly characteristic style during the latter half of the century among these Scandinavian playwrights was the realistic, but since the majority of the authors did not succeed in enlarging their vision as Ibsen had done, and since they could not improve upon Ibsen's technique, their works have now become little more than historical curiosities. The Norwegian Knut Hamsun is remembered as a novelist, not as the author of *Livets spil* (*The Game of Life*, 1896); novelist rather than dramatist, too, is Jonas Lie, whose *Lystige koner* (*Merry Wives*, 1894), despite its effectively ironic tone, is by no means a great play; Alexander Kielland is barely to be remembered for his *Tre par* (*Three Couples*, 1886) and *Professoren* (*The Professor*, 1888). Just a trifle better equipped for the stage is Gunnar Heiberg, a dramatist who has at least a considerable local reputation. Starting in the problem-play tradition with *Tante Ulrikke* (*Aunt Ulrikke*, 1884), he soon proceeded to move from the discussion of social problems to treatment of human emotions, reaching his greatest success in two related dramas, *Balkonen* (*The Balcony*, 1894) and *Kjærlighedens tragedie* (*Love's Tragedy*, 1904). In both of these it is the nature of love, not the quality of social evils, that occupies his attention. He still remains aware of political and other similar issues, but his main interest lies in probing the complexities of the individual human soul.

Among these dramatists, however, stands one man of more than common quality, Björnstjerne Björnson, a Norwegian whose life. is closely associated with that of Ibsen. Had Ibsen not been, Björnson's reputation assuredly would have stood high; as it is, he has been fated ever to be compared, and always to his disadvantage, with his greater compatriot and contemporary. This has been due, partly to the circumstances that threw them together, partly to the fact that in their dramatic art a peculiar parallelism prevails, and partly because Björnson, while seeing many of the errors in social life that were so patent to Ibsen, inclined to adopt an optimistic and compromising attitude that has little pleased the intellectual or other rebels during the past decades.

His earliest works were composed in the familiar historical mould so popular in his time. From the barbaric Viking material of *Mellem slagene* (*Between the Battles*, 1857), *Halte-Hulda* (*Hulda the Halt*, 1858), *Kong Sverre* (*King Sverre*, 1861), and the long series of episodes in *Sigurd Slembe* (*Sigurd the Bastard*, 1862) he moved to the ever-fascinating topic of *Maria Stuart i Skotland* (*Mary Stuart in Scotland*, 1864). The year following the appearance of the last of this series, however, saw the production of a play in an entirely different style, *De nygifte* (*The Newly Married Couple*, 1865), in which Björnson definitely aligned himself with the realists. Its tone is light and its conclusion happy, but the subject is definitely a 'problem'—that of the young man (in this case a worthy fellow named Axel) who finds his whole being fettered by a child-like wife, Laura, who, in turn, has not sufficiently grown beyond babyhood to escape from the loving chains set about her by her parents. There is a good deal that is artificial about Björnson's comedy, yet one can feel here an easy strength and an agreeable liberalism of outlook eminently admirable.

After nearly a decade of active political work, when Björnson returned to the theatre it was the style set in *The Newly Married Couple* that he pursued. A lone *Sigurd Jorsalfar* (*Sigurd the Crusader*, 1872) testified to his earlier interests; *Redaktören* (*The Editor*, 1874) and *En fallit* (*A Bankruptcy*, 1874) demonstrated clearly that in realism he had found his most effective medium. The former attacked bitterly the weaknesses of journalism; in the business-man Tjaelda of the latter play he reveals the dishonesties which may enter into commercial life, and, through this character's conversion to integrity, trumpets forth the claims of standards based more deeply upon true moral values.

The dull demand for respectability ruling in the society of his time was further pilloried in the interesting *Leonarda* of 1879, in which a woman of sincerest virtue is seen cold-shouldered by society. Leonarda's niece, Aagot, falls in love with Hagbart, nephew of the local bishop, and when this young man shifts his affections to her she deliberately sacrifices herself for the girl's sake. The play contains one particularly interesting character, the old Grandmother, first of a lengthy theatrical progeny of octogenarians, very wise and very tolerant, who are rather amused at youth's belief that they alone have the secrets of freedom, frankness, and independence. Following an unimportant *Det ny system* (*The New System*, 1879) came what is probably Björnson's best-known drama, *En hanske* (*A Gauntlet*, 1883), where a simple question is asked: has a girl the right to demand from her fiancé the same premarital purity he demands from her? The author has been blamed for leaving his answer unsure, but perhaps such criticism is misplaced: what Björnson was interested in was the voicing of the problem itself, and the fact that he leaves his own answer in doubt makes his play maybe more in tune with the reality than any doctrinaire pronouncement could have made it. The young Alfred Christensen loves Svava Riis, and is repentant on account of an earlier *affaire* of his own, yet not so repentant as to permit him to believe he would have condoned any similar escapade on Svava's part; she is horrified at this realization of the 'double morality,' and her intellect tells her to break the match, yet her affections prevent her from wholly closing the door; her mother is inclined to side with her, yet realizes that the setting up of such severe standards as Svava's would wreck social life entirely.

Over ævne (*Beyond our Strength*, or *Beyond Human Might*, 1883) enters into the realm of religious faith, and presents a tragic picture of the simple Pastor Sang, who believes he has been gifted with the power to work miracles. Extraordinary examples of his healing skill persuade the countryside that he is blessed by God with supernatural talents; only his bedridden wife, although she loves him, sets her will, almost unconsciously, against his, and in the end he dies, broken by the knowledge that his power is not what he has deemed. Perhaps in this drama Björnson has reached his highest and deepest dramatic utterance. Two years later came *Geografi og kjærlighed* (*Geography and Love*, 1885), depicting the utter selfishness of a scholar, Professor Tygesen, who demands that his whole household should be subservient to his needs: although much in the play is feeble, there are several scenes here—notably those in which Tygesen and his rival Turman appear—that are rich in sly, comic values. In 1895 came a second play entitled *Over ævne*, a drama dealing with the problems of capital and labour, introducing four characters from the former play, but fundamentally standing distinct from it. Designed to defy the forces of superstition and to call for a rational planning of human life, Björnson here has entered into the symbolic realm inhabited by the aging Ibsen. The two persons who testify to hope for the future, Credo and Spera, are as much personifications as any allegorical figures in the medieval moralities. A similar style appears in *Laboremus* (1901) and *Naar den ny vin blomstrer* (*When the Vineyards are in Blossom*, 1909). In the former, a powerful play, Björnson castigates in Lydia not merely a woman but a principle—the principle of aggressive individualism which is associated with the Nietzsche cult; the latter drama, infinitely weaker in concept and execution, gives one last fling at the Ibsenian new woman, and shows a middle-aged husband seeking in the love of a young girl for that which his wife is too busily occupied to give him.

In these and other dramas we may, if we will, find much shallowness and perhaps not a trifle of sentimentalism, yet Björnson's works are of value for their healthy sanity, their breezy good-humour, and their constant sympathy even for those characters whom he most condemned. If Ibsen is the Puritan of the nineteenth-century theatre, Björnson is one of its truest humanitarians.

THE EARLY STRINDBERG

Greater by far than Björnson—and, indeed, a man whose genius, although erratic and strangely tormented by grotesque fancies, may be thought more intense than that of Ibsen itself—was the Swede August Strindberg. His fiery career has been narrated by himself and often retold by others, and from the record it is apparent that his creative career is sharply split in two by the complete breakdown which he suffered in his late forties; in a sense there are two Strindbergs, and, although there are ties binding the man who wrote before the year 1897 with the man whose work appeared after that date, these two may be regarded almost as separate entities.

Among the qualities held in common by the early Strindberg and the late, chief in significance is the intense 'subjectivity' in his art. It was as though he saw the whole of life focused upon himself, as though nothing existed save for the purpose of impinging on his personality. Oppressed by this concept, he continually interpreted events, not in relation to other events, but in relation to things that had happened to him: in his play *After the Fire* the Stranger speaks in the author's name when he declares that

> however life shaped itself, I always became aware of connexions and repetitions. I saw in one situation the result of another earlier one. Or meeting *this* person I was reminded of *that* one whom I had met in the past.

The result is that every one of his plays is a kind of reflection of himself: of the purely objective style in dramatic art he is entirely innocent.

Along with this must be noted a peculiar attitude towards reality which, although appearing in an intensified form only among his later plays, is early adumbrated in diverse scenes. For Strindberg material reality does not possess the same significance it did for Ibsen, and this expresses itself both by a greater selectivity and by a tendency to allow appearances, phenomena, to dominate in his plays. Not only is the spiritual of greater consequence to him than the physical, the physical at times almost seems to cease to exist, to prove itself merely a figment of the mind.

A third characteristic is the fact that, while his genius was a forceful one, hardly any other author of equivalent stature has shown himself so strongly and yet fitfully influenced by others as he has. In philosophy he passes under the spell of Buckle, Kierkegaard, and Swedenborg; in art he is swayed by a variety of writers from Byron to Maeterlinck. The consequence of this is twofold: that often two diametrically opposed styles are apparent at one single period of his career, and that that career exhibits a variety far greater than what is usually to be found in the work of a great dramatic author.

His first compositions intended for theatrical representation were romantic in tone (showing clearly the influence of the Byron-Schiller tradition). For his earliest dramas he made selection of classical subject-matter, but soon, like so many other Scandinavian authors, he turned to the history of his own land, and in *Mäster Olof* (*Master Olof*, 1872) produced his first notable dramatic work. While almost entirely neglected or condemned on its first appearance, this play shows the hand of genius at work, and was destined to win later esteem. The central figure is Olaus (Olof) Petri, the founder of the Swedish Reformation; he is associated with Gustavus Vasa and the Anabaptist Gert, a fanatic printer. The historical plot is concerned with the first struggles that Olof has with the priesthood, his acceptance by Gert as a kindred revolutionary soul, his patronage by the King, and his pursuit of his ideal in compromise manner. Apart from this plot, however, the drama may be looked upon subjectively, and in this manner Strindberg himself probably conceived it. Seen thus, the three persons of Olof, the practical idealist, Gustavus Vasa, the man of affairs who allows no ideal to deflect him from his purpose, and the utterly impractical visionary Gert take shape as projections of parts of Strindberg's own self— for thus early in his career did he recognize in himself a split individuality. The double quality gives to the work, crude though it may be, a distinction among the historical dramas of the time.

A few other similar plays followed, including *Gillets hemlighet* (*The Secret of the Guild*, 1880) and *Herr Bengts hustru* (*Sir Bengt's Lady*, 1882), and then came the satirical fairy-tale *Lycko-Pers resa* (*The Wanderings of Lucky Per*, 1882). This, Strindberg insisted, was intended as a play for children, and, even although it has won much success on the stage among adult audiences, it would seem that his assertion ought to be taken literally. If we judge it as, for example, we judge the similar *Peer Gynt*, then the fairy machinery and the obvious allegory must be condemned as childish; but if it was indeed Strindberg's purpose to make it so, our estimate of the drama's worth inevitably will be of a different kind, and we shall find in its satire of social life a subtle adjustment of means to ends. Particularly effective from this point of view is the scene in the third act wherein we find ourselves in a market-square: in the middle are a Pillory and a Statue of the Mayor. These suddenly become animate and hold a conversation:

PILLORY [*bows to the* STATUE]: Good morning, Statue! Did you sleep well last night?
STATUE [*nods*]: Good morning, Pillory; did you sleep well yourself?
PILLORY: I slept all right, but I dreamt too; can you guess what I dreamt?
STATUE [*testily*]: How should I be able to guess?
PILLORY: Well, I dreamt—can you imagine?—that a reformer had come to the town!
STATUE: A reformer? What! [*Stamps.*] It's deuced cold for the feet standing here, but what does one not do for honour's sake! A reformer? Well, I suppose he will have a statue too?
PILLORY: Statue! Statue indeed! No! He had to stand here at my feet himself like a statue, and I took him by the throat with my two arms! [*The neck-irons rattle.*] You see, he was a real reformer and not one of those charlatans you were when you were alive.

This introduces us effectively to a developing action wherein Strindberg's fantastically conceived satire is displayed with skill and precision.

THE VIOLENCE OF REALISM

From the tone of this play it is indeed a far cry to the tortured misery of *Fadren* (*The Father*, 1887), through which Strindberg inaugurated his trenchant series of darkly pessimistic and tortured realistic dramas. The theme of this tragic action is bare, almost gaunt. A Captain, characteristically left without a name, finds his strength and his reason sapped by his wife, Laura. With diabolical cruelty she separates him from his only friend, Dr Östermark, and then proceeds by insinuations deliberately to drive him insane. Beyond and around this bitter tale of two sex-enemies is the atmosphere of feminine power—the monstrous regiment of women—that Strindberg sets as background for the action. The Captain's household is dominated and ruled not only by his wife, but also by those associated with her, and there is a bitter irony in the fact that, at the very conclusion of the play, the strait-jacket is slipped upon him by his old Nurse as she bends over him, whispering motherly words into his ears. Without a doubt this is among the greatest dramas produced by the late-nineteenth-century theatre: its very simplicity of aim gives it a peculiar distinction.

In connexion with this simplicity of aim there should be noted one basic difference between the methods and the concepts of Ibsen and Strindberg. If, for example, we take *Hedda Gabler* for comparison with *The Father* we find that the Ibsen play starts with a meticulously described interior setting, and that as the action unfolds very considerable reference is made to the material surroundings of the characters. *Things* were for Ibsen of tremendous import, and frequently he makes his most telling points by relating his persons to furniture and properties. We can hardly think of this, or of any other of his realistic dramas, separated from the settings. To such a dramatic method *The Father* presents a complete contrast. The room in which the Captain sits—and the very fact that he is called simply the Captain and not given an individual name is in keeping—is described in general terms; almost the only two objects of which dramatic use is made in the whole course of the action are the lamp he hurls after his wife and the strait-jacket by which he is bound at the end. In effect, *The Father* could quite easily, and perhaps might most effectively, be played on a completely bare stage. With this quality in Strindberg's work may be associated both his reduction of the plot element and his several experiments in writing plays which, unbroken by scene divisions, present one unified action from start to finish, with all stress upon the

passions, none upon the intrigue. Strindberg's concentration is
wholly on the world of the spirit: his action is of the soul, not of
the body.

Precisely similar in character to *The Father* is *Kamraterna* (*Comrades*, 1888), in which a talented artist, Axel, sacrifices his genius for
his wife, Berta. During several years of marriage, which she likes
to describe as "comradeship," she has forced him to debase his
talents by the turning out of commercial work, while she, an artist
also, is free to give her time to painting what she likes. So devoted
is he to her that when they both prepare pictures for the Salon and
when he realizes that his unquestionably will be accepted, hers
rejected, he sends his canvas in under her name. When news comes
that Berta's picture has been accepted she openly exults, and with
unparalleled cruelty arranges that the rejected work should be
returned to him, humiliatingly, in the midst of a party. This action
finally brings him to a realization of her true nature and of the
quality of their relationship: although she pleads with him, he
determines that their marriage must be dissolved. He will, he says,
take a mistress: "I like to meet a comrade at a café; at home I
want a wife," are his final words. Strindberg's genius is nowhere
more clearly demonstrated than by the fact that this is one of the
few plays in the entire history of the drama that truly conveys the
impression of an artist's life. Ibsen's Rubek is by comparison a
synthetic composition.

Even more bitter is the tormenting *Fröken Julie* (*Miss Julie*, 1888).
The heroine of this terrible "naturalistic tragedy" Strindberg himself describes as a "half-woman, the man-hater"—a tragic type,
"offering the spectacle of a desperate fight with nature"; she is a
neurotic child of a degenerate aristocracy, proud and yet willing to
sink her pride in the frenzied attempt to satisfy her love of sensation.
Centuries before, Middleton had depicted just such a character in
the heroine of *The Changeling*. Almost hysterically she makes love
and gives herself to her valet, Jean, finds herself in his power, and is
forced by him to steal money from her own father; in the end Jean
callously suggests that her only remedy is to commit suicide, and,
as in a trance, she obeys. In telling this gruesome tale Strindberg
deliberately sets himself to plan a technique harmonious with his
central purpose.

"I have rather broken with tradition," he says,

in not making my characters catechists who sit asking foolish questions
in order to elicit a smart reply. I have avoided the mathematically
symmetrical construction of French dialogue and let people's brains

work irregularly, as they do in actual life, where no topic of conversation is drained to the dregs, but one brain receives haphazard from the other a cog to engage with. Consequently, my dialogue too wanders about, providing itself in the earlier scenes with material which is afterwards worked up, admitted, repeated, developed and built up, like the theme of a musical composition.

The plot is full of possibilities, and since it really concerns only two characters I have confined myself to these, merely introducing one minor character, the cook, and allowing the father's unfortunate spirit to hover over and behind the whole. This is because I thought I had noticed that the psychological process is what chiefly interests the newer generation; our inquisitive souls are not content with seeing a thing happen; they must also know how it happens. What we want to see is the wires, the machinery; we want to examine the box with the false bottom, to handle the magic ring and find the joint, to haxe a look at the cards and see how they are marked.

In addition he has abolished the act division, an experiment made in the belief "that our decreasing capacity for illusion was possibly weakened by intervals in which the spectator has time to reflect and thereby escape from the suggestive influence of the author-mesmerist."

From these remarks, made by the author himself, it is obvious that the 'naturalism' of *Miss Julie* is something that goes far beyond earlier naturalistic endeavours. There are none of Zola's "supernumerary fools" here: indeed, Strindberg deliberately rejects "the so-called 'folk-scene'" as being something likely to destroy the illusion. And as for scenery, he declares that he has "borrowed from impressionist painting its asymmetry and its abruptness." Already the stage was moving beyond the limits of Ibsenian realism.

In *Fordringsägare* (*Creditors*, 1888) the sex-war is still further developed, and in a form even more abstract. Here, again, only three persons are introduced: Tekla, a predatory woman writer; Adolph, her husband, an artist; and Gustav, her former husband, a teacher. The lesson of the play is that the woman has made her reputation by sucking the strength of Gustav, and is now similarly sapping Adolph's power. Hardly any drama of Strindberg's is more compact than this one, and the author's skill is displayed no less by the incisive etching of his characters than by the tensity of the emotional atmosphere evoked.

The same year saw the composition of *Paria* (*Pariah*, 1889), a drama in which for the first time the influence of Poe becomes dominant. Two middle-aged characters—again typically called simply Mr X (an archæologist) and Mr Y (an American traveller)

—appear, set almost *in vacuo*. The former, poor yet holding in his hands a priceless treasure he has unearthed, wonders why he cannot bring himself to take some of the antique golden ornaments and melt them down for his own use. Something he cannot himself understand, an inner compulsion, holds him back. His companion turns out to have been guilty of a forgery; and, as for himself, Mr X reveals that he has been guilty of murder. On hearing this Mr Y tries to blackmail him, but his strength is petty compared with that of the archæologist, and it is the man who will not steal who remains the victor. The play is interesting for its deliberate seeking after an effective and sensational curtain, and for its early treatment of a theme later to press heavily on Strindberg's mind— that of justice.

The sensationalism reappears in the still more Poe-esque *Samum* (*Simoom*; written 1888, printed 1890), where, in the midst of the simoom, an Arabian girl, Biskra, aided by her lover, Yusuf, suc- ceeds by tricks in so working upon the mind of Guimard, a lieutenant of the Zouaves, as to drive him to his death. Another, and even shorter, one-act play of the same time is *Den starkare* (*The Stronger*, 1890), interesting technically because, although it presents two characters, Mrs X and Miss Y, the latter remains silent, and the piece thus takes shape as a kind of monologue. With consummate skill Strindberg succeeds in focusing attention more on the woman who does not speak than on the one who does.

During the following years many other plays succeeded, diverse influences, chief among them that of Nietzsche, ever bringing fresh tones and colours to their composition. *Debet och kredit* (*Debit and Credit*; printed 1893) introduces a kind of bitter laughter in its delineation of Axel, a teacher who, by relying on help from others, has gained a high reputation, but who has no financial means at his command. Pestered by those who think he owes them a return for services rendered, he prepares a set of cynically worded letters, leaving thus the country of his birth and his creditors. Closely akin in spirit are *Första varningen* (*The First Warning*, 1893), in which marital relationships in middle age are treated with a crackling and ironic laughter, and *Leka med elden* (*Playing with Fire*, 1892), where an artist's wife nearly goes off with her husband's best friend. In *Moderskärlek* (*Mother Love*, 1893) he turns to the problem of children and parents, a theme further developed in *Bandet* (*The Link*, or *The Bond*, 1893), which also deals with the question of justice. Here a young Judge is forced to fine a farmer for libel when he knows that the man is perfectly innocent, and then is confronted by the perplexing case of the Baron and the Baroness who seek separation, bitterly accuse each other, and yet are tied together by thought of the child they have brought into the world. In this work the 'abstract' quality of Strindberg's art is more than ever apparent: his mind increasingly is being drawn within itself.

THE LATER HISTORICAL PLAYS

After he had recovered from his mental breakdown Strindberg's writings assumed diverse forms. Rather peculiarly, one set of dramas is a series of historical studies which catch up, as it were, his earliest efforts. In *Gustav Vasa* (1899), indeed, he actually took over the characters whom, years before, he had shown in *Master Olof*, revealing them now in their middle age. *Erik XIV* came the same year, with, as its central figure, Erik, the son of Gustavus. Perhaps the most interesting of all his historical works, its atmosphere is that of "a mad world, my masters." The King lives with his devoted mistress, Karin, but dreams of becoming the husband of Queen Elizabeth of England. His eccentricities, by no means unlovable, drive him into opposition with his hard-headed, ambitious nobles, and the drama ends with a magnificent scene in which Erik's miserable and pathetic Court is shattered by the heavy tread of the Dukes who are to usurp his rule.

In *Folkunga-sagan* (*The Saga of the Folkungs*, 1899) Strindberg turned farther back in the pages of history, and wrote a fascinating study of the weakly tolerant Magnus, setting this King against a background of sex-passions. He is married to Blanche, but she has a 'servant' in Bengt Algotson, while the Queen Mother, Ingeborg, keeps a lover in Knut Porse: against these is set the pathetic child-marriage of the boy Erik and his bride, Beatrix. With extraordinary vigour the author reveals to us this wretched palace, concentrating with particular delight on delineating the vicious Ingeborg and her Porse:

PORSE [*brutally*]: Can I rely on you?
INGEBORG: You don't love me!
PORSE: Nonsense! Is it for elderly people like us to waste our time on lovers' tiffs? I suppose you expect me, the Duke of Halland, to squat on my knees and pluck the lute while women and boys snatch away the crowns! Be yourself, Ingeborg; be rough, as nature and life has made you; fire for the hovel and axe for the head, mirror of my own soul! Love? Really I never expected that word from you. If we feel drawn to each other, that is not love, but a common hate, hate, hate!

INGEBORG: You frighten me!

PORSE: Are you so easily frightened? I shouldn't have thought so!— Tell me: why won't you marry me? It would make our position safer and dearer!

INGEBORG: I don't see that.

PORSE: Don't you? But consider what may happen. When I have thrown out Erik the crown is mine; I can't offer to share it with you as my mistress, but as my wife I could!

INGEBORG: Time enough to think about that when . . .

PORSE: It's too late . . .

INGEBORG: First do your knightly service and clear the way to the throne.

PORSE: For two, or for one?

INGEBORG: That depends on . . .

PORSE: Whether you have to kick me aside then. Show your cards! You want to use me as a broom and then throw me into the fire. It's Aunt Britta's great idea come up again: the sisters are to rule over the brothers; but the brothers are to look after mass, confession, preaching, choir duty, housekeeping, instruction,—in a word—do the brain work, while ignorance and incompetence sit at the helm.

INGEBORG: I hate you!

PORSE: Go on!

INGEBORG: So much that I should like to see your eyes on a fish-hook and your liver chopped up for the cats! I loathe you like garbage and filth; you sicken me like unkempt hair and black finger-nails; I curse the hour your feet brought you my way, and I wish your mother had thrown you on a dung-heap one dark night, to be eaten by the swine!

PORSE: Bravo! Splendid! There speaks my Ingeborg again; the royal mother, the strong, the red-hot. If you knew how beautiful you are now you would never prattle of love. When you talk like this, your words are drums and trumpets, the music of battle in my ear. And now for my knightly guard—even if it means fighting with ghosts and Satan! Hail, Queen!

[*He seizes her and throws himself on her to steal a kiss.*

In this series of dramas, which includes the strong *Gustav Adolf* (*Gustavus Adolphus*, 1900), *Engelbrekt* (1901), *Carl XII* (1901), *Gustav III* (1903), and *Kristina* (*Queen Christina*, 1903)—the last a skilful study of a neurotic and half-deranged woman—Strindberg revealed the power of his dramatic conceptions and the mastery he had acquired of his craft. These later historical dramas are among the most powerful plays of the kind produced in modern times.

THE LATER REALISTIC PLAYS

Another group of plays written at this time recalls, but afar off, the style of his middle period. Typical of these is the strange 'comedy' *Brott och brott* (*There are Crimes and Crimes*), published in 1899 with *Advent* under the general title of *Vid högre rätt* (*In a Higher Court*). Here the theme of justice is caught up with the religious trend, which had already, in 1892, found expression in *Himmelrikets nycklar* (*The Keys of the Kingdom of Heaven*). The scene of *There are Crimes and Crimes* is Paris; but it is a Paris of the mind, not the city of actuality, and the action is one in which the real is subordinated to the imaginative. The main character is Maurice, a playwright who, after years of poverty, is expecting success from a drama about to be produced. He has received devoted love from his mistress, Jeanne, by whom he has a dearly beloved daughter, Marion. On the eve of his victory he meets Henriette, the mistress of his friend Adolphe, and, consumed by a wild passion, goes off with her. The child Marion, however, is a bar to their happiness, and when it dies he accuses Henriette of committing murder, while he himself is looked upon by the law as the probable criminal. The world, which had seemed so full of promise, turns against him, and only at the close is it discovered that Marion had died naturally, with the consequence that he is relieved of the nightmare into which he had sunk. The whole drama, of course, is a kind of impressionistic study of thought, and its ironic conclusion, wherein Maurice agrees to divide his life between prayer and acceptance of the worldly joys now restored to him, is deliberately planned.

Its companion piece, *Advent* (1899), departs entirely from even a semblance of realism, and is replete with Swedenborgian symbolism. The main characters are, on the one hand, a Judge and an Old Lady, essentially evil, accompanied by the Other One, the devil who feels pain in the task assigned to him, and, on the other, by two children, befriended by the Playmate, who is in reality the Christ Child. This entire piece is wrought with a dream-like atmosphere; we are withdrawn entirely from the world of reality; it is a realm of magic we inhabit where objects pass through apparently solid walls: in the court-room scene,

The bell rings. The gavel raps once on the table. All the chairs are pulled up to the table at once. The Bible is opened. The candles on the table become lighted.

Peculiarly effective is the macabre devil-dance episode, in which appear the Prince, Lucifer himself, and the Satanic Master of Ceremonies. The Prince demurs at taking part in the masquerade:

MASTER OF CEREMONIES: Try to do anything but what you must, and you'll experience an inner discord that you cannot explain.

PRINCE: What does it mean?

MASTER OF CEREMONIES: It means that you cannot all of a sudden cease to be what you are: and you are what you have wanted to become.

To this section of his writings belong the several 'chamber plays' that Strindberg wrote specifically for August Falck's Intimate Theatre at Stockholm—a tiny structure that became, to all intents, a Strindberg playhouse. In these dramas the author sought to carry out his original dream of abolishing intermissions, and pursued farther his characteristic treatment of the scenic accompaniment of his actions. The scenery he reduced to quickly interchangeable backgrounds with a few stage properties—just sufficient and no more to provide his characters with a barely indicated *milieu*. Among these chamber plays *Oväder* (*The Thunderstorm*; printed 1907) is notable for its effective picture of old age, presented in a study of the Master, living in an apartment of the house where he had once been happy with his divorced wife, Gerda. To her image he clings, and only gradually does it lose its power as his passions sink to resignation. In the conduct of this piece there is more than a suggestion of a Pirandellesque treatment, with people and their actions viewed from differing standpoints.

Another play of the same kind is *Brända tomten* (*After the Fire*, or *The Burned Lot*; printed 1907). As in *The Thunderstorm* a house of several apartments stood behind the characters, so here the background is composed of the ruins of a burned home, set in a street which, as Anderson the Mason tells the Detective, has the peculiar quality that the people who move from it always must return. "We call it the Bog," he says. "And all of us hate each other, and suspect each other, and blackguard each other, and torment each other." The fire has started gossip, and gossip has widened into accusation: all that is rotten has been exposed to the light; symbolically, a pitiful pile of salvaged goods lies open for all to gaze at. Into this picture steps the Stranger—a portrait of Strindberg himself—philosophically moving amid the wreckage of his world.

Sometimes dark, sometimes with a breaking of light, Strindberg's mind during these years passed in review the fundamental problems of man's life. In *Påsk* (*Easter*, 1901) a religious spirit prevails; the darkness and cold of winter, the dark depression of Elis, burdened with a sense of guilt because of his father's actions, are dissipated as the warmth of the spring sun enters into his life. But the shadows are impenetrable in the terrible *Dödsdansen* (*The Dance of Death*, 1901), which some critics, not without justice, regard as Strindberg's greatest work. Here, in an isolated fort, Edgar, a captain of artillery, and Alice, his wife, have lived for twenty-five years, hating each other with a deadly venom and each wishing for the other's death. Their home becomes peopled with devils, and when Curt, Edgar's friend, comes to stay in it he is caught up in the atmosphere of evil: he falls in love with the wife and becomes her associate in a plot designed to destroy her husband. During a stroke, however, Edgar suddenly gains a new vision of life. He realizes his own errors and pleads for a reconciliation. Thus ends the first part of the drama. The second shows the final triumph of the wife. Remorselessly she drives Edgar to his death—although in the very process of doing so a bitter doubt enters her mind:

> ALICE: Do you notice that there is peace in the house now? The wonderful peace of death. Wonderful as the solemn anxiety that surrounds the coming of a child into the world. I hear the silence —and on the floor I see the traces of the easy-chair that carried him away—— And I feel now that my own life is ended, and I am starting on the road to dissolution! . . . While we have been talking here, the image of him as he was in his younger years has come back to me—I have seen him, I see him—now, as when he was only twenty—I must have loved that man!
>
> CURT: And hated him!
>
> ALICE: And hated!—Peace be with him!

THE DEVELOPMENT OF A NEW FORM: "THE DREAM PLAY"

It is the third type of play developed by Strindberg during this time that is most interesting, because most new. Even in *Advent* Strindberg had kept some slight hold on the objective. In *Till Damaskus* (*To Damascus*; Parts 1 and 2, 1898; Part 3, 1904) something different appeared. Here is the true theatre of surrealism, the presentation on the stage of the wholly subjective—the theatrical representation of the dream. This was followed in the same style by *Ett drömspel* (*The Dream Play*, 1902) and *Spöksonaten* (*The Spook Sonata*, 1907).

In writing these Strindberg worked quite deliberately. He had, he declared, "tried to imitate the disconnected but seemingly logical form of the dream":

Anything may happen; everything is possible and probable. Time and space do not exist. On an insignificant background of reality, imagination designs and embroiders novel patterns: a medley of memories, experiences, free fancies, absurdities and improvisations. The characters split, double, multiply, vanish, solidify, blur, clarify. But one consciousness reigns above them all—that of the dreamer; and before it there are no secrets, no incongruities, no scruples, no laws. There is neither judgment nor exoneration, but merely narration. And as the dream is mostly painful, rarely pleasant, a note of melancholy and of pity with living things runs right through the wabbly tale. Sleep, the liberator, plays often a dismal part, but when the pain is at its worst, the awakening comes and reconciles the sufferer with reality, which, however distressing it may be, nevertheless seems happy in comparison with the torments of the dream.

To attempt to describe the kaleidoscopic 'plots' of these works would be futile. *The Dream Play* opens with conversation between a Glazier and his Daughter, looking upon a castle that is growing ever higher and higher "because they have manured it," and that "ought to be blooming soon, as we are already past midsummer." Soon an Officer and his sick Mother are introduced, and before long the stage is peopled with a medley collection of variegated characters —a Singer, a Portress, a Bill-poster. In the midst of these the Prompter enters, followed by a Lawyer and a *corps de ballet*. Poets and miners, personifications of Theology, Philosophy, and Medicine, these are jumbled together with all the inconsequence of a nightmare; yet beyond them all lies the dreamer himself, seeing evil come of the incorporation of the pure intelligence in fleshly form.

In *The Spook Sonata* a similar atmosphere prevails—with an apparition of a Milkmaid, the ghost of a Consul, a Mummy (the Colonel's wife). We are in a world of spectres here, not less terrible and not less real because they are figments of the imagination. The world is one of illusion, guilt, suffering, and death, with only the fitful light of faith to give it feeble illumination. Youth and age alike are bound in a circle of evil, and although the action ends with a strange vision in which "the whole room disappears, and in its place appears 'The Island of the Dead' by Boecklin as background," while "soft music, very quiet and pleasantly sad, is heard" from the distance, the mood is pessimistic, modified only by a kind of Buddhistic resignation towards the miseries of the flesh. The young Student, Arkenholtz, and his sweetheart are as tightly shackled by the terrors around them as the old Hummel and the whitehaired crone who had once been his love.

Closely associated with these dramas is the fairy-tale *Svanevit* (*Swanwhite*; printed 1902), in which the influence of Maeterlinck is, confessedly, dominant. Among the most successful theatrically of all Strindberg's plays, it substitutes the pleasant dream for the nightmare, drawing its portraits of little Swanwhite and her Prince with infinite compassion, though with the same unreality as distinguishes the other plays. With it may be placed another 'folk-play,' *Kronbruden* (*The Bridal Crown*, 1902), of kindred spirit. Here the legend is told of two shepherd lovers, separated by family feuds, but pursuing their life of mutual passion amid a world peopled with characters human and supernatural.

In these dramas, as in the others written during his tempestuous career, Strindberg reveals a power which can barely be matched elsewhere in the nineteenth-century theatre. Even when he is contrasted with Ibsen the impression of this power remains distinct and emphatic. Indeed, it is Ibsen, not Strindberg, who suffers in the comparison. No doubt the Norwegian author is the more accomplished playwright, assured in his craftsmanship, while the Swede is erratic and sometimes fumbling; yet the fact remains that after reading or seeing Strindberg's plays Ibsen's seem to us not a trifle dull and dowdy, adolescent, facile, lacking in deep passion. What appeared to us to be granite suddenly assumes the softness of putty. Where Ibsen's scenes are sometimes ordinary, Strindberg's are extraordinary and demonic. His characters possess almost superhuman proportions, and his masculinity triumphs over Ibsen's feminism.

While it is certain that Ibsen writes works better calculated for commercial production, and that most of Strindberg's plays are likely to remain somewhat caviare to the general, these latter plays forge far ahead of the former in vision and concept. Three things in especial Strindberg did. First, in the supreme concentration of the dramas of his middle period, he showed how much even the closely packed realistic plays of Ibsen lacked of essential dramatic economy. Secondly, he came as near as any man towards creating a modern social tragedy. And, thirdly, in his latest works he achieved what might have seemed the impossible—producing theatrical compositions that in effect are wholly subjective. In the long range of his writings his hands touch now the early romantics, now the realists and naturalists, now the expressionists, now the surrealists, and now the existentialists. There is no author whose range is wider or more provocative. In him the entire history of the stage from 1800 to the present day is epitomized.

THE INDEPENDENT THEATRE IN GERMANY

THE FORCE that had produced Schiller and Goethe and that later was to foster the works of Hebbel, Ludwig, and Wagner was not yet spent; in Gerhart Hauptmann Germany was to welcome a dramatist only slightly less powerful than the Scandinavian masters.

To a large extent his genius was inspired by the opportunities offered to him by the Freie Bühne, which, created under the enthusiasm of Otto Brahm, first came before the public with a production of Ibsen's *Ghosts* in 1889. Although this venture succeeded in maintaining life for only three seasons, its impetus was perhaps of even greater influence than its own intrinsic efforts. Directly arising out of its example came Bruno Wille's proletarian playhouse, the Freie Volksbühne, of 1890, and the same director's Neue Freie Bühne of 1892; later, in 1895, came the inauguration of the Workman's Theatre of Vienna, modelled on the People's Independent Theatre Society of Berlin. Through these efforts of the original Freie Bühne the ordinary stages were opened to works written by the new realistic playwrights, and from them sprang, indirectly at least, the manifold activities of Max Reinhardt.

HAUPTMANN'S PREDECESSORS AND COMPANIONS

Besides the influence exerted upon Hauptmann by this theatrical movement, he owed much to his immediate predecessors in dramatic writing. The works of Hebbel, Ludwig, and their companions have already been noted: slightly later came Ludwig Anzengruber, whose importance lies chiefly in his deliberate attempt to develop a form of dramatic dialogue suited to the new realistic stage which, while based on the forms of speech current in various spheres of ordinary life, should still avoid the monotony consequent upon mere phonographic reproduction of the common tongue.

In structure Anzengruber's dramas are based on the popular and rather melodramatic 'Wiener Volksstück,' from which he borrows sensational effects, looseness of structure, and rapid changes of scene.

Thence, too, came his love of music, sometimes introduced merely as background accompaniment, sometimes built into the body of a play. Fundamentally, however, he is interested in developing a realistic form of theatrical expression somewhat along the lines of the experiments made fully a generation earlier by Hebbel and Ludwig. His themes are diverse. In his first drama of this kind, *Der Pfarrer von Kirchfeld* (*The Kirchfeld Priest*, 1870), he chooses a religious subject, showing a young idealistic pastor, Hell, in conflict both with the church authorities and with a local dignitary, Count Finsterberg. Having taken into his service a girl, Anna, he is traduced by evil-minded neighbours and removed from his cure, but, rising out of despair, determines to carry on the good fight. For *Heimg'funden!* (*Home at Last*, 1885) he introduces as the main figure a Dr Hammer who deserts his old mother in order to devote himself to money-making, who is ruined and is on the point of committing suicide when he is persuaded to return to the scenes of his boyhood, there achieving peace of soul. Often Anzengruber strikes a note of sardonic laughter, as in *Der G'wissenswurm* (*The Worm of Conscience*, 1874), with its old farmer, Grillhofer, his poor brother-in-law, Dusterer, and Grillhofer's bright, joyous illegitimate daughter, Liese Horlacher. The scene in which the farmer, persuaded that it is his duty to visit the girl whom he had seduced in his youth, finds in his former flame a termagant mother of a dozen children, has genuine verve and spirit. Clearly, however, this author felt more at ease when his subjects were melodramatically full of exciting incident or when they were dark with disaster. Typical is *Der Meineidbauer* (*The Perjurer*, 1871), in which the main plot is based on the perjury whereby the wicked Ferner robs the heroine, Vroni, of her just inheritance, and which gloomily combines with this dark romantic tale equally dark romantic scenes in the mountains among the haunts of smugglers. Typical in another way is the burlesquely titled *Der Doppelselbstmord* (*The Double Suicide*, 1875), where a pair of rustic lovers, compelled by circumstances, end their lives in a death pact. This is the mood that dominates in Anzengruber's most famous drama, *Das vierte Gebot* (*The Fourth Commandment*, 1877), a play which, because of its bitter attack on the crushing of youthful spirit by the old, was seized upon eagerly by Otto Brahm when he first opened the doors of his Freie Bühne. In this play still another theme much to be exploited by the realistic dramatists of the end of the century— what may be styled the 'generations' theme—made its appearance. The same year that *Das vierte Gebot* was thus introduced to a

Berlin audience the work of two younger writers, *Die Familie Selicke* (*The Selicke Family*, 1890), by Arno Holz and Johannes Schlaf, was produced at the Freie Bühne. Here misery prevails. The family circle is made up of a weak-willed mother whose whole interest is focused on her dying youngest daughter, a father besotten with drink, and a girl who is forced to break her engagement for the sake of her parents. Naturalism of the gloomiest kind is now being introduced to the German stage. In a work of similar tone Schlaf produced later his tortured portrait of a criminal in *Meister Ölze* (*Master Olze*, 1892), thus establishing yet another model for the naturalistic drama.

Others during these years eagerly and viciously pursued similar ideas. Max Halbe, in whom is to be discerned a theatrical power beyond that of most of his companions, delineates a doomed household in *Emporkömmling* (*The Upstart*, 1889), where a son, instead of a daughter, is ruined by a hard, obstinate father—a descendant of Anthony in Hebbel's *Maria Magdalena*. Halbe's most influential plays, however, came only in the nineties—*Der Eisgang* (*The Ice Floe*, 1892), *Jugend* (*Youth*, 1893), and *Mutter Erde* (*Mother Earth*, 1897). Over the German-Polish lovers, Paul and Antoinette, in the first of these heavily burdened dramas hangs the menace of heredity, and in the conflict of son and father clashing social concepts are embodied. *Jugend* tells a terrible story of a girl, Annchen, who, falling in love with a young student, is murdered by her imbecile half-brother, Amandus, who aims his gun at the man and by mistake shoots her dead. In the third play romantic love, carried from youth to middle age, yields nothing but bitterness, and the familiar double suicide closes the action. Equally violent are the dismal themes of *Die tausendjährige Reich* (*The Thousand-year Reich*, 1900) and of *Der Strom* (*The Stream*, 1903). Although Halbe possesses some power, and although his example was of considerable influence during these formative years, there is little likelihood, now that this gloomy naturalism has lost its force, that he will be remembered otherwise than as a writer of temporary appeal. All that can be said is that he is outspoken in his championing of the poor, although generally this championing assumes rather crude form—as in *Die gerechte Welt* (*The Just World*, 1897), where, artificially, the miseries of the simple mechanic Hügel and his sister, Anna, are contrasted with the evil machinations of the capitalistic Grossmann brothers.

Among these revolutionaries, most of them so extreme that their writings could be expected to make appeal only in limited circles, two men in particular were responsible for bringing the naturalistic problem play to the attention of more general audiences. The first of these, Hermann Sudermann, once was hailed as among the greatest of the realistic playwrights of these years, but time has not dealt gently with him, and his reputation now has become rather sadly tarnished. Serious in aim, he is yet seen to have sacrificed honesty of purpose to theatrical effect: the insincerities that were not so obvious to his contemporaries have been blatantly revealed by the light of passing decades.

Die Ehre (*Honour*, 1889), his first play, won him considerable esteem. Presented not in an independent theatre but on a public stage, it must have appeared daring indeed to an ordinary audience. Its object was to delineate, in sensational terms, the vast cleavage in viewpoint between the code of the upper-middle class and that of the proletariat. There is nothing startling here in the discussion of a problem still potent in Germany; there is no vision; there is but mediocre development of character; but unquestionably this young author displayed considerable perspicacity in seizing on the kind of problem for which his audience were eagerly expectant.

If in this play he turned a satiric pen upon a current social code, in his second drama, *Sodoms Ende* (*The Destruction of Sodom*, 1891), he attacked the vices rampant in aristocratic circles. The hero is an artist who is taken up by a rich woman, is seduced by her, and is instrumental in causing misery to more than one of his companions as he sinks lower and lower in the moral scale. A providential, poetic-justice death immediately following a scene of repentance brings to a neat conclusion a play honest in parts and clumsily spurious in others. This work, moderately successful though it was, brought less attention to Sudermann than his once-famous *Die Heimat* (*Home*; usually played as *Magda*, 1893), which might be regarded as *La dame aux camélias* of the nineties. Here a heroine dominates the play—a girl who rebels against the strait-laced morality of her home, works out a life of her own as a concert singer, has an *affaire* with a local dignitary, and bears an illegitimate child; in melodramatic manner her father demands that she marry her seducer and, on her refusal, has an apoplectic stroke and dies.

Illicit love has a fascination for Sudermann. In *Das Glück im Winkel* (*The Vale of Content*, 1896) the heroine, who has married the headmaster of a school, encounters her former lover, who urges her to go off with him. Amid a welter of confused hopes and fears, she confides in her husband, and the curtain falls on a reasonably happy domestic fireside. Less fortunate is Countess Beata in

Es lebe das Leben (*Long Live Life*, or *The Joy of Living*, 1902): she too has had her lover, but abandons the *affaire* when her husband and he become friends. Most of the plot is taken up with a complicated endeavour to still the voice of slander, and at the end, when the endeavour has proved successful, Beata, rather unnecessarily, puts poison in her glass and dies immediately after proposing a toast to the joy of life.

This last play suggests that when Sudermann treats of upper-class existence he is somewhat out of his element: only when his main characters are of lower-middle class does he reach even slight honesty in portraiture. His picture, in *Die Schmetterlingsschlacht* (*The Battle of the Butterflies*, 1895), of the struggle waged by the courageous widow Frau Hergentheim to preserve a semblance of respectability for her family is of moderate merit. There is fairly vigorous ironic comedy in *Der Sturmgeselle Sokrates* (*Socrates, Companion of the Storm*, 1903), where the democratic dreams of 1848 are shown amusingly, yet pathetically, pursued by old men, once young and ardent revolutionaries, now washed by time into a backwater. What approaches tragic tension appears in the fated loves of Georg and Marikke in *Johannisfeuer* (*Midsummer Eve's Fire*, 1900), and in the equally dark theme of *Morituri* (1896). This last-mentioned play really consists of three connected one-act pieces, *Teja*, *Fritschen*, and *Das ewig Männliche* (*The Eternal Male*). In each the hero is destined to die. The first deals with a gloomy King of the Goths, trapped near Vesuvius by Byzantine forces; from this barbaric atmosphere we are carried in *Fritschen* to the modern world where a young officer is forced into a duel from which, we understand, he will not come alive; in the third play the central figure perishes because of a jest undertaken in all mirthfulness.

By no means a genius of the calibre of Ibsen or Strindberg, Sudermann yet deserves perhaps more praise than critics and historians of the theatre have been prepared to grant him. He may have sought mainly for commercial success, but the stage needs men who, determined to appeal to the general public, are still determined to provide that public with something more than common entertainment.

It is, of course, true that his often sentimental treatment of current problems appears superficial when we compare it with the bold ideas put forward by such men as Otto Erich Hartleben and Georg Hirschfeld. The former approaches the entire subject of moral concepts with a questioning and even anarchic spirit. Indeed, in *Die sittliche Forderung* (*The Moral Demand*, 1896) his heroine, a concert singer like the heroine of *Magda*, laughs at her lover when he urges her to marry him, stating her preference for a life free from the ties of marriage. Like several of his companions, Hartleben exercises his mind mightily over the way in which youth is prevented, through economic necessity, from marrying until an age when healthy passion has become vitiated and dulled. This is the topic that occupies his attention in *Die Erziehung zur Ehe* (*Education for Marriage*, 1893). *Rosenmontag* (*Rose Monday*, or *Love's Carnival*, 1900) attacks the Prussian military code by showing a young officer who feels himself forced to shoot the girl he loves because his colleagues have, in their conversation, spoken slightingly of her virtue. In the same questioning spirit he approaches the entire social life of man in what is his most interesting drama, *Hanna Jagert* (1893), wherein he traces the struggles of a poor girl who moves from the haranguing of a socialistic soap-box to the polite conversation of a baron's hall. Georg Hirschfeld's claim to attention among this group of writers depends partly on his technical skill and dramatic experiments, partly on his power of delineating, in incisive terms, the social *milieu* of his time. His experimental spirit is well illustrated in *Agnes Jordan* (1898), the first drama to attempt the plan—later popularized by twentieth-century playwrights—of presenting a family through the passage of decades. The first act of this work is set in 1865, and the young, optimistic Agnes Jordan introduced to us here is shown as she passes through disillusioned middle life (with scenes in 1873 and 1882) until she reaches the serenity of age in 1896. In the one-act *Zu Hause* (*At Home*, 1893) Hirschfeld displays his extraordinary ability to reveal domestic interiors: this household of Doergens, a goodwilled, hard-working tradesman, with its selfish wife, its tragically debilitated daughter, and mean-spirited son, is etched in gloomy but memorable terms. A similar atmosphere is presented in *Die Mütter* (*The Mothers*, 1895), which shows a young artist introducing to his family the mistress whom he has found in a social circle lower than his own; with perhaps slightly unnatural perspicacity she decides that she will merely be a drag upon him, and, without letting him know that she is to bear his child, she pathetically departs.

Among these authors Max Dreyer also deserves mention, both because of the manner in which he explored the possibilities of what may be called the drama of atmospheric realism in *Winterschlaf* (*Hibernation*, 1895), and because of his extending the field of the social-problem play into the sphere of philosophic thought. His *Der Probekandidat* (*The Practice Teacher*, 1899), the first of many works in many tongues dealing with educational problems, takes as hero a young biology teacher, Dr Heitmann, who finds himself forced either to palter with the truth and abandon his Darwinian beliefs or else to lose his position. With this may be associated *Flachsmann als Erzieher* (*Flachsmann the Teacher*, 1900), a witty treatment of scholastic life by Otto Ernst (Otto Ernst Schmidt). For his *Drei* (*Three*, 1892) Dreyer won some fame, and, indeed, this drama—which takes its title from a trio consisting of the nervous *littérateur* Karl Genzmer, his wife, Susanne, and his friend Hans Martiensson—has some value. With skill Dreyer develops his theme—the way in which Susanne is led to fall in love with Hans because of the suspicions expressed by her husband; yet, when the last curtain falls, there is little of abiding interest left in our minds, largely because of the realistic sentimentalism that colours so much of the action.

Although by no means a follower of current Ibsenite ideas, Ludwig Fulda essayed the realistic style in his own way. *Die Kamaraden* (*Comrades*, 1894) is an amusing satire, almost Molièresque in its proportions, of the 'new woman.' When Frau Thekla Hildebrand, wife of a rich merchant, leaves his house because it fetters her soul all she gets is a divorce and the chagrin of seeing her husband marry her young friend. Less gay by far are Fulda's earlier writings, *Die Sklavin* (*The Slave-girl*, 1892) and *Das verlorene Paradies* (*The Lost Paradise*, 1890)—plays which, even if not of prime value, served to extend the confines of the social theatre. It is noteworthy that, in addition to penning such works, this author could also produce a romantic *Der Talisman* (*The Talisman*, 1892) and an Arabian Nights tale of the kind represented in *Der Sohn des Kalifen* (*The Caliph's Son*, 1896), where social purpose is clad in richly Eastern robes. In Austria Karl Schoenherr extended the stage's confines still farther, although the finest of his dramas, coming after the turn of the century, were rather elaborations of hints put before him by his predecessors than excitingly fresh experiments. In *Die Bildschnitzern* (*The Wood-carvers*, 1900) he early displayed his tragically ironic mood by dealing with a plot in which a husband consciously seeks death in order to bring happiness to his wife and his dearly loved friend. It was the tragic bitterness of life that appealed to this author—the compelling power of hunger that drives a young boy in *Karrnerleut'* (*Caravan Folk*, 1904) to betray his own father for the pitiful reward of a loaf of bread; the sardonic situation in *Erde* (*Earth*, 1907) where an old peasant causes his coffin to be made while the family quarrel over the disposal of his goods even before he is dead; the infatuation of a woman, in *Der Weibsteufel* (*The She-devil*, 1914), for a man with whom she has been toying in order to protect her husband; the fate of three children, in *Die Kindertragödie* (*The Children's Tragedy*, 1919), as they watch their mother engaging in a love-affair. About all of Schoenherr's work lingers a peculiar bitterness and a mood of miserable resignation, made endurable only by his undoubted skill in character-portrayal. With almost adolescent sentiment his companion Felix Dörmann, once one of Vienna's literary lights, treats in *Sein Sohn* (*His Son*, 1896) the story of a maladjusted young sculptor who is obsessed by the thought that his greater sculptor father has by the power of his art deprived him of glory. There is a bottle of poison conveniently handy for the final act.

Hauptmann's eclecticism and Sudermann's flair for the popularizing of the new meet in the work of another Austrian author, Hermann Bahr. Bahr can be amusing in an almost Shavian manner, as in *Josephine* (1898); he can deal comically with social problems, as in *Das Konzert* (*The Concert*, 1909), which presents a portrait of a musician, in love with his wife yet demanding the excitement of other love-affairs; in other plays, such as *Der Meister* (*The Master*, 1903), he can pursue a serious course, in this drama presenting a study of a doctor who, proud of his intellect, seeks to be master of the world surrounding him. Among his dramatic works not least notable is *Das Tschaperl* (*The Fellow*, 1897), in which two contrasting couples are presented: in each case a husband has a wife who wins fame and fortune, one by writing an opera, the other by acting. Jealousy and shattered affection result in the first household; in the other the husband complacently accepts the advantages accruing from the wealth and patronage his wife's beauty brings. It is interesting to note how frequently this theme of the woman artist appears in plays (particularly German and Austrian) of this time: attention may here be called to one other drama of the kind, *Ewige Liebe* (*Eternal Love*, 1897), by Hermann Faber, which deals with the passion of a young professor for a violinist who, although attracted by him, wishes, like the heroines of Sudermann and Hartleben, to be independent and to lead her own life.

All these authors, however, fade in importance when they are put alongside the German Wedekind and the Austrian Schnitzler, and even these two must obviously cede place to the still greater Hauptmann. With Frank Wedekind the realistic drama is seen, as in the writings of Strindberg, to be at the point of shattering its restraining walls. Like Strindberg, he moves from naturalism of the starkest kind to symbolic abstractions; at one moment we are confronted with merciless pictures of the world around us; at the next we are drawn into the haunted realm of the nightmare. Like Strindberg's, too, his dramas are obsessed by thoughts of those sexual relationships which he sees determining men's lives by their terrible power.

Wedekind will certainly never prove a popular playwright: his methods are too blunt and too personal to receive wide acceptance, yet no one can read his plays without feeling that here indeed was a man of genius, even if that genius lacks the balance of form and the assured harmony from which alone true mastery springs. Coming before the world with *Die junge Welt* (*The World of Youth*) in 1890, he showed, in this drama of adolescent dreams in a girls' boarding-school, what was to prove his lifelong obsession. Then, the following year, he startled even the revolutionary enthusiasts with his utterly frank, incredibly brutal, and still strangely beautiful *Frühlings Erwachen* (*Spring's Awakening*), with its mixture of appearance and reality, its naturalism and its symbolism, its lyrical chant of love and its tortured depiction of adolescent imaginings. Suicide, misery, joy, are presented here in a flame of outpouring words. Basically, the story is that of two boys: one, Moritz, commits suicide because of his brooding over sex; the other, Melchior, gets a young girl with child. In a final scene of fantasy Melchior comes to the graveyard, where his friend's ghost bids him take his own life, but from such thoughts he is drawn by a symbolic figure, the Man with the Mask, who leads him back to life. The world of adolescence is changed in *Erdgeist* (*Earth Spirit*, 1895) into the world of later youth, with a tragically symbolic heroine in Lulu, who, evil incarnate, lusts instead of loves; her diabolic power causes her first husband to die by a stroke, her second to commit suicide, while she herself murders her third after she has had an *affaire* with his son. In a sequel, *Die Büchse der Pandora* (*Pandora's Box*; printed 1904), peculiarly written with one act in German, one in French, one in English, this wretched woman is shown moving to a dismal end, even while a spirit greater than hers arises in the person of her Lesbian devotee, the Countess Geschwitz. Equally violent is the action of *Totentanz* (*The Dance of Death*, 1906); of the three connected plays—*Der Kammersänger* (*The Tenor*, 1899), *Musik* (*Music*, 1907), and *Schloss Wetterstein* (*Castle Wetterstein*, 1910); and of *Der Marquis von Keith* (1901). In all of these love, natural and degenerate, and lust are the dominating forces, while the style moves erratically and erotically from the real to the allegoric, with a kind of spluttering lunacy gradually becoming more and more evident. In others of Wedekind's dramas, such as *So ist das Leben* (*Such is Life*, 1902), *Karl Hetmann* (1908), *Simson, oder Scham und Eifersucht* (*Samson; or, Shame and Jealousy*, 1914), and *Herakles* (1917), the lunacy becomes predominant, and we move in a wild, fantastic nightmare of sexual imaginings. Although it is impossible to aver that Wedekind has been grossly underrated, and although much of his would-be tragic vaporizings become simply amusing in their immaturity of expression, it must be confessed that in his dramas resides an inchoate strength and a peculiar intensity of spirit.

Love too dominates in the writings of Arthur Schnitzler, albeit in a vastly different manner. Wedekind was a man who never, in thought, got beyond the sexual torments of a hypersensitive eighteen or twenty; Schnitzler's world is that of disillusioned middle life. He has long passed the adolescence that keeps Wedekind so firmly in its grip; he has acquired the wisdom that recognizes how darkly we are surrounded by illusions, and how much more terrible it is to live without these illusions than to accept them frankly for what they are. In style Wedekind was the type of irritated artist who impatiently shatters existing forms; Schnitzler is of the company of those who frankly accept such existing forms, even although they may realize their inadequacy, and endeavour to put into them fresh content. From one point of view his dramatic structure appears antiquated and artificial, from another its quality is richer than the erratic and discordant venturings which dictated Wedekind's latter plays. Wedekind is the wild-eyed, propagandist rebel; Schnitzler is the sad-eyed, compassionate poet of resignation.

His introduction to the literary world came in the form of a series of one-act plays (perhaps dramatic sketches would be a better description) under the general title of *Anatol* (1893), slightly sentimental, delicately flavoured, the gentle reminiscences of diverse affections. These were followed by a play, *Liebelei* (*Light o' Love*, 1895), by which he is perhaps best known to the outside world. The hero of this drama is a young Fritz Loheimer, whose *affaire* with a married woman, Catherine Binder, is becoming so serious that his light-hearted friend introduces him to a girl of lower-middle-class surroundings, Christine, in the hope that a little philandering with her will cure him of his obsession. Fritz lightly toys with Christine, and his shallow love-making is exquisitely contrasted with the deep affection which is awakened in her heart. In the end he is killed in a duel by Binder, Catherine's husband, and gradually the wretched Christine learns the truth. He is dead,

he has been killed on account of another woman; he has left her
no note; before he went to the duel he had merely casually spoken
of Christine among other things. Yet, knowing all this, her loyalty
to him still makes life seem meaningless without his presence.
Suddenly she turns to his friend Theodore:

> CHRISTINE [*with sudden resolve*]: Theodore, take me to him—I want to
> see him—once more I want to see him—his face—— Theodore,
> take me to him.
> THEODORE [*with a gesture, hesitatingly*]: No. . . .
> CHRISTINE: Why 'no'? You can't refuse me that! Surely I can see
> him once more?
> THEODORE: It is too late.
> CHRISTINE: Too late? To see his corpse . . . is it too late? Yes. . . .
> Yes. . . .   [*She does not understand.*
> THEODORE: He was buried this morning.
> CHRISTINE [*with the greatest horror*]: Buried. . . . And I didn't know
> about it? They shot him . . . and put him in his coffin and carried
> him out and buried him down in the earth—and I couldn't even see
> him once more? He's been dead two days—and you didn't come
> and tell me?
> THEODORE [*moved*]: In these two days I have. . . . You cannot dream
> all that I . . . Consider that it was my duty to notify his parents—
> I had to think of many things—and then my own state of mind.
> CHRISTINE: Your . . .
> THEODORE: And then the . . . it was done very quietly. . . . Only
> the closest relatives and friends . . .
> CHRISTINE: The closest——? And I——? . . . What am I?

In spite of all, she bids to be taken to his grave, and there she dies.
About the entire play, realistic though it is, breathes a peculiar air
of melancholy poetry.

Liebelei is thoroughly typical of Schnitzler's art as a whole.
Four years before, in *Das Märchen* (*The Fairy-tale*, 1891), he had
written a play of social ideas, and a similar style appeared in *Freiwild*
(*Free Game*, 1896) and *Das Vermächtnis* (*The Legacy*, 1897); in these
questions were asked such as were being asked by his companions:
can a girl who has committed an error in her youth ever be rehabi-
litated? and, what is honour? But fundamentally such themes were
alien to Schnitzler's spirit. Basically alien, too, was the kind of
objective case-study of sex which appears in *Reigen* (*Hands Around*;
written 1896–97, printed 1900): these were merely pages from the
doctor's diary. Much more characteristic were *Der grüne Kakadu*
(*The Green Cockatoo*, 1898) and the strangely appealing *Der einsame
Weg* (*The Lonely Way*, 1904). In the latter of these two dramas

Schnitzler carries his method one stage farther: action almost disappears, and what is set before us is a study, entirely unsentimental yet sadly gracious, of the loneliness of age. Pursuing this actionless theatre, Schnitzler, like his contemporary Maeterlinck, found the one-act form peculiarly suited to his genius, and many of his writings, from this time on, are cast in that shape. In *Der Ruf des Lebens* (*The Call of Life*, 1905) he expresses, even more forcibly than in his earlier dramas, his belief in life, in the open-armed acceptance of experience, and at the same time his belief in the power of devoted self-sacrifice. *Lebendige Stunden* (*Living Hours*, 1901) tells the story of a woman who, realizing that her ill-health is ruining her son's artistic powers, commits suicide: what her death means is trenchantly presented in a contrast provided by the son and by an older man, who had been the mother's lover.

The extraordinary power of Schnitzler's dramatic writing rests in the fact that in it three qualities are merged. He is the scientific observer, objective, unimpassioned; he is the cynic, who sees the follies and the meannesses of the world; and he is the poet, his heart filled with compassion, a love of beauty, and faith. Thus at one moment he can write his *Reigen*, at another his *Lebendige Stunden*, and at a third sardonically witty studies such as *Zwischenspiel* (*Interlude*, or *Intermezzo*, 1904). His best work is achieved when, subtly uniting these qualities, he depicts the intimacies of the human soul, not in tortured spirit like Strindberg, not blatantly like some of his German companions, but with a strange, resigned, melancholy mood unique in its tone. Such plays as *Komtesse Mizzi* (*Countess Mizzi*, 1909) and *Das weite Land* (*The Vast Domain*, 1910) most perfectly offer him opportunity for the exercise of his peculiar power—a power that draws its strength not from violence and sensationalism, but from quietness and reflection. The same power allows him to create impressive scenes in his *Professor Bernhardi* (1912), where a Jewish doctor refuses to permit a Roman Catholic priest to administer the last sacrament to a dying girl, because she pathetically believes she has been cured and the doctor has not the heart to shatter her illusions. Towards the end of his life, in a manner reminiscent of the pattern set by many another playwright, he tended to let the symbolic and the fantastic take possession of him—witness his *Fink und Fliederbusch* (1917), *Der Gang zum Weiher* (*The Pathway to the Pond*, 1925), and *Im Spiel der Sommer-lüfte* (*In the Play of the Summer's Breezes*, 1930)—but these rather tedious works should not allow us to forget the inimitable quality of his writings during youth and middle age.

GERHART HAUPTMANN

Titanic as is Wedekind in his frenzied sex obsession, nobly resigned and artistically gracious as is Schnitzler, the writings of both men fall below the broad, if strangely disappointing, accomplishment of Gerhart Hauptmann, the only German dramatist of this period who is worthy of being associated in name with Ibsen and Strindberg.

Hauptmann's contributions to the theatre depend, like Ibsen's, primarily upon the fact that, gifted with keen powers of observation, he succeeded, at one and the same time, in developing his own individual style and in bringing to culmination the best qualities of his predecessors. His sense of dialect variations was extraordinary; he knew how to construct his scenes so as to give the impression of reality, and at the same time arrest the attention of an audience; he carried a stage farther the Ibsen development of the descriptive and atmospheric stage direction. From Hebbel he inherited the tradition of the bourgeois tragedy; from later naturalistic authors he derived the concept of objective depiction of life, so that he could speak of himself as an Æolian harp whose strings are stirred by every slightest breeze; from others he gained the concept of the social problem drama; and from others still he got the idea of the vaster philosophic theatre, exploring the deeper roots of our being.

His advent was meteoric. In the year 1889 the Freie Bühne staged *Vor Sonnenaufgang* (*Before Sunrise*), and this, his first play, immediately created a stir in intellectual circles. The *Tobacco Road* of its day, it presented an utterly sordid scene of degradation. Two characters only are raised above the bestial level—the young Alfred Loth, who is visiting a Silesian village in pursuit of his economic studies, and Helene Krause, a girl who, though born there, has been educated outside it. Her father is a besotten wretch, who falls so low as to assault his own daughter; Martha, Helene's sister, married to an engineer, is tainted with the taste for drink; her stepmother is carrying on an *affaire* with her nephew, Wilhelm Kahl. Out of this desperate atmosphere Helene hopes to escape with Loth, but he is so shocked by thought of the hereditary vices which must be implanted in her that he departs. The closing of the entire action by means of stage direction is so characteristic of atmosphere and technique that it may be quoted in full. Helene enters the empty room:

She looks about her and calls softly: "Alfred! Alfred!" As she receives no answer, she calls out again more quickly: "Alfred! Alfred!" She has

DEGAS:
"FOUR DANCERS"

By courtesy of the National Gallery
of Art, Washington, Chester Dale
Collection (Loan)

TOULOUSE-LAUTREC: "QUADRILLE AT THE MOULIN-ROUGE"

By courtesy of the National Gallery of Art, Washington, Chester Dale Collection (Loan) hurried to the door of the conservatory, through which she gazes anxiously. She goes into the conservatory, but reappears shortly. *"Alfred!"* Her disquiet increases. She peers out of the window. *"Alfred!"* She opens the window and mounts a chair that stands before it. At this moment there resounds clearly from the yard the shouting of the drunken farmer, her father, who is coming home from the inn. *"Hay-hee! Ain' I a han'some feller? Ain' I got a fine-lookin' wife? Ain' I got a couple o' han'some gals? Hay-hee!"* HELEN utters a short cry and runs, like a hunted creature, towards the middle door. From there she discovers the letter which LOTH has left lying on the table. She runs to it, tears it open, feverishly takes in the contents, of which she audibly utters separate words. *"'Insuperable!' . . . 'Never again.' . . ."* She lets the letter fall and sways. *"It's over!"* She steadies herself, holds her head with both hands, and cries out in brief and piercing despair. *"It's over!"* She rushes out through the middle door. The farmer's voice without, drawing nearer. *"Hay-hee! Ain' the farm mine? Ain' I got a han'some wife? Ain' I a han'some feller?"* HELEN, still seeking LOTH half-madly, comes from the conservatory and meets EDWARD, who has come to fetch something from HOFFMANN'S room. She addresses him: *"Edward!"* He answers: *"Yes, Miss Krause."* She continues: *"I'd like to . . . like to . . . Dr Loth . . ."* EDWARD answers: *"Dr Loth drove away in Dr Schimmelpfennig's carriage."* He disappears into HOFFMANN'S room. *"True!"* HELEN cries out and holds herself erect with difficulty. In the next moment a desperate energy takes hold of her. She runs to the foreground and seizes the hunting-knife with its belt which is fastened to the stag's antlers above the sofa. She hides the weapon and stays quietly in the dark foreground until EDWARD, coming from HOFFMANN'S room, has disappeared through the middle door. The farmer's voice resounds more clearly from moment to moment. *"Hay-hee! Ain' I a han'some feller?"* At this sound, as at a signal, HELEN starts and runs, in her turn, into HOFFMANN'S room. The main room is empty, but one continues to hear the farmer's voice: *"Ain' I got the finest teeth? Ain' I got a fine farm?"* MIELE comes through the middle door and looks searchingly about. She calls: *"Miss Helen! Miss Helen!"* Meanwhile the farmer's voice: *"The money'sh mi-ine!"* Without further hesitation MIELE has disappeared into HOFFMANN'S room, the door of which she leaves open. In the next moment she rushes out with every sign of insane horror. Screaming, she spins around twice—thrice—screaming, she flies through the middle door. Her uninterrupted screaming, softening as it recedes, is audible for several seconds. Last there is heard the opening and resonant slamming of the heavy house door, the tread of the farmer stumbling about in the hall, and his coarse, nasal, thick-tongued drunkard's voice echoes through the room: *"Hay-hee! Ain' I got a couple o' han'some gals?"*

CURTAIN

The following year appeared *Das Friedensfest* (*The Feast of Reconciliation*, or *The Reconciliation*, 1890), almost equally sombre in

T

theme and tone, while in 1891 came *Einsame Menschen* (*Lonely Men*, or *Lonely Lives*), in which, with subtle skill, Hauptmann reveals the way in which the ordinary circumstances of life, without the incursion of any evil forces, can suck away joy and creative power. In *Before Dawn* Helene had stood, dismayed, among a group of dipsomaniacs and perverted souls; in *Lonely Lives* Johannes Vockerat is enveloped by the shallowly good. His father and mother, unlike the Krauses, are morally respectable, and they have a real interest in furthering their son's career; his wife, Käthe, is the very embodiment of good nature. What he lacks in his family circle is intellectual companionship: he tries to think for himself, and his thoughts appear merely shocking to these worthy burghers reared in a safe conservative tradition. Into his life comes a young girl, Anna Mahr, attuned to him in spirit, and through association with her he might have risen to something greater; but such intellectual companionship is not understood by his family. Anna has to go, and in despair he commits suicide.

After producing an unimportant *Kollege Crampton* (*Colleague Crampton*, 1892) Hauptmann turned to a new sphere in *Die Weber* (*The Weavers*, 1892), and at once demonstrated that in him lay a quality beyond that possessed by any of his companions. Those earlier plays of his might have been written by one of the others: *The Weavers* was utterly unique both in concept and technique. In general the realistic drama had been tending in the direction of economy in the use of characters; it was no uncommon thing to find, in the early nineties, dramas restricted to three or four main persons; here Hauptmann suddenly set a whole crowd upon the stage, and, in addition, made that crowd the hero of his drama. Even although both Schiller and Büchner had suggested the making of the crowd the central collective figure in a play, new ground unquestionably was being broken here; and new ground too was being broken by the combination of the realistic method and of the historical theme. For the most part, with the exception of Büchner's *Dantons Tod*, the many historical dramas produced during the seventies and eighties had searched far back into the almost legendary past and had treated their characters 'poetically': in *The Weavers* Hauptmann returns to the year 1844, taking his inspiration confessedly from his own father's accounts of the author's grandfather, "who in his young days sat at the loom, a poor weaver like those here depicted," and he deals with these persons as though they were contemporaries. Fundamentally his theme is revolution. The terrible conditions amid which the weavers live are depicted with grim anger; the manner in which the traditional subservience of the mass of the men is changed—partly by the pressure of circumstance, partly by the righteous indignation of Moritz Jaeger, who has returned to his native village after service in the army—into fiery revolt is carefully traced; and the play ends with the crowd sacking the home of the 'capitalist' Dreissiger and meeting the soldiery with volleys of stones.

Nothing quite like *The Weavers* had ever appeared on the stage before, and with it Hauptmann opened up vast possibilities. Hitherto the theatre of the realists had been documentary or concerned with bourgeois problems: Hauptmann first introduced the proletariat on to the boards and suggested a revolutionary theme. Here, however, enters a paradox: a lesser author, thus having accomplished something new, would have proceeded to turn out other *Weavers* by the dozen, and we cannot declare that we should have esteemed Hauptmann more had he pursued such a course. At the same time, when we look at the erratic path of his later career, during which he moved restlessly from style to style, we are almost bound to acknowledge that his violent artistic see-sawing is indicative of a less assured sense of purpose than that we discern in Ibsen or in Strindberg. His next play was "a thieves' comedy," *Der Biberpelz* (*The Beaver Coat*, 1893). With richly ironic comedy, much of the kind that Gay exploited in *The Beggar's Opera*, Hauptmann here takes as his heroine a thoroughly disreputable washerwoman, Mrs Wolff, who, in league with her equally disreputable husband, steals a fur coat and proceeds thoroughly to baffle the addle-pated justice von Wehrhahn. She stands, as the curtain falls, in meek humility while Wehrhahn lauds her honesty and, shaking her head resignedly, murmurs: "Well, then, I don't know no more what to think. . . ." From this atmosphere Hauptmann next moved into the symbolic and poetic realm of *Hanneles Himmelfahrt* (*The Assumption of Hannele*, or *Hannele*, 1893), a complete departure from his earlier styles. Amid the sordid surroundings of a dirty hospital peopled by the very scum of Berlin's underworld, there mysteriously blossoms forth a strange vision in which the real becomes the ideal, in which concepts of formal Christianity mingle with the spirit of Hans Andersen's fairy-tales. The effect is achieved by introducing into the wretched *milieu* of the outcasts a little girl, Hannele, who, after having been brutally ill-treated and neglected by her besotted stepfather, has been brought there to die. As she lies on her cot she dreams—and the visions that come to her are, quite naturally, a far-rago of all she has known and heard. Heaven and Hell are there, the devil and God's angels, the palace of the fairy prince and the glories of paradise. In effect, Hauptmann is employing here the basic methods used in Strindberg's final plays, except that the dream, instead of being presented in itself, becomes a kind of play within a play.

Pursuing his avid search for new forms, Hauptmann next proceeded into the realm of the historical drama, producing in *Florian Geyer* (1894) another play where an attempt is made to treat the life of former generations in a 'realistic' spirit. We are far here from earlier romantic styles; all the flamboyance of the Schiller school has gone, and instead we are regaled with dialogue which the author tries to render at once historically correct and true to life. The treatment of the theme too is different. *Florian Geyer* takes shape as a social drama, with the peasantry of the sixteenth century the hero, and with plentiful display of revolutionary sentiment.

This effort was, to Hauptmann's anger and dismay, ill-received by the public; but he was amply compensated by the acclaim which greeted still another experiment, this time in the style of the symbolic, *Die versunkene Glocke* (*The Sunken Bell*, 1896). The power of this play derives in no little measure from the manner in which it reflects the author's own aspirations and doubts, although in the very process of doing so it indirectly reveals his weaknesses.

In *The Sunken Bell* this reflection of the author's own uncertainty is presented through the medium of a fairy-tale. Attempts have been made to interpret the drama as illustrating the general problem of the modern artist: rather is it to be regarded as applying solely to Hauptmann's own personality. The action opens with a scene introducing Rautendelein, a sprite of the woods, with some of her elvish companions; one of these, a hob-goblin creature, tells how some men have been dragging a great bell to the church, but have been cheated of their object: the bell has been tipped over a gulf and now is lying at the bottom of a lake. At this enters Heinrich, the maker of the bell, faint and weary; Rautendelein succours him. "Thou art not used to mountain ways," she tells him,

> Thy home
> Lies in the vale below, where mortals dwell.
> And, like a hunter who once fell from the cliff
> While giving chase to some wild mountain fowl,
> Thou hast climbed far too high. And yet . . . that man
> Was not quite fashioned as the man thou art.

From this point the symbolic allegory develops. Heinrich is an artist, and he stretches out arms imploringly to this forest maiden, calling her his fantasy. Heinrich is married to Magda, but she cannot share his visions: when he is brought down on a litter from the mountainside she can only rejoice at his being saved, what the loss of the bell means to him she cannot fathom, and when he tells her that his work was faulty, that the bell now lying at the bottom of the lake "was not made for the heights," she is merely puzzled. This was a fine bell, she avers, and fails to understand as he insists that it was merely for the valley, not for the mountain-top. Rautendelein comes to him and saves him from despair, and he goes to the mountains with her, but the ties of the valley are still strong upon him, and in the end he dies, hearing "the Sun-bell's song." The skill by which Hauptmann has invigorated the scenes of this morality play keeps it from being tedious, but as a whole it is sadly representative of his own failure: the varied claims of valley and hill were too strong for his spirit.

After an unimportant *Elga* (1896) and *Das Hirtenlied* (*Pastoral*, 1898) he returned once more to the realistic style in *Fuhrmann Henschel* (*Drayman Henschel*, 1898), a grim, tragic essay in the breaking of a vital soul. Henschel, the central figure, is a sturdy, good-natured, lusty, vigorous man; his wife, dying, makes him promise that when she goes he will not marry another. Soon, however, he is caught in the toils of the ambitious maidservant Hanne Schäl, and by her tormenting cruelty is driven to suicide. There is a powerful economy here, and a directness of aim that wins our admiration, even although the characteristic German violence makes the entire action darkly sensational.

As though his restless spirit could find no peace anywhere, in his next play Hauptmann veered off again into the realms of the fantastic. *Schluck und Jau* (1899) is "an ironical masque with five interruptions," an elaboration of the ever-popular theme that Shakespeare had exploited in the Christopher Sly scenes of *The Taming of the Shrew*. Jau and Schluck, two peasants, are transformed by a nobleman into a 'prince' and his 'princess.' Out of this story the author extracts much opportunity for philosophizing on the nature of life, with plentiful suggestion taken from Calderón's *Life is a Dream*. When Jau has been returned to his normal state, at first he cannot quite believe that his glory has been taken from him; then slowly the truth penetrates his brains:

JAU: Ay, ay, tha's right.
    These ain't nothin' but ol' patched rags!
KARL: Be thou content, my man! Thou hast but dreamed.
    Yet I, even as thou seest me, and the prince
    And all his huntsmen and his serving-men—

> We dream! And to each one the moment comes,
> Seven times upon each day, in which he says:
> Thou wakest now and hitherto hast dreamed. . . .

JAU: So I just dreamed that there business! Well, well, well, well! You don't say! Well, I'll be damned! All right then! Things is as they is! How! Tell me this: Ain't I as good as him? He's got a good stomack! I got one, too. Better mebbe 'n his. He's got two eyes. All right. I ain't blind, neither. Has he got four stomacks or six eyes? I sleep all right; I c'n drink my whiskey. I c'n draw my breath as good as him! What? Ain't I right? . . . I tell you, I know, Schluck! I'm a prince an' I'm Jau too. Come, lil' brother. Even if I'm a prince, we'll go over to the inn now an' sit down with plain people an' I'll be reel condescending, reel friendly like!

Back to the darkly realistic came Hauptmann again in *Michael Kramer* (1900), in which, once more, suicide closes the action. The hero is a teacher of painting, who realizes that his own talents have never reached their hoped-for ends, and who dreams of so inspiring his son, Arnold, as to create in him the artist he himself would have wished to be. Unfortunately Arnold's spirit is incapable of scaling the heights. He is a weak, ineffective lad, who makes ridiculous love to a cheaply pert Liese Bäusch, and, mocked by his fellows, tormented at home, ends his miserable life by suicide.

With *Der rote Hahn* (*The Red Cock*, or *The Conflagration*, 1901) we return to the mood of the 'thieves' comedy. Frau Wolff of *The Beaver Coat* is now Frau Fielitz, wife of an elderly shoemaker, and, pursuing her earlier activities, decides to set fire to her house in order to collect the not inconsiderable insurance money. In this case the imbecilic Gustav Rauchhaupt is accused of the crime, and until the end Frau Fielitz cleverly keeps attention from herself—but that end is a grimmer one than the comically ironic lines of *The Beaver Coat*; a bitter sadness envelops the final scene as Rauchhaupt mourns for his boy and the dishonest old woman passes from this life.

The to-and-fro movement of Hauptmann's artistic development (perhaps 'groping' would be the better word) is shown by the strange mixture of styles in his next three plays—*Der arme Heinrich* (*Poor Heinrich*, or *Henry of Auë*, 1902), *Rose Bernd* (1903), and *Und Pippa tanzt!* (*And Pippa Dances!*, 1906). The first meanders into the world of medieval legend, telling the story of a knight afflicted with leprosy who can be cured only if a virgin is willing to give her blood for him. Ottegebe is prepared to make this sacrifice, and he, after much doubt, at last consents, only to reject the offer when he truly realizes what it means. As a result comes a miracle; he is cured by an act of God, and, restored to his former health, takes Ottegebe as his bride. In this play we are thoroughly immersed in romantic sentiment. Our immersion in the realistic when we turn to *Rose Bernd* is no less complete. Here is nothing but stark misery and sensational violence. Rose Bernd is a young peasant girl who has an *affaire* with a neighbouring landowner, Christopher Flamm, and who later is forced to give herself to the despicable Arthur Streckmann. Her guilty liaisons are made public; she bears a child and smothers it; she makes confession of her crime; only in the final words of her fiancé, August Keil, do we rise out of the dark pessimism surrounding all the action. "That girl," he says to the police constable, "what she must have suffered!" —and his simple phrase lets loose a wealth of pity. *And Pippa Dances!* moves again into the symbolic sphere. The first act is realistic enough, with its noisy scene in old Wende's tavern, but very soon we move among shadowy abstractions. Pippa becomes the symbol of beauty sought in diverse ways by diverse men. Old Huhn is the primitive man who wants her simply as a wife; the unnamed Manager of a factory wants her merely as a plaything; for herself, she is attracted by the self-centred artist Michael Hellriegel, while the wise Wann, described as "a mythological character," glimpses something of her mystery. This is a strange drama and perhaps not a very good one: the symbols are at once crude and synthetic, the atmosphere childishly clear in parts, in others mistily obscured.

The truth is that by this time Hauptmann was coming to the end of whatever true artistic power he possessed, and for the most part his erratic questing becomes henceforth blundering and ineffectual. *Die Jungfern vom Bischofsberg* (*The Maidens of Bischofsberg*, 1907) and *Kaiser Karls Geisel* (*Charlemagne's Hostage*, 1908) are of minor interest; *Griselda* (1909) is an uninspired treatment of a theme which, though basically absurd and not a trifle distasteful, has made a deep impress on the romantic imagination In 1911 came, disconcertingly, *Die Ratten* (*The Rats*), a "Berlin tragicomedy," with its degraded atmosphere and tone of dejection. Suicide (so familiar a device in Hauptmann's theatre) closes the action, yet many scenes, particularly those in which the irrepressible Harro Hassenreuter appears, are rich in bitter, earthy comedy. Complex in plot, the play suggests that modern style of dramaturgy in which several entirely separate plots run their course with little to unite them save the physical proximity of the characters living in city tenements. Suicide likewise was Hauptmann's solution for the hero of *Gabriel Schillings Flucht* (*Gabriel Schilling's Flight*, 1912), in which an artist is set between the opposing claims of wife and mistress.

A medley of mainly mediocre work followed: *Festspiel in deutschen Reimen* (*The Festival Play*, 1913), *Der Bogen des Odysseus* (*Ulysses' Bow*, 1914), *Winterballade* (*Winter Ballad*, 1917), *Der weisse Heiland* (*The White Saviour*, 1920), *Dorothea Augermann* (1926), *Die schwartze Maske* (*The Black Mask*, 1930), and so on to *Ulrich von Lichtenstein* in 1939 and *Iphigenia in Delphi* in 1941. Among these perhaps the only dramas of any interest are *Der Bogen des Odysseus*, where the Homeric hero is delineated in modern spirit as a man afraid to return home lest, having been forgotten by his friends there, he may be deprived of his illusions; and *Hamlet in Wittenberg* (1935), which essays to show the young Dane at the university immediately before news comes to him of his father's death. A democratically minded young idealist who has some theatrical and dramatic skill, author of a play on King Cophetua, he is outlined in such a way as to make probable the effect on his nature of the rude shock from outside reality. As friends he has his countryman Horatio, a young Danish student, Wilhelm, and a German aristocrat, Balthasar von Flachus, while among his acquaintances are the ribald vagrants Paulus and Achazius, as well as a riotous swaggerer, Juan Pedro de León. In the first act Hamlet rescues a pretty young gipsy girl, Hamida, with whom he falls in love, but who proves to be one of Hauptmann's characteristic faithless temptress women. The play is interesting rather than appealing.

Hauptmann's career, even up to his latest embracing of the Nazi philosophy, is peculiarly symbolic of the entire German genius. He has inventiveness and the flash of inspiration, but of that deeper desire to reach uttermost perfection in any one style or of consistency in patterning there is in his work no sign. The German drama of the nineteenth century consists largely of a long line of unfinished or shattered monuments, some of them strong, but strong largely by means of their violence. We cannot deny that Hauptmann possesses those qualities that warrant our putting him alongside Ibsen and Strindberg; the structural perfection of the one, however, and the deep intensity of the other fail to find expression in his writings, nor does he provide anything of value to take their place. Among all his plays there is hardly a character whom we can admire; the good characters are weak and pathetic, the strong are brutal. We can have nothing but praise for his energy and his craftsmanship, nothing but regret that that energy and craftsmanship have not been put to service in the creation of something more than the sorry world of his realistic dramas, something firmer than the nebulous realm of his fantasies.

THE PLAY OF IDEAS IN FRANCE

FRANCE presents a startling contrast to Germany during these years. The German theatre wins attention because of the contributions made by a number of highly individual playwrights: in Paris there is no single dramatist during these years who deserves to be put alongside even Hauptmann—far less alongside Ibsen or Strindberg—yet the cumulative efforts of a group of late-nineteenth-century writers unquestionably make the French stage of this time assume a position of considerable importance. Although these writers may not have been linked together under a single banner, they did express common ideals, and each in his own way gave something to the development of that play of ideas that had already been adumbrated by Augier and Dumas *fils*.

THE ETERNAL TRIANGLE

When Georges de Porto-Riche published some of his dramas in a collected volume he found for them the general title of *Théâtre d'amour*, and this is symbolic of one extremely characteristic feature of at least a large section of the late-nineteenth-century Parisian stage. As often as not the 'problem' dealt with by the playwright was the problem of wife and mistress: the eternal triangle loomed heavily over the proscenium. It proved both a source of strength and a source of weakness—of weakness because it tended to circumscribe and to fetter, of strength because it led to the development of a number of exceedingly subtle character studies and of skilful analysis of emotional situations.

In this field Porto-Riche is supreme. Essentially a poet, he is obsessed by the omnipresence and predominance of passion. Love is both sunshine and lowering tempest in his dramas. Of these *La chance de Françoise* (*The Luck of Françoise*, 1889)—the story of a wife who, forgiving a husband for his infidelity, saves him from possible death in a duel—was the first to attract wide attention, *Amoureuse* (*A Loving Wife*, 1891) was unquestionably the most effective, and *Le vieil homme* (*The Old Man*, 1911) was the most carefully wrought. In all of his plays appears a woman whose whole being is set upon passion, and who either destroys herself or finds complete satisfaction in the world of the emotions. This passion he often brings into association with other interests, as, for example, he does in *Amoureuse*, where his heroine dominates all the scenes of the drama. Germaine is the wife of a man, Dr Étienne Feriaud, considerably older than herself; wearied of the amorous adventures of his youth, he now hopes for calm and the leisure to work in the warmth of a domestic fireside. This hope, however, is dashed, for Germaine, loving him, makes large demands: he cannot concentrate on his studies; he is forced by her to break his ties with colleagues. The situation becomes so intolerable that he proceeds, quite deliberately, to throw her into the embraces of his friend Pascal—yet at the end, even after she has openly told him of her infidelity, he finds himself so deeply impelled by her physical attractions that he is forced to bid her stay with him. In the unexpected close the ironic spirit of Porto-Riche is perfectly expressed. Fundamentally a dramatist of inner action, he remains uninterested in intrigue for itself, and consequently his plays are cast mainly in the form of discussion pieces: in the ceaseless, subtly delicate play of words rests his dramatic strength.

Emphasis on dialogue and avoidance of violent physical action characterize, too, the plays of Maurice Donnay, a dramatist of wider powers and broader interests. Where Porto-Riche remains baffled by the passions he has observed and portrayed, Donnay presents a wise and half-smiling tolerance. His *milieu* is much the same, but it is noticeable that while Porto-Riche tends to concentrate his focus on one or two characters, in Donnay's hands a definite segment of life, carefully modelled, is set before us like a set of Dresden figurines. There is ironic humour in his eyes, and a sense of almost Grecian proportion keeps him from entering the realm of hysteria; not without significance is the fact that his first play was a modern version of the *Lysistrata* (1893). The choice of *La patronne* (*The Proprietress*, 1908) as a theme is also typical of his interests; here the life of the *pension* gives him an opportunity of peopling his stage with numerous characters, and likewise offers him the chance of giving concrete expression to his own philosophy of love: love is a pleasant thing, but if the object of one's adoration prove disloyal one should not wreck one's life over the defection or indulge in useless heroics. This is the central theme of the play through which Donnay first came to public attention—*Amants* (*Lovers*, 1896), a study of a youth and a girl, Vetheuil and Claudine Rozay, who, passionately devoted to each other in lyrical ecstasy, yet find themselves prevented by external circumstance from marriage. Many another dramatist would have made of this a tragedy; Donnay, with quiet calm, allows his lovers to separate and each marry another. A series of similarly toned plays followed— *La douloureuse* (*The Aching Heart*, 1897); *L'affranchie* (*The Emancipated Woman*, 1898), wherein a philosopher expresses the belief that women should be kept in the realm of emotion, to which they properly belong, and not introduced into the world of reason; *Georgette Lemeunier* (1898), which presents a variant of the theme otherwise developed by Porto-Riche in *La chance de Françoise*; and *Le torrent* (*The Torrent*, 1899), less successful because the author here has carried his favourite story of unfaithfulness to tragic realms, wherein he moves manifestly out of ease. Then, in 1902, came what is unquestionably his best work, *L'autre danger* (*The Other Danger*). The 'other danger' is revealed in the story of Claire Jadin, who, wearying at last of a husband cowardly, petty, and mean-spirited, finds a new joy in life through the love of Freydières. To her dismay, however, her daughter, Madeleine, meets this man, and rapturously tells her mother of her devotion to him. In order to give Madeleine her happiness Claire renounces the one thing that had made her own existence tolerable. In this play Donnay's attitude to life's problems is made clear: happiness, although the most precious possession, is short-lived, and the wise human being is the one who is ever ready to seize the joy when it comes and to accept with calmness its inevitable loss. While perhaps he is not an outstanding genius, there is a peculiar quality, introducing mingled passion and philosophical resignation, which gives an individual tone to all this dramatist's work.

For *Le mariage de Télémaque* (*The Marriage of Telemachus*, 1910) this author took as collaborator Jules Lemaître, a man of not dissimilar qualities, evenly balanced, widely observant, gifted with a kind of sadly ironic acceptance of life's vagaries. After a rather uncertain beginning with *Révoltée* (*Insurgent Woman*) in 1889, he produced in *Le député Leveau* (*Deputy Leveau*, 1890) a well-written and characteristic drama, essentially true to life and made theatrically interesting only by the extreme skill with which the characters are delineated and their inner motives revealed. *Mariage blanc* (*White Marriage*, 1891) tells a strained and peculiar story of a consumptive girl, who, about to marry an old roué, is driven to her death on seeing him make love to her half-sister. *L'âge difficile* (*The Difficult Years*, 1895) deals with the problems of middle age, and to this adds satire directed at an attractive 'new woman' whose husband, realizing what advantages she brings him, encourages her in her career as an adventuress. *Le pardon* (*The Pardon*, 1895) essays to give a fresh twist to the triangle. Suzanne, the young wife of Georges, a husband whose work takes him much away from home, finds joyless amusement for her idle hours in a rather pathetic intrigue. Georges behaves in conventional manner, drives her from his house, and sets off to tell his woes to a former friend of his, Thérèse, now herself a married woman. For a time Thérèse vainly tries to soften his anger and to persuade him to pardon his wife, but, as these two are so closely thrown together, the inevitable happens, with the result that the pardon which could not come before now is easily found. Georges realizes that he has sinned as well as Suzanne, and the play ends as they agree to restart their lives on a fresh basis. Irony enters into *La massière* (*The Studio Assistant*, 1905), when a mother who has objected to the marriage of her son with a girl engaged as assistant to her artist husband hastens to approve the match when she finds the latter much attracted by this lady. Lemaître, brilliant as a critic, was gifted with no more dramatic genius than Donnay, but once more we must recognize in his plays suggestions at least of true virtue. His vision is wide and his sense of inner reality by no means despicable.

THE PASSING OF JOYOUSNESS

Dozens of other dramas by diverse authors, some of them to be noted below, were devoted to such themes of love, and almost always the sadness of the contemplative mind rather than the lyricism of unreflective youth colours their scenes. Alongside this another current of thought is devoted to consideration either of the changing social world or of the joyless search for pleasure on the part of men and women wearied and forlorn.

In the works of François de Curel, an author of much more distinguished gifts than those possessed by any of the playwrights already mentioned, there breathe constantly a sad nostalgia and a melancholy induced by viewing the decay of ancient culture. His advent upon the stage (that of the Théâtre Libre) was startling: a young dramatist who could present, in the same year (1892), two such powerful and interesting plays as *L'envers d'une sainte* (*The Reverse of a Saint*) and *Les fossiles* (*The Fossils*) obviously was a man of more than common attainments. The first of these narrates a strange story—the story of a woman who, deserted by her lover

and driven by her jealous passion to make an attempt on the life of
his young wife, enters a convent and lives there for many years.
Learning that her former lover has died, she returns once more
to the world and seeks to steal away from the hated wife her beloved
daughter, only to be thwarted by learning of an affectionate farewell left her by the dead husband. Moved by this, she abandons
her vengeance, and the convent embraces her once more. A mere
outlining of the plot is unjust to the keen psychological penetration
with which the heroine's character is drawn and which gives
distinction to the peculiar theme. *L'envers d'une sainte* concentrates
its attention wholly upon psychological analysis: in *Les fossiles* the
theme of love is allied to contemplation of the decaying aristocracy
to which Curel himself belonged. The scene is the country house
of the Duc de Chantenelles, who lives there with his duchess and
his two children, Robert and Claire. Over the household hangs a
heavy shadow, for the heir to the dukedom is dying of consumption.
As his end approaches he begs that his mistress, Hélène Vatrin, be
permitted to come to him. Claire objects, but his mother tends to
welcome the suggestion—the more so as, having formerly suspected
a liaison between her husband and this girl, she is relieved to think
that her fears were false. When Hélène arrives it is found that she
has a child, a boy, and a marriage is planned in order that the
tradition of the ancient house be preserved. After several scenes in
which the honour of this house emerges more than a trifle tarnished,
and the Duke confesses to Robert that in reality Hélène had been
his mistress, the dying man discovers a new vision. "Let us forget
ourselves for the time being," he says, "and save little Henri: he is
the family: think of him!" He himself goes to his death, while
Hélène and Claire pledge themselves to devoted care of his son,
aiming "to make him first an honest man, and, better, a man
capable of dying for the sake of an idea."

The theme of the child, combined with the lengthy dramatic
interval used in *L'envers d'une sainte*, reappears in *L'invitée* (*The
Guest*, 1893), where a woman abandons her home on learning of
her husband's intrigues with other women, only to return after the
passing of nearly two decades in order to protect her children,
dangerously apt to be ruined by his influence. That Curel was
capable of writing scenes of high comedy is proved in *L'amour brode*
(*Love Embroiders*, 1893), in which a widow and her lover play a
game of pretence until both get what they want—a marriage. The
same mood gives quality to a much later play, *La comédie du génie*
(*The Comedy of Genius*, 1918), where a young man becomes a

famous dramatist just because one day he sees an actress rehearsing her part at an open window and thinks that her gestures are an invitation to him to enter her apartment. In *La figurante* (*The Ballet Dancer*, 1896) an ironically conceived situation is saved from sentimentalism only by the author's delicate style, and even so there is a sense of strain in the achieving of the effect. If this was somewhat of a failure, *Le repas du lion* (*The Lion's Feast*, 1898) was an unquestioned triumph, perhaps not in the grand style, but at least in a style interesting and not without its own power. Here the atmosphere of *Les fossiles* is further pursued in a form which, abandoning the theme of love, involves the author's entry into the sphere of the social-problem play. The hero, Jean de Miremont, is an aristocrat who, having been inadvertently responsible for killing a drunken workman, is driven by a sense of guilt to devote his life to ameliorating the conditions of the proletariat. By turns Christian socialist and revolutionary, he ends ironically as a great factory-owner, satisfying himself by developing the theory that the workers can best be aided by the expansion of industrialism. This play was followed by *La nouvelle idole* (*The New Idol*, 1899), in which Curel, choosing as his hero a scientist, Dr Donnat, interestingly strives, by showing the struggle within this man's mind between his scientific denial of God and the persistence with which his mind demands belief in a divinity, to suggest the ever-questing spirit of the human race. The plot deals with a doctor who inoculates with cancer a girl whom he (wrongly) has believed dying of tuberculosis, and not the least effective scene of the drama is that in which the victim, learning the truth, accepts her sacrifice for the sake of humanity. Equally interesting is the kindred study of a woman, the heroine of *La fille sauvage* (*The Savage Girl*, 1902), who finds herself between the spirit of animalism and a mystic faith.

In all these plays symbolism is constantly intruding, although it is symbolism of a peculiar kind. When Ibsen or Hauptmann introduce symbols into a drama we can remain in no doubt as to the fact that they are symbols; one of the most perplexing elements in Curel's art is the half-light in which many of his scenes and characters are set, so that we can never be entirely sure when we are on the plane of objective reality and when we move on to a plane of allegory. We see this no less in *La fille sauvage* than in *La danse devant le miroir* (*The Dance before the Mirror*, 1914), *L'ivresse du sage* (*The Wise Man's Rapture*, 1922), *La terre inhumaine* (*No Man's Land*, 1922), and *L'orage mystique* (*The Mystic Storm*, 1927). Of these latter plays perhaps the most interesting is *La danse devant le miroir*, which might almost be regarded as a precursor of psychological dramas to come. Here a man and woman, in love with each other, are yet tortured by doubts, and in the end the former kills himself at the very moment when he sees in the woman's eyes her true devotion to him: he prefers to die on this second of untrammelled joy rather than descend once more into his spiritual hell of uncertainty.

A peculiar inner quality distinguishes Curel's work, and along with that an equally peculiar fastidiousness. He will not stoop to win applause by the introduction of sensational incident, nor will he even pay attention to the commonly accepted conventions of dramatic technique, and consequently his dramas may gather less applause than those of his companions—but there can be no doubt that his influence was strong upon those who in the twentieth century sought to develop the theatre of inner realism.

Closely associated with Curel, yet profoundly removed from him in outlook, is Henri Lavedan. Often the themes chosen by these two dramatists have a passing similarity, but when we search deeper we realize that where Curel's are tortuously composed psychological studies, Lavedan's are competently written surface sketches; a comparison of the two men reveals the distinction between the artist (however minor in worth) and the craftsman. This does not mean that Lavedan's plays are characterless—simply that their characters do not have that brilliant flame that irradiates so many of Curel's scenes which without it would be flat and dull. In *Le Prince d'Aurec* (1892) and *Les deux noblesses* (*The Two Nobilities*, 1894) he surveys the fate of the aristocracy as Curel had done, and perhaps the difference between the two men is shown most clearly by the contrast between their respective methods. Lavedan's plays are well constructed, and the fact that he seems to owe a debt to Augier places him in the tradition that stretches forward from Scribe. The first of the two dramas shows a young aristocrat wasting his patrimony in senseless gambling and finally approaching almost complete ruin, to be saved only through the instrumentality of his mother, who, it is stressed, was born not of an aristocratic family, but of good bourgeois stock. In the second play the fortunes of the d'Aurec family are shown progressing in the hands of a scion of the house who, making a success of business ventures, carries the name of d'Aurec to the plebeian levels of Roche.

In *Viveurs* (*The Rakes*, 1895) Lavedan discovered his true métier. When he tries to be philosophic and to present problems he seems rather out of his element, but when he casts his observant eye upon the jaded, restless troops of Parisian pleasure-hunters and describes their wretched intrigues, their crackling, mirthless laughter, and their inner dejection of spirit, he is thoroughly in his element. The play vastly appealed to contemporaries when they saw on the stage the realistic scenes of a fashionable ladies' tailor's 'studio' and the exact representation of a well-known Parisian restaurant. His attempt in *Catherine* (1898) to contrast aristocratic and middle-class manners is of little worth, but when he carries on from *Viveurs* to pen *Le nouveau jeu* (*The Latest Craze*, 1898), *Le vieux marcheur* (*The Old Reprobate*, 1895), and *Le goût du vice* (*The Taste for Vice*, 1911) he strikes an individual note. The first and the last of these well illustrate his characteristic attitude. In the society he depicts men and women must, in order to be fashionable, profess to be vicious. In *Le nouveau jeu* he shows men and women following society's tone in regarding marriage as a thing to be lightly undertaken and as lightly dropped. Among his characters in *Le goût du vice* are two—a girl, Mirette, who pretends to be as fast as any one of her set, and a man, Lortay, who writes fiction which is on the borderland of the obscene. These two fall in love, and gradually they discover that neither is really vicious, that neither takes pleasure in the evils they talk about so freely. Their taste for vice is merely pretence, imposed upon them by their social surroundings.

THE PLAY OF IDEAS

In Lavedan's work a moral purpose is obviously present, but that purpose is subordinate to the presentation of sensational scenes. In the writings of the other authors mentioned above the introduction of problems is patent, but in general the problem is subordinate to character. Alongside these men there were others to whom the idea, the social view, was of greater importance than either the development of the intrigue or psychological analysis.

Within this group comes Paul Hervieu, an author of some considerable distinction who permitted his love of the intellectually conceived 'thesis' to rule both the course of his plots and the treatment of his characters. That Hervieu had, in spite of this, the ability to pen dramas of interest and even of warmth demonstrates the amount of genuine talent concealed behind his somewhat frigid façade.

His problems are at once varied and restricted. He confines himself almost entirely to the world of 'society,' but within that field he ranges widely. In *Les paroles restent* (*Words Remain*, 1892) it is his object to show that gossip, however innocently retailed, has a power of destruction: words are easily spoken and seem to be slight, evanescent things, yet words can murder on occasion. *Les tenailles* (*The Pincers*, 1895), his next play, and the first of his successes, illustrates well the intellectual patterning of plot that is so typical of his art. This play falls into two parts, perfectly balanced. A wife, tortured by her marriage, seeks divorce, is refused, and takes a lover: such is the theme of the first part. In the second her husband, who for diverse reasons has changed his mind, proposes a legal separation; but now the wife, for the sake of her child (who, ironically, is the son not of the husband, but of the lover), refuses to grant him his wish. The same theme of divorce is dealt with in *La loi de l'homme* (*Man-made Law*, 1897), where a woman is compelled to sacrifice herself for the sake of a daughter. Laure de Raguais discovers that her husband is having an *affaire* with her friend Mme d'Orcieu, and, later, that her daughter, Isabel, and this lady's son have fallen in love. In an attempt to break this proposed marriage she reveals her husband's faithlessness to M. d'Orcieu, but he, to save himself from society's gibes, insists on absolute silence. The woman is beaten by the man-made law.

With *L'énigme* (*The Riddle*, 1901), Hervieu makes a departure almost in the direction of the Pirandellesque concept, but in writing *La course du flambeau* (*The Passing of the Torch*, 1901) he comes back to the same problem, evidently one that affected him deeply, which he had exploited in *Les tenailles* and *La loi de l'homme*. Basically *La course du flambeau* is written to prove that, as generation succeeds generation, the parents always sacrifice themselves in the interests of the young, and that the young, for the most part, accept these sacrifices as their right. The central figure is Savine Revel, a mother with one daughter, Marie-Jeanne, who first puts aside thoughts of a second marriage, next is prepared to steal her own mother's money in order to save this girl and her husband from financial disaster, and finally goes so far as to allow the mother to die simply that Marie-Jeanne may be happy. Naturally the author endeavours to hide the mechanical nature of the theme by every means in his power, but nothing can conceal the fact that the play has been evolved not out of an imaginative concept, but out of a desire to prove a case.

The problem of divorce in a household where there are children occupies his attention in the fairly powerful *Le dédale* (*The Maze*, 1903); the eternal triangle appears in *Le réveil* (*The Awakening*, 1905); the guilty wife once more is introduced into *Connais-toi* (*Know Thyself*, 1909), where a further ironic twist is given to the familiar theme by contrasting a military man's advice regarding the obligations of 'honour,' given to a friend, with his own common-sense complacency when he finds himself confronted by similar circumstances. In all of these there is a contrast set up between social convention on the one hand and natural feeling on the other; in all the basic intellectual problem is the core of the action.

What Hervieu lacks above all is variety of mood. In every scene his style is the same, and as a consequence, despite our feeling that he possesses some strength, we are oppressed by his monotony of conception and utterance. The same judgment might be passed on Henry Becque, were it not that his dramas are illuminated by a peculiar sombre and bitter irony. Where Hervieu possesses a certain calm when confronting his problems, Becque displays irritation, anger, and disgust: throughout his scenes burns a black and turgid fire. It is true that he rarely is successful in penning a drama capable of giving us an harmonious and consistently sustained impression, yet maybe *Les corbeaux* (*The Vultures*, 1882) and *La Parisienne* (*The Woman of Paris*, 1885) are more powerful plays than any written by Hervieu. Whether Becque was acquainted with Jonson's *Volpone* we cannot tell: the fact is that *Les corbeaux* takes shape as a kind of naturalistic bourgeois replica of that bitter comedy. We are introduced here to the household of a hardworking paterfamilias, Vigneron by name, who, dying suddenly, leaves his wife and three daughters, Judith, Marie, and Blanche, at the mercy of the vultures who eagerly descend to pick at the carcass. Chief of these vultures is Vigneron's rapacious business partner, Teissier. With remorseless truth to the sordid reality, Becque makes scene follow scene in the depiction of the doom settling on this once happy family. The lives of all these helpless women are broken, and in the end Marie, the frankest and most open-eyed of them all, is forced to marry the odious Teissier in order that he may turn on the other vultures, drive them off, and so rescue what little has been left. A similarly gloomy atmosphere pervades *La Parisienne*, which presents, not without genuine comic verve of the mordant sort, a portrait of what Becque regards as a typical Parisian woman, eminently respectable, yet in heart and in action hopelessly depraved.

The last of this group of dramatists is the most extreme. In the work of Eugène Brieux France saw the play of ideas carried to its final conclusion and the stage turned into a platform for the reformer. According to Bernard Shaw, who in 1911 sponsored the publication of three of his plays in translation, "after the death of Ibsen, Brieux confronted Europe as the most important dramatist west of Russia." The claim is a large one, and may hardly be accepted if we look upon the theatre not as a sounding-board for the presentation of ideas, but as a place for the exhibition of artistry. Brieux, it is true, possesses the necessary qualities for putting a story into dramatic terms, but without a doubt his own real interests, and the source of any esteem to be granted to his writings, rests in the boldness with which he put upon the boards vivid representations of broader problems than those which had formed the themes of Hervieu and his companions. The trouble is that these problems, if boldly conceived, are dealt with in a somewhat juvenile spirit: his plays read rather like fiery prize essays written by revolutionary-minded undergraduates upon the enormities of the civilization of their times. With disconcerting fervour, he seizes upon topic after topic, as though his one object was to reveal as many as possible of the errors in life around him. Starting with a rather clumsy series of efforts, he won attention first with *Blanchette* in 1892, produced at the Théâtre Libre, a play designed to demonstrate the difficulties arising from the widespread education of girls. In *Les bienfaiteurs* (*The Philanthropists*, 1896) he proceeds to attack fashionable charity, claiming that the giving of alms without love is worse than futile. In *Les trois filles de M. Dupont* (*The Three Daughters of Mr Dupont*, 1897) it is the loveless marriage imposed by society's conventions that arouses his anger, the theme being revealed through the story of the three daughters—Angèle, who has been forced into a life of prostitution, Caroline, the ugly, soured old maid, and Julie, attractive, driven into a loveless marriage and impelled by circumstance to indulge in sordid intrigues. In *La robe rouge* (*The Red Robe*, 1900) he melodramatically castigates the errors apparent to him in the exercise of justice, by showing a group of provincial judges, all eager for promotion, and the fate of an innocent man who gets caught in the legal machinery. This was followed by *Les remplaçantes* (*The Substitutes*, 1901), where the thesis is directed against mothers who permit their babies to be reared by peasant wet-nurses; and by the best known of his dramas, *Les avariés* (*Damaged Goods*, 1902), where venereal disease is made the subject of a dramatic essay. In it Georges Dupont, just about to be married, discovers that he has syphilis: he undergoes a short treatment by a quack doctor and weds; a child is born, diseased like himself; when the wife at last discovers his fatal secret she is beside herself with angry horror, and only the advice of a *raisonneur* doctor, who suggests that a permanent cure may be effected, prevents the action closing in sensational melodrama.

Brieux' next two plays, *La petite amie* (*The Little Sweetheart*, 1902) and *Maternité* (*Maternity*, 1903), have virtually the same basic subject-matter. In the latter drama two themes run parallel courses, the one depicting the misery of a woman, Lucie Brignac, forced by her husband to have a child every year, and the terrors of Annette, who, about to become an unmarried mother, goes to a quack in order to have an abortion. Annette dies, and the woman-quack is brought to trial, when counsel for the defence causes a sensation by delivering a fiery attack on the girl's lover and on the hypocrisy of society. *Les hannetons* (*The May Bugs*, 1906) demonstrates, with bitter humour, that unmarried love may be more enfettering and enfeebling than a burdensome marriage, the hero, Pierre, being completely enthralled by a woman from whom he could escape—so far as legal ties are concerned—but who maintains her hold fast upon him.

In such wise, with plays coming from his pen in almost annual progression, Brieux ranged over the social vices and the creaking flaws in civilization's machinery. Perhaps he would have achieved more had he himself practised a kind of artistic birth-control: as it is, his dramatic progeny is too numerous and ill-reared. There is a want of classic restraint in his work, a reliance on crude effects, a descent to the use of the melodramatic, a spurious theatricalization of commonplace doctrines. It is to be feared that Bernard Shaw was mistaken.

Brieux' position in the history of drama is symbolic of what the French theatre achieved, in general, during these years. Much of interest is to be found here, yet we can hardly believe that the plays of this period, even the best of them, will continue to give pleasure on the stage. Less than a half-century has passed since once they were applauded, and already they are damned by that most devastating critical judgment—the accusation of being old-fashioned.

REALISM IN DIVERSE LANDS: ITALY, SPAIN, ENGLAND, RUSSIA

THE OTHER countries of Europe during the last years of the century all were influenced by the movements which produced Ibsen, Strindberg, Hauptmann, and the French playwrights of the 'problem' variety, but hardly anywhere else was anything of real and characteristic value contributed to the stage.

Italy presents a picture as typical as may be found. Into the midst of romantic melodrama intrudes the spirit of Scribe, and soon plays *a tesi* are being written, with naturalism, in the guise of *verismo*, capturing all the attention of the younger intellectuals and artists.

The movement starts with romantically conceived dramas into which enters a dash of the realistic—such as *Una donna di quarant' anni* (*A Woman of Forty*, 1853) or *Il cavaliere d'industria* (*The Captain of Industry*, 1854), by Vincenzo Martini. In *Il marito e l'amante* (*The Husband and the Lover*, 1855) this author dares (for the first time in the Italian theatre) to deal seriously with the theme of adultery. The conflict between natural sentiment and social convention is the theme of *Il misantropo in società* (*The Misanthrope in Society*, 1858). The development of the new realism may well be traced in the work of his companion, Tommaso Gherardi del Testa. At the start this author's style is fundamentally based on that of Goldoni—as in *Con gli uomini non si scherza* (*Don't Play with Men*, 1848). Then gradually this style becomes altered by contact with the French stage. The *nouveaux riches* form the centre of the picture in *La moda e la famiglia* (*Manners and the Family*, 1848). In *La carità pelosa* (*Selfish Charity*, 1860) a self-seeking philanthropist has his inherent inhumanity unmasked. A kindred mixture of styles is displayed in the writings of Achille Torelli—for example, *I mariti* (*The Husbands*, 1867), a study of social follies. Most of this author's writings deal with the familiar problems of love, sometimes expressed in an appealing manner: *La moglie* (*The Wife*, 1868) presents a vivid picture of a woman's devotion, and *L'ultimo convegno* (*The Last Meeting*, 1898) gives us an understanding portrait of an understanding husband. In the work of Leo di Castelnuovo (Conte Leopoldo Pullè) the moral note is strongly stressed. His *Impara d'arte* (*Getting a Job*, 1872) shows an impoverished nobleman trying to earn a living by learning a craft. Thence the new style develops in the hands of Paolo Ferrari and others during the second stage of its progress. Typical are this author's *Il duello* (*The Duel*, 1868) and his *Cause ed effetti* (*Causes and Effects*, 1871), in both of which appears a mixture of sentimentalism, Scribe-like intrigue, and serious purpose, the amalgam being rendered into a unity by the author's keen interest in character and by the verve he inherits from the Goldoni tradition. With what force that tradition operates on his mind is indicated in the title of one of his best-known plays, *Goldoni e le sue sedici commedie nuove* (*Goldoni and his Sixteen New Plays*, 1851), at once an historical study and an autobiographical document.

After these come the plays of Giuseppe Giacosa. This author began with a series of plays in which he exploited historical and legendary material, principally from the medieval period. Among these perhaps the best are *Il conte Rosso* (1880), *Il fratello d'armi* (*The Brother-in-arms*, 1877), and the delightfully fantastic *Una partita a scacchi* (*A Game of Chess*, 1873). This preoccupation with themes from the past, however, gave way to other interests, and soon he made himself one of the leading exponents of the new realistic drama. His *Tristi amori* (*Sad Loves*, 1888) is a well-wrought play rather in the manner of the French school. The basic situation might be paralleled by reference to half a dozen contemporary Parisian dramas —a wife, who does not obtain all the attention she desires, drifting into a love-affair—although the solution, through which husband and wife agree to live together for the sake of their child, has an individual flavour. *I diritti dell' anima* (*The Rights of the Soul*, 1894) tells of a husband who is full of pride when he finds that his wife's loyalty has succeeded in withstanding the wooing of an ardent lover, but who discovers later that, while her physical loyalty remained unimpaired, in her soul she had responded to the courtier's advances. In *Come le foglie* (*Like Falling Leaves*, or *As the Leaves*, 1900) a lower-middle-class family is presented in the midst of financial decay, while in *Il più forte* (*The Stronger*, 1904) there is a companion picture of a skilful and ruthless business man who, having no scruples, is well qualified to succeed in the money-making world.

Next to Giacosa in importance is Girolamo Rovetta, whose collected dramas, from *La moglie di Don Giovanni* (*Don Juan's Wife*), of 1877, to *Molière e sua moglie* (*Molière and his Wife*), of 1909, although none of them masterpieces, contain vividly written and well-imagined scenes. Not without human understanding he depicts the little bank clerk Carlo Moretti in *I disonesti* (*The Dishonest*, 1892), and shows him gradually forced into a series of crimes until, no longer able to stand the weight upon his conscience and the fear of discovery, he abandons his beloved family and flees abroad. On account of its unusual theme, *Il poeta* (*The Poet*, 1897) has interest, with its caustic attack on a thoroughly selfish and basically evil youth, Paolo Sardi, who sponges on a worthy humanitarian, Giovanni Vandoni, until his excesses become so foul as to lead to his exposure and dismissal from grace.

With Rovetta is to be associated another author, Roberto Bracco, whose work carries us well into the twentieth century. In *Una donna* (*A Woman*, 1892) he fashions a play which, manifestly influenced by the work of the French school, presents a dismal picture of a woman of easy virtue who falls in love with a poor painter, has a child by him, and eventually, after many trials, commits suicide. Something of the same spirit dominates in *Maschere* (*Masks*, 1893). The influence of Schnitzler becomes evident in *L'infidele* (*The Unfaithful*, 1894). Out of a combination of these two, together with a vivid observation of Neapolitan life, Bracco creates his own characteristic style in *Don Pietro Caruso* (1895). Pietro Caruso is an ordinary little man whose one joy is his daughter, Margherita, and the play concerns itself with showing how this girl, protected by him from reality, becomes the mistress of one of his acquaintances. With an interesting mixture of ironic comedy and seriousness Bracco succeeds in drawing an appealing picture of this couple. The combination of ruthless realism and widespread human sympathy appears also in *Sperduti nel buio* (*Lost in Darkness*, 1901), with its touching picture of a blind man's hopeless passion for a girl who, he thinks, may respond to his affection because he believes her ill-featured, but who in reality is an outstanding beauty. The central figures of these two dramas are of the kind Bracco knows best how to paint, for he is a man of infinite pity for the humble soul—for such a hero as appears, for example, in *Il piccolo santo* (*The Little Saint*, 1909), a man who, having loved and lost, becomes a priest, and years later has the memory of his sorrow return. Bracco is at his best in such 'tragedies of the soul' as are represented in this play or in *I fantasmi* (*The Phantoms*, 1906) and the later *I pazzi* (*The Fools*, 1921). The former shows a widow who has promised her dying husband not to remarry falling in love and finding her vow an impassable barrier between her and a man with whom she might have secured happiness. All this author's characters are simple folk, the sufferers on earth rather than the wilful seekers of power.

Bracco is delicate, reflective, sympathetic in his realism: Giovanni Verga prefers, like the Germans, scenes of brutal violence, of the kind introduced into *Cavalleria rusticana* (*Rustic Chivalry*, 1884—better known in its operatic version), *La Lupa* (*The She-wolf*, 1896), *La caccia alla volpe* (*The Fox-hunt*, 1902), *La caccia al lupo* (*The Wolf-hunt*; printed 1902), and *Dal tuo al mio* (*From Thine to Mine*, 1903). All these are dramas passionate, dark, pessimistic in tone. Less violent, but bitter, are the plays of Marco Praga, a competent craftsman who yet lacks inspiration. Influenced by Ibsen, his drama *Le vergini* (*The Virgins*, 1889) first brought him to notice. The title is ironic, for the 'virgins' of the play are girls who, to serve their purposes, are willing to make any concessions to the men they meet; out of this atmosphere of outward respectability and inner corruption arises a dramatic situation in which one of the women falls genuinely in love, is compelled by a sense of honesty to confess to her fiancé, and remains abandoned by him. Like some, indeed most, of the French playwrights, Praga is deeply obsessed by the question of sexual relationships, although his manner of dealing with these presents nothing startlingly novel. *La moglie ideale* (*The Ideal Wife*, 1890) sardonically treats its heroine as an 'ideal wife' because she so carefully conceals a liaison from the husband for whom she has affection. The secret of an *affaire* is concealed for different reasons in *La morale della favola* (*The Moral of the Fable*, 1904), while in *La porta chiusa* (*The Closed Door*, 1913) the results of such adventures are shown when a son escapes from his mother's fond clutches by revealing his knowledge of the fact that he is illegitimate. Both the uncertainty of Praga's philosophic approach and his power of evoking strong scenes is shown well in *La crisi* (*The Crisis*, 1901), with its portraits of the weakly besotted Piero, his strong-minded wife, Nicoletta, and his stern brother, Raimondo.

Something of the same preoccupation with sexual relationships dominates in the rather unsatisfactory realistic dramas penned by Sabatino Lopez, an author whose dramatic career extends from a *Di notte* (*At Night*) in 1890 to a *Luce* (*Light*) in 1937.

Dark pessimism characterizes the plays of Camillo Antona-Traversi, best known for his *Le Rozeno* (*The Rozeno Family*, 1891), but probably reaching greater artistic success in *I parassiti* (*The Parasites*, 1899), a vigorous attack on those members of society who, outwardly respectable, make their fortunes by preying on others worthier than themselves. Camillo's brother Giannino likewise turned his pen, with a lighter satiric touch, against society's villains and fools, achieving his greatest success in *La scuola del marito* (*The School for Husbands*, 1899), a study of a man and woman of the upper class losing their lives in the idle pursuit of pleasure. His work continues well into the modern period.

Such success, however, was at its best but slight. The truth is that *verismo*, or naturalism of the kind exploited abroad, was alien to the spirit of the Italian theatre, which, from earliest days to latest, found its most effective expression in the realm of open and obvious theatricality: the spirit of the *commedia dell' arte* and of the opera suited its temper better than the painful naturalism exploited by these followers of French, German, and Scandinavian masters.

To a certain extent the Spanish stage exhibits similar qualities. Born of romance in the days of Lope da Vega, it never took kindly to the incipient realism of the sentimental movement, and when the influence of later realists came to exert itself the imitation of their methods was either hesitating and unsure or suffered a sea-change. Only one playwright of any distinction appeared in Madrid to cultivate this form of dramatic composition, and even he betrays in his writing dissatisfaction with the style of his adoption; the romantically melodramatic constantly causes his steps to stray from the path of naturalism. This man, José Echegaray y Elizaguirre, once had a wide reputation; nowadays his esteem is moderately low. A romanticist at heart—as is demonstrated not only by his early 'cloak-and-sword' dramas, but by kindred pieces produced throughout his entire career—he endeavoured to capitalize on the new style, as in *El hijo de Don Juan* (*The Son of Don Juan*, 1892), but without achieving more than temporary success. Although in Spain his most famous play is *O locura o santidad* (*Lunatic or Saint*, 1877), in which a generously minded man is hurried to an asylum by his relations, of his works only *El gran Galeoto* (*The Great Galeoto*, or *The World and his Wife*, 1881) has succeeded in winning an international reputation; and even so perhaps its real interest lies less in fineness of craftsmanship and in true vision than in the fact that, historically, it is among the first dramas to suggest, albeit vaguely, the method later to be more fully exploited by Pirandello. Taking a common theme, that of the eternal triangle and the concept of honour, Echegaray gives it a new orientation. The triangle is there, not in reality, but in imagination. The wife, Teodora, is pure-minded: gossip, however, couples her name with that of a protégé, Ernesto, of her husband, Don Julian; at last the husband comes to believe that she has been unfaithful to him, and Teodora is forced, by this pressure of opinion, to take Ernesto as her lover. Outwardly the play shapes itself as a fairly uninspired re-treatment of an old theme, but the operation of public thought, instituting an opposition between what is in reality and what exists no less firmly in imagination, is so far made the core of the plot as to give the action a peculiar flavour of its own.

Echegaray's other plays hardly merit much attention. Desperately he tried to develop new themes in the manner of the French playwrights or of Ibsen. Their problems, however, seem synthetic, the result rather of a desire to make profit out of a new style than of a deeply felt urge to explore fresh territory. Greater sincerity of purpose appears in the peculiar writings of Benito Pérez Galdós— Spain's François de Curel—lacking Echegaray's theatrical sense, although gifted with an appreciation of social values and of character utterly wanting in the other. In his plays the heroine usually takes precedence of the hero, and it is through her eyes that the author presents his view of the world. *Electra* (1900) discusses the problem of the girl who is being impelled towards a convent life for which she is entirely unsuited; *La [Duquesa] de San Quintín* (*The Duchess of San Quintín*, 1894) poses the problem of a young duchess, early left a widow, who has as choice for a second husband a spiritless, conventional nobleman, who has no susbtance on which to exist save his traditions, and a vigorous, keen-witted, idealistic member of the bourgeoisie; to the horror of her relations, she chooses the latter. Not only domestic and social problems attract his attention: he is prepared also to enter into the then less-explored realm of politics, producing in *La fiera* (*The Beast*, 1896) an interesting dramatic work anticipatory of Spain's civil war, pleading for compromise and common sense in the bitter conflict between the Absolutists and the Liberals. Author of a considerable number of dramas, including *La loca de la casa* (*The Family Lunatic*, 1893), *Mariucha* (1903), *El abuelo* (*The Grandfather*, 1904)—a Curel-like study of an aging aristocrat who finds peace of spirit in the love of an illegitimate child—and *Alceste* (1914), Galdós certainly is a man of considerable power, although his hesitant handling of dramatic form and his concentration upon purely Spanish questions take from his work the possibility of wide appeal.

Much more sensational, not to say melodramatic, situations appear in the work of Joaquín Dicenta, whose *Juan José* (1895) is a powerful study of a labourer, become a thief through his love of a fickle Rosa and roused at the end to murder both her and her rich admirer. The impress of realism was, however, most clearly to be found during those years in the specifically and intensely patriotic Catalan theatre organized by Frederick Soler, himself author of a number of unimportant pieces. More gifted than he was José Feliu y Codina, author, among several other dramas, of the racily authentic *La Dolores* (1892), the heroine of which is a lovely barmaid pursued by many men, and giving her heart only to one, who is slain by a rival. The outstanding playwright of this movement was Ángel Guimerá, whose works show the familiar pattern in their progress from romantic sentiment, through realism, to symbolic experiments. Among his earlier works *Judith de Welp* (1883) and *Mar y cielo* (*Sea and Sky*, 1888) have some value; in the second style he produced *María Rosa* (1894) and *Terra baixa* (*Lowlands*, 1896)—the latter a strong naturalistic study in which a labourer, Mannelich, takes vengeance upon his master, a wealthy farmer named Sebastian, when the latter, after foisting off on him his mistress, Marta, seeks to resume his former intrigue after the girl's marriage; in the third style he wrote *Andrónica* (1905), a play of manifest weaknesses, yet aiming at effects beyond those attempted in his more youthful essays.

Although, naturally, a vast gulf separates these Spanish plays from contemporary English productions, there is a certain historical kinship between the works of Echegaray and the writings of the once famous, now rather despised Sir Arthur Wing Pinero and Henry Arthur Jones. Like him, both these men were professional dramatic authors intent upon theatrical success; like him, both turned to exploit the new realism; like him, both failed to produce any work of sterling quality worthy of being compared with Continental masterpieces.

Once more we are confronted by the equivocal position occupied by these men. Of their great importance in the development of the English stage there can be no doubt; of their insignificance in the great march of the modern theatre there is equal certainty. Their plays materially aided in the development of the English drama in the twentieth century, yet not one, even the once-lauded *The Second Mrs Tanqueray* (1893), has qualities of permanence.

Pinero and Jones gained much strength from the fact that both allowed their art to grow out of an essentially popular stage tradition. The former's earliest writings were farces—some of them very good ones, such as *The Magistrate* (1885) and *The Squire* (1881); the latter began in the melodramatic tradition and won considerable success with his *The Silver King* (1882), distinguished from none of its predecessors save by a greater tightness of structure and incisiveness of dialogue. From these beginnings each proceeded, with characteristic mildness and lack of revolutionary fervour, to exploit the potentialities of the play of ideas. With *The Second Mrs Tanqueray* Pinero startled London society and was acclaimed by the critics as responsible for having produced the greatest drama of his age. Regarding it now from the standpoint of fifty years later, we may agree that, while it possesses unquestioned virtues, its worth appears markedly less than was once imagined There is not a little of the sentimental in this treatment of a woman with a past who finds that her now grown daughter has fallen in love with her own former lover. Suicide suitably brings the plot to a would-be 'tragic' conclusion, without in the least arousing in us that admiration and that sense of wonder out of which alone the true tragic passion can be evoked. The same judgment must be passed on such an ambitious effort as *Iris* (1901), where the heroine is a woman who, while not natively vicious, has no will-power to keep her on the straight path and gradually deteriorates into a creature of vice. In Pinero's last important drama, *Mid-Channel* (1909), a kindred atmosphere prevails. Here we are presented with a middle-aged couple, Theodore and Zoe Blundell, who after fourteen years of marriage are becoming constantly involved in quarrels and recriminations. They part: Zoe goes off to Italy with a friend of her husband's on a perfectly virtuous and platonic tour, but, learning that Theodore is having an *affaire* of his own, she takes this friend as a lover. On her return home she finds to her dismay that, while she is willing to pardon her husband, he angrily drives her from the house. The result is suicide from a balcony.

Jones was much less interested in the woman who sins, much more in social and religious ideas. These ideas, however, he handled in a manner which showed that, while he had the will to be a thinker, he entirely lacked the ability. *Saints and Sinners* (1884) is both melodramatic and sentimental, and something of those qualities mars the much finer, and relatively significant, *Michael and his Lost Angel* (1896), a drama in which the soul of a Puritanical clergyman is bared for us. Perhaps Jones' importance lies less in what he actually achieved in dramatic form than in his ceaseless and effective championing of a new modern theatre in London. His collected critical studies, animated by a fine enthusiasm, published under the title of *The Renascence of the English Drama* (1895), were of no little importance in directing men's minds towards the potentialities of the realistic stage.

During these years Wilde was penning his witty comedies, and the Independent Theatre Society was discovering the genius of a fiery-headed young Irishman resident in London, George Bernard Shaw; but the former is to be considered rather as a comic writer than as a contributor to the realistic drama, while the latter's greatest achievements belong to the period after 1900. As companions, Jones and Pinero had, during the nineteenth century, only worthy but wholly uninspired writers such as Sydney Grundy, author of the sentimental *A Pair of Spectacles* (1890) and the peculiarly confused *A Fool's Paradise* (1887). It must sadly be confessed that in this kind the English stage had little to offer during the final decades of the century.

In Holland arose one writer of slightly greater promise, Herman Heijermans. Although it is impossible to associate his name with those of Ibsen or Hauptmann, there can be no doubt that he possessed sterling qualities. He has a sure grasp of dramatic technique; he has an observant eye and a reflective mind; and he has true sincerity. On the other hand, all his work has now an old-fashioned flavour: far less than the others was he possessed of the power to incorporate into his realistic scenes elements of an enduring quality. The reason, perhaps, may lie in what was his chief virtue as a man. Where Ibsen, Strindberg, and Hauptmann were self-centred, Heijermans has a broadly humanitarian outlook upon the world; infinite pity is his, and he looks upon the men and women around him with genuine sorrow when he sees them involved in misery and torment. The result is that, even while we appreciate the qualities that animate his nature, we feel in his plays a lack of strength and a want of deeper intensity.

His first success was secured with *Ahasuerus* (1893), and his fame definitely established with *Ghetto* (1899), in which an attempt is made to depict the atmosphere of a typical Dutch Jewish home— the world of youth, inspired by new dreams, rebelling against the Puritan conservatism of the elders. After this exploration of Jewish life Heijermans turned, like the other realists, to deal with a variety of social problems, from those of wide extent, involving whole classes, to those of individuals wrecked by the civilization around them. In 1900 came an effective study of the thwarted, twisted soul of a young servant—*De Meid* (*The Maid*)—a girl who, having found a compromising letter belonging to her mistress, derives an evil joy in the sense of power thus given to her. The same year saw the appearance of *Op Hoop van Zegen* (*The Good Hope*), a drama in which, with his characteristic tenderness and understanding, he deals with a fishing community where men's lives are sacrificed to add to the wealth of a callous shipowner. While there is little value in the 'social' message of this drama, Heijermans' skill is evident in the atmospheric quality of the scenes. A similar mood prevails in *Ora et labora* (1903), a miserable picture of small tenant-farmers; in the characteristically named *Shakels* (*Shackles*, 1904); and in *De opgaande Zon* (*The Rising Sun*, 1908), where his dark-glassed microscope is turned upon the petty shopkeeper.

In all his writings Heijermans betrays the same qualities—a competent knowledge of stagecraft, a sympathetic understanding of character, a genuine sympathy with the underdog, and a complete lack of that spark from which alone can come real and continuing dramatic interest.

To Russia, as has been noted above, the realistic style that was sweeping the Continent during the latter years of the nineteenth century had already been introduced by such men as Alexis Feofilaktovich Pisemski, whose *Gorkaia sudbina* was as violent and gloomy as any naturalistic study by Hauptmann. This style, which in effect ran parallel and sometimes clashed with the tradition set by Gogol and Griboedov and carried on by Turgenev and Ostrovski, found a powerful exponent in Count Lev, or Leo, Nikolaevich Tolstoi. Fundamentally, of course, Tolstoi's genius gained deepest expression through the medium of the novel, where the vaster canvas permitted him to reveal his characteristic breadth of vision, and where no narrowly circumscribing conventions detracted from the vigour of his character conceptions. When he approaches the theatre there is amply evident in his scenes an impatience with stage restrictions, so that his plays are often marred by weakness in dramatic structure and by a certain spluttering incoherence. At the same time, the vigour of his own personality and his burning sincerity give to his characters a peculiar intensity and to his scenes a lurid grandeur.

His first approach to the theatre came in 1887, when he wrote a sketch called *Pervii vinokur* (*The First Distiller*), designed as a moral tract whereby to reveal the evils consequent upon drunkenness among the peasantry, and followed this with the tragic naturalistic drama, *Vlast tmi* (*The Power of Darkness*, 1889). In general the atmosphere of this work is akin to that of Hauptmann's *Before Sunrise*—sensational in episode and brutal in conception—to it, however, is given a typically Tolstoian conclusion that removes its Christian fervour from the agnostic pessimism of the German author. The central character is a peasant, Nikita, who has an *affaire* with the wife of the man for whom he works. In order to profit from this situation Nikita's mother, an evil-spirited and avaricious woman, persuades the wife to kill her husband. Thus freed, she marries her young lover, but he now proceeds to seduce her stepdaughter. Once more the mother enters the scene: the child born of this intrigue must die, she declares, and the girl be married off. To her promptings are added those of the wife, who realizes that if Nikita can be persuaded to undertake this crime his soul will be stained by the same guilt as has besmirched her. Eventually Nikita consents, crushes the child under a board, and inters it in a cellar. Almost immediately, however, his conscience begins to work, and, in order to free himself from the weight of his crime, he takes the occasion of the marriage of his mistress to announce publicly what he has done.

In Tolstoi's hands, accordingly, the stark depiction of life's brutalities serves a purpose different from that which it had in the hands of others. The entire drama is shot through with a moral, or religious, concept of a kind which but rarely is apparent even in vaguest form among the works of the realists. The larger social world is depicted in *Plodi prosveshcheniya* (*The Fruits of Enlightenment*, 1891), where Tolstoi takes up—although in vastly diverse terms—a theme dealt with in one of the early comedies of Catherine the Great, that of the toying with the supposedly supernatural. Catherine had laughed satirically at those who followed the lead of Cagliostro; Tolstoi bitterly attacks the parlour spiritualism of his age, and adroitly mingles this topic with the larger one of opposition between peasants and landowners. It is a peasant girl who, pretending to have the powers of a medium, succeeds in helping her fellows to purchase a tract of land from a proprietor who hitherto had refused to sell it to them; it is through the spiritualistic scenes that these peasants are brought to a dim realization of the profitless lives of the aristocracy. Already in 1891 Tolstoi sensed that the class to which he belonged was rudderlessly drifting to disaster.

After this play there was a long dramatic silence. Over twenty years were to elapse before *Zhivoi trup* (*The Living Corpse*, or *Redemption*, 1911; written 1900) and *I svet vo tme tsvetit* (*And Light shines in Darkness*) were published. The hero of the former is a true Tolstoian figure—a man, Fedia, who, discovering his wife's intrigue with one of his companions and himself deeply oppressed by a feeling of his own inner weakness, abandons his home, leaves his coat by the side of a stream, and is consequently thought to have been drowned. Unfortunately one man knows the secret and villainously exposes the deception. Lisa, the wife, and her lover are arrested as accom-

SKETCH BY HENRIK IBSEN

From the original in the Fylkesmuseet, Skien.

THE CHINESE
STAGE: HEROINE
IN A GARDEN

609

plices in a supposed attempt to thwart the marriage laws: these laws prohibit divorce, and it is thought that the entire trick was a conspiracy designed to allow a bigamous remarriage. In the end Fedia decides, both to satisfy his own sense of unworthiness and to give happiness to his wife and her lover, that his death is the only solution. In *And Light shines in Darkness* Tolstoi gives a dramatic picture of his own tortured soul. The story of the man who wants to give away his wealth and is thus brought into opposition with his wife, who seeks to inculcate the ideal of pacificism and finds his preaching resultant in disaster, is quite clearly a reflection of the struggles of his own latter days. As might be expected, its action has a luminous intensity, although the nearness of the theme to the author's own personal experiences manifestly detracts—quite apart from the unfinished state in which it was left—from its dramatic value.

During these years when Tolstoi was writing a far greater play-wright, Anton Chekhov, was experimenting in still newer forms of realism. Although his earliest dramas belong to the eighties, it may, however, be better to postpone an account of these until an opportunity arises for discussion of the significant productions of the Moscow Art Theatre. Chekhov died ere the twentieth century had passed the half of its first decade, yet, despite that fact, he belongs in spirit rather to the realism of that age than to the realism of the century in which most of his life was passed. In the closely related Slavonic country of Poland Stanisław Przybyszewski contributed to the realistic movement another individualistically conceived treatment. A daimonic spirit somewhat akin to Strindberg, he was a man at once deeply oppressed by sexual preoccupations and one whose soul fared into dim metaphysical realms. Out of the combination of these elements was wrought his series of realistic-symbolic dramas—*Dla szczęścia* (*For Happiness*, 1902), *Złote runo* (*The Golden Fleece*, 1902), *Goście* (*The Guests*, 1902), *Matka* (*The Mother*, 1903), *Śnieg* (*Snow*, 1903), *Odwieczna baśń* (*The Eternal Fable*, 1906), and *Gody życia* (*The Feast of Life*, 1907). In these he expresses forcibly his sense of the sorrows, the confusions, the inconsistencies, of the world. It is himself who appears as the hero of his dramas: he is his own Zdżarski in *For Happiness*, Ruszczyc in *The Golden Fleece*, Kazimierz in *Snow*. To a large extent, therefore, his realism approaches the inward style of Strindberg; the external events of *Snow*, for example, have very much less import than what is symbolized of subjective emotions and of the despairs of dreams. Although an author almost unknown outside of Poland, and

U

although himself a strangely tortured and erratic soul, Przybyszewski possesses a power of no ordinary measure.

The new French realism captured the attention of several other Polish authors during these years, but without enabling them to produce plays powerful enough to appeal beyond their own time and country. Among them Józef Narzymski is worthy of mention because of the extreme enthusiasm with which he embraced the realistic creed and of the way in which he used its style—as, for example, in *Pozytywni* (*The Positivists*, 1872)—for idealistic purposes. Further advanced on the path towards naturalism were the plays of Gabrjela Zapolska, in whom resided a power both of serious purpose and of comic conception; her later *Moralność pani Dulskiej* (*The Morals of Mme Dulska*, 1913) is still remembered. For his *Rozbitki* (*The Wreck*, 1882) Józef Bliziński is also to be remembered in this company.

To the other countries of Eastern Europe also came the new style, although usually the familiar form of the realistic problem play was transformed there by the inclusion of elements of the sentimental, the legendary, or the fantastic. The sentimental is to be seen, for example, in such a play as *A nagymama* (*The Grandmother*, 1891), by the Hungarian Gergely Cziky, with its 'thesis' set against an old-fashioned plot of a long-lost daughter and a lover who, in order to see the girl he adores, disguises himself as a teacher of French. In Czechoslovakia Alois Jirásek oscillates between drama of a like kind and historical works such as *Lucerna* (*The Lantern*, 1905), while Ladislav Stropežnický develops a sort of Ostrovski-like realism in pieces like *Naši furianti* (*Our Swaggerers*, 1887), where, instead of a formally developed plot, we see our entire community set in confusion over a dispute concerning a dowry. Rumania produced Joan Luca Cargiale, locally famed both for his problem plays and for his more individually flavoured social satires. In Jugoslavia Branislav Nušich applied the satiric method to the life of his native land, and Ivan Cankar aimed his shafts at local political corruption. None of these, however, produced playwrights worthy on account of their individual forms of expression to stand alongside either the great trio or the host of lesser masters whom the movement called into being elsewhere. Something of consequence was to come from diverse parts of the world during the twentieth century, but nineteenth-century realism flourished freely and fruitfully only in Scandinavia, Germany, France, and the Slavonic lands.

CHAPTER VI

NEO-ROMANTICISM IN THE THEATRE

ONE THING must never be lost sight of in surveying the fortunes of the drama during these years. Ibsen and Ibsenism loom up as the great force of the time; the work of the independent theatres, almost wholly devoted to the cultivation of the violently naturalistic stage, seizes primarily upon our attention. Yet, even in the very days when the culmination of this style had barely been reached, there is amply evident a counter-movement designed to combat and, if possible, to destroy the very tenets of naturalism.

This, we must remember, was the age that produced the 'symbolist' movement in poetry, a school adumbrated by the appearance of Mallarmé's *L'après-midi d'un faune* in 1876, and definitely launched as a 'movement' by a manifesto published in *Figaro* during the year 1886. From its inspiration came plays wherein the external reality ceded to the inner. In the original manifesto it was stated that "symbolist poetry seeks to clothe the Idea with a sensory form which, however, would not be its own end." Here logic is completely banished, and Zola's belief that the naturalistic method of composition could ever possess the exactitude of science is utterly denied: words are used not to reproduce life, but to evoke emotions, and objectivity is abandoned in favour of the subjective.

THE NEO-ROMANTICISM OF GERMANY

Almost every country during the latter years of the nineteenth century can exhibit dramatic movements of an anti-realist kind, sometimes taking shape as revivals of the earlier romantic styles, sometimes expressive of this later poetic inspiration. Not only so: often these dramatic movements are to be found even among the works of those authors most closely associated with the growth of naturalism. Ibsen thus starts his career with the penning of historical dramas clearly inspired by previous experiments in that form; in *Peer Gynt* he veers off into the world of the fantastic; while the impress of the symbolic sheds a quivering poetic light on his later compositions. His companion Strindberg begins with the historical and fantastic and later returns to both styles. Perhaps most characteristic of this development, however, is Gerhart Hauptmann.

Hauptmann is chief of the realistic school in Germany: he is also the chief exponent of the neo-romantic movement there. *The Sunken Bell, Henry of Auë, And Pippa Dances!*, are landmarks in the history of romanticism on the stage, and in these plays he was expressing a need felt by his contemporaries; he was giving the public that for which, in addition to the realistic, it sought. The truth of this assertion is demonstrated by even the most cursory glance at theatrical development from the nineties of the century onward. When Ludwig Fulda presented his *Talisman* in 1892 its success was so emphatic that no doubt could remain concerning the will of the playgoers to welcome something poetic and colourful, and, as a result, the immediately following years show a succession of efforts to provide these elements in stage form—efforts that gave inspiration to a number of dramatists who, coming to the theatre after the year 1900, pursued the same path and sought to reach further goals.

Dominant among Hauptmann's companions is the Austrian poet Hugo von Hofmannsthal, one who sought through the medium of romance to provide for the world a great vision of life. In his earliest plays he wanders lyrically and beautifully in a realm of subjectively conceived romantic dreams. From *Gestern* (*Yesterday*, 1891) he moves to *Der Tor und der Tod* (*The Fool and Death*, 1893), eventually collecting together in his *Theater in Versen* (1899) and in his *Kleine Dramen* (1906) a series of such studies, mainly short, one-act pieces—such as *Der Abenteurer und die Sängerin* (*The Adventurer and the Singing-girl*; written 1899) and *Der Kaiser und die Hexe* (*The Emperor and the Witch*; written 1895).

At the beginning he is the exponent of the ideal of 'sensations'—the passive acceptance of experience and of such emotions experience may bring with it. Gradually this philosophy gives way to an appreciation of higher and less selfish values, so that *Der Tor und der Tod* is an essay in the futility of concentration upon those secret passions that were so precious to the æsthetes of the nineties; while in his latest works he passes into a sphere where the elements of classical thought are allied to the concepts of Christian belief. It is somewhat remarkable that on this final level the poet found the most fitting medium for the expression of his moods in the re-handling of ancient themes. For *Elektra* (1903) and *Ödipus und die Sphinx* (*Œdipus and the Sphinx*, 1905) and *Ariadne auf Naxos* (1912) he turned to Athens, making the classical figures into tortured neurotics; for *Das gerettete Venedig* (*Venice Preserved*, 1905) he found the source in Otway's play; for *Jedermann* (1912) he sought inspiration in the morality of *Everyman*; and for *Das grosse Salzburger Welttheater* (*The Great Theatre of the World*, 1922) the Spanish *autos* form a source. Fate looms darkly in all of these; death is omnipresent; and the dream that is life leaves man strangely insecure—a creature stumbling his way along paths that lead he knows not where. The author of the delightfully romantic *Der Rosenkavalier* (1911) found his true realm in the world of spiritual torment. *Elektra* is a study of the frenzied psychology of a woman whom hate has made mad; *Ödipus* presents a strange treatment of the Greek theme, with Œdipus hailed as deliverer and the atmosphere of "the blind deed of the gods" about him.

In all his work Hofmannsthal reveals himself as a poet of high distinction, although a poet whom sheer love of beauty frequently leads astray and whose writings have but little message of hope. Despite his 'philosophy,' he is only a blind prophet whose ears are intoxicated with music, and at the end of his life, as is shown in *Der Schwierige* (*The Fastidious Man*, 1921) and in *Der Turm* (*The Tower*, 1925), with its plot developed out of Calderón's *La vida es sueño*, he felt out of touch with his time, preferring the dream to the after-war reality.

In developing this atmosphere Hofmannsthal is the typical poet of the entire school, finding exquisite expression for the common thoughts and emotions of his companions—such men as the German Karl Gustav Vollmoeller, whose dramatic work, starting in 1903 with *Katharina, Gräfin von Armagnac, und ihre beiden Liebhaber* (*Catherine, Countess of Armagnac, and her Two Lovers*), includes a *Turandot* (1912), based on Gozzi, and the famous *Das Mirakel* (*The Miracle*, 1912), the pantomimic production that gave Max Reinhardt international fame; Eduard Stucken, who exploited the Grail legend in *Gawan, Lanval*, and *Lanzelot* (1902–9); and Ernst Hardt, author of *Tantris der Narr* (*Tantris the Fool*, 1908). Besides these avowed disciples of the school were numerous others who, influenced by the wave of enthusiasm that greeted its efforts, essayed individual works in this style. The weathervane that was Sudermann thus produced his *Johannes* and *Die drei Reiherfedern* (*The Three Feathers*) in 1898, while in 1892 Schnitzler caught the mood in *Paracelsus*, and in 1898 followed this with *Der Schleier der Beatrice* (*The Veil of Beatrice*). Later Herbert Eulenberg, after dealing unromantically with an incest theme in *Anna Walewska* (1899), penned his *Kassandra* (1903) in the symbolist style, and neo-classicist

Wilhelm von Scholz, whose *Vertauschte Seelen* (*Bartered Souls*) appeared in 1901, was sufficiently influenced to write his mythological *Meroe* (1906), in which father and son are tormented rivals in love. Effectively, although painfully, Richard Voss wrought out of Hans Andersen an engrossing fairy-play in *Die Blonde Kathrein* (*Fair Kathrein*, 1894). Obviously influenced by Hauptmann, he here tells the story of a poor mother's sacrifice to prolong her suffering child's pilgrimage on earth. The older style of romanticism is pursued by Adolf Willbrandt in *Der Königsbote* (*The King's Messenger*, 1894), an historical drama set in eleventh-century Norway.

It cannot be claimed that, except for the plays of Hauptmann and Hofmannsthal, the German theatre produced much of permanent worth in this kind, but assuredly considerable historical interest attaches to these works produced in the very midst of enthusiasm for the realistic. Hardly anywhere more clearly are the trends of the time thus demonstrated in concrete productions. The works of the neo-romantic school when placed alongside the contemporaneous naturalistic dramas help to explain the peculiar eclecticism of the greatest stage director of that time, Max Reinhardt, who seized variously upon the ultra-realistic and the fantastic, the prosaically objective and the subjectively lyrical, who found inspiration alike in the tiny Kleines Theater and in the vast Grosses Schauspielhaus.

Before leaving the German neo-romantic theatre one other thing should be observed. The antagonism towards the naturalistic led some of the younger spirits through incipient romanticism to a new kind of classicism. Typical here is Paul Ernst, who, starting in the realistic camp, soon moved over to the world of romance in *Der Tod* (*Death*, 1900), and thence shifted to a style in art which is definitely based on classical models, tending to rely on intellectual ideas rather than on emotions and to preach the cult of civilization based on order imposed upon the individual. Neither his works nor those of his companions merit the esteem in which they were held in Hitler's Germany, yet the trend marked in them deserves attention, particularly if it is related to the contemporary resuscitation of the classical tragedy in France.

FRENCH FANTASY AND FLAMBOYANCE: ROSTAND AND MAETERLINCK

During the years before the appearance of the Symbolist manifesto various playwrights in Paris had been attempting to keep alive the spirit of the poetic theatre. Vicomte Henri de Bornier thus won considerable success with *La fille de Roland* (*Roland's Daughter*, 1875), a vigorous treatment of heroic material, while François Coppée attempted to give new form to the romantic historical drama in such works as *Severo Torelli* (1883), *Les Jacobites* (1885), and *Pour la couronne* (*For the Crown*, 1895). The first, set in fifteenth-century Pisa, tells a melodramatic story of a mother who saves her son from parricide by herself stabbing her former lover; and the other plays introduce similar sensational situations covered with the rich colours of romantic verse. Manifestly stimulated by the writings that had stirred France during the thirties of the century, Coppée brought to the theatre a skilled dramatic craftsmanship, a true sense of effective situation, a bold if not very subtle understanding of character, and a rich poetic eloquence. His *Pour la couronne* is Victor Hugo modernized and tightened in structure. With admirable economy he keeps his eyes fixed on his central situation—that of a son, Constantin, who is faced with the terrible problem of murdering his own father, Michel Brancomir, or of permitting his father to sacrifice his country and his honour. In others of his dramatic compositions, such as the one-act pieces *Le passant* (*The Passer-by*, 1869), *Le luthier de Crémone* (*The Lute-maker of Cremona*, 1876), and *Le trésor* (*The Treasure*, 1879), Coppée shows a grace and delicacy which give to his works their peculiar flavour.

These writings, however, fade in importance when put alongside those of Edmond Rostand, an author of considerably greater strength, and one who has succeeded in gaining both a national and an international reputation. Rostand's success depends upon a number of very definite qualities. He was, first of all, a consummately skilful playwright; indeed, some of his dramas might almost be taken by apprentice writers as models of craftsmanship. To this he added a genuine, if not extraordinary, poetic gift: his words sing, and he combines a skilful handling of words with flamboyant passion. Still further, he succeeds in making the most of two worlds, taking from the older romanticism its vigour and from neo-romanticism its delicacy and novel soul-searching. It was the combination of these diverse elements in his work that gave to him his peculiar position.

His first play, *Les Romanesques* (*The Romancers*, 1894), is a joyous lyrical essay written in a frankly escapist mood—a glove laughingly cast down at the feet of the dismal followers of Zola. This was succeeded by *La princesse lointaine* (*The Far-away Princess*, 1895), in which the medievalism of the neo-romantic movement is exploited. In an almost pre-Raphaelite manner the tale is retold of the troubadour Rudel whose heart is dominated by a hopeless passion for the distant Mélisande, and who makes his last journey to her Court, there to die in the ecstasy of his bliss. With medieval themes the neo-romanticists frequently combined treatment of themes based on Christ's life, and we need not be surprised to find Rostand next composing *La Samaritaine* (*The Woman of Samaria*, 1897), where the idealistic love of Rudel is translated into divine devotion. The plot is simple: among the Samaritans Christ makes his appearance, and by his gentle words instantly converts the beautiful Photina, who becomes one of his most devoted proponents, one who succeeds in bringing all the natives of Samaria to the worship of the new God.

Perhaps realizing that his true métier did not lie in such realms, Rostand proceeded, immediately after the production of this piece, to startle Parisian society with his swaggering *Cyrano de Bergerac* (1897). In this he abandoned the stained-glass effects of the preceding two plays and developed his theme against a background, carefully and minutely studied, of life in seventeenth-century France. That vivid opening scene set in the theatre, with its teeming humanity and its contrast between the real and the artificial, strikes at once a note entirely fresh. Rudel had no substance, and the Christ of *La Samaritaine* was but a figment of the imagination: in the depiction of the historical Cyrano and his comrades there is solidity and life, so that even when the theme introduces the same story of hopeless passion as already had been dealt with in *La princesse lointaine* we are prepared to listen with a fresh interest and to be moved. It is true that the devotion of Cyrano for Roxane is like that of Rudel for his lady, but the hero is different. Skilfully, Rostand has altered his pattern and found as a barrier to love's fulfilment not an external obstacle, but a characteristic of the hero himself. Rudel's story was a pitiful one of a moth and a flame; that of Cyrano is the story of a man proud, courageous, and witty, doomed by fate to have his spirit encased in a ridiculous frame. About the treatment of the tale too there is an expansive gaiety. Fundamentally the play relates the sad tale of Cyrano, in love with Roxane and driven by that very love to aid the handsome young Christian de Neuvillette towards possessing her, until he dies with his own passion unspoken: it is consequently 'tragic.' Yet our general impression of the action is not one of gloom: rather do we recall such episodes as that in which Cyrano contemptuously teaches the impertinent Valvert a lesson and runs him through with his rapier to the riming music of a ballade.

THE VICOMTE: I shall fling at him now some of my wit! [*Advances towards* CYRANO, *who is watching him, and takes his place in front of him with a silly air.*] You—your nose is—nose is—very large.

CYRANO [*gravely*]: Very!

THE VICOMTE [*smiling*]: Ha!

CYRANO [*imperturbable*]: That is all?

THE VICOMTE: But——

CYRANO: No, young man.
> That is somewhat too brief. You might say—Lord!—
> Many and many a thing, changing your tone.
> As, for example, these:—Aggressively:
> "Sir, had I such a nose I'd cut it off!"
> Friendly: "But it must dip into your cup.
> You should have made a goblet tall to drink from."
> Descriptive: "'Tis a crag—a peak—a cape!
> I said a cape?—'tis a peninsula."
> Inquisitive: "To what use do you put
> This oblong sheath; is it a writing-case
> Or scissors-box?" Or, in a gracious tone:
> "Are you so fond of birds, that like a father
> You spend your time and thought to offer them
> This roosting-place to rest their little feet?" . . .

THE VICOMTE [*in a temper*]: Buffoon!

CYRANO [*giving a cry like one who feels a sudden pain*]: Oh!

THE VICOMTE [*who was going off, turning about*]: What's he saying now?

CYRANO [*with grimaces of pain*]: I must
> Shake it, because it falls asleep—the fault
> Of leaving it long idle——

THE VICOMTE: What's the matter?

CYRANO: My sword-blade tingles!

THE VICOMTE [*drawing his own sword*]: Very well, come on!

CYRANO: I shall give you a charming little stroke.

THE VICOMTE [*with disdain*]: Poet!—

CYRANO: A poet, yes! and such a one,
> That, while I fence with you, I'll improvise
> A ballade for you.

THE VICOMTE: A ballade?

CYRANO: I suppose
> You do not e'en imagine what that is?

THE VICOMTE: But——

CYRANO [*as if reciting a lesson*]: The ballade, then, is made up of three stanzas,
> Of eight lines——

THE VICOMTE [*shuffling his feet*]: Oh!

CYRANO [*continuing*]: And a refrain of four.

THE VICOMTE: You——

CYRANO: I'll make one and fight you, both at once.
And at the last verse touch you, sir.

THE VICOMTE: No!

CYRANO: No?
*The Ballade of Monsieur de Bergerac's Duel
At the Hôtel de Bourgogne with a Booby.*

THE VICOMTE: What is that, if you please?

CYRANO: That is the title.

THE HALL [*excited to the highest pitch*]: In place!—
No noise!—In line!—This is amusing.

[*Tableau. A circle of curious onlookers in the parterre, the* MARQUISES *and the* OFFICERS *mixed in with the* TRADESMEN *and common people. The* PAGES *climb on people's shoulders to see better. All the women stand up in the boxes. To the right* DE GUICHE *and his gentlemen. To the left* LE BRET, RAGUENEAU, CUIGY, *etc.*

CYRANO [*closing his eyes for a moment*]: Wait, let me choose my rhymes
—I have them now:

> My hat I toss lightly away;
> From my shoulders I slowly let fall
> The cloak which conceals my array,
> And my sword from my scabbard I call;
> Like Céladon, graceful and tall,
> Like Scaramouche, quick hand and brain,—
> And I warn you, my friend, once for all,
> I shall thrust when I end the refrain.

[*The swords meet.*

> You were rash thus to join in the fray;
> Like a fowl I shall carve you up small,
> Your ribs, 'neath your doublet so gay,
> Your breast, where the blue ribbons fall.
> Ding dong! ring your bright trappings all;
> My point flits like a fly on the pane,
> As I clearly announce to the hall
> I shall thrust when I end the refrain.
> I need one more rhyme for 'array'—
> You give ground, you turn white as the wall,—
> And so lend me the word 'runaway.'
> There! you have let your point fall
> As I parry your best lunge of all;
> I begin a new line, the end's plain,
> Your skewer hold tight, lest it fall.
> I shall thrust when I end the refrain.

[*Announces solemnly*]

REFRAIN.

Prince, on the Lord you must call!
I gain ground, I advance once again,
I feint, I lunge [*lunging*]. There! that is all!
[*The* VICOMTE *staggers.* CYRANO *salutes.*
For I thrust as I end the refrain.

It proved hard for Rostand to equal this masterpiece of the colourfully romantic. *L'Aiglon* (1900) deals with the 'eaglet,' the son of Napoleon, who, inspired to recapture the empire of his father, has no strength of will or of body to carry out his aims. This play was a manifest failure. Something near to success, however, comes with *Chantecler* (1910) and *La dernière nuit de Don Juan* (*Don Juan's Last Night*; printed 1921). The former, with its richly satirical verse and its general symbolic character, introduces a new element in Rostand's art. His old power of dramatic construction is there, and every scene is carefully planned for its effect: one after another—the coming of the Pheasant, the incursion of the Hunting-dog, the bliss of love, the flight, the despair, and the new-found hope—each aids in contributing to the general impression. The main story is properly simple—the tale of the renowned barnyard cock who believes in his soul that the very sun rises at the command of his proud crowing. Detested by the creatures of night, he is in a dangerous position: if his dream is shattered his sense of the value of life itself will be gone. The Pheasant with whom he goes off wishes to destroy this dream, for she is jealous of Chantecler's devotion to it, but even after she has succeeded in this plot Chantecler regains his confidence in himself, although with a wisdom deepened by experience, and the Pheasant herself, won by his strength of spirit, is content to accept his vision of life. There is nothing very profound in the play's theme or in the hundreds of minute episodes through which the allegory is pursued: nevertheless *Chantecler*, because of its richly lyrical utterance, its vivid sense of character values, and its skilful construction, is one of the most interesting dramas of its period.

Rostand's last play, left unfinished by his death, deals interestingly with the eternally fascinating theme of Don Juan. Opening with a scene in which Don Juan is being taken to Hell by the Statue—and in which the dialogue is, as it were, a continuation of the last lines of Molière's drama—the action presents the hero as granted, like Faust, a respite of ten years ere the Devil calls on him, and finding, again like Faust, that he has gained nothing. At the conclusion he is forced ignominiously into taking a part in the Devil's puppet-show. "I long to suffer!" cries the romantically disposed hero.

> I've never suffered! I've a right to hell!
> I've earned my hell!

To which the Devil makes reply:

> Hell is where I decree;
> I fix its place. Some celebrated men
> Are damned within their statues; thou art damned
> Within thy puppet!

Rostand's gaiety, satire, and irony, combined with his rich appreciation of romantic heroics, give him a secure position in the theatre. He may not have contributed much towards the dramatic interpretation of the neo-romanticism of his time, yet we gladly exonerate him for this, in view of the breezy freshness and vivid colouring that is spread over his three greatest dramas.

For the dramatic interpretation of neo-romanticism the Parisian stage had in the Belgian Maurice Maeterlinck a man who in his youth distinguished himself as a poet of the Symbolist school, and who later deliberately set about the task of translating the quality of this poetry into theatrical terms. Both because he was a pioneer in this realm and because he was possessed of a true, if limited, genius, his influence upon the theatre of the present century has been widespread. We may perhaps have grown out of the mood from which his plays were constructed; his scenes may no longer have the excitement and magic they had for an earlier generation; these things can be readily admitted without our forgetting the debt that the modern stage owes to his work.

In the year 1889 appeared his first drama, characteristically titled *La Princesse Maleine*, and this was followed by a series of similar plays—*L'intruse* (*The Intruder*, 1890), *Les aveugles* (*The Blind*, or *The Sightless*, 1890), *Pelléas et Mélisande* (1892), *Alladine et Palomides* (1894), *L'intérieur* (*The Interior*, 1894), *La morte de Tintagiles* (*The Death of Tintagiles*, 1894), *Aglavaine et Sélysette* (1896). The last of this series was *Sœur Béatrice* (*Sister Beatrice*) in 1899.

All of these, whether exploiting medieval themes or not, are characterized by the same qualities. A thin veil separates us from the characters; a dreaming inactivity replaces the richly moving action of a Rostand; a sense of fatal destiny removes the slightest vestige of human responsibility. Of the medieval-set dramas, *Pelléas et Mélisande* is the finest—a variant of the Paolo and Francesca story placed in a world of dreams. The opening scene strikes the note that is to be heard throughout its entire length. We are placed before a castle gate, and voices are heard within:

MAIDSERVANTS: Open the gate! Open the gate!

PORTER: Who is there? Why do you come and wake me up? Go out by the little gates; there are enough of them.

A MAIDSERVANT: We have come to wash the threshold, the gate and the steps; open, then! open!

Clearly we are in a world beyond reality, and in that world we remain until the doomed lovers are finally laid to rest.

Medieval themes, however, were common among the writings of the romantic poet-dramatists, and Maeterlinck showed far greater originality in his attempt to create a "static theatre" in *L'intruse*, *Les aveugles*, and *L'intérieur*. The first introduces us to death, the intruder in the family circle. There is no plot in the ordinary sense of the word—just a picture of a little group sitting in a small room, while beyond a woman lies in childbirth. Fitfully the talk drifts, ebbs lightly, and falls silently back, while all the time we feel death's presence drawing closer:

THE GRANDFATHER: Are the windows open, Ursula?

THE DAUGHTER: The glass door is open, Grandfather.

THE GRANDFATHER: It seems to me the cold is entering the room.

THE DAUGHTER: There is a little wind in the garden, Grandfather, and the rose leaves are falling.

THE FATHER: Well, shut the door, Ursula. It is late.

THE DAUGHTER: Yes, Father. I cannot shut the door, Father.

THE TWO OTHER DAUGHTERS: We cannot shut the door.

In *Les aveugles* the situation is equally static—just a group of blind men, lost in a forest and desperate because their guide, a priest, has died in their midst. Even less of dramatic action is involved in *L'intérieur*. Here we stand outside a house and look in through a window at a happy, quiet, peaceful family scene within. But a girl belonging to this family has been drowned, and the dialogue of the play comes from one or two neighbours whose duty it is to break the sad news and who stand hesitating outside. The real persons of the drama are not these neighbours: they are the members of the family circle whom we cannot see, whom we never hear speak: the veil is drawn between us and them.

For the subtlety of these pieces there can be nothing save admiration. In them Maeterlinck has fully and delicately realized his dream of a new stage. "There is," he says,

an everyday tragedy which is more real, deeper and more in keeping with our true existence than the tragedy of great adventures. . . . I

have come to think that an old man, seated in his armchair, simply
waiting beside the lamp, listening, without knowing it, to all the
eternal laws that reign about him, interpreting, without understanding
it, what there is in the silence of the doors and windows and in the
small voice of the light, undergoing the presence of his soul and of his
destiny, leaning a little his head, without suspecting that all the powers
of this world are intervening and watching in his room like attentive
servants, not knowing that the sun itself sustains the little table on
which he rests his elbows and that there is not a planet in heaven nor
a power of the soul which is indifferent to the dropping of an eyelid
or the disclosure of a thought—I have come to think that this motionless old man was living in reality a deeper, more human and more
general life than the lover who strangles his mistress, the captain who
wins a victory or the 'husband who avenges his honour.'

In his dream of a static theatre Maeterlinck may have been anticipated by predecessors such as Norwid, but his enunciation of this
theatre's aims no less than his creative interpretation of them still
justify us in styling him an innovator.

From this style Maeterlinck moved, with the production of
Monna Vanna in 1902, to another less individual in concept, yet
more likely to win popular esteem. The story here has a ring
familiar to those versed in the romantic drama of the time. The
city of Pisa is besieged and starving: to save it from destruction
Monna Vanna agrees to give herself to the general, Prinzivalle,
commanding the investing forces, but to her amazement finds in
him a chivalrous lover who freely proposes to release her from her
promise. When he is about to be arrested as a traitor she brings this
hero to her house; her husband suspects the worst; she declares she
has not been seduced, but at the threat of torture being applied to
Prinzivalle she lies boldly, and we are left to believe that she will
rescue him from prison and go off with him. Here is something
vastly less interesting than Maeterlinck's earlier work. Unquestionably, despite its theatrical success, this play marks a retrogression in
his art: there is some beauty in it, yet there is an irritating quality
combined of sexual suggestiveness and vague mysticism.

Joyzelle (1903) introduces more of the mystical, although here
too the themes of love and of sexual sacrifice are once more pursued; and both reappear in *Marie Magdaleine* (1910), a somewhat
unsatisfactory piece, in which the characters are obvious stereotypes—the Roman soldier Lucius Verus, Marie Magdaleine, the
courtesan who becomes devoted to Christ, and the philosopher
Annæus Silanus, who quests solely after wisdom.

In *L'oiseau bleu* (*The Blue Bird*, 1908) Maeterlinck discovered fresh and fruitful territory, and the appeal of this play must be fully recognized, even if we may now find much of its allegory childish and most of its philosophy spurious. Perhaps it is best to accept it for what it truly is—a rather sentimental children's fantasy, skilfully planned and expressed with not a little beauty of language. It is easy to sneer at *The Blue Bird*: nevertheless it possesses its own virtues and is a play which, even although its bloom of novelty is now worn off, has an enduring appeal. Not so successful is *Les fiançailles* (*The Betrothal*, 1918), in which the author tried to provide a kind of sequel to his earlier fantasy.

To reach an objective estimate of Maeterlinck's contribution to the theatre is difficult. Posing as a philosopher, he can win little esteem for his thoughts about the mystery of life; beginning his career with a bold new theory of dramatic expression, he abandoned his own position and ended by supplying the public with rather cheap theatrical effects. Yet in the end it is in these early dramas, and the theory out of which they grew, that we find the truest evidence of his genius. No doubt the theatre is too rough and vulgar a place for the exploitation of the purely static drama that he desired to encourage: no doubt the veils he places between his characters and ourselves occasion, if they do not justify, accusations that his art is inherently 'escapist.' On the other hand, those who condemn or dismiss these works will neglect at their peril observation of the wide influence Maeterlinck's style has had on dozens of twentieth-century authors, many of them working in realms apparently far removed from his, and they will fail to assess at its real worth the truly exquisite craftsmanship that these dramas display.

Beyond the writings of the French Rostand and the Belgian Maeterlinck the theatre of Paris has nothing of consequence to offer in the field of romanticism, unless we except *Le chemineau* (*The Tramp*, 1897) of Jean Richepin, that interestingly ironic idyllic picture of a tinker's life, and the dramas, such as *Le cloître* (*The Cloister*, 1900), written in the lyrical strain by Maeterlinck's fellow-countryman Émile Verhaeren. But more was not needed. Rostand and Maeterlinck between them gave to the French romantic play a paramount international import.

PART X

THE DRAMA OF THE ORIENT

THE DRAMA OF THE ORIENT

To INTRODUCE a summary account of the theatres of the East at this particular point in a general history of the stage may seem to be preposterous. We have just surveyed the age of Ibsen and we are approaching the age of Shaw: to divide these epochs by passing in imagination to the countries washed by the waters of the warm Pacific does indeed appear at first glance to be absurd. Chronologically the dramas of China, Japan, and India took their rise during the centuries we style the Middle Ages and the Renaissance; it was at that time that they achieved their richest power of expression; and since that expression commonly was devoted to truths religious, metaphysical, and philosophical, it might well be thought that more appropriately these Oriental plays might have been dealt with in association with the mysteries and miracles of the Catholic Church.

As a justification for the placing of the present section it may be argued that every work of wide general scope—whether it be a universal history of human events or of literature—must select some definite orientation, and clearly what we are most interested in is the development of the Western theatre from its earliest-known days in Greece to its latest manifestations in the playhouses with which we ourselves are currently familiar. If we had turned to treat the Eastern drama along with the medieval mysteries solely because, across a waste of several thousand miles, unknown poets of China, Japan, and India were engaged at the same time in producing religious dramas, we should unquestionably have been falsifying the composition of the picture being painted. The focal point is the theatre of the West, and everything must be dependent upon that fact.

To the Western stage Oriental drama remained almost utterly unknown until the early part of the nineteenth century, and even then its impact on the playwrights was but slight. True, Goethe and others among the German romantics raved over the beauties of Kalidasa's works in the ecstatic terms of praise which they found for all objects of their adoration, but direct influence of these works on contemporary dramatic form is still to seek. All through

627

the century increased knowledge of the Oriental stages was brought to men's attention; from the specialized library of the scholar this knowledge was passed to the theatrical library; and gradually, towards the end of the century, we begin to discern faint signs of an impact being made by the East upon the West. Linnebach is sufficiently acquainted with certain features of the Japanese stage to borrow from it the device of the revolving platform; the public is being made acquainted with the forms of the plays by a series of translations. India, China, and Japan, with their theatres, are drawing closer to the Occident.

It is, however, only during the present century that this knowledge becomes intimate and begins to influence our drama directly. A Chinese company comes to Paris in 1895, a Japanese to London in 1900; the ancient Sanskrit plays are being looked upon not merely as curiosities or as storehouses of Oriental philosophy: they are adapted to the stage and performed, and even if nearly all these performances make their appeal to limited audiences the fashion has been set for other more popular productions to come. Even in the nineties *The Toy Cart* was something of a success in France: *The Yellow Jacket* (1913), fashioned in Chinese style for the American playhouse by J. H. Benrimo, finds commercial acclaim, and is followed by the frequently acted *The Circle of Chalk* (originally adapted as *Der Kreidekreis*, 1923, by Klabund) and by *Lady Precious Stream* (1938), wherein, with subtle skill, S. I. Hsiung has so adapted the Oriental style to Western needs as to have created a work whose general appeal has made it one of the best-known dramas of our times.

Along with these developments comes an awakening of interest on the part of the poets in the conventionalities of the Oriental stage. Arthur Waley's renderings of the Japanese Nō dramas are eagerly welcomed, and so, too, are works describing the methods of acting used in the presentation of these and kindred plays. As will be seen, the impress made by the Oriental theatre on the writings of poetic dramatists—particularly in the twenties and the thirties of our century—is by no means negligible.

All of this offers ample justification for the treatment of the stage of the East at this particular position in the general account of the theatre. In a work written by a Chinese theatrical historian concerning dramatic development in his own country Shakespeare and his fellows might occupy a corresponding place, coming along with the record of such native works as first displayed Elizabethan influence. We are dealing here not with actual but with spiritual time.

THE SANSKRIT DRAMA

THE THEATRE of India, as has been noted above, first among the Oriental stages impinged itself on the attention of the West. Precisely when the Sanskrit drama arose we do not know, largely because of that almost complete lack of any chronological interest so characteristic of early Indian literature. Traditional myth asserts that the joys of the stage were brought to men by Urvasi, condemned to descend from heaven to earth because, her mind confused by thoughts of her human lover, she had failed to exhibit her accustomed skill before the great god Indra. But when this supposedly supernatural event occurred and who were Urvasi's immediate successors remains utterly unknown. All that can be said even with the faintest measure of assurance is that already towards the beginning of our era a scholar, Bharata, had in front of him a sufficient body of material to be able, Aristotle-like, to compose his exhaustive *Science of Dramaturgy*; that the most famous of all Sanskrit playwrights, Kalidasa, apparently flourished in the fourth and fifth centuries; that before his time there had already been at least one successful playwright, Bhasa (some of whose work may perhaps be included among the dozen early Sanskrit dramatic works discovered some thirty years ago); and that the theatre long remained a distinguished and noble form of artistic expression in Indian Courts.

Concerning the stage used for these productions, much rests unsure, yet a fairly vivid general picture can still be formed both of the methods used and of the social background against which the dramas were enacted. The first thing we have to do in order to place Kalidasa in his setting is to allow our imaginations to carry us back to an ancient Indian palace Court, gorgeous in its appointments, replete with glistening adornments. Within this palace a theatre has been erected, with care and devotion. Prayers have been spoken; the very site has been selected only after meticulous consideration; the ground has been measured out in its minutest proportions; four pillars, symbolic of the four castes, have been erected at each corner to provide the main supports of the building;

preceding the ritual when the foundations are laid, the man in charge of the performances has fasted for three full days. The whole atmosphere connected with the establishment of this play-house is solemn and majestic.

We may imagine erected in this area so carefully chosen a hall about a hundred feet long and about half as wide, divided into two equal parts, the one designed for the King and his courtiers, the other for the performers. Facing the audience is a platform stage, with two compartments at the sides, backed by a curtain which can be drawn when necessary, revealing behind it another stage area ending in a magnificently decorated scenic back-wall.

What is peculiarly characteristic of this theatre, however—and, indeed, of all the theatres of the Orient—is not its physical shape, but rather the conventions on which the entire art of the perform-ance depends. Costumes, make-up, gestures, all are highly stylized, and, since dance and music play a significant part in the production, this stylization is harmonized with the other elements to make one unified whole. Movement of head, eyes, limbs, fingers. all is strictly set. The gestures may or may not approximate to what we should expect in reality: the important thing is that the highly select and cultured audience knows how to interpret the minutest indications given by the actors, translating these into terms of mood or situation. In *Sakuntala* the heroine is called upon to express fear of a bee that is buzzing round her head: this the performer does by moving his head quickly to and fro, while his lips quiver and his hands, with the palms held inward, are pressed unsteadily against his face. In the same drama a character has to pretend to be gather-ing flowers: here the left hand is extended horizontally in a set position, to symbolize the holding of a basket, while the position of the right is so devised as to suggest the motion of plucking the blossoms and carefully placing them in the basket.

In imagining a performance of a Sanskrit play as it was originally produced we must, therefore, place ourselves within the closely guarded precincts of an ancient and splendid Court and endeavour o think ourselves trained members of an alert audience. The joy of the spectacle will come, not so much from what is new, but rather from the delight in watching highly expert preformers reproducing with their bodies the time-honoured gestures appro-priate to the scenes in which they appear.

Perhaps Italian audiences in the early seventeenth century derived just such joy from seeing the histrionic exhibitions of a fresh Arlec-chino or Pantalone, although in such farcical episodes as were presented by the *commedia dell' arte* companies greater latitude and more individual freedom could be permitted than was possible in the presentation of the seriously conceived romantic plays which formed the dramatic fare of the early Indian Courts. In so far as the emotional content of these plays is concerned, the nearest parallel offered by the Western theatre is perhaps the type of comedy which became so popular in England during the reign of James I, and which may be exemplified by Shakespeare's last writings—*Cymbeline, A Winter's Tale,* and *The Tempest.* Within the Sanskrit theatre there could be no tragedy, since the very concept of the tragic, as interpreted in the West, would have been utterly alien to the philosophic and metaphysical beliefs of this age and clime. The result is that nearly all the plays produced on the Indian stage belong to what we should call romantic tragi-comedy, of a strongly poetic, even lyrical, tone. Serious and distressing scenes are introduced here, but softened in their colouring; comic scenes appear along with them, but with their realism decently veiled.

From the critical writings on the theatre that have been preserved for us it would seem that both structure and characterization were as conventionally controlled as was the actor's gesture. Individuality of conception was achieved by the dramatist through variations in the set pattern rather than through boldness of composition. Of special significance here was the elaboration of what may be styled dramatic moods (*rasas*), each distinct, yet capable of being employed in combination, which the playwright had to try to express. Every play, it was argued, must have its dominant impression—whether of love or of the marvellous or of the heroic—and, even if some scenes might awaken other impressions, the total harmony demanded that these scenes be treated as subordinate to the mood which had been conceived as the major theme. By means of these *rasas* men might classify the plays set before them, and by appreciation of the *rasa* aimed at they could gain delight from contemplation of each production. Again, as with the conventions of histrionic performance, we must assume and make all allowance for a deep and intimate basis of appreciative knowledge on the part of the audience: each drama must have been regarded, not separately, but in association with other dramas of a similar kind and with the vast body of critical precept that presented, in codified form, the principles upon which the whole of the dramatic art was founded.

KALIDASA

The flower of Sanskrit drama appears in the work of Kalidasa, an author whose dates are unknown: some would place him in the fourth century; others aver that he lived in the first century of our era. Of his plays three have been preserved—*Malavikagnimitra* (*Malavika and Agnimitra*), *Vikramorvasiya*, and, the best-known of them all, *Sakuntala*.

Neither of the first two—thought to have been respectively among the earliest and the latest of Kalidasa's compositions—is of any great value. *Malavika and Agnimitra* tells a romantic story of love set against a background of war. The heroine is Malavika, really a princess, but at the moment living unknown as a maid in the service of Queen Dharini, the chief wife of King Agnimitra. Having seen Malavika's portrait, the monarch has fallen madly in love with her, but the Queen's jealousy forbids his meeting her. By a trick of the clown Gautama, however, an interview is effected, although this is in turn interrupted by the angry arrival of one of the young Queens, who sharply upbraids her lord for his defections. Once more Gautama arranges a love-tryst; once more the young Queen, Iravati, intervenes. In the end it is Dharini who gives way and announces that Agnimitra may have his Malavika; while general joy comes to all (save the ousted Iravati) by the discovery that the maid is a princess in disguise.

The main lines of the plot demonstrate clearly how close in spirit is this ancient Sanskrit play to the romantic comedies of the early seventeenth century, even to those produced by Shakespeare towards the close of the century previous. Allowance being made for the social custom of polygamy, the love theme is developed in a manner startlingly akin to these, and there are even some scenes—such as that wherein Agnimitra and Gautama hide in a grove in order to see Malavika, while Iravati and her maid similarly conceal themselves—which seem almost identical to episodes of the kind made memorable by Shakespeare in *Love's Labour's Lost* and *Twelfth Night*.

One particular device used in all Kalidasa's dramas strikes an especially 'modern' note. Before the action of *Malavika and Agnimitra* begins the stage-director enters, gives out the title of the piece, and bids the music begin—only to be interrupted by his assistant, who conservatively demands to know whether the writings of the classical masters shall be neglected in favour of the work of a modern author. To him the director replies with epigrammatic verse:

> Not all is good that bears an ancient name,
> Nor need we every modern poem blame:
> Wise men approve the good, or new or old;
> The foolish critic follows where he's told.

This introductory device has the ring of Ben Jonson—and perhaps, too, of still later authors who, stepping outside the frame of their dramatic action, speak to the audience directly. The familiar tone, apparent in the entire handling of the plot material, is here symbolized.

If the chief *rasa* of *Malavika and Agnimitra* is that of love the chief *rasa* of *Vikramorvasiya* (*Urvashi won by Valour*) is that of the marvellous. In it the legend is told of the divine nymph who, famed for her skill in acting before the gods, brings the joys of the drama to human realms, although in treating it Kalidasa has laid less stress on the art, more on the human passion. After rescuing Urvashi and her friend Chitralekha from the power of a demon, King Pururavas finds his heart smitten with love of the celestial maiden. Likewise moved by love of him, Urvashi descends, invisible, to earth and leaves him a message written on a birch-leaf; this is unfortunately found by Queen Aushinari, who indulges in the usual scene of jealousy. From this episode on earth we are now carried back to Paradise, where Urvashi is in disgrace. While acting in a play she is asked, "On whom is your heart set?" and, forgetting her rôle, replies, "On Pururavas." As a result she is condemned to abandon Paradise, being permitted to return only after her lover shall have seen a child born of her human union. The pair are joined in marriage, Queen Aushinari having magnanimously withdrawn her objections, and for a time they live happily. Trouble comes, however, when Urvashi, entering a grove forbidden to women, is changed into a vine, and for long Pururavas is forced in vain to seek her. All the animals he meets he questions, but none of these can help him, and he succeeds in his quest at last only after finding the magical ruby of reunion. Once more united with his love, he is entirely contented, save for one thing, that he has had no son by Urvashi. By a wonderful coincidence, however, a youth is discovered who turns out to be in reality his child: for Urvashi, dreading the decree that will call her back to Paradise, has chosen to abandon her offspring rather than lose her husband. Touched by her devotion, the gods now rescind their order, and she, to her joy, is not only privileged to welcome her child, but also to remain joined till death with her beloved Pururavas.

There is much charm in this dramatic tale, and certain scenes are brilliantly designed, but its theme makes far less appeal to us than that of the better-known *Sakuntala*, which relates another story of a King's love of a beautiful maiden. King Dushyanta, during a hunting expedition, catches a glimpse of Sakuntala, the daughter of a famous sage and foster-child of a hermit. As she is watering the shrubs she is attacked by a bee, and in her attempts to escape it she encounters the monarch:

SAKUNTALA: This impertinent bee will not rest quiet. I must move elsewhere. [*Moving a few steps off, and casting a glance around*] How now! he is following me here. Help! my dear friends, help! deliver me from the attacks of this troublesome insect. . . .

KING: An excellent opportunity for me to show myself. Fear not—— [*Checks himself when the words are half uttered. Aside*] But stay, if I introduce myself in this manner, they will know me to be the King. Be it so, I will accost them, nevertheless.

SAKUNTALA [*moving a step or two further off*]: What! it still persists in following me.

KING [*advancing hastily*]: When mighty Puru's offspring sways the earth,
And o'er the wayward holds his threatening rod,
Who dares molest the gentle maids that keep
Their holy vigils here in Kanwa's grove?

Of course, the pair fall in love, and the King decides to encamp near the hermit's cell:

I have no longer any desire to return to the city. I will therefore rejoin my attendants, and make them encamp somewhere in the vicinity of this sacred grove. In good truth, Sakuntala has taken such possession of my thoughts that I cannot turn myself in any other direction.

My limbs drawn onward leave my heart behind,
Like silken pennon borne against the wind.

The King marries her, but departs for the city, and there a curse is laid upon him: all memory of his wedding vanishes from his mind. By good fortune, however, a ring belonging to Sakuntala and given her by the King is found by a common fisherman in the body of a carp he has caught: on seeing it memory comes surging back to him, and, after a series of romantic adventures (some of them, like those in *Vikramorvasiya*, set in celestial regions), he regains both his bride and the son to whom she has given birth.

In this drama, wherein elements of love and wonder, the comic and the pathetic, are mingled in admirable profusion, wherein time is ideal and the scenes move easily from earth to heaven and back again, is a quality thoroughly typical of the Sanskrit theatre as a whole. The atmosphere is lyrically fantastic, yet reality intrudes and forms a contrast with the more imaginative passages; in general the tone is one of intent seriousness, yet cynical reflections are not unheard from the lips of clowns and jesters.

Since in structure the play bears a close resemblance to the forms assumed by the Western drama (even being composed in the five-act pattern favoured by the Sanskrit critics), and since its spirit is prevailingly romantic, there need be no wonder that when Sir William Jones issued his translation in 1789 it was eagerly seized upon by those young talents who, in love with everything opposed to classical precision, were searching for new objects of admiration. Goethe's praise may be a trifle exaggerated, but it was assuredly sincere and it was characteristic of his age:

> Willst du die Blüte des Frühen, die
> Früchte des späteren Jahres,
> Willst du, was reizt und entzückt,
> Willst du, was sättigt und nährt,
> Willst du den Himmel, die Erde mit
> Einem Namen begreifen,
> Nenn' ich, Sakuntala, dich, und
> Dann ist alles gesagt.

OTHER SANSKRIT DRAMATISTS

Kalidasa's works do not stand alone, but, with one exception, they remain virtually neglected save by specialists in Sanskrit literature. That exception is *Mrichhakatika*, known as *The Little Clay Cart*, traditionally attributed to King Shudraka—an attribution, however, not supported by modern scholarly opinion. By whomsoever it was written, there is no doubt but that it is a later elaboration of a much earlier work, attributed to Bhasa, called *Daridracharudatta* (*The Poor Charudatta*), which presents an identical main plot without the embellishments of *The Little Clay Cart*. Here, instead of a royal romance, we are introduced to the story of a poor Brahman, Charudatta by name, who falls in love with a courtesan, Vasantasena. This lady comes under the gaze of an evil prince, and the exigencies of the plot force her to bring her jewels for safety to Charudatta's house: the gems are stolen, and the worthy wife of the hero nobly hands over to him her own jewels in order that he may make restitution. From this point on the adventures become complex and involved. The title of the drama comes from an episode when Vasantasena generously fills with diamonds the little toy cart belonging to Charudatta's son; another line of plot development relates how she saves from wrongful punishment a poor peasant, who later turns out to be the true heir to the throne; a third tells how, rejecting the evil prince's advances, she is apparently strangled by him. Charudatta is accused of the crime: he is led off to be executed; in the nick of time witnesses appear in his defence; the true heir seizes the throne; the hero is rewarded by being made a provincial governor; he and his loyal Vasantasena are, at long last, happily united.

This is a composition of a somewhat different cast from that of Kalidasa's plays. The technique is similar and the romantic episodes, although brought nearer to the levels of domesticity, are akin; but the dialogue displays a surprising number of remarks of the kind we should now call 'social comment.' Indeed, an entire section of the work—that in which a judge, although convinced of Charudatta's innocence, is prepared to sentence him to death because he fears the power of the evil prince—is devoted to an exposure of the ways of justice in ancient days: for this is *La robe rouge* of the Orient. Because of these qualities, perhaps, *The Little Clay Cart* won not a little esteem when, heavily adapted, it was first acted in America some twenty years ago.

Among the followers of Kalidasa is numbered another royal dramatist, Harsha by name, who has left three plays, two of which are patterned much on this model. In *Ratnavali* (*The Pearl Necklace*) the device is used of a parrot repeating a love message and so revealing to a monarch a girl's devotion to him; in *Priyadarsika* there is a play within the play. *Nagananda* stands distinct, since, unlike the others, it treats of a religious concept. Here a Buddhist saint, Jimutavahana, seeing that his people are being consumed by a devil-monster in the shape of a horrendous vulture, voluntarily sacrifices himself for their sake. In the end he is saved by the fact that this evil creature, converted through his noble action, suddenly has a change of heart and agrees to undo all the depredations of which it had been guilty.

Some centuries later came Bhavabhuti, and with him the classical stage virtually ceased to be. Rather less variegated in their tone than the earlier dramas, his plays are again romantic tragi-comedies—as, for example, the *Malatimadhava* (*Malati and Madhava*), which narrates the crossed loves of a youth and a girl separated by their families. For his style he is praised, but there is less quality in his work likely to appeal to audiences ignorant of Sanskrit. Plays continued to be written in Sanskrit for many years after this date, but all the evidence seems to indicate that after reaching its flower in Kalidasa the drama of India rapidly declined.

Before leaving these plays, however, note must be taken of two works of entirely different kinds. The first is the farcical comedy called *Bhagavadajjukiya* (*The Ascetic transmuted into a Courtesan*), by an otherwise unknown author, Bodhayana. In its intrigue this play sharply recalls the adventures of Puck in *A Midsummer Night's Dream*, for the whole action is based on the mistake of a supernatural messenger of the god Yama. The chief character is a holy hermit who, at the very beginning of the piece, is shown talking to a not-so-holy disciple, Sandilya by name. During this talk the courtesan Vasantasena enters; Sandilya is much attracted by her, when, to his dismay, she suddenly falls dead—for the celestial messenger, bidden to kill a certain woman and mistaking Vasantasena for his victim, has changed himself into a serpent and stung her. Hereupon the hermit, by the force of his art, causes his own soul to enter the body of the woman: when the girl's mother and her lover arrive they are utterly baffled by the sanctimonious discourses that come from the courtesan's lips. Meanwhile the messenger has been severely reprimanded by Yama for having made a mistake: back to earth he is sent to restore Vasantasena's soul, but, finding her body occupied, he inserts it in the body of the hermit, who now begins to talk in the language of courtesans. The theme is amusing, and without doubt the author displays a rich and racy sense of the comic in the handling of his scenes.

The second play mentioned above is the first known example of Buddhist mystery-morality drama—*Prabodhacandrodaya* (*The Rise of Conscience*, eleventh century). Its plot, involving characters all of whom bear names similar to those appearing in medieval English moralities, shows that besides the familiar tragi-comedies the Indian theatre produced dramas of diverse sorts. At the same time, it is the tragi-comedies which, in the end, are of chief significance for us.

As has been observed, most of these dramas, although dealing with social life and episodes far different from our own, do not materially differ in style and structure from Western tragi-comedies and comedies—particularly those of the kind produced by the English Elizabethan and Jacobean playwrights or by Lope de Vega and Calderón in Spain. The result is that, althouhg Kalidasa's works have for long been known and admired, their influence on the West has been but slight. Knowledge of the highly conventional ballet-like methods of performance on their original production has come to us only within comparatively recent years, and, in the absence of such knowledge, the general tendency has been to interpret these Indian plays in terms of the stage known in the Occident. Only within the last few decades has an appreciation of the unrealistic stylization in histrionic method caused them to be related to the kindred style of dramatic artistry created in China and in Japan.

THE DRAMA OF CHINA

As in other lands, the drama in China seems to owe its origin to religious exercises, although the records of the stage there leave many things uncertain and render any attempt at dogmatic assertion dangerous. Apart from the loss of documentary evidence, the relative disesteem in which the theatre has been held in Chinese literary circles has tended to obscure both the story of its development and the account of its growth in later times.

Legend asserts that stage productions began in the Chow dynasty (1122–255 B.C.), and the Emperor Ming Huang of the Tang dynasty was reputedly an eager patron of such shows in the eighth century of our era. The truth is, however, that not until we reach the hundred and thirty-odd dramas preserved from the Yuan dynasty (A.D. 1280–1368) do we have certain evidence on which to base any firm judgments: most of these plays are included in a famous collection titled "The Hundred Yuan Plays," printed about the year 1600. They belong to the highly refined classical tradition.

Popular elements were introduced into the *kun chü*, several centuries later, and further popularization, with the assimilation of certain forms of rustic drama, appears in the modern 'Peking Opera.' In noting these types of play it is important to remember that, while the Yuan dramas provide the basis for much later endeavour, they themselves are now only reading works, in a language which only a few can understand, and that the 'Peking Opera' for the most part is a thing purely of the theatre, rarely put in reading form.

THE CHINESE THEATRE

Perhaps to us the most interesting feature of China's theatrical activity is not the drama itself but the stage.

The actors appear on a platform which, like that of the Elizabethan playhouse, is surrounded by spectators on three sides, the men formerly on the floor and the women in boxes slightly elevated. Above and behind the players occasionally appears a balcony, reserved for the use of heavenly visitants. There is no scenery, although a heavily and richly embroidered curtain forms a background for the action.

Peculiarly characteristic of the performance in this theatre is the appearance on stage of the property-man, who unconcernedly brings on and removes the few pieces of furniture necessary for the progress of the pieces, hands small properties to the actors during the course of their performance, or even attends to their costumes as they proceed with their parts. His presence there indicates at once that for Chinese spectators realism is not only unnecessary but undesired. In the property-man's appearance among the players is, as it were, a visible and constant testimony to the imaginative quality of the entire production.

This imaginative quality controls, too, the use of such furniture as is supplied and governs the histrionic movements. A chair set on its side will serve to represent a rock; a flowered carpet will become a garden; a table will be taken as a mountain. All sorts of symbolic or conventional gestures provide indication of movements not shown in actuality. If an actor has to go through water he displays a little flag painted with fishes: if he is supposed to be riding a horse he takes long strides and flourishes a whip. Instead of imitating reality, the Chinese actor presents a conventional symbol by which the reality may be imagined.

In harmony with this approach, the rôles appearing on the stage are carefully classified, with four main types—the heroic 'baritone,' or 'tenor,' the 'soprano,' the 'bass,' and the clown. To each of these and to others are apportioned certain characteristic tones of voice and gestures. Where the *tan*, or young girl, sways rhythmically in body, the *lao tan*, or old lady, has a conventionalized palsy shake and bending movements. The hero walks in one way, the villain in another, so that, immediately the spectators see a character enter, even before they hear him say a word, they know his rôle in the drama.

The costumes are rich, although not always governed in colour or shape by the requirements of the particular drama being enacted, and the make-up used is so heavy and so stylized as to make some players seem to be using masks. So complex are the indications given to the audience of age, character, and mood by these means that the theatres have before them some two hundred models of facial presentation, each line and each colour having its own special significance.

THE JAPANESE KABUKI STAGE: TWO ORIGINAL DESIGNS FOR SETS

THE JAPANESE KABUKI STAGE: ORIGINAL DRAWING OF A PERFORMANCE

THE JAPANESE NŌ STAGE:
ANCIENT MASK

THE JAPANESE NŌ STAGE:
ANCIENT MASK

Black behind.

Coutinued stripes as opposite

GORDON CRAIG:
DESIGN FOR
"MACBETH"

From *Theatre Arts
Monthly*, November
1928.

THE CHINESE DRAMAS

Fundamentally the Chinese plays may be likened rather to Western opera than to ordinary tragedies or comedies with spoken dialogue (whether prose or poetic). Music, too loud and clamorous for most ears, accompanies much of the action, and the performers, originally all male, chant their parts in conventional tones and with long monologues. There is some spoken dialogue (sometimes improvised), but the lyrical portions are those on which main attention is set. Like the Sanskrit plays, the Chinese all assume the character of tragi-comedies, although the mixed elements that make up this type of drama appear in forms much coarser than those provided for the highly refined Indian Courts. Pathos is more deeply stressed, clownery is more absurd, sensational incident is more blatant.

Generally short, these tragi-comedies are usually played in series; so that in such a well-known production as *Hsi hsiang chi* (*The Western Chamber*), for example, we have, not one single play, but in reality five plays linked together in general theme. The style prevailing in these pieces may be assessed from such adaptations as S. I. Hsiung's *Lady Precious Stream*, taken from the original *Wang pao ch'mau*, or *The Circle of Chalk*, as devised by Ethel van der Veer from *Hoei lan kia*. The latter tells the ancient, and universal, story which is familiar to us in the Biblical story of the judgment of Solomon. Hai-t'ang is a beautiful girl who, after a miserable youth, becomes the Second Wife of Ma Chun-shing. This gentleman's First Wife, however, has fallen in love with Ch'ao, a Government clerk, and with her lover she poisons her husband. At the same time, in order to obtain Ma's money, she seizes Hai-t'ang's child, claims it as her own, bribes witnesses to appear in her support, and, by giving a present to the corrupt governor So-shun, obtains an order in her favour. Poor Hai-t'ang is arrested and put in chains. Now enters a *deus ex machina*—the supreme judge Pao-ch'ing. Hearing the statements of the two women, he commands a circle of chalk to be inscribed on a bench; the child is placed thereon and the pair of claimants bidden to pull it out of the marked space. Twice Hai-t'ang fails to hold on to the child, and the judge, realizing that this failure is due to her unwillingness to give hurt, decides that her claim is just: Ch'ao is arrested and the wicked governor So-shun deprived of his offices.

In form, all is wrought in conventional manner. Each character on entering announces his or her name, ancestry, upbringing, and present position. Problems are directly outlined in monologue. Villains have no scruples in telling the audience their inmost secrets. Time passes with bewildering rapidity, and localities are established, as need arises, by the words of the characters. These words vary from prose passages to lyrical, the commonest device being the presentation of some informatory lines followed and broken by a chant. Thus, for example, Hai-t'ang appears after her marriage:

I am named Hai-t'ang. It is five years since I was married to my lord Ma. My Venerable Mother has long ago departed to the Land of the Gods. I do not know the whereabouts of my brother, as since his departure I have received no news of him. The child which I had from my marriage is called Shiu-lang. Since he was three years of age he has stayed by the side of Mrs Ma, who took him to bring up. As to-day is the anniversary of his birth, my lord and Mrs Ma have taken him to all the temples in the city to burn sweet perfumes and to gild the image of Fu. I go now to prepare rice and tea to receive them as soon as they shall have returned. . . . Hai-t'ang, since you have espoused the lord Ma, nothing has interfered with your happiness.

> Through the silken curtains
> At my window
> I contemplate the moon
> And its cold shadows.
> It shines alike without reproach or passion
> Upon my richly embroidered curtains
> And upon that street which is the abode of vice.
> Could I ever have hoped one day
> To abandon that degrading profession,
> The companionship of rakes and their mistresses,
> With their orgies and licentious songs?
> Yet I have for ever said farewell
> To that theatre of pleasure.
> Let them follow me if they will
> With railleries and aspersions.
> Never again will I make advances for gain
> Nor stretch forth a seducing hand to noblemen.
> No more will I make traffic with my beauty
> Nor return to the follies of the gay life. . . .
> Untroubled by the wickedness of the world outside,
> I live the long hours through in tranquil peace.
> Even as the wild duck seeks its mate in the grass,
> I have found a husband
> Whose heart accords happily with mine,
> And who each day begs me
> To recompense his tenderness.

And so that I may taste with him
The sweetness of slumber
Ere the moon silvers the edges
Of my window curtains.
I send back to her own apartment
That woman so jealous of my serenity.

I await the return of my lord and Mrs Ma. . . . But they do not come. . . . Let us go out for a moment and look for them in the distance.

The romantic tragi-comedy tone is akin to that of the Sanskrit plays, but there are several differences. In style the dialogue is much more conventional and the transitions from one part of the action to another more sharply abrupt. The supernatural is less in evidence, and the atmosphere, instead of being courtly fanciful, descends more commonly to the levels of ordinary ilfe. Rags and poverty make their gaunt appearance on this stage, whereas in the Indian plays they appear only by implication or in forms made gracious by the play of the imagination.

Above all, where the dramas of Kalidasa possess a poetic quality which, if it does not justify, at least explains the enthusiasm of Goethe, very rarely in the Chinese stage pieces do we find flashes of penetrating insight and the thrill of the poetic vision. The charm of the theatre of China lies not so much in the dramatic style as in the total effect of the entire production.

It is this total effect that has, indeed, caught the attention of some at least among those interested in the development of a non-realistic theatre in the West. These productions have taught men that it is not necessary, in order to capture the minds of audiences, to depend wholly upon the naturalistic conventions of the fourth-wall stage; they have indicated that it is possible to find in those other conventions of the Oriental theatre different methods for the setting forth of situation, character, and emotional concept.

We should not, of course, assume from the example of *The Circle of Chalk* that the Chinese drama habitually deals with matters of domestic import; indeed, the precise opposite is true. On the stage regularly appear stage representations of the most famous events in the history of the country, sometimes modified by the introduction of legendary material, often keeping with reasonable accuracy to the progress of actual events. The very earliest Chinese play known in the West, *Chao shih ku erh* (*The Orphan of China*), from which Voltaire wrought his *L'orphelin de la Chine*, is of this kind. Although its most impressive scenes have a kind of 'domestic' quality, the main action, recording the brutal persecution of the Chao family by the wicked T'u Anku and the strange manner in which the little orphan is preserved to wreak his vengeance, has an historical flavour. Of such dramas *Hān koong tseu* (*The Sorrows of Hān*) may be taken as typical. The action is opened by some verses spoken by the Khan of the Tartars, Hanchenyu by name, followed by a simple prose statement of his position, the association of his tribes with China, and preceding political events. He has come to demand an alliance with Yuente, the Emperor, one of the Hān dynasty. Immediately thereafter enters the corrupt, self-seeking, and ambitious Minister Mao Yen-shou, who confesses that he has won his present position of importance by deliberately persuading his master to spend all his time, not with his counsellors, but with the women of the palace, and in a following conversation with the Emperor himself we hear him making arrangements for obtaining many pretty girls for the latter's enjoyment. After this prologue the first section, or act, of the play shows the Minister deliberately disfiguring a portrait of a beautiful maiden (who might have been introduced to the palace) because her father has no bribe to give him, and later comes a scene in which the Emperor chances to encounter this lady, Chao-chün by name, who has been brought to [the] royal household, but kept jealously from the eyes of the Emperor by his avaricious Minister. Order is given for the Minister's execution. In the second act the Khan reveals that the alliance has been refused; Mao Yen-shou enters—having escaped from the palace—and advises him to ask for Chao-chün by name; this message is transmitted to the Emperor, who is swayed by love on the one hand and on the other by fear of the Tartar host now on his borders. The sacrifice is made, but Chao-chün finds she cannot give herself to another and commits suicide. The fourth act shows the Emperor mourning in his palace:

EMPEROR: Since the princess was yielded to the Tartars, we have not held an audience. The lonely silence of night increases our melancholy. We take the picture of that fair one and suspend it here, as some small solace to our griefs. [*To the* ATTENDANT] Keeper of the yellow gate, behold, the incense in yonder vase is burnt out; hasten then to add some more——

Though we cannot see her, we may at least retain this shadow; and, while life remains, betoken our regard.

But oppressed and weary, we would fain take a little repose.

[*Lies down to sleep. The* PRINCESS *appears before him in a vision.*
PRINCESS: Delivered over as a captive to appease the barbarians, they

would have conveyed me to their northern country: but I took an occasion to elude them, and have escaped back. Is not this the Emperor, my sovereign? Sir, behold me again restored.

[*A* TARTAR SOLDIER *appears in the vision.*

SOLDIER: While I chanced to sleep, the lady, our captive, has made her escape, and returned home. In eager pursuit of her, I have reached the imperial palace. Is not this she?

[*Carries her off. The* EMPEROR *starts from his sleep.*

EMPEROR: We just saw the princess returned—but, alas, how quickly has she vanished!——

In bright day she answered not to our call—but when morning dawned on our troubled sleep, a vision presented her in this spot. [*Hears a wild-fowl's cry.*] Hark, the passing fowl screamed twice or thrice!—Can it know there is one so desolate as I? [*Cries repeated.*] Perhaps worn out and weak, hungry and emaciated, they bewail at once the broad nets of the south and the tough bows of the north. [*Cries repeated.*] The screams of those water-birds but increase our melancholy.

In bitter sorrow, he mourns, and finds satisfaction only in learning that the evil Minister has been captured. "Strike off the traitor's head," he cries,

and be it presented as an offering to the shade of the princess! Let a fit banquet be got ready for the envoy, preparatory to his return.

[*Recites these verses.*

At the fall of the leaf, when the
 wild fowl's cry was heard in the
 recesses of the palace,
Sad dreams returned to our lonely
 pillow; we thought of her
 through the night:
Her verdant tomb remains—but where
 shall we seek herself?
The perfidious painter's head shall
 atone for the beauty which he wronged.

One other example may be taken: in the Chinese repertoire no play is more famous than one which goes under a variety of names —*The Ch'ingting Pearl*, *Demanding the Fish-tax*, or *Fishing and Massacre*—but which is better titled (as it is by its translator, Yao Hsin-nung) *The Right to Kill*. There is at once appeal and an alienating sense of strangeness here. The idea that a poor man, exploited by those granted power beyond his own, has the right to take justice into his own hands is understandable, even if we may not accept the principle involved: what is alien is the Chinese concept that an entire family must be condemned for the excesses of one of its members. Central in this drama is an old fisherman, Hsiao En, with his daughter, Kuei-ying: desperately poor, he is compelled to pay to a local landowner an exorbitant tax on the fish he catches. So hard are his straits that he resists the landowner's minions by force, and as a result is severely punished by the law. In a scene by no means without crude emotional strength we are shown Hsiao En's final decision being made and the timorous, devoted complicity of his daughter:

KUEI-YING: Father, you have suffered from injustice.

HSIAO EN: You call this injustice! [*Vehemently*] In addition to this, that thief of a magistrate ordered me to go to Squire Ting's house to-morrow and beg his pardon. Then, I shall have a more complete injustice!

KUEI-YING [*eagerly*]: Are you going or not?

HSIAO EN: What are you talking—going or not! I only wish there were a pair of wings under my shoulders. [*Stares straight before him, with an upswelling rage.*] I want to fly! I want to *kill*——!!!

Terrified though she is, Kuei-ying insists on accompanying him. We see them going down to the river to their boat; in midstream her heart almost fails her, then once more she steels herself; they reach the big house and achieve their vengeance.

It is obvious that, while in these episodes resides an unquestioned emotional quality, the dramatic form itself has little to offer to Western playwrights. The Chinese plays possess charm—and, in their methods of production, inspirational quality—but in themselves they present no peculiar qualities likely to stimulate experiment in European tongues. The conventionalism is appealing, but fundamentally the method of outlining the plot is the same as that habitual in the West. For novelty of technical approach men had to wait until the Japanese Nō plays became available in translation.

THE JAPANESE DRAMA

IF THE conventionalism of the Chinese stage has made its impress felt during recent years, an even greater impress has been exerted by these Japanese Nō plays, which, still further stylized, possess the literary qualities lacking in the others. Since the appearance in 1921 of Arthur Waley's *The Nō Plays of Japan* the influence on many Western poets of this ancient aristocratic theatre has been widespread.

KABUKI: THE POPULAR DRAMA

The Japanese playhouse presents to us two distinct types of entertainment. Of these the Kabuki is at once the more popular, the later in origin, and the less significant. Developed towards the beginning of the seventeenth century, to a certain extent it relates itself to the Chinese, although many of its conventions are utterly distinct and its general orientation is different.

For a stage the Kabuki actors use a platform which characteristically was at first surrounded by spectators on three sides. Into the midst of these spectators are thrust two narrow raised *hanamichi*, or 'flower-ways,' regularly used by the players for entrance upon the stage proper. By this means not only is the drama brought within the auditorium, but the acting-areas at the command of the performers are materially increased. As in China, so in Japan the property-man, clad in black, appears alongside the actors, performing much the same duties, although, in view of the greater amount of scenic display presented in Kabuki, employing methods of which the Chinese stage is ignorant.

This scenic display is of a peculiar kind. A great part of the action is, it is true, conducted by means of familiar, conventionalized movements and gestures. The actors indulge in make-up that is fully as complex and stylized as the Chinese. Villains are ruddy, heroes are basically white, but here too every line tells its story of age, social position, temperament, and even of the present situation in which the character may find himself. Many actions are carried out by means of expressive mimicry, without the use of properties.

A duel may be fought in a kind of dance movement so that one sword sweeps close to, but never touches, the other; tea may be drunk from cups that are non-existent.

At the same time the Japanese spectators seek for more in the way of scenic decoration than that with which Chinese audiences are content. Behind the actors, in a kind of frame surmounted by a sloping roof, sets of a mixed realistic-conventional sort are presented to feast the eyes. By using a revolving stage and a complicated system of traps changes of locality can easily and quickly be effected, and in general no scene, whether interior or exterior, is permitted to be shown without an attempt to reproduce—mainly through the employment of flat wings—the semblance of reality.

In content and form the plays produced on this stage are, again like the Chinese, operatic, with chanted lyrics and the constant accompaniment of music. Some deal with subjects from common life; most are historical, with frequent use of the popular theme of the forty-seven Ronins. Among the many dramas produced for the Kabuki stage from its origins, and for the very closely related Jōruri, or puppet stage, those of one author, Chikamatsu Monzaemon, have achieved something of an international reputation, although those who call him the Japanese Shakespeare perhaps permit their fancies somewhat to run away with them. With him is frequently associated a later prolific author, Takeda Izumo, who with his collaborators ran what amounted to a play-factory. What we do find in these works is melodrama, sensational tragi-comedy, and crude supernatural incident, inventive and vigorous, no doubt, but lacking in any qualities of greatness. Exciting scene is heaped on exciting scene in admirable confusion, and although here and there we come upon situations that make direct appeal, it must be confessed that most of this Kabuki playwriting is vulgar and lacking in true interest. From study of the highly traditional skill of the actors and of the exquisitely planned performances we may gain much of interest and profit, but from the dramas in which these actors appear there is little indeed that can be extracted of worth.

A few typical examples may serve to illustrate their scope. *Chushingura* (1748), written by Takeda Izumo along with a couple of coadjutors, tells in sensational wise the tale of the forty-seven Ronins. Starting with a scene in which a lord commits hara-kiri immediately after giving his final commands to Yuranosuke, the loyal retainer, it proceeds to narrate excitingly the adventures o this band of desperate, masterless men, moving from episode to episode with such bewildering rapidity that only those spectators especially well versed in the ancient legends or in national history could be expected to follow the action as a whole.

Perhaps because of this, many of these dramas seem to exist rather as a series of only slightly related scenes than as artistic wholes. They are written mainly for the purpose of providing opportunities for the actors, and, as the actor depends upon the scene rather than on the whole play for the demonstration of his traditional points, quite naturally emphasis is laid upon the action immediately before us at any one moment instead of upon the relationship between this action and situations following or preceding, Thus it is entirely possible to extract one episode from Takeda Izumo's lengthy *Sugawara denju tenarai kagami* (*Sugawara's Instruction in Calligraphy*), to call it *The Village School*, and treat it as a separate work. Its story is really complete in itself, narrating how Genzo, the faithful retainer of the exiled Sugawara Michizane, in order to protect and conceal the latter's son, disguises himself as a teacher and puts the boy among a group of others in the classroom. By force of circumstance he is compelled to produce the head of his pupil—for his enemies have become aware of the trick. Another retainer, however, with supreme loyalty, has brought his son to Genzo, prepared to allow him to be sacrificed in place of the heir or Sugawara. In a terrible yet intensely dramatic scene this retainer stands with the official while Genzo goes to a room within: a blow is heard and Genzo returns with a box. The retainer opens it, and, though what he sees within is his own son's head, he bravely asserts that this is the young prince. Sugawara's heir has been saved.

To what extent this episodic treatment extended is to be seen in Chikamatsu Monzaemon's classic *Kokusenya kassen* (*The Battles of Kokusenya*, 1710), in which appears a wild story of conflict, murder, treachery, loyalty, and torture. To and fro the events connected with a Chinese Emperor and his Ministers surge on the stage, introducing scenes of a brutal kind apt to turn the stomach of any Western audience, and finally bringing in the great Japanese hero, Watonai, son of the faithful Minister by a woman of Kyushu, a fearful avenging spirit, monstrous in a make-up of fierce black-and-red streaks. To wrest a sense of unity from such a work is a virtual impossibility.

Sometimes the themes embrace the world of the supernatural, as in *Yotsuya kaidan* (*Yotsuya's Ghost*), by Tsuruya Namboku. Here the beautiful neglected wife of Iyemon has her face hideously disfigured through a poison administered by another woman who is in love with her husband. Worn out by her miseries, O-Iwa commits suicide, and Iyemon marries again; but when he raises his new bride's veil, there is O-Iwa's disfigured countenance staring at him. Spectral visitation followed by spectral visitation eventually drives him to his end.

This drama, it is true, has a fairly direct and consecutive plot, but even when we encounter something of such a kind we cannot persuade ourselves that in these popular Japanese dramas is to be found anything likely to inspire fresh dramatic effort in the West. For that we must seek on the exclusively aristocratic Nō stage.

THE NŌ PLAYS

Developed during the fourteenth and fifteenth centuries by Kanami Kiyotsugu and his son Seami Motokiyo, the Nō drama was born of the temple, and in latter times became the pastime of the cultured nobility. Some of its elements were later assimilated into the popular Kabuki, but it itself retained all the exact and precise qualities of a specialized form, bound closely by rules rigorous and unbreakable.

The stage used for these Nō productions is of the simplest. About eighteen feet square, it is almost surrounded by the audience; on the right a narrow platform is designed for a singing chorus, at the rear is another platform for an orchestra. The dressing-room is a separate structure on the left, connected with the main stage by a passage, called the *hashigakari*, or bridge, along which the players make their appearances.

Probably because the performances originally took place in a grove, some small trees invariably are set on the *hashigakari*, or bridge, while the 'scenery' consists simply of a wooden panel at the rear, painted on one side with the representation of a pine-tree and on the other with bamboos. Three pine-branches are also attached to the *hashigakari*.

The costumes of the actors are rich and colourful, and the masks worn by the chief characters are marvels of artistry. Some of those made in early times have been preserved, either as heirlooms or as museum objects, and in them is exhibited a care and a skill which demonstrates the devoted, painstaking efforts that went to produce the polished and assured perfection for which the Nō performances are famous. The actors, all men, have been trained in their art from infancy; every smallest gesture is made to yield significance; by the subtlest movement of a fan an emotion is conveyed and an inner story revealed by a stylized movement of the arm. Although there are several officially recognized 'schools' of the Nō, all agree in insisting upon the utmost fidelity to traditional practice, partly handed down from actor-father to actor-son, partly described and codified in written texts. This traditional practice insists, like the Chinese, on the utmost of conventionalism, with the use of properties which merely suggest, and by no means represent, the real objects supposed to be involved in the action.

The effect created by these means is vividly suggested in a letter written by Oswald Sickert to Charles Ricketts in 1916. He is describing the performance of a play in which an angel, descending to earth, loses her flying robe:

> The best single moment I have seen was the dance of thanks to the fisherman who returns to the divine lady the Hagoromo, the robe without which even an angel cannot fly. It seemed to me an example of the excellent rule in art that, if a right thing is perhaps rather dull or monotonous lasting five minutes, you will not cure the defect by cutting the performance to two and a half minutes; rather give it ten minutes. If it's still perhaps rather dull, try twenty minutes or an hour. This presupposes that your limitations are right and that you *are* exploiting them. The thing may seem dull at first because at first it is the limitations the spectator feels; but the more these are exploited the less they are felt to be limitations, and the more they become a medium. The divine lady returned on her steps at great length and fully six times after I had thought I could not bear it another moment. She went on for twenty minutes, perhaps, or an hour or a night; I lost count of time; but I shall not recover from the longing she left when at last she floated backwards and under the fatal uplifted curtain.

Sickert's prose record of the impression made on a Western mind may be related to a poetic reflection by Eunice Tietjens occasioned by a similar performance:

> In a band of perfect silence the Noh dancer is coming.
>
> The air is still, stirred by the small sounds of the musicians, and the bar of afternoon sunlight between the stage and people is warm with overtones of sound.
>
> Yet the dancer has wrapped silence about him, and time stands back as he moves.
>
> On the narrow raised bridge he is between Here and There, between this world and the next.
>
> Presently, in an æon, when he has reached the stage, he will speak in a strange high treble, at once chant and wail. The words will be

unintelligible. Even his own countrymen must know them to understand.

Then he will be the spirit revenant, ghost of a dead princess, returned at moonrise to lead her lord to the shadow of Buddha.

But now, on the narrow bridge, he is a presence only, a rhythm incarnate, abstraction visible.

His rich brocaded silks flow stiffly, as stone might flow. The mask of the dead princess might be the moon, so pale, so eerily remote. . . .

The gestures of his coming are complete, each in itself a whole. Perceptibly they shift into one, held into rhythm by his presence.

Tidally he moves, slow as a planet, ultimate as beauty.

In a band of perfect silence the Noh dancer comes.

Such an art obviously must depend upon not merely long individual training, but upon extensive tradition as well. The Nō stage is one that has passed down with only the barest of modifications from the time of its first development, and even the plays themselves are largely hallowed by antiquity. Of the eight hundred-odd extant scripts (of which about two hundred and fifty are regularly played) nearly half were written before the seventeenth century; compositions in the style of the older masters are still created in modern times, and numerous texts come from the eighteenth century, but Kwanami Kiyotsugu and Seami Motokiyo remain still the dominant literary figures in this composite form of artistry. The only thing, perhaps, that has fundamentally changed is the general appeal of the performance. Originally hieratic, and hence fairly widely popular, so that Seami could declare that "the perfect actor is he who can win certain praise alike in palaces, temples or villages, or even at festivals held in the shrines of the remotest provinces," the Nō productions have become almost exclusively aristocratic, even while retaining their antique forms.

These antique forms control even the plays' order of performance. Although now three pieces are usual in one 'bill,' originally tradition classified the Nō dramas into five categories and insisted that in one performance a play from each category, culled in a recognized order, must be presented, with a *kyōgen*, or humorous piece, separating each successive play from that which immediately precedes it. After a prefatory sketch, in which the sun-goddess is the main character, there first comes a play (*shura-mono*) in which the ghost of a warrior is presented, next one featuring some noble lady (*kazura-mono*), next a supernatural piece, and finally a play dealing with human passions or teaching some specific virtue.

In general, from two to six characters only are allowed to appear on the stage—the hero, or *shite*; his close companion, or *tsure*; the *waki*, or secondary character with his companion; a child (*kokata*); and, when necessary, a supplementary actor, or *ai*. Some of the plays have a structure which, albeit conventional and compressed, deals with their material in what may be called a normal dramatic manner. In these the regular form is for a *waki* to introduce an opening poetic couplet, to announce his identity, and to describe a journey in which he is engaged, and for the hero thereupon to make his appearance and engage in conversation with him, the events proceeding as though they took place in reality. In other dramas, however, appears a method far at variance with this, and so distantly removed from normal dramatic methods as to have made a deep impress on the minds of many modern poets. Here the dramatic action, as it were, unfolds itself in retrospect and, by the introduction of a ghost, joins past and present in one. It is this type of play that has laid deepest spell on the West during recent years.

An example both of the warrior drama and of this dramatic method appears in Seami's *Atsumori*. A priest, Rensei, enters and recites:

> Life is a lying dream, he only wakes
> Who casts the World aside.

In a succeeding speech he reveals that he had been a warrior who has become a priest because of the grief he suffers for the death of Atsumori, who had fallen in battle by his hand. He makes his conventional journey and encounters a chorus of reapers, with one of whom he stands talking. Suddenly this Reaper turns into the ghost of Atsumori. During their conversation the past reshapes itself imaginatively before our eyes; Atsumori's death is re-enacted. Just as Atsumori advances with sword upraised against his foe comes the chant of the chorus:

> "There is my enemy," he cries, and would strike.
> But the other is grown gentle
> And calling on Buddha's name
> Has obtained salvation for his foe;
> So that they shall be re-born together
> On one lotus-seat.
> "No, Rensei is not my enemy.
> Pray for me again, oh, pray for me again."

A peculiar twilight atmosphere, wherein real and ideal become undistinguishable, breathes in the poetic action.

In all this, strange subdued emotional quality resides, as it does, to take another example, in Seami's *Hagoromo*, wherein a Fisherman, Hakuryō by name, picks up the feather robe of an Angel who has come down to earth. Pathetically the Angel pleads:

> Oh pitiful! How shall I cloakless tread
> The wing-ways of the air, how climb
> The sky, my home?
> Oh, give it back, in charity give it back.

At first obdurate, Hakuryō is at last moved by these entreaties. The Angel dances while the chorus records her flight until her form becomes faint,

> Mingled with the mists of heaven;
> Now lost to sight.

This is the drama that Sickert describes.

Hatsuyuki, by Komparu Zembō Motoyasu, tells the story of an Abbot's daughter who has a beloved white bird that she has named "Early Snow." It vanishes from its cage, and in grief its mistress sings a Mass in its memory, whereupon the bird's soul appears in the sky. "Look! Look!" the chorus cries,

> A cloud in the clear mid-sky!
> But it is not a cloud.
> With pure white wings beating the air
> The Snow-bird comes!
> Flying towards our lady
> Lovingly he hovers,
> Dances before her.

THE BIRD'S SOUL: Drawn by the merit of your prayers and songs.

CHORUS: Straightway he was reborn in Paradise.

> By the pond of Eight Virtues he walks abroad:
> With the Phœnix and Fugan his playtime passing.
> He lodges in the sevenfold summit of the trees of Heaven.
> No hurt shall harm him
> For ever and ever.
> Now like the tasselled doves we loose
> From battlements on holy days
> A little while he flutters;
> Flutters a little while and then is gone
> We know not where.

The subject-matter of these plays is various. Seami's *Haku Rakuten* might be styled patriotic, since it shows the Chinese poet

Haku Rakuten coming to Japan to subdue that country by the exercise of his art and driven back in his ship by the winds raised during a dance executed by the Japanese god of poetry and his companions. Many themes are Buddhistic, as, for example, *Ukai* (*The Cormorant Fisher*), by Enami no Sayemon, in which a Priest rebukes a Fisherman for his cruel trade, and in which this Fisherman reveals himself as the ghost of Yama, the lord of hell. "Hell," he says,

> is not far away:
> All that your eyes look out on in the world
> Is the Fiend's home.

It is interesting to observe that, while such Buddhistic concepts form a staple theme of the Nō dramas, quite frequently these very concepts are chosen in the *kyogen* for parody. Thus *Ukai* is burlesqued in *The Bird-catcher in Hell*, where Yama catches the evil bird-catcher Kiyoyori, who argues so well and gives the demon such a delicious tit-bit that he is sent back to earth to go on with his trade. As in other lands where burlesque has co-existed with serious effort, however, no farcical scenes of this kind take from the deeply imaginative serious appreciation of the deeper and profounder plays.

In this whole sphere of dramatic activity there is so much that is new, together with such a vivid poetic imagination, that we need not wonder at the way in which it has seized upon the spirit of Western artists.

THE CONVENTIONALISM OF THE EAST

It is obvious, too, that the quality of the Nō drama, once appreciated, was of a kind likely to draw men's attentions to other different, though intimately related, theatrical activities of the Orient: to the Sanskrit drama and the Chinese, and, as well, to the entire vast realm of the marionette stage, which, spread over every Asiatic land, achieves its highest form in those half-lifesize Japanese puppets of the so-called Bunraku-za, which are so complex in their manipulation that each has to be controlled by no less than three or four individual attendants. Here, too, is a highly developed, intricate, conventional, and traditional technique, of the perfection of which numerous Western observers have written in glowing terms. "The artists," declares Paul Schiffer,

> are so skilful in their manipulation and directing, in the profound
> godlike attitude they assume toward the creatures in their control,

that after a moment they succeed in making us forget their own presence. . . . Delicately and with a sure touch, they pour their very being and whatsoever of thoughts they may have concerning life and human passions and human moods into the puppets which they move. . . . They do not hide, as we do, that they have to make a thousand movements; the puppets are always openly surrounded by these mechanical devices, and because of that they become uncanny. Before our eyes is clearly revealed the means by which the figure nods, rises angrily, throws a sharp glance to the side, or seems to laugh sneeringly. . . . The boundaries between mechanism and inspired existence are, as it were, obliterated.

For these marionettes plays are written not dissimilar from those composed for living actors: many of the dramatists, indeed, applied themselves to works of both kinds, and some of their works— among them the most famous of Chikamatsu Monzaemon's writings, the *Kokusenya kassen* (*The Battle of Kokusenya*)—are performed now on the puppet stage, now on that of the living actors.

The importance of the Oriental puppet theatre lies in the fact that it is, as it were, a concrete symbol of the conventionalism that has everywhere ruled, at least until latest times, on the stages of India, China, and Japan: and it is precisely this conventionalism that has made its appeal during the past few decades in the West. True, conventional forms have not made any very great incursions on to the commercial stages of Europe or America, yet the influence of the Orient has laid its hand upon the Western playhouse and is likely to inspire further stylized productions in the future. As will be seen, such a popular drama as Thornton Wilder's *Our Town* openly reveals the source of its being, while in the field of the poetic drama writers such as W. B. Yeats and Gordon Bottomley have been led, from study of Asiatic technique, to devise new technical devices suited to their own ends. In seeking for an escape from naturalism they have imaginatively started to explore the possibilities of that theatre which forms the utter antithesis of naturalism—and in this exploration they have discovered a method distinct from that of the Shakespearian. During the earlier romantic period the excitement over Kalidasa brought nothing new, for the style of Kalidasa's plays merely corroborated that of Shakespeare, Calderón, and Fletcher; in this latest interest in the theatre of the Orient it is not subject-matter that has attracted attention, but basic dramatic form. To realize the impress the conventional stage has made on the modern mind we need only note Lion Feuchtwanger's adaptation of Sanskrit drama, Berthold Brecht's utilization of

Chinese plays, and Paul Claudel's experimentation in the style of the Nō stage.

The force exerted by this Oriental theatre is well expressed in some passages of a private letter by Gordon Bottomley. Referring to the "dissociations and symbolisms" of the Nō dramas, "which have given a few poets hope for a renewed poetic drama in which poetry will master the form as well as content," he tells how, about the time of the First World War, these Japanese plays first impinged on his imagination and on the imagination of W. B. Yeats, and how they were made real by the demonstrations of ritual dramatic dance given in London by Ito. After he had been stirred to write his *Four Plays for Dancers* Yeats urged his friends to pursue this style further, with the ultimate result that both Bottomley and Laurence Binyon began, about the year 1927, to experiment in the writing of Japanese-inspired plays for John Masefield's garden theatre:

> That stage lent itself to the Nō conceptions. In using it, our lack of a dancer could, we found, be replaced by an element of narrative poetry (thus integrating the poetic content of the stage more completely)—in the person of the Greek messenger.

Thus, in our times, was a deliberate effort made to naturalize an Oriental form in a Western land, and thus was the symbolic ceremonial of the Nō theatre related to the conventions of that theatre which is the fount of all Occidental drama, the theatre of Æschylus and Sophocles.

PART XI

ENTERING THE TWENTIETH CENTURY

ENTERING THE TWENTIETH CENTURY

THERE can be established, of course, no neat break in Western dramatic affairs between the nineteenth and the twentieth centuries. The year 1900 by no means marks the end of the old and the beginning of something new; many dramatists, as has already been sufficiently indicated, whose most important works belong to the period before 1900 continued to produce work for the theatre after that date, while not a few, including among them no less a figure than George Bernard Shaw, whose chief contributions were made in the present era, had already approached the stage before the previous century had run its course.

At the same time, some justification does exist for making a pause at the century's end—even if only because Ibsen's last play came in the year 1899. With his departure from the scene new forces, adumbrated perhaps in the earlier years, found freedom of expression, and the theatres of 1920 had before them a variety of styles vastly different from those available to the dramatists of 1900 or of 1890. The first two decades of the new century saw the birth or the maturing of a considerable group of playwrights—Yeats and Synge, Benavente and Sierra, Gorki and Andreev, Lenormand and Bernard—who were destined to enrich the playhouse during the period immediately before or during the First World War, and whose influence was to lead the drama in new directions.

For the most part these first two decades of our century are a time of continual searching and of constant, violent experimentation. New ideas of stagecraft are now beginning to modify the prevailing trends towards the naturalistic and the colourful romantic. In 1895 Adolphe Appia, a Swiss artist and admirer of Wagner, published his *La mise en scène du drame Wagnérien*, and followed this, in 1899, with the more important *Die Musik und die Inscenierung*. Pleading for a theatrical art wherein light and basic form should be combined with the poet's words and the composer's music, he presented in these books a series of designs in which effects were to be secured through the placing on the stage of series of long, low platforms, essentially non-realistic, designed to offer full opportunities for the play of light. The year after the publication of *Die Musik und die*

Inscenierung Gordon Craig produced Purcell's *Dido and Æneas* in London, thus launching his long, inspired efforts to startle his contemporaries to an appreciation of theatrical values beyond the realistic. His epoch-making volume *The Art of the Theatre* was issued five years later, the first of a series of studies in which, with fervent enthusiasm, burning words, and soaring imagination, he pleaded for the theatre theatrical and poetic.

While neither Appia nor Craig succeeded in making much direct impact on the commercial playhouse within these years, the ideas they expressed were finding reflection in a diversity of quarters. The Moscow Art Theatre, born of the enthusiasm of Stanislawski and Nemirovich-Danchenko, opened its doors in 1897; Jacques Copeau's Théâtre du Vieux Colombier was established in 1913; the famous Granville-Barker seasons at the Court Theatre were inaugurated in 1904; in Germany and Austria Max Reinhardt gave opportunity to dozens of young men eager to present new stage ideas; during the first years of the century Meierhold was striving to find a fitting medium for his anti-naturalistic visions. Although these various activities assumed many contrasting forms, and although some (such as the work of the Moscow Art Theatre) seemed to be engaged in furthering the cause of the naturalistic, in effect they all combined in enlarging, extending, and pressing beyond the sphere of nineteenth-century realism. The typical independent theatre of the nineties fixed its gaze on the naturalistic presentation of the darker sides of existence; the typical independent theatre at the beginning of the twentieth century was largely engaged in the exploitation of the beautiful and the artistically conventional.

Especially noteworthy during these years is the growth of the repertory theatre, particularly in the English-speaking countries. In effect these playhouses marked a realization on the part of those truly interested in the stage of the peculiar needs of the modern period. Until the second half of the nineteenth century 'provincial' towns had been fairly well served by a widespread, sometimes crude, but always vigorous ring of stock-company theatres and of accompanying touring 'circuits.' Here young men and women planning to devote themselves to the boards might win experience; hereby audiences throughout the country were kept acquainted with the best the metropolitan theatres had to offer. From the recognition that with the disappearance of these older stock-company traditions a great void had been left in the world of the stage, the impulse towards the establishment of the repertory playhouse—generally associated in the first instance with the enthusiastic devotion of amateurs—took its being. The first years of the twentieth century show this impulse in its primal, formative period, while the century's second decade presents it in the full flush of excited achievement. In England the Birmingham Repertory Theatre opened its doors in 1913, just before the outbreak of war, while in America those stages which were to be responsible for the arising of O'Neill came in the very midst of international hostilities.

Mention of O'Neill reminds us that these repertory ventures exerted great influence on playwriting during this time. Again and again we meet with authors whose genius was first fed by the enthusiastic support of some non-commercial theatre. The flowering of Chekhov is associated with the Moscow Art Theatre; Synge comes from Dublin's Abbey; Shaw originally finds an audience among the members of the Independent Stage Society; O'Neill in his youth acts and writes for the Provincetown Players; while both in England and America there begins to emerge, largely sponsored by the little theatres, a long line of local playwrights who seek to exploit the events and characters of the diverse areas in which they live.

The twentieth century, therefore, introduces us to the development of a new theatrical force—the non-commercial stage—which, although shadowed forth during the final years of the nineteenth century, finds fruition only in our own times. In any survey of the contemporary drama the significance of this force must be kept fully in mind.

THE RELICS OF THE OLDER REALISM

In the commercial playhouses during these years, and even in some advanced playhouses, the earlier styles of realism still attracted wide attention. What had been the cult of the intelligentsia of the nineties gradually became the joy of a larger public, and in some areas where 'Ibsenism' had barely made an impact even on the more progressive the realistic medium was taken up with all the enthusiasm that comes from the delight of discovery. Thus such plays as *A Doll's House* and *Ghosts*, which had been caviare to the general at the time of their composition, came to be accepted without qualms by a later theatre-going public, while the slowly emergent drama of the United States (to take the most characteristic example), which had so far remained only slightly touched by the revolutionary movements in Europe, found its first inspiration at this time from cultivation of the realistic style. In surveying the fortunes of the stage between 1900 and 1920 it is important to remember that all the many experiments in new forms were set, as it were, against the solid background of 'Ibsenism.'

THE ENGLISH CONTRIBUTION

In England Pinero and Jones, rather sentimentally and without any singular boldness of purpose, had essayed the new form before the opening of the century, and both pursued their dramatic careers in the years immediately following. Their efforts, however, were soon outdistanced by others, and notably by John Galsworthy, who exhibited the rare ability of mastering the divergent techniques of the vast canvas of fiction and of the more economic way of the stage.

Galsworthy's plays are thoroughly typical of what the realistic mood meant to England. There is no violent *Tobacco Road* atmosphere here; there is no self-tortured misery of the kind purveyed by Strindberg; there is no sensationalism of effect: no brutal villain darkens with his shadow the scenes of this author's plays; no doctrinaire preachments colour the development of the action. In

Galsworthy we find a perfect mastery of the naturalistic method, a compassionate depiction of humanity, a fine humanitarianism of spirit. Although one of the most famous of his plays effected much-needed reforms in the penal code, his dramas are not designed to argue any case, and it is indeed ironic that, where so many of the Continental plays of ideas passed by without materially influencing the ways of society, *Justice* should be a prime example of a drama which wrought a mighty change in social conditions.

Galsworthy first came to the notice of the playgoing public in 1906 with the production of *The Silver Box*, in which he established a contrast between the comfortable, fashionable household of Mr Barthwick, a thoroughly respectable Member of Parliament, and that of Mrs Jones, the charwoman. Barthwick's son, Jack, is a scapegrace who steals a girl's purse; Mrs Jones' husband, bringing Jack home after a debauch, steals a silver box. In the one case a cheque easily settles the matter; in the other the law is set heavily in motion. In telling this story Galsworthy never permits the introduction of any direct comment, nor does he darken any of his characters in order to point a lesson. Characteristically, he simply sets forward the theme with as exact faithfulness to reality as he can: we are made aware that there is one law for the rich and one for the poor, but that does not imply by any means that Barthwick is a villain or Jones a blameless hero. Similarly, Galsworthy refuses to admit the easy solution of a suicide (so beloved of the German authors) and the absurd attempt to weave a tragic pattern out of untragic material: his play is frankly and professedly a 'drama,' and gains in strength from recognition of the limitations of its kind.

In *Justice* (1910) we may perhaps detect more of a burning emotion, yet even here, where the dramatist's anger is obviously aroused, the method remains the same. In the central figure, William Falder, we are given no 'hero'; instead we have a weak-willed, ineffective little law-clerk who falls pathetically in love with a married woman, forges a cheque in order to obtain money wherewith to go off with her to South America, and is arrested. Condemned to prison, he is put in solitary confinement, and here Galsworthy introduces the wordless scene which so startled contemporaries:

FALDER'S *cell, a whitewashed space thirteen feet broad by seven deep, and nine feet high, with a rounded ceiling. The floor is of shiny blackened bricks. The barred window, with a ventilator, is high up in the middle of the end wall. In the middle of the opposite end wall is the narrow door. In a corner are the mattress and bedding rolled up (two blankets, two sheets, and a coverlet). Above them is a quarter-circular wooden shelf, on which is a Bible and several little devotional books, piled in a symmetrical pyramid; there are also a black hairbrush, tooth-brush, and a bit of soap. In another corner is the wooden frame of a bed, standing on end. There is a dark ventilator under the window, and another over the door.* FALDER'S *work (a shirt to which he is putting button-holes) is hung to a nail on the wall over a small wooden table, on which the novel "Lorna Doone" lies open. Low down in the corner by the door is a thick glass screen, about a foot square, covering the gas-jet let into the wall. There is also a wooden stool, and a pair of shoes beneath it. Three bright round tins are set under the window.*

In fast-failing daylight, FALDER, *in his stockings, is seen standing motionless, with his head inclined towards the door, listening. He moves a little closer to the door, his stockinged feet making no noise. He stops at the door. He is trying harder and harder to hear something, any little thing that is going on outside. He springs suddenly upright—as if at a sound—and remains perfectly motionless. Then, with a heavy sigh, he moves to his work, and stands looking at it, with his head down; he does a stitch or two, having the air of a man so lost in sadness that each stitch is, as it were, a coming to life. Then turning abruptly, he begins pacing the cell, moving his head, like an animal pacing its cage. He stops again at the door, listens, and, placing the palms of his hands against it with his fingers spread out, leans his forehead against the iron. Turning from it, presently, he moves slowly back towards the window, tracing his way with his finger along the top line of the distemper that runs round the wall. He stops under the window, and, picking up the lid of one of the tins, peers into it, as if trying to make a companion of his own face. It has grown very nearly dark. Suddenly the lid falls out of his hand with a clatter—the only sound that has broken the silence—and he stands staring intently at the wall where the stuff of the shirt is hanging rather white in the darkness—he seems to be seeing somebody or something there. There is a sharp tap and click; the cell light behind the glass screen has been turned up. The cell is brightly lighted.* FALDER *is seen gasping for breath.*

A sound from far away, as of distant, dull beating on thick metal, is suddenly audible. FALDER *shrinks back, not able to bear the sudden clamour. But the sound grows, as though some great tumbril were rolling towards the cell. And gradually it seems to hypnotize him. He begins creeping inch by inch nearer to the door. The banging sound, travelling from cell to cell, draws closer and closer;* FALDER'S *hands are seen moving as if his spirit had already joined in this beating, and the sound swells till it seems to have entered the very cell. He suddenly raises his clenched fists. Panting violently, he flings himself at his door, and beats on it.*

THE CURTAIN FALLS

This scene, entirely devoid of dialogue, indicates both Galsworthy's own inventive power and the general manner in which the elaborated, 'literary' stage direction, introduced by Ibsen for the purpose of giving realistic background to his characters, was being further developed in the twentieth century. The year before *Justice* appeared Galsworthy had produced his *Strife* (1909), a drama in which again he displays his broad humanitarian sympathies and his wise impartiality. In *Justice* there was no blackening of those responsible for Falder's imprisonment—indeed, there are scenes in that drama obviously planned for the purpose of being utterly fair to such persons as the Governor of the gaol: similarly, in *Strife* the claims of workers and of masters alike are presented with sympathy, the whole work being designed to show the fatal consequences and the waste resultant from the strife between them. Galsworthy's world knows few villains and few heroes: over all his characters he broods with understanding and pity, baffled by the circumstances that produce misery and disaster without the active operation of human evil.

All his plays have a kindred atmosphere, even as he turns from aspect to aspect of the little universe around him. When he tries to plead too strongly for a particular individual, as he does in *The Pigeon* (1912), *The Fugitive* (1913), and *The Mob* (1914), he seems a trifle out of his element, but when he essays, as in his one-act *The Little Man* (1915) and *Loyalties* (1922), to present his broad, kindly philosophy—the philosophy of the humanitarian gentleman —he exhibits a quality all too frequently lacking in this age of fierce conflicts and melodramatic concepts—applied, not as they properly may be in the theatre, but disastrously in terms of real life.

Along with him stands Harley Granville-Barker, a man of similar broad sympathies and one who vitally influenced the stage by his creative literary efforts, by his new visions of what should be the functions of the theatrical producer, and by his alert critical studies. Starting with an unimportant *The Weather Hen* (written in collaboration with Berte Thomas, 1899), he brought forward during the first decade of the century four particularly interesting plays—*The Marrying of Ann Leete* (1901), *The Voysey Inheritance* (1905), *Waste* (1907), and *The Madras House* (1910)—in all of which he sought to extend the realistic form beyond its Ibsenite bounds. All tend to neglect plot in favour of atmosphere and character: indeed, basically, their stories are of no importance. Ann Leete shocks social conventions because she, well-born, marries her gardener; Mr Voysey, a prosperous solicitor, is found by his son to owe his fortune to the result of successful gambling with his clients' money; a young politician is ruined when his mistress dies in trying to destroy the child he has given her: such are the simple themes Granville-Barker deals with; yet the general impression we have of his plays, because of the subtle detail introduced by the author, is one of complex structure rather than of simplicity.

There can be no doubt but that here realism is carried almost to its extreme verge, yet it is interesting to observe that for such a writer as Granville-Barker realism was not enough. In 1904 he wrote, in collaboration with Laurence Housman, the delicately idealistic *Prunella*; later came *Rococo* (1911) and *The Harlequinade* (in collaboration with D. C. Calthrop, 1913); later still, in *The Secret Life* (1923), the outer is sacrificed completely for the inner vision. Beyond that Granville-Barker the critic has shown in many essays that his true ideal is, not the realistic prose drama, but the drama of poetic concept. No clearer example could be found of realism's shattering of its own confining walls.

Within these years many other authors, with varying degrees of success, explored the reaches of the realistic social stage, most of them, however, tending to deal rather with provincial life than with studies of a more general kind. The use of dialect, the association of the events with a particular limited area, best harmonized with their purposes and at the same time met the needs of the slowly arising local 'repertory theatres.' From Northern Ireland came St John Ervine with his *Mixed Marriage* (1911), a kind of modern realistic *Romeo and Juliet*, in which the son of a fanatic Orangeman falls in love with a Catholic girl; *Jane Clegg* (1913), a study of a woman who, after trying her best to act as helpmeet to her spineless husband, eventually is forced for the sake of her own self-respect to leave him; and *John Ferguson* (1915), a powerful portrait of a worthy man who finds his whole world crumbling about him. Hardly any other realistic dramatic author exhibited at this time greater vigour or intensity of purpose than he—nor have many others carried their active careers over so many decades. Always a fighter, Ervine has given us in his latest drama, *Private Enterprise* (1947), a vigorous polemic against nationalization.

In England itself the 'repertory' playwrights eagerly assayed the form. St John Hankin produced, among other theatrical writings, *The Cassilis Engagement* (1907), a much-discussed drama of ideas in which a wise mother, objecting to her son's choice of a fiancée, invites the girl for a week-end to her home, guessing that the discrepancy between her ways and theirs will result in the breaking of the match. With her *Chains* (1909) Elizabeth Baker travelled into a London suburb to draw a depressing picture of a poor little clerk whose visions of escape are thwarted by his wife's announcement that she is to bear a child. Famous in his time was Stanley Houghton, whose *The Younger Generation* (1910) is a cynical study of puritanical middle age in conflict with oat-sowing youth, and whose *Hindle Wakes* (1912) fluttered conventional circles by introducing a determined young 'new woman' of the working class who goes off for a week-end with the son of a factory-owner and then refuses to marry him even when both her parents and the parents of the youth are determined that marriage is the only honourable solution for her escapade.

For Lancashire Harold Brighouse did what others had done for their areas, reaching a true depth of passion in *The Price of Coal* (1909).

Memorable among these plays are *Milestones* (1912), by Arnold Bennett and Edward Knoblock, which treats a basic theme by making the action move through several generations; *Rutherford and Son* (1912), by Githa Sowerby, with its study of the bleakness of spirit that comes from industrialism; *A Bill of Divorcement* (1921), by Clemence Dane (Winifred Ashton), where a popular problem is handled tensely and with originality; and *The Mollusc* (1907), by Hubert Henry Davies, a brilliantly constructed comedy-drama.

THE PLAYWRIGHTS OF FRANCE, RUSSIA, AND SPAIN

There can be no doubt but that the English contributions to the realistic stage during the first two decades of the present century were materially finer both in craftsmanship and concept than those made by their predecessors during the latter years of the century previous—and this even omitting the works of Sir J. M. Barrie and George Bernard Shaw, which, although closely associated with the work of the realistic movement, are obviously of a kind different from that of *Chains* or *Justice*. Yet, when we survey the entire field of the drama at this time it is obvious that the primal force of the older realism was spent. The truth of this assertion is amply apparent when we turn to survey the work of authors in France, Germany, and Scandinavia.

Many of the dramas penned by the French playwrights already examined were, of course, written after 1900. At the same time it is possible, and for critical purposes desirable, to differentiate those authors who had already established their reputations during the last century from others who first came to recognition in our own era. Of the latter group there are many, and only a few of these can here be singled out for mention.

The Franco-Belgian Henry Kistemaeckers may be taken first, not because of the worth of his plays, but because he was the purveyor of pouplar pieces in which a dash of the drama of ideas was used to flavour well-made works fashioned according to the old nineteenth-century formulas. *La flambée* (*The Blaze*, 1912) might have been written by Sardou, and his other pieces demonstrate clearly that, despite the achievements of Antoine's Théâtre Libre, there was an ample public for the exhibition of scenes in which no more of 'reality' was presented than might serve to give a surface appearance of life. Just a trifle deeper is the work of Henry Bernstein, an author who knows all the tricks of the stage and who skilfully can combine a suggestion of a problem with melodramatic incident. The modern Scribe, he can turn out a sensational *Le voleur* (*The Thief*, 1906) or direct his hand to the exploitation of current psychology, as in *L'elévation* (*The Height*, 1917) or *Mélo* (1929); he is at home in many theatrical realms.

Bernstein's style, though effective, is apt to be sensationally heavy; that of Alfred Savoir is treacherously light, the bright play of a rapier with point sometimes buttoned, sometimes sharply dangerous; while in Alfred Capus appears an ironic resignation concealed by outward jesting. There is more than meets the eye in such brittle plots as serve *Brignol et sa fille* (*Brignol and his Daughter*, 1894)—a tale of how a man near financial ruin is saved when his daughter happens to fall in love with, and marry, his chief creditor's nephew —or *Monsieur Pégieois* (1905). The same ironic jesting appears in *L'habit vert* (*The Green Uniform*, 1912), by Gaston-Armand de Caillavet and Robert de Flers, with its mixture of the triangle theme and satire directed against the Academicians. A lighter cynicism colours the writings of Romain Coolus (René Weill). Something of the same admixture of apparent triviality and inner depth gives quality to many of the plays contributed to the French stage by Pierre Wolff and Georges Courteline. Outwardly their plays may resemble such popular farces as were being currently produced by a Tristan Bernard or a Georges Feydeau, but spiritually they are born of a different mood.

In the eternal triangle Félix-Henry Bataille finds his opportunity for the writing of plays outwardly more serious : play after play he turns out with variants on the same theme—extending from *Maman Colibri* in 1904, on through *La femme nue* (*The Naked Woman*, 1908) and *L'Amazone* (*The Amazon*, 1916), to *La chair humaine*

(*Human Flesh*, 1922)—a rather tedious collection of pieces monotonously beating the same rhythm on the erotic drum. True, he varies the environment of his plots, as in *Ton sang* (*Thy Blood*, 1897), where the appearance of novelty is given by the fact that the heroine is blind and that the lovers are brothers, but the central theme is nearly always the same. And often the inner action is accompanied by outer violence, as in *La marche nuptiale* (*The Wedding March*, 1905), where an aristocratic girl, marrying her piano-teacher, finds him wanting and dismally commits suicide. Émile Fabre is more obviously the follower of Becque and Brieux. *Le bien d'autrui* (*The Property of Others*, 1897) presents an idealistic young hero who, on discovering that some property left to him was given in a later will to another, and after searching in vain for a means of giving it to the one whom he regards as its rightful owner, proposes to hand it over to the Government. Political ambition dominates in *Les vainqueurs* (*The Conquerors*, 1908), where the central figure is a man who, to further his ends, is content to indulge in blackmail and to accept a sum of money from the lover of his own wife. Seriousness of purpose, with a definitely 'labour' slant, characterizes, too, the plays of Octave Mirbeau, as represented, for example, by *Les affaires sont les affaires* (*Business is Business*, 1903), which shows a wealthy industrialist engaged in seeking means of adding to his wealth even while his domestic life is crashing about him. No less serious, though not so socialistic in his attitude, is Jean Jullien, whose *L'écolière* (*The Girl Student*, 1901) carries the style of Brieux into other realms.

This record of realism on the Paris stage is, at best, a sorry affair, nor is it bettered by the German theatre's record—indeed, there not even so much was on offering, and we need not pause to consider any individual authors. Almost the only writer here who calls for attention is the Austrian Thaddeus Rittner, an author gifted with a gentle talent which enables him to create a peculiar atmosphere not unreminiscent of the quality investing Schnitzler's plays. In Scandinavia the great wave that had come with Ibsen and Strindberg was losing its force. Ibsen's son, Sigurd, produced one play of slightly more than mediocre quality, *Robert Frank* (1914), but there is little to be found in the realistic essays of other Norwegian dramatists, such as Nils Kjaer and Oskar Braaten, or in those of the Swedish, such as Tor Hedberg, although the last-named author's *Johan Ulfstjerna* (1907), telling the tale of a Finnish patriot, has a few strong scenes. In *Gertrud* (1906) Hjalmar Söderberg produces a tense drama of the sexes that for the darkness of its spirit almost rivals the frenzies of Strindberg. Writing in Swedish, the Finnish Mikall Dybeck infused into the Ibsenian formula a peculiarly poetic spirit of his own, but one too national in inspiration to bear transference abroad. Denmark gave the theatre one writer of talent, Gustav Wied, but even his best plays, such as *Dansemús* (*Dancing Mice*, 1905), can be accepted as no more than second-rate and rather precious. Reminiscent of Ibsen and wholly lacking Ibsen's subtlety is the style of *En martyr* (*A Martyr*, 1896), by another Danish author, Sven Lange, while Hjalmar Bergström develops further the Ibsenian concept of the 'new woman,' who can have *affaires* if she wants to, in *Karen Borneman* (1907). More primitive passion is infused by the Icelandic Gudmundur Kamban into his *Hadda Padda* (1914), a love-story in which attempted murder is followed by suicide, and into his *Vi mordere* (*We Murderers*, 1920). Surveying the Scandinavian stage as a whole during these years, we realize that most of its vitality went into plays of fantastic, historical, or poetic style rather than into dramas of realism.

In Belgium the current vogue of realism produced the plays of Gustave Vanzype and influenced the writing of Paul Spaak. The romantic meets, and clashes with, the realistic in the dramas of the Latvian Jānis Rainis. Ibsen's influence is clearly marked on the Greek playwright Gregori Xenopoulos, and it crosses the oceans to cast its spell on the Uruguayan Florencio Sánchez and Ernesto Herrera. In none of these, however, do we encounter much, if anything, of permanent and general value.

In Italy Enrico Annibale Butti, who had early essayed the Ibsenite path with *La fine di un ideale* (*The End of an Ideal*, 1898), and who had drawn in *La corsa al piacere* (*The Race for Pleasure*, 1900) a vivid picture of a life devoid of spiritual aims, produced in 1904 his by no means negligible *Fiamme nell' ombra* (*Flames in Darkness*), a study of a pious priest and his sister impatient of convention. As in *Il vortice* (*The Vortex*, 1892) and *L'Utopia* (1894), Butti's philosophy suggests that it is wiser for man to accept than to beat against society's conventions.

The only other Italian 'realistic' author of the time who deserves mention is Dario Niccodemi, and his work can hardly be accepted as anything save the purveying of popular sensationalism with a veneer of *verismo*. An accomplished craftsman, he succeeded by knowing well how to compromise: a cosmopolitan, who could as easily pen a play in French as in Italian, he provided for the public dozens of dramas in which current stage fashions were adroitly dished up in pleasing or thrilling forms. *L'aigrette*, for example,

ADOLPHE APPIA: DESIGN FOR "HAMLET"
From *Theatre Arts Monthly*, January 1925.

THE THÉÂTRE DU VIEUX-COLOMBIER, PARIS
From *Theatre Arts Monthly*, October 1924.

composed in 1912 specifically for production in Paris, and translated by the author for the first Italian performance in the following year, is a somewhat sensational satire in which the 'aigrette' worn habitually by the Countess of Saint-Servan is regarded by her son, Henri, as a symbol of their family honour. Actually the Countess finds it impossible to keep up her estate and indulges in divers tricks to obtain money; in particular she persuades Madame Leblanc, the wife of a banker, to 'lend' her money. This lady has young Henri as her lover, and in the discovery of the Countess's financial intrigues he is so shocked out of his complacency and so involved in a situation of apparently inevitable disaster that only a violent wrenching of the plot enables the author to bring his curtain down on a stage not darkened by suicide or death in duel. Typical of Niccodemi's writing at its best is his achievement in *L'alba, il giorno, la notte* (*Dawn, Noon, and Night*, 1921), where he keeps three entire acts alive with interest although only two characters, Anna and Mario, are on the stage. At dawn, in a forest, Mario meets a girl and follows her to her house: from their conversation it emerges that he is about to fight a duel with a man with whom he has quarrelled because he had insisted he had seen a ghost in the wood; now it turns out that this 'ghost' was Anna. At noon Mario turns up and expresses his astonishment at finding her, instead of wracked with anxiety on his behalf, engaged in eating lunch; since she has found out that before leaving for the duel he has written a letter to a certain Marion, her replies are tinged with asperity, while he displays jealousy on believing that she is affianced to a certain Paolino. In anger, Mario departs, but, returning at night, he declares his love and is accepted; all the causes of daytime quarrel are found to have been mere figments: Marion never had any existence and Paolino is a brother, not a lover.

Without doubt Niccodemi possesses extreme skill in weaving his scenes delicately together; his dialogue is vividly precise; and he succeeds in presenting lively pictures of the bourgeois world of his time. We cannot, however, place him very high among dramatic authors: he is of the company of the talented, not of the geniuses. A slightly greater interest attaches to one play, *Addio, giovinezza!* (*Adieu, Youth!*, 1911), by Sandro Camasio and Nino Oxilia, but even this capably written and thoughtful study of adolescent intrigue set against a darker background displays little of the quality demanded of greatness. The truth is, of course, that realism of this sort ill-suited the Italian spirit and consequently yielded few fruitful results.

Y

Two countries only have much to offer in this style. In Russia Tolstoi's mantle was cast on the shoulders of Maxim Gorki (Alexei Maxsimovich Peshkov), who, after one or two early experiments, succeeded in fashioning out of the bitterness of his heart the one work by which he will assuredly continue to be known. *Na dne* (*The Lower Depths*, 1903) hardly resembles in technique any of the realistic plays of the earlier years, save, perhaps, Tolstoi's *The Power of Darkness*. It is not described by its author as a drama: rather he prefers to follow the Ostrovski tradition and styles it "Scenes from Russian Life." In these scenes the author descends to "a basement resembling a cavern," where a miserable group of waifs of all ages are wretchedly huddled together. Of plot there is virtually nothing; of plots there are many. The only real 'story' in the work is that which concerns Vassili, who, having an *affaire* with Vaska, the wife of the lodging-house keeper Kostilev (Mishka), is persuaded to leave her and go off with her sister, Natasha: angered, Vaska comes to blows with Natasha, and Vassili, trying to protect the girl, accidentally kills Kostilev. If, however, this is the only apparent plot, Gorki has succeeded in presenting us with an entire series of stories connected with his characters. Imaginatively, from the hints given to us, we follow the degeneration of the broken-down actor until he has reached this pit of horror; we fill in the grim biographies of the out-of-work locksmith Kleshch and his consumptive wife, Anna, of the 'Baron' and the prostitute Nastia, of Kvashnia, the market woman, of Aliosha, the shoemaker. Into this group of cold and hungry derelicts comes an elderly pilgrim, Luka, and it is through him that most of the atmosphere is revealed. His wanderings have given him a philosophy of life. "We're all pilgrims in this world," he says. "I've heard tell that even the globe we're on is just a pilgrim in the heavens." His secret is revealed when he answers the dying Anna:

ANNA: My name is Anna . . . When I look at you . . . you are so much like my own father . . . my own dear father . . . you, too, are so kind and soft . . .

LUKA: The world has kneaded me for a long time, that's why I'm soft.

He knows all the despair of life, yet hope is still in him. "Human beings?" he asks. "They will find. He who seeks will find. He who earnestly desires will find!" Yet in the end Luka's words are at variance with reality; nothing is found here; these wretched creatures have passed through a night of misery, and their misery stretches on into an indefinite future.

In *The Lower Depths* Gorki produced a masterpiece, but, unfortunately, not so much may be said of his later writings for the stage. None is without interest, none without that peculiar bitter strength which was his greatest characteristic, yet not one of his other plays quite captures the magnificent quality that gives to this drama its unique distinction. Against the cosmopolitan intellectuals he directed his *Dachniki* (*Summer Visitors*, 1903), declaring in it that these men, instead of being integrated in Russian life, were merely tourists in their native land. In *Deti solntsia* (*Children of the Sun*, 1904) he turned, rather futilely, to a mixture of an ordinary domestic theme and a larger political problem. Class conflict is the theme of *Vragi* (*Enemies*, 1906), wherein an attempt is made to demonstrate that inevitably an impassable chasm separates capitalists and workers. In *Starik* (*The Old Man*, or *The Judge*, 1915) he wrote a sombre drama showing a man with another (a former fellow-convict) in his power; the latter is driven remorselessly to his death. Plays of these kinds came from his pen between the beginning of the century and the time of the First World War, all interesting and all essentially mediocre.

Then, almost three decades after the composition of *The Lower Depths*, came *Egor Bulichov i drugie* (*Egor Bulichov and Others*, 1932), in which some of his old magic, but by means of a different formula, was recaptured. This play is designed to present a picture of the collapse of the middle class on the approach of the Revolution. Taking as central figure the capitalist Egor Bulichov, Gorki shows the inherent rottenness pervading the Russian society of the time immediately preceding the outbreak of civil violence. For Bulichov we cannot help feeling some admiration: he is a man of character, will, and ability; but his riches are the result of exploitation; the cancer from which he suffers does not prevent him from seeking to add to his wealth; around him are none save fools and leeches. His relatives are self-seeking and credulously stupid; the Church eagerly eyes his fortune. Although the settings are vastly different from that degrading basement in which the lowest depths were reached, the spiritual atmosphere is no less wretched and despairing. Only towards the close of the drama does a note of hope approach. As the dying Egor stands at his window the singing of revolutionaries can be heard from the streets: for him it is an ironic requiem.

Egor Bulichov and Others was planned by its author as the first part of a great trilogy, representing dramatically the early course of the Revolution. That trilogy was rudely broken by Gorki's death: whether it could have been successfully carried out to completion if he had lived we cannot tell, but certainly the second portion,

Dostigaev i drugie (*Dostigaev and Others,* 1933), displays nothing of the vigour of its predecessor. As a record of historical events it is interesting; drama, however, to be great needs to be more than mere record, and it must be confessed that of true dramatic vigour this last of Gorki's plays has nothing to give to us.

Besides Gorki, the naturalistic or Ibsenian styles inspired no notable works on the Russian stage. There was one realistic writer, it is true, Michael Petrovich Artzibashev, whose writings once had a scandalous success, but he has long been forgotten. The hysterical exploitation of frantic eroticism and sensational episode that luridly illuminates *Revnost* (*Jealousy,* 1913) is not of a sort destined to endure: it is easy to see why when these works were new they excited young men's minds; it is equally easy, now, to discern their inherent absurdity.

To turn from Gorki and Artzibashev in Russia to Sierra and Benavente in Spain is to journey from the bitter North to the warmth of the South. Jacinto Benavente y Martínez in fertility almost equalled the records set by Lope de Vega and his followers. (It would be interesting to inquire and to discover, if possible, why the greater Spanish dramatists have been granted so overwhelmingly fecund talents as to make the totality of their works far outdistance the writings of any of their contemporaries in other countries.) From the year 1892, when four short pieces were issued under the general title of *Teatro fantástico*, he has contributed hundreds of diverse dramas to the stage, some of them, it is true, adapted from the plays of other writers, but most of his own invention. Here is Dionysus' plenty—plays short and plays long, plays romantic and plays realistic, farces and fairy-plays, plays sentimental and plays static.

The very variety of Benavente's contributions to the stage indicates that he is no faithful follower of the realistic tradition. Rather might it be said that on the stock of the traditional vigorous Spanish poetic drama he grafts the twig of Ibsen and his followers. His quality, therefore, depends less on his pursuit of the realistic problem play in itself than upon the strength that comes to him from outside that particular sphere; and this fact reminds us that Gorki too owed his power largely to his inheriting, from Ostrovski and Tolstoi, a theatrical form which may have run parallel with but ever remained essentially distinct from the line leading back to the Scandinavian authors and the French problem dramatists.

Even to enumerate the titles of all Benavente's plays would occupy several pages of this volume, and consequently nothing more can be done here than to indicate in general terms the main characteristics of his dramatic work. First is to be noted in him an element of the fantastic, the love for which no doubt led him towards an appreciative interest in the Oriental stage, expressed in such writings as *El dragón de fuego* (*The Fire Dragon*, 1903), inspired by an Indian theme, and *La túnica amarilla* (*The Yellow Jacket*, 1916), adapted from Benrimo's Chinese drama. This fantastic element already was expressed in his first dramatic writings; among the four dramas making up the *Teatro fantástico* is *El encanto de una hora* (*The Magic of an Hour*), which uses the device of animating some statuettes and of playing with their cold passions until one, attempting to kiss the lady of his choice, chips a piece out of her cheek. Throughout Benavente's career the mood that produced this one-act sketch continued to flower, giving us now the *Cuento de amor* (*The Love-story*, 1899), adapted from *Twelfth Night*, now *La princesa sin corazón* (*The Heartless Princess*, 1907), now *El hijo de Polichinela* (*The Son of Pulcinella*, 1927) and *La novia de nieve* (*The Snow Bride*, 1935).

From these it is but a step to the romanticized, artificial, and sentimental comedies of manners represented by *La Princesa Bebé* (*Princess Bebé*, 1904), and the satirically conceived comedies such as *Los malhechores del bien* (*The Evildoers of Good*, 1905). Romantic passion of a stronger kind enters into some of these dramas, but in general his true strength lies rather in the gentler emotions and in the exercise of concealed irony than in the exploitation of burning fervour.

Among such works Benavente included numbers based on the current naturalistic and realistic efforts outside Spain. The life of the peasantry and the farmers, which had attracted the attention of Hauptmann and others, is dealt with in *Señora Ama* (1908) and *La malquerida* (*The Passion Flower*, 1913). In the former a wife who had previously taken pride in the affairs of the heart pursued by her husband changes her ideas when she finds she is to have a child. The latter is one of those rarer plays from his pen in which passion, usually subdued in the Benavente theatre, bursts forth in a torrent of fury. The central figure is a girl, Acacia, who finds herself, hardly realizing the force that possesses her, enamoured of her stepfather, Esteban, a well-to-do farmer. Like a flame, this incestuous frenzy consumes the pair until Raimunda, the mother, deliberately provokes Esteban into killing her, conscious that now Acacia can never give herself to the man who has murdered her parent.

This reads almost like one of the more violent specimens of the naturalistic German theatre. Powerful as it is, other realistic efforts by Benavente are, however, more characteristic and finer in texture. Already in 1896 with *Gente conocida* (*People of Importance*) he had turned his gaze on the aristocratic world of his time; in 1903, with *El hombrecito* (*The Little Man*), he was exploring the life of the bourgeoisie. These realms attracted much of his attention throughout his career, and out of them he wrought what unquestionably are his finest dramas. Peculiarly typical is *Los intereses creados* (*The Bonds of Interest*, 1907). The plot is confessedly derived from the *commedia dell' arte*, testifying to that love of the fantastic that ever coloured Benavente's work; the theme is a social one, testifying to the influence upon him of the realistic theatre. While the atmosphere may be imaginary, the problems are real. Leandro and Crispin arrive, with little money between them, at a strange city. "This is a little play of puppets, impossible in theme, without any reality at all," says Crispin ironically in speaking the prologue. The city is really two cities—"one for people who arrive with money and the other for persons who arrive like us." Crispin pretends to be Leandro's servant, and starts actively to promote that young gentleman's marriage to an heiress. First they put up an outward show by entertaining the Captain and Harlequin; then Crispin starts to foment his intrigue, which, however, is somewhat upset by Leandro's genuinely falling in love with the fair Silvia. The end of the piece shows a happy union, achieved, thinks Crispin, by the material bonds of interest that unite men, by the principles of self-interest, and by the foundations of the market-place:

> CRISPIN: And believe me now, when you are getting on in the world, the ties of love are as nothing to the bonds of interest.
>
> LEANDRO: You are wrong. For without the love of Silvia I should never have been saved.
>
> CRISPIN: And is love a slight interest? I have always given due credit to the ideal, and I count upon it always. With this the farce ends.

Silvia now turns to the audience. "You have seen in the play," she says,

> how these puppets have been moved by plain and obvious strings, like men and women in the farces of our lives—strings which were their interests, their passions, and all the illusions and petty miseries of their state. Some are pulled by the feet to lives of restless and weary wandering; some by the hands, to toil with pain, to struggle with bitterness, to strike with cunning, to slay with violence and rage. But into the hearts of all there descends sometimes from heaven an invisible thread, as if it were woven out of the sunlight and the moonbeams, the invisible thread of love, which makes these men and women, as it does

these puppets which seem like men, almost divine, and brings to our foreheads the smile and splendours of the dawn, lends wings to our drooping spirits, and whispers to us still that this farce is not all a farce, that there is something noble, something divine, in our lives which is true and which is eternal, and which shall not close when the farce of life shall close.

Obviously this is not a realistic drama; as obviously it is a drama of ideas, and the ideas are those that colour all Benavente's 'social' works, even although there occasionally creeps into the optimistic philosophy a faint note of scepticism—such, for example, as appears in the sequel to *The Bonds of Interest*—*La ciudad alegre y confiada* (*The Joyous and Confident City*, 1916)—wherein Leandro is shown in a less sympathetic light than he was in the earlier play.

Benavente's studies of the social life of his time are numerous. In *La comida de las fieras* (*The Banquet of Wild Beasts*, 1898) the basic theme of *Timon of Athens* is transferred to modern surroundings. *La gobernadora* (*The Governor's Wife*, 1901) satirizes society's manners, as does *Lo cursi* (*Vulgarity*, 1901). No revolutionary, he reveals his basic attitude in *Campo de armiño* (*Field of Ermine*, 1916), wherein a noble lady takes a boy into her house in the belief that he is the bastard son of her brother, discovers that he has been foisted on her by a group of grasping lower-class characters, in anger dismisses him from her palace, and then finds that love of him compels her to adopt him as her own: the field of ermine in her coat-of-arms is left pure by her yielding to her better emotions. For Benavente love is the mystery of life and the hope of mankind.

The author's dramatic career has been a long one—and peculiarly fortunate. After the performance of his latest drama in Madrid (1947) the audience rose in a mass, raised the aged playwright on their shoulders, and in triumphant procession bore him from the theatre to his home. Benavente at least is one philosopher who has won fame, while living, in his own country.

Next to Benavente in this new flourishing of the Spanish stage stands Gregorio Martínez Sierra, in whose works, with gentle melancholy, much the same atmosphere prevails. He too is influenced by the social drama of the age; he too brings to that realism a peculiar flavour of his own. From his very first play he exhibited the quality that was to dominate in his work throughout the whole of his career—the quality of penetrating sympathy. This quality is carried to full expression in *Canción de cuna* (*Cradle Song*, 1911), a tender, sensitive study of quiet emotion in a Spanish nunnery; a baby girl left in a basket at the gate is reared, under the sisters' care, by their gardener's wife; at the age of eighteen she becomes betrothed to a young man, and in the play we see him visiting the convent to thank the nuns for the care of his future wife. There is no more plot than that, and Sierra's skill is demonstrated clearly by the way in which, with such slender material, he keeps our interest alert and our sympathies keen, yet untouched by the sentimental. A kindred spirit hovers over *El Reino de Dios* (*The Kingdom of God*, 1916), which consists merely of three episodes in a nun's life—as a girl just before taking her vows, as a woman crushing from her heart a human love, and as an elderly woman commanding by her wisdom a crowd of unruly and half-starved orphans. The power of understanding love, in which Sierra believes as fervently as does Benavente, is revealed in *Los pastores* (*The Shepherds*, 1913), where a priest and a doctor, although neither is capable of passing the examinations which authority deems necessary, are shown as true shepherds protecting the souls and bodies of the country people of their rural area.

Even when Sierra turns from the religious field to the secular he bears with him his own characteristic mood. In *Sueño de una noche de Agosto* (*A Dream of an August Eve*, or *The Romantic Young Lady*, 1918), where a girl, grieved because she cannot have adventures like a man, finds such adventure coming her way when the wind carries a straw hat into her room, and when the hat is merely an introduction to the young novelist who has lost it. No matter how flimsy and artificial the plot, Sierra can hold us intent. *El enamorado* (*The Lover*, 1912) tells merely of a self-made factory-owner whose romantic adoration of his queen is such that he follows in her train wherever she goes. One day her carriage is overturned, and he rescues her: she offers to grant him whatever he asks; and his plea is for a railway pass which will allow him always to be close to her. We may smile in superior manner at such fancies, but if we do we smile at something rather fragrant and lovely.

Fragrance and loveliness too, combined with gentle laughter, appear in the writings of the Quintero brothers—Serafín and Joaquín Alvarez—who, like Benavente, have contributed to the theatre several hundred dramas, from short sketches to full-length plays. Best-known of these outside Spain is the delightful *La consulesa* (*The Lady from Alfáqueque*, 1914), with its magnificently drawn picture of an appealing rascal whose manners are so perfect that hardly anyone can take offence at his shameless sponging on others. Closely akin in spirit is *El genio alegre* (*The Merry Heart*, 1906), wherein the austere household of Donna Sacramento is transformed when her orphan niece, Consolación, comes to stay with her, bringing to the house her canaries, her parrots, and her light-hearted *joie de vivre*. The individual flavour of the Quintero stage is likewise fully revealed in *Papá Juan, centenario (A Hundred Years Old, 1909)*, in which Papa Juan by his wisdom resolves the perplexing difficulties in his large household; chuckling, he pulls the strings so as to engineer a wedding between his beloved great-granddaughter and her gay blade of a cousin. Sometimes their scenes grow darker, as in *Los Galeotes (The Two Galeotes, 1900)*, which shows ingratitude rampant—even though good triumphs in the end. Even when they introduce evil it is with a gentle smile. In *Malvaloca* (1912), for example, Salvador has seduced the girl Malvaloca. He and his brother, Leonardo, are at the time of the action engaged in remoulding the cracked bell of the convent, and Malvaloca comes to love and to be loved by Leonardo. In the end, as the task is finished and the bell rings out clearly, Salvador is shown ready to depart, while Leonardo protests to Malvaloca that he will seek to recast her life with his love. Somewhat similar to this play is *Amores y amoríos* (*Loves and Intrigues*, 1908). Here the heroine, Isabel, falls in love with a roué, Juan Maria, who, charmed by the atmosphere of an Andalusian spring, makes her a promise of marriage. Back in cold Madrid, he abandons her, but eventually true love conquers over his libertine affections, and in the end the pair are united.

Besides these major authors the Spanish stage produced many other interesting playwrights at this time. Thoughtful comedy is provided by Manuel Linares Rivas, who, as in *La garra* (*The Claws*, 1914), embodies his problems in scenes of laughter; a gloomier note intrudes into the *Esclavitud* (*Slavery*, 1918) of José López Pinillos; the social conflict is dramatized seriously by Federico Oliver in *El crímen de todos* (*A Common Crime*, 1916) and *Los pistoleros* (*The Bandits*, 1931). None of these, however, is of any great individual significance: their value rests rather in their collective worth, demonstrating that after its long period of hibernation the Spanish drama once more was recapturing its pristine strength. That strength, however, obviously lies in qualities which, even in plays that seem to follow the lines of French, German, or Scandinavian realism, carry the dramatists far into other realms.

CHAPTER II

THE EXTENSION OF THE REALISTIC

IT HAS been noted above that both Gorki and Benavente—each in his own way—introduce into their plays qualities of a kind distinct from those associated with the direct naturalistic tradition and with the tradition of the drama of ideas. Indeed, we might almost aver that the worth of their writings depends basically upon their divergence from, rather than upon their imitation of, the style of theatrical composition established by Ibsen. Their works thus serve as a kind of transition from the typical *Ghosts* and *A Doll's House* to the various experiments made during the years that followed the appearance of these dramas towards the building of still newer dramatic forms.

THE POETIC REALISM OF CHEKHOV

Already in the last two decades of the nineteenth century a fresh impulse was being felt in the plays of Anton Pavlovich Chekhov, and, so far as strict chronology is concerned, there would have been every justification for dealing with his work alongside Ibsen's dramas. Although Chekhov started writing for the theatre in 1884, however, and although he himself died ere the twentieth century had passed four years of its course, the fact that his fame did not reach fruition until the production, in 1898, of *The Seagull* by the Moscow Art Theatre warrants consideration of his peculiar contributions to the stage, not among nineteenth-century, but among twentieth-century dramas. Chekhov was well ahead of his time, and the qualities of his plays find harmony rather with what men were trying to do a dozen years after Ibsen's death than with what they actually accomplished during his lifetime.

For the first years of his dramatic career Chekhov restricted himself to the one-act play form, gaining mastery of situation and of character by means of short sketches of life. His first composition was a sketch, or 'dramatic study,' entitled *Na bolshoi doroge* (*On the High Road*; written in 1884, but for a time denied theatrical representation because of the opposition of the censorship). There is no plot here, just a picture of a number of ill-assorted characters lodged temporarily in a roadside inn. There are touches of laughter, but the atmosphere in general is one of gloom. Quiet, resigned acceptance of life's despairs is the mood of *Lebedinaia pesnia* (*Swan-song*, 1889), in which an aging comic actor, left alone on the stage of a small theatre, dreams of his past life, of the visions that once were his, and of the reality before him.

This sadness, generally induced by contemplation of life's failures, is an inherent part of Chekhov's being, yet his real strength comes from his mastery of laughter. In one of his earliest sketches, *Medved* (*The Bear*, 1888), an irate young landowner calls on a neighbour lady to demand repayment of a debt: there is a violent quarrel between them, yet before the half-hour's action is over they have become engaged. Here the spirit of Musset is being transformed into Russian terms. *Predlozhenie* (*The Marriage Proposal*, 1889) shows a timorous young suitor calling on the lady of his choice and becoming so involved in an acrimonious debate concerning the ownership of some worthless land as almost to wreck his hopes—and the girl's. For *Svadba* (*The Wedding*, 1890) Chekhov takes as setting a bridal feast, and derives much merriment from the contrasting characters introduced—particularly from those of a retired naval captain who is mightily aggrieved because, snobbishly, he is being introduced to the company as a general and a nobleman, and of a self-effacing clerk who, himself wishing to have been the bridegroom, seeks to pacify his anger by pretending that after all her family is vulgar and ignorant. *Zhubilei* (*The Anniversary*, 1892) is a hilarious study of the celebrations attendant upon the fiftieth anniversary of the founding of a bank—celebrations considerably interrupted by the love-affairs of the bank manager. Laughter too predominates in *Tragik ponevole* (*A Tragedian in spite of Himself*, 1893), where the wretched husband Tolkachov, burdened with commissions imposed upon him by members of his family comfortably established in a country cottage, seeks sympathy from his friend Murashkin. After listening to the tale of woe Murashkin adds a commission of his own, and the sketch ends with poor Tolkachov madly losing his temper, attacking his friend, and crying out hysterically for blood.

An appreciation of these one-act pieces is absolutely essential for an understanding of Chekhov's full-length plays. While it is true that some of these latter works end with suicide and that all introduce an atmosphere of darkness, it would seem that a true interpretation of their spirit demands a full acceptance of the humorous qualities inherent in their being. There is nothing here of the gloomy pessimism characteristic of Hauptmann's *Before Sunrise*, nothing of the frenzied self-centredness of Strindberg's work. A deep understanding of human souls is Chekhov's prime quality, and, together with that, an ability to view life ironically. He is deeply moved as he contemplates his scenes, yet no bitterness, no fervent anger, stirs his being.

In 1887 he first tried his hand at the composition of a long play, and succeeded in turning out what must be regarded, in every respect, as a failure. *Ivanov* nowhere reveals Chekhov's genuine spirit. Unsuited to the expression of his genius is this story of a spineless man who marries a Jewess, finds his love for her depart, and falls in love with a neighbour's daughter. The wife, he knows, is dying of consumption, and in one terrible scene, when she upbraids him for his intrigue, he flings the knowledge of her close-approaching death in her face. Shortly after this she departs from life: Ivanov, though racked by conscience, plans to go ahead with a second marriage, but when the doctor declares he will publicly expose him he seeks release in suicide.

Except for the fact that Ivanov himself is akin to other characters in the later plays who fail in their adjustment to life, this drama has but little in common with Chekhov's masterpieces. It aims at creating a tragic impression, and for that his powers were eminently unsuited.

His first true triumph came with *Chaika* (*The Seagull*), unsuccessfully produced in 1896, and two years later destined to become the primal glory of the Moscow Art Theatre. *Ivanov* had been constructed more or less along traditional lines, and all stress was laid on one central figure. In *The Seagull* Chekhov abandoned the traditional formulas and set himself to depict a group rather than an individual. To narrate the plot of such a work is almost impossible, so closely intertwined are the characters with one another. Four persons in particular concern us—the successful actress Irina Arkadina, who, despite her reputation, is obsessed by fears of becoming too old for the stage; her son, Konstantin Treplev, gifted with literary powers, yet submerged by the dominant personality of his mother; Trigorin, a fashionable and successful novelist, conscious of the fact that for all his esteem his genius is not of the highest; and Nina, a young idealistic girl who dreams of a great theatrical career. These are the central figures, but even these four cannot be considered in isolation as a group, for their lives are intimately associated with, and illuminated by, other characters—Irina's good-humoured, slightly soured brother, Piotr Nikolaevich Sorin; his steward, Ilia

Shamraev; his wife, Polina Andreevna, and daughter, Masha; the doctor, Evgeni Dorn; and the schoolmaster, Semion Medvedenko. All these persons Chekhov has wrought into a harmonious whole, while apparently allowing his action to drift and even to stagnate.

This play too ends with suicide (Treplev's), but it cannot be styled a tragedy. Throughout its length, despite the many soul sorrows that are revealed by the various persons in the action, ironic laughter is rippling: it was, indeed, Chekhov's unique discovery that the spirit of high comedy could be evoked by means of effects which in the hands of another author might have led only to the tragic or the melodramatic. "Why do you always wear black?" asks Medvedenko of Masha at the very beginning of the play, but the reference to her black dress is not, as one might have thought, a symbolic introduction to a tragic theme. Her reply—"I am in mourning for my life. I am unhappy"—at once reveals to us the mood in which we are to accept the following scenes. This is serious, but somehow not tragically serious. Medvedenko is a sorry creature, and so is Masha; when, however, the two start to argue fitfully on which is the more miserable, while each, despite the fact that they are conversing, remains inwardly intent on his or her own thoughts, the mood evoked is an ironically comic one:

MEDVEDENKO: Why? [*Hesitatingly*] I don't understand. . . . You're in good health; perhaps your father isn't very rich, but he's got enough. My life's very much harder than yours. I get twenty-three roubles a month in all, and from that a deduction's made for pension, and yet I don't go about in mourning. [*They sit down.*

MASHA: It isn't a question of money. Even a beggar can be happy.

MEDVEDENKO: In theory, yes, but in practice it's like this: I, and my mother and my two sisters and my little brother—with a total income of twenty-three roubles. I suppose we must eat and drink, mustn't we? I suppose we must have some tea and sugar? And tobacco? There's the rub.

MASHA [*glancing at the platform*]: The play will begin soon.

MEDVEDENKO: Yes. Miss Zarechni will act, and the play is by Konstantin Gavrilovich. They're in love with each other, and to-day their souls will unite in the effort to present one and the same artistic image. But my soul and yours do not have any common point of contact. I love you; I'm so miserable I can't stay at home; every day I walk six versts here and six back again, and from you I get only indifference. That, of course, is to be understood. I am without means, I've a big family on my hands. . . . What inducement is there to marry a man who hasn't enough to live on?

MASHA: Nonsense. [*Takes a pinch of snuff.*] Your love touches me, but I can't return it, that's all. [*Offers him her snuff-box.*] Have some?

MEDVEDENKO: I don't want any.

The quality that is in *The Seagull* also renders this play essentially poetic. Here is life apparently depicted with an utterly naturalistic pen, and yet the impression we have in our minds is entirely imaginative. Partly this comes from the way in which unobtrusively Chekhov weaves symbol into reality, so that what in Ibsen remains something tacked on to the action is here so integrated with the outward movement that the two cannot be disentangled. Partly it comes from the sharp juxtaposition of different thoughts uttered by two or more characters as each remains involved in his own meditations: the effect occasionally is akin to the juxtaposition of images in a passage of lyrical poetry: it is as though the imaginative quality of a Hamlet soliloquy were orchestrated for a quartette; it is as though Hamlet and many Hamlets, their tongues incapable of fully expressing their thoughts, were desperately trying to make others listen, without anyone to heed them or to understand.

How difficult was the task that Chekhov had set himself is revealed in his next play, *Diadia Vania* (*Uncle Vanya*, 1899). Already in 1888 he had tried his hand at dealing with the theme here presented, in his *Leshii* (*The Wood Demon*). The character of Professor Serebriakov is common to both plays, and Uncle Vanya appears in the former as Uncle George, killing himself at the end of the third act. There is, however, in *The Wood Demon* a jangling of notes, a lack of a central tune, and it is easy to see why Chekhov himself was dissatisfied with it. Even in the rewriting, or rather re-creation, *Uncle Vanya* may be regarded as less powerful than *The Seagull*.

The central figure here is the retired and widowed Professor Serebriakov, who lives on his small estate with his daughter, Sofia, and his brother-in-law, Ivan Petrovich Voinitski, known as Uncle Vanya. Into this circle the Professor brings a young wife, a woman of twenty-seven, Elena Andreievna. With her Vanya falls in love, and at the same time the man whom Sofia loves, Dr Astrov, is also attracted by her. Serebriakov is a pompous, fussy egoist; Vanya is a man who has sacrificed everything for his dead sister's estate, which he manages; Sofia is a woman, unattractive, to whom the joys of life have been denied; Astrov is a strange mixture of the cynic and the idealist, a drunkard who yet has a great vision of afforestation designed to change Russia's climate and better her peoples; Elena is a woman who, after marrying the Professor, discovers that she does not love him and yet is resolved to remain faithful to him. When Vanya learns that Serebriakov intends to sell the estate to which he himself has given his whole life he tries, unsuccessfully, to shoot him, and in the last act we are back, as it were, at the beginning. Vanya and Sofia are left alone; the vision that was Elena has gone; for Vanya there may be release in carrying on the work that no longer gives him satisfaction, for Sofia there is hope only of happiness in a life other than this:

> We shall go on living, Uncle Vanya. We shall live on through a great, great line of days, of long evenings; we shall patiently endure the trials our fate brings us; we shall toil for others, now and when we are old, without rest; and when our time comes we shall die submissively, and there beyond the grave we shall say that we have suffered, that we have wept, that our lives were bitter, and God will take pity upon us, and I and you, uncle, dear uncle, shall see a life that is luminous, beautiful, splendid. . . . In your life you have not known any joy, but wait, Uncle Vanya, wait. . . . We shall have rest.

After this exploration of the human soul Chekhov had acquired sufficient power to create his two outstanding final dramas—*Tri sestri* (*The Three Sisters*, 1901) and *Vishnevii sad* (*The Cherry Orchard*, 1904). Here the plots are even less firm and at the same time, paradoxically, more complex. All that *The Three Sisters* has to tell is the story of Olga, Masha, and Irina, three sisters living in a small provincial town and ever dreaming of escaping to the joys of Moscow life. In the action of the play we see nothing more than the slow, gradual fracturing of these dreams. What is remarkable in this play is the quality—still more marked in *The Cherry Orchard* —of a strange mood born out of nostalgia for the lovely things of life that are passing and of some dim hope of future happiness. Men and women are at odds here, with one another, with themselves, with their circumstances. Colonel Vershinin, whose own life is a failure, considers the problems of existence: "Well, I don't know," he says:

> It seems to me that everything on this earth must change little by little, that it's actually changing as we look at it. In two hundred years, three hundred, maybe a thousand years—how long doesn't matter— a new, happy life will arise. We shan't be able to share in that life, of course, but we are living for it now, we're working for it, yes, suffering for it: we are creating it—and in this one effort is the reason for our existence and, if you like, our happiness.

And, as if in comment, comes the stage-direction—"Masha laughs softly." "What is it?" she is asked. "I don't know," she replies.

"I've been laughing all day." The close of the play is in keeping with this tone.

Finally comes *The Cherry Orchard*, in which Chekhov finds complete mastery of his medium. The last scene shows the old Firs left alone in a dark and shuttered house, there presumably to die: throughout the course of the action a sad, nostalgic sorrow prevails for the beautiful things that are being sacrificed. "My dear, my tender, beautiful orchard!" sighs Lubov as she leaves. "My life, my youth, my happiness, good-bye! . . . Good-bye!" But before that the student has been speaking to Anya:

> All Russia is our orchard. The land is great and beautiful, there are many wondrous places in it. [*A pause.*] Think, Anya: your grand-father, your great-grandfather and all your ancestors were owners of serfs, holders of living souls—and can you fail to see something human looking at you from every cherry in the orchard, from every leaf, from every stem? Don't you hear voices there? . . . Oh, your orchard is fearsome and frightening; and when in the evening or at night you walk through it, then the old bark on the trees glows dimly and the old cherry-trees seem to be dreaming of all that was a hundred, two hundred years ago, and their visions weigh them down. Well, then, we have remained for at least two hundred years, it means nothing to us, we don't realize our relationship to the past—we can only philosophize, complain of boredom or drink vodka. And yet it's so clear: in order to begin to live in the present we must first pay for the past, make our peace with the past, and that payment can be made only through suffering, through extraordinary, uninterrupted toil. . . . I feel that happiness is coming, Anya, I see it already.

Not that such a speech by Trofimov makes *The Cherry Orchard* into a thesis play. There is nothing intellectual and rational here: all is imaginative and emotional. As the characters are seated outside by the bank of a river, "suddenly a distant sound is heard as from the sky, the sound of a breaking harp string, sadly dying away." "What's that?" asks Lubov, the graciously useless owner of the orchard. "I don't know," replies the wealthy peasant Lopakhin. "A bucket's fallen down a shaft somewhere far off. It's certainly far off." "Or perhaps it's some bird . . . like a heron," hazards the drifting intellectual Gaev. "Or an owl," adds Trofimov satirically. Lubov shudders: "It's unpleasant, somehow," she remarks, and there is a pause. Then the old Firs speaks, he who had been a slave in the days before the emancipation of the serfs: "Before the mis-fortune the same thing happened. An owl screamed and the samovar simmered without stopping." "Before what misfortune?"

Gaev asks, and the old man's answer comes from the depth of memory—"Before the Emancipation."

In this drama, where tears are blended with laughter, hope with despair, Chekhov carries to the farthest limit his peculiar power of suggesting the inner loneliness of his characters. Each one speaks for himself, and there is no one to listen. The talk drifts on, thoughts welling up from within the breasts of these waifs, tossed on the air and vanishing like bubbles. We know these people as we do not know even the strongly delineated types created by Ibsen, for Chekhov's art is a poetic art where implications and associative values fire the creative process in our own minds.

It has taken many years for Chekhov's peculiar artistry to win general acceptance, but that acceptance has now come, and the success which has attended the many productions of his dramas during recent years seems to indicate that he possesses that almost indefinable quality which alone can win universal and enduring life in the theatre. His world is in truth far farther removed from that of London and New York than the provincial-city flavour set as a background to most of Ibsen's plays, and one might well have thought that things so strange could never have been successful outside of Russia. The fact is, however, that, whenever produced, *The Cherry Orchard* and *The Seagull* have demonstrated their power of making a direct appeal in spite of the strangeness of their atmosphere: by some magic, the precise operation of which baffles our intelligence, Chekhov has been able to invest the particular with universal attributes, so that even when his delicately poised dialogue suffers inevitable coarsening in being transformed into another tongue the play of his creative imagination still casts a warm glow over his characters. Although his dramatic work falls quantitatively far below that of Ibsen, of Strindberg or of Hauptmann, perhaps future historians of the theatre, surveying the fortunes of the stage at the turn of the century, may decide that so far as quality is concerned no other author can vie with him: his subtlety is supreme.

THE IRISH SCHOOL

Chekhov wrote his plays in prose, yet in speaking of his writings the epithet 'poetic' constantly comes to our lips. His imaginative process succeeds in transforming the real into the ideal, the particular into the universal. A somewhat similar process was at work during those years in another centre from which hitherto little of dramatic value had come.

It is true that Ireland had made many contributions to the English stage. Numerous dramatic authors whose plays were produced in the London theatres from the beginning of the eighteenth century onward were Irishmen who had settled in England: scores of Irishmen won success as actors during these centuries. For the most part, however, neither playwrights nor actors had anything peculiarly their own, with a national flavour, to give to the stage. We may discern, in both, elements of characteristic Irish humour, but it is clothed in an English dress. Only in the time of Dion Boucicault was there any exploiting of Irish themes and dialect, and even then little more than an external veneer was given to melodramatic situations that might have emanated from almost any land or time.

Occasionally original dramas appeared from the pens of Irish authors on the Dublin boards: some have historical interest and a few exhibit intrinsically interesting scenes, but none break away from the basic patterns derived from outside. These earlier Irish comedies are framed on the current moulds of English comedy; Irish melodramas have precisely the same sensational episodes and the same stereotyped figures as may be found associated with *milieux* of an entirely different kind.

When, in 1899, a small band of enthusiasts set up the Irish Literary Theatre something entirely new was in process of being born. Aided by the munificent patronage of Miss Horniman, they were able to establish themselves, barely three years later, in the famous Abbey playhouse, with the poet W. B. Yeats and the versatile Lady Gregory as their leaders. Yeats' entire spirit was, of course, devoted to the purely poetic, but in his protégé, John Millington Synge, appeared a writer, destined to be of great influence both in Ireland and abroad, who made a contribution to the stage by no means dissimilar to that of the Russian Chekhov. In the writings of the two men, far removed from each other in space, strength came through the exploitation of ways of life distinct from those to be found in the larger centres of Western Europe and through the transmutation of the real world around them into something rich in imaginative quality.

It was in 1897 that Yeats, finding Synge wasting his talents in the Bohemian circles of Paris, persuaded him to return to his native country and, in particular, to dwell for a space in the most isolated areas of that land. The life of the Aran islanders entered into his very being: their speech made music in his ears; their simplicity brought to him a deep sense of essential human emotion. As strange to a citizen of London, of Paris, or of Berlin was this primitive existence as the world out of which Chekhov evoked his tragic comedies, and Synge, gifted with something of the Russian dramatist's power, succeeded similarly in so dealing with his material as to make it of appeal and interest to those utterly ignorant of its customs and essentially alien to its spirit. In his own way Synge pursued Chekhov's path—he remained, of course, wholly without knowledge of the Russian's dramatic work—in extending the confines of the realistic, although his steps led him into more diversified territory, where the starkly tragic exists alongside the comic.

His first two theatrical essays, produced in 1903 and in 1904 respectively, were a cynically kindly little folk-sketch, *In the Shadow of the Glen*, and the short tragic essay, unrelieved in its tension, *Riders to the Sea*. The former is to be associated with *The Well of the Saints* (1905) and *The Playboy of the Western World* (1907); the latter, although realistically dealing with contemporaries, has affinities in spirit with the uncompleted legendary drama, *Deirdre of the Sorrows* (1910). In none of these plays, serious or humorous, does Synge deal, even by implication, with the social-political themes so beloved by the stage of the first years of our century. In Holland Ibsen's follower Heijermans can take the tragedies of fisher-folk and make of their story an indictment of the grasping capitalist: Synge's *Riders to the Sea* confines itself entirely to the relations of men with the nature around them. So far as spirit is concerned, for Synge Ibsen and his companions might never have been: although his dramas could not have taken such shape as they did had it not been for the development of a realistic theatrical technique during the latter years of the nineteenth century, the atmosphere he evokes is strangely unlike anything to be found elsewhere, unless perhaps it be in Chekhov's writings—and even there the changing social-economic conditions operative at this time were scenically introduced either directly or indirectly. Synge has no character in any of his plays corresponding to the Lopakhin of *The Cherry Orchard*: no hint of life altering under the impact of industrialism intrudes into his episodes.

Riders to the Sea and *Deirdre of the Sorrows* unite in demonstrating what formed a great measure of Synge's strength. He realized to the full that if the dramatist could produce nothing but pale and pallid words his writings would possess only ephemeral worth, and he early set himself to master a prose style that had within it the richer cadences we associate with the poet while at the same time retaining ties with the common speech of men. In this task he was materially aided by the subject-matter with which he had chosen to deal. In Ireland, among the western peasantry, he could listen to a language which, because it remained close to the soil, because it was enriching itself by borrowings of phrase and rhythm from the neighbouring Erse, provided a basis far stronger and far more flexible than anything that might be heard in England. The result was that he found himself in a peculiarly fortunate position and was enabled to develop a style of dramatic dialogue at once realistic and poetic—uniquely his own, yet gaining strength from the fact that it was not merely the invented form of utterance devised by a single individual.

Without such a dialogue medium as Synge evolved, *Riders to the Sea* would be of little worth: expressed in bare naturalistic tones it could arouse in us no vital response. As it is, the atmosphere evoked here comes close to the true spirit of the tragic. The haunting cadences of the prose speech not only harmonize with the theme, but are inseparable from that theme:

CATHLEEN [*begins to keen*]: It's destroyed we are from this day. It's destroyed, surely.

NORA: Didn't the young priest say the Almighty God wouldn't leave her destitute with no son living?

MAURYA [*in a low voice, but clearly*]: It's little the like of him knows of the sea. . . . Bartley will be lost now, and let you call in Eamon and make me a good coffin out of the white boards, for I won't live after them. I've had a husband, and a husband's father, and six sons in this house—six fine men, though it was a hard birth I had with every one of them and they coming into the world—and some of them were found and some of them were not found, but they're gone now the lot of them. . . . There were Stephen and Shawn were lost in the great wind, and found after in the Bay of Gregory of the Golden Mouth, and carried up the two of them on one plank, and in by that door.

There is exquisite music here, a music that works upon our senses and charms us into viewing the dark disaster that has fallen on Maurya's little household not with the dark despair which alone the naturalistic playwrights know how to evoke, but with deeper vision.

Riders to the Sea is one of the best-known of all short plays; not so well known is the longer tragedy *Deirdre of the Sorrows*, although Synge's drama of the love of the fair Deirdre, betrothed to King Conchubor, but intoxicated by the passion in her heart for Naisi, is a true masterpiece of the romantic theatre. In itself it combines the best qualities of two worlds: there is about it the twilight spirit of Celtic myth combined with the more flaming emotions of the earlier romantic movement, and at the same time the handling of the characters has a firmness demonstrating Synge's determined grip upon reality: its language is both beautiful and taut.

While Synge thus won success in the sphere of the tragic, perhaps his spirit found most fitting opportunity for expression in the realm of comedy—a peculiar realm of his own invention where cynicism meets and harmonizes with sympathy. *In the Shadow of the Glen* takes us to a small cottage in the west where a young wife, Nora, her heart full of visions that carry her far from her home, discovers a certain satisfaction when her husband decides to lie down in his bed and die. To her comes the Tramp, a rascally fellow whom she invests with the robes of her fancy, seeing in him a symbol of all the fun and adventure she has missed in her life. Pleasantly they chat and make plans, when a sudden sneeze from the 'corpse' reveals that the good husband has been merely pretending illness. All irate, he drives Nora from his house, and we are left to imagine her trudging down the road to meet her Tramp at the foot of the hill. A kindred atmosphere enwraps *The Well of the Saints*, wherein a couple of aged blind beggars, husband and wife, come to a well blessed by a saint, the waters of which have the power of giving sight to the sightless. Their eyes are opened, and each gazes with horror and dismay at the lined and ugly countenance of the other: in anger, they come to blows. Once more the blindness returns, and the good saint, pitying them, proposes to repeat the miracle; now, however, the thought of being able to see brings them nothing save fear, and the husband desperately dashes the charmed water to the ground. He prefers to go through the world with his illusory visions rather than have the advantages of sight accompanied by spiritual despair.

The mood of these two short plays is intimately associated with that of *The Playboy of the Western World*, with its delightfully cynical and humorous plot, telling how Christy Mahon, a weak and worthless fellow, becomes a hero among those who have heard that he has had the daring to kill his own father. Pegeen Flaherty decides that her loutish fiancé, Shawn, is but a block in comparison with this mighty man; Shawn is thrown off even although her father tries desperately to speed up her marriage to him:

CHRISTY: And you'll be wedding them this day, is it?

MICHAEL [*drawing himself up*]: Aye. Are you thinking, if I'm drunk itself, I'd leave my daughter living single with a little frisky rascal is the like of you?

PEGEEN [*breaking away from* SHAWN]: Is it the truth the dispensation's come?

MICHAEL [*triumphantly*]: Father Reilly's after reading it in gallous Latin, and "It's come in the nick of time," says he; "so I'll wed them in a hurry, dreading that young gaffer who'd capsize the stars."

PEGEEN [*fiercely*]: He's missed his nick of time, for it's that lad, Christy Mahon, that I'm wedding now.

MICHAEL [*loudly with horror*]: You'd be making him a son to me, and he wet and crusted with his father's blood?

PEGEEN: Aye. Wouldn't it be a bitter thing for a girl to go marrying the like of Shaneen, and he a middling kind of a scarecrow, with no savagery or fine words in him at all.

MICHAEL [*gasping and sinking on a chair*]: Oh, aren't you a heathen daughter to go shaking the fat of my heart, and I swamped and drownded with the weight of drink? Would you have them turning on me the way that I'd be roaring to the dawn of day with the wind upon my heart? Have you not a word to aid me, Shaneen? Are you not jealous at all?

SHAWN [*in great misery*]: I'd be afeard to be jealous of a man did slay his da.

PEGEEN: Well, it'd be a poor thing to go marrying your like. I'm seeing there's a world of peril for an orphan girl, and isn't it a great blessing I didn't wed you before himself came walking from the west or south?

SHAWN: It's a queer story you'd go picking a dirty tramp up from the highways of the world.

PEGEEN [*playfully*]: And you think you're a likely beau to go straying along with, the shiny Sundays of the opening year, when it's sooner on a bullock's liver you'd put a poor girl thinking than on the lily or the rose?

SHAWN: And have you no mind of my weight of passion and the holy dispensation, and the drift of heifers I am giving, and the golden ring?

PEGEEN: I'm thinking you're too fine for the like of me, Shawn Keogh of Killakeen, and let you go off till you'd find a radiant lady with droves of bullocks on the plains of Meath, and herself bedizened in the diamond jewelleries of Pharaoh's ma. That'd be your match, Shaneen. So God save you now!

Of course, the supposedly dead father turns up; of course, Christy is shamed, and, when he tries to rehabilitate himself by attacking the old man again, the entire village, which had been charmed by the vision of heroism afar off, is horrified. By twists and turns of the humorously comic imagination and by the enriching of his scenes with his treasury of language Synge has created here one of the finest plays that the twentieth century has to offer.

Once more we encounter, in the fortunes of the Irish theatre at this time, the same phenomenon already observed in other lands. The awakening of dramatic impulse is by no means restricted to the work of one man. Although up to these years there had been no school of Dublin playwriting, Synge does not stand alone: a whole group of writers for the stage are his companions. Yeats' writings fall almost wholly within the sphere of the romantically poetic, but close to Synge's humorous spirit is the mood with which Lady Gregory gives colour to many of her short plays. Like him she is closely in touch with the simple folk whom she introduces into her scenes; like him she allows her fancy to give deeper quality to the world of actuality. Again and again she exploits the situation out of which grew *The Playboy of the Western World*—the contrast between the real and what men think is the real. In *Hyacinth Halvey* (1906) a young man struggles in vain against the common belief that he is an image of virtue; in *Spreading the News* (1904) opinion, based on gossip, has a greater power than truth; in *The Jackdaw* (1907) an entire village community is cast into disorder because its men and women come to believe a wholly impossible tale about an easy way of making money. A basically similar contrast provides the pattern for *The Workhouse Ward* (1908), where the kindly efforts of a niece to take her uncle out of the workhouse (an eminently sensible idea) are thwarted by the old man's desire to remain—because in the workhouse there is a crony-enemy of his with whom he has had a lifelong quarrel. Such a concept is carried even farther in *The Image* (1909), which, through a plot telling how a group of villagers lose a couple of whales that have been cast up on the sands because of their interminable debates as to what to do with the oil, deliberately exploits the belief that in the heart of every man there is an ideal, an image, constantly at odds with reality.

We cannot claim Lady Gregory to be a great dramatist, although we must accept her plays as charmingly delightful sketches of life and as indicative in their style of fundamental qualities informing much of the work of her companions. Yeats' early *The Pot of Broth* (1902) was built on the same pattern, narrating how two beggars succeed in convincing a number of peasants that the boiling of a certain stone in the pot will produce a nice thick steaming soup. With more bitter emphasis Edward Martyn selected the contrast between the real and the ideal as the foundation for his tragic *The Heather Field* (1899). Here a landowner, Carden Tyrrell, is dominated by one consuming desire—to make a great waste of heathery moor into fertile fields; into this effort he throws all his money and sinks into debt; even when at the end, a broken man, he dreams that the ideal has been translated into reality he finds the vision shattered. The heather, he thinks, has been conquered, and, lying ill in his house, he lets his mind dwell fondly on what he has accomplished, when, ironically, his little son runs in, flushed and happy, with a bunch of heather he has gathered from the fields. Without a doubt in this drama Martyn is more deeply influenced than Synge or Lady Gregory by the Ibsen style of realistic play, yet the spirit that informs it is typically Irish. The close contact with nature, the flavour of poetic conception, the symbolic connotations are its own. These qualities are even more marked in *Maeve* (1900), where a woman, Maeve O'Heynes, is summoned from the world of actuality into a vision-world, where reigns Queen Maeve, the fairy of the moors and mistress of all things lovely. Maybe the essential difference between Ibsen and such a writer as Martyn is revealed most clearly by a comparison between *The Lady from the Sea* and *An Enchanted Sea* (1902): Ellida is caught merely by a fancy; the kin of Guy Font is of the realm of fairies and the mermen.

Slightly later than Martyn came Lennox Robinson, whose *The Clancy Name* appeared in 1908. A young man, John Clancy, has killed another in a fit of passion: his mother, intent on keeping unstained the family name, tries to prevent him from confessing, but his conscience is so moved that he determines to give himself up, when by chance he is given the opportunity of saving, at the cost of his own life, a child from a runaway horse. He himself dies a hero, and the name of the Clancys is saved. A peculiar cynicism detracts from the value of this drama. Happily, however, Robinson soon evolved a dramatic concept of greater worth. In *The Dreamers* (1915) he essayed, not very successfully, the sphere of the political-historical play, and in *The Patriots* (1912) he had already presented a bitter portrait of an aging revolutionary who, newly released from prison and expecting to be greeted with enthusiasm by his fellow-patriots, is met with indifference and cold neglect. Out of the spirit of these two comes *The Lost Leader* (1918), a clever exercise in dramatic suspense. For years popular belief credited the story that the unfortunate Irish leader Parnell was not dead, but living under an assumed name somewhere in Ireland. In a decayed old innkeeper, Lucius Lenihan, Parnell's features are discovered, and adroitly Robinson keeps us guessing: there are many arguments which seem to prove that he is no other than merely Lucius Lenihan, yet other evidence seems to prove that he is Parnell. Just as final demonstration is about to be made the old man is accidentally killed, and the curtain falls on a question. While this work perhaps has no great depth of character-drawing, its dramatic skill is subtle and assured.

This dramatic skill has enabled Robinson to produce in *The Whiteheaded Boy* (1916) a delightful comedy, almost worthy of comparison with Synge's masterpiece. The central figure here is Denis Geoghan, a light-hearted youth for whom every sacrifice is made by his family. With sparkling humour and pleasantly cynical laughter Robinson traces his adventures until in the end, when all his relatives have been forced to make contributions towards a sum designed to repay John Duffy for the youth's trifling with the affections of his daughter, it is gaily revealed that Denis and she are in reality married: the money goes to the pair as a wedding present, and the merry of heart are suitably rewarded. A companion picture appears in *The Far-off Hills* (1928), still another study of dream and reality.

With these writers may be noted, too, the author of *Maurice Harte* (1912), T. C. Murray. Although, like most Irish dramatists, Murray cannot keep the lilt of poetic utterance completely banished from his stage, the strength of this drama lies in its unflinching display of the thwarted ambitions and useless strivings so common amid the drudgery of ordinary life. The same quality animates *Birthright* (1910) and, richer and more mature, gives to *Autumn Fire* (1924) its peculiar atmosphere of intensity.

Yet another playwright of this school who succeeded in combining diverse qualities in his work is Padraic Colum, a man who, while by no means an important author, has succeeded in *The Fiddler's House* (1907; a revised version of *The Broken Soil*, 1903) in giving his drunken Conn Hourican a certain distinction; in *The Land* (1905) he essays a more realistic study, and by dwelling on the contrast between the call of the city and the ancient appeal of the soil introduces a social note unheard in Synge and his companions; in *Thomas Muskerry* (1910) he descends still farther towards the level of the naturalistic, writing a play which, except for the character of the old piper Myles Gorman, might have been penned by an uninspired Hauptmann. Colum is by way of being a poet, but he differentiates himself from his companions by keeping his whimsy for children's books, by holding his poetic imagination apart from his study of life, and by proving over-serious in his professional patriotism. It is characteristic that he departed from the Abbey Theatre on account of *The Playboy of the Western World* and that the call of another civilization took him to America in 1914. In his work there are already signs of the disintegration of that fertile movement of which Yeats and Synge were the literary leaders.

BARRIE AND SCOTS SENTIMENTALISM

From Scotland hailed an author once spoken of in terms of rapturous praise, now almost completely under a mist of neglect. To assess correctly the position of Sir James M. Barrie assuredly is a difficult task: it is very easy to dismiss him as a mere sentimentalist without worth; it is as easy to allow his charm to persuade us into believing him an author far greater than he actually was. Perhaps a middle course is best, whereby we recognize qualities in his nature which (however admirable in him as a man) will prevent his finding an enduring place on the stage, while at the same time we give due acclaim both to his dramatic skill and to his ability in extending the field of the realistic theatre.

Of his large dramatic output much may be completely neglected; on the other hand, even when this is done, there remain sufficient plays of genuine interest to merit individual attention. *Peter Pan* (1904) may be merely a children's piece, but *The Admirable Crichton* (1902), *Dear Brutus* (1917), and *What Every Woman Knows* (1908) are plays of which no dramatist need have been ashamed. The first adroitly deals with society's conventions. In Lord Loam's household is an ideal butler, Crichton, polite, imperturbable, deferential. With his master and some others of the family this paragon of servants is shipwrecked on a desert island; through his ingenuity and adaptability to circumstances he becomes lord of the altered society imposed on the group by the power of nature. A rescue ship arrives, and the last act carries us back to Lord Loam's domain, with Crichton once more the model domestic. Outwardly the play is simply a charming whimsy; beneath it has all the characteristics of Barrie's philosophy. His mind was essentially childlike, and this story is one such as a child would love and appreciate. He has an observant eye, and he can well pierce beneath the butler's dark uniform to the man below; at the same time what he sees does not set him mounting soap-boxes and attacking the aristocracy. He recognizes that Lord Loam's position is founded wholly on convention, yet such convention he is perfectly willing to accept. In all his outlook on the world there is a kind of sadly resigned humour, an almost pathetic willingness to be content, and a smiling tolerance of pretension.

What Every Woman Knows reminds us that Barrie's entire temperament was feminine rather than masculine. It is on his heroine, Maggie Shand, that he lavishes all his affectionate attention here. John Shand is a capable enough man in the rough-and-tumble of political life, but in his immediate relations with others he is a bit of a fool, and it is only through Maggie's astutely discreet guidance that he is prevented from revealing this folly to the world. Through her he rises up the political ladder; through her he escapes ruining himself by having an *affaire* with an aristocratic charmer. Barrie never saw his women as objects of passion: the motherly invariably loomed more significant in his vision than the qualities of the mistress.

In *Dear Brutus* his philosophy of life is most completely revealed. Taking his cue from some famous lines in *Julius Cæsar*, he evolves a poetic-realistic plot in which the central figure is Mr Lob, who is Puck, middle-aged and in modern dress. Mr Lob is host of a week-end party, and all his guests have one thing in common: each is dissatisfied with his lot and deems that, if only he could be granted a second chance, greater things by far might be attained. They are granted their common wish. On midsummer eve they enter an enchanted wood—and find that, released from reality, they remain themselves. It is not in our stars, declares Barrie, but in ourselves that our faults lie. Purdie, who has thought himself unhappily married and who has been indulging in an *affaire* with Mabel, is now married to the latter, with his real wife as the object of his attentions. The butler Matey, who had proclaimed that his dishonesty was merely the result of poverty, is just as dishonest now that he has become a rich capitalist. So it is for all of them, and, as the charm is dissipated, each returns dazed and a trifle chagrined to the world of reality.

The sheer skill with which Barrie has dealt with his material in these three plays demonstrates the quality of his craftsmanship, and his success in putting before us characters so intimately studied proves how penetrating was his vision. These comedies have nothing to say to us about the iniquities of the social world; in such iniquities Barrie was not interested, since he disbelieved in the thesis that man is made by his surroundings. In a civilization highly conscious of economic conditions and dominated by behaviouristic psychology his is a lonely figure, yet no other dramatist of his time was more adroit than he, no other fixed his gaze so intimately upon the vagaries of human nature viewed, not at moments of tempestuous passion, but by the light of the desert island's camp-fire, the gentle glow of the parlour fire, or the moonlight of the enchanted forest.

Barrie has not had many followers, although one other author, Alan Alexander Milne, has essayed the same sentimentally whimsical path. Typical of his work are *Mr Pim Passes By* (1919), *The Truth about Blayds* (1921), and *The Dover Road* (1922). The first deals, in charmingly comic terms, with the flutter in George Marden's family circle when a Mr Pim casually declares that Mrs Marden's former husband (long since presumed dead) is still alive; in the second, a ninety-year-old Oliver Blayds, for years revered by his family as the solitary remaining major poet of Victorian days, announces that all his fame was based on poems stolen from a deceased friend; while in *The Dover Road* appears a Mr Latimer, not unlike Barrie's Mr Lob, who takes a house on the Dover road where he welcomes lovers posting towards France, hoping that by throwing them together for a time they may consider whether indeed they are being wise in abandoning their marriage ties. There is charm here rather than strength.

THE TEATRO GROTTESCO: THE PREDECESSORS OF PIRANDELLO

In all these playwrights from Chekhov to Barrie there is one common theme: each in his own way is intent upon the conflict between reality and the dream. The three sisters live in a world dominated by their thoughts of going to Moscow; Madame Ranevski dwells in the realm of the idealized cherry orchard; Christy Mahon becomes a hero of illusion; Mr Lob puckishly pierces the dreams of his guests. In all of these there is emphasis on the distinction between what a man is in reality, what he thinks he is, and what others think of him. From this mood easily arises a fundamental question: what, we ask, is reality?

It was through the dramatic exploitation of this query that Pirandello made his international reputation; nor was it surprising that an Italian dramatist should have been the man to discover the full potentialities of this theme. As has been already observed, the Italian temperament was basically antagonistic towards dramatic realism. In the theatres of Rome and Florence and Milan the stage is characteristically the home of the theatrical: we need not wonder that the opera, with its frank artificiality, found its true home in the peninsula or that the spirit of the *commedia dell' arte* has ever haunted its stage. As a result, the endeavours on the part of Italian playwrights to emulate the styles of Ibsen or of Hauptmann were almost all either half-hearted or expressive of a desire essentially alien to the demands of their audiences.

Throughout, opposition was evident to the realistic trend, opposition that sometimes took the form of a revival of poetic romanticism, sometimes veered off in the direction of more original forms. Already, in 1909, 'Futurism' was born, and by 1915 Filippo Tommaso Marinetti had established his 'synthetic' drama. Besides this, however, was another movement not heralded by any glowing manifesto, that was to prove more harmoniously associated with the Italian spirit.

In various Italian cities, notably Venice, Milan, Florence, Naples, and Bologna, and in the island of Sicily, the long-established native dialect theatres were beginning to display a new lease of life. Venice's lively and delicate civic comedy had been largely dormant since the time of Goldoni: now it started to display a fresh vigour, and in Giacinto Gallina produced a playwright of more than common talent. With his *Una famegia in rovina* (*A Family in Ruin*, 1872), *Barufe in famegia* (*Family Quarrels*, 1872), *La chitara del papà* (*Father's Guitar*, 1875), *Così va il mondo, bimba mia* (*The Way of the World, My Child*, 1880), *Amor in paruca* (*Love in a Wig*, 1880), and *La base de tuto* (*The Root of Everything*, 1894) he exhibited a keen theatrical sense and a unique depth of perception. The plot of *Barufe in famegia* is based on Goldoni's *La famiglia dell' antiquario*, and breathes the very spirit of that eighteenth-century master. With wit and a true understanding of stage requirements Gallina gaily carries us from scene to scene in which gossip and misconception set the fact in conflict with fiction. A quarrel between the young Toni and Orsolina is fanned to a flame by the chatterings of the maidservant Bettina until these characters, Momolo, the father, Emilia, his wife, and Rosa, his mother, are all involved in violent confusion. *La chitara del papà* almost reminds us of Goldoni's *Il ventaglio* because of the device by which the author has bound his plot together by the use of an inanimate object—here a guitar instead of a fan. Similarly derived from a Goldoni comedy, *Amor in paruca* merely tells how Giulia puts tests upon her lover Andrea to see how far he truly loves her. Tiring of this series of adventures and beginning to guess what is afoot, the latter engages in a counter-stratagem when Giulia writes to tell him that through an illness all her hair has come out. He himself puts on a bald-pated wig and calls on her. Before seeing his head, with pretended tears she offers to release him from his promise of marriage: he accepts the offer, and when she flies into a fury, believing that at last she has discovered his perfidy, he sadly declares that he has done so only because he has gone bald. Thereupon she shows him that her story about her own hair was merely a trick and assures him that, despite the loss of his, she loves him sincerely. By removing his wig Andrea ends both the comedy and his series of tests. A different note, however, enters into *Così va il mondo, bimba mia*, where the story is told, sympathetically yet with a certain bitterness, of a child's emotions when she finds her widowed mother about to take a second husband. Even more bitter, and showing awareness of changing social conditions, is the comedy-drama *La base de tutto*. Vidal is a noble-minded father whose morals are based on ancient traditions, but his son, Alviso, has the standards of a new age. The latter seduces a girl, Cecilia, whom he marries off to an unsavoury Carlo Scamoffietoli, and is quite content to consider the affair settled by payment of some money. Old Vidal is scandalized, and finds it hard to realize that gold, in this new age, has become "the root of everything." Gallina's genius is perhaps not outstanding, but in these and other plays he has shown ability to give fresh life to the Venetian dialect theatre, and has hinted, at least, at the fundamental cleavage between appearance and reality, between fact and belief.

For the Florentine stage, much the same was being done by Augusto Novelli, among whose many plays one, *L'acqua cheta* (*Still Waters*, 1908), stands out as the finest. Against a background of Florentine life a family picture is presented, with two girls each in love with a young man. One of the lovers is a sincere, honest fellow who, because he is a socialist, finds little favour from the girl's father; the other is a seemingly good match, although in reality all he wants is to get the second daughter into his clutches. The young socialist, of course, proves hero in the end and succeeds both in gaining his own happiness and in rescuing his sister-in-law from the hands of a would-be seducer. In similar wise Aniello Costagliola devoted his attention to the re-creating of a Neapolitan dialect theatre.

Still more important was the development of native Sicilian drama as a direct result of the enthusiasm of Nino Martoglio, who in 1903 realized his dream of setting up a dialect repertory troupe. Here, in place of Venetian gaiety and Florentine seriousness of purpose, theatrical sensationalism found freest scope, although a characteristic kind of comedy too found expression on its stage. Typical of the latter is Martoglio's own *L'aria del continente* (*The Metropolitan Spirit*, 1915), in which a Sicilian Don Cola Dosciu, after having been forced to spend some months in Rome, returns to his native village the complete 'continental' and starts to reform the habits of his neighbours. In this attempt he puts himself thoroughly to shame, and the final scene shows him angrily reverting to the ways of life that he had so lately been treating with scorn.

Already in the last decades of the nineteenth century the Sicilian 'Renaissance' was in the making. Giovanni Verga's *Cavalleria rusticana* had appeared in 1884, and Luigi Capuana, besides making many contributions to native prose fiction and to the stage, had led a crusade for the encouragement of dialect drama, declaring that, while some might argue that broad social movements were the most significant characteristics of the time, more important were the vast psychological and spiritual gulfs existing not only between the peoples of different countries, but also between the inhabitants of regional areas within Italy itself. For the most part Capuana himself keeps to the brutally sensational side of Sicilian existence, where consuming passions are permitted full scope. A wife is murdered by an injured husband in one of his plays; in another the plot tells of the murder of a woman possessed by an evil spirit. It is the flame of strange passion that inspires this author rather than the irony of life.

The influence of these Sicilian dramatists upon Pirandello was direct and strong: at the same time he received inspiration and suggestions from other playwrights who stood outside the dialect theatre movement. One of these is the Neapolitan Salvatore di Giacomo, who exhibits, albeit in lurid flashes, a certain quality of power. Such dramas as *A San Francisco* (*To San Francisco*, 1896), with its ghastly tale of horror and passion, and *Assunta Spina* (1910), with its powerfully drawn portrait of a woman led by her instincts to betray two men, have a vigour of their own and an individual style. Similar individuality of style is obvious in the work of Sem Benelli, an author who, despite the fact that he displays clearly enough the romantic-poetic influence of D'Annunzio, must be definitely taken into account in any consideration of the antecedents of Pirandello. Without doubt the taffetaed *La cena delle beffe* (*The Jest*, 1909) could not have been penned had D'Annunzio not shown the way, yet here and in others of Benelli's dramas are introduced characters who adumbrate the persons who move on the Pirandello stage. The contrast between the vision and reality was suggested in Benelli's early prose-play *La tignola* (*The Bookworm*, 1908), in which a young librarian dreams of abandoning the world of books and living dangerously: the dream realized, the uninspiring desk, where there is at least security, claims its errant wanderer again. In the very title of *La maschera di Bruto* (*The Mask of Brutus*,

1908) the mood of Pirandello's theatre-world is suggested, and
something more of that mood appears in *L'amore dei tre re* (*The Love
of Three Kings*; printed 1915).

Throughout these and other dramatic essays produced in Italy
during these years hints of the style later to be given the title of
'grottesco' may be discerned—sometimes merely faint wisps, sometimes, as in Niccodemi's *Acidalia* (1919), decisively moving from the
ordinary realism popularized by Ibsen into an entirely new world.
This 'Teatro del grottesco,' however, was not formally established
as a separate form until Luigi Chiarelli came forward in 1916 with
La maschera e il volto (*The Mask and the Face*), a brilliantly clever
extravaganza of human follies. Taking as his central figure a man
who professes to live by the ancient code of honour, the author
shows him faced with reality (or, rather, for we are now entering
the realm of Pirandello, with what he thinks is reality): he believes
his wife has been unfaithful to him. The trouble, however, is that
this Paolo really loves his Savina, or at least depends on her, and
that his loud protestations are merely a robe covering weakness of
nature. Not wanting to kill her, and at the same time afraid of
being ridiculed, he packs Savina off, giving out that he has taken
her body and cast it in a lake. Arrested and brought to trial, he is
the occasion of a famous case: he knows, of course, although he
hardly admits the knowledge to his consciousness, that Savina is
alive and could at the last resort save him, but he puts up a brave
show as the husband who has dared to protect his honour, and is
acquitted amid the plaudits of the crowd. The town band greets
him on his return home; the mayor gives him a civic welcome;
one of his friends, who has hitherto resignedly winked at the giddy
flirtations of his wife, assumes a new sternness and is tearfully
obeyed; ladies send flowers and marriage proposals to Paolo. But
new trouble for the hero now arises. Savina's scarf has been found
in the lake, and it is decided that she must be given a suitable burial
service: despite Paolo's protests, society demands the ritual. As the
mourners gather Savina, completely veiled in black, arrives, determined to be at her own funeral. Paolo locks her up in his room,
thereby arousing not a little gossip, and, at last realizing that she is
necessary for his happiness, decides that, whatever society says, he
must have her as his wife again.

In this grotesquely humorous work the cynical humour of
The Playboy of the Western World was carried one stage farther, and
Italian dramatists realized that a new medium was being put at their
command. Chiarelli himself pursued the method of his invention

in *La scala di seta* (*The Silken Ladder*, 1917), introducing still another element in the form of what is almost allegory. Contrasted with the sincerely honest man is a male dancer on whom the world showers honours and riches. It is, says Chiarelli, the dancers of life who alone are likely to succeed, and this concept is demonstrated in action when the dancer, created a Minister of State and delivering his inaugural address to the populace, mouths out impeccable platitudes while his feet keep moving in rhythmic steps. The structure and tone of this drama reveal one other feature of Chiarelli's work: with no change in dialogue and merely an alteration of character names, *The Silken Ladder* could almost be taken for a *fiaba* by Gozzi. There can be no doubt but that the 'Teatro del grottesco' is a lineal descendant of the ancient *commedia dell' arte*. The masks that so often are referred to in these plays are the masks of Pulcinella and Arlecchino and Pantalone.

In *Chimere* (*Chimeras*, 1919) a darker tone prevails, although the technique is the same. By taking a Claudio who professes, like Paolo, the sternest rectitude and a Marina who avers she could never be unfaithful to her husband, and by showing this couple faced with financial disaster, Chiarelli demonstrates how the ideal is rudely dissipated when confronted by the real. Salvation can come to Claudio and Marina if she consents to give herself to a wealthy banker: she agrees, and her husband is content. The farcically ironic mood of Chiarelli's first play reappears in *La morte degli amanti* (*The Lovers' Death*, 1921), in which a romantically inclined Eleanora arranges a death-pact with her lover, Alfredo, only to be thwarted of her heroic end by the unfortunate (or fortunate) arrival of her husband, who turns off the gas in good, practical, bourgeois manner. For the theme of *Fuochi d'artificio* (*Fireworks*, 1923) he turns to a story very close to that used by Benavente in *Los intereses creados*. Gerardo and Scaramanzia have returned to Italy from America absolutely broke: the former, an honest fellow, thinks there is nothing for the future save suicide, but Scaramanzia, posing as Gerardo's secretary, allows every one to think he serves a millionnaire, and public opinion creates the lie into the truth.

Even further than Chiarelli went Luigi Antonelli with his *L'uomo che incontro sè stesso* (*The Man who Met Himself*, 1918), *La fiaba dei tre maghi* (*The Fable of the Three Wise Men*, 1919), and *L'isola delle scimmie* (*The Island of the Monkeys*, 1919). The first of these has the advantage of casting a certain illumination on a dramatist whose work has previously been considered. It will be

z

recalled that in dealing with Barrie an attempt was made to indicate the way in which his plays, although now so freely dismissed as merely sentimental, reveal the same features that give distinction to these grotesque plays of Italy: this judgment is concretely illustrated by the fact that the plots of two of his comedies are reflected in that of *L'uomo che incontro sè stesso*, where Luciano, in despair because he has found that his wife has a lover and chiding himself for not warning her against the wiles of her seducer, laments that he cannot be given a second chance. Fate brings him to a lonely island, and there his wish is fulfilled. He warns his wife, and she behaves just as she had done before. We are close, indeed, here to *Dear Brutus* and *The Admirable Crichton*.

The use of the term 'fiaba' in the title of the second drama once more reminds us of the indebtedness of this whole school to the work of Gozzi, while the third play illustrates well the bitter disillusionment that is a component of nearly all these writings. When monkeys accept the guidance of men and establish what we style civilization they open their lives to all the misery and evil that surrounds humanity—this is Antonelli's thesis.

Much the same quality informs the work of Cesare Vico Ludovici, an author who won some fame for *La donna di nessuno* (*Nobody's Wife*, 1919), and of Carlo Veneziani, whose disillusionment in *La finestra sul mondo* (*The Window opening on the World*, 1918), and *Io prima di te* (*I before You*, 1919) is even deeper than that exhibited by Antonelli. Symbolism tends to become dominant here, as it does in the work of Enrico Cavacchioli. *L'uccello del paradiso* (*The Bird of Paradise*, 1919), by the last-named author, introduces a central character called He who is in part a mere figment of the mind, in part a kind of allegorical abstraction of fate. Similarly, in *La danza del ventre* (*The Belly Dance*, 1920) a typical mixture of morality drama and of the *commedia dell' arte* produces a strange world peopled by Arlecchino, the sexless dancer Nadir, and the symbol of passion, Pupa. Here the 'Teatro del grottesco' is becoming a trifle absurd.

One writer, however, besides Pirandello remains to be considered, and in his work something of true genius is apparent. Piermaria Rosso di San Secondo, an offshoot of the Sicilian school, brings to the grotesque drama a quality intensely original, vivid, and bizarre. In 1918 he came before the public with his ironic *Marionette, che passione!* (*Marionettes, What Passion!*), in which three characters, wholly unrelated, are thrown together in a telegraph office. All are lonely, suffering souls—a girl who is abandoning a cruel lover, a betrayed husband, and a second man whose heart is torn by some secret inner torment. They arrange to meet at a café: the girl's lover enters and drags her off, the second man takes poison, and the husband is left in his dejection. The mere outlining of the plot must inevitably be inadequate to suggest the strange, haunting, tortured spirit that the author calls forth from his characters, who, puppet-like, are moved jerkily by forces they cannot control.

Throughout all Rosso di San Secondo's score or so of dramas runs a constant disharmony, as though sweet music were being rudely jangled and strings pulled awry. Mystical allegories are woven into plots in which sensationalism is mingled with the symbolic. The season following that in which his first play appeared saw the production of *La bella addormentata* (*The Sleeping Beauty*, 1919), in which the fairy-tale princess becomes a prostitute, but a prostitute who herself is a symbol of beauty desecrated by humanity. With a strange intoxicating mixture of *commedia dell' arte* figures and of poetic fantasy, wherein colours—blue and grey and yellow —assume almost living qualities, the author guides us through a vision fully as inward in its nature as the dream plays of Strindberg. *La roccia e i monumenti* (*The Rock and the Monuments*) came in 1923, and in it a certain alteration in style is apparent. The rock is the marble of Carrara, and there, in the house of the owner of a great quarry, the action takes place. On the surface the characters are ordinary men and women, but as the scenes unfold themselves we realize that the author's purpose is to use his basic setting in order to demonstrate the difference between primitive man, ignorant of any ties beyond those of his own nature, and the marble that has been chiselled by civilization into a new shape. The real and the symbolic, the living things and the inanimate or dead, are united here, as in *Febbre* (*Fever*, 1927), *La Madonnina di Belvento* (*The Little Madonna of Belvento*, 1928), and *L'avventura terrestre* (*The Terrestrial Adventure*, 1925), into a single strange atmosphere where wisdom and folly, deep thought and vulgar rhetoric, sincerity of purpose and frank theatricalism of the cheapest sort, are incongruously jumbled together.

LUIGI PIRANDELLO

From this atmosphere arose Luigi Pirandello, already well known as a novelist long before he turned to the stage with his first full-length play, *Se non così* (*If Not So*), in 1915—even long before he had written his first one-act piece, *Lumíe di Sicilia* (*Sicilian Limes*, 1910). From that time on he tended more and more to devote himself to the theatre, and soon became one of the most widely discussed of modern playwrights. Although it is to be confessed that throughout his dramatic writing he tends to harp on the same string, ever evolving fresh plots founded on the same basic principle, we must at the same time recognize both the sincerity of his aim (for this repetition of theme is not merely the lazy pursuit of a pattern which had already proved itself successful) and the skill through which he continually finds fresh facets of his theme to display to the world.

Essentially Pirandello is a realist whose realism questions the very fact of reality. For Ibsen a character might be complex, but the character was always one despite the complexity: Pirandello splits the atom that is man, and with explosive results. "Each one of us," he says, "believes himself to be one, but that is a false assumption: each of us is so many, so many—as many as are all the potentialities of being that are in us. . . . We ourselves know only one part of ourselves, and in all likelihood the least significant." The concept of the mask and the face is here taken one stage farther.

But the mask has another aspect. There is, as it were, an internal mask seen only by the person who wears it: there is also the external mask, or masks, by which he is known to his companions. This outer mask may be something he himself has created, or, on the other hand, it may be a thing imposed on him by society, which perhaps he would gladly doff, but which the imposition of public opinion insists that he shall wear. Where, asks Pirandello, in this maze are we to find any objective truth or reality? If all is relative —not merely with respect to an individual, but also with respect to different parts, or aspects, of an individual—surely there can be found no certainty anywhere?

From such thoughts he passes to others concerned with the relationship between art and nature. An author, we say, 'creates' a character; in what sense do we use that word? What hope is there for any writer to depict the shifting sands of character? What bearing have these figments of the imagination, the persons who move and speak on the stage, upon the real individuals whom they are supposed to represent? We speak of theatrical 'naturalism,' but if the stage is manifestly false and if in any case we cannot fathom the substance of the natural, the theatre surely can hardly dare to prate of realism.

While it must be confessed that such ideas are reiterated over and over again in Pirandello's long series of dramas, we must, at the same time, recognize that his inventive skill in finding interestingly varied plots through which to give concrete expression to his intellectual concepts gives to the body of his work a variety which we might well have deemed it could not possibly possess. His early plays, including, besides the already-mentioned *Lumíe di Sicilia*, *La morsa* (*The Vice*, 1913) and the undated *Il dovere de medico* (*The Doctor's Duty*), *Cecè* and *L'imbecile* (*The Imbecile*), may be neglected: his first essay in the style he was to make his own was *Pensaci, Giacomino!* (*Think it over, Giacomino!*), which appeared in 1916. Here no more than the bare outlines of his later philosophy are presented, but clearly the basis is being firmly set. An elderly teacher named Toti exhibits a peculiar whim: finding that his school board is compelled to pay a pension to the widow of a deceased member of its staff, he deliberately marries a young girl, Lillina, who is about to have a child by Giacomino. Toti makes no attempt to take his place as husband: rather does he do all in his power to cement the ties between his wife and her lover. Gossip buzzes, but he remains content: has he not, he asks serenely, acted much more logically and humanely than the wiseacres would admit—has he not succeeded both in deriving pleasure for himself from the satisfaction consequent on doing a good deed and in protecting a girl from being broken on the wheels of the world?

The same year saw the production of two other plays, *All'uscita* (*At the Gate*) and *Così èse vi pare* (*Right You Are—If You Think You Are*), the latter of which carries us fully into the world of the fantastically rational irrational. So tangled is the plot that a précis is barely possible; yet certain dominant concepts clearly make their appearance. A husband, Signor Ponza, has supposedly lost his first wife in an earthquake and marries again. However, he carefully keeps this second wife apart from the supposed mother-in-law, Signora Frola, of his first wife. This, he explains, is because Signora Frola thinks her daughter is still alive, still Signora Ponza. The mother-in-law, however, has a different story: she says that Signora Ponza is really her daughter, who is forced to pretend to be a second wife in order to humour a whim of her husband's. As for Signora Ponza herself, she is prepared at one moment to tell Signora Frola she is her daughter and at the next to agree with her husband she is his second wife. Wherein lies the truth? We cannot tell, for the arguments used by each one of these persons are so logical, so plausible, that as we listen to them we are compelled to accept each separate interpretation of events, and, in order the further to make his purpose plain, Pirandello introduces a kind of *raisonneur* in

Laudisi, a man whose only function in the drama is to underline the author's basic purpose.

Having thus set the stage with this question-mark of a play, Pirandello gave it further movement in his next two works, both produced in 1917, *Il berretto a sonagli* (*Cap and Bells*) and *Il piacere dell' onesta* (*The Pleasure of Honesty*). *Cap and Bells* introduces a fresh motif. Outwardly throughout most of its action it is a typical Sicilian drama, half amusing, half tragic, of jealous passion. In this outward drama the key figure is Beatrice Fiorica, who, owing to the malicious tattle of an old crone, "La Saracena," is consumed with frenzied anger when she believes her husband to be having an *affaire* with the wife of an ugly, almost grotesque-looking, clerk, Ciampa. In order to catch her husband, she gets Ciampa sent off to a neighbouring city and tells the police to raid his house after he has gone. Fiorica is caught there, but now the stratagem recoils on Beatrice's head: if her husband is proved guilty she will have to leave him and her estate will not be an enviable one. To add to this thought there is the unexpected attitude of Ciampa—and there we move from the outward story to the inner. Ciampa is ugly and he knows it: the only thing he could do to keep his self-respect was to overlook his wife's peccadilloes and put up a brave front to the world. Although he might suspect, even know, the truth, all was well with him just so long as common opinion thought her faithful. The logical solution, he declares, is for Beatrice to let herself be certified insane: it will mean only a few months in an asylum, there will be no case against her husband, no need of senseless heroics, no tearing off of the mask. In the development of the latter part of the action Pirandello indulges in much talk of 'puppets,' and these references serve at once to indicate the deep impress made on his mind by the *commedia dell' arte*—particularly by its still-living descendant, the marionette show—and to prepare the way for many other plays in which a contrast is effected between the world of life and that of the stage. The real Ciampa has his existence underneath the puppet figure on which his neighbours look.

The Pleasure of Honesty has a different concept to convey. The story tells of life in aristocratic Society. A young girl, Agata Renni, has been seduced by a fashionable married man-about-town, the Marquis Fabio Colli. To hush up a scandal he approaches an impoverished friend, Angelo Baldovino, with the proposal that he should marry Agata—in the hopeful expectation, of course, that under the cover of this wedding he may pursue his *affaire*. Baldovino accepts the proposal, but, once married, declares that his wife must conduct herself with rigid propriety. Enraged, Fabio plans a stratagem through which the husband shall appear to be a thief: the stratagem, however, is perceived by the intended victim and the tables are turned. Baldovino, however, assures the lover that, so long as his name is cleared, he is content to depart; and in this assurance a new note is seen to intrude. Up to now Baldovino has been only a puppet husband; but to his inner dismay he finds himself, as a man, truly falling in love with his wife. This dismay is turned into a kind of regretful joy when he later discovers that Agata herself, deeply influenced by his pronouncements of rectitude, has likewise come to regard him as her husband in fact. From one world, the world from which he had endeavoured to shut out all emotion, Baldovino is drawn into the other world of human passion.

In *L'innesto* (*Grafting*), also produced in 1917, Pirandello has hardly succeeded in making his strained psychological analysis either palatable or credible. His next play, however, *Il giuoco delle parti* (*His Part in the Game*, 1918), presents a grippingly interesting situation—that of a husband, Leone Galla, who so complacently accepts the intrigue of his wife, Silia, with Guido that, enraged, she manœuvres to get her husband killed. Claiming that she has been insulted by a young nobleman, a noted duellist, she declares that Leone must send a challenge in order to protect her honour; in equally complacent manner he does so, naming Guido as his second, but when the time for the combat arrives he refuses to go, knowing that in such cases the second is bound by convention to take the place of the principal. Guido is thus driven into the trap he and Silia have set; he, not the husband, dies.

Ma non è una cosa seria (*He didn't mean it*, or *But it is not a Serious Affair*) came the same year, and was followed by *L'uomo, la bestia e la virtù* (*Man, Beast, and Virtue*, or *Say it with Flowers*, 1919), a play in which Pirandello shows how deeply his dramatic style, for all its novelty, was implanted in native traditions. In effect we are back in the world of *La mandragola*, with all the apparatus of Renaissance intrigue: the difference lies in the bitter twisting of the plot from what would have been a trick designed by a lover to obtain his mistress into a cruelly savage paradox: instead of using a drug to gain his own pleasure, the lover here is forced to employ it for the purpose of throwing his lady into the arms of her husband. This husband, a sea-captain, rarely comes home to his wife, Signora Perrella, and, when he does, he is so afraid of having another child that he seeks immediate opportunity of quarrelling with her and leaving his house. Signora Perrella, however, has been consoling herself with the little schoolteacher Paolino, and unfortunately finds herself pregnant. In order to save appearances, the lover Paolino is thus forced into devising a stratagem (including the use of an aphrodisiac) whereby Perrella will be induced to lie with his wife. The whole situation is farcical, but the farce is typically Pirandellian; the laughter is torn by an almost hysterical bitterness.

With *Tutto per bene* (*All for the Best*, 1920) Pirandello returns to the contrast between the image and reality, and in handling this theme he here produces one of his most incisive and moving dramas. Three or four levels of belief confront us. First there is the common belief that the girl who passes as Palma Lori is in reality the daughter of Senator Manfroni: Manfroni has provided the money for her education, and every one accepts this as right and proper. Secondly there is the belief that Martino Lori, her theoretical 'father,' knows of this common opinion and merely pretends to be devoted to Palma, merely simulates the grief he outwardly shows for the memory of his dead wife: he is, accordingly, treated with scant attention by others, and his expressions of love for his daughter are met by her with obvious irritation—for she too thinks that he is aware of what all accept to be true. Thirdly there is Martino's own belief, genuine and deeply felt, that his deceased wife was a saint: his love of Palma is now the only joyous thing in his life. When he first learns of what has been happening his whole world comes crashing down on him: ideas of revenge fill his mind and have to be rejected; and in the end the old position is restored—but with a vast inner distinction. So far as society is concerned, Martino continues his former pretence, but now he does so deliberately, with conscious knowledge; while that which he had lost before, his daughter's love, is now freely given to him, since, in the realization that he had not formerly been merely play-acting, she discovers in her heart admiration and affection for a man deeply wronged and tormented. The surface is the same, but in the depths all is altered.

To deal with all Pirandello's many variations on this concept of the mask and the face would be impossible here, since his output is so large: no more can be done than to take a few characteristic specimens of his later dramas, as examples of the diverse ways in which he explores, now satirically, now with almost tragic intensity, the possibilities of his chosen realm. One line of development is marked by *La Signora Morli una e due* (*Signora Morli Two in One*, 1920; revised in 1926 as *Due in una*), where the author examines the different personalities embraced within a single human being.

In the central character of this play he shows us a woman almost equally divided between the gay, thoughtless, frivolous creature who had been the wife of Ferrante Morli and the serious, cautious, respectable housewife she has become in her association with Lello Carpani. Ironically Pirandello makes the former side of her character associate itself with a husband, the latter with a lover, and he is at pains to demonstrate that these two sides are not due merely to change in circumstance, the one following and as it were supplanting the other, but that they co-exist at the same time in her nature.

Immediately after the production of this study in double personality came the famous *Sei personaggi in cerca d'autore* (*Six Characters in Search of an Author*, 1921). The plot of this drama is well known. We are in a theatre as a new play is being rehearsed (the play, indeed, is one of Pirandello's own). Suddenly, illuminated by a light of their own, Six Characters enter. These were creatures of an artist's imagination, some fully developed in personality, others only half developed, and, searching for an author, they are desperately anxious to realize their destiny. The Father, chief of the group, tries stumblingly to explain to the puzzled theatrical director:

> Oh, sir, you are well aware that life is full of infinite absurdities which, since they are true, do not need to seem plausible. . . . I tell you that to try and reverse the process, to aim at verisimilitude, to make these things appear true, is nothing but folly. Yet you will allow me to remark that if this is folly, it is the sole justification for your profession.

In these words Pirandello carries us into the world of appearance and reality, but with a different purpose. These characters have been side-tracked,

> in the sense, you see, that the author who gave us vitality no longer wished or was not able materially to introduce us to the world of art. And this was a real crime, sir; because he who has the good fortune to be born a living character can laugh even at death. He is beyond death! The man, the writer, the instrument of the creation, will die, but his creation never dies. And for this eternal life no extraordinary gifts, no working of wonders, are needed. Who was Sancho Panza? Who was Don Abbondio? Yet they live eternally because—living germs—they had the good fortune to find a fruitful womb, a fantasy that could rear and nourish them—make them live for eternity!

By contrasting the real and the imagined, the genuine passion and its theatrically simulated counterpart, Pirandello directs our gaze

upon the inadequacy of the supposed 'realism' that has so long
dominated on our stage. In the fantastic outlining of the plot in
which the Six Characters are involved he shows the utter impossibility of neatly ascribing 'motives' to their actions and of hoping
that their lives can be adequately translated into playhouse terms.
The Director is tempted to act their drama and calls to the Property
Man for a sofa:

PROPERTY MAN: Yes, sir, there's that green one.
THE STEPDAUGHTER: No, no, not green! It was yellow, ornamented
 with flowers—very large! Very soft.
PROPERTY MAN: We haven't one like that.
THE DIRECTOR: But it doesn't matter! Bring the one you've got!
THE STEPDAUGHTER: What do you mean—'doesn't matter'?

The Director proceeds to try to cast the characters: he turns to the
Leading Lady:

THE DIRECTOR: You, of course, are the Stepdaughter . . .
THE STEPDAUGHTER [*laughing*]: What? what? I that woman there?
 [*Bursts out laughing.*
THE DIRECTOR [*angrily*]: What is there to laugh at?
LEADING LADY [*indignantly*]: Nobody has ever dared to laugh at me!
 I insist on being treated with respect—or I'll go.
THE STEPDAUGHTER: No, no, excuse me. I'm not laughing at you at all.
THE DIRECTOR [*to* STEPDAUGHTER]: You ought to feel honoured to be
 played by——
LEADING LADY [*angrily*]: 'That woman there . . .'
THE STEPDAUGHTER: But I wasn't speaking of you, believe me! I was
 speaking of myself. I don't somehow . . . I don't *see* myself in
 you at all.
THE FATHER: There! That's the point, you see, sir! What we have
 to express——
THE DIRECTOR: What you have to express! Do you really think you
 have any power of expression in you? Nothing of the kind!
THE FATHER: What! We don't have something of our own to express?
THE DIRECTOR: Not a bit of it! You can find expression only when
 the actors give body and form, voice and gesture, to your beings.
 And these actors, each in his own line, have been able to give expression to much finer material. Yours is so thin that if it does
 succeed on the stage, the merit, believe me, will rest entirely in
 my actors.

To and fro the argument goes until at the end a shot rings out and
the Boy falls:

THE LEADING LADY [*entering in tears*]: He's dead! Poor boy! He's
 dead! Oh, how terrible!

THE LEADING MAN [*running in, laughing*]: He isn't dead! Pretence! Pretence! Don't you believe it.

SOME ACTORS: Pretence? Reality! Reality! He's dead!

OTHER ACTORS: No! Pretence! Pretence!

THE FATHER [*rising, with a cry*]: Pretence is it? Reality, reality, sir! Reality! [*He rushes desperately behind the curtain.*

THE DIRECTOR [*unable to stand it any longer*]: Pretence! Reality! To hell with all of it! Lights! Lights! Lights! [*Immediately the whole theatre is illuminated. The* DIRECTOR *takes a deep breath as though he had been freed from an incubus, and all the actors look at each other, puzzled and bewildered.*] Ah! I've never known such a thing! They've made me lose a whole day's rehearsal!

This might well have been the culmination of Pirandello's work, but the year following appeared another, and a diverse, study of a variant aspect of his problem—*Enrico Quarto* (*Henry IV*, 1922). During the celebration of a pageant the hero of this play has fallen from his horse and has been living for years under the delusion that he is, in fact, the character he had represented in the pageant itself. Surrounded by a bevy of servants, he maintains a royal state appropriate to the position of the eleventh-century German monarch. After some years, however, his insanity passes: he realizes who he is, but he realizes too that he so hates the ordinary world that he prefers to maintain the illusion of his madness among others. Into this strange Court, wherein 'Henry IV' quite deliberately keeps up his pretence and wherein his attendants comply in the belief that he is mad, come the Marchioness Matilda Spina, whom 'Henry IV' had loved in the past, her daughter, Frida, and Baron Tito Belcredi, who had caused the accident responsible for the delusion suffered by the main character. These persons appropriately disguise themselves so as to fit in with the eleventh-century atmosphere, but Matilda has the uneasy suspicion that he has pierced through their deception. At the end of the play Henry, after denouncing all of them, snatches a sword and stabs Belcredi, and the final words suggest that now, sane though he is, he must continue in his pretence if his life is to be safe. Left on the stage with his three valets, he gazes round desperately, "with his eyes almost starting out of his head, terrified by the life of his own masquerade which has driven him to crime":

HENRY IV: Ah, now . . . yes, now . . . inexorably [*gathers his* VALETS *around him as if to protect him*] together . . . here together . . . for ever . . . for ever.

This study of insanity was accompanied the same year by the

study of what might be styled a characterless personality in *Vestire gli ignudi* (*Naked*, or *Clothing the Naked*, 1922), where Ersilia Drei, a governess whose drab life has been interrupted by a passing flirtation with a young naval officer and by an *affaire* with her master, takes poison, and, in the belief that she will die, gives a highly romantic story of her adventures to a journalist. An elderly novelist, Ludovico Nota, impressed by this account, takes her from hospital to his rooms. There she pathetically tries to create a personality for herself, clinging anxiously to the novelist's interpretation of her actions, but life will not let her be. Nota sees in her one thing, the young naval officer sees another, and her former master still a third. Each of these has before him the same set of outward appearances; these appearances each interprets in his own way. The officer tells Nota he is ignoring the facts, and the latter, speaking for the author, makes reply:

Facts! Facts! My dear sir, facts are what we assume them to be; and then, in their essence, they are no longer facts, but phenomena of life that take on one or another semblance.

Deprived of her attempt to create a being for herself, poor Ersilia takes poison a second time and dies, clearly revealing in her last words the longings she has had. Her fallacious record of her life was made because she had felt herself naked, never had anything beautiful to put on:

And then . . . and then I wanted at least to have a decent dress for my burial. You see why I lied? For this, I assure you. Never in my whole life have I been able to have a decent dress to make a good appearance in.

Even this is torn from her. "Go and tell it to them," she cries, "that this dead woman—this dead woman here—could not find a dress for herself."

This drama was followed by the effective one-act *L'uomo dal fiore in bocca* (*The Man with a Flower in his Mouth*, 1923) and by another essay in the nature of truth, *Ciascuno a suo modo* (*Each in his own Way*, 1924), in which again the worlds of 'reality' and of the theatre are intermingled. The first act shows a play being enacted on the stage: this finished, we move to the foyer and listen to the members of the audience commenting upon it, and in particular drawing attention to the fact that the fictional story bears a close resemblance to the 'real' story of a woman who sits in the stalls, Delia Moreno. Pirandello himself provides an understanding of what he was attempting to do:

With this presentation of the foyer and of the spectators attending the first act of the play, what appeared on the stage in the first plane as the representation of a segment of life will now assume shape as an artistic fiction; hence it will accordingly be distanced and pushed back into a second plane. Later, at the close of this first interlude, it will become clear that even the foyer and the spectators will also be, in their turn, pushed back into a plane yet further removed: this will be realized when it is seen that the play presented on the stage is a *comédie à clef*—that is to say, a drama composed by the author on an event supposed to have occurred in real life and currently in the news.

The entirely fictional, the translation on to the stage of 'real' events, and the 'real' itself are thus completely confounded, and, although Pirandello does not specifically refer to this, yet a fourth plane enters in through the fact that the foyer represented on the stage is the image of the foyer used by the audience who have come to see *Ciascuno a suo modo*.

In the plays written after this date the repetition of forms already exploited tends to take from the characters such glow of sympathy as was apparent in the earlier works, while a movement towards the exploitation of symbolic elements brings to their scenes a rather cold, abstract quality. The earlier concepts are pursued in a number of dramas, but only *Questa sera si recita a soggetto* (*To-night We Improvise*, 1930) and *Come tu mi vuoi* (*As You Desire Me*, 1930) warrant particular mention. The former is a further essay on the subject of *Six Characters*, contrasting the actor's pretence of emotion with the emotion itself; the latter reminds us of the theme of *Right You Are*, introducing a woman whom Bruno Pieri thinks is his long-lost wife, Lucia: her memory seems to be returning to her after a fit of amnesia just when another woman is found and claimed by the family to be the true Lucia. A question-mark ends this play, and we are left with the impression so frequently conveyed by Pirandello's dramas that personality is a thing either built up by ourselves or else imposed from without by others.

The symbolic style may be exemplified by such works as *La sagra del Signore della Nave* (*Our Lord of the Ship*, 1925) and *I giganti della montagna* (*The Giants of the Mountain*, 1937). *La sagra del Signore della Nave* presents a single long scene of massed humanity shown in pagan celebration on a saint's-day, with a strong contrast set between the licence of the secular and the solemnity of the ecclesiastical. Written especially for the Teatro Odescalchi, which came under Pirandello's direction in 1925, the play introduces a style distinct from that of his earlier dramas. In *I giganti della montagna* something still farther removed makes its appearance. This, his last play, introduces to us a group of wretched human creatures who live in some hovels under the spell of a Magician, and to them come a number of characters, half real, half illusionary—a Countess who bears with her a play written by a dead poet, a troupe of actors, and a set of figures of a purely allegorical sort, spirits of the mountain who apparently symbolize bestial power. Despite some scenes of haunting if puzzling beauty, the drama shows a disintegration of strength: without being able to capture the imaginative vision that could come only from a poetic treatment of his material, Pirandello here allows his intellectual fantasies to carry him into a world beyond the reach of artistic harmony.

What judgment ultimately will be passed on his work as a whole is hard to guess. One thing, however, is certain: no other author so clearly, and with such skill, has given expression to this contrast between the appearance and the reality which forms a kind of *leitmotiv* in almost the whole of the serious theatre of the between-war period. Pirandello thus assumes a key position in the history of the modern stage. Apart from this, there can be no doubt but that his analysis of the human personality is acute, that he shows a brilliant mastery of his craft, and that he possesses the power to give emotional connotations to concepts which at first seem wholly intellectual. The likelihood is that he is a dramatic artist who will remain long in the memory of the stage.

THE THEATRE SYMBOLIC AND THEATRICAL

PIRANDELLO's dramas suggest that symbols might better convey dramatic truth than living characters; they suggest also by implication that the theatre might as well forget its endeavour to reproduce 'reality' and be content with its theatricalism. Neither suggestion was carried to fulfilment in his own work, since he himself was concerned rather with displaying the inadequacy of certain established forms than with the pursuit of other forms likely to lead to concrete, positive achievement. That task was undertaken during these years by two Russian playwrights, Leonid Nikolaevich Andreev and Nikolai Nikolaevich Evreinov.

Neither perhaps can be esteemed a really great writer; but both are of considerable historical interest, and, even although their works are now but rarely presented on the stage, their influence may still be traced in many quarters. In thus linking them together, however, there is no intention to suggest that their styles are the same: indeed, their aims were so entirely at variance that we might well have dealt with them in wholly different sections. The justification for bringing them under one heading here rests on a single consideration, and on a single consideration only—that both endeavours, each in his own way, to release the stage from the incubus of realism.

Andreev's work is best to be understood by thinking of him as standing between Gorki and Maeterlinck. With the former he is bound by his experiments in realistic drama; with the latter he stands because of his several symbolic plays. Introspective, discouraged, fundamentally pessimistic, he is thoroughly characteristic of the period when Russian intellectuals, after the failure of the 1905 revolution, could see no hope in the future and tended to turn in on themselves. Writing a "Letter on the Theatre" in 1913, he clearly revealed his ultimate desires in pleading for a "theatre panpsyche," imagining—like Maeterlinck—that action, "in the accepted sense of movements and visible achievements on the stage," might well be dispensed with and that the dramatists to come ought to concentrate upon the workings of the soul.

His first four plays—*K zvezdam* (*To the Stars*, 1905), *Savva*

(1906), *Zhizn cheloveka* (*The Life of Man*, 1906), and *Tsar-Golod* (*King Hunger*, 1907)—fully illustrate the nature of his questing for form and substance. *To the Stars* is a peculiarly effective drama in which realism and symbolism are combined. The setting is an observatory situated just beyond the Russian frontier; there live Inna Alexandrovna and her husband, an astronomer, Sergei Ternovski. From across the boundary-line shots can be heard, and Ternovski's rapt absorption in his studies, whereby the affairs of men are viewed as infinitesimal when considered *sub specie æternitatis*, is contrasted with the passions of the young Nikolai, an active revolutionary, and his fiancée, Marusia. Although the play has manifold weaknesses, it possesses, by reason both of its theme and of its sharply delineated characters, the true quality of strength. In *Savva* the method employed is more strictly realistic and the endeavour more consciously intellectual: it is, indeed, a kind of propaganda play designed as an attack upon the superstitions encouraged by the Orthodox Church. Realism, however, could not give Andreev what he wanted, and in *The Life of Man* he discovered a style more intimately harmonized with his aims. Even although we have passed beyond the spiritual atmosphere out of which this symbolic fantasy was created, even although we can now discern how trite are some of its philosophical pronouncements, Andreev's achievement must receive at least qualified praise. Man is born in darkness; as he traces his path upon the earth the Being in Grey, a symbol of inexorable fate, stands constantly by his side; and in darkness man dies. The whole spirit of the drama breathes despair and bitterness, and the final scene is a fitting close to the action:

BEING IN GREY: Silence! Man is dead!

[*Silence, absolute quiet. And the same cold, emotionless voice repeats the words from afar off, like an echo:*

Silence! Man is dead!

[*Silence, absolute quiet. Slowly the darkness thickens, but still the mouse-like figures of the attendant* OLD WOMEN *are visible. Quietly and silently they begin to gather round the corpse—then they begin to sing quietly—the musicians begin to play. The darkness thickens, and the music and the singing grows ever louder, the wild dance becomes more impetuous. Now they are hardly dancing; rather they madly fling themselves around the corpse, stamping their feet, shrieking, uttering wild, continuous sounds of laughter. It is completely dark, save that the face of the dead man grows luminous; then that light too disappears. Black, opaque darkness.*

And in the darkness are heard the movements of the mad dancers, the screams, the laughter, the discordant, desperately loud music of the orchestra.

When they reach their highest note all these sounds, all these noises, swiftly pass somewhere afar off and die away. . . . Silence.

Man expires amid the cacophony of jazz and swing.

The same symbolic style dominates in *King Hunger*, where the figure of Hunger appears before the toiling poor, while above their heads the wealthy move in a constant, dancing round of gaiety. Less successful as a whole than *The Life of Man*, this was followed by the extraordinary drama called *Cherniya maski* (*The Black Maskers*, 1908), strangely beautiful and perplexing, where something of the Pirandellian concept is added to the morality atmosphere that Andreev had cultivated in his two preceding compositions. The Black Maskers are the powers whose field of action is the soul of man and whose mysterious nature no one can ever fathom. When they come seeping into the palace the entire stage becomes as it were a concrete image of the human being, although the symbolism is double in that the main plot deals with the fate of Duke Lorenzo, who, oppressed by dark thoughts, has created a kind of evil double of himself. Only when he rises at the end and slays this second self, thus taking action against the besieging forces of despair and dejection, does he come to a vision of what life may be. Lorenzo himself perishes at the end, but in dying he is a soul who, after a frenzied, nightmarish battle with himself, has gained mastery over his fate.

In *Dni nashei zhizni* (*The Days of Our Life*, 1908), *Anfisa* (1909), and *Gaudeamus* (1910) Andreev returns to a more realistic atmosphere, but at the same time continues actively his exploration of the soul. Of these plays the second is without question the more impressive. The dark theme, involving the treatment of incest, is developed with tense and impressive vigour. The central figure, Anfisa, is a widow, the sister of Alexandra, wife of the erratically brilliant but basically weak Feodor Kostomarov. Alarmed at his excesses, Alexandra has brought Anfisa into her home, hoping that her influence will have the effect of restraining him: instead Anfisa herself comes under his influence, and the greater part of the play is devoted to an analysis of the tortured emotions of these three characters—Anfisa, intoxicated by passion and tormented by Kostomarov's cruelty to her, Alexandra, not certain of the truth yet strongly suspecting, and Kostomarov, a creature swayed like a piece of flotsam by his emotions.

The only symbolic element in this drama is the figure of the old nurse, whose presence introduces a faint suggestion of the supernatural and gives a universality to the story it otherwise would have lacked. The supernatural, however, flows in and engulfs the stage in *Anathema* (1909), a rather unsuccessful development of the age-old theme of the Devil descended to earth for the purpose of plaguing an individual human soul. Equally unsuccessful is the satirically comic *Prekrasnie Sabiniaki* (*The Sabine Women*, 1912), wherein contemporary politics are clothed in Roman dress. Possibly dissatisfied with these, Andreev tended in most of his later works to content himself with the infusion of a slight element of the symbolic into scenes that outwardly at least were realistic. Such a drama, for example, as *Sobachii vals* (*The Waltz of the Dogs*; written 1914, printed 1922) is thoroughly in the Gorki manner, while *To, kto poluchaet poshchetschini* (*He Who Gets Slapped*, 1915) introduces symbolic connotations only by implication. If *The Waltz of the Dogs* reminds us of earlier Russian realistic efforts, this last play clearly has affiliations with the Italian 'Teatro del grottesco.' The concept of the mask and the face is inherent in its theme of the lonely intellectual who deliberately covers his personality with the ridiculous make-up of a clown and permits himself to appear before the public as the wretched zany, the man who arouses laughter because he appears as the absurd simpleton, the butt for the jests and the blows of his companions. Even further is the concept carried through the love awakened in the clown's heart by the lovely Consuelo: when he sees her about to be condemned to what he regards as a living death he gives her poison, and is content to think that thus he has saved her spirit.

A good deal of the sentimental enters into this would-be tragedy, and maybe it is this quality in Andreev that is most likely to deny him permanence. He would have liked to have written plays powerful as *Œdipus Rex*, overwhelming as *King Lear*: instead he succeeded only in creating scenes either of a baffling or of a slightly spurious kind. At the same time, he is by no means to be neglected. If he failed he failed because he aimed high and gloriously.

While Andreev was thus struggling to invest the realistic drama with qualities deeper and more penetrating, Evreinov consciously sought to exploit the theatrical. Andreev's mind was oriented towards the tragic; Evreinov's was inclined towards the comic, even if often his comedy was bitter. The former sought for truth in the theatre; the latter believed not only in making the theatre theatrical, but also in exploiting to the full that theatrical quality which he saw everywhere in nature. At the same time he shared with Andreev interest in the complexities of the mind, and succeeded in mingling with his 'theatricalism' not a little of the quality that was expressed in *The Black Maskers*.

For realism Evreinov has utter contempt. In his book *The Theatre in Life* he makes fun of the famous production of *The Three Sisters* at the Moscow Art Theatre. When he saw it, he tells us, he laughed because he realized that this solemnly naturalistic performance was still conventional and theatrical. In order to be thoroughly naturalistic Stanislavski should, he suggests, have rented a small house in the suburbs of Moscow:

> You, a spectator, would come with the other spectators under the pretext of looking for apartments. At the gate leading into the courtyard you would buy an admission ticket. You would be accompanied to the house by a janitor who would give you in a low voice all explanations needed (that is to say, the full text of the playwright's remarks, uttered, if possible, in a 'Chekhovian' tone). In order to see through the keyhole, or through a half-open door, all the scenes of the play (for even in such stage setting one could not very well do without a bit of conventionality), you would have to visit the house quite a few times—in the morning, in the afternoon, and even in the night, when you would behold it in flames (for the fire which must take place in the abode of the three sisters would be, of course, a one hundred per cent. 'real' one).

This concept he treats dramatically in an entertaining two-act comedy *Chetvertaia stena* (*The Fourth Wall*, 1915), where an ultra-naturalistic Assistant Producer casts doubt into the mind of a Director who is preparing a production of *Faust*. The operatic form has to be given up; the Russian text has to be abandoned in favour of German; the furniture has to be authentic; the contents of the bottles in Faust's workroom have to be filled with 'real' liquids, including poisons; in the end even a fourth wall has to be built up and Faust seen merely by glimpses at the window of his study. The play ends when the wretched actor who takes Faust's part, unable to stand this any longer, comes out before the audience and, crying "I can't bear it! I can't bear it!" swallows a fatal draught and dies on the attenuated stage.

This piece, besides presenting characteristically Evreinov's contempt for the realistic, well exhibits the qualities of his style. There is a touch of Pirandello here; there is a suggestion of the symbolic quality associated with Andreev's work; and along with this, strangely, there is a flavour of Chekhov. Had Chekhov opposed realism as does Evreinov, this is precisely the kind of play he would have written: its technique and atmosphere recall nothing so markedly as the spirit of the earlier author's one-act comedies.

At the opposite extreme from *The Fourth Wall*, yet closely bound to it in method of composition and in general texture, is another short piece, *V kulisakh dushi* (*In the Wings of the Soul*, or *The Theatre of the Soul*, 1912), a 'monodrama' introduced by a Professor, who carefully explains to us that, instead of there being, as is commonly supposed, a single 'I' for each individual, a human personality is built up of numerous entities—I_1, I_2, I_3, and so on:

> 'I' is not 'I,' because 'I' consists of several 'I's.' In practice we may treat 'I' as consisting of three 'I's.'

> [*He writes on the blackboard:* "$I = \dfrac{x}{3}$."

The first is reason, the second is emotion, the third is the eternal. After this introduction we move to a scene within a single human being, with a great heart pulsating in the middle of the stage, and within this scene the various 'I's' play their part in such a manner as to make the man to whom they belong wander distractedly through a maze of a world. Like Pirandello, but in a slightly different way, Evreinov strives to show us, not only that material objects appear to different persons in different ways, but also that even a single person views these objects differently on different occasions. Thus the Woman with whom this man is in love assumes one form when he applies his reason to her, another when his emotional 'I' is dominant. With skilled hand and witty dialogue Evreinov here presents what might be regarded as the seriously comic counterpart of *The Black Maskers*. In the end the Man shoots himself, but the general atmosphere of the piece summons forth laughter rather than tears. At the end the third 'I' "puts on his hat, picks up his portmanteau, yawns," and leaves the empty stage.

Among the shorter plays of this author, *Revizor* (1912) may be noted as a lively skit on diverse productional methods, showing how Gogol's play would be presented by a 'classic' director, by Stanislavski, by Reinhardt, and by Gordon Craig. Akin in spirit is *Kukhnia smecha* (*A Feast of Fun*, 1913), described as an "International Competition in Wit," wherein the same plot is supposed to be dramatized by a German, a Frenchman, and an American. In the symbolist style *Vesdaia smert* (*A Merry Death*) ironically plays with characters from the *commedia dell' arte*. More interesting is *Krasivii despot* (*The Beautiful Despot*), which shows an intellectual who, tiring of liberal sentiment, deliberately sets himself back into the year 1808, surrounds himself with servants who are content to be serfs, and goes so far as to be provided even with newspapers of the period in which he is living his dream existence.

In such short plays Evreinov was thoroughly in his element. He failed, however, to translate his buoyant, mordantly satirical spirit into larger terms. Neither his earlier full-length dramas nor his later *Samoe glavnoe* (*The Chief Thing*, 1919), with its symbolic Paraklete who tries to put the author's theories into practice and to bring the drama out of the theatre into life, have much real value, although this last play, developing the idea of happiness being brought to a number of wretched souls through the building of illusions by theatrical means, has both an original concept and some interestingly penned scenes.

The links that bind Andreev and Evreinov to Pirandello and the whole Italian 'Teatro del grottesco' are obvious. In noting them, however, we should not overlook the links that join all of these to that fantastic comedy strain which already has been noted as one of the chief elements in the nineteenth-century theatre, and which stems back ultimately to the *commedia dell' arte*. There is something in common between Gozzi's *fiabe* and Tieck's purposeful fairy-tales; and qualities inherent in these plays are clearly reflected in Evreinov's scenes. Even more clearly are they mirrored in the poetic dramas of Alexander Alexandrovich Blok, where the play of imagination mingles with satirical laughter and ironic fancies. Typical are his *Balaganchik* (*The Puppet Show*, 1906)—which, with its Pierrot and Columbine, its suggestion of the contrast between appearance and reality, and its symbolist tone, obviously is to be related to Evreinov's *A Merry Death*—and *Neznakomka* (*The Stranger*, 1907). Some of the same elements intrude into the 'tragedy' *Roza i krest* (*The Rose and the Cross*, 1913), a rather weak medieval-set drama of a great lady and her hopeless lover. To the same symbolist school belongs Feodor Sologub (Feodor Kuzmich Teternikov), whose *Pobeda smerti* (*The Triumph of Death*, 1907) and other dramas are clearly cast in the same mould as produced the works of Evreinov.

With these Russian dramas may be associated the peculiar 'Marionette Plays' (1917), by the Swedish author Hjalmar Bergman. After starting his career with realistic works heavily influenced by Ibsen, such as *Familjens renhet* (*The Purity of the Family*, 1907), Bergman came under the spell of the symbolists and wrote a series of short realistic-poetic pieces of the kind of *Dödens Arlekin* (*Death's Harlequin*), *En skugga* (*A Shadow*), and *Herr Sleeman kommer* (*Mr Sleeman is coming*)—the last a simple story of a girl,

Marie-Antoinette, who is forced by her aunts into a marriage with an old, lecherous Mr Sleeman while her heart is given to a young Hunter. Here too belongs the series of experimental dramas with which the Belgian Herman Teirlinck sought, in the twenties, to revitalize his native stage, and to these may be related such plays as the *Comedia del arte* (1927), by the Spanish Azorín (José Martínez Ruiz).

When we observe how such men as Azorín, Bergman, Evreinov, and Blok experimented with their Pierrots, their Harlequins, and their Columbines we realize how deeply the whole of the theatre theatrical was impregnated with memories of the *commedia dell' arte*. The mask-and-face concept, whether Italian, Russian, or Scandinavian, is an organic development from the comedy of Pulcinella and Arlecchino. We need not wonder that these characters are continually coming before us in recent dramas: their authors had found their imaginations fired by the improvised comedy and the posturings of the clown.

THE VOGUE OF THE 'ISMS'

Realism, naturalism, symbolism, theatricalism—these movements have been seen to play a prominent part in the theatre's world during the last years of the nineteenth century and the first years of our own era. Even more pronounced 'isms,' however, were still to come.

Closely connected with Evreinov in Russia was Vladimir Vladimirovich Maiakovski, whose *Misteriya-Buf* (*Mystery-Bouffe*, 1921) won him some fame in the early days of the Revolution, partly because it is an effective piece of propaganda, partly because its fantastic style is handled with consummately skilful showmanship. Maiakovski, however, is admittedly a Futurist, and here we are carried back once more to Italy—not the Italy of Pirandello, but that of Filippo Tommaso Marinetti, who first formulated and defined the movement. Futurism itself gave little to the stage, yet an understanding of its tenets is important if only for the reason that within Futurism is to be found the extreme expression of many of the mood-qualities animating men who are otherwise set widely apart. To a large extent Futurism is a destructive force in that it rejects the 'beauty' of the past and endeavours to overthrow completely that romantic cult of loveliness which, in its eyes, is nothing save futile escapism. At the same time, it attempts to be constructive by clamouring for a new art from which these romantic delicacies have been banished, an art which will reflect the mechanical civilization surrounding us. In place of the rounded line so characteristic of romantic artistry Marinetti boldly demands the straight line of girders and factories; in place of the haunting charms of the poetic he asks for a blatant, staccato form of expression that, if need be, will substitute mere sounds for the richer tones of the human voice.

In so far as the theatre was concerned, these Futuristic tenets obviously tended to lead in three directions: first, towards the substitution of 'mechanical' form in place of the current types of scenery; secondly, towards the subordination of the playwright to the director; and, thirdly, towards an emphasis in acting upon physical movement. All three trends were carried to ultimate fulfilment in Russia.

Trained in the Moscow Art Theatre, Vsevolod Meierhold gradually moved over to the embracing of non-realistic styles of production. 'Stylization' became with him a watchword, and, in his attempt to break down the convention of the fourth wall, he moved easily from experimentation with Maeterlinckian symbolism to more original and daring adventures. In the actor he found the core of the dramatic performance, and, since a group of actors must clearly be guided by one person, he began to elevate the director into a position higher even than any he had reached before this time. If the actor were indeed the core of the production, he further argued, then clearly the performer should be permitted to exercise to the full all his athletic skill. In the performances he directed theatricalism went rampant.

About the same time came Alexander Tairov, equally opposed to realism, equally intent upon theatricality, and sufficiently influenced by Futuristic doctrines to set his plays on a stage in which platforms, scaffoldings, and ladders at once reflected the 'mechanical' shapes so familiar to us in our daily lives and provided opportunities for actors to run up and down, to demonstrate their agility, to behave like acrobats. Thus Constructivism came into being.

As both Meierhold and Tairov set the actor and the production above and beyond the play, naturally this movement, although it is associated with the work of Evreinov and Blok, did little to encourage the dramatists; but elsewhere than in Russia the impulse that moved the Constructivists was destined to develop, under the name of Expressionism, a new kind of playwriting which, although in its pure form it was short-lived, has wielded a considerable influence during the past twenty years on writers who otherwise remained far outside the pure Expressionist cult. This, however, is a development which best may be dealt with in a later section. All we need do at the moment is to note the appearance of these diverse theatrical 'isms,' to recognize that in essence they were anti-dramatic, and, at the same time, to see in them a force which, directed into different channels, was to prove of potent influence in later years.

THE POETIC STAGE

ALEXANDER BLOK was a poet, but the trends that led to the efforts of Meierhold and Tairov were in essence so deliberately opposed to romantic aspirations that they may be regarded as a direct attack upon the literary theatre. In stressing the importance of the actor and of the director, in cultivating athleticism and acrobatics among the performers, and in extolling the virtues of improvization, they clearly aimed at taking the theatre out of the hands of the dramatic authors.

This was, in effect, one way of attacking realism. Another way, however, was found in the equally deliberate exaltation of the word instead of the action. When Synge wrote of Ibsen's pallid dialogue and pleaded for the reintroduction to the stage of verbal terms richer and more powerful he expressed what was beginning to trouble many minds, and within a few concise phrases formulated a programme which numerous authors, in diverse ways, were to follow during the twentieth century.

IRISH AND ENGLISH CONTRIBUTIONS

The Abbey Theatre in Dublin was, we must ever remember, inspired and directed in its first years by the man who is likely to be regarded by future historians of literature as the greatest poet of our time. William Butler Yeats, throughout the whole of the extraordinarily lengthy period of his creative career, was passionately devoted to the stage, and, although his own plays cannot be extolled as works of supreme dramatic mastery, his influence has been widespread and his example powerful.

At the beginning of his theatrical career he sought to establish a new kind of romantic drama which, intensely lyrical, should combine within itself something of the strength of the older romantic stage, something of the qualities associated with the more recent symbolist movement, and something of an individual atmosphere borrowed from the folk-memories of his native Ireland. Thus inspired, he composed *The Countess Cathleen* (printed 1892, acted

1899), wherein a noble heroine offers herself in sacrifice when, during a time of terrible famine, the Demon Merchants are moving about the land mercilessly purchasing souls for the price of bread. Now that fifty years have passed since the publication of this work, its loveliness may seem a trifle precious, its rhythms too exquisitely beautiful, its theme too far removed into a world of the romantic imagination. Nevertheless Yeats' effort must be esteemed as one of the most worthy among the many attempts, made over numerous generations, to bring new life to the poetic drama. Unlike most of the poetic dramatists of the nineteenth century, the poet has here abandoned the Shakesperian music and sought to compose a new music of his own.

From the same period come *The Land of Heart's Desire* (1894), in which a mortal woman is shown listening to the call of fairies' horns; *Cathleen Ni Houlihan* (1902), wherein the spirit of Ireland, eternally lovely and incredibly old, is symbolized in the figure of an old crone who becomes transformed into a young girl with the walk of a queen; *The Shadowy Waters* (printed 1900; acted 1904); *The Hour Glass* (1903), in which a Wise Man finds his reason powerless to aid him when confronted with the mystery of life and death; and *The King's Threshold* (1904). In this last play a master-musician, Seanchan, being affronted by his king, Guaire, decides to sit at the royal threshold without food or drink until he dies, thus bringing shame upon the palace. The affront rests in Seanchan's dismissal by the King from the council of state. King Guaire explains:

> Three days ago
> I yielded to the outcry of my courtiers—
> Bishops, Soldiers, and Makers of the Law—
> Who long had thought it against their dignity
> For a mere man of words to sit amongst them
> At the great council of the State and share
> In their authority.

Seanchan's pupils, instead of persuading their master to save his life, support him in his proclamation of the poets' rights, and the little drama closes with a kind of pæan chanted over the dead body of the poet-musician as it is carried away on a litter.

In all probability Yeats soon recognized that he could not proceed much farther along this particular romantic path, and we need not therefore be surprised to find that, as he advanced in his art and in years, other forms came to be adopted for his models. Such a play as *The King's Threshold*, apart from its strongly lyrical note, is cast in a perfectly familiar form. When he pens his *Four Plays for Dancers* (1920) the poet's aims have altered: now he seeks to make use of all the conventionalism that is associated with the theatre of the Orient. The theatrical use of the mask arouses his imagination; the dance-movement of the Japanese Nō drama he endeavours to harmonize with his words; he even attempts to introduce that retrospective element which is such a characteristic feature of this Eastern stage. The result is the creation of something utterly unlike any previous Western plays. In *At the Hawks' Well* (1920), for example, an Old Man, moving with stylized gestures to the tapping of a drum, makes as if to prepare a fire, the while Musicians describe his actions and chant in chorus:

> FIRST MUSICIAN [*speaking*]:
> He has made a little heap of leaves;
> He lays the dry sticks on the leaves
> And, shivering with cold, he has taken up
> The fire-stick and socket from its hole.
> He whirls it round to get a flame;
> And now the dry sticks take the fire
> And now the fire leaps up and shines
> Upon the hazels and the empty well.
> MUSICIANS [*singing*]:
> "O wind, O salt wind, O sea wind!"
> Cries the heart, "it is time to sleep;
> Why wander and nothing to find?
> Better grow old and sleep."

The entire atmosphere is extra-naturalistic. In searching for escape Yeats has boldly gone for inspiration, back beyond the romantic tradition, to that type of play wherein conventionalism is not merely a useful device, but the very basis of the dramatic movement.

A similar development from work cast in earlier romantic forms to work even more heavily influenced by the Oriental theatre is to be viewed in the writings of Gordon Bottomley. From *The Crier by Night* (printed 1902, acted 1916) to *Britain's Daughter* (1922) this poet, the inheritor of the traditions of the nineteenth century, experimented in an endeavour to develop a style which, while borrowing from the Shakespearian model alertness and vigour, should be more harmoniously bound to the actual utterance of our own times than were the imitative measures of so much of the poetic dialogue penned during the years from Wordsworth to Swinburne. Bottomley's strength here lay in his refusal to wander, as Yeats had done, into a misty world of symbolic shapes. He unquestionably possessed the power to evoke an impression of the shadowy and to make the mysterious seem real, but in his works too there appears an earthy, almost barbaric, strength which gives them a unique quality. It is characteristic of his earlier style that, when he essayed to write two dramas which should, as it were, present the atmosphere out of which the tragic action of a couple of Shakespeare's had been wrought, he selected, in *King Lear's Wife* (1915) and *Gruach* (printed 1921, acted 1923), themes which permitted him to depict an ancient world of bitter struggle and fierce emotion. Like Yeats, however, Bottomley moved from such plays to the deliberate cultivation of a kind of drama based on the structure of the Japanese Nō. Whereas, however, Yeats had dreamed of rather precious productions in drawing-rooms, Bottomley deliberately oriented himself towards the innumerable non-commercial acting-groups which have sprung up so freely during recent years, believing that a revival of the poetic theatre might be effected by interesting these groups in verse plays and so by providing later an appreciative audience for the professional presentation of poetic dialogue on the commercial stage. Nearly all his writings during the twenties and thirties were guided by this purpose, and the structure of the Nō in his hands was wrought to a form adapted for the treatment of Western themes and calculated for less precious productions and for more general audiences than Yeats' drawing-room performances.

As an example of the dramatic method he made his own we may take *Fire at Callart* (1939). The plot is taken from a sixteenth-century legend of a Mairi Cameron who, having angered her family, is not allowed to go down to visit a newly arrived Spanish ship and like her cousins amuse herself in the purchasing of some of the fine silks which the sailors have on display. Locked in her room at home, she hears the gay voices of her relatives on their return, but in the morning there is a dull silence. Terrified, she breaks open her door and finds nothing save bloated corpses: the Black Death has come with the silks. Neighbours arrive with orders to burn the house, but they consent, before doing so, to summon her affianced lover, Diarmid of Lochawe. He arrives, rescues her, and carries her off. In telling this tale Bottomley introduces three men in Spanish costume who, announcing that they "are nameless men in Spain," unfold and fold a curtain patterned with flames. In general terms they outline the plot, fold up their curtain, and move to the side of the stage. After this the story is revealed in a series of episodes, broken and expanded by choral elements. When the family returns, Mairi's little sister, Griatach, comes to bid her good-night. In the darkness

> *The* CURTAIN ATTENDANTS *speak without moving.*
> THE CURTAIN-BEARER: Is that something in the night?
> THE FIRST FOLDER: What do you hear?
> THE CURTAIN-BEARER: I hear nothing.
> THE SECOND FOLDER: Yet you speak as though in fright.
> THE CURTAIN-BEARER: There is no sound—but is there no sound?
>   In the air, though not on the ground,
>   Something stirs: is it breath or clothing?
> THE FIRST FOLDER: Is it the murmur of very earth
>   After midnight, in the hush?
> THE CURTAIN-BEARER: At a time of death or birth
>   There's a tension, there's a massing
>   Of strong silence, moving, passing:
>   Stillness is on us with that rush.
> THE SECOND FOLDER: Something happens; I cannot bear it.
>   Agony makes the darkness deeper,
>   Yet is soundless——
> THE FIRST FOLDER: For that I fear it.
> THE SECOND FOLDER: It goes on: by hour and hour
>   This dread night piles up its power.
> THE CURTAIN-BEARER: Slow—slow—slow and slower
>   Alike to sleepless and to sleeper.
> *The darkness yields a little, the* CURTAIN ATTENDANTS *are visible again.*

And the way is prepared for Mairi's grim discovery in the dawning. By such means Bottomley sought to link past and present, the real and the symbolic, the fact and the poetic comment.

Along with this poet stands Lascelles Abercrombie, who in the course of his poetic career likewise tried, equally deliberately, to establish new rhythmic measures apt to be welcomed by modern ears. His approach is somewhat different from those of Yeats and Bottomley. For the most part he turns, as in *Deborah* (1913), to deal with contemporary subject-matter, seeking to evolve a dialogue-form based on the music of common speech. While there can be no doubt but that his experiments have had a considerable (and perhaps not always fully acknowledged) influence, his impress on the theatre has, unfortunately, not been great. More immediate success greeted the efforts of John Drinkwater, who, after writing several impressive early plays, such as *Rebellion* (1914), *The Storm* (1915), and *X=O* (1917), suddenly achieved international fame with his *Abraham Lincoln* (1918). Drinkwater, by no means so powerful a poet as the others mentioned above, possesses the quality that Abercrombie lacks: as a dramatist he has sureness of aim and knows how to concentrate upon the more important elements in his theme. At the same time, despite the extraordinary success of *Abraham Lincoln*, it may be questioned whether his work is likely to stand the test of time. There is virtue here, but it is a virtue of limited appeal.

Still another English poet, John Masefield, applied himself at this time to the stage, but, except for *The Tragedy of Nan* (1908), it cannot be claimed that his dramatic contributions are either of any outstanding importance or are likely to exert any great influence in the future. He too was impressed by the recently discovered Japanese drama, and in *The Faithful* (1915) he wrote a verse play on one of its most famous themes. It is typical, however, that not the structure but the subject-matter of the Nippon stage has here been used: where Yeats and Bottomley endeavoured to find new forms in the conventionalism of the East, Masefield saw there mainly a source for such strong, brutal plots as he has always loved. Typical also is the fact that in *The Tragedy of Nan* he wrote a drama which, despite its unquestioned power, must be regarded as a *tour de force* rather than as a work belonging to any clearly marked tradition or destined to inaugurate a new style. In effect, *The Tragedy of Nan* may be regarded less as a play written for the purpose of revitalizing the theatre by the application to a given theme of the poetically imaginative purpose than as the composition by a man of poetic powers who has been stimulated by the naturalistic style. The dialogue is in prose, and although Masefield invests the speeches of the old Gaffer with a rich, broken music of their own the impression given to us is one of the starkly realistic. His plot Masefield has succeeded in raising above the sordid, so that the roaring of the Severn waters assumes an element of universal, almost supernatural, power; but we cannot believe that other writers would be apt to find in this play any qualities likely to inspire them to further efforts. The truth is that *The Tragedy of Nan*, like its own heroine, is a beautiful but lonely denizen in an alien world.

THE FLAMBOYANCE OF D'ANNUNZIO

All the pent-up romanticism of these decades found flaming expression not in the English theatre (although the *Hassan* (printed 1922, produced 1923) of J. Elroy Flecker came near to giving full scope to the ecstatic luxuries of the late romantic spirit), but in

Italy. Gabriele D'Annunzio may not have been so great an author as he thought he was, and we may utterly condemn his philosophy of life, but no one can deny the sharp surge of his enthusiasm and the fervour of his passions. No Pirandellian doubts trouble his soul: for him conscience is an illness from which man should seek to cure himself: a kind of flaring amoral sensuality colours all his scenes. All is fire, all is burning passion, all is vital energy in his theatre.

D'Annunzio first came before the public with *La città morta* (*The Dead City*) in 1898, and at once showed the main trends of his art in the peculiar treatment he gave to an ancient theme. Although he had already written some five other plays, the daring of *La città morta* came as a shock to his contemporaries and immediately set him in the forefront of the young literary rebels of this time. Here the past is carried into the present, the present confounded with the past; here the modern searching of the soul's innermost reaches is allied to the presentation of bold emotionalism; here the prevailing romantic obsession with fate is given a new treatment. In the devising of his plot D'Annunzio undoubtedly displays extreme adroitness. He tells how, living in the country of Mycenæ, a poet, Alessandro, married to a blind wife, is infatuated with a girl, Bianca Maria, who in turn has aroused the incestuous passion of her own brother, Leonardo. On the site of the dead city Leonardo murders his sister, his soul infected by the atmosphere of the ancient curse on Atreus' house. No doubt it is possible to see many absurd situations in the play, yet we must confess that in its tense, brooding atmosphere it creates just that impression of impending doom which it was the author's object to evoke.

The same year (1898) saw the appearance of *La Gioconda*, in which D'Annunzio turns to pen a realistic-symbolic study of love and art. Lucio Settala, the central figure in this drama, is a sculptor, married to Silvia: although she gives him all her devotion, the inspiration he needs is lacking in her motherly being, and he is forced to turn for this life-giving force to his model, Gioconda Danti. The scene that has most deeply impressed itself upon all those familiar with the drama is that wherein Silvia and Gioconda confront each other in Lucio's studio; Gioconda loses her temper and rushes towards his latest marble in a frenzied desire to destroy it. Silvia cries out and attempts to save the work of art, sacrificing herself so much as to let the stone fall upon and crush her beautiful hands. Even this, however, is not enough to bring Lucio back to her: by a force beyond himself, even though his very soul is torn, he finds himself driven to desert her for Gioconda: his art is a force greater than any common human passion.

Such a man as D'Annunzio could not escape writing a *Francesca da Rimini* (1902), and this he did with frank delight in the penning of the more sensuous episodes. More original is *La figlia di Jorio* (*Jorio's Daughter*, 1904), which carries us far into the mountain lands of the primitive and only half-christianized peasantry of the Abruzzi. Mila, the daughter of Jorio, a noted sorcerer, after being protected by a young shepherd, Aligi, goes to live with him in a hilltop fastness. Days of idyllic happiness follow until Lazaro, Aligi's father, comes, attacks the girl, and is killed by his own son. The youth is condemned to a lingering death as punishment for his parricide, when Mila voluntarily takes the guilt on herself and even pleads that she used black magic to conceal her evil from her lover. As a result she is reviled by all as a witch, hauled off to be burned at the stake, and cursed by the very man whose life she had saved by her tragic lies. Perhaps in the end, despite the brutality of many of its scenes, this drama will be recognized by future historians of the drama as D'Annunzio's most powerful play.

There is no need to survey individually his other works: lust, uninhibited exhibition of passion, physical torment, appear as strains in them all, and the constant iteration of the same subjects makes any continuous reading of his work a descent from reluctant admiration to a boredom that cannot even find amusement in those scenes wherein the tumultuous frenzy seems to become almost a travesty of itself. Whatever his limitations, however, D'Annunzio must, if only for the few plays mentioned above, be recognized as a by no means unimportant figure in the European theatre towards the beginning of our century.

The colourful romanticism that he so vigorously made his own was reflected in some of the writings of Sem Benelli, an author whose other affiliations with Pirandello have already been noted. *La cena delle beffe* (*The Jest*, 1909) demonstrates this patently in its story of Giannetto, the butt for the cruel jests of his brothers, Neri and Gabriello, who succeeds in turning the tables in such a manner as to leave him victor with Gabriello killed through a mistake by Neri, and Neri languishing lunatic in a cell. There is here, in spite of the melodramatic episodes and the obvious spectacularism, a genuine force which gave to the play at least a passing international reputation.

Rather different in style, although animated by some of the same motifs, are the allegorical dramas written by Ercole Luigi Morselli,

"CARMENCITA": MUSICAL STUDIO OF THE MOSCOW ART THEATRE
From *Theatre Arts Monthly*, December 1925.

"GORE OT UMA": MEIERHOLD PRODUCTION
From *The Seven Soviet Arts*, by Kurt London (Faber, 1937).

"THE CRADLE SONG": CIVIC REPERTORY THEATRE, NEW YORK
Setting by G. E. Calthrop. From *Theatre Arts Monthly*, March 1927.

"THE ADDING MACHINE": BOSTON REPERTORY THEATRE
Setting by Jonel Jorgulesco. From *Theatre Arts Monthly*, March 1927.

notably the mythological *Orione* (1910), where the son of Earth, the symbol of instinctive desire, miserably perishes, and the rather more subtle *Glauco* (1919). In this company, too, may be mentioned Federico Valerio Ratti, whose plays—*Il solco quadrato* (*The Square Furrow*, 1911), *Bruto* (1924), and *Socrate* (1927)—employ historical subject-matter for the purpose of giving symbolic dramatic expression to the tortured soul of man in conflict with society.

There is not much of permanent worth in these Italian experiments, yet they express so vigorously and in such an extreme manner at least one of the main spiritual currents of the age that they deserve attention perhaps beyond their actual accomplishment.

THE POETIC-HISTORICAL DRAMA FROM SCANDINAVIA TO SLAVONIA

The impulse that drove D'Annunzio to his frenzied ecstasies and that led Yeats to a richly new field of poetic endeavour found a voice in almost every country of Europe, without, however, yielding much that was capable of being translated from the land of its birth on to alien soil.

The Norwegian Hans E. Kinck emulated D'Annunzio and Benelli in his *Agilulf den vise* (*Agilulf the Wise*, 1906), *Bryllupet i Genua* (*The Wedding at Genoa*, 1911), *Mot karneval* (*Towards Carnival Time*, 1915), and *Den sidste gjest* (*The Last Guest*, 1910)—in all of which flaring colours and fiery passions find full scope. The choice of Italian subject-matter in most of Kinck's dramatic work was something of an innovation in the Scandinavian theatre, but this shifting from saga material to Italianate love and intrigue was not entirely an individual idiosyncrasy: when we find the Swedish Per Hallström writing a *Bianca Capello* (1900) alongside *Karl den elfte* (*Charles XI*, 1918), Hjalmar Bergman producing a *Parisina* (1915), and the Danish Sophus Michaëlis writing a *Giovanni* (1901), we realize that in the life of the Renaissance men were finding qualities of peculiar and immediate appeal. Throughout these decades the efforts to establish a poetic drama on the Scandinavian stage were vigorous, although in general these efforts, while eminently laudable, failed to rise above mediocrity. We can hardly find much of universal dramatic value in the *Solsagn* (*Sun Legends*, 1904) of the Danish Helge Rode; and, despite Masefield's interest in it, the *Anne Pedersdotter* (1910), by the Norwegian Hans Wiers-Jenssen, a tale of sixteenth-century witchcraft wherein a wife wins a stepson's love by sorcery, cannot be esteemed a masterpiece. The 'poetic' stage in Iceland, also, found enthusiastic exponents at this

2A

time, although none have a very great general interest. Following the lead of Indridi Einarsson, whose lyrical *Nýársnóttin* (*New Year's Eve*) appeared in 1872 and legendary *Dansinn í Hruna* (*The Dance at Hruni*) in 1921, Jóhann Sigurjónsson produced his well-known tragic drama *Bjaerg-Ejvind og hans hustru* (*Ejvind of the Hills*, 1911) and his less familiar dramatic treatment of local folk-tales, *Galdra Loftur* (*Loft's Wish*, 1915). It is in the fantastic, the mythical, and the historic that the Icelandic theatrical genius seems to find its most harmonious setting, and the style thus established by these two men has been carried on by such later authors as Sigurdur Eggerz, with his *Líkkistusmidurinn* (*The Coffin-maker*, 1938), and Davíd Stefánsson, with his *Vopn gudanna* (*The Weapons of the Gods*, 1943).

What is important in these imaginatively inspired historical and folk-lore dramas is not the individual excellence of any particular plays, but the extraordinarily wide vogue accorded to them. In Czechoslovakia Jaroslav Vrchlický (Emil Bohuš) exercised his lyric talents in several not very inspiring scenes, his most ambitious effort being the romantically conceived trilogy *Hippodamie* (*Hippodamia*, 1889–91); Jaroslav Hilbert varied his excursions into the Ibsenite drama by experiments in the historical style; while Arnošt Dvořák incorporated modern concepts into a series of dramas mostly based on episodes in Bohemian history. The Slovak Jozef Gregor Tajovský, produced *Smert Durka Langsfelda* (*The Death of Durko Langsfeld*, 1922), a drama noteworthy for its realistic treatment of past events. Much of twentieth-century Bulgarian theatrical writing, too, has dealt with the past, generally in poetic terms. In Rumania Lucian Blaga has found his themes mainly in the realm of folk-myth; the symbolic mingles with the historical in the plays of the Croat Ivo Vojnović. Even from distant Armenia there comes to us an interesting play of this kind—*Hin astvadzner* (*Ancient Gods*, 1912), by Levon Sciant. Set in a medieval community inhabiting an island on a lake, it deals with a convent built on the site of an antique temple and subtly reveals the conflict between instinctive pagan passions and superimposed Christian ideals. An interesting companion piece to this Armenian drama is *Advokat Martian* (*The Advocate Martianus*; printed 1913), by the Ukrainian authoress Lesia Ukrainka, where a similar contrast is presented. The action takes place in the third century, and the Christian Martianus, a brilliant advocate, is engaged in defending a number of his coreligionists. To make his pleading the more effective he is bidden by the Church to pretend to be a pagan, and the conflict here is between his desire to confess openly to his faith and the duty imposed on him by those with whom he is associated. At the end, faced with the need of saving a bishop, he not only allows a complete cleavage to separate him from his sons, but even sacrifices a youth who has fled to his house seeking sanctuary. More interesting is this authoress's dramatic poem *Cassandra* (printed 1908), in which the characters of Greek myth are translated into terms of twentieth-century political and social aspiration.

A kindred spirit animates the work of the Lettish playwright Jānis Rainis; his *Zelta zirgs* (*The Golden Horse*, 1910) is a symbolic mythical drama in which national aspirations are clothed in allegoric forms. Similar in treatment is his *Uguns un nakts* (*Fire and Night*, 1900), also based on local legend. Famous in Estonia is the *Libahunt* (*The Werewolf*, 1912) of August Kitzberg—a dramatization of a sensational folk-tale. The Greek playwright Demetrios Tango-poulos produces an interestingly symbolic *Zontani kai pethameni* (*The Quick and the Dead*, 1905), while Rumania contributes Victor Eftimiu's *Inšira-te, mărgărite* (*A Tale with No Ending*, 1911), an imaginative fantasy woven out of folk-tale material.

In Hungary Jenö Rákosi, Lajos Dóczy, and the better-known Ferenc Herczeg had applied themselves to the exploitation of native folk-legends or local history, and something of the quality they succeeded in bringing into their scenes gives colour to the best of Molnar's work, even although his chosen sphere is that of the common and familiar. National sentiment colours all these works, as it does Kálmań Harsány's dramatic treatment of the Attila legend, *Ellák* (1923). The poetic-historical and the poetic-fantastic found many other exponents in the eastern countries of Europe, but only one author showed any real power. Stanisław Wyspiański in Poland alone infused into his writings an element of true originality. This originality derived largely from the fact that to native influences he added the strong impress of both the Greek dramatists and of Shake-speare: from these three he wrought a peculiar atmosphere charac-teristically his own, but unfortunately too deeply encased with national sentiment to permit it to be carried beyond the bounds of his native country. His unquestioned strength still fails to gather sufficient power to transmute the local into the universal.

Although much of Wyspiański's work was accomplished during the last years of the nineteenth century, the special nature of his genius and the appearance of several of his most important writings after the year 1900 gives authority for discussing him here. It was precisely in the first year of the century, indeed, that his finest drama, *Wesele* (*The Wedding*), made its appearance. Outwardly this is a simple folk-drama, similar in kind to many peasant pieces turned out in half a score of countries during these romantic years, but Wyspiański has introduced into the folk-canvas individual elements of his own. The subjective and the objective are inextricably intertwined in its action, and the symbolic boldly takes its place along with the realistic depiction of a rustic interior: even the sheaves of corn, the very basis of life for the peasant community, live and move in the appearance of the *chochoł*.

Wesele demonstrates that Wyspiański's genius is peculiarly fitted to weld together elements of the most diverse—indeed, seemingly irreconcilable—kinds, and it is from just such a process of fusion that his better plays derive their interest. In both *Akropolis* (printed 1904) and *Noc listopadowa* (*A November Night*, 1904), for example, figures taken from classic myth appear in a Polish setting, and the walls of Cracow's Wawel are peopled by ghosts of the past: it is as though the ramparts of Troy were superimposed upon the medieval fortress. In these and in his other plays Wyspiański shows himself a master of stage effects: a painter himself, he builds many of his scenes with their decorative appearance in view, and at the same time he engages in interesting dramatic experiments, such as the use of crowds in *Legjon* (*Legion*, 1904). This last-mentioned drama, however, serves to indicate why his fame will always remain localized. In creating it the author frankly indicates that he has been dominated by one basic concept—the idea that "Poland is the Christ of Nations"—and at once we realize that such a theme, although it might give him added power as a national writer, is bound so to restrict his appeal as to make his work assume no more than historical interest for others. Wyspiański, indeed, may perhaps be taken as the supreme example of the poet, undoubtedly gifted with genius, who is so rooted in his own land that transplantation is impossible.

PURPOSEFUL LAUGHTER: GEORGE BERNARD SHAW

DESPITE the innumerable experiments in divesre directions made during this time, and despite all the would-be tragic tension, the gloom, the bitterness, and the romantically flamboyant, this age is likely to be recorded in the annals of the theatre as the age of one man—and that man a master of laughter—George Bernard Shaw. Like a mobile and restless colossus, he carelessly straddles over the lesser figures beneath him, and his laughter pricks many a pretentious bubble, whether blown from Ibsen's hard kitchen-soap or from the more perfumed toilet varieties favoured by Maeterlinck and D'Annunzio.

Not, of course, that Shaw stands alone in his world of penetrating laughter. Amid the prevailing darkness of the naturalistic drama and the often absurdly serious efforts of the neo-romanticists some scenes of laughter were permitted to intrude into the theatre of the time, and it is interesting to observe that for the most part these experiments in comedy during the latter years of the century tended to move into the realm of the fantastic—not necessarily the fantastic as exemplified in the invention of an utterly imaginary world of fairy, rather the playing of fancy upon characters and episodes that outwardly have the appearance of the real.

The tone is set, perhaps, in Ibsen's *Love's Comedy*, with its tinkling verse and its fantastification of persons who bear a likeness to those introduced in other dramas more solemn in style. With this play may be associated some of Strindberg's, darker in spirit, it is true, yet clearly exhibiting the operation of the comic mood. Laughter of a bitter sort appears too among the writings of many other authors of the time. There is a play of wit in the work of Arthur Schnitzler; Hermann Bahr's *Das Konzert* is a comedy.

Animated by an original tone is the group of comedies fathered by the German Ludwig Thoma, of which *Moral* (1908) and *Die Lokalbahn* (*The Branch Line*, 1902) may be taken as representative. The former displays the worthy dignitaries of a small town aghast at realizing that all their names are recorded in the account-books belonging to a bawd who has lately been arrested and whom they are consequently now anxious to protect. The same spirit animates *Die Lokalbahn.* The mayor of a little town interviews a high official concerning a proposed extension of a local railway and reports back to his fellow-aldermen how courageously he confronted this dignitary; awed by his courage, they organize a parade in his honour, but, on thinking over the matter, they later decide that he may have harmed the township by his domineering manner; sensing the change in attitude, the mayor promptly modifies his story, and a second parade is organized. Noteworthy, too, is the vigorous little sketch called *Erster Klasse (First Class*, 1910), where the scene is a first-class carriage and where the socially important passengers are made wroth by the entry of a loud-mouthed peasant—who turns out to be a Member of Parliament. Somewhat akin in spirit is *Der kleine Mann (The Little Man*, 1894), where the Austrian playwright Edouard Karlweis (Karl Weiss) satirizes the way in which the wealthy solicit the working-class vote before elections and then promptly forget the 'little man' when the elections are over.

Much more important than Thoma is Karl Sternheim, the nineteenth- and early-twentieth-century master of acidulous mockery, his jests constantly being directed at bourgeois respectability and the unco guid. Nothing quite like the tone of his collected sketches, published as *Portraits of Bourgeois Heroes* (1908–22), is to be met with elsewhere in this period. *Bürger Schippel* tells the amusing tale of an ambitious young workman who adroitly ascends the social ladder, first by gaining admission to the civic orchestra, next by showing his willingness to aid a middle-class widow in her need, and lastly by having the good luck to be victorious in a duel. In *Die Hose (The Trousers)* the adventures of a married lady's pants are hilariously recounted; *Der Snob (The Snob)* introduces a middle-class hero in Christian Maske, who carries Schippel's social climbing a stage higher by marrying into a noble house and winning respect there by hinting that blue blood, even if illegitimate, flows in his veins, that he has right to a coat-of-arms with the bar sinister; *Die Marquise von Arcis* (adapted as *The Mask of Virtue*) delicately pierces the pretensions of society; in *Die Cassette (The Treasure Chest)* a little schoolmaster dreams of inheriting his aunt's riches even while she is writing a will leaving all her possessions to the Church.

In England these were the Gilbert and Sullivan decades, when the mood of the century's earlier fairy comedy and extravaganza was transmuted into the delicate style of the Savoy operas. And, above all, these were the years when Oscar Wilde introduced his own inimitable brand of the comic. Wilde's position is thoroughly characteristic. A poet of the art-for-art's-sake school, he could toy with flamboyant romanticism in *The Duchess of Padua* (1891) and deal with the decadently suggestive in *Salome* (1893); at the same time, he yet finds his fame as a dramatist resting securely on exercises in the realm of the witty and fantastic. *Lady Windermere's Fan* appeared in 1892, *A Woman of No Importance* in the following year, *An Ideal Husband* and *The Importance of Being Earnest* in 1895.

In *Lady Windermere's Fan* Wilde showed clearly what was his aim. This and the immediately following plays outwardly accept the prevailing themes of the current realistic drama. The drama introduces a 'problem'—that of Mrs Erlynne, a woman with a past who is in reality the mother of the proud young Lady Windermere; the woman with a past, together with concealed parentage, re-appears in *A Woman of No Importance*; and a somewhat similar person is the main character in *An Ideal Husband*. Obviously, however, Wilde is dealing with these topics with his tongue in his cheek. He makes no serious attempt to follow the new dramaturgy of the revolutionary intellectuals. Asides and soliloquies are used when they can serve his turn, and he permits the machinery to creak. What he is interested in is the play of wit which his scenes of high life permit him to exploit, and it is for the irridescence of epigram and of lightly turned phrase, not for their solemn problems, that these plays are now remembered.

The Importance of Being Earnest sheds all pretence. Here a wholly farcical plot offers gay opportunity for the flinging of jest after jest before the audience. Wilde has now found the perfect medium for the display of his wit, and that wit continually shatters the conventions of the society he depicts. In his art-for-art's-sake æstheticism he had shocked comfortable respectability: his witty farce is simply the obverse of the medal he ironically hung around his contemporaries' necks. Algernon is making love to Cecily:

ALGERNON: I hope, Cecily, I shall not offend you if I state quite frankly and openly that you seem to me to be in every way the visible personification of absolute perfection.

CECILY: I think your frankness does you great credit, Ernest. If you will allow me, I will copy your remarks into my diary.
    [*Goes over to table and begins writing in diary.*

ALGERNON: Do you really keep a diary? I'd give anything to look at it. May I?

CECILY: Oh, no. [*Puts her hand over it.*] You see, it is simply a very young girl's record of her own thoughts and impressions, and consequently meant for publication. When it appears in volume form I hope you will order a copy.

These sallies are constant from the very opening of the play:

ALGERNON: Did you hear what I was playing, Lane?

LANE: I didn't think it polite to listen, sir.

ALGERNON: I'm sorry for that, for your sake. I don't play accurately —anyone can play accurately—but I play with wonderful expression. As far as the piano is concerned, sentiment is my forte. I keep science for life.

LANE: Yes, sir.

ALGERNON: And, speaking of the science of Life, have you got the cucumber sandwiches cut for Lady Bracknell?

LANE: Yes, sir.

ALGERNON: Oh! . . . by the way, Lane, I see from your book that on Thursday night, when Lord Shoreman and Mr Worthing were dining with me, eight bottles of champagne are entered as having been consumed.

LANE: Yes, sir; eight bottles and a pint.

ALGERNON: Why is it that in a bachelor's establishment the servants invariably drink the champagne? I ask merely for information.

LANE: I attribute it to the superior quality of the wine, sir. I have often observed that in married households the champagne is rarely of a first-rate brand.

ALGERNON: Good heavens! Is marriage so demoralizing as that?

LANE: I believe it *is* a very pleasant state, sir. I have had very little experience of it myself up to the present. I have only been married once. That was in consequence of a misunderstanding between myself and a young person. . . .

ALGERNON: . . . That will do, Lane, thank you.

LANE: Thank you, sir.   [*He goes out.*

ALGERNON: Lane's views on marriage seem somewhat lax. Really, if the lower orders don't set us a good example, what on earth is the use of them? They seem, as a class, to have absolutely no sense of moral responsibility.

Here is the spirit of topsy-turviness, the characteristic of the fairy play, transformed into a new medium; here is the social question treated not with dull seriousness of purpose, but with irreverent gaiety.

THE PLAY OF IDEAS

So much has been written on almost every conceivable aspect of Shaw's career, and he himself has so copiously annotated his own purposes, that any brief general survey of his work must inevitably prove impossible. At the same time it may be worth while to emphasize here, not the social ideas about which so much has been said, but rather the purely dramatic significance of his plays.

Many of his contemporaries have been taken in by his own emphatic assurances that he has applied himself to the stage only because he finds there the best platform for the preaching of certain moral or social truths and that he is much more of the prophet than the playwright. Undoubtedly there resides a modicum of truth in these assertions. Shaw has thought more vigorously, more alertly, and with more penetrating insight about the social problems of our day than any other living author. In play after play, in preface after preface, he has presented his analysis of the evils and errors of the time and has indicated his own solutions. From his early study of the circumstances surrounding professional prostitution in *Mrs Warren's Profession* (1898) to the vast survey of human failure in *Back to Methuselah* (1919-20) he has constantly infused into his action ideas of a philosophical and sociological kind, and there can be no doubt but that the stage-platform has given him the opportunity of shattering numerous false idols and of awakening minds to thoughts beyond the shallowly conventional.

At the same time, even while recognizing these facts, we cannot accept the Shavian assurances at their face-value. If, indeed, Shaw's reputation is to stand on his 'prophecy,' its endurance is set on a shaky foundation. The discussion of war in *Arms and the Man* may have seemed incisive and full of basic truth when this play appeared in 1894, but the experiences of two great wars have cut away the very premises on which the author erected his ideas. When we start to analyse the thought in *Back to Methuselah* all we are left with is the often expressed regret that the ass that is man lies down and dies just when he is beginning to learn some lessons.

In writing his preface to the English translation of some of Brieux' plays Shaw gives the impression that this French writer is his ideal of a dramatist and that he himself is doing in London what Brieux was doing in Paris. Fortunately the truth lies far otherwise. Brieux is certainly the sociological dramatist, but there is not the most tenuous connexion between his works and those of his adulator. *Damaged Goods* and the rest of the plays of ideas that Brieux turned out are dictated by central 'thoughts': they are admittedly thesis plays: their ideas might just as easily have been formulated in pamphlet prose: the author clearly indicates just precisely where he stands and creates puppet figures, poor, flat pasteboard puppets, for the purpose of driving his lesson home.

True, the same has been said of Shaw, but it has been falsely said; in reality his method is far different. Had he worked as Brieux did, then his fame, even now, would have similarly sunk. The fact that Shaw's plays still hold the stage demonstrates that we must look in them for something more, and this something more obviously has to be a quality distinct from either analysis of social evil or suggestion for its remedy. What we need to do, in fact, is to forget the prefaces and consider the plays.

Exactly how the prefaces are written in time-relation to the dramas they profess to elucidate is not known, and does not matter: the impression they give is that they are, if not afterthoughts, essays penned separately in spirit from the composition of the stage scenes. We might put this in another way by saying that, unlike Brieux, Shaw succeeds, when he is engaged in dramatic composition, in dividing the pamphleteer from the playwright. In the preface he is the pamphleteer, presenting a reasoned argument and pressing home upon us his own particular point of view. Here Shaw the individual and the sociologist is in the ascendant. Never for a moment are we in doubt as to what he thinks and what he wants us to do. The same impression, however, is not with us when we contemplate the plays: in these the pamphleteer, with his clear, incisive reasoning, gives way to another kind of writer.

This other kind of writer is a man who possesses, or is afflicted by, the dramatist's objectivity. When a true dramatist (not a Brieux) lets his mind play over his chosen plot and its characters he enters into a paradoxical state: on the one hand, he is the god-creator, master of these figures of his imagination; on the other, the persons he has evoked out of the unknown begin to assume their own life. The dramatist's task, in effect, is to give as much free play as possible to the various characters and yet guide them all home to a successful conclusion. It is not simply that he keeps some half a dozen different persons in view all the time that he is writing, but rather that, even while remaining the god-creator, he gives himself to each one of the persons as he or she is made to speak. Within a single individual scene, so to say, Shakespeare is at once consistently and continuously absolute lord of the stage and successively Hamlet, Polonius, Ophelia, when these characters are made to utter their lines. Precisely in this paradox rests the peculiar quality of dramatic art.

Frequently the accusation has been brought against Shaw that his characters are not living beings, with the conclusion that because of this his dramatic artistry is of a sort not destined to endure. The truth of the observation may be accepted, without endorsement of the conclusion. We may agree that in the whole range of Shavian drama there are no characters who assume such breathing vitality as we find in the persons of Sophocles or of Shakespeare: but that is because Shaw's approach to his characters is of a different kind. His theatre might well be described as the theatre of ideas, not in the sense that a single thought is imposed, Brieux-wise, on the entire action, but rather in the sense that Shaw possesses the supreme and well-nigh unique power of making the most diverse ideas take on human semblance. His characters are the embodiments of intellectual concepts; his dramas are ceaseless dances of thoughts.

What requires to be stressed is that, precisely as Shakespeare gives himself to his 'living' characters, so Shaw gives himself to his ideas. When Shakespeare throws himself into Claudius he still retains his comprehensive view of *Hamlet* and of Claudius' position in the story of that play: when Shaw throws himself into the embodiment of a particular thought he similarly remains at once true to the thought itself and to the general plan of which the thought forms merely one part. Unconsciously he has described his own power in his *Too True to be Good* (1932). Aubrey is talking to the Patient:

AUBREY: I am a born preacher, not a pleader. The theory of legal procedure is that if you set two liars to expose one another, the truth will emerge. That would not suit me. I greatly dislike being contradicted; and the only place where a man is safe from contradiction is in the pulpit. I detest argument: it is unmannerly, and obscures the preacher's message. Besides, the law is too much concerned with crude facts and too little with spiritual things; and it is in spiritual things that I am interested: they alone call my gift into full play.

THE PATIENT: You call preaching things you don't believe spiritual, do you?

AUBREY: . . . My gift is divine: it is not limited by my petty personal convictions. It is a gift of lucidity as well as of eloquence. Lucidity is one of the most precious of gifts: the gift of the teacher: the gift of explanation. I can explain anything to anybody; and I love doing it. I feel I must do it if only the doctrine is beautiful and subtle and exquisitely put together. I may feel instinctively that it is the rottenest nonsense. Still, if I can get a moving dramatic effect out of it, and preach a really splendid sermon about it, my gift takes possession of me and obliges me to sail in and do it.

Had Shaw been merely a Brieux all we should have had would have been a series of Shavian sermons; but, Shaw being Shaw, what happens is that, as each idea presents itself, the playwright's gift of lucidity and sensitivity to dramatic effect make him devote all his strength and skill, for the moment, to the one object of producing conviction in the readers or in the audience. The idea steps out of the *corps de ballet* and executes a *pas seul* in mid-stage.

All Shaw's plays reveal this power, but none more clearly than *Androcles and the Lion* (1913), where the concepts of paganism, meek Christianity, and muscular Christianity are each put forward with such vigour, wit, and charm that while we listen to each sermon we are convinced that in it and in it alone must reside eternal truth. From this derives, ultimately, the interest of *Saint Joan* (1923). These are not living characters who inhabit here: they are all incorporations of spiritual things, the embodiments of faiths and beliefs, the human semblances of rationalizations. That extraordinarily powerful tent scene, wherein the Bishop of Beauvais confronts Warwick, gains its stageworthiness, not from such qualities as Shakespeare would have put there, the vivid illumination cast upon human character; not on such qualities as Jonson would have displayed, the juxtaposition of symbols of classes within the body of humanity; not on such qualities as Ibsen would have used, the subtle building-up of character by the light of a Norwegian table-lamp rather than by that of the sunshine flooding in upon an Elizabethan stage; but from the skill through which Shaw makes two ideas assume the medieval garbs of layman and ecclesiastic, take on material form, and confront each other. The Bishop's arguments are so clearly and so trenchantly expressed that it seems they are irrefutable:

> Catholic courts are composed of mortal men, like other courts, however sacred their function and inspiration may be. And if the men are Frenchmen, as the modern fashion calls them, I am afraid the bare fact that an English army has been defeated by a French one will not convince them that there is any sorcery in the matter. . . . Sir John Talbot, we all know, is a fierce and formidable soldier, Messire; but I have yet to learn that he is an able general. And although it pleases you to say that he has been defeated by this girl, some of us may be disposed to give a little of the credit to Dunois.

But we have only to listen for a moment to another speaker to hear a sermon equally true and equally sincere. In the final scene of the play the idea that is Joan and the idea that is the Inquisitor are both presented with absolute assurance.

THE COMEDY OF FUN

It is this quality that explains most of the peculiarities of the Shavian drama. Because of this his scenes often rightly become debates, since the spiritual essences with which he deals are more important than their material semblances. Shaw knows usually when to break a scene with the introduction of some flash of colour or rush of physical business, but these are no more than clowneries devised to provide variety of interest. Because his characters are ideas, too, the atmosphere he invokes is of a kind absolutely distinct from anything the theatre has had in the past. *Saint Joan* ends with the burning of the heroine, but it is not a tragedy: our hearts are, again perfectly rightly, untouched, our withers unwrung. When Joan sits before the Inquisitor's court it is not a girl who is being tried: it is an idea that is being examined. Concepts of tragedy and comedy need never trouble our minds when we enter the doors of this theatre. Even in the most intellectual, the most unemotional, comic drama of the past a faint call of sympathy has come for the characters. We speak of the Restoration comedy of manners as an amoral creation of wit where we are never summoned to praise or blame save in intellectual terms, where we are never induced to feel for any of the dramatist's persons. This is true when the comedy of manners is compared with such plays as the romantic comedies of Shakespeare's middle period, but the truth is, after all, only relative, since in the end we realize that even Congreve's scenes are peopled with living beings. Millamant may be a cold creation compared with Rosalind, yet still there is warmth beneath her brilliant mask of affectation. In Shaw's dramas there is nothing beneath the mask: the mask is the character, of face there is none.

To sport with ideas in this way is fun, and the term 'comedy of fun' seems best to describe Shaw's peculiar contribution to the stage. One play, *Candida* (1895), he wrote in a more conventional style, and it accordingly has perhaps received more praise than most (for we are ever inclined to run in grooves and more readily welcome the known than the unknown): but it may seriously be questioned whether this is, as some have averred, his best play. There are other dramatists who could have written *Candida*: his best plays are utterly unique. In a sense *Candida*, too, is a play wherein the dramatist has fun with the confrontation of ideas, but it is not a pure specimen of the type. Much more individual among the early dramas, and one wherein we can see adumbrated much of Shaw's later style, is *The Devil's Disciple* (1897). This is called a melodrama, and the very designation reminds us that Shaw's lineage stems from that theatre of the nineteenth century which revelled in stage forms innocent of the living character. Melodrama, opera, extravaganza, flourished then, and in none appeared more than pasteboard figures: melodrama's persons were stereotypes, opera's were inflated balloons, extravaganza's were *commedia dell' arte* caricatures. What Shaw did was to take these and make them spiritually interesting. He could treat them with a disrespect which might be permitted towards the creatures of his imagination by no playwright whose object it was to make his inventions seem real. Hence *The Devil's Disciple* can be full of slapstick: *Saint Joan* can start with a frantic cry on the part of Robert de Baudricourt for eggs, and its most serious scenes can be broken by the English chaplain's loyal platitudes; *Back to Methuselah* can move at times into sheer farce of a kind which H. J. Byron and J. R. Planché would have recognized as akin to their own. In *Cæsar and Cleopatra* (1899) Britannus is made to utter sentiments of a purely modern sort, and Shaw's own comment on those who had taken exception to this character's lines demonstrates patently the mood in which these scenes were written:

I find among those who have read this play in manuscript a strong conviction that an ancient Briton could not possibly have been like a modern one. I see no reason to adopt this curious view. It is true that the Roman and Norman conquests must have for a time disturbed the normal British type produced by the climate. But Britannus, born before these events, represents the unadulterated Briton who fought Cæsar and impressed Roman observers much as we should expect the ancestors of Mr Podsnap to impress the cultivated Italians of their time.

I am told that it is not scientific to treat national character as a product of climate. This only shows the wide difference between common knowledge and the intellectual game called science. We have men of exactly the same stock, and speaking the same language, growing in Great Britain, in Ireland, and in America. The result is three of the most distinctly marked nationalities under the sun. Racial characteristics are quite another matter. . . . The characteristics of Britannus are local characteristics, not race characteristics. In an ancient Briton they would, I take it, be exaggerated, since modern Britain, disforested, drained, urbanified and consequently cosmopolized, is presumably less characteristically British than Cæsar's Britain.

And again I ask does anyone who, in the light of a competent knowledge of his own age, has studied history from contemporary documents, believe that sixty-seven generations of promiscuous marriage have made any appreciable difference in the human fauna of these isles? Certainly I do not.

Playing with ideas is certainly fun.

FROM MRS WARREN TO GOOD KING CHARLES

During the earlier part of his career, from *Mrs Warren's Profession*, through *Arms and the Man*, *Candida*, *You Never Can Tell* (1898), *The Devil's Disciple*, *Cæsar and Cleopatra*, *Man and Superman* (1903), *Major Barbara* (1905), *The Doctor's Dilemma* (1906), and *Androcles and the Lion*, on to *Pygmalion* (1913), Shaw's models were obviously those mentioned above. In each of these appeared an apotheosis of melodrama, opera, and extravaganza. The structure is familiar, although we hardly recognize old friends when they appear before us in fantastic Shavian dress, brilliant of tongue, daring in the expression of idea, and tricked out with the characteristically voluble stage-directions which, instead of serving (as in the melodrama) to describe actions, now describe thoughts. "Surmising that he has no valet," writes Shaw at the beginning of *Man and Superman*,

> and seeing that he has no secretary with a shorthand notebook and a typewriter, one meditates on how little our great burgess domesticity has been disturbed by new fashions and methods, or by the enterprise of the railway and hotel companies which sell you a Saturday to Monday of life at Folkestone as a real gentleman for two guineas, first-class fares both ways included.

By the use of such devices, by the incisiveness of his thought, and, above all, by the exquisitely modulated prose of which he is such a complete master Shaw gave to the old devices a gloss of novelty and established himself as the most important dramatic author of his time.

In 1912 came a break in his service to the theatre. War was to shatter men's lives within less than a couple of years, and it was not until 1919 that his next full-length play, *Heartbreak House* (1919), made its appearance. Here a new element has been incorporated into his art. The picture of Captain Shotover's ship-like home with its strange collection of drifting inhabitants points unmistakably to the influence on Shaw's mind of the Chekhovian pattern. It is as though, in place of the individualized persons whom the Russian dramatist had loved to gather together in one limited locale, Shaw had taken his method and peopled his house with ideas—the idea of the out-of-date conservative, the idea of the new financier, the idea of the purposeless woman of the world. In the atmospheres of *The Cherry Orchard* and of *Heartbreak House* there is much in common—a mingled nostalgia for something rather lovely that is perishing and a dim hope for the future, a combination of contempt for moral helplessness and of admiration for courage; but whereas we come from Chekhov's play with certain human characters indelibly implanted in our minds, from Shaw's we come with vivid memories of basic philosophies trenchantly expressed.

Back to Methuselah again brings something new: hardly any dramatic work of our time can be compared with it. Here is a vastness of concept akin to that of *The Dynasts*, and at the same time a vivid theatrical power. The philosophy may be of little account, but the experience of seeing, in sequence, the five plays which make up this enormous work is like no other experience to be gained in the theatre.

This was followed by *Saint Joan* (1923), in which the new lessons he had learned were put to fresh use. There is a subtlety here and a breadth of vision beyond anything in his earlier work. Almost the only inharmonious note is the epilogue—not because it introduces a modern strain into an historical theme, but because the trend it displays runs counter to the main trend of the drama as a whole. Its symbolic saint is at odds with the girl possessed of belief in her own righteousness and determined, in the manner of all dangerous fanatics, to press others into her own mould.

In *Saint Joan* Shaw reaches the peak of his art. Thereafter discursiveness, an increasing tendency towards the use of symbols, and a failure to bring his themes to any logical conclusion have been evident. There are brilliant scenes in *The Apple Cart* (1929), but these scenes are isolated, not firmly bound together in a single unity; *Too True to be Good* (1932) opens magnificently and drifts inconsequentially away; *On the Rocks* (1933) is hopelessly chaotic, as is *The Simpleton of the Unexpected Isles* (1935). Weaker still are *The Millionairess* (1936) and *Geneva* (1938). Only in *In Good King Charles's Golden Days* (1939) does something of the old glitter return.

The truth, of course, is that when a dramatist essays the bold and hazardous path of building his plays out of ideas rather than out of persons he denies himself the possibility of achieving anything between complete success and failure. Shakespeare may not succeed in creating a masterpiece in *Measure for Measure*, but the fact that our sympathies have been excited for an apparently living Isabella,

Claudio, and Angelo permits us to overlook the serious structural weaknesses in the drama. Where we have been moved even by a few scenes we are prepared to accept the play in its entirety and are content to view it with interest whenever it is presented before us. In the Shavian type of theatre we cannot do this. None of the characters in these last plays can make appeal to us as human beings: even King Magnus, the most vital of them all, is cast in Shaw's familiar mould. The result is that, without human warmth to inspire us towards liking, structural weaknesses become more than commonly apparent, and these are made the more obvious in that, without realizing it consciously, we feel that the figures moving before us are rationalizations, and consequently that any logical failure in the conduct of the action is a betrayal of its very fabric. Logical errors may be condoned—indeed, freely accepted—in Shakespeare because the foundation of his work is emotional; in Shaw they must be condemned.

Despite the decline from the *Saint Joan* of 1923, however, Shaw takes his throne amid modern dramatists without the slightest fear of being challenged by any pretender. He has brought to a glorious consummation that strain of comic fantasy that we have seen threading its way through the vast-spreading territory of nineteenth-century romanticism. For all we know, he may be utterly ignorant of the very names of Gozzi and of Raimund, yet there can be no doubt but that he is their descendant, the splendid triumph of their lineage.

PART XII

DRAMA BETWEEN TWO WARS

DRAMA BETWEEN TWO WARS

THE SECOND decade of our century was rudely broken by the First World War, and as a result many movements within the theatrical realm became straddled, as it were, between the years before 1914 and the years after 1918. Thus, to take two examples, Italian Futurism, heralded by Marinetti's manifestoes in the earlier period, was not fully developed until the twenties, while French Surrealism, anticipated in the first decades of the century and formally exploited as a dramatic form in 1916, had to wait until 1924 before it was developed into a 'school.' In one sense, therefore, the story of the stage after 1920 might well be regarded as a true continuation of what went immediately before with merely a lapse in time during which the work of the enthusiasts remained largely dormant and the playhouses in many countries were given over to plays of an 'escapist' kind.

While this is undoubtedly true, the advent of such a war as that of 1914–18 could not at its end leave the mood of the dramatists quite identical with their mood at its beginning, while it is obvious that, entirely apart from this general change in mental atmosphere, the theatres and audiences came under the sway of social conditions of a sort entirely undreamed of in those years when Victorianism seemed an affair no further removed than yesterday. The social interests that had been introduced to the theatre in the late nineteenth century suddenly assumed a new intensity, and the play of ideas was transformed into a propagandist drama.

At the same time a sort of counter-movement may readily be traced during these years. Many dramatists concentrated their attention on larger social issues where men became symbolized as Man, but others turned from the macrocosm and sought to make explorations not outward but inward. Hence, alongside the theatre that dealt largely with economic conditions, there came into being the theatre that sought to penetrate within the individual soul more deeply than any of the psychological playwrights who had immediately followed Ibsen.

These two forces in themselves are sufficient to give the two decades a quality of their own, but besides these there exist other conditions serving to mark the post-war from the pre-war. Not least of such conditions is what may be called the shifting of the theatrical balance. Before the war had ended Russia, the home of Chekhov, had become the U.S.S.R., and as a result its stage completely changed character. Just at first, in the primal flush of revolutionary enthusiasm, the styles of Meierhold and Tairov were given free play, but these were early curbed and methods more staid and stern took their place. As has already been observed, the aims of Meierhold and Tairov were essentially anti-literary, and as a consequence the years when they flourished had little to give in the way of new dramatic work. After their time the propagandist aims so fully pressed since the early thirties have subordinated the æsthetic to the practical, so that a peculiar paradox has come into being. The theatre in the U.S.S.R. is possibly more alive than that of any other country, yet even the most enthusiastic must admit that of fine dramas (as distinct from interesting productions) very little has come from the stages of Moscow and Leningrad. If we look upon the drama as an art and not simply as a useful means towards a political end we have to decide that, to all intents, one of the largest European countries has had little to contribute worthy of a high place in the world's theatrical repertory. Such contributions may come in the future, but guessing is useless, and the present fact is all that we have before us.

If Russia has thus been removed from the dramatically productive field, two other lands have had even less to offer. Very soon after the cessation of hostilities Italy came under the grip of Fascism, and, although Pirandello continued writing, although other playwrights developed their own styles, the Fascist culture was obviously not one apt to encourage much creative endeavour. Even so, a little more was produced there than Nazi Germany had to present, which was absolutely nothing. Only during the first post-war years did the German stage provide anything of interest. Throughout part of this time, too, Spain was in the toils of civil war; the confusions resultant ill-served the theatre, and the only young writer of unquestioned promise died in a prison courtyard with the bullets of Franco's ruffians in his breast.

To counterbalance this the United States of America, which hitherto had offered nothing save mediocre copies of prevailing European styles, suddenly demonstrated a vigorous creative spirit —indeed, it is certain that theatre historians of the future will discern there the mid-twentieth-century home of that errant dramatic spirit which we have watched through long ages moving from Greece to England, from England to France, from France to Germany, and from Germany to Scandinavia and Russia. While the American theatre has so far failed to develop any fresh dramatic form, and while it has no individual author to show as great as Ibsen, there can be no doubt but that its surprisingly rapid growth after 1918 and its many varied contributions to all kinds of theatrical styles will give it a not unimportant place in theatrical records.

The large scope and the diversity of forms exhibited in this American theatre, however, present a serious problem to anyone who tries to gain a perspective view of the stage from 1920 to 1940. What may be called the American dramatic impulse deserves to be treated as a complete whole: on the other hand, the very mixture of elements within that whole prevents us from seeing in the New York stage such a coherent unity in variety as, for example, emerges from our contemplation of the English Elizabethan theatre. Moreover, complete segregation of the American drama from the drama of other countries would be unquestionably false to the spirit of the age, since many of the most able and characteristic developments of particular dramatic styles have come from the western shores of the Atlantic.

For this problem one solution only seems possible. It is important for us to trace the larger currents of the time; it is equally important to recognize the worth of the American contribution. Therefore, it would appear, we may best deal with the former first, trying to gain a general perspective view of the development of the New York stage without examining the works of any individual dramatists, and then proceed to view the exemplification of the larger dramatic currents in their plays. One author alone, Eugene O'Neill, deserves to be given special treatment. This implies a logical break between discussion of subject-matter according to prevailing styles and discussion of it according to national or individual contribution, but no other method seems quite to satisfy the difficult theatrical conditions confronting us during these two decades—and the treatment of O'Neill's work by itself has the advantage of providing us with a kind of mirror of the period's dramatic trends, for in the plays of this typically eclectic author we have influences from almost every quarter, from sombre realism to the abstractions of expressionism.

These twenty years, perhaps because of the variety of effort within them, bring before us a series of paradoxes. Not least of these is the paradox occasioned by the vast amount of experimentation in new theatrical forms and the staid continuance in our midst of the type of stage characteristic of 1880. Gordon Craig's ideas were widely discussed during the inter-war decades; from the example of a proscenium-less playhouse established by Jacques Copeau in the Théâtre du Vieux Colombier (1913) much later effort resulted; in Germany Max Reinhardt, with his vast productions in the Grosses Schauspielhaus and his intimate chamber-theatre productions, expressed movements which may be traced in many another land. Despite all of this, the fact remains that when, in London, New York, or Paris, we go to see a play we are rather surprised if that play is not presented before us in a frame, with painted scenery, on a stage separated from the auditorium. After long ages of constant change the ordinary commercial theatre has become fixed in shape and function.

No doubt the reasons for this are many, although maybe most potent among them are the facts that the costs involved in theatrical construction are now so enormous as to impose cautious conservatism on the builders of new playhouses, and that, with the application of modern safety rules, these structures have a measure of permanency denied to the playhouses of the past. Seventeenth- and eighteenth-century conflagrations provided wonderful opportunities for successive experimentation. It will certainly be interesting to see what happens when some of the theatre buildings destroyed in the bombings of 1939–45 are restored; already in Genoa there is active debate, for example, as to whether the famous Teatro Fenice should be made to rise again exactly as it was or whether something entirely novel ought to take its place.

Whatever the reason, the fact is certain, and no doubt the continued existence of such theatres explains the prevalence of the ordinary realistic play in our midst. These picture-frame theatres are best calculated for the production of realistic scenes, and thus a dramatic form which thoughtful observers of the stage in the nineties of the last century deemed to have reached its culmination has, by a combination of circumstance, been dragged on into our own time.

This process has been further strengthened by two entirely opposed forces. It is during these years that the film has assumed its universal prominence, and, as the cinematographic form is so closely associated with realism, and as it is, at the same time, so closely akin to the art of the stage, no surprise is to be felt at observing the strong influence of the extraordinarily popular two-dimensional film upon the three-dimensional theatre. This was an unconscious influence, of course, and due simply to prevailing conditions: with it goes the entirely deliberate efforts on the part of many writers to establish a new realism, mainly for the purpose of devising a means of disseminating social ideas. When we consider the confluence of these streams of influence we certainly need not be astonished at the current exploitation of the realistic scene.

At the same time, it must be observed that nearly all the authors (except those most intent on their social message) most clearly gifted with individuality and the fire of creative talent have, in one way or another, striven to escape from these bonds. Sometimes the striving takes shape as the exploitation of expressionistic or poetic forms, sometimes it displays itself as the infusing of a kind of symbolic content into an apparently realistically conceived plot, but, whether the method be overt or concealed, we cannot escape recognition of the fact that within those circles most animated by interest in the theatre's future and vigour of creative imagination there is evident a restlessness under curbs which delay or prevent a movement forward into fresh dramatic territory.

One further general development of these years deserves special attention. Without doubt the decades from 1920 to 1940 formed the period of the amateur, particularly in the United States of America and in Britain. It was not long after 1918 that the British Drama League was founded, less to encourage the development of amateur stage activity than to meet the needs of the scores of amateur theatrical groups already in existence; and since that time the movement has grown to enormous dimensions, so that whereas national 'tournaments' could be thought of in the twenties, regional tournaments be planned in the early thirties, by 1939 there could be tournaments organized within the area of single cities and even smaller towns. Britain's example has, of course, been far surpassed by American example. There the development of the Little Theatre movement is so characteristic that we may best defer consideration of it until we come to deal with the American theatre as a whole. From village communities to communities in the largest cities, from university students to factory workers, hardly an area exists that has not seen the ardent application, often with standards close to the professional, of effort in this direction.

Although this movement has reached its greatest proportions in the English-speaking countries, we must not lose sight of the fact that similar adventurings are to be found in nearly all lands. Alongside the immense development of the professional stage in the U.S.S.R. amateur activities, in the form of workers' theatres, are eagerly encouraged. Italy's 'carri di Tespi,' by means of which the drama was carried to remotest villages, were paralleled by numerous little-theatre efforts, such as the well-known Teatro degli Indipendenti, directed by Anton Giulio Bragaglia, in Rome. In Madrid the little theatres assumed peculiar importance during these years, and Lorca's genius was, at least partly, inspired by their work.

Nor, when we look at the achievements of the amateur groups and at the related achievements of those who, because of their opposition to the commercial stage, may be called the professional-amateurs, should we forget the diverse experiments in hitherto undreamed-of productional methods carried out by men sympathetic towards the spirit from which the little theatre drew its strength. When, in 1934, Gino Rocca presented Goldoni's *La bottega del caffè* in a small square of Venice and Max Reinhardt brought Shakespeare's Shylock on to the very paving-stones of the Rialto they were expressing in their own way the need and the desire which were responsible for the founding of so many non-commercial stages. The same needs and desires too may be found seeking release in the notable productions of Racine's tragedies in the ruins of ancient Roman theatres, in the productions of Greek dramas at Delphi, and in the presentation of Sicilian mimes within the precincts of Pæstum's dreaming temple.

Up till 1939 this amateur and non-commerical professional movement had not succeeded thoroughly in integrating itself into the larger world of the stage. At the same time its service in extending the potential theatre audience must, even within the two decades with which we are concerned, be taken fully into consideration, while consequences resultant during and after the Second World War suggest that perhaps, when we can obtain sufficient perspective in time, we shall have to recognize in this force one of the chief conditioning elements making for the development of the twentieth-century drama.

CHAPTER I

THE AMERICAN ADVENT

WITHOUT a doubt among the dramatists who first arose during these decades the author who most impresses upon us a sense of power and daimonic genius is Eugene O'Neill, and in his writings we have a kind of vast symbol of the power of the American stage.

THE FORERUNNERS

Up to the time of the First World War, as we have seen, the playhouses of the United States, although active and yielding profit, had failed to produce any theatrical literature of importance. For the history of the American stage itself there are many nineteenth-century works which well deserve remembrance, but the best will in the world cannot sincerely argue that even the worthiest of these productions are of wide general, as opposed to local national, significance. All we can say is that as the nineteenth century was drawing to its close and during the first years of the present era definite signs of a stirring of spirit may be discerned, and although no great work immediately resulted, we can recognize that within these decades the largely somnolent American drama was nearing its awakening.

The signs, however, were undoubtedly faint, so that the awakening, when it came, was all the more surprising in view of the lack of dramatic energy preceding it. If England, with her Jones and Pinero, lagged behind the rest of Europe during the period of Ibsen, the United States lagged as far behind England. It is only now, with our advantage in time, that we can discern the faint premonitions of something notable to come. Of such premonitions three in especial are of historical significance.

First, there is evident in the American theatre from 1890 to 1914 an even greater love of surface realism (the old Crummles variety brought up to date) than is to be found in any other country. David Belasco becomes the grand master of the spuriously authentic, making a fortune from the public's willingness to pay money in order to see in the playhouse replicas of scenes they might easily have viewed for nothing outside the auditorium. It is true that Belascoism, dominant within the period 1890–1914, was to become rapidly outmoded in succeeding years, yet its influence, both positive and negative, has by no means disappeared: it forms one of the foundation-stones of the modern American theatre.

In its own time, of course, it served to prevent the growth of a deeper realism, and this force was augmented by a second. There can be no doubt but that American playwrights during these decades were apt pupils in the school of the 'well-made play.' Scores of melodramas and farce-comedies written from 1870 onward exhibit considerable technical ability within the limits of that particular form. The immediate effect of this was to encourage among the public a love of the sensational and of the sentimentally adroit: when plays are 'slick' and trapped out in outward realism of the Belasco kind there is little call for audiences to question their inner truth. Beyond this, however, we must observe that, even although later authors came to express contempt for mechanical stagecraft, the long training in this style was not without its importance for later generations. There are many who would sneer at Scribe who borrow from his treasury of theatrically effective situations.

The emphasis on outward realism is further intensified at this time by a third element. Playwrights from 1870 on are mightily engaged in putting on the boards scenes that at least purport to represent the ways of life to be found in diverse states of the Union or to reproduce fairly recent historical events in these areas. Sufficient evidence of such a trend is to be found in the mentioning of four dramas—one each from the four authors whose names come most readily to our minds when we think of these earlier years. Bronson Howard deals in *Shenandoah* (1888) with an episode in the Civil War; James A. Herne composes, in *Shore Acres* (1893), a melodrama of New England life; *Barbara Frietchie* (1899) is one of the most successful dramas of Clyde Fitch; Augustus Thomas, starting his career with *In Mizzoura* (1893), ends it with another Civil War piece in *The Copperhead* (1918). We may readily appreciate the inevitable effect of these and of other kindred works. The very novelty of seeing stage characters of native American flavour, of hearing in their speeches the tones of the American voice, hoodwinked even the most astute into believing that the farcical, the sentimental, and the melodramatic situations were realistic, thus once more setting up a barrier in the way of something worthier. On the other hand, this exploitation of native material served a purpose in directing the public's attention away from decayed classicism or romanticism towards elements of greater potential power.

As the twentieth century moved past its first decade a slow change is observable—but still so slow as to be notable not in itself, but only in relation to what remains to come. As yet no dramatic work of outstanding excellence or of penetrating integrity of spirit makes its appearance. Edward Sheldon pens, in *Salvation Nell* (1908), a sensational study of a woman who clings to her ne'er-do-well sweetheart and eventually succeeds in reclaiming him from sin, and, in *The Nigger* (1909), produces one of the very first of many dramatic essays designed to awaken men's minds to the Negro problem; but when we remember that he was also the author of *Romance* (1913) we feel no surprise in finding that his treatment of the plots of those two plays is slabbily thick with sentimentalism. Sentimentalism and melodramatic sensationalism colour, too, the episodes of *The Great Divide* (1906) of William Vaughan Moody, a play in which a relatively bold effort is made to combine two themes—that of the gentle-born New England woman who forsakes the comforts of civilization in order to be with the man she loves, and that of the woman who, violated by a man, comes to feel affection for him growing in her heart. Equally artificial in treatment, although introducing new topics, are the numerous lighter plays of Rachel Crothers, extending from the early study of man-made social conventions, *A Man's World* (1909), to the facile satire directed at the Oxford Movement, *Susan and God* (1937).

THE AWAKENING

During this second decade of the century, however, other things —some of them hardly noticed by the public at large—were happening. In circles entirely unassociated with the commercial playhouses efforts are being made to establish a fresh foundation. Winthrop Ames' attempt to set up a great American repertory theatre fails, but other endeavours of a less spectacular kind are more fruitful. At Harvard University Professor George Pierce Baker starts to give encouragement to a small group of young writers, and in other centres outside of New York similar activities are being eagerly sponsored. Meanwhile two companies of enthusiastic amateurs arise out of the metropolitan artists' colonies. The first is the Washington Square Players, which, inaugurated in 1915 through the apostolic fervour of Theresa Helburn, Robert Edmond

Jones, Lawrence Langner, Philip Moeller, Lee Simonson, Maurice Wertheim, and Helen Westley, advances from a tiny makeshift stage in Greenwich Village to become the once highly important Theatre Guild. The second is the so-called Provincetown Players, also started in 1915, not fated like its companion to develop into a permanent organization, but distinguished by the fact that one of its members is Eugene O'Neill and that his first dramatic experiments are presented on its stage.

Excitement was in the air during those early months of the First World War. Almost contemporaneously with the establishing of these two producing groups Arthur Hopkins had the hardihood to organize the first American drama festival, and the enthusiasts found a journal for the expression of their dreams in *The Theatre Arts Monthly*, a long-lived journal. The impact of war on the United States did, it is true, temporarily delay further realization of the ideals animating these endeavours, but no sooner had peace come than the seeds already sown began to blossom luxuriantly. In 1914 O'Neill had published his first volume of one-act plays: between 1916 and 1918 four of his sea-pieces were acted; in 1920 came his first truly important work, *Emperor Jones*. During those same years a noble band of supporting playwrights were starting their careers, and were preparing to form a kind of phalanx, with O'Neill at their head, taking the New York theatres by storm. By the mid-twenties their works were ousting nearly all other dramas from the stage. During the years 1923, 1924, and 1925, for example, came O'Neill's *All God's Chillun Got Wings*, *Desire under the Elms*, and *The Fountain*, Elmer Rice's *The Adding Machine*, Philip Barry's *The Youngest* and *In a Garden*, Maxwell Anderson's *What Price Glory*, *First Flight*, and *The Buccaneer*, Paul Green's *The Scuffletown Outlaws*, *Fixin's*, and *The No 'Count Boy*, Marc Connelly's and George S. Kaufman's *Beggar on Horseback*, George Kelly's *Craig's Wife*, and Sidney Howard's *They Knew What They Wanted* and *Lucky Sam McCarver*. Before 1927, besides other contributions by these authors, Sam Behrman had come forward with *The Second Man*, Robert Sherwood with *The Road to Rome*, and Dubose Heyward with *Porgy*. These dramas alone would make any theatre rich, and when we remember how many other works accompanied them we fully realize the force of the dramatic impulse thus released in the United States.

Nor was the impulse confined to the creation of drama alone. A new enthusiastic group of scene-designers had sprung up, and appropriately the first exhibition of American stage-designs was opened in 1919—an exhibition that showed the public the work of Robert Edmond Jones, Joseph Urban, Lee Simonson, and Norman Bel Geddes.

These were undoubtedly exciting and adventuresome years.

THE MOVEMENT FORWARD

Equally exciting and adventuresome years were to follow.

American life was doomed to feel the impact of a great depression at the beginning of the century's third decade, but out of that a new endeavour came. We can note now how in these years a fresh sociological content was being introduced into the theatre and how the efforts of the early Provincetown Players were being paralleled by those of the Group Theatre and the Theatre Union; and we can observe how from out of such efforts new dramatists were arising.

Their work, however, calls for fuller attention in a later section: here we may pause for a moment to observe the development of one of the most extraordinary theatrical ventures in the history of the playhouse—the Federal Theatre Project, a Government-sponsored and Government-supported scheme (involving the expenditure of millions) set up in 1935 under the direction of Hallie Flanagan, head of the drama department of Vassar College. The first purpose of the Project was to provide relief for thousands of theatre-workers thrown out of employment during the depression. At the same time the whole concept of the W.P.A. (under which the Federal Theatre Project operated) was to provide relief which—unlike the British 'dole'—should be productive: hence the scheme was launched with the idea of stimulating the theatre generally, and those who were in charge of it eagerly sought to further this end. Operating in areas representative of more than half the country, the acting groups formed under these auspices sought to reintroduce among communities everywhere a knowledge of and interest in the drama such as had been almost wholly lost since the time of the nineteenth-century stock and touring companies. Besides this, money was expended in the restoration of old playhouses and in the erection of new ones: the building of the Park Theatre at Charleston, on the site of a once-famous eighteenth-century structure, is a typical example. New experiments were tried out—among the most notable being the Negro productions of *Macbeth* and the *Swing Mikado*, in the former of which Shakespeare's tragedy was made into a kind of voodoo-drama of extraordinarily effective quality, and in the latter Sullivan's music was treated to the re-fashioning of 'swing.'

For nearly four years the Project flourished. By the middle of 1939, however, a new spirit was animating Congress, and, despite frenzied appeals, the entire vast machinery thus set up was permitted to become idle and to rust.

In this endeavour perhaps there lies a moral. While it may be agreed that the evidence brought forward before the notorious Dies Committee of Congress in the summer of 1939 was much of it exaggerated and some of it absurd, any fair-minded observer must confess that on the whole the Project failed. It failed, first, because it would seem to be impossible to combine a cultural end with a scheme whose primary aim is the providing of immediate relief. Because it was a relief measure, hundreds of individuals who, although genuinely out of work, possessed no talent for the stage had to be borne as a huge burden by a rapidly improvised and creaking piece of administrative machinery. There were many persons of talent, perhaps of genius, connected with the Federal Theatre Project, but there were many more who could be regarded as no more than unsuccessful playwrights, scene-designers, actors. A second cause of failure may be discerned in the manner by which the whole scheme was compelled to operate. Again, it would seem to be utterly useless to suppose that a great deal of work of sterling quality can come from a venture of such vast proportions and centrally administered, no matter how much local autonomy is given to its component parts. The third reason is that a number of social revolutionaries endeavoured, and to a certain extent succeeded, in capturing diverse 'units' and in employing the theatrical means thus set at their disposal for the purpose of inculcating their own beliefs. Maybe what they succeeded in accomplishing was no danger to the American Constitution, but the fact remains that there was some justification for the complaint of the conservatives—that what had been designed as a relief measure with a secondary cultural objective was, in fact, being used as an instrument of socialistic or communistic propaganda.

The measure of the failure of the Federal Theatre Project is to be realized when we note that hardly anything of a permanent nature has remained after its income was cut off and that practically no original dramatic work was encouraged through its efforts. Stimulating experiments were made in production; nothing of any interest came from its efforts in the direction of 'creative writing.' The entire endeavour thus stands as a bold—indeed, a noble—device

"THE GREAT GOD BROWN": GREENWICH VILLAGE THEATRE
From *Theatre Arts Monthly*, April 1926.

DESIRE UNDER THE
ELMS": GREENWICH
VILLAGE THEATRE

ing by Robert Edmond
nes. From *Theatre Arts
onthly*, December 1924.

"THIS WAY TO THE TOMB": PILGRIM PLAYERS, MERCURY THEATRE, LONDON

Photo D. Beck

"ŒDIPUS THE KING": ABBEY THEATRE, DUBLIN

From *Theatre Arts Monthly*, March 1927.

designed (at least indirectly) to revitalize the stage, which yet found it impossible to produce results in any respect comparable with what had been produced in ancient Athens by civic support. After a spectacular display of firework stars it went out as rapidly as a spent rocket.

AMERICAN ECLECTICISM

One thing, however, remains to be said. The very fact of this Project testifies to the significant place the theatre had come to occupy in American society by the thirties of this century, while its magnitude of effort serves as a symbol of the enormous latent power in the United States. It may be that the American drama has already given us of its best—for history teaches us that these theatrical impulses tend to be short-lived—but at any rate for the period between the two wars the American effort far surpasses anything accomplished, during the same years, by any other country. Bernard Shaw is certainly the greatest living playwright, and his work alone serves to give the Anglo-Irish drama a position of major importance; but the totality of the American contribution to the theatre between 1920 and 1940 must be deemed to go considerably beyond the British or the French contributions of the same decades.

What, at the same time, is significant is that, despite the power inherent in this totality of effort, the American drama has offered us no characteristically new style. There is no Ibsen, there is no Strindberg, there is no Shaw, to be found on this stage. Rather has the American playwright tended to be thoroughly eclectic and to have built his work on suggestions, often fused together, taken from elsewhere. It is for this reason that, as has been indicated in the preface to this chapter, we cannot profitably discuss these American plays within one section, as, for example, we can discuss the Elizabethan English, the seventeenth-century Spanish, or the nineteenth-century Scandinavian. No doubt, in those periods there was variety; yet a great central core gave individual quality to the dramatic productivity of each separate age. In the modern American theatre, while power is manifest and individual accomplishment constant, such a characteristic core does not exist. The various movements, or styles, used by the playwrights have not been invented by them.

O'Neill, because of his pre-eminence, demands treatment of a special kind (although even with his works the diversity of styles presents difficulties): for the other authors who are his companions we must, if we are to try to get a clear picture of general theatrical

2B

trends, seek to relate them to their appropriate 'schools' of endeavour rather than link them together. Thus to link them could only serve to distort a wider perspective. It is more important to associate Barry and Saroyan with impressionism, Howard Lawson and Elmer Rice with expressionism, than to consider these four authors collectively as 'American.'

THE DRAMA OF THE INDIVIDUAL

IN THE development of dramatic trends after the cessation of hostilities in 1918 the first broad movement which we must consider is that which inclines towards the focusing of attention upon the individual. This is the subjective theatre and may be associated with at least some of the main qualities characterizing the impressionistic school in the sister art of painting.

The word 'subjective' may, of course, be applied to the theatre in a variety of different ways, and it is important that these should not be confused. A play is subjective when all its scenes and characters, the entirety of its theme, are consistently coloured by the author's own personality: thus, for example, Maeterlinck's *Pelléas et Mélisande* is subjectively conceived in that over the whole of the action is cast one prevailing spirit, persons of the drama appearing, as it were, through a veil, which is the personality—or at least the particular mood—of Maeterlinck himself. *Pelléas et Mélisande* is utterly unlike Strindberg's *The Spook Sonata*, yet the latter, too, can be described as subjective. In using the word for Strindberg, however, we mean that the writer has permitted himself to attempt the dramatic exploitation of his own inner self: he is not merely letting his subject-matter be coloured by a particular sentiment, rather is he putting his soul's adventures on the stage. Nor is this all: in yet a third kind of play the author may select an individual character (not a reflection of himself) and, as it were, present the rest of the play as though it were a projection of that character's mind. A good example occurs in *Beggar on Horseback*, an American comedy written in 1924 by George S. Kaufman and Marc Connelly. Here the central figure is a man, Neil McRae, by nature a musician, but prevented from applying himself to his art because of lack of money. Although in love with Cynthia, he is toying with the idea of marrying the rich Gladys. Up to this point the scenes provide a kind of introduction to what forms the real core of the drama, wherein a nightmare experienced by Neil takes the place of 'real' episodes. Dreaming, he marries a Gladys whose bridal bouquet is made up of banknotes: he is asked to play something for the guests and his hands refuse to turn out anything save jazz; money is showered upon him, yet when a friend advises him to murder all his wife's family he does so with glee, and at his trial he vigorously defends himself; finally condemned to punishment, he is placed in a prison-like Cady Consolidated Art Factory, where the convicts hammer out music and poetry and painting as though they were breaking stones, picking oakum, sewing mailbags.

Clearly these three species of subjective drama are connected, and equally clearly we must hold them distinct in our minds even while, for the purpose of tracing larger dramatic trends, we are forced to link them together. They are not, of course, entirely new trends belonging specifically to these between-war years; although they reach a culmination in this period, each had been adumbrated during the opening decades of the century. The first, the *Pelléas et Mélisande* type, we have already seen fully developed by the neo-romantic symbolist poets; the second finds characteristic expression in Strindberg; the third finds expression in such works as Ibsen's *Peer Gynt*, Hauptmann's *Die versunkene Glocke*, and Evreinov's 'monodramas.'

There are, however, two further services to which the word 'subjective' can be, and frequently is, put. In Vienna, during the early years of the present century, Sigmund Freud was engaged in revolutionizing previous concepts of human behaviour, in stressing the importance of the subconscious, and in developing the 'science' of psychoanalysis. Naturally his investigations were bound to exert very considerable influence on the creative arts, particularly upon those of narrative fiction and of drama wherein supposedly living persons are presented. Here older ideas of character-portrayal were put aside and an effort was made to probe more deeply below the surface, to make explicit what is generally concealed, to give expression, directly or indirectly, to those elements in the human soul which remain hidden even from their possessor. In dramatic form this endeavour leads, on the one hand, to a kind of theatrical case-history of clinical tendency and, on the other, to studies such as those of the French playwright Jean-Jacques Bernard—and of both the stage between 1920 and 1940 can produce innumerable examples. For many dramatists psychology has been dismissed in favour of psychoanalysis.

Along with this may be taken a trend exemplified in the work at least of a few dramatists who, dissatisfied with the application of reason to all aspects of human existence, seek once more to testify to the predominance of the spirit and introduce religious themes to the stage. During the nineteenth century and the first decades of our own age the theme of religion was almost entirely banished from the theatre, and when it did make its appearance it usually took the form of vast poetic dramas in which the 'gods' were much spoken of and man's life was symbolically set against a great infinitude of empty space. What is interesting during recent years is the development of a dramatic style wherein matters of the spirit are brought into close association with ordinary life, and wherein a quiet utterance, sometimes even moving into the sphere of the comic, is substituted for the grandiose romantic eloquence of earlier writers.

For convenience all these diverse movements may here be assembled under the single heading of impressionism: although varied in character, they manifest certain qualities in common, and it is perhaps more important that we should recognize these bonds between them by thus connecting them all with the attempt to enter inside the human soul, than that we should divide them into separate categories.

THE VOGUE OF SURREALISM

The most extreme form may be considered first. In the year 1896 Alfred Jarry produced his strong satirical drama *Ubu roi*, destined to be treated by many later writers as a prime essay in the surrealist style; in 1917 Guillaume Apollinaire presented his *Les mamelles de Tirésias* (*The Breasts of Tiresias*) to the public as a "drame surréaliste"; eight years later André Breton published the first of his surrealistic manifestoes. In surrealism we may see both a destructive and a constructive force. The year when *Les mamelles de Tirésias* appeared the nihilistic Dadaist movement was founded in Zurich by Tristan Tzara, Hans Arp, and their companions, and its first manifesto was issued two years later. Between Dadaisme and surréalisme there is a close connexion, and when we observe that the former is a perfectly deliberate denial of all values, an anarchistic attempt to mock at everything in life, we recognize that for some of the followers of surrealism the movement meant no more than an excuse for the cynical expression of disbelief in all and everything.

Beyond this, however, the surrealistic enthusiasts, unlike the Dadaists, had a core of positive endeavour in their theories. Having become acquainted with the subconscious, they declared, in effect, that the only true art, and, incidentally, the only true realism, could lie in those regions of the human mind which hitherto had been explored only occasionally in the past (by such artists, for example, as the fifteenth-century Hieronymus Bosch or the eighteenth-century William Blake). In effect, they took the division of the soul outlined by Evreinov, separated man into the rational and the irrational self, and declared that only in the operation of the latter could the source of art be found.

A few of the extremists went so far as to plead that 'art' should consist merely in (a) automatic writing or (b) the faithful recording of dreams; but the cleverer among the adherents of the movement, realizing that if such a doctrine were adopted, then anybody's dream is as good as anybody else's, and that hence the position of the 'artist' becomes imperilled, allowed themselves to admit an element of the ordering imagination, without, however, abandoning their belief in the fundamental importance, for the creative writer, of the realm of the subconscious.

We all know the kind of paintings produced under the spell of this theory, and, whether we sympathize or not with the æsthetic aims, we cannot deny that some of the artists, such as Salvador Dali, are men highly gifted with technical ability and power of expression. We all know, too, the manifestations of this style of artistic creation in the works of James Joyce and his followers. What is not so well known are the plays executed in an attempt to put on to the boards the subject-matter of the subconscious.

Perhaps we need feel no surprise at this, since fundamentally the theatre would seem to provide a means singularly unfitted for such an endeavour. The dream is always characterized by its shifting forms: one thing fades into another; nothing keeps its shape for long; in sharp juxtaposition appear images of startling clarity and shadowy essences whose lineaments fade perplexingly into their backgrounds. Such things may be able to find expression in the cinema; in general, the theatre is too hard and fixed a medium for their exhibition. As a result, none of the several dramatic essays penned by the avowed adherents of the school has any lasting, intrinsic significance.

Against that, however, we must weigh two considerations: first, that one or two other writers have succeeded in taking the general spirit of the surrealist mood and in producing works of some interest, and, secondly, that elements of the surrealistic style have found their way into many dramas otherwise not in any respect associated with the aims of Apollinaire and Breton.

In the former category stand forward the perplexing plays of that extraordinary French author Jean Cocteau, a man so various that he seems to be, not one, but all mankind's epitome. Starting his career with *Les mariés de la Tour Eiffel* (*The Couple of the Eiffel Tower*, 1921), he has turned out a *Roméo et Juliette* (1924), *Orphée* (1926), *La voix humaine* (*The Human Voice*, 1934), *Les chevaliers de la Table Ronde* (*The Knights of the Round Table*, 1937), *L'aigle à deux têtes* (*The Eagle with Two Heads*, 1946), and many others in a confusing mixture of styles. In general—and despite the fact that he lately turned to the realistic in *Les parents terribles* (*The Terrible Relations*, 1938) and *La machine à écrire* (*The Typewriter*, 1941)—he stands as the spearhead of that phalanx of writers who demand that the theatre should turn from the realistic style and evolve fresh forms of expression. In general, too, he demands that all the thought processes, all the ratiocination associated with the play of ideas should be abandoned, that the theatre should once more become true to itself and recognize that in pure theatricality resides a virtue with its own inherent value. At the same time he keeps to no set path, and even within the framework of single plays he startles us by the introduction of inconsistencies and disharmonies. At times he can be almost melodramatically realistic, as when in *La voix humaine* he introduces one long monologue spoken by a character into the telephone, ending the flow of words by means of a suicide effected with the flex of the instrument. At other moments, as in *L'aigle à deux têtes*, his mood turns Websterian and romantic. Here he spins a dark fantasy of a peasant-poet who comes to a palace with the intent of murdering his Queen. Seeing her, he falls under her spell and is drawn into a passionate love romance. She and he are wrapped in a passion beyond which there can be nothing of any worth, and the Queen, realizing that on earth their love cannot find consummation, yet that life without him would be empty, goads him into committing the assassination he had come to effect. In another mood he turns to the style of surrealism, and proceeds to take a number of ancient Greek themes for a treatment far removed from that which they had received in Athenian days. *Orphée* has all the inconsequence of a dream, introducing a bizarre mixture of the gay and the terrible, allowing its characters to defy at once the dictates of reason and the laws of gravitation. The same process is followed in *Antigone* (1922), and is carried to most satisfying form in *La machine infernale* (*The Infernal Machine*, 1934). This last play, based on the ever-fascinating myth of Œdipus, presents the gods before us, in the words of its title, as naught save an 'infernal machine,' a vicious power intent on the creating of misery for man. In narrating his story Cocteau completely abandons any attempt to startle his audience by any surprises except those achieved by his own nimble imaginative dialogue and by the contrast between the Greek story and his chosen method of treatment: he causes his chorus not merely to outline the plot, but also to elucidate the course of the spiritual movement of the play. That spiritual movement aims, albeit by means strange and unfamiliar, at the evoking of a tragic mood by showing a human character who, while not himself of great stature, achieves unwonted dignity by passing through the fire of torment. In this effort Cocteau has displayed consummate skill in craftsmanship, power over words, and innate wisdom in his choice of material. The surrealist (and other anti-realistic) styles can easily lose themselves in an incomprehensible medley of subjectively conceived imaginings: in selecting stories well-known and hallowed by previous handling the author at once permits himself the opportunity of achieving effects from the contrast between the old and the new, and secures a firm basis in dramatic unity and in fundamental clarity of purpose. At the same time in Cocteau's work we always feel that something is lacking. Without doubt he has the power to create scenes which, even when not fully intelligible, are instinct with emotional quality, but it must be admitted that throughout his work we are uneasily conscious of a certain insincerity: we suspect that the surrealistic technique is employed, not because of a deeply felt belief in its virtue, but because, handled with his adroit skill, its very novelty is bound to attract attention.

Another dramatist, the Franco-Belgian Fernand Crommelynck, has likewise found the surrealistic methods of some service. From that school he learned how to mix scenes of violently contrasting qualities, to set crudest farce alongside potentially tragic material, to make a dream sequence follow or precede a scene of almost naturalistic kind. Outside of France he is best known for the overflowing vitality and gusty humour of *Le cocu magnifique* (*The Magnificent Cuckold*, 1920), but others of his plays perhaps may be considered in the future as even richer in quality and more vivid in execution. An irrepressibly eccentric author, he has an extended career from the beginning of the century on to the thirties—from *Le sculpteur de masques* (*The Maker of Masks*, 1908) and *Le marchand de regrets* (*The Merchant of Regrets*, 1913), through *Les amants puérils* (*The Childish Lovers*, 1921), *Carine* (1930), and *Tripes d'or* (*Golden Tripe*, 1930), to *Une femme qu'a le cœur trop petit* (*The Woman whose Heart is Too Small*, 1934) and *Chaud et froid* (*Hot and Cold*, 1934). In all of these the same qualities are apparent—the rich outpouring of words, the skilful theatrical situations, the intermingling of the rational and the irrational. In *Une femme qu'a le cœur trop petit*, a strange play that takes as its heroine a woman, Balbine, whose emotional life is suppressed by her concentration on the petty things of domestic existence, we move from scenes of the outward to scenes of the inward, while in others we can hardly tell which particular region we inhabit at any precise moment. In this connexion it is interesting to compare the methods of *Beggar on Horseback* and *Tripes d'or*. Both present fundamentally the same theme—that of a young man in love with a girl, yet prepared to forsake her for money. Whereas Kaufman and Connelly, however, never leave us in doubt concerning the nature of their scenes and eventually reach a nice sentimental conclusion, Crommelynck brings the inner and the outer together and produces a bitter irony all his own. One of the most effective scenes in this play shows the hero, Hormidas, in his room. We know that he adores Azelle, but adroitly Crommelynck has kept her off the stage: we know her, we feel, but only through what others have said of her. Now we learn that she is coming to see her Hormidas, and her knock sounds on the door. In silence he pretends not to hear, and for a brief space we are kept in suspense, then we listen to her steps retreating. The scene is real and yet it is symbolic; it is outward and yet it concerns rather the adventures of the soul than those of the body.

Other authors in France have occasionally borrowed directly from the surrealistic, notably Roger Vitrac, whose works go directly back to Jarry. His *Les mystères d'amour* (*The Mysteries of Love*, 1927) exists only to present the confused dreams of a lover. In *Victor, ou les enfants du pouvoir* (*Victor; or, Children in Power*, 1928) he satirizes society's follies by creating an impossible world in which a child nine years old speaks and acts like a man. In general, however, the borrowings from the surrealistic rarely go beyond the seizing of its devices for a bare scene or two, and consequently the works in which they appear may better be considered elsewhere than here. Cocteau and Crommelynck may be permitted to stand by themselves as two playwrights illustrating the manner in which this influence can appear, the one deliberately taking over much of the eccentric dream machinery, but enclosing it in the tight frame of classical myth, and the other rarely using the more obvious tricks of surrealistic technique, but clearly introducing into his plays something of its spirit. Perhaps, when the dramatic works of this period can be viewed in the perspective of time, it will be agreed that the latter rather than the former approach is of greater significance.

THE ENTRY OF PSYCHOANALYSIS INTO THE THEATRE

More common is the introduction to the stage of psychoanalytic method, and here Henri-René Lenormand stands forth as a prime representative of a loosely affiliated school of writers. Lenormand comes before us as the brutal naturalistic dramatist turned inward. In his scenes are sensational crudities that remind us of the early Hauptmann's imaginings—with this difference, that the focus is always less on the events themselves than upon the subconscious workings of his characters' beings. One of his better-known dramas, *Le mangeur de rêves* (*The Eater of Dreams*, 1922), indeed, goes so far as to psychoanalyse a psychoanalyst, the central figure being a professional exponent of this 'science' who himself is so unbalanced as deliberately to drag from his patients' souls secrets which should never have been brought to light: he thus demonstrates to a young girl that a display of jealousy in her childhood (which she had entirely forgotten) was responsible for her mother's death. In *Les ratés* (*The Failures*, 1920) two wretched people, an author and his actress wife, both of them wholly unsuccessful, are relentlessly brought from step to step down the ladder until the man murders the woman and commits suicide. The inner life of a Don Juan is revealed in *L'homme et ses fantômes* (*Man and his Phantoms*, 1924), with the psychoanalytic explanation that the hero has passed restlessly from one mistress to another because all his life he has been unconsciously seeking his mother; a perverted soul is dissected in *L'ombre du mal* (*The Shadow of Evil*, 1924); while in *La dent rouge* (*The Red Tooth*, 1925) the story is told of a sophisticated girl's marrying an unlettered mountaineer, finding herself surrounded by the fantastic demons of the popular imagination as she sits virtually alone in her snow-bound hut, and finally being accused of witchcraft. *Le simoun* (1920) narrates, in the arid setting of the Arabian desert, the story of a father's incestuous love of his daughter; *Le lâche* (*The Coward*, 1926) cruelly analyses the soul terrors and weaknesses of a man who, during the war, has sought escape in Switzerland. There is not, perhaps, very much of real worth in Lenormand's work, and occasionally we may suspect there is a good deal of nonsense, but his position in the history of the drama is an important one and his influence has not been by any means meagre.

Not unlike in spirit is Paul Raynal, author of *Le maître de son cœur* (*The Master of his Heart*, 1920), *Le tombeau sous l'Arc de Triomphe* (*The Tomb beneath the Arc de Triomphe*, or *The Unknown Warrior*, 1924), *Au soleil de l'instinct* (*In the Sunshine of Instinct*, 1932), and

La Francerie (1933). The first of these deals trenchantly with the affection of two friends broken by the machinations of a woman; the second, a more powerful drama, shows a soldier on leave from the front and carries its tense scenes forward with merely three persons—the soldier himself, the girl to whom he is betrothed, and his father. Unlike Lenormand, Raynal is rather the romanticist of psychoanalysis than its naturalist. Lenormand's words are bare; Raynal's pour forth in a wild torrent; his figures, although also laid on the dissecting table, have their nakedness wrapped up in the rich folds of his lyrical utterance.

It is interesting to observe here that at this time in Paris a peculiar recrudescence of crude violence, whether naturalistic or romantic, appeared in the works of several dramatists. To those mentioned above may be added the names of two other authors—Steve Passeur and the Belgian Michel de Ghelderode. Passeur, whose *Suzanne* (1929), *L'acheteuse* (*The Woman Buys*, 1930), *La chaîne* (*The Chain*, 1931), *Les tricheurs* (*The Cheats*, 1933), *Je vivrai un grand amour* (*I shall have a Great Love*, 1935), and *Le château de cartes* (*The House of Cards*, 1937) all present dismal, brutal pictures of life, with love a kind of frenzied hatred, has carried his earlier style into the post-war period with his melodramatic *La traitresse* (*The Traitress*, 1946). Ghelderode enters into this sphere with the tumultuous scenes of his *Hop, Signor!* (1938).

THE PSYCHOANALYSIS OF LOVE

There are others, however, who take a quieter course, and here the once esteemed but now somewhat neglected Jean-Jacques Bernard may be taken as typical. Some few years ago critics were raving about his works: later re-reading suggests that, despite the unquestioned skill of his dramas, their themes are a trifle thin and their characters too delicate to be real. Take, for example, *L'âme en peine* (*The Soul in Pain*, or *The Unquiet Spirit*, 1926), where an attempt is made to show a woman, Marceline, married to a man she loves, yet strangely tortured in mind, restless, losing energy she knows not why: the explanation is that she has a twin-soul, a man she never meets, but whom we see drifting near to her on several occasions; and we are given to understand that her separation from him torments her subconscious spirit. There is some subtlety here, yet, when we have done with the play, we realize that it is no more than a new treatment of Maeterlinck's neo-romantic *Blue Bird* fantasy of boy and girl souls being divided by the exigencies of their incorporation in human bodies. All Bernard's dramas are of a similar kind: like Maeterlinck, he argues for a 'static' drama; like Norwid, he believes in the drama of silences. *L'invitation au voyage* (*The Invitation to a Voyage*, 1924) shows a young wife morbidly dreaming of a young engineer who has gone off to the Argentine; she is shocked into a realization of fact when she meets him again on one of his visits home. In *Le feu qui reprend mal* (*The Sulky Fire*, 1921) a soldier returns from the front and is racked by jealousy because his wife has had an American billeted in the house; in *Martine* (1922) a country girl, married later, finds her heart throbbing for a youth whom she had met casually years before; in *Le printemps des autres* (*The Springtime of Others*, 1924) a mother finds herself moved, beyond her will, to love her daughter's husband, until, in the end, she forces herself to separate from her child (as the two women part there is "a very long silent gaze between them, the understanding gaze of woman to woman"); *Denise Marette* (1925) narrates the story of an artist's daughter who puts forth her work as his and is visited by a perplexing ghost who appears now as an angry stranger, now as the father whom she had idolized. It is all very pretty, all very sentimental, and all very thin.

Closely associated with Bernard is Charles Vildrac (Charles Messager), author of *Le Paquebot Tenacity* (*S.S. Tenacity*, 1920), *Madame Béliard* (1925), *Le pélerin* (*The Pilgrim*, 1926), *La brouille* (*The Estrangement*, 1930), and *L'air du temps* (*The Atmosphere of the Times*, 1938). Intimate in portraiture, gentle in emotion, sad of mood, he has turned out some appealing plays, although not such as are likely to endure. *Le pélerin* is a kind of tender *Three Sisters* in which the impact of the outside world impinges on a narrow provincial home: listening to her uncle's stories of life in Paris, an awakening dream and a wonder comes to birth in the heart of the little Denise. In *Le Paquebot Tenacity* two ex-soldiers, waiting for the ship that will carry them to Canada, are shown in love with a pretty waitress at a café: the more idealistic of the pair loses her, his bolder friend carries her off. Such simple situations appeal to Vildrac, and he makes them appealing to others by means of a skill in the revealing of secret sentiments and in the evoking of mood.

The psychology of love is the general theme also of nearly all the rather disappointing works of Paul Géraldy. In *Les noces d'argent* (*The Silver Wedding*, or *The Nest*, 1917) he returns to the problem which had so exercised the thought of some nineteenth-century authors and treats of the neglect of the middle-aged and the old by their children. *Aimer* (*To Love*, 1921) interestingly deals with the eternal triangle by concentrating the whole of the attention not on the woman and the lover, but upon the husband and wife. This concentration on a couple of persons appears again in *Robert et Marianne* (1925), where the contrast between sexual desire and love is handled with some real penetration. So he proceeds with similar themes in the bitter *Christine* (1932) and in the less gloomy *Do-mi-sol-do* (1934) and *Duo* (1938), without achieving more than the fashioning of sincere, yet uninvigorating, dramas of meagre worth.

Among all these authors one more stands out—Jean Sarment. There are others, such as Jean-Victor Pellerin, with his interesting study of a will-less character who cannot take his part in life in *Têtes de rechange* (*Spare Heads*, 1926), or Simon Gantillon, with his once much-discussed *Maya* (1924), in which a Marseilles prostitute becomes to diverse men what they desire her to be—but the one man who seems to have the qualities necessary for enduring worth is the creator of *Le pêcheur d'ombres* (*The Fisher of Shades*, 1921), an amazing study of insanity, in which a poet, whose memory has gone, can find peace for his spirit only by remaining, deliberately, within his world of shadows. The play recalls the psychological studies of Pirandello, but still more it savours of the spirit that produces the *proverbes dramatiques* of Musset. Pirandello's music may be 'cerebral' and sometimes hard to follow, but his notes are clear: Sarment plays continuously on muted strings. All his plays have similar qualities. In his first piece, *La couronne de carton* (*The Pasteboard Crown*, 1920), the Pirandellesque quality is shown in the story of a woman who does not appreciate a man when he is himself; he can arouse her love only when he pretends to be what she thinks he ought to be; and, so far as he is concerned, the confusion of appearance and reality brings to his heart wisdom, perhaps, but also, and more powerfully, a great weariness of spirit. The connexion between Pirandello and Barrie has already been noted; Sarment too becomes Barrieesque in *Le mariage d'Hamlet* (*Hamlet's Marriage*, 1922), where Ophelia, her father, and the hero are given a second chance; Hamlet endeavours to accept his trials less passionately, but soon tires of his static rôle. The contrast between the ideal and reality gives the sadly resigned theme of *Je suis trop grand pour moi* (*I am Too Noble for Myself*, 1924), and variations on such contrasts furnish the mainsprings of *Les plus beaux yeux du monde* (*The Most Beautiful Eyes in the World*, 1925), *Madelon* (1925), *Léopold le Bien-Aimé* (*Leopold the Beloved*, 1927), *As-tu du cœur?* (*Have you No Feelings?*, 1926), *Le plancher des vaches* (*Terra Firma*, 1931), *Le voyage à Biarritz* (*The Trip to Biarritz*, 1936), *Othello*

(1937), and *Mamouret* (1941). In all of these are men and women haunted by visions whose airy wraiths are dissipated by reality, shattered by the breaking of their ideals, yet finding the best part of themselves in the sorry remnants of what they had dreamed. There may be no great strength here, but there is undoubtedly magic of a kind.

The English dramatist who perhaps approaches more closely than any other to these French playwrights is Charles Morgan. Although better-known as a novelist, he has contributed to the theatre one interesting drama, *The Flashing Stream* (1938), wherein he subtly contrasts and compares the imaginatively rational appeal of science with the appeal of the emotions. It is worthy of note that this play seems to have had a greater success in Paris than it had in London: it springs more from the French tradition than from the English.

THE PLAY OF FAITH, SPACE, AND TIME

For some authors the search inward implies a hard, sometimes cruel, scientific dissection of the soul; for others it implies an exploration of that irrational quality of mankind to which we give the name of faith. This may take the form either of excursions into the field of the religious drama or else of experiments in the writing of plays which, outwardly realistic, concentrate attention on the spirit.

The former endeavour obviously carries us close to the mood of earlier romanticism, although the demands of the modern world call for scenes less flamboyant and decidedly less rhetorical. Thoroughly characteristic of this sphere of dramatic writing is Paul Claudel, whose *L'ôtage* (*The Hostage*, 1911) presents a heroine set in much the same situation as some heroines of Maeterlinck, faced with the dilemma of carrying out her duty or of forgetting duty in abandonment to love. Essentially Claudel is a poet who finds himself most at home with figments of his own imagination. Early in his career he penned a strange drama, *La ville* (*The City*, 1893), which indicated the general trend of his art. In the midst of the abstractions with which he peoples this play we move darkling; any attempt to find rational explanations of the scenes presented results in a breaking of the charm; only through a frank devotion to the emotional can we hope to sense the author's purpose. Hardly less abstract are the figures introduced into his study of profane and spiritual love, *Partage de midi* (*The Midday Break*; printed 1906). It is true that in his later dramas the characters assume more of human semblance, but always in Claudel's work we sense the hovering of invisible presences, and, at the same time, we feel that within any single one of his works there is incorporated a wealth of imaginative experience which only vaguely is expressed in the plot before us. Perhaps his imagination is too fertile to permit its flourishing satisfactorily within the walls of the theatre. Most appealing of all his works is unquestionably *L'annonce faite à Marie* (*The Tidings brought to Mary*, 1912), in which the author's simple faith makes memorable a play of quiet emotion. Through her unquestioning assurance in the all-loving God the leprous Violaine effects a miracle and brings back to life the dead child of her sister Mara. Claudel's later *Le soulier de satin* (*The Satin Slipper*; printed 1930, acted 1943) presents to the public a perplexing double action which, however, becomes irradiated by the peculiarly imaginative style and by the almost mystical philosophic emotion cast upon its scenes and characters. Spiritual devotion, too, is the theme of his latest work, *Le père humilié* (*The Father Humiliated*, 1946).

For Henri Ghéon (Henri Vanglon) the medieval period, with its orthodox faith, proves happy hunting-ground: typical are his *Le mystère de l'invention de la Croix* (*The Mystery of the Finding of the Cross*, 1932), *Violante* (1933) and *L'histoire du jeune Bernard de Menthon* (1925)—the last of which has gained fame in the version produced by Sir Barry Jackson as *The Marvellous History of St Bernard* (1926). For a Biblical drama *Noé*, (*Noah*, 1931), André Obey won considerable attention when it was toured through various countries during the thirties by the Compagnie des Quinze, an offshoot of Jacques Copeau's venture at the Vieux Colombier. Obey's other writings, however, carry us out of the religious field: *Le viol de Lucrèce* (*The Rape of Lucrèce*, 1931) is a stylized modernistic treatment of the story that Shakespeare immortalized; *Maria* (1945) is a kind of mixture of Thornton Wilder and Pirandello, the action taking place on a bare stage while a play is being rehearsed, and introducing the familiar contrast between the world of reality and the theatre's fictional realm; in *Œdipe* (*Œdipus*, 1948) he turns Sophocles into modern form. Clearly associated with Claudel and other playwrights of this group is another French author, Boussac de Saint Marc, with his peculiar *Le loup de Gubbio* (*The Wolf of Gubbio*, 1921), in which a wild outcast is cared for by a girl strong in her unquestioning faith, and *Moloch* (1929), a drama that seeks to delineate the all-devouring maw of the artistic impulse. With these dramas may be associated *L'autre Messie* (*The Other Messiah*, 1923) of the Belgian Henri

Soumagne, an author responsible also for a less successful, although still interesting, drama of the Resurrection, *Madame Marie* (1928).

In Germany the *Totentanz* (*Dance of Death*, 1921) of Leo Weismantel springs from the same impulse that led French experimenters to make use of medieval material. A similar trend appears in the work of the Austrian Max Mell, the title of whose *Das Wiener Kripperl von 1919* (*The Viennese Manger of 1919*, 1921) sufficiently indicates its inspiration. The same mood is present also in the earlier dramas of Hermann Heinz Ortner, notably *Sebastian-legende* (*The Legend of Sebastian*, 1929). The way in which this exploration of the supernatural meets with the widespread dramatic interest in the folk is made apparent in the writings of another Austrian author, Richard Billinger, in whose works the ideas of Christianity are mingled with the pagan memories jealously guarded by the peasants of the Tyrol. *Das Perchtenspiel* (*The Perchten Play*, 1928) thus bases its plot on the operation of the powers possessed by the 'Perchten' who haunt the mountainside; *Rauhnacht* (1931) celebrates that December eve when these and other supernatural creatures roam the land; while *Die Hexe von Passau* (*The Witch of Passau*, 1935), although it does not deal with material of quite the same kind, introduces the same atmosphere by dealing with a religious conversion occasioned by the presentation of a mystery drama.

The range of this religious drama is to be realized when we set these imitations of the medieval theatre and these explorations of folk myth alongside such Catholic essays as come from the pen of the Spanish José María Pemán and such symbolic works as *La morte in vacanze* (*Death takes a Holiday*, 1924), by the Italian Alberto Casella, which in turn leads us to a series of plays wherein the metaphysical is theatrically exploited in terms not specifically associated either with Christian dogma or pagan legend.

In England Sutton Vane created something of a lively stir with *Outward Bound* (1923), a skilful, but perhaps not very profound or sincere, presentation of the world after death as a ship carrying souls from the country of the living to heaven's custom-house. Since then, both in England and in America, many experiments have been made in this sphere, and perhaps one of the most notable things about the modern stage has been the freedom with which it has seriously exploited the supernatural. Except for some melodramatic experiments made during the early nineteenth century, it might almost be said that the European and American drama remained entirely ghostless from just after the time of Shakespeare until our own period; we think nothing now of accepting a blithe spirit from the other world in a Noel Coward comedy or of welcoming the presence of the devil in a James Bridie fantasy. Thoroughly characteristic is *Father Malachy's Miracle* (1937) by the Canadian author Brian Doherty. With charming power, this author persuades us that little Father Malachy is truly gifted with the miracle-maker's gifts. Declaring that a night club of which he disapproves will be removed from the city of Edinburgh to the lonely Bass Rock, he finds, to his dismay, that his prophecy has been taken by the heavenly powers at face-value. For himself only trouble can come from this manifestation of supernatural power: the Church will certainly want to know all about it, and charlatans will plague him. In despair he racks his brains for a solution and finds it in uttering a second declaration to the effect that the night club will be removed back to Edinburgh again: it is, and the curtain descends on a Father Malachy mightily relieved in spirit.

The mood animating *Father Malachy's Miracle* is somewhat akin to that from which the plays of the Irish dramatist Paul Vincent Carroll draw their distinction, although in this author we sense the · presence of a strange dichotomy. On the one hand, we feel that the impulse which has driven him to turn to the theatre is the desire to preach a message of liberal thought; on the other, his most memorable scenes are those wherein his message is forgotten and the light hovering of supernatural wings trembles above his human characters. This dichotomy is to be seen nowhere more clearly than in the play, *Shadow and Substance* (1934), which, after the relatively unsuccessful *Things that are Cæsar's* (1932), brought him to fame. In one sense *Shadow and Substance* may be regarded as a realistic problem drama in which the author contrasts the narrow, reactionary clericalism of Canon Skerritt and the broad-minded, forward-looking idealism of the liberal teacher O'Flingsley. What gives to the play its peculiar intensity, however, and raises it far beyond the reach of the ordinary play of ideas is the imaginative quality that surrounds the character of Brigid, an unlettered country girl on whom the hand of the eternal spirit has descended. Like Joan of Arc, Brigid sees visions beyond the limits of the phenomenal world, and in listening to her words we are rapt into the realm of faith.

Most unfortunately Carroll has not succeeded in rising again to the quality of this drama. The *White Steed* (1938) is disappointing, partly because it does not have the richness of texture that makes *Shadow and Substance* memorable, partly because its 'problem' theme is virtually the same as that of the earlier play, and partly because the sense of the miraculous is summoned forth with far less subtlety. Even weaker seems the confused and confusing *The Wise have not Spoken* (1944), a play in which incoherency beautifully reigns.

Closely associated with such plays are those in which exploration is made of space-time concepts or of subject-matter in which, without the direct or indirect interposition of divine powers, the normal sequence of events in real life is interrupted. A typical example may be found in the play *On Borrowed Time* (1938), wherein the American Paul Osborn tells a strange story of a man who succeeds in temporarily staying the power of death. The author, however, who has most consistently applied himself to this field is the English John Boynton Priestley. His earliest theatrical essays, such as *Dangerous Corner* (1932) and *Laburnum Grove* (1933), give no more than a hint of what he was to make his later speciality. These works indicated that he possessed (rather surprisingly, in view of the large canvas of his novels) the true dramatist's gift: *Laburnum Grove* is a skilfully constructed work in which the contrast between crime and quiet suburbia is excellently handled, and *Dangerous Corner*, with a greater anticipation of his later style, is inherently of the theatre. So, too, is his later *The Linden Tree* (1947), a study of ordinary life amid modern doubts and the clashing of values.

Priestley's 'speciality,' if so it may be called, appeared first full shaped in four dramas released in 1937 and 1938—*Time and the Conways, I Have Been Here Before, I'm a Stranger Here,* and *Music at Night*: in diverse ways the same 'time continuum' concept provides the mainspring for *They Came to a City* (1942), *Desert Highway* (1944), and *An Inspector Calls* (1946), although in a later work, *Ever since Paradise* (1947), he has moved into a different kind of experimentation, bringing characters in and out of a play-within-the-play being enacted in their midst. Without doubt all of these possess individual and appealing qualities. In *Music at Night* the playing of a violin concerto releases a group of characters from their outer selves and permits the author to make stage presentation of the subconscious. The plot of *Time and the Conways* allows him to build his scenic picture of life independent of the commonly accepted sequence of minutes, days, and hours. In *Desert Highway* past and present meet on one plane; the action of the first part, involving the adventures of a tank crew stuck in the illimitable waste of sands, is related to action belonging to the eighth century before Christ. Fully into the realm of the imaginative he moves in *They Came to a City*, which shows a crowd of diversely assorted characters, each representative of a class within the community, coming to a great majestic walled town. They find that here civilization has reached perfection. Work is play here; there are no wars; bitterness of spirit is a thing unknown. As Priestley develops the action he seeks to show how the diverse persons from our imperfect social world react to the wonders of this world of wonders. For some it is bliss; for some it is hell. Still another experiment is tried in *An Inspector Calls*. Here a family circle is presented before us. From outside the walls of their home comes a piece of news, the death of a girl, which at first sight seems to have no more to do with them than a mere item of interest in a newspaper. When an Inspector calls, however, he gradually relates each member of this comfortable group to the girl's fate; inner secrets are dragged to light, concealed hopes and fears are laid bare on the dissecting table. After he has gone one of the family telephones to headquarters, but the police know nothing about it. This was an Inspector of whom the police have no knowledge.

It is too early yet to pass any general judgment on Priestley's position as a dramatist, but this at least may be said, that among the playwrights of the past ten years he is, without doubt, one of the most ambitious in his aims and the most skilled in his handling of scenic material. Perhaps he has not yet succeeded in passing beyond the stage of experimentation, but, even if so, what he has already accomplished shows a scope, a vigour, and a sense of theatrical effectiveness that put him in the vanguard of English playwrights.

A consideration of these dramas reminds us that similar topics were being dealt with during these years, and even earlier, on several European stages. In the year following the Armistice (1919) Henri Lenormand in France produced *Le temps est un songe* (*Time is a Dream*). This drama clearly anticipates Priestley's exploitation of the time-continuum concept when it shows the suicidal death of the hero revealed, some time before its actual occurrence, to the girl with whom he is in love. The English author's *An Inspector Calls* reminds us too that there are several present-day dramatists who, interested in personality, employ the device of inserting into a chosen *milieu* some person, such as Priestley's Inspector, who possesses a catalytic force almost supernatural in its capabilities. Very close to *An Inspector Calls*, for example, are several plays by the Italian Ugo Betti. Betti's form is, like Priestley's, outwardly realistic, yet his characters and plots are constantly shot through with symbolic significance. Representative of his style is

Frana allo scalo Nord (*Landslide at the North Slope*, 1935), *Notte in casa del rico* (*Night in the Rich Man's House*, 1942), and *Ispezione* (*Inspection*, or *The Inspector Calls*, 1947). The first introduces an accident during civic excavations; even as each person involved endeavours to disclaim responsibility, the circle widens until the entirety of the city is involved, even while the secret souls of the individuals directly concerned are bared. Into the realistic setting something of the supramundane enters: the victims of the accident appear to rise again, and the advocate is transmogrified into the judge; for human errors only pity remains. As the play ends Parsc, a counsellor, speaks in a thundering voice, giving judgment:

> PARSC: Taking into consideration that they suffer, yet wish to suffer; they suffer when they own their land and when they work for others; when they are reputed good and when they are reputed evil, when they oppress and when they are oppressed, when they cheat and when they are cheated; they suffer, yet they wish to suffer because they breathe, because they are men, because they wish to live, weep, hope and advance their interests. . . .
>
> GOETZ: For these reasons . . . [*All remain motionless, with heads bowed.*
>
> PARSC [*stretches forth his hand, takes the documents, raises them*]: For these reasons. In the name of God; in the name of the law; we declare that these men . . .
>
> GOETZ [*provokingly*]: Proceed, Parsc. Pronounce the sentence!
>
> PARSC: We declare that these men have pronounced—that every day they pronounce—through their lives, through their labour, the just sentence; they themselves will find their own certitude. And maybe from the hands of justice they may have something else, something higher—pity. Pity.
>
> ALL [*in a low tone*]: Pity . . . Pity . . .

About the whole of his action Betti throws this veil of uncertainty, doubt, condemnation, and compassion.

Notte in casa del ricco shows Betti developing the idea that all our present is bound up in the past. Tito expresses its philosophy. "Yes," he says,

> For example, I want to go there. [*Points in one direction.*] But I cannot. Because of an action that I committed long ago, here I am now; almost without realizing it, without having the freedom to go where I want to go, I find myself *there*.   [*Points in another direction.*

Ispezione draws this author nearest to Priestley. Into a household come two inspectors; they rake up things hidden, and depart. "We are going," declares one of them at the end of the drama.

THE INSPECTOR: We are going. We have nothing more to do here.

ANDREA: You're going?

THE INSPECTOR: Yes.

ANDREA: You're leaving us in this way?

THE INSPECTOR: What do you mean?

ANDREA [*suddenly, with anger*]: And the dispositions? The directives?
At least we can learn why you came here? You'll surely tell us
something!

THE INSPECTOR [*suddenly, with sombre vehemence*]: You yourself don't
know what you want, and you have the impertinence to think you
know what others want? Very convenient! These are your affairs:
and you must puzzle them out alone: reach to an understanding of
them all alone. Every one by himself alone. [*With a thunderous tone*]
By himself alone! You can be assured that no one will help you!
[*Goes to the door and disappears with his companion.*

If we have been led to a consideration of Betti's work through
consideration of Priestley's plays, Betti in turn leads us to Jules
Romains (Louis Farigoule). Like his Italian fellow-dramatist,
Romains stylizes reality, and, like him, he sees the individual human
being at once as a lonely entity and as a mere part of a larger whole.
His philosophy is that of 'Unanimism'—the invisible society that
exists among men united by a physical or a spiritual link. A family
circle is an example of unanimism; so is a nation, a church, the community of a city—even the passengers in a bus, if something happens
to make them conscious of their common interests, can become
such a unit. In his plays Romains constantly provides, generally in
mocking tones, examples of such unanimity. In *L'armée dans la
ville* (*The Army in the Town*, 1911), a play dealing with the question
of resistance to imposed authority, the occupying forces form one
unit, the townspeople another. Characteristically, *Cromedeyre-le-
vieil* (1920) is given a title from the name of the village in which
the fantastic action takes place, and the better-known *Knock, ou le
triomphe de médecine* (*Knock; or, The Triumph of Medicine*, or *Dr
Knock*, 1923) gains all its comic power from exploitation of this
concept. The little village of Saint-Maurice here is at once recognizable and a figment of the imagination: Romains' hero, Dr
Knock, who comes to take the place of the old-fashioned Dr Parpa-
laid, and who succeeds in persuading all the people in this community that they are ill, is both man and symbol. Human beings
are thus given unanimity in that every healthy man becomes a
potential patient.

The same spirit animates the two plays dealing with *Monsieur Le
Trouhadec* (1923 and 1925); in the former we are presented with the

'unanimisme' of the Casino at Monte Carlo; in the latter the hero of the play ironically is shown founding and leading "The Honest Men's Party." Irony colours the whole of *Musse, ou l'école de l'hypocrisie* (*Musse; or, The School of Hypocrisy*, 1930), wherein the little man, Musse, in discovering that a great philanthropist is a completely selfish libertine, comes to the conclusion that the only way of living a quiet life is to be a hypocrite himself; more bitter is *Le dictateur* (*The Dictator*, 1926), which shows an erstwhile revolutionary accepting a king's commission to form a strong (and therefore dictatorial) government. These, unfortunately, are less powerful plays than the brilliant *Knock*; even the film-like satire *Donogoo* (1931), telling how a number of crack-pots try to establish a town in America, although interesting, lacks the graceful verve of that comedy, while *Boën* (1931), displaying the effects of sudden wealth upon a relatively honest middle-class man, wants both vigour and clarity of orientation. In *L'an mil* (*The Year One Thousand*, 1947), one of his most powerful plays, he pursues his aims by taking us far back into the past and by relating that past to the present.

PLAYS OF THE SOUL

Romains probably takes us rather far from the impressionism from which we started, but in the work of an American playwright, Philip Barry, we clearly find ourselves in close association with the most characteristically 'impressionistic' writers, and from a consideration of his writings we realize the ties that bind together those who are led into the dim regions of the psyche and those who are drawn within the equally dim regions of the symbolic. About Barry there is an aura that reminds us of his Scottish namesake Barrie; that aura, however, also reveals shades reminiscent of Maeterlinck, Pirandello, Bernard, and Sarment. Barry secures an individual note by taking symbolic forms and clothing them with delicate laughter. Often he is spoken of in terms that suggest that his chief interest lies in the development of a modern comedy of manners; in reality his spirit is close to those writers of the 'impressionistic' tradition with whom we have just been dealing. *Hotel Universe* (1930) is a strictly psychoanalytic and 'time-space' play which shows a group of tortured souls gathered together in a house inhabited by a (supposedly) great scientist whose views on the nature of man and of the universe have made him seem mad to his relatives. However, by his influence all the tormented characters, by having their thoughts turned to persons whom they had loved

and forgotten, are brought back to mental health. There is no depth
in this drama, and (despite the esteem in which it has been held)
there is a vast amount of absurdity in its dialogue. No one can
deny, perhaps, the simple-minded sincerity that gave it birth, but
in the theatre neither simple-mindedness nor sincerity alone is likely
to achieve anything of worth. The title of *Hotel Universe* itself
well displays Barry's attraction towards the almost childishly
'symbolic,' and this tendency is further exemplified in the Globe
Theatre wherein the persons of *Here Come the Clowns* (1938) indulge
in their metaphysical meanderings. Some good theatricalism is
present in its scenes, but we shall err sadly if we assume that its story
of a scene-shifter seeking God and much impressed by the tricks of a
charlatan who seems to be an embodiment of the Devil has any
profundity of thought or intensity of emotion. On analysis the
entire content of the drama is found to be mushy; there is no firm
substance fit for dissection. Even a clearer example of the juvenile
symbols so dear to Barry appears in *Liberty Jones* (1941), in which
Uncle Sam and Liberty rather tediously give expression to the very
best, and the most obvious, of sentiments.

Along with these plays Barry has penned many others, and in
some at least he happily forgets the pseudo-mystical and engages
in purely comic exercise. *The Animal Kingdom* (1932), with its
triangle and its paradoxical treatment of the mistress who takes on
the qualities of a wife, might have been written by one of Paris's
lesser playwrights; *Paris Bound* (1927) unites a Catholic concept to
a theme apt for comic treatment in emphasizing that a little defection
on the part of a husband need not, and should not, ruin a marriage;
Holiday (1928) is a rather thin study of love and life cast in sentimental terms, but made gracious by its delicate dialogue; in *Phila-
delphia Story* (1939), more successfully, he pens a comedy which
perhaps may be regarded as the peak of his achievement as an artist.

In general, we may say that Barry is an author some of whose
scenes are enjoyable, whose skill in writing we may admire, but
whose spirit is apt uneasily to stray into realms he is utterly un-
qualified to understand or appreciate. Akin to him in some respects,
yet outwardly far apart, is William Saroyan, whose continual
reiteration of facile philosophic sentiments and apparently novel
methods of play construction once persuaded many critics that in
him great genius was to be found. It is observable, however, that
after the excitement of *My Heart's in the Highlands* (1939) his
enthusiastic supporters have tended to become ever less and less
vociferous. This, his first play, characteristically mingles together

an outwardly realistic scene with elements of the symbolic and with a method of episodical display of material which has the appearance of being new: colloquial dialogue, suggesting naturalistic effort, is set close against flights in a poetic vein. But on reflection we can find but little in these sentimental pictures of poverty-stricken young poets and of broken-down actors who play on trumpets with such Orphean charm that all the neighbourhood comes rapt to listen. This drama was followed by the more ambitious *The Time of Your Life* (1939), where again the scene, a wretched San Francisco saloon, gives the semblance of reality. Following the line of Chekhov, Saroyan here dispenses with plot and causes his characters to philosophize mightily and mistily about life, its wonders and its despairs, its sorrows and its joys. In the centre of the motley group of characters drifts a person named Joe, eternally drunk and eternally buying toys: we learn that this is so since he remembers that as a child he once stopped crying because a toy was given to him. In addition the spectators are provided with a diversity of other strange oddities, for Saroyan also brings in a number of broken-down 'bums,' a prostitute, and a midget barely three feet in height. In *The Beautiful People* (1941) once more a philosopher and a poet are introduced (this time father and son), with a plot which tells of a family living on pension cheques due to the defunct owner of the house in which they dwell. During the next season (1942) a Saroyan Theatre, presenting *Across the Board on To-morrow Morning* and *Talking to Yoy*, was opened in New York, and closed rapidly. His latest play, *Jim Dandy* (1947), has as its setting

> all or part of a transparent egg shell which is broken and open along one side. Inside the shell are miserable and majestic ruins. These ruins represent immemorial and immediate reality, as thrown together by time, nature, art, religion, labour, science, invention, plan, accident, violence of war, and wear and tear of weather.

This is all very mysterious, but at least it may be said that these plays have more substance than the shadow that was Gertrude Stein's *Four Saints in Three Acts* (1934)—a musical play that uses four acts to present fifteen saints uttering sentiments wholly incomprehensible.

In diverse ways and in several lands these styles have been cultivated. The plays of Miguel de Unamuno, known as one of the foremost of Spanish philosophers, delve far within the recesses of the soul. Of external action in *Fedra* (1917)—a modern-dress and modern-spirit reworking of the perennially interesting Greek myth

—there is virtually nothing, and the very title of *Sombras de sueño* (*Dream Shadows*, 1931) indicates its quality: this is a kind of mystical essay in Pirandello's favourite theme of double personality.

In Italy itself Pirandello's mantle has been given a fresh satirical twist in the writings of Massimo Bontempelli, whose *Nostra dea* (*Our Goddess*, 1925) is an outwardly farcical, inwardly bitter, revelation of a woman who, naked, is nothing, but who assumes diverse personalities in accordance with the dresses she chooses to wear. A kindred mood animates *Il calzolaio di Messina* (*The Shoemaker of Messina*, 1925), by Alessandro di Stefani: here the central figure is a man who, obsessed with the concept of justice and angered because he sees so many criminals escape the law, himself assumes the rôle of judge and executioner. In one instance, however, he finds he has made a mistake, killing an innocent victim, and as a result, his ideal broken, he takes his own life. The same author's *Pazzi sulla montagna* (*Madmen on the Mountains*, 1926) seeks to demonstrate that only the fools among men are wise. Another Pirandellesque author is Guglielmo Zorzi: his *La vita degli altri* (*The Life of Others*, 1926) is a study of a woman who wears like a cloak the personality of her husband, and *La vena d'ora* (*The Vein of Gold*, 1919) contrasts a young mother as she really is with what her son deems her to be. In *Fiore sotto gli occhi* (*Circles under the Eyes*, 1921), by Fausto Maria Martini, a strange story is told of a poor school-teacher and his wife who, terrified of the monotony of their lives, start deliberately to live the fiction that they are passionate lovers; similarly, in *L'altra Nanetta* (*The Other Nanette*, 1923) the contrast is presented of a woman as she is and as she pretends herself to be. These themes are obviously Pirandellian in character, although Martini succeeds in giving them his own individual flavour by the subtlety of his character delineation and by his technique of understatement.

The Pirandellian style is obvious also in Denmark's *Circus Juris* (1935), by Svend Borberg, an interesting drama dealing with the several 'individualities' within a single individual. Among other contributions in this kind may be noted those of two Polish authoresses, Marja Pawlikowska-Jasnorzewska and Zofja Nałkowska, both of whom, profiting from the earlier example of Przybyszewski, followed a line parallel with that taken by Lenormand, Bernard, and others. The former's *Niebiescy zalotnicy* (*Heavenly Lovers*, 1933) and the latter's *Dzień jego powrotu* (*The Day of His Return*, 1931) are by no means unworthy examples of psychological 'impressionism.'

THE EXPRESSIONISTIC MOVEMENT

IMPRESSIONISM is characteristically French: expressionism is characteristically Germanic. Impressionism is a term that applies to a mood, or to an æsthetic endeavour merely: there is no particular dramatic form or technique (if we except the theories concerning 'static drama' and the 'drama of silences') associated with its aims. Expressionism, on the other hand, implies both a definite manner of approach towards theatrical material and a fresh means of treating this material.

Such distinctions between the two movements would suggest that expressionism might be explained and defined in simpler and clearer terms than is possible where we are concerned with the diverse schools of dramatic inwardness, yet, strangely, the precise opposite is true. Developed in Berlin between 1910 and 1920, the expressionistic style has embraced within itself the most varied talents, and, by concentrating on one or another of these talents, the several critics who have applied themselves to analysing the general qualities of the style as a whole find themselves seriously at odds both with regard to their diagnosis of the movement's origins and with regard to its particular manifestations.

For the most part the divergences in opinion are due to two causes: first, a confusion between the means and the aims; and, second, a failure to see that the expressionist movement, fundamentally anti-realistic in its objectives, gathered to itself a considerable number of adherents whose ideals were far other than those of the men who stood at the core of the school. Thus, for example, it is easy to see that some of the *methods* used by Strindberg and Wedekind anticipate the methods which the expressionists eagerly adopted as their own, but any attempt to prove that the aims of these two earlier authors were 'expressionistic' is false and confusing. In searching for a true definition of what these German revolutionaries sought when they established Expressionismus as an artistic objective we must, therefore, endeavour at once to separate in our minds the technical devices they employed and the ideals for which these devices were but the means, and to track down the core of the true expressionistic spirit amid the confusion of contradictory aims apparent in the works of those who attached themselves directly or indirectly to the school.

THE AIMS OF THE EXPRESSIONISTS

In general the expressionist dramatists seized upon and developed further the kind of dramatic technique in which diverse experiments had already been made by Hauptmann, Wedekind, and Strindberg. Short scenes took the place of longer acts; dialogue was made abrupt and given a staccato effect; symbolic (almost morality-type) forms were substituted for 'real' characters; realistic scenery was abandoned, and in its place the use of light was freely substituted; frequently choral, or mass, effects were preferred to the employment of single figures, or else single figures were elevated into positions where they became representative of forces larger than themselves.

These means, being new, exercised a peculiar fascination on many minds during the twenties, and often we find them employed for purposes far removed from those which explicitly were announced as the aims of expressionism. In particular they were seized upon eagerly and exploited by some writers who, excited by the new psychoanalytic researches, sought to develop a 'subjective' theatre. What we have to recognize—if the picture is to be kept clear—is that, so far from aiming at the subjective, the true expressionists are in conscious revolt against the whole impressionistic theatre of inwardness. Instead of searching into the reaches of the individual soul, they seek to put upon the stage representations of man in the mass: if they are influenced by psychoanalysis it is the crowd emotions they desire to display. Indeed, we might almost say that, while the impressionists are the last descendants of the romantic poets, the expressionists belong to a modern classicism.

Fundamentally, what these men sought to do was to escape from the detailed exploration of the psyche and from the rounded, indirect methods implied in the entirety of neo-romantic endeavour, and to substitute therefor the typical representation of humanity along with a sharp, economic, straight-line effect. In method the expressionists are closely associated with the school of cubism, which, born at Paris in 1908, endeavoured to get beneath the curves of reality to express basic flat planes, and with Italian futurism, which, established by F. T. Marinetti in 1909, similarly aimed at the exploitation of the straight line and the 'synthetic.' In 1915 the first of futurism's theatre manifestoes stressed these qualities: it was specifically called a "Manifesto del teatro futuristo sintetico." Out of the futurist movement developed two cardinal concepts: the idea or sense of space based on appreciation of flat planes, and the idea or sense of function, wherein all romantic ornament was stripped away until only the absolutely essential (the typical) remained. The connexion between these various movements has been well summarized by Anton G. Bragaglia in *La maschera mobile* (1926). Trenchantly he stresses there the connexion between the German revolutionaries and those men—Marinetti, Boccioni, Carrà, Soffici, Depero—who headed the Italian futurist school. In both, he notes, is apparent an antagonism to 'verismo' (realism or naturalism); in both an attempt at the synthetic is the dominant aim. "By the word synthetic," he adds, "is not meant the gallery scene of one colour to which this word is often applied, but those scenes which, by an admixture of design and colour, provide a disciplined and stylized representation of reality, recorded, not re-copied—what Boccioni called the ideal abstraction of typical forms." With minor changes that sentence might have been applied to the aims of classical art two hundred years before.

The development of the new style is intimately bound up with a realization of the mechanistic nature of our civilization. For the neo-romanticist there is always the desire to escape from the machine —escape into a world inhabited by Pelléas and Mélisande, escape into the realm of vague emotional symbols, escape into the misty reaches of the human soul. In effect, the mechanistic is here deliberately avoided and, if possible, forgotten. The true expressionist takes a different line. Whether he shares Marinetti's enthusiasm for the machine or whether he stands aghast at the way in which the machine is gradually imposing itself on the living organism, he accepts its existence and endeavours to deal boldly with the problems it raises. The expressionist often is a tortured, sometimes a desperate soul, but he does not wish to abnegate the world he lives in, and thus, so far from exploiting the dream realm in Strindbergian style (as some critics of expressionism have averred), he takes a firm stand in a position diametrically opposed to that of the subjective impressionist.

GERMAN EXPRESSIONISMUS

In the theatre the expressionistic style is clearly exemplified in the work of Georg Kaiser, and particularly in his *Gas* (two parts,

1918 and 1920), a drama which provides a kind of vast morality showing the effect of industrialism on society. The very title of the play indicates its purpose and demonstrates that the author's object, instead of being directed towards the exhibition of individual characters, is to portray the larger elements of collective man. After a kind of prelude in *Die Koralle* (*The Coral*, 1917), in which a former labourer is shown building up a vast factory, the two sections of *Gas* trace the fate of the industry in the hands of this man's son and grandson: both try to help the workers, both are thwarted, until in the end only annihilation of the human race seems left as a solution for a problem thus symbolically presented in a concrete instance.

Kaiser is not a great dramatist, but he is one characteristic of his time, and although he makes free use of effects which would have been styled melodramatic had they appeared in plays of earlier vintage, there does exist in him a kind of tormented daimonic force. Starting with a relatively unimportant satiric *Die jüdische Witwe* (*The Jewish Widow*) in 1911, he produced a not ineffective *Die Bürger von Calais* (*The Citizens of Calais*) three years later, and then, in 1916, startled his contemporaries by the boldness of his *Von Morgens bis Mitternacht* (*From Morn to Midnight*). In this last work he takes as central figure a petty bank-clerk, but in true expressionistic manner makes this character a symbol of a large class rather than an individual. Stealing some of his employers' money, the clerk is shown, in violently anti-realistic scenes, passing through a series of adventures in which his dreams of a fine and exciting life gradually crumble or are rudely shattered. All the persons he meets are symbols or type-representations of human groups: to condemn the author for failing to draw interesting individual characters here is absurd, since his central aim is to avoid that method of dramatic composition and to achieve, by other means, a larger concept than could otherwise be attained. We may legitimately condemn the object: we have no right to seek in such a work something which the playwright specifically sought to exclude.

Beyond these plays Kaiser has little to offer to us. His *Der Brand im Opernhaus* (*The Fire in the Opera House*, 1916) is unimportant; no vigour appears in *Kolportage* (*Hawking*, 1924) or *Zweimal Oliver* (*Twice Oliver*, 1926); a faint sign only of the quality animating *Von Morgens bis Mitternacht* appears in *Gats* (1928). Among his various posthumous works acted in recent years, perhaps only *Der Floss der Medusa* (*The Medusa's Lifeboat*, 1948) calls for attention, and that rather on account of its form than because of its excellence in style. This play is almost unique in that it is written for a company of thirteen children—their adventures in shipwreck being used to suggest the evils in the world surrounding us. Interesting though *Der Floss der Medusa* is, however, it is by no means a masterpiece. The truth is, of course, that Kaiser was one of those dramatists who, having said one thing, has nothing more to say.

Closely associated with his writing is the work of Ernst Toller, whose first play, *Die Wandlung* (*The Transformation*), a study of the growth of revolutionary sentiment in an artist's being, appeared in 1919. This made no particular stir, but excited enthusiasm greeted *Masse-Mensch* (*Man and the Masses*) two years later. Here, again, the typical takes the place of the particular. "These pictures of 'reality' are not realism," writes Toller, "are not local colour; the protagonists are not individual characters." Sonia, the chief person in the drama, is a representative of all idealistic revolutionaries, a woman who leads the crowd of slave-workers to throw off their chains, who tries in vain to curb them when they institute a social rebellion, and who in the end is executed for a movement she had done her best to check. The language used is violently staccato; all shadings are abandoned; the characters appear violently illuminated against a Cimmerian background; exhortation and exclamation are substituted for ordinary conversation; scenes of fantasy are intermingled with scenes of stylized 'reality.' Over the entire action breathes an atmosphere of hysteria. Characteristic is the end of the third 'picture,' in which the heroine speaks to The Nameless One, who is the spirit of the mob, and the beginning of the fourth 'picture,' a dream fantasy:

THE NAMELESS ONE: Keep silent, comrade!
　　　　　　　The cause demands it.
　　　　　　　What does one person matter?
　　　　　　　His feelings? or his conscience?
　　　　　　　Only the Mass must count!
　　　　　　　Just think of it: a single bloody battle
　　　　　　　And then, eternal peace.
　　　　　　　No empty peace, a mask of mockery,
　　　　　　　Hiding the face of war,
　　　　　　　War of the strong against the weak,
　　　　　　　War of exploiters, war of greed.
　　　　　　　Think of it: the end of misery!
　　　　　　　Think of it: crime a half-remembered fable!
　　　　　　　It is the dawn of freedom for all people! . . .
　　　　　　　You think I reckon lightly?
　　　　　　　It is no longer a matter of choice.

War's a necessity for us.
Your advice means discord.
For the sake of the cause,
Keep silent.

THE WOMAN: You . . . are . . . Mass.
You . . . are . . . right.

THE NAMELESS ONE: Beat in the pillars of the bridge, O comrades!
Drive over every one who stands in our way,
Mass is action!

CROWD IN THE HALL [*as they storm out*]: Action!   [*The stage darkens.*

FOURTH PICTURE
(Dream-picture)

A court with a high wall is suggested. On the ground in the middle of the court, a lantern which gives a miserable light. WORKER GUARDS *suddenly emerge from the corners of the court.*

FIRST GUARD [*sings*]: My mother
Bore me
In the mud of a trench.
Lalala, la,
H'm, H'm.

SECOND GUARD: My father
Lost me
In a brawl with a wench.

ALL THE GUARDS: Lalala, la,
H'm, H'm.

After some more singing The Nameless One confronts a Prisoner:

THE NAMELESS ONE: Condemned
By the tribunal?

A GUARD: He brought death
Upon himself.
He shot at us.

THE PRISONER: Death?

THE NAMELESS ONE: It frightens you?
Listen:
Guard! Answer me.
Who taught us
Capital punishment?
Who gave us weapons?
Who said "Hero" and "noble deed"?
Who glorified violence?

THE GUARDS: Schools.
Barracks.
War.
Always.

In such wise is the basic theme revealed in jerky progress of dialogue and scene, the angularity of the whole assuming features that are precisely parallel to those aimed at in contemporary cubist and futurist painting.

The year following the appearance of *Masse-Mensch* came *Die Maschinenstürmer* (*The Machine-wreckers*, 1922), wherein Toller turns to write of the Luddite riots of 1812–15 in terms outwardly more realistic, but basically wrought out of the same artistic desire. In *Der deutsche Hinkemann* (*The German Hinkemann*, 1923) the story is bitterly told of an ex-soldier (again a type-figure, not an individual) who returns home sexually incapable and finds his wife accepting the caresses of another man. Toller's anti-realistic tendencies well up once more in the strange, and not very successful, *Die Rache des verhöhnten Liebhabers, oder Frauenlist und Männerlist: ein galantes Puppenspiel* (*The Revenge of the Rejected Lover; or, Male and Female Craftiness: A Puppet-show of Gallantry*, 1925), as well as in *Hoppla, wir leben* (*Hurrah! We Live!*, 1927), a disillusioned picture of post-war existence.

This last play, which shows a revolutionary returning from a spell in an asylum only to find his comrades turned sadly respectable, is interesting because of the introduction into it of a device which came to be rather freely employed in the expressionistic theatre— whereby dramatic scenes were accompanied by the sporadic display of cinematographic films. The object of this device is amply patent, and, although it must be confessed that hitherto no satisfactory fusion of the two forms has been achieved, we can easily see how tempting must have seemed the use of the film among those authors who aimed at the creation of this vast theatre of humanity.

The 'epic drama' has gained no more enthusiastic a proponent than Bertolt Brecht. This author's seriousness of purpose and untutored strength have won him a number of adherents, but it is more than doubtful whether either his works or the style he cultivates are likely to cause more than an idle ripple on the surface of the dramatic current. We may sincerely praise the mordant satire and racy wit apparent in *Die Dreigroschenoper* (*The Twopence-halfpenny Opera*, 1928), a modern version of *The Beggar's Opera*, without feeling ourselves impelled towards the discovery of any rich qualities in his other plays. *Trommeln in der Nacht* (*Drums in the Night*, 1922) is a fairly effective—and now sadly dated—study of the contrast between the hard trials of a soldier at the front and the easy life of those who have made fortunes from the war, and in some of his other plays no doubt there are scenes of occasional vigour, but in general we may say that his writings present a rather inchoate mixture of almost every possible style animating the theatre of the twenties and thirties. He tries to make the drama subserve 'social' truth, thus following the production methods used by the communistic Erwin Piscator; like Piscator, he loves to secure effects by novel theatrical means and the employment of unexpected tricks; he takes from the Chinese theatre some ideas and from the Russian many; he flatters the anti-realists by rejecting the set scene and the formal dialogue; the support of the naturalists he seeks by claiming that his plays, instead of arousing emotions, endeavour to present truth. From the earlier work of the expressionists he takes much; Marxist concepts colour many of his scenes; and his appeal to the intellect flows from the tradition set by Zola and others. It is all very new, and at the same time very old-fashioned.

Brecht, of course, carries us well past the period when expressionism was most rampant, and for consideration of the others it is necessary to move back a number of years. One of the earliest on the stage was Reinhard Sorge, whose *Der Bettler* (*The Beggar*), an hysterical portrait of a poet to whom men will not listen, appeared in 1912, followed by diverse other similar dramas, ending with *König David* (*King David*) in 1916. Violent effects and equally violent emotions were infused into *Vatermord* (*Parricide*, 1925), by the Austrian Arnolt Bronnen, a man who continued to vex the theatre with pretentious sensationalism in such plays as *Rheinische Rebellen* (*Rebels in the Rhineland*, 1925) and *Reparationen* (*Reparations*, 1926). *Mörder, Hoffnung der Frauen* (*Murderer, Hope of Women*, 1907) and *Orpheus und Eurydike* (1918), by Oskar Kokoschka, indicate how closely associated is the expressionist movement with the effort to explore what might be called the hidden wells of humanity. Something of the same quality, although with a more assured lyrical tone, appears in *Himmel und Hölle* (*Heaven and Hell*, 1919), by Paul Kornfeld, and in *Liebe* (*Love*, 1916), by Anton Wildgans. Wildgans perhaps deserves a trifle more attention than some of his fellows because of the imaginative atmosphere he can at times evoke: he has, too, an innate sympathy with individual human beings of a kind often lacking amid the vaster concepts of the expressionists. *Armut* (*Poverty*, 1914), for example, despite its sentimentalism and rhetorical excesses, does succeed in making us believe in its wretched hero, Spuller. In *Die Seeschlacht* (*The Seabattle*, 1918) Reinhard Göring cleverly causes reality to subserve expressionistic aims by making his sailor characters appear in monstrous-seeming 'mechanistic' gas-masks. In many of these dramas,

2C

which remind us of nothing so much as the absurd early efforts of the 'Sturm und Drang' period, the expressionistic devices were used most commonly for non-expressionistic ends; here psychoanalysis was rampant and complexes had the time of their lives.

The company exploiting the new style was numerous, and, although the most talented of its members later sloughed off the more blatant wrappings of the expressionistic style, few who were caught in its delirious ecstasy succeeded in returning to sanity. Some of the group, such as Julius Maria Becker, were inspired by highest humanitarian concepts; some, like Ernst Barlach, were moved by the indignation of the intellectual adolescent against the thoughtless, money-seeking man of business; some, like Lothar Schreyer, author of *Nacht* (*Night*, 1919), appeared to be animated largely by a simple desire for novelty; nearly all shared a spirit likely to carry them to the extremes of political conviction. Like Becker, a few writers, among whom may be numbered the Austrian Franz Csokor, author of *Die rote Strasse* (*The Red Road*, 1918), and Hans Kaltneker, whose trilogy of *Das Bergwerk* (*The Mine*), *Die Opferung* (*The Offering*), and *Die Schwester* (*The Sister*), all printed in 1919, seeks to base religious faith and purity on a previous embracing of evil, search out—albeit in strained and neurotic terms—for a spiritual end; but obviously the excesses of expressionism could easily lead to the goal reached by Hans Johst, who moved from a mood of rebellion to an acceptance of Nazi philosophy, or to that of Friedrich Wolf, whose *Die Matrosen von Cattaro* (*The Sailors of Cattaro*, 1931) once captured the acclaim of the enthusiasts.

Among the motley host there may perhaps be singled out a few other names. There is something of virtue in the dramas of the poet Fritz von Unruh, notably *Ein Geschlecht* (*One Race*, 1918), wherein the author ironically sets a graveyard scene of a Mother burying her Son against a background of distant battle, and those of Walter Hasenclever, notably *Der Sohn* (*The Son*, 1914), *Die Menschen* (*Humanity*, 1918), *Gobseck* (1921), and *Mord* (*Murder*, 1926). To assess Hasenclever's worth is difficult. He has his follies. Towards the beginning of his career he permitted the extravagant to lead him into strange paths, as when, in *Der Sohn*, he upholds a youth's right to murder his parents. (Why, forsooth? Simply because he thinks they prohibit the free expression of his being.) Even later, in *Die Menschen*, the macabre note appears in the introduction of a corpse as a hero, while in *Jenseits* (*Beyond*, 1920) the ghost of a dead husband plays a dominant rôle. On the other hand, there is a vigour in his writing denied to many of his companions, while the fact must be noted that he later cast off the absurdities of the expressionistic style and turned to comedy. The trouble is that, although gifted with some genius, he never seems to have known quite what he wanted to do or in which camp he proposed to abide. At one moment he is weltering in the dark joys of the psychoanalytic or among the spectres of the later romantic imagination; at the next he is pursuing a definitely expressionistic path, writing dramas such as *Die Entscheidung* (*The Decision*, 1919); at the next he is laughing sardonically, as in *Zero* (1932).

And, finally, there is the later Austrian Hans Chlumberg (Hans Bardach von Chlumberg), whose *Wunder um Verdun* (*Miracle at Verdun*, 1930) shows how the expressionistic style, in its basic elements, continued to exert its influence long after the first flush of enthusiasm was over. This drama, unquestionably invested with power, sardonically shows the distress of the living when thirty-two million dead soldiers rise from their graves. The directness of purpose and the trenchant style of *Miracle at Verdun* deservedly gave it an international reputation.

A consideration of all these plays demonstrates two things: first, that the expressionistic technique, appealing because of its novelty, could be applied for a diversity of ends, and, second, that the expressionistic objective, while no doubt helping to extend the narrowing confines of the drama, was apt in its purer form to lead towards just such absurdities as characterized the excesses of the early romantic poets. In some of the devices used by the expressionists still resides an element of potential strength, but that strength will probably be found rather in an indirect acceptance of the expressionist objective than in its bolder and unchastened exploitation. It is likewise clear that, although such aims as those put forward by Brecht may be of service in theatres devoted entirely to social propaganda, they tend to deny the very being of the drama as an art.

THE SPREAD OF EXPRESSIONISM

In France the expressionistic movement found little support, but in Eastern Europe it served to stimulate the genius of Karel Čapek, whose *R.U.R.* (1921), written in a modified form of the technique of expressionism, well reveals the central objectives of that movement in its imaginative picture of a world mechanized. *R.U.R.* is Rossum's Universal Robots, an industrial organization that mass-produces mechanical figures capable of acting as slaves of men. Gradually something begins to stir in the chill beings of these automata: they rise in rebellion against man: apparently the world is doomed to an existence completely controlled by the mechanical when, at the very end, the playwright shows the first glimmerings of love stirring the mechanized hearts of two of these monsters and, with the arising of love, the growth of alien sentiments of self-sacrifice and loyalty. Out of the mechanistic, life is being reborn. Although expressionistic in origin and choice of theme, *R.U.R.* possibly owes its success largely to the fact that here Čapek has succeeded in moulding well-established melodramatic practice to the needs of his own generation and school.

That Čapek too was gifted with a vision which sets him apart from most of the rather callow Germanic philosopher-dramatists from Kaiser to Brecht is shown clearly in *Vec Makropulos (The Macropulos Secret,* 1922). Such a work as *Ze zivota hmyzu (The Insect Comedy,* or *The Life of the Insects,* 1921) may seem on reflection somewhat obvious in its symbolism and shallow in its thought, but the man who could argue that the lengthening of life would be a curse, and not, as Shaw thought, a blessing, was certainly gifted with an independent mind. In collaboration with his brother Josef he penned a possibly over-ambitious philosophical drama entitled *Adam stvoritel (Adam the Creator,* 1927), wherein Adam, having blown the world to dust in a fit of horror at its errors, is bidden, ironically, by God to refashion it anew. Despite his efforts and enthusiasm, the new earth is found to be precisely similar to the old. This is by no means a great work, and the truth seems to be that Čapek's genius exhausted itself in *R.U.R.,* with only just sufficient left to give some colouring to a couple of other plays. By himself Josef Čapek penned his *Zeme mnoha jmen (Land of Many Names,* 1923), but this satirical essay presenting the discovery of a new continent and showing what it means to various persons (romance, economic freedom, opportunity for financial exploitation) barely reaches above the ordinary.

Amid plays of other styles, in which the lyrical sharply confronts the naturalistic, a Polish dramatist, Karol Rostworowski, has presented one drama of the expressionistic kind, *Milosierdzie (Charity,* 1920), wherein the problem of the poor in modern society is dealt with in symbolic style. In Sweden Pär Lagerkvist, a disciple of Strindberg, has turned out his expressionistically inclined *Sista människan (The Last Man,* 1917), and *Himlens hemlighet (The Secret of Heaven;* printed 1919; 1921); but this style he has tended to abandon in favour of a fairy-tale fantasy shot through with realistic elements. And in Lauri Haarla the Finnish stage finds its counterpart.

In the English-speaking theatre several of these Continental plays have been given notable productions, and the expressionistic style has been attempted by a considerable number of dramatists—although it is observable that in England itself only one author, C. K. Munro (Charles Kirkpatrick MacMullan), and then only in a single work, has succeeded in producing an expressionistic play of any worth. *The Rumour* appeared in 1922 and attracted some attention, partly because it introduced the new technique to London, and partly because its author had discovered an interestingly novel idea—the tracing, through a series of short scenes, of a rumour, idle and relatively innocent, which eventually leads two countries into war. When he tried to capitalize on his first success, however, Munro found that his *Progress* (1924) sadly failed to recapture the first enthusiasm out of which *The Rumour* was born.

More emphatically, expressionism made appeal among the young theatrical (and social) revolutionaries of America. From the time when John Howard Lawson presented his *Processional* (1925) sporadic utilization of the German methods have appeared on the American stage, the more particularly on those boards dedicated to the inculcation of radical ideas. *Processional* is an unquestionably effective drama, in which, ironically set against a background of jazz, Lawson deals with a bitter and bloody strife between a group of miners and the police-supported owners. Central in the picture are the symbolic figures of Sadie Cohen and her seducer, Dynamite Jim, with the child to be born of them, the future leader of the workers. Although the social philosophy is crude and several scenes somewhat absurd, *Processional* has a sincere, burning power in it that holds our attention. Less effective, yet still noteworthy, is the *Machinal* (1928) of Sophie Treadwell, a thoroughly characteristic work, in which the heroine, called simply The Young Woman, vainly seeks for romance in a world of machines and commerce.

With much greater result, the expressionistic form seized on the ever-questing imagination of Elmer Rice, one of that powerful group of young playwrights who so ably provided a rich background for Eugene O'Neill in and around the years of the First World War. From the very beginning of his career Rice exhibited an eagerness for any new devices likely to make his themes more effective, and from the beginning, too, he showed a strong, constant sympathy with the oppressed. In his first play, *On Trial* (1914), he indicated without doubt what were his aims when he dealt boldly with a social problem and gave novelty to his treatment of it by introducing a trick—the 'flash-back'—borrowed from the cinema.

It was no wonder, therefore, that when knowledge of the expressionistic style came to America he should seize upon it with avidity. In *The Adding Machine* (1923) we are given a vigorous and effective theatrical study akin in spirit to the writings of Toller and Kaiser. The hero is an elderly clerk, Mr Zero, who, when dismissed from his post because mechanical adding machines can do his work more accurately and more economically, goes mad and murders his employer. For this crime he is executed, and his spirit wanders through eternity until, reaching heaven, he is set to work on a monstrous adding machine. This was undoubtedly Rice's most powerful essay in this particular kind of dramatic technique, but the expressionistic method, although not in such extreme terms, has ever laid its spell upon him. Something of the method he had learned in *The Adding Machine* is utilized in his *Judgment Day* (1934), based on the Reichstag Fire trial; signs of its operation are evident in *A New Life* (1943), an allegory of a child surrounded by good (the friends of its mother, honest, hardworking folk) and evil (its father's relatives, idle, rich, and reactionary), as well as in *The Dream Girl* (1946), wherein the expressionistic technique is used, as so often it had been used before, for the purpose of exploiting psychoanalytical scenes. All of these dramas have quality, although all are rendered less interesting because of Rice's tendency to see everything in terms of white and black: his anger at social evils inclines him both to lose objectivity of approach and to obscure a sense of colour values.

The expressionistic aims and methods are to be found in many quarters. They have influenced considerably the writings of several poets, in particular Archibald MacLeish and W. H. Auden; they are plainly evident in such a work as *Johnny Johnson* (1936), Paul Green's plea for pacifism; and they have played their part in forming the styles of other authors, such as Thornton Wilder, whom we should not normally think of as belonging to this school. Thornton Wilder, indeed, may well provide for us an example of the spirit out of which expressionism grew: although he himself is not swayed towards embracing the more bizarre among the technical devices cultivated by the followers of Kaiser, his whole creative work is animated by a desire to escape from the trammels of particularized realism, and a consideration of the ways in which he has sought to effect this escape helps to explain the aberrations of the extreme revolutionaries. Gifted with a fine sense of style and a wisely humanitarian outlook upon life, his theatrical writings show that consistently he has endeavoured to find means whereby the modern stage can be released from the narrowness of the ordinary domestic scene and at the same time can be revitalized by the introduction of appropriate conventionalism. For that reason various manifestations of dramatic form have particularly appealed to him—the Elizabethan, the Oriental, and the expressionistic. On the other hand, he does not wish to set any one of these in imitative fashion on the modern boards: rather does he try to employ their principles in an individual manner. *Our Town* (1938) is not, as some critics were inclined to think, a play written in a manner designed merely to excite by reason of its novelty. When Wilder takes a story of characters belonging to a small New England town and sets it forth without the slightest vestige of scenery he is not playing any tricks; nor is he playing tricks when he causes these characters to be introduced by a stage-manager, who, standing at the very edge of the proscenium, addresses the audience directly. These things are introduced because what Wilder wishes to do is to present not merely a particular story of Grover's Corners, New Hampshire, but a typical picture of New England life, because he desires his public, not to sit back and objectively observe the action, but to be drawn over the footlights among the actors. In effect, Wilder is aiming at imaginative participation. Still further, although he is animated by no doctrinaire social theories, he seeks to deal both with the general social life of man and with the deepest, most universal things in man's existence—love and birth and death.

We may be far off here from the staccato rhythms of *Masse-Mensch*, of *Gas*, of *The Adding Machine*, but there is still something in common between the spirit of these plays and Wilder's work; and the connexion becomes clearer still in that strange, exciting, yet by no means wholly satisfying later play, *The Skin of Our Teeth* (1942), which, by its story of Mr and Mrs Antrobus and Sabina, the maid, seeks to put the entire history of mankind into a single dramatic framework. Without a doubt *The Skin of Our Teeth* could not have been written had Toller and Kaiser not shown the way.

SEAN O'CASEY

Much of Wilder's writing is cast in a strictly realistic form; besides *The Adding Machine*, Rice pens the ultra-naturalistic *Street Scene*; expressionism and realism meet also in the work of that great Irish successor of Synge, Sean O'Casey.

When *The Shadow of a Gunman* appeared at the Abbey Theatre in 1923 there was general recognition that a new star had come into the theatrical firmament. Here was the advent of a young author whose rich sense of language, keen insight into character, and broad, firm handling of dramatic material immediately set him forth as a worthy successor to the first playwrights of the Irish renaissance. And, in succeeding to this tradition, he indicated, with bold, strong fervour, that he was not prepared merely to follow: if to the tradition he owed his being, he was determined to add to it and enlarge its confines. Yeats had brought the poetic drama to Ireland: Synge had explored the realms of the peasantry: O'Casey set himself the task of interpreting the lower-class life of the city. A born fighter, he had identified himself both with the Irish labour struggle and with the national uprising, yet, despite his direct involvement in these tumultuous movements, he retained a vigorous independence of mind and was prepared to startle his fellow-associates by his unflinching condemnation of some among their most deeply cherished fancies. A man with a definitely tragic attitude towards existence, he has shown himself capable of producing scenes of gorgeous laughter, deep-rooted in a profound knowledge of human life.

The Shadow of a Gunman reveals clearly the chief qualities of his early style. Irony appears in this tale of a loud-mouthed, self-esteeming revolutionary whose romantic pose takes in his associates and, with more serious consequence, leads to the death of a brave young girl. Even finer in quality were the two plays soon to follow, *Juno and the Paycock* (1924) and *The Plough and the Stars* (1926). In these the comic scenes are more harmoniously woven into the tragic texture, the characters are more sharply etched, the episodes more skilfully wrought. Once more, the former introduces a romantic boaster, the 'Paycock' himself, Captain Jack Boyle, fit companion for the lovable yet utterly useless Joxer Daly. Round these persons the family circle is drawn—a fatal circle, poverty-stricken, with death and the breaking of dreams leaving it shattered at the end, yet strangely ennobled by the figure of Juno, the Paycock's wife, a figure into whom O'Casey has cast all his pity and his love. As a background to the action of this drama is set the Irish revolutionary movement: this is brought to the front of the stage in *The Plough and the Stars*, where, almost without a plot, the author has created a series of vivid scenes of darkness irradiated by bitter laughter. There appears, however, to be a change in spirit from *The Shadow of a Gunman*. While still O'Casey is sympathetic towards those who had the courage to fight for the ideal of national independence, we realize that he is becoming more intent upon the general evils in our civilization, deeper and more vicious than those evils against which Jack Clitheroe takes active battle and over which Fluther Good wastes many besotted words. His vision has grown wider and deeper; it is no longer merely Irish.

With this inner development it is not surprising to find him turning from the realistic style to the expressionistic in *The Silver Tassie* (1928). No play better than this illustrates the spiritual essence of the latter form or demonstrates more clearly the impulse that has led so many moderns to seek in it a medium for the display of their dramatic truths. O'Casey's object in *The Silver Tassie* is to show a man of powerful physique broken by the war and turned from a being proud of his healthy body into a cripple. The first act places him: hilariously acclaimed by his friends for having won the 'silver tassie,' the football trophy cup, he has just played his last game before setting off with the army. Another dramatist with aims less wide than O'Casey's would have proceeded throughout in a realistic manner, but for O'Casey the problem of the individual man is dwarfed by the problem of men. After this first act he wants to show the horror of war. Were he to do this in the style of *Journey's End* our attentions would still be riveted on the single hero, and the breadth of effect desired would be lost. Hence abruptly O'Casey changes his method: from the realism of the opening scenes he moves to an expressionistic, symbolic treatment of the trenches. This done, and the background set, he is free to turn back to the particular, knowing that, if we have imaginatively given ourselves to his vision and have been willing to accept the sharp juxtaposition of dramatic methods, the story of his hero will have been enlarged because of what we have heard and seen of the hell through which he has passed.

Having thus experimented with a single scene in the expressionistic manner, O'Casey has found that only this form can give him the opportunity he seeks of presenting his vision of life. *Within the Gates* (1934) is written entirely in the anti-realistic manner. We are within the gates of Hyde Park, but the characters, instead of being individualized, are type creations—a Poet Dreamer, a Young Whore, a Bishop and his Sister. As the scenes develop we learn that the Whore is the illegitimate daughter of the Bishop: sick and near to death, she finds consolation and a spirit of hope not in the dogmas of the Church, but in the arms of the Poet. While this play may be by no means entirely successful, it possesses a wealth of imaginative power and a richness of utterance such as few modern plays have to offer us.

From this time on the expressionistic has been O'Casey's chosen form of dramatic composition, his torrential outpouring of words finding fitting channel in those freer and uninhibited realms which Toller and Kaiser had substituted for the tight and economical Ibsenian structure. In 1940 he wrote for the Unity Theatre *The Star turns Red*, and followed that with *Purple Dust* (1945) and *Red Roses for Me* (1943)—the last a magnificent colourful fantasy, with a poetic dialogue that soars and sears, with a fine distillation of that tragic sense, that irony, and that comedy he is so skilful in intermingling into an impressive whole. There is a central figure here in Ayamonn, but again the vision goes beyond the individual. What is memorable in the play is the mass effect of the whole, the miseries and the splendours of the unemployed and the flower-girls, the quiet searching of the uttermost reaches in the ironic graveyard scene, the philosophical atmosphere which enwraps the entirety of the action. O'Casey has no need to prate about an epic theatre: by his genius, whatever its failures, he has succeeded in creating a theatrical impression of the epic sweep which goes far beyond anything achieved by any of his contemporaries.

The movement called expressionism would have fully justified its existence even if O'Casey's plays alone were the products of its germinating impulse.

REALISM, SOCIAL AND OTHERWISE

WHILE the expressionistic movement thus rebelliously set out to hatter the realistic form of drama the various influences, already discussed in brief outline, tending towards a retention of the late-nineteenth-century pattern were being augmented by developments such as the nineteenth century could not have dreamed of. The result has been the paradoxical coexistence of the most bizarre forms the theatre has ever known and of the continued popularity of one of its most narrowly restricted genres.

SOCIALIST REALISM IN RUSSIA

When the Revolution first laid its impress on the stages of Moscow and Leningrad enthusiastic producers indulged in a riot of eccentric styles which, stemming ultimately from the more radical works of the immediate pre-war years, embraced all the 'isms' and added some more to their number. These were the heydays of Meierhold and Tairov.

Soon, however, violent changes arrived. Partly impressed by the need of utilizing the theatre as a kind of lecture platform and of making plays serve the needs of mass education, the authorities proceeded to curb the excesses and to demand the realistic. This statement, of course, must not be taken to imply that there has been a complete reversion to the old proscenium-frame, peep-show type of stage. The exact opposite is the case. All kinds of methods of production are employed. It is true that Meierhold's 'biomechanical' stylization has fallen by the wayside and that Tairov's 'synthetic' theatre is no longer looked upon with favour, but we have only to consider the various experiments made by Nikolai Okhlopkov at the Realistic Theatre or by Alexei Popov at the Central Theatre of the Red Army in Moscow to recognize that, in so far as productional methods are concerned, there is no tying of actors or directors to a set pattern; and it is in the U.S.S.R. that experimental forms of theatre construction find their freest scope.

Method, however, is one thing and basic aim another; there may exist a vast difference in the impress of an idea upon the literary art of the drama and upon the interpretative art of the stage. In imposing Socialist Realism on the arts in Russia the central authoritics, beyond curbing extreme naturalism on the one hand and extreme stylization on the other, may have left room for a considerable amount of diversity in the manner of presenting plays, but on the playwrights themselves they set a firm decree. According to the manifesto issued in 1932 by the All-Union Congress of Soviet Writers, this Socialist Realism,

> being the fundamental method of Soviet writing, whether creative or critical, demands from the author a truthful, historically concrete representation of actuality in its revolutionary development. Above all, the truthfulness and historical concreteness of the artist's representation of actuality must be united with the problem of the spiritual fashioning and educating of the workers in the concept of socialism.

This means, when applied to dramatic art, that all plays must be both informative and propagandist. They have to be propagandist because their object is to educate the workers: at the same time they ought not to distort their subject-matter (whether that be contemporary material or historical), but endeavour to be true to all aspects of life in a given period, interpreting these, of course, in communist terms. In effect, what this implies is that the old Russian theatrical ideal of *byt* has been extended and applied to the newer Marxist ideals.

We are not, however, so much concerned with theory as with results, and the results indicate that the application of the dogma of socialist realism has the effect of compelling the authors to produce dramas which seek to combine a whiff of the schoolroom with a steady breeze of Marxist propaganda, and that in style these authors are forced to follow realistic methods of character-displayal and development of dialogue.

From the statistics that are available no country shows a greater wave of theatrical activity than the U.S.S.R. Native-language stages have multiplied themselves constantly during the past decades, and even in Great Russia itself the expansion has been extraordinary. By 1936 it was calculated that, apart from several hundred workers' playhouses, there existed more than six hundred and fifty theatres spread over the whole of the country, with an audience throughout the year of fifty million persons. In these theatres scores of new plays are presented annually, and, as has often been justifiably pointed out, the young dramatist in Russia is offered material opportunities that might well make him an object of envy to his Western colleagues. The fact remains, however, that during these twenty-odd years few Soviet dramas have risen above mediocrity, and none, apparently, have been produced of a kind likely to achieve an international reputation. Symbolic is the fact that a State competition of 1934 yielded 1200 plays, of which not one was deemed worthy of an award.

Among the authors certain major distinctions can be made. First come those who, having had their training before the Revolution, adapted themselves, sometimes enthusiastically and sometimes with effort, to the new conditions. Of this group Alexei Nikolaevich Tolstoi and Anatoli Vasilevich Lunacharski have contributed little of any consequence, but some quality resides in the writings of two of their companions. Early in the recent war a German bomb was responsible for the death of Alexander Nikolaevich Afinogenov, undoubtedly one of the most gifted of modern Russian dramatists, but at the same time one who, in 1938, fell under the dire suspicion of the Government. With ardent revolutionary enthusiasm, this writer started his career by the penning of dramas which were designed either to show the development of the social struggle in various countries or to give simple admonishments to his audiences. Most of these early works, although wrought with some skill, are negligible. Nothing much of value can be expected of a theme indicated by a title such as *Keep Your Eyes Open* (1927), a play wherein the story is told of a young communist student who carelessly allows his party card to be used by an acquaintance, and who is aghast to find that it has subserved counter-revolutionary purposes. In 1931, however, came a much more important drama, *Shtrakh* (*Fear*), in which appears an interesting and sympathetic study of an old-time scientist, Professor Borodin, who finds himself so surrounded by Marxist inhibitions that he deems the whole of Russian life to be dominated by fear. The interest of the play consists in the fact that, although the ending demonstrates that the hero is wrong, the analysis of his mood is executed with deep sympathy and alert understanding. Some of Afinogenov's work reminds us of antiquated formulas for play construction, and other dramas, like *Saliut, Ispaniya!* (*Salute, Spain!*, 1936), are, as their titles indicate, largely hysterical *pièces d'occasion*. With *Dalekoe* (*Distant Point*, 1935) we fortunately move back to the mood of *Fear*. In a manner that indicates how deeply he has been influenced by Chekhov, Afinogenov here presents a quiet picture rich in emotional power. The locale is a small Siberian village far removed from wider civilization: its inhabitants quarrel and are at odds with one another. Hither arrives, in the course of a journey from the East, a Soviet general, and through his greatness of soul and sympathetic understanding the confused community life is directed towards a universal united endeavour. Whether in Afinogenov's return to communist grace he would have been likely, had he lived, to enrich his art further, we cannot tell: his comic *Mashenka* (1940) is negligible, and *Nakanune* (*On the Eve*, 1943), while interesting, does not measure up to *Fear*.

Konstantin Andreivich Trenev, a younger contemporary of Afinogenov, is worthy of mention because of his *Liubov Iarovaia* (1925, original version; rewritten 1936). In essence this is a good old melodrama, with a heroine perplexed as to whether she shall save her husband—whom she still loves, but who has joined the Whites—or, by denouncing him, save her comrades. No doubt the thrills and the scenes of suspense are exciting, but, beyond the introduction of some boldly drawn character types, we can hardly esteem the play an important work of dramatic art.

About the same time Michael Afanasevich Bulgakov produced in *Dni Turbinikh* (*The Days of the Turbins*, 1926) another essay in Chekhovian style, one distinguished by its skilful, sympathetic study of an old-time family confronted by the Revolution. For one man the Revolution means the complete negation of all he has known and loved; for another it means simply confusion of spirit, where ancient loyalties batter against human sympathy; for a third it implies a fresh challenge. The final lines in effect tell its story. "Gentlemen," says Nikolka, "do you know, this evening is a great prologue to an historical play"—to which Studzinsky replies, "For some a prologue—for me an epilogue." This is at once among the most powerful and the least typical of Soviet theatrical productions.

Companions of Bulgakov are Alexei Mikhailovich Faiko, author of *Chelovek s portfelem* (*The Man with a Portfolio*, 1928), Vsevolod Viacheslavovich Ivanov, whose most important play is *Bronepoezd No. 14–69* (*The Armoured Train*, 1927), and Valentin Petrovich Kataev, distinguished for his comedy *Kvadratura kruga* (*Squaring the Circle*, 1928). None of these plays is truly valuable, but all are interesting. *The Man with a Portfolio* is a kind of melodramatic *Fear*, and does succeed in presenting, albeit with many sensational incidents, the progress of an intellectual during the first years of the Revolution. Born in an aristocratic circle, Professor Gratanov starts by secretly doing all he can to sabotage the communist government. As he advances in honour and position, however, his sentiments change, and he becomes sincerely anxious to work for the common good. Friends from his past now bring him new dangers, and in desperation he resorts to murder, endeavouring thus to obliterate what he thinks will ruin him, and in the end is forced into confessing his crimes. Crude though portions of this play are, Faiko comes very close to arousing a genuine tragic mood; but very close is not final achievement, and the scenes remain in the melodramatic, not in the tragic, realm. Even more melodramatic is *The Armoured Train*, which does little more than narrate, excitingly, the adventures of a trainload of revolutionary soldiers in conflict with the Whites. *Squaring the Circle* deserves its place in the list because it is one of Russia's few modern comedies: here the fortunes of two ill-assorted couples who are compelled to inhabit a single room is told with gaiety, but at the same time in terms which savour rather of antiquated farce than of recent experiments. It is with some surprise that we find in this proletarian *milieu* precisely the same theme as that which appears in Noel Coward's *Private Lives*.

Beyond a few sensational propaganda pieces apt to arouse political emotions in the audience this first group of authors has not much to contribute to the stage. For the most part their minds were too confused, or else they strove too hard towards a semblance of conforming with the new conditions to permit them to develop a free and unhampered form of expression.

But if they have failed, an even greater failure must be recorded for their successors. Their many patriotic-historical studies are dull, and their dramas of contemporary life wholly propagandist. There is a strange coldness about the majority of these works, as though all the shadings that humanity can give to a work of art were banished in favour of metallic and mechanical darkness and light. Some acclaim has been given to Nikolai Fedorovich Pogodin, but his *Tempo* (1930) rather crudely draws in Boldyrev a portrait of the spotless communist hero; *Aristokrati* (*Aristocrats*, 1935) inclines to creak; and although there is some humour and understanding of humanity in *Chelovek s ruzhem* (*The Man with a Gun*, 1938), we seek in vain here for anything apt to arouse our deeper praise: this also is a drama made to order wherein characters behave, not as they do in real life, but as they ought to do according to Marxist theory. *Inga* (1929), by Anatol Glebov, finds its main interest in discussing the position of woman in the new socialist society. *Konstantin Terekhin* (translated as *Red Dust*, 1927), by Vladimir Mikhailovich Kirshon, gives a tantalizing glimpse of possibilities as each scene moves on its predetermined propagandist way. *Khleb* (*Bread*, 1930) has some effective short scenes, but as a whole is nothing more than a tract preaching the necessity of following the party line.

Though the very latest plays produced in Russia are not available for critical analysis, such information of them as comes to us suggests that no new masterpieces are being brought to birth. While we can understand the enthusiastic reception given to *Russkie liudi* (*The Russian People*, 1942), by Konstantin Simonov, we can hardly attribute this reception to its artistic qualities. It may be that in the future the many theatres of the Union will stimulate a great dramatic impulse: at the moment, however, all we can say is that, unless some masterpieces have appeared so recently as to be yet unavailable outside the U.S.S.R., the thirty years of the Revolution have succeeded in producing little more than a series of informative and doctrinaire dramas, realistically and melodramatically old-fashioned in technique. So far the tale of the Soviet stage has been six hundred theatres in search of an author.

THE REALISTIC DRAMA IN AMERICA

Realism is deeply implanted in the theatre of the United States, and during the thirties of the present century the natural predisposition towards the realistic has been markedly augmented by the arising of a group of young enthusiasts eager, like their Russian colleagues, to use the stage for social purposes.

Despite the fact that the various Continental 'isms' were joyously seized upon and exploited by the leaders of what may be called the American Renaissance, realism and naturalism remained to dominate most of their work. We may think of O'Neill chiefly as the author of stylized and symbolic dramas, yet it was by writing a series of one-act studies of life that he first made his name. If the name of Elmer Rice associates itself with *The Adding Machine*, equally fittingly is it associated with *Street Scene* (1929) and *Counsellor-at-Law* (1931). The former play, as its title clearly indicates, is an essay in locale. It is the street that acts as hero, and the several characters—Frank Moran and his wife, the happy-natured Italian musician, the Swedish janitor, the old folks and the children—serve only to enrich the painting of the setting. Here is an exceedingly effective experiment in a naturalistic form familiar to us from other examples produced during the years 1890 1910. In the second play Rice reverses his technique, throwing all stress on one central figure

—the successful attorney whose past error leads to his professional and social disgrace. How closely Rice copies life may be realized from such a passage as the following—the chatter of Bessie Green, switchboard girl for Simon and Tedesco, lawyers, as she answers calls, talks on another line to an admirer, and occasionally throws a reprimand at the office-boy:

> Say, listen, how many people's work do you think I'm goin' to do around here? . . . Simon and Tedesco—Oh, it's you, is it?—Why, I thought you was dead and buried—No, I don't look so good in black—Yeah, sure I missed you: like Booth missed Lincoln—Well, what do you think I've been doing: sittin' home embroiderin' doilies? Gee, I'm glad I'm wearin' long sleeves, so's I can laugh in 'em—All right, now I'll tell one. [*A buzz.*] Wait a minute—Simon and Tedesco— Mr Tedesco hasn't come in yet—Any minute—What is the name, please?—How do you spell that?—Napoli Importing Company?— All rightee, I'll tell him—Hello—Yeah, I had another call—No, I can't to-night—I can't, I'm tellin' you—I got another date—Ask me no questions and you'll hear no lies—How do you know I want to break it?—Say, you must have your hats made in a barrel factory.

Hardly any American dramatist has his ear more closely attuned to the rhythms of metropolitan speech than Rice.

Another, but a less vigorous, playwright of the same generation, George Kelly, has (among other lesser works which extend as far as the rather futile *The Fatal Weakness* of 1947) contributed one effective drama in this style, *Craig's Wife* (1925), a study of a domineering wife who keeps her husband securely under her thumb until by chance she acts in such a way as to show him precisely in what bonds of slavery he dwells. Similar in tone are the works of Susan Glaspell, who, early on the scene with her *Trifles* (1917), won success as late as 1930 with her play on a poetess, *Alison's House*. Sherwood Anderson first appeared about the same time as Susan Glaspell's début, and, without ever achieving greatness, succeeded in giving to the stage a number of at least capably written dramas, mostly reportorial in kind. Local realism displaying the American West appears in the plays of Lynn Riggs, whose best play, *Green Grow the Lilacs* (1931), with its sentimental flavour, gives a measure of his importance; similarly local in atmosphere is the once bepraised *Hell-bent fer Heaven* (1923), a naturalistic study of a religious enthusiast among the mountaineers, by Hatcher Hughes.

Sternly realistic in tone and treatment is Sidney Howard's *The Silver Cord* (1926), a vigorous essay in the terrors of mother-love, showing a Mrs Phelps who breaks the engagement of one of her sons and nearly shatters the married happiness of his brother. Although gifted with no very great power as a dramatist, Howard has succeeded in leaving behind him a number of fairly memorable plays, works hardly likely to find a permanent place in the repertory, yet possessed of such seriousness of purpose and such integrity as to mark them out from the run of their companions. Intimate pictures of California life are painted in *They Knew What They Wanted* (1924), a play marked by kindly understanding; *The Late Christopher Bean* (1932), adapted, like Emlyn Williams' similarly named play, from René Fauchois' *Prenez garde à la peinture*, ironically deals with the fate of an artist who has become famous in death; *Alien Corn* (1933) narrates the romance of a mid-Western piano-teacher; in *Dodsworth* (1934) the impossible almost reaches achievement and the widespread canvas of Sinclair Lewis' novel is compressed, with moderate success, into the more restricted framework of the stage. Superior to these is *Yellow Jack* (1934), where again a broad area is covered, Howard's endeavour being to put into dramatic terms the long, painful, and at times seemingly hopeless struggle of man against the malaria-carrying mosquito. It is a high testimony to Howard's skill that he has been able to wrest so much of warm human interest from a theme essentially historical and scientific.

Yellow Jack reminds us of *Men in White* (1933), by a younger contemporary of Howard's, Sidney Kingsley. Kingsley's most successful play was *Dead End* (1935), a work in which, with a strange reversion to almost Belascoish methods of handling material, he endeavoured, starkly and yet sentimentally, to prove that criminals are made, not born. Despite the acclaim that greeted this drama, however, it is perhaps in *Men in White* that he has exhibited most dramatic power, and, apart from the interest inherent in his treatment of his subject, there is here the added interest that rests in his choice of theme. When we look at the plays of the latter part of the nineteenth century and of the first decades of our own era we must be struck by the extraordinary appeal made to the dramatists by what may be called the artist hero. Ibsen, Strindberg, Hauptmann, together with dozens of their companions, have put painters, writers, and sculptors upon the stage, frequently—indeed, generally—endeavouring to present a contrast between the claims of a consuming passion for artistic creation and the claims of ordinary life. The trailing relics of this tradition are clearly to be viewed in the artist of *The Late Christopher Bean* and the musician of *Alien Corn*. *Yellow Jack* and *Men in White* carry us into another world wherein the scientist, whether he be hardworking general practitioner, aspiring young medical genius, or great inventor, becomes the hero. No doubt Kingsley allows more than a dash of that sentimentalism which ever seems to be the companion of the realistic to enter into his theme of a doctor who has to choose between the claims of romance and the demands of his career, but at least in his choice of that theme he shows himself attuned to the spirit of the thirties.

Something finer in texture and more philosophic in outlook appears in the writings of Robert Emmet Sherwood, who inaugurated his theatrical career with *The Road to Rome* in 1927. From this comedy-drama on to his latest work we have the impression that here walks a thoughtful playwright puzzled by the contours of the land he is traversing, anxious to discover his orientation yet lost without a compass, and inclining to steer his steps now towards one landmark, now towards another. In *The Road to Rome* Shaw's influence is obvious, and the action takes shape as a modernistic treatment of a section of classical history, inspired not merely by the detestation of war, but also by the sentimental assumptions that wars are caused by stupid individual heroics and that the bubble of these heroics can be easily pricked by common sense. Rome, threatened by the might of Hannibal, is protected from ruin by the realistic wit of Amytis, wife of Fabius, not by Fabius' armies. The gay spirit of thoughtful wit also animates *Reunion in Vienna* (1931), a delightful fantasy which presents a gathering of Habsburgs, now scattered over the earth and sadly decayed in grandeur, in the home of their former colourful existence. Adroitly Sherwood, in this latter comedy, contrasts both the relics of aristocratic pride with existing poverty and the relics of the code of honour with bourgeois morality, wrapping the entire action in a vesture as witty as it is colourful.

This author's purpose, however, is too serious to permit him to find full satisfaction in the comic realm, even although the laughter be shot through with grave reflection. Already in *Waterloo Bridge* (1930), with its story of a young soldier and a prostitute, he had essayed something darker, and five years later he reached mastery of expression when he turned to write *The Petrified Forest* (1935). With a peculiarly appealing style, he here depicts, in Alan Squire, an unsuccessful, highly cultured poet wandering wearily over the Arizona desert, symbolizing the sense of spiritual disillusionment out of which the entire drama grows. Every one of the characters, indeed, is symbolic; yet every one is real. Duke Mantee, the gangster, stands for the new spirit of adventure, adventure that has been forced to become evil; Gabby, the girl with whom Squire falls in love, represents the hope that lies, rather precariously, in the future. Despairing though the spirit of this play is, it has a warmth and a breadth wanting in many other realistic works of the age. At least Sherwood does not concentrate his attention on eternal triangles, neurotics, or criminals created by society. *Idiot's Delight* (1936) carries on and perfects the style of *The Petrified Forest*. Again the characters are both real and symbols—the German scientist, the French munitions manufacturer, the American 'hoofer,' the English honeymoon couple—and again the emotional tension rises steadily until it ends in the staccato of explosions. Only this time the explosions are not the petty gunfire between gangsters and police, but the dull echoing of bombs amid the mountains. There can be no doubt that this is one of the most effective realistic dramas the twentieth-century theatre has to offer us.

Much less satisfactory, *Abe Lincoln in Illinois* (1938) turns to explore the early life of a recent yet already mythical American president. Then in 1940 Sherwood produced, in a white heat of passion, *There shall be No Night*, a grimly tense testimonial to the Finns in their struggle to preserve their independence. Perhaps it is typical of the author's wandering path that, soon after the appearance of this work, he found himself as passionately aroused by the German menace, so that, while he was himself devoting his time to the war effort, he allowed the subject-matter of *There shall be No Night* to be translated into terms of invaded Greece. There is probably something of a spiritually autobiographical character in Sherwood's later play, *The Rugged Path* (1945), which shows a liberal newspaperman, Vinion, who, after roaming far through the world, returns to edit his home-town newspaper, becomes involved in a struggle with conservative, 'isolationist' elements, and only by enlisting in the navy succeeds in recapturing his faith in humanity.

THE THEATRE OF THE 'SOCIALLY CONSCIOUS'

With the coming of the depression diverse social strains, amply evident in the earlier American drama, came to the surface. Class-consciousness developed rapidly, and most of the younger theatre enthusiasts were prepared to mingle admiring imitation of Stanislawski with ardent inculcation of socialism. The Group Theatre was thus formulated out of a Theatre Guild Studio; more radical in aim, the Theatre Union bravely struggled on for some years;

a New Theatre League came into being; at the extreme left agitated the Theatre of Action and the Labour Stage (the theatre unit of the International Ladies Garment Workers Union). Not only did these organizations present their own repertory (and in one instance develop their own playwright), but the spirit they so eagerly expressed spread over to influence the current fare in the commercial theatres.

Naturally the dramatic results of this movement were various and of varying quality. At the Theatre Union the dramas inclined to be solemnly sincere, melodramatic, sensational, and sentimental. Here appeared *Peace on Earth* (1933), by Albert Maltz and George Sklar, who had already collaborated in a tense and in its way effective indictment of the iniquities of American justice in *Merry-go-Round* (1932). Although the theme of *Peace on Earth* has virtue—it is an attack on munitions-makers and their influence—the handling of the plot is reminiscent of nineteenth-century melo-drama. A similar criticism may be passed on *Stevedore* (1934), written by Sklar in conjunction with Paul Peters, and on *Black Pit* (1935), by Maltz. Characteristic of the qualities introduced into these plays is the Theatre Union's final production—*Marching Song* (1937), by John Howard Lawson, author of the expressionistic *Processional* of 1925. Taking as centre of his picture a wretched family, compelled to live in a disused factory building because they have been turned out of their home by the 'capitalists' (who dis-approve of the father's radical agitation), Lawson develops his story along familiar lines. The other workers go on strike; the father is given the alternative of having his job back and betraying his fellows or of living with his family at starvation's edge; gunmen engaged by the factory owners resort to murder; the strike spreads, and amid cries of jubilation the capitalists are brought to their knees in abject surrender.

Something rather richer in texture appears in *Let Freedom Ring* (1935), by Albert Bein, chiefly because the setting—a mill located in the Kentucky mountains—permits of the introduction of a more variegated dramatic personnel than can appear in a city-set labour drama. Still richer is *The Cradle will Rock* (1937), by Marc Blitz-stein, a play to which flavour is given through the employment of the operatic technique for the expressing of socialistic propaganda. Richer yet is the long one-act drama by Irwin Shaw called *Bury the Dead* (1936), with its gripping (and almost expressionistically developed) theme of the soldiers rising from their trenches and being frantically told by all the living—from their generals to their relatives—that they must remain in the land of the lifeless. Irwin Shaw unquestionably has an original talent denied to most of his fellow-enthusiasts, as is shown by one of his following plays, *The Gentle People* (1939), the tender fantasy of which contrasts vividly with the white-hot bitterness of his first work. The gentle people are two cronies, a Jew and a Greek, desperately poor yet gathering money gradually wherewith to purchase a boat large enough to allow them to fulfil their dream of sailing off far into a warm South. A gangster appears and demands tribute from them, whereupon this innocent and mild-mannered and timorous pair lure him into their little fishing-skiff, row him out to sea, and drown him: the curtain falls upon them as, returned home, they sit, quiet and satisfied, dreaming their dreams.

While the Federal Theatre Project (1935–39) stimulated the labour theatre, in itself it did not do much to encourage dramatic talent. Under its auspices appeared interesting productions—such as the Negro *Macbeth* and the *Swing Mikado*—but of new plays there was a dearth. For the Project Sinclair Lewis and John C. Moffitt wrote the anti-fascist *It Can't Happen Here* (1936): this, however, is a rather lonely effort, and most of the playwrights' energies went into the preparation of 'Living Newspaper' material of Soviet style (such as *One Third of a Nation*, 1938).

For writers of power we must look beyond this venture, and particularly to the talent sponsored by the Group Theatre. This unit brought forward a dramatist with a peculiar quality of his own in Robert Ardrey, author of a fairly feeble 'labour' play *Casey Jones* (1938) and of a truly interesting *Thunder Rock* (1939). The latter, which strangely failed to win any acclaim in America, but was a great success in London, displays extraordinary power and deep-searching vision in its picture of the lonely lighthouse and the shades of the past meeting the forms of the living. Ardrey is a playwright who yet may have much to give us, although his recent Negro drama, *Jeb* (1946), hardly fulfils the promise of *Thunder Rock*.

Beyond all others of this group, however, towers Clifford Odets. When his *Waiting for Lefty* appeared in 1935 it was easy to see that the labour stage had gained a literary artist whose abilities carried him beyond the cliché and the hysterical appeal towards 'action.' No doubt the emotional effect of this one-act drama depends more on the author's skill in arousing political emotion than upon his æsthetic effects, but, even so, the arousing of the political emotion is achieved by means far subtler than had been used in the Theatre

Union's melodramas. With skill, Odets has raised before us a vivid picture of the absent Lefty, so that when news comes of his murder by agents of the capitalistic owners we feel almost as though we had heard of the death of a friend. Odets' second play, *Awake and Sing* (1935), demonstrated equally clearly that here was an author not content to rely on the facile sentiments of the ordinary propagandist drama. No doubt the flame at the heart of these bitter scenes is the flame of anger; at the same time, the picture of the Berger family circle, impoverished and destined by circumstance to have all its dreams broken, gains its power from the author's grasp of character and his almost Chekhovian sense of human relationships. One by one, we see these characters going their ways—the old grandfather, to his death; the son Ralph, to a shattering of his romance; his sister, Hennie, to a loveless intrigue. The atmosphere is thoroughly realistic, yet Odets has the power to make his words sing; here is a force akin to that of the young O'Casey.

In *Paradise Lost* (1935) something of the magic vanishes, but sufficient remains to make this too a notable drama: what is missing here is the power so markedly present in the earlier plays whereby the individual action was given general overtones. There is a descent to the melodramatic in *Paradise Lost*, and we feel that the cards have been carefully stacked: in the story of Ben Gordon and his ending under police gunfire we are given something that strains our belief and renders us unable to accept either the characters or the plot as representative in the larger sense. *Golden Boy* (1937) is also melodramatic, particularly towards the conclusion of the piece, yet in this play we sense a return to the quality that gave distinction to *Awake and Sing*. Joe Bonaparte is drawn in terms that bring him to life on the stage, a character at once admirable and weak, a study unmarred by the black-and-white portraiture so often found in the theatre of social realism. This man, a violinist, with the soul of a musician, gives up his art to become a prize-fighter. Money is in the ring, and money he craves, both because he can give of it to the woman he loves and because deep within himself resides a passion for the worldly power that riches can procure. Throughnut the play Joe's mental agonies are skilfully revealed in taut, oervous dialogue that, when need arises, has the strength to borrow the qualities of music and to sing. In the end the strain on him is so great that he feels the desire to fly from the world of his own creating, and to crash. He has killed a man in a contest; he has abandoned his violin; his hands, trained to fight, have no longer the skill to play; and in the wild motor-drive which brings death

to Lorna and himself he seeks his release. Odets' power of rising to
the demands of an emotional climax is revealed nowhere more
vividly than in his hero's despairing and exalted pæan in praise of
speed:

JOE: But I *did* it! That's the thing—I *did* it! What will my father say
when he hears I murdered a man? Lorna, I see what I did. I murdered myself, too! I've been running around in circles. Now I'm
smashed! That's the truth. Yes, I was a real sparrow, and I wanted
to be a fake eagle! But now I'm hung up by my finger-tips—I'm
no good—my feet are off the earth!

LORNA [*in a sudden burst, going to* JOE]: Joe, I love you! We love each
other. Need each other!

JOE: Lorna darling, I see what's happened!

LORNA: You wanted to conquer the world——

JOE: Yes——

LORNA: But it's not the kings and dictators who do it—it's that kid in
the park——

JOE: Yes, that boy who might have said, "I have myself; I am what
I want to be!"

LORNA: And now, to-night, here, this minute—finding yourself again
—that's what makes you a champ. Don't you see that?

JOE: Yes, Lorna—yes!

LORNA: It isn't too late to tell the world good-evening again!

JOE: With what? These fists?

LORNA: Give up the fighting business!

JOE: To-night!

LORNA: Yes, and go back to your music——

JOE: But my hands are ruined. I'll never play again! What's left,
Lorna? Half a man, nothing, useless . . .

LORNA: No, *we're* left! Two together! We have each other! Somewhere there must be happy boys and girls who can teach us the
way of life! We'll find some city where poverty's no shame—
where music is no crime!—where there's no war in the streets—
where a man is glad to be himself, to live and make his woman
herself!

JOE: No more fighting, but where do we go?

LORNA: To-night? Joe, we ride in your car. We speed through the
night, across the park, over the Triboro Bridge——

JOE [*taking* LORNA'S *arms in his trembling hands*]: Ride! That's it, we
ride—clear my head. We'll drive through the night. When you
mow down the night with headlights nobody gets you! You're
on top of the world then—nobody laughs! That's it—speed!
We're off the earth—unconnected! We don't have to think! That's
what speed's for, an easy way to live! Lorna darling, we'll burn
up the night!

Although this scene betrays the weakness common to many young American dramatic authors of the thirties—an inordinate tendency to feel sorry for themselves in the midst of plenty—yet Odets' power is sufficient to carry us past and above the rather lachrymose sentimentalizing. These few lines of dialogue alone are sufficient to testify to his power over theatrical words.

In *Rocket to the Moon* (1938) Odets turned to write a play more puzzling than any he had previously composed. The plot drifts along with the inconsequentiality of a Chekhovian drama, although we feel that it lacks that essential quality which makes Chekhov's plays great. In the works of the Russian dramatist an inner symphonic harmony gives purpose to the least (and perhaps, at first sight, meaningless) episode; in *Rocket to the Moon* we are troubled by a sense of confusion—and for this the cause is to be sought in what Harold Clurman has to tell us of its inception. *Rocket to the Moon*, he comments,

> contained some of Odets' most mature writing and two of his finest characters. The play as written, however, was thematically quite different from what had been implied in Odets' original sketch of it. . . .
> As originally planned, the play was about a meek little dentist ravaged through the love of a silly girl. Regardless of its object, love was to give this man a depth of experience and thus a stature beyond his normal scope. The dentist then was the central character, and the play was his play. In the actual writing of the play the theme was transformed to that of the difficult quest for love in the modern world. The person who embodied this quest was the little girl, uneducated, childish, rattle-brained, and true. She had become the centre of the play, a person who despite her 'ordinariness' was what the author called a moral idealist, whose pathos arises from an inability to find realization through connexion with any of the representative middle-class men she meets in the course of her quest.

As a result, Clurman points out, the original scheme was to present a man with a choice of women—a nagging wife and a trivial child mistress. But

> when the girl at the end of the play matured sufficiently to express the essence of her experience—and the playwright's thought—a good part of the audience was bewildered by her transformation and the unexpected turn the play had taken.

This example, perhaps, has the quality of illustrating Odets' main dramatic weakness. He has power over character and his words are rich, but he has not that larger constructive sense which alone can produce unity of impression and of concept.

What he may accomplish in the future it is hard to say. *Night Music* (1940), although its sense of comic values is delicate and fine, although its picture of youth lost in the industrial jungle has strength and vision, suffers from the same failings as his other dramas: it too lacks the core of an imaginative idea to which all other elements are rigorously sacrificed. Equally difficult to assess is *Clash by Night* (1941), with its rather dreary solemnity. To achieve dramatic greatness demands infinite patience and the willingness to subordinate the will to the exactions of a jealous art: perhaps, for all his gifts, Odets is too impatient and is not prepared wholly to accept the inevitable restrictions of the stage.

In one particular realm the socially conscious theatre of the United States has found a native theme whose seriousness and dramatic potentialities have been diversely exploited. The Negro problem is one unique to that country, and it is not surprising that almost every one of her playwrights, each in his own way, has tried to set some of its perplexing issues upon the stage. Far back in the nineteenth century the ever-inventive Boucicault won success by his melodramatic treatment of *The Octoroon* (1859), and since then scores of dramas have set the opposition of whites and blacks upon the stage. Even those authors who show themselves intent on larger questions feel impelled to turn to this subject: O'Neill pens his *Emperor Jones* and *All God's Chillun Got Wings*, while Anderson gives us his *Wingless Victory*.

The variety of approach here is, naturally, great. Some authors burn with a sense of immediate and urgent purpose. Thus John Wexley, who had, very melodramatically, attacked capital punishment in *The Last Mile* (1930) and ill-treatment of workers in *Steel* (1931), was inspired by a notorious trial of Negroes to write his would-be flaming, but in actuality merely spluttering, *They Shall Not Die* (1934). At the opposite extreme comes the attempt simply to present a theatrical record of Negro psychology. Of this kind of play the delightful *Green Pastures* (1930) of Marc Connelly easily ranks highest—a skilful and sympathetic presentation of a Negro minister's idea of heaven and the history of the world. With a deep understanding of the primitive mind, in which the abstractly symbolic disconcertingly jostles against the common things of the day, Connelly has produced a play that assuredly will remain among the treasures of the world's lesser drama. There is a peculiar direct simplicity of appeal here that captures our attention. "I kin out-trick you an' de Lawd too!" cries Pharaoh, and Moses replies:

MOSES [*angrily*]: Now you done it, ol' King Pharaoh. You been mean to de Lawd's people, and de Lawd's been easy on you caize you didn't know no better. You been givin' me a lot of say-so and no do-so, and I didn' min' dat. But now you've got to braggin' dat you's better dan de Lawd, and dat's too many.

PHARAOH: You talk like a preacher, an' I never did like to hear preachers talk.

MOSES: You ain't goin' to like it any better, when I strikes down de oldes' boy in every one of yo' people's houses.

PHARAOH: Now you've given up trickin' and is jest lyin'. [*He rises.*] Listen, I'm Pharaoh. I do de strikin' down yere. I strike down my enemies, and dere's no one in all Egypt kin kill who he wants to, 'ceptin' me.

MOSES: I'm sorry, Pharaoh. Will you let de Hebrews go?

PHARAOH: You heard my word. [AARON *is lifting his rod again at a signal from* MOSES.] Now, no more tricks or I'll——

MOSES: Oh, Lawd, you'll have to do it, I guess. Aaron, lift de rod. [*There is a thunderclap, darkness, and screams. The lights go up. Several of the younger men on the stage have fallen to the ground or are being held in the arms of the horrified elders.*]

PHARAOH: What have you done yere? Where's my boy? [*Through the door come four men bearing a young man's body.*]

FIRST OF THE FOUR MEN: King Pharaoh. [PHARAOH *drops into his chair, stunned, as the dead boy is brought to the throne.*]

PHARAOH [*grief-stricken*]: Oh, my son, my fine son. [*The courtiers look at him with mute appeal.*]

MOSES: I'm sorry, Pharaoh, but you cain't fight de Lawd. Will you let his people go?

PHARAOH: Let them go. [*The lights go out. The* CHOIR *begins,* "*Mary Don't You Weep,*" *and continues until it is broken by the strains of* "*I'm Noways Weary and I'm Noways Tired.*"]

Between the extremes of *They Shall Not Die* and *Green Pastures* rest most of the works of Paul Green, a Southerner who has made the depiction of the Negro and of the 'poor white' his life's task. When his *In Abraham's Bosom* appeared in 1926 it was immediately realized that its author was a man of no common ability. Taking as his hero a half-caste who determines that the only hope for the Negroes lies in their fuller education, Green shows his Abraham McCranie struggling both against the indifference of his black cousins and against the evil animosity of his white, until, driven desperate by the callousness and evil around him, he is led to murder his own half-brother, a man from whom he had sought aid and

who had betrayed his trust by stealing from him his few last possessions. This drama was followed several years later by *The House
of Connelly* (1931), in which the crumbling of the old Southern
aristocracy is displayed in the gradual disintegration of one single
great estate. Through the marriage of Will Connelly, weak-willed
and decadent, and Patsy Tate, a girl belonging to the 'poor white
trash' whom the Connellys despise, but who possesses vigour and
initiative, Green seems to suggest that only through an infusion of
new blood into the dry veins of the aristocrats can there be any
hope of saving a dying segment of the nation. In a sense Green is
thus merely transferring to an American *milieu* what had been
hinted by Goldoni nearly two hundred years before, and what had
formed the major theme, in the late nineteenth century, of plays
by Augier and Lavedan. In subsequently written dramas, many of
them one-acts, Green has sought to explore further diverse aspects
of life in the South, but without achieving unquestioned success.
There is in Green a burning sincerity unfortunately not accompanied
by that technical mastery and abounding strength which are required by the most exacting of all literary arts.

Along with Green may be associated Du Bose Heyward, famous
for his *Porgy* (1927), dramatized from his own novel and later made
into operatic form (1935), with music by George Gershwin. The
importance of this work rests in its departure from themes of miscegenation, of sharecroppers and the like, depicting instead Negro
life as it is carried on in Charleston. There is no colour problem
here, simply a well-wrought drama with the crippled Porgy as its
hero, surrounded by the self-seeking Bess, the flashy Sportin' Life,
the murderous Crown, and a variety of other characters making
up a vividly drawn picture of a kind that hitherto the American
stage had not known. Another drama on similar lines, *Mamba's
Daughters*, a collaborative work of Dorothy and Du Bose Heyward,
appeared in 1939.

Through these and other plays the Negro has definitely entered
the New York theatre. *Cabin in the Sky* (1940), by Lynn Root
and John La Touche, shows an imaginative sense and suggests fresh
proportions; although melodramatic, *Native Son* (1941), by Richard
Wright, possesses a vigour of peculiar intensity; Hall Johnson's
Run, Little Chillun (1933) has an intimate quality that demonstrates
how far the drama of colour has moved from the artificialities of
The Octoroon. All-Negro casts are now by no means rare, and in
1946 theatrical history was made when a Negro actor, Canada Lee,
reversed a tradition of generations and, after essaying the rôle of

Caliban in *The Tempest*, played a part in *The Duchess of Malfi* in white-face. Now that coloured actors have won a distinguished position on the serious stage and Negro authors are having their plays produced, it may be that this particular kind of drama will show marked development in years to come.

CURRENT AMERICAN REALISM

With the Negro, as has been indicated, is connected the poor white, and for a time the rage of New York was a rather sordid piece called *Tobacco Road* (1933), adapted by John Kirkland from a novel by Erskine Caldwell. The authors may have been inspired by the desire to present a sociological document: audiences almost certainly flocked to see the play out of itching curiosity. This is the *Before Sunrise* of the thirties.

The writer who has most specialized in gaunt, stark pictures of depressed areas and depressing types is John Steinbeck, a novelist who won some theatrical fame when his *Of Mice and Men* was turned into a play in 1937 and when his *The Grapes of Wrath* was made into a film in 1940. Steinbeck has all the true characteristics of the naturalist—his love of the gloomy *milieu*, his implied sense of social purpose, and his inescapable sentimentalism. *Of Mice and Men* is typical, with its deceptively objective yet sentimentally weak portrait of the gentle-hearted, half-witted giant who kills unwittingly the things he loves. The same sentimentalism runs amok in the popular but trivial *The Moon is Down* (1941), which demonstrates in its strained action a worthy idea, no doubt, but one which startlingly fails to do justice to the real events it celebrates: larger problems cannot, it would appear, come satisfactorily within the framework of the realistic drama. This attempt in the American theatre to reproduce the tough naturalism of the Hauptmann period does not seem to offer much hope of worthy results. Even the novelist Ernest Hemingway's *The Fifth Column* (published 1938; acted 1940), although it does succeed in painting a powerful portrait of Philip Rawlings and in making us understand his actions, is vitiated by the same weaknesses as mar Steinbeck's work.

Within the realm of what may be called commercial realism no author has recently shown more skill or won more fame than Lillian Hellman, who first came before the public with *The Children's Hour* in 1934 and followed this with *Days to Come* (1936), *The Little Foxes* (1939), *Watch on the Rhine* (1941), and *The Searching Wind* (1944). In these she stands about midway between the social playwrights and those realistic writers who are intent upon depiction of character. Her not very powerful *Days to Come* deals with labour problems, but obviously this is not the sphere in which she is most at home, and her best, most characteristic scenes appear in such works as *The Children's Hour* and *The Little Foxes*. It is the vicious soul that attracts her most: her understanding of human evil is acute, and she knows how to make it theatrically effective. Indeed, we might almost say that she has won her success by devising a formula for an up-to-date melodrama where the villain, instead of being a black-moustached squire or factory owner, is revealed unexpectedly as a child possessed of inherent wickedness and where the dialogue is impeccably true to the tones of current speech. The theme of *The Children's Hour* might perhaps be described as the effect of an original lie working on a gossip-ridden community, but the real dramatic interest of the play lies in its vicious little Mary Tilford, whose original hint that her school-teachers, Karen Wright and Martha Dobie, have Lesbian relations succeeds not only in arousing this community's anger against a couple of largely innocent women, but also in infecting their souls with ugly thoughts. This is by no means so great or so original a drama as was once thought; we cannot, however, deny its impressive technical ability. *The Little Foxes* varies the pattern slightly. Here the evil force is a woman, Regina Giddens, who practically murders her husband and robs her brothers in order to gain control of a factory. For *Watch on the Rhine* the villain becomes a more familiar figure—a Rumanian count who is in reality a Fascist agent and who is killed by the worthy hero, a mild-mannered German refugee. Perhaps because she was dealing here with somewhat alien matter, Lillian Hellman's hand seems not so steady and her scenes not so effective, nor has she succeeded in rehabilitating herself in *The Searching Wind*. Perhaps in *The Children's Hour* and *The Little Foxes* she has exhausted her treasury of wickedness: this, indeed, is suggested when we find her, in her very latest play, *Another Part of the Forest* (1947), returning to the latter's domestic *milieu*.

A companion authoress, but one less gifted with original vision, is Rose Franken, whose *Another Language* won some attention in 1932. Later her *Claudia* (1941) attracted audiences not so much because of its dramatic power as because its subject—the difficulty experienced by a girl in casting off her mother's influence and becoming a responsible wife—seemed to many to be new. In *Soldier's Wife* (1944) the problem of the readjustment of the army man to civilian life is discussed, while *Outrageous Fortune* (1944) runs through a gamut of problems from homosexuality to anti-Semitism.

Besides these authors numerous others have contributed to the New York stage plays, objective or intense, in the realistic kind. Most of them assuredly will be forgotten a few decades hence, yet in several reside qualities which we might well have wished to be incorporated in less mortal shapes. There is, for example, an element of strength in *The Criminal Code* (1929), a study by Martin Flavin of honour among thieves; sympathetic portraiture appears in *The Barker* (1927), by Kenyon Nicholson; an affecting story of the impress of divorce on a child's mind is told by Leopold Atlas in *Wednesday's Child* (1934)—we might extend the list by enumerating scores of titles, all worthy yet all certainly lacking the quality of permanence. Once more we are confronted by the fact that, in general, the realistic drama but seldom rises (and then usually by means of extra-realistic elements) to a plane above that of the immediately popular.

THE CONTINUANCE OF THE REALISTIC IN ENGLAND

In England the realistic strain has been carried on during these years with far less vigour and far less fervency than in the United States. Young American dramatists in the twenties found all the excitement of handling a form new to them, and in the thirties there was the socially conscious theatre to urge them forward: by comparison their English companions in this field seem just a trifle bored and consequently unable to wrest virtue from a long-tried style.

Among these writers John Van Druten takes prominence, if only because of the consistency in his application to the stage. His formula is composed of an apparently realistic setting, characters apparently true to life, the suggestion of a problem, and a strong dash of genteel sentimentalism; through the handling of this material with an undeniably skilled hand, he has won success for many of his pieces. *Young Woodley* (1928), his first, captured attention because of its interesting theme of an elder schoolboy's infatuation for the young wife of his master and because of its excellence of construction. Since then he has produced numerous similarly conceived dramas—*Diversion* (1928), *After All* (1929), *There's Always Juliet* (1931), *The Distaff Side* (1933), *Old Acquaintance* (1939), *The Voice of the Turtle* (1943)—wherein we constantly feel that the author, while gifted with a strength out of the ordinary, always fails to bring to the stage more than a series of relatively trivial plays, each likely to be a current success and each likely to be forgotten once its run is over.

At one moment it looked as though, with the appearance of *Journey's End* (1928), by R. C. Sherriff, a brilliant new dramatist had entered the theatre's doors: his later works, however, have failed to capture the truly extraordinary success of this his first play. The same judgment must unfortunately also be passed on J. R. Ackerley, whose *The Prisoners of War* (1925), a study of conditions in a military camp, possesses real tension and sense of character values. Still another war play that remains the solitary notable achievement of its author (H. B. Trevelyan) is *The Dark Angel* (1928), in which a blinded soldier returns to find his sweetheart devoted to a second man.

The 'repertory' tradition during these years was carried on by Allan N. Monkhouse, with ability but without high distinction. *The Conquering Hero* (1924) is a good play of its kind—a kind that is not good; and *First Blood* (1924) seems a very tame study of strike conditions when we compare it with its American cousins. The early death of Ronald Mackenzie may have cut off (as some think) a true dramatic promise, yet objective analysis of *Musical Chairs* (1931) suggests that it is not nearly so fine a play as many critics once thought it, while *The Maitlands* (1934) hardly suggests developing talent. Slightly more difficult is it to estimate the value of the numerous contributions to the theatre made by Emlyn Williams. Starting with a couple of sensational pieces, expertly planned, *A Murder has been Arranged* (1930) and *Night Must Fall* (1935), he showed even in his first works a firm grasp of character values and an adroitness in the devising of stage situations. *The Corn is Green* (1938), with its interesting treatment of a village teacher and her prize pupil, seemed to set him on a higher level, although we can hardly maintain that his subsequent dramas, all of them marked by a sentimental flavour, have served to keep him there. The study of the drunken actor in *The Light of Heart* (1940) does not penetrate very deeply; *The Morning Star* (1941) is obviously a *pièce d'occasion*; *The Wind of Heaven* (1945) offers somewhat more, with its *Here Come the Clowns* atmosphere, although perhaps it has been over-praised; *Spring 1600* (latest version, 1945) merely presents a pleasing dream of Elizabethan London; and *Trespass* (1947) is a somewhat artificial theatrical essay in ghosts and mediums.

There is entertainment in this realm; what is lacking is broader vision. C. L. Anthony (Dodie Smith) can turn out a graceful

BASIC SETTING BY PETER GOFFIN FOR THE TRAVELLING REPERTORY
THEATRE PRODUCTION OF "IN TIME TO COME"

Photo John Vickers

"WAITING FOR LEFTY":
GROUP THEATRE, NEW YORK
Photo Vandamm, New York
833

Autumn Crocus (1931) and an equally graceful *Dear Octopus* (1938);
Mordaunt Shairp can engage in psychological studies in *The Offence*
(1925) or, more brilliantly, in *The Green Bay Tree* (1932); Keith
Winter can pen a would-be tragic study of the grand passion in
The Shining Hour (1934); others there are who might similarly be
recorded—and when the catalogue is done we must acknowledge
that, despite the excellencies apparent in diverse individual dramas,
we are left in the end with nothing of enduring force. The field
is barren and can produce no satisfying crops.

FURTHER RELICS OF THE REALISTIC

The same story must be told of the progress of the realistic play
in Ireland. O'Casey and Carroll, by infusing into the form elements
of another character, have achieved some considerable distinction,
but because of these other elements they have called for discussion
in earlier sections of this survey. Among the Irish authors who
have pursued the strictly realistic path hardly any can be esteemed
to have produced work likely to remain. Best of them is George
Shiels, a man who gained some success with *The New Gossoon*
(1930), *The Rugged Path* (1940), *The Summit* (1941), and *Tenants-at-
Will* (1942). The first of these is a comedy, defending youthful
gaiety against age's solemnity; the last grimly deals with a period
of famine. Between these two extremes come the companion plays,
The Rugged Path and *The Summit*, concerned with the way in
which a lonely Irish community is tyrannized over by the members
of a ne'er-do-well and criminal family—a study that is highly
reminiscent of the many American between-war dramas that deal
with life in the Kentucky mountains. In *Marrowbone Lane* (1946)
Robert Collis deals with Dublin's slums; the potato famine of 1847
is the theme of Gerard Healey's *The Dark Stranger* (1947).

Greater value attaches to a few plays in which the approach is more
fanciful. Anthony Wharton (Alister McAllister) produces in *The
O'Cuddy* (1943) a pleasingly satiric picture of a stupid man who is
argued into believing that he is the heir to a long line of Irish kings,
and Brinsley MacNamara presents a series of hilarious dramatic
escapades from *The Rebellion in Balleycullen* (1919) to *The Three
Thimbles* (1942). A kindred mood prevails in the plays of Denis
Johnston, who first acquired fame with *The Moon in the Yellow
River* in 1931. This is an interesting drama, concerned mainly with
the struggle of an idealistic Irish revolutionary to prevent the
erection of a power plant near Dublin; he has fought for the freedom

2D

of his country, but he wants her freedom to be more than political; Ireland, he dreams, should be the one place on God's earth which remains green and unpolluted by industrialism's evils. Unfortunately Johnston's later plays have hardly approached the brilliance of this early work. *A Bride for the Unicorn* (1933) is confused in its mingling of common reality and of symbolism; neither *Blind Man's Buff* (1936) nor *The Golden Cuckoo* (1938) possesses the peculiar appeal of the visionary who follows the moon's gleams in the muddy waters. The Irish genius finds its spirit expressed perhaps more freely in the imaginative than in the realistic style, and maybe its mood is better caught in Micheál MacLiammóir's *Ill Met by Moonlight* (1946), with its modern atmosphere charmed into strangeness because the house in which the characters dwell has been built upon a fairy ring.

Just before the outbreak of war a revival of dramatic power seemed imminent in Scandinavia, but not sufficient of worth came from that area before 1939 to warrant any sure guess as to what might have been achieved had Norway and Denmark not been rudely occupied by Teutonic forces. Apart from Helge Krog, whose work is referred to elsewhere, the most important writer here is the Norwegian Nordahl Grieg. In all, his writings suggest that, had his short life not unfortunately been ended in the War, he might have proved the greatest dramatist of his generation. Starting his career obviously influenced by Ibsen and Pirandello, he first produced *En ung manns kjærlighet* (*A Young Man's Love*, 1927) and *Barrabas* (1927). Then, some five years later, he essayed a new style in *Atlanterhavet* (*The Atlantic Ocean*, 1932), where a striking contrast is drawn between the fate of those engaged in a dangerous transatlantic flight and the preoccupations of a newspaper editor interested only in the publicity values of their exploit. *Vår ære og vår makt* (*Our Honour and Our Might*, 1935) similarly introduces vivid contrasts—in this case between a German submarine crew and their hapless victims. In his last play, *Nederlaget* (*The Defeat*, 1936), he turned to deal with an historical theme of the time of the Paris Commune, but obviously his interest in this powerful drama lay not in illustrating the past, but in giving himself an opportunity for commenting indirectly on current life. Very close in spirit and atmosphere are the plays of the Danish Kaj Munk, an author who also perished during the War. His career started with a drama on Herod the Creat, *En idealist* (*An Idealist*, 1928), was carried on in *Ordet* (*The Word*, 1932) and the patriotic *Egelykke* (1940), and closed with a vigorous drama, *Niels Ebbesen* (1942), which deals with a

Danish hero who kills a brutal German officer. Among these dramas interesting, too, is the work of Kjeld Abell, whose rather immature *Melodien, der blev væk* (*The Melody which was Lost*, 1935) found an abler successor in *Anna Sophie Hedvig* (1938), a strange drama in which the chief character, a rather timorous rural school-teacher, is shown murdering an evil-minded woman who is about to be made director of her school, and who, in that position, would be likely to ruin the lives of the children placed in her care. The murder is clearly symbolic, and the symbolism becomes manifest when at the end we find the heroine, along with a soldier, waiting for a firing-squad in Spain. There is virtue also in his *Silkeborg* (1946), a play wherein middle-aged bourgeois prudence under the occupation is contrasted with youthful defiance. Less likely to pass beyond the bounds of their own country are the numerous plays, including *Ledaren* (*The Leader*, 1935) and *Modern och stjärnen* (*The Mother and the Star*, 1940), in which the Swedish Rudolf Värnlund has found expression for social-realistic studies: these can hardly be esteemed richer in content, deeper in psychological penetration, or more exciting in form than the hundreds of other similar plays with which the twentieth century has provided us.

In France during these years most of the writers for the theatre have avoided what may be called straight realism. Of the minority, Gabriel Marcel, an exponent of "existentialisme chrétien," may be noted for his exposure of an artist's selfishness in *Le cœur des autres* (*The Heart of Others*, 1920) and for his analysis of conflicting ideologies in *Le dard* (*The Spear*, 1937); so too may be noted Denys Amiel for his *La souriante Madame Beudet* (*The Smiling Madame Beudet*, 1921; written in collaboration with André Obey), *M. et Mme Un Tel* (*Mr and Mrs So-and-so*, 1925), and *Le mouton noir* (*The Black Sheep*, 1946). The first two are rather dark studies of marital animosity and infidelity; the last deals with the love of a husband for his stepdaughter. Although there is some quality here, little of vigour and less of enduring interest make their appearance.

Elsewhere there is little of consequence to be found—whether among the old-fashioned new-woman dramas of F. X. Svoboda and the racy comedy-dramas of Frantiçek Langer in Czechoslovakia, the labour plays of G. Ciprian in Rumania, the social-problem dramas of Stanko Majcen in Jugoslavia, the bitingly sardonic pieces of Karl Kraus in Austria, or, in Hungary, the peasant studies of Zsigmond Móricz, the middle-class pictures presented by Sándor Bródy, and the half-romantic, half-realistic nationalistic essays of Lajos Zilahy.

No doubt each one of these authors has had considerable significance for his time and people; not one can be considered to possess significance for those outside his country and living in a later period. Over practically all recent realistic theatre writings hangs the shadow of death.

THE COMIC SPIRIT AND SOCIAL UNREST

ALTHOUGH most of the more ambitious authors who devoted their attention to the between-war stage tended to be bitter, over-serious, or hysterical in their denunciations of society's errors, there still were among them some prepared to take a gayer path, and others anxious to laugh even while engaged in their task of castigation.

LAUGHTER MERELY

By a somewhat strange paradox the socially conscious comedy flourished little in London. It was for the English stage that Bernard Shaw poured forth the iridescent stream of his Irish wit, and one might have thought that his influence would have encouraged many young English dramatists to imitate his peculiar style, wherein laughter joins hands with serious purpose. The exact opposite is true. When we compare the contributions to comedy made during these years by playwrights on the two Atlantic coasts we recognize that, whereas New York witnessed the production of numerous excellent 'social' comedies and farces, in London older traditions tended to prevail.

Typical is the contrast between American and English farce. Whereas, as we shall see, the former has found it difficult to escape from the building of its merry episodes around a serious concept, the latter has, for the most part, continued the style set in the nineteenth century. The spirit of *Charley's Aunt* and *The Private Secretary* still remains vital in the long series of such plays which extends on to *French without Tears* (1936), by Terence Rattigan, and beyond.

If we shift our gaze a trifle farther the same prospect stretches out before us. A. P. Herbert permits but little of the serious concept to intrude into *La Vie Parisienne* (1929), *Tantivy Towers* (1931), and *Derby Day* (1932). When C. K. Munro, St John Ervine, and John Drinkwater enter into the comic realm they write, respectively, *At Mrs Beam's* (1921), *The First Mrs Fraser* (1928), and *Bird in Hand* (1928)—comedies that are all entirely free of any social revolutionary message. Among the most successful plays of the kind produced within this period are *The Farmer's Wife* (1916) and *Yellow Sands* (1926), by Eden Phillpotts, and contemporary audiences have given warm welcome to the airy nothingnesses of Noel Coward.

Noel Coward may be taken, indeed, as a symbol of twentieth-century English comedy. Although at the beginning of his career he produced a spuriously serious psychological study of a mother and a son, *The Vortex* (1924), and a tense domestic drama, *The Rat Trap* (1924), and although in later years he has sporadically turned to such patriotic efforts as *Cavalcade* (1931), what strength he has lies obviously in the easy persiflage of his comic writing or in the lyrical trivialities of his revues. *The Young Idea* (1921) shows this style at its earliest stage; *Private Lives* (1930) reveals it in maturity; and its final graces appear in *Blithe Spirit* (1941). The words that Congreve used of Cibber might well apply to Coward: he has many things in his comedies that seem like wit and are not. Here, for example, are Amanda and Elyot, in *Private Lives*, seated at the dinner-table, she wearing pyjamas, he in "a comfortable dressing-gown":

AMANDA: I'm glad we let Louise go. I am afraid she is going to have a cold.

ELYOT: Going to have a cold; she's been grunting and snorting all the evening like a whole herd of bison.

AMANDA [*thoughtfully*]: Bison never sounds right to me somehow. I have a feeling it ought to be bisons, a flock of bisons.

ELYOT: You might say a covey of bisons, or even a school of bisons.

AMANDA: Yes, lovely. The Royal London School of Bisons. Do you think Louise is happy at home?

ELYOT: No, profoundly miserable.

AMANDA: Family beastly to her?

ELYOT [*with conviction*]: Absolutely vile. Knock her about dreadfully, I expect, make her eat the most disgusting food, and pull her fringe.

AMANDA [*laughing*]: Oh, poor Louise.

ELYOT: Well, you know what the French are.

AMANDA: Oh, yes, indeed. I know what the Hungarians are, too.

ELYOT: What are they?

AMANDA: Very wistful. It's all those Pretzles, I shouldn't wonder.

ELYOT: And the Poostza; I always felt the Poostza was far too big, Danube or no Danube.

AMANDA: Have you ever crossed the Sahara on a camel?

ELYOT: Frequently. When I was a boy we used to do it all the time. My grandmother had a lovely seat on a camel.

AMANDA: There's no doubt about it, foreign travel's the thing.

ELYOT: Would you like some brandy?

AMANDA: Just a little.

So it goes on; amusing, no doubt, yet hardly moving farther below the surface than a paper boat in a bath-tub, and, like the paper boat, ever in imminent danger of becoming a shapeless sodden mass. Of Coward's skill there is no doubt, and we may joyously acclaim *Blithe Spirit* as a minor comic masterpiece of the lighter sort. He is, however, a dallier with light words and situations rather than a creator of memorable lines, characters, or concepts.

In Paris a kind of Noel Coward appears in the person of Sacha Guitry, facile creator both of a series of biographical plays (which merit attention later) and of a number of lightly witty comedies— extending from *Nono* (1906), *La prise de Berg-op-Zoom* (*The Taking of Berg-op-Zoom*, 1912) on to *Le nouveau testament* (*Where There's a Will*, or *The New Testament*, 1934) and *Quand jouons-nous la comédie?* (*When do we begin to Play?*, 1935). All these works are of a piece, cleverly turned, skilfully constructed, wholly unbelievable, and for the most part lacking entirely any foundation of thought. As typical as any is *Le veilleur de nuit* (*The Night Watchman*, 1911), in which the author delicately plays on the conventions connected with the eternal triangle and shows a professor who, on discovering that his mistress is being unfaithful to him, acts most magnanimously.

Sacha Guitry's style is crisp and incisive; with him may be considered the skilful and facile but rather puzzling Jacques Deval, creator of *Une faible femme* (*A Weak Woman*, 1920), a study reminiscent of the style of Jean-Jacques Bernard, of *Mademoiselle* (1932), a brilliant portrait of a private teacher, and of *Tovaritch* (1933), an effervescent fantasy which shows the gay Grand Duchess Tatania and Prince Mikhail Alexandrovitch merrily applying themselves to their domestic duties in the house of the bourgeois M. Dupont.

Invested with a gentler spirit are the light extravaganzas of Léopold Marchand, a writer welcome in the world of modern cynicism, but the cynical reappears in the equally extravagant scenes devised by René Fauchois, such as *Le singe qui parle* (*The Monkey who Talks*, 1924) and *Prenez garde à la peinture* (*Watch the Picture!*, 1932), and in the less ambitious but eminently popular farce-comedies of Louis Verneuil.

THE COMEDY OF MANNERS

With Deval we move close to the spirit of the comedy of manners and to that kind of high comedy where occasionally the very ripple of laughter dies away, where a chastened mood brings serious reflection. In Coward's works even we feel ourselves close to the kind of comedy for which the Restoration dramatists won fame, although when we watch his scenes there is the impression that Congreve's heady port, which can bring moments of reflection as well as of merriment, has been replaced by a carelessly tossed-off cocktail or a glass of champagne, possibly not of the finest vintage.

Nearer to the atmosphere of English Restoration comedy—to Wycherley if not to Congreve—stands Somerset Maugham. Some of his earlier plays, including the popular *East of Suez*, which came in 1922, will almost certainly be forgotten; but with equal certainty he will be remembered for *Our Betters* (1917), *The Circle* (1921), and *The Constant Wife* (1927). Despite the air of easy sophistication that enwraps the action of these plays, their author has succeeded in giving an edge to their wit and a depth to their situations of which Coward is incapable. The basic plot of *Our Betters*, in which an American girl, Elizabeth, turns back to her honest American sweetheart, Fleming Harvey, after she has been shocked by the escapades of her cosmopolitanized sister, Lady George Grayson, is trite: the dialogue, however, possesses a peculiar brilliance and gives to a stock situation a quality of bitterly amusing interest. The same interest attaches to *The Circle*, with its magnificently planned parallelism in structure, and to *The Constant Wife*, with its novel interpretation of that theme so beloved of modern playwrights, the double standard in marriage. Maugham is on safer ground here than when he tries to deal with serious scenes: such a play as *For Services Rendered* (1932) seems sadly exaggerated and melodramatic, indicating that for the successful treatment of potentially 'tragic' material its author's talent is nowise fitted.

Close to Maugham stands Frederick Lonsdale, whose *The Last of Mrs Cheyney* (1925) deservedly is remembered as a skilful exercise in comic antitheses and in slightly acidulous irony. Here, too, may be mentioned J. B. Fagan, skilful applier, in *And So to Bed* (1926), of modern society's facile witticisms to the age of Charles II.

In Italy something of the style of Maugham, modified by memories of Pirandello and insensibly influenced by native comic tradition, appears reflected in the works of several authors. Obviously Pirandellian in concept is the *Il cuore in due* (*The Double Heart*, 1926) of Cesare Giulio Viola, which deals entertainingly with the story of two men, brothers, who collaborate in the writing of novels: together they present a whole and interesting human personality, but separately each is only half of a man. How potent even yet is the long-enduring dialect-theatre tradition is to be seen in the work of Gino Rocca, whose several plays include comedies written both in standard Italian and, more characteristically, in his native Venetian speech, wherein he amply pays tribute to the still-abiding and vital influence of Goldoni. The comedy-drama style is preferred by Giuseppe Lanza, who might perhaps most properly be called the Italian Somerset Maugham. *Esilio* (*Exile*, 1929), with its tale of the sarcastic Conte Enrico Sanfiorenzo, his wife, Marta, and the young writer, Luciano Vergati, might easily be related to the high-comedy forms cultivated by that English writer; something of the same quality pervades *Ritorni* (*Returns*, 1929). Perhaps Lanza's most interesting play is *La buona sementa* (*The Good Seed*, 1934), wherein a wisely observant magistrate, Sademo, penetrates to the secret of the shooting of a man, Ranza, who has been found seriously wounded in the house of his friend Viario. Sademo knows that the person directly responsible is Viario's wife, Irene, yet he succeeds in convincing the husband that ultimately his was the fault. At the end of the drama Viario, under Sademo's influence, is ready to start a new life with Irene, but she rejects his offer, declaring that she must sacrifice the rest of her life to caring for Ranza.

Elsewhere, in Norway, Helge Krog has tried to develop a style of love comedy of his own, a kind of sophisticated modern version of Marivaux. He is much concerned with the ages of his lovers, and takes pains to indicate not merely the diverse shapes that love assumes at different periods in a man's or woman's life, but also the call of one generation to another. This is revealed trenchantly in *På Solsiden* (*Happily Ever After*, 1927), where the heroine is shown at the age of seventeen attracted by the nineteen-year-old Axel; at twenty she is the mistress of Inge, thirty-five years old; at twenty-two she has become the mistress of twenty-six-year-old Gustav; and at twenty-three she finds her Axel again (now aged twenty-five) and presumably will be happy ever after. Something of the same pattern is used for *Treklang* (*Triad*, 1933), where Agnete, aged thirty-four and married to the forty-three-year-old Georg, becomes the mistress first of Emile, in his thirties, and later of a young architect. Krog's philosophy, such as it is, is expressed in a scene which shows Georg, Emile, Peter, and Agnete seated at a café table:

EMILE [*drinking deeply*]: The wandering of souls. . . . Do you remember what you said once about the wandering of souls, Agnete? From woman to woman. From man to man. Hop-skip-and-jump. The fable of the three billy-goats. You know that little fable? Well, once upon a time three billy-goats, one ordinary-sized, one big, and one *tremendous*, were crossing a bridge one after the other; the first explained to the hungry giant that met him there, that there was a bigger one coming behind, and so went free. The second did the same. Same result. But when the *third* one came along— why, it simply put down its head, and flattened him out! Your health, Mr Malling!   [*Drinks.* PETER *does not touch his glass.*

GEORG: Migration of souls. Do you travel in souls, Agnete?

EMILE: Yes, and it's like walking on treacle! The soul sticks; it clings fast. And therefore a man meets many men in every woman, and a woman meets many women in every man. . . . Your health again, Mr Malling!

PETER: And yours! [*Takes just barely a sip from his glass.*] By the way, do you know the story of the boy and the worm?

EMILE [*uninterested*]: The boy and the . . . ? No.

PETER: The boy finds a worm and feels sorry for it because it looks so lonely. So he cuts it in two in order that it may have company. Is that clear?

EMILE [*laughing*]: As clear as daylight!

PETER [*slowly and deliberately*]: But there are people who are so deadly afraid of being alone that they cut themselves in two in order to have company.

In Krog's work there appears an able handling of dramatic material and an interesting diversity in treatment—qualities that enable him to deal with situations hovering between the comic and the psychologically serious.

The essays in the comic spirit during the twenties and the thirties have been various, much of them tinged with the tone of cynicism, it is true, yet, perhaps because of that, making definite contributions to the style of the comedy of manners. In Germany, Bruno Frank is perhaps too seriously aroused to permit him to catch the right quality in his *Perlenkomödie* (*Pearl Comedy*, 1929), or *Sturm im Wasserglas* (*Storm in a Teacup*, 1930), but Austria and the eastern lands of Europe still preserved sufficient balance to capture the elusive comic mood. Nostalgically, Stephan Kamare (Cokorac von Kamare) turns back to a gayer Vienna of the past in *Der junge Baron Neuhaus* (*Young Baron Neuhaus*, 1933); a more bitter laughter invests *Die Gartenlaube* (*The Summerhouse*, 1929), by Hermann Ungar. Neighbouring Hungary produces the sardonic Lajos Biró and the wittily accomplished Melchior Lengyel; incisive satire distinguishes the writings of the Czechoslovak Edmund Konrád and those of the Jugoslav Ivan Stodola; while in Poland the native tradition that stems from the time of Fredro gives in these years, despite a general decline in dramatic standards, at least a glimmer of animation. Even further afield we may go for examples of this kind of drama. In distant Mexico, for example, Rodolfo Usigli and Xavier Villaurrutia, amid their many experiments, have turned to exploit this territory: the latter's *Parece mentira* (*It's Incredible,* 1934) is well worthy of notice.

To find a richer manifestation of the spirit of the comedy of manners, however, we must turn to the American Samuel N. Behrman, a man who, despite the unevenness of his accomplishment, manifestly possesses true dramatic strength. Behrman's great achievement is to have established an American comedy of manners, but, characteristically, that comedy, even when it deals with those upper-class persons amid whom flourish the social conventions out of which this kind of drama grows, is built upon a seriously conceived foundation—so serious, indeed, that sometimes the rocky basis on which his houses are set is permitted to jut through the ballroom floor. He starts his career with *The Second Man* (1927), a comedy-drama showing a successful novelist who, facing a dilemma in his life, elects to take the safe path rather than to essay one which, while perhaps more heroic, might lead him to disaster. Already a social interest is apparent in Behrman's work, and this becomes further marked in *Meteor* (1929), in which the story is told of a man, Raphael Lord, who rises to self-made wealth, fails, is deserted by his friends, and, undaunted, starts on his own to retrieve his fortunes. In *Brief Moment* (1931) we have a study of a wealthy young man who weds a night-club singer precisely because she does not have the manners of his set, and to his dismay finds her, after marriage, imitating badly all the social tricks from which he had hoped to escape. The political world intrudes, in the person of Leander Nolan, into *Biography* (1932), a rather overpraised comedy concentrating upon the character of a woman painter, Marian Froude. If, however, this comedy ranks not quite so high among Behrman's works as some critics were inclined to believe on its first appearance, it does mark a very definite development in the author's work, since it brings into play the quality which was destined to give distinction to all his later works—the weaving into the action of a great deal of philosophical and social discussion. The truth is that Behrman is a man who, gifted with the truly comic view, is puzzled by life and desperately seeks an answer to his puzzlement. Like all those gifted (or cursed) by the comic mood, he sees that man has made a stupid mess of his existence, and yet, at the same time, he realizes that recognition of man's follies is not enough, since besides folly there is evil, and evil must be combated.

We can follow this progress of thought in Behrman through *Rain from Heaven* (1934)—a play which is really an essay in political discussion—and *End of Summer* (1936)—wherein the opportunistic doctor is contrasted with the honest, socialistic, poverty-stricken young novelist—on to *Wine of Choice* (1938) and the characteristically titled *No Time for Comedy* (1939), wherein the author almost pathetically displays his own realization of the dilemma in which he is placed: his talent is a talent for comedy, yet there are things in the world so dark and menacing that he would fain take sword in hand to fight them. Behrman's provisional answer, in *The Talley Method* (1941), was not successful: the attempt made here to identify discipline and Fascism failed precisely because Fascism and discipline, contrary to his philosophy, lie poles apart. In *Jakobowsky and the Colonel* (1944), he suggests that he is on the way towards finding a satisfactory compromise, whereby the content of his work may be harmonized with the style of which he is a master. True, we may with justice complain that the subject-matter of his play (based on a piece by Franz Werfel) is no matter for laughter: but, if we can succeed in separating the worlds of reality and of the theatre, we may well agree that *Jakobowsky and the Colonel* is one of the most adroit and delightful comedies of modern times. Unfortunately his latest play, *Jane* (1947), adapted from a short story by Somerset Maugham, can hardly be rated so high. The plot of a middle-aged woman who is turned into the toast of the town simply because her young husband happens to be a skilful dress-designer capable of giving her fashionable clothes is either eminently undramatic or else suited only for farcical treatment.

SOCIAL COMEDY

Behrman's interest in social conditions is thoroughly symbolic of the American stage. His fellow-authors can, on occasion, turn out farcical comedies which aim at no more than the arousing of thoughtless laughter. Thus J. C. Holm and George Abbott, in *Three Men on a Horse* (1935) present their delightfully impossible and mirth-moving story of a timid little non-betting clerk who discovers in himself the power of correctly guessing the winners on the racecourse. This is a successor to the record-breaking *Abie's Irish Rose* (1922) of Anne Nichols and a partner to the hilarious presentation of Hollywood's absurdities in *Boy Meets Girl* (1935) by Bella and Samuel Spewack. Here the typical American crackle of fantastic laughter is to be seen at its most typical. The story-writers are in conference with a film producer:

BENSON [*crosses back to desk; sighs; indicates script*]: You were saying that this is one of the greatest picture scripts ever written.

C.F. [*with a superior smile*]: Now, just a minute——

LAW [*quickly*]: And do you know why? Because it's the same story Larry Toms has been doing for years.

BENSON: We *know* it's good.

LAW: Griffith used it. Lubitsch used it. And Eisenstein's coming around to it.

BENSON: Boy meets girl. Boy loses girl. Boy gets girl.

LAW: The great American fairy-tale. Sends the audience back to the relief rolls in a happy frame of mind.

BENSON: And why not?

LAW: The greatest escape formula ever worked out in the history of civilization. . . .

C.F.: Of course, if you put it that way . . . but, boys, it's hackneyed.

LAW: You mean classic.

C.F. [*triumphantly*]: *Hamlet* is a classic—but it isn't hackneyed!

LAW: *Hamlet* isn't hackneyed? Why, I'd be ashamed to use that poison gag. He lifted that right out of the Italians. [PEGGY *enters and crosses to her chair and sits.*] Ask Peggy.

[PEGGY *puts the bowl now half filled with water down on the desk.*]

BENSON: Yes, let's ask Peggy . . . if she wants to see Larry Toms in a different story. She's your audience.

PEGGY: Don't ask me anything, Mr Benson. I've got the damnedest toothache. [*She takes* C.F.'s *hand and looks up at him suddenly.*] Relax!

[*She begins filing.*]

BENSON [*wheedling*]: But, Peggy, you go to pictures, don't you?

PEGGY: No.

BENSON: But you've seen Larry's pictures and enjoyed them?

PEGGY: No.

BENSON: . . . As millions of others have . . .

LAW: Why, one man sent him a rope all the way from Manila—with instructions.

C.F.: Boys, this isn't getting us anywhere.

In many of these comedy-farces, however, even in *Boy Meets Girl*, an underlying social purpose is apparent. What on the surface seems nothing but gaiety reveals on examination a kind of crude philosophy—at times, perhaps, a concealed bitterness. A single example will illustrate this clearly. In 1936 Moss Hart and George S. Kaufman collaborated in producing *You Can't Take It with You*. Outwardly this is a piece penned according to early recipes and well flavoured with just such indigenous exaggeration as had animated the plays of American popular comedians, like Edward Harrigan, more than half a century previously. *You Can't Take It with You* is, however, not a simple farce. No doubt it exists primarily for the purpose of arousing laughter; no doubt the aim of its creators was to win immediate popular success. Nevertheless the action of this crazy comedy has a purpose, and that purpose is definitely drawn to our attention in the title. There is almost as much 'philosophy' here as in any of the solemnly serious melodramas produced by the Theatre Union.

Nor is *You Can't Take It with You* an aberration on the part of Kaufman and Hart. This pair of writers, either in collaboration with each other or separately in collaboration with others, have made the New York stage gay with many another merry piece in which the sense of fun is associated with social or political satire. *Once in a Lifetime* (1930) turns the spotlight on Hollywood just at the time when that city of silent lots was fluttered by the sudden irruption of sound. How basically serious are the two authors appears in the fact that within a few years of the writing of this joyous onslaught on the films they joined in composing *Merrily We Roll Along* (1934), a play in which a story with a goodly message is told backward. As the curtain rises we find ourselves at a party given by a successful playwright, who, despite his success, is seen by his friends to have sacrificed integrity for the sake of money. Having thus set the scene, Kaufman and Hart carry us back seven years to 1927, and so by a series of reverse chronological steps we end in 1916 and listen to the future playwright as he stands delivering the valedictory address in the chapel of his college, and ending with the words—"This above all, to thine own self be true."

The spirit in which this drama is written must be borne in mind when we turn to those musical burlesques *Of Thee I Sing* (1931; by Kaufman and Morrie Ryskind) and *I'd Rather be Right* (1937), which were among the most original contributions of the New York stage during the thirties. Taking a suggestion from Gilbert and Sullivan and applying the style of burlesque musical comedy to contemporary politics, the authors here present a parody of the life of their time. In *Of Thee I Sing*—the title is, of course, taken from the American national anthem—John P. Wintergreen is hustled into the Presidency through his slogan, "Love is sweeping the Country." His excesses, however, are discovered, and he is on the point of being impeached when it is learned that Mrs Wintergreen is about to have a baby; on the basis of the slogan that "Posterity is just around the corner," Congress permits them to remain in the White House. In *I'd Rather be Right* Phil Barker meets Roosevelt in Central Park and puts to him his dilemma: he cannot marry Mary Jones unless he gets an increase in salary; he cannot get that increase in salary until his employer's business gets better; the business cannot get better unless the country's budget is balanced. Roosevelt is touched and convinced: he goes off determined to balance his budget so that Phil and Mary may wed.

In the collaboration of Kaufman and Hart we have the modern American counterpart of the seventeenth-century collaboration of Beaumont and Fletcher, and the facts that they are both so thoroughly identified with the ordinary commercial playhouse, that they are so obviously in harmony with each other, and that beneath their outward merriment courses such a clear current of serious purpose make their works of considerable historical importance. To the writings mentioned above should be added two (quite diversely styled) 'dinner' comedies—the satirically serious *Dinner at Eight* (1932), by Kaufman and Edna Ferber, and the wickedly hilarious *The Man Who Came to Dinner* (1939), by the familiar partners.

Something of the same current flows through dozens of other American comedies and farces, variously displaying itself, for example, in *Having Wonderful Time* (1937), by Arthur Kober, a comedy-drama of life in Camp Care-Free, or in *The Pursuit of Happiness* (1933), by Lawrence Langner and Arminia Marshall, which, though set in Revolutionary times, has obvious contemporary implications. As characteristic as any is the long series of comedies contributed by Rachel Crothers, from *The Three of Us* (1906) to *Susan and God* (1937).

Another style of American realistic comedy displays its interest in the social scene in a diverse manner. From the time when Ben Hecht and Charles MacArthur won resounding success for their noisy, quick-tempo *The Front Page* (1928) to the appearance of *The Women* (1936), by Clare Boothe, the American theatre has developed one peculiar kind of drama of its own—a kind wherein sensational scenes are scrambled up with scenes of raucous laughter, wherein the actions and the characters are given a spurious air of naturalistic authenticity, and wherein vituperative rudeness of phrase is substituted for wit. Although we may readily conceive that journalists testify to the exactitude with which *The Front Page* reproduces American newspaper life and that Clare Boothe has faithfully recorded the conversation of the ladies' retiring-room in *The Women*, both of these thoroughly typical plays are to be seen, on examination, as conceived in terms of modern melodrama. How true this is becomes apparent when we see Clare Boothe, after the incivilities of *Kiss the Boys Good-bye* (1938), turning to write her anti-Nazi thriller, *Margin for Error* (1939).

These plays, while they may contain matter fit for satire, are not created in the true satiric mood. For that bitter ingredient we must turn to France. There, for example, Marcel Pagnol is coldly enflamed to use laughter for purposes wholly satiric. His first success, written in collaboration with Paul Nivoix, was a bitter attack on war profiteers, *Les marchands de gloire* (*The Merchants of Glory*, 1924), in which an ambitious father is shown in dismay when his soldier son, supposed dead, returns; for the sake of his own career, largely based on the esteem given to the 'dead' hero, he persuades the youth to remain unknown and to live under another name. *Jazz* (1926), ironically vivacious, sufficiently indicates its theme by its very title. In *Topaze* (1928) the charlatanism of the world of modern finance is revealed; disillusionment colours the depiction of the ironically conceived action in the later *Marius* (1930) and *Fanny* (1931), where Pagnol uses his art to depict a section of Marseilles life.

Satirical purpose of an equally bitter sort inspires Édouard Bourdet, a purpose so bitter that his comedies often have the flavour of tragedy. He started his career with a cheerless love tale, *L'heure de berger* (*The Gloaming*, 1922), and four years later won international fame, or notoriety, for *La prisonnière* (*The Prisoner*, 1926), a study of homosexuality in which a heroine is shown powerless to escape from the chains of her unnatural passion. Since then he has devoted himself mainly to the darkly comic exposure of society's errors: true, his last piece, *Hyménée* (1941), deals almost entirely with a love theme, but this is in marked contrast to his more typical writings—*Le sexe faible* (*The Gentler Sex*, 1930), *Les temps difficiles* (*The Difficult Years*, 1934), and *Fric-frac* (1936). We cannot claim this author as a great artist: on the other hand, his keen eye—particularly for things on the darker side of life—and his unquestionably skilled hand merit our giving him at least a measure of attention.

GROTESQUE COMEDY

At a pole diametrically opposed to such comedies as endeavour to hold the mirror rudely before society's unmade-up face there are others, equally characteristic of these our times, which thrive in the realms of the fantastic and eagerly seek for the grotesque.

In France a kind of link between the two kinds appears in the brilliant comic essays of Alfred Savoir, witty, mordant, with concealed barbs underneath their cloak of hilarious laughter. Most characteristic and interesting among his works is the series of allegorical farces which he penned towards the close of his career —notably *La huitième femme de Barbe bleue* (*Bluebeard's Eighth Wife*, 1921) and *Le dompteur, ou l'anglais tel qu'on mange* (*The Lion-tamer; or, English as it is Eaten*, 1925), wherein an English lord goes round with a circus, always hoping that he will see the lions eat their trainer; it is he himself who in the end is eaten. The trainer is, of course, the symbol of Fascist tyranny; the English lord is the image of philosophic liberalism.

The circus atmosphere, treated more sentimentally and with no political connotations, appears also in the first play, *Voulez-vous jouer avec moi?* (*Will You Play with Me?*, 1924), in which Marcel Achard came to public attention. This study of three clowns and a poet possesses a peculiar limpidity and sensitiveness in character presentation and adumbrates the style which reached fruition in *Jean de la Lune* (1929), a study of touching faith, with Jean de la Lune absolutely devoted to his Marceline, even although she tricks him continually, and eventually conquering her admiration. The same qualities—of delicate poetic fantasy and a delineation of sentiment that ever hovers on the border of the sentimental without crossing that treacherous boundary—are carried on in *La belle marinière* (*The Pretty Fisher Lass*, 1929), with its memorable heroine, and in *Domino* (1931), a fanciful picture of the world of roués. *Le corsaire* (*The Pirate*, 1938) introduces something different: partly this play is a satiric comedy directed at Hollywood; partly it is an imaginative, almost Barrie-esque fantasy of a pirate's love for a girl he has captured and of the repetition of that love when the pirate's story is being made into a film. Achard loves to play with time in his comedies, and in this manner his later play, *Auprès de ma blonde* (*Beside My Blonde*, 1945), is thoroughly characteristic—a comedy of marriage which starts in the old age of the present and moves back to the youth of sweetheart days.

Satirical extravaganza of a more bitter sort appears in the work of Bernard Zimmer, notably in *Bava l'Africain* (1926), in which a little clerk with dreams succeeds in persuading the world that he is a great explorer; the fairy-tale takes theatrical form in the fantasies of Alexandre Arnoux, of whose writing *Petite Lumière et l'ourse* (1924) and *Huon de Bordeaux* (1922) are perhaps most characteristic; in the plays of Jean Giono, such as *Lanceurs de graines* (*The Sowers*,

1932) and *Le bout de la route* (*Journey's End*, 1941), a poetic mood enwraps all the action—the former presenting a contrast between true love of nature and the desire to exploit nature, and the latter treating with strange and appealing delicacy a simple story of the heart.

Among the writers who have most powerfully contributed to this style of drama is the Scots James Bridie (O. H. Mavor), an author who, although by no means all his works are comedies, clearly demands attention here, since even his most gruesome scenes are inspired rather by the comic than by the tragic muse. Although he has not succeeded in producing any single play to mark him out for secure fame, the totality of his writings are such as to make him the one modern British dramatist who merits a place close to that of Shaw. He has, like Shaw, a deep foundation of philosophical (rather than social) purport, which gives both a firmness and an interest to his dramas, and he shares in Shaw's sense of fun. What prevents his plays from having attained a greater position than they at present occupy is a tendency, apparent in almost all, to bring a promising action to an inconclusive end: we almost have the impression that his mind is so alert, his spirit so inventive, that before one theme has been completed another has sprung into being in the author's vivid imagination, and that, as a result, he would fain be off from the old, before the old is done with, to the new.

His entry into the theatre was made in 1930 with a drama, *The Anatomist*, which was by no means a comedy. This rueful work tells of the body-snatchers of Edinburgh, engaged in their dark task at a time when the law prevented medical workers from obtaining the bodies they required for their training and experiments. From this he moved to *Tobias and the Angel* (1931), followed by *Jonah and the Whale* (1932), and it was immediately apparent that in these plays he had found the proper medium for his genius. The Biblical stories and atmosphere permitted him to introduce an element of the philosophic; the fantastic quality of both the tales accorded with his own love of the extravagant; while the contrast between the ancient world inhabited by his characters and the modern implications of their adventures offered full scope for the exercise of his own peculiar style in comedy.

In *A Sleeping Clergyman* (1933) Bridie returns, in a way, to the mood of *The Anatomist*, essaying the difficult task of demonstrating the close connexion of genius and criminality in the human soul. This he does by opening the action with a brilliantly sordid scene in which a poverty-stricken medical student, gifted with a vision beyond that of his age, but at the same time utterly without any ordinary sense of moral values, is shown dying of tuberculosis. He leaves behind him an illegitimate daughter, who inherits only the criminal side of his nature, but she is succeeded in her turn by twins, a man and a woman, in whom the vision is renewed and who succeed in saving the world from the menace of a new plague. Except for the final scenes set in the future—and scenes placed in the future hardly ever can be made convincing in the theatre—this play deserves to be regarded as one of the boldest, most satisfying, and most powerfully conceived dramas of our time.

When we consider the scenes of *Tobias and the Angel* along with those of *A Sleeping Clergyman* we obtain a measure of Bridie's wide dramatic range. In the former he can let his fancy play lightly with the episodes of the journey undertaken by the timorous young Tobias and his guide, Raphael in disguise. The latter has encouraged the boy to use his own initiative in killing a great monster of a mud-fish and has further incited him into outfacing a Kurdish bandit. Tobias boasts of what he has done to the fish. "And," he adds,

> what I did to that atrocious, fire-breathing river demon I shall do to you, you hairy-toed polecat, you son of a burnt father, for I am only beginning the carnage I feel I must make before sunset.
> THE BANDIT: Who are you, my lord?
> TOBIAS: I am Suleiman-ibn-Daoud, and this is one of my Afreets.

The bandit slinks off, and, left alone, Tobias turns exultantly to Raphael:

> TOBIAS: I certainly seemed to be able to speak up to that bandit once I got started. I told him off properly, I think. The words seemed to come, somehow. I heard them at the jetty, but I hoped I had forgotten them. And I did very well with the fish too, didn't I?
> RAPHAEL: Yes. But there was no need to lie to the bandit.
> TOBIAS: I didn't lie to him.
> RAPHAEL: You did. Your story of the fish I forgive you. Everybody exaggerates about fish. But you said you were Solomon. That is very far from being true.
> TOBIAS: I didn't know what I was saying. I was excited. I wish I weren't such a coward. . . . I was right in one thing I said to the bandit.
> RAPHAEL: What was that?
> TOBIAS: I said you were an old Afreet. So you are.
> RAPHAEL: There are no such things as Afreets. Come along.

This scene has but to be compared with the terrible and powerful opening episode of *A Sleeping Clergyman* for a realization of the ample stops in Bridie's organ. The tubercular genius Cameron is lying near death in his wretched Glasgow lodgings, and with conscious irony he makes a promise to marry a girl, Harriet, whom he has got with child. Harriet goes, and Cameron is left alone:

> Most touching. Most affecting. What memories to weep over, my dear, twenty years ahead. Your miserable, begrutten face! And now I'm going to die. I've bilked you, you bitch.

His landlady comes in and threatens to send him away:

> You'll go out of here to-morrow, so you will. How I'll ever let this room again, I'm sure I don't know. A perfect pigsty. I'm sure I don't know what sort of home you come out of. And that young lady, too, that I was in the house of the day she was born. I little knew, I've kept myself decent and my premises decent till the black burning day you came, Mister Cameron. Never mind. Out you go to-morrow's morning. And you'll pay for the carpet, and the clock you broke, and the holes in the mantelshelf you burned with your pipe, and the antimacassar you tore. You'll pay. And you needna pretend to be asleep. You know as well as I do . . . as I do . . . Jesus, Mary, and Joseph. He's dead.

From the thirties onward Bridie contributed many plays of diverse kinds to the stage. Among them may particularly be mentioned *The King of Nowhere* (1938), a comedy in which a study of insanity is combined with an analysis of the Fascist mentality, and *Mr Bolfry* (1943), a delightful essay in the fantastic, wherein the devil is charmed up from the nether regions in the likeness of a Protestant minister. Laughter and philosophic purpose meet in both of these, and in their combination amply testify to the originality of talent and to the technical skill of their author.

Allowing for the vast differences in intellectual climate, the mood out of which these plays are built may be related to that inspiring Ferenc Molnár, the dramatist who stands most clearly as the theatrical representative of his native Hungary. He too has his serious pieces; he too succeeds best when laughter and fantasy meet. One of his first works was *Az Ördög* (*The Devil*, 1907), in which the satanic agent appears garbed as a man of the world, while the play on which the author's fame principally rests, *Liliom* (1909), exists in the main for the sake of the scene in heaven when the hero, an unsuccessful waif who has committed suicide, is arraigned before a higher court. Pathos rules here, and some others of Molnár's dramas are tragically or philosophically conceived—witness the symbolic *A vörös malom* (*The Red Mill*, 1923), the characters of which are God, Lucifer, and a perfect human being, and *Az üvegcipö* (*The Glass Slipper*, 1924), in which fantasy of a sentimental sort enriches an outwardly realistic action. Usually, however, at its finest Molnár's talent, like Bridie's, finds itself oscillating between philosophic seriousness and incisive wit. In *A testör* (*The Guardsman*, 1910) laughter triumphs in the plot devised by a jealous husband to test his wife, the curtain ironically falling at the end on a man thoroughly baffled by woman's wit. *A hattyú* (*The Swan*, 1914) pursues a skilful way between ironic comedy and sentiment, telling the story of a princess who, falling in love with her tutor, decides to remain a swan majestically floating on her own watery element rather than step in awkward manner on to common ground:

DOMINICA: I fancy he has had enough. But I shall kiss . . . your daughter.

ALEXANDRA: Dear Aunt . . . if you deem me worthy . . .

DOMINICA: Entirely, my dear daughter, with only this suggestion: that you remember now and again that your sainted father used to call you his swan. Think often of what it means to be a swan . . . gliding proudly . . . majestically . . . where the moon gleams on the mirror of the water . . . gliding always in that purple radiance . . . and never coming ashore. For when a swan walks, my daughter . . . when she waddles up the bank . . . then she painfully resembles another bird.

ALEXANDRA [*softly ironical at her own expense*]: A goose?

DOMINICA: Almost, my girl. Natural history teaches that the swan is nothing but an aristocratic duck. That is why she must stay on the mirror of the water. She is a bird, but she may never fly. She knows a song, but she may never sing until she is about to die. Yes, dear, glide on the water . . . head high . . . stately silence . . . and the song—never! [*There is a pause.*

CÆSAR [*entering at right*]: Breakfast is served.

Uri-divat (*Fashions for Men*, 1915) is an ironic comedy of a hero, Peter, who acts with magnanimity when his wife runs away. His reputation for saintliness, however, brings its own rewards, and his business is shown prospering mightily from the esteem he has won for himself. The general mood which had led the author on the one hand to the gay cynicism of *The Guardsman* and on the other to the fantasy of *Liliom* finds final expression in *Játék a kastélyban* (*The Play's the Thing*, or *The Play in the Castle*, 1925). In this last piece we are, indeed, almost completing the circle and returning to

Pirandello. Albert Adam, the young fiancé of the actress Llona Szabo, by chance overhears her making love to another man, whereupon one of his friends, a dramatist, hastily concocts a one-act play in the dialogue of which the overheard words are included. The result is that when he listens to the rehearsal of this piece Albert is happily convinced that the love-scene was fictional, not real, and thus for him the imaginary becomes the actual.

The spirit of the grotesque is to be widely traced during these between-war years. From Germany Carl Zuckmayer brings, besides his fantastic *Der Schelm von Bergen* (*The Rascal from Bergen*, 1934) and his rustic comedy, *Der fröhliche Weinberg* (*The Joyous Vineyard*, 1926), an excellent satire, *Der Hauptmann von Koepenick* *The Captain of Koepenick*, 1930), which aptly takes off the pretensions of the old German Junker class. His latest drama, *Der Teufels General* (*The Devil's General*, 1948), made memorable by its vivid portrait of the ice-cold Oderbruch, has lately won attention because of its delineation of the Nazi hierarchy. In Spain, alongside comic dramatists such as Pedro Muñoz Seca and Enrique Suárez de Dezo, who follow more realistic methods, the fantastic appears in diverse quarters. Among writers in this style Carlos Arniches and Ramón del Valle-Inclán deserve particular mention, the former because of the verve with which he presents his extraordinary situations and eccentric characters, and the latter for his 'comedias bárbaras' and for the other poetically conceived dramas that spring from their spirit. In the work of Ramón del Valle-Inclán appears in an extreme form that love of the fantastic, that fascination for the man or woman whose personality deviates from the commonplace, and that tendency towards the introduction of a lyrical quality into the treatment of the action which may be found expressed in diverse ways on the Spanish stage. Whether we look at the almost wholly 'literary' *Cara de plata* (*Face of Silver*, 1923) or at the fantastic *Farsa y licencia de la reina castiza* (*The Farce of the True Spanish Queen*, 1920) these qualities are amply apparent.

With this variety of kindred works before us, from countries as far removed from each other as Scotland and Spain, we cannot escape the conclusion that in the comic grotesque (as opposed to Victor Hugo's tragic grotesque) there lies a quality apt to appeal to, and well calculated to express, the spirit of our age.

THE VOGUE OF THE HISTORICAL PLAY

LOGICALLY it is incorrect to set a discussion of the historical drama in juxtaposition to discussions of such dramatic styles as impressionism and expressionism or of such forms as comedy. Historical subject-matter may be, and has been, used for a diversity of purposes: the poets have found therein opportunities for the revealing of their imaginative concepts; some authors have employed historical themes for the exercise of psychoanalysis; there are historical comedies, tragedies, and problem plays.

At the same time the vogue of the historical drama during the between-war years is so marked that it positively demands independent examination: exhibiting itself in all lands, it forms one of the chief trends in the twentieth-century theatre and testifies to the fervent seeking on the part of our contemporaries for comfort or for help in the past. This trend is potent no matter what political systems or social conventions the countries concerned may have. With the historical play in France, Britain, America, we are familiar: equally widespread has been the invocation of former times in Soviet lands. The long series of Russian dramas dealing with the revolutionary years were already 'historical plays' when they appeared in the late twenties and early thirties: Trenev takes an eighteenth-century theme for *Pugachevshchina* (*The Pugachov Rebellion*, 1925), Alexander Evdokimovich Korneichuk, whose *Gibel eskadri* (*The Sinking of the Squadron*, 1934) had dealt with the scuttling of the Black Sea fleet in 1918, goes a century earlier for the plot of his *Bogdan Kmelnitski* (1939), and numerous other authors similarly explore episodes of bygone times.

The prevalence of this almost universal interest, therefore, justifies our considering the historical drama by itself, although, in doing so, we must remember that in the examination of impressionism, expressionism, comedy, and the like we have already covered part of the field. Several of Bridie's plays and of Sherwood's, for example, seek their plots in recorded history, and even such a composition as *And So to Bed* is an historical comedy.

THE HISTORICAL PLAY IN FRANCE

The fortunes of this type of drama in France are typical, clearly revealing that which is most significant in the modern development of the form—its sudden departure from a generally misty and often 'escapist' handling of colourful material, and the evident endeavour of the authors to bring their selected actions into association with the events of to-day. A new note is struck here, a note different from that which Schiller and his followers made resonant.

Take, for example, the *Elizabeth, la femme sans homme* (*Elizabeth, the Woman without a Husband*, 1935), by André Josset, wherein, as it were, the psychoanalyst's piercing eye is turned on the Queen's escapades with her Essex. By leaving out the novel trappings and cutting down on the familiar doublet and hose, Josset succeeds in isolating his characters and giving them human proportions. The theme of Elizabeth and Essex has been put upon the stage many times, but rarely with such vigour. Although the same author's *Les Borgia, étrange famille* (*The Borgias, a Strange Family*, 1938) hardly captures the intensity of his *Elizabeth*, there is no doubt but that, even if for this one play alone, Josset is a dramatist worthy of our attention.

Something of a quality different in kind yet akin in virtue appears in the *Napoléon unique* (*The One and Only Napoleon*, 1936), by Paul Raynal, an author already noted in another connexion. Here too the supernumeraries are all dismissed, and attention is focused on the Emperor and his Joséphine. Action disappears; two souls are drawn out of the past, and are revealed to us with dazzling and even disconcerting clarity.

Into this realm the Belgian Herman Closson brings a spirit of daring, of adventure, of joyous quest, and at the same time of satire. His *Godefroid de Bouillon* (1933) and *Les quatre fils Aymon* (*The Four Sons of Aymon*, 1941) stand out among other works of the kind for their colour, their vivacity, and their wit. A later play by this author is a picture of Elizabethan life—*Shakespeare ou la comédie de l'aventure* (*Shakespeare; or, The Comedy of Adventure*, 1946).

In this particular style no writer has achieved more during recent years than François Porché. His earlier pieces are unimportant, but when we come to *Un roi, deux dames et un valet* (*A King, Two Ladies, and a Valet*), in 1934, we recognize that we are in the presence of a play to be remembered. The King (Louis XIV) is kept off stage during the entire action, and the focus is upon Madame de Maintenon, Madame de Montespan, and the valet Bontemps. Under the most delicate Court polish, emotions struggle to be given birth; indeed, the tension of the drama comes from the manner in which Porché has secured a kind of ironic counterpoint between the artificial manners of Louis' entourage and the passions concealed under flowered brocades and impeccable courtesies. The same treatment gives distinction to his *La vierge au grand cœur* (*The Great-hearted Maid*, 1925), wherein his choice of a theme already well familiar to the stage—that of Jeanne d'Arc—is justified by the imaginative penetration into the inner emotions of the heroine. Another notable piece is his *Le lever de soleil* (*Sunrise*, 1946), written in collaboration with Mme Simone.

From dozens of hands the Parisian stage has been supplied with works of this kind. The plays of Romain Rolland, almost all historical in subject-matter and, for preference, dealing with the period of the French Revolution, extend from a *Danton* of 1901 to *Le jeu de l'amour et de la mort* (*The Play of Love and Death*) in 1925. The general trend of this author to make his subject-matter serve symbolic purposes is shown clearly when we compare his historical pieces with the strange farrago of imaginative type characters who inhabit his satirical extravaganza *Liluli* (1922). Sacha Guitry interrupts his series of comedies to produce *Deburau* (1918), *Pasteur* (1919), *Béranger* (1920), and *Mozart* (1925), just as Édouard Bourdet varies his satirical career by dealing, in *Margot* (1935), with the reign of Henri III, as Jean Sarment casts in among his other plays a *Madame Quinze* (1935), and as Jules Supervielle presents us with his *Bolivar* (1936). With these authors may be mentioned Paul Demasy, on account of his series of Biblical and classically inspired dramas—of which *Dalilah* (1926) and *La tragédie d'Alexandre* (*The Tragedy of Alexander*, 1933) are the most important.

One principal interest for these dramatists in themes taken from the past lies, of course, in the manner through which comment on the present day may be made through the choice of subject-matter from past ages, and for some there is the added incentive which comes from realization that only through the handling of a 'distanced' story can there be even a hope of approaching the quality of tragedy. It is obvious, therefore, that the same motives which lead some authors to select actual historical events will induce others to turn to ancient legend. Realizing this, we may well feel justified in associating with the authors mentioned above the name of that playwright who has so distinguished himself for his treatment of the legendary, and who, in the end, will perhaps be recognized as the greatest French dramatic writer of the thirties—Jean Giraudoux.

Giraudoux' plays have taken diverse forms. In 1928 he first appeared before the public with a strange allegorical drama called *Siegfried*, in which he tells the story of a wounded French soldier who, rescued by a German woman and on his recovery utterly forgetful of his former life, so identifies himself with his new country that he becomes a prominent leader in a reviving Reich. Such a theme, however, obviously does not offer to this author the scope best calculated to bring forth his talents: that scope is seen immediately we turn from his first play to his second, *Amphitryon 38* (1929). Since then he has contributed to the stage numerous dramas, among which may be mentioned *Judith* (1931), *Intermezzo* (1933), *La Guerre de Troie n'aura pas lieu* (*The Trojan War will not Take Place*, 1935), *Électre* (1937), *L'impromptu de Paris* (1937), *Cantique de cantiques* (*Song of Songs*, 1937), *Sodome et Gomorrhe* (1943), and *La folle de Chaillot* (*The Madwoman of Chaillot*, 1945). Varied as these are, from the artificial comedy of *Amphitryon 38* to the essay in theatrical imagination that appears in *L'impromptu de Paris*, from the bitter reflection of *La Guerre de Troie n'aura pas lieu* to the tragic sentiment of *Électre*, there runs through all a single though complex strain, composed of a precise and penetrating inellectualism and a richly poetic emotion. The range of his work can perhaps best be appreciated by taking in conjunction those two plays of his that are based on classic legend—*Amphitryon 38* and *Électre*.

In the former Giraudoux takes the myth which has so often seized upon the imagination of playwrights in the past; this version of his he believes must be the thirty-eighth treatment of the theme —hence the title of his piece—and to it he brings both a graciously piercing wit and a fine sense of character values. Anyone who had seen the brilliant original performance of this play, in which the acting, direction, and décor were all harmonious with the dramatist's purpose, will agree that *Amphitryon 38* has been but ill-served by its production in English. The adaptation was one of S. N. Behrman's less inspired efforts, and on the stage the heavy-handed treatment of the action, for which presumably Alfred Lunt and Lynn Fontanne must share the blame, somewhat dissipated the peculiar grace investing the French scenes. Something very delicate and exquisite in its proportions was here brought to earth and vulgarized.

From the comic action of this play we move to the tragic of *Électre*, which, besides the time-honoured characters of the ancient story, introduces a number of persons of Giraudoux' own invention. The mood of the play is well suggested at the very start when a

Stranger (Oreste) enters escorted by three little girls, the young Eumenides, and meets the Gardener of the palace:

FIRST LITTLE GIRL: How handsome the gardener's looking!

SECOND LITTLE GIRL: Why not? He's to be married to-day.

THIRD LITTLE GIRL: There it is, sir, your palace of Agamemnon!

THE STRANGER: A curious façade! . . . Isn't it out of balance?

FIRST LITTLE GIRL: No. The right wing isn't there. You think you see it, but it's just a mirage. It's like the gardener who comes here to speak to you. He doesn't come. He can't say a word.

SECOND LITTLE GIRL: He'll just bray or mew.

THE GARDENER: The façade is in balance, sir. Don't pay any attention to these little liars. What cheats the eye is the fact that the right wing is built of stones from Gaul that sweat during certain periods of the year. The villagers say then that the palace is weeping. The left wing is made of Argive marble which—no one knows why— sometimes shines of a sudden, even at night. When that happens they say that the palace is laughing. What's happening now is that the palace is laughing and crying at the same time.

As they talk the little girls demand leave to act a piece of their own:

FIRST LITTLE GIRL: Are we to act or not?

THE STRANGER: Let them act their piece, gardener.

FIRST LITTLE GIRL: We shall act Clytemnestra, mother of Electra. Are you ready for Clytemnestra?

SECOND LITTLE GIRL: We're ready.

FIRST LITTLE GIRL: *Queen Clytemnestra has a bad complexion. She puts rouge on her face.*

SECOND LITTLE GIRL: *She has a bad complexion because she sleeps badly.*

THIRD LITTLE GIRL: *She sleeps badly because she's afraid.*

FIRST LITTLE GIRL: *Of what is Queen Clytemnestra afraid?*

SECOND LITTLE GIRL: *Of everything.*

FIRST LITTLE GIRL: *What is everything?*

SECOND LITTLE GIRL: *The silence. The silences.*

THIRD LITTLE GIRL: *The noise. The noises.*

FIRST LITTLE GIRL: *The idea that midnight is coming. That the spider on his web is about to move from the part of the day which brings happiness to that which brings misfortune.*

SECOND LITTLE GIRL: *Everything red because it is blood.*

FIRST LITTLE GIRL: *Queen Clytemnestra has a bad complexion. She puts blood on her face.*

THE GARDENER: What stupid stories!

SECOND LITTLE GIRL: It's very nice, isn't it?

FIRST LITTLE GIRL: The way we catch up the end with the beginning, it couldn't be more poetic, could it?

The play develops as a tense study of a woman's hate for a woman, told in a series of passionate scenes, of which, in particular, the conversation of Oreste and Électre in the first act and the confrontation of Egisthe by Électre in the second reach a height of true tragic utterance. As the plot develops the Eumenides grow from children to womanhood, while the theme of the action is symbolically revealed in the speeches of the Beggar, a kind of one-man chorus. In choosing the legend of Electra Giraudoux dared boldly, and his daring has been justified.

WERFEL AND OTHERS

Emotions and artistic needs not dissimilar seem to have driven the Austrian Franz Werfel to the writing of historical plays. Better known, perhaps, as a novelist, he has still devoted considerable time to the theatre, where he has veered from experiments in poetic drama to attempts in the direction of revitalizing bygone ages.

Towards the beginning of his career he was caught up in the expressionistic movement, and under this influence produced a fairy romance entitled *Die Mittagsgöttin* (*The Goddess of Noon*, 1919) and a nobly ambitious but rather boring work entitled *Der Spiegelmensch* (*The Man in the Mirror*, 1920), which confusedly sought to reveal the duality of human nature, one part extending love towards fellow-creatures, another part selfish and enclosed within itself. The dual personality, treated almost clinically, is the theme likewise of *Schweiger* (1922), in which we find a Franz Schweiger who is really a child-murderer, Franz Forster, cured from his madness by hypnosis: his wife discovers the truth, leaves him, and returns after he has heroically rescued a group of children—too late, however, for she finds he has committed suicide. Neither of these is particularly important, but *Bocksgesang* (*The Goat Song*, 1921) introduces us to something different. In this peculiarly effective tale of a monster who springs from the loins of a normal man and who, although slain, leaves his seed to carry on his terrible race, Werfel presents an effective picture of the beast that lurks under the semblance of human civilization. The symbolism is clear and simple, perhaps even over-obvious, but it is not the quality of the symbols that gives this play distinction: what raises it above the mediocre mass of its companions is its genuine, intense theatricality and its power to rise, at least in certain scenes, towards the rarely scaled heights of the tragic.

Hardly the same may be said of *Juarez und Maximilian* (1924) and *Paulus unter den Juden* (*Paul among the Jews*, 1926), while the spectacularism of *The Eternal Road* (1935)—for which, of course, Max Reinhardt must be held mainly responsible—can readily be forgotten. The first of these is a sincere attempt to portray the combined idealism and ineffectiveness of the unhappy Maximilian, caught in the web of his own blind liberalism, of European politics, and of incipient Mexican nationalism: what is lacking is the quality of strength that fired the scenes of *Goat Song*. Werfel forgot that a play on this subject which does not introduce Juarez is equivalent to *Hamlet* without the prince, and that tragedy demands admiration as well as sympathy. Philosophic concepts take, likewise, from the strength of *Paulus unter den Juden*, a study of the differing attitudes towards the new Christian religion exemplified by Paul on the one hand and by Peter on the other.

Far less successful are the plays of Werfel's compatriot and fellow-novelist, Emil Ludwig (Emil Cohn): although sincerely wrought, and although presenting some interesting scenes, his *Bismarck* (1922–24) and *Versailles* (1931) make but dull reading to-day. Nor can a higher judgment be made of the *Kalkutta, 4 Mai* (*Calcutta, May 4th* or *Warren Hastings*, 1916), of still another German author, Lion Feuchtwanger. A trifle more of interest attaches to the Austrian historical studies of Hans Sassmann, Ferdinand Bruckner (Theodore Tagger), Friedrich Schreyvogl, and Erwin Kolbenheyer. Of these Bruckner is probably the most important, if only because of his *Elizabeth von England* (1930); his latest play, *Heroische Komödie* (*Heroic Comedy*, 1948), is, like most of his others, an historical piece —here dealing with Mme de Staël and Napoleon.

So widespread has been the cultivation of such historical material in numerous countries that, apart from those who have explored this realm in England and America, no attempt can be made here to do other than mention briefly a few dramatists who may be regarded as representative of the movement as a whole. In Spain the historical playwrights are headed by the two brothers Manuel and Antonio Machado, whose first drama, *Desdichas de la fortuna ó Julianillo Valcárcel* (*The Blows of Fortune; or, Julianillo Valcarcel*, 1926), set in the times of Philip IV, immediately demonstrated their unquestioned gifts—a rich sense of verbal values, a keen penetration into character, and a power to make their situations bold and interesting. For Poland we may turn to Adolf Nowaczyński, whose *Car Samozwaniec* (*The Pretender*, 1908) treats of a theme which has inspired many Slav authors, and whose *Wiosna ludów w cichym zakątku* (*The People's Springtime in a Quiet Corner of the World,*

1929) has the merit of originality in that it treats of an abortive revolution, not in terms of tragic gloom, but with infective gaiety. In Czechoslovakia the same trend leads to the writings of Stanislav Lom (Stanislav Mojžiš), such as the historical-legendary *Devín* (1919) and *Žižka* (1925).

Italy presents us with several dramatists of this order. Giovanni Cavicchioli turns for inspiration to the half-barbaric times of early Rome in his *Romolo* (1924) and *Lucrezia* (1925). Less gifted with literary talent than Cavicchioli, but a far more accomplished craftsman, Giovacchino Forzano became at one time the most commercially popular of modern Italian playwrights, and in his latter years he achieved notoriety, if not fame, by collaborating with none other than Benito Mussolini. Among his many works the most outstanding is the set of four dramas dealing with the progress of the French Revolution—*Il conte di Bréchard* (1923), *I fiordalisi d'oro* (*The Golden Fleur-de-lis*, 1925), *Danton* (1930), and, with Mussolini, *Campo di Maggio* (*The Hundred Days*, 1931). None of these possesses any permanent value, but all are written with assured theatrical skill.

THE HISTORICAL PLAY IN ENGLAND

As in France and other European lands, so in England the predilection for historical themes has proved a marked feature of theatrical activity from 1920 to 1940, and it is clear that the impulse has not yet died out. Here, however, a peculiar paradox is to be observed. In Drinkwater's *Abraham Lincoln* and Shaw's *Saint Joan* the English stage gave the world two dramas obviously inspired by the desire to use historical material for the purpose of illustrating a philosophy; in the events of the American Civil War and in the conflict between France and England during the fifteenth century these two authors saw characters and issues such as would meet their larger needs. The paradox enters in when we note that, despite the two great examples, English playwrights as a whole have not sought, when treating historical subjects, to make the past a commentary on the present. What characterizes their plays is, in general, their frank endeavour simply to revivify the past or to use the historical method for the purpose of finding escape from the trammels of realism.

The Barretts of Wimpole Street (1930), by Rudolph Besier, and the *Victoria Regina* (1934) of Laurence Housman are thoroughly representative of this trend. The first is an excellently planned work which seeks to do no more than create an appealing drama out of the Browning-Barrett romance; the second seeks only to present, in a series of episodes, the career of the great Queen from her accession to the throne until her last days. In precisely similar manner Gordon Daviot (Elizabeth Mackintosh) covers the ground already trodden by Shakespeare in *Richard II*, presenting a coulouful and sympathetic portrait of that unfortunate monarch in *Richard of Bordeaux* (1932); her latest drama, *The Little Dry Thorn* (1947), goes far further back in history to deal with the Biblical story of Abraham and Sarah. The life of Charles Lamb is dramatized by Joan Temple in *Charles and Mary* (1930) and that of Henry VII in *The Patched Cloak* (1947); Reginald Berkeley brings Florence Nightingale to theatrical life in *The Lady with a Lamp* (1929); in *The Brontës* (1933) Alfred Sangster turns to present portraits of a famous literary family; Norman Ginsbury, after dealing with the Duchess of Marlborough in *Viceroy Sarah* (1934), moves a century forward in time to depict the Prince Regent in *The First Gentleman* (1945).

In not one of these plays is there any 'social criticism'; in not one is an effort made to make the recorded events commentaries on our own existence. The authors are all intent, first, on producing effective dramas, second, on revealing character, and, thirdly, on faithfully evoking the spirit of the times with which they deal. In addition, most of them clearly manifest a joy in finding themselves amid surroundings where style in conversation and grace in living are more apparent than they are amid the life we presently lead.

This last quality becomes even more evident when we move from the realm of the authentic historical to that of the imaginative —for English between-war playwrights, not satisfied with what history could in fact give them, frequently proceeded to create episodes for themselves, fancifully set in some past age, or else sported with characters such as had already been given imaginative being. In this way St John Ervine took the persons of *The Merchant of Venice* and carried them a stage farther on their life's journey in *The Lady of Belmont* (1925). Thoroughly characteristic of these trends are the works of Ashley Dukes, who, besides penning a *Tyl Ulenspiegel* (1927), gave to the theatre one of the most graciously written and fancifully conceived of recent period comedies in *The Man with a Load of Mischief* (1924).

In his search for style and in his discovery that the opportunity for exercising style is to be found in settings from the past, Dukes is companioned by an author, Clifford Bax, who more consistently than any other has sought departure from the contemporary scene.

His work extends from free fantasies of the kind represented in *Midsummer Madness* (1924), through historical dramas like *The Rose without a Thorn* (1932), a memorable play on the subject of Henry VIII, on to such experimental essays as *Socrates* (1930), wherein an attempt is made to grant theatrical quality to the Socratic dialogue. As this last-mentioned drama suggests, Bax is less interested in action than in words. It is on his dialogue he concentrates, and few writers of the present day have a finer sense of the jewelled phrase than he. The trouble is that, as was shown recently in his *The Golden Eagle* (1946), yet another drama on Mary Queen of Scots, he is inclined to lose dramatic effectiveness for the sake of rich words.

MAXWELL ANDERSON AND THE HISTORICAL PLAY IN AMERICA

No less than in other countries the popularity of the historical drama is to be seen in the American theatre. Despite the strong impress of the realistic style on the New York stage, playwright after playwright has turned to the past. It is, however, to be noted that, whereas in general the English writers tended to avoid using material from the past as commentary on the present, American authors have tended to pursue a path diametrically opposed to this and to seek for themes which might aid them in expressing social judgments on the twentieth century.

All through these decades this nostalgic interest in bygone years has given colour to a stage that otherwise might have been severely drab. Sometimes this takes fantastic shape of the kind exemplified in the *Berkeley Square* (1926) of John Balderston, wherein a man of to-day is sent magically back into the eighteenth century; sometimes it finds expression in such musicals as the radiant *Oklahoma!* (1945); occasionally, as in Dorothy Gardner's *Eastward in Eden* (1947)—a study of Emily Dickinson—it merely seeks to record; most frequently it assumes the form of reasonably faithful recordings of past events with stress laid on those features of the selected episodes which appear to offer contemporary parallels. E. P. Conkle thus writes his *Prologue to Glory* (1938), which deals with the adolescence of Abraham Lincoln; in *The Patriots* (1943) Sidney Kingsley selects the times of Jefferson and Hamilton for his theme; *Harriet* (1944), by Florence Ryerson and Colin Clemens, treats of Harriet Beecher Stowe. These three examples may be taken as typical of numerous others produced during the two decades from 1920 to 1940.

In this sphere one particular author calls for special examina-

"RAZBEG": OKHLOPKOV'S
REALISTIC THEATRE, MOSCOW
From *The Seven Soviet Arts*, by
Kurt London (Faber, 1937).

864

GEORGE BERNARD SHAW

Photo H. E. Brooks

tion. As a whole, the plays of Maxwell Anderson may be considered disappointing, but they are disappointing in a grand way. No dramatic author of our age has higher or clearer concepts of what he wants the theatre to be; no other author has made more determined efforts to replace the figure of tragedy in the niche that for so long has been left empty. "I have found my religion in the theatre," he has said recently, "where I least expected to find it, and where few will credit that it exists. But it is there, and any man among you who tries to write plays will find himself serving it, if only because he can succeed in no other way. He will discover, if he works through his apprenticeship, that the theatre is the central artistic symbol of the struggle of good and evil within men." Anderson has the true vision. He recognizes that our present-day playhouse has sacrificed broader interests to the presentation of merely passing entertainment, and he is convinced that unless the quality that evoked an *Œdipus Rex* or a *Hamlet* can be restored to it the theatre will die of inanition or sink to becoming a thing of no consequence in our lives. Even those writers who have most at heart the desire to introduce things vital and appealing have, as he sees it, failed to do more than bring to the stage the elements of journalism.

Throughout his career as a dramatist Anderson has sought, in diverse ways, to realize this vision. His very first play, *White Desert* (1923), was an essay in the tragic. When this failed he set himself to pen a number of dramas in a more realistic style—*What Price Glory* (with Laurence Stallings, 1924), a bitter unveiling of the 'heroic' soldier, *Saturday's Children* (1927), a bourgeois comedy, and *Gods of the Lightning* (with Harold Hickerson, 1928), in which his anger over the Sacco-Vanzetti case makes some of his scenes almost incoherent.

During this time, however, an inward dissatisfaction with realistic prose dialogue makes itself apparent, so that we feel no surprise in finding Anderson turn, in 1930, to history and verse in *Elizabeth the Queen*, followed in 1933 by a companion piece, *Mary of Scotland*. Between these comes an Indian play, *Night over Taos* (1932), also in the poetic style, and a sudden incursion into the mood of political satire, *Both your Houses* (1933). In *Valley Forge* (1934) he again seeks historical subject-matter, this time in the life of George Washington, and the following year he startles theatre-goers and critics by presenting a gangster drama in verse (*Winterset*, 1935). *Wingless Victory* (1936), a poetic study of the colour problem placed in the nineteenth century, proves thoroughly unsuccessful, but

2E

again something new is attempted in the verse comedy *High Tor* (1936). In *The Masque of Kings* (1937) he seeks his theme in Vienna and the unsolved question of how Prince Rudolph came to die; *Knickerbocker Holiday* (1938) is a gay, yet indirectly biting, musical fantasy of old New York; for the story of *Key Largo* (1939) he goes to the Spanish Civil War; *Journey to Jerusalem* (1940) carries us back to Biblical Palestine; *Candle in the Wind* (1941) deals with an imagined episode in the Second World War, and this war also provides the setting for *The Eve of St Mark* (1942) and *Storm Operation* (1944); the difficulties experienced by the young in finding readjustment to civilian life is the topic of *Truckline Café* (1946); in *Joan of Lorraine* (1947) an experiment is made in a kind of Pirandellian style, with a play in rehearsal while the actors discuss the way in which the characters shall be treated.

There is an almost disconcerting variety here, and the variety itself is symbolic of Anderson's failure to discover a medium that shall thoroughly satisfy his needs. He is a prophet vainly dreaming of the temple appropriate to his vision and visiting now one and now another among many houses of worship. What we have here is not a shifting of aim such as marred the creative work of Hauptmann, but rather the restless search for a means wherewith a single dominant purpose may find realization.

In general, perhaps we can admit that the main reason why the purpose has not found concrete embodiment in dramatic form rests rather in our present age than in Anderson himself. No doubt there are among his plays many pieces of lesser import. No doubt his Elizabethan dramas are vitiated by Shakespearian echoes. No doubt his last works in particular fail to rise to the majesty of the occasion they celebrate—so that we are compelled to admit that the story of the American actress, in *Candle in the Wind*, who saves her French officer lover and remains herself in the hands of the Gestapo, seems artificially conceived, and that the theme of *The Eve of St Mark*, with its central figure of Quizz West, appears rather sentimental in concept. No doubt, too, the philosophic speeches in several of the dramas must strike us as lacking in firmness and, so far as the expression is concerned, framed in words which produce a static effect rather than the dynamic impression which greater authors know how to evoke by means of moving imagery and the use of restless words.

All these things can readily be admitted, yet the fact remains that the man who created the Esdras scenes in *Winterset* has in him a vision and a strength denied to most of his companions:

ESDRAS: Yes, if you hold with the world that only
those who die suddenly should be revenged.
But those whose hearts are cancered, drop by drop
in small ways, little by little, till they've borne
all they can bear, and die—these deaths will go
unpunished now as always. When we're young
we have faith in what is seen, but when we're old
we know that what is seen is traced in air
and built on water. There's no guilt under heaven,
just as there's no heaven, till men believe it—
no earth, till men have seen it, and have a word
to say this is the earth.

GARTH: Well, I say there's an earth,
and I say I'm guilty on it, guilty as hell.

ESDRAS: Yet till it's known you bear no guilt at all—
unless you wish. The days go by like film,
like a long written scroll, a figured veil
unrolling out of darkness into fire
and utterly consumed. And on this veil,
running in sounds and symbols of men's minds
reflected back, life flickers and is shadow
going toward flame. Only what men can see
exists in that shadow. Why must you rise and cry out:
That was I, there in the ravelled tapestry,
there, in that pistol flash, when the man was killed.
I was there, and was one, and am blood-stained!
Let the wind
and fire take that hour to ashes out of time
and out of mind! This thing that men call justice,
this blind snake that strikes men down in the dark,
mindless with fury, keep your hand back from it,
pass by in silence—let it be forgotten, forgotten!—
Oh, my son, my son—have pity!

Maybe there is in these speeches a sign why Anderson has been prevented from achieving more. "There's no heaven," says Esdras, "till men believe it"—and men in our days have ceased to believe. We might almost say that there can be no tragedy without belief, for tragic drama is essentially metaphysical and religious. Thus, in the want of a common faith in our midst, the playwright who aims at tragic expression is given no basis on which to stand. One phrase that, slightly varied, finds continual echo in Anderson's plays is that of Mio's in *Winterset*: "The bright ironical gods!" he cries. "Dark gods," "cruel gods," they appear elsewhere, and the very fact that divinity is thus spoken of in the plural tells its tale.

The phrase is empty of meaning because there is no belief behind it, and as a result when Anderson confronts life's miseries he can only sink into despair. When Lear addresses the heavenly powers in the storm scene we know that his arms are stretched upward towards a real presence; when Mio addresses the bright ironical gods he is turning towards a great empty void of interstellar space. The conditions of the world in which we live well-nigh deny the playwright to reach, as Anderson would fain have reached, the exhilarating terror and the agonized serenity of the true tragic concept.

Yet the desire is there; and, noting its presence in Anderson's work, we are reminded once more of that tendency, already discussed, on the part of many writers of the twenties and thirties to explore the realms of religious faith and metaphysical questioning. In the course of this study several dramas based on Biblical or related legendary themes have been chronicled, and when we add to these many others, such as the *Joseph d'Arimathée* (1898), by Gabriel Trarieux, *L'amante du Christ* (*The Lover of Christ*, 1888), by Rodolphe Darzens, *Jaakobs Traum* (*Jacob's Dream*, 1918), by the Austrian Richard Beer-Hofmann, and *La cattura di Sansone* (*Samson's Betrayal*, 1923), by the Italian Alberto Spaini, we must recognize that in this realm resides one of the most characteristic developments of the stage since the time of Ibsen's *Emperor and Galilean*. Men may find it difficult to believe in a world beset by the materialistic, but they would fain believe; they may have difficulty in escaping from the trammels of dramatic realism, yet the will to seek expression in forms apart from the realistic is everywhere present.

THE REVIVAL OF POETIC DRAMA

IN ATTEMPTING to create a tragic drama out of contemporary subject-matter Maxwell Anderson dared more courageously than any playwright of the past. From Æschylus onward the playwrights have found that distance in time or place is well-nigh essential for the full and satisfying exposition of tragedy's spirit, and perhaps even Anderson himself was conscious of the unlikelihood of his achieving perfection of utterance in a theme selected from the underworld of his own day.

Yet the attempt forms a symbol and a challenge. Through writing *Winterset* Anderson has shocked many of his companions into a recognition that the theatre of our time, if it is to win greatness, must once again be prepared to welcome the poetic imaginative processes couched in appropriate language; and there is no other modern playwright who has done more towards trying to bring this poetic concept within the framework of the common commercial playhouse.

POETIC EXPERIMENT IN AMERICA

Although Anderson himself is rather heavily influenced by Shakespeare, he realizes that if this attempt is to succeed some other form than the Shakespearian must be found. Even in *Winterset*, with its modern gangster story, echoes of *Hamlet* are plainly visible in the creation of Mio; one of the chief scenes in the drama is modelled upon the storm scene in *King Lear*; while the Mio-Miriamne story bears close connexions with *Romeo and Juliet.* Despite this, Anderson has sought, in his four-beat line with all the licences which he permits himself, to develop an instrument better harmonized to the speech of to-day than the blank-verse line of the Elizabethans—and in the fashioning of this instrument he shows himself in accord with what must be regarded as among the most hopeful portents of our stage.

It is only within the past few years that poet-playwrights have come to understand that before there can be any revival of poetic drama in our midst a medium of expression must be found which shall bear the same relationship to our current speech as the sixteenth-century blank verse bore to the current speech of Shakespeare's companions. All the efforts to re-establish the poetic drama in the nineteenth century failed precisely because the Elizabethan rhythms were regarded as a model towards which later writers should work, and, as a consequence, what once had been vital because organically bound to living reality became artificial, dull, or, at its best, falsely rhetorical.

Anderson's experimentation in technical form of expression is, therefore, of prime importance; and our sense of the importance of his effort is increased when we observe how his work is companioned by that of many others. In *Panic* (1935) Archibald MacLeish consciously set himself the task of listening to current American talk and of fashioning a verse formula harmonized with it. The result, perhaps, was not entirely successful; what was significant was the recognition of the need and the deliberate attempt to meet it. Since then MacLeish has further experimented in the field of radio drama, producing in *The Fall of the City* (1937) and *Air Raid* (1938) two memorable works, in both of which he has succeeded admirably in evoking an impression of mounting terror.

Earlier than this Edna St Vincent Millay had sought, in the style of an earlier generation, to start a new poetic drama in her *Aria da Capo* (1921), a rather artificial but still graceful one-act piece in which Pierrot and Columbine, lightly dallying, are set in juxtaposition with the tragic actors Thyrsis and Corydon. This first effort, however, was not followed by any notable successors. *The Lamp and the Bell* and *Two Slatterns and a King* (both 1921) are negligible as plays, and only *The King's Henchman* (1927), a libretto written for the music of Deems Taylor, warrants even modified praise—and that rather for her originality in selecting Saxon England for her subject than for the excellence of her treatment of the plot. Edna Millay is decidedly rather poet than playwright.

Despite all the numerous experiments, however, and despite the fact that Maxwell Anderson has succeeded in winning popular success with his several poetic dramas deliberately penned for the commercial stage, it must be agreed that the American drama is still heavily dominated by the realistic pattern. A revulsion may come, but until that happens we can record only brave attempts such as *Winterset*, largely isolated from the world in which they make their appearance.

T. S. ELIOT AND THE REVIVAL OF THE POETIC PLAY IN ENGLAND

We must note, however, that the writer who has been most markedly responsible both for the development of a new poetic orientation in England and for encouraging a rebirth of verse drama there—T. S. Eliot—was born an American. Already in 1928 he had published an important *Essay of Poetic Drama*; seven years later, in 1935, he produced a play, *Murder in the Cathedral*, which at once was hailed as a work better fitted than any other twentieth-century composition to mark the foundation of a modern poetic theatre. Although penned for, and originally produced at, Canterbury Cathedral, it proved its stage-worthiness when transferred from these ecclesiastical surroundings to the public playhouse, and since its appearance it has clearly exercised a widespread influence.

What distinguishes *Murder in the Cathedral* from all preceding verse plays is its method of approach. So far as the subject is concerned, it is just another historical drama, telling of the assassination, at Canterbury's high altar, of Thomas à Becket, the archbishop who had dared to oppose King Henry II. This ancient tale, however, Eliot has raised to the level of the philosophic. Thomas is a man fated for martyrdom, yet conscious that under the cloak of the martyr many evils may lie hid. Four tempters come to him. Three of these he easily thrusts aside, but the fourth, almost a replica of himself, he finds difficult to reject, for this figure dangles before his eyes an intangible bait—the hope of heavenly glory after death. At last Thomas reaches his decision:

> Now is my way clear, now is the meaning plain:
> Temptation shall not come in this kind again.
> The last temptation is the greatest treason:
> To do the right deed for the wrong reason.

So he goes to his death, while the Knights who have slain him attempt, in almost burlesque manner, to justify their action, and from the chorus of the women of Canterbury comes a great piercing cry of lamentation and self-abasement. In this chorus Eliot has sought to symbolize the cheap, common world, intent on its own safety, unable to reach to the vision of its Thomases:

> Forgive us, O Lord, we acknowledge ourselves as type of the common man,
> Of the men and women who shut the door and sit by the fire;
> Who fear the blessing of God, the loneliness of the night of God, the surrender required, the deprivation inflicted;

Who fear the injustice of men less than the justice of God;
Who fear the hand at the window, the fire in the thatch, the fist in the
tavern, the push into the canal,
Less than we fear the love of God.

By reintroducing the use of the chorus Eliot has taught his
companions what virtues this dramatic device can bring with it.
A whole human background is provided by these old women of
Canterbury for the figure of Thomas; the commonplace unanimity
of the mass is, through them, set against the extraordinary stature of
the hero; by means of the chorus the poet gains a means of presenting indirect commentary on his action; and, above all, the
lyrical opportunities thus offered give excellent means both of
enriching the speech of the play and of arousing imaginative recep-
tivity on the part of the audience. When, for example, just before
the murder, Eliot desires to awaken in us a sense of invading, invisible evil it is the chorus that supplies him with his instrument:

We have not been happy, my Lord, we have not been too happy.
We are not ignorant women, we know what we must expect and not
expect.
We know of oppression and torture,
We know of extortion and violence,
Destitution, disease,
The old without fire in winter,
The child without milk in summer,
Our labour taken away from us,
Our sins made heavier upon us.
We have seen the young man mutilated,
The torn girl trembling by the mill-stream.
And meanwhile we have gone on living,
Living and partly living,
Picking together the pieces,
Gathering faggots at nightfall,
Building a partial shelter,
For sleeping, and eating and drinking and laughter.

God gave us always some reason, some hope; but now a new terror
has soiled us, which none can avert, none can avoid, flowing under
our feet and over the sky;
Under doors and down chimneys, flowing in at the ear and the mouth
and the eye.
God is leaving us, God is leaving us, more pang, more pain than birth
or death.
Sweet and cloying through the dark air
Falls the stifling scent of despair;

The forms take shape in the dark air;
Puss-purr of leopard, footfall of padding bear,
Palm-pat of nodding ape, square hyæna waiting
For laughter, laughter, laughter. The Lords of Hell are here.
They curl round you, lie at your feet, swing and wing through the
  dark air.
O Thomas Archbishop, save us, save us, save yourself that we may be
  saved;
Destroy yourself and we are destroyed.

There is to be found no nobler language in the theatre of our times. *Murder in the Cathedral* was followed, in 1939, by *The Family Reunion* and, in 1949, by *The Cocktail Party*. Both of these have won success, yet it may be questioned whether Eliot's bold endeavour to build a poetic theatre out of the common, everyday life is likely to produce the results desired. The fact remains that the history of the stage shows that, in those ages when the imaginative verse drama flourished, it sought for themes and characters removed from the ordinary world of its time. True, the theme of *The Family Reunion* is based on the antique legend of Orestes, and the juxtaposing of the modern on the ancient produces a peculiar imaginative tension; but the endeavour itself is so much more difficult and hazardous than any task set to himself by a Sophocles or by a Shakespeare that one questions whether this is the path which the poetic drama will take in the days immediately to come.

Somewhat in the same mood that inspired Eliot to write *Murder in the Cathedral*, Dorothy L. Sayers has penned her *The Zeal of Thy House* (1937) and *The Devil to Pay* (1939). More significant are the plays of Eliot's follower, W. H. Auden, who has reversed the elder poet's career by moving from England to America. In 1935 he collaborated with Christopher Isherwood in producing *The Dog beneath the Skin; or, Where is Francis?* in which still another approach is made to the revivification of verse drama. Here fantastic satire takes the place of tragic tension. The chorus in melodious verse introduces us to a kind of idyllic Auburn, village of our dreams, and then harshly shatters the dreams by hinting that here too

Corruption spreads its peculiar and emphatic odours
And Life lurks, evil, out of its epoch.

In telling his story of the man who disguises himself as a dog Auden endeavours to make dramatic use of diverse measures and, in particular, to employ for his own purposes both popular jingles and forms of verse already associated with special situations. The first act, with its stanzaic forms, suggests the opening of a medieval morality play; a moment later we are listening to octosyllabic couplets; these change to dimeters; prose and a kind of blank verse follow. Witty, impudent, embittered, the play breathes the spirit of the intellectual who has just looked upon the world and found it wanting. *The Ascent of F.6* (1936), once more written in collaboration with Isherwood, has more of a story to narrate—that of an expedition sent out by the British Government to scale a mountain, marked F.6 on the maps and never yet conquered. Since the natives of the region regard it as sacred, and since Britain's rival, Ostnia, is proposing to mount to its summit, the expedition headed by Michael Ransom thus has a political significance—and the two authors seize every opportunity of indulging in vicious, embittered satire at political chicanery and intrigue. Unfortunately they also introduce a strain of the psychoanalytical, which serves to confuse a drama that otherwise might have had considerable directness of appeal.

A third play by the same authors, *On the Frontier* (1938), hardly improves upon these earlier efforts. The story of how war between a Fascist and a democratic nation is prevented by the will of the people has in it more sentimental wishful-thinking than sense. Where Auden fails is in his subject-matter. Not one of these plays presents a strongly imagined theme, and each one is cluttered up with inconsequentialities. This fact is peculiar in that the two poets, deeply concerned about the fate of the world, would wish to make direct appeal to their contemporaries, and we may well deem it ironically paradoxical that the writers most anxious to have their words heard and most intent on utilizing every possible device, including popular songs, to capture public attention should remain farther removed from the public stage than Eliot, with his medieval theme wrought into a drama for presentation in a cathedral.

Several other English poets have applied themselves similarly to the stage during recent years. Louis MacNeice, besides having made numerous contributions to the poetic radio play, and besides having prepared one of the finest existing translations of Æschylus' *Agamemnon*, produced one interesting drama of this kind, *Out of the Picture* (1937), a study of a young artist and the girl by whom he is killed. The year following the appearance of this work Stephen Spender published his *The Trial of a Judge*, a bitter and at times even hysterically violent denunciation of Nazi ideology and practice.

Nor, in dealing with this movement, must we forget how

materially the poets have been aided during the past twenty years by numbers of other dramatists who, while eschewing the use of verse, have sought to prepare audiences for acceptance of the imaginative in treatment and of the majestic in language by presenting fanciful themes in a richly heightened prose. Of this kind of writing the plays of Lord Dunsany (Edward Plunkett, Baron Dunsany)—who, although Irish, has identified himself rather with England's stage than with that of his native country—are noteworthy. He is by no means a great dramatist, yet we must acknowledge that his consistent application to themes strange and out of this world has had considerable influence in awakening the audience's willingness to accept other than realistic scenes upon the stage. In *The Glittering Gate* (1909) he carries us to the very portals of whatever heaven may be; *The Gods of the Mountain* (1911) shows a group of vagrants who are punished for pretending to be gods by themselves being struck into chill idol-images. Less entirely in the realm of the supernatural is Dunsany's most effective work, *If* (1921). Here, almost in the manner of Barrie's *Dear Brutus*, the hero, a little London clerk, is presented with a series of adventures, rising to chieftaincy of a Middle Eastern tribe and descending to poverty, that might have come to him had he not missed his 8.10 train on one particular morning.

Dunsany may be a playwright without enough strength to keep his plays permanently in the theatre, but he certainly deserves to be given an honourable place among those between-war playwrights who have sought to make the theatre once more a home for the imagination.

THE POETIC DRAMA IN FRANCE AND SPAIN

Some of the French writers, such as Claudel and Giraudoux, whose works have been considered elsewhere, might well have found fitting place in an examination of the poetic theatre. *Électre* is written in prose, but its conception is imaginative, and it carries us far from that theatrical realm which Maxwell Anderson has labelled the 'journalistic.'

With Giraudoux may be associated here Jules Supervielle, whose *La belle au bois* (*The Sleeping Beauty*, 1931) is rich with lyrical beauty; while several other French authors have shown, during recent decades, a desire similar to that which has inspired Anderson, Eliot, and Auden.

At the same time we must admit, first, that so far the Parisian stage has not succeeded in evolving a form for the verse play that is in any respect satisfying, and, second, that 'poetic' plays in prose cannot be regarded as having achieved harmony of expression. Poetry is not to be confused with verse, yet only through the employment of the regular rhythmical pattern we call 'verse' can a poet-playwright hope to have at his command an instrument capable of rising to the heights of his more passionate scenes.

Greater achievement in this direction comes from Spain. Already in the first years of the century Eduardo Marquina was vigorously engaged in an effort to revive the glories of the native poetic play, and around him circled a little group of authors inspired by a kindred purpose. As we look upon this group one interesting observation may be made—that gradually, almost insensibly, the scenes, which at the start are imitative of the romantic style, begin to change shape and to become modern. Where the aim of a dramatist writing in 1900 was to select a past theme and to make it as colourful or as authentic as possible, a dramatist of 1920 is thinking of ways by which this theme can be related to contemporary affairs.

This movement can be observed even within the work of the one writer already mentioned. There is a considerable measure of difference between the earlier *El pastor* (*The Shepherd*, 1902) or *Las hijas del Cid* (*The Daughters of the Cid*, 1908), the latter with its romantic treatment of a twelfth-century theme, and such a later play as the more richly imaginative *Fuente escondida* (*The Hidden Spring*, 1931). At the same time the influence of the Golden Age is deeply implanted in his work. Such plays as *Las flores de Aragón* (*The Flowers of Aragon*, 1915) are obviously based on the writings of Lope de Vega, and even those (for example, *En Flandes se ha puesto el sol* (*The Sun has Set in Flanders*, 1910) or *El gran capitán* (*The Great Captain*, 1916)) which do not outwardly recall the seventeenth-century works are warmed inwardly by their memory.

With Marquina may be associated Jacinto Grau, less lyrical in his orientation, but winning success by means of his fertile imaginative processes. Among his dramas *El señor de Pigmalión* (1923), a fantastic story of a collection of marionettes who rebel against their own master and demand a free, independent existence, brought him some international fame. Interesting, too, is the *Ollontay* (1938) of the Argentine Riccardo Rojas, a drama based on an ancient Inca play of the same title. Numerous other writers, both in Spain itself and in South America might be mentioned here, but among them perhaps only one demands individual attention.

This author, Federico García Lorca, is, however, of major stature, and the quality of his genius we are now slowly coming to recognize. True, his style is marked by a certain artificiality; the earlier symbolist movement has clearly laid its impress upon him; and his themes are apt to be a trifle precious or thin. Nevertheless there can be no doubt that he is among the most original and the most interesting of twentieth-century dramatic authors, even although the lyrical quality of his writing will always present a barrier between those to whom Spanish is a native language and those who must read his plays in translation.

Bitterness and fire breathe in all his writings. Starting with a surrealistic and allegorical *El maleficio de la mariposa* (*The Butterfly's Crime*, 1920), he moves on to *La zapatera prodigiosa* (*The Shoemaker's Prodigious Wife*, 1930), which shows an elderly shoemaker who, marrying late in life, finds he has a shrew for a mate—a woman who rates at him because he does not come up to her romantic ideal, and who creates a scandal in the village by reason of her constant revilings. At last the shoemaker leaves his house, and, returning disguised, finds to his joy that, whatever her previous treatment of him, she loves him truly. After he hears her say she would be mad with joy were he to come back to her he casts off his disguise, and she staggers back speechless:

SHOEMAKER: Pardon me, my heart. I ought to have prepared you for this. . . . But I wasn't able to wait. I was so happy!

THE WIFE [*regaining her self-possession and crying out*]: Oh, my God!
　　　　　　　[*She is still dazed, and stands as though paralysed.*

SHOEMAKER: Pardon me, darling. I've suffered so much. . . .
　　　　　　　[*He embraces her. She still remains motionless.*

SHOEMAKER: Pardon me. Even if the neighbours were right, I would have returned. I couldn't have done otherwise.
　　　　　　　[*Outside a song is heard to the accompaniment of tambourines.*

THE WIFE [*as if awakening from a dream*]: You hear? That is on your account—you scamp, you rogue, you scoundrel!
　　　　　　　[*She knocks over chairs and tables. The chairs crash on the floor.*

SHOEMAKER [*with delight*]: My dear little wife!

THE WIFE: Vagabond! You've come back? I'm so glad!

SHOEMAKER [*picking up the chairs*]: How sweet life is in one's own home!

And the last words of this ironic symbolic comedy are those she utters to the assembled neighbours:

You get off to your pigs of husbands! Here, I am with mine—with this scamp, with this tyrant that the good Lord has given me. Oh! how unhappy I am!

The mixture of the real and the symbolic here is thoroughly typical of Lorca's art. Even when he takes such a passionate theme as appears in *Bodas de sangre* (*The Fatal Wedding*, or *Bitter Oleander*, 1933) he succeeds in voyaging from such scenes as other authors would have made brutal, sensational, and merely trivial into a realm of his own devising. The same admixture of the realistic and the imaginatively poetic appears in *Yerma* (1934). Outwardly this is the drama of a woman who seeks for, and is denied, a child; inwardly it is a study of the constant clash between the reason and the instinct; between civilization's ideal of order and primitive orderless passion. Most moving of all his dramas is *La casa de Bernarda Alba* (*The House of Bernarda*, 1935), which shows a household doomed by a widow to the seven years' mourning that custom dictates. Against the black-robed gloom is set the spirit of youth, fain to be freed from these restraints and developing, within this unnatural environment, evil emotions. The youngest daughter, Adela, gives herself to the fiancé of her elder sister, Augusta; Bernarda shoots this man, whom she regards as the ravisher of her girl, and Augusta commits suicide. It is a dark tale, but narrated with such skill and so illuminated by the almost symbolic figure of the wise old grandmother as to assume the beauty of ebony.

Before leaving these diverse approaches made towards the creation of a modern, imaginative, poetic theatre we may finally note briefly the recent contributions made to it by the Jewish stage —the more particularly since it is only within recent years that the dramas written for this stage have come to be known outside the environment of the Yiddish and Hebrew playhouses. Here the supernatural has flourished and the world of wonder found harmony with the world of actuality. The best-known Jewish play, *The Dybbuk* (1914), by S. Ansky (S. A. Rappaport), illustrates this well. The immediate setting is realistic, showing a young student, Channon, dying when he hears that a girl, Leah, is to be given to another man; but soon we move into a region of unearthly presences. A strange voice speaks from Leah's lips, and it is discovered that her body is inhabited by a dybbuk, the soul of her lover—a man to whom she had been betrothed at birth, but whom her father has thrust aside in favour of a richer bridegroom. Although the dybbuk is taken from her by means of appropriate ritual, she dies, listening to the summons of the affianced husband who has gone before her in death. Over the whole of this strange drama, one of the most notable in the repertory of Vakhtangov's Habimah Theatre, spreads an imaginative spirit of peculiar power.

Not unlike in atmosphere, although far less inspired by vital power, is *Der Oytser* (*The Treasure*, 1906), by David Pinski, a tale of buried treasure, in which again the supernatural meets the natural. The world of superstition serves as a background for *The Haunted Inn* (1911), by Peretz Hirschbein, while the finer plays of Sholom Asch, such as *The God of Vengeance* (printed 1918), gain their effect by the way in which the naturalistic scenes are invested with imaginative and symbolic connotations.

In the general picture of the poetically conceived drama of our time these plays too deserve their place.

CHAPTER VIII

EUGENE O'NEILL

IF WE put aside Bernard Shaw as an author who, while producing some of his finest work during the twenties and thirties of this century, established himself on the stage before the outbreak of the First World War, we must all recognize that the only between-war playwright endowed with those virtues which are the mark of true genius was a scion of the American stage. Eugene O'Neill is not only a symbol of the dramatic movement that flourished so rapidly and with such resultant fruitfulness during the century's third and fourth decades; he also stands, a powerful and vibrant figure, over all his playwriting colleagues throughout the world.

He has genuine dramatic stature, yet the colossus does not by any means plant itself firmly upon the soil, nor is it lacking in cracks and fissures. Richly endowed with genius, O'Neill presents himself as a man who, whatever his strength, is wanting in that one final element of power and balance out of which greatness is born. He has strength of passion; he is not content to serve the stage merely with trivial themes of domestic interest; he ponders deeply upon man in relation to the universe in which he lives; more nearly than any author writing in English he approaches the great entrance-hall to tragedy's temple.

Two things only are lacking. First, we sense in O'Neill's career a strangely uneasy relationship between the man and the theatre of his time. When we confront such dramatists as Sophocles, Shakespeare, Molière, Racine, we feel that there is a perfect adjustment between their desires and the stage for which they write. At times they may endeavour to seize from the theatre effects almost beyond its reach, but in general they restrain themselves, with apparent content and harmony, within limits set by the very nature of the theatrical art of their ages. Not so does O'Neill impress us. All too often he suggests that he is impatient of the restrictions and that he is attempting to shatter them or to wrest from within them something the theatre is incapable of yielding. Frantically, almost hysterically, he turns from style to style, from device to device. Realism, expressionism, impressionism—all these paths are tried; he experiments with the use of masks and of the chorus; he takes the old theatrical convention of the aside and seeks to force from it new dramatic effect. Not content with the play of normal length, he pens a work which takes many hours to set upon the stage, and then proceeds farther towards the design of penning nine dramas as a kind of long-drawn-out theatrical cycle reminiscent of medieval amplitude.

This constant and restless movement in his career, this phrenetic seizing upon new devices, maybe ultimately depends upon his unconscious recognition of the essential lack in him of what is the essential instrument of the great playwright. With the deepest regret we must confess that O'Neill is not a finished literary artist. No words of rich import and beauty wing themselves from his pages; we remember his scenes but not the language in which they are couched; again and again as we reach an emotional climax in one or another of his dramas a wave of disappointment comes flooding in upon us. Where we had confidently expected to find lines instinct with loveliness and majesty all we have heard are sharp cries, broken phrases, the clichés rather than the originalities of expressive language. How far and how deep this defect in O'Neill's writing extends may be realized fully if we open any one of his printed plays at an episode of intense emotion: like a schoolgirl sending an epistle to her friend and conscious that she has not the power to wield her words so as to wring from them true record of sentiment or emotion, O'Neill falls back on the useless device of spattering his speeches with exclamation-marks. As a sort of short-hand stage direction for the actor the use of such exclamation-marks may be justified; but that use is not justified when it is a symbol of all that an author would have liked to say and cannot.

The whole trouble is that O'Neill has been at once fortunate and unfortunate in his training and in his career. A playwright can ask no better destiny than to be born the son of an actor, and from James O'Neill his son must have learned much. We observe, however, that the future author of *Mourning Becomes Electra* soon absented himself from the theatre's realm and spent several years in adventure afloat and ashore. No doubt these years yielded him much experience which later he put to use, but the fact remains that during the formative years when he ought to have been training himself as a writer his time was dissipated far from the stage or the study. True, he endeavoured to remedy this by attending, for a brief period, Professor G. P. Baker's "47 Workshop" at Harvard; by that time, however, the damage had been done.

To this we may add something more. A young dramatist is always blessed by the stars when he finds easy access to a theatre, and in this respect it was lucky that, in the years of the First World War, O'Neill found, in the Provincetown Players, an acting group ready to present his earliest efforts. At the same time we must remember that this was a collection of amateurs, and the fact that O'Neill began with them is likely to have intensified his own inherent aloofness (despite his having been born 'in the profession') from the commercial theatre. Instead of being forced to adapt his visions to the requirements of the ordinary playhouse, O'Neill began by finding a group of enthusiastic but technically inexperienced amateurs of the stage anxious to present his pieces as they were written and eager to idolize this young genius of their very own finding.

FROM "THIRST" TO "ALL GOD'S CHILLUN GOT WINGS"

The first play of O'Neill's to be produced was *Bound East for Cardiff* (1916), but two years previously there had appeared at Boston a volume now excessively scarce, entitled *Thirst and Other One-Act Plays*. Of its contents *Thirst* and *Fog* were given by the Provincetown Players in 1916 and 1917 respectively: the other dramas in the collection never saw stage performance.

All of these belong to one style, and that style appears also as the dominant force in several other apprentice works of these years. *Bound East for Cardiff* is related in subject-matter and characters to *In the Zone* (1917), *The Long Voyage Home* (1917), and *The Moon of the Caribbees* (1918); and as a result these have occasionally been grouped together and given a general title, *S.S. Glencairn*. In addition, several other one-act dramas of kindred mood saw early production by the amateurs with whom O'Neill was associated— *'Ile* (1917), *The Rope* (1918), and *Where the Cross is Made* (1918).

The general judgment which can be passed on these works is that they are strong, sometimes melodramatic, authentic studies of human passion, unflinching in their delineation of rougher, though not necessarily darker, scenes of human life. Of the four *S.S. Glencairn* playlets the first concentrates on a sailor, Yank, who, dying on board his ship, dreams of the peaceful farm he would have wished to have; the second shows a dim-witted but sympathetic Swede, dreaming of visiting his mother after long absence, shanghaied for a vessel bound across the Atlantic; the third reveals a group of sailors in the war zone desperately afraid of sabotage and suspicious of a black box owned by one of their number—till they find it contains nothing more explosively inflammatory than love-letters; in *The Moon of the Caribbees* nothing happens save the coming on board a ship of a group of native women who are entertained by all the sailors except one—Smithy, who sits by himself reading a love-letter. *'Ile* is a trifle more complex—the study of a whaling captain whose wife, nervously ill, begs him to return to port: after long pleading he agrees, but suddenly another whale is sighted and he turns his ship back again; the curtain falls on his wife gone utterly insane. More conscious irony appears in *The Rope*, where children avid of gold search for a miser's treasure, and where, at the end, one lad, not knowing the value of money, sends the coins skipping out over the calm sea-water immediately beyond the barn in which the treasure has been located. The same theme occurs in *Where the Cross is Made*, a play later expanded into *Gold* (1921).

What we have here is either melodramatically conceived irony, as in the last dramas mentioned, or else gripping studies of situations —the fear of the black box, the riotous orgy of sailors and native women, a sailor's dying aboard ship far from home. The language is sincere and realistic, the characters well known to the author. Over all the episodes hovers a highly charged atmosphere, tense and sometimes ominous: throughout these episodes we feel the presence of an author intent on saying more to his audiences than the pretty nothings of social comedy or the trivialities of the domestic problem drama. Even at the very beginning of his career O'Neill is intent on the eternal verities: the sea is as much his hero as man, and the gold of *The Rope* and *Where the Cross is Made* assumes symbolic quality.

In 1920 his first full-length play was produced—*Beyond the Horizon*—a work clearly born out of his experimental essays. In effect this drama takes shape as an extended study of one character, Robert, who, reversing Yank's dreams in *Bound East for Cardiff*, would fain have been a sailor, set against the foil that is his brother, Andrew. The pair are farmers: Robert is about to realize his dream of voyaging when he falls in love with Ruth, marries her, and prepares to settle down on the farm. Andrew goes in his place aboard ship, but when he returns, instead of having let the sea liberate his soul, it is found that his interest has been in amassing a hoard of money in the Argentine. Robert, thwarted, and his visions shattered, dies gladly, and finds in death the joy denied him in life of sailing 'beyond the horizon.' The symbolic use of the sea and of gold, representing good and evil; the nature of the characterization; the overlying mood of irony—all these recall the spirit of the experimental one-acts.

Then came the exciting *The Emperor Jones* (1920), in which a new style was tried: expressionism takes the place of realism in a drama which is, in effect, one long dramatic soliloquy revealing the terror that enters a Negro's soul as, driven into the jungle, he flies in terror from the beating of the drums. Already, however, in this play O'Neill was beginning to let his weaknesses take hold of him. In an interview he stated that, having read of the Congo drums, he immediately asked himself: How would this sort of thing work on an audience in a theatre? The question is revealing, since it indicates the beginning of his search for theatrical means outside the use of words for the arousing of imaginative impression; and when we observe how carefully he has sought to build up his effect by other non-literary means—scenery, lighting, and so on—we realize that, effective as is *The Emperor Jones*, its author was stepping out on a dangerous path.

Like Hauptmann, however, O'Neill was not prepared to move from one kind of endeavour to another in artistic progress. Although he had turned here to the expressionistic style, he was by no means done with realism. A month after the appearance of *The Emperor Jones*, *Diff'rent* was given by the Provincetown Players; six months later came *Gold*; and six months after that appeared *Anna Christie* (1921). The first of these is an unsatisfactory piece of work, a rather crudely artificial study of sex-suppression that becomes either brutal or absurd. Briefly the story tells of a woman, Emma, who, believing that her sweetheart, Caleb Williams, is "diff'rent" from other men, breaks off her engagement when she hears that he has had an *affaire* with another woman. The second part of the play shows her a woman of fifty who, because of her suppressed desires, allows herself to be taken in by a self-seeking young soldier just returned from France. For good measure O'Neill throws in a double suicide at the close. If *Diff'rent* is unsatisfactory *Gold* may be called disappointing. The theme is interesting, but the machinery creaks, and the dialogue fails to illuminate this tale of a sea-captain who, again despite the pleadings of a wife, is proposing to set sail in search of buried treasure and is bilked by his companions and even by his own son. The trouble here—as so often in O'Neill—is that there is a great yawning gulf between conception and achievement. Stevenson's *Treasure Island* is a thoroughly satisfying masterpiece because it does exactly what it sets out to do: it is a romantic story of adventure told with the consummate skill of a man who knows that the first duty of a writer is to learn how to write, that no artist is any good unless, by diligent application, he makes himself an able craftsman. O'Neill obviously wishes to invest his story of a desert island, a treasure-chest, and a ship of ill-assorted gold-seekers with a symbolic and tragic significance, and because he has failed to make himself a craftsman and because he merely blunders his way through the scenes, the discrepancy between aim and execution becomes often ludicrous.

Anna Christie is more harmonious in its parts, since it is nothing beyond what it sets out to be, because it avoids the sensational, and because from such a realistic theme as it presents we ask in words no more than the actual speech of common life. The play is deservedly popular, yet we may well inquire whether this is the kind of drama we expect from a man of O'Neill's unquestioned genius. There are other playwrights who might have written this rather mediocre sentimental tale of a golden prostitute. At the beginning we are shown the heroine as a cheap, vulgar streetwalker; then we learn that she has had to adopt this profession because of circumstances; and later we discover that, in spite of all the filth through which she has passed, her soul is pure within her. This is simply the eighteenth-century sentimental libertine-hero who sins not from innate evil, but because he has had bad associates. No doubt O'Neill intended more than the play presents, but it is the play, after all, upon which alone we can base our judgments; and the judgment that must be passed on *Anna Christie* is that, although effective as a stage piece, it is no great contribution to the theatre's treasury.

Amid some other writings of lesser import—*The Straw* (1921), with its scene in a sanatorium, *The First Man* (1922), the study of married torment, *Welded* (1924), and the rather weak *The Ancient Mariner* (1924)—O'Neill turned back from the realistic to the expressionistic style in *The Hairy Ape* (1922) and, at least in parts, in *All God's Chillun Got Wings* (1924). The former is a long character portrait somewhat in the style of *The Emperor Jones*, showing Yank, a person so dark on his chest that he is nicknamed "The Hairy Ape," trying to find out where he belongs. Again the symbol intrudes. Writing about this drama in 1924, O'Neill asserted that the play was intended as "a symbol of man, who has lost his old harmony with nature, the harmony he used to have as an animal and has not yet acquired in a spiritual way." In a series of scenes, some of which are 'realistic' and some cast in a form akin to that of other 'expressionistic' dramas, we see Yank moving from stokehole to Fifth Avenue and from there to a branch office of the I.W.W., until eventually he gets to the Zoo, tries to shake hands with a gorilla, and is crushed to death. There is strength of conception here, yet, when all is said, *The Hairy Ape* is not a play we would care to see often. At its first impact it impresses us by its novelty and by the obvious sincerity of the author, but once we have heard the lines there is no point in our hearing them a second time. In the scene on the upper deck of the ship we get dialogue like this:

AUNT: But don't you have to have the captain's—or some one's—permission to visit the stokehole?

MILDRED [*with a triumphant smile*]: I have it—both his and the chief engineer's. Oh, they didn't want to at first, in spite of my social-service credentials. They didn't seem a bit anxious that I should investigate how the other half lives and works on a ship. So I had to tell them that my father, the president of Nazareth Steel, chairman of the board of directors of this line, had told me it would be all right.

Down below there is a babel of noise:

VOICES: He ain't ate nothin'.
Py golly, a fallar gat to gat grub in him.
Divil a lie.
Yank feeda da fire, no feeda da face.
Ha-ha.
He ain't even washed hisself.

And so on. At the end Yank's long soliloquy before the apes' cage is nothing but a series of staccato phrases and sentences freely bespattered with exclamation-marks:

What de hell! T'hell wit it! A little action, dat's our meat! Dat belongs! Knock 'em down and keep bustin' 'em till dey croaks yuh wit a gat—wit steel! Sure!

We certainly gain nothing from listening to such dialogue twice.

All God's Chillun Got Wings has the virtue that, while dealing with a question, miscegenation, that stirs human passions to white heat in America, O'Neill has with almost Olympian wisdom concentrated his attention, not on the social problem, but upon his chief characters. Had it not been that such a story as he has selected here cannot hope to escape from being interpreted in social and political terms, it might almost have been said that in this play he came as near to complete fusing of concept and execution as he did in the

entire course of his work. There is a peculiar intensity and a directness of purpose in its scenes that carry us triumphantly onward from
the opening episodes, wherein we see black and white children
playing thoughtlessly together, on to the painful last moments
when Ella, half recovered from the fit of insanity during which she
has tried to murder her Negro husband Jim, sits with him on his
knees before her:

JIM: Forgive me, God, for blaspheming You! Let this fire of burning
suffering purify me of selfishness and make me worthy of the child
you send me for the woman you take away!

ELLA: Don't cry, Jim! You mustn't cry! I've got only a little time
left and I want to play. Don't be old Uncle Jim now. Be my little
boy, Jim. Pretend you're Painty Face and I'm Jim Crow. Come
and play!

JIM: Honey, Honey, I'll play right up to the gates of Heaven with you!

These lines, however, in themselves indicate what the drama is not.
It has been described as a tragedy, but in tragedy, in addition to
pain, we want to experience an emotion of admiration, of wonder.
Jim is a kindly-souled Negro who at the same time is a failure;
Ella is an ordinary girl who, broken in the world, has found temporary refuge in Jim's love. Neither character has the least glimpse
of greatness, and, as a consequence, while we may hail *All God's
Chillun Got Wings* as an affecting play, we cannot in any wise
relate it to those dramatic works of the past to which we give the
name of tragedy.

FROM "DESIRE UNDER THE ELMS" TO "THE ICEMAN COMETH"

The excitement occasioned by *All God's Chillun Got Wings* was
repeated when *Desire under the Elms* appeared in 1924. Here O'Neill
turns to the stark New England countryside and presents to us the
Puritanical old farmer Ephraim Cabot, married to the much
younger Abbie. Between Abbie and Cabot's thirty-two-year-old
son Eben there is strife, for he feels that she has stolen what should
have been his birthright: but this strife Abbie turns aside by deliberately enticing him to become her lover, proceeding thereafter
to get her husband to sign a deed granting the farm to the child
which Ephraim believes to be his. Enraged, Eben tells his father
what has happened, while she, now consumed by a genuine passion
for her lover, murders her own babe to prove her devotion to him.
In the end Eben and Abbie, arrested for the crime of child-murder,
go together to gaol, intent only on one another.

There can be no doubt but that *Desire under the Elms* possesses an almost daimonic strength, and O'Neill has been completely successful in presenting his contrast between the hard religious atmosphere, so thoroughly in keeping with the rocky soil, and the volcanic passion aroused in this pair of semi-incestuous lovers. At the same time we do not have here anything that surpasses some of the earlier works in the naturalistic style, while, once more, it must be emphasized that to call this drama a tragedy is completely to deny the only true meaning of that term. *Desire under the Elms* is a powerful play of sex-repression and of sex-satisfaction; of the metaphysical qualities out of which tragedy arises it has none.

A peculiar, romantically conceived piece, *The Fountain* (1925), followed, illustrative of O'Neill's own restless quest. In effect it is a fairy-tale, of almost Maeterlinckian sentimentality, narrating how Juan Ponce de Leon dedicates his life to a search for the Fountain of Youth, and ends, not by discovering it, but by coming to realize that love is the secret of youth. Again the exclamation-marks bespatter the scene of climax:

> Juan Ponce de Leon is past! He is resolved into the thousand moods of beauty that make up happiness—colour of that sunset, of to-morrow's dawn, breath of the great Trade Wind—sunlight on the grass, an insect's song, the rustle of leaves, an ant's ambitions. I shall know eternal becoming—eternal youth!

Then came *The Great God Brown* (1926), in which O'Neill tries another device—the use of masks—for the purpose of presenting what he obviously intended to be a great philosophic drama, but which can only confuse and perplex. His hero is Dion Anthony, a man within whose self, as the author explains, is combined the quality of Dionysus—"the creative pagan acceptance of life" —and of St Anthony—"the masochistic, life-denying spirit of Christianity." For heroine he has a Margaret, Faust's Marguerite, "the eternal girl-woman with a virtuous simplicity of instinct, properly oblivious to everything but the means to her end of maintaining the race." Brown "is the visionless demi-god of our new materialistic myth—a Success—building his life of exterior things, inwardly empty and resourceless, an uncreative creature of superficial preordained social grooves, a by-product forced aside into slack waters by the deep main current of life-desire." With these and other characters, each possessing masks and donning first one and then another, we get a drama, animated no doubt by the highest motives, that seeks to do in the theatre what the theatre by the very nature of its being cannot attain.

Much the same impression is provided by *Lazarus Laughed* (1926). Here also O'Neill has a basic philosophy to present. Lazarus, having died and returned to earth, has a message to give to men: death is not to be feared, and in God's house there is only laughter. The trouble is that this idea is so constantly driven at us in each scene of the play, and that O'Neill, not possessing literary means to arouse our emotions, so constantly falls back on hysterical outbursts of staccato phrases as to make the entire play a wearisome series of echoes of itself. When it first appeared its novelty must have been appealing, but now that the novelty has worn off, *Lazarus Laughed* can be accounted nothing save another grand failure. Even while rejoicing that a playwright of our time has such vision as is exhibited in this play, we are forced to acknowledge O'Neill's inability to incorporate the vision in theatrical form likely to make enduring appeal.

The attack on the materialistic is carried a stage farther in *Marco Millions* (1928), where the famous Italian venturer to the East is shown, with mordant satire, passing on his way through the ancient world of the Orient blind of eye and heart, intent only on his own commercial advancement. To point his message O'Neill causes an epilogue to carry the spiritual action into the present. As the spectators rise they find to their surprise that one of their number is, in fact, Marco Polo. Dressed in Venetian garments, he "conceals a yawn in his palm, stretches his legs as if they had become cramped by too long an evening," and moves towards the exit door, looking a trifle puzzled. Then, as he nears the street and he finds himself in his familiar materialistic surroundings, his countenance clears. A luxurious limousine arrives: "he gets in briskly, the door is slammed, the car edges away into the traffic, and Marco Polo, with a satisfied sigh at the sheer comfort of it all, resumes his life."

Once more a novel theatrical device is introduced into *Strange Interlude* (1928), a drama made extraordinarily long by its somewhat tedious and fundamentally undramatic elaboration of the quite worthy convention of the 'aside' into a pretentious artistic instrument. The story of this play is, in the main, concerned with the heroine, Nina Leeds, who, having lost in the war the one man who might have satisfied her whole nature, drifts from male to male. Finally we find her with her three lovers—her husband, Sam, Dr Darrel, by whom she has had a son, and Charles Norsden, a novelist who tends to look on her as though she were his mother. It is all very psychoanalytical and very subtle and very long.

With *Dynamo* (1929) we are back again in the mood of *The Great*

God Brown, with an increase in the use of symbolism. The son of a Christian rejects his father's religion and goes out into the world to seek a god: this he finds in Electricity. He is, however, in love with the daughter of an Atheist, and, having been cheated by her, he kills her and finally electrocutes himself in the great Dynamo which is the idol of his faith. A tragic dramatist is always unfortunate when one of his chosen themes reminds us of a similar theme comically treated, and O'Neill's Electricity has an uncomfortable resemblance to the hilariously conceived Clouds which Aristophanes makes an earlier truth-quester adopt as his god.

Dynamo is one of O'Neill's mistakes: in *Mourning Becomes Electra* (1931), however, he comes as close to realization of his tragic purposes as in any of his works. Here he escapes from the rather jejune allegory of the machine; here his modern characters are ennobled by their association with that story which, above all others, has seized on the imagination of successive dramatists from the majestic times of Æschylus to the not-so-majestic of Sartre. Composed in trilogy form, the play takes shape as one long drama with three separate parts, *The Homecoming*, *The Hunted*, and *The Haunted*, narrating a story set just after the close of the American Civil War. Head of the Mannon household in New England is General Mannon, married to a woman, Christine, who is a stranger to the district: there is a son, Orin, passionately devoted to his mother, and a daughter, Lavinia, as passionately devoted to her father. During the General's absence at the war Christine has had a love affair with a certain Adam Brant, one of O'Neill's men of the sea, who turns out to be the illegitimate son of Lavinia's grandfather and thus half-brother to the General. Terrified of her husband's homecoming, Christine poisons him and departs to live with Brant. Her crime might have lain unsuspected had it not been for Lavinia's hate. The girl discovers the dark secret and, with much difficulty, convinces Orin of the truth; he shoots Brant almost before the very eyes of Christine, who, her life broken, takes her own life. In order to escape from these memories, brother and sister go away on a long voyage, but during this time Orin finds all the devotion that was once given to his mother turned upon Lavinia, and when he learns that she proposes to marry he is horrified. In the end he commits suicide, while she, her heart torn, shuts herself up in the ill-fated Mannon house and settles down there to self-tormented solitude.

The scheme of the drama is excellent, and O'Neill has been successful in making us believe in the terrible story. Subtly, yet boldly, the characters are revealed before us; although no concrete representation of the Eumenides appear on the stage, the author almost makes them seem to live upon the stage. At the same time we do not encounter here that great vision which we look for in tragedy. O'Neill has presented a memorable picture of a sex-repressed family finding its passions released in strange, dark, ugly ways, but the mood in which the action opens is carried through to the very end without relief or the enlarging of outlook. This is rather a magnificently presented case-study than a powerful tragic drama. Almost the last words are those of Lavinia addressed half to herself, half to her faithful servant Seth:

> Don't be afraid. I'm not going the way Mother and Orin went. That's escaping punishment. And there's no one left to punish me. I'm the last Mannon. I've got to punish myself! Living alone here with the dead is a worse act of justice than death or prison! I'll never go out or see anyone! I'll have the shutters nailed close so no sunlight can ever get in. I'll live alone with the dead, and keep their secrets, and let them hound me, until the curse is paid out and the last Mannon is let die! [*With a strange, cruel, smile of gloating over the years of self-torture*] I know they will see to it I live for a long time! It takes the Mannons to punish themselves for being born!

In this speech is a symbol of O'Neill's final inadequacy in language. As in his earlier plays, the multitude of exclamation-marks is a confession of weakness—nor do these appear only in passages that are almost soliloquy. Here, for example, is the scene, towards the end of *The Hunted*, wherein Orin tells his mother of Brant's death:

CHRISTINE [*stupidly*]: You didn't go—to Blackridge?
ORIN: We took the train there but we decided to stay right on and go to Boston instead.
CHRISTINE [*terrified*]: To—Boston——?
ORIN: And in Boston we waited until the evening train got in. We met that train.
CHRISTINE: Ah!
ORIN: We had an idea you would take advantage of our being in Black-ridge to be on it—and you were! And we followed you when you called on your lover in his cabin!
CHRISTINE [*with a pitiful effort at indignation*]: Orin! How dare you talk——! [*Then brokenly*] Orin! Don't look at me like that! Tell me——
ORIN: Your lover! Don't lie! You've lied enough, Mother! I was on deck, listening! What would you have done if you had dis-covered me? Would you have gotten your lover to murder me,

Mother? I heard you warning him against me! But your warning was no use!

CHRISTINE [*chokingly*]: What——? Tell me——!

ORIN: I killed him!

CHRISTINE [*with a cry of terror*]: Oh—oh! I knew! [*Then clutching at* ORIN] No—Orin! You—you're just telling me that—to punish me, aren't you? You said you loved me—you'd protect me—protect your mother—you couldn't murder——?

This is not such language as we look for from a truly great dramatist.

After this work O'Neill somewhat surprised his public by writing a comedy, *Ah, Wilderness!* (1933), in which he returns to a period of twenty-five years before. In Richard he draws the portrait of a boy endowed with love of literature and romance who shocks his staid neighbours and is sympathetically counselled by an understanding father. No doubt this is a fairly well-constructed play, but half a dozen other living playwrights might have penned its scenes. The solemn strain returns in *Days without End* (1934), wherein still another rather forced theatrical device is used. In order to present his 'tragedy' of John Loving, a man who has forgotten his early visions and is, as it were, shocked back to his God, O'Neill uses the trick of having two actors portray a single character (for the purpose of revealing different aspects of his being). It can hardly be claimed that the means designed to secure his end is anything save cumbersome and artificially conceived.

Immediately following the appearance of *Days without End* O'Neill let it be known that he was engaged in penning a great cycle of dramas depicting a section of American life. What this will be like we cannot, of course, even guess at: all we may say is that his first contribution to this his latest work, *The Iceman Cometh* (1946), is a vastly disappointing play. The characters talk too much; we become wearied with the constant repetition of the phrase "pipe-dreams"; the philosophy of the scenes is confused. Set in a wretched saloon where the flotsam and jetsam of society gather, it concentrates attention upon a certain travelling salesman, Hickey, who is accustomed to come there at periodic intervals for a drinking-bout. The usual habitués are eagerly awaiting his appearance as the play opens, but when he arrives he announces that he has been reformed and proceeds to try to reform them also, thus incidentally stripping them of the illusions and fancies that have made their lives endurable. It appears that Hickey, realizing that he has given pain and sorrow to his wife, has murdered her in order to put her out of her misery, although at the close of the play we discover that the murder has been committed because, in reality, he hated her. What this farrago of despairing scenes implies no one can tell: O'Neill's latest play is perhaps his poorest.

In a sense the dramatic career of this strange author is representative of the American theatre as a whole. From about 1918 to the present time the New York stage has been one of the most vital in the world, and when we consider its contributions collectively we may readily admit that it has exhibited a vitality and a strength which cannot be matched anywhere else within these years. On the other hand, those last refinements which alone can bring greatness are lacking. It is as though we were constantly approaching and never arriving at our destination.

PART XIII

THE THEATRE IN THE MIDST OF WAR, AND AFTER

THE THEATRE IN THE MIDST OF WAR, AND AFTER

FROM 1939 to 1945, of course, the progress of the theatre was completely disrupted by the conflict which shattered the whole of civilized life throughout the entirety of the world, and since 1945 not sufficient time has elapsed for us to determine what may be the chief trends of the immediate future. At the same time, amid the darkness there are at least some streaks of light to be discerned.

First, an important fact is the continued activity of the serious theatre in those centres wherein such activity was possible, even under conditions that might well have yielded nothing at all or, at the best, merely light-hearted entertainment. Under the German occupation the French stage still kept alive, while in London the theatrical fare presented in the midst of bombings was far other than what had been characteristic of the years 1914–18. During the First World War the London actors, for the most part, gave themselves over to the frothiest of shows, and for four long years audiences were denied the opportunity of seeing plays of worthier purpose. To the surprise of many, the six years from 1939 to 1945 were marked, if not by the appearance of new dramas (for most of the playwrights were otherwise engaged), at least by a truly extraordinary series of interesting revivals. Shakespeare proved suddenly popular: Donald Wolfit's repertory company found eager audiences; important productions were given of *King Lear*, *The Tempest*, *Macbeth*, *Othello*, *Hamlet*, and *Richard III*; into the reaches of Welsh mining villages Dame Sybil Thorndike, with success, took her versions of *Macbeth* and *Medea*.

These tours of Sybil Thorndike are symptomatic, for perhaps English theatre historians of the future will find as the most notable feature of these war years the extraordinary development of dramatic interest in areas which before had been served by nothing save the films. In December 1939 a small group of enthusiasts, fearing lest the arts should be completely blacked out, obtained a grant from the Pilgrim Trust and established C.E.M.A.—the Council for the Encouragement of Music and the Arts. At the beginning their activities were naturally restricted in scope, but the start of bombing in 1941 revealed, with surprising suddenness, the value to the community of the small touring companies—such as Martin Browne's

Pilgrim Players—that these enthusiasts had been sponsoring. Very soon C.E.M.A. received a Treasury grant, and was transformed into a permanent, officially supported organization as the Arts Council of Great Britain. Through its efforts what approaches a provincial 'national theatre' has been set up in the happily preserved eighteenth-century Theatre Royal in Bristol, while in diverse parts of the country new civic playhouses have, through its help, been opened.

It must be confessed that so far the efforts of the Arts Council have been directed towards the presentation of old plays rather than towards the encouragement of new dramatic talent, but no doubt this was inevitable, and, no doubt, too, the prime necessity is the establishment of means to fill the vast yawning gap between the theatre-going public in London and the rest of the country. When we remember that since the breakdown of the stock-companies in the nineteenth century scores of reasonably important towns and cities, despite the efforts of the repertory theatres, have been for generations without the opportunity of seeing any plays at all, the service rendered by the Arts Council must indeed assume in our minds considerable significance.

Along with the Arts Council, although operative in an entirely different sphere, may be mentioned the rather remarkable growth of Unity Theatre, established originally in 1936 and gaining prominence during the years just before and during the War. The "political pantomime" called *Babes in the Wood* drew attention to their efforts in 1938, and this was followed by another similar revue in 1939, *Sandbag Follies*. In 1941 Unity put on Sean O'Casey's *The Star Turns Red*, acquiring thereby added fame, while in 1944 came a joyous extravaganza telling the story of the music-halls, *Winkles and Champagne*.

Originally a purely amateur organization, in its growth Unity has tended ever more and more towards the professional, and we need not doubt that its increasing activity is supplementing the work of the Arts Council by spreading interest in the drama among sections of the community for whom the theatre has long been dead.

Very similar movements are afoot in the United States. Throughout the thirties valiant endeavours were made to encourage the local theatre everywhere throughout the Union, and, with the cessation of hostilities, these endeavours are once more being pursued with added enthusiasm. There may be nothing quite comparable with the Arts Council, but in the National Theatre Conference, sponsored by the Rockefeller Foundation, exists a body which may at least be associated with that out of which the Arts Council grew;

and besides this body there are others of more recent foundation intent upon enriching and widening the dramatic fare presented to the public. In America as in Britain there is evident an extensive and enthusiastically pressed desire both to enlarge the playhouse audience and to see that, amid theatrical conditions which have tended to become more and more commercial, the best in the theatre's treasury shall not be forgotten.

THE NEW DRAMA IN THE UNITED STATES

Our interest, however, lies not so much in the sphere of the revival as in that of the original play. Obviously the consideration of new contributions to the drama made since 1939 cannot be separated from what went immediately before the outbreak of war. Within the last few years, as has been seen, many of the playwrights, including O'Neill, most prominent in the twenties and thirties have presented their later works, and even some of the youngest writers who seem to belong to the war and post-war years had been experimenting on the stage before peace was shattered by the German march on Poland. We can, nevertheless, make a general division among these authors and segregate for present consideration those whose first productions arrived within the last eight years or who first came to public attention during that time.

So far as dramatic form is concerned, the young American dramatists do not have anything to offer us. Their work is almost uniformly realistic, and, although we meet with some strong scenes, we have the impression that they are mainly working along lines which forbid them to reach, as O'Neill tried to reach, beyond their immediate material environment. Several of them are bitterly angry at social errors around them, but we look in vain for any larger vision. Their theatre we might call critical and negative rather than creative and positive.

The Negro problem has attracted several authors. Lilian Smith presents in *Strange Fruit* (1946) a study of the love of a rather feckless youth for a dark-skinned girl. In *Jeb* (1946) Robert Ardrey rather ineffectively discusses Negro questions. Perhaps the finest recent drama on this subject is *Deep are the Roots* (1945), by James Gow and Arnaud d'Usseau. These collaborators had swum into prominence in 1943 with *To-morrow the World*, a play which, although maybe a trifle reminiscent of *The Children's Hour*, effectively gave us a terrible picture of a German boy in whom evil is so deeply implanted that even change of environmental climate cannot alter its quality. Both the technical skill of the authors and their firm handling of dramatic character are further revealed in their second play, wherein is discussed the problem of the Negro officer who returns to a civilian *milieu* where the ribbons on his breast and the pips on his shoulder mean nothing to a white society steeped in prejudice and hate.

Not dissimilar in tone is *Decision* (1944), by Edward Chodorov, a tense drama which shows a young soldier returning from the front only to discover that his hometown is riddled with just such oppressive, fascistic sentiment as he has been combating abroad. This author, already well known for his *Kind Lady* (1935), possesses undoubted theatrical skill. Diverse in theme but born of the same mood is Arthur Miller's *All My Sons* (1947). Here indignation breathes fiercely in a story that tells of a worthy father who makes his money from a small motor-engine-producing factory. In his desire to provide the better for his family he is content to permit defective machines to be shipped for use in war, and is shocked into a sense of duties beyond the reach of his immediate family circle only when one of his soldier-sons comes home. This is by no means a great play, although it has the merit of vigour and youthful enthusiasm. Here, too, may be mentioned *The State of the Union* (1945), by Howard Lindsay and Russel Crouse, the two authors who in 1939 produced the long-running comedy *Life with Father*. *The State of the Union* is an embittered attack on American party politics, showing how a wealthy industrialist is encouraged by his mistress, owner of a number of Republican newspapers, to aim at the presidency, and how in this venture he is seized upon and moulded by the party machine—an interesting document, hardly a noteworthy play. In *The Magnificent Yankee* (1946) Emmet Lavery turns to deal with the life of the great Oliver Wendell Holmes.

Much fame has come in the last few years to Tennessee Williams, but it is as yet too soon to say whether he has the elements of true greatness in him. *The Glass Menagerie* (1944), by which, after having obscurely experimented in playwriting for some years, he came to public attention, is well written, but its theme and characterization are heavily tinged with sentimental colourings. Maybe there are deeper overtones in *A Streetcar named Desire* (1947), yet this sordid tale of sex in New Orleans has but little to offer to a world craving for things that are broader and more spacious. It is the direct descendant of Hauptmann's *Before Sunrise*.

I then realm of comedy two works claim passing attention — *The Male Animal* (1940), by James Thurber and Elliott Nugent, and

Mary Chase's *Harvey* (1944). Although neither is likely to become a lasting monument in the theatre, the former wrests a good deal of serious gaiety out of the figure of Professor Tommy Turner, who becomes a male animal when he thinks his wife is infatuated with Joe Ferguson, a prosperous business-man; while the latter shows skill in the delicate handling of that lovable drunkard Elwood Dowd, who tells us with such conviction about his friend the tall white rabbit that we are almost prepared to accept his hallucinations as reality.

On the whole this is a meagre collection of dramatic canvases, and among them there is not one whose creator impresses us with a feeling of true strength. Some are sincere, others are indignant, still others have a mildly humorous view of human follies, but sincerity, indignation, and mild humour are not enough to produce notable plays.

THE DRAMA IN ENGLAND

From London the story is even less rosy, although if we include the work of one or two authors who were beginning to establish themselves immediately before 1939 the record becomes not quite so dark as otherwise it would be.

Such men as Priestley, Bridie, O'Casey, Coward, and Williams, since they had all won full recognition in the thirties, are, of course, dealt with elsewhere, although we may observe that each one of them found new strength during these latter years. *They Came to a City, Mr Bolfry, Red Roses for Me, Blithe Spirit,* and *Wind of Heaven* all belong to the forties. The enumeration of these titles suggests that the English stage is not so heavily bound by the realistic convention as is the American. The gay introduction of the supernatural into Bridie's and Coward's comedies, the rich outpouring of O'Casey's eloquence, and Priestley's experiments in time and space philosophies tell a different story.

It is true that one of the most popular of recent plays has been *The Winslow Boy* (1946), by Terence Rattigan, an author who, after having made his name by writing a series of light farces, is clearly now aiming at higher things. *The Winslow Boy* is thoroughly realistic, as is Rattigan's later *The Browning Version* (1948), a moving picture of a thwarted schoolmaster. The emphasis on school and children, we may note, is repeated by other dramatists of the time: Reginald Beckwith deals in *Child's Play* (1947) with the fate of youth in a loveless home, while W. Chetham Strode provides us with his rather sentimentally conceived *The Guinea-pig* (1945), an essay on the theme of the poor-born boy at a public school, as well as with his returned-soldier drama, *Young Mrs Barrington* (1945) and his sociological study, *The Gleam* (1947). Peter Powell's *The Two Children* (1943) deals with family life in war-time, and the popular *Edward, My Son* (1947), by Robert Morley and Noel Langley, weaves dramatic tension from the contrast between ambitious father and worthless progeny. In the realistic style Joan Temple treats of the problems of billeting in *No Room at the Inn*, while Ronald Adam provides an Air Force documentary in *An English Summer* (1947). James Parrish's *Message for Margaret* (1947) and Mary Hayley Bell's *Duet for Two Hands* (1947) illustrate the manner in which this style is being still allied, but in a 'psychological' manner, with melodramatic forms.

Among these writers two in particular have attracted considerable attention. Peter Ustinov, after capturing critical esteem for his *House of Regrets* (1942), a play concerned with Russian exiles in London, produced in *The Banbury Nose* (1944) an interesting, if not wholly satisfying, study of a military family, tracing its generations backward from present to past. Similar esteem was won by William Douglas Home for his prison drama *Now Barabbas* (1946), and his later plays, including the political satire *The Chiltern Hundreds* (1946), demonstrate his true flair for the stage.

Nothing in this realm, however, can equal the interest attaching to the extraordinary upsurge in popularity of the verse drama. Immediately after the cessation of hostilities a Poets' Theatre was established, and since then several of London's most distinguished actors have won success and acclaim in the works of contemporary poets. During the years 1945-46 a small but powerful public hailed such plays as Peter Yates' *The Assassin*, a skilful treatment of Lincoln's murderer, Norman Nicholson's modern version of the Elijah and Ahab story, *The Old Man of the Mountain*, Ronald Duncan's St Anthony drama, *This Way to the Tomb*, and Anne Ridler's *The Shadow Factory*, a kind of up-to-date Nativity play. Then came the theatrical advent of Christopher Fry. Already in 1939 this poet had published *The Boy with a Cart*, a short religious choral work somewhat reminiscent of Eliot's style; in 1936 *A Phœnix Too Frequent*, on the 'Widow of Ephesus' theme, showed in its witty lines that the author was possessed both of wide range and marked originality; and then during 1949 and 1950 came the triumph of *The Lady's not for Burning*, *Venus Observed*, and (adapted from Anouilh) *Ring round the Moon*. No doubt part of the popular acclaim given to these works must be attributed to such star performers as John Gielgud, Sir Laurence Olivier, and Paul Scofield; through the instrumentality of the actors the plays have been brought to a larger audience; but it is essentially their inherent virtue which has won them their popularity.

What Fry has done is to evoke verse rhythms which at the same time are apt for the actors' utterance and make direct appeal to the modern consciousness, to demonstrate that poetic drama need not keep within the narrow range of tragic and religious themes, and to bring within the theatre a boisterous air of imaginative vitality. Not without reason have several critics spoken of his 'Elizabethanism.' That label, of course, was attached also to the dramatic work of the early romantic poets; but for them the plays we have in mind are *Macbeth* and *Hamlet*; for Fry our thoughts go to the youthful cleverness and adroit lines of *Love's Labour's Lost*. For them the label implies the presence in their dialogue of imitative echoes; for Fry we think rather of a likeness of mood. Replete with rich evocative imagery, his verses sing a modern tune; there is nothing in vocabulary, rhythm, or syntax to suggest the copying of Shakespearian melodies in such lines as

> Flattery, Jessie; for years the frost has lain
> On my stubble beard. The swallows and other such
> Migratory birds have left me months ago—

or

> Dignity has dropped upon all fours.
> Indeed there's hardly to be seen
> One intense perpendicular
> In all the streets of men—

or

> Astrology, then. You can't
> Throw someone against the sky and not expect
> A certain vapour of magic to condense
> In moisture on their lashes.[1]

Perhaps, like *Love's Labour's Lost*, his plays as yet show greater skill in the patterning of words and dexterous juggling of ideas than in the development of plot material, but the progress of dramatic art demonstrates that before a new kind of play can be born the form of its being must first be shaped. As we listen to Eliot's searing lines and to the scintillating brilliance of Fry's, we may well believe that London's stage is nearer to recapturing the true poetic drama than it has been through all the long centuries from the death of Shakespeare.

[1] *Venus Observed.*

DIVERSE EXPERIMENTS

In mentioning these efforts in the poetic style allusion should be made to kindred endeavours in neighbouring Dublin. From Ireland come such gay fantastic plays as Donagh MacDonagh's *Happy as Larry* (1947), "a melodrama in ballade." This play emanates from the Lyric Theatre, an organization directed by Austin Clarke, whose activities have all been directed towards arousing public interest in the poetic drama. Among Clarke's own works—mostly one-acts—the "poetic farce," *Black Fast* (1941), and *The Viscount of Blarney* (1944) are particularly noteworthy. Much has already been achieved by the Lyric Theatre, and more may be expected from it in the future.

These endeavours, of course, must be regarded as somewhat akin to those of London's Mercury Theatre. For the most part, the majority of recent Irish dramas have been cast in the familiar realistic form. Walter Macken's *Mungo's Mansions* (1946) deserves notice: although lacking O'Casey's richness of dialogue, this story of a Mungo King who wins a sweepstake and has his life transformed exhibits vigour and incisiveness. Worthy of mention, too, is Frank Corvey's tale, in *The Righteous are Bold* (1945), of an Irish girl who, visiting England, returns possessed of a devil.

In diverse countries the drama is being actively cultivated, although perhaps only one European capital suggests that a true theatrical renaissance is in the making. From Germany one would not expect much under present-day conditions: indeed, it is rather surprising that so many new plays have been written there during the past three years. A continued interest in the historical theme constitutes the most interesting feature of this modern German dramaturgy. Josef Nowak deals with Joan of Arc in *Johanna in Rouen* (*Joan in Rouen*, 1948), Paul Helwig treats of Attila's descent on Rome in *Der Barbar* (*The Barbarian*, 1948), and Günther Weisenborn evokes the spirit of Renaissance Spain in *Spanische Hochzeit* (*Spanish Wedding*, 1948). Even for a comedy-farce Theo Lingen and Franz Gribitz return to the past with their *Theophanes* (1948). This last play shows an author engaged in the study of ancient Rome; suddenly the telephone rings, and soon he finds himself first conversing with, and then actually meeting Cicero and his companions. As might have been anticipated, alongside these historical dramas appear others in which an attempt is made to deal with various aspects of modern life. Of these the latest is Wolfgang Borchert's *Draussen vor der Tür* (*Outside the Door*, 1948), which deals frenziedly with the fate of the returned soldier much in the manner of such earlier dramas as the *Douaumont* (1924) of Eberhard Möller.

The Scandinavian countries show kindred interests, with (as is natural) much attention given to the theme of collaboration and resistance. Bitter attacks on those who were prepared, if not to act with the Germans, at least to take no active part against them appear in the Norwegian Hans Heiberg's *Minnefesten* (*The Feast of Commemoration*, 1946) and in Arthur Omre's *Linedansere* (*The Tightropewalkers*, 1945). Something of the same mood animates the Swedish *Rid i natt* (*To Horse!*, 1946) of Vilhelm Moberg. In Denmark Carl Erik Soya, an author who began his career in the thirties, is currently engaged on a vast tetralogy of modern life, of which *To traade* (*Two Threads*, 1943) and the psychological *30 aars henstand* (*Thirty Years of Respite*, 1944) have been completed. A study of a mother's evil influence on her children is presented by Knud Sonderby in *En kvinde er overflodig* (*A Superfluous Woman*, 1942). In Finland Maria Jetuni produces an effective fifteenth-century study, *Klaus Louhikkon Herra* (*Klaus, Lord of Louhikko*, 1941). Most significant of all these dramatists seems to be the Swedish Stig Dagerman, whose striking modern allegory, *Den dödsdömde* (*Condemned to Death*, 1944), and whose picture, in *Skuggan av Mart* (*The Shadow of Mart*, 1948), of a youth eclipsed in the shadow of an elder brother killed in the war have rich promise.

With the possible exception of the last-named author, however, these various efforts hardly suggest either that a new individual style in drama is being evolved or that any new star is about to make its appearance in the theatrical heavens.

THE DRAMA IN FRANCE

In Paris, however, we do feel the presence of a dramatic movement which, because searching out new ways, promises fresh vision for the future.

During the long German occupation, of course, the progress of the Parisian stage was seriously interrupted, but even within that time a truly surprising vitality is apparent, while the post-war seasons have brought forward numerous dramas which, even if we do not like the tone of all of them, are interesting in form and content. So diverse, indeed, are the methods taken by the playwrights that it is difficult to know how best to deal with them.

Perhaps for convenience we may start with that author who has, of late, been more than any other in the field of public discussion, Jean-Paul Sartre. The 'existentialism' with which his name is associated does not have much consequence. Rather an attitude than a definite philosophy, the existentialist creed may be regarded as being, to a large extent, a development from the creeds of the surrealists and others who made strident the between-war years. In effect it recognizes, like them, the presence in man of powers wholly outside the range of the reason, but at the same time it does not propose to concentrate all its attention upon such powers. Rather, the existentialist declares that as man applies himself rationally to the consideration of any aspect of life he is constantly being confronted, to his dismay, by concepts which, so far from merely being outside the range of reason, are utterly opposed to it. In human life, therefore, there is an ever-present irony and paradox. It is precisely this paradoxical irony that the existentialists claim should be the subject-matter of art.

In arguing thus they are introducing nothing new. When Shakespeare makes Hamlet think of the wonder of man which is, after all, a mere quintessence of dust he is being a true existentialist, so far as the basic 'philosophy' is concerned—for Kierkegaard, on whom the moderns so often rely, founded most of his thought on the one essential paradox of the finiteness allied to the eternal nature of man. What distinguishes Sartre is the peculiar bitterness with which the paradox is expressed and, as it were, the concentration rather on the quintessence of dust than on the wonder of man. Unquestionably gifted with high talent and with a flair for the devising of effective dramatic scenes, Sartre chooses to employ these in the interests of ugliness. He loves all that is damp, oily, and viscous: in his imagery he displays a strange devotion to metaphors and similes taken from the processes of digestion. We get the impression that while Hamlet primarily thought of Alexander Sartre thinks primarily of the bung-hole.

A further series of paradoxes clearly animates this author's thought. Man makes the social world in which he lives, and yet each individual finds himself set in a situation over which he has no control, and there he is forced to act (if he would live), not necessarily doing the things he would have liked to do, but, instead, doing things which seem to offer the best alternatives. The individual thus is set before a great roulette table and gambles according to his intuition; the ball that spins on the edge of the wheel may stop at his number; as likely as not it will pass it by. To this is added another reflection. Man is a social animal, yet again each individual is a lonely entity, his heaven and his hell within him. This paradox means that, while we are gregarious, our souls always remain lonely entities.

These fragments of philosophy find expression in Sartre's plays and give them their peculiar tone. In *Huis clos* (*Vicious Circle*, or *No Exit*, 1944) three dead people, Garcin, Estelle, and Inez, are presented as in hell; but hell has no fires, it is a Second Empire drawing-room, and the torments of the damned are the torments created by the fact that these three are doomed for ever to live together in nerve-strung misery. The cruel Garcin, the homosexual Inez, and Estelle, the child-murderess, now can never hope to escape from one another. For Sartre "Hell is . . . other people." Even more characteristic is *Les mouches* (*The Flies*, 1943), since here the author has taken the Orestes story for retreatment, and in his handling of the theme so often put upon the stage we can readily mark the qualities of his style. The Furies here are become flies— flies that plague Argos, that bring putrefaction in their midst, and that are reflections of the human beings inhabiting the city's confines. "This Argos is a nightmare city," says the Tutor;

> Squeals of terror everywhere, people who panic the moment they set eyes on you, and scurry to cover, like black beetles, down the glaring streets.

Other cities in Greece have happiness; here only is the cult of the dead and the constant confession of sin; Electra herself has as her duty the washing of the palace's dirty linen. Orestes would fain do nothing, yet he feels an urgent need to 'belong'; in his native town he walks a stranger. "But, mind you," he remarks,

> if there were something I could do, something to give me the freedom of the city; if, even by a crime, I could acquire their memories, their hopes and fears, and fill with these the void within me, yes, even if I had to kill my own mother——

And later he puts this thought into even clearer terms:

> What do I care for happiness? I want my share of memories, my native soil, my place amongst the men of Argos.

Thus he goes to his mission. Desperately the Furies, ministers of the gods, try to divide Orestes and Electra. Her they spare because she offers to give up her life to atonement, but he refuses the throne that is offered to him if he will repudiate his crime. He alone stands defying the gods, and is consequently the object of their jealous hate.

Other aspects of Sartre's interests are shown in *Morts sans sépulture* (*Unburied Dead*, 1946), wherein every device is used to portray the utmost in stage horror, including the torture of a Resistance prisoner by the Vichy police, and in *La putain respectueuse* (*The Law-abiding Whore*, 1946), with its sardonic treatment of lynching in the southern states of America. Here, as elsewhere in his work, there is an inordinate attraction towards the torment of life—a tendency that, in its exaggeration, might well seem to put him on a level with some of the gloomier naturalists of the turn of the century. In Sartre, however, does appear a genuine passion for the creation of a new kind of tragedy, wherein situation rather than character is the dominant force. "A man who is free within the circle of his own situations," he says, "who chooses, whether he wishes to or not, for every one else when he chooses for himself—that is the subject-matter of our plays. . . . In this we return to the concept of tragedy as the Greeks saw it." The characters in these ancient dramas, as he asserts, combine in themselves "transports of feeling which have their origin deep within us and expressions of impregnable will which are affirmations of systems of values and rights such as the rights of citizenship, the rights of the family, individual ethics, collective ethics, the right to kill, the right to reveal to human beings their pitiable condition, and so forth." His vision at least is the vision of the tragic.

Closely associated with Sartre is Albert Camus, author of *Le malentendu* (*Cross Purpose*, 1944) and *Caligula* (1945). The former is a not very inspiring drama based on the old legend, already familiar in stage form, of the unwitting murder by parents of their son, returned after long absence. In Camus' hands the story takes shape as a tale of an elderly woman living alone with her daughter. They dream of one thing only—amassing sufficient money to get away from the town in which they dwell and to spend the rest of their lives by the seashore. Running a boarding-house, they have murdered several travellers and stolen their goods; now only a little more is needed. A young man arrives: the sister, through some intuition she cannot explain to herself, would spare him, but the mother is adamant. In the morning, the deed done, they discover that he was the son of the house, who had concealed his identity in order not to give his mother and sister too great a shock. *Caligula* has more originality, and there is a strange tension in this powerful study of a man granted power of life and death who pursues a phrenetic course of complete nihilism. He dreams of having the moon, and, knowing that that is impossible, madly seeks to dominate over the men who are his subjects. This indeed is the world of lunacy. In his madness Caligula tries to demonstrate to all men the absurdity of living. There is a simple strength here in the presentation of the idea. Caligula's first entry is characteristic of the author's style:

> *The stage remains empty for a moment.* CALIGULA *enters furtively at the left. He has a distraught air; he is dirty; his hair is wet, his legs are filthy. Frequently he puts his hand to his mouth. He goes up to the mirror and stops when he sees his reflection. He mumbles something indistinctly, then sits down at the right, his knees far apart and his arms hanging between them.* HÉLICON *enters at the left. Seeing* CALIGULA, *he stops at the side of the stage and watches him in silence.* CALIGULA *turns and catches sight of him. A pause.*

> HÉLICON [*to some one offstage*]: Good–day, Caius.
> CALIGULA [*simply*]: Good–day, Hélicon. [*A pause.*
> HÉLICON: You seem tired?
> CALIGULA: I've walked a lot.
> HÉLICON: Yes, you've been away a long time. [*A pause.*
> CALIGULA: It was hard to find.
> HÉLICON: What?
> CALIGULA: What I was looking for.
> HÉLICON: And what were you looking for?
> CALIGULA [*still speaking simply*]: The moon.

Through the long horrors of a play, in which this madman has power of life and death over the whole of the civilized world, this image of the moon remains before us. As Caligula first appeared before us so we leave him. Haggard in visage, he talks at the end to his mirrored image:

> Caligula! You also, you also, you are to blame. A little more, a little less. But who can dare to condemn me in this world without a judge, where no one is innocent? [*In a piteous tone, close to the mirror*] You see? Hélicon hasn't come. I shan't have the moon. . . . If I had had the moon . . .

Another author adhering to the existentialist group is Simone de Beauvoir, whose *Les bouches inutiles* (*The Useless Mouths*, 1945) gives as good an example as any of what Sartre describes as the aim of his fellows in presenting dramatic figures on the stage: the authors seek, Sartre says, to show "the anguish of a man who is both free and of good will, who in all sincerity is trying to find out the side he must take, and who knows that when he chooses the lot of others he is at the same time choosing his own pattern of behaviour." In de Beauvoir's story of a mayor who, when his city is besieged, is faced with the dilemma of getting rid of the 'useless mouths' (the old men, the children, the women) or of letting the entire citizenry starve, de Beauvoir gives us a primal type of the situation that oppresses the imagination and disturbs the dreams of the existentialists. Kierkegaard's famous "Either—or" is here incorporated in dramatic form.

What will come of this new kind of drama we cannot tell: undoubtedly, however, the existentialist style has some of its course still to run in France, and already there are signs of its influence abroad. Perhaps we may not be wrong in suggesting that something of its spirit appears in O'Neill's latest work: he may not have been directly influenced by Sartre, yet there is something in common between the dark irony of *The Iceman Cometh* and the bitterness that breathes a plague on Argos. It is probable that this latest artistic fashion will have a force in the theatre akin to that of surrealism—proving more important for its indirect influence than for what is composed confessedly in the existentialist form.

ANOUILH AND OTHERS

Experimentation in form, the quest for the impossible, the dissatisfaction with the present, have all been marked features of the Parisian theatre during recent years. Life's torment dominates in *Les vivants* (1946), by Henri Troyat, although a philosophy less dark than Sartre's colours his story of men and women in early Renaissance Florence surrounded by the menace of the Black Death. Bitterness that expresses itself in harshly incisive scenes appears in the *Asmodée* (1937) of François Mauriac, wherein the portrait of the tutor Couture, with his mixture of evil and good, has strength even if we may find that strength distasteful. This author later turns to compose, in *Les mal aimés* (*The Ill-beloved*, 1945), a tense prose tragedy which clearly demonstrates its indebtedness to the Racine tradition. An elderly man, de Virelade, depends on his daughter, Élisabeth; she falls in love with Alain, a man six years her junior; her father practically forces a marriage between him and her younger sister, Marianne, without, however, succeeding in breaking the passion that he has for Élisabeth and she for him. At the end it seems as though she is to go off with her lover, but unexpectedly she returns, weary, prepared to sacrifice herself and take up her burden once more.

Pessimism once more intrudes into another of those many

modern French plays based on ancient classical material—the *Megarée* (1946) of Maurice Druon, wherein the prophet Tirésias is made into a politician who invents a premonitory dream simply because he needs to inspire a hero to animate the flagging powers of the Theban army. For *La course des rois* (*The Sport of Kings*, 1947) Thierry Maulnier takes the myth of Hippodamia, the princess whose hand is to be given to the man who can outdistance her father Œnomaos at the races. All the suitors fail until Pelops suborns the King's charioteer, Myrtilos, whom later he slays. Here the stress is rather on the psychological relation between the monarch and his daughter than upon political implications, although these too play their part in the development of the action.

Irony rules in the fifteenth-century fantasy of René Laporte, *Fédérigo* (1945), wherein a lord gambles with others' lives until he loses his own. It is indeed interesting to see how, in vastly different ways and in situations taken from all periods of history, this concept of the individual in relation to society and of the contrast between man's aspirations and his ability has laid its spell on the Parisian stage. Numerous other single plays of related interest might here be recorded—such as Maurice Clavel's powerful study of ordinary human beings under the impact of war, *Les incendiaires* (*The Incendiary Bombs*, 1946), or the strange psychological melodrama by Pierre Montazel, *Le Fauteuil Voltaire* (1945), wherein a character murdered at the beginning of the action pursues with his spirit the other persons in the play, or Roger Ferdinand's study of children in the black market (*J 3*, 1947), or Pierre-Maurice Richard's tense prisoner-of-war play, *Le retour* (*The Return*, 1947)—but here perhaps it is sufficient to close this rapid survey of modern French playwriting by alluding to the work of a few authors who for diverse reasons seem to merit individual attention. In *L'immaculée* (*The Virgin Mother*, 1947) Philippe Hériat draws a peculiar picture of a woman who wants a child without a man, is given her wish by the skill of a doctor, and finds that the daughter thus born to her is so horrified that she is prepared to give herself to the first man she encounters. Rigid austerity and religious thought dominate in the work of Henry de Montherlant. Montherlant is an aristocrat, and in the interests of the aristocratic cult of perfection he is willing to sacrifice all, going so far, indeed, in *Fils de personne* (*No One's Son*; printed 1944) to show a father who, looking upon his mediocre son and feeling that no such vulgar thing should belong to him, permits the youth to die. More impressive, although less theatrical, is *Le maître de Santiago* (1947), which presents an interesting and strongly drawn portrait of a Spanish grandee who finds himself almost alone in his passionate devotion to the ancient code, and who sees in the discovery of the Indies the ruination of all that Spain means to him. The same atmosphere is present in *La reine morte* (*The Dead Queen*, 1942), a drama dealing with Inez de Castro. A similar preoccupation with religious concepts, it may be observed, comes into the interesting scenes of Fabien Reignier's *À l'approche du soir du monde* (*Nearing the World's End*, 1945), set in the period of Calvinism.

Much more fully gifted with theatrical qualities is Armand Salacrou, who, after several early essays, began to attract attention when his surrealistically inclined drama of passion, *Patchouli*, appeared in 1930. This was followed by the strange *Atlas-Hôtel* (1931), by the study of a big-business man in *Les frénétiques* (*Frenzy*, 1934), and by the analysis of a girl's fear of bourgeois domesticity in *Une femme libre* (*A Free Woman*, 1934). Then came the much more important and distinguished *L'inconnue d'Arras* (*The Unknown Woman of Arras*, 1935), with its highly original plot in which, again in a modified surrealistic manner, a man who has shot himself finds all his life and his dreams passing before him. His family, his mistresses, appear in his visions, and among them figures centrally in his mind the Arras girl of whom he does not even know the name. After an experimental *Un homme comme les autres* (*A Man like the Others*, 1936) Salacrou greatly added to his fame with *La terre est ronde* (*The Earth is Round*, 1938), an interesting play in which a technical novelty is introduced in the form of what might almost be called entr'acte prayers by Savonarola, and in which an attempt is made to reveal certain eternal conflicts present now, as in the past, among human beings. The action here takes place in the year 1492, and the tone of the drama, with its contemporary implications, is revealed by the very first words we hear as the curtain rises. Manente, a rich middle-aged apothecary, is speaking:

> No! No! No! I shan't let you talk in 1492 as we talked in 1482. Even stupidity, sir, must have its limits. . . . In ten years there have been great changes, sir! Progress——

In an interesting manner Salacrou proceeds to present a picture of Florence in the time of Savonarola, when men to their amazement learned that the earth, instead of being flat, was round, and when great disturbances of soul swept the land:

> SILVIO: I've just heard an extraordinary thing. Just think, Luciana, it seems that the earth is round.
> LUCIANA: What earth?

SILVIO: Ours.

LUCIANA: I don't understand.

SILVIO: Beyond Florence, there is Fiesole, Monte Cassino, the mean city of Pisa, and then savage lands and great dark seas. Well, all these things are nothing but a globe in the heavens.

LUCIANA: This is a joke?

SILVIO: Listen: some sailors set out from the south of Spain towards the setting sun. They spread out their sails and went straight westwards, and one morning these sails appeared among the islands of Greece.

This geographical fact Salacrou renders into a spiritual symbol: the earth is round, he hints, and what happened yesterday will come again to-day or to-morrow.

In *Histoire de rire* this ironically solemn style gives place to acidulous laughter, in which a story of two wives with lovers is told as though by a Noel Coward with a philosophy. Its last words are those of Gérard and Adélaide. "Their grand passion?" says he. "Nothing but a matter for laughter." "A matter for laughter?" she answers. "How sad!" Like others of his period Salacrou is continually searching and hoping to find absolute truth, absolute devotion, and absolute integrity.

In 1946 appeared another expression of Salacrou's philosophy, *L'Archipel Lenoir, ou, il ne faut pas toucher aux choses immobiles* (*The Lenoir Archipelago; or, Fixed Ideas shouldn't be Interfered With*). This is an amusingly satiric and penetrating scene of a family conference in the Lenoir household. The main title is explained by Victor Lenoir's comment on his relatives: "We are," he says, "exactly like little islands, separated from each other, living each for himself. . . . However, when a number of little islands get together they form an archipelago. The Archipelago Lenoir." The archipelago in this instance is created when it is discovered that Grandfather Paul-Albert Lenoir has attempted to ravish a young girl: the girl's father is adamant—Paul-Albert will be brought to court; and as a result the family faces shame and probably loss of revenue from the source of their fortunes, the famous Lenoir wine, concocted according to a secret recipe. The police are waiting downstairs, and they discuss what they should do. They first think how good it would be if Grandpapa were to die; then they toy with the idea of killing him; and finally they argue him into committing suicide. Adolphe hands him a revolver. Grandpapa hesitates. "But," says Adolphe, "you will always live in our memory."

GRANDFATHER: Yes, when I'm dead, I'll live a little so far as you're concerned, but for my part I'll be quite dead. . . .

ADOLPHE: I've never admired you so much. Take this revolver, and in a moment of courage——

GRANDFATHER: But an eternity of courage is needed for suicide. . . .

ADOLPHE: They're knocking at the door. Take this revolver——

[GRANDFATHER *takes the revolver. Silence.*

GRANDFATHER: What if I shoot at you instead of at myself?

ADOLPHE: Are you crazy?

Calmly the old man explains that if he were to shoot them all they would not have to suffer from his dishonour. In a frenzy Adolphe demands the revolver back, and the play ends in a tumultuous question-mark:

A struggle begins. The curtain begins to descend slowly. GRANDFATHER'S *voice is heard calling:* "Valentine! Valentine!" *Then there is a shot. And the*

CURTAIN

reaches the stage.

This author's later play, *Les nuits de la colère* (*Nights of Wrath*, 1947), essays, perhaps not with complete success, to reveal the meannesses of life by dealing with a theme of the Occupation and by giving it novelty through a theatrical trick. As the curtain rises we find ourselves in the midst of a fight between members of the Resistance and their opponents. This done, the play then moves to another atmosphere, wherein the dead and the living take part in a controversy, through which the dramatist seeks, as it were, to penetrate into the hearts of some of those left living and to demonstrate how the petty affections and the trivial calls of the selfish mood can be as potent for evil as positive wickedness. So much of life for Salacrou is a matter for laughter and regret, the world a place where but to think is to be full of sorrow.

Somewhat of the same spirit, but deepened and made tragic, appears in the works of the third author, perhaps the most original dramatist of our present generation, Jean Anouilh. Anouilh started his stage career as far back as 1932 with *L'Hermine*, but it is only during recent years that he has come to his own and that his genius has been fully recognized. Characteristically this recognition has come through appreciation of his skill and his power in the exploitation of the ancient world of classical legend. In 1941 appeared his *Eurydice*, in 1942 *Léocadia*, in 1944 *Antigone*, and in 1946 *Médée*. The individual quality of these works derives from a strange mingling of ironic sarcasm and of healthy assurance, from a sense that, more than many of his companions, this author is searching passionately for the truth, and from a flexible style that moves from quiet limpidity to torrential force.

In general, we may follow the author himself in dividing his works into "pièces noires," where the tragic sentiment reigns, and "pièces roses," where the fantastic is allowed free sway. Among the latter are *Le bal des voleurs* (*The Thieves' Ball*, 1938), a clever comedy-ballet, in which a trio of thieves pose as gentlemen of Spain and disport themselves hilariously and ironically in the fashionable villa of an English lady, *Le rendez-vous de Senlis* (1941), and *Léocadia*. Both of the last-mentioned comedies introduce the familiar play-within-the-play technique. The first shows a young Georges who has married, for money, a girl he does not love, but whose money serves to supply the needs of his disreputable parents and of his friend Robert, whose wife, Barbara, is his mistress. To the distress of these characters, Georges falls in love with Isabelle. He tells her of his family, paints them in glowing colours, and then is forced to engage a couple of actors to impersonate his father and mother. His family, however, summon him back to town at the crucial moment: Isabelle learns the truth, and, on his promise to reform, goes off with him. *Léocadia* tells the story of a young nobleman who, mourning the death of an actress whom he loved, is surrounded with a theatrically contrived environment recalling her being, but when a young midinette is engaged to take the rôle of the lost mistress she shatters the fabric of the dream and a new love enters.

These plays are charmingly fantastic, and it is with justice that some spectators have seen here a re-evocation of the spirit of Musset, but it is not in them that Anouilh's genius most clearly is exhibited. In his tragic plays, his "pièces noires," he shows his full strength. Here he takes from Pirandello's interest in the complexities of human personality, from Bernard's concentration upon analysis of the human soul, from Racine's precision and his appreciation of sentiment, from Sophocles' majestic grandeur, and creates a dramatic world all his own.

His earliest dramas, *L'Hermine*, *Mandarine* (1933), *Le voyageur sans bagages* (*The Traveller without Luggage*, 1937), and *La sauvage* (*The Savage*, 1938), indicate his almost pessimistic attitude towards life. He sees men and women surrounded by pettiness and meanness. The poor young lover, Franz, in *L'Hermine* is forced into committing murder in order to obtain his aristocratic sweetheart, and even then he loses her; the heroine of *La sauvage* finds herself compelled, because of her parents' disreputable lives, to give up her love; in *Le voyageur sans bagages* a soldier who has lost his memory discovers a past, vicious and disgusting, of which he has no recollection.

In *Eurydice* this atmosphere reappears, but with a completer mastery and a deeper vision. Here enters in Anouilh's most characteristic concept. Happiness is for him an illusory thing, and the soul's deepest satisfaction often, perhaps always, comes when we sacrifice what seems to be our happiness. Orphée is a violinist in a saloon, Eurydice a third-rate actress. Meeting on a station platform, they find they are both searching pathetically for a purity of spirit beyond their reach. Eurydice, however, cannot escape from her sordid past, and death, in the shape of Henri, a commercial traveller, takes her. Orphée is given the chance of bringing her back to life, but he tries too soon to penetrate her secret, and she passes back into death's hands. In the end he goes to seek her:

MONSIEUR HENRI [*going towards him, smiling*]: You always want to know everything, little man. . . . I like you. I've been sorry to see you suffer. But that'll soon be done with. You'll see how everything will become pure, luminous, limpid. . . . A world for you, little Orphée. . . .

ORPHÉE: What have I to do?

MONSIEUR HENRI: Take your coat, it's cold outside. Go out of town by the road lying before you. Where the houses become fewer and farther between, you'll come to a cliff, near a little olive grove. It's there.

ORPHÉE: What?

MONSIEUR HENRI: Your rendezvous with death. At nine o'clock. It's nearly that time now; don't keep it waiting.

ORPHÉE: I'll see Eurydice again?

MONSIEUR HENRI: At once.

ORPHÉE [*taking his coat*]: Then I'll go. Adieu.

MONSIEUR HENRI: Au revoir, little man.

There is an infinite pity here, and a profound repose. "My dear," cries Eurydice when she sees him, "how long you've been," but now, in death, the pair will never part.

Antigone presents a similar picture. Antigone goes, as in the Sophoclean drama, to bury her brother, Polyneices, but this she does, not so much because of devotion to his memory, but because of her dissatisfaction with the crass, timorous, unadventuresome society around her. Even when she is offered mercy by Créon she refuses it; for her, too, death alone can hold inviolate the serenity of spirit that has come to her from her daring. She goes, as she tells Créon, to "a realm which you cannot enter with all your wrinkled wisdom."

The themes of *Eurydice* and of *Antigone* present, as it were, the quintessence of Anouilh's philosophy—the concept that the most precious things can be found only in a realm beyond the limits of this terrestrial existence. Such a philosophy, however, leads towards the cult of death, and perhaps there are signs in his two latest plays, *Roméo et Jeannette* and *Médée* (both 1947), that his ideas are changing shape. The former shows a young boy, engaged to a thoroughly 'nice' and respectable girl, Julia, suddenly falling tempestuously and tragically in love with his fiancée's sister, Jeannette; but Jeannette is neither 'nice' nor respectable—she is depraved and violent in her passions. In some respects she is akin to the Medea who is painted in *Médée*, and when we see Jason, worn out with the wild criminality into which this witch has led him, seeking escape in the quiet conventional love of Creusa we recognize that Anouilh's latest steps are leading him towards a goal somewhat different from that which was his objective in *Eurydice*.

Although there are still things wanting in Anouilh's art, he has a truer sense than any other playwright belonging to the latest generation of what tragedy means, and to its noble confines he approaches nearer than any. In melodrama, as he sees clearly, and in the ordinary drama we have merely a series of common things— of villains, distressed maidens, revengers. In melodrama there are "glimmers of hope" and "men are afraid of death as they are afraid of accidents." As we follow the plot we are ever waiting for the hero to dash in with the police on the nick of time. "In the tragic realm," says Anouilh, "we are quiet of heart." Here is no record of a killer and of one who is killed. "Tragedy, above all, is reposeful, because we know that there is no more hope." In the ordinary drama men struggle because there is always the thought that there may be an escape: in tragedy all is resignation.

Remembering the success of Anouilh's *Antigone* in Paris, remembering that an *Œdipus* was one of the theatrical triumphs of London's 1946 season, and that an *Orestes* has lately found welcome in Warsaw's Teatr Polski, noting, too, the long series of dramas from many lands which have sought to reinterpret the ancient classical myths—plays as diverse as Werfel's *Die Troerinnen* (*The Trojan Women*, 1913), Mell's *Die Sieben gegen Theben* (*The Seven against Thebes*, 1931), and *Le roi Candule* (1901) of André Gide—may we not see in this return to the concepts of Greek tragedy one of the most potent forces in the theatre of our age? And for an age that finds within itself the strength to embrace the tragic concept there is the hope which, paradoxically, it is the very mission of tragedy to deny.

During those years which, for convenience, may be called the Ibsen years the ancient and hallowed forms of tragedy and comedy were completely confounded and the prophecy uttered in the eighteenth-century sentimental drama was fulfilled. Men could not laugh without weeping, they could find nothing at which their mockery could not be directed; they lost the power to see life in the clear terms of a *Lysistrata* or of an *Antigone*. In rediscovering the meaning of tragedy—even when the ultimate power of the universe is viewed as an infernal machine or as a jealous Jupiter—the French authors of our time are suggesting a new future for the theatre. In disregarding all the long course of the theatre from the end of the eighteenth century to the beginning of our own era they are testifying to the strength and integrity of their spirit. By finding inspiration in some of the most powerful myths of the human race they are once more bringing upon the stage the whole long pageant of humanity, instead of merely offering peep-show views of domestic interiors decorated with modern furniture and fashioned with ideas of merely temporary significance.

PART XIV

CONCLUSION

CONCLUSION

FROM Æschylus to Anouilh, from Sophocles to Shaw and Sartre, we have followed the wandering steps of the drama through a period of nearly two thousand five hundred years. Within these ages we have seen four great peaks of accomplishment—the ancient Greek, including the work of four authors (Æschylus, Sophocles, Euripides, and Aristophanes); the Elizabethan English, with Shakespeare shining as a major planet in a brilliant galaxy; the seventeenth-century French, with Molière and Racine; and the late nineteenth-century Scandinavian, dominated by the achievements of Ibsen and Strindberg.

Beside these peaks stand many other eminences, not so lofty, perhaps, yet all rising sharply above the vast undulating plain made up of the current fare provided by the playhouses. The first of these is the New Comedy of Menander and the closely related dramatic work of Plautus and Terence. Next comes the international and almost wholly anonymous theatre of the Middle Ages, noteworthy rather for the extent of its scope and the cumulative effect of its innumerable pageant-scenes than for any individual masterpieces. The mystery play, like the ballad, exists as a corporate, communal whole; even the most appealing scenes or stanzas derive their emotional power rather from the common soil out of which they spring than from their own brilliance. During the period of the Renaissance, while France and Italy failed to produce any literary work of interest, the Spanish drama almost vies with the Elizabethan English and certainly has a worth easily commensurate with the immediately contemporary achievements of the Jacobean playwrights. At the same time Italy, whose dramatists produced nothing of consequence, gives birth to a form of stage entertainment —the *commedia dell' arte*—which by a strange magic not only captures the attention of every theatre in that time, but also lays its spell on later stages.

From the time of Racine and Molière on to the days of Ibsen, diverse dramatic developments attract our attention. In England the Restoration comedy of manners produces something strictly limited in scope, but unique in flavour. Half a century later Venice suddenly sponsors a rich flowering in the work of Gozzi and Goldoni, while only a few decades after that time a uniting Italy finds in Alfieri a poet who, while not of the highest rank, displays a strength and vigour in the neo-classic style such as meets with only one rival—the French Voltaire. From Italy the impulse moves to Germany, with Lessing and Schiller wresting dramatic form out of romantic sentiment, and then once more reverts to France, first expressing itself in the neo-romantic flamboyance of Victor Hugo, and afterwards finding opportunity in the play of ideas as cultivated by Dumas *fils* and Augier.

Ibsen's power makes the earlier realistic efforts seem feeble, while alongside Ibsen appears the still stronger but less essentially theatrical genius of Strindberg. Hauptmann vies with these, but, having a less assured sense of purpose and a weaker spirit, falls below their efforts. In contrast with Strindberg, George Bernard Shaw handles his dramatic material with consummate ease and to a certain extent shifts the theatre's focus back again to the playhouses of London. Characteristic of the modern movement in stage affairs, however, is the wide area it embraces. Hitherto one country at any particular time had tended to take the lead: now, in addition to London, we find other centres producing work of peculiar excellence: Russia with her Chekhov, Ireland with Synge—and of course it need not be said that Shaw, although writing chiefly for the English stage, is an Irishman—Spain with Benavente, Italy with Pirandello, Austria with Schnitzler, the United States with Eugene O'Neill—and even such a list does not take into account the inspirational quality of numerous playwrights from many lands whose achievements, while perhaps not rivalling in quality the work of those mentioned above, have had the power to suggest fresh methods of dramatic treatment or unexplored territory to be exploited. One thinks, for example, of the Russian Andreev, the German Toller, the Czech Čapek, the Hungarian Molnár, the French Cocteau, the Belgian Maeterlinck, and a host of others, each with an individual approach towards theatrical form. Even without alluding to those belonging to the latest generations, we can readily admit that the sweep and the range here are unequalled by anything in the past, even while at the same time we are forced to confess that no single plays of these years are worthy of being set against an *Antigone*, a *Birds*, a *Hamlet*, or a *Tartuffe*.

To devise any neat formula which may explain the shifting fortunes of the theatre among these various countries is, of course, an impossible task. Not any formula can show us precisely why certain countries, such as Portugal, Mexico, Brazil, and Switzerland, have yielded little of real worth to the stage; not any formula can provide a complete explanation of the sudden dying away of the dramatic impulse in one area and of its equally sudden quickening elsewhere. At the same time a few general observations can be made, and from some of these conclusions may be drawn.

THE DRAMATIST

First we may consider the characteristics of the greater dramatic authors. One thing immediately attracts our attention: in general these authors have shown themselves to be late starters and long endurers. Shakespeare in this is typical. His first theatrical essays cannot have come much before he reached the age of twenty-seven; he must have been in his thirties when he was attaining mastery; his great tragedies came when he was about forty, and one of his most lovely plays, *The Tempest*, was presumably written as he approached his fiftieth year. A similar pattern is exhibited elsewhere. So many of the early Greek dramas have perished that we cannot speak of their creators' development with great assurance, but sufficient facts remain to yield at least a general picture. Æschylus was nearly thirty before he became a playwright; his *Oresteia* came when he was in his sixties. Sophocles produced his first play at the age of twenty-five, and when fifty-eight defeated Euripides in contest. At the age of twenty-five Euripides presented his first play, but had to wait another fourteen years before he won a victory; he was seventy-four when his last was written. Aristophanes began earlier, but his highest achievements came about the time he was over thirty, and he continued his career until he was sixty.

In seventeenth-century France, Racine was twenty-five when his first play appeared, but he was close to thirty before *Andromaque* brought him success. Molière's first triumph came when he was thirty-seven, and he was over fifty when he wrote *Le malade imaginaire*. Ibsen, born in 1828, produced *The Feast at Solhaug* in 1856; *When We Dead Awaken* was penned in 1899. Shaw did not start writing plays until he was in his middle thirties, *St Joan* came when he was aged sixty-seven, and *King Charles's Golden Days* when he was eighty-three.

The pattern is, of course, by no means complete. There are, indeed, violent exceptions, such as Schiller's schoolboy experiments in penning *Die Räuber*. Yet the outline is sufficiently constant to indicate that it is rare for extreme youth to produce dramatic work of quality, that mastery of theatrical form commonly comes in an author's mid-career, and that age may, and often does, yield masterpieces in this kind.

For these qualities of playwriting endeavour the causes would appear to lie in two things—the necessity for the incorporation within the dramatic framework of human character closely and maturely observed, and the very considerable technical demands made by theatrical form. The dramatic is distinguished from the lyrical in that the latter depends almost wholly on the expression of the poet's personality, whereas the former must ever fuse into a single unity the objective and the subjective. From the novel the drama is distinguished by the fact that the requirements of the stage impose on a play a tightness of structure such as narrative fiction need never have. A novel may ramble; a play must move forward with assured gait, conscious of its path, and with an end exactly timed.

While there can be no doubt but that certain authors are able almost by instinct to grasp the essentials of this dramatic form, an examination of the works of the more notable playwrights indicates clearly that attainment of mastery is no easy thing and that every great theatrical author has had to add to his instinctive divinations of stage effect by the exercise of hard and tedious experiment. There is some truth buried in the Russian remark that for a man who would make a success in the theatre the first thirty years are always the most difficult.

In addition to these requirements—the mastery of form and the mature observation of human thought and emotion—there is another. No doubt the excellence of a play depends very largely upon the skill with which its plot is wrought and upon the vividness with which the author conceives his characters; but beyond such things, and still more important, is the command of effective words. Dramatic style is not easily attained, since once more it must create a double impression. Just as the great dramatist must give free play to his characters and yet introduce the flavouring of his own personality to the action in which these characters appear, so he must evolve for himself such a style as will give the double impression of individuality (his own individuality) and of appropriateness to the person into whose mouth the particular lines are put. We thus speak of a passage as essentially 'Shakespearian' and at the same time recognize that the words are entirely fitting for a Hamlet, a Lear, a Falstaff or a Dame Quickly. The consequence is that a playwright who starts in the lyrical vein, evolving a language suited to the expression of his own individuality, must seek, by painful endeavour, to hammer or mould that language so that, without losing the qualities which make it unique, it enlarges its scope and becomes richer in potentiality.

There is still another thing to be observed in connexion with this question of language. It may perhaps be averred that no true greatness in the world of drama can be attained unless an author, through the combination of native talent and laborious application to his art, devises for himself a form of language which for convenience may be called 'poetic.' For the poor journeyman or the realist wandering in confused error through these realms there can be no hope of endurance. When we think of those playwrights whose names are mightiest in the theatre, in the end we think of them as stylists. Æschylus, Sophocles, Euripides, Aristophanes, were all poets; preeminently a poet is Shakespeare. Congreve lingers in our minds because of his prose poetry, and Shaw has secured greatness above his fellows not only by the play of his wit, but also, and more potently, by the brilliance of his language and its peculiar flexibility. Goldoni sinks below Molière because he does not have the French author's sense of word values; in our own day O'Neill fails of greatness because he has not magical power over the words he employs. It cannot be too strongly stressed that fundamentally the art of the drama is a branch of the art of poetry.

Another observation can be made concerning the pattern of the playwright's work. Again and again we can find a movement which may be described as a passage from the historical-poetic or fanciful-poetic through the realistic on to the symbolic. *Richard II* and *A Midsummer Night's Dream*; *Othello* and *Measure for Measure*; *A Winter's Tale* and *The Tempest*—these plays may be related to Ibsen's series—*Peer Gynt* and *Lady Inger*; *Ghosts* and *A Doll's House*; *The Master Builder* and *When We Dead Awaken*. Shaw has *The Devil's Disciple*, *The Doctor's Dilemma*, and *On the Rocks*; even if we move back to ancient Greek days we see something of the same pattern in Euripides, with its symbolic ending in *The Bacchæ*.

It is not suggested here, of course, that this pattern is exact or universally applicable—such an effort would mean hopeless twisting of the facts. At the same time there is sufficient indication to show that quite commonly a great dramatic author starts by letting his imagination play colourfully upon life, moves from that to a sphere wherein, as it were, the imaginative process is tempered and restrained by observation of things perhaps hitherto ignored, and then travels forward in an attempt to make the theatre yield maybe more than it can possibly give. At the beginning of his career the playwright sees his *dramatis personæ* as airy fancies; in his middle career reality weighs on him more heavily; at the end of his life men and women become symbols of larger concepts.

Because the fancies, the realistically conceived portraits, and the symbols have to be dressed in theatrical clothes, the dramatist usually finds himself most fortunate if he is in some way connected with the stage, but this does not imply that he must be an actor or a producer. Indeed, it might almost be said that too close association with the practical theatre may do more harm than good. We speak of Shakespeare as an actor, and it is obviously impossible to deny that he was one; there is, on the other hand, every reason to believe that from his earliest associations with the Lord Chamberlain's men he was regarded by his fellows as more valuable in his capacity of playwright than in that of player. Racine was not a theatre man if Molière was; Shaw came to the stage from outside, and has proved a more successful creator of dramas than O'Neill, who was almost born on the boards. The truth is that, while clearly knowledge of theatrical practice is demanded of a playwright, too much of a mystery can be made of that practice, and if an author does not from the very beginning show an innate sense of stage requirement, no amount of acting or scene-shifting, no long training as player or producer, can hope to make of him more than a journeyman writer for the stage.

CHARACTERISTICS OF THE GREATER AGES OF THE DRAMA

If we turn from the particular author to consider the qualities animating those periods when the drama rose to special heights of expression some further observations can be made and conclusions reasonably drawn.

First we recognize immediately that, while dramatic power almost always appears in the midst of a general flowering of literature, the fact that a particular time and place are artistically productive by no means is a guarantee that the theatre of that place and time will yield work of true value. The truth of this observation is demonstrated sufficiently by the single example of the Romantic Revival in England: during those years, when poets from Wordsworth to Byron were exhibiting an imaginative intensity greater than anything that had been witnessed since Milton's days, the rama sank to levels almost incredibly abject. There was inspiration ere for the lyrical poet, for the novelist, for the author of creative criticism, but clearly some elements necessary for the encouragement of literature for the stage were lacking.

To declare, as is sometimes done, that the cause of this discrepancy between the poetic and the dramatic writings of the time is to be found in the 'lyrical' quality of these decades from 1790 to 1830 is by no means a sufficient answer. During this time there was a lively and widespread interest in the theatre both among the general unliterary public and among those professionally associated with the writer's craft. Hazlitt, Lamb, and, later, Dickens were thoroughly typical of their age in their frequenting of the playhouses and in their keen appreciation of theatrical values. Nor did the romantic period throw all its creative being into the composition of lyrics. From Scott through Jane Austen to Thackeray and Dickens the prose writers carried the novel to new levels, and, when we remember how anxiously Dickens dreamed of applying his talents to the service of the theatre, we might well have thought that the fictional technique, involving the presentation of diverse characters and the making of these characters speak in their own tongues, would, thus combined with interest in the drama, have yielded plays of more than common quality. Yet Scott could reach in this way no farther than the dully mediocre *The House of Aspen*, and Dickens could not rise above the trivial playlet of *The Lamplighter*. The dismal failure of the romantic poets must therefore be considered along with a corresponding failure on the part of the novelists; and these, taken in combination, certainly demand that the cause of the debility be sought elsewhere than in the 'lyrical' qualities of the time.

One further remark may be made in this connexion. Occasionally we find it stated that an age of great actors is *ipso facto* an age that produces little of worth in the dramatic kind. For evidence those who argue in this way point to the days of Garrick and, for the early nineteenth century, to the histrionic excellencies of Edmund Kean, Mrs Siddons, and Macready. We may, however, suggest that such arguments are based on insufficient authority and on insecure conjecture. In the first place, since the art of the actor has obviously no permanency, there can be no possibility of comparing one player's skill with the skill of another performer living at a different time. Who is to say that Betterton was greater than Burbage, Kean than Kemp? Who can aver with any assurance that the histrionic art of one period was superior to that of another? Here we move in a realm of uncertainties, and the endeavour to explain the dearth of dramatic genius, for example, in England during the eighteenth and early nineteenth centuries may well be casting unfair reflections on the ability of the Lord Chamberlain's company in the sixteenth century. The truth seems rather to be that when an age has little to offer in the way of powerful new plays contemporaries naturally tend to focus their attention on the non-literary parts of the performance in the theatres and in their comments give to these an emphasis possibly out of proportion to their worth. There can be no doubt that Edmund Kean was a very great actor, yet, even while fully recognizing his greatness, we are not in a position either to laud his genius above the genius of an Alleyn or to attribute to his power the weakness of contemporary playwrights.

In searching for the cause of dramatic flowering—or, at least, in seeking for a suggestion of some of the elements apparently essential to such flowering—another thing may be observed. When a rich dramatic productivity arises in any country it is usually of fairly short duration and is rarely expressed through the work of a single author. Sophocles, Shakespeare, Lope de Vega, Ibsen—these men do not stand alone. Sophocles had Æschylus, Euripides, and Aristophanes as companions; Shakespeare is merely the central figure in a great surge of theatrical energy that embraces, besides himself, men as various as Marlowe and Jonson, Beaumont and Fletcher, Webster and Shirley, Massinger and Middleton; Lope de Vega has Calderón by his side, and many others as well; Ibsen is not a solitary Scandinavian giant, but is supported by a Björnson and a Strindberg. Wherever we look, this is true: Etherege, Wycherley, Congreve; Racine and Molière; Gozzi, Goldoni, Metastasio, Alfieri; Lessing, Schiller, Goethe; Dumas *fils* and Augier; Synge and Yeats; Benavente and the Quintero brothers; O'Neill, Maxwell Anderson, Sherwood, Behrman: the association of groups of noteworthy dramatists at the same time indicates that whatever conditions are ultimately responsible for the development of richer styles in the theatre we need not look simply for the emergence of one man influencing others. In the Elizabethan age the circumstances are typical: Shakespeare is manifestly the greatest playwright-poet of his time, and no doubt his impress is firmly set on his successors, but before Shakespeare there was Marlowe, there was Lyly, there were Lodge and Greene and Peele. This at once suggests to us that, besides looking at the personal qualifications of individual authors, we ought to search for qualities animating the entire theatrical world of particular epochs.

If this is true, equally true is the rapidity with which a theatre will rise to prominence and decline. Æschylus' first play comes about the year 500 B.C.; before a century has passed all the glory of the Greek stage is gone. The Elizabethan drama takes characteristic form in the eighties of the sixteenth century; already by 1610 it has passed its peak, and it is vanished by 1640. Etherege and his companions endure for only about thirty years. The Golden Age in Spain has little longer a date. Between *Le Cid* of 1637 and the seventies of the seventeenth century Corneille, Racine, and Molière have accomplished and ended their task. Italy's dramatic flowering in the century following is embraced within a few brief decades; so, too, is the German romantic theatre of slightly later date. The realistic drama reaches culmination about 1880, and by 1900 it is virtually done. Much more than in any other field of literary endeavour, the playwriting impulse seems to move rapidly to a culmination, to die out in the place of its birth, and to be reborn elsewhere.

Pursuing this line of inquiry, we observe something more. All these periods of outstanding dramatic activity develop their own special styles, and their finest writers, building upon the achievements of their immediate predecessors, bring these styles to such a culmination as to leave little for their successors to do. Usually sufficient remains to permit of a short continuation of the effort, but in this continuation there are always evident the clear signs of deterioration. After Sophocles comes Euripides, after Shakespeare comes Fletcher. Perhaps the culmination is not so much a matter of subject and character as it is a matter of words. Dramatic writing is a peculiar thing: it must give the audience an impression of reality, and yet it must have within itself the power of transcending reality; it must have at its command all the resources of poetic speech, and yet it can never escape, as non-dramatic poetry so easily and so effectively may, into a realm wholly divorced from common utterance. The power of Shakespeare's dialogue rests in the fact that it is timeless even while it bears an obvious and a close relationship to the common language of his day. Thus the task of the dramatist becomes one different from that of the lyric poet. No doubt the latter is ever seeking for fresh means of expression; no doubt certain harmonies become, after a time, cloying, old-fashioned, powerless to inspire, gilt-o'er-dusted—as, for example, the music of the romantics became in the earlier years of the present century. At the same time, we do not find a Wordsworthian sonnet powerless to appeal because it borrows from Milton's music. No such borrowing is possible in drama: the theatrical efforts of the early-nineteenth-century poets are lifeless largely because these poets took Shakespeare as their model, without realizing that what was

2G

eminently proper for the sixteenth century had completely lost its balance with current speech after the passage of more than two hundred years.

What is required by the drama is a form of utterance which shall have a definite connexion with the ordinary speech of the period in which it is used. Shakespeare's blank verse had ceased to be an inspiring force in 1800 partly because this one author had explored all, or nearly all, its possibilities, but partly also because the current language of common existence had changed, so that, instead of having a close relationship to each other, a great chasm yawned between the speech familiar to the audiences of Drury Lane and the language they heard delivered on the stage.

This observation must, of course, be closely related to what we have already noted in the work of individual playwrights. As we have seen, the importance of style in dramatic dialogue becomes immediately apparent when we consider that every one of those dramatic authors who have raised their heads above the level of ordinary theatrical attainment either have been distinguished by the fact that the form of their utterance at once possesses a distinctive quality and is related by clear bonds to the speech of the time, or have failed to reach the heights they aimed at precisely because, like O'Neill, their means of expression proved inadequate to render in fitting terms the scenic concepts they wished to convey.

If, however, a particular form of dramatic speech ceases after a time to possess the inspirational power necessary to encourage the creation of new masterpieces, it does not by any means follow either that masterpieces of the past lose their appeal or that inspiration in general is not be to gained from contemplation of these masterpieces. The precise opposite, indeed, is true, and the modern dramatist who neglects his Shakespeare and his Sophocles does so at his soul's peril and to the detriment of his own art. It is obvious that there are certain plays wherein their authors have so perfectly harmonized concept and expression that their theatrical presentation, even in ages far removed in time and spirit, has the power to evoke enthusiasm and complete acceptance of their scenes. In this sense Shakespeare continues to live on the stage and to give delight. Even beyond this we may go, and declare that the history of the theatre has constantly shown how certain dramatic themes, already dealt with powerfully by playwrights of the past, have laid their eternal spell on succeeding authors. Whether Shakespeare was conscious that in his *Hamlet* the shade of Orestes walked the boards of the Globe Theatre we cannot tell, but we may not escape from believing that at least unconscious memories of the Agamemnon story were in his mind when he wrote of his Prince of Denmark. Concerning the deliberate endeavour of Eliot, O'Neill, Giraudoux, Sartre, and Anouilh to reframe some of these ancient dramatic themes there can be no doubt, and unquestionably among the most impressive of modern plays are those in which the authors, instead of inventing new plots, have taken their themes from their predecessors. The pathway to the temple of Thespis is liberally and graciously adorned with many statues raised in the images of Electra and of Œdipus.

Nor has this inspiration from past endeavour related itself only to the exploitation of certain themes which, for some strange reason, appear to be peculiarly fitted for dramatic treatment. As we look at those periods where the drama most freely flourished we can discern a kind of double germinating force wherein the excited rediscovery of some earlier effort that temporarily had been forgotten or that suddenly has assumed a fresh radiance is associated with a concept wholly novel. Shakespeare himself once more provides a prime example, with his wedding of Senecan and Plautan form to the romantic ideas of a new age; but the same double force may be found in an examination of the works of all dramatists who stand highest in the theatre's rolls. Racine unites an intense appreciation of what the Greeks had accomplished with a fresh aim; Goldoni marries the spirit of the *commedia dell' arte* to an eighteenth-century philosophical outlook. Even if we were merely to consider the manner in which Shakespeare's works have operated on the spirits of successive playwrights this judgment would be fully proved—although, again, we may note that the more likely the later dramatists are to be swayed by the Shakespearian form of expression the less fecund is the Elizabethan author's influence. Neither the romantic writers nor such moderns as Maxwell Anderson have profited by being so close to Shakespeare's language as to have their own dialogue pregnant with its echoes: where Shakespeare's works have proved most fruitful inspirers has been in countries of an alien tongue. Shakespeare could effectively and to good purpose arouse a Victor Hugo to fresh effort when he utterly failed to stimulate the English authors of the early nineteenth century, and even might be said to have had a blighting influence upon their spirits.

Commonly the union of the twin forces comes to yield fruitful results at times when the mood of the romantic overlaps the mood of the classicist. It is indeed rare that the stricter forms of classicism or the libertine shapes of romanticism offer dramatic work of worth. Greek classicism includes within itself many elements which, had they exhibited themselves in a later period, we should unhesitatingly have hailed as belonging to the world of romance: the surge of the surf in *Philoctetes* brings to the mind haunting shapes of a kind we do not associate with the colder forms of the classic imagination. Shakespeare gains part of his strength from his arrival at a time when the rediscovery of the classic genius was being superimposed upon and integrated with the medieval romantic spirit, and Ibsen comes at a time when a classical reaction is opposing itself to the fervours of a romanticism which, although decaying, still possesses elements of power.

The classical tempering of romantic enthusiasm seems demanded in the theatre by the severe restrictions that accompany stage representation. Lyrical abandon will not serve the playhouse; the author must ever keep his rational self master of his scenes and characters. When we encounter dramatic greatness the impression we receive is always one of emotional intensity restrained by the rigorous control of the author's mind. Dramas become weak when, on the one hand, excessive control sends a chill through the entire production or when, on the other, the writer so identifies himself emotionally with his creations as to become lost in their midst. The most powerful masters are those who, like God, are transcendant lords of the world of their imagination, yet immanent in this realm they themselves have wrought.

THEATRICAL CONDITIONS

But drama is, of course, not merely a thing of writing, and its flourishing depends as largely on the development of suitable theatrical forms as on the achievement of an appropriate literary style. It is, indeed, not too much to say that Sophocles depends upon the establishment of the Greek open-air playhouse, Shakespeare upon the evolution, just before his time, of the arena-like Elizabethan stage, and Ibsen upon the setting-up of the modern proscenium-frame peep-show. Just as no one form of dramatic dialogue will suit all ages, so all ages can never be satisfied with one single type of theatre; and it is noteworthy that almost always the great playwrights have appeared shortly after the creation of some new kind of stage or after some readjustment of the relationship between actors and audience. For the Greeks the theatre of Dionysus was precisely adjusted to their desires and their needs; the same structure would not have been in harmony with the spirit of the Renaissance. Out of neither the Greek nor the Elizabethan playhouse could Ibsen have wrought his greatest plays: either might have served for *Lady Inger of Ostrât*, but not for *The Wild Duck*. It will not, therefore, be far wrong to say that almost always we find dramatic genius flowering when a particular land in a particular age discovers a theatrical form that is new, adjusted to its demands, and hitherto not fully exploited. The only formidable exceptions to this generalization are those provided by certain smaller countries, such as Ireland at the beginning of the present century, when the theatre —any theatre—becomes for the first time associated with native aspirations.

This consideration leads to the thought that dramatic progress is likely to be inhibited during any lengthy period when a single theatrical form endures comparatively unaltered. This happened in ancient Greece, when the monumental stone playhouses retained their essential features (despite minor alterations) long after fresh demands called imperiously for other shapes. So, too, in the eighteenth century the familiarly established theatrical edifice, with its formalized auditorium and its wing-and-border stage, lasted too long to yield inspiration to the playwrights. Only with the development of such technical devices as allowed this kind of proscenium theatre to be used for realistic effects could it be invested with the power of stimulation. In our own times, when our theatres are built to last for decades, we are in danger of finding ourselves in a similar area of dramatic desolation.

All this is not to say, of course, that every theatre form, even when fully in accord with the spirit of its own period, has the same inspiring force at its command. The Elizabethan stage, for example, was a peculiarly flexible instrument, and because of its flexibility offered to the dramatists of the late sixteenth century peculiar opportunities. In it the actors were at once close to and distanced from the audience; action could take place on various planes; there could appear in it both scenes wherein the actors were concerned entirely with each other and scenes wherein the players made direct contact with the audience. In Ibsen's time the proscenium-frame playhouse was as well harmonized with the ideals of the age as Shakespeare's was harmonized with the ideals of the age of Elizabeth, but this playhouse was far less flexible than its predecessor. Here the actors were removed into a territory of their own; lateral action alone could be employed; and the opportunity of introducing scenes in which the stage characters might address the audience directly was denied to the playwrights. Thus, purely because of theatrical conditions, Ibsen found himself vastly less free than Shakespeare had been three hundred years before. What he actually accomplished could not, clearly, have been done in the Elizabethan framework, yet this fact should not blind us to the fact that the Elizabethan framework allowed Shakespeare to achieve things far beyond Ibsen's scope.

In this connexion another consideration must be put under review. A theatrical performance is manifestly something more than the uttering of a dramatist's lines by a group of actors. The appeal of the theatre is to the eye as well as to the ear, and producers are completely justified in employing every means at their command for the purpose of producing a unified impression. We may go even further and observe that, at certain times, new scenic devices may have the strength to stimulate dramatic effort: Ibsen's realistic plays are thus to be connected with the development of new methods for the securing of realistic visual effects, and the dramas of the expressionists were born of electricity. At the same time we cannot avoid noting that in those ages when a great dramatic movement is in decline scenery, show, 'productional' elements, take control of the stage. Scenic effects were rapidly being developed as the Greek drama faded away; scenery came to the English theatre just as Shakespeare's work was drawing to its close; after Chekhov in Russia came Meierhold and Tairov. Certainly it seems that overgreat emphasis on the productional elements is, in general, inimical to the creation of great drama and that the more famous plays in the theatre's repertory were written with no specially elaborate scenic effects in mind. An age of great actors may be also an age of great plays; an age of producers is hardly so likely to yield important dramatic work.

The reason would seem to be that whereas the actors are associated with what is the spiritual core of a drama, its characters, the scenic effects are connected only with the material surroundings of the action. When a true dramatist frames in his mind's eye a picture of his stage action he thinks almost entirely of the 'living' persons who have sprung from his Jove-like brain: it is the lesser playwright who clutters his mental image with visions of scenic embellishments. The actor can thus prove an inspiration to the literary artist where the scene-designer cannot. It is worthy of note how closely so many dramatic authors of the past have written their works to fit a particular company of players and how so many modern writers of prominence have deliberately penned their plays for particular actors or actresses. The process has frequently had the virtue of giving solidity and substance to what might otherwise have been airy and insubstantial. While it is difficult to determine the process of dramatic invention exactly, we may perhaps be near the mark if we say that an author, such as Shakespeare, is aroused, for one reason or another, to pen a play on some particular theme: he lets his imagination play with the characters and the action, and suddenly that which had come to him in monochrome begins to glow with colour, while at the same time the probably confused elements of the original concept become fashioned into a compositional pattern. At this moment he starts to write; but the characters he sees are not real men and women moving amid scenes of nature; they take shape as personifications treading the boards of a stage, and inevitably they thus become identified with actors. If the actors are there—as in the Elizabethan company—all ready to take their rôles, and if the author is familiar with their respective capacities, he is in an advantageous position, for in the process of creation his imaginative vision is, as it were, given body and substance by a mental fusing of the player's personality and the part he will be expected to take. We may suspect, on grounds quite other than bibliographical, that for the intrusion of actors' names into the text of some of Shakespeare's dramas the author himself was responsible: we need not doubt that in his mind Dogberry was at one and the same time a creature of his fancy and the player Kemp, who, Shakespeare knew, would certainly perform the rôle.

The actors, therefore, definitely are linked with the dramatist and contribute materially to the composition of his plays. It is far other when we turn to the scene-designer. Not only is this artist in the theatre concerned with the background of the action rather than with its spiritual core, he is not able to offer to the writer anything so concrete, constant, and stimulating as the player's personality. What he has to contribute must inevitably come after the drama has been wrought, whereas any competent author is able to guess precisely at the scope which a particular actor can command, and, consequently, even before the rehearsals, before the making-up and the costuming, the personality of this actor will be present in the writer's mind, consciously or unconsciously influencing him in the process of creation. Hence the distinction that must be drawn between an actors' theatre and a theatre of producers: the former, as any survey of the drama must reveal, has an inspirational value;

the latter, except in certain periods, tends to be negative in its effect on dramatic writing or to lead away from the full exploitation of literary elements in the performance.

THE AUDIENCE IN THE THEATRE

The theatre is a building intended for an audience, and there can be no doubt but that one of the chief determining factors in dramatic art is that a play is written, not primarily for reading, but for histrionic interpretation before an assembled body of spectators. Moreover, since the dramatist must ever adjust his conceptions to the theatre of his own time, it follows that he must seek to pen his works in such a way as to make appeal, not vaguely to 'an audience' in general, or to some imagined audience of after-times, but to the only audience he knows—that of his own period. Thus to a very large extent he is dependent upon the kind of playgoers frequenting the theatre during the years that he is writing.

This is a matter of very considerable importance, since one thing an historical survey of the theatre indicates clearly: that the theatre acquires its greatest strength when the spectators form a cross-section of the entire community of their age. The more universal the audience is in this sense, the more latent power seems to inhabit the auditorium. This does not mean, of course, that in such a period every one in the community goes to the playhouse. That may happen in certain places, as, for example, in ancient Athens, but representative, not necessarily all-inclusive, quality is all that is needed. We may be sure that not every one of the citizens of Elizabethan London went to the Globe and its companion houses of entertainment: at the same time it is equally certain that if we could be privileged to pass back in time in order to witness the original productions of *Julius Cæsar* or *Hamlet* we should have found ourselves set among two thousand-odd persons from every rank of London's society and extending from the literate to the illiterate. From the fact that he had to appeal to all levels of taste and interest Shakespeare drew inspiration and strength.

While in general this widely representative audience seems to form a necessary basis for the production of highest excellency in the drama, we may, however, observe two things. On occasion some periods when the theatre makes limited appeal and some playhouses that deliberately aim at the presentation of dramatic work of a special character may yield results which, if not of the profoundest, at least have elements of worth. If they do, however, they achieve their effects because of the association of their specialized interests with other elements. When, for example, the English theatre in the early nineteenth century was attended largely by the rougher and less literate members of society it could encourage little save crude melodrama, which, even when it did not become positively ungrammatical, was entirely devoid of grace and distinction. This crude audience could stimulate nothing more. A different picture is presented to us when we turn to the period of the Restoration. In those days the playhouses of London made their appeal only to the aristocrats, and at first glance we might well have supposed that these gallants would have been unlikely to encourage any dramatic work of consequence. Since, however, the society attending the theatres was one assured of its own conventions and its peculiar interests, and since, above all things, it was devoted to ease of conversation and delighted in the rapier-play of wit, the Restoration playhouses succeeded in producing perfect examples of a kind of comedy which, if restricted in scope, nevertheless possessed an æsthetic value, a precision, and a delicacy worthy of esteem.

More important is it to estimate aright the force of a relatively modern development—the independent and usually non-commercial theatre. To a certain extent these ventures appealing to a small minority audience find adumbrations in the groups of literary amateurs who, during the time of Shakespeare, sought to cultivate the classical kind of play-construction and to present models better fitted, in their opinion, to stimulate the stage than the romantically conceived dramas presented by the professional players. The heyday of the independents, however, does not come until our own times, when, with a record stretching back to Antoine's Théâtre Libre and extending to Martin Browne's Poets' Playhouse, they have played a by no means inconsiderable rôle. That rôle, where it is vital, has been to provide opportunities for playwrights whose form or content step a little way in advance of that which the ordinary theatre public is willing to accept. For the independent theatre that goes too far in the van there can be but little hope of abiding success; the road the stage has taken during the past fifty years is littered with the shattered wrecks of ventures that were over-impatient of current theatrical fare and strove, vainly, to impose on the spectators something alien to their wishes. The truth, of course, is that the really strong playwright is the man who is in tune with his audience, but who may perhaps desire to play some melodies for the reception of which the audience is nearly, but not quite, ready. Here the independent theatres have recently shown

what they can effectively accomplish; by going just a trifle ahead
they can familiarize their select audiences with the kind of production which in a few years' time will be common property. This
was the mission of the Théâtre Libre, of the Freie Bühne, of the
Provincetown Players.

The danger in their being rests in the fact that a young writer of
promise may, unless he is wise and careful, tend so to identify himself with the limited objectives of an 'independent playhouse' as to
injure his later writing. It is only when a dramatist, such as Shaw,
finds his first opportunities in the small house and then moves on
to the larger commercial stage that value accrues from his earlier
experimentation before a carefully selected group of advanced
enthusiasts. Shaw soon found that, with growing skill, he did not
require to have this prop for his genius. In his subsequent career he
ever shocked his general audiences by his seeming daring, but he
was skilful enough not to go too far and to give the public what it
wanted, even though perhaps that public could not have put its
wants into words. In *Pygmalion* Shaw made news by introducing
a "bloody" into his dialogue; spectators were startled, but pleasantly
so; for that "bloody" they had been waiting.

The allusion to *Pygmalion* reminds us that in hardly any period of
the theatre's history has the censorship hurt the dramatists. There
was censorship in Athens, and Aristophanes continued writing;
there was censorship in Elizabethan England, and Shakespeare's
genius flourished unchecked; there is censorship in modern England,
and Shaw can effervesce without hindrance. Perhaps, however, a
distinction should be made between a censorship that is negative
and a censorship that is positive. If authors are told that there are
certain things they must not do no harm arises: they will find other
ways of accomplishing their ends, and probably benefit from the
enforced imaginative exercise involved. The English censorship
says that God must not appear on the stage; but a religious play can
be written, and finely written, without introducing the Deity in
person. When, on the other hand, a censorship, instead of declaring
that certain things must not be done, demands that the playwrights
do certain things only, then, it would seem, the artistic excellence
is bound to be impaired, unless the dramatists are so thoroughly in
accord with the objectives in view that compliance is desire. You
can lead a horse to water; you cannot force him to drink.

One further thing becomes plain from a survey of the theatre's
history. The playhouse is a thing partly of entertainment, partly of
devotional ritual, and unless the age allows for the exercise of both,

little of value is likely to result. "As everybody knows," says Maxwell Anderson,

> the great plays of the world—those accepted by civilization as part of a great heritage and played for centuries—these are almost all concerned with the conduct of exceptional men or women in positions of great responsibility, men with tragic faults and weaknesses but with mind and strength enough to overcome in the struggle with evil forces, both those within themselves and those without. . . . In such cases it is obvious that some kind of religious ritual is involved in reviving these symbols of national or cultural faith in a public performance.

When the theatre becomes merely a playhouse, a building to which men and women go for laughter or sensation, little is likely to result of fine dramatic craftsmanship.

The ritual that produces greatness is one essentially metaphysical in its nature, and it is this kind of ritual which Marxist critics are most inclined to deny. We can, if we like, interpret *Othello* in terms of money and explain away Sophocles by referring to the economic condition of ancient Athens; but when we do so we either are merely touching with forced fingers rude the fringe of a mystery or completely falsify the truth. Of course, the playwrights of any particular age are influenced by that age's spirit, but the economic life of man is not the whole of man's existence.

In these greater dramas of the world there is little to be found of what for convenience may be called 'propaganda.' Contemporary material may enter in, but the authors are not engaged in any preachments: rather do they conceive their task to be the imaginative reflection of experience. Shakespeare's history plays provide an excellent example of this. Having noted that the theme of these dramas is closely bound up with the philosophy of the Tudors, some recent critics have tended to claim that their author was deliberately presenting a philosophy, was engaged in an attempt to educate the people. The truth seems rather to be that he was reflecting an experience—not inculcating a course of action or presenting a thesis. Because he was doing so his plays have remained of constant interest and of enduring value. There is, thus, in the theatre a sharp distinction to be made between two kinds of dramatic work which may at first sight appear identical. Nowhere more clearly does the distinction between them appear than in an examination of recent Russian plays. Those which are fashioned merely to educate the public are easily seen to be of no permanent worth; the plays that stand out, if not as masterpieces at least as dramas possessing greater quality than the others, are those wherein an experience has been recorded. *Bread* is temporary; *Fear* has something of the quality of which great works of the theatre are made.

It has something, but by no means all, for a survey of the drama shows that true greatness can be secured only when the lambent flame of the poetic imagination is allowed to caress and sear, and in searing to transmute, the forms of the actual. It may be that the world may decide that it has no more use for the enduring monument of art and that drama, like the other arts, is useless unless as a propagandist or educative force. If that view be accepted, then we are not interested in whether another *Hamlet*, another *Antigone*, can be created. We have chosen our star and by its light have fixed our course. But if we still hope, whatever our views on the social life of the future, that the theatre may still yield us dramas of such universal scope as to make them of enduring appeal, then the concepts on which the Russian Socialist Realism and other Socialist Realisms are based must be regarded as trends inimical to our desire. The 'truthfulness' aimed at there is at variance with the truthfulness of the poetic imagination, and from that alone things permanent may spring.

The enduring theatre is educative, no doubt, but it is educative not in the manner of the reasoning lecturer or of the political orator; it is educative only in the sense that it arouses our interests and stimulates our imagination, that it penetrates deep into the heart of humanity and draws the very gods from the height of heaven or the depth of hell to walk upon the boards. The vulgar chink of money echoes through all the drama of realism, whether the realism be bourgeois or socialistic; in the realms of tragedy and of comedy inspired by the true poetic concept the gold is the gold of the spirit.

DRAMATIC FORM

In saying that the greatest drama enshrines a vividly felt imaginative experience we must recognize that in the theatre this experience has tended to develop strength when, instead of being any experience, it restricts itself in scope and fits itself into a pattern. The classical division of plays into the tragic, the comic, and the satiric may have derived in origin from cultural and religious exercise, but the endurance of these forms long after the civilization of Athens had become merely a memory seems to indicate that in them some peculiar virtue lies. In a recent volume on *The American Drama since 1918* Joseph Wood Krutch observes that it is worthy of remark that the playwrights whose names most persistently reappear in any discussion of the possibly permanent achievements of the contemporary drama are those in whose work the formal element is conspicuous. It is true that Eugene O'Neill, Maxwell Anderson and S. N. Behrman have all dealt sometimes with current topics. It is also true that they could not have been so important as they are had they not been unmistakably of our day. But it is not primarily of their timeliness that one thinks; they are, first of all, a writer of tragedies, a poetic dramatist and a creator of comedies, respectively. That means that each has thought his way through his material with such thoroughness that he has been able to give it one of the forms eternally appropriate to the drama. It also suggests that such a process is necessary before any play can achieve permanent interest and that we have, perhaps, been too ready to assume that intellectual honesty in the presentation of contemporary themes is in itself all-sufficient.

We may well believe that there is fundamental truth in these words. As Krutch shows, O'Neill's plays, whatever their shortcomings in expression, are tragedies and Behrman's are comedies "because, despite the fact neither could have been written in any age except this, they achieve the formal perfection of one of the classic patterns and produce an effect of completeness and finality possible only when such a pattern has been evolved." These dramas "owe their effectiveness to the fact that they make possible a maximum of intensity while at the same time they provide for orderly progress toward a clear conclusion."

The truth is, of course, that the dramatist, working within the scope of a highly restricted art, must, if he wishes for success, give to his imaginative vision a clearer and closer focus than another literary artist need have. In the Greek classical division of kinds exists something beyond the merely temporary, and what is revealed here finds corroboration in the Sanskrit doctrine of *rasas*. When Bharata presents his eight 'sentiments' and declares that, although these may be mingled or associated with other subsidiary sentiments, each play must aim fundamentally at the arousing of one dominant emotion, he is recognizing the quality that, in a different way, was recognized by Aristotle and inspired his arguments in the *Poetics*. If this judgment has validity, then obviously much of the amorphous realistic drama of our time can have little hope of permanence. It may please temporarily because of its depiction of current affairs, but its life-span is destined to be short.

This question of form must, naturally, be associated with the question of the audience, since here the dramatist is completely in the hands of those to whom his works are addressed. If the spectators are not willing to rise to an appreciation of scenic intensity in clearly formalized terms the playwright can do little. Neither the middle-class audience in England during the eighteenth century, nor the aristocratic audience preceding it—nor, one might add, the 'popular' audience succeeding—was prepared to embrace the rigours of the tragic, and as a result the Restoration period could produce only the love-and-honour dramas, the sentimental age could yield only dully fashioned and imitative would-be tragic plays in which there was no virtue, the age of romanticism could make only a few faint gestures towards the poetically tragic.

If there is hope for a revival of dramatic power in our times, that hope is to be found mainly in the fact that in some quarters at least this formalized intensity is being welcomed. Theatrical conditions, perhaps, are not on the whole very propitious just at present, but when we observe what considerable steps in advance have been taken by the poetic play, when we see how the ancient themes are being given new meanings in modern works, and, particularly, when we note how French dramatists are striving passionately to create a new foundation for tragedy, the noblest form that the theatre knows, we may well be justified in wondering whether a fresh glory is not near at hand. Our peep-show stage holds us back; emphasis on the productional elements is a hindrance; the general decay of the stock company gives the playwright in our midst a harder task than he need have; but when we consider what important suggestions for the future have been variously exhibited by *Murder in the Cathedral*, *Électre*, and *Eurydice* we may perhaps be justified in letting our imaginations move forward with pleasant anticipation into the realm of the theatre to come. In certain circles, at least, a renewed interest in form—the be-all and the end-all of dramatic art—is being born.

INDEX

Dates of birth and death are inserted after the names of dramatists.